A PEOPLE & A NATION

A PEOPLE & A NATION

A History of the United States

EIGHTH EDITION

Volume Two: Since 1865

Mary Beth Norton
Cornell University

Carol Sheriff
College of William and Mary

David M. Katzman
University of Kansas

David W. Blight
Yale University

Howard P. Chudacoff
Brown University

Fredrik Logevall
Cornell University

Beth Bailey
Temple University

HOUGHTON MIFFLIN COMPANY   Boston   New York

Publisher: *Suzanne Jeans*
Senior Sponsoring Editor: *Ann West*
Marketing Manager: *Katherine Bates*
Senior Developmental Editor: *Jeffrey Greene*
Senior Project Editor: *Jane Lee*
Art and Design Manager: *Jill Haber*
Cover Design Director: *Tony Saizon*
Senior Photo Editor: *Jennifer Meyer Dare*
Composition Buyer: *Chuck Dutton*
New Title Project Manager: *James Lonergan*
Editorial Associate: *Adrienne Zicht*
Marketing Assistant: *Lauren Bussard*
Editorial Assistant: *Carrie Parker/Anne Finley*

Cover image: *Julianita* by Robert Henri, ca. 1917. Private Collection, courtesy Gerald Peters Gallery, New York and John G. Hagan.

Chapter opener montage (pp. 435, 467, 497, 529, 563, 591, 621, 647, 677, 707, 739, 766, 795, 825, 857, 889, 921, 951): American Indian, far left: Northwestern University Library, Edward S. Curtis's *The North American Indian: Photographic Images, 2001*; second from left: *Women of Protest: Photographs from the Records of the National Woman's Party*, Manuscript Division, Library of Congress, Washington, DC; center, second from right, and far right: Courtesy of the Library of Congress, Washington, DC.

Printed in the U.S.A.

Library of Congress Catalog Number: 2007936065

Instructor's exam copy:
ISBN 13: 978-0-547-05241-0
ISBN 10: 0-547-05241-3

For orders, use student text ISBNs:
ISBN 13: 978-0-618-94777-5
ISBN 10: 0-618-94777-9

1 2 3 4 5 6 7 8 9-WEB-11 10 09 08 07

Brief Contents

Contents

16   Reconstruction: An Unfinished Revolution, 1865–1877   434

17   The Development of the West, 1865–1900   466

18   The Machine Age, 1877–1920   496

19   The Vitality and Turmoil of Urban Life, 1877–1920   528

20   Gilded Age Politics, 1877–1900   562

21   The Progressive Era, 1895–1920   590

22 The Quest for Empire, 1865–1914   620

23 Americans in the Great War, 1914–1920   646

24 The New Era, 1920–1929   676

32 Conservatism Revived, 1980–1992   920

33 Into the Global Millennium: America Since 1992   950

Special Features

MAPS

FIGURES

TABLES

LINKS TO THE WORLD

LEGACY FOR A PEOPLE AND A NATION

In this eighth edition, *A People and a Nation* has undergone both reorganization and revision, while still retaining the narrative strength and focus that have made it so popular with students and teachers alike. In the years since the publication of the seventh edition, new materials have been uncovered, new interpretations advanced, and new themes have come to the forefront of American historical scholarship. All the authors—joined by one new member, Carol Sheriff—have worked diligently to incorporate those findings into this text.

Like other teachers and students, we are always recreating our past, restructuring our memory, and rediscovering the personalities and events that have influenced us, injured us, and bedeviled us. This book represents our continuing rediscovery of America's history—its diverse people and the nation they created and have nurtured. As this book demonstrates, there are many different Americans and many different memories. We have sought to present as many of them as possible, in both triumph and tragedy, in both division and unity.

About *A People and A Nation*

A People and a Nation, first published in 1982, was the first major textbook in the United States to fully integrate social and political history. From the outset, the authors have been determined to tell the story of *all* the people of the United States. This book's hallmark has been its melding of social and political history, its movement beyond history's common focus on public figures and events to examine the daily life of America's people. All editions of the book have stressed the interaction of public policy and personal experience, the relationship between domestic concerns and foreign affairs, the various manifestations of popular culture, and the multiple origins of America and Americans. We have consistently built our narrative on a firm foundation in primary sources—on both well-known and obscure letters, diaries, public documents, oral histories, and artifacts of material culture. We have long challenged readers to think about the meaning of American history, not just to memorize facts. Both students and instructors have repeatedly told us how much they appreciate and enjoy our approach to the past.

As has been true since the first edition, each chapter opens with a dramatic vignette focusing on an individual or a group of people. These vignettes introduce key themes, which then frame the chapters in succinct introductions and summaries. Numerous maps, tables, graphs, and charts provide readers with the necessary geographical and statistical context for observations in the text. Carefully selected illustrations—many of them unique to this book—offer readers visual insight into the topics under discussion, especially because the authors have written the captions. In this edition, as in all previous ones, we have sought to incorporate up-to-date scholarship, readability, a clear structure, critical thinking, and instructive illustrative material on every page.

Themes in This Book

Several themes and questions stand out in our continuing effort to integrate political, social, and cultural history. We study the many ways that Americans have defined themselves—gender, race, class, region, ethnicity, religion, sexual orientation—and the many subjects that have reflected their multidimensional experiences. We highlight the remarkably diverse everyday lives of the American people—in cities and on farms and ranches, in factories and in corporate headquarters, in neighborhoods and in legislatures, in love relationships and in hate groups, in recreation and in work, in the classroom and in military uniform, in secret national security conferences and in public foreign relations debates, in church and in voluntary associations, in polluted environments and in conservation areas. We pay particular attention to lifestyles, diet and dress, family life and structure, labor conditions, gender roles, migration and mobility, childbearing, and child rearing. We explore how Americans have entertained and informed themselves by discussing their music, sports, theater, print media, film, radio, television, graphic arts, and literature, in both "high" culture and popular culture. We study how technology has influenced Americans' lives, such as through the internal combustion engine and the computer.

Americans' personal lives have always interacted with the public realm of politics and government. To understand how Americans have sought to protect their different ways of life and to work out solutions to thorny problems, we emphasize their expectations of governments at the local, state, and federal levels; governments' role in providing answers; the lobbying of interest groups; the campaigns and outcomes of elections; and the hierarchy of power in any period. Because the United States has long been a major participant in world affairs, we explore America's participation in wars, interventions in other nations, empire-building, immigration patterns, images of foreign peoples, cross-national cultural ties, and international economic trends.

What's New in This Edition

Planning for the eighth edition began at a two-day authors' meeting at the Houghton Mifflin headquarters in Boston. There we discussed the most recent scholarship in the field, the reviews of the seventh edition solicited from instructors, and the findings of our own continuing research. For this edition, we added a new colleague, Carol Sheriff, who experienced the intellectual exhilaration and rigor of such an authors' meeting for the first time. Sheriff, a member of the History Department at the College of William and Mary, has written extensively on antebellum America, especially in the North, and she has taken on the responsibility for those chapters in the eighth edition.

This edition builds on its immediate predecessor in continuing to enhance the global perspective on American history that has characterized the book since its first edition. From the "Atlantic world" context of European colonies in North and South America to the discussion of international terrorism, the authors have incorporated the most recent globally oriented scholarship throughout the volume. Significantly, the eighth edition includes an entirely new chapter on the American West in the years before the Civil War and the discussion of the West has been expanded throughout. The treatment of the history of children and childhood has been increased, as has the discussion of environmental history, including the devastating impact of hurricanes in North America and in the Caribbean from the earliest days of European settlement. As in the seventh edition, we have worked to strengthen our treatment of the diversity of America's people by examining differences within the broad ethnic categories commonly employed and by paying greater attention to immigration, cultural and intellectual infusions from around the world, and America's growing religious diversity. We have also stressed the incorporation of different peoples into the United States through territorial acquisition as well as through immigration. At the same time, we have integrated the discussion of such diversity into our narrative so as not to artificially isolate any group

from the mainstream. We have added three probing questions at the end of each chapter's introduction to guide students' reading of the pages that follow.

As always, the authors reexamined every sentence, interpretation, map, chart, illustration, and caption, refining the narrative, presenting new examples, and bringing to the text the latest findings of scholars in many areas of history, anthropology, sociology, and political science. More than one-third of the chapter-opening vignettes are new to this edition.

"Legacies" and "Links to the World"

Each chapter contains two brief feature essays: "Legacies for a People and a Nation" (introduced in the sixth edition) and "Links to the World" (introduced in the seventh edition). Legacies appear toward the end of each chapter and offer compelling and timely answers to students who question the relevance of historical study by exploring the historical roots of contemporary topics. New subjects of Legacies are: Kennewick Man/Ancient One, Blue Laws, women's political activism, the township and range system, descendants of early Latino settlers, "Big Government," the Lost Cause, the Cowboy myth, recorded music, Guantánamo Bay, nuclear proliferation, and the all-volunteer force. Numerous other Legacies have been updated.

"Links to the World" examine both inward and outward ties between America (and Americans) and the rest of the world. The Links appear at appropriate places in each chapter to explore specific topics at considerable length. Tightly constructed essays detail the often little-known connections between developments here and abroad. The topics range broadly over economic, political, social, technological, medical, and cultural history, vividly demonstrating that the geographical region that is now the United States has never lived in isolation from other peoples and countries. New to this edition are Links on smallpox inoculations, the Amistad case, Russian Populism, European influence on American workers' compensation, and *National Geographic*. Each Link highlights global interconnections with unusual and lively examples that will both intrigue and inform students.

Section-by-Section Changes in This Edition

Mary Beth Norton, who had primary responsibility for Chapters 1 through 8 and served as coordinating author, augmented her discussion of the age of European expansion with new information on Muslim power and the allure of exotic spices; she also expanded the treatment of Spanish colonization and settlements in the Caribbean. She incorporated extensive new scholarship on early Virginia into Chapter 2. In addition to reorganizing part of Chapter 3 to bring more coherence to the discussion of the origins of slavery in North America, she added demographic information about enslaved peoples (both Indians and Africans) and those who enslaved and transported them, stressing in particular the importance of African women in South Carolina rice cultivation. She added material on transported English convicts, Huguenot immigrants, Acadian exiles, iron-making, land riots, the Stono Rebellion, the Seven Years' War in western Pennsylvania, the experiences of common soldiers in the Revolution, Shays's Rebellion, and the Jay Treaty debates. In Chapter 8 she created new sections on Indians in the new nation and on revolutions at the end of the century, including among them the election of Thomas Jefferson.

Carol Sheriff completely reorganized the contents of Chapters 9, 11, and 12, clarifying chronological developments and including much new material. Chapter 9 now covers politics through 1823 in order to emphasize the impact of the War of 1812 in accelerating regional divisions. It has expanded coverage of popular political practice (including among non-voters), the separation of church and state, the Marshall Court, the First and Second Barbary Wars, and the incorporation of the Louisiana Territory and its residents into the United States. Chapter 11, retitled "The Modernizing North," consolidates information previously divided between two chapters and augments it with new discussions of daily life before commercial and industrial expansion, rural-urban contrasts, children and youth culture, male and female common laborers, and the origins of free-labor ideology. Chapter 12 focuses on reform and politics in the age of Jackson, with expanded attention to communitarian experiments, abolitionism (including African Americans in the movement), women's rights, and religion (including revivalism in general and the Second Great Awakening in particular). The entirely new Chapter 13, "The Contested West," combines material that was previously scattered in different locations with a great deal of recent scholarship on such topics as the disjunction between the ideal and reality of the West, exploration and migration, cultural diversity in the West, cooperation and conflict among the West's peoples, and the role of the federal government in regional development. In all of her reorganized chapters she relied on a base created by David M. Katzman, an original member of the author team who had responsibility for this section in the seven earlier editions.

David W. Blight, who had primary responsibility for Chapter 10 and Chapters 14 through 16, extensively reorganized Chapter 10 (previously Chapter 13), on the South, in part to reflect its new chronological placement in the book. The chapter now covers material beginning in 1815 rather than in 1830 and contains a section on Southern expansion and Indian removal. In his chapters he has added material on the Taos revolt, enslaved children, "Bleeding Kansas," Harriet Scott, Louisa May Alcott, union sentiment in the South, the conduct of the war, and economic and social conditions in the postwar North and South. He has revised Chapter 16 to emphasize economic as well as political change in the era of Reconstruction.

Howard P. Chudacoff, responsible for Chapters 17 through 21 and Chapter 24, has increased the coverage of Indians, Exodusters, and Hispanics in the West, and of western Progressivism. His treatment of popular culture now stresses its lower-class, bottom-to-top origins. He has added information on the history of childhood, vaudeville, and the movies; and he revised discussions of monetary policy, Progressivism, Populism, and urban and agrarian protests. He also has included more coverage of racism and those who combated it, such as Ida B. Wells, and of women and the Ku Klux Klan. Business operation and regulation receive new attention in his chapters, as do Calvin Coolidge, consumerism, and baseball.

Fredrik Logevall, with primary responsibility for Chapters 22, 23, 26, and 28, has continued to work to establish the wider international context for U.S. foreign affairs throughout his chapters. He has added considerable new material on the Middle East (especially in Chapter 28) and has incorporated recent scholarship on the Vietnam War. He also has updated the treatment of the Spanish-American War with new information on the sinking of the *Maine* and on the Philippine insurrection. His discussion of World War I now includes consideration of the antagonistic relationship of Woodrow Wilson and V. I. Lenin; and he has given more attention to American economic and cultural expansion in the 1920s and 1930s. Furthermore, he has expanded his treatment of American reactions to the Spanish Civil War.

Beth Bailey, primarily responsible for Chapters 25, 27, and 29, has added information on women, the left, and popular culture (especially film and the production code) during the 1930s. She has expanded coverage of the European front in World War II and of divisions within the United States during the war. In Chapter 29, she has thoroughly reorganized the section on civil rights to clarify the chronology and key points of development, and she also has included new information on emerging counter-cultures and the beats, union activities, and the Eisenhower administration.

Bailey and Logevall shared responsibility for Chapters 30 through 33. In Chapter 30 Freedom Summer is given enhanced attention and the section on civil rights has been reorganized to emphasize a clear chronology. These chapters contain new material on the women's movement and the barriers women faced before 1970s reforms, recent immigration, neoconservatism, anti-Vietnam War protests, Nixon's presidency, the Supreme Court, the 1982 Israeli invasion of Lebanon, and the 1991 Iraq War. Chapter 33, in particular, has been thoroughly revised to include the latest demographic data on Americans and their families, along with discussions of the struggles over science and religion, Hurricane Katrina, the Bush administration's domestic policies, and especially the Iraq War.

Teaching and Learning Aids

The supplements listed here accompany the eighth edition of *A People and a Nation*. They have been created with the diverse needs of today's students and instructors in mind.

For the Instructor

- Houghton Mifflin's **HistoryFinder** is a new online tool developed to help instructors create rich and exciting presentations for the U.S. history survey class. History-Finder offers thousands of online resources, including art, photographs, maps, primary sources, multimedia content, Associated Press interactive modules, and ready-made PowerPoint slides. HistoryFinder's assets can be searched easily by keyword topic, media type, or by textbook chapter. It is then possible to browse, preview, and download resources straight from the website into the instructor's own PowerPoint collection.

- The **Instructor Website** at HM HistorySPACE™, which is accessible by visiting college.hmco.com/pic/norton8e, includes a variety of resources that will help instructors engage their students in class and assess their understanding inside and outside the classroom. The Instructor Website includes the **Instructor's Resource Manual,** written by George C. Warren of Central Piedmont Community College. For each chapter there is a brief list of learning objectives, a comprehensive chapter outline, ideas for classroom activities, discussion questions, several suggested paper topics, and a lecture supplement. Also available on the Instructor Website is a complete set of PowerPoint slides created by Barney Rickman of Valdosta State University to assist in instruction and discussion of key topics and materials for each chapter.

- The **HM Testing™ CD-ROM** provides flexible test-editing capabilities for the test items written by George Warren of Central Piedmont Community College. Included in the Test Bank are multiple-choice, identification, geography, and essay questions.

- Houghton Mifflin's **Eduspace Course** for *A People and a Nation* offers a customizable course management system powered by Blackboard along with homework assignments that engage students and encourage in-class discussion. Assignments include gradable homework exercises, writing assignments, primary sources with questions, and Associated Press Interactives. Eduspace also provides a gradebook and communication capabilities, such as live chats, threaded discussion boards, and announcement postings. The Eduspace course also includes an interactive version of *A People and a Nation* with direct links to relevant primary sources, quizzes, and more.

For the Student

- The **Student Website** at HM HistorySPACE™, also accessible by visiting college.hmco.com/pic/norton8e, contains a variety of review and self-assessment resources to help students succeed in the U.S. history survey course. ACE quizzes with feedback, interactive maps, primary sources, chronology exercises, flashcards, and other activities are available for each chapter. Audio files provide chapter summaries in MP3 format for downloading and listening to at any time.

- **Study Guides** (Volumes I and II), written by George Warren, provide learning objectives, vocabulary exercises, identification suggestions, skill-building activities, multiple-choice questions, essay questions, and map exercises in two volumes.

Please contact your local Houghton Mifflin sales representative for more information about these learning and teaching tools in addition to the **Rand McNally Atlas of American History,** WebCT and Blackboard cartridges, and transparencies for United States history. Your sales representative can also provide more information about **BiblioBase for U.S. History,** a database of hundreds of primary sources from which you can create a customized course pack.

||||||||||||||||||||||||||||||

Acknowledgments

The authors would like to thank the following persons for their assistance with the preparation of this edition: Shawn Alexander, Marsha Andrews, Edward Balleisen, Philip Daileader, Katherine Flynn, John B. Heiser, Danyel Logevall, Daniel Mandell, Clark F. Norton, Mary E. Norton, Anna Daileader Sheriff, Benjamin Daileader Sheriff, Selene Sheriff, and Seymour Sheriff.

At each stage of this revision, a sizable panel of historian reviewers read drafts of our chapters. Their suggestions, corrections, and pleas helped guide us through this momentous revision. We could not include all of their recommendations, but the book is better for our having heeded most of their advice. We heartily thank:

Marynita Anderson, *Nassau Community College/SUNY*

Stephen Aron, *UCLA and Autry National Center*

Gordon Morris Bakken, *California State University, Fullerton*

Todd Forsyth Carney, *Southern Oregon University*

Kathleen S. Carter, *High Point University*

Robert C. Cottrell, *California State University, Chico*

Lawrence Culver, *Utah State University*

Lawrence J. DeVaro, *Rowan University*

Lisa Lindquist Dorr, *University of Alabama*

Michelle Kuhl, *University of Wisconsin, Oshkosh*

Martin Halpern, *Henderson State University*

John S. Leiby, *Paradise Valley Community College*

Edwin Martini, *Western Michigan University*

Elsa A. Nystrom, *Kennesaw State University*

Chester Pach, *Ohio University*

Stephen Rockenbach, *Northern Kentucky University*

Joseph Owen Weixelman, *University of New Mexico*

The authors once again thank the extraordinary Houghton Mifflin people who designed, edited, produced, and nourished this book. Their high standards and acute attention to both general structure and fine detail are cherished in the publishing industry. Many thanks, then, to Patricia Coryell, vice president and publisher, history and social science; Suzanne Jeans, publisher, history and political science; Sally Constable and Ann West, senior sponsoring editors; Ann Hofstra Grogg, freelance development editor; Jeff Greene, senior development editor; Jane Lee, senior project editor; Katherine Bates, senior marketing manager; Pembroke Herbert, photo researcher; Jill Haber, art and design manager; Charlotte Miller, art editor; and Evangeline Bermas, editorial assistant.

M. B. N.
C. S.
D. B.
H. C.
F. L.
B. B.

Mary Beth Norton

Born in Ann Arbor, Michigan, Mary Beth Norton received her B.A. from the University of Michigan (1964) and her Ph.D. from Harvard University (1969). She is the Mary Donlon Alger Professor of American History at Cornell University. Her dissertation won the Allan Nevins Prize. She has written *The British-Americans* (1972), *Liberty's Daughters* (1980, 1996), *Founding Mothers & Fathers* (1996), which was one of three finalists for the 1997 Pulitzer Prize in History, and *In the Devil's Snare* (2002), which was one of five finalists for the 2003 *LA Times* Book Prize in History and which won the English-Speaking Union's Ambassador Book Award in American Studies for 2003. She has coedited *Women of America* (with Carol Berkin, 1979), *To Toil the Livelong Day* (with Carol Groneman, 1987), and *Major Problems in American Women's History* (with Ruth Alexander, 2007). She was general editor of the *American Historical Association's Guide to Historical Literature* (1995). Her articles have appeared in such journals as the *American Historical Review, William and Mary Quarterly,* and *Journal of Women's History.* Mary Beth has served as president of the Berkshire Conference of Women Historians, as vice president for research of the American Historical Association, and as a presidential appointee to the National Council on the Humanities. She has received four honorary degrees and in 1999 was elected a fellow of the American Academy of Arts and Sciences. She has held fellowships from the National Endowment for the Humanities, the Guggenheim, Rockefeller, and Starr Foundations, and the Henry E. Huntington Library. In 2005–2006, she was the Pitt Professor of American History and Institutions at the University of Cambridge and Newnham College.

Carol Sheriff

Born in Washington, DC, and raised in Bethesda, Maryland, Carol Sheriff received her B.A. from Wesleyan University (1985) and her Ph.D. from Yale University (1993). Since 1993, she has taught history at the College of William and Mary, where she has won the Thomas Jefferson Teaching Award, the Alumni Teaching Fellowship Award, and the University Professorship for Teaching Excellence. Her publications include *The Artificial River: The Erie Canal and the Paradox of Progress* (1996), which won the Dixon Ryan Fox Award from the New York State Historical Association and the Award for Excellence in Research from the New York State Archives, and *A People at War: Civilians and Soldiers in America's Civil War, 1854–1877* (with Scott Reynolds Nelson, 2007). Carol has written sections of a teaching manual for the New York State history curriculum, given presentations to a Teaching American History grant project, consulted on an exhibit for the Rochester Museum and Science Center, appeared in the History Channel's Modern Marvels show on the Erie Canal, and is serving as a consultant for "The Inland Voyage," a forthcoming television documentary on the Erie Canal. At William and Mary, she teaches the U.S. history survey as well as upper-level classes on the Early Republic, the Civil War Era, and the American West.

David W. Blight

Born in Flint, Michigan, David W. Blight received his B.A. from Michigan State University (1971) and his Ph.D. from the University of Wisconsin (1985). He is now professor of history and director of the Gilder Lehrman Center for the Study of Slavery, Resistance, and Abolition at Yale University. For the first seven years of his career, David was a public high school teacher in Flint. He has written *Frederick Douglass's Civil War* (1989) and *Race and Reunion: The Civil War in American Memory, 1863–1915* (2000). His most recent book is *A Slave No More: the Emancipation of John Washington and Wallace Turnage* (2007). His edited works include *When This Cruel War Is Over: The Civil War Letters of Charles Harvey Brewster* (1992), *Narrative of the Life of Frederick Douglass* (1993), W. E. B. Du Bois, *The Souls of Black Folk* (with Robert Gooding Williams, 1997), *Union and Emancipation* (with Brooks Simpson, 1997), and *Caleb Bingham, The Columbian Orator* (1997). David's essays have appeared in the *Journal of American History, Civil War History,* and Gabor Boritt, ed., *Why the Civil War Came* (1996), among others. In 1992–1993 he was senior Fulbright Professor in American Studies at the University of Munich, Germany. A consultant to several documentary films, David appeared in the 1998 PBS series, *Africans in America.* In 1999 he was elected to the Council of the American Historical Association. David also teaches summer seminars for secondary school teachers, as well as for park rangers and historians of the National Park Service. His book, *Race and Reunion: The Civil War in American Memory* (2000), received many honors in 2002, including The Bancroft Prize, Abraham Lincoln Prize, and the Frederick Douglass Prize. From the Organization of American Historians, he has received the Merle Curti Prize in Social History, the Merle Curti Prize in Intellectual History, the Ellis Hawley Prize in Political History, and the James Rawley Prize in Race Relations.

Howard P. Chudacoff

Howard P. Chudacoff, the George L. Littlefield Professor of American History and Professor of Urban Studies at Brown University, was born in Omaha, Nebraska. He earned his A.B. (1965) and Ph.D. (1969) from the University of Chicago. He has written *Mobile Americans* (1972), *How Old Are You?* (1989), *The Age of the Bachelor* (1999), *The Evolution of American Urban Society* (with Judith Smith, 2004), and *Children at Play: An American History* (2007). He has also co-edited with Peter Baldwin *Major Problems in American Urban History* (2004). His articles have appeared in such journals as the *Journal of Family History, Reviews in American History,* and *Journal of American History.* At Brown University, Howard has co-chaired the American Civilization Program, chaired the Department of History, and serves as Brown's faculty representative to the NCAA. He has also served on the board of directors of the Urban History Association. The National Endowment for the Humanities, Ford Foundation, and Rockefeller Foundation have given him awards to advance his scholarship.

Fredrik Logevall

A native of Stockholm, Sweden, Fredrik Logevall received his B.A. from Simon Fraser University (1986) and his Ph.D. from Yale University (1993). He is professor of history at Cornell University. He is the author of *Choosing War: The Lost Chance for Peace and the Escalation of War in Vietnam* (1999), which won three prizes, including the Warren F. Kuehl Book Prize from the Society for Historians of American Foreign Relations (SHAFR). His other publications include *The Origins of the Vietnam War* (2001), *Terrorism and 9/11: A Reader* (2002), as coeditor, the *Encyclopedia of American For-eign Policy* (2002), and, as co-editor, *The First Vietnam War: Colonial Conflict and Cold War Crisis* (2007). Fred is a past recipient of the Stuart L. Bernath article, book, and lecture prizes from SHAFR and is a member of the SHAFR Council, the Cornell University Press faculty board, and the editorial advisory board of the Presidential Recordings Project at the Miller Center of Public Affairs at the University of Virginia. In 2006–2007 he was Leverhulme Visiting Professor at the University of Nottingham and Mellon Senior Fellow at the University of Cambridge.

Beth Bailey

Born in Atlanta, Georgia, Beth Bailey received her B.A. from Northwestern University (1979) and her Ph.D. from the University of Chicago (1986). She is now a professor of history at Temple University. Her research and teaching fields include American cultural history (nineteenth and twentieth centuries), popular culture, and gender and sexuality. She is the author of *From Front Porch to Back Seat: Courtship in 20th Century America* (1988), a historical analysis of conventions governing the courtship of heterosexual youth; *The First Strange Place: The Alchemy of Race and Sex in WWII Hawaii* (with David Farber, 1992), which analyzes cultural contact among Americans in wartime Hawai'i; *Sex in the Heartland* (1999), a social and cultural history of the post-WWII "sexual revolution"; *The Columbia Companion to America in the 1960s* (with David Farber, 2001); and is co-editor of *A History of Our Time* (with William Chafe and Harvard Sitkoff, 6th ed., 2002). Beth has served as a consultant and/or on-screen expert for numerous television documentaries developed for PBS and the History Channel. She has received grants from the ACLS and NEH, was the Ann Whitney Olin scholar at Barnard College, Columbia University, from 1991 through 1994, where she was the director of the American Studies Program, and held a senior Fulbright lectureship in Indonesia in 1996. She teaches courses on sexuality and gender, war and American culture, research methods, and popular culture.

A PEOPLE & A NATION

Reconstruction: An Unfinished Revolution
1865-1877

The lower half of the city of Charleston, South Carolina, the seedbed of secession, lay in ruin when most of the white population evacuated on February 18, 1865. A prolonged bombardment by Union batteries and gunboats around Charleston harbor had already destroyed many of the lovely town homes of the low-country planters. Then, as the city was abandoned, fires broke out everywhere, ignited in bales of cotton left in huge stockpiles in public squares. To many observers the flames were the funeral pyres of a dying civilization.

Among the first Union troops to enter Charleston was the Twenty-first U.S. Colored Regiment, which received the surrender of the city from its mayor. For black Charlestonians, most of whom were former slaves, this was a time of celebration. In symbolic ceremonies they proclaimed their freedom and announced their rebirth. Whatever the postwar order would bring, the freedpeople of Charleston converted Confederate ruin into a vision of Reconstruction based on Union victory and black liberation.

Still, in Charleston as elsewhere, death demanded attention. During the final year of the war, the Confederates had converted the planters' Race Course, a horseracing track, and its famed Jockey Club, into a prison. Union soldiers were kept in terrible conditions in the interior of the track, without shelter. The 257 who died there of exposure and disease were buried in a mass grave behind the judges' stand. After the fall of the city, Charleston's blacks organized to create a proper burial ground for the Union dead. During April, more than twenty black workmen reinterred the dead in marked graves and built a high fence around the cemetery. On the archway over the cemetery's entrance they painted the inscription "Martyrs of the Race Course."

◀ "Entrance of the 55th Massachusetts (Colored) Regiment into Charleston, S. C., February 21, 1865." Thomas Nast, pencil, oil, and wash on board, 1865. Black troops celebrated as they marched into the Confederate stronghold, hoisting their caps on their bayonets, and singing "John Brown's Body" as they marched up Meeting Street, Charleston's main thoroughfare. *(Museum of Fine Arts, Boston)*

CHRONOLOGY

1865 ■ Johnson begins rapid and lenient Reconstruction
- ■ White southern governments pass restrictive black codes
- ■ Congress refuses to seat southern representatives
- ■ Thirteenth Amendment ratified, abolishing slavery

1866 ■ Congress passes Civil Rights Act and renewal of Freedmen's Bureau over Johnson's veto
- ■ Congress approves Fourteenth Amendment
- ■ In *Ex parte Milligan* the Supreme Court reasserts its influence

1867 ■ Congress passes First Reconstruction Act and Tenure of Office Act
- ■ Constitutional conventions called in southern states

1868 ■ House impeaches and Senate acquits Johnson
- ■ Most southern states readmitted to Union under Radical plan
- ■ Fourteenth Amendment ratified
- ■ Grant elected president

1869 ■ Congress approves Fifteenth Amendment (ratified in 1870)

1871 ■ Congress passes second Enforcement Act and Ku Klux Klan Act
- ■ Treaty with England settles *Alabama* claims

1872 ■ Amnesty Act frees almost all remaining Confederates from restrictions on holding office
- ■ Grant reelected

1873 ■ *Slaughter-House* cases limit power of Fourteenth Amendment
- ■ Panic of 1873 leads to widespread unemployment and labor strife

1874 ■ Democrats win majority in House of Representatives

1875 ■ Several Grant appointees indicted for corruption
- ■ Congress passes weak Civil Rights Act
- ■ Democratic Party increases control of southern states with white supremacy campaigns

1876 ■ *U.S. v. Cruikshank* further weakens Fourteenth Amendment
- ■ Presidential election disputed

1877 ■ Congress elects Hayes president

And then they planned an extraordinary ceremony. On the morning of May 1, 1865, a procession of ten thousand people marched around the planters' Race Course, led by three thousand children carrying armloads of roses and singing "John Brown's Body." The children were followed by black women with baskets of flowers and wreaths, and then by black men. The parade concluded with members of black and white Union regiments, along with white missionaries and teachers led by James Redpath, the supervisor of freedmen's schools in the region. All who could fit assembled at the gravesite; five black ministers read from Scripture, and a black children's choir sang "America," "We'll Rally 'Round the Flag," "The Star-Spangled Banner," and Negro spirituals. When the ceremony ended, the huge crowd retired to the Race Course for speeches, picnics, and military festivities.

The war was over in Charleston, and "Decoration Day"—now Memorial Day, the day to remember the war dead and decorate their graves with flowers—had been founded by African Americans. Black people—by their labor, their words, their songs, and their marching feet on the old planters' Race Course—had created an American tradition. In their vision, they were creating the Independence Day of a Second American Revolution.

Reconstruction would bring revolutionary circumstances, but revolutions can also go backward. The Civil War and its aftermath wrought unprecedented changes in American society, law, and politics, but the underlying realities of economic power, racism, and judicial conservatism limited Reconstruction's revolutionary potential. As never before, the nation had to determine the nature of federal-state relations, whether confiscated land could be redistributed, and how to bring justice to both freedpeople and aggrieved white southerners whose property and lives had been devastated. Americans faced the harrowing challenge of psychological healing from a bloody and fratricidal war. How they would negotiate the tangled relationship between healing and justice would determine the extent of change during Reconstruction.

Nowhere was the turmoil of Reconstruction more evident than in national politics. Lincoln's successor, Andrew Johnson, fought bitterly with Congress over the shaping of Reconstruction policies. Although a southerner,

Johnson had always been a foe of the South's wealthy planters, and his first acts as president suggested that he would be tough on "traitors." Before the end of 1865, however, Johnson's policies changed direction, and he became the protector of southern interests. Jefferson Davis stayed in prison for two years, but Johnson quickly pardoned other rebel leaders and allowed them to occupy high offices. He also ordered the return of plantations to their original owners, including abandoned coastal lands of Georgia and South Carolina on which forty thousand freed men and women had settled early in 1865, by order of General William Tecumseh Sherman.

Johnson imagined a lenient and rapid "restoration" of the South to the Union rather than the fundamental "reconstruction" that Republican congressmen favored. Between 1866 and 1868, the president and the Republican leadership in Congress engaged in a bitter power struggle over how to put the United States back together again. Before the struggle ceased, Congress had impeached the president, enfranchised freedmen, and given them a role in reconstructing the South. The nation also adopted the Fourteenth and Fifteenth Amendments, ushering equal protection of the law, a definition of citizenship, and universal manhood suffrage into the Constitution. But little was done to open the doors of economic opportunity to black southerners, and the cause of equal rights for African Americans fell almost as fast as it had risen.

By 1869 the Ku Klux Klan employed extensive violence and terror to thwart Reconstruction and undermine black freedom. As white Democrats in the South took control of state governments, they encountered little opposition from the North. Moreover, the wartime industrial boom had created new opportunities and priorities. The West, with its seemingly limitless potential and its wars against Indians, drew American resources and consciousness like never before. Political corruption became a nationwide scandal, and bribery a way of doing business.

Thus Reconstruction became a revolution eclipsed. The white South's desire to reclaim control of its states and of race relations overwhelmed the national interest in stopping it. But Reconstruction left enduring legacies with which the nation has struggled ever since.

- Should the Reconstruction era be considered the Second American Revolution? By what criteria should we make such a judgment?
- What were the origins and meanings of the Fourteenth Amendment in the 1860s? What is its significance today?
- Reconstruction is judged to have "ended" in 1877. Over the course of the 1870s, what caused its end?

WARTIME RECONSTRUCTION

Civil wars leave immense challenges of healing, justice, and physical rebuilding. Anticipating that process, reconstruction of the Union was an issue as early as 1863, well before the war ended. Many key questions loomed on the horizon when and if the North succeeded on the battlefield: How would the nation be restored? How would southern states and leaders be treated—as errant brothers or as traitors? What was the constitutional basis for readmission of states to the Union, and where, if anywhere, could American statesmen look for precedence or guidance? More specifically, four vexing problems compelled early thinking and would haunt the Reconstruction era throughout. One, who would rule in the South once it was defeated? Two, who would rule in the federal government—Congress or the president? Three, what were the dimensions of black freedom, and what rights under law would the freedmen enjoy? And four, would Reconstruction be a preservation of the old republic or a second Revolution, a reinvention of a new republic?

Abraham Lincoln had never been anti-southern, though he had become the leader of an antislavery war.

Lincoln's 10 Percent Plan

He lost three brothers-in-law, killed in the war on the Confederate side. His worst fear was that the war would collapse at the end into guerrilla warfare across the South, with surviving bands of Confederates carrying on resistance. Lincoln insisted that his generals give lenient terms to southern soldiers once they surrendered. In his Second Inaugural Address, delivered only a month before his assassination, Lincoln promised "malice toward none; with charity for all," as Americans strove to "bind up the nation's wounds."

Lincoln planned early for a swift and moderate Reconstruction process. In his "Proclamation of Amnesty and Reconstruction," issued in December 1863, he proposed to replace majority rule with "loyal rule" as a means of reconstructing southern state governments. He proposed pardons to all ex-Confederates except the highest-ranking military and civilian officers. Then, as soon as 10 percent of the voting population in the 1860 general election in a given state had taken an oath to the United States and established a government, the new state would be recognized. Lincoln did not consult Congress in these plans, and "loyal" assemblies (known as "Lincoln governments") were created in Louisiana, Tennessee, and Arkansas in 1864, states largely occupied by Union troops. These governments were weak and dependent on northern armies for survival.

Congress responded with great hostility to Lincoln's moves to readmit southern states in what seemed such a premature manner. Many Radical Republicans, strong proponents of emancipation and of aggressive prosecution of the war against the South, considered the 10 percent plan a "mere mockery" of democracy. Led by Thaddeus Stevens of Pennsylvania in the House and Charles Sumner of Massachusetts in the Senate, congressional Republicans locked horns with Lincoln and proposed a longer and harsher approach to Reconstruction. Stevens advocated a "conquered provinces" theory, arguing that southerners had organized as a foreign nation to make war on the United States and, by secession, had destroyed their status as states. They therefore must be treated as "conquered foreign lands" and returned to the status of "unorganized territories" before any process of readmission could be entertained by Congress.

Congress and the Wade-Davis Bill

In July 1864, the Wade-Davis bill, named for its sponsors, Senator Benjamin Wade of Ohio and Congressman Henry W. Davis of Maryland, emerged from Congress with three specific conditions for southern readmission.

1. It demanded a "majority" of white male citizens participating in the creation of a new government.
2. To vote or be a delegate to constitutional conventions, men had to take an "iron-clad" oath (declaring that they had never aided the Confederate war effort).
3. All officers above the rank of lieutenant, and all civil officials in the Confederacy, would be disfranchised and deemed "not a citizen of the United States."

The Confederate states were to be defined as "conquered enemies," said Davis, and the process of readmission was to be harsh and slow. Lincoln, ever the adroit politician, pocket-vetoed the bill and issued a conciliatory proclamation of his own, announcing that he would not be inflexibly committed to any "one plan" of Reconstruction. This exchange came during Grant's bloody campaign against Lee in Virginia, when the outcome of the war and Lincoln's reelection were still in doubt. On August 5, Radical Republicans issued the "Wade-Davis Manifesto" to newspapers. An unprecedented attack on a sitting president by members of his own party, it accused Lincoln of usurpation of presidential powers and disgraceful leniency toward an eventually conquered South. What emerged in 1864–1865 was a clear debate and a potential constitutional crisis. Lincoln saw Reconstruction as a means of weakening the Confederacy and winning the war; the Radicals saw it as a longer-term transformation of the political and racial order of the country.

In early 1865, Congress and Lincoln joined in two important measures that recognized slavery's centrality to the war. On January 31, with strong administration backing, Congress passed the Thirteenth Amendment, which had two provisions: first, it abolished involuntary servitude everywhere in the United States; second, it declared that Congress shall have the power to enforce this outcome by "appropriate legislation." When the measure passed by 119 to 56, a mere 2 votes more than the necessary two-thirds, rejoicing broke out in Congress. A Republican recorded in his diary, "Members joined in the shouting and kept it up for some minutes. Some embraced one another, others wept like children. I have felt ever since the vote, as if I were in a new country."

Thirteenth Amendment

But the Thirteenth Amendment had emerged from a long congressional debate and considerable petitioning and public advocacy. One of the first and most remarkable petitions for a constitutional amendment abolishing slavery was submitted early in 1864 by Elizabeth Cady Stanton, Susan B. Anthony, and the Women's Loyal National League. Women throughout the Union accumulated thousands of signatures, even venturing into staunchly pro-Confederate regions of Kentucky and Missouri to secure supporters. It was a long road from the Emancipation Proclamation to the Thirteenth Amendment—through treacherous constitutional theory about individual "property rights," a bedrock of belief that the sacred document ought never to be altered, and partisan politics. But the logic of winning the war by crushing slavery, and of securing a new beginning under law for the nation that so many had died to save, won the day.

Potentially as significant, on March 3, 1865, Congress created the Bureau of Refugees, Freedmen, and Abandoned Lands—the Freedmen's Bureau, an unprecedented agency of social uplift necessitated by the ravages of the war. Americans had never engaged in federal aid to cit-

Freedmen's Bureau

izens on such a scale. With thousands of refugees, white and black, displaced in the South, the government continued what private freedmen's aid societies had started as early as 1862. In the mere four years of its existence, the Freedmen's Bureau supplied food and medical services, built several thousand schools and some colleges, negotiated several hundred thousand employment contracts between freedmen and their former masters, and tried to manage confiscated land.

The Bureau would be a controversial aspect of Reconstruction—within the South, where whites generally hated it, and within the federal government, where politicians divided over its constitutionality. Some Bureau agents were devoted to freedmen's rights, whereas others were opportunists who exploited the chaos of the postwar South. The war had forced into the open an eternal question of republics: what are the social welfare obligations of the state toward its people, and what do people owe their governments in return? Apart from their conquest and displacement of the eastern Indians, Americans were relatively inexperienced at the Freedmen's Bureau's task—social reform through military occupation.

In 1865, due to the devastation of the war, America was now a land with ruins. Like the countries of Europe, it now seemed an older, more historic landscape. It had torn itself

Ruins and Enmity

asunder—physically, politically, spiritually. Some of its cities lay in rubble, large stretches of the southern countryside were depopulated and defoliated, and thousands of people, white and black, were refugees. Some of this would in time seem romantic to northern travelers in the postwar South.

Thousands of yeoman farmer-soldiers, some paroled by surrenders and others who had abandoned Confederate ranks earlier, walked home too late in the season to plant a crop in a collapsed economy. Many white refugees faced genuine starvation. Of the approximately 18,300,000 rations distributed across the South in the first three years of the Freedmen's Bureau, 5,230,000 went to whites. In early 1866, in a proud agricultural society, the legislature of South Carolina issued $300,000 in state bonds to purchase corn for the destitute.

In October 1865, just after a five-month imprisonment in Boston, former Confederate Vice President Alexander H. Stephens rode a slow train southward. In Virginia he found "the desolation of the country . . . was horrible to behold." When Stephens reached northern Georgia, his native state, his shock ran over: "War has left a terrible impression. . . . Fences gone, fields all a-waste, houses burnt." A northern journalist visiting Richmond that same fall observed a city "mourning for her sins . . . in dust and ashes." The "burnt district" was a "bed of cinders . . . broken and blackened walls, impassable streets deluged with debris." Above all, every northern traveler encountered a wall of hatred among white southerners for their conquerors. An innkeeper in North Carolina told a journalist that Yankees had killed his sons in the war, burned his house, and stolen his slaves. "They left me one inestimable privilege," he said, "to hate 'em. I git up at half-past four in the morning, and sit up 'til twelve at night, to hate 'em."

THE MEANINGS OF FREEDOM

Black southerners entered into life after slavery with hope and circumspection. A Texas man recalled his father's telling him, even before the war was over, "Our forever was going to be spent living among the Southerners, after they got licked." Freed men and women tried to gain as much as they could from their new circumstances. Often the changes they valued the most were personal—alterations in location, employer, or living arrangements.

For America's former slaves, Reconstruction had one paramount meaning: a chance to explore freedom. A southern white woman admitted in her diary that the black people

The Feel of Freedom

"showed a natural and exultant joy at being free." Former slaves remembered singing far into the night after federal troops, who confirmed rumors of their emancipation, reached their plantations. The slaves on a Texas plantation shouted for joy, their leader proclaiming, "We is free—no more whippings and beatings." A few people gave in to the natural desire to do what had been impossible before. One angry grandmother dropped her hoe and ran to confront her mistress. "I'm free!" she yelled. "Yes, I'm free! Ain't got to work for you no more! You can't put me in your pocket now!" Another man recalled that he and others "started on the move," either to search for family members or just to exercise the human right of mobility.

Many freed men and women reacted more cautiously and shrewdly, taking care to test the boundaries of their new condition. "After the war was over," explained one man, "we was afraid to move. Just like terrapins or turtles after emancipation. Just stick our heads out to see how the land lay." As slaves they had learned to expect hostility from white people, and they did not presume it would instantly disappear. Life in freedom might still be a matter of what was possible, not what was right. Many freedpeople evaluated potential employers with shrewd caution.

▲ *The Armed Slave,* William Sprang, oil on canvas, c. 1865. This remarkable painting depicts an African American veteran soldier, musket with fixed bayonet leaning against the wall, cigar in hand indicating a new life of safety and leisure, reading a book to demonstrate his embrace of education and freedom. The man's visage leaves the impression of satisfaction and dignity. *(The Civil War Library and Museum, Philadelphia)*

that continued to appear in black newspapers well into the 1880s, some succeeded in their quest, while others searched in vain.

Husbands and wives who had belonged to different masters established homes together for the first time, and, as they had tried under slavery, parents asserted the right to raise their own children. A mother bristled when her old master claimed a right to whip her children. She informed him that "he warn't goin' to brush none of her chilluns no more." The freed men and women were too much at risk to act recklessly, but, as one man put it, they were tired of punishment and "sure didn't take no more foolishment off of white folks."

Many black people wanted to minimize contact with whites because, as Reverend Garrison Frazier told General

Blacks' Search for Independence

Sherman in January 1865, "There is a prejudice against us . . . that will take years to get over." To avoid contact with overbearing whites who were used to supervising them, blacks abandoned the slave quarters and fanned out to distant corners of the land they worked. "After the war my stepfather come," recalled Annie Young, "and got my mother and we moved out in the piney woods." Others described moving "across the creek" or building a "saplin house . . . back in the woods." Some rural dwellers established small, all-black settlements that still exist along the back roads of the South.

Even once-privileged slaves desired such independence and social separation. One man turned down his master's offer of the overseer's house and moved instead to a shack in "Freetown." He also declined to let the former owner grind his grain for free because it "make him feel like a free man to pay for things just like anyone else."

In addition to a fair employer, what freed men and women most wanted was the ownership of land. Land

Freedpeople's Desire for Land

represented self-sufficiency and a chance to gain compensation for generations of bondage. General Sherman's special Field Order Number 15, issued in February 1865, set aside 400,000 acres of land in the Sea Islands region for the exclusive settlement of freedpeople. Hope swelled among ex-slaves as forty-acre plots, mules, and "possessary titles" were promised to them. But President Johnson ordered them removed in October and the land returned to its original owners under army enforcement. A northern observer noted that slaves freed in the Sea Islands of South Carolina and Georgia made "plain, straight-forward" inquiries as they settled on new land. They wanted to be

"Most all the Negroes that had good owners stayed with 'em, but the others left. Some of 'em come back and some didn't," explained one man. After considerable wandering in search of better circumstances, a majority of blacks eventually settled as agricultural workers back on their former farms or plantations. But they relocated their houses and did their utmost to control the conditions of their labor.

Throughout the South, former slaves devoted themselves to reuniting their families, separated during slavery by sale or hardship, and during

Reunion of African American Families

the war by dislocation and the emancipation process. With only shreds of information to guide them, thousands of freedpeople embarked on odysseys in search of a husband, wife, child, or parent. By relying on the black community for help and information, and by placing ads sure the land "would be theirs after they had improved it." Everywhere, blacks young and old thirsted for homes of their own.

But most members of both political parties opposed genuine land redistribution to the freedmen. Even northern reformers who had administered the Sea Islands during the war showed little sympathy for black aspirations. The former Sea Island slaves wanted to establish small, self-sufficient farms. Northern soldiers, officials, and missionaries of both races brought education and aid to the freedmen but also insisted that they grow cotton. They emphasized profit, cash crops, and the values of competitive capitalism.

"The Yankees preach nothing but cotton, cotton!" complained one Sea Island black. "We wants land," wrote another, but tax officials "make the lots too big, and cut we out." Indeed, the U.S. government eventually sold thousands of acres in the Sea Islands, 90 percent of which went to wealthy investors from the North. At a protest against evictions from a contraband camp in Virginia in 1866, freedman Bayley Wyatt made black desires and claims clear: "We has a right to the land where we are located. For why? I tell you. Our wives, our children, our husbands, has been sold over and over again to purchase the lands we now locates upon; for that reason we have a divine right to the land."

Ex-slaves everywhere reached out for education. Blacks of all ages hungered for the knowledge in books that had been permitted only to whites. With freedom, they started schools and filled classrooms both day and night. On log seats and dirt floors, freed men and women studied their letters in old almanacs and in discarded dictionaries. Young children brought infants to school with them, and adults attended at night or after "the crops were laid by." Many a teacher had "to make herself heard over three other classes reciting in concert" in a small room. The desire to escape slavery's ignorance was so great that, despite their poverty, many blacks paid tuition, typically $1 or $1.50 a month. These small amounts constituted major portions of a person's agricultural wages and added up to more than $1 million by 1870.

The federal government and northern reformers of both races assisted this pursuit of education. In its brief life the Freedmen's Bureau founded over four thousand schools, and idealistic men and women from the North established others funded by private northern philanthropy. The Yankee schoolmarm—dedicated, selfless, and religious—became an agent of progress in many southern

Black Embrace of Education

▲ African Americans of all ages eagerly pursued the opportunity to gain an education in freedom. This young woman in Mt. Meigs, Alabama, is helping her mother learn to read.
(Smithsonian Institution, photo by Rudolf Eickemeyer)

communities. Thus did African Americans seek a break from their past through learning. More than 600,000 were enrolled in elementary school by 1877.

Blacks and their white allies also saw the need for colleges and universities to train teachers, ministers, and professionals for leadership. The American Missionary Association founded seven colleges, including Fisk and Atlanta Universities, between 1866 and 1869. The Freedmen's Bureau helped to establish Howard University in Washington, D.C., and northern religious groups, such as the Methodists, Baptists, and Congregationalists, supported dozens of seminaries and teachers' colleges.

During Reconstruction, African American leaders often were highly educated individuals; many were from the prewar elite of free people of color. Francis Cardozo, who held various offices in South Carolina, had attended universities in Scotland and England. P. B. S. Pinchback, who became lieutenant governor of Louisiana, was the son of a planter who had sent him to school in Cincinnati. Both of the two black senators from Mississippi, Blanche K. Bruce and Hiram Revels, possessed privileged educations. Bruce was the son of a planter who had provided tutoring at home; Revels was the son of free North Carolina blacks who had sent him to Knox College in Illinois. These men and many self-educated former slaves brought to political office not only fervor but education.

Freed from the restrictions and regulations of slavery, blacks could build their own institutions as they saw

Growth of Black Churches

fit. The secret churches of slavery came into the open; in countless communities throughout the South, ex-slaves "started a brush arbor." A brush arbor was merely "a sort of . . . shelter with leaves for a roof," but the freed men and women worshiped in it enthusiastically. "Preachin' and shouting sometimes lasted all day," they recalled, for the opportunity to worship together freely meant "glorious times."

Within a few years, independent branches of the Methodist and Baptist denominations had attracted the great majority of black Christians in the South. By 1877 in South Carolina alone, the African Methodist Episcopal (A.M.E.) Church had 1,000 ministers, 44,000 members, and its own school of theology, while the A.M.E. Zion Church had 45,000 members. In the rapid growth of churches, some of which became the wealthiest and most autonomous institutions in black life, the freedpeople demonstrated their most secure claim on freedom and created enduring communities.

► Churches became a center of African American life, both social and political, during and after Reconstruction. Churches large and small, like this one, Faith Memorial Church in Hagley Landing, South Carolina, became the first black-owned institutions for the postfreedom generation.

(Aunt Phebe, Uncle Tom and Others: Character Studies Among the Old Slaves of the South Fifty Years After by Essie Collins Matthews)

The desire to gain as much independence as possible also shaped the former slaves' economic arrangements.

Rise of the Sharecropping System

Since most of them lacked money to buy land, they preferred the next best thing: renting the land they worked. But the South had a cash-poor economy with few sources of credit, and few whites would consider renting land to blacks. Most blacks had no means to get cash before the harvest, so other alternatives had to be tried.

Black farmers and white landowners therefore turned to sharecropping, a system in which farmers kept part of their crop and gave the rest to the landowner while living on his property. The landlord or a merchant "furnished" food and supplies, such as draft animals and seed, needed before the harvest, and he received payment from the crop. Although landowners tried to set the laborers' share at a low level, black farmers had some bargaining power, at least at first. Sharecroppers would hold out, or move and

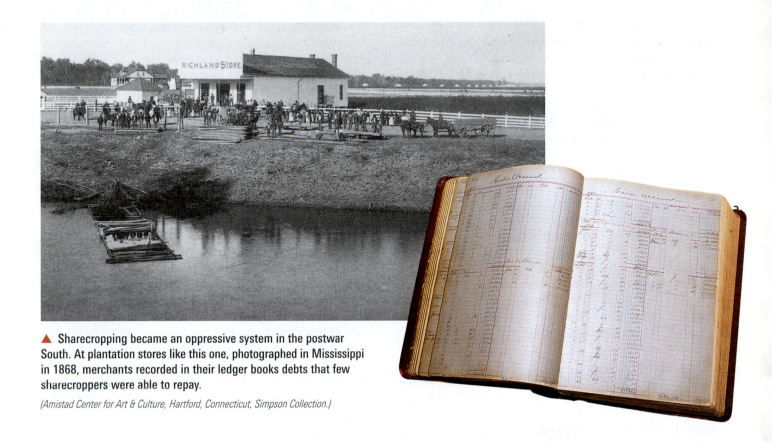

▲ Sharecropping became an oppressive system in the postwar South. At plantation stores like this one, photographed in Mississippi in 1868, merchants recorded in their ledger books debts that few sharecroppers were able to repay.

(Amistad Center for Art & Culture, Hartford, Connecticut, Simpson Collection.)

try to switch employers from one year to another. As the system matured during the 1870s and 1880s, most share-croppers worked "on halves"—half for the owner and half for themselves.

The sharecropping system, which materialized as early as 1868 in parts of the South, originated as a desirable compromise between former slaves and white landown-ers. It eased landowners' problems with cash and credit, and provided them a permanent, dependent labor force; blacks accepted it because it gave them freedom from daily supervision. Instead of working in the hated gangs under a white overseer, as in slavery, they farmed their own plots of land in family groups. But sharecropping later proved to be a disaster. Owners and merchants developed a monopoly of control over the agricultural economy, as sharecroppers found themselves riveted in ever-increasing debt (see page 576).

The fundamental problem, however, was that southern farmers as a whole still concentrated on cotton. In free-dom, black women often chose to stay away from the fields and cotton picking, to concentrate on domestic chores. Given the diminishing incentives of the system, they placed greater value on independent choices about gender roles and family organization than on reaching higher levels of production. By 1878 the South had recovered its prewar share of British cotton purchases. But even as southerners grew more cotton than ever, their reward diminished. Cot-ton prices began a long decline, as world demand fell off.

Thus southern agriculture slipped deeper and deeper into depression. Black sharecroppers struggled under a growing burden of debt which reduced their independence and bound them to landowners and to furnishing mer-chants almost as oppressively as slavery had bound them to their masters. Many white farmers became debtors, too; gradually lost their land; and joined the ranks of share-croppers. By the end of Reconstruction, over one-third of all southern farms were worked by sharecropping ten-ants, white and black. This economic transformation took place as the nation struggled to put its political house back in order.

JOHNSON'S RECONSTRUCTION PLAN

When Reconstruction began under President Andrew Johnson, many expected his policies to be harsh. Throughout his career in Tennessee he had criticized the wealthy planters and championed the small farmers.

When an assassin's bullet thrust Johnson into the presidency, many former slaveowners shared the dismay of a North Carolina woman who wrote, "Think of Andy Johnson [as] the president! What will become of us—'the aristocrats of the South' as we are termed?" Northern Radicals also had reason to believe that Johnson would deal sternly with the South. When one of them suggested the exile or execution of ten or twelve leading rebels to set an example, Johnson replied, "How are you going to pick out so small a number? . . . Treason is a crime; and crime must be punished."

Like his martyred predecessor, Johnson followed a path in antebellum politics from obscurity to power. With

Andrew Johnson of Tennessee

no formal education, he became a tailor's apprentice. But from 1829, while in his early twenties, he held nearly every office in Tennessee politics: alderman, state representative, congressman, two terms as governor, and U.S. senator by 1857. Although elected as a southern Democrat, Johnson

▲ Combative and inflexible, President Andrew Johnson contributed greatly to the failure of his own Reconstruction program.

(Library of Congress)

was the only senator from a seceded state who refused to follow his state out of the Union. Lincoln appointed him war governor of Tennessee in 1862; hence his symbolic place on the ticket in the president's bid for reelection in 1864.

Although a Unionist, Johnson's political beliefs made him an old Jacksonian Democrat. And, as they said in the mountainous region of east Tennessee, where Johnson established a reputation as a stump speaker, "Old Andy never went back on his 'raisin'." Johnson was also an ardent states' rightist. Before the war, he had supported tax-funded public schools and homestead legislation, fashioning himself as a champion of the common man. Although he vehemently opposed secession, Johnson advocated limited government. He shared none of the Radicals' expansive conception of federal power. His philosophy toward Reconstruction may be summed up in the slogan he adopted: "The Constitution as it is, and the Union as it was."

Through 1865 Johnson alone controlled Reconstruction policy, for Congress recessed shortly before he became president and did not reconvene until December. In the following eight months, Johnson formed new state governments in the South by using his power to grant pardons. He advanced Lincoln's leniency by extending even easier terms to former Confederates.

Johnson had owned house slaves, although he had never been a planter. He accepted emancipation as a result

Johnson's Racial Views

of the war, but he did not favor black civil and political rights. Johnson believed that black suffrage could never be imposed on a southern state by the federal government, and that set him on a collision course with the Radicals. When it came to race, Johnson was a thorough-going white supremacist. He held what one politician called "unconquerable prejudices against the African race." In perhaps the most blatantly racist official statement ever delivered by an American president, Johnson declared in his annual message of 1867 that blacks possessed less "capacity for government than any other race of people. No independent government of any form has ever been successful in their hands; . . . wherever they have been left to their own devices they have shown a constant tendency to relapse into barbarism."

Such racial views had an enduring effect on Johnson's policies. Where whites were concerned, however, Johnson seemed to be pursuing changes in class relations. He proposed rules that would keep the wealthy planter class at least temporarily out of power.

White southerners were required to swear an oath of loyalty as a condition of gaining amnesty or pardon, but

Johnson's Pardon Policy

Johnson barred several categories of people from taking the oath: former federal officials, high-ranking Confederate officers, and political leaders or graduates of West Point or Annapolis who joined the Confederacy. To this list Johnson added another important group: all ex-Confederates whose taxable property was worth more than $20,000. These individuals had to apply personally to the president for pardon and restoration of their political rights. The president, it seemed, meant to take revenge on the old planter elite and thereby promote a new leadership of deserving yeomen.

Johnson appointed provisional governors, who began the Reconstruction process by calling state constitutional conventions. The delegates chosen for these conventions had to draft new constitutions that eliminated slavery and invalidated secession. After ratification of these constitutions, new governments could be elected, and the states would be restored to the Union with full congressional representation. But only those southerners who had taken the oath of amnesty and had been eligible to vote on the day the state seceded could participate in this process. Thus unpardoned whites and former slaves were not eligible.

If Johnson intended to strip former aristocrats of their power, he did not hold to his plan. The old white

Presidential Reconstruction

leadership proved resilient and influential; prominent Confederates won elections and turned up in various appointive offices. Then Johnson started pardoning planters and leading rebels. He hired additional clerks to prepare the necessary documents and then began to issue pardons to large categories of people. By September 1865, hundreds were being issued in a single day. These pardons, plus the rapid return of planters' abandoned lands, restored the old elite to power and quickly gave Johnson an image as the South's champion.

Why did Johnson allow the planters to regain power? Personal vanity may have played a role, as he turned proud planters into pardon seekers. He was also determined to achieve a rapid Reconstruction in order to deny the Radicals any opportunity for the more thorough racial and political changes they desired in the South. And Johnson needed southern support in the 1866 elections; hence, he declared Reconstruction complete only eight months after Appomattox. Thus, in December 1865, many Confederate congressmen traveled to Washington to claim seats in the U.S. Congress. Even Alexander Stephens, vice president of the Confederacy, returned to Capitol Hill as a senator-elect from Georgia.

The election of such prominent rebels troubled many northerners. Some of the state conventions were slow to repudiate secession; others admitted only grudgingly that slavery was dead and wrote new laws to show it.

Furthermore, to define the status of freed men and women and control their labor, some legislatures merely revised large sections of the slave

Black Codes

codes by substituting the word *freedmen* for *slaves*. The new black codes compelled former slaves to carry passes, observe a curfew, live in housing provided by a landowner, and give up hope of entering many desirable occupations. Stiff vagrancy laws and restrictive labor contracts bound freedpeople to plantations, and "anti-enticement" laws punished anyone who tried to lure these workers to other employment. State-supported schools and orphanages excluded blacks entirely.

It seemed to northerners that the South was intent on returning African Americans to servility and that Johnson's Reconstruction policy held no one responsible for the terrible war. But memories of the war—not yet even a year over—were still raw and would dominate political behavior for several elections to come. Thus the Republican majority in Congress decided to call a halt to the results of Johnson's plan. On reconvening, the House and Senate considered the credentials of the newly elected southern representatives and decided not to admit them. Instead, they bluntly challenged the president's authority and established a joint committee to study and investigate a new direction for Reconstruction.

THE CONGRESSIONAL RECONSTRUCTION PLAN

Northern congressmen were hardly unified, but they did not doubt their right to shape Reconstruction policy. The Constitution mentioned neither secession nor reunion, but it gave Congress the primary role in the admission of states. Moreover, the Constitution declared that the United States shall guarantee to each state a "republican form of government." This provision, legislators believed, gave them the authority to devise policies for Reconstruction.

They soon found that other constitutional questions affected their policies. What, for example, had rebellion done to the relationship between southern states and the Union? Lincoln had always believed secession impossible—the Confederate states had engaged in an "insurrection" within the Union in his view. Congressmen who favored vigorous Reconstruction measures argued that the war had broken the Union and that the South was subject to the victor's will. Moderate congressmen held that the states had forfeited their rights through rebellion and thus had come under congressional supervision.

These theories mirrored the diversity of Congress itself. Northern Democrats, weakened by their opposition to the war in its final year, denounced any idea of racial equality and supported Johnson's policies. Conservative Republicans, despite their party loyalty, favored a limited federal role in Reconstruction. The Radical Republicans, led by Thaddeus Stevens, Charles Sumner, and George Julian, wanted to transform the South. Although a minority in their party, they had the advantage of clearly defined goals. They believed it was essential to democratize the South, establish public education, and ensure the rights of the freedpeople. They favored black suffrage, supported some land confiscation and redistribution, and were willing to exclude the South from the Union for several years if necessary to achieve their goals.

The Radicals

Born of the war and its outcome, the Radicals brought a new civic vision to American life; they wanted to create an activist federal government and the beginnings of racial equality. A large group of moderate Republicans, led by Lyman Trumbull, opposed Johnson's leniency but wanted to restrain the Radicals. Trumbull and the moderates were, however, committed to federalizing the enforcement of civil, if not political, rights for the freedmen.

One overwhelming political reality faced all four groups: the 1866 elections. Ironically, Johnson and the Democrats sabotaged the possibility of a conservative coalition. They refused to cooperate with conservative or moderate Republicans and insisted that Reconstruction was over, that the new state governments were legitimate, and that southern representatives should be admitted to Congress. Among the Republicans, the Radicals' influence grew in proportion to Johnson's intransigence and outright provocation.

Trying to work with Johnson, Republicans believed a compromise had been reached in the spring of 1866. Under its terms Johnson would agree to two modifications of his program: extension of the Freedmen's Bureau for another year and passage of a civil rights bill to counteract the black codes. This bill would force southern courts to practice equality under the ultimate scrutiny of the federal judiciary. Its provisions applied to public, not private, acts of discrimination. The Civil Rights Bill of 1866 was the first statutory definition of the rights of American citizens and is still on the books today.

Congress Versus Johnson

Johnson destroyed the compromise, however, by vetoing both bills (they later became law when Congress overrode the president's veto). Denouncing any change in his program, the president condemned Congress's action and

▲ The Memphis race riots during Reconstruction. Unarmed blacks are gunned down by well-armed whites in this scene, reinforced by a Congressional investigation. *(Library of Congress)*

revealed his own racism. Because the civil rights bill defined U.S. citizens as native-born persons who were taxed, Johnson claimed that it discriminated against "large numbers of intelligent, worthy, and patriotic foreigners . . . in favor of the negro." The bill, he said, operated "in favor of the colored and against the white race."

All hope of presidential-congressional cooperation was now dead. In 1866 newspapers reported daily violations of blacks' rights in the South and carried alarming accounts of antiblack violence—notably in Memphis and New Orleans, where police aided brutal mobs in their attacks. In Memphis, forty blacks were killed and twelve schools burned by white mobs, and in New Orleans, the toll was thirty-four African Americans dead and two hundred wounded. Such violence convinced Republicans, and the northern public, that more needed to be done. A new Republican plan took the form of the Fourteenth Amendment to the Constitution.

Of the five sections of the Fourteenth Amendment, the first would have the greatest legal significance in later

Fourteenth Amendment

years. It conferred citizenship on "all persons born or naturalized in the United States" and prohibited states from abridging their constitutional "privileges and immunities" (see the Appendix for the Constitution and all amendments). It also barred any state from taking a person's life, liberty, or property "without due process of law" and from denying "equal protection of the laws." These resounding phrases have become powerful guarantees of African Americans' civil rights—indeed, of the rights of all citizens, except for Indians, who were not granted citizenship rights until 1924.

Nearly universal agreement emerged among Republicans on the amendment's second and third sections. The fourth declared the Confederate debt null and void, and guaranteed the war debt of the United States. Northerners rejected the notion of paying taxes to reimburse those who had financed a rebellion, and business groups agreed on the necessity of upholding the credit of the U.S. government. The second and third sections barred Confederate leaders from holding state and federal office. Only Congress, by a two-thirds vote of each house, could remove the penalty. The amendment thus guaranteed a degree of punishment for the leaders of the Confederacy.

The second section of the amendment also dealt with representation and embodied the compromises that produced the document. Northerners disagreed about whether blacks should have the right to vote. As a citizen of Indiana wrote to a southern relative, "Although there is a great deal [of] profession among us for the relief of the darkey yet I think much of it is far from being cincere. I guess we

want to compell you to do right by them while we are not willing ourselves to do so." Those arched words are indicative not only of how revolutionary Reconstruction had become, but also of how far the public will, North and South, lagged behind the enactments that became new constitutional cornerstones. Many northern states still maintained black disfranchisement laws during Reconstruction.

Emancipation finally ended the three-fifths clause for the purpose of counting blacks, which would increase southern representation. Thus the postwar South stood to gain power in Congress, and if white southerners did not allow blacks to vote, former secessionists would derive the political benefit from emancipation. That was more irony than most northerners could bear. So Republicans determined that, if a southern state did not grant black men the vote, their representation would be reduced proportionally. If they did enfranchise black men, their representation would be increased proportionally. This compromise avoided a direct enactment of black suffrage but would deliver future black southern voters to the Republican Party.

The Fourteenth Amendment specified for the first time that voters were "male" and ignored female citizens, black and white. For this reason it provoked a strong reaction from the women's rights movement. Advocates of women's equality had worked with abolitionists for decades, often subordinating their cause to that of the slaves. During the drafting of the Fourteenth Amendment, however, female activists demanded to be heard. Prominent leaders, such as Elizabeth Cady Stanton and Susan B. Anthony, ended their alliance with abolitionists and fought for women, while others remained committed to the idea that it was "the Negro's hour." Thus the amendment infused new life into the women's rights movement and caused considerable strife among old allies. Many male former abolitionists, white and black, were willing to delay the day of woman suffrage in favor of securing freedmen the right to vote in the South.

In 1866, however, the major question in Reconstruction politics was how the public would respond to the

The South's and Johnson's Defiance

congressional initiative. Johnson did his best to block the Fourteenth Amendment in both North and South. Condemning Congress for its refusal to seat southern representatives, the president urged state legislatures in the South to vote against ratification. Every southern legislature except Tennessee's rejected the amendment by a wide margin.

To present his case to northerners, Johnson organized a National Union Convention and took to the stump himself. In an age when active personal campaigning was rare for a president, Johnson boarded a special train for a "swing around the circle" that carried his message into the Northeast, the Midwest, and then back to Washington. In city after city, he criticized the Republicans in a ranting, undignified style. Increasingly, audiences rejected his views, hooting and jeering at him. In this whistle-stop tour, Johnson began to hand out American flags with thirty-six rather than twenty-five stars, declaring the Union already restored. At many towns he likened himself to a "persecuted" Jesus who might now be martyred "upon the cross" for his magnanimity toward the South. And, repeatedly, he labeled the Radicals "traitors" for their efforts to take over Reconstruction.

The elections of 1866 were a resounding victory for Republicans in Congress. Radicals and moderates whom Johnson had denounced won reelection by large margins, and the Republican majority grew to two-thirds of both houses of Congress. The North had spoken clearly: Johnson's official policies of states' rights and white supremacy were prematurely giving the advantage to rebels and traitors. Although the Radicals may have been out ahead

of public opinion, most northerners feared Johnson's approach more. Thus Republican congressional leaders won a mandate to pursue their Reconstruction plan.

But Johnson and southern intransigence had brought the plan to an impasse. Nothing could be accomplished as long as the "Johnson governments" existed and the southern electorate remained exclusively white. Republicans resolved to form new state governments in the South and enfranchise the freedmen.

After some embittered debate in which Republicans and the remaining Democrats in Congress argued over the meaning and memory of the Civil War itself, the First Reconstruction Act passed in March 1867. This plan, under which the southern states were actually readmitted to the Union, incorporated only a part of the Radical program. Union generals, commanding small garrisons of troops and charged with supervising elections, assumed control in five military districts in the

Reconstruction Acts of 1867–1868

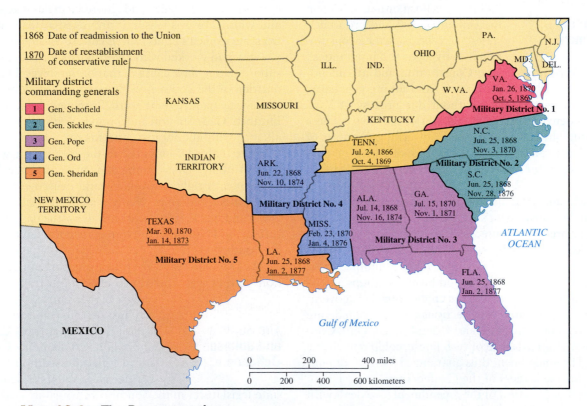

Map 16.1   The Reconstruction

This map shows the five military districts established when Congress passed the Reconstruction Act of 1867. As the dates within each state indicate, conservative Democratic forces quickly regained control of government in four southern states. So-called Radical Reconstruction was curtailed in most of the others, as factions within the weakened Republican Party began to cooperate with conservative Democrats.

South (see Map 16.1). Confederate leaders designated in the Fourteenth Amendment were barred from voting until new state constitutions were ratified. The act guaranteed freedmen the right to vote in elections for as well as serve in state constitutional conventions and in subsequent elections. In addition, each southern state was required to ratify the Fourteenth Amendment, to ratify its new constitution by majority vote, and to submit it to Congress for approval (see Table 16.1).

Thus African Americans gained an opportunity to fight for a better life through the political process, and ex-Confederates were given what they interpreted as a bitter pill to swallow in order to return to the Union. The Second, Third, and Fourth Reconstruction Acts, passed between March 1867 and March 1868, provided the details of operation for voter registration boards, the adoption of constitutions, and the administration of "good faith" oaths on the part of white southerners.

In the words of one historian, the Radicals succeeded in "clipping Johnson's wings." But they had hoped Congress could do much more. Thaddeus Stevens, for example, argued that economic opportunity was essential to the freedmen. "If we do not furnish them with homesteads from forfeited and rebel property," Stevens declared, "and hedge them around with protective laws . . . we had better left them in bondage." Stevens therefore drew up a plan for extensive confiscation and redistribution of land, but it was never realized.

Failure of Land Redistribution

Racial fears among whites and an American obsession with the sanctity of private property made land redistribution unpopular. Northerners were accustomed to a limited role for government, and the business community staunchly opposed any interference with private-property rights, even for former Confederates. Thus black farmers were forced to seek work in a hostile environment in which landowners opposed their acquisition of land.

Congress's quarrels with Andrew Johnson grew still worse. To restrict Johnson's influence and safeguard its plan, Congress passed a number of controversial laws. First, it limited Johnson's power over the army by requiring the president to issue military orders through the General of the Army, Ulysses S. Grant, who could not be dismissed without the Senate's consent. Then Congress passed the Tenure of Office Act, which gave the Senate power to approve changes in the president's cabinet. Designed to protect Secretary of War Stanton, who sympathized with the Radicals, this law violated the tradition that a president controlled appointments to his own cabinet.

Constitutional Crisis

All of these measures, as well as each of the Reconstruction Acts, were passed by a two-thirds override of presidential vetoes. The situation led some to believe that the federal government had reached a stage of "congressional tyranny" and others to conclude that Johnson had become an obstacle to the legitimate will of the people in reconstructing the nation on a just and permanent basis.

TABLE 16.1	Plans for Reconstruction Compared			
	Johnson's Plan	**Radicals' Plan**	**Fourteenth Amendment**	**Reconstruction Act of 1867**
Voting	Whites only; high-ranking Confederate leaders must seek pardons	Give vote to black males	Southern whites may decide but can lose representation if they deny black suffrage	Black men gain vote; whites barred from office by Fourteenth Amendment cannot vote while new state governments are being formed
Officeholding	Many prominent Confederates regain power	Only loyal white and black males eligible	Confederate leaders barred until Congress votes amnesty	Fourteenth Amendment in effect
Time out of Union	Brief	Several years; until South is thoroughly democratized	Brief	3–5 years after war
Other change in southern society	Little; gain of power by yeomen not realized; emancipation grudgingly accepted, but no black civil or political rights	Expand public education; confiscate land and provide farms for freedmen; expansion of activist federal government	Probably slight, depending on enforcement	Considerable, depending on action of new state governments

Johnson took several belligerent steps of his own. He issued orders to military commanders in the South, limiting their powers and increasing the powers of the civil governments he had created in 1865. Then he removed military officers who were conscientiously enforcing Congress's new law, preferring commanders who allowed disqualified Confederates to vote. Finally, he tried to remove Secretary of War Stanton. With that attempt the confrontation reached its climax.

Impeachment is a political procedure provided for in the Constitution as a remedy for crimes or serious abuses of power by presidents, federal judges, and other high government officials.

Impeachment of President Johnson

Those who are impeached (judged or politically indicted) in the House are then tried in the Senate. Historically, this power has generally not been used as a means to investigate and judge the private lives of presidents, although in recent times it was used in this manner in the case of President Bill Clinton.

Twice in 1867, the House Judiciary Committee had considered impeachment of Johnson, rejecting the idea once and then recommending it by only a 5-to-4 vote. That recommendation was decisively defeated by the House. After Johnson tried to remove Stanton, however, a third attempt to impeach the president carried easily in early 1868. The indictment concentrated on his violation of the Tenure of Office Act, though many modern scholars regard his efforts to obstruct enforcement of the Reconstruction Act of 1867 as a far more serious offense.

Johnson's trial in the Senate lasted more than three months. The prosecution, led by Radicals, attempted to prove that Johnson was guilty of "high crimes and misdemeanors." But they also argued that the trial was a means to judge Johnson's performance, not a judicial determination of guilt or innocence. The Senate ultimately rejected such reasoning, which could have made removal from office a political weapon against any chief executive who disagreed with Congress. Although a majority of senators voted to convict Johnson, the prosecution fell one vote short of the necessary two-thirds majority. Johnson remained in office, politically weakened and with less than a year left in his term. Some Republicans backed away from impeachment because they had their eyes on the 1868 election and did not want to hurt their prospects of regaining the White House.

In the 1868 presidential election, Ulysses S. Grant, running as a Republican, defeated Horatio Seymour, a New York Democrat. Grant was not a Radical, but his platform supported congressional Reconstruction and endorsed black suffrage in the South.

Election of 1868

▲ Thomas Waterman Wood, who had painted portraits of society figures in Nashville before the war, sensed the importance of Congress's decision in 1867 to enfranchise the freedmen. This oil painting, one in a series on suffrage, emphasizes the significance of the ballot for the black voter. *(Cheekwood Museum of Art, Nashville, Tennessee)*

(Significantly, Republicans stopped short of endorsing black suffrage in the North.) The Democrats, meanwhile, vigorously denounced Reconstruction and preached white supremacy. Indeed, in the 1868 election, the Democrats conducted the most openly racist campaign to that point in American history. Both sides waved the "bloody shirt," accusing each other as the villains of the war's sacrifices. By associating themselves with rebellion and with Johnson's repudiated program, the Democrats went down to defeat in all but eight states, though the popular vote was fairly close. Participating in their first presidential election ever on a wide scale, blacks decisively voted en masse for General Grant.

In office Grant acted as an administrator of Reconstruction but not as its enthusiastic advocate. He vacillated

▲ A Republican Party brass band in action during the 1868 election campaign in Baton Rouge, Louisiana. The Union regimental colors and soldiers' caps demonstrate the strong federal presence in the South at this pivotal moment in radical Reconstruction.

(Andrew D. Lytle Collection, Louisiana and Lower Mississippi Valley Collections, LSU Libraries, Louisiana State University, Baton Rouge, Louisiana.)

in his dealings with the southern states, sometimes defending Republican regimes and sometimes currying favor with Democrats. On occasion Grant called out federal troops to stop violence or enforce acts of Congress. But he never imposed a true military occupation on the South. Rapid demobilization had reduced a federal army of more than 1 million to 57,000 within a year of the surrender at Appomattox. Thereafter, the number of troops in the South continued to fall, until in 1874 there were only 4,000 in the southern states outside Texas. The later legend of "military rule," so important to southern claims of victimization during Reconstruction, was steeped in myth.

In 1869 the Radicals pushed through the Fifteenth Amendment, the final major measure in the constitutional revolution of Reconstruction. This measure forbade states to deny the right to vote "on account of race, color, or previous condition of servitude." Such wording did not guar-

Fifteenth Amendment

antee the right to vote. It deliberately left states free to restrict suffrage on other grounds so that northern states could continue to deny suffrage to women and certain groups of men—Chinese immigrants, illiterates, and those too poor to pay poll taxes.

Although several states outside the South refused to ratify, three-fourths of the states approved the measure, and the Fifteenth Amendment became law in 1870. It, too, had been a political compromise, and though African Americans rejoiced all across the land at its enactment, it left open the possibility for states to create countless qualification tests to obstruct voting in the future.

With passage of the Fifteenth Amendment, many Americans, especially supportive northerners, considered Reconstruction essentially completed. "Let us have done with Reconstruction," pleaded the *New York Tribune* in April 1870. "The country is tired and sick of it. . . . Let us have Peace!" But some northerners, like abolitionist Wendell Phillips, worried. "Our day," he warned, "is fast slipping away. Once let public thought float off from the great issue of the war, and it will take . . . more than a generation to bring it back again.”

POLITICS AND RECONSTRUCTION IN THE SOUTH

From the start, Reconstruction encountered the resistance of white southerners. In the black codes and in private attitudes, many whites stubbornly opposed emancipation, and the former planter class proved especially unbending because of their tremendous financial loss in slaves. In 1866 a Georgia newspaper frankly observed that “most of the white citizens believe that the institution of slavery was right, and . . . they will believe that the condition, which comes nearest to slavery, that can now be established will be the best.” And for many poor whites who had never owned slaves and yet had sacrificed enormously in the war, destitution, plummeting agricultural prices, disease, and the uncertainties of a growing urban industrialization, drove them off land, toward cities, and into hatred of the very idea of black equality.

Fearing loss of control over their slaves, some planters attempted to postpone freedom by denying or misrepresenting events. Former slaves reported that their owners “didn’t tell them it was freedom” or “wouldn’t let [them] go.” Agents of the Freedmen’s Bureau reported that “the old system of slavery [is] working with even more rigor than formerly at a few miles distant from any point where U.S. troops are stationed.” To hold onto their workers, some landowners claimed control over black children and used guardianship and apprentice laws to bind black families to the plantation.

White Resistance

Whites also blocked blacks from acquiring land. A few planters divided up plots among their slaves, but most condemned the idea of making blacks landowners. A Georgia woman whose family was known for its support of religious education for slaves was outraged that two property owners planned to “rent their lands to the Negroes!” Such action was, she declared, “injurious to the best interest of the community.”

Adamant resistance by whites soon manifested itself in other ways, including violence. In one North Carolina town, a local magistrate clubbed a black man on a public street, and in several states bands of “Regulators” terrorized blacks who displayed any independence. Amid their defeat, many planters believed, as a South Carolinian put it, that blacks “can’t be governed except with the whip.” And after President Johnson encouraged the South to resist congressional Reconstruction, many white conservatives worked hard to capture the new state governments, while others boycotted the polls in an attempt to defeat Congress’s plans.

Very few black men stayed away from the polls. Enthusiastically and hopefully, they voted Republican. Most agreed with one man who felt he should “stick to the end with the party that freed me.” Illiteracy did not prohibit blacks (or uneducated whites) from making intelligent choices. Although Mississippi’s William Henry could read only “a little,” he testified that he and his friends had no difficulty selecting the Republican ballot. “We stood around and watched,” he explained. “We saw D. Sledge vote; he owned half the county. We knowed he voted Democratic so we voted the other ticket so it would be Republican.” Women, who could not vote, encouraged their husbands and sons, and preachers exhorted their congregations to use the franchise. Zeal for voting spread through entire black communities.

Black Voters and the Southern Republican Party

▲ Southern blacks attempting to vote are halted by White Leaguers in this engraving by J. H. Wares. The black man doffing his cap holds a “Republican ticket” but it will not get him to the ballot box, guarded by the election judge with a loaded pistol.

(Granger Collection)

Thanks to a large black turnout and the restrictions on prominent Confederates, a new southern Republican Party came to power in the constitutional conventions of 1868–1870. Republican delegates consisted of a sizable contingent of blacks (265 out of the total of just over 1,000 delegates throughout the South), some northerners who had moved to the South, and native southern whites who favored change. The new constitutions drafted by this Republican coalition were more democratic than anything previously adopted in the history of the South. They eliminated property qualifications for voting and holding office, and they turned many appointed offices into elective posts. They provided for public schools and institutions to care for the mentally ill, the blind, the deaf, the destitute, and the orphaned.

The conventions broadened women's rights in property holding and divorce. Usually the goal was not to make women equal with men but to provide relief to thousands of suffering debtors. In white families left poverty-stricken by the war and weighed down by debt, it was usually the husband who had contracted the debts. Thus giving women legal control over their own property provided some protection to their families.

Under these new constitutions the southern states elected Republican-controlled governments. For the first time, the ranks of state legislators in 1868 included black southerners. It remained to be seen now how much social change these new governments would foster. Contrary to what white southerners would later claim, the Republican state governments did not disfranchise ex-Confederates as a group. James Lynch, a leading black politician from Mississippi, explained why African Americans shunned the "folly" of disfranchising whites. Unlike northerners who "can leave when it becomes too uncomfortable," landless former slaves "must be in friendly relations with the great body of the whites in the state. Otherwise . . . peace can be maintained only by a standing army." Despised and lacking material or social power, southern Republicans strove for acceptance, legitimacy, and safe ways to gain a foothold in a depressed economy.

Triumph of Republican Governments

Far from being vindictive toward the race that had enslaved them, most southern blacks treated leading rebels with generosity and appealed to white southerners to adopt a spirit of fairness. In this way the South's Republican Party condemned itself to defeat if white voters would not cooperate. Within a few years most of the fledgling Republican parties in the southern states would be struggling for survival against violent white hostility. But for a time some propertied whites accepted congressional Reconstruction as a reality.

Reflecting northern ideals and southern necessity, the Reconstruction governments enthusiastically promoted industry. Accordingly, Reconstruction legislatures encouraged investment with loans, subsidies, and short-term exemptions from taxation. The southern railroad system was rebuilt and expanded, and coal and iron mining made possible Birmingham's steel plants. Between 1860 and 1880, the number of manufacturing establishments in the South nearly doubled.

Industrialization and Mill Towns

This emphasis on big business, however, produced higher state debts and taxes, drew money away from schools and other programs, and multiplied possibilities for corruption in state legislatures. The alliance between business and government took firm hold, often at the expense of the needs of common farmers and laborers. It also locked Republicans into a conservative strategy and doomed them to failure in building support among poorer whites.

Poverty remained the lot of vast numbers of southern whites. On a daily basis during the Reconstruction years, they had to subordinate politics to the struggle for livelihood. The war had caused a massive one-time loss of income-producing wealth, such as livestock, and a steep decline in land values. From 1860 to 1880, the South's share of per capita income fell from nearly equal to only 51 percent of the national average. In many regions the old planter class still ruled the best land and access to credit or markets.

As many poor whites and blacks found farming less tenable, they moved to cities and new mill towns. Industrialization did not sweep the South as it did the North, but it certainly laid deep roots. Attracting textile mills to southern towns became a competitive crusade. "Next to God," shouted a North Carolina evangelist, "what this town needs is a cotton mill!" In 1860 the South counted some 10,000 mill workers; by 1880, the number grew to 16,741 and by the end of the century, to 97,559. In thousands of human dramas, poor southerners began the multigenerational journey from farmer to mill worker and other forms of low-income urban wage earner.

Policies appealing to African American voters never went beyond equality before the law. In fact, the whites who controlled the southern Republican Party were reluctant to allow blacks a share of offices proportionate to their electoral strength. Aware of their weakness, black leaders

Republicans and Racial Equality

▲ One notable success in Reconstruction efforts to stimulate industry was Birmingham, Alabama. Here workers cast molten iron into blocks called pigs. *(Birmingham Public Library)*

did not push very far for revolutionary economic or social change. In every southern state, they led efforts to establish public schools, although they did not press for integrated facilities. In 1870 South Carolina passed the first comprehensive school law in the South. By 1875, 50 percent of black school-age children in that state were enrolled in school, and approximately one-third of the three thousand teachers were black.

Some African American politicians did fight for civil rights and integration. Many were from cities such as New Orleans or Mobile, where large populations of light-skinned free blacks had existed before the war. Their experience in such communities had made them sensitive to issues of status, and they spoke out for open and equal public accommodations. Laws requiring equal accommodations won passage, but they often went unenforced.

The vexing questions of land reform and enforcement of racial equality, however, all but overwhelmed the Republican governments. Land reform largely failed because in most states whites were in the majority, and former slaveowners controlled the best land and other sources of economic power. Economic progress was uppermost in the minds of most freedpeople. Black southerners needed land,

and much land did fall into state hands for nonpayment of taxes. Such land was offered for sale in small lots. But most freedmen had too little cash to bid against investors or speculators. South Carolina established a land commission, but it could help only those with money to buy. Any widespread redistribution of land had to arise from Congress, which never supported such action.

Within a few years, as centrists in both parties met with failure, white hostility to congressional Reconstruction began to dominate. Some conservatives had always wanted to fight Reconstruction through pressure and racist propaganda. They put economic and social pressure on blacks: one black Republican reported that "my neighbors will not employ me, nor sell me a farthing's worth of anything." Charging that the South had been turned over to ignorant blacks, conservatives deplored "black domination," which became a rallying cry for a return to white supremacy.

Such attacks were inflammatory propaganda and part of the growing myth of "Negro rule," which would serve as a central theme in battles over the memory of Recon-

Myth of "Negro Rule"

struction. African Americans participated in politics but hardly dominated or controlled events. They were a majority in only two out of ten state constitutional writing conventions (transplanted northerners were a majority in one). In the state legislatures, only in the lower house in South Carolina did blacks ever constitute a majority. Sixteen blacks won seats in Congress before Reconstruction was over, but none was ever elected governor. Only eighteen served in a high state office, such as lieutenant governor, treasurer, superintendent of education, or secretary of state.

In all, some four hundred blacks served in political office during the Reconstruction era, a signal achievement by any standard. Although they never dominated the process, they established a rich tradition of government service and civic activism. Elected officials, such as Robert Smalls in South Carolina, labored tirelessly for cheaper land prices, better healthcare, access to schools, and the enforcement of civil rights for their people. For too long the black politicians of Reconstruction were the forgotten heroes of this seedtime of America's long civil rights movement.

Conservatives also assailed the allies of black Republicans. Their propaganda denounced whites from the North as "carpetbaggers," greedy crooks planning to pour stolen tax revenues into their sturdy luggage made of carpet material. Immigrants from the North, who held the largest share of Republican offices, were all tarred with this rhetorical brush.

Carpetbaggers and Scalawags

In fact, most northerners who settled in the South had come seeking business opportunities, as schoolteachers, or to find a warmer climate; most never entered politics. Those who did enter politics generally wanted to democratize the South and to introduce northern ways, such as industry and public education. Carpetbaggers' ideals were tested by hard times and ostracism by white southerners.

In addition to tagging northern interlopers as carpetbaggers, conservatives invented the term *scalawag* to discredit any native white southerner who cooperated with the Republicans. A substantial number of southerners did so, including some wealthy and prominent men. Most scalawags, however, were yeoman farmers, men from mountain areas and nonslaveholding districts who had been Unionists under the Confederacy. They saw that they could benefit from the education and opportunities promoted by Republicans. Sometimes banding together with freedmen, they pursued common class interests and hoped to make headway against the power of long-dominant planters. Such cooperation led to genuine hopes for black-white coalitions, but most of these efforts in the long run floundered in the quicksand of racism.

Taxation was a major problem for the Reconstruction governments. Republicans wanted to repair the war's destruction, stimulate industry, and support such new ventures as public schools. But the Civil War had destroyed much of the South's tax base. One category of valuable property—slaves—had disappeared entirely. And hundreds of thousands of citizens had lost much of the rest of their property—money, livestock, fences, and buildings—to the war. Thus an increase in taxes (sales, excise, and property) was necessary even to maintain traditional services. Inevitably, Republican tax policies aroused strong opposition, especially among the yeomen.

Tax Policy and Corruption as Political Wedges

Corruption was another serious charge levied against the Republicans. Unfortunately, it was often true. Many carpetbaggers and black politicians engaged in fraudulent schemes, sold their votes, or padded expenses, taking part in what scholars recognize was a nationwide surge of corruption in an age ruled by "spoilsmen" (see pages 566–567). Corruption carried no party label, but the Democrats successfully pinned the blame on unqualified blacks and greedy carpetbaggers among southern Republicans.

All these problems hurt the Republicans, whose leaders also allowed factionalism along racial and class lines to undermine party unity. But in many southern states the deathblow came through violence. The Ku Klux Klan (its members altered the Greek word for "circle," *kuklos*), a secret veterans' club that began in Tennessee in 1866, spread through the South and rapidly evolved into a terrorist organization. Violence against African Americans occurred from the first days of Reconstruction but became far more organized and purposeful after 1867. Klansmen sought to frustrate Reconstruction and keep the freedmen in subjection. Nighttime harassment, whippings, beatings, rapes, and murders became common, as terrorism dominated some counties and regions.

Ku Klux Klan

Although the Klan tormented blacks who stood up for their rights as laborers or individuals, its main purpose was political. Lawless nightriders made active Republicans the target of their attacks. Leading white and black Republicans were killed in several states. After freedmen who worked for a South Carolina scalawag started voting, terrorists visited the plantation and, in the words of one victim, "whipped every . . . [black] man they could lay their hands on." Klansmen also attacked Union League

IF HE IS A UNION MAN OR A FREEDMAN.

"VERDICT", HANG THE D— YANKEE AND NIGGER".

▲ During Reconstruction, especially the years 1868–1871, the Ku Klux Klan, and other groups like them, terrorized and murdered blacks as well as white unionists or Republicans. Their goals were to destroy black community development and Republican political power. *(Harper's Weekly, March 23, 1867)*

▲ Albion Winegar Tourgée, a former Union soldier severely wounded at the Battle of Bull Run in 1861, became a carpetbagger and was elected a district judge in North Carolina during Reconstruction. In 1879 he published a bestselling novel, *A Fool's Errand,* which told his own story of travail as a Yankee immigrant in the South confronting the Ku Klux Klan and implementing freedmen's rights.

(Chautauqua County Historical Society, Westfield, N.Y.)

clubs—Republican organizations that mobilized the black vote—and schoolteachers who were aiding the freedmen.

Klan violence was not a spontaneous outburst of racism; very specific social forces shaped and directed it. In North Carolina, for example, Alamance and Caswell Counties were the sites of the worst Klan violence. Slim Republican majorities there rested on cooperation between black voters and white yeomen, particularly those whose Unionism or discontent with the Confederacy had turned them against local Democratic officials. Together, these black and white Republicans had ousted officials long entrenched in power. The wealthy and powerful men in Alamance and Caswell who had lost their accustomed political control were the Klan's county officers and local chieftains. They organized a deliberate campaign of terror, recruiting members and planning atrocities. By intimidation and murder, the Klan weakened the Republican coalition and restored a Democratic majority.

Klan violence injured Republicans across the South. One of every ten black leaders who had been delegates to the 1867–1868 state constitutional conventions was attacked, seven fatally. In one judicial district of North Carolina, the Ku Klux Klan was responsible for twelve murders, over seven hundred beatings, and other acts of violence, including rape and arson. A single attack on Alabama Republicans in the town of Eutaw left four blacks dead and fifty-four wounded. In South Carolina, five hundred masked Klansmen lynched eight black prisoners at the Union County jail, and in nearby York County, the Klan committed at least eleven murders and hundreds of whippings. According to historian Eric Foner, the Klan "made it virtually impossible for Republicans to campaign or vote in large parts of Georgia."

Thus a combination of difficult fiscal problems, Republican mistakes, racial hostility, and terror brought down the Republican regimes. In most southern states, Radical Reconstruction lasted only a few years (see Map 16.1). The most enduring failure of Reconstruction, however, was not political; it was social and economic. Reconstruction failed to alter the South's social structure or its distribution of wealth and power.

RETREAT FROM RECONSTRUCTION

During the 1870s, northerners increasingly lost the political will to sustain Reconstruction in the South, as a vast economic and social transformation occurred in their own region as well as in the West. Radical Republicans like Albion Tourgée, a former Union soldier who moved to North Carolina and was elected a judge, condemned Congress's timidity. Turning the freedman out on his own without protection, said Tourgée, constituted "cheap philanthropy." Indeed, many African Americans believed that, during Reconstruction, the North "threw all the Negroes on the world without any way of getting along." As the North underwent its own transformations and lost interest in the South's dilemmas, Reconstruction collapsed.

In one southern state after another, Democrats regained control, and they threatened to defeat Republicans in the North as well. Whites in the old Confederacy referred to this decline of Reconstruction as "southern redemption," and during the 1870s, "redeemer" Democrats claimed to be the saviors of the South from alleged "black domination" and "carpetbag rule." And for one of only a few times in American history, violence and terror emerged as a tactic in normal politics.

Political Implications of Klan Terrorism

In 1870 and 1871 the violent campaigns of the Ku Klux Klan forced Congress to pass two Enforcement Acts and an anti-Klan law. These laws made actions by individuals against the civil and political rights of others a federal criminal offense for the first time. They also provided for election supervisors and permitted martial law and suspension of the writ of habeas corpus to combat murders, beatings, and threats by the Klan. Federal prosecutors used the laws rather selectively. In 1872 and 1873, Mississippi and the Carolinas saw many prosecutions; but in other states where violence flourished, the laws were virtually ignored. Southern juries sometimes refused to convict Klansmen; out of a total of 3,310 cases, only 1,143 ended in convictions. Although many Klansmen (roughly 2,000 in South Carolina alone) fled their state to avoid prosecution, and the Klan officially disbanded, the threat

of violence did not end. Paramilitary organizations known as Rifle Clubs and Red Shirts often took the Klan's place.

Klan terrorism openly defied Congress, yet even on this issue there were ominous signs that the North's commitment to racial justice was fading. Some conservative but influential Republicans opposed the anti-Klan laws. Rejecting other Republicans' arguments that the Thirteenth, Fourteenth, and Fifteenth Amendments had made the federal government the protector of the rights of citizens, these dissenters echoed an old Democratic charge that Congress was infringing on states' rights. Senator Lyman Trumbull of Illinois declared that the states remained "the depositories of the rights of the individual." If Congress could punish crimes like assault or murder, he asked, "what is the need of the State governments?" For years Democrats had complained of "centralization and consolidation"; now some Republicans seemed to agree with them. This opposition foreshadowed a more general revolt within Republican ranks in 1872.

Both immigration and industrialization surged in the North. Between 1865 and 1873, 3 million immigrants entered the country, most settling in the industrial cities of the North and West. Within only eight years, postwar industrial production increased by 75 percent. For the first time, nonagricultural workers outnumbered farmers, and wage earners outnumbered independent craftsmen. And by 1873 only Britain's industrial output was greater than that of the United States. Government financial policies did much to bring about this rapid growth. Low taxes on investment and high tariffs on manufactured goods aided the growth of a new class of powerful industrialists, especially railroad entrepreneurs.

Industrial Expansion and Reconstruction in the North

Railroads became the symbol of and the stimulus for the American age of capital. From 1865 to 1873, 35,000 miles of new track were laid, a total exceeding the entire national rail network of 1860. Railroad building fueled the banking industry and made Wall Street the center of American capitalism. Eastern railroad magnates, such as Thomas Scott of the Pennsylvania Railroad, the largest corporation of its time, created economic empires with the assistance of huge government subsidies of cash and land. Railroad corporations also bought up mining operations, granaries, and lumber companies. In Congress and in every state legislature, big business now employed lobbyists to curry favor with government. Corruption ran rampant, with some congressmen and legislators were paid annual retainers by major companies.

This soaring capitalist-political alliance led as well to an intensified struggle between labor and capital. As captains of industry amassed unprecedented fortunes in an age with no income tax, gross economic inequality polarized American society. The work force, worried a prominent Massachusetts business leader, was in a "transition state . . . living in boarding houses" and becoming a "permanent factory population." In Cincinnati, three large factories employed as many workers as the city's thousands of small shops. In New York or Philadelphia, workers increasingly lived in dark, unhealthy tenement housing. Thousands would list themselves on the census as "common laborer" or "general jobber." Many of the free labor maxims of the Republican Party were now under great duress. Did the individual work ethic guarantee social mobility in America or erode, under the pressure of profit making, into a world of unsafe factories, child labor, and declining wages? In 1868 the Republicans managed to pass an eight-hour workday bill in Congress that applied to federal workers. The "labor question" (see Chapter 18) now preoccupied northerners far more than the "southern" or the "freedmen" question.

Then the Panic of 1873 ushered in over five years of economic contraction. Three million people lost their jobs as class attitudes diverged, especially in large cities. Debtors and the unemployed sought easy-money policies to spur economic expansion (workers and farmers desperately needed cash). Businessmen, disturbed by the widespread strikes and industrial violence that accompanied the panic, fiercely defended property rights and demanded "sound money" policies. The chasm between farmers and workers on the one hand, and wealthy industrialists on the other, grew ever wider.

Disenchanted with Reconstruction, a largely northern group calling itself the Liberal Republicans bolted the party in 1872 and nominated Horace Greeley, the famous editor of the *New York Tribune,* for president. The Liberal Republicans were a varied group, including foes of corruption and advocates of a lower tariff. Normally such disparate elements would not cooperate with one another, but two popular and widespread attitudes united them: distaste for federal intervention in the South and an elitist desire to let market forces and the "best men" determine policy and events.

Liberal Republican Revolt

The Democrats also gave their nomination to Greeley in 1872. The combination was not enough to defeat Grant, who won reelection, but it reinforced Grant's desire to avoid confrontation with white southerners. Greeley's campaign for North-South reunion, for "clasping hands across the bloody chasm," was a bit premature to win at the polls but was a harbinger of the future in American politics. Organized Blue-Gray fraternalism (gatherings of Union and Confederate veterans) began as early as 1874. Grant continued to use military force sparingly and in 1875 refused a desperate request from the governor of Mississippi for troops to quell racial and political terrorism in that state.

Dissatisfaction with Grant's administration grew during his second term. Strong-willed but politically naive, Grant made a series of poor appointments. His secretary of war, his private secretary, and officials in the Treasury and Navy Departments were involved in bribery or tax-cheating scandals. Instead of exposing the corruption, Grant defended the culprits. In 1874, as Grant's popularity and his party's prestige declined, the Democrats recaptured the House of Representatives, signaling the end of the Radical Republican vision of Reconstruction.

The effect of Democratic gains in Congress was to weaken legislative resolve on southern issues. Congress had already lifted the political disabilities of the Fourteenth Amendment from many former Confederates. In 1872 it had adopted a sweeping Amnesty Act, which pardoned most of the remaining rebels and left only five hundred barred from political office holding. In 1875 Congress passed a Civil Rights Act, partly as a tribute to the recently deceased Charles Sumner, purporting to guarantee black people equal accommodations in public places, such as inns and theaters, but the bill was watered down and contained no effective provisions for enforcement. (The Supreme Court later struck down this law; see page 573.)

General Amnesty

Democrats regained control of four state governments before 1872 and a total of eight by the end of January 1876 (see Map 16.1). In the North, Democrats successfully stressed the failure and scandals of Reconstruction governments. As opinion shifted, many Republicans sensed that their constituents were tiring of southern issues and the legacies of the war. Sectional reconciliation now seemed crucial for commerce. The nation was expanding westward rapidly, and the South was a new frontier for investment.

Nowhere did the new complexity and violence of American race relations play out so vividly as in the West. As the Fourteenth Amendment and other enactments granted to blacks the beginnings of citizenship, other nonwhite peoples faced continued persecution. Across the West, the federal government pursued a policy of containment against Native Americans. In California, where white farmers and ranchers often forced Indians into captive labor, some civilians practiced a more violent form of "Indian hunting." By 1880,

The West, Race, and Reconstruction

The Grants' Tour of the World

On May 17, 1877, two weeks after his presidency ended, Ulysses S. Grant and his wife Julia embarked from Philadelphia on a grand tour of the world that would last twenty-six months. Portrayed as a private vacation, the trip was a very public affair. The taint of corruption in Grant's second term could be dissipated only in the air of foreign lands reached by steamship. The small entourage included John Russell Young, a reporter for the *New York Herald* who recorded the journey in the two-volume, illustrated *Around the World with General Grant*. The Grants' expenses were paid by banker friends and by Grant's personal resources, accumulated in gifts.

The Grants spent many months in England attending a bewildering array of banquets, one with Queen Victoria. In Newcastle, thousands of workingmen conducted a massive parade in Grant's honor. He was received as the odd American cousin, simple and great, the conqueror and warrior statesman. In an age that worshiped great men, Grant was viewed as the savior of the American nation, the liberator of slaves, and a celebrity—a measure of the American presence on the world stage.

On the European continent the pattern continued, as every royal or republican head of state hosted the Grants. In Belgium, France, Switzerland, Italy, Russia, Poland, Austria, and Spain, the Grants reveled in princely attentions. In Berlin, Grant met Otto von Bismarck, the chancellor of Germany. The two got along well discussing war, world politics, and the abolition of slavery.

The Grants next went to Egypt, where they rode donkeys into remote villages along the Nile and then traveled by train to the Indian Ocean, where they embarked for India. They encountered British imperialism in full flower in Bombay, and that of the French in Saigon. Northward in Asia, the grand excursion went to China and Japan. In Canton, Grant passed before an assemblage of young men who, according to a reporter, "looked upon the barbarian with . . . contempt in their expression, very much as our young men in New York would regard Sitting Bull or Red Cloud." In Japan, the Grants had a rare audience with Emperor Mutsuhito in the imperial palace. Grant found Japan "beautiful beyond description," and the receptions there were the most formal of all.

"I am both homesick and dread going home," Grant wrote in April 1879. Sailing across the Pacific, the Grants landed in San Francisco in late June. Why had Grant taken such a prolonged trip? Travel itself had its own rewards, but the tour became an unusual political campaign. Grant sought publicity abroad to convince his countrymen back home that they should reelect him president in 1880. But the strategy failed; Grant had developed no compelling issue or reason why Americans should choose him again. He would spend his final years, however, a war hero and a national symbol. No American president would again establish such personal links to the world until Woodrow Wilson at the end of World War I.

▲ On their tour of the world, Ulysses and Julia Grant sat here with companions and guides in front of the Great Hypostyle Hall at the Temple of Amon-Ra in Karnak at Luxor, Egypt, 1878. The Grants' extraordinary tour included many such photo opportunities, often depicting the plebeian American president's presence in exotic places with unusual people. Whether he liked it or not, Grant was a world celebrity. *(Library of Congress)*

▲ Anti-Chinese cartoon, "Every Dog (No Distinction of Color) Has His Day." The imagery here links Native Americans, African Americans, and Chinese immigrants in the same racist and xenophobic fear. *(Granger Collection)*

thirty years of such violence left an estimated 4,500 California Indians dead at the hands of white settlers.

In Texas and the Southwest, the rhetoric of national expansion still deemed Mexicans and other mixed-race Hispanics to be debased, "lazy," and incapable of self-government. And in California and other states of the Far West, thousands of Chinese immigrants became the victims of brutal violence. Few whites had objected to the Chinese who did the dangerous work of building railroads through the Rocky Mountains. But when the Chinese began to compete for urban, industrial jobs, great conflict emerged. Anti-coolie clubs appeared in California in the 1870s, seeking laws against Chinese labor, fanning the flames of racism, and organizing vigilante attacks on Chinese workers and the factories that employed them. Western politicians sought white votes by pandering to prejudice, and in 1879 the new California constitution denied the vote to Chinese.

If we view America from coast to coast, and not merely on the North-South axis, the Civil War and Reconstruction years both dismantled racial slavery and

fostered a volatile new racial complexity, especially in the West. During the same age when early anthropologists employed elaborate theories of "scientific" racism to determine a hierarchy of racial types, the West was a vast region of racial mixing and conflict. Some African Americans, despite generations of mixture with Native Americans, asserted that they were more like whites than the nomadic, "uncivilized" Indians, while others, like the Creek freedmen of Indian Territory, sought an Indian identity. In Texas, whites, Indians, blacks, and Hispanics had mixed for decades, and by the 1870s forced reconsideration in law and custom of who was white and who was not.

During Reconstruction, America was undergoing what one historian has called a reconstruction of the very idea of race itself. As it did so, tumbling into some of the darkest years of American race relations, the turbulence of the expanding West reinforced the new nationalism and the reconciliation of North and South based on a resurgent white supremacy.

Following the Civil War, pressure for expansion reemerged (see Chapter 22), and in 1867 Secretary of State William H. Seward arranged a vast addition of territory to the national domain through the purchase of Alaska from Russia. Opponents ridiculed Seward's $7.2 million venture, calling Alaska "Frigidia," "the Polar Bear Garden," and "Walrussia." But Seward convinced important congressmen of Alaska's economic potential, and other lawmakers favored the dawning of friendship with Russia.

Foreign Expansion

Also in 1867 the United States took control of the Midway Islands, a thousand miles northwest of Hawai'i. And in 1870 President Grant tried unsuccessfully to annex the Dominican Republic. Seward and his successor, Hamilton Fish, also resolved troubling Civil War grievances against Great Britain. Through diplomacy they arranged a financial settlement of claims on Britain for damage done by the *Alabama* and other cruisers built in England and sold to the Confederacy. They recognized that sectional reconciliation in Reconstruction America would serve new ambitions for world commerce and expansion.

Meanwhile, the Supreme Court played its part in the northern retreat from Reconstruction. During the Civil War, the Court had been cautious and inactive. Reaction to the *Dred Scott* decision (1857) had been so vehement, and the Union's wartime emergency so great, that the Court had avoided interference with government actions. The justices breathed a collective sigh of relief, for example, when legal technicalities prevented them from reviewing the case of Clement Vallandigham,

Judicial Retreat from Reconstruction

a Democratic opponent of Lincoln's war effort who had been convicted by a military tribunal of aiding the enemy. But in 1866 a similar case, *Ex parte Milligan,* reached the Court.

Lambdin P. Milligan of Indiana had plotted to free Confederate prisoners of war and overthrow state governments. For these acts a military court sentenced Milligan, a civilian, to death. Milligan challenged the authority of the military tribunal, claiming that he had a right to a civil trial. The Supreme Court declared that military trials were illegal when civil courts were open and functioning, and its language indicated that the Court intended to reassert its authority.

In the 1870s the Court successfully renewed its challenge to Congress's actions when it narrowed the meaning and effectiveness of the Fourteenth Amendment. The *Slaughter-House* cases (1873) began in 1869, when the Louisiana legislature granted one company a monopoly on the slaughtering of livestock in New Orleans. Rival butchers in the city promptly sued. Their attorney, former Supreme Court justice John A. Campbell, argued that Louisiana had violated the rights of some of its citizens in favor of others. The Fourteenth Amendment, Campbell contended, had revolutionized the constitutional system by bringing individual rights under federal protection. Campbell thus articulated an original goal of the Republican Party: to nationalize civil rights and guard them from state interference.

But in the *Slaughter-House* decision, the Supreme Court dealt a stunning blow to the scope and vitality of the Fourteenth Amendment. Refusing to accept Campbell's argument, the Court declared state citizenship and national citizenship separate. National citizenship involved only matters such as the right to travel freely from state to state, and only such narrow rights, held the Court, were protected by the Fourteenth Amendment.

The Supreme Court also concluded that the butchers who sued had not been deprived of their rights or property in violation of the due-process clause of the amendment. Shrinking from a role as "perpetual censor upon all legislation of the States, on the civil rights of their own citizens," the Court's majority declared that the framers of the recent amendments had not intended to "destroy" the federal system, in which the states exercised "powers for domestic and local government, including the regulation of civil rights." Thus the justices severely limited the amendment's potential for securing and protecting the rights of black citizens—its original intent.

The next day the Court decided *Bradwell v. Illinois,* a case in which Myra Bradwell, a female attorney, had been denied the right to practice law in Illinois because she was a married woman, and hence not considered a free agent. Pointing to the Fourteenth Amendment, Bradwell's attorneys contended that the state had unconstitutionally abridged her "privileges and immunities" as a citizen. The Supreme Court rejected her claim, declaring a woman's "paramount destiny . . . to fulfill the noble and benign offices of wife and mother."

In 1876 the Court weakened the Reconstruction era amendments even further by emasculating the enforcement clause of the Fourteenth Amendment and revealing deficiencies inherent in the Fifteenth Amendment. In *U.S. v. Cruikshank* the Court overruled the conviction under the 1870 Enforcement Act of Louisiana whites who had attacked a meeting of blacks and conspired to deprive them of their rights. The justices ruled that the Fourteenth Amendment did not give the federal government power to act against these whites. The duty of protecting citizens' equal rights, the Court said, "rests alone with the States." Such judicial conservatism had a profound impact down through the next century, blunting the revolutionary potential in the Civil War amendments.

As the 1876 elections approached, most political observers saw that the nation was increasingly focused on economic issues and that the North was no longer willing to pursue the goals of Reconstruction. The results of a disputed presidential election confirmed this fact. Samuel J. Tilden, the Democratic governor of New York, ran strongly in the South and needed only one more electoral vote to triumph over Rutherford B. Hayes, the Republican nominee. Nineteen electoral votes from Louisiana, South Carolina, and Florida (the only southern states not yet under Democratic rule) were disputed; both Democrats and Republicans claimed to have won in those states despite fraud committed by their opponents (see Map 16.2).

Disputed Election of 1876 and Compromise of 1877

To resolve this unprecedented situation Congress established a fifteen-member electoral commission. Membership on the commission was to be balanced between Democrats and Republicans. Because the Republicans held the majority in Congress, they prevailed, 8 to 7, on every attempt to count the returns, with commission members voting along strict party lines. Hayes would become president if Congress accepted the commission's findings.

Congressional acceptance was not certain. Democrats controlled the House and could filibuster to block action on the vote. Many citizens worried that the nation would slip once again into civil war, as some southerners vowed, "Tilden or Fight!" The crisis was resolved when Democrats acquiesced in the election of Hayes based on a "deal" cut in a Washington hotel between Hayes's supporters and southerners who wanted federal aid to railroads,

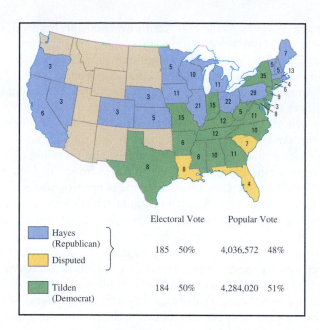

	Electoral Vote		Popular Vote	
Hayes (Republican)	185	50%	4,036,572	48%
Disputed				
Tilden (Democrat)	184	50%	4,284,020	51%

Map 16.2   Presidential Election of 1876 and the Compromise of 1877

In 1876 a combination of solid southern support and Democratic gains in the North gave Samuel Tilden the majority of popular votes, but Rutherford B. Hayes won the disputed election in the electoral college, after a deal satisfied Democratic wishes for an end to Reconstruction.

internal improvements, federal patronage, and removal of troops from southern states. Northern and southern Democrats simply decided not to contest the election of a Republican who was not going to continue Reconstruction policies in the South. Thus Hayes became president, inaugurated privately inside the White House to avoid any threat of violence. Southerners relished their promises of economic aid, and Reconstruction was unmistakably over.

Southern Democrats rejoiced, but African Americans grieved over the betrayal of their hopes for equality. The Civil War had brought emancipation, and Reconstruction had guaranteed their rights under law. But events and attitudes in larger white America were foreboding. In a Fourth of July speech in Washington, D.C., in 1875, Frederick Douglass anticipated this predicament. He reflected anxiously on the American centennial to be celebrated the following year. The nation, Douglass feared, would "lift to the sky its million voices in one grand Centennial hosanna of peace and good will to all the white race . . . from gulf to lakes and from sea to sea." Douglass looked back on fifteen years of unparalleled change for his people and worried about the hold of white supremacy on America's historical memory: "If war among the whites brought peace and liberty to the blacks, what will peace among the whites bring?" Douglass's question would echo down through American political culture for decades.

SUMMARY

Reconstruction left a contradictory record. It was an era of tragic aspirations and failures but also of unprecedented legal, political, and social change. The Union victory brought about an increase in federal power, stronger nationalism, sweeping federal intervention in the southern states, and landmark amendments to the Constitution. But northern commitment to make these changes endure had eroded, and the revolution remained unfinished. The mystic sense of promise for new lives and liberties among the freedpeople, demonstrated in that first Decoration Day in Charleston, had fallen into a new, if temporary, kind of ruin.

The North embraced emancipation, black suffrage, and constitutional alterations strengthening the central government. But it did so to defeat the rebellion and secure the peace. As the pressure of these crises declined, Americans, especially in the North, retreated from Reconstruction. The American people and the courts maintained a preference for state authority and a distrust of federal power. The ideology of free labor dictated that property should be respected and that individuals should be self-reliant. Racism endured and transformed into the even more virulent forms of Klan terror and theories of black degeneration. Concern for the human rights of African Americans was strongest when their plight

Legacy FOR A PEOPLE AND A NATION

The Lost Cause

All major wars and their aftermath compel a struggle over their memory. Sometimes losers prevail over winners in contests to shape historical memory. After the Civil War, white southerners and their northern allies constructed a "Lost Cause" tradition, a potent and racially exclusive version of the war and Reconstruction which persists in American culture today.

The Lost Cause emerged among ex-Confederates as a mourning ritual and a psychological response to the trauma of defeat. But with time it also took root in selective reinterpretations of the war's causes, in southern resistance to Reconstruction, in doctrines of white supremacy, and in a mythic, nostalgic popular culture enjoyed and promoted by northerners and southerners alike. Lost Cause advocates—from high-ranking officers to common soldiers writing reminiscences to women leading memorial associations—argued that the war had never been about slavery, that the Confederates had only lost to Yankee numbers and resources, and that the nation should reconcile by equally honoring both southern and northern sacrifice. In the industrial, urban, multi-ethnic America of the emerging twentieth century, an Old South of benevolent masters and faithful slaves, of Robert E. Lee portrayed as America's truest Christian soldier, provided a romantic, sentimentalized road to reunion. These images reverberated in the very heartbeat of Jim Crow America, and they endure in modern tastes for Civil War memorabilia, such as the epic *Gone with the Wind,* the 2003 film *Gods and Generals,* and uses of the Confederate flag to oppose civil rights and affirmative action.

From 1865 to the 1880s, this Confederate legend had been forged by wartime participants determined to vindicate the Confederacy. By the 1890s, however, Lost Cause culture emerged especially with the United Daughters of the Confederacy. Elite southern white women built monuments, lobbied congressmen, delivered lectures, ran essay contests for schoolchildren, and strove to control the content of history textbooks, all in the service of an exalted South. Above all, Lost Causers advocated a story not at all about loss, but about what one historian has called a "victory narrative." This new victory was the nation's triumph over the racial revolution and constitutional transformations of Reconstruction. In his 1881 memoir, Jefferson Davis argued that slavery "was in no wise the cause of the conflict" and that slaves had been "contented with their lot." He also declared the Lost Cause not lost: "Well may we rejoice in the regained possession of self-government. . . . This is the great victory . . . a total non-interference by the Federal government in the domestic affairs of the States."

threatened to undermine the interests of whites, and re-form frequently had less appeal than moneymaking in an individualistic, industrializing society.

New challenges to American society and values began to overwhelm the aims of Reconstruction. How would the country develop its immense resources in an increasingly interconnected national economy? Could farmers, industrial workers, immigrants, and capitalists co-exist in harmony? Industrialization not only promised prosperity but also wrought increased exploitation of labor. Moreover, industry increased the nation's power and laid the foundation for an enlarged American role in international affairs. The American imagination again turned to the conquest of new frontiers.

In the wake of the Civil War, Americans faced two profound tasks—the achievement of healing and the dispensing of justice. Both had to occur, but they never developed in historical balance. Making sectional reunion compatible with black freedom and equality overwhelmed the imagination in American political culture, and the nation still faced much of this dilemma more than a century later.

SUGGESTIONS FOR FURTHER READING

David W. Blight, *Race and Reunion: The Civil War in American Memory* (2001)

W. E. B. Du Bois, *Black Reconstruction in America* (1935)

Eric Foner, *Reconstruction: America's Unfinished Revolution, 1863–1877* (1988)

William Gillette, *Retreat from Reconstruction, 1869–1879* (1980)

Steven Hahn, *A Nation Under Our Feet: Black Political Struggles in the Rural South from Slavery to the Great Migration* (2003)

Gerald Jaynes, *Branches Without Roots: The Genesis of the Black Working Class in the American South, 1862–1882* (1986)

Michael Perman, *The Road to Redemption* (1984)

George Rable, *But There Was No Peace* (1984)

Heather Richardson, *The Death of Reconstruction* (2001)

Elliot West, "Reconstructing Race," *Western Historical Quarterly* (Spring 2003)

For a more extensive list for further reading, go to college.hmco.com/pic/norton8e.

CHAPTER

17

The Development of the West 1865-1900

𝓘n 1893 a young historian named Frederick Jackson Turner delivered a stunning lecture at the Columbian Exposition in Chicago. In it, Turner expounded a theory that would shape views of the American West for several generations. Titled "The Significance of the Frontier in American History," the paper argued that the existence of "free land, its continuous recession, and the advancement of American settlement westward" had created a distinctive spirit of democracy and egalitarianism. The settlement of a succession of frontier Wests from colonial times onward, in other words, explained American progress and character.

At a covered arena across the street from the Chicago world's fair, the folk character Buffalo Bill Cody staged two performances daily of an extravaganza called "The Wild West." Although Cody also dramatized the conquest of frontiers and the creation of an American identity, his perspective differed markedly from Turner's. Whereas Turner described a relatively peaceful settlement of largely empty western land, Cody portrayed violent conquest of territory occupied by savage Indians. Turner's heroes were persevering farmers who tamed the wilderness with axes and plows. Buffalo Bill's heroes were rugged scouts who braved danger and vanquished Indians with firepower and blood. Turner used images of log cabins, wagon trains, and wheat fields to argue that the frontier fashioned a new, progressive people. Cody, who employed a cast of actual Indians and soldiers (plus himself) to stage scenes of clashes between native warriors and white cavalry, depicted the West as a place of brutal aggression and heroic victory.

Turner's thesis and Cody's spectacle contained exaggerations and inaccuracies, yet both Turner and Cody were to some degree correct. The American West inspired material

◄ Thomas Moran (1837–1926) painted numerous scenes like this one of a lone Indian dwarfed by nature. Yet the West's raw bounty was luring countless white settlers even as Moran depicted the region's wilderness and immensity.

(Mist in Kanab Canyon, Utah, *Thomas Moran, 1892, oil, Smithsonian American Art Museum, Bequest of Mrs. Bessie B. Croffut*)

467

CHRONOLOGY

1862 ■ Homestead Act grants free land to citizens who live on and improve the land
■ Morrill Land Grant Act gives states public land to sell in order to finance agricultural and industrial colleges

1864 ■ Chivington's militia massacres Black Kettle's Cheyennes at Sand Creek

1869 ■ First transcontinental railroad completed

1872 ■ Yellowstone becomes first national park

1876 ■ Lakotas and Cheyennes ambush Custer's federal troops at Little Big Horn, Montana

1877 ■ Nez Percé Indians under Young Joseph surrender to U.S. troops

1878 ■ Timber and Stone Act allows citizens to buy timberland cheaply but also enables large companies to acquire huge tracts of forest land

1879 ■ Carlisle School for Indians established in Pennsylvania

1880–81 ■ Manypenny's Our Indian Wards and Jackson's A Century of Dishonor influence public conscience about poor government treatment of Indians

1881–82 ■ Chinese Exclusion Acts prohibit Chinese immigration to the United States

1883 ■ National time zones established

1884 ■ U.S. Supreme Court first denies Indians as wards under government protection

1887 ■ Dawes Severalty Act ends communal ownership of Indian lands and grants land allotments to individual native families

1887–88 ■ Devastating winter on Plains destroys countless livestock and forces farmers into economic hardship

1890 ■ Final suppression of Plains Indians by U.S. Army at Wounded Knee
■ Census Bureau announces closing of the frontier
■ Yosemite National Park established

1892 ■ Muir helps found Sierra Club

1902 ■ Newlands Reclamation Act passed

progress, and it also witnessed the forceful domination of one group of humans over another and over the environment. Both Turner and Cody believed that by the 1890s the frontier era had come to an end. In fact, Turner's essay had been sparked by an announcement from the superintendent of the 1890 census that "at present the unsettled area [of the West] has been so broken into by isolated bodies of settlement that there can be hardly said to be a frontier line." Over time, Turner's theory was abandoned (even by Turner himself) as too simplistic, and Buffalo Bill was relegated to the gallery of rogues and showmen. Yet the depictions of both Wests persist in the romance of American history, even while they obscured the complex story of western development in the late nineteenth century.

One fact is certain. Much of the West was never empty, and its inhabitants built communities and utilized its resources in quite different ways. Indians had managed the environment and sustained their needs long before white settlers arrived on the scene. On the Plains, for example, the Pawnees planted crops in the spring, left their fields in summer to hunt buffalo, then returned for harvesting. They sometimes battled with Cheyennes and Arapahos, who wanted hunting grounds and crops for their own purposes. The technology of Plains Indians was simple. Although they sometimes splurged, feasting on buffalo, they survived by developing and using natural resources in limited ways. In what now is the American Southwest, including southern California, natives shared the land and sometimes integrated with Hispanic people, who were descendants of Spanish colonists. Most Hispanics farmed small plots or worked for large landowners who had only limited access to outside markets.

As white immigrants built new communities in the West in the late nineteenth century, however, they exploited the environment for profit far more extensively than did Indians. They excavated deep into the earth to remove minerals, felled forests for timber to construct homes, pierced the countryside with railroads to carry goods and link markets, and dammed rivers and plowed soil with machines to grow crops. Their goal was not mere survival; it included buying and selling in regional, national, and international markets. As they transformed the landscape, the triumph of their market economies transformed the nation.

The West, which by 1870 referred to the expanse between the Mississippi River and the Pacific Ocean, actually consisted of several regions and a variety of economic potential. Abundant rainfall along the northern Pacific coast fed huge forests. Farther south into California, woodlands and grasslands provided fertile valleys suitable for vegetable fields and orange groves. Eastward, from the Cascades and the Sierra Nevada to the Rocky Mountains, is a series of deserts and plateaus known as the Basin and Range province, where gold, silver, and other minerals lay buried. East of the Rockies, the Great Plains divided into a semiarid western side of few trees and tough buffalo grass and an eastern sector of ample rainfall and tall grasses which could support grain crops and livestock.

Much of the West had long been the scene of migrations. Before contact with whites, Indian peoples had moved around and through the region. As they searched for food and shelter, they warred, traded, and negotiated with one another. In parts of the Southwest, Hispanics had moved north and south between Mexican and American territory, and they built towns, farms, and ranches. After the Civil War, white Americans flooded into the West, overwhelming the native and Hispanic peoples. Between 1870 and 1890, the white population living in the region swelled from 7 million to nearly 17 million.

The West's abundance of exploitable land and raw materials filled white Americans with faith that anyone eager and persistent enough could succeed. But this confidence rested on a belief that white people were somehow superior, and individual advantage often asserted itself at the expense of people of color as well as the environment. Although eventually some people came to realize the benefits of protecting the environment, Americans rarely thought about conserving resources because there always seemed to be more territory to develop and bring into the market economy.

By 1890 communities of farms, ranches, mines, towns, and cities could be found in almost every corner of the present-day continental United States, but vast stretches of land remained unsettled. Although it may have been of symbolic importance to Frederick Jackson Turner, the fading of the frontier had little direct impact on people's behavior. Pioneers who failed in one locale rarely perished;

they moved on and tried again elsewhere. Although life in the West could be challenging, a surplus of seemingly uninhabited land gave Americans a feeling that they would always have a second chance. It was this belief in an infinity of second chances, more than Turner's theory of frontier democracy or Cody's reenactments of heroic battles, that left a deep imprint on the American character.

- How did the interaction between people and the environment shape the physical landscape of the West and the lives of the region's inhabitants?
- How did the U.S. government's relations with Native Americans change over time throughout the late nineteenth century?
- Describe the societal and technological changes that revolutionized the lives of farmers and ranchers on the Great Plains.

THE ECONOMIC ACTIVITIES OF NATIVE PEOPLES

Native Americans settled the West long before other Americans migrated there. Neither passive nor powerless in the face of nature, Indians had been shaping their environment—for better and for worse—for centuries. Nevertheless, almost all native economic systems weakened in the late nineteenth century. Several factors explain why and how these declines happened.

Western Indian communities varied. Some natives inhabited permanent settlements; others lived in a series of temporary camps. Seldom completely isolated, most Indians were both participants and recipients in a large-scale flow of goods, culture, language, and disease carried by bands that migrated from one region to another. Regardless of their type of community, all Indians based their economy to differing degrees on four activities: crop growing; livestock raising; hunting, fishing, and gathering; and trading and raiding. Corn was the most common crop; sheep and horses, acquired from Spanish colonizers and from other Indians, were the livestock; and buffalo (American bison) were the primary prey of hunts. Indians raided one another for food, tools, hides, and horses, which in turn they used in trading with other Indians and with whites. They also attacked to avenge wrongs and to drive out competitors from hunting grounds. To achieve their

Subsistence Cultures

▲ Using buffalo hides to fashion garments, Indians often exhibited artistic skills in decorating their apparel. This Ute Indian hide dress shows symbolic as well as aesthetic representations. *(Denver Art Museum)*

cally setting fire to tall-grass prairies. The fires burned away dead plants, facilitating the growth of new grass in the spring so that horses could feed all summer.

In the Southwest, Indians were herders and placed great value on sheep, goats, and horses. Old Man Hat, a Navajo, explained, "The herd is money. . . . You know that you have some good clothing; the sheep gave you that. And you've just eaten different kinds of food; the sheep gave that food to you. Everything comes from the sheep." He was not speaking of money in a business sense, though. To Navajos, the herds provided status and security. Like many Indians, the Navajos emphasized generosity and distrusted private property and wealth. Within the family, sharing was expected; outside the family, gifts and reciprocity governed personal relations. Southwestern Indians, too, altered the environment, building elaborate irrigation systems to maximize use of scarce water supplies.

What buffalo were to Plains Indians and sheep were to southwestern Indians, salmon were to Indians of the Northwest. Before the mid-nineteenth century, the Columbia River and its tributaries supported the densest population of native peoples in North America, all of whom fished the river for salmon in the summer and stored dried fish for the winter. To harvest fish, the Clatsops, Klamath, and S'Klallams developed technologies of stream diversion, platform construction over the water, and special baskets. Like natives of other regions, many of these Indians traded for horses, buffalo robes, beads, cloth, and knives.

On the Plains and in parts of the Southwest, this native world began to dissolve after 1850, when white migrants entered and competed with Indians for access to and control over natural resources. Perceiving buffalo and Indians as hindrances to their ambitions, whites endeavored to eliminate both. The U.S. Army refused to enforce treaties that reserved hunting grounds for exclusive Indian use, so railroads sponsored buffalo hunts in which eastern sportsmen shot at the bulky targets from slow-moving trains. Some hunters collected from $1 to $3 from tanneries for hides that were sent east for use mainly as belts to drive industrial machinery; others did not even stop to pick up their kill.

Unbeknownst to both Indians and whites, however, a complex combination of circumstances had already doomed the buffalo before the slaughter of the late 1800s. Natives themselves were contributing to the depletion of the herds by increasing their kills, especially to trade hides with whites and other Indians. Also, a period of generally dry years in the 1840s and 1850s had forced Indians to

Slaughter of Buffalo

standards of living, Indians tried to balance their economic systems. When a buffalo hunt failed, they subsisted on crops. When crops failed, they could still hunt buffalo and steal food and horses in a raid or trade livestock and furs for necessities.

For Indians on the Great Plains, whether nomads, such as the Lakotas (or "Sioux"), or village dwellers, such as the Pawnees, everyday life focused on the buffalo. They cooked and preserved buffalo meat; fashioned hides into clothing, shoes, and blankets; used sinew for thread and bowstrings; and carved tools from bones and horns. Buffalo were so valuable that the Pawnees and Lakotas often fought over access to herds. Plains Indians also depended on horses, which they used for transportation and hunting, and as symbols of wealth. To provide food for their herds, Plains Indians altered the environment by periodi-

◀ Horses, sometimes numbering more than one hundred, and women and children, usually twenty or thirty, were a liability as well as a help to a Plains Indian camp. The horses competed with buffalo for valuable pasturage, and the women and children made camps vulnerable when white soldiers attacked.

(Denver Public Library, Western History Division)

set up camps in river basins, where they competed with buffalo for space and water. As a result, the buffalo were pushed out of nourishing grazing territory and faced threats of starvation. When whites arrived on the Plains, they, too, sought to settle in the same river basin areas, thereby further forcing buffalo away from nutritious grasslands. At the same time, lethal animal diseases, such as anthrax and brucellosis, brought in by white-owned livestock, decimated buffalo already weakened by malnutrition and drought. Increased numbers of horses, oxen, and sheep, owned by white newcomers as well as by some Indians, also upset the buffalo's grazing patterns by devouring grasses that they depended on at certain times of the year. In sum, human and environmental shocks created vulnerability among the buffalo, to which mass killing only struck the final blow. By the 1880s only a few hundred of the 25 million buffalo estimated on the Plains in 1820 remained.

In the Northwest, the basic wild source of Indian food supply, salmon, suffered a fate similar to that of the buffalo, but for different reasons.

Decline of Salmon

White commercial fishermen and canneries moved into the Columbia and Willamette River valleys during the 1860s and 1870s, and they harvested increasing numbers of salmon running upriver to spawn before laying their eggs, so the fish supply was not being replenished. By the 1880s they had greatly diminished the salmon runs on the Columbia, and by the early 1900s, the construction of dams on the river and its tributaries further impeded the salmon's ability to reproduce. The U.S. government protected Indian fishing rights, but not the supply of fish on the river. Hatcheries helped restore some of this supply, but dams built to provide power, combined with overfishing and pollution, diminished salmon stocks.

THE TRANSFORMATION OF NATIVE CULTURES

Buffalo slaughter and salmon reduction undermined Indian subsistence, but a unique mix of human demography contributed as well. For most of the nineteenth century, the white population that migrated into western lands inhabited by Indians was overwhelmingly young and male. In 1870 white men outnumbered white women by three to two in California, two to one in Colorado, and two to one in Dakota Territory. By 1900, preponderances of men remained throughout these places. Most of these males were unmarried and in their twenties and thirties, the stage of life when they were most prone to violent behavior. In other words, the whites with whom Indians were most likely to come into contact first were explorers, traders, trappers, soldiers, prospectors, and cowboys—almost all of whom possessed guns and had few qualms about using their weapons against animals and humans who got in their way.

Moreover, these men subscribed to prevailing attitudes that Indians were primitive, lazy, devious, and cruel.

Western Men

Such contempt made exploiting and killing natives all the easier, and whites often justified violence against Indians by claiming preemptive defense of threats to life and property. When Indians raided white settlements, they sometimes mutilated bodies, burned buildings, and kidnapped women, acts that were embellished in campfire stories, pamphlets, and popular fiction—all of which reinforced images of Indians as savages. Among the bachelor society of saloons and cabins, men boasted of their exploits in Indian fighting and showed off trophies of scalps and other body parts taken from victims.

Indian warriors, too, were young, armed, and prone to violence. Valuing bravery and vengeance, they boasted of fighting white interlopers. But Indian communities contrasted with those of whites in that they contained excesses of women and children, making native bands less mobile and therefore vulnerable to attack. They also were susceptible to the bad habits of bachelor white society. Indians copied white behavior of bingeing on cheap whiskey and indulging in prostitution. The syphilis and gonorrhea that Indian men contracted from Indian women infected by white men killed many and reduced natives' ability to reproduce, a consequence that their populations, already declining from smallpox and other diseases spread by whites, could not afford. Thus the age and gender structure of the white frontier population, combined with attitudes of racial contempt, created a further threat to Indian existence in the West.

Government policy reinforced efforts to remove Indians from the path of white ambitions. North American natives were organized not so much into tribes, as whites believed, as into hundreds of bands and confederacies in the Plains and into villages in the Southwest. Some two hundred languages and dialects separated these groups, making it difficult for Indians to unite against white invaders. Although a language group could be defined as a tribe, separate bands and clans within each language group had their own leaders, and seldom did a tribal chief hold widespread power. Moreover, bands often spent more time quarreling among themselves than with white settlers.

Lack of Native Unity

Nevertheless, the U.S. government needed some way of categorizing Indians so as to fashion a policy toward them. It did so by imputing more meaning to tribal organization than was warranted. After the Treaty of Greenville in 1795, American officials considered Indian tribes to be separate nations with which they could make treaties that ensured peace and defined boundaries between Indian and white lands. But the government did not understand that a chief or chiefs

Territorial Treaties

who agreed to a treaty did not speak for all members of a band and that the group would not necessarily abide by an agreement. Moreover, white settlers seldom accepted treaties as guarantees of Indians' future land rights. In the Northwest, whites considered treaties protecting Indians' fishing rights on the Columbia River to be nuisances and ousted Indians from the best locations so that they could use mechanical devices that harvested thousands of fish a day. On the Plains, whites assumed that they could settle wherever they wished, and they rarely hesitated to commandeer choice farmland along river basins. As white migrants pressed into Indian territories, treaties made one week were violated the next.

Prior to the 1880s, the federal government tried to force western Indians onto reservations, where, it was thought, they could be "civilized." Reservations usually consisted of those areas of a group's previous territory that were least desirable to whites. When assigning Indians to such parcels, the government promised protection from white encroachment and agreed to provide food, clothing, and other necessities.

Reservation Policy

The reservation policy helped make way for the market economy. In the early years of contact in the West, trade had benefited both Indians and whites and had taken place on a nearly equal footing, much as it had between eastern Indians and whites in the years before the American Revolution. Indians acquired clothing, guns, and horses from whites in return for furs, jewelry, and, sometimes, military assistance against other Indians. In the West, however, whites' needs and economic power grew disproportionate to Indians' needs and power. Indians became more dependent, and whites increasingly dictated what was to be traded and on what terms. For example, white traders persuaded Navajo weavers in the Southwest to produce heavy rugs suitable for eastern customers and to adopt new designs and colors to boost sales. Meanwhile, Navajos raised fewer crops and were forced to buy food because the market economy undermined their subsistence agriculture. Soon they were selling land and labor to whites as well, and their dependency made it easier to force them onto reservations.

Reservation policy had degrading consequences. First, Indians had no say over their own affairs on reservations. Supreme Court decisions in 1884 and 1886 defined them as wards (falling, like helpless children, under government protection) and denied them the right to become U.S. citizens. Thus they were unprotected by the Fourteenth and Fifteenth Amendments, which had extended to African Americans the privileges and legal protections of citizenship. Second, pressure from white farmers, miners, and herders who continually sought Indian lands made it difficult for the government to preserve reservations intact. Third, the government ignored native history, even combining on the same reservation Indian bands that habitually had waged war against each other. Rather than serving as civilizing communities, reservations weakened every aspect of Indian life, except the resolve to survive.

Not all Indians succumbed to market forces and reservation restrictions. Apache tribes in the Southwest

Native Resistance

long had raided settlers and migrants passing through their lands and continued to battle whites even after most of their people had been forced onto reservations. Their raiding ended only after the last of their leaders, the Chiricahua insurgent Geronimo, was captured in 1886. Pawnees in the Midwest resisted the disadvantageous deals that white traders tried to impose on them. In the Northwest, Nez Percé Indians tried to prevent being forced onto a reservation by fleeing to Canada in 1877. They successfully eluded U.S. troops and their Crow and Cheyenne scouts over 1,800 miles of rugged terrain, but when they reached Montana, their leader, Young Joseph, decided that they could not succeed, and he ended the flight. Sent to a reservation, Joseph repeatedly petitioned the government for a return of his ancestral lands, but his appeals went unheeded.

As they had done earlier in the East, whites responded to western Indian defiance with military aggression. In

Indian Wars

1860, for example, Navajos, reacting to U.S. military pressure, carried out a destructive raid on Fort Defiance in Arizona Territory. In reprisal, the army eventually attacked and starved the Navajo into submission, destroying their fields, houses, and livestock, and in 1863–1864 forced them on a "Long Walk" from their homelands to a reservation at Bosque Redondo in New Mexico. Also in 1864, in order to eliminate Indians who blocked white ambitions in the Sand Creek region of Colorado, a militia led by Methodist minister John Chivington attacked a Cheyenne band under Black Kettle, killing almost every Indian. In 1879, 4,000 U.S. soldiers forced a surrender from Utes who already had given up most of their ancestral territory in western Colorado but were resisting further concessions.

▲ Plains Indians did not write books or letters as whites did, but they did tell stories and spread news through art. They painted scenes in notebooks and on hides, like this one which depicts the Indians' annihilation of General George A. Custer's soldiers at Little Big Horn in 1876.

(Smithsonian Institution, Western History Division)

The most publicized of Indian battles occurred in June 1876, when 2,500 Lakotas and Cheyennes led by Chiefs Rain-in-the-Face, Sitting Bull, and Crazy Horse surrounded and annihilated 256 government troops led by the rash Colonel George A. Custer near the Little Big Horn River in southern Montana. Although Indians consistently demonstrated military skill in such battles, shortages of supplies and relentless pursuit by U.S. soldiers, including all–African American units of Union Army veterans called Buffalo Soldiers (so named by the Cheyennes and Comanches they fought), eventually overwhelmed armed Indian resistance. Native Americans were not so much conquered in battle as they were harassed and starved into submission.

In the 1870s and 1880s, government officials and reformers sought more purposely than in the past to "civilize" and "uplift" natives through landholding and education. This meant changing their identities and outlawing customs deemed to be "savage and barbarous." In this regard, the United States copied imperialist policies of other nations, such as the French, who banned native religious ceremonies in their Pacific island colonies, and the British, who jailed African religious leaders. The American government determined to persuade Indians to abandon their traditional cultures and adopt American values of ambition, thrift, and materialism.

Reform of Indian Policy

At the same time, other groups argued for sympathetic—and sometimes patronizing—treatment. Reform treatises, such as George Manypenny's *Our Indian Wards* (1880) and Helen Hunt Jackson's *A Century of Dishonor* (1881), and unfavorable comparison with Canada's management of Indian affairs aroused the American conscience. Canada had granted native peoples the rights of British subjects and proceeded more slowly than the United States in efforts to acculturate Indians. A high rate of intermarriage between Indians and Canadian whites also promoted smoother relations.

In the United States, the two most active Indian reform organizations were the Women's National Indian Association (WNIA) and the Indian Rights Association (IRA). The WNIA, composed mainly of white women who sought to use domestic skills to help people in need, urged gradual assimilation of Indians. The IRA, which was more influential but numbered few Native Americans among its members, advocated citizenship and landholding by individual Indians. Most reformers believed Indians were culturally inferior to whites and assumed Indians could succeed economically only if they embraced middle-class values of diligence and education.

Reformers particularly deplored Indians' sexual division of labor. Women seemed to do all the work—tending crops, raising children, cooking, curing hides, making tools and clothes—while being servile to men, who hunted but were otherwise idle. Ignoring the fact that white men sometimes mistreated white women, groups such as the WNIA and IRA wanted Indian men to bear more responsibilities, to treat Indian women more respectfully, and to resemble male heads of white middle-class households. But when Indian men and women adopted the model of white society, in which women were supposed to be submissive and private, Indian women lost much of the economic independence and power over daily life that they once had.

Some exceptional Indians managed to use white-controlled education to their advantage. Zitkala-Sa (Red Bird) was a Yankton Sioux born on the Pine Ridge reservation in South Dakota in 1876. At age twelve, she was sent to a Quaker boarding school in Indiana and later attended Earlham College and the Boston Conservatory of Music. She became an accomplished orator and violinist, but her major contribution was her writing on behalf of her people's needs and the preservation of their cultures. In 1901 Zitkala-Sa published a work of fiction titled *Old Indian Legends,* in which she translated Sioux oral tradition into stories. She wrote other pieces for *Harper's* and *Atlantic Monthly,* and served in various capacities on the Standing Rock and Ute reservations. Zitkala-Sa married a Sioux who had taken the name Ray Bonnin and became known as Gertrude Bonnin. Subsequently, she was elected the first full-blooded Indian secretary of the Society of American Indians (see page 606) and served as editor of *American Indian Magazine,* all the while advocating for Indian rights and cultural respect.

Zitkala-Sa

In 1887 Congress reversed its reservation policy and passed the Dawes Severalty Act. The act, supported by reformers, authorized dissolution of community-owned Indian property and granted land allotments to individual Indian families. The government held that land in trust for twenty-five years, so families could not sell their allotments. The law also awarded citizenship to all who accepted allotments (an act of Congress in 1906 delayed citizenship for those Indians who had not yet taken their allotment). It also entitled the government to sell unallocated land to whites.

Dawes Severalty Act

Indian policy, as implemented by the Interior Department, now took on two main features, both of which aimed at assimilating Indians into white American culture.

▲ White reformers believed children at Indian boarding schools needed to adopt "civilized" dress as necessary to their education. Thus the eleven Chirachua Apache girls and boys who were wearing native dress when they reached the Carlisle (Pennsylvania) School in November 1883 (top) had their hair cut and wore uniforms and dresses for the (bottom) photograph taken after their supposed transformation four months later.

(Both photos: Cumberland County Historical Society, Carlisle, PA)

First and foremost, as required by the Dawes Act, the government distributed reservation land to individual families in the belief that the American institution of private property would create productive citizens and integrate Indians into the larger society. As one official stated, the goal was to "weaken and destroy [Indians'] tribal relations and individualize them by giving each a separate home and having them subsist by industry." Second, officials believed that Indians would abandon their "barbaric" habits more quickly if their children were educated in boarding schools away from the reservations.

The Dawes Act reflected a Euro-American and Christian world-view, an earnest but narrow belief that a society of families headed by men was the most desired model.

Government agents and reformers were joined by educators who viewed schools as tools to create a patriotic, industrious citizenry. Using the model of Hampton Institute, founded in Virginia in 1869 for the education of newly freed slaves, educators helped establish the Carlisle School in Pennsylvania in 1879, which served as the flagship of the government's Indian school system. In keeping with European American custom, the boarding schools imposed white-defined sex roles: boys were taught farming and carpentry, and girls learned sewing, cleaning, and cooking.

In 1890 the government made one last show of force. With active resistance having been suppressed, some Lakotas and other groups turned to the religion of the Ghost Dance as a spiritual means of preserving native culture. Inspired by a Paiute prophet named Wovoka, the Ghost Dance consisted of movement in a circle until the dancers reached a trancelike state and envisioned dead ancestors. Some dancers believed these ancestral visitors heralded a day when buffalo would return to the Plains and all elements of white civilization, including guns and whiskey, would be buried. The Ghost Dance expressed this messianic vision in a ritual involving several days of dancing and meditation.

Ghost Dance

Ghost Dancers forswore violence but appeared threatening when they donned sacred shirts that they believed would repel the white man's bullets. As the religion spread, government agents became alarmed about the possibility of renewed Indian uprisings. Charging that the cult was anti-Christian, they began arresting Ghost Dancers. Late in 1890, the government sent the Seventh Cavalry, Custer's old regiment, to detain Lakotas moving toward Pine Ridge, South Dakota. Although the Indians were starving and seeking shelter, the army assumed they were armed for revolt. Overtaking the band at a creek called Wounded Knee, the troops massacred an estimated three hundred men, women, and children in the snow.

The Indian wars and the Dawes Act effectively accomplished what whites wanted and Indians feared: it reduced native control over land. Eager speculators induced Indians to sell their newly acquired property, in spite of federal safeguards against such practices. Between 1887 and the 1930s, Indian landholdings dwindled from 138 million acres to 52 million. Land-grabbing whites were particularly cruel to the Ojibwas of the northern plains. In 1906 Senator Moses E. Clapp of Minnesota attached to an Indian appropriations bill a rider declaring that mixed-blood adults on the White Earth reservation were "competent" (meaning educated in white ways)

The Losing of the West

enough to sell their land without having to observe the twenty-five-year waiting period stipulated in the Dawes Act. When the bill became law, speculators duped many Ojibwas into signing away their land in return for counterfeit money and worthless merchandise. The Ojibwas lost more than half their original holdings, and economic ruin overtook them.

The government's policy had other injurious effects on Indians' ways of life. The boarding-school program enrolled thousands of children and tried to teach them that their inherited customs were inferior, but most returned to their families demoralized rather than ready to assimilate into white society. Polingaysi Qoyawayma, a Hopi woman forced to take the Christian name Elizabeth Q. White, recalled after four years spent at the Sherman Institute in Riverside, California, "As a Hopi, I was misunderstood by the white man; as a convert of the missionaries, I was looked upon with suspicion by the Hopi people."

Ultimately, political and ecological crises overwhelmed most western Indian groups. White violence and military superiority alone did not defeat them. Their economic systems had started to break down before the military campaigns occurred. Buffalo extinction, enemy raids, and disease, as well as force, combined to hobble subsistence culture to the point where Native Americans had no alternative but to yield their lands to market-oriented whites. Believing their culture to be superior, whites determined to transform Indians into successful farmers by teaching them the value of private property, educating them in American ideals, and eradicating their "backward" languages, lifestyles, and religions. Although Indians tried to retain their culture by both adapting to the various demands they faced, by the end of the century they had lost control of the land and were under increasing pressure to shed their group identity. The West was won at their expense, and to this day they remain casualties of an aggressive age.

THE EXTRACTION OF NATURAL RESOURCES

In contrast to Indians, who used natural resources to meet subsistence needs and small-scale trading, most whites who migrated to the West and the Great Plains were driven by the desire for material success. To their eyes, the vast stretches of territory lay as untapped sources of wealth that could bring about a better life (see Map 17.1). Extraction of these resources advanced settlement and created new markets at home and abroad; it also fueled revolutions in transportation, agriculture, and industry that swept across the United States in the late nineteenth century.

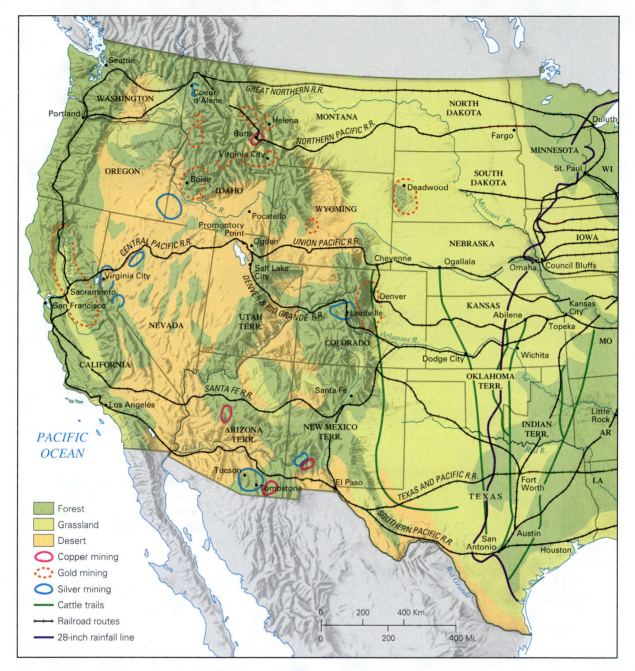

Map 17.1 The Development and Natural Resources of the West

By 1890, mining, lumbering, and cattle ranching had penetrated many areas west of the Mississippi River, and railroad construction had linked together the western economy. These activities, along with the spread of mechanized agriculture, altered both the economy and the people who were involved in them.

This same extraction of nature's wealth also gave rise to wasteful interaction with the environment and fed habits of racial and sexual oppression.

In the mid-1800s, eager prospectors began to comb western forests and mountains for gold, silver, copper, and

Mining and Lumbering

other minerals. The mining frontier advanced rapidly, drawing thousands of people to Nevada, Idaho, Montana, Utah, and Colorado. California, where a gold rush helped populate a thriving state by 1850, furnished many of the miners, who traveled to nearby states in search of riches. Others seeking mineral riches followed traditional routes, moving from the East and Midwest to western mining regions.

Prospectors tended to be restless optimists, willing to climb mountains and trek across deserts in search of a telltale glint of precious metal. They shot game for food and financed their explorations by convincing merchants to advance credit for equipment in return for a share of the as-yet-undiscovered lode. Unlucky prospectors whose credit ran out took jobs and saved up for another search.

Digging for and transporting minerals was extremely expensive, so prospectors who did discover veins of metal seldom mined them. Instead, they sold their claims to large mining syndicates, such as the Anaconda Copper Company. Financed by eastern capital, these companies brought in engineers, heavy machinery, railroad lines, and work crews, and helped boost populations in cities such as El Paso and Tucson. In doing so, they made western mining corporate just like eastern manufacturing. Although discoveries of gold and silver first drew attention to the West and its resources, mining companies usually exploited less romantic but equally lucrative bonanzas of lead, zinc, tin, quartz, and copper.

Unlike mining, cutting trees for lumber to satisfy the demand for construction and heating materials required vast tracts of forest land to be profitable. Because tree supplies in the upper Midwest and South had been depleted—aided by such inventions as bandsaws and feeding machines, which quickened the pace of timber cutting—lumber corporations moved into the forests of the Northwest. They often grabbed millions of acres under the Timber and Stone Act, passed by Congress in 1878 to stimulate settlement in California, Nevada, Oregon, and Washington. It allowed private citizens to buy, at a low price, 160-acre plots "unfit for cultivation" and "valuable chiefly for timber." Lumber companies hired seamen from waterfront boarding houses to register claims to timberland and then transfer those claims to the companies. By 1900 private citizens had bought over 3.5 million acres, but most of that land belonged to corporations.

While mining corporations were excavating western mineral deposits and lumber corporations were cutting down Northwest timberlands, oil companies were beginning to drill wells in the Southwest. In 1900 most of the nation's petroleum still came from the Appalachians and the Midwest, but rich oil reserves had been discovered in southern California and eastern Texas, creating not only new wealth but also boosting boom cities, such as Los

▲ By the 1880s, large-scale operations had replaced solitary prospectors in the extraction of minerals from western territories. Here, powerful sprays of water are being used to wash silver from a deposit in Alma, Colorado. *(Colorado Historical Society)*

Angeles and Houston. Although oil and kerosene were still used mostly for lubrication and lighting, oil discovered in the Southwest later became a vital new source of fuel.

As the West developed, it became a rich multiracial society, including not only Native Americans and native-born white migrants but also Mexicans, African Americans, and Asians, all involved in a process of community building. A crescent of territory, a borderland stretching from western Texas through New Mexico and Arizona to northern California, supported Mexicano ranchers and sheepherders, descendants of the Spanish who had originally claimed the land. In New Mexico, Spaniards mixed with Indians to form a mestizo population of small farmers and ranchers. All along the Southwest frontier, Mexican immigrants moved into American territory to find work. Some returned to Mexico seasonally; others stayed.

Complex Communities

Although the Treaty of Guadalupe Hidalgo (1848) had guaranteed property rights to Hispanics, "Anglo" (the Mexican name for a white American) miners, speculators, and railroads used fraud and other means to steal much of Hispanic landholdings. As a result, many Mexicanos moved to cities such as San Antonio and Tucson, and became wage laborers.

Before the Chinese Exclusion Act of 1882 prohibited the immigration of Chinese laborers, some 200,000 Chinese—mostly young, single males—came to the United States and built communities in California, Oregon, and Washington. Many came with five-year contracts to work on railroad construction, then return home, presumably with resources for a better life. They also worked in the fields. By the 1870s, Chinese composed half of California's agricultural work force. The state's farms and citrus groves demanded a huge migrant work force, and Chinese laborers moved from one ripening crop to another, working as pickers and packers. In cities such as San Francisco, they labored in textile and cigar factories, and lived in large boarding houses. Few married because Chinese women were scarce.

Like Chinese and Mexicans, Japanese and European immigrants moved from place to place as they worked in mining and agricultural communities. The region consequently developed its own migrant economy, with workers shifting communities within a large geographical area as they took short-term jobs in mining, farming, and railroad construction.

African Americans tended to be more settled, many of them "exodusters" who built all-black western towns. Nicodemus, Kansas, for example, was founded in 1877 by black migrants from Lexington, Kentucky, and grew to 600 residents within two years. Early experiences were challenging, but eventually the town developed newspapers, shops, churches, a hotel, and a bank. When attempts to obtain railroad connections failed, however, the town declined, as many of its businesses moved across the Solomon River to the town of Bogue, where a Union Pacific Railroad camp was located.

The major exodus occurred in 1879, when some 6,000 blacks, many of them former slaves, moved from the South to Kansas, aided by the Kansas Freedmen's Relief Association. Other migrants, encouraged by newspaper editors and land speculators, went to Oklahoma Territory. In the 1890s and early 1900s, African American settlers founded thirty-two all-black communities in Oklahoma, and the territory boasted several successful black farmers.

Although unmarried men numerically dominated the western natural-resource frontier, many communities

Western Women

contained populations of white women who had come for the same reason as men: to make their fortune. But on the mining frontier as elsewhere, women's independence was limited; they usually accompanied a husband or father and seldom prospected themselves. Even so, many women used their labor as a resource and earned money by cooking and laundering, and in some cases providing sexual services for the miners in houses of prostitution. In the Northwest, they worked in canneries, cleaning and salting the fish that their husbands caught. Mexicano women took jobs in cities as laundresses and seamstresses.

A number of white women helped to bolster family and community life as members of the home mission movement. Protestant missions had long sponsored benevolent activities abroad, such as in China, and had aided the settlement of Oregon in the 1830s and 1840s. But in the mid-nineteenth century, a number of women broke away from male-dominated missionary organizations. Using the slogan "Woman's work for women," they sought to help women wherever polygamy and female infanticide existed. In the West, they exerted moral authority by establishing missionary societies and aiding women—unmarried mothers, Mormons, Indians, and Chinese—who they believed had fallen prey to men or who had not yet accepted the principles of Christian virtue.

To control labor and social relations within this complex population, white settlers made race an important

Significance of Race

distinguishing characteristic. They usually classified people into five races: Caucasians (themselves), Indians, Mexicans (both Mexican Americans, who had originally inhabited western lands, and Mexican immigrants), "Mongolians" (a term applied to Chinese), and "Negroes." In applying these categories, whites imposed racial distinctions on people who, with the possible exception of African Americans, had never before considered themselves to be a "race." Whites using these categories ascribed demeaning characteristics to all others, judging them to be permanently inferior. In 1878, for example, a federal judge in California ruled that Chinese could not become U.S. citizens because they were not "white persons."

Racial minorities in western communities occupied the bottom half of a two-tiered labor system. Whites dominated the top tier of managerial and skilled labor positions, while Irish, Chinese, Mexican, and African American laborers held unskilled positions. All non-Anglo groups, in addition to the Irish, encountered prejudice,

▲ Born in China, Polly Bemis, pictured here, came to America when her parents sold her as a slave. An Idaho saloonkeeper bought her, and she later married a man named Charlie Bemis, who won her in a card game. Her life story was common among the few Chinese women who immigrated to the United States in the 1860s and 1870s (most Chinese immigrants were men). Unlike many Chinese, however, she lived peacefully after her marriage until her death in 1933.

(Idaho Historical Society Library and Archives)

especially as dominant whites tried to reserve for themselves whatever riches the West might yield. Anti-Chinese violence erupted during hard times. When the Union Pacific Railroad tried to replace white workers with lower-waged Chinese in Rock Springs, Wyoming, in 1885, whites invaded and burned down the Chinese part of town, killing twenty-eight. Mexicans, many of whom had been the original owners of the land in California and elsewhere, saw their property claims ignored or stolen by white miners and farmers.

The multiracial quality of western communities, however, also included a cross-racial dimension. Because so many white male migrants were single, intermarriage with Mexican and Indian women was common. Such intermarriage was acceptable for white men, but not for white women, especially where Asian immigrants were involved. Most miscegenation laws passed by western legislatures were intended to prevent Chinese and Japanese men from marrying white women.

As whites were wresting control of the land from the Indian and Mexican inhabitants of the West, questions

Conservation Movement

arose over control of the nation's animal, mineral, and timber resources. Much of the remaining undeveloped territory west of the Mississippi was in the public domain, and some people believed that the federal government, as its owner, should limit its exploitation. Others, however, believed that their own and the nation's prosperity depended on unlimited use of the land.

Questions about natural resources caught Americans between a desire for progress and a fear of spoiling nature. After the Civil War, people eager to protect the natural landscape began to organize a conservation movement. Sports hunters, concerned about loss of wildlife, opposed market hunting and lobbied state legislatures to pass hunting regulations. Artists and tourists in 1864 persuaded Congress to preserve the beautiful Yosemite Valley by granting it to the state of California, which reserved it for public use. Then, in 1872, Congress designated the Yellowstone River region in Wyoming as the first national park. And in 1891 conservationists, led by naturalist John Muir, pressured Congress to authorize President Benjamin Harrison to create forest reserves—public lands protected from private-interest cutting.

Such policies met with strong objections from lumber companies, lumber dealers, railroads, and householders accustomed to cutting timber freely for fuel and building material. Despite Muir's activism and efforts by the Sierra Club (which Muir helped found in 1892) and by such corporations as the Southern Pacific Railroad, which supported rational resource development, opposition was loudest in the West, where people remained eager to take advantage of nature's bounty. Ironically, however, by prohibiting trespass in areas such as Yosemite and Yellowstone, conservation policy deprived Indians and white settlers of the wildlife, water, and firewood that they had previously taken from federal lands.

Admission of New States

Development of mining and forest regions, as well as of farms and cities, brought western territories to the economic and population threshold of statehood (see Map 17.2). In 1889 Republicans seeking to solidify control of Congress passed an omnibus bill granting statehood to North Dakota, South Dakota, Washington, and Montana. Wyoming and Idaho, both of which allowed women to vote, were admitted the following year. Congress denied statehood to Utah until 1896, wanting assurances from the Mormons, who constituted a majority of the territory's population and controlled its government, that they would give up polygamy.

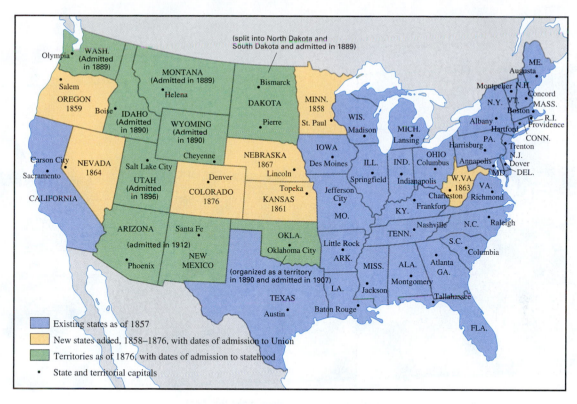

Map 17.2   The United States, 1876–1912
A wave of admissions between 1889 and 1912 brought remaining territories to statehood and marked the final creation of new states until Alaska and Hawai'i were admitted in the 1950s.

Western states' varied communities spiced American folk culture and fostered a "go-getter" optimism that distinguished the American spirit. The lawlessness and hedonism of places such as Deadwood, in Dakota Territory, and Tombstone, in Arizona Territory, gave their region notoriety and romance. Legends grew up almost immediately about characters whose lives both typified and magnified the western experience, and promoters such as Buffalo Bill enhanced the appeal of western folklore.

Arizona's mining towns, with their free-flowing cash and loose law enforcement, attracted gamblers, thieves, and opportunists whose names came to stand for the Wild West. Near Tombstone, the infamous Clanton family and their partner John Ringgold (known as Johnny Ringo) engaged in smuggling and cattle rustling. Inside the town, the Earp brothers—Wyatt, Jim, Morgan, Virgil, and Warren—and their friends William ("Bat") Masterson and John Henry ("Doc") Holliday operated on both sides of the law as gunmen, gamblers, and politicians. A feud between the Clantons and the Earps climaxed on October 26, 1881, in a shootout at the OK Corral, where three

Clantons were killed and Holliday and Morgan Earp were wounded. These characters and their exploits provided material for countless future novels, movies, and television programs.

Writers Mark Twain, Bret Harte, and others captured the flavor of western life, and characters such as Buffalo Bill, Annie Oakley, Wild Bill Hickok, and Poker Alice became western folk heroes. But violence and eccentricity were far from common. Most miners and lumbermen worked long hours, often for corporations rather than as rugged individuals, and had little time, energy, or money for gambling, carousing, or gunfights. Women worked as long or longer as teachers, laundresses, storekeepers, and housewives. Only a few were sharpshooters or dance-hall queens. For most, western life was a matter of adapting and surviving.

IRRIGATION AND TRANSPORTATION

Glittering gold, tall trees, and gushing oil shaped popular images of the West, but water gave it life. If western territories and states promised wealth from mining, cutting,

▲ Water, aided by human resolve, coaxed crops from the dry soil and helped make the West habitable for whites. On this Colorado farm, a windmill pumps water for irrigation.

(Longmont Museum, Longmont, Colorado)

and drilling, their agricultural potential promised more— but only if settlers could find a way to bring water to the arid land. Western economic development is the story of how public and private interests used technology and organization to develop the region's river basins and make the land agriculturally productive. Just as control of land was central to western development, so, too, was control of water.

For centuries, Indians irrigated southwestern lands to sustain their subsistence farming. When the Spanish arrived, they began tapping the Rio Grande River to irrigate farms in southwest Texas and New Mexico. Later they channeled water to the California mission communities of San Diego and Los Angeles. The first Americans of northern European ancestry to practice extensive irrigation were the Mormons. Arriving in Utah in 1847, they quickly diverted streams and rivers into networks of canals, whose water enabled them to farm the hard-baked soil. By 1890 Utah boasted over 263,000 irrigated acres supporting more than 200,000 people.

Efforts at land reclamation through irrigation in Colorado and California sparked conflict over rights to

Rights to Water

the precious streams that flowed through the West. Americans had inherited the English common-law principle of riparian rights, which held that only those who owned land along a river's banks could appropriate from the water's flow. The stream itself, according to riparianism, belonged to God; those who lived near it could take water for normal needs but were not to diminish the river. This principle, intended to protect nature, discouraged economic development because it prohibited each property owner from damming or diverting water at the expense of others who lived downstream.

Americans who settled the West rejected riparianism in favor of the doctrine of prior appropriation, which awarded a river's water to the first person who claimed it. Westerners, taking cues in part from eastern Americans who had diverted waterways to power mills and factories, asserted that water, like timber, minerals, and other natural resources, existed to serve human needs and advance profits. They argued that anyone intending a "reasonable" or "beneficial" (economically productive) use of river water should have the right to appropriation, and the courts generally agreed.

Under appropriation, those who dammed and diverted water often reduced the flow of water downstream. People disadvantaged by such action could protect their interests either by suing those who deprived them of water or by establishing a public authority to regulate water usage. Thus in 1879 Colorado created several water divisions, each with a commissioner to determine and regulate water rights. In 1890 Wyoming enlarged the concept of control with a constitutional provision declaring that the state's rivers were public property subject to state supervision.

Destined to become the most productive agricultural state, California devised a dramatic response to the problem of water rights, sometimes called the California Solution. In the 1860s, a few individuals controlled huge tracts of land in the fertile Sacramento and San Joaquin River valleys, which they used for speculating in real estate, raising cattle, and growing wheat. But around the edges of the wheat fields lay unoccupied lands that could profitably support vegetable and fruit farming if irrigated properly.

Unlike western states that had favored appropriation rights over riparian rights, California maintained a mixed legal system that upheld riparianism while allowing for some appropriation. This system disadvantaged irrigators and prompted them to seek to change state law. In 1887 the legislature passed a bill permitting farmers to organize into districts that would construct and operate irrigation projects. An irrigation district could use its public authority to purchase water rights, seize private property to build irrigation canals, and finance projects through taxation or by issuing bonds. As a result of this legislation, California became the nation's leader in irrigated acreage, with more than 1 million irrigated acres by 1890, making the state's fruit and vegetable agriculture the most profitable in the country.

Although state irrigation provisions stimulated development, the federal government still owned most of western lands in the 1890s, ranging from 64 percent of California to 96 percent of Nevada. Prodded by land-hungry developers, states wanted the federal government to transfer to them at least part of the public domain lands. States claimed that they could make these lands profitable through reclamation—providing them with irrigated water. Congress generally refused such assignments because of the controversies they raised. If one state sponsored irrigation to develop its own land, who would regulate waterways that flowed through more than one

Newlands Reclamation Act

state? If, for example, California assumed control of the Truckee River, which flowed westward out of Lake Tahoe on the California-Nevada border, how would Nevadans be assured that California would give them sufficient water? Only the federal government, it seemed, had the power to regulate regional water development.

In 1902, after years of debates, Congress passed the Newlands Reclamation Act. Named for Nevada congressman Francis Newlands, the law allowed the federal government to sell western public lands to individuals in parcels not to exceed 160 acres and to use proceeds from such sales to finance irrigation projects. The Newlands Act provided for control but not conservation of water, because three-fourths of the water used in open-ditch irrigation, the most common form, was lost to evaporation. Thus the legislation fell squarely within the tradition of development of nature for human profit. Often identified as an example of sensitivity to natural-resource conservation, the Newlands Reclamation Act in fact represented a decision by the federal government to aid the agricultural and general economic development of the West, just as state and federal subsidies to railroads during the 1850s and 1860s aided western settlement.

Between 1865 and 1890, railroad expansion boomed, as total track in the United States grew from 35,000 to 200,000 miles, mostly from construction west of the Mississippi River (see Map 17.1). By 1900 the United States contained one-third of all railroad track in the world. A diverse mix of workers made up construction crews. The Central Pacific, built eastward from San Francisco, employed thousands of Chinese to build its tracks; the Union Pacific, extending westward from Omaha, Nebraska, used mainly Irish construction gangs. Workers lived in shacks and tents that were dismantled, loaded on flatcars, and relocated each day.

Railroad Construction

Railroad construction had powerful economic effects. After 1880, when steel rails began to replace iron rails, railroads helped to boost the nation's steel industry to international leadership. Railroad expansion also spawned related industries, including coal production, passenger- and freight-car manufacture, and depot construction. Influential and essential, railroads also gave important impetus to western urbanization. With their ability to transport large loads of people and freight, lines such as the Union Pacific and the Southern Pacific accelerated the growth of western hubs, such as Chicago, Omaha, Kansas City, Cheyenne, Los Angeles, Portland, and Seattle.

Railroads accomplished these feats with help from some of the largest government subsidies in American

The Australian Frontier

America's frontier West was not unique. Australia, founded like the United States as a European colony, had a frontier society that resembled the American West in several ways, especially in its mining development, its folk society, and its treatment of indigenous people. Australia experienced a gold rush in 1851, just two years after the United States did, and large-scale mining companies quickly moved into its western regions to extract lucrative mineral deposits. In 1897 future U.S. president Herbert Hoover, who at that time was a twenty-two-year-old geology graduate, went to work in Australia and began his successful career as a mining engineer.

A promise of mineral wealth lured thousands of immigrants to Australia in the late nineteenth century. Many of the newcomers arrived from China, and, as in the United States, these immigrants, most of them men, encountered abusive treatment. Anti-Chinese riots erupted in debarkation ports in New South Wales in 1861 and 1873, and beginning in 1854, the Australian government passed several laws restricting Chinese immigration. When the country became an independent British federation in 1901, one of its first acts applied a strict literacy test that virtually terminated Chinese immigration for over fifty years.

As in the American West, the Australian frontier bred folk heroes who came to symbolize white masculinity. In a society where men vastly outnumbered women, Australians glorified the tough, aggressive individual who displayed self-reliance and quick judgment. As an ethos of freedom and opportunity intertwined with the idea of masculine ruggedness, the Australian backcountry man soon became as idealized as the American cowboy. Australian outlaws (called "bushrangers") such as Ned Kelly, an infamous bandit who was hanged in 1880, achieved the same notoriety as Americans Jesse James and Billy the Kid.

Although Australians lauded white men who brought a spirit of personal liberty and opportunism to a new country, they also considered indigenous peoples, whom they called "Aborigines" rather than Indians, as savages needing to be conquered and civilized. Christian missionaries viewed aborigines as lost in pagan darkness and tried to convert them. In 1869 the government of Victoria Province passed an Aborigine Protection Act that, like American policy toward Indians, encouraged removal of native children from their families so they could learn European customs in schools run by whites. Aborigines adapted in their own ways. They formed cricket teams, and those with light skin sometimes hid their identity by telling a census taker they were white. In the end, though, assimilation did not work, and Australians resorted to reservations as a means of "protecting" Aborigines, just as Americans isolated native peoples on reserved land. Like the Americans, white Australians could not find a place for indigenous people in a land of opportunity.

Much like the American counterpart, the Australian frontier was populated by natives before Anglo colonists arrived. The Aborigines, as the Australian natives were called, lived in villages and utilized their own culture to adapt to the environment. This photo shows a native camp in the Maloga Reserve.
(National Library of Australia)

▲ This ad from 1882 shows a steam engine of the Illinois Central Railroad pulling into a station and admired by all. The ad boasts of how the I.C.R.R. not only linked the growing city of Chicago with numerous places all the way south to New Orleans but also replaced old methods of transportation such as the stagecoach and barge pictured in the small insets on the right side of the illustration. *(Library of Congress)*

Railroad Subsidies

history. Promoters argued that, because railroads were a public benefit, the government should aid them by giving them land from the public domain, which they could then sell to finance construction. During the Civil War, Congress, dominated by business-minded Republicans and in the absence of representatives from the seceded southern states, was sympathetic, as it had been when it aided steamboat companies earlier in the nineteenth century. As a result, the federal government granted railroad corporations over 180 million acres, mostly for interstate routes. These grants usually consisted of a right of way, plus alternate sections of land in a strip 20 to 80 miles wide along the right of way. Railroads funded construction by using the land as security for bonds or by selling it for cash. States and localities heaped on further subsidies. State legislators, many of whom had financial interests in a railroad's success, granted some 50 million acres. Cities and towns also assisted, usually by offering loans or by purchasing railroad bonds or stocks.

Government subsidies had mixed effects. Although capitalists often opposed government involvement in the economic affairs of private companies, privately owned railroads nevertheless accepted public aid and pressured governments into meeting their needs. The Southern Pacific, for example, threatened to bypass Los Angeles unless the city paid a bonus and built a depot. Localities that could not or would not pay suffered. Without public help, few railroads could have prospered sufficiently to attract private investment, yet such aid was not always salutary.

During the 1880s, the policy of generosity haunted communities whose zeal had prompted them to commit too much to railroads that were never built or that defaulted on loans. Some laborers and farmers fought subsidies, arguing that companies such as the Southern Pacific would become too powerful. Many communities boomed, however, because they had linked their fortunes to the iron horse. Moreover, railroads helped attract investment into the West and drew farmers into the market economy.

Railroad construction brought about important techological and organizational reforms. By the late, 1880s, almost all lines had adopted

Standard Gauge, Standard Time

standard-gauge rails so that their tracks could connect with one another. Air brakes, automatic car couplers, standardized handholds on freight cars, and other devices made rail transportation safer and more efficient. The need for gradings, tunnels, and bridges spurred the growth of the American engineering profession. Organizational advances included systems for coordinating passenger and freight schedules, and the adoption of uniform freight-classification systems. Railroads also, however, helped reinforce racial segregation by separating black from white passengers on railroad cars and in stations.

Rail transportation altered conceptions of time and space. First, by surmounting physical barriers to travel, railroads transformed space into time. Instead of expressing the distance between places in miles, people began to refer to the amount of time it took to travel from one place to another. Second, railroad scheduling required nationwide standardization of time. Before railroads, local church bells and clocks struck noon when the sun was directly overhead, and people set clocks and watches accordingly. But because the sun was not overhead at exactly the same moment everywhere, time varied from place to place. Boston's clocks, for instance, differed from those in New York by almost twelve minutes. To impose regularity, railroads created their own time zones. In 1883, without authority from Congress, the nation's railroads agreed to establish four standard time zones for the country. Most communities adjusted their clocks accordingly, and railroad time became national time.

FARMING THE PLAINS

While California emerged as the nation's highest-yielding agricultural state, extraordinary development occurred in the Great Plains. There, farming in the late nineteenth century exemplified two important achievements: the transformation of arid, windswept prairies into arable land that would yield crops to benefit humankind, and the transformation of agriculture into big business by means of mechanization, long-distance transportation, and scientific cultivation. These feats did not come easily. The climate and terrain of the Great Plains presented formidable challenges, and overcoming them did not guarantee success. Irrigation and the mechanization of agriculture enabled farmers to feed the nation's burgeoning population and turned the United States into the world's breadbasket, but the experience also scarred the lives of countless men and women who made that accomplishment possible.

During the decades of the 1870s and 1880s, more acres were put under cultivation in states such as Kansas,

Settlement of the Plains

Nebraska, and Texas than in the entire country during the previous 250 years. The number of farms tripled from 2 million to over 6 million between 1860 and 1910, as hundreds of thousands of hopeful farmers streamed into the Plains region. The Homestead Act of 1862 and other measures to encourage western settlement offered cheap or free plots to people who would reside on and improve their property. Land-rich railroads were especially aggressive, advertising cheap land, arranging credit terms, offering reduced fares, and promising instant success. Railroad agents—often former immigrants—traveled to Denmark, Sweden, Germany, and other European nations to recruit settlers and greeted newcomers at eastern ports.

Most families who settled western farmlands migrated because opportunities in the West seemed to promise a second chance, a better existence than their previous one. Railroad expansion gave farmers in remote regions a way to ship produce to market, and the construction of grain elevators eased problems of storage. As a result of worldwide as well as national population growth, demand for farm products burgeoned, and the prospects for commercial agriculture—growing crops for profit and for shipment to distant, including international, markets—became more favorable than ever.

Life on the farm, however, was much harder than advertisements and railroad agents insinuated. Migrants

Hardship on the Plains

often encountered scarcities of essentials that they had once taken for granted, and they had to adapt to the environment. The prairies contained insufficient lumber for housing and fuel, so pioneer families had to build houses of sod and burn buffalo dung for heat. Water for cooking and cleaning was sometimes scarce also. Machinery for drilling wells was expensive, as were windmills for drawing water to the surface.

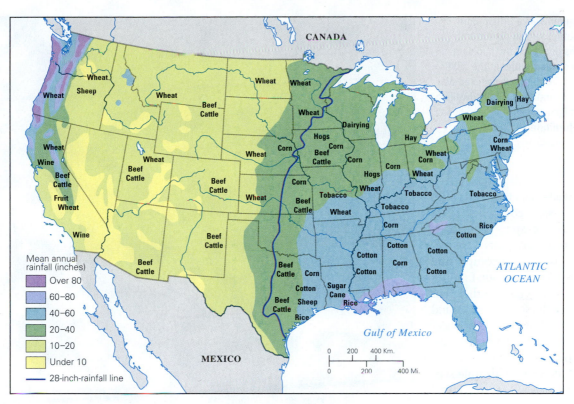

Map 17.3   Agricultural Regions of the United States, 1890

In the Pacific Northwest and east of the twenty-eight-inch-rainfall line, farmers could grow a greater variety of crops. Territory west of the line was either too mountainous or too arid to support agriculture without irrigation. The grasslands that once fed buffalo herds could now feed beef cattle.

The weather was even more formidable than the terrain. The climate between the Missouri River and the Rocky Mountains divides along a line running from Minnesota southwest through Oklahoma, then south, bisecting Texas. West of this line, annual rainfall averages less than twenty-eight inches, not enough for most crops or trees (see Map 17.3), and even that scant life-giving rain was never certain. Heartened by adequate water one year, farmers gagged on dust and broke plows on hardened limestone soil the next.

Weather seldom followed predictable cycles. Weeks of torrid summer heat and parching winds suddenly gave way to violent storms that washed away crops and property. The wind of frigid winter blizzards piled up mountainous snowdrifts that halted outdoor movement. During the Great Blizzard that struck Nebraska, Wyoming, and the Dakota Territory in the winter of 1886–1887, the temperature plunged to 36 degrees below zero. In springtime, melting snow swelled streams, and floods threatened millions of acres. In fall, a week without rain turned dry grasslands into tinder, and the slightest spark could ignite a raging prairie fire. A severe drought in Texas between 1884 and 1886 drove many farmers off the land, and a more widespread drought in 1886 struck areas as diverse as Dakota, Wyoming, and California

Nature could be cruel even under good conditions. Weather that was favorable for crops was also good for breeding insects. Worms and flying pests ravaged fields. In the 1870s and 1880s, grasshopper swarms virtually ate up entire farms. Heralded only by the din of buzzing wings, a mile-long cloud of insects would smother the land and devour everything: plants, tree bark, and clothing. As one farmer lamented, the "hoppers left behind nothing but the mortgage."

Settlers also had to cope with social isolation. In New England and Europe, farmers lived in villages and

Social Isolation

traveled daily to nearby fields. This pattern of community building was rare in the vast expanses of the Plains—and in the Far West and

Evelyn Cameron was a British-born ▶
Montana settler whose diaries and
photographs portrayed the hardship
and beauty of the frontier in the 1890s
and early 1900s. Here she depicted two
homesteaders and their simple dwelling
with its dirt floor, wood stove, and boxes
serving as furniture.
(Montana Historical Society)

South as well—where peculiarities
of land division compelled rural
dwellers to live apart from each
other. Because most plots were rec-
tangular—usually encompassing
160 acres—at most four families
could live near one another, but
only if they built homes around
their shared four-corner intersection. In practice, farm families usually lived back from their boundary
lines, and at least a half-mile separated farmhouses. Men might find
escape by working in distant fields
and taking occasional trips to sell
crops or buy supplies. Women were
more isolated, confined by domestic chores to the household. They
visited and exchanged food and
services with neighbor women when they could, but, as one
writer observed, a farm woman's life was "a weary, monotonous round of cooking and washing and mending."

Letters that Ed Donnell, a young Nebraska home-
steader, wrote to his family in Missouri reveal how time
and circumstances could dull optimism. In the fall of 1885,
Donnell rejoiced to his mother, "I like Nebr first rate. . . .
I have saw a pretty tuff time a part of the time since I have
been out here, but I started out to get a home and I was
determined to win or die in the attempt. . . . Have got a
good crop of corn, a floor in my house and got it ceiled
overhead." Already, though, Donnell was lonely. He went
on, "There is lots of other bachelors here but I am the only
one I know who doesn't have kinfolks living handy. . . .
You wanted to know when I was going to get married.
Just as quick as I can get money ahead to get a cow."

A year and a half later, Donnell's dreams were dis-
solving and, still a bachelor, he was beginning to look for
a second chance elsewhere. He wrote to his brother, "The
rats eat my sod stable down. . . . I may sell out this summer, land is going up so fast. . . . If I sell I am going west
and grow up with the country." By fall, conditions had

worsened. Donnell lamented, "We have been having wet
weather for 3 weeks. . . . My health has been so poor this
summer and the wind and the sun hurts my head so. I
think if I can sell I will . . . move to town for I can get $40
a month working in a grist mill and I would not be exposed to the weather." Donnell's doubts and hardships,
shared by thousands of other people, fed the cityward migration of farm folk that fueled late-nineteenth-century
urban growth (see Chapter 19).

Farm families survived by sheer resolve and by organizing churches and clubs where they could socialize a few
times a month. By 1900 two de-
velopments had brought rural settlers who lived east of the rainfall
line into closer contact with modern consumer society.

**Mail-Order
Companies and
Rural Free Delivery**

First, mail-order companies,
such as Montgomery Ward and Sears, Roebuck, made
new products attainable by the 1870s and 1880s. Emphasizing personal attention to customers, Ward and Sears
received letters that often reported family news and sought
advice on needs from gifts to childcare. A Washington man

▲ By the late nineteenth century, the industrial revolution was having a significant impact on farming. This scene from a Colorado wheat farm shows a harvest aided by a steam tractor and a belt-driven thresher, equipment that made large-scale commercial crop production possible.

(Colorado Historical Society)

wrote to Mr. Ward, "As you advertise everything for sale that a person wants, I thought I would write you, as I am in need of a wife, and see what you could do for me." Another reported, "I suppose you wonder why we haven't ordered anything from you since the fall. The cow kicked my arm and broke it and besides my wife was sick, and there was the doctor bill. But now, thank God, that is paid, and we are all well again, and we have a fine new baby boy, and please send plush bonnet number 29d8077."

Second, after farmers petitioned Congress for extension of the postal service, in 1896 the government made Rural Free Delivery (RFD) widely available. Farmers previously had to go to town to pick up mail. Now they could receive letters, newspapers, and catalogues in a roadside mailbox nearly every day. In 1913 the postal service inaugurated parcel post, which enabled people to receive packages, such as orders from Ward and Sears, more cheaply.

As with industrial production (see Chapter 18), the late-nineteenth-century agricultural revolution was driven by the expanded use of machinery.

Mechanization of Agriculture

When the Civil War drew men away from farms in the upper Mississippi River valley, women and older men who remained behind began using reapers and other mechanical implements to satisfy demand for food and take advantage of high grain prices. After the war, continued demand encouraged farmers to utilize machines, and inventors developed new implements to facilitate planting and harvesting. Seeders, combines, binders, mowers, and rotary plows, carried westward by railroads, improved grain growing on the Plains and in California. Technology also aided dairy and poultry farming. The centrifugal cream separator, patented in 1879, sped the process of skimming cream from milk, and a mechanized incubator, invented in 1885, made chicken raising more profitable.

For centuries, the acreage of grain a farmer planted was limited by the amount that could be harvested by hand. Machines—driven first by animals, then by steam—significantly increased productivity. Before mechanization, a farmer working alone could harvest about 7.5 acres of wheat. Using an automatic binder that cut and bundled the grain, the same farmer could harvest 135 acres. Machines dramatically reduced the time and cost of farming other crops as well.

Meanwhile, Congress and scientists worked to improve existing crops and develop new ones. The 1862

Legislative and Scientific Aids

Morrill Land Grant Act gave each state federal lands to sell in order to finance agricultural research at educational institutions. The act prompted establishment of public universities in Wisconsin, Illinois, Minnesota, California, and other states. A second Morrill Act in 1890 aided more

TABLE 17.1	Summary: Government Land Policy
Railroad land grants (1850–1871)	Granted 181 million acres to railroads to encourage construction and development
Homestead Act (1862)	Gave 80 million acres to settlers to encourage settlement
Morrill Act (1862)	Granted 11 million acres to states to sell to fund public agricultural colleges
Other grants	Granted 129 million acres to states to sell for other educational and related purposes
Dawes Act (1887)	Allotted some reservation lands to individual Indians to promote private property and weaken tribal values among Indians and offered remaining reservation lands for sale to whites (by 1906, some 75 million acres had been acquired by whites)
Various laws	Permitted direct sales of 100 million acres by the Land Office

Source: Goldfield, David; Abbott, Carl; Anderson, Virginia Dejohn; Argersinger, Jo Ann; Argersinger, Peter H.; Barney, William L.; and Weir, Robert M., *The American Journey, Volume II*, 3rd ed., © 2004. Reproduced by permission of Pearson Education, Inc., Upper Saddle River, New Jersey.

schools, including several all-black colleges. The Hatch Act of 1887 provided for agricultural experiment stations in every state, further encouraging the advancement of farming science and technology.

Science also enabled farmers to use the soil more efficiently. Researchers developed dry farming, a technique of plowing and harrowing that minimized evaporation of precious moisture. Botanists perfected varieties of "hard" wheat whose seeds could withstand northern winters, and millers invented a process for grinding the tougher wheat kernels into flour. Agriculturists also adapted new varieties of alfalfa from Mongolia, corn from North Africa, and rice from Asia. Horticulturist Luther Burbank developed hundreds of new food plants and flowers at a garden laboratory in Sebastopol, California. George Washington Carver, a son of slaves who became a chemist and taught at Alabama's Tuskegee Institute, created hundreds of new products from peanuts, soybeans, and sweet potatoes. Other scientists developed means of combating plant and animal diseases. Just as in mining and manufacturing, science and technology provided American farming with means for expanding productivity in the market economy.

THE RANCHING FRONTIER

While commercial farming was overspreading the West, it ran headlong into one of the region's most romantic industries—ranching. Beginning in the sixteenth century, Spanish landholders had engaged in cattle raising in Mexico and what would become the American Southwest.

They employed Indian and Mexican cowboys, known as *vaqueros*, who tended the herds and rounded up cattle to be branded and slaughtered. Anglo ranchers moving into Texas and California in the early nineteenth century hired *vaqueros*, who in turn taught their skills in roping, branding, horse training, and saddle making to white and African American cowboys. About one-fourth of all cowboys were black. Although black cowboys probably experienced less discrimination than other African American laborers did on the job, off the trail they had to sit in separate sections in saloons and endured derogatory names and other mistreatment.

By the 1860s, cattle raising became increasingly profitable, as population growth boosted the demand for beef and railroads simplified the transportation of food. By 1870 drovers were herding thousands of Texas cattle northward to Kansas, Missouri, and Wyoming (see Map 17.1). At the northern terminus, the cattle were sold to northern ranches or loaded onto trains bound for Chicago and St. Louis, for slaughter and distribution to national and international markets.

The long drive gave rise to romantic lore of bellowing cattle, buckskin-clad cowboys, and smoky campfires under starry skies, but the process was not very efficient. Trekking 1,000 miles or more for two to three months made cattle sinewy and tough. Herds traveling through Indian lands and farmers' fields were sometimes shot at and later prohibited from such trespass by state laws. Ranchers adjusted by raising herds nearer to railroad routes. When ranchers discovered that crossing Texas longhorns with heavier Hereford and Angus breeds produced animals better able to survive harsh winters, cattle raising expanded northward, and proliferating herds in Kansas, Nebraska, Colorado, Wyoming, Montana, and the Dakotas crowded out already declining buffalo populations. Profits were considerable. A rancher could purchase a calf for $5, let it feed at no cost on the Plains for a few years, recapture it in a roundup, and sell it at a market price of $40 or $45.

Cattle raisers needed vast pastures to graze their herds while incurring as little expense as possible. Thus

The Open Range

they often bought a few acres bordering a stream and turned their herds loose on adjacent public domain that no one wanted because it lacked water access. By this method, called open-range ranching, a cattle raiser could utilize thousands of acres by owning only a hundred or so. Neighboring ranchers often formed associations and allowed herds to graze together. Owners identified their cattle by burning a brand into each animal's hide. Each ranch had its own brand—a shorthand method for labeling movable property. But as

▲ A group of cowboys prepare for a roundup. Note the presence of African Americans, who, along with Mexicans, made up one-fourth of all cowboys. Though they rarely became trail bosses or ranch owners, black cowboys enjoyed an independence on the trails that was unavailable to them on tenant farms and city streets. *(Nebraska State Historical Society)*

demand for beef kept rising and as ranchers and capital flowed into the Great Plains, cattle began to overrun the range, and other groups' interests began challenging ranchers over use of the land.

Sheepherders from California and New Mexico were also using the public domain, sparking territorial clashes. Ranchers complained that sheep ruined grassland by eating down to the roots and that cattle refused to graze where sheep had been. Occasionally ranchers and sheepherders resorted to armed conflict rather than settle disagreements in court, where a judge might discover that both were using public land illegally.

More important, however, the advancing farming frontier was generating new demands for land. Devising a way to organize property resulted in an unheralded but highly significant change in land management. The problem was fencing. Lacking sufficient timber and stone for traditional fencing, western settlers could not easily define and protect their property. Tensions flared when farmers accused cattle raisers of allowing their herds to trespass on cropland and when herders in turn charged that farmers should fence their property against grazing animals. But ranchers and farmers alike lacked an economical means of enclosing their herds and fields.

The solution was barbed wire. Invented in 1873 by Joseph F. Glidden, a DeKalb, Illinois, farmer, this fencing consisted of wires held in place by sharp spurs twisted around them.

Barbed Wire

Mass-produced by the Washburn and Moen Manufacturing Company of Worcester, Massachusetts—80.5 million pounds worth in 1880 alone—barbed wire provided a cheap and durable means of enclosure. It opened the Plains to homesteaders by enabling them to protect their farms from grazing cattle. It also ended open-range ranching and made roundups unnecessary, because it enabled large-scale ranchers to enclose their herds within massive stretches of private property. In addition, the development of the round silo for storing and making feed (silage) enabled cattle raisers to feed their herds without grazing them on vast stretches of land.

By 1890 big businesses were taking over the cattle industry and applying scientific methods of breeding and feeding. Corporations also used

Ranching as Big Business

technology to squeeze larger returns out of meatpacking. Like buffalo, all parts of a cow had uses. Only about half of it consisted of salable meat. Meatpackers' largest profits came from

▲ Bordered by the product it was promoting, this advertisement conveyed the message that railroads and farmers could protect their property from each other by utilizing a new type of fencing. *(Elwood House Museum, DeKalb, Illinois)*

livestock by-products: hides for leather, blood for fertilizer, hooves for glue, fat for candles and soap, and the rest for sausages. But cattle processing also had harmful environmental impact. What meatpackers and leather tanners could not sell was dumped into rivers and streams. By the late nineteenth century, the Chicago River, which flowed past the city's mammoth processing plants, created such a powerful stench that nearby residents became sick in the summer.

Open-range ranching made beef a staple of the American diet and created a few fortunes, but its features could not survive the spurs of barbed wire and the rush of history. During the 1880s, overgrazing destroyed nourishing grass supplies on the Plains, and the brutal winter of 1886–1887 destroyed 90 percent of some herds and drove small ranchers out of business. By 1890, large-scale ranchers owned or leased the land they used, though some illegal fencing persisted. Cowboys formed labor organizations and participated in strikes for higher pay. The myth of the cowboy's freedom and individualism lived on, but ranching, like mining and farming, quickly became a corporate business.

Legacy FOR A PEOPLE AND A NATION

The Myth of the Cowboy

The image of the cowboy has been one of America's most distinctive icons. Yet its legacy reveals much about how the nation's culture has transformed an ordinary phenomenon into a myth. The actual American cowboys, whose heyday lasted only twenty-five years, about 1865–1890, were poorly paid, poorly fed, poorly dressed, illiterate young men who sometimes stole cattle from their employers. They were, as one Wyoming newspaper called them, "rough men with shaggy hair and wild staring eyes in butternut trousers stuffed into great rough boots." From a total of about 35,000 cowboys, 25 percent were black and another 15 percent were Mexican, Indians, and Chinese, all of whom their employers treated even more unfairly than they did white cowboys. Working at dirty jobs and often unemployed, some white and nonwhite cowboys joined unions and went on strike for job security and better wages. Mostly, however, cowboys got drunk more often than (as the myth suggests) they engaged in gunfights, enforced the law, or defended a woman's honor.

Yet the apparently independent, highly masculine, outdoor existence that cowboys led fueled a romantic notion that they somehow embodied the true American. Buffalo Bill Cody was one of the first to create this image by featuring in his Wild West shows a cattle herder named Buck Taylor, whom Cody glamorized as "King of the Cowboys." Shortly thereafter, fiction writers and artists began depicting cowboys as valiant characters. A best-selling novel, *The Virginian* (1902) by Owen Wister, about a Wyoming cowboy, helped reinforce the image of a rugged, self-reliant individualist who took the law into his own hands, and thereafter myriad films, radio, and television programs turned what once was a common laborer into a hero. A new "King of the Cowboys," Roy Rogers, who acted in hundreds of movies and TV shows between 1938 and 1964, was just one of many media characters who enlarged the myth, aided by the rise of the cowboy theme in country and western music. Gone was the ill-fitting, makeshift clothing of the past, now replaced by fancy boots, huge belt buckles, Stetson hats, and blue jeans, all of which became popular American fashion, worn at home and exported abroad.

Equally important, the disreputable, low-life reality was replaced by a no-nonsense lawman battling evil. President Ronald Reagan, a Californian, embellished his image by wearing western clothing and being photographed on horseback. And President George W. Bush, a Texan, stirred patriotism by assuming the role of a "good cowboy" after September 11, 2001, while opponents of his Iraq invasion criticized America's "bad cowboy" tactics of recklessly using violence to achieve a quick solution. The cowboy myth has consequently left a legacy not only of images but also of actions.

SUMMARY

The reality of history revealed that both Frederick Jackson Turner's image of the West as the home of democratic spirit and Buffalo Bill's depiction of the West as the battlefield of the white man's victory were incomplete at best. Interaction between people and the environment proved to be far more intricate than either understood.

The landscape of the American West exerted lasting influence, through both its dominance and its fragility, on the complex mix of people who built communities there. Indians, the original inhabitants, had used, and sometimes abused, the land to support subsistence cultures that included trade and war as well as hunting and farming. Living mostly in small groups, they depended on delicate resources, such as buffalo herds and salmon runs. When they came into contact with commerce-minded, migratory European-Americans, their resistance to the market economy, diseases, and violence that whites brought into the West failed.

Mexicans, Chinese, African Americans, and Anglos discovered a reciprocal relationship between human activities and the nonhuman world which they had not always anticipated. Miners, timber cutters, farmers, and builders extracted raw minerals to supply eastern factories, used irrigation and mechanization to bring forth agricultural abundance from the land, filled pastures with cattle and sheep to expand food sources, and constructed railroads to tie the nation together. In doing so, they transformed half of the continent within a few decades. But the environment also exerted its own power over humans, through its climate, its insects and predators, its undesirable plant growth, and its impenetrable hazards and barriers to human movement and agriculture.

The West's settlers, moreover, employed force, violence, and greed that sustained discrimination within a multiracial society; left many farmers feeling cheated and betrayed; provoked contests over use of water and pastures; and sacrificed environmental balance for market profits. The region's raw materials and agricultural products improved living standards and hastened the industrial progress of the Machine Age, but not without human and environmental costs.

SUGGESTIONS FOR FURTHER READING

William Cronon, *Nature's Metropolis: Chicago and the Great West* (1991)

Albert L. Hurtado and Peter Iverson, *Major Problems in American Indian History: Documents and Essays,* 2d ed. (2001)

Karl Jacoby, *Crimes Against Nature: Squatters, Poachers, Thieves and the Hidden History of American Conservation* (2001)

Patricia Nelson Limerick, *The Legacy of Conquest: The Unbroken Past of the American West* (1987)

Eugene P. Moehring, *Urbanism and Empire in the Far West, 1840–1890* (2004)

Alan Trachtenberg, *The Incorporation of America: Culture and Society in the Gilded Age* (1982)

Robert M. Utley, *The Indian Frontier of the American West, 1846–1890* (1984)

Richard White, *"It's Your Misfortune and None of My Own": A New History of the American* (1991)

For a more extensive list for further reading, go to college.hmco.com/pic/norton8e.

The Machine Age

1877-1920

*I*n 1911 iron molders at the Watertown Arsenal, a government weapons factory near Boston, went on strike after a fellow worker, Joseph Cooney, was fired. Cooney had objected when an efficiency expert timed his work with a stopwatch, and the molders feared that such a time study was the first step in management's imposition of new standards on their labor. Iron molders' union president John Frey explained, "The workman believes when he goes on strike that he is defending his job." Frey meant that the molders felt a property right to their labor, that a job was not something that could be changed or removed from them without their consent.

The army officers who ran the factory believed differently. They thought that they owned the molders' labor and that the output was "not much more than one-half what it should be." To increase production, they hired Dwight Merrick, an expert in a new field called "scientific management," to time workers and suggest ways to speed their performance.

The day Merrick began his study, a molder named Perkins secretly timed the same task that Merrick did. Merrick reported that the job should take twenty-four minutes; Perkins found that to do the job right required fifty minutes. Merrick concluded that the workers were wasting time and materials in making molds; Perkins maintained that the molders knew more about making molds than Merrick did. That evening, the molders met to discuss how they should respond to the discrepancy between Merrick's report and their own sense of their job. Joseph Cooney argued that they should not submit to the system of scientific management, and the workers drew up a petition expressing their views. When Cooney confronted Merrick the next day, the molders were ready to walk out.

◄ Building parts for mowing machines at the McCormick farm implements factory, these workers are engaged in mechanized, mass production. Machines, standardized parts, and assembly-line production transformed American industrialization, the status of labor, and the availability of consumer goods. *(Navistar Archives)*

CHRONOLOGY

1869 ■ Knights of Labor founded

1873–78 ■ Economy declines

1876 ■ Bonsack invents machine for rolling cigarettes

1877 ■ Widespread railroad strikes protest wage cuts

1878 ■ Edison Electric Light Company founded

1879 ■ George's *Poverty and Progress* argues for taxing unearned wealth

1881 ■ First federal trademark law begins spread of brand names

1882 ■ Standard Oil Trust founded

1884–85 ■ Economy declines

1886 ■ Haymarket riot in Chicago protests police brutality against labor demonstrations
■ American Federation of Labor (AFL) founded

1890 ■ Sherman Anti-Trust Act outlaws "combinations in restraint of trade"

1892 ■ Homestead (Pennsylvania) steelworkers strike against Carnegie Steel Company

1893–97 ■ Economic depression causes high unemployment and business failures

1894 ■ Workers of Pullman Palace Car Company strike

1895 ■ *U.S. v. E. C. Knight Co.* limits Congress's power to regulate manufacturing

1896 ■ *Holden v. Harcy* upholds law regulating miners' working hours

1903 ■ Women's Trade Union League (WTUL) founded

1905 ■ *Lochner v. New York* overturns law limiting bakery workers' working hours and limits labor protection laws
■ Industrial Workers of the World (IWW) founded

1908 ■ *Muller v. Oregon* upholds law limiting women to ten-hour workday
■ First Ford Model T built

1911 ■ Triangle Shirtwaist Company fire in New York City leaves 146 workers dead

1913 ■ Ford begins moving assembly-line production

1919 ■ Telephone operators strike in New England

Eventually, molders and their bosses at the Watertown Arsenal compromised and settled the strike, but this incident reveals one of the important consequences of the industrialization that was making countless new products available in the late 1800s. Four themes characterized the era. First, inventors and manufacturers harnessed technology in ways never before imagined. Second, the new economic order had a profound impact on production and labor. To increase production and maximize use of machines, factory owners divided work routines into minute, repetitive tasks and organized them according to the dictates of the clock. Workers (employees) like the Watertown molders, who had long thought of themselves as valued for their skills, now struggled to avoid becoming slaves to machines. Third, a new consumer society took shape as goods that had once been accessible to a few became available to many. Products such as canned foods and machine-made clothing, which had hardly existed before the Civil War, became common by the turn of the century. Finally, in their quest for growth and profits, corporation owners (employers) amassed great power. Defenders of the new system devised theories to justify it, while critics and laborers tried to combat what they thought were abuses of power.

Industrialization is a complex process whose chief feature is production of goods by machine rather than by hand. In the mid-nineteenth century, an industrial revolution had swept through parts of the United States, and the mechanization that characterized it powered a second round in the late 1800s and early 1900s. Three technological developments characterized this new process: electricity, the internal-combustion engine, and new applications in the use of chemicals. These technologies followed from earlier industrialization. Electricity provided a needed alternative to steam engines, which had reached their peak of utility. The demand for transportation to supplement railroads spurred progress in automobile manufacture. And the textile industry's experiments with dyes, bleaches, and cleaning agents advanced chemical research.

Until the late nineteenth century, the United States was just another developing nation. In 1860 only one-fourth of the American labor force worked in manufacturing and transportation; by 1900 over half did so. As the twentieth century dawned, the United States had become

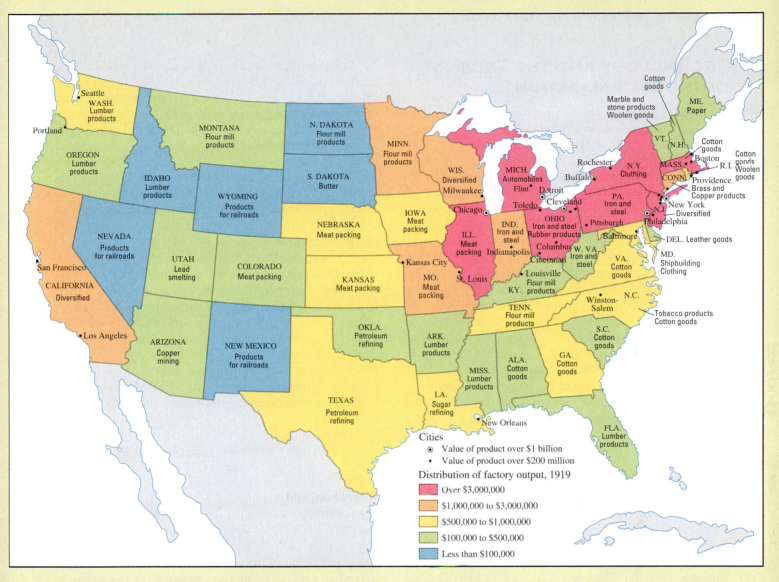

Cotton goods — ME. Paper

Marble and stone products Woolen goods — VT.

Seattle — WASH. Lumber products

Portland

OREGON Lumber products

IDAHO Lumber products

MONTANA Flour mill products

N. DAKOTA Flour mill products

MINN. Flour mill products

WIS. Diversified Milwaukee

MICH. Automobiles Flint

Detroit

Rochester

Buffalo

N.Y. Clothing

N.H.

Cotton goods

Boston

MASS.

R.I.

Cotton goods

Woolen goods

S. DAKOTA Butter

WYOMING Products for railroads

NEVADA Products for railroads

San Francisco

CALIFORNIA Diversified

Los Angeles

UTAH Lead smelting

COLORADO Meat packing

ARIZONA Copper mining

NEW MEXICO Products for railroads

IOWA Meat packing

NEBRASKA Meat packing

KANSAS Meat packing

Chicago

ILL. Meat packing

Toledo

Cleveland

IND. Iron and steel

Indianapolis

Columbus

Cincinnati

OHIO Iron and steel Rubber products

PA. Iron and steel

Pittsburgh

W. VA Iron and steel

Baltimore

New York

Philadelphia

CONN.

Providence Brass and Copper products

N.J. Diversified

DEL. Leather goods

MD. Shipbuilding Clothing

Kansas City

MO. Meat packing

St. Louis

Louisville

KY. Flour mill products

VA. Cotton goods

N.C.

Winston-Salem

Tobacco products Cotton goods

OKLA. Petroleum refining

ARK. Lumber products

TENN. Flour mill products

S.C. Cotton goods

TEXAS Petroleum refining

MISS. Lumber products

LA. Sugar refining

New Orleans

ALA. Cotton goods

GA. Cotton goods

FLA. Lumber products

Cities

◉ Value of product over $1 billion
• Value of product over $200 million

Distribution of factory output, 1919

▮ Over $3,000,000
▮ $1,000,000 to $3,000,000
▮ $500,000 to $1,000,000
▮ $100,000 to $500,000
▮ Less than $100,000

Map 18.1   Industrial Production, 1919

By the early twentieth century, each state could boast at least one kind of industrial production.
Although the value of goods produced was still highest in the Northeast, states such as Minnesota
and California had impressive dollar values of outputs.

(Source: *Data from U.S. Bureau of the Census,* Fourteenth Census of the United States, 1920, *Vol. IX, Manufacturing*
[Washington, D.C.: U.S. Government Printing Office, 1921].)

not only the world's largest producer of raw materials and food, but also the most productive industrial nation (see Map 18.1). Between 1877 and 1920, migrants from farms and abroad swelled the industrial work force (see Chapter 19), but labor-saving machines, more than people, boosted productivity. Innovations in business organization and marketing also fueled the drive for profits.

These developments had momentous effects on standards of living and everyday life. The accomplishments of industrialization provided a complementary episode to the extraction of natural resources and the expansion of agriculture (see Chapter 17). Together, these processes combined people, the environment, and technology in a mix that gave rise to both constructive and destructive forces.

• How did mechanization affect the lives of average workers and the makeup of the labor force?
• In what ways did technological innovation alter the American standard of living?
• What ideas did some Americans use to justify industrialization, and how did others criticize it?

TECHNOLOGY AND THE TRIUMPH OF INDUSTRIALIZATION

While some people pursued opportunity in the American West, others sought new ways of doing things with technology. Thomas Edison was one such person. In 1876 he and his associates opened an "invention factory" in Menlo Park, New Jersey, where they intended to turn out "a minor invention every ten days and a big thing every six months or so." If Americans wanted new products, Edison believed, they had to organize and work purposefully to bring about progress. His attitude reflected the spirit that enlivened American inventiveness, which in turn propelled industrialization in the late nineteenth century. Activity at the U.S. Patent Office, created by the Constitution to "promote the Progress of science and useful Arts," reflects this spirit. Between 1790 and 1860 the government granted a total of 36,000 patents. In the next seventy-year span, between 1860 and 1930, it registered 1.5 million. Inventions often sprang from a marriage between technology and business organization. The harnessing of electricity, internal combustion, and industrial chemistry illustrates how this marriage worked.

Most of Edison's more than one thousand inventions used electricity to transmit light, sound, and images. His

Birth of the Electrical Industry

biggest "big thing" project began in 1878 when he embarked on a search for a cheap, efficient means of indoor lighting. After tedious experiments, Edison perfected an incandescent bulb that used tungsten to prevent the filament from burning up when electrical current passed through it. At the same time, his Edison Electric Light Company devised a system of power generation and distribution that could provide electricity conveniently to a large number of customers. To market his ideas, Edison acted as his own publicist. During the 1880 Christmas season he illuminated Menlo Park, and in 1882 he built a power plant that lighted eighty-five buildings on New York's Wall Street. A *New York Times* reporter marveled that working in his office at night now "seemed almost like writing in daylight."

Edison's system of direct current could transmit electric power only a mile or two, because it lost voltage the farther it was transmitted. George Westinghouse, an inventor from Schenectady, New York, who had previously created an air brake for railroad cars, solved the problem. Westinghouse purchased European patent rights to generators that used alternating current and to transformers that reduced high-voltage power to lower voltage levels, thus making long-distance transmission more efficient.

Other entrepreneurs utilized new business practices to market Edison's and Westinghouse's technological breakthroughs. Samuel Insull, Edison's private secretary, organized Edison power plants across the country, amassing an electric utility empire. In the late 1880s and early 1890s, financiers Henry Villard and J. P. Morgan bought up patents in electric lighting and merged small equipment-manufacturing companies into the General Electric Company. Equally important, General Electric and Westinghouse Electric encouraged practical applications of electricity by establishing research laboratories that paid scientists to create electrical products for everyday use.

While corporations organized company labs, individual inventors continued to work independently and tried, sometimes successfully and sometimes not, to sell their handiwork and patents to manufacturers. One such inventor, Granville T. Woods, an engineer sometimes called "the black Edison," patented thirty-five devices vital to electronics and communications. Among his inventions, most of which he sold to companies such as General Electric, were an automatic circuit breaker, an electromagnetic brake, and instruments to aid communications between railroad trains.

Early innovations in the technology of the internal-combustion engine took place in Europe. In 1885 a German

Henry Ford and the Automobile Industry

engineer, Gottlieb Daimler, built a lightweight engine driven by vaporized gasoline. This development inspired one of America's most visionary manufacturers, Henry Ford. In the 1890s, Ford, an electrical engineer in Detroit's Edison Company, experimented in his spare time with using Daimler's engine to power a vehicle. George Selden, a Rochester, New York, lawyer, had already been tinkering with such technology, but Ford applied organizational genius to this invention and spawned a massive industry.

Like Edison, Ford had a scheme as well as a product. In 1909 he declared, "I am going to democratize the automobile. When I'm through, everybody will be able to afford one, and about everyone will have one." Ford proposed to reach this goal by mass-producing thousands of identical cars in exactly the same way. Adapting the methods of the meatpacking and metalworking industries, Ford engineers set up assembly lines that drastically reduced the time and cost of producing autos. Instead of performing numerous tasks, each worker was assigned only one task, performed repeatedly, using the same specialized machine. In this way, workers assembled the entire car as it passed by them on a conveyor belt.

The Atlantic Cable

During the late nineteenth century, as American manufacturers expanded their markets overseas, their ability to communicate with customers and investors improved immeasurably as a result of a telegraph cable laid beneath the Atlantic Ocean. The telegraph was an American invention, and Cyrus Field, the man who thought up the idea to lay a cable across the ocean, was an American. Yet most of the engineers who worked on the Atlantic cable, as well as most of the capitalists involved in the venture, were British. In 1851 a British company laid the first successful undersea telegraph cable from Dover, England, to Calais, France, proving that an insulated wire could carry signals underwater. The effectiveness of this venture, which connected the Reuters news service to the European continent and allowed French investors to receive instantaneous messages from the London Stock Exchange, inspired British and American businessmen to attempt a larger project across the Atlantic.

The first attempts to build a transatlantic cable failed, but in 1866 a British ship, funded by British investors, successfully laid a telegraph wire that operated without interruption. The project was designed by cooperative efforts of American and British electrical engineers. Thereafter, England and the United States grew more closely linked in their diplomatic relations, and citizens of both nations developed greater concern for each other as a result of their ability to receive international news more quickly. When American president James Garfield was assassinated in 1881, the news traveled almost instantly to Great Britain, and Britons mourned the death more profusely than they had mourned the passing of Abraham Lincoln, whose death was not known in England until eleven days after it had occurred, because transatlantic messages at that time traveled by steamship.

Some people lamented the stresses that near-instant international communications now created. One observer remarked that the telegraph tended "to make every person in a hurry, and I do not believe that with our business it is very desirable that it should be so." But financially savvy individuals experienced welcome benefits as a result of the cable's link. Rapid availability of stock quotes boomed the businesses of the New York and London stock exchanges, much to investors' delight. Newspaper readers enjoyed reading about events on the other side of the ocean the next day, instead of a week after they had occurred. And the success of the Atlantic cable inspired similar ventures in the Mediterranean Sea, the Indian Ocean, and, eventually, across the Pacific. By 1902 underwater cables circled the globe, and the age of global telecommunications had begun.

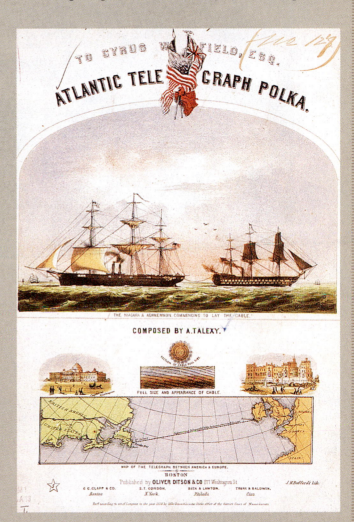

▲ Laid by British ships across the ocean in 1866, the Atlantic cable linked the United States with England and continental Europe so that telegraph communications could be sent and received much more swiftly than ever before. Now Europeans and Americans could exchange news about politics, business, and military movements almost instantly, whereas previously such information could take a week or more to travel from one country to another. *(Library of Congress)*

▲ The assembly line broke the production process down into simple tasks that individual workers could efficiently repeat hour after hour. Here, assembly-line workers at the Ford plant in Highland Park, Michigan, outside Detroit, are installing pistons in engines of the Model T around 1914.

(Henry Ford Museum and Greenfield Village)

In 1913 the Ford Motor Company's first full assembly line began operation in Highland Park outside Detroit, Michigan, and the next year, Ford sold 248,000 cars. Soon, other manufacturers entered the field. Rising automobile output created more jobs, higher earnings, and greater profits in such companies, but also in related industries, such as oil, paint, rubber, and glass, which in turn necessitated increased extraction of resources from the West and abroad. Moreover, assembly-line production in these and many other industries would not have been possible without precision machine tools to create standardized parts. Advances in grinding and cutting technology in this era made production processes accurate to one-thousandth of an inch.

By 1914 a Ford car cost $490, about one-fourth of the price a decade earlier. Yet even $490 was too expensive for many workers, who earned at best $2 a day. That year, however, Ford tried to spur productivity, prevent high labor turnover, head off unionization, and better enable his workers to buy the cars they produced by offering them the Five-Dollar-Day plan—a combination of wages and profit sharing.

The du Pont family did for the chemical industry what Edison and Ford did for the electrical and automobile industries. The du Ponts began

The Du Ponts and the Chemical Industry

manufacturing gunpowder in Delaware in the early 1800s. In 1902, fearing antitrust prosecution for the company's near monopoly of the American explosives industry, three cousins, Alfred, Coleman, and Pierre, took over E. I. du Pont de Nemours and Company, and broadened production into fertilizers, dyes, and other chemical products. In 1911 du Pont scientists and engineers working in the nation's first corporate research laboratory adapted cellulose to the production of such consumer goods as photographic film, lacquer, textile fibers, and plastics. In 1914 Pierre du Pont invested $25 million in fledgling automobile manufacturer General Motors, helping that company rise to compete with Ford. The du Pont company also pi-

▲ Tobacco production was one southern industry that traditionally hired African American laborers. This scene from a Richmond tobacco factory around 1880 shows women and children preparing leaves for curing by tearing off the stems. *(Library of Congress)*

oneered methods of management, accounting, and reinvestment of earnings, all of which contributed to efficient production, better recordkeeping, and higher profits.

The South's major staple crops, tobacco and cotton, drew industry to the region after the Civil War, and other forms of production grew as well. Before the 1870s, Americans used tobacco mainly for snuff, cigars, and chewing. But in 1876 James Bonsack, an eighteen-year-old Virginian, invented a machine for rolling cigarettes. In 1885 James B. Duke, owner of a North Carolina tobacco company, licensed Bonsack's machine and began mass-production. Like Edison and Ford, Duke marketed what he manufactured. Sales soared when he began enticing consumers with free samples, trading cards, and billboard ads. By 1900 his American Tobacco Company was a global business, dominating sales in England and Japan as well

Technology and Southern Industry

as the United States. Duke's and other cigarette factories employed black and white workers (including women), though in separate locations of the plant.

New technology helped relocate the textile industry to the South, as electricity made New England's water-powered mills obsolete. Factories with electric looms were more efficient, because they needed fewer workers with fewer skills, and electric lighting expanded the hours of production. Investors built new plants in southern communities, where a cheap labor force was available. By 1900 the South had more than four hundred textile mills, with a total of 4 million spindles. Women and children who worked in these mills earned 50 cents a day for twelve or more hours of work—about half the wages that northern workers received. Most mills refused to hire black workers except as janitors. Many companies built villages around their mills, where they controlled housing, stores, schools, and churches. Inside these towns, owners banned criticism of the company and squelched attempts at union organization.

Northern and European as well as the region's own investors financed other southern industries. During the 1880s, northern capitalists developed southern iron and steel manufacturing, much of it in the boom city of Birmingham, Alabama. Between 1890 and 1900, northern lumber syndicates moved into the pine forests of the Gulf states, boosting production 500 percent. Southern wood production not only advanced the construction industry but also prompted the relocation of furniture and paper production from the North to the South.

Encouraged by industrial expansion, boosters heralded the emergence of a New South. Challenging the power of the planter class, a business class of manufacturers, merchants, and financiers were making southern cities the nerve centers of a new economic order (see Chapter 19). These promoters believed that the South should put the military defeat of the Civil War behind it—though never forget the heroism of Confederate soldiers—and emulate the North's economic growth. Henry Grady, editor of the *Atlanta Constitution* and a passionate advocate of southern progress, proclaimed, "We have sowed towns and cities in the place of theories, and put business in place of politics. We have challenged your spinners in Massachusetts and your iron-makers in Pennsylvania. . . . We have fallen in love with work."

In all regions, the timing of technological innovation varied from one industry to another, but machines broadly altered the economy and everyday life. Telephones and typewriters made face-to-face communication less important and facilitated correspondence and recordkeeping in growing insurance, banking, and advertising firms. Electric sewing machines made mass-produced clothing available to almost everyone. Refrigeration changed dietary habits by enabling the preservation and shipment of meat, fruit, vegetables, and dairy products. Cash registers and adding machines revamped accounting and created new clerical jobs. At the same time, American universities established programs in engineering, enabling manufacturers such as Edison and the du Ponts to hire new graduates in chemistry and physics.

Profits resulted from higher production at lower costs. Small crafts, such as cabinet making and metalworking, persisted, but as technological innovations made large-scale production more economical, owners replaced small factories with larger ones. Between 1850 and 1900, average capital investment in a manufacturing firm increased by 250 percent. Only large companies could afford to buy

Consequences of Technology

▲ Taken at the historic moment of liftoff, this photograph shows the first airplane flight at Kitty Hawk, North Carolina, on December 17, 1903. With Orville Wright lying at the controls and brother Wilbur standing nearby, the plane was airborne only twelve seconds and traveled 120 feet. Even so, the flight marked the beginning of one of the twentieth century's most influential industries.

(Library of Congress)

complex machines and operate them at full capacity. And large companies could best take advantage of discounts for shipping products in bulk and for buying raw materials in quantity. Economists call such advantages economies of scale.

Profitability depended as much on how production was arranged as on the machines in use. Where once shop-floor workers such as the Watertown molders controlled the methods and timing of production, by the 1890s engineers and managers with specialized, "scientific" knowledge had assumed this responsibility. They planned every task to increase output. Through standardization, they reduced the need for worker skills and judgment, boosting profits at the expense of worker independence.

The most influential advocate of efficient production was Frederick W. Taylor. As foreman and engineer for the Midvale Steel Company in the 1880s, Taylor concluded that the best way a company could reduce fixed costs and increase profits was to apply systematic studies of "how quickly the various kinds of work . . . ought to be done." The "ought" in Taylor's formulation signified producing more for lower cost per unit, usually by eliminating unnecessary workers. Similarly, "how quickly" meant that time and money were equivalent. He called his scheme "scientific management."

Frederick W. Taylor and Efficiency

In 1898 Taylor took his stopwatch to the Bethlehem Steel Company to illustrate how his principles worked. His experiments, he explained, required studying workers and devising "a series of motions which can be made quickest and best." Applying this technique to the shoveling of ore, Taylor designed fifteen kinds of shovels and prescribed the proper motions for using each one, thereby reducing a crew of 600 men to 140. Soon other companies, including the Watertown Arsenal, began applying Taylor's theories to their production lines.

As a result of Taylor's writings and experiments, time, as much as quality, became the measure of acceptable work, and management accumulated knowledge of and power over the ways of doing things. As integral elements of the assembly line, which divided work into specific time-determined tasks, employees such as the Watertown molders feared that they were becoming another kind of interchangeable part.

MECHANIZATION AND THE CHANGING STATUS OF LABOR

By 1900, the status of labor had shifted dramatically in just a single generation. Technological innovation and

▲ The combination of machines and workers still required meticulous hand-work in some industries. Often women with nimble fingers could find jobs in industries such as jewelry and watch-making where, as at this room at the Elgin National Watch Company, they could swiftly manipulate tiny production processes. *(Chicago Historical Society)*

assembly-line production created new jobs, but because most machines were labor saving, fewer workers could produce more in less time. Moreover, workers could no longer accurately be termed producers, as farmers and craftsmen had traditionally thought of themselves. The working class now consisted mainly of employees—people who worked not on their own but when someone hired them. Producers had been paid in accordance with the quality of what they produced; employees received wages for time spent on the job.

By subdividing manufacturing into small tasks, mass production required workers to repeat the same standardized operation all day every day. One investigator found that a worker became

Mass Production

a mere machine. . . . Take the proposition of a man operating a machine to nail on 40 to 60 cases of heels in a day. That is 2,400 pairs, 4,800 shoes in a day. One not accustomed to it would wonder how a man could pick up and lay down 4,800 shoes in a day, to say nothing of putting them . . . into a machine. . . . That is the driving method of the manufacture of shoes under these minute subdivisions.

Assembly lines and scientific management also deprived employees of their independence. Workers could no longer decide when to begin and end the workday, when to rest, and what tools and techniques to use. The clock regulated them. As a Massachusetts factory laborer testified in 1879, "During working hours the men are not allowed to speak to each other, though working close together, on pain of instant discharge. Men are hired to watch and patrol the shop." And employees now were surrounded by others who labored at the same rate for the same pay, regardless of the quality of their effort.

Workers affected by these changes, such as the Watertown iron molders, struggled to retain autonomy and self-respect in the face of employers' ever-increasing power. Artisans such as glass workers and coopers (barrel makers), caught in the transition from hand labor to machine production, fought to preserve their work pace and customs—say, by appointing a fellow worker to read a newspaper aloud while they worked. When immigrants went to work in factories, they tried to persuade foremen to hire their relatives and friends, thus preserving on-the-job family and village ties. Off the job, workers gathered in saloons and parks for such leisure-time activities as social drinking and holiday celebrations, ignoring employers' attempts to control their social lives as well.

Employers, concerned with efficiency, wanted certain standards of behavior upheld. Ford Motor Company re-

quired workers to satisfy the company's behavior code before becoming eligible for a part of the Five-Dollar-Day plan. To increase worker incentives, some employers established piecework rates, paying laborers an amount per item produced rather than an hourly wage. These efforts to increase productivity and maximize use of machines were intended to make workers perform like the machines they operated.

As machines and assembly lines reduced the need for skilled workers, employers found that they could cut labor costs by hiring women and children, and paying them low wages. Between 1880 and 1900, the numbers of employed women soared from 2.6 million to 8.6 million. At the same time, their occupational patterns underwent striking changes (see Figure 18.1). The proportion of women in domestic service (maids, cooks, laundresses)—the most common and lowest-paid form of female employment—dropped as jobs opened in other sectors. In manufacturing, women usually held menial positions in textile mills and food-processing plants that paid as little as $1.56 a week for seventy hours of labor. (Unskilled men received $7 to $10 for a similar workweek.) Although the number of female factory hands tripled between 1880 and 1900, the proportion of women workers in these jobs remained about the same.

Restructuring of the Work Force

General expansion of the clerical and retail sectors, however, greatly boosted the numbers and percentages of women who were typists, bookkeepers, and sales clerks. Previously, men with accounting and letter-writing skills had dominated sales and office positions. New inventions, such as the typewriter, cash register, and adding machine, simplified these tasks, and employers replaced males with lower-paid females, many of whom had taken courses in typing and shorthand, and were looking for the better pay and conditions that clerical jobs offered compared with factory and domestic work. By 1920, women filled nearly half of all clerical jobs; in 1880 only 4 percent had been women. An official of a sugar company observed in 1919 that "all the bookkeeping of this company . . . is done by three girls and three bookkeeping machines . . . one operator takes the place of three men." Although poorly paid, women were attracted to sales jobs because of the respectability, pleasant surroundings, and contact with affluent customers that such positions offered. Nevertheless, sex discrimination persisted. In department stores, male cashiers took in cash and made change; women seldom were given responsibility for billing or for counting money. Women held some low-level supervisory positions, but males dominated the managerial ranks.

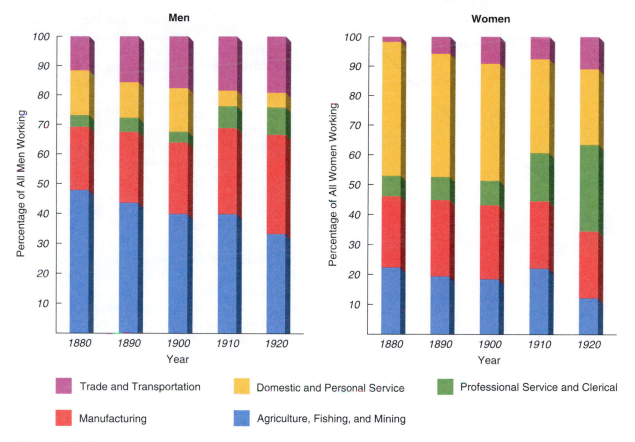

Figure 18.1 **Distribution of Occupational Categories Among Employed Men and Women, 1880–1920**

The changing lengths of the bar segments of each part of this graph represent trends in male and female employment. Over the forty years covered by this graph, the agriculture, fishing, and mining segment for men and the domestic service segment for women declined the most, whereas notable increases occurred in manufacturing for men and professional services (especially store clerks and teachers) for women.

(Source: *U.S. Bureau of the Census,* Census of the United States, 1880, 1890, 1900, 1910, 1920 *[Washington, D.C.: U.S. Government Printing Office].)*

Although most children who worked toiled on their parents' farms, the number in nonagricultural occupations tripled between 1870 and 1900. In 1890 over 18 percent of all children between ages ten and fifteen were gainfully employed (see Figure 18.2). Textile and shoe factories in particular employed young workers. Mechanization created numerous light tasks, such as running errands and helping machine operators, which children could handle at a fraction of adult wages. Conditions were especially hard for child laborers in the South, where growing numbers of textile mills needed unskilled hands. Mill owners induced white sharecroppers and tenant farmers, who desperately needed extra income, to bind their children over to factories at miserably low wages.

Several states, especially in the Northeast, passed laws specifying minimum ages and maximum workday hours for child labor. But large companies could evade regulations because such statutes regulated only firms operating within state borders, not those engaged in interstate commerce. Enforcing age requirements proved difficult because many parents, needing income from child labor, lied about their children's ages, and employers rarely asked. After 1900, state laws and automation, along with compulsory school attendance laws, began to

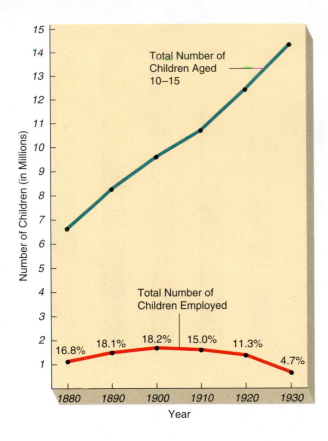

Figure 18.2   Children in the Labor Force, 1880–1930

The percentage of children in the labor force peaked around the turn of the century. Thereafter, the passage of state laws requiring children to attend school until age fourteen and limiting the ages at which children could be employed caused child labor to decline.

(Source: *Data from* The Statistical History of the United States from Colonial Times to the Present *[Stamford, Conn.: Fairfield Publishers, 1965].)*

reduce the number of children employed in manufacturing, and Progressive era reformers sought federal legislation to restrict child labor (see Chapter 21). Still, many children continued to work at street trades—shining shoes and peddling newspapers and other merchandise—and as helpers in stores. The poorest children also scavenged city streets for pieces of coal and wood, discarded clothing and furniture, and other items that their families could use.

For all workers, industrial labor was highly dangerous. Repetitive tasks using high-speed machinery dulled concen-

Industrial Accidents

tration, and the slightest mistake could cause serious injury. Industrial accidents rose steadily before 1920, killing or maiming hundreds of thousands of people each year. In 1913, for example, even after factory owners had installed safety devices, some 25,000 people died in industrial mishaps, and 1 million were injured. For those with mangled limbs, infected cuts, and chronic illnesses, there was no disability insurance to replace lost income, and families stricken by such misfortunes suffered acutely.

Sensational disasters, such as explosions and mine cave-ins, aroused outcries for better safety regulations. The most notorious tragedy was a fire at New York City's Triangle Shirtwaist Company in 1911, which killed 146 workers, most of them teenage immigrant women trapped in locked workrooms. Despite public clamor, prevailing free-market views hampered passage of legislation that would regulate working conditions, and employers denied responsibility for employees' well-being. As one railroad manager declared, "The regular compensation of employees covers all risk or liability to accident. If an employee is disabled by sickness or any other cause, the right to claim compensation is not recognized."

To justify their treatment of workers, employers asserted the principle of "freedom of contract." The relation-

Freedom of Contract

ship between an employee and an employer, according to this principle, resembled one between a customer and a seller. Like the price of an item for sale, wages and working conditions were the result of a free market in which laws of supply and demand prevailed. In addition, employers asserted, workers entered into a contract with bosses, either explicit or assumed, in which they "sold" their labor. If a worker did not like the contract's provisions, such as the wages and hours, the worker was free to decline and seek another job elsewhere, just as the customer was free to buy a product somewhere else. In practice, however, employers used supply and demand to set wages as low as laborers would accept, causing workers to conclude that the system trapped them. A factory worker told Congress in 1879, "The market is glutted, and we have seasons of dullness; advantage is taken of men's wants, and the pay is cut down; our tasks are increased, and if we remonstrate, we are told our places can be filled. I work harder now than when my pay was twice as high."

Reformers and union leaders lobbied Congress for laws to improve working conditions, but the Supreme Court,

▲ As textile mills often employed young children, so too did the food-processing industry. In 1913, Rosie, age seven, worked full time at the Varn & Platt Canning Company, in Bluffton, South Carolina. She started at 4 a.m. every day and did not go to school. *(Library of Congress)*

Court Rulings on Labor Reform

agreeing with business interests, limited the scope of such legislation by narrowly defining which jobs were dangerous and which workers needed protection. In *Holden v. Hardy* (1896), the Court upheld a law regulating miners' working hours, concluding that an overly long workday would increase the threat of injury. In *Lochner v. New York* (1905), however, the Court voided a law limiting bakery workers to a sixty-hour week and ten-hour day. Offsetting the argument that states had authority to protect workers' health and safety, the Court ruled that baking was not a dangerous enough occupation to justify restricting workers' right to sell their labor freely. Such restriction, according to the Court, violated the Fourteenth Amendment's guar-

antee that no state could "deprive any person of life, liberty, or property without due process of law."

In *Muller v. Oregon* (1908), the Court used a different rationale to uphold a law limiting women in laundries to a ten-hour workday. In this case the Court set aside its *Lochner* argument that a state could not interfere with an individual's right of contract, asserting instead that a woman's well-being "becomes an object of public interest and care in order to preserve the strength and vigor of the race." The case represented a victory for reform groups such as the Consumers' League, which had sought government regulation of women's hours and working conditions. As a result of the *Muller* decision, however, labor laws effectively barred women from occupations, such as in printing and transportation, that

On March 25, 1911, the worst factory ▶
fire in U.S. history occurred at the Triangle
Shirtwaist Company, which occupied the
top three floors of a building in New York
City. Fed by piles of fabric, the fire spread
quickly, killing 146 of the 500 young women,
mostly Jewish immigrants, employed in the
factory. Many of the victims, lined up at the
morgue in this scene, were trapped inside
rooms locked by their employer; others
plunged to their death out of the upper-
story windows.

*(Juanita Hadwin Collector. Triangle Fire Lantern Slides,
Kheel Center, Cornell University, Ithaca, NY 14853-3901)*

required heavy lifting, long hours, or
night work, further confining women
to low-paying, dead-end jobs.

LABOR VIOLENCE
AND THE UNION MOVEMENT

Workers adjusted to mechanization as best they could.
Some people submitted to the demands of the factory, machine, and time clock. Some tried to blend old ways of
working into the new system. Others turned to resistance.
Individuals challenged the system by ignoring management's orders, skipping work, or quitting. But also, anxiety over the loss of independence and a desire for better
wages, hours, and working conditions drew disgruntled
workers into unions. Organized labor was not new in the
late nineteenth century. Trade unions for skilled workers in
crafts such as printing and iron molding dated from the
early 1800s, but their influence was limited. The National
Labor Union, founded in 1866, claimed 640,000 members
from a variety of industries, but it collapsed in 1873 when it
failed to convince Congress to legislate a shorter workday.

In the economic slump that followed the Panic of
1873, railroad managers cut wages, increased workloads,
and laid off workers, especially
those who had joined unions. Such
actions drove workers to strike and
riot. The year 1877 marked a crisis.
In July, unionized railroad workers
organized a series of strikes to protest wage cuts. Venting
pent-up anger, rioters attacked railroad property from Pennsylvania and West Virginia to the Midwest, Texas, and

**Railroad Strikes
of 1877**

California, derailing trains and burning rail yards. State
militia companies, organized and commanded by employers, broke up picket lines and fired into threatening crowds.
In several communities, factory workers, wives, and merchants aided the strikers, while railroads enlisted strikebreakers to replace union men.

The worst violence occurred in Pittsburgh, where on
July 21 state troops bayoneted and fired on rock-throwing
demonstrators, killing ten and wounding many more. In-
furiated, the mob drove the troops into a railroad roundhouse and set fires that destroyed 39 buildings, 104 engines,
and 1,245 freight and passenger cars. The next day, the
troops shot their way out of the roundhouse and killed
twenty more citizens before fleeing the city. After more than
a month of unprecedented violence, President Rutherford B. Hayes sent in federal soldiers—the first significant use of the army to quell labor unrest. Throughout
the strike, emotions ran high. A Pennsylvania militiaman,
ordered out to break the 1877 strike, recalled, "I talked to
all the strikers I could get my hands on, and I could find
but one spirit and one purpose among them—that they
were justified in resorting to any means to break down
the power of the corporations."

Although they sometimes spoke for all laborers, railroad workers had struck in 1877 in their own interest.

Knights of Labor

About the same time, however, an organization called the Knights of Labor tried to attract a broad base of laborers. Founded in 1869 by Philadelphia garment cutters, the Knights began recruiting other workers in the 1870s. In 1879 Terence V. Powderly, a machinist and mayor of Scranton, Pennsylvania, was elected grand master. Under his forceful guidance, Knights membership grew rapidly, peaking at 730,000 in 1886. In contrast to most craft unions, Knights welcomed unskilled and semiskilled workers, including women, immigrants, and African Americans (but not Chinese laborers).

The Knights tried to avert the bleak future that they believed industrialism portended by building an alliance that offered an alternative to profit-oriented industrial capitalism. They intended to eliminate conflict between labor and management by establishing a cooperative society in which laborers, not capitalists, owned factories, mines, and railroads. The goal, argued Powderly, was to "eventually make every man his own master—every man his own employer." This view had its drawbacks. The cooperative idea, attractive in the abstract, was unattainable because employers held the economic leverage and could outcompete laborers who might try to establish their own businesses. Strikes offered one means of achieving immediate goals, but Powderly and other Knights leaders argued that strikes tended to divert attention from the long-term goal of a cooperative society and that workers tended to lose more by striking than they won.

Some Knights, however, did support militant action. In 1886 the Knights demanded higher wages and union recognition from railroads in the Southwest. Railroad magnate Jay Gould refused to negotiate, and a strike began in Texas and spread to Kansas, Missouri, and Arkansas. As violence increased, Powderly met with Gould and called off the strike, hoping for a settlement. But Gould again rejected concessions, and the Knights gave in. Militant craft unions began to desert the Knights, upset by Powderly's compromise and confident that they could attain more on their own.

After the Haymarket riot (see below), Knights membership dwindled, although the union and its cooperative vision survived in a few small towns, where it made a brief attempt to unite with Populists in the 1890s (see Chapter 20). The special interests of craft unions replaced the Knights' broad-based but often vague appeal, and dreams of labor unity faded.

Haymarket Riot

At the same time that Knights went on strike in the Southwest, workers both inside and outside of formal labor organizations generated mass strikes in favor of an eight-hour workday. On May 1, 1886, in Chicago, some 100,000 workers turned out for the largest labor demonstration in the country's history. Their numbers included anarchists who believed in using violence to replace all government with voluntary cooperation. Chicago police, fearing that European radicals were transplanting a tradition of violence to the United States, mobilized to prevent disorder, especially among striking workers at the huge McCormick reaper plant. The day passed calmly, but two days later, police stormed an area near the factory and broke up a battle between striking unionists and nonunion strikebreakers. Police shot and killed two unionists and wounded several others.

The next evening, laborers rallied at Haymarket Square near downtown Chicago, to protest police brutality. As a

▲ The Haymarket riot of 1886 was one of the most violent incidents of labor unrest in the late nineteenth century. This drawing, from *Frank Leslie's Illustrated Newspaper*, shows workers fleeing while police beat demonstrators with nightsticks. As this clash was occurring, a bomb, allegedly set off by anarchists, exploded, killing both police and workers. *(Library of Congress)*

police company approached, a bomb exploded, killing seven and injuring sixty-seven. In reaction, authorities made mass arrests of anarchists and unionists. Eventually a court convicted eight anarchists of the bombing, though evidence of their guilt was questionable. Four were executed, and one committed suicide in prison. The remaining three received pardons in 1893 from Illinois governor John P. Altgeld, who believed they had been victims of the jurors' "malicious ferocity." Denounced by capitalists as a friend of anarchy, Altgeld found that his act of conscience ruined his political career.

The Haymarket bombing, like the 1877 railroad strikes, drew attention to labor's growing discontent and heightened fear of radicalism. The participation of anarchists and socialists, many of them foreign-born, created a feeling that forces of law and order must act swiftly to prevent social turmoil. To protect their interests, private Chicago donors helped to establish a military base just outside the city. Elsewhere, governments strengthened police forces and armories. Employer associations, coalitions of manufacturers in the same industry, countered labor militancy by circulating blacklists of union activists whom they would not employ and by hiring private detectives to guard company property and suppress strikes.

The American Federation of Labor (AFL), founded in 1886, emerged from the upheavals of that year as the major workers' organization. An alliance of national craft unions, the AFL had about 140,000 members, most of them skilled workers. Led by Samuel Gompers, former head of the Cigar Makers' Union, the AFL avoided the Knights' and anarchists' idealism to press for concrete goals: higher wages, shorter hours, and the right to bargain collectively. Born in London to German Jewish parents, Gompers developed his commitment to unionism from interactions with émigré socialists, but he was more of a pragmatist than a radical. In contrast to the Knights, Gompers and the AFL accepted capitalism and worked to improve conditions within it.

American Federation of Labor

AFL member unions retained autonomy in their own areas of skill but tried to develop a general policy that would suit all members. The national organization required constituent unions to hire organizers to expand membership, and it collected dues for a fund to aid members on strike. The AFL avoided party politics, adhering instead to Gompers's dictum of supporting labor's friends and opposing its enemies, regardless of party.

AFL membership grew to 1 million by 1901 and 2.5 million by 1917, when it consisted of 111 national unions and 27,000 locals. But because member unions organized by craft rather than by workplace, they had little interest in recruiting unskilled workers. Nor did they recruit women. Of 6.3 million employed women in 1910, fewer than 2 percent belonged to unions. Male unionists often rationalized women's exclusion by insisting that women should not be employed. According to one labor leader, "Woman is not qualified for the conditions of wage labor. . . . The mental and physical makeup of woman is in revolt against wage service. She is competing with the man who is her father or husband or is to become her husband." Mostly, unionists worried that, because women were paid less, men's wages would be lowered or they would lose jobs if women invaded the workplace. Moreover, male workers, accustomed to sex segregation in employment, could not imagine working side by side with women.

Organized labor also excluded most immigrant and African American workers. Many white workers feared that such groups would depress wages, but long-standing nativism and racism also influenced union policies. Only a few trade unions in which foreign-born craftsmen were leaders welcomed immigrants. Blacks were prominent in the coal miners' union and were partially unionized in such trades as construction, barbering, and dock work, which employed large numbers of African American workers. But they could belong only to segregated local unions in the South, and the majority of northern AFL unions had exclusion policies. Long-held prejudices were reinforced when blacks and immigrants, eager for any work they could get, were hired as strikebreakers to replace striking whites.

The AFL and the labor movement suffered a series of setbacks in the early 1890s, when once again labor violence stirred public fears. In July 1892 the AFL-affiliated Amalgamated Association of Iron and Steelworkers refused to accept pay cuts and went on strike in Homestead, Pennsylvania. In response, Henry C. Frick, president of the Carnegie Steel Company, closed the plant. Shortly thereafter, Frick hired three hundred guards from the Pinkerton Detective Agency to protect the factory and floated them in by barge under cover of darkness. Lying in wait on the shore of the Monongahela River, angry workers attacked and routed the Pinkertons. State troops intervened, and after five months the strikers gave in. By then public opinion had turned against the union, after a young anarchist who was not a striker attempted to assassinate Frick.

Homestead Strike

In 1894 workers at the Pullman Palace (railroad passenger) Car Company walked out in protest over ex-

Pullman Strike

ploitative policies at the company town near Chicago. The paternalistic owner, George Pullman, provided everything for the twelve thousand residents of the so-called model town named after him. His company controlled all land and buildings, the school, the bank, and the water and gas systems. It paid wages, fixed rents, and spied on disgruntled employees. As one laborer grumbled, "We are born in a Pullman house, fed from the Pullman shop, taught in the Pullman school, catechized in the Pullman church, and when we die we shall be buried in the Pullman cemetery and go to the Pullman hell."

One thing Pullman would not do was negotiate with workers. When hard times hit in 1893, Pullman tried to protect profits and stock dividends by cutting wages 25 to 40 percent while holding firm on rents and prices in the town. Hard-pressed workers sent a committee to Pullman to protest his policies. He reacted by firing three committee members. Enraged workers, most of them from the American Railway Union, called a strike; Pullman retaliated by closing the factory. The union, led by the charismatic Eugene V. Debs, voted to aid strikers by refusing to handle any Pullman cars attached to any trains anywhere. Pullman rejected arbitration. The railroad owners' association then enlisted aid from U.S. Attorney General Richard Olney, a former railroad lawyer, who obtained a court injunction to prevent the union from "obstructing the railways and holding up the mails." President Grover Cleveland ordered federal troops to Chicago, ostensibly to protect rail-carried mail, but in reality to crush the strike. Within a month strikers gave in, and Debs went to prison for defying the court injunction. The Supreme Court upheld Debs's six-month sentence on grounds that the federal government could legally remove obstacles to interstate commerce.

IWW

In the West, Colorado miners engaged in several bitter struggles and violent strikes. In 1905 they helped form a new, radical labor organization, the Industrial Workers of the World (IWW). Unlike the AFL but like the Knights of Labor, the IWW strove to unite all laborers of all races who were excluded from craft unions. Its motto was "An injury to one is an injury to all," and its goal was "One Big Union." But the "Wobblies," as IWW members were known, exceeded the tactics of the Knights by espousing violence and sabotage.

Embracing the rhetoric of class conflict—"The final aim is revolution," according to IWW creed—and an ideology of socialism, Wobblies believed workers should seize and run the nation's industries. Leaders such as Mary "Mother" Jones, an Illinois coalfield union organizer; Elizabeth Gurley Flynn, a fiery orator known as the "Joan of Arc of the labor movement"; Italian radical Carlo Tresca; Swedish-born organizer and songwriter Joe Hill; and William D. (Big Bill) Haywood, the brawny, one-eyed founder of the Western Federation of Miners, headed a series of strife-torn strikes. Demonstrations erupted in western lumber and mining camps, in the steel town of McKees Rocks, Pennsylvania (1907), and in the textile mills of Lawrence, Massachusetts (1912). Although the Wobblies' anticapitalist goals and aggressive tactics attracted considerable publicity, IWW membership probably never exceeded 150,000. The organization collapsed during the First World War when federal prosecution sent many of its leaders to jail and local police forces violently harassed IWW members.

Women Unionists

Despite their general exclusion from unions, some women employees did organize and fight employers as strenuously as men did. The "Uprising of the 20,000" in New York City, a 1909 strike by male and female immigrant members of the International Ladies' Garment Workers' Union (ILGWU), was one of the country's largest strikes to that time. Women were also prominent in the 1912 Lawrence, Massachusetts, textile workers' "Bread and Roses" strike. Female trade-union membership swelled during the 1910s, but men monopolized national leadership, even in industries with large female work forces, such as garment manufacturing, textiles, and boots and shoes.

Women, however, did dominate one union: the Telephone Operators' Department of the International Brotherhood of Electrical Workers. Organized in Montana and San Francisco early in the twentieth century, the union spread throughout the Bell system, the nation's monopolistic telephone company and single largest employer of women. To promote solidarity among their mostly young female members, union leaders organized dances, excursions, and bazaars. They also sponsored educational programs to enhance members' leadership skills. The union focused mainly on workplace issues. Intent on developing pride and independence among telephone operators, the union resisted scientific management techniques and tightening of supervision. In 1919 several militant union branches paralyzed the phone service of five New England states, but the union collapsed after a failed strike, again in New England, in 1923.

A key organization seeking to promote interests of laboring women was the Women's Trade Union League

▲ In 1919 telephone operators, mostly female, went out on strike and shut down phone service throughout New England. The male-dominated leadership of the International Brotherhood of Electrical Workers, to which the operators belonged, opposed the strike, but the women refused to back down and eventually achieved several of their demands against the New England Telephone Company. *(Corbis-Bettmann)*

(WTUL), founded in 1903 and patterned after a similar organization in England. The WTUL sought workplace protection legislation and reduced hours for female workers, sponsored educational activities, and campaigned for woman suffrage. It helped telephone operators organize their union, and in 1909 it supported the ILGWU's massive strike against New York City sweatshops. Initially the union's highest offices were held by middle-class women who sympathized with female wage laborers, but control shifted in the 1910s to forceful working-class leaders, notably Agnes Nestor, a glove maker; Rose Schneiderman, a cap maker; and Mary Anderson, a shoe worker. The WTUL advocated opening apprenticeship programs to women so they could enter skilled trades and training female workers to assume leadership roles. It served as a vital link between the labor and women's movements into the 1920s.

The dramatic labor struggles in the half-century following the Civil War make it easy to forget that only a

The Experience of Wage Work

small fraction of American wage workers belonged to unions. In 1900 about 1 million out of a total of 27.6 million workers were unionized. By 1920 union membership had grown to 5 million, still only 13 percent of the work force. Unionization was strong in construction trades, transportation, communications, and, to a lesser extent, manufacturing. For many workers, getting a job and keeping it took priority over bargaining for higher wages and shorter hours. Job instability and the seasonal nature of work seriously hindered union-organizing efforts. Few companies employed a full work force year-round; most employers hired during peak seasons and laid workers off during slack periods. The 1880 census showed that in some communities 30 percent of adult males had been jobless at some time during the previous year. Moreover, union organizers took no interest in large segments of the industrial labor force and intentionally barred others.

The millions of men, women, and children who were not unionized tried in their own ways to cope with the pressures of the machine age. Increasing numbers, both native-born and immigrant, joined fraternal societies, such as the Polish Roman Catholic Union, the African American Colored Brotherhood and Sisterhood of Honor, and the Jewish B'nai B'rith. For small monthly or yearly contributions these organizations, widespread by the early twentieth century, provided members with life insurance, sickness benefits, and burial costs.

For most American workers, then, the machine age had mixed results. Industrial wages, though rarely generous, rose between 1877 and 1914, boosting purchasing power and creating a mass market for standardized goods. Yet in 1900 most employees worked sixty hours a week at wages that averaged 20 cents an hour for skilled work and 10 cents an hour for unskilled. And workers found that, even as their wages rose, living costs increased even faster.

STANDARDS OF LIVING

Some Americans, like the Watertown molders, distrusted a system that treated them like machines, but few could resist the experts' claims that efficiency and mechanization were improving everyday life. The expansion of railroad, postal, and telephone service drew even isolated communities into the orbit of a consumer society. American ingenuity combined with mass production and mass marketing to make available myriad goods that previously had not existed or had been the exclusive property of the wealthy. As a result, Americans were better fed, better clothed, and better housed than ever before. The new material well-being, symbolized by canned foods, ready-made clothing, and home appliances, had a dual effect. It blended Americans of differing status into consumer communities defined not by place of residence but by possessions, and it accentuated differences between those who could afford goods and services and those who could not.

If a society's affluence is measured by how it converts luxuries into commonplace articles, the United States was indeed becoming affluent in the years between 1880 and 1920. In 1880 smokers rolled their own cigarettes; only wealthy women could afford silk stockings; only residents of Florida, Texas, and California could enjoy fresh oranges; and people made candy and soap at home. By 1899 manufactured goods and perishable foodstuffs had become increasingly available. That year Americans bought 2 billion machine-produced cigarettes and 151,000 pairs of silk stockings, consumed oranges at the rate of 100

Commonplace Luxuries

crates for every 1,000 people, and spent averages of $1.08 per person on store-bought candy and 63 cents per person on soap. By 1921 the transformation had advanced further. Americans smoked 43 billion cigarettes that year (403 per person), bought 217 million pairs of silk stockings, ate 248 crates of oranges per 1,000 people, and spent $1.66 per person on confectionery goods and $1.40 on soap.

What people can afford obviously depends on their resources and incomes. Data for the period show that incomes rose broadly. At the top of society, the expanding economy spawned massive fortunes and created a new industrial elite. An 1891 magazine article estimated that 120 Americans were worth at least $10 million ($250 million in current dollars). By 1920 the richest 5 percent of the population received almost one-fourth of all earned income. Incomes also rose among the middle class. For example, average pay for clerical workers rose 36 percent between 1890 and 1910 (see Table 18.1). At the turn of the century, employees of the federal executive branch averaged $1,072 a year, and college professors, $1,100 (around $25,000 in modern dollars)—not handsome sums, but much more than manual workers received. With such salaries, the middle class, whose numbers were increasing as a result of new job opportunities, could afford relatively comfortable housing. A six- or seven-room house cost around $3,000 to buy or build (about $65,000 in current

TABLE 18.1	American Living Standards, 1890–1910	
	1890	**1910**
Income and Earnings		
Annual income		
Clerical worker	$848	$1,156
Public school teacher	256	492
Industrial worker	486	630
Farm laborer	233	336
Hourly wage		
Soft-coal miner	0.18[a]	0.21
Iron worker	0.17[a]	0.23
Shoe worker	0.14[a]	0.19
Paper worker	0.12[a]	0.17
Labor Statistics		
Number of people in labor force	28.5 mil.	41.7 mil.[b]
Average workweek in manufacturing	60 hrs.	51 hrs.

[a]1892
[b]1920

dollars) and from $15 to $20 per month ($400 to $500 in current dollars) to rent.

Although hourly wages for industrial employees increased, workers had to expend a disproportionate amount of income on necessities. On average, annual wages of factory laborers rose about 30 percent, from $486 in 1890 (about $12,000 in modern dollars) to $630 in 1910 (about $15,500 in current dollars). In industries with large female work forces, such as shoe and paper manufacturing, hourly pay rates remained lower than in male-dominated industries, such as coal mining and iron production. Regional variations were also wide. Nevertheless, as Table 18.1 shows, most wages moved upward. Income for farm laborers followed the same trend, though wages remained relatively low because farm workers usually received free room and board.

Wage increases mean little, however, if living costs rise as fast or faster. That is what happened. In few working-class occupations did incomes rise

Cost of Living

as fast as prices. The weekly cost of living for a typical wage earner's family of four rose over 47 percent between 1889 and 1913. In other words, a combination of housing, food, and other goods that cost $68 in 1889 increased, after a slight dip in the mid-1890s, to $100 by 1913.

How, then, could working-class Americans afford machine-age goods and services? Many could not. The daughter of a textile worker, recalling her school days, described how "some of the kids would bring bars of chocolate, others an orange. . . . I suppose they were richer than a family like ours. My father used to buy a bag of candy and a bag of peanuts every payday. . . . And that's all we'd have until the next payday." Another woman explained how her family coped with high prices and low wages: "My mother made our clothes. People then wore old clothes. My mother would rip them out and make them over."

Still, a family could raise its income and partake modestly in consumer society by sending children and women into the labor market (see pages

Supplements to Family Income

506–508). In a household whose main breadwinner made $600 a year, wages of other family members might lift total family income to $800 or $900. Many families also rented rooms to boarders and lodgers, a practice that could yield up to $200 a year. These means of increasing family income enabled people to purchase important services. Between 1889 and 1901, working-class families markedly increased expenditures for life insurance and funeral policies, as well as for new leisure activities (see Chapter 19). Workers were thus able to improve their living standard, but not without sacrifices.

More than ever, American working people lived within a highly developed money economy. Between 1890 and 1920, the labor force increased by 50 percent, from 28 million workers to 42 million. These figures, however, are misleading: in general, they represent a change in the nature of work as much as an increase in the number of available jobs. In the rural households that predominated in the nineteenth century, women and children performed tasks crucial to a family's daily existence—cooking, cleaning, planting, and harvesting—but these jobs seldom appeared in employment figures because they earned no wages. As the nation industrialized and the agricultural sector's share of national income declined, paid employment became more common. Jobs in urban industries and commerce were easier to define and easier to count. The proportion of Americans who worked—whether in fields, households, factories, or offices—probably did not increase markedly. Most Americans, male and female, had always worked. What was new was the increase in paid employment, making purchases of consumer goods and services more affordable.

Science and technology eased some of life's struggles, and their impact on living standards strengthened after 1900. Medical advances, better diets, and improved housing sharply

Higher Life Expectancy

reduced death rates and extended life. Between 1900 and 1920, life expectancy rose by fully six years, and the death rate dropped by 24 percent. Notable declines occurred in deaths from typhoid, diphtheria, influenza (except for a harsh pandemic in 1918 and 1919), tuberculosis, and intestinal ailments—diseases that had been scourges of earlier generations. There were, however, significantly more deaths from cancer, diabetes, and heart disease, afflictions of an aging population and of new environmental factors, such as smoke and chemical pollution. Americans also found more ways to kill one another: although suicide rates remained stable, homicides and automobile-related deaths—effects of a fast-paced urban society—increased dramatically.

Not only were amenities and luxuries more available than in the previous half-century, means to upward mobility seemed more accessible as well. Although inequities that had pervaded earlier eras remained in place, and race, gender, religion, and ethnicity still affected access to opportunity, education increasingly became the key to success. Public education, aided by construction of new schools and passage of laws that required children to stay in school to age fourteen, equipped young people to achieve a living standard higher than their parents'. Between 1890 and 1922, the number of students enrolled in public high schools rose dramatically, though by today's standards graduation rates among young people were low—16.3 percent in 1920, up from 3.5 percent in 1890. The creation of managerial and sales jobs in service industries helped to counter the downward mobility that resulted when mechanization pushed skilled workers out of their crafts. And the resulting goods of mass production meant that even workers found life more convenient.

At the vanguard of a revolution in lifestyles stood the toilet. The chain-pull, washdown water closet, invented in England around 1870, reached the

Flush Toilets and Other Innovations

England around 1870, reached the United States in the 1880s. Shortly after 1900, the flush toilet appeared; thanks to mass production of enamel-coated metal fixtures, it became common in American homes and buildings. The toilet, cheap and easy to install, brought about a shift in habits and attitudes. Before 1880 only luxury hotels and wealthy families had private indoor bathrooms. By the 1890s the germ theory of disease was raising fears about carelessly disposed human waste as a source of infection and water contamination. Much more rapidly than Europeans did, Americans combined a desire for cleanliness with an urge for convenience and began installing modern toilets in middle-class urban houses. By the 1920s, they were prevalent in many working-class homes, too. Bodily functions took on an unpleasant image, and the home bathroom became a place of utmost privacy. Edward and Clarence Scott, who manufactured white tissue in perforated rolls, provided Americans a more convenient form of toilet tissue than the rough paper they had previously used. At the same time, toilets and private bathtubs gave Americans new ways to use—and waste—water. Plumbing advances belonged to a broader democratization of convenience that accompanied mass production and consumerism.

The tin can also altered lifestyles. Before the midnineteenth century, Americans typically ate only foods that were in season. Drying, smoking, and salting could preserve meat for a short time, but the availability of fresh meat and milk was limited; there was no way to prevent spoilage. A French inventor developed the cooking-and-sealing process of canning around 1810, and in the 1850s an American man named Gail Borden devised a means of condensing and preserving milk. Sales of canned goods and condensed milk increased during the 1860s, but processing some foods was difficult, and cans had to be made by hand. In the 1880s, technology solved production problems. Inventors fashioned machines to peel fruits and veg-

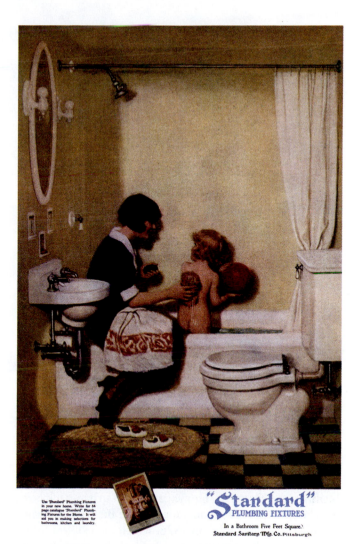

"**Standard**" PLUMBING FIXTURES

In a Bathroom Five Feet Square.
Standard Sanitary Mfg. Co. Pittsburgh

▲ The modern bathroom, with sink, tub, and flush toilet, marked an unheralded but noteworthy feature of American living standards. It improved habits of personal hygiene, increased household water consumption, altered patterns of waste disposal, and occupied a new and private realm of domestic space.
(Picture Research Consultants and Archives)

etables and to process salmon, as well as stamping and soldering machines to mass-produce cans from tin plate. Now, even people remote from markets, like sailors and cowboys, could readily consume tomatoes, milk, oysters, and other alternatives to previously monotonous diets. Housewives preserved their own fruits and vegetables, "putting up" foods in sealed glass jars.

Other trends and inventions broadened Americans' diets. Growing urban populations created demands that encouraged fruit and vegetable farmers to raise more produce. Railroad refrigerator cars enabled growers and meatpackers to ship perishables greater distances and to preserve them for longer periods. By the 1890s, northern city dwellers could enjoy southern and western strawberries, grapes, and tomatoes for several months of the year. Home iceboxes enabled middle-class families to store perishables. An easy means of producing ice commercially was invented in the 1870s, and by 1900 the nation had two thousand ice plants, most of which made home deliveries.

Availability of new foods also inspired health advocates to reform American diets. In the 1870s, John H. Kellogg, nutritionist and manager of the Western Health Reform Institute in Battle Creek, Michigan, began serving patients health foods, including peanut butter and wheat flakes. Several years later, his brother, William K. Kellogg, invented corn flakes, and another nutritionist, Charles W. Post, introduced Grape-Nuts, revolutionizing breakfast by replacing eggs, potatoes, and meat with ready-to-eat cereal, which supposedly was healthier. Like Edison and Ford, Post believed in the power of advertising, and he personally wrote ads for his products. His company became one of fastest growing in the country.

Dietary Reform

Other developments affected the ways people prepared and consumed food. Just before the First World War, scientists discovered the dietetic value of vitamins A and B (C and D were discovered later). Growing numbers of published cookbooks and the opening of cooking schools reflected heightened interest in food and its possibilities for health and enjoyment. Home gardens in urban backyards also became easier to tend, aided by the Burpee Company, founded in Philadelphia in 1876, which mailed flower and vegetable seeds to gardeners who bought them through mail-order catalogues—just as they bought goods from Sears, Roebuck.

As in the past, the poorest people still consumed cheap foods, heavy in starches and carbohydrates. Southern textile workers, for example, ate corn mush and fatback (the strip of meat from a hog's back) almost every day. Poor urban families seldom could afford meat. Now, though, many of them could purchase previously unavailable fruits, vegetables, and dairy products. Workers had to spend a high percentage of their income on food—almost half of a breadwinner's wages—but they never suffered the severe malnutrition that plagued other developing nations.

Just as cans and iceboxes made many foods more common, the sewing machine and standardized sizes sparked a revolution in clothing. The sewing machine, invented in Europe but refined in the mid-nineteenth century by Americans Elias Howe Jr. and Isaac M. Singer, came into

Ready-Made Clothing

▲ Using color, large-scale scenes, and fanciful images, manufacturers of consumer goods advertised their products to a public eager to buy. This ad from the W. K. Kellogg Company, maker of breakfast foods, shows the increasingly common practice of using an attractive young woman to capture attention.

(Picture Research Consultants & Archives)

use in clothing and shoe manufacture. Demand for uniforms during the Civil War boosted the ready-made (as opposed to custom-made) clothing industry, and by 1890 annual retail sales of machine-made garments reached $1.5 billion. Mass production enabled manufacturers to turn out good-quality apparel at relatively low cost and to standardize sizes to fit different body shapes. By 1900 only the poorest families could not afford "ready-to-wear" clothes. Tailors and seamstresses were relegated to repair work. Many women continued to make clothing at home, to save money or as a hobby, but commercial dress patterns intended for use with a sewing machine simplified home production of apparel and injected another form of standardization into everyday life.

Mass-produced garments altered clothing styles and tastes. Restrictive Victorian designs still dominated female fashion, but women were abandoning the most burdensome features. As women's participation in work and leisure activities became more active, dress designers placed greater emphasis on comfort. In the 1890s, long sleeves

◀ Offering a wide variety of goods and services, such as prescriptions, meats, furniture, loans, medical help, and restaurants, this late-nineteenth-century department store in Chicago epitomized the new conveniences of consumerism. It even featured a grand fountain as an easily recognized meeting place.

(Chicago Historical Society)

classes would have owned two suits: one for Sundays and special occasions, and one for everyday wear. After 1900, however, manufacturers began producing inexpensive garments from fabrics of different weights and for different seasons. Men replaced derbies with felt hats, and stiff collars and cuffs with soft ones; somber, dark-blue serge gave way to lighter shades and more intricate weaves. Workingmen still needed durable, inexpensive overalls, shirts, and shoes. But even for males of modest means, clothing was becoming something to be bought instead of made and remade at home.

and skirt hemlines receded, and high-boned collars disappeared. Women began wearing tailored blouses called shirtwaists, manufactured by such companies as the Triangle Shirtwaist Factory. Designers used less fabric; by the 1920s a dress required three yards of material instead of ten. Petite prevailed as the ideal: the most desirable waist measurement was eighteen to twenty inches, and corsets were big sellers. In the early 1900s, long hair tied up behind the neck was the most popular style. By the First World War, when many women worked in hospitals and factories, shorter and less hindering hairstyles had become acceptable.

Men's clothes, too, became lightweight and stylish. Before 1900, men in the middle and well-off working

Department stores and chain stores helped to create and serve this new consumerism. Between 1865 and 1900, Macy's Department Store in New York, Wanamaker's in Philadelphia, Marshall Field in Chicago, and Rich's in Atlanta became urban landmarks. Previously, working classes bought goods in stores with limited inventories, and wealthier people patronized fancy shops; prices, quality of goods, and social custom discouraged each from shopping at the other's establishments. Now, department stores, with their open displays of clothing, housewares, and furniture—all available in large quantities to anyone

Department and Chain Stores

with the purchase price—caused a merchandising revolution. They offered not only variety but also home deliveries, exchange policies, and charge accounts.

Meanwhile, the Great Atlantic Tea Company, founded in 1859, became the first grocery chain. Renamed the Great Atlantic & Pacific Tea Company in 1869 (and known as A&P), the firm's stores bought in volume and sold to the public at low prices. By 1915 there were eighteen hundred A&P stores, and twelve thousand more were built over the next ten years. Other chains, such as Woolworth's dime stores, which sold inexpensive personal items and novelties, grew rapidly during the same period.

A society of scarcity does not need advertising: when demand exceeds supply, producers have no trouble selling

||||||||||||||||||||||||||||||||

Advertising

what they market. But in a society of rising abundance, such as industrial America, supply frequently outstrips demand, necessitating a means to increase and create demand. Advertising assumed this function. In 1865 retailers spent about $9.5 million on advertising; that sum reached $95 million by 1900 and nearly $500 million by 1919.

In the late nineteenth century, companies that mass-produced consumer goods hired advertisers to create "consumption communities," bodies of consumers loyal to a particular brand name. In 1881 Congress passed a trademark law enabling producers to register and protect brand names. Thousands of companies registered products as varied as Hires Root Beer, Uneeda Biscuits, and Carter's Little Liver Pills. Advertising agencies—a service pioneered by N. W. Ayer & Son of Philadelphia—in turn offered expert advice to firms that wished to cultivate brand loyalty. Newspapers served as the prime instrument for advertising. In the mid-nineteenth century, publishers began to pursue higher revenues by selling more ad space. Wanamaker's placed the first full-page ad in 1879, and advertisers began using large print and including elaborate illustrations of products. Such attention-getting techniques transformed advertising into news. More than ever before, people read newspapers to find out what was for sale as well as what was happening.

Outdoor billboards and electrical signs rivaled newspapers as important selling devices. Billboards on city buildings, in railroad stations, and alongside roads promoted such products as Gillette razors, Kodak cameras, Wrigley chewing gum, and Budweiser beer. In the mid-1890s, electric lights made billboards more dynamic and appealing. Commercial districts sparkled under what one observer called "a medium of motion, of action, of *life,* of *light,* of compulsory attraction." The flashing electrical signs on New York City's Broadway—including a forty-

▲ Advertising, which developed into a powerful medium in the late nineteenth century, used explicit and implicit domestic images to reinforce a wife's role as homemaker. This ad implies that a devoted wife lovingly assumes such tasks as sewing and mending clothing, guided into her role by a strong and superior husband.

(Library of Congress)

five-foot Heinz pickle in green bulbs and dazzling theater marquees—gave the street its label "the Great White Way." Soon, "talking" signs were installed, with words moving along signboards providing news as well as advertising copy in a multitude of colors. Americans now had an enticing variety of inducements to consume.

THE CORPORATE CONSOLIDATION MOVEMENT

Neither new products nor new marketing techniques could mask unsettling factors in the American economy. The huge capital investment needed for new technology meant that factories had to operate at near capacity to recover costs. But the more manufacturers produced, the more they had to sell. To sell more and outdo competitors, they had to advertise and reduce prices. To increase profits and compensate for advertising costs and low prices, they further expanded production and often reduced wages. To expand, they borrowed money. And to repay loans, they had to produce and sell even more. This spiraling process strangled small firms that could not keep pace and thrust workers into constant uncertainty. The same cycle affected commerce, banking, and transportation as well.

In this environment, optimism could dissolve at the hint that debtors could not meet their obligations. Economic downturns occurred with painful regularity—1873, 1884, 1893. Business leaders disagreed on what caused economic strains. Some blamed overproduction; others pointed to underconsumption; still others blamed lax credit and investment practices. Whatever the explanation, businesspeople began seeking ways to combat the uncertainty of boom-and-bust business cycles. Many adopted centralized forms of business organization, notably corporations, pools, trusts, and holding companies.

Unlike laborers, industrialists never questioned the capitalist system. They sought new ways to build on the base that had supported economic growth since the early 1800s, when states revised incorporation laws to encourage commerce and industry.

Rise of Corporations

Under such laws, almost anyone could start a company and raise money by selling stock to investors. Stockholders shared in profits without personal risk, because laws limited their liability for company debts to the amount of their own investment; the rest of their wealth was protected should the company fail. Nor did investors need to concern themselves with a firm's day-to-day operation; responsibility for company administration rested with its managers.

Corporations proved to be the best instruments to raise capital for industrial expansion, and by 1900 two-thirds of all goods manufactured in the United States were produced by corporate firms such as General Electric and the American Tobacco Company. Corporations won judicial protection in the 1880s and 1890s when the Supreme Court ruled that they, like individuals, are protected by the Fourteenth Amendment. In other words, states could not deny corporations equal protection under the law and could not deprive them of rights or property without due process of law. Such rulings insulated corporations from government interference in their operations.

To combat downward swings of the business cycle, corporation managers sought stability in new and larger forms of economic concentration.

Pools

Between the late 1880s and early 1900s, an epidemic of business consolidation swept the country, resulting in massive conglomerates that have since dominated the nation's economy. At first such alliances were tentative and informal, consisting mainly of cooperative agreements among firms that manufactured the same product or offered the same service. Through these arrangements, called pools, competing companies tried to control the market by agreeing how much each should produce and by sharing profits. Used by railroads (to divide up traffic), steel producers, and whiskey distillers, pools depended on their members' honesty. Such "gentlemen's agreements" worked during good times when there was enough business for all; but during slow periods, desire for profits often tempted pool members to secretly reduce prices or sell more than the agreed quota. The Interstate Commerce Act of 1887 outlawed pools among railroads (see page 567), but by then the pool's usefulness was already fading.

John D. Rockefeller, founder of Standard Oil, disliked pools, calling them weak and undependable. In 1879 one of his lawyers, Samuel Dodd, devised a more stable means of dominating the market. Because state laws prohibited one corporation from holding stock in another corporation, Dodd suggested utilizing an old device called a trust, a legal arrangement whereby a responsible individual would manage the financial affairs of a person unwilling or unable to handle them alone. Dodd reasoned that one company could control an industry by luring or forcing stockholders of smaller companies in that industry to yield control of their stock "in trust" to the larger company's board of trustees. This device allowed Rockefeller to achieve horizontal integration—the acquisition of similar companies—of the profitable petroleum industry in 1882 by combining his corporation with other refineries that he bought up.

Trusts and Holding Companies

In 1888 New Jersey adopted laws allowing corporations chartered there to own property in other states and to own stock in other corporations. (Trusts provided for trusteeship, not ownership.) This liberalization facilitated creation of the holding company, which owned a partial or complete interest in other companies. Holding companies could in turn merge all their holdings' assets (buildings, equipment, inventory, and cash) as well as their management. Under this arrangement, Rockefeller's holding company merged forty formerly independent operations into Standard Oil of New Jersey. By 1898 Standard Oil refined 84 percent of all oil produced in the nation, controlled most pipelines, and engaged in natural-gas production and ownership of oil-producing properties.

Standard Oil's expansion into operations besides refining exemplified a new form of economic combination. To

▲ Believing that Rockefeller's Standard Oil monopoly was exercising dangerous power, this political cartoonist depicts the trust as a greedy octopus whose sprawling tentacles already ensnare Congress, state legislatures, and the taxpayer, and are reaching for the White House.

(Library of Congress)

dominate their markets, many holding companies sought control over all aspects of the industry, including raw-materials extraction, product manufacture, and distribution. A model of such vertical integration, which fused related businesses under unified management, was Gustavus Swift's Chicago meat-processing operation. During the 1880s, Swift invested in livestock, slaughterhouses, refrigerator cars, and marketing to ensure profits from the sale of beef at prices he could control. With their widespread operations, both Swift & Company and Standard Oil extended the economic tentacles of single companies to all regions of the nation.

Mergers provided answers to industry's search for order and profits. Between 1889 and 1903, some three hundred combinations were formed, most of them trusts and holding companies. The most spectacular was U.S. Steel Corporation, financed by J. P. Morgan in 1901. This enterprise, made up of iron-ore properties, freight carriers, wire mills, and other firms, was capitalized at over $1.4 billion (more than $35 billion in current money). Other mammoth combinations included Amalgamated Copper Company,

American Sugar Refining Company, and U.S. Rubber Company. In 1896 fewer than a dozen corporations were worth over $10 million; by 1903 three hundred were worth that much, and seventeen had assets exceeding $100 million. At the same time, these huge companies ruthlessly put thousands of small firms out of business.

The merger movement created a new species of businessman, one whose vocation was financial organizing rather than producing a particular good. Shrewd investors sought opportunities for combination, formed a holding company, then persuaded producers to sell their firms to the new company. These financiers raised money by selling stock and borrowing from banks. Their attention ranged widely. W. H. Moore organized the American Tin Plate Company, Diamond Match Company, and National Biscuit Company, and he acquired control of the Rock Island Railroad. Elbert H. Gary similarly participated in consolidation of the barbed-wire industry and of U.S. Steel. Investment bankers such as J. P. Morgan and Jacob Schiff piloted the merger move-

Financiers

ment, inspiring awe with their financial power and organizational skills.

Growth of corporations turned stock and bond exchanges into hubs of activity. In 1886 trading on the New York Stock Exchange passed 1 million shares a day. By 1914 the number of industrial stocks traded reached 511, compared with 145 in 1869. Between 1870 and 1900, foreign investment in American companies rose from $1.5 billion to $3.5 billion, as the country's economy assumed the image of a safe and lucrative investment. Assets of savings banks, concentrated in the Northeast and on the West Coast, rose by 700 percent between 1875 and 1897. States loosened regulations to enable banks to invest in railroads and industrial enterprises. Commercial banks, insurance companies, and corporations also invested heavily. As one journal, exaggerating the optimism of capitalists, proclaimed, "Nearly the whole country (including the typical widow and orphan) is interested in the stock market."

THE GOSPEL OF WEALTH AND ITS CRITICS

Business leaders used corporate consolidation to minimize competition. To justify their tactics, they invoked the doctrine of Social Darwinism. Developed by British philosopher Herbert Spencer and preached in the United States by Yale professor William Graham Sumner, Social Darwinism loosely grafted Charles Darwin's theory of survival of the fittest onto laissez faire, the doctrine that government should not interfere in private economic matters. Social Darwinists reasoned that, in a free-market economy, wealth would flow naturally to those most capable of handling it. Acquisition and possession of property were thus sacred and deserved rights. Civilization depended on this system, explained Sumner. "If we do not like the survival of the fittest," he wrote, "we have only one possible alternative, and that is survival of the unfittest." In this view, large corporations represented the natural accumulation of economic power by those best suited for wielding it.

Social Darwinists reasoned, too, that wealth carried moral responsibilities to provide for those less fortunate or less capable. Steel baron Andrew Carnegie asserted what he called "the Gospel of Wealth," meaning that he and other industrialists were guardians of society's wealth and as such had a duty to serve society in humane ways. Over his lifetime, Carnegie donated more than $350 million to libraries, schools, peace initiatives, and the arts. Such philanthropy, however, also implied a right for benefactors such as Rockefeller and Carnegie to define what was good and necessary for society; it did not translate into paying workers decent wages.

Like western entrepreneurs who lauded rugged individualism while seeking public subsidies in their mining, transportation, and agricultural businesses, leaders in the corporate consolidation movement extolled initiative and independence but also pressed for government assistance. They denounced efforts to legislate maximum working hours or to regulate factory conditions as interference with natural economic laws, but they lobbied forcefully for public subsidies, loans, and tax relief to encourage business growth. Grants to railroads (see Chapter 17) were one form of such assistance. Tariffs, which benefited American products by placing import taxes on imported products, were another. Since the inception of tariffs in the early nineteenth century, industrialists argued that tariff protection encouraged the development of new products and new enterprises. But tariffs also forced consumers to pay artificially high prices for many goods (see page 568).

Government Assistance to Business

While defenders such as Carnegie and Rockefeller insisted that trusts and other forms of big business were a natural and efficient outcome of economic development, critics charged that these methods were unnatural because they stifled opportunity and originated from greed. Such charges, emanating from farmers, workers, and intellectuals, reflected an ardent fear of monopoly—the domination of an economic activity (such as oil refining) by one powerful company (such as Standard Oil). Those who feared monopoly believed that large corporations fixed prices, exploited workers by cutting wages, destroyed opportunity by crushing small businesses, and threatened democracy by corrupting politicians—all of which was not only unnatural but immoral.

Dissenting Voices

Critics believed they knew a better, more ethical path to progress. For example, by the mid-1880s, a number of intellectuals began to challenge Social Darwinism and laissez-faire economics. Sociologist Lester Ward, in his book *Dynamic Sociology* (1883), argued that human control of nature, not natural law, accounted for civilization's advance. A system that guaranteed survival only to the fittest was wasteful and brutal; instead, Ward reasoned, cooperative activity fostered by government intervention was more just. Economists Richard Ely, John R. Commons, and Edward Bemis agreed that natural forces should be harnessed for the public good. They denounced the laissez-faire system for its "unsound morals" and praised the positive assistance that government could offer to ordinary people.

Whereas academics endorsed intervention in the natural economic order, writers such as Henry George and Edward Bellamy questioned why the United States had to have so many poor people while a few became fabulously wealthy. Henry George was a San Francisco printer with only a seventh-grade education but an avid reader of economic theory. Alarmed at the existence of abject poverty among working people like himself, he came to believe that inequality stemmed from the ability of a few to profit from rising land values. George argued that such profits made landowners rich from ever-higher rents charged by them because of increased demand for living and working space, especially in cities. Unlike wages paid to workers, wealth from landowning was created without any productive effort. To prevent profiteering, George proposed to replace all taxes with a "single tax" on the "unearned increment"—the rise in property values caused by increased market demand rather than by owners' improvements. George's scheme, argued forcefully in *Progress and Poverty* (1879), had great popular appeal and almost won him the mayoralty of New York City in 1886.

Unlike George, who accepted private ownership, novelist Edward Bellamy believed that competitive capitalism promoted waste. Instead, he proposed a state in which government owned the means of production. Bellamy outlined his dream in *Looking Backward* (1888). The novel, which sold over a million copies, depicted Boston in the year 2000 as a peaceful community where everyone had a job and a council of benevolent elders managed the economy according to scientific principles. Although ordinary people could not vote in this utopia, Bellamy tried to convince readers that a "principle of fraternal cooperation" could replace vicious competition and wasteful monopoly. His vision, which he called "Nationalism," sparked formation of Nationalist clubs across the country and kindled popular appeals for political reform, social welfare measures, and government ownership of railroads and utilities.

Few people supported the universal government ownership envisioned by Bellamy, but several states took steps to prohibit monopolies and regulate business. By 1900 twenty-seven states had laws forbidding pools, and fifteen had constitutional provisions outlawing trusts. Most were agricultural states in the South and West that were responding to antimonopolistic pressure from farm organizations (see Chapter 20). But state governments lacked the staff and judicial support for an effective attack on big business, and corporations found ways to evade restrictions. Only national legislation, it seemed, could work.

Antitrust Legislation

Congress moved hesitantly toward such legislation but in 1890 passed the Sherman Anti-Trust Act. Introduced by Senator John Sherman of Ohio, the law made illegal "every contract, combination in the form of trust or otherwise, or conspiracy in the restraint of trade." Those found guilty of violating the law faced fines and jail terms, and those wronged by illegal combinations could sue for triple damages. However, the law was left purposely vague, watered down when it was rewritten by pro-business eastern senators. It did not clearly define "restraint of trade" and consigned interpretation of its provisions to the courts, which at the time were allies of business.

Judges used the law's vagueness to blur distinctions between reasonable and unreasonable restraints of trade. When in 1895 the federal government prosecuted the so-called Sugar Trust for owning 98 percent of the nation's sugar-refining capacity, eight of nine Supreme Court justices ruled in *U.S. v. E. C. Knight Co.* that control of manufacturing did not necessarily mean control of trade. According to the Court, the Constitution empowered Congress to regulate interstate commerce, but manufacturing (which in the *Knight* case took place entirely within the state of Pennsylvania) did not fall under congressional control.

Between 1890 and 1900, the federal government prosecuted only eighteen cases under the Sherman Anti-Trust Act. The most successful involved railroads directly involved in interstate commerce. Ironically, the act equipped the government with a tool for breaking up labor unions: courts that did not consider monopolistic production a restraint on trade willingly applied antitrust provisions to boycotts encouraged by striking unions.

Legacy FOR A PEOPLE AND A NATION

Technology of Recorded Sound

Today's widespread markets for iPods and digital recorders derive from a combination of technology, chemistry, and human resourcefulness that came together in the late nineteenth century. In 1877, even before he invented the light bulb, Thomas Edison devised a way to preserve and reproduce his own voice by storing it on indentations made in tin foil. At first, Edison intended his "speaking machine" to help businesses store dictation and replace undependable secretaries. But in 1878 he was stirred by a rivalry with Alexander Graham Bell, inventor of the telephone who also was working on a device that reproduced sounds, to invent a phonograph that played recorded music. By the 1890s, entrepreneurs were charging audiences admission to hear recorded sounds from these machines.

By 1901, companies such as the Columbia Phonograph Company and Victor Talking Machine Company began to produce machines that played music recorded on cylinders molded from a chemical wax compound more durable than the metal cylinders that Edison had used. Over the next ten years, various inventors improved the phonograph so that it played back sound from a stylus (needle) vibrating in grooves of a shellac disc. These developments increased the playing time of records from two minutes to four.

Phonograph records now replaced sheet music as the most popular medium of popular music, but soon another technological wonder, radio, rose to prominence and helped boost record sales. The popularity of the radio could not have been possible without another feat of electronic acoustic technology: the microphone. The microphone achieved better sound quality over previously used megaphones by picking up sound from a performance and turning it into electrical currents that were transmitted via radio wire from the microphone to a radio station, which then broadcast the sound. As phonograph prices declined and sound quality improved, more records became available.

The invention in 1938 of the idler wheel, which enabled a phonograph turntable to spin a disk at the exact speed necessary for the stylus to pick up the sound accurately, brought an important advance. Shortly thereafter, more significant inventions in sound recording, such as the magnetic tape recorder, allowed for more manipulation of sound in the recording studio than ever before. Tape and slower-speed turntables lengthened play time, and in 1963 Philips, a Dutch electronics firm, introduced the compact audio cassette. Two decades later, Philips joined with the Japanese corporation Sony to adapt digital laser discs, which an American had invented to store video images, to store music by transforming sound into sequences of numbers. The compact disc (CD) was born, and from there it was a short step for the Apple Computer Company to create the iPod, which stored CD-quality music on an internal hard drive.

SUMMARY

Mechanization and new inventions thrust the United States, once just a developing country, into the vanguard of industrial nations. By the early twentieth century, American industrial output surpassed that of Great Britain, France, and Germany combined. Industrial growth transformed the national economy and freed the United States from dependence on European capital and manufactured goods. Imports and foreign investments still flowed into the United States. But by 1900, factories, stores, and banks were converting America from a debtor agricultural nation into an industrial, financial, and exporting power. In addition, developments in electrical power, internal-combustion engines, and chemistry immeasurably altered daily life at home and abroad.

But in industry, as in farming and mining, massive size and aggressive consolidation engulfed the individual, changing the nature of work from individual activity undertaken by skilled producers to mass production undertaken by wage earners. Laborers fought to retain control of their work and struggled to organize unions that could meet their needs. The outpouring of products created a mass society based on consumerism and dominated by technology and the communications media.

The problems of enforcing the Sherman Anti-Trust Act reflected the uneven distribution of power. Corporations consolidated to control resources, production, and politics. Laborers and reformers had numbers and ideas but lacked influence. They benefited from material gains that technology and mass production provided, but they accused businesses of acquiring too much influence and profiting at their expense. In factories and homes, some people celebrated the economic transformation, while others struggled with the dilemma of industrialism: whether the new accumulations of wealth would undermine the ideal of a republic based on republicanism, democracy, and equality.

The march of industrial expansion proved almost impossible to stop, however, because so many people, powerful and ordinary, were benefiting from it. Moreover, the waves of newcomers pouring into the nation's cities were increasingly furnishing both workers and consumers for America's expanding productive capacity. The dynamo of American vitality now rested in its urban centers.

SUGGESTIONS FOR FURTHER READING

Edward L. Ayers, *The Promise of the New South: Life After Reconstruction* (1992)

Ileen A. DeVault, *United Apart: Gender and the Rise of Craft Unionism* (2004)

Steven J. Diner, *A Very Different Age: Americans of the Progressive Era* (1998)

John F. Kasson, *Civilizing the Machine: Technology and Republican Values in America, 1776–1900* (1976)

Alice Kessler-Harris, *Out to Work: A History of Wage-Earning Women in the United States* (2003)

T. J. Jackson Lears and Richard W. Fox, eds., *The Culture of Consumption: Critical Essays in American History, 1880–1980* (1983)

David Montgomery, *The Fall of the House of Labor: The Workplace, the State and American Labor Activism, 1865–1925* (1987)

Jeffrey Sklansky, *The Soul's Economy: Market Society and Selfhood in American Thought, 1820–1920* (2002)

For a more extensive list for further reading, go to college.hmco.com/pic/norton8e.

The Vitality and
Turmoil of Urban Life
1877-1920

rowds on the street gasped as they looked upward. There he was! A man, tightly bound in a straitjacket, hanging by his heels high above New York's Times Square. Suddenly, he began wriggling wildly. In seconds he was free, spreading his arms in an upside-down bow. Harry Houdini, the most celebrated showman of the early twentieth century, had escaped. As he had done so many times before, Houdini had fed the public taste for suspense, courage, and entertainment with a death-defying feat.

Harry Houdini's life epitomized both the symbol and the reality of escape from hardship and injustice. Born as Erich Weiss in Hungary in 1874, he and his family emigrated to the United States in 1878. After Erich's father lost his job as a rabbi, the family moved again, this time to seek opportunity in New York City, where they first lived in a boarding house. Erich and his father found work in a necktie factory, but when Erich's father died in 1892, the young man decided to escape factory work and become an entertainer. After a few lackluster years as a magician, Erich discovered his true talent as an illusionist and escape artist. He changed his name, remaking himself into Harry Houdini, after a French magician named Houdin, and became one of America's most enthralling performers.

By the early 1900s, "The Great Houdini" was a featured act in vaudeville, a new form of urban entertainment. His specialty was escaping from elaborate and dangerous confinements: ropes, manacles, padlocked crates, and jail cells. Like Thomas Edison and Henry Ford, Houdini not only accomplished something but also was a skillful self-publicist, advertising his act with myriad posters and leaflets. Around 1913 Houdini introduced his

◀ "Houdini's Escape Act." High above Broadway and 46th Street in New York City, Harry Houdini, the world-famous immigrant-American escape artist, hangs upside down while bound in a straitjacket. Crowds watch breathlessly, wondering whether or how he will free himself. New people, bustling cities, mass entertainment, and the quest for freedom symbolized by Houdini's act characterized American society at the end of the nineteenth century and beginning of the twentieth.

(Bettmann/Corbis)

529

CHRONOLOGY

1867 ■ First law regulating tenements passes in New York State

1870 ■ One-fourth of Americans live in cities

1876 ■ National League of Professional Baseball Clubs founded

1880s ■ "New" immigrants from eastern and southern Europe begin to arrive in large numbers

1883 ■ Brooklyn Bridge completed
■ Pulitzer buys *New York World,* creating major publication for yellow journalism

1885 ■ Safety bicycle invented

1886 ■ First settlement house opens in New York City

1889 ■ Edison invents motion picture and viewing device

1890s ■ Electric trolleys replace horse-drawn mass transit

1893 ■ Columbian Exposition opens in Chicago

1895 ■ Hearst buys *New York Journal,* which becomes another popular yellow-journalism newspaper

1898 ■ Race riot erupts in Wilmington, North Carolina

1900–10 ■ Immigration reaches peak
■ Vaudeville rises to popularity

1903 ■ Boston beats Pittsburgh in baseball's first World Series

1905 ■ Intercollegiate Athletic Association, forerunner of National Intercollegiate Athletic Association (NCAA) is formed, restructuring rules of football

1915 ■ Griffith directs *Birth of a Nation,* one of first major technically sophisticated movies

1919 ■ Race riot erupts in East St. Louis, Illinois

1920 ■ Majority (51.4 percent) of Americans live in cities

while he twisted and stretched. Although he constantly defied death in his act, Houdini could not escape the abdominal infection that took his life in 1926.

He became extraordinarily successful, both in the United States and in Europe, but Houdini initially followed a path taken by many people at the end of the nineteenth century and the beginning of the twentieth. The Weiss family were immigrants who fled poverty and tried to remake themselves in a burgeoning American city where life was not easy for them and for countless other newcomers. They faced daunting challenges of where to live, where to work, how to deal with a cash-based economy, how to preserve their ethnic consciousness amid bigotry, how to achieve independence and respectability. And, like Houdini, they somehow needed to use escape and remaking as means to succeed. These challenges made cities places of hope, frustration, achievement, and conflict, where clanging trolleys, smoky air, crowded streets, and a jumble of languages saturated the senses.

Cities had influenced the nation's history since its inception, serving as marketplaces and forums that amassed people, resources, and ideas, but not until the 1880s did the United States begin to become a fully urban nation. The technological innovations and industrialization of the late nineteenth century sparked widespread economic and geographical expansion which funneled millions of people into cities. By 1920 a milestone of urbanization was passed: that year's census showed that, for the first time, a majority of Americans (51.4 percent) lived in cities (settlements with more than 2,500 people). This new fact of national life was as symbolically significant as the Census Bureau's announcement in 1890 that the frontier had disappeared.

Cities were filled with new kinds of consumerism, commercial amusement, and politics. Urban dwellers patronized dance halls, theatrical performances, vaudeville, movies, and sporting events in record numbers. By idolizing Houdini, sports heroes, and movie celebrities, or by benefiting from the largesse of a political boss, ordinary working- and middle-class people could experience the feeling that individuals could free themselves from the constraints of an emerging technological and urban society. But at the same time, poverty and discrimination haunted the lives of countless urban dwellers, combining

famous "Chinese water torture cell" escape, in which he extracted himself from being bound and suspended upside down in a water-filled, locked glass-and-steel cabinet. Houdini succeeded in these escapes not only by manipulating his five-foot-five frame in unusual ways but also by concealing picks and keys, sometimes regurgitating them opportunities of the era with the persistence of inequality and prejudice. Whatever people's personal experiences, cities had become central to American life, and the ways people built cities and adjusted to the urban environment have shaped modern American society.

- What were the most important factors contributing to the urban growth of the period 1877–1920?
- How did immigrants adjust to and reshape their adopted homeland?
- How did industrialization and urbanization affect patterns of family life and leisure time?

GROWTH OF THE MODERN CITY

Although their initial functions had been commercial, cities became the main arenas for industrial growth in the late nineteenth century. As centers of labor, transportation, and communication, cities supplied everything factories needed. Capital accumulated by urban mercantile enterprises fed industrial investment. City dwellers also acted as consumers for myriad new products. Thus urban growth and industrialization wound together in a mutually advantageous spiral. The further industrialization advanced, the more opportunities it created for jobs and investment. Increased opportunities in turn drew more people to cities; as workers and as consumers, they fueled yet more industrialization. Urban growth in modern America was a dynamic process involving all groups of Americans, including those already settled and new arrivals from Europe and Asia.

Most cities housed a variety of industrial enterprises, but product specialization became common. Mass pro-

Industrial Development

duction of clothing concentrated in New York City, the shoe industry in Philadelphia, and textiles in New England cities such as Lowell. Other cities created goods derived from surrounding agricultural regions: flour in Minneapolis, cottonseed oil in Memphis, beef and pork in Chicago. Still others processed natural resources: gold and copper in Denver, fish and lumber in Seattle, coal and iron in Pittsburgh and Birmingham, oil in Houston and Los Angeles. Such activities increased cities' magnetic attraction for people in search of steady employment.

At the same time, the compact city of the early nineteenth century, where residences mingled among shops, factories, and warehouses, burst open. From Boston to

Los Angeles, the built environment sprawled several miles beyond the original settlement. No longer did walking distance determine a city's size. No longer did different social groups live close together. Instead, cities subdivided into distinct districts: working-class neighborhoods, commercial strips, downtown, and a ring of suburbs. Two forces were responsible for this new arrangement. One, mass transportation, was centrifugal, propelling people and enterprises outward. The other, economic change, was centripetal, drawing human and material resources inward.

Mass transportation moved people faster and farther. By the 1870s, horse-drawn vehicles began sharing city streets with motor-driven conveyances.

Mechanization of Mass Transportation

At first, commuter railroads carried commuters to and from outlying communities, but soon mechanical vehicles were moving people from one part of the city to another. In the 1880s, cable cars (carriages that moved by clamping onto a moving underground wire) started operating in Chicago, San Francisco, and other cities. Then, in the 1890s, electric-powered streetcars began replacing horse cars and cable cars. Designed in Montgomery, Alabama, and Richmond, Virginia, electric trolleys spread to nearly every large American city. In a few cities, companies raised track onto trestles, enabling "elevated" vehicles to travel above jammed downtown streets. In Boston, New York, and Philadelphia, transit firms dug underground subway tunnels, also to avoid traffic congestion. Because "els" were extremely expensive to construct, they appeared only in the few cities where companies could amass necessary capital and where there were enough riders to ensure profits.

Another form of mass transit, the electric interurban railway, linked nearby cities. Usually built over shorter distances than steam railroads, interurbans operated between cities with growing suburban populations and furthered urban development by making outlying regions attractive for home buyers and businesses. The extensive Pacific Electric Railway network in Southern California, for example, facilitated travel and economic progress in that region.

Mass transit launched urban dwellers into remote neighborhoods and created a commuting public. The re-

Urban Sprawl

sulting urban sprawl benefited the urban public unevenly and was essentially unplanned. Streetcar lines serviced mainly districts that promised the most riders—those whose fares would increase company revenues. Working-class families, who needed

▲ Electric trolley cars and other forms of mass transit enabled middle-class people such as these women and men to reside on the urban outskirts and ride into the city center for work, shopping, and entertainment. *(Library of Congress)*

every cent, found streetcars unaffordable. But those of the growing middle class who could afford the fare— usually 5 cents a ride—could escape to quiet, tree-lined neighborhoods on the outskirts, live in bungalows with their own yards, and commute to the inner city for work, shopping, and entertainment. A home several miles from downtown was inconvenient, but benefits outweighed costs. As one suburbanite wrote in 1902, "It may be a little more difficult for us to attend the opera, but the robin in my elm tree struck a higher note and a sweeter one yesterday than any prima donna ever reached."

Streetcars, els, and subways altered commercial as well as residential patterns. When consumers moved outward, businesses followed, locating at trolley-line intersections and near elevated-railway stations. Branches of department stores and banks joined groceries, theaters, taverns, and shops to create neighborhood shopping centers, forerunners of today's suburban malls. Meanwhile, the urban core became a work zone, where tall buildings loomed over streets clogged with people, horses, and vehicles. Districts such as Chicago's Loop and New Orleans's Canal Street employed thousands in commerce and finance.

Between 1870 and 1920, the number of Americans living in cities increased from 10 million to 54 million.

Population Growth

During this period, the number of cities with more than 100,000 people swelled from fifteen to sixty-eight; the number with more than 500,000 rose from two to twelve (see Map 19.1). These figures, dramatic in themselves, represent millions of stories of dreams and frustration, coping and confusion, success and failure.

American urban growth derived not from natural increase (excess of births over deaths) but through the annexation of bordering land and people, and mostly by net migration (excess of in-migrants over out-migrants). Every city grew territorially. The most notable enlargement occurred in 1898, when New York City, which previously consisted of only Manhattan and the Bronx, merged with Brooklyn, Staten Island, and part of Queens, and doubled from 1.5 million to 3 million people. Elsewhere, central cities gobbled up miles of surrounding area. Suburbs often desired annexation for the schools, water, fire protection, and sewer systems that cities could

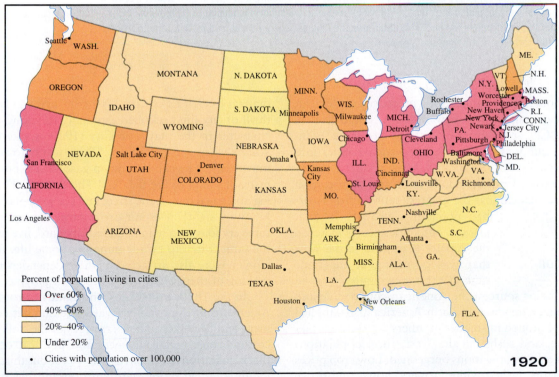

Map 19.1   Urbanization, 1880 and 1920

In 1880 the vast majority of states were still heavily rural. By 1920 only a few had less than 20 percent of their population living in cities.

▲ Along with mass-produced consumer goods, such as clothing and appliances, Sears, Roebuck and Company marketed architectural plans for middle-class suburban housing. This drawing, taken from the Sears catalogue for 1911, illustrates the kind of housing developed on the urban outskirts in the early twentieth century. *(Sears, Roebuck and Company)*

provide. Sometimes annexation preceded settlement, adding vacant land where new residents could live. In the 1880s, Chicago, Minneapolis, and Los Angeles incorporated hundreds of undeveloped square miles into their borders.

In-migration from the countryside and immigration from abroad made by far the greatest contribution to urban population growth. In fact, movement to cities nearly matched the massive migration to the West that was occurring at the same time. Urban newcomers arrived from two major sources: the American countryside and Europe. Asia, Canada, and Latin America also supplied immigrants, though in smaller numbers.

Urban In-Migration

Despite land rushes in the West, rural populations declined as urban populations burgeoned. Low crop prices and high debts dashed white farmers' hopes and drove them toward opportunities that cities seemed to offer. These migrants filled major cities, such as Detroit, Chicago, and San Francisco, but also secondary cities, such as In-dianapolis, Salt Lake City, Nashville, and San Diego. The thrill of city life beckoned especially to young people. A character in the play *The City* (1920) spoke for many youths when she exclaimed, "Who wants to smell new-mown hay, if he can breathe in gasoline on Fifth Avenue instead! Think of the theaters! The crowds! Think of being able to go out on the street and see someone you didn't know by sight!" Despair drove farm boys to cities, but for every four men who migrated cityward, five women did the same, often to escape unhappy home life. But young women were also attracted by the independence—the remaking of themselves—that urban employment offered.

In the 1880s and 1890s, thousands of rural African Americans also moved cityward, seeking better employment and fleeing crop liens, ravages of the boll weevil on cotton crops, racial violence, and political oppression. Black migration accelerated after 1915, but thirty-two cities already had more than ten thousand black residents by 1900. African American populations rose in southern cities, such as Baltimore, Atlanta, and Birmingham, but northern places, such as New York, Cleveland, and Chicago, also received thousands of black migrants. These newcomers resembled other migrants in their rural backgrounds and economic motivations, but they differed in several important ways. Because few factories would employ African Americans, most found jobs in the service sector—cleaning, cooking, and driving—rather than in industrial trades. Also, because most service openings were traditionally female jobs, black women outnumbered black men in cities such as New York, Baltimore, and New Orleans. In the South, blacks migrating from the countryside became an important source of unskilled labor in the region's growing cities. By 1900, almost 40 percent of the total population of both Atlanta, Georgia, and Charlotte, North Carolina, was black.

In the West, many Hispanics, once a predominantly rural population, also moved into cities. They took unskilled construction jobs previously held by Chinese laborers who had been driven from Southern California cities, and in some Texas cities, native Mexicans (called *Tejanos*) held the majority of all unskilled jobs. In Los Angeles and other cities, Hispanic males often left home for long periods to take temporary agricultural jobs, leaving behind female heads of household.

Even more newcomers were foreign immigrants who had fled villages and cities in Europe, Asia, Canada,

Foreign Immigration

and Latin America for the United States. Many never intended to stay; they wanted only to make enough money to return home and live in greater comfort and security. For every hundred foreigners who entered the country, around thirty ultimately left. Still, like Houdini and his family, most of the 26 million immigrants who arrived between 1870 and 1920 remained, and the great majority settled in cities, where they helped reshape American culture.

Immigration to the United States was part of a worldwide movement pushing people away from traditional

The New Immigration

means of support and pulling them toward better opportunities. Population pressures, land redistribution, and industrialization induced millions of peasants, small landowners, and craftsmen to leave Europe and Asia for Canada, Australia, Brazil, and Argentina, as well as the United States. Religious persecution, too, particularly the merciless pogroms and military conscription that Jews suffered in eastern Europe, forced people to escape across the Atlantic. Migration has always characterized human history, but in the late nineteenth century, technological advances in communications and transportation spread news of opportunities and made travel cheaper, quicker, and safer.

▲ The Caribbean as well as Europe sent immigrants to the United States. Hopeful that they were leaving their homeland of Guadeloupe for a better life, these women were perhaps unprepared for the disadvantages they faced as blacks, foreigners, and women.

(William Williams Papers, Manuscripts & Archives Division, The New York Public Library)

Immigrants from northern and western Europe had long made the United States their main destination, but after 1880 economic and demographic changes propelled a second wave of immigrants from other regions. People from Ireland, England, and Germany continued to arrive, but increased numbers came from eastern and southern Europe, plus smaller bands from Canada, Mexico, and Japan (see Map 19.2 and Figure 19.1). Between 1900 and 1909, when the new wave peaked, two-thirds of immigrants came from Italy, Austria-Hungary, and Russia. By 1910 arrivals from Mexico outnumbered arrivals from Ireland, and numerous Japanese had moved to the West Coast and Hawai'i. Foreign-born blacks, chiefly from the West Indies, also came. (See website for the nationalities of immigrants.)

Many long-settled Americans feared those whom they called "new immigrants," whose folk customs, Catholic and Jewish faiths, and poverty made them seem more

Country of Origin of Foreign-Born Population in U.S.
1/4" = 500,00 people
■ 1900
■ 1920
—— Boundary, 2000

Map 19.2   Sources of European-Born Population, 1900 and 1920

In just a few decades, the proportion of European immigrants to the United States who came from northern and western Europe decreased (Ireland and Germany) or remained relatively stable (England and Scandinavia), while the proportion from eastern and southern Europe increased dramatically.

(Source: Data from U.S. Census Bureau, "Historical Census Statistics on the Foreign-Born Population of the United States: 1850–1990," February 1999, http://www.census.gov/population [accessed February 12, 2000].)

alien than previous newcomers. Unlike earlier groups from Great Britain and Ireland, new immigrants did not speak English, and more than half worked in low-skill occupations. Yet old and new immigrants closely resembled each other in their strategies for coping. The majority of both groups hailed from societies that made family the focus of all undertakings. As in the case of Erich Weiss's family, whether and when to emigrate was decided in light of family needs, and family bonds remained tight after immigrants reached America. New arrivals usually knew

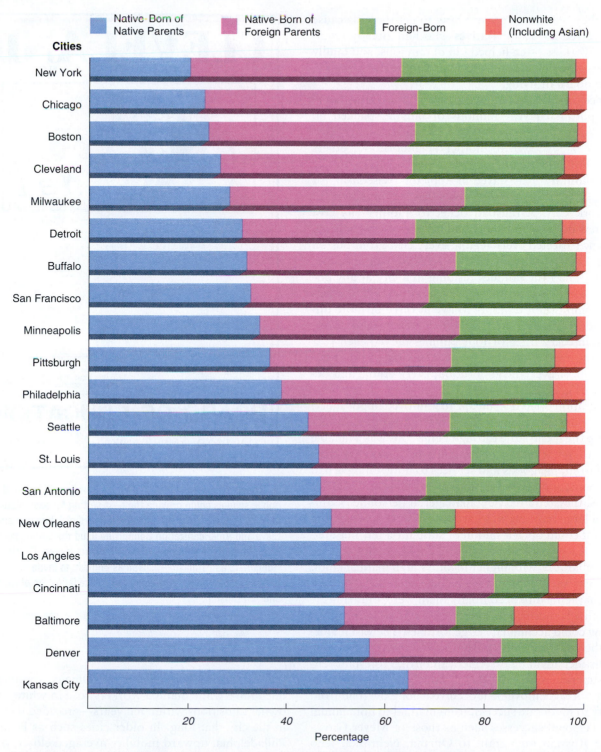

Figure 19.1   Composition of Population, Selected Cities, 1920

Immigration and migration made native-born whites of native-born parents minorities in almost every major city by the early twentieth century. Moreover, foreign-born residents and native-born whites of foreign parents (combining the purple and green segments of a line) constituted absolute majorities in numerous places.

where they wanted to go and how to get there, because they received aid from relatives who had already immigrated. Workers often helped kin obtain jobs, and family members pooled resources to maintain, if not improve, their standard of living.

Once they arrived, in-migrants and immigrants rarely stayed put. Each year millions of families packed up and moved elsewhere. Some moved to another neighborhood; others left town. Thus the Weiss family stayed in Appleton, Wisconsin, for only a few years before moving to New York City. A railroad ticket to another city cost only a few dollars, and many had little to lose by moving. Transience affected every region, every city. From Boston to San Francisco, from Minneapolis to San Antonio, more than half the families residing in a city at any one time were gone ten years later. Even within a city, it was not uncommon for a family to live at three or more different addresses over a ten- or fifteen-year period. Overall, one in every three or four families moved each year (today the rate is one in five). Population turnover affected almost every neighborhood, every ethnic and occupational group.

Geographic and Social Mobility

Migration offered an escape to improved opportunity; remaking oneself occupationally offered another. An advance up the social scale through better jobs was available mostly to white males. Thousands of businesses were needed to supply goods and services to burgeoning urban populations, and as corporations grew and centralized operations, they required new managerial personnel. Capital for a large business was hard to amass, but an aspiring merchant could open a saloon or shop for a few hundred dollars. Knowledge of accounting could qualify one for white-collar jobs with higher incomes than manual labor. Thus nonmanual jobs and the higher social status and income that tended to accompany them were attainable.

Such advancement occurred often. To be sure, only a very few could accumulate large fortunes. The vast majority of the era's wealthiest businessmen began their careers with distinct advantages: American birth, Protestant religion, superior education, and relatively affluent parents. Yet considerable movement occurred along the road from poverty to moderate success, from manual to nonmanual work. Personal successes such as those of Meyer Grossman, a Russian immigrant to Omaha, Nebraska, who worked as a teamster before saving enough to open a successful furniture store, were common.

Rates of upward occupational mobility were slow but steady between 1870 and 1920. In fast-growing cities

▲ Those who wished to Americanize immigrants believed that public schools could provide the best setting for assimilation. This 1917 poster from the Cleveland Board of Education and the Cleveland Americanization Committee used the languages most common to the new immigrants—Slovene, Italian, Polish, Hungarian, and Yiddish—as well as English, to invite newcomers to free classes where they could learn "the language of America" and "citizenship."

(National Park Service Collection, Ellis Island Immigration Museum. Photo: Chermayeff & Geismar/ MetaForm)

such as Atlanta, Los Angeles, and Omaha, approximately one in five white manual workers rose to white-collar or owner's positions within ten years—provided they stayed in the city that long. In older cities such as Boston and Philadelphia, upward mobility averaged closer to one in six workers in ten years. Some men slipped from a higher to a lower rung on the occupational ladder, but rates of upward movement usually doubled those of downward movement. Although patterns were not consistent, immigrants generally experienced less upward and more downward mobility than did the native-born. Still, regardless of birthplace, the chances for a white male to rise occupationally over the course of his career or to hold a higher-status job than his father were relatively good.

What constitutes a better job, however, depends on one's definition of improvement. Many immigrant artisans, such as a German carpenter or an Italian shoemaker, considered an accountant's job unmanly. People with traditions of pride in working with their hands neither desired nonmanual jobs nor encouraged their children to seek them. As one Italian tailor explained, "I learned the tailoring business in the old country. Over here, in America, I never have trouble finding a job because I know my business from the other side [Italy]. . . . I want that my oldest boy learn my trade because I tell him that you could always make at least enough for the family."

Business ownership, moreover, entailed risks. Failure rates were high among saloon owners and other small proprietors in working-class neighborhoods, because the low incomes of their customers made profits uncertain. Many manual workers sought security rather than mobility, preferring a steady wage to the risks of ownership. A Sicilian who lived in Bridgeport, Connecticut, observed that "the people that come here they afraid to get in business because they don't know how that business goes. In Italy these people don't know much about these things because most of them work on farms or in [their] trade."

Many women held paying jobs and, like men, migrated within and between cities, but they often moved with fathers or husbands whose economic standing usually defined their social position. Women could improve their status by marrying men with wealth or potential, but other avenues were mostly closed to them. Laws limited what women could inherit; educational institutions blocked their training in such professions as medicine and law; and prevailing assumptions attributed higher aptitude for manual skills and business to men than to women. For African Americans, American Indians, Mexican Americans, and Asian Americans, opportunities were even scarcer. Assigned to the lowest-paying occupations by prejudice, they could make few gains.

In addition to advancing occupationally, a person might achieve social mobility by acquiring property, such as building or buying a house. But home ownership was not easy to achieve. Banks and savings-and-loan institutions had strict lending practices, and mortgage loans carried high interest rates and short repayment periods. Thus renting, even of single-family houses, was common, especially in big cities. Nevertheless, many families were able to amass savings, which they could use as down payments on property. Ownership rates varied regionally—higher in western cities, lower in eastern cities—but 36 percent of all urban American families owned their homes in 1900, the highest homeownership rate of any western nation except for Denmark, Norway, and Sweden.

Many who migrated, particularly unskilled workers, did not improve their status; they simply floated from one low-paying job to another. Others could not maintain their Old World occupations; Erich Weiss's father had to accept manual labor employment because he could not continue being a rabbi. Still others, however, did find greener pastures. Studies of Boston, Omaha, Atlanta, and other cities show that most men who rose occupationally or acquired property had migrated from somewhere else. Thus, although cities frustrated the hopes of some, they offered opportunities to others. The possibilities for upward mobility seemed to temper people's dissatisfaction with the tensions and frustrations of city life. For every story of rags to riches, there were a multitude of small triumphs mixed with dashed hopes and discrimination. Although the gap between the very rich and the very poor widened, for those in between, the expanding economies of American cities created room.

URBAN NEIGHBORHOODS

Despite the constant turnover that made them dynamic places, American cities were characterized by collections of subcommunities where people, most of whom had migrated from somewhere else, coped with daily challenges to their cultures. Rather than yield completely to pressures to assimilate, migrants and immigrants interacted with the urban environment in a complex way that enabled them to retain their identity while also altering both their own outlook and the social structure of cities themselves.

In their new surroundings—where the English language was a struggle, where the clock regulated their workday, and where housing and employment were uncertain—immigrants first anchored their lives to the root they knew best: their culture. Old World customs persisted in immigrant districts of Italians from the same province, Japanese from the same island district, and Russian Jews from the same *shtetl*. Newcomers re-created mutual aid societies they had known in their homeland. For example, in western cities Japanese transferred *ken* societies, which organized social celebrations and relief services, and Chinese used loan associations, called *whey,*

Cultural Retention and Change

which raised money to help members acquire businesses. Chinese also transplanted village associations called *fongs,* which rented apartments to homeless members; *kung saw,* assistance organizations of people with the same family name regardless of what part of China they came from; and *tongs,* secret societies designed to aid people but which often acted as gangs that extorted protection money from businesses. Southern Italians transplanted the system whereby a *padrone* (boss) found jobs for unskilled workers by negotiating with—and receiving a payoff from—an employer. People practiced religion as they always had, held traditional feasts and pageants, married within their group, and pursued long-standing feuds with people from rival villages.

In large cities, such as Chicago, Philadelphia, and Detroit, European immigrants initially clustered in inner-city neighborhoods where low-skill jobs and cheap housing were most

Urban Borderlands

available. These districts often were multi-ethnic, places historians have called "urban borderlands," where a diversity of people, identities, and lifestyles coexisted. To be sure, members of the same group often tried to exclude outsiders from their neighborhood space and institutions, but even within districts identified with a certain group, such as Little Italy, Jewtown, Polonia, or Greektown, rapid mobility constantly undermined residential homogeneity, as former inhabitants dispersed to other neighborhoods and new inhabitants moved in. Often a particular area was inhabited by several ethnic groups, while the local businesses and institutions, such as bakeries, butcher shops, churches, and club headquarters—which usually were operated by and for one ethnic group—gave a neighborhood its identity.

For first- and second-generation immigrants, their neighborhoods acted as havens until individuals were ready to cross from the borderland into the majority society. But borderland experiences often dissolved, sometimes in a generation, sometimes in just a few years. The expansion of mass transportation and outward movement of factories enabled people to move to other neighborhoods, where they interspersed with families of their own socioeconomic class but not necessarily of their own ethnicity. European immigrants did encounter prejudice, such as the exclusion of Jews from certain neighborhoods, professions, and clubs, or the inability of Italians to break into urban politics, but discrimination rarely was systematic or complete. For people of color, however—African Americans, Asians, and Mexicans—the borderlands kept a more persistent character which, because of discrimination, became less multiethnic over time.

Although the small numbers of African Americans who inhabited American cities in the eighteenth and early

Racial Segregation and Violence

nineteenth centuries may have lived near or interspersed with whites, by the late nineteenth century rigid racial discrimination forced them into relatively permanent, highly segregated ghettos. By 1920 in Chicago, Detroit, Cleveland, and other cities where tens of thousands of blacks now lived, two-thirds or more of the total African American population inhabited only 10 percent of the residential area. Within their neighborhoods, African Americans, like other urban dwellers, nurtured cultural institutions that helped them cope with city life: shops, schools, clubs, theaters, dance halls, newspapers, and saloons. Churches, particularly those of the Baptist and African Methodist Episcopal (AME) branches of Protestantism, were especially influential. Pittsburgh blacks boasted twenty-eight such churches in the early 1900s. Membership in Cincinnati's black Baptist churches doubled between 1870 and 1900. In Louisville, blacks pooled their resources and built their own theological institute. In virtually all cities, black religious activity not only dominated local life but also represented cooperation across class lines.

In most cities, the only way blacks could relieve the pressures of crowding that resulted from increasing migration was to expand residential borders into surrounding, previously white neighborhoods, a process that often resulted in harassment and attacks by white residents whose intolerant attitudes were intensified by fears that black neighbors would cause property values to decline. Moreover, the increased presence of African Americans in cities, North and South, as well as their competition with whites for housing, jobs, and political influence, sparked a series of race riots. In 1898 white citizens of Wilmington, North Carolina, resenting African Americans' involvement in local government and incensed by an editorial in an African American newspaper accusing white women of loose sexual behavior, rioted and killed dozens of blacks. In the fury's wake, white supremacists overthrew the city government, expelling black and white officeholders, and instituted restrictions to prevent blacks from voting. In Atlanta in 1906, newspaper accounts alleging attacks by black men on white women provoked an outburst of shooting and killing that left twelve blacks dead and seventy injured. An influx of unskilled black strikebreakers into East St. Louis, Illinois, heightened racial tensions in 1917. Rumors that blacks were arming themselves for an attack on whites resulted in numerous attacks by white mobs on black neighborhoods. On July 1, blacks fired back at a car whose occupants they believed

▲ Although Chinese immigrants, like other immigrants, struggled to succeed in American society, they often faced severe discrimination because of their different lifestyle. As this photo of a San Francisco grocery shows, Chinese looked, dressed, and ate differently than did white Americans. Occasionally, they suffered from racist violence that caused them to fear not only for their personal safety but also for the safety of establishments such as this one that might suffer damage from resentful mobs. *(The Bancroft Library, University of California)*

had shot into their homes and mistakenly killed two policemen riding in the car. The next day, a full-scale riot erupted which ended only after nine whites and thirty-nine blacks had been killed and over three hundred buildings destroyed.

Asians also encountered discrimination and an isolated residential experience. Although Chinese immigrants often preferred to live apart from Anglos, in Chinatowns of San Francisco, Los Angeles, and New York City, where they created their own business, government, and social institutions, Anglos also made every effort to keep them separated. In San Francisco, anti-Chinese hostility was fomented by Denis Kearney, an Irish immigrant who blamed Chinese for unemployment in California in the late 1870s. Using the slogan "The Chinese must go," Kearney and his followers intimidated employers into refusing to hire Chinese, and drove hundreds of Asians out of the city. San Francisco's government prohibited Chinese laun-

dries (which were social centers as well as commercial establishments) from locating in white neighborhoods and banned the wearing of queues, the traditional Chinese hair braid. In 1882 Congress passed the Chinese Exclusion Act, which suspended immigration of Chinese laborers and prohibited naturalization of those Chinese already residing in the United States. And in 1892 Congress approved the Geary Act, which extended immigration restriction and required Chinese Americans to carry certificates of residence issued by the Treasury Department. A San Francisco–based organization called the Chinese Six Companies fought the law, but in 1893 the U.S. Supreme Court upheld the Geary Act in *Fong Yue Ting v. United States*. Japanese immigrants, called Issei, most of whom settled in or near Los Angeles, were prevented by law from becoming American citizens and, like the Chinese, developed communities with their own economic and residential character.

Mexicans in southwestern cities experienced somewhat more complex residential patterns. In places such as

Mexican Barrios

Los Angeles, Santa Barbara, and Tucson, Mexicans had been the original inhabitants, and Anglos were migrants who overtook the city, pushing Mexicans into adjoining areas. Here, Mexicans became increasingly isolated in residential and commercial districts called barrios. Frequently, real-estate covenants, by which property owners pledged not to sell homes to Mexicans (or to African Americans, or to Jews), kept Mexican families confined in barrios of Los Angeles, Albuquerque, and San Antonio. These areas tended to be located away from central-city multiethnic borderlands housing European immigrants. To a considerable extent, then, racial bias, more than any other factor, made urban experiences of African Americans, Asians, and Mexicans unique and hindered their opportunities to remake their lives.

Virtually everywhere immigrants lived, Old World culture mingled with New World realities. On one hand,

Cultural Adaptation

people often found their local identities eclipsed by national identities. Although many foreigners identified themselves by their village or region of birth, native-born Americans simplified by categorizing them by nationality. People from County Cork and County Limerick, for example, were merged into Irish; those from Schleswig and Württemberg into Germans; those from Calabria and Campobasso into Italians. Immigrant institutions, such as newspapers and churches, found they had to appeal to the entire nationality in order to survive.

Moreover, the diversity of American cities prompted foreigners to modify their attitudes and habits. With so many people interacting on streets and in workplaces, few newcomers could avoid contact with groups different from themselves, and few could prevent such contacts from altering old ways of life. Although many immigrants tried to preserve their native language, English, taught in schools and needed on the job, soon penetrated nearly every community. Foreigners fashioned garments in homeland styles but had to use American rather than traditional fabrics. Italians went to American doctors but still carried traditional amulets to ward off evil spirits. Unavailability of Asian vegetables and spices forced Chinese American cooks to improvise by using local ingredients in a new dish they called "chop suey." Music especially revealed adaptations. Polka bands entertained at Polish social gatherings, but their repertoires blended American and Polish folk music Mexican ballads acquired new

themes that described adventures of border crossing and hardships of labor in the United States.

The influx of so many immigrants between 1870 and 1920 transformed the United States from a basically Protestant nation into a diverse collection of Protestants, Catholics, Orthodox Christians, Jews, Buddhists, and Muslims. Newcomers from Italy, Hungary, Polish lands, and Slovakia joined Irish and Germans to boost the proportion of Catholics in many cities. In Buffalo, Cleveland, Chicago, and Milwaukee, Catholic immigrants and their offspring approached a majority of the population. Catholic Mexicans constituted over half of the population of El Paso. German and Russian immigrants gave New York City one of the largest Jewish populations in the world.

Partly in response to Protestant charges that their religions prevented them from assimilating, many Catholics and Jews tried to accommodate their faiths to the new environment. Catholic and Jewish leaders from earlier immigrant groups supported liberalizing trends—use of English in services, the phasing out of such Old World rituals as saints' feasts, and a preference for public over religious schools. As long as new immigrants continued to arrive, however, these trends met stiff resistance. Catholics, for example, supported parochial schools and occasionally campaigned for public funding for them. In some cases, Catholic children's attendance at parochial schools prevented public schools from becoming even more crowded than they already were.

Newcomers usually held onto familiar religious practices, whether the folk Catholicism of southern Italy or the Orthodox Judaism of eastern Europe. Because Catholic parishes served distinct geographic areas, immigrants wanted parish priests of their own "kind," in spite of church attempts to make American Catholicism more uniform. Bishops acceded to pressures from predominantly Polish congregations for Polish rather than German-born priests. Eastern European Jews, convinced that Reform Judaism sacrificed too much to American ways, established the Conservative branch, which retained traditional ritual though it abolished the segregation of women in synagogues and allowed English prayers. But, in addition, the tendency of second-generation Catholics and Jews to marry coreligionists of other ethnic groups—an Italian Catholic marrying a Polish Catholic, for example—kept religious identity strong while undercutting ethnic identity.

Each of the three major migrant groups that peopled American cities—native-born whites, foreigners of various races, and native-born blacks—created the pluralism of modern American culture. The country's cultural diversity prevented domination by a single racial or ethnic majority. The cities nurtured rich cultural variety: American folk music and literature, Italian and Mexican cuisine, Irish comedy, Yiddish theater, African American jazz and dance, and much more. Newcomers in the late nineteenth century changed their environment as much as they were changed by it.

LIVING CONDITIONS IN THE INNER CITY

Although filled with inhabitants rich in varied cultures, the central sections of American cities also seemed to harbor every affliction that plagues modern society: poverty, disease, crime, and the tensions that occur when large numbers of people live close together. City dwellers coped as best they could, and technology, private enterprise, and public authority achieved some remarkable successes. But many of their problems still await solution.

One of the most persistent shortcomings—the scarcity of adequate housing—has its origins in nineteenth-

Inner-City Housing

century urban development. In spite of massive construction in the 1880s and early 1900s, population growth outpaced housing supplies. Lack of inexpensive living quarters especially afflicted working-class families who, because of low wages, had to rent their homes. As cities grew, landlords took advantage of shortages in inexpensive rental housing by splitting up existing buildings to house more people, constructing multiple-unit tenements, and hiking rents. Low-income families adapted to high costs and short supply by sharing space and expenses. It became common in many cities for a one-family apartment to be occupied by two or three families, or by a single family plus several boarders.

The result was unprecedented crowding. In 1890 New York City's immigrant-packed Lower East Side averaged 702 people per acre, one of the highest population densities in the world. Inner districts had distinctive physical appearances in different cities: six- to eight-story

▲ Inner-city dwellers used not only indoor space as efficiently as possible, but also what little outdoor space was available to them. Scores of families living in this cramped block of six-story tenements in New York strung clotheslines behind the buildings. Notice that there is virtually no space between buildings, so only rooms at the front and back received daylight and fresh air.

(Library of Congress)

barracks-like buildings in New York; dilapidated row houses in Baltimore and Philadelphia; converted slave quarters in Charleston and New Orleans; and crumbling two- and three-story frame houses in Seattle and San Francisco. But everywhere crowding was common.

Inside these structures, conditions were harsh. The largest rooms were barely ten feet wide, and interior rooms either lacked windows or opened onto narrow shafts that bred vermin and rotten odors. Describing such a duct, one immigrant housekeeper revealed, "It's damp down there, and the families, they throw out garbage and dirty papers and the insides of chickens, and other unmentionable filth. . . . I just vomited when I first cleaned up the air shaft." Few buildings had indoor plumbing; residents had to use privies (outdoor toilets) in the back yard or basement. Often, the only source of heat was dangerous, polluting coal-burning stoves.

Housing Reform

Housing problems sparked widespread reform campaigns. New York State took the lead by passing laws in 1867, 1879, and 1901 that established light, ventilation, and safety codes for new tenement buildings. These and similar measures in other states could not remedy ills of existing buildings, but they did impose minimal obligations on landlords. A few reformers, such as journalist Jacob Riis and humanitarian Lawrence Veiller, advocated housing low-income families in "model tenements," with more spacious rooms and better facilities. Model tenements, however, required landlords to accept lower profits, a sacrifice few were willing to make. Both reformers and public officials opposed government financing of better housing, fearing that such a step would undermine private enterprise. Still, housing codes and regulatory commissions strengthened the power of local government to oversee construction.

New Home Technology

Eventually, technology brought about important changes in home life. Advanced systems of central heating (furnaces), artificial lighting, and indoor plumbing created more comfort, first for middle-class households and later for most others. Whereas formerly families had bought coal or chopped wood for cooking and heating, made candles for light, and hauled water for bathing, their homes and apartments increasingly connected to outside pipes and wires for gas, electricity, and water. Central heat and artificial light made it possible for residents to enjoy a steady, comfortable temperature and to turn night into day, while indoor plumbing removed the unpleasant experiences of the outhouse. Moreover, these utilities helped create new attitudes about privacy among those who could afford the technology. Middle-class bedrooms and bathrooms became private retreats. Even children could have their own bedrooms, complete with individualized decoration.

Scientific and technological advances eventually enabled city dwellers and the entire nation to live in greater safety. By the 1880s, doctors had begun to accept the theory that microorganisms (germs) cause disease. In response, cities established more efficient systems of water purification and sewage disposal. Although disease and death rates remained higher in cities than in the countryside, and tuberculosis and other respiratory ills continued to plague inner-city districts, public health regulations as applied to water purity, sewage disposal, and food quality helped to control such dread diseases as cholera, typhoid fever, and diphtheria.

Meanwhile, street paving, modernized firefighting equipment, and electric street lighting spread rapidly across urban America. Steel-frame construction, which supports a building with a metal skeleton rather than with masonry walls, made possible the erection of skyscrapers—and thus more efficient vertical use of scarce and costly urban land. Electric elevators and steam-heating systems serviced these buildings. Steel-cable suspension bridges, developed by John A. Roebling and epitomized by his Brooklyn Bridge (completed in 1883), replaced ferry boats and linked metropolitan sections more closely.

Poverty Relief

None of these improvements, however, lightened the burden of poverty. The urban economy, though generally expanding, advanced erratically. Employment, especially for unskilled workers in manufacturing and construction, rose and fell with business cycles and changing seasons. An ever-increasing number of families lived on the margins of survival.

Since colonial days Americans have disagreed about how much responsibility the public should assume for poor relief. According to traditional beliefs, still widespread at the beginning of the twentieth century, anyone could escape poverty through hard work and clean living; indigence existed only because some people were morally weaker than others. Such reasoning bred fear that aid to poor people would encourage paupers to rely on public support rather than their own efforts. As business cycles fluctuated and poverty increased, this attitude hardened, and city governments discontinued direct grants of food, fuel, and clothing to needy families. Instead, cities provided relief in return for work on public projects and sent special cases to state-run almshouses, orphanages, and homes for the blind, deaf, and mentally ill.

Efforts to rationalize relief fostered some changes in attitude. Between 1877 and 1892, philanthropists in ninety-two cities formed Charity Organization Societies, an attempt to make social welfare (like business) more efficient by merging disparate charity groups into coordinated units. Believing poverty to be caused by personal defects, such as alcoholism and laziness, members of these organizations spent most of their time visiting poor families and encouraging them to be thriftier and more virtuous. These visits were also intended to identify the "deserving" poor.

Close observation of the poor, however, prompted some humanitarians to conclude that people's environments, not their shortcomings, caused poverty and that society ought to shoulder greater responsibility for improving social conditions. These reformers had faith that they could reduce poverty by improving housing, education, sanitation, and job opportunities rather than by admonishing the poor to be more moral. This attitude fueled campaigns for building codes, factory regulations, and public health measures in the Progressive era of the early twentieth century (see Chapter 21). Still, most middle- and upper-class Americans continued to endorse the creed that in a society of abundance only the unfit were poor and that poverty relief should be tolerated but never encouraged. As one charity worker put it, relief "should be surrounded by circumstances that shall . . . repel every one . . . from accepting it."

Crime and disorder, as much as crowding and poverty, nurtured fears that cities, especially their slums, threatened the nation. The more cities grew, it seemed, the more they

Crime and Violence

shook with violence. While homicide rates declined in industrialized nations such as England and Germany, those in America rose alarmingly: 25 murders per million people in 1881; 107 per million in 1898. In addition, innumerable disruptions, ranging from domestic violence to muggings to gang fights, made cities scenes of constant turbulence. Pickpockets, swindlers, and burglars roamed every city. Urban outlaws, such as Rufus Minor, acquired as much notoriety as western desperadoes. Short, stocky, and bald, Minor resembled a shy clerk, but one police chief labeled him "one of the smartest bank sneaks in America." Minor often grew a beard before holding up a bank, then shaved afterward to avoid identification by eyewitnesses. Minor was implicated in bank heists in New York City, Cleveland, Detroit, Providence, Philadelphia, Albany, Boston, and Baltimore—all between 1878 and 1882.

Despite fears, however, urban crime and violence may simply have become more conspicuous and sensational rather than more prevalent. To be sure, concentrations of wealth and the mingling of different peoples provided opportunities for larceny, vice, and assault. But urban lawlessness and brutality probably did not exceed that of backwoods mining camps and southern plantations. Nativists were quick to blame immigrants for urban crime, but the law-breaking population included native-born Americans as well as foreigners. One investigation of jails in 1900 concluded that "we have ourselves evolved as cruel and cunning criminals as any that Europe may have foisted upon us."

MANAGING THE CITY

Those concerned with managing cities faced daunting challenges in the late nineteenth century. Burgeoning populations, business expansion, and technological change created urgent needs for sewers, police and fire protection, schools, parks, and other services. Such needs strained municipal resources beyond their capacities, and city governments were poorly organized to handle them. In addition to a mayor and a city council, governmental responsibilities typically were scattered among independent boards that administered health regulations, public works, poverty relief, and other functions. Philadelphia at one time had thirty such boards. State governments also often interfered in local matters, appointing board members and limiting cities' abilities to levy taxes and borrow money.

Finding sources of clean water and a way to dispose of waste became increasingly pressing challenges. In the

Water Supply and Sewage Disposal

early nineteenth century, urban households used privies to dispose of human excrement, and factories dumped untreated sewage into rivers, lakes, and bays. By the late nineteenth century, most cities had replaced private water companies with public water supplies, but these services did not guarantee pure water. The installation of sewer systems and flush toilets, plus use of water as a coolant in factories, overwhelmed waterways, contaminating drinking-water sources and sending pollution to communities downstream. The stench of rivers was often unbearable, and pollution bred disease. Memphis and New York experienced severe yellow-fever epidemics in the 1870s and 1880s, and typhoid fever threatened many cities. By 1900, the Passaic River in northern New Jersey, once a popular recreation and fishing site, had been ruined by discharge from the cities along its banks.

Acceptance in the 1880s of the germ theory of disease prompted city health officials to take steps to reduce chances that human waste and other pollutants would endanger water supplies, but the task proved difficult. Some states passed laws prohibiting discharge of raw sewage into rivers and streams, and a few cities began the expensive process of chemically treating sewage. Gradually,

This scene, captured by a Philadelphia ▶ photographer sent to record the extent of trash that was littering city streets and sidewalks, illustrates the problems of disposal confronting inner-city, immigrant neighborhoods and the necessity for some form of public service to remove the refuse. Seemingly oblivious to the debris, the residents pose for the photographer.

(Philadelphia City Archives, Department of Records)

water managers installed mechanical filters, and cities, led by Jersey City, began purifying water supplies by adding chlorine. These efforts dramatically reduced death rates from typhoid fever.

But waste disposal remained a thorny problem. Experts in 1900 estimated that every New Yorker generated annually some 160 pounds of garbage (food and bones); 1,200 pounds of ashes (from stoves and furnaces); and 100 pounds of rubbish (shoes, furniture, and other discarded items). Europeans of that era produced about half as much trash. Solid waste dumped from factories and businesses included tons of scrap metal, as well as wood. In addition, each of the estimated 3.5 million horses in American cities in 1900 daily dropped about 20 pounds of manure and a gallon of urine that rain washed into nearby water sources. When horses died, the disposal of their carcasses brought more environmental problems. In past eras, excrement, trash, and dead animals could be dismissed as nuisances; by the twentieth century they had become health and safety hazards.

Citizens' groups, led by women's organizations, began discussing these dilemmas in the 1880s, and by the turn of the century urban governments began to hire sanitary engineers, such as New York's George Waring, to design efficient systems to collect garbage and dispose of it in incinerators and landfills. Engineers also were solving other urban problems and making cities more livable. Street lighting, bridge and street construction, fire protection, and other vital services required technological creativity, and in addressing these issues, the American engineering profession developed new systems and standards of worldwide significance. Elected officials came to depend on the expertise of engineers, who seemed best qualified to supervise a city's expansion. In-

Urban Engineers

sulated within bureaucratic agencies away from tumultuous party politics, engineers generally carried out their responsibilities efficiently and made some of the most lasting contributions to urban management.

After the mid-nineteenth century, urban dwellers increasingly depended on professional police to protect life and property, but law enforcement became complicated and controversial, as various urban groups differed in their views of the law and how it should be enforced. Ethnic and racial minorities were more likely to be arrested than those with economic or political influence. And police officers applied the law less harshly to members of their own ethnic groups and to people with power or those who bought exemptions with bribes.

Law Enforcement

As law enforcers, police, often poorly trained and prone to corruption, were caught between demands for swift and severe action on the one hand and for leniency on the other. As urban society diversified, some people clamored for police crackdowns on saloons, gambling halls, and houses of prostitution; at the same time, others who profited from and patronized such customer-oriented criminal establishments favored loose law enforcement. Achieving balance between the idealistic intentions of criminal law and people's desire for individual freedom grew increasingly difficult, and it has remained so to this day.

Out of the apparent confusion surrounding urban management arose political machines, organizations whose

▲ "Big Tim" Sullivan, a New York City ward boss, rewarded "repeat voters" with a new pair of shoes. Sullivan once explained, "When you've voted 'em with their whiskers on, you take 'em to a barber and scrape off the chin fringe. Then you vote 'em again. . . . Then to a barber again, off comes the sides and you vote 'em a third time with the mustache. . . . [Then] clean off the mustache and vote 'em plain face. That makes every one of 'em for four votes." *(Library of Congress)*

Political Machines

main goals were the rewards—money, influence, and prestige—of getting and keeping power. Machine politicians routinely used fraud and bribery to further their ends. But they also provided relief, security, and services to the crowds of newcomers who voted for them and kept them in power. By meeting people's needs, machine politicians accomplished things that other agencies had been unable or unwilling to attempt.

Machines bred leaders, called bosses, who built power bases among urban working classes and especially among new immigrant voters. Most bosses knew their constituents' needs firsthand; they had immigrant backgrounds and had grown up in the inner city. Bosses held power because they tended to problems of everyday life. Martin Lomasney, boss of Boston's South End, explained, "There's got to be in every ward somebody that any bloke can come to—no matter what he's done—and get help. Help, you understand, none of your law and justice, but help." In return for votes, bosses provided jobs, built parks and bathhouses, distributed food and clothing to the needy, and

helped when someone ran afoul of the law. New York's "Big Tim" Sullivan, for example, gave out free shoes and sponsored annual picnics. Such personalized service cultivated mass attachment to the boss; never before had public leaders assumed such responsibility for people in need. Bosses, moreover, made politics a full-time profession. They attended weddings and wakes, joined clubs, and held open houses in saloons where neighborhood folk could speak to them personally. According to George Washington Plunkitt, a neighborhood boss in New York City, "As a rule [the boss] has no business or occupation other than politics. He plays politics every day and night in the year and his headquarters bears the inscription, 'Never closed.'"

To finance their activities and election campaigns, bosses exchanged favors for votes and money. Power over local government enabled machines to control the awarding of public contracts, the granting of utility and streetcar franchises, and the distribution of city jobs. Recipients of city business and jobs were expected to repay the machine with a portion of their profits or salaries and to cast supporting votes on election day. Critics called this process graft; bosses called it gratitude.

Bosses such as Philadelphia's "Duke" Vare, Kansas City's Tom Pendergast, and New York's Richard Croker lived like kings, though their official incomes were slim. Yet machines were rarely as dictatorial or corrupt as critics charged. Rather, several machines, like businesses, evolved into tightly structured operations, such as New York's Tammany Hall organization (named after a society that originally began as a patriotic and fraternal club), which wedded public accomplishments with personal gain. The system rested on a popular base and was held together by loyalty and service. A few bosses had no permanent organization; they were freelance opportunists who bargained for power, sometimes winning and sometimes losing. But most machines were coalitions of smaller organizations that derived power directly from inner-city neighborhoods. Bosses also could boast major achievements. Aided by engineers, machine-led governments constructed the urban infrastructure—public buildings, sewer systems, schools, bridges, and mass-transit lines—and expanded urban services—police, firefighting, and health departments.

Machine politics, however, was rarely neutral or fair. Racial minorities and new immigrant groups, such as Italians and Poles, received only token jobs and nominal favors, if any. And bribes and kickbacks made machine projects and services costly to taxpayers. Cities could not ordinarily raise enough revenue for their construction projects from taxes and fees, so they financed expansion with loans from the public in the form of municipal bonds. Critics of bosses charged that these loans were inflated or unnecessary. Necessary or not, municipal bonds caused public debts to soar, and taxes had to be raised to repay their interest and principal. In addition, payoffs from gambling, prostitution, and illicit liquor traffic often became important sources of machine revenue. But in an age of economic individualism, bosses were no more guilty of discrimination and self-interest than were business leaders who exploited workers, spoiled the environment, and manipulated government in pursuit of profits. Sometimes humane and sometimes criminal, bosses acted as brokers between various sectors of urban society and an uncertain world.

While bosses were consolidating their power, others were trying to destroy them. Many middle- and upper-class Americans feared that immigrant-based political machines menaced democracy and that unsavory alliances between bosses and businesses wasted municipal finances. Anxious over the poverty, crowding, and disorder that accompanied city growth, and convinced that urban services were making taxes too

Civic Reform

high, civic reformers organized to install more responsible leaders at the helm of government. Civic reform arose in part from the industrial system's emphasis on eliminating inefficiency. Business-minded reformers believed government should run like a company. The way to achieve this goal, they concluded, was to elect officials who would hold down expenses and prevent corruption.

To implement business principles in government, civic reformers supported structural changes, such as city-manager and commission forms of government, which would place administration in the hands of experts rather than politicians, and nonpartisan citywide rather than neighborhood-based election of officials. Armed with such strategies, reformers believed they could cleanse city government of party politics and weaken bosses' power bases. They rarely realized, however, that bosses succeeded because they used government to meet people's needs. Reformers noticed only the waste and dishonesty that machines bred.

A few reform mayors moved beyond structural changes to address social problems. Hazen S. Pingree of Detroit, Samuel "Golden Rule" Jones of Toledo, and Tom Johnson of Cleveland worked to provide jobs to poor people, reduce charges by transit and utility companies, and promote governmental responsibility for the welfare of all citizens. They also supported public ownership of gas, electric, and telephone companies, a quasi-socialist reform that alienated their business allies. But Pingree, Jones, and Johnson were exceptions. Civic reformers could not match the bosses' political savvy; they achieved some successes but rarely held office for very long.

A different type of reform arose outside politics. Driven to improve as well as manage society, social reformers—mostly young and middle class—embarked on campaigns to investigate and solve urban problems. Housing reformers pressed local governments for building codes to ensure safety in tenements. Educational reformers sought to use public schools as a means of preparing immigrant children for citizenship by teaching them American values. Health reformers tried to improve medical care for those who could not afford it.

Social Reform

Perhaps the most ambitious urban reform movement was the settlement house, a place located in inner-city neighborhoods and established mostly by young, middle-class women who hoped to bridge the gulf between social classes by living among and directly helping immigrants and poor people. The first American settlement, patterned after London's Toynbee Hall, opened in New York City in 1886, and others quickly followed, including Hull

House, founded in Chicago in 1889. To help immigrants adapt to American urban life, settlements offered vocational classes, lessons in English, and childcare, and they sponsored programs to improve nutrition and housing.

As settlement-house workers such as Jane Addams and Florence Kelley of Chicago and Lillian Wald of New York broadened their scope to fight for school nurses, factory safety codes, and public playgrounds, they became reform leaders in cities and in the nation. Their efforts to involve national and local governments in the solution of social problems made them key contributors to the Progressive era, when a reform spirit swept the nation (see Chapter 21). Moreover, settlement-house programs created new professional opportunities for women in social work, public health, and child welfare. These professions enabled female reformers to build a dominion of influence over social policy independent of male-dominated professions and to make valuable contributions to national as well as inner-city life.

Like much in American life, however, settlement houses were segregated. White female reformers lobbied for government programs to aid mostly white immigrant and native-born working classes. Black women reformers, excluded from white settlements, raised funds from private donors and focused on helping members of their own race. African American women were especially active in founding schools, old-age homes, and hospitals, but they also worked for racial advancement and protection of black women from sexual exploitation. Their ranks included Jane Hunter, who founded a home for unmarried black working women in Cleveland in 1911 and inspired the establishment of similar homes in other cities, and Modjeska Simkins, who worked to overcome health problems among blacks in South Carolina.

While female activists tried to assist people in need and revive neighborhoods, a group of male reformers or-

The City Beautiful Movement

ganized the City Beautiful movement to improve cities' physical organization. Inspired by the Columbian Exposition of 1893, a dazzling world's fair built on Chicago's South Side, architects and planners, led by architect Daniel Burnham, urged the construction of civic centers, parks, and boulevards that would make cities economically efficient as well as beautiful. "Make no little plans," Burnham urged. "Make big plans; aim high in hope and work." This attitude spawned beautification projects in Chicago, San Francisco, and Washington, D.C., in the early 1900s. Yet most big plans existed mostly as big dreams. Neither government nor private businesses could finance large-scale projects, and planners disagreed among themselves

and with social reformers over whether beautification would truly solve urban problems.

Regardless of their focus, urban reformers wanted to save cities, not abandon them. They believed they could improve urban life by achieving cooperation among all citizens. They often failed to realize, however, that cities were places of great diversity and that different people held very different views about what reform actually meant. To civic reformers, appointing government workers on the basis of civil service exams rather than party loyalty meant progress, but to working-class men, civil service signified reduced employment opportunities. Moral reformers believed that restricting the sale of alcoholic beverages would prevent working-class breadwinners from squandering wages and ruining their health, but immigrants saw such crusades as interference in their private lives. Planners saw new streets and buildings as modern necessities, but such structures often displaced the poor. Well-meaning humanitarians criticized immigrant mothers for the way they shopped, dressed, did housework, and raised children, without regard for these mothers' inability to afford products that the consumer economy created. Thus urban reform merged idealism with naiveté and insensitivity.

FAMILY LIFE

Although the vast majority of Americans lived within families, this basic social institution suffered strain during the era of urbanization and industrialization. New institutions—schools, social clubs, political organizations, unions—increasingly competed with the family to provide nurture, education, and security. Clergy and journalists warned that the growing separation between home and work, rising divorce rates, the entrance of women into the work force, and loss of parental control over children spelled peril for home and family. Yet the family retained its fundamental role as a cushion in a hard, uncertain world.

Throughout modern western history, most people have lived in two overlapping social units: household

Family and Household Structures

and family. A household is a group of people, related or unrelated, who share the same residence. A family is a group related by kinship, some members of which typically live together. In the late nineteenth and early twentieth centuries, different patterns characterized the two institutions.

Until the present, when high divorce rates and relatively late age at first marriage have increased the percentage of one-person households, most American households (75 to 80 percent) have consisted of nuclear families—usually a married couple, with or without children. About 15 to 20 percent of households consisted of extended families—usually a married couple, their children, and one or more relatives, such as parents of the husband or wife, adult siblings, aunts, uncles, or other kin. About 5 percent of households consisted of people living alone. Despite slight variations, this pattern held fairly constant among ethnic, racial, and socioeconomic groups.

Several factors explain this pattern. Because immigrants tended to be young, the American population as a whole was young. In 1880 the median age was under twenty-one, and by 1920 it was still only twenty-five. (Median age at present is above thirty-five.) Moreover, in 1900 the death rate among people aged forty-five to sixty-four was double what it is today. As a result, there were few elderly people: only 4 percent of the population was sixty-five or older, compared with almost 13 percent today. Thus few families could form extended three-generation households, and fewer children than today had living grandparents. Migration split up many families, and the ideal of a home of one's own encouraged nuclear household organization.

The average size of nuclear families also changed over time. Most of Europe and North America experienced falling birth rates in the nineteenth century. The decline in the United States began early in the 1800s and accelerated toward the end of the century. In 1880 the birth rate was 40 live births per 1,000 people; by 1900 it had dropped to 32; by 1920, to 28. Although fertility was higher among black, immigrant, and rural women than among white native-born urban females, birth rates of all groups fell.

Declining Birth Rates

Several factors explain this decline. First, as the United States became more urbanized, the economic value of children lessened. On farms, where young children worked at home or in the fields, each child born represented an addition to the family labor force. In the wage-based urban economy, children could not contribute significantly to the family income for many years, and a new child represented a draw on family income. Second, infant mortality fell as diet and medical care improved, and families did not have to bear many children to ensure that some would survive.

Perhaps most importantly, as economic trends changed, attitudes toward children changed. No matter what the era, parents always cherished their children. But as American society industrialized and urbanized, the idea of a child as a pure, innocent being who not only needed shelter from society's corruptions but who also could provide parents with emotional rewards spread, first among the middle class and gradually to the working class as well. A mother's investment of care and attention could be more focused and effective if she had fewer rather than more children. Such an attitude seems to have stimulated decisions by parents to limit family size—either by abstaining from sex during the wife's fertile period or by using contraception. Families with six or eight children became rare; three or four became more usual. Birth-control technology—diaphragms and condoms—had been utilized for centuries, but in this era new materials made devices more convenient and dependable. Use of rubber rather than animal membranes for condoms after 1869 inspired British playwright and philosopher George Bernard Shaw to exclaim that new birth-control devices were "the greatest invention of the nineteenth century."

Although the family remained resilient and adaptable, notable changes began to occur in individual life patterns. Before the late nineteenth century, stages of life were less distinct than they are today, and generations blended together with relatively little differentiation. Childhood, for instance, had been regarded as a period during which young people prepared for adulthood by gradually assuming more roles and responsibilities. Subdivisions of youth—toddlers, schoolchildren, teenagers, and the like—were not recognized or defined. Because married couples had more children over a longer time span than is common today, active parenthood occupied most of adult life. Older children might begin parenting even before reaching adulthood by caring for younger siblings. And because relatively few people lived to advanced age or left work voluntarily, and because old-age homes were rare, older people were not isolated from other age groups. By the late nineteenth century, however, decreasing birth rates shortened the period of parental responsibility, so more middle-aged couples experienced an "empty nest" when all their children had grown up and left home. Longer life expectancy and a tendency by employers to force aged workers to retire separated the old from the young.

Stages of Life

New patterns of childhood also emerged. The separation of home and work, especially prevalent in cities, meant that children were less likely than previously to be involved in producing income for the family. To be sure, youngsters in working-class families still helped out—working in factories, scavenging streets for scraps of wood and coal, and peddling newspapers and other goods—but generally youngsters had more time for other activities. As states passed compulsory school attendance laws in the

▲ As cities grew and became increasingly congested, children in immigrant and working-class neighborhoods used streets and sidewalks as play sites. Activities of youngsters such as these, playing unsupervised in front of a Polish saloon, prompted adults to create playgrounds, clubs, and other places where they could protect children's safety and innocence and where they could ensure that play would be orderly and obedient. *(Chicago Historical Society)*

Although marriage rates were high, large numbers of city dwellers were unmarried, largely because many people waited to wed until they were in their late twenties. In 1890 almost 42 percent of adult American men and 37 percent of women were single, almost twice as high as the figures for 1960 but slightly lower than they are today. About half of all single people still lived in their parents' household, though they led independent working and social lives, but many others inhabited boarding houses or rooms in the homes of strangers. Mostly young, these men and women constituted a separate subculture that helped support institutions such as dance halls, saloons, cafés, and the Young Men's Christian Association (YMCA) and Young Women's Christian Association (YWCA).

The Unmarried

Some unmarried people were part of the homosexual populations that especially thrived in large cities such as New York, San Francisco, and Boston. Although numbers are difficult to estimate, gay men had their own subculture of clubs, restaurants, coffeehouses, theaters, and support networks. A number of same-sex couples, especially women, formed lasting marital-type relationships, sometimes called "Boston marriages." People in this subculture were categorized more by how they acted—men acting like women, women acting like men—than by who their sexual partners were. The term *homosexual* was not used. Men who dressed and acted like women were called "fairies," and men who displayed masculine traits could be termed "normal" even though they might have sexual relations with fairies. Gay women remained even more hidden, and a lesbian subculture of clubs and commercial establishments did not develop until the 1920s. The gay world, then, was a complex one that included a variety of relationships and institutions.

In every city, large numbers of young people—and some older people—lived as boarders and lodgers. (Boarders usually received meals along with a room; lodgers only rented a room.) Boarding houses and lodging hotels were common, but families also commonly took in boarders to occupy rooms vacated by grown children and to get additional income. By 1900 as many as 50 percent of city residents, including Erich Weiss's family, had lived either as, or with, boarders at some point during their lifetime. Housing reformers charged that boarding and lodging caused overcrowding and loss of privacy. Yet the practice was highly useful. For people on the move, boarding or lodging was a transitional stage, providing a quasi-family environment until they set up their

Boarding and Lodging

1870s and 1880s, education occupied more of children's daily time than ever before, keeping them in school nine months of the year until they were teenagers and strengthening peer rather than family influence over their behavior. Also, in keeping with the scientific spirit of the era, physicians and psychologists began studying children in order to help shape them into moral, productive adults. Researchers such as G. Stanley Hall and Luther H. Gulick advocated that teachers and parents should match education and play activities to the needs that children had at different stages of their development. Anxious that children be protected from city streets, "child-saving" advocates asserted that adult-supervised playgrounds should be established to give children alternatives to dangerous activities.

own households. Especially in communities where economic hardship or rapid growth made housing expensive or scarce, newlyweds sometimes lived temporarily with one spouse's parents. Families also took in widowed parents or unmarried siblings who otherwise would have lived alone.

At a time when welfare agencies were scarce, the family was the institution to which people could turn in times

Functions of Kinship

of need. Even when relatives did not live together, they often resided nearby and aided one another with childcare, meals, advice, and consolation. They also obtained jobs for each other. Factory foremen who had responsibility for hiring often recruited new workers recommended by their employees. According to one new arrival, "After two days my brother took me to the shop he was working in and his boss saw me and he gave me the job."

But obligations of kinship were not always welcome. Immigrant families pressured last-born female children to stay at home to care for aging parents, a practice that stifled opportunities for education, marriage, and independence. As an aging Italian American father confessed, "One of our daughters is an old maid [and] causes plenty of troubles. . . . it may be my fault because I always wished her to remain at home and not to marry for she was of great financial help." Tensions also developed between generations, such as when immigrant parents and American-born children clashed over the abandonment of Old World ways or over the amount of wages that employed children should contribute to the household. Nevertheless, for better or worse, kinship provided people a means of coping with stresses caused by urban-industrial society. Social and economic change did not sever family ties.

Thus, by 1900, family life and functions were both changing and holding firm. New institutions were assuming tasks formerly performed by the family, and people's roles in school, in the family, on the job, and in the community came to be determined by age more than by any other characteristic. Schools made education a community responsibility. Employment agencies, personnel offices, and labor unions were taking responsibility for employee recruitment and job security. Age-based peer groups exerted greater influence over people's values and activities. Migration and divorce seemed to be splitting families apart. Yet, in the face of these pressures, the family adjusted by expanding and contracting to meet temporary needs, and kinship remained a dependable though not always appreciated institution.

An emphasis on family togetherness became especially visible at holiday celebrations. Middle-class moralists

Holiday Celebrations

helped make Thanksgiving, Christmas, and Easter special times for family reunion and child-centered activities, and female relatives made special efforts to cook and decorate the home. Birthdays, too, took on an increasingly festive quality, both as an important family occasion and as a milestone for measuring the age-related norms that accompanied intensified consciousness of life stages. In 1914 President Woodrow Wilson signed a proclamation designating the second Sunday in May as Mother's Day, capping a six-year campaign by Anna Jarvis, a schoolteacher who believed grown children too often neglected their mothers. Ethnic and racial groups made efforts to fit national celebrations to their cultures, using holidays as occasions for preparing special ethnic foods and engaging in special ceremonies. For many, holiday celebrations were a testimony to the vitality of family life. "As I grew up, living conditions were a bit crowded," one woman reminisced, "but no one minded because we were a family . . . thankful we all lived together."

THE NEW LEISURE AND MASS CULTURE

On December 2, 1889, as hundreds of workers paraded through Worcester, Massachusetts, in support of shorter working hours, a group of carpenters hoisted a banner proclaiming "Eight Hours for Work, Eight Hours for Rest, Eight Hours for What We Will." That last phrase was significant, for it laid claim to a special segment of daily life that belonged to the individual. Increasingly, among all urban social classes, leisure activities, doing "what we will," filled this time segment.

American inventors had long tried to create labor-saving devices, but not until the late 1800s did technology

Increase in Leisure Time

become truly timesaving. Mechanization and assembly-line production cut the average workweek in manufacturing from sixty-six hours in 1860 to sixty in 1890 and forty-seven in 1920. These reductions meant shorter workdays and freer weekends. White-collar employees spent eight to ten hours a day on the job and often worked only half a day or not at all on weekends. Laborers in steel mills and sweatshops still endured twelve- or fourteen-hour shifts and had no time or energy for leisure. But as the economy shifted from one of scarcity and production to one of sur-

SHOOTING THE CHUTES, CONEY ISLAND, N. Y.

▲ Amusement centers such as Luna Park at Coney Island in New York City, became common and appealing features of the new leisure culture. One of the most popular Coney Island attractions was a ride called Shooting the Chutes, which resembled modern-day giant water slides. In 1904 Luna Park staged an outrageous stunt of an elephant sliding down the chute. The creature survived, apparently unfazed. *(Picture Research Consultants and Archives)*

plus and consumption, more Americans began to engage in a variety of recreations, and a substantial segment of the economy provided for—and profited from—leisure. By 1900 many Americans were enmeshed in the business of play.

Amusement became an organized, commercial activity, as the introduction of games, toys, and musical instruments for indoor family entertainment expanded. Improvements in printing and paper production, and the rise of manufacturers such as Milton Bradley and Parker Brothers, increased the popularity of board games. Significantly, the content of board games shifted from moral lessons to topics involving transportation, finance, and sports. Middle-class families were also buying mass-produced pianos and sheet music which made the singing of popular songs a common form of home entertainment. The vanguard of new leisure pursuits, however, was sports. Formerly a fashionable indulgence of elites, organized sports became a favored pastime of all classes, attracting countless participants and spectators. Even those who could not play or watch got involved by reading about sports in the newspapers.

The most popular sport was baseball. Derived from older bat, ball, and base-circling games, baseball was formalized in 1845 by the Knickerbocker Club of New York, which standardized the rules of play. By 1860 at least fifty baseball clubs existed, and youths played informal games on city lots and rural fields across the nation. In 1869 a professional club, the Cincinnati Red Stockings, went on a national tour, and other teams followed suit. The National League of Professional Baseball Clubs, founded in 1876, gave the sport a stable, businesslike structure. Not all athletes benefited, however; as early as 1867 a "color line" excluded black players from professional teams. Nevertheless, by the 1880s professional baseball was big business. In 1903 the National League and the competing American League (formed in 1901) began a World Series between their championship teams, entrenching baseball as the

Baseball

Japanese Baseball

Baseball, the "American pastime," was one of the new leisure-time pursuits that Americans took with them into different parts of the world. The Shanghai Base Ball Club was founded by Americans in China in 1863, but few Chinese paid much attention to the sport, largely because the Imperial Court denounced the game as spiritually corrupting. However, when Horace Wilson, an American teacher, taught the rules of baseball to his Japanese students around 1870, the game received an enthusiastic reception as a reinforcement of traditional virtues. In fact, baseball quickly became so much a part of Japanese culture that one Japanese writer commented, "Baseball is perfect for us. If the Americans hadn't invented it, we probably would have."

During the 1870s, scores of Japanese high schools and colleges sponsored organized baseball, and in 1883 Hiroshi Hiraoka, a railroad engineer who had studied in Boston, founded the first official local team, the Shimbashi Athletic Club Athletics. Fans displayed wild devotion to this and similar teams as they developed over the next several years.

Before Americans introduced baseball to Japan, the Japanese had no team sports and no predilection for recreational athletics. Once they learned about baseball, they found that the idea of a team sport fit their culture very well. But the Japanese had difficulty applying the American concept of leisure to the game. For them, baseball was serious business, involving hard and often brutal training. Practices at Ichiko, one of Japan's two great high school baseball teams in the late nineteenth century, were dubbed "Bloody Urine" because many players passed blood after a day of drilling. There was a spiritual quality as well, linked to Buddhist values. According to one Japanese coach, "The purpose of [baseball] training is not health but the forging of the soul, and a strong soul is only born from strong practice. . . . Student baseball must be the baseball of self-discipline, or trying to attain the truth, just as in Zen Buddhism." This attitude prompted the Japanese to consider baseball as a new method to pursue the spirit of Bushido, the way of the samurai.

When Americans played baseball in Japan, the Japanese found them to be strong and talented but lacking in discipline and respect. Americans insulted the Japanese by refusing to remove their hats and bow when they stepped up to bat. An international dispute occurred in 1891 when William Imbrie, an American professor at Tokyo's Meijo University, arrived late for a game. Finding the gate locked, he climbed over the fence in order to enter the field. The fence, however, had sacred meaning, and Japanese fans attacked Imbrie for his sacrilege. Imbrie suffered facial injuries, prompting the American embassy to lodge a formal complaint. Americans assumed that their game would encourage Japanese to become like westerners, but the Japanese transformed the American pastime into an expression of team spirit, discipline, and nationalism that was uniquely Japanese.

▲ Replete with bats, gloves, and uniforms, this Japanese baseball team of 1890 very much resembles its American counterpart of that era. The Japanese adopted baseball soon after Americans became involved in their country but also added their cultural qualities to the game. *(Japanese Baseball Hall of Fame)*

national pastime. The Boston Red Sox beat the Pittsburgh Pirates in that first series.

Baseball appealed mostly to men. But croquet, which also swept the nation, attracted both sexes. Middle- and upper-class people held croquet parties and outfitted wickets with candles for night contests. In an era when the departure of paid work from the home had separated men's from women's spheres, croquet increased opportunities for social contact between the sexes.

Croquet and Cycling

Meanwhile, cycling achieved a popularity rivaling that of baseball, especially after 1885, when the cumbersome velocipede, with its huge front wheel and tall seat, gave way to safety bicycles with pneumatic tires and wheels of identical size. By 1900 Americans owned 10 million bicycles, and clubs such as the League of American Wheelmen were petitioning state governments to build more paved roads. African American cyclists were allowed to compete as professionals, unlike baseball. One black rider, Major Taylor, won fame in Europe and the United States between 1892 and 1910. Like croquet, cycling brought men and women together, combining opportunities for exercise and courtship. Moreover, the bicycle played an influential role in freeing women from the constraints of Victorian fashions. In order to ride the dropped-frame female models, women had to wear divided skirts and simple undergarments. As the 1900 census declared, "Few articles . . . have created so great a revolution in social conditions as the bicycle."

American football, as an intercollegiate competition, attracted mostly players and spectators wealthy enough to have access to higher education. By the late nineteenth century, however, the game was appealing to a broader audience. The 1893 Princeton-Yale game drew fifty thousand spectators, and informal games were played in yards and playgrounds throughout the country. Soon, however, football became a national scandal because of its violence and use of "tramp athletes," nonstudents whom colleges hired to help their teams win. Critics accused football of mirroring undesirable features of American society. An editor of *The Nation* charged in 1890 that "the spirit of the American Youth, as of the American man, is to win, to 'get there,' by fair means or foul; and the lack of moral scruple which pervades the struggles of the business world meets with temptations equally irresistible in the miniature contests of the football field."

Football

The scandals climaxed in 1905, when 18 players died from game-related injuries and 159 were seriously injured.

President Theodore Roosevelt, a strong advocate of athletics, convened a White House conference to discuss ways to eliminate brutality and foul play. The gathering founded the Intercollegiate Athletic Association (renamed the National College Athletic Association in 1910) to police college sports. In 1906 the association altered the game to make it less violent and more open. New rules outlawed "flying-wedge" rushes, extended from five to ten yards the distance needed to earn a first down, legalized the forward pass, and tightened player eligibility requirements.

As more women enrolled in college, they pursued physical activities besides croquet and cycling. Believing that intellectual success required active and healthy bodies, college women participated in such sports as rowing, track, and swimming. Eventually women made basketball their most popular intercollegiate sport. Invented in 1891 as a winter sport for men, basketball received women's rules (which limited dribbling and running, and encouraged passing) from Senda Berenson of Smith College.

Three branches of American show business—popular drama, musical comedy, and vaudeville—matured with the growth of cities. New theatrical performances offered audiences escape into melodrama, adventure, and comedy. Plots were simple, heroes and villains recognizable. For urban people unfamiliar with the frontier, popular plays made the mythical Wild West and Old South come alive through stories of Davy Crockett, Buffalo Bill, and the Civil War. Virtue and honor always triumphed in melodramas such as *Uncle Tom's Cabin* and *The Old Homestead*, reinforcing faith that, in an uncertain and disillusioning world, goodness would prevail.

Show Business

Musical comedies entertained audiences with song, humor, and dance. The American musical derived from lavishly costumed operettas common in Europe. The introduction of American themes (often involving ethnic groups), folksy humor, and catchy tunes in the late nineteenth century helped these shows spawn the nation's most popular songs and entertainers. George M. Cohan, a singer, dancer, and songwriter born into an Irish family of entertainers, became master of American musical comedy after the turn of the century. Drawing on patriotism and traditional values in songs such as "Yankee Doodle Boy" and "You're a Grand Old Flag," Cohan helped bolster morale during the First World War. Comic opera, too, became popular. Initially, American comic operas imitated European musicals, but by the early 1900s composers such as Victor Herbert were writing for American audiences.

Vaudeville was probably the most popular mass entertainment in early-twentieth-century America because

▲ Joe Weber and Lew Fields were one of the most popular comic teams in vaudeville. They and similar comedians used fast-paced dialogue to entertain audiences with routines like this one: *Doctor:* Do you have insurance? *Patient:* I ain't got one nickel insurance. *Doctor:* If you die, what will your wife bury you with? *Patient:* With pleasure.   *(Corbis-Bettmann)*

its variety offered something for everyone. Shows, whose acts followed a fixed schedule just like trains and factory production, included jugglers, magicians, puppeteers, acrobats, comedians, singers, dancers, and specialty acts like Houdini's escapes. Around 1900, the number of vaudeville theaters and troupes skyrocketed, and big-time operators such as Tony Pastor (who gave Houdini his first vaudeville job) and the partnership of Benjamin Keith and Edward Albee consolidated theaters and acts under their management in the same manner that other businessmen were consolidating factory production. Marcus Loew, an owner of theaters that attracted working-class audiences, was known as "the Henry Ford of show business." Producer Florenz Ziegfeld brilliantly packaged shows in a stylish format—the Ziegfeld Follies—and gave the nation a new model of femininity, the Ziegfeld Girl, whose graceful dancing and alluring costumes suggested a haunting sensuality.

Show business provided economic and social mobility to female, African American, and immigrant performers, but it also encouraged stereotyping and exploitation.

Opportunities for Women and Minorities

Comic opera diva Lillian Russell, vaudeville singer-comedienne Fanny Brice, and burlesque queen Eva Tanguay attracted intensely loyal fans, commanded handsome fees, and won respect for their talents. In contrast to the demure Victorian female, they conveyed an image of pluck and independence. There was something both shocking and confident about Eva Tanguay when she moved energetically around the stage singing earthy songs like "It's All Been Done Before but Not the Way I Do It" and "I Don't Care." But lesser female performers and showgirls (called "soubrettes") were often exploited by male promoters and theater owners, many of whom wanted only to profit by titillating the public with the sight of scantily clad women.

Before the 1890s, the chief form of commercial entertainment that employed African American performers had been the minstrel show, but vaudeville opened new opportunities to them. As stage settings shifted from the plantation to the city, music shifted from sentimental folk tunes to the syncopated rhythms of ragtime. Pandering to the prejudices of white audiences, composers ridiculed blacks, and black performers were forced to portray demeaning characters. In songs such as "He's Just a Little Nigger, But He's Mine All Mine" and "You May Be a Hawaiian on Old Broadway, But You're Just Another Nigger to Me," blacks were degraded on stage much as they were in society. Burt Williams, a talented black comedian and dancer who had graduated from high school at a time when most whites did not, achieved success by wearing blackface (black makeup) and playing stereotypical roles of a smiling fool and dandy, but was tormented by the humiliation he had to suffer.

An ethnic flavor gave much of American mass entertainment its uniqueness. Like Houdini, many performers were immigrants, and their stage acts reflected their experiences. Vaudeville in particular utilized ethnic humor and exaggerated dialects. Skits and songs were fast-paced, replicating the tempo of factories, offices, and the streets. Performances reinforced ethnic stereotypes, but such distortions were more self-conscious and sympathetic than those directed at blacks. Ethnic humor often involved everyday difficulties that immigrants faced. A typical scene involving Italians, for example, highlighted a character's uncertain grasp of English, which caused him to confuse *diploma* with *the plumber* and *pallbearer* with *polar bear*. Other scenes included gags about dealing with modern society. Thus, when a stage doctor required ten dollars for his advice, the patient responded, "Ten dollars is too much. Here's two dollars. Take it, that's *my* advice." Such scenes allowed audiences to laugh with, rather than at, foibles of the human condition.

Shortly after 1900, live entertainment began to yield to a more accessible form of commercial amusement: mo-

Movies

tion pictures. Perfected by Thomas Edison in the 1880s, movies began as slot-machine peepshows in arcades and billiard parlors. Eventually, images of speeding trains, acrobats, and belly dancers were projected onto a screen so that large audiences could view them, and a new medium was born. Producers, many of them from Jewish immigrant backgrounds, soon discovered that a film could tell a story in exciting ways and, like vaudeville performers, catered to viewers' desires. Using themes of patriotism and working-class experience, early filmmakers helped shift American culture away from its more straitlaced Victorian values to a more cosmopolitan outlook.

As they expanded from minutes to hours in length, movies presented controversial social messages as well as innovative technology and styles of expression. For example, the film *Birth of a Nation* (1915), by the creative director D. W. Griffith, was a stunning epic film about the Civil War and Reconstruction, but it also fanned racial prejudice by depicting African Americans as threats to white moral values. The National Association for the Advancement of Colored People (NAACP), formed in 1909, led organized protests against it. But the film's ground-breaking techniques—close-ups, fade-outs, and battle scenes—heightened the drama.

Technology and entrepreneurship also made news a mass consumer product. Using high-speed printing presses, cheaply produced paper, and profits from growing advertisement revenues, shrewd publishers created a medium that made people crave news and ads just as they craved amusements. City life and increased leisure time seemed to nurture a fascination with the sensational, and from the 1880s onward popular urban newspapers increasingly whetted that appetite.

Joseph Pulitzer, a Hungarian immigrant who bought the *New York World* in 1883, pioneered journalism by

Yellow Journalism

making news a mass commodity. Believing that newspapers should be "dedicated to the cause of the people," Pulitzer filled the *World* with stories of disasters, crimes, and scandals. Screaming headlines, set in large, bold type like that used for advertisements, attracted readers. Pulitzer's journalists not only

▲ Dick Merriwell and his brother, Frank, were fictional heroes of hundreds of stories written in the early 1900s by Burt Standish (the pen name used by Gilbert Patten). In a series of adventures, mostly involving sports, these popular character models used their physical skills, valor, and moral virtue to lead by example, accomplish the impossible, and influence others to behave in an upstanding way.

(Collection of Picture Research Consultants, Inc.)

reported news but also sought it out and created it. *World* reporter Nellie Bly (real name, Elizabeth Cochrane), for example, faked her way into a mental asylum and wrote a brazen exposé of the sordid conditions she found. Other reporters staged stunts and hunted down heart-rending human-interest stories. Pulitzer also popularized comics, and the yellow ink in which they were printed gave rise to the term *yellow journalism* as a synonym for sensationalism.

Pulitzer's strategy was immensely successful. In one year the *World*'s circulation increased from 20,000 to 100,000, and by the late 1890s it reached 1 million. Other publishers, such as William Randolph Hearst, who bought the *New York Journal* in 1895 and started an empire of mass-circulation newspapers, adopted Pulitzer's techniques. Pulitzer, Hearst, and their rivals boosted circulation further by making sports and women's news a mass commodity. Newspapers had previously reported sporting events, but yellow-journalism papers gave such stories greater prominence by printing separate, expanded sports pages. Sports news re-created a game's drama through narrative and statistics, and promoted sports as a leisure-time attraction. To capture female readers, newspapers also added special sections devoted to household tips, fashion, etiquette, and club news.

By the early twentieth century, mass-circulation magazines overshadowed the expensive elitist journals of earlier eras. Publications such as *McClure's, Saturday Evening Post,* and *Ladies' Home Journal* offered human-interest stories, muckraking exposés (see page 594), titillating fiction, photographs, colorful covers, and eye-catching ads to a growing mass market. Meanwhile, the total number of published books more than quadrupled between 1880 and 1917. Rising consumption of news and books reflected growing literacy. Between 1870 and 1920, the proportion of Americans over age ten who could not read or write fell from 20 percent to 6 percent.

Other Mass-Market Publications

Other forms of communication also expanded. In 1891 there was less than 1 telephone for every 100 people in the United States; by 1901 the number had grown to 2.1, and by 1921 it swelled to 12.6. In 1900 Americans used 4 billion postage stamps; in 1922 they bought 14.3 billion. The term *community* took on new dimensions, as people used the media, mail, and telephone to extend their horizons far beyond their immediate locality.

More than ever before, people in different parts of the country knew about and discussed the same news event, whether it was a sensational murder, a sex scandal, or the fortunes of a particular entertainer or athlete. America was becoming a mass society where the same products, the same technology, and the same information dominated everyday life, regardless of region.

American mass culture, perhaps more than any other factor, represented democracy, because influences flowed upward from the experiences and desires of ordinary people as much as, if not more than, they were imposed from above by the rich and powerful. The popularity of sports, the themes depicted in movies and on stage, and the content of everyday publications reveal not only that Americans in the urban-industrial era had time to patronize leisure-time activities but also that savvy entrepreneurs understood that what they produced needed to meet the needs of the new consumers. At the same time, producers helped people adapt by providing lessons about new social and economic conditions and by making some of the disruptive factors more tolerable through drama and humor. The major exception was the portrayal and treatment of African Americans with a viciousness that did not diminish as entertainment expanded.

To some extent, then, the cities' new amusements and media had a homogenizing influence, allowing ethnic and social groups to share common experiences. Parks, ball fields, vaudeville shows, movies, and the feature sections of newspapers and magazines were nonsectarian and apolitical. Yet different consumer groups adapted them to their own cultural needs. Immigrant groups, for example, often used parks and amusement areas as sites for special ethnic gatherings. To the dismay of reformers who hoped that public recreation and holidays would assimilate newcomers and teach them habits of restraint, immigrants converted picnics and Fourth of July celebrations into occasions for boisterous drinking and sometimes violent behavior. Young working-class men and women resisted parents' and moralists' warnings, and frequented urban dance halls, where they explored forms of courtship and sexual behavior free from adult oversight. And children often used streets and rooftops to create their own entertainment rather than participate in adult-supervised games in parks and playgrounds. Thus, as Americans learned to play, their leisure—like their work and politics—expressed, and was shaped by, the pluralistic forces that thrived in urban life.

Legacy FOR A PEOPLE AND A NATION

Ethnic Food

Today, an American might eat a bagel for breakfast, a gyro sandwich for lunch, and wonton soup, shrimp creole, and rice pilaf for dinner, followed by chocolate mousse and espresso. An evening snack might consist of nachos and lager beer. These items, each identified with a different ethnic group, serve as tasty reminders that immigrants have made influential and lasting contributions to the nation's culinary culture. The American diet also represents one of the few genuine ways that the multicultural nation has served as a melting pot.

The American taste for ethnic food has a complicated history. Since the nineteenth century, the food business has offered immigrant entrepreneurs lucrative opportunities, many of which involved products unrelated to their own ethnic background. The industry is replete with success stories linked to names such as Hector Boiardi (Chef Boyardee), William Gebhardt (Eagle Brand chili and tamales), Jeno Paulucci (Chun King), and Alphonse Biardot (Franco-American), all of whom immigrated to the United States in the late nineteenth or early twentieth century. But Americans have also supported unheralded local immigrant merchants and restaurateurs who have offered special and regional fare—German, Chinese, Italian, Tex-Mex, "soul food," or Thai—in every era.

Unlike the strife that occurred over housing, jobs, schools, and politics when different nationalities and racial groups collided, the evolution of American eating habits has been peaceful. Occasionally criticisms developed, such as when dietitians and reformers in the early twentieth century charged that Mexican immigrants were harming their digestion by overusing tomatoes and peppers, and that the rich foods of eastern European Jews made them overly emotional and less capable of assimilating. But relatively conflict-free sharing and borrowing have characterized American food ways far more than "food fights" and intolerance. The sensory pleasure of eating has always overridden cultural loyalty, and mass marketers have been quick to capitalize.

As each wave of immigrants has entered the nation—and especially as these newcomers have occupied the cities, where cross-cultural contact has been inevitable—food has given them certain ways of becoming American, of finding some form of group acceptance, while also giving them a means of confirming their identity. At the same time, those who already thought of themselves as Americans have willingly made the newcomers' gastronomic legacy a part of the existing culture and a part of themselves.

SUMMARY

People and technology made the late nineteenth and early twentieth centuries the "age of the city." Flocking cityward, migrants already in America and those coming from foreign parts remade themselves, like Houdini, and remade the urban environment as well. Although they may have escaped their places of residence, they also brought with them cultures that in turn enriched American culture. They also found new escape in new and expanded forms of mass leisure and entertainment. Cities were dynamic places, where everyday life brought new challenges, where politics and reform took on new meanings, and where family life reflected both change and continuity.

Although their governments and neighborhoods may have seemed chaotic, American cities experienced an "unheralded triumph" by the early 1900s. Amid corruption and political conflict, engineers modernized sewer, water, and lighting services, and urban governments made cities safer by expanding professional police and fire departments. When native inventiveness met the traditions of European, African, and Asian cultures, a new kind of society emerged. This society seldom functioned smoothly; there really was no coherent urban community, only a collection of subcommunities. The jumble of social classes, ethnic and racial groups, political and professional organizations, sometimes lived in harmony, sometimes not. Generally, cities managed to thrive because of, rather than in spite of, their diverse fragments.

Optimists had envisioned the American nation as a melting pot, where various nationalities would fuse into a unified people. Instead, many ethnic groups proved unmeltable, preferring—and sometimes forced—to pursue their own ways of acting, and racial minorities got burned on the bottom of the pot. As a result of immigration and urbanization, the United States became a pluralistic society in which cultural influences moved in both directions: imposed from above by people with power and influence, and adopted from below through the traditions and tastes brought to cities by disparate peoples. When the desire to retain one culture met with the need to fit in, often the results were compound identifications: Irish American, Italian American, Polish American, and the like.

By 1920, immigrants and their offspring outnumbered the native-born in many cities, and the national economy depended on these new workers and consumers. Migrants and immigrants transformed the United States into an urban nation. They gave American culture its rich and varied texture just by living their lives but also, like Harry Houdini, by changing the course of entertainment and consumerism, and they laid the foundations for the liberalism that would characterize American politics in the twentieth century.

SUGGESTIONS FOR FURTHER READING

John Bodnar, *The Transplanted: A History of Immigrants in Urban America* (1985)

Howard P. Chudacoff and Judith E. Smith, *The Evolution of American Urban Society*, 6th ed. (2005)

John D'Emilio and Estelle Freedman, *Intimate Matters: A History of Sexuality in America* (1988)

Nancy Foner and George M. Frederickson, eds., *Not Just Black and White: Historical and Contemporary Perspectives on Immigration, Race, and Ethnicity in the United States* (2004)

Kenneth T. Jackson, *The Crabgrass Frontier: The Suburbanization of the United States* (1985)

Matthew Frye Jacobson, *Whiteness of a Different Color: European Immigrants and the Alchemy of Race* (1998)

Erika Lee, *At America's Gates: Chinese Immigration During the Exclusion Era, 1882–1943* (2003)

Martin V. Melosi, *The Sanitary City: Urban Infrastructure in America from Colonial Times to the Present* (2000)

Robyn Muncy, *Creating a Female Dominion in American Reform, 1890–1935* (1991)

Kathy Peiss, *Cheap Amusements: Working Women and Leisure in Turn-of-the-Century New York* (1986)

For a more extensive list for further reading, go to college.hmco.com/pic/norton8e.

Gilded Age Politics

1877-1900

𝒮he had a sharp tongue and a combative spirit. Known to friends as the "People's Joan of Arc" and to enemies as the "Kansas Pythoness," Mary Elizabeth Lease was such an electrifying orator that, according to one observer, "she could recite the multiplication table and set a crowd hooting and harrahing at her will." Born in 1853 in Pennsylvania, she lived most of her adult life in Kansas. Married at age twenty, she bore five children but somehow found time to study law while she took in washing, pinning her notes above her washtub.

In 1885 Mary became the first woman admitted to the Kansas bar and began an activist career. Joining the Woman's Christian Temperance Union and an organization called the Farmers' Alliance, she served as spokesperson for the new Populist party and made more than 160 speeches in 1890 on behalf of downtrodden rural folk and laboring people. She later ran for the U.S. Senate and campaigned for Populist presidential candidate James B. Weaver. Lease unleashed powerful language in support of her causes, which ranged beyond Populism to prohibition, woman suffrage, and birth control. She once proclaimed, "This is a nation of inconsistencies. . . . We fought England for our liberty and put chains on four million blacks. We wiped out slavery and [then] by our tariff laws and national banks began a system of white wage slavery worse than the first." Although she denied ever making the oft-quoted suggestion that Kansas farmers should "raise less corn and more hell," she admitted that it "was a good bit of advice."

Mary Lease's turbulent career paralleled an eventful era, one that can be characterized by three themes: special interest ascendancy, legislative accomplishment, and political

◀ Politics in the late nineteenth century was a major community activity. In an age before movies, television, shopping malls, and widespread professional sports, forceful orators, such as Socialist Party leader Eugene V. Debs, shown speaking in a railroad yard, attracted large audiences for speeches that sometimes lasted for hours. *(Brown Brothers)*

CHRONOLOGY

1873 ■ Congress ends coinage of silver dollars

1873–78 ■ Economic hard times hit

1877 ■ Georgia passes poll tax, disfranchising most African Americans

1878 ■ Bland-Allison Act requires Treasury to buy between $2 and $4 million in silver each month

1881 ■ Garfield assassinated; Arthur assumes presidency

1883 ■ Pendleton Civil Service Act introduces merit system
■ Supreme Court strikes down 1883 Civil Rights Act

1886 ■ *Wabash* case declares that only Congress can limit interstate commerce rates

1887 ■ Farmers' Alliances form
■ Interstate Commerce Commission begins regulating rates and practices of interstate shipping

1890 ■ McKinley Tariff raises tariff rates
■ Sherman Silver Purchase Act commits Treasury to buying 4.5 million ounces of silver each month
■ "Mississippi Plan" uses poll taxes and literacy tests to prevent African Americans from voting
■ National Woman Suffrage Association formed

1890s ■ Jim Crow laws, discriminating against African Americans in legal treatment and public accommodations, passed by southern states

1892 ■ Populist convention in Omaha draws up reform platform

1893 ■ Sherman Silver Purchase Act repealed

1893–97 ■ Major economic depression hits United States

1894 ■ Wilson-Gorman Tariff passes
■ Coxey's Army marches on Washington, D.C.

1896 ■ *Plessy v. Ferguson* establishes separate-but-equal doctrine

1898 ■ Louisiana implements "grandfather clause," restricting voting by African Americans

1899 ■ *Cummings v. County Board of Education* applies separate-but-equal doctrine to schools

exclusion. Her fiery speeches voiced the growing dissatisfaction with the ways in which powerful private interests—manufacturers, railroad managers, bankers, and wealthy men in general—were exercising greed through large corporations and political power. The era's obsession with riches seemed so widespread that, when Mark Twain and Charles Dudley Warner satirized America as a land of shallow money grubbers in their novel *The Gilded Age* (1874), the name stuck. Ever since, historians have used the expression "Gilded Age" to characterize the late nineteenth century.

At the same time, Lease's rhetoric obscured economic and political accomplishments at both national and state levels. Between 1877 and 1900, large corporations and allies of big business influenced politics and government as much as they shaped everyday life. Yet, in spite of partisan and regional rivalries, Congress achieved legislative landmarks in railroad regulation, tariff and currency reform, civil service, and other important issues. Meanwhile, the judiciary countered reform by supporting big business and defending property rights against state and federal regulation. The presidency was occupied by honest, respectable men who, though not as exceptional as Washington, Jefferson, or Lincoln, attempted to assert their authority and independence. Amid these trends, exclusion prevented the majority of Americans—including women, southern blacks, Indians, uneducated whites, and unnaturalized immigrants—from voting and from access to the tools of democracy. This exclusion deeply concerned Mary Elizabeth Lease and many others.

Until the 1890s, a stable party system and a balance of power among geographic sections kept politics in a delicate equilibrium. Then, in the 1890s, rural discontent rumbled through the West and South, and a deep economic depression bared flaws in the industrial system. Mary Lease and others like her helped awaken rural masses with her fiery rhetoric. A presidential campaign in 1896 stirred Americans as they had not been stirred for a generation. A new party arose, old parties split, sectional unity dissolved, and fundamental disputes about the nation's future climaxed. The nation emerged from the turbulent 1890s with new economic configurations and new political alignments.

- What were the functions of government in the Gilded Age, and how did they change?
- How did policies of exclusion and discrimination make their mark on the political culture of the age?
- How did the economic climate give rise to the Populist movement?

THE NATURE OF PARTY POLITICS

At no other time in the nation's history was public interest in elections more avid than between 1870 and 1896. Consistently, around 80 percent of eligible voters (white and black males in the North, somewhat lower rates among mostly white males in the South) cast ballots in local, state, and national elections. (Under 50 percent typically do so today.) Politics served as a form of recreation, more popular than baseball or circuses. Actual voting provided only the final step in a process that included parades, picnics, and speeches. As one observer remarked, "What the theatre is to the French, or the bull fight . . . to the Spanish . . . [election campaigns] and the ballot box are to our people."

Cultural-Political Alignments

In recent times, more voters have considered themselves independents than have identified with one political party or another. But in the Gilded Age, party loyalty was often vigorous and emotional. With some exceptions, people who opposed government interference in matters of personal liberty identified with the Democratic Party; those who believed government could be an agent of reform identified with the Republican Party. Democrats included foreign-born and second-generation Catholics and Jews, who followed rituals and sacraments to guide personal behavior and prove one's faith in God. Republicans consisted mostly of native-born Protestants, who believed that salvation was best achieved by purging the world of evil and that legislation could protect people from sin. Democrats would restrict government power. Republicans believed in direct government action.

There was also a geographic dimension to these divisions. Well into the 1880s, northern Republicans capitalized on bitter memories of the Civil War by "waving the bloody shirt" at northern and southern Democrats. As one Republican orator scolded in 1876, "Every man that tried to destroy this nation was a Democrat. . . . Soldiers, every scar you have on your heroic bodies was given you by a Democrat." Democrats in the north tended to focus more on urban and economic issues, but southern Democratic candidates waved a different bloody shirt, calling Republicans traitors to white supremacy and states' rights.

At state and local levels, partisan politicians often battled over how much government should control people's lives. The most contentious issues were use of leisure time and celebration of Sunday, the Lord's day. Protestant Republicans tried to keep the Sabbath holy through legislation that prohibited bars, stores, and commercial amusements from being open on Sundays. Immigrant Democrats, accustomed to feasting and playing after church, fought saloon closings and other restrictions on the only day they had free from work. Similar splits developed over public versus parochial schools and over prohibition versus unrestricted availability of liquor.

These issues made politics a personal as well as a community activity. In an era before media celebrities occupied public attention, people formed strong loyalties to individual politicians, loyalties that often overlooked crassness and corruption. James G. Blaine—Maine's flamboyant and powerful Republican congressman, senator, presidential aspirant, and two-time secretary of state—typified this appeal. Followers called him the "Plumed Knight," composed songs and organized parades in his honor, and sat mesmerized by his long speeches, while disregarding his corrupt alliances with businessmen and his animosity toward laborers and farmers.

Allegiances to national parties and candidates were so evenly divided that no faction gained control for any sustained period of time. Between 1877 and 1897, Republicans held the presidency for three terms, Democrats for two. Rarely did the same party control both the presidency and Congress simultaneously. From 1876 through 1892, presidential elections were extremely close. The outcome often hinged on the vote in a few populous northern states—Connecticut, New York, New Jersey, Ohio, Indiana, and Illinois. Both parties tried to gain advantages by nominating presidential and vice-presidential candidates from these states (and also by committing vote fraud on their candidates' behalf).

Party Factions

Factional quarrels split both the Republican and the Democratic Party. Among Republicans, New York's pompous senator Roscoe Conkling led one faction, known as "Stalwarts." A physical fitness devotee labeled "the finest torso in public life," Conkling worked the spoils system to win government jobs for his supporters. The Stalwarts' rivals were the "Half Breeds," led by James G. Blaine, who pursued influence as blatantly as Conkling did. On the sidelines stood more idealistic Republicans, or "Mugwumps" (supposedly an

Indian term meaning "mug on one side of the fence, wump on the other"). Mugwumps, such as Senator Carl Schurz of Missouri, scorned the political roguishness that tainted Republican leaders and believed that only righteous, educated men like themselves should govern. Republican allies of big business supported the use of gold as the standard for currency, whereas those from mining regions favored silver. Meanwhile, Democrats subdivided into white-supremacist southerners, immigrant-stock and working-class supporters of urban political machines, business-oriented advocates of low tariffs and the gold standard, and debtor-oriented advocates of free silver. Like Republicans, Democrats avidly pursued the spoils of office.

In each state, one party usually dominated, and within that party a few men typically held dictatorial sway. Often the state "boss" was a senator who parlayed his state power into national influence and command over federal jobs. (Until the Seventeenth Amendment to the Constitution was ratified in 1913, state legislatures elected U.S. senators.) Besides Conkling and Blaine, the senatorial ranks included Thomas C. Platt of New York, Nelson W. Aldrich of Rhode Island, Mark A. Hanna of Ohio, Matthew S. Quay of Pennsylvania, and William Mahone of Virginia. These men exercised their power brazenly. Quay once responded to an inquiry about using secret information from a Senate investigation to profit from an investment in the American Sugar Refining Company by pronouncing, "I do not feel that there is anything in my connection with the Senate to interfere with my buying or selling stock when I please, and I propose to do so in the future."

ISSUES OF LEGISLATION

In Congress, the issues of sectional controversies, patronage abuses, railroad regulation, tariffs, and currency provoked heated debates, and several times partisan discord was so fierce that it prevented passage of legislation. From the end of the Civil War into the 1880s, Congress spent much time discussing soldiers' pensions. The Grand Army of the Republic, an organization of 400,000 Union Army veterans, allied with the Republican Party and cajoled Congress into providing generous pensions for former Union soldiers and their widows. Many pensions were deserved: Union troops had been poorly paid, and thousands of wives had been widowed. But for some veterans, the war's emotional memories furnished an opportunity to profit at public expense. Although the Union Army spent $2 billion to fight the Civil War, pensions to veterans ultimately cost $8 billion, one of the largest welfare commitments the federal government has ever made. By 1900 soldiers' pensions

accounted for roughly 40 percent of the federal budget. Confederate veterans received none of this money, though some southern states funded small pensions and built old-age homes for ex-soldiers.

Few politicians dared oppose pensions, but some attempted to dismantle the spoils system. During the

Civil Service Reform

Civil War, the federal government had expanded considerably, and the practice of awarding government jobs to the party faithful (regardless of their qualifications), which had taken root before the Civil War, flourished afterward. As the postal service, diplomatic corps, and other government agencies expanded, so did the public payroll. Between 1865 and 1891, the number of federal jobs tripled, from 53,000 to 166,000. Elected officials scrambled to control these jobs as a means to benefit themselves and their party. In return for comparatively short hours and high pay, appointees to federal positions pledged votes and a portion of their earnings to their patrons.

Shocked by such corruption, especially after the revelation of scandals in the Grant administration, some reformers began advocating appointments and promotions based on merit—civil service—rather than on political connections. Support for change accelerated in 1881 with formation of the National Civil Service Reform League, led by editors E. L. Godkin and George W. Curtis. That year, the assassination of President James Garfield by a distraught job seeker hastened the drive for reform. The Pendleton Civil Service Act, passed by Congress in 1882 and signed by President Chester Arthur in 1883, created the Civil Service Commission to oversee competitive examinations for government positions. The act gave the commission jurisdiction over only 10 percent of federal jobs, though the president could expand the list. Because the Constitution barred Congress from interfering in state affairs, civil service at state and local levels developed in a more haphazard manner. Nevertheless, the Pendleton Act marked a beginning and provided a model for further reform.

Veterans' pensions and civil service reform were not the main issues of the Gilded Age, however. Rather, economic policy occupied congressional concerns more than ever before. Railroads particularly provoked controversy. As rail networks spread, so did competition. In their quest for customers, railroad lines reduced rates to outmaneuver rivals, but rate wars hurt profits, and inconsistent freight charges angered shippers and farmers. On noncompetitive routes, railroads often boosted charges as high as possible to compensate for unprofitably low rates on competitive routes, making pricing disproportionate to distance. Charges on short-distance shipments served by only one

▲ The patronage system—the practice of rewarding political supporters with jobs and favors— reached such extent during the Gilded Age that critics likened it to the stock exchange where traders clamored to be heard. President James A. Garfield is shown on a pedestal in the center of this cartoon surrounded by pleading job-seekers while on the left, Senator Thomas C. Platt, Republican leader from New York State, is handcuffed to a man handing "orders from the boss" to Vice President Chester A. Arthur. The Pendleton Civil Service Act of 1883 was intended to replace patronage by making federal appointments based on merit rather than on political connections.

(Library of Congress)

line could exceed those on long-distance shipments served by competing lines. Railroads also played favorites, reducing rates to large shippers and offering free passenger passes to preferred customers and politicians.

Such favoritism stirred farmers, small merchants, and reform politicians to demand rate regulation. Their efforts succeeded first at the state level. By 1880 fourteen states had established commissions to limit freight and storage charges of state-chartered lines. Using corrupt lobbyists and a variety of pressure tactics, railroads fought these measures, arguing that the Fourteenth Amendment to the Constitution guaranteed them freedom to acquire and use property without government restraint. But in 1877, in *Munn v. Illinois,* the Supreme Court upheld the principle of state regulation, declaring that grain warehouses owned by railroads acted in the public interest and

Railroad Regulation

therefore must submit to regulation for "the common good."

State legislatures, however, could not regulate interstate lines, a limitation affirmed by the Supreme Court in the *Wabash* case of 1886, in which the Court declared that only Congress could limit rates involving interstate commerce. Reformers thereupon demanded action by the federal government. With support from some businessmen who believed that they, like farmers, were suffering from discriminatory rates, Congress passed the Interstate Commerce Act in 1887. The law prohibited pools, rebates, and long-haul/short-haul rate discrimination, and it created the Interstate Commerce Commission (ICC), the nation's first regulatory agency, to investigate railroad rate making, issue cease-and-desist orders against illegal practices, and seek court aid to enforce compliance. The legislation's weak provisions for enforcement, however, left railroads room for evasion, and federal judges chipped away at ICC powers. In the *Maximum Freight Rate* case (1897), the Supreme Court ruled that the ICC lacked power to set rates, and in the *Alabama Midlands* case (1897), the Court overturned prohibitions against long-haul/short-haul discrimination. Even so, the principle of regulation, though weakened, remained in force.

The economic issue of tariffs carried strong political implications. From 1789 onward, Congress had created tariffs, which levied duties (taxes) on imported goods, to protect American manufactures and agricultural products from European competition. But tariffs quickly became a tool by which special interests could enhance their profits. By the 1880s these interests had succeeded in obtaining tariffs on more than four thousand items. A few economists and farmers argued for free trade, but most politicians insisted that tariffs were a necessary form of government assistance to support industry and preserve jobs.

Tariff Policy

The Republican Party put protective tariffs at the core of its political agenda to support economic growth. Democrats complained that tariffs made prices artificially high by keeping out less expensive foreign goods, thereby benefiting domestic manufacturers while hurting farmers whose crops were not protected and consumers who had to buy manufactured goods. For example, a yard of flannel produced abroad might cost 10 cents, but an 8-cent import duty raised the price paid by American consumers to 18 cents. An American manufacturer of a similar yard of flannel, also costing 10 cents, could charge 17 cents, underselling foreign competition by 1 cent yet still pocketing a 7-cent profit.

During the Gilded Age, revenues from tariffs and other levies created a surplus in the federal budget. Most Republicans liked the idea that the government was earning more than it spent and hoped to keep the extra money as a Treasury reserve or to spend it on projects such as harbor improvements, which would aid commerce. Democrats, however, asserted that the federal government should not be a profit-making operation. They acknowledged a need for protection of some manufactured goods and raw materials, but they favored lower tariff duties to encourage foreign trade and to reduce the Treasury surplus.

Manufacturers and their congressional allies firmly controlled tariff policy. The McKinley Tariff of 1890 boosted already-high rates by another 4 percent. When House Democrats supported by President Grover Cleveland passed a bill to trim tariffs in 1894, Senate Republicans, aided by southern Democrats eager to protect their region's infant industries, particularly textiles and steel,

added six hundred amendments restoring most cuts (the Wilson-Gorman Tariff). In 1897 the Dingley Tariff raised rates further. Attacks on duties, though unsuccessful, made tariffs a symbol of privileged business in the public mind and a continuing target for reformers.

Monetary policy inflamed even stronger emotions than tariffs did. When increased industrial and agricultural production caused prices to fall after the Civil War, debtors and creditors had opposing reactions.

Monetary Policy

Farmers suffered because the prices they received for crops were dropping, but because high demand for a relatively limited supply of money in circulation raised interest rates on loans, it was costly for them to borrow funds to pay mortgages and other debts. They favored schemes like the coinage of silver to increase the amount of currency in circulation. An expanded money supply, they reasoned, would reduce interest rates, making their debts less burdensome. Small businessmen, also in need of loans, agreed with farmers. Large merchants, manufacturers, and bankers favored a more stable, limited money supply backed only by gold. They feared that the value of currency not backed by gold would fluctuate; the resulting uncertainty would threaten investors' confidence in the U.S. economy.

Arguments over the quantity and quality of money, however, transcended economics. Creditor-debtor tension translated into class divisions between haves—those with easy access to money—and have-nots—those who had problems borrowing. The debate also reflected sectional cleavages: western silver-mining areas and agricultural regions of the South and West against the more conservative industrial Northeast. And the issue carried moral, almost religious, overtones. Some Americans believed that the beauty, rarity, and durability of gold gave it magical potency. Others believed the gold standard for currency was too limiting; sustained prosperity, they insisted, demanded new attitudes.

By the 1870s, the currency controversy boiled down to which precious metal should be used to back national paper money (dollar bills): gold or silver? Previously, the government had bought both gold and silver, setting a ratio that made a gold dollar worth sixteen times more than a silver dollar. In theory, a person holding a specific sum of dollar bills could exchange them for one ounce of gold or sixteen ounces of silver. Mining discoveries after the gold rush of 1848, however, increased the gold supply and lowered its market price relative to that of silver. Consequently, silver dollars disappeared from circulation—because of their inflated value relative to gold, owners

▲ Taking advantage of the new fad of bicycling (see Chapter 19), a cartoonist in an 1886 issue of the humor magazine *Puck* illustrates the controversy over silver coinage. Depicting two uncoordinated wheels, one a silver coin and the other a gold coin, the illustration conveys the message of how hard it was to proceed with conflicting kinds of currency. *(Private Collection)*

rency supply. They joined silver producers to press for resumption of silver coinage at the old sixteen-to-one ratio.

With both parties split into silver and gold factions, Congress first tried to compromise. The Bland-Allison Act (1878) authorized the Treasury to buy between $2 million and $4 million worth of silver each month, and the Sherman Silver Purchase Act (1890) increased the government's monthly silver purchase by specifying weight (4.5 million ounces) rather than dollars. Neither measure satisfied the different interest groups. Creditors wanted the government to stop buying silver, whereas for debtors, the legislation failed to expand the money supply satisfactorily and did not erase the impression that the government favored creditors' interests. The issue would become even more emotional during the presidential election of 1896 (see pages 584–587).

Members of Congress dealt with such thorny issues as civil service, railroad regulation, and monetary policy under

Legislative Accomplishments

difficult conditions in the Gilded Age. Senators and representatives earned small salaries and usually had the financial burden of maintaining two residences: one in their home district and one in Washington. Weather in the nation's capital was sweltering in summer, muddy and icy in winter. Most members of Congress had no private office space, only a desk. They worked long hours responding to constituents' requests, wrote their own speeches, and paid for staff out of their own pocket. Yet, though corruption and greed tainted several, most politicians were principled and dedicated. They managed to deal with important issues and pass some significant legislation.

TENTATIVE PRESIDENTS

Operating under the cloud of Andrew Johnson's impeachment, Grant's scandals, and doubts about the legitimacy of the 1876 election (see Chapter 16), American presidents between 1877 and 1900 moved gingerly to restore authority to their office. Proper and honest, Presidents Rutherford Hayes (1877–1881), James Garfield (1881), Chester Arthur (1881–1885), Grover Cleveland (1885–1889 and 1893–1897), Benjamin Harrison (1889–1893), and William McKinley (1897–1901) tried to act as legislative as well as administrative leaders. Like other politicians, they used symbols. Hayes served lemonade at the White House to emphasize that he, unlike his predecessor Ulysses Grant, was no hard drinker. McKinley set aside his cigar in public so photographers would not catch him setting a bad example for youth. More important, each president made

hoarded them—and in 1873 Congress officially stopped coining silver dollars. European governments also stopped buying silver, and the United States and many of its trading partners unofficially adopted the gold standard, meaning that their currency was backed chiefly by gold.

But within a few years, new mines in the American West began to flood the market with silver, and its price dropped. Because gold now was relatively less plentiful, worth more than sixteen times the value of silver (the ratio reached twenty to one by 1890), it became worthwhile for people to spend rather than hoard silver dollars. Silver producers wanted the government to resume buying silver at the old sixteen-to-one ratio, which amounted to a subsidy because they could sell silver to the government above its market price. Debtors, hurt by the economic hard times of 1873–1878, saw silver as a means of expanding the curcautious attempts to initiate legislation and use vetoes to guide national policy.

Rutherford B. Hayes had been a Union general and an Ohio congressman and governor before his disputed

Hayes, Garfield, and Arthur

election to the presidency, an event that prompted opponents to label him "Rutherfraud." Although his party expected him to serve business interests, Hayes played a quiet role as conciliator. He emphasized national harmony over sectional rivalry and opposed racial violence. He tried to overhaul the spoils system by appointing civil service reformer Carl Schurz to his cabinet and by battling New York's patronage king, Senator Conkling. (He fired Conkling's protégé, Chester Arthur, from the post of New York customs house collector.) Though averse to using government power to aid the oppressed, Hayes believed society should not ignore the needs of the American Chinese and Indians, and after retiring from the presidency he worked to aid former slaves.

When Hayes declined to run for reelection in 1880, Republicans nominated another Ohio congressman and Civil War hero, James A. Garfield, who defeated Democrat Winfield Scott Hancock, also a Civil War hero, by just 40,000 votes out of 9 million cast. By winning the pivotal states of New York and Indiana, however, Garfield carried the electoral college by a comfortable margin, 214 to 155. A solemn and cautious man, Garfield spent most of his brief presidency trying to secure an independent position among party potentates. He hoped to reduce the tariff and develop economic relations with Latin America, and he pleased civil service reformers by rebuffing Conkling's patronage demands. But his chance to make lasting contributions ended in July 1881 when Charles Guiteau shot him in a Washington railroad station. Garfield lingered for seventy-nine days while doctors tried vainly to remove a bullet lodged in his back, but he succumbed to infection and died September 19.

Garfield's successor was Vice President Chester A. Arthur, the New York spoilsman whom Hayes had fired in 1878. Republicans had nominated Arthur for vice president only to help Garfield win New York State's electoral votes. Although his elevation to the presidency made reformers shudder, Arthur became a dignified and temperate executive. He signed the Pendleton Civil Service Act, urged Congress to modify outdated tariff rates, and supported federal regulation of railroads. He wielded the veto aggressively, killing several bills that excessively benefited railroads and corporations. But congressional partisans frustrated his plans for reducing the tariff and strengthening the navy. Arthur wanted to run for president in 1884

but lost the nomination to James G. Blaine at the Republican national convention.

To oppose Blaine, Democrats named New York's governor, Grover Cleveland, a bachelor who had tainted his reputation when he fathered an out-of-wedlock son—a fact he admitted during the campaign. Both parties focused on the sordid. (Alluding to Cleveland's son, Republicans chided him with catcalls of "Ma! Ma! Where's my pa?" to which Democrats replied, "Gone to the White House, Ha! Ha! Ha!") Distaste for Blaine prompted some Mugwump Republicans to desert their party for Cleveland. On election day, Cleveland beat Blaine by only 29,000 popular votes; his tiny margin of 1,149 votes in New York gave him that state's 36 electoral votes, enough for a 219-to-182 victory in the electoral college. Cleveland may have won New York thanks to last-minute remarks of a Protestant minister, who equated Democrats with "rum, Romanism, and rebellion." Democrats eagerly publicized the slur among New York's large Irish-Catholic population, urging voters to protest by supporting Cleveland.

Cleveland, the first Democratic president since James Buchanan (1857–1861), tried to exert vigorous leadership.

Cleveland and Harrison

He expanded civil service, vetoed hundreds of private pension bills, and urged Congress to cut tariff duties. When advisers warned that his stand might weaken his chances for reelection, the president retorted, "What is the use of being elected or reelected, unless you stand for something?" But the Mills tariff bill of 1888, passed by the House in response to Cleveland's wishes, died in the Senate. When Democrats renominated Cleveland for the presidency in 1888, businessmen in the party convinced him to moderate his attacks on high tariffs.

Republicans in 1888 nominated Benjamin Harrison, former senator from Indiana and grandson of President William Henry Harrison (1841). During the campaign, some Republicans manipulated a British diplomat into stating that Cleveland's reelection would be good for England. Irish Democrats, who hated England's colonial rule over Ireland, took offense, as intended, and Cleveland's campaign was weakened. Perhaps more beneficial to Harrison were the bribery and multiple voting that helped him win Indiana by 2,300 votes and New York by 14,000. (Democrats also indulged in such cheating, but Republicans proved more successful at it.) Those states' electoral votes ensured Harrison's victory. Although Cleveland outpolled Harrison by 90,000 popular votes, Harrison carried the electoral college by 233 to 168.

The first president since 1875 whose party had majorities in both houses of Congress, Harrison used a variety

▲ During the Gilded Age, political events provided opportunity for elaborate spectacle, and office-holders occupied the limelight as major celebrities. A presidential inauguration, such as that of Rutherford B. Hayes, though perhaps no less lavish than one of the current era, functioned as a public festival at a time when mass entertainment was far less prevalent than in recent times. During a political campaign a candidate's supporters wore colorful emblems, such as the brooch pictured in the corner, reminding voters of Hayes's Civil War record.

(Left: National Archives; Right: Collection of Janice L. and David J. Frent)

of methods, ranging from threats of vetoes to informal dinners and consultations with politicians, to influence the course of legislation. Partly in response, the Congress of 1889–1891 passed 517 bills, 200 more than the average passed by Congresses between 1875 and 1889. Harrison showed support for civil service by appointing reformer Theodore Roosevelt as civil service commissioner, but neither the president nor Congress could resist pressures from special interests, especially those waving the bloody shirt. Harrison signed the Dependents' Pension Act, which provided pensions for Union veterans who had suffered war-related disabilities and granted aid to their widows and children. The bill doubled the number of welfare recipients from 490,000 to 966,000.

The Pension Act and other appropriations in 1890 pushed the federal budget past $1 billion for the first time in the nation's history. Democrats blamed the "Billion-Dollar Congress" on spendthrift Republicans. Voters reacted by unseating seventy-eight Republicans in the congressional elections of 1890. Seeking to capitalize on voter unrest, Democrats nominated Grover Cleveland to run against Harrison in 1892. This time Cleveland attracted large contributions from business and beat Harrison by 370,000 popular votes (3 percent of the total), easily winning the electoral vote.

In office again, Cleveland addressed problems of currency, tariffs, and labor unrest, but his actions reflected a narrow orientation toward business and bespoke political weakness. During his campaign Cleveland had promised sweeping tariff reform, but he made little effort to line up support in the Senate, where protectionists undercut efforts to reduce rates. And when 120,000 boycotting railroad workers paralyzed commerce in the Pullman strike of 1894, Cleveland bowed to requests from railroad managers and Attorney General Richard Olney (a former railroad lawyer) to send in troops. In spite of Cleveland's attempts at initiative, major events—particularly economic downturn and agrarian ferment—shoved him from the limelight.

DISCRIMINATION, DISFRANCHISEMENT, AND RESPONSES

Although speechmakers often spoke of freedom and opportunity during the Gilded Age, policies of discrimination and exclusion continued to haunt more than half of the nation's population. Just as before the Civil War, issues of race shaped politics in the South, home to the vast majority of African Americans. Southern white farmers and workers, facing economic insecurity, feared that newly enfranchised African American men would challenge whatever political and social superiority (real and imagined) they enjoyed. Wealthy landowners and merchants fanned these fears, using them to divide the races and to distract poor whites from protesting their own economic subjugation. Even some white feminists, such as Susan B. Anthony, opposed voting and other rights for blacks on the grounds that white women deserved such rights before black men did.

The abolition of slavery altered the legal status of African Americans, but it did not markedly improve their

Violence Against African Americans

economic opportunities. In 1880, 90 percent of all southern blacks depended for a living on farming or personal and domestic service—the same occupations they had held as slaves. Discrimination was rampant. Some communities considered themselves "sundown towns," places where only whites were allowed on the streets at night. The New South, moreover, proved to be as violent for blacks as the Old South had been. Between 1889 and 1909, more than seventeen hundred African Americans were lynched in the South. Most lynching victims were accused of assault—rarely proved—on a white woman. These acts of terror occurred often, but by no means exclusively, in sparsely populated districts where whites felt threatened by an in-

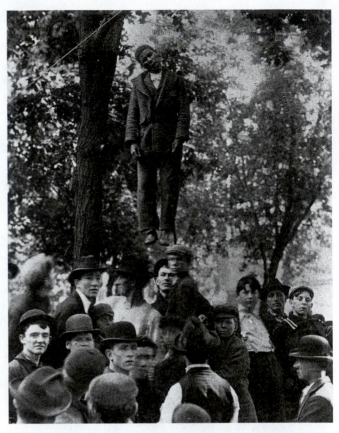

▲ In the years after Reconstruction, lynchings of African American men occurred with increasing frequency, chiefly in sparsely populated areas where whites looked on strangers, especially black strangers, with fear and suspicion.

(© R. P. Kingston/Index Stock Imagery, Picture Cube Division)

flux of migrant blacks who had no friends, black or white, to vouch for them.

Blacks did not suffer such violence silently, however. The most notable activist at this time was Ida B. Wells, a Memphis schoolteacher. In 1884, when she was twenty-two years old, Wells was forcibly removed from a railroad car when she refused to give up her seat to a white man. The incident sparked her career as a forceful and tireless spokesperson against white supremacy and violence. In 1889 Wells became a partner of a Memphis newspaper, the *Free Speech and Headlight,* in which she published attacks against white injustice, especially in the case of three black grocers lynched in 1892 after defending themselves against whites who had attacked them. Wells wrote an editorial urging local blacks to migrate to the West. She herself was forced to flee to England to escape threats against her life. But she soon returned and lived in Chicago, where she wrote *A Red Record* (1895), which tabulated statistics on racial lynchings and served as a foundation for further protest campaigns.

With slavery abolished, white supremacists fashioned new ways to keep blacks in an inferior position. Southern

||||||||||||||||||||||||||||||

Disfranchisement

leaders, eager to reassert authority over people whom they believed to be inferior, instituted measures to prevent blacks from voting and to segregate them legally from whites. The end of Reconstruction had not stopped blacks from voting and holding office. Despite threats and intimidation, blacks still formed the backbone of the southern Republican Party and won numerous elective positions. In North Carolina, for example, eleven African Americans served in the state Senate and forty-three in the House between 1877 and 1890. In reaction, white politicians sought to impose restrictions that would disfranchise blacks; that is, deprive them of their right to vote. Beginning with Tennessee in 1889 and Arkansas in 1892, southern states levied taxes of $1 to $2 on all citizens wishing to vote. These poll taxes proved prohibitive to most blacks, who were so poor and deeply in debt that they rarely had cash for any purpose. Other schemes disfranchised blacks who could not read.

Disfranchisement was accomplished in other devious ways. The Supreme Court determined in *U.S. v. Reese* (1876) that Congress had no control over local and state elections other than the explicit provisions of the Fifteenth Amendment, which prohibits states from denying the vote "on account of race, color, or previous condition of servitude." State legislatures found ways to exclude black voters without mentioning race, color, or servitude. For instance, an 1890 state constitutional convention established the "Mississippi Plan," requiring all voters to pay a poll tax eight months before each election, present the tax receipt at election time, and prove that they could read and interpret the state constitution. Registration officials applied stiffer standards to blacks than to whites, even declaring black college graduates ineligible on grounds of illiteracy. In 1898 Louisiana enacted the first "grandfather clause," which established literacy and property qualifications for voting but exempted sons and grandsons of those eligible to vote before 1867. Other southern states initiated similar measures.

Such restrictions proved highly effective. In South Carolina, for example, 70 percent of eligible blacks voted in the 1880 presidential election; by 1896 the rate had dropped to 11 percent. By the 1900s African Americans had effectively lost political rights in the South. More importantly, because voting is often considered a common right of citizenship, disfranchisement stripped African American men of their social standing as U.S. citizens. Disfranchisement also affected poor whites, few of whom could meet poll tax, property, and literacy requirements. Thus the total number of eligible voters in Mississippi shrank from 257,000 in 1876 to 77,000 in 1892.

Racial discrimination also stiffened in areas beyond voting, as existing customs of racial separation were

||||||||||||||||||||||||||||||

Legal Segregation

expanded. In a series of cases during the 1870s, the Supreme Court opened the door to discrimination by ruling that the Fourteenth Amendment protected citizens' rights only against infringement by state governments. The amendment, according to the Court, lacked authority over what individuals or organizations might do. If blacks wanted legal protection from discriminatory behavior by individuals or companies, the Court said, they must seek it from state laws because under the Tenth Amendment states retained all powers not specifically assigned to Congress. These rulings climaxed in 1883 when, in the *Civil Rights* cases, the Court struck down the 1875 Civil Rights Act, which prohibited segregation in public facilities, such as streetcars, theaters, and parks. Again the Court declared that the federal government could not regulate private behavior in matters of race relations. Thus railroads, such as the Chesapeake & Ohio Railroad, which had forced Ida B. Wells out of her seat, could maintain discriminatory policies.

At the state level, segregation could legally occur on a "separate-but-equal" basis, as upheld by the Supreme Court in the case of *Plessy v. Ferguson* (1896). This case began in 1892 when a New Orleans organization of prominent African Americans chose Homer Plessy, a dark-skinned creole who was only one-eighth black (but still considered black by Louisiana law), as a volunteer to violate a state law by sitting in a whites-only railroad car. As expected, Plessy was arrested, and the appeal of his conviction reached the U.S. Supreme Court in 1896. Hopes for justice faded when the Court affirmed that a state law providing for separate facilities for the two races was reasonable because it preserved "public peace and good order." Writing for the Court, Associate Justice Billings Brown said that legislation could not overcome prejudice. "If the two races are to meet upon terms of social equality," he wrote, "it must be the result of . . . a voluntary consent of individuals." Thus, in the court's mind, a law separating the races did not necessarily "destroy the legal equality of the races." Although the ruling did not use the phrase "separate but equal," it made legal separate facilities for black and white people as long as they were equal.

In 1899 the Court applied the separate-but-equal doctrine to schools in *Cummins v. County Board of Education*, legalizing school segregation until it was overturned by *Brown v. Board of Education* in 1954.

Segregation laws—known as Jim Crow laws—multiplied throughout the South, confronting African Americans with daily reminders of inferior status. State and local statutes, most of which were passed in the 1890s, restricted blacks to the rear of streetcars, to separate public drinking fountains and toilets, and to separate sections of hospitals and cemeteries. A Birmingham, Alabama, ordinance required that the races be "distinctly separated . . . by well defined physical barriers" in "any room, hall, theatre, picture house, auditorium, yard, court, ballpark, or other indoor or outdoor place." Mobile, Alabama, passed a curfew requiring blacks to be off the streets by 10 p.m., and Atlanta mandated separate Bibles for the swearing-in of black witnesses in court.

African American women and men challenged prejudice in several ways. Some organized boycotts of segregated streetcars and discriminatory businesses; others considered moving to Africa. Still others promoted "Negro enterprise." In 1898, for example, Atlanta University professor John Hope called on blacks to become their own employers and supported formation of Negro Business Men's Leagues. In the optimistic days following Reconstruction, a number of blacks used higher education as a means of elevating their status. In all-black teachers' colleges, young men and women sought opportunities for themselves and their race. Education also seemed to present a way to foster interracial cooperation. But the white supremacy campaigns that Jim Crow laws reflected taught southern blacks that they would have to negotiate in a biracial, rather than an interracial, society.

While disfranchisement pushed African American men, who in contrast to women had previously been able to vote, out of public life, African American women used traditional roles as mothers, educators, and moral guardians to uplift the race and seek better services for black communities. Their efforts signified a kind of political activity that was more subtle than voting—though they also did fight for the vote. They successfully lobbied governments in the South for cleaner city streets, better public health, expanded charity services, and vocational education. In these efforts, black women found ways to join with white women in campaigns to negotiate with the white

African American Activism

▲ Livingstone College in North Carolina was one of several institutions of higher learning established by and for African Americans in the late nineteenth century. With a curriculum that emphasized training for educational and religious work in the South and in Africa, these colleges were coeducational, operating on the belief that both men and women could have public roles.

(Courtesy of Heritage Hall, Livingstone College, Salisbury, North Carolina)

male power structure to achieve their goals. In many instances, however, white women sympathized with men in support of white-supremacist campaigns.

In the North, white women contended head-on with male power structures. Their goal was the vote; their successes in reaching this goal were limited. Prior to 1870, each state determined voting qualifications.

Woman Suffrage

The Fifteenth Amendment, ratified that year, forbade states to deny the vote "on account of race, color or previous condition" but omitted any reference to sex. For the next twenty years, two organizations, the National Woman Suffrage Association (NWSA) and the American Woman Suffrage Association (AWSA), crusaded for female suffrage. The NWSA, led by Elizabeth Cady Stanton and Susan B. Anthony, advocated women's rights in courts and workplaces as well as at the ballot box. The AWSA, led by former abolitionists Lucy Stone and Thomas Wentworth Higginson, focused more narrowly on suffrage. Congress failed to heed either group. Anthony's effort to get a constitutional amendment for woman suffrage never received support. On the few occasions when a bill for the amendment reached the Senate floor, senators voted it down, claiming that suffrage would interfere with women's family obligations. While the NWSA fought for suffrage on the national level, the AWSA worked to amend state constitutions. (The groups merged in 1890 to form the National American Woman Suffrage Association.) Although these campaigns succeeded only slightly, they helped train a corps of female leaders in political organizing and public speaking.

Women did win partial victories. Between 1870 and 1910, eleven states (mostly in the West) legalized limited woman suffrage. By 1890 nineteen states allowed women to vote on school issues, and three granted suffrage on tax and bond issues. The right to vote in national elections awaited a later generation, but the activities of women like Mary Lease, Ida B. Wells, Susan B. Anthony, and Lucy Stone proved that women did not have to vote to be politically active.

AGRARIAN UNREST AND POPULISM

While voting and racial segregation concerned those suffering from political exclusion, economic inequities sparked a mass movement that would shake American society. Despite rapid industrialization and urbanization in the late nineteenth century, the United States remained an agrarian society. In 1890, 64 percent of the total population lived in rural areas, many of which seethed under economic pressures and were primed for protest. The expression of farmers' discontent—a mixture of strident rhetoric, nostalgic dreams, and hard-headed egalitarianism—began in Grange organizations in the early 1870s. It accelerated when Farmers' Alliances formed in Texas in the late 1870s and spread across the Cotton Belt and Great Plains in the 1880s. The Alliance movement flourished chiefly in areas where tenancy, debt, weather, and insects endangered struggling farmers. Once under way, the agrarian rebellion inspired visions of a cooperative and democratic society.

HOW WOMEN'S SUFFRAGE WILL INCREASE THE POWER OF THE WARD HEELER.

◄ This anti–woman suffrage cartoon implies that, if women were to be allowed to vote, the inferior types among them—in this case, ugly, slovenly immigrants—would outweigh and outvote their more distinguished sisters. The artist, drawing for *Judge* magazine in 1894, was not only expressing anti-female and anti-immigrant views but also using a fear that female voters would only entrench corrupt politicians.

(William L. Clements Library)

Southern agriculture, unlike that of the Midwest, did not benefit much from mechanization (see Chapter 17).

||||||||||||||||||||||||||||||
Sharecropping and Tenant Farming in the South

Tobacco and cotton, the principal southern crops, required constant hoeing and weeding by hand. Tobacco required careful harvesting, because the leaves matured at different rates and because the stems were too fragile for machines. Also, mechanical devices were not precise enough to pick cotton. Thus, in former plantation areas after the Civil War, southern agriculture remained labor-intensive, and labor-lords, who had once utilized slaves, were replaced by landlords, who employed sharecroppers and tenant farmers.

Sharecropping and tenant farming—meaning that farmers rented their land rather than owned it—entangled millions of black and white southerners in webs of debt and humiliation, at whose center loomed the crop lien. Most farmers, too poor to have ready cash, borrowed in order to buy necessities. They could offer as collateral only what they could grow. A farmer in need of supplies dealt with a "furnishing merchant," who would exchange supplies for a lien, or legal claim, on the farmer's forthcoming crop. After the crop was harvested and brought to market, the merchant collected his debt by claiming the portion of the crop that would repay the loan. All too often, however, the debt exceeded the crop's value. The farmer could pay off only part of the debt to the merchant but still needed food and supplies for the coming year. The only way he could get these supplies was to sink deeper into debt by reborrowing and giving the merchant a lien on his next crop.

Merchants frequently took advantage of indebted farmers' powerlessness by inflating prices and charging excessive interest on the advances farmers received. Suppose, for example, that a cash-poor farmer renting some land needed a 20-cent bag of seed or a 20-cent piece of cloth. The furnishing merchant would sell him the goods on credit but would boost the price to 28 cents. At year's end, that 28-cent loan would have accumulated interest of 50 percent or more, raising the farmer's debt to 42 cents—more than double the item's original cost. The farmer, having pledged more than his crop's worth against scores of such debts, fell behind in payments and never recovered. If he fell too far behind, he could be evicted.

In the southern backcountry, which in antebellum times had been characterized by small, family-owned farms, few slaves, and diversified agriculture, the crop-lien problem was compounded by other economic changes. New spending habits of backcountry farmers illustrate these changes. In 1884 Jephta Dickson, who farmed land in the northern Georgia hills, bought $55.90 worth of flour, potatoes, peas, meat, corn, and syrup from merchants. Such expenditures would have been rare before the Civil War, when farmers grew almost all the food they needed. But after the war, yeomen like Dickson shifted to commercial farming; in the South that meant raising cotton. This move to the market economy came about for two reasons: constant debt forced farmers to grow crops that would bring in cash, and railroads enabled them to transport cotton to market more easily than before. As backcountry yeomen devoted more acres to cotton, they raised less of what they needed on a daily basis and found themselves more frequently at the mercy of merchants.

In the Midwest, as growers cultivated more land, as mechanization boosted productivity, and as foreign competition increased, supplies of agricultural products exceeded national and worldwide demand. Consequently, prices for staple crops dropped steadily. A bushel of wheat that sold for $1.45 in 1866 brought only 80 cents in the mid-1880s and 49 cents by the mid-1890s. Meanwhile, transportation and storage fees remained high relative to other prices. Expenses for seed, fertilizer, manufactured goods, taxes, and mortgage interest trapped many farm families in stressful and sometimes desperate circumstances. In order to buy necessities and pay bills, farmers had to produce more. But the spiral wound ever more tightly: the more farmers produced, the lower crop prices dropped (see Figure 20.1).

||||||||||||||||||||||||||||||
Hardship in the Midwest and West

The West suffered from special hardships. In Colorado, absentee capitalists seized control of access to transportation and water, and concentration of technology in the hands of large mining companies pushed out small firms. Charges of monopolistic behavior by railroads echoed among farmers, miners, and stockmen in Wyoming and Montana. In California, Washington, and Oregon, wheat and fruit growers found their opportunities blocked by railroads' control of transportation and storage rates.

Even before they felt the full impact of these developments, farmers began to organize. With aid from Oliver H. Kelley, a clerk in the Department of Agriculture, farmers in almost every state during the 1860s and 1870s founded a network of local organizations called Granges, dedicated to improving economic and social conditions. By 1875 the national Grange had twenty thousand branches and a million members. Like voluntary organizations throughout the country,

||||||||||||||||||||||||||||||
Grange Movement

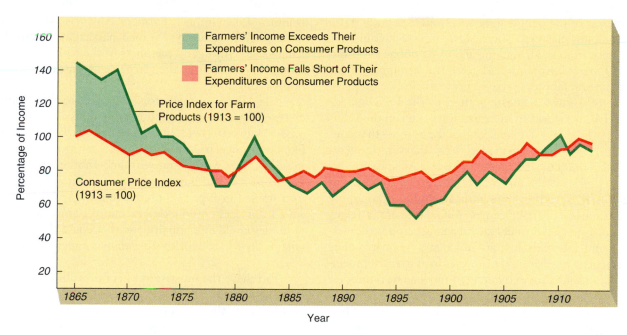

Figure 20.1   **Consumer Prices and Farm Product Prices, 1865–1913**
Until the late 1870s, in spite of falling farm prices, farmers were able to receive from their crops
more income than they spent on consumer goods. But beginning in the mid-1880s, consumer prices
leveled off and then rose, while prices for farm products continued to drop. As a result, farmers
found it increasingly difficult to afford consumer goods, a problem that plagued them well into the
twentieth century.

Granges had constitutions, elected officers, and membership oaths. Strongest in the Midwest and South, Granges
sponsored meetings and educational events to relieve the
loneliness of farm life. Family-oriented local Granges welcomed women's participation.

As membership flourished, Granges turned to economic and political action. Many Grange members joined
the Greenback Labor Party, formed in 1876 to advocate
expanding the money supply by keeping "greenbacks"—
the paper money created by the government during the
Civil War to help pay costs—in circulation. Local Grange
branches formed cooperative associations to buy supplies
and to market crops and livestock. In a few instances,
Grangers operated farm-implement factories and insurance companies. Most enterprises failed, however, because
farmers lacked capital for large-scale buying and because
competition from large manufacturers and dealers undercut them. For example, the mail-order firm Montgomery
Ward could furnish rural customers with cheaper products
more conveniently than could Granges.

Despite their efforts, Granges declined in the late
1870s. They achieved some political successes, convincing
states to establish agricultural colleges, electing sympathetic legislators, and pressing state legislatures for so-
called Granger laws to regulate transportation and storage
rates. But these ventures faltered when, in the *Wabash* case
of 1886, the U.S. Supreme Court overturned Granger
laws by denying states the power to regulate railroad rates.
Granges disavowed party politics and thus would not challenge the power of business interests within the two major
parties. After a brief assertion of economic and political
influence, Granges again became farmers' social clubs.

In the Southwest, migrations of English-speaking
ranchers into pastureland used communally by Mexican
farmers and villagers sparked an-
other kind of agrarian protest. In
the late 1880s, a group calling itself
Las Gorras Blancas, or the White
Hats, struggled to control lands that their Mexican ancestors had once held. They harassed Anglo ranchers and
destroyed fences that Anglos had erected on public land.
Sounding like the Grangers and Knights of Labor before
them and the Populists after them, the White Hats proclaimed in 1889, "Our purpose is to protect the rights

The White Hats

and interest of the people in general and especially those of the helpless classes." Their cause, however, could not halt Anglos from legally buying and using public land, and by 1900 many Hispanics had given up farming to work as agricultural laborers or to migrate to cities.

By 1890, rural activism shifted to the Farmers' Alliances, two networks of organizations—one in the Great Plains, one in the South—that constituted a new mass movement.

Farmers' Alliances

(The West also had Alliance groups, but they tended to be smaller and more closely linked to labor radicals and antimonopoly organizations.) The first Farmers' Alliances arose in Texas, where hard-pressed farmers rallied against crop liens, merchants, and railroads in particular, and against money power in general. Using traveling lecturers to recruit members, Alliance leaders extended the movement into other southern states. By 1889 the southern Alliance boasted 2 million members, and a separate Colored Farmers' National Alliance claimed 1 million black members. A similar movement arose in the Plains, which in the late 1880s organized 2 million members in Kansas, Nebraska, and the Dakotas. Like Granges, Farmers' Alliances tried to foster feelings of community. Women participated actively in Alliance activities, and members of the Knights of Labor were invited to join in the "struggle against monopolistic oppression."

The Alliance remedy for economic woes combined a culture of generosity with government assistance. To bypass corporate power and to control markets, Alliances, like the Grange, proposed that farmers form cooperatives, in which they would join with one another to sell crops and livestock, and buy supplies and manufactured goods, as a unified group. By pooling resources, Alliances reasoned, farmers could exert far more economic pressure than they could individually, and they could share the benefits of their hard work rather than competing with each other.

To relieve the most serious rural problem, shortages of cash and credit, Alliances put forward a system of government aid called a subtreasury. The plan had two parts. One called for the federal government to construct warehouses where farmers could store nonperishable crops while awaiting higher market prices; the government

▲ Exhibited at the Chicago World's Fair of 1893, this cabin was the site of the first Farmers' Alliance meeting in Lampasas County, Texas. Using recruiters, rallies, and meetings replete with slogans like "We Are All Mortgaged But Our Votes," the organization voiced the grievances of rural America and laid the groundwork for formation of the Populist party in the 1890s. *(Private Collection)*

would then loan farmers Treasury notes amounting to 80 percent of the market price that the stored crops would bring. Farmers could use these notes as money to pay debts and make purchases. Once the stored crops were sold, farmers would repay the loans plus small interest and storage fees. This provision would enable farmers to avoid the exploitative crop-lien system.

The subtreasury plan's second part would provide low-interest government loans to farmers who wanted to buy land. These loans, along with the Treasury notes loaned to farmers who temporarily stored crops in government warehouses, would inject cash into the economy and encourage the kind of inflation that advocates hoped would raise crop prices without raising other prices. If the government subsidized business through tariffs and land grants, reasoned Alliance members, why should it not help farmers earn a decent living, too?

If all Farmers' Alliances had been able to unite politically, they could have been a formidable force; but racial and sectional differences and personality clashes thwarted early attempts at merging. Racial barriers weakened Alliance voter strength because, as noted earlier, southern white Democrats had succeeded in creating voting restrictions that prevented African Americans from becoming a political force. In addition, raw racism impeded acceptance of blacks by white Alliances. Some southern leaders, such as Georgia's Senator Tom Watson, tried to unite distressed black and white farmers, realizing that both races suffered from similar burdens. But poor white farmers could not forgo their prejudices. Many came from families that had once owned slaves; they considered African Americans an inferior people and took comfort in the belief that there always would be people worse off than they were. At an 1889 meeting in St. Louis, white southerners rejected uniting with northern Alliances because such a merger would have ended secret Alliance activities and whites-only membership rules.

Problems in Achieving Alliance Unity

Differences on regional issues also prevented unity. Northern Alliances declined to merge with southerners, fearing domination by more experienced southern leaders. Northern farmers also favored protective tariffs to keep out foreign grain, whereas white southerners wanted low tariffs to hold down costs of imported manufactured goods. Northern and southern Alliances agreed on some issues, however: both favored government regulation of railroads, equitable taxation, currency reform, an end to alleged election frauds that perpetuated special interests in office, and prohibition of landownership by foreign investors.

In spite of their initial divisions, growing membership and rising confidence drew Alliances into politics. By 1890, farmers had elected several officeholders sympathetic to their cause, especially in the South, where Alliances controlled four governorships, eight state legislatures, and forty-seven seats in Congress (forty-four in the House, three in the Senate). In the Midwest, Alliance candidates often ran on third-party tickets, such as the Greenback Party, and achieved some success in Kansas, Nebraska, and the Dakotas. Leaders crisscrossed the country organizing meetings to recruit support for a new party. During the summer of 1890, the Kansas Alliance held a "convention of the people" and nominated candidates who swept the state's fall elections. Formation of this People's, or Populist, Party gave a title to Alliance political activism. (Populism, derived from populus, the Latin word for "people," is the political doctrine that asserts the rights and powers of common people in their struggle against the privileged elite.) The Alliance election successes in 1890 energized efforts to unite Alliance groups into a single Populist party. By 1892, southern Alliance members were ready to leave the Democratic Party and join northern counterparts in summoning a People's Party convention to draft a platform and nominate a presidential candidate. The gathering met in Omaha, Nebraska, on July 4.

Rise of Populism

The new party's platform was a sweeping reform document, reflecting its goals of moral regeneration, political democracy, and antimonopolism. Its preamble charged that the nation had been "brought to the verge of moral, political, and material ruin. Corruption dominates the ballot box, the legislatures, the Congress, and . . . even the [courts]." Charging that inequality (between white classes) threatened to splinter society, the platform declared, "The fruits of the toil of millions are boldly stolen to build up colossal fortunes for a few," and that "wealth belongs to him that creates it." The document addressed three central sources of rural unrest: transportation, land, and money. Frustrated with weak state and federal regulation, Populists demanded government ownership of railroad and telegraph lines. They urged the federal government to reclaim all land owned for speculative purposes by railroads and foreigners. The monetary plank called on the government to expand the currency by making more money available for farm loans and by restoring free and unlimited coinage of silver. Other planks advocated a graduated income tax, postal savings banks, direct election of U.S. senators, and a shorter workday. As its presidential candidate, the party nominated James B. Weaver of Iowa, a former

Russian Populism

Before American Populism arose late in the nineteenth century, a different form of populism took shape in another largely rural country: Russia. Whereas American Populism emerged from the Alliance organizations of farmers, Russian populism was the creation of intellectuals who wanted to educate peasants to agitate for social and economic freedom.

Propelled by reforms imposed by Czar Alexander II, Russian society had begun to modernize in the mid-nineteenth century. Government administration and the judiciary were reformed, town governments were given control of local taxation, and education became more widespread. Perhaps most importantly, in 1861 Alexander signed an Edict of Emancipation, freeing Russian serfs (slaves attached to specific lands) and granting them compensation to buy land from their landlords. The reforms were slow to take hold, however, prompting some young, educated Russians, called nihilists because they opposed the czar and feudalism, to press for more radical reforms, including socialism. The reformers became known as *narodniki,* or populists, from *narod,* the Russian term for "peasant."

Narodniki envisioned a society of self-governing village communes, somewhat like the cooperatives proposed by American Farmers' Alliances, and in the 1870s they visited Russian villages attempting to educate peasants to their ideas. One of their leaders, Peter Lavrov, believed that intellectuals needed to narrow the gap between themselves and the people, and help the masses improve their lives. This message, however, included a more radical tone than the American Populists' campaign for democracy, because Russian populists believed that only a social revolution, an uprising against the czar, could realize their goals. When Alexander instituted repressive policies against the *narodniki* in the late 1870s, many of them turned to terrorism, a move that resulted in the assassination of Alexander II in 1881.

Russian populism failed in different ways than American Populism. Russian peasants were not receptive to the intervention of educated young people, and many peasants remained tied to tradition and could not abandon their loyalty to the czar. Government arrests and imprisonments after Alexander's assassination discouraged populists' efforts, and the movement declined. Nevertheless, just as many of the aims of American Populists were adopted by reformers after the turn of the century, the ideas of Russian populism became the cornerstone of the Russian Revolution of 1917 and of Soviet social and political ideology that followed.

Russian peasants, like American tenant farmers and owners of small landholdings, suffered from poverty and pressures of the expanded market economy. The plight of struggling Russian farm families stirred up empathy from young populist intellectuals, who adopted radical solutions that did not capture as much political fervor among farmers as American populism did. *(Bettmann/Corbis)*

Union general and supporter of an expanded money supply, who already had run for the presidency when he was the Greenback Party's candidate in 1880.

The Populist campaign featured dynamic personalities and rousing rhetoric. The Kansas plains rumbled with speeches not only by Mary Lease but also by "Sockless Jerry" Simpson, an unschooled but canny rural reformer who got his nickname after he ridiculed silk-stockinged wealthy people, causing a reporter to muse that Simpson probably wore no stockings at all. The South produced equally dynamic leaders, such as Texas's Charles W. Macune, Georgia's Tom Watson, and North Carolina's Leonidas Polk. Colorado's governor, Davis "Bloody Bridles" Waite, attacked mine owners with prolabor and antimonopoly rhetoric. Texas's Governor James Hogg battled railroads and other corporations. Minnesota's Ignatius Donnelly, pseudoscientist and writer of apocalyptic novels, became chief visionary of the northern plains and penned the Omaha platform's thunderous language. The cam-

Populist Spokespeople

paign also attracted opportunists, such as one-eyed, sharp-tongued "Pitchfork Ben" Tillman of South Carolina, who were not genuine Populists but used agrarian fervor for their own political ends.

In the 1892 presidential election, Populist candidate James Weaver garnered 8 percent of the popular vote, majorities in four states, and twenty-two electoral votes. Not since 1856 had a third party done so well in its first national effort. Nevertheless, the party faced a dilemma of whether to stand by its principles at all costs or compromise in order to gain power. The election had been successful for Populists only in the West. The vote-rich Northeast ignored Weaver, and Alabama was the only southern state that gave Populists as much as one-third of its votes.

Still, Populism gave rural dwellers in the South and West faith in a future of cooperation and democracy. Although Populists were flawed egalitarians—they mistrusted blacks and foreigners—they sought change in order to fulfill their version of American ideals. Amid hardship and desperation, millions of people came to believe that a cooperative democracy in which government would ensure equal opportunity could overcome corporate power. A banner draped above the stage at the Omaha convention captured the movement's spirit: "We do not ask for sympathy or pity. We ask for justice." With this goal in mind, Populists looked ahead to the presidential election of 1896 with hope.

THE DEPRESSION AND PROTESTS OF THE 1890s

Before that election took place, however, the nation suffered a major economic disruption. In 1893, shortly before Grover Cleveland's second presidency began, the Philadelphia & Reading Railroad, once a thriving and profitable line, went bankrupt. Like other railroads, it had borrowed heavily to lay track and build stations and bridges. But overexpansion cut into profits, and ultimately the company was unable to pay its debts.

The same problem beset manufacturers. For example, output at McCormick farm machinery factories was nine times greater in 1893 than in 1879, but revenues had only tripled. To compensate, the company bought more equipment and squeezed more work out of fewer laborers. This strategy, however, increased debt and unemployment. Jobless workers found themselves in the same plight as employers: they could not pay their bills. Banks suffered, too, when their customers defaulted. The failure of the National Cordage Company in May 1893 sparked a chain reaction of business and bank closings. By year's end,

▲ Mary Elizabeth Lease (1850–1933) was one of the founders of the Populist party in Kansas. Tall and intense, she had a deep, almost hypnotic voice which made her an effective publicist for the farmers' cause. She gave a seconding speech to the presidential nomination of James B. Weaver in 1892.

(The Kansas State Historical Society, Topeka, Kansas)

five hundred banks and sixteen hundred businesses had failed. An adviser warned President Cleveland, "We are on the eve of a very dark night." He was right. Between 1893 and 1897, the nation suffered a devastating economic depression.

Personal hardship followed business collapse; nearly 20 percent of the labor force was jobless for a significant time during the depression. Falling demand caused prices to drop between 1892 and 1895, but layoffs and wage cuts more than offset declining living costs. Many people could not afford basic necessities. The New York police estimated that twenty thousand homeless and jobless people roamed the city's streets. Surveying the impact on Boston, Henry Adams wrote, "Men died like flies under the strain, and Boston grew suddenly old, haggard, and thin."

As the depression deepened, the currency dilemma reached a crisis. The Sherman Silver Purchase Act of 1890

Continuing Currency Problems

had committed the government to use Treasury notes (silver certificates) to buy 4.5 million ounces of silver each month. Recipients could redeem these certificates for gold, at the ratio of one ounce of gold for every sixteen ounces' worth of silver. But a western mining boom made silver more plentiful, causing its market value relative to gold to fall and prompting holders of Sherman silver notes and greenback currency issued during the Civil War to cash in their notes in exchange for more valuable gold. As a result, the nation's gold reserve dwindled, falling below $100 million in early 1893.

The $100 million level had psychological importance. If investors believed that the country's gold reserve was disappearing, they would lose confidence in America's economic stability and refrain from investing. British capitalists, for example, owned some $4 billion in American stocks and bonds. If dollars were to depreciate because there was too little gold to back them up, the British would stop investing in American economic growth. In fact, the lower the gold reserve dropped, the more people rushed to redeem their money—to get gold before it disappeared. Panic spread, causing more bankruptcies and unemployment.

Vowing to protect the gold reserve, President Cleveland called a special session of Congress to repeal the Sherman Silver Purchase Act. Repeal passed in late 1893, but the run on gold continued through 1894. In early 1895, reserves fell to $41 million. In desperation, Cleveland accepted an offer of 3.5 million ounces of gold in return for $65 million worth of federal bonds from a banking syndicate led by financier J. P. Morgan. When

the bankers resold the bonds to the public, they made a $2 million profit. Cleveland claimed that he had saved the reserves, but discontented farmers, workers, silver miners, and even some of Cleveland's Democratic allies saw only humiliation in the president's deal with big businessmen. "When Judas betrayed Christ," charged Senator Tillman, "his heart was not blacker than this scoundrel, Cleveland, in betraying the [Democratic Party]."

Few people knew what the president was privately enduring. At about the time Cleveland called Congress into special session, doctors discovered a tumor on his palate that required immediate removal. Fearful that publicity of his illness would hasten the run on gold, and intent on preventing Vice President Adlai E. Stevenson, a silver supporter, from gaining influence, Cleveland kept his condition a secret. He announced that he was going sailing, and doctors removed his cancerous upper left jaw while the yacht floated outside New York City. Outfitted with a rubber jaw, Cleveland resumed a full schedule five days later, hiding terrible pain to dispel rumors that he was seriously ill. He eventually recovered, but those who knew of his surgery believed it had sapped his vitality.

The deal between Cleveland and Morgan did not end the depression. After improving slightly in 1895, the economy plunged again. Farm income, declining since 1887, continued to slide; factories closed; banks that remained open restricted withdrawals. The tight money supply depressed housing construction, drying up jobs and reducing immigration. Cities like Detroit encouraged citizens to cultivate "potato patches" on vacant land to help alleviate food shortages. Each night, urban police stations filled up with homeless persons who had no place to stay.

The depression ultimately ran its course. In the final years of the century, gold discoveries in Alaska, good harvests, and industrial growth brought relief. But the downturn

Consequences of the Depression

hastened the crumbling of the old economic system and the emergence of a new one. The American economy had expanded well beyond local and sectional bases; the fate of a large business in one part of the country had repercussions elsewhere. When farmers in the West fell into debt and lost purchasing power, their depressed condition in turn affected the economic health of railroads, farm-implement manufacturers, and banks in other regions. Moreover, the trend toward corporate consolidation that characterized the new business system had tempted many companies that had expanded too rapidly. When contraction occurred, as it did in 1893, their reckless debts dragged them down, and they pulled other industries with them.

At the same time, a new global marketplace was emerging, forcing American farmers to contend not only with discriminatory transportation rates and falling crop prices at home, but also with Canadian and Russian wheat growers, Argentine cattle ranchers, Indian and Egyptian cotton manufacturers, and Australian wool producers. More than ever before, the condition of one country's economy affected the economies of other countries. In addition, the glutted domestic market persuaded American businessmen to seek new markets abroad (see Chapter 22).

The depression exposed fundamental tensions in the industrial system. Technological and organizational

Depression-Era Protests

changes had been widening the gap between employees and employers for half a century, and an upsurge of dissent emerged from this gap. The era of labor protest began with the railroad strikes of 1877. The vehemence of those strikes, and the support they drew from working-class people, raised fears that the United States would experience a popular uprising like one in France in 1871, which had briefly overturned the government and introduced communist principles. The Haymarket riot of 1886, a general strike in New Orleans in 1891, and a prolonged strike at the Carnegie Homestead Steel plant in 1892 heightened anxieties. In the West, embittered workers also rebelled. In 1892 violence erupted at a silver mine in Coeur d'Alene, Idaho. Angered by wage cuts and a lockout, striking miners seized the mine and battled federal troops sent to subdue them.

To many middle- and upper-class people, it seemed as if worker protests portended an economic and political explosion. In 1894, the year the economy plunged into depression, there were over thirteen hundred strikes and countless riots. Contrary to accusations of business leaders, few protesters were anarchists or communists come from Europe to sabotage American democracy. Rather, the disaffected included thousands of men and women who believed that in a democracy their voices should be heard.

Small numbers of socialists participated in these and other confrontations. Some socialists believed that work-

Socialists

ers should control factories and businesses; others supported government ownership. All socialists, however, opposed the private enterprise of capitalism. Their ideas derived from the writings of Karl Marx (1818–1883), the German philosopher and father of communism, who contended that who-

ever controls the means of production determines how well people live. Marx wrote that industrial capitalism generates profits by paying workers less than the value of their labor and that mechanization and mass production alienate workers from their labor. Thus, Marx contended, capitalists and laborers engage in an inescapable conflict over how much workers will benefit from their efforts. According to Marx, only by abolishing the return on capital—profits—could labor receive its true value, an outcome possible only if workers owned the means of production. Marx predicted that workers worldwide would become so discontented that they would revolt and seize factories, farms, banks, and transportation lines. This revolution would establish a socialist order of justice and equality. Marx's vision appealed to some workers, including many who did not consider themselves socialists, because it promised independence and abundance. It appealed to some intellectuals as well, because it promised to end class conflict and crass materialism.

In America, socialism suffered from disagreement over how to achieve Marx's vision. Much of the movement consisted of ideas brought in by immigrants, first from Germany but also by Russian Jews, Italians, Hungarians, and Poles. Although American socialism splintered into small groups, one of its main factions was the Socialist Labor Party, led by Daniel DeLeon, a fiery editor and lawyer born in Curacao and educated in Germany, who criticized American labor organizations like the AFL as too conservative. Yet, as he and other socialist leaders argued fine points of doctrine, they ignored workers' everyday needs and thus failed to attract the mass of laborers. Nor could they rebut the clergy and business leaders who celebrated opportunity, self-improvement, and consumerism. Social mobility and the philosophy of individualism also undermined socialist aims. Workers hoped that they or their children would benefit through education and acquisition of property or by becoming their own boss; most American workers sought individual advancement rather than the betterment of all.

As the nineteenth century closed, however, American socialism generated a new and inspiring leader. Indiana-

Eugene V. Debs

born Eugene V. Debs headed the newly formed American Railway Union which had carried out the 1894 strike against the Pullman Company. Jailed for defying the injunction against striking rail workers, Debs read works of Karl Marx in prison. Once released, he flirted briefly with Populism, then became the leading spokesman for American socialism, combining visionary Marxism with Jeffersonian and Populist antimonopolism. Debs captivated audiences with passionate eloquence and indignant attacks on the free-enterprise system. "Many of you think you are competing," he would lecture. "Against whom? Against Rockefeller? About as I would if I had a wheelbarrow and competed with the Santa Fe [railroad] from here to Kansas City." By 1900 the group soon to be called the Socialist Party of America was uniting around Debs. It would make its presence felt more forcefully in the new century.

In 1894, however, not Debs but rather a quiet businessman named Jacob Coxey from Massillon, Ohio, captured public attention with his act of protest. Coxey had a vision. He was convinced that, to aid debtors, the government should issue

|||||||||||||||||||||||||||||||
Coxey's Army

$500 million of "legal tender" paper money and make low-interest loans to local governments, which would in turn use the funds to pay the unemployed to build roads and other public works. He planned to publicize his scheme by leading a march from Massillon to Washington, D.C., gathering a "petition in boots" of unemployed workers along the way. Coxey even christened his newborn son Legal Tender and proposed that his teenage daughter lead the procession on a white horse.

Coxey's army, about 200 strong, left in March 1894. Moving across Ohio into Pennsylvania, the marchers received food and housing in depressed industrial towns and rural villages, and they attracted additional recruits. Elsewhere, a dozen similar processions from places such as Seattle, San Francisco, and Los Angeles also began the trek eastward. Sore feet prompted some marchers to commandeer trains, but most marches were peaceful and law-abiding.

Coxey's band of 500, including women and children, entered Washington on April 30. The next day (May Day, the anniversary of the Haymarket violence), the group, armed with "war clubs of peace," advanced to the Capitol. When Coxey and a few others vaulted the wall surrounding the Capitol grounds, mounted police moved in and routed the demonstrators. Coxey tried to speak from the Capitol steps, but police dragged him away. As arrests and clubbings continued, Coxey's dream of a demonstration of 400,000 jobless workers dissolved. Like the strikes, the first people's march on Washington yielded to police muscle.

Unlike socialists, who wished to replace the capitalist system, Coxey's troops merely wanted more jobs and better living standards. Today, in an age of union contracts, regulation of business, and government-sponsored unemployment relief, their goals do not appear radical. The brutal reactions of officials, however, reveal how threatening

dissenters like Coxey and Debs seemed to defenders of the existing social order.

THE SILVER CRUSADE AND THE ELECTION OF 1896

Amid the tumult of social protest and economic depression, it appeared that the presidential election of 1896 would be pivotal. Debates over money and power were climaxing, Democrats and Republicans continued their battle over control of Congress and the presidency, and the Populists stood at the center of the political whirlwind. The key question was whether or not voters would abandon old party loyalties for the Populist party.

The Populist crusade against "money power" settled on the issue of silver, which many people saw as a simple solution to the nation's complex ills. To them, free coinage of silver symbolized an end to special privileges for the rich and the return of

|||||||||||||||||||||||||||||||
Free Silver

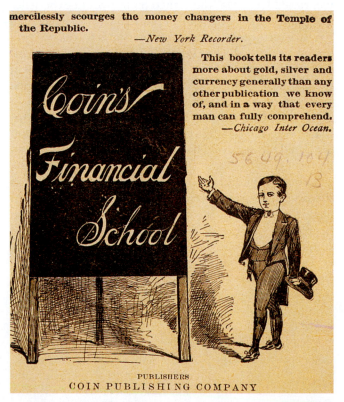

mercilessly scourges the money changers in the Temple of the Republic.
—*New York Recorder.*

This book tells its readers more about gold, silver and currency generally than any other publication we know of, and in a way that every man can fully comprehend.
—*Chicago Inter Ocean.*

Coin's Financial School

PUBLISHERS
COIN PUBLISHING COMPANY

▲ Published in 1894, *Coin's Financial School* by William H. Harvey expressed the position of free silver in simple language and illustrations. Written in the form of lectures on the money question given by "Professor Coin," Harvey's book had enormous appeal to distressed farmers. *(Trustees of the Boston Public Library)* government to the people, because it would lift the common people out of debt, increase the amount of cash in circulation, and reduce interest rates. Populists made free coinage of silver their political battle cry.

As the election of 1896 approached, Populists had to decide how to translate their few previous electoral victories into larger success. Should they join with sympathetic factions of the major parties, thus risking a loss of identity, or should they remain an independent third party and settle for minor wins at best? Except in mining areas of the Rocky Mountain states, where free coinage of silver had strong support, Republicans were unlikely allies because their support for the gold standard and their big-business orientation represented what Populists opposed.

In the North and West, alliance with Democrats was more plausible. There, the Democratic Party retained vestiges of antimonopoly ideology and sympathy for a looser currency system, though "gold Democrats," such as President Cleveland and Senator David Hill of New York, held powerful influence. Populists assumed they shared common interests with Democratic urban workers, who they believed suffered the same oppression that beset farmers. In the South, Alliances had previously supported Democratic candidates, but the failure of these candidates to carry out their promises once in office caused southern farmers to feel betrayed. Whichever option they chose, fusion (alliance with Democrats) or independence, Populists ensured that the election campaign of 1896 would be the most issue oriented since 1860.

As they prepared to nominate their presidential candidate, both parties were divided internally. Republicans were guided by Ohio industrialist Marcus A. Hanna, who for a year had been maneuvering to win the nomination for Ohio's governor, William McKinley. By the time the party convened in St. Louis, Hanna had corralled enough delegates to succeed. "He had advertised McKinley," quipped Theodore Roosevelt, "as if he were a patent medicine." The Republicans' only distress

Republican Nomination of McKinley

THE LOCKOUT IS ENDED; HE HOLDS THE KEY.

▲ During the 1896 presidential campaign, Republicans depicted their candidate, William McKinley, as holding the key to prosperity for both the working man and the white-collar laborer, shown here raising their hats to the candidate. Republicans successfully made this economic theme, rather than the silver crusade of McKinley's unsuccessful opponent, William Jennings Bryan, the difference in the election's outcome. *(Collection of David J. and Janice L. Frent)* occurred when they adopted a moderate platform supporting the gold standard, rejecting a prosilver stance proposed by Colorado senator Henry M. Teller. Teller, who had been among the party's founders forty years earlier, walked out of the convention in tears, taking a small group of silver Republicans with him.

At the Democratic convention, prosilver delegates wearing silver badges and waving silver banners paraded through the Chicago Amphitheatre. Observing their tumultuous demonstrations, one delegate wrote, "For the first time I can understand the scenes of the French Revolution!" A *New York World* reporter remarked that "all the silverites need is a Moses." They found one in William Jennings Bryan.

Bryan arrived at the Democratic convention as a member of a contested Nebraska delegation. A former congressman whose support for coinage of silver had annoyed President Cleveland, Bryan found the depression's impact on midwestern farmers distressing. Shortly after the convention seated Bryan and his colleagues instead of a competing faction that supported the gold standard, Bryan joined the party's resolutions committee and helped write a platform calling for unlimited coinage of silver. When the committee presented the platform to the full convention, Bryan rose to speak on its behalf. His now-famous closing words ignited the delegates.

|||||||||||||||||||||||||||||||||

William Jennings Bryan

> Having behind us the producing masses of this nation and the world, supported by the commercial interests, the laboring interests, and the toilers everywhere, we will answer [the wealthy classes'] demand for a gold standard by saying to them: You shall not press down upon the brow of labor this crown of thorns, you shall not crucify mankind upon a cross of gold.

The speech could not have been better timed. Delegates who backed Bryan for president now began enlisting support. It took five ballots to win the nomination, but the magnetic "Boy Orator" proved irresistible. In accepting the silverite goals of southerners and westerners, and repudiating Cleveland's policies in its platform, the Democratic Party became more attractive to discontented farmers. But, like the Republicans, it, too, alienated a minority wing. Some gold Democrats withdrew and nominated their own candidate.

Bryan's nomination presented the Populist party convention meeting in St. Louis with a dilemma. Should Populists join Democrats in support of Bryan, or should they nominate their own candidate? Tom Watson, who opposed fusion with Democrats, warned that "the Demo-

▲ William Jennings Bryan (1860–1925) posed for this photograph in 1896, when he first ran for president at the age of thirty-six. Bryan's emotional speeches turned agrarian unrest and the issue of free silver into a moral crusade. *(Library of Congress)*

cratic idea of fusion [is] that we play Jonah while they play whale." Others reasoned that supporting a separate candidate would split the anti-McKinley vote and guarantee a Republican victory. In the end the convention compromised, first naming Watson as its vice-presidential nominee to preserve party identity (Democrats had nominated Maine shipping magnate Arthur Sewall for vice president) and then nominating Bryan for president.

The campaign, as Kansas journalist William Allen White observed, "took the form of religious frenzy . . . as the crusaders of the revolution rode home, praising the people's will as though it were God's will and cursing wealth for its iniquity." Bryan preached that "every great economic question is in reality a great moral question." Republicans countered Bryan's attacks on privilege by predicting chaos if he won. While Bryan raced around the country giving twenty speeches a day, Hanna invited thousands of people to McKinley's home in Canton, Ohio, where the candidate plied them with homilies on moderation and prosperity, promising something for everyone. In an appeal to working-class voters, Republicans stressed the new jobs that a protective tariff would create.

The election results revealed that the political standoff had finally ended. McKinley, symbol of urban and

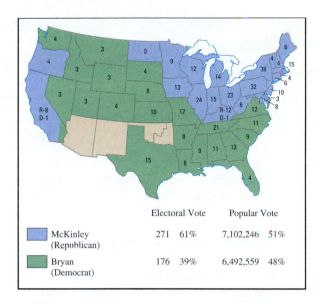

	Electoral Vote	Popular Vote
■ McKinley (Republican)	271 61%	7,102,246 51%
■ Bryan (Democrat)	176 39%	6,492,559 48%

Map 20.1   **Presidential Election, 1896**

William Jennings Bryan had strong voter support in the South and West, but the numerically superior industrial states, plus California, created majorities for William McKinley.

Election Results

corporate ascendancy, beat Bryan by 600,000 popular votes and won in the electoral college by 271 to 176 (see Map 20.1). It was the most lopsided presidential election since 1872.

Bryan worked hard to rally the nation, but obsession with silver prevented Populists from building the urban-rural coalition that would have expanded their political appeal. The silver issue diverted voters from focusing on broader reforms of cooperation and government aid deriving from the Alliance movement and the 1892 Omaha platform. Urban workers, who might have benefited from Populist goals, feared that silver coinage would shrink the value of their wages. Labor leaders, such as the AFL's Samuel Gompers, though partly sympathetic, would not commit themselves fully because they viewed farmers as businessmen, not workers. And socialists like Daniel DeLeon denounced Populists as "retrograde" because they, unlike socialists, believed in free enterprise. Thus the Populist crusade collapsed. Although Populists and fusion candidates won a few state and congressional elections, the Bryan-Watson ticket of the Populist party polled only 222,600 votes nationwide.

As president, McKinley reinforced his support of business by signing the Gold Standard Act (1900), requiring that all paper money be backed by gold. A seasoned and personable politician, McKinley was best known for crafting protective tariffs; as a congressman, he had guided passage of record-high tariff rates in 1890. He accordingly supported the Dingley Tariff of 1897, which raised duties even higher. Domestic tensions subsided as prosperity returned. A believer in opening new markets abroad to sustain profits at home, McKinley encouraged imperialistic ventures in Latin America and the Pacific. Good times and victory in the Spanish-American War enabled him to beat Bryan again in 1900.

The McKinley Presidency

SUMMARY

Politicians during the Gilded Age succeeded in making many modest, and some major, accomplishments. Guided by well-meaning, generally competent people, much of what occurred in statehouses, the halls of Congress, and the White House prepared the nation for the twentieth century. Laws encouraging economic growth with some principles of regulation, measures expanding government agencies while reducing crass patronage, and federal intervention in trade and currency issues all evolved during the 1870s and 1880s.

True to Mary Lease's characterization, the United States remained a "nation of inconsistencies." Those who supported disfranchisement of African Americans and continued discrimination against both blacks and women still polluted politics. People in power, often representing special-interest groups, could not tolerate radical views like those expressed by socialists, Coxey, or Populists, but many of the ideas raised by these groups continued to find supporters as the new century dawned.

The 1896 election realigned national politics. The Republican Party, founded in the 1850s amid a crusade against slavery and benefiting from northern victory in the Civil War, became the majority party by emphasizing government aid to business, expanding its social base among the urban middle class, and playing down its moralism. The Democratic Party miscalculated on the silver issue but held its traditional support in the South and in urban political machines. At the national level, however, loyalties lacked the potency they once had. Suspicion of party politics increased, and voter participation rates declined. The Populists tried to energize a third-party movement, but their success was fleeting. A new kind

Legacy FOR A PEOPLE AND A NATION

Interpreting a Fairy Tale

The Wizard of Oz, one of the most popular movies of all time, began as a work of juvenile literature penned by journalist L. Frank Baum in 1900. Originally titled *The Wonderful Wizard of Oz,* the story used memorable characters to create a fun-filled and adventurous quest.

Although children have viewed the tale and film as a fantasy, adults have been tempted to seek hidden meanings. In 1964 one scholar, Henry M. Littlefield, published an article in which he asserted that Baum really intended to write a Populist parable about the conditions of overburdened farmers and laborers. The characters in *The Wonderful Wizard,* Littlefield opined, supported his theory. Dorothy symbolized the well-intentioned common person; the Scarecrow, the struggling farmer; the Tin Man, the industrial worker. Hoping for a better life, these friends, along with the Cowardly Lion (William Jennings Bryan with a loud roar but little power), followed a yellow brick road (the gold standard) that led nowhere. The Emerald City that they find is presided over by a wizard, who rules from behind a screen. A typical politician, the wizard tries to be all things to all people, but Dorothy reveals him as a fraud. Dorothy is able to leave this muddled society and return to her simple Kansas farm family of Aunt Em and Uncle Henry by using her magical silver slippers (representing coinage of silver, though the movie made them red).

Subsequent theorists, though sometimes qualifying Littlefield, identified additional symbols, such as Oz being the abbreviation for ounces (oz.), the chief measurement of gold. The Wicked Witch of the East—who, Baum wrote, kept the little people (Munchkins) "in bondage, . . . making them slaves for her night and day"—could be seen as representing the force of industrial capitalism. Baum's story, seen in film by most Americans, became a tool for explaining Populism to students, and by the 1970s its apparent message had strong appeal to critics of "the Establishment."

But then investigators began to take another look and to offer different conclusions. In 1983 historian William R. Leach asserted that Baum's tale actually was a celebration of urban consumer culture. Its language exalted the opulence of Emerald City, which to Leach resembled the "White City" of the Chicago World's Fair of 1893, and Dorothy's upbeat nature symbolized the optimism of the industrial era. Moreover, Baum's career supported this new interpretation. Before he was a writer, he had designed display windows and was involved in theater—activities that gave him an appreciation of modern urban life.

Rather than confusion, the real legacy of *The Wonderful Wizard of Oz* has been its ability to provoke differing interpretations. What matters is that Baum's fairy tale, the first truly American work of this sort, has bequeathed to the present so many fascinating images about the diversity and contradictions of American culture.

of politics was brewing, one in which technical experts and scientific organization would attempt to supplant the backroom deals and favoritism that had characterized the previous age.

Although the silver issue faded, by 1920 many Populist goals had been incorporated by the major parties, including regulation of railroads, banks, and utilities; shorter workdays; a variant of the subtreasury plan; a graduated income tax; and direct election of senators. These reforms succeeded because a variety of groups united behind them. Immigration, urbanization, and industrialization had transformed the United States into a pluralistic society in which compromise among interest groups had become a political fact of life. As the Gilded Age ended, business was still in the ascendancy, and large segments of the population were still excluded from political and economic opportunity. But the winds of dissent and reform had begun to blow more strongly.

SUGGESTIONS FOR FURTHER READING

Edward L. Ayers, *The Promise of the New South: Life After Reconstruction* (1992)

Nancy Cohen, *The Reconstruction of American Liberalism, 1865–1914* (2002)

Glenda Elizabeth Gilmore, *Gender and Jim Crow: Women and the Politics of White Supremacy in North Carolina, 1896–1920* (1996)

Steven Hahn, *A Nation Under Our Feet: Black Political Struggles in the Rural South, from Slavery to the Great Migration* (2003)

Michael Kazin, *The Populist Persuasion: An American History* (1995)

Jean V. Matthews, *The Rise of the New Woman: The Women's Movement in America, 1875–1930* (2003)

Nick Salvatore, *Eugene V. Debs: Citizen and Socialist* (1992)

The Progressive Era *1895-1920*

*H*hat Ben Lindsey saw made him furious. As a young Colorado lawyer in the 1890s, he had been asked by a judge to defend two boys, about twelve years old, accused of burglary. The boys had already been imprisoned for sixty days without a trial and did not understand what the word *burglary* meant, let alone how the justice system worked. When he went to visit them in jail, Lindsey found the youngsters playing poker with two older cellmates, one a safe cracker and the other a horse thief. Lindsey asked the warden how many other boys were in the jail. "Oh, quite a number" was the answer. Outraged that "good-natured" children were housed with hardened criminals, Lindsey later wrote, "Here were two boys, neither of them serious enemies of society, who were about to be convicted of burglary and have felony records for the rest of their lives. . . . I had made up my mind to smash the system that meant so much injustice to youth."

In 1901 Lindsey ran for county judge and began a long career fighting on behalf of juvenile protection. He spoke and wrote extensively about protecting children from criminal prosecution, exploitative labor practices, and the burdens of poverty. He and his wife, Henrietta, worked ceaselessly to spread the idea of a separate juvenile court system and to aid families whose children they thought might be at risk of becoming criminals. They wrote reform laws that were adopted by many states and foreign countries. The Lindseys' efforts to abolish injustice showed both genuine compassion and middle-class bias, and they occupied a part of a broader movement aimed at finding solutions to the social and economic problems of modern American society.

During the 1890s, economic depression, labor violence, political upheaval, and foreign entanglements shook the nation. Technology had fulfilled many promises, but great

◄ Judge Ben Lindsey (1869–1943) of Denver was a Progressive reformer who worked for children's legal protection. Like many reformers of his era, Lindsey had an earnest faith in the ability of humankind to build a better world. *(Library of Congress)*

591

CHRONOLOGY

1895 ■ Booker T. Washington gives Atlanta Compromise speech

■ National Association of Colored Women founded

1898 ■ *Holden v. Hardy* upholds limits on miners' working hours

1901 ■ McKinley assassinated; T. Roosevelt assumes presidency

1904 ■ *Northern Securities* case dissolves railroad trust

1905 ■ *Lochner v. New York* removes limits on bakers' working hours

■ NCAA founded

1906 ■ Hepburn Act tightens ICC control over railroads

■ Meat Inspection Act passed

■ Pure Food and Drug Act Passed

1908 ■ *Muller v. Oregon* upholds limits on women's working hours

1909 ■ NAACP founded

1910 ■ Mann-Elkins Act reinforces ICC powers

■ White Slave Traffic Act (Mann Act) prohibits transportation of women for "immoral purposes"

■ Taft fires Pinchot

1911 ■ Society of American Indians founded

1913 ■ Sixteenth Amendment ratified, legalizing income tax

■ Seventeenth Amendment ratified, providing for direct election of senators

■ Underwood Tariff institutes income tax

■ Federal Reserve Act establishes central banking system

1914 ■ Federal Trade Commission created to investigate unfair trade practices

■ Clayton Anti-Trust Act outlaws monopolistic business practices

■ Adamson Act mandates eight-hour workday for railroad workers

1919 ■ Eighteenth Amendment ratified, establishing prohibition of alcoholic beverages

1920 ■ Nineteenth Amendment ratified, giving women the vote in federal elections

numbers of Americans continued to suffer from poverty and disease. Business and politics seemed out of control. Some critics regarded industrialists as monsters who controlled markets and prices for the sole purpose of maximizing profits. Others believed government was corroded by bosses who enriched themselves through politics. Still others felt that the needs of the laboring classes were being overlooked. Tensions created by urbanization and industrialization seemed to be fragmenting society into conflicting interest groups.

By 1900, however, the previous decade's political tumult had calmed, and economic depression seemed to be over. The nation emerged victorious from a war against Spain (see Chapter 22), and a new era of dynamic political leaders, such as Theodore Roosevelt and Woodrow Wilson, was dawning. A sense of renewal served both to intensify anxiety over continuing problems and to raise hopes that somehow these problems could be fixed and democracy could be reconciled with capitalism.

From these circumstances there emerged a complex and many-sided reform campaign. By the 1910s, reformers from both Republican and Democratic Parties were calling themselves Progressives; in 1912 they formed a political party by that name to embody their principles. Historians have uniformly used the term *Progressivism* to refer to the era's spirit, while disagreeing over its meaning and over which groups and individuals actually were Progressive. Nonetheless, the era between 1895 and 1920 included a series of movements, each aiming in one way or another to renovate or restore American society, values, and institutions by imposing change from above and by exercising influence from below.

The reform impulse had many sources. Industrial capitalism had created awesome technology, unprecedented productivity, and a cornucopia of consumer goods. But it had also brought harmful overproduction, domineering monopolies, labor strife, and the destruction of natural resources. Burgeoning cities facilitated the amassing and distribution of goods, services, and cultural amenities; they also bred poverty, disease, and crime. The influx of immigrants and the rise of a new class of managers and professionals reconfigured the social order. And the depression of the 1890s forced leading citizens to realize what working people already knew: the central promise of American life was not being kept; equality of opportunity was elusive.

These problems galvanized members of both the middle class and the working class to work toward change, though in differing ways. Middle-class reformers organized their ideas and actions around three goals. First, they sought to end abuses of power. Attacks on privilege, monopoly, and corruption were not new; Jacksonian reformers of the 1830s and 1840s, as well as Populists of the 1890s, belonged to the same tradition. Progressives, however, broadened the offensive. Trustbusting, consumers' rights, and good government became compelling political issues.

Second, Progressives like Ben Lindsey wished to supplant corrupt power with humane institutions, such as schools, courts, and medical clinics. Though eager to protect individual rights, they abandoned individualistic notions that hard work and good character automatically ensured success, and that the poor had only themselves to blame for their plight. Instead, Progressives acknowledged that society had responsibility and power to improve individual lives, and they believed that government, acting for society at large, must intervene in social and economic affairs to protect the common good and elevate public interest above self-interest. Their revolt against fixed categories of thought challenged entrenched views on women's roles, race relations, education, legal and scientific thought, and morality.

Third, Progressives wanted to apply scientific principles and efficient management to economic, social, and political institutions. Their aim was to establish bureaus of experts who would end wasteful competition and promote social and economic order. Science and the scientific method—planning, control, and predictability—were their central values. Just as corporations applied scientific management techniques to achieve economic efficiency, Progressives advocated expertise and planning to achieve social and political efficiency.

Another kind of reform arose from the everyday needs and problems of urban working classes. Reformers representing the interests of this group sometimes allied with others interested in broad social welfare and sometimes worked on their own to promote greater public responsibility for the health, safety, and security of families and workers at risk in the new urban industrial world.

Befitting their name, Progressives had faith in the ability of humankind to create a better world. They voiced such phrases as "humanity's universal growth" and "the upward spiral of human development." Rising incomes, new educational opportunities, and increased availability of goods and services created an aura of confidence that social improvement would follow. Judge Ben Lindsey of Denver, who spearheaded reform in the treatment of juvenile delinquents, expressed the Progressive creed when he wrote, "In the end the people are bound to do the right thing, no matter how much they fail at times."

- What were the major characteristics of Progressivism?
- In what ways did Progressive reform succeed, and in what ways did it fail?
- How did women and racial minorities challenge previous ways of thinking about American society?

THE VARIED PROGRESSIVE IMPULSE

Progressive reformers addressed vexing issues that had surfaced in the previous half-century, but they did so in a new political climate. After the heated election of 1896, party loyalties eroded and voter turnout declined. In northern states, voter participation in presidential elections dropped from the 1880s' levels of 80 percent of the eligible electorate to less than 60 percent. In southern states, where poll taxes and literacy tests excluded most African Americans and many poor whites from the polls, it fell below 30 percent. Parties and elections, it seemed, were losing influence over government policies. At the same time, new interest groups, which championed their own special causes, gained influence.

Many formerly local organizations that had formed to shape public policy in a specific area became nationwide after 1890. These organizations included professional associations, such as the American Bar Association; women's organizations, such as the National American Woman Suffrage Association; issue-oriented groups, such as the National Consumers League; civic-minded clubs, such as the National Municipal League; and minority-group associations, such as the National Negro Business League and the Society of American Indians. Because they usually acted independently of established political parties, such groups made politics more fragmented and issue focused than in earlier eras.

National Associations and Foreign Influences

American reformers also adapted foreign models and ideas. A variety of proposals traveled across the Atlantic; some were introduced by Americans who had been exposed to reforms while studying in England, France, and Germany; others, by foreigners visiting the United States. (Europeans also learned from Americans, but the balance of the idea flow tilted toward the United States.) Americans copied from England such ideas as the settlement house, in which reformers went to live among and aid the urban poor, and workers' compensation for victims of industrial accidents. Other reforms, such as old-age insurance, subsidized workers' housing, city planning, and rural reconstruction, originated abroad and were adopted or modified in America.

Issues and methods arising from a new age distinguished Progressive reform from the preceding Populist movement. Although goals of the rural-based Populists—moral regeneration, political democracy, and antimonopolism—continued after the movement faded, the Progressive quest for social justice, labor laws, educational and legal reform, and government streamlining had a largely urban bent. Utilizing advances in mail, telephone, and telegraph communications, urban reformers could exchange information and coordinate efforts more easily than rural reformers could.

Progressive goals—ending abuse of power, protecting the welfare of all classes, reforming social institutions, and promoting bureaucratic and scientific efficiency—existed in all levels of society. But a new middle class of men and women in professions of law, medicine, engineering, social service, religion, teaching, and business formed an important vanguard of reform. Offended by inefficiency and immorality in business, government, and human relations, these people determined to apply the rational techniques that they had learned in their professions to problems of the larger society. They also believed that they could create a unified society by transforming immigrants and Indians—"Americanizing" them through education and other means—to conform to middle-class customs and ideals.

The New Middle Class and Muckrakers

Indignation motivated many middle-class reformers to seek an end to abuses of power. Their views were voiced by journalists whom Theodore Roosevelt dubbed muckrakers (after a character in the Puritan allegory *Pilgrim's Progress,* who, rather than looking heavenward at beauty, looked downward and raked the muck to find what was wrong with life). Muckrakers fed public tastes for scandal and sensation by exposing social, economic, and political wrongs. Their investigative articles in *McClure's, Cosmo-*

politan, and other popular magazines attacked adulterated foods, fraudulent insurance, prostitution, and political corruption. Lincoln Steffens's articles in *McClure's,* later published as *The Shame of the Cities* (1904), epitomized muckraking style. Steffens hoped his exposés of bosses' misrule would inspire mass outrage and, ultimately, reform. Other well-known muckraking works included Upton Sinclair's *The Jungle* (1906), a novel that disclosed outrages of the meatpacking industry; Ida M. Tarbell's disparaging history of Standard Oil (first published in *McClure's,* 1902–1904); Burton J. Hendrick's *Story of Life Insurance* (1907); and David Graham Phillips's *Treason of the Senate* (1906).

To improve politics, these Progressives advocated nonpartisan elections to prevent fraud and bribery bred by party loyalties. They also promoted direct primaries, in which all voters could participate, instead of party caucuses, in which only insiders had influence. To make officeholders more responsible, they urged adoption of the initiative, which permitted voters to propose new laws; the referendum, which enabled voters to accept or reject a law (Oregon was first to introduce these measures); and the recall, which allowed voters to remove offending officials and judges from office. The goal, like that of the business-consolidation movement, was efficiency: middle-class Progressives would reclaim government by replacing the boss system with accountable managers chosen by a responsible electorate.

The Progressive spirit also stirred some male business leaders and wealthy females. Executives like Alexander Cassatt of the Pennsylvania Railroad supported some government regulation and political reforms to protect their interests from more radical reformers. Others, like E. A. Filene, founder of a Boston department store, and Tom Johnson, a Cleveland streetcar magnate, were humanitarians who worked unselfishly for social justice. Business-dominated organizations like the Municipal Voters League and the U.S. Chamber of Commerce thought that running schools, hospitals, and local government like efficient businesses would help stabilize society. Elite women led organizations like the Young Women's Christian Association (YWCA), which aided unmarried working women, and they joined middle- and working-class women in the Woman's Christian Temperance Union (WCTU), the largest women's organization of its time, which supported numerous causes besides abstinence from drinking.

Upper-Class Reformers

Vital elements of what became modern American liberalism derived from working-class urban experiences.

Workers' Compensation

During the Progressive era, the volume and extent of industrial accidents attracted considerable attention from muckraking journalists and academic researchers. At the dawn of the twentieth century, accident rates on American railroads and in American mines and factories far exceeded those in Great Britain and Germany, the other two major industrial nations. In 1911 one study concluded that the accident rate in the nation's industries "equals the average yearly casualties of the American Civil War, plus all of those of the Philippine War, plus all of those of the Russo-Japanese War." The United States was, said one reformer, creating an "army of cripples." Prevailing American legal theory protected employers from liability and prevented workers from recovering medical costs and lost income when injured on the job. Progressives challenged that theory and proposed that employers, guided by government, should shoulder the obligation.

The principle that employers should be legally responsible for compensating victims of industrial accidents emerged most strongly in Germany and Britain. In 1884 the German government began requiring employers and wage earners to contribute to quasi-public funds that could be used to provide for those injured at work. In England, an 1897 law compelled employers to create some form of payment through contributions to an insurance company or from their own funds. Shortly thereafter, variations appeared in Denmark, France, and Italy. But not until 1907 did the reform find influential support in the United States. That year, President Theodore Roosevelt began advocating employers' liability legislation. The next year, two different Progressive organizations, the social reform–minded Russell Sage Foundation and the business-oriented National Civic Foundation, took up the cause.

Most American Progressives favored the German system because it operated more under government administration than the British method and because it encouraged industrial safety. But states, rather than the federal government, assumed responsibility for the exact form of a program. By 1911, Ohio and Washington had state-administered insurance funds into which employers made contributions, and between 1911 and 1913, twenty other states enacted some form of workers' compensation laws. Private insurance companies, however, strongly opposed state monopolies on compensation insurance, and by 1919, though employers were still required to make contributions, the majority of workers' compensation funds were in the hands of private firms. American legislators, propelled by Progressive arguments, had borrowed an insurance system from abroad but applied their own imprint of private enterprise.

A SUCCESSFUL WORKMAN

This man who lost an arm in an industrial accident in Cleveland, invented a good substitute arm, wears it at work, and uses it in earning his living. He has made good by his own unaided efforts. The average man, however, needs a lift in the way of training.

▲ In the early twentieth century, industrial accidents continued to kill and maim thousands of workers. Without insurance to support them when they were disabled, some employees created aids to enable them to continue on the job. This man, who lost an arm in a factory mishap, invented his own artificial limb. Other victims of misfortune, however, were not so handy and could receive compensation only if their state or their employer adopted the European model and instituted a workers' insurance program. *(Library of Congress)*

Working-Class Reformers

By 1900 many urban workers were pressing for government intervention to ensure safety and security. They advocated such "bread-and-butter reforms" as safe factories, shorter workdays, workers' compensation, protection of child and women laborers, better housing, health safeguards, and a more equitable tax structure. Politicians like Senator Robert F. Wagner of New York and Governor Edward F. Dunne of Illinois worked to alleviate hardships that resulted from urban-industrial growth. They trained in the trenches of machine politics, and their constituents were the same people who supported political bosses, supposedly the enemies of reform. Yet bossism was not necessarily at odds with humanitarianism. When "Big Tim" Sullivan, an influential boss in New York City's Tammany Hall political machine, was asked why he supported a shorter workday for women, he explained, "I had seen me sister go out to work when she was only fourteen and I know we ought to help these gals by giving 'em a law which will prevent 'em from being broken down while they're still young." Reformers who represented working-class interests did not subscribe to all reforms. As protectors of individual liberty, they opposed reforms such as prohibition, Sunday closing laws, civil service, and nonpartisan elections, which conflicted with their constituents' interests. On the other hand, they joined with other reformers to pass laws aiding labor and promoting social welfare.

Much of Progressive reform rested on religious underpinnings. The distresses of modern society especially sparked new thoughts about how to fortify social relations with moral principles. In particular, a movement known as the Social Gospel, led by Protestant ministers Walter Rauschenbusch, Washington Gladden, and Charles Sheldon, would counter competitive capitalism by interjecting Christian churches into practical, worldly matters, such as arbitrating industrial harmony and improving the environment of the poor. Believing that service to fellow humans provided the way to securing individual salvation and to creating God's kingdom on earth, Social Gospelers actively participated in social reform and governed their lives by asking, "What would Jesus do?" Other Progressives had more secular influences. Ben Lindsey's battle for juvenile justice, for example, derived in part from the democratic ideals of Populism.

The Social Gospel

Those who believed in service to all people tried to "Americanize" immigrants and Indians by expanding their educational, economic, and cultural opportunities. But at times, by imposing their own values on people of different cultures, they undermined their efforts to help. Catholic and Jewish immigrants, for example, sometimes rejected the Protestant creed and Americanization efforts of Social Gospelers, settlement-house workers, and other reformers. Working-class families, too, often resented middle-class reformers' interference in their prerogative to raise their children according to their own beliefs.

Some disillusioned people wanted a different society altogether. A blend of immigrant intellectuals, industrial workers, Populists, miners, and women's rights activists, they turned to socialism. Taking a cue from European counterparts, especially in Germany, England, and France, where the government sponsored such socialist goals as low-cost housing, workers' compensation, old-age pensions, public ownership of municipal services, and labor reform, they advocated that similar measures be adopted in the United States. By 1912, the Socialist Party of America, a merger of several groups and founded in 1901, claimed 150,000 members, and the socialist newspaper *Appeal to Reason* achieved the largest circulation—700,000 subscribers—of any weekly newspaper in the country. But American socialism had difficulty sustaining widespread acceptance. Although some AFL unions supported socialist goals and candidates, many unions opposed a reform like social insurance because it would increase taxes on members' wages. Moreover, private real-estate interests opposed any government intervention in housing, and manufacturers blacklisted militant socialist laborers.

Socialists

In politics, many socialists united behind Eugene V. Debs, the American Railway Union organizer who drew nearly 100,000 votes as the Socialist presidential candidate in the 1900 presidential election. A spellbinding orator who was able to appeal to urban immigrants and western farmers alike, Debs won 400,000 votes in 1904 and polled 900,000 in 1912, at the pinnacle of his and his party's career. Although Debs and other Socialist leaders, such as Victor Berger of Wisconsin, the first Socialist to be elected to the U.S. Congress, and New York's Morris Hillquit, did not always agree on tactics, they made compelling overtures to reform-minded people. Some Progressives joined the Socialist Party, but most Progressives had too much at stake in capitalism to want to overthrow it. Municipal ownership of public utilities represented their limit of drastic change. In Wisconsin, where Progressivism was most advanced, reformers refused to ally with Berger's more radical group. California Progressives temporarily allied with conservatives to prevent Socialists from gaining power in Los Angeles. And few

▲ Although their objectives sometimes differed from those of middle-class Progressive reformers, socialists also became a more active force in the early twentieth century. Socialist parades on May Day, like this one in 1910, were meant to express the solidarity of all working people.
(Library of Congress)

Progressives objected when Debs was jailed in 1918 for giving an antiwar speech.

In some ways, Progressive reform in the South resembled that in other regions. Essentially urban and middle class in nature, it included the

Southern and Western Progressivism

same goals of railroad and utility regulation, factory safety, pure food and drug legislation, and moral reform as existed in the North. The South pioneered some political reforms; the direct primary originated in North Carolina; the city-commission plan arose in Galveston, Texas; and the city-manager plan began in Staunton, Virginia. Progressive governors, such as Braxton Bragg Comer of Alabama and Hoke Smith of Georgia, introduced business regulation, educational expansion, and other reforms that duplicated actions taken by northern counterparts.

In the West, several politicians championed humanitarianism and regulation, putting the region at the forefront of the campaign to expand functions of federal and state governments. Nevada's Progressive Senator Francis Newlands advocated national planning and federal con-

trol of water resources. In California, Governor Hiram Johnson fought for direct primaries, regulation of child and women's labor, workers' compensation, a pure food and drug act, and educational reform. Montana's Senator Thomas J. Walsh fought against corruption and for woman suffrage.

Southern and western women, white and black, made notable contributions to Progressive causes, just as they did in the North and the East. In western states, women could vote on state and local matters, so that they could participate directly in political reform. But the more effective women's reform efforts in both regions took place outside of politics, and their projects remained racially distinct. White women crusaded against child labor, founded social service organizations, and challenged unfair wage rates. African American women, using a nonpolitical guise as homemakers and religious leaders—roles that whites found more acceptable than political activism—served their communities by acting as advocates for street cleaning, better education, and health reforms.

It would be a mistake to assume that a Progressive spirit captivated all of American society between 1895 and

Opponents of Progressivism

1920 Large numbers of people, heavily represented in Congress, disliked government interference in economic affairs and found no fault with existing power structures. Defenders of free enterprise opposed regulatory measures out of fear that government programs undermined the initiative and competition that they believed were basic to a free-market system. "Old-guard" Republicans, such as Senator Nelson W. Aldrich of Rhode Island and House Speaker Joseph Cannon of Illinois, championed this ideology. Outside of Washington, D.C., tycoons like J. P. Morgan and John D. Rockefeller insisted that progress would result only from maintaining the profit incentive and an unfettered economy.

Moreover, prominent Progressives were not "progressive" in every respect. Their attempts to Americanize immigrants reflected prejudice as well as naiveté. As governor, Hiram Johnson promoted discrimination against Japanese Americans, and whether Progressive or not, most southern governors, such as Smith, Comer, Charles B. Aycock of North Carolina, and James K. Vardaman of Mississippi, rested their power on appeals to white supremacy. In the South, the exclusion of blacks from voting through poll taxes, literacy requirements, and other means meant that electoral reforms affected only whites—and then only white men with enough cash and schooling to satisfy voting prerequisites. Settlement houses in northern cities kept blacks and whites apart in separate programs and buildings.

Progressive reformers generally occupied the center of the ideological spectrum. Moderate, socially aware, sometimes contradictory, they believed on one hand that laissez faire was obsolete and on the other that a radical departure from free enterprise was dangerous. Like Thomas Jefferson, they expressed faith in the conscience and will of the people; like Alexander Hamilton, they desired a strong central government to act in the interest of conscience. Their goals were both idealistic and realistic. As minister-reformer Walter Rauschenbusch wrote, "We shall demand perfection and never expect to get it."

GOVERNMENT AND LEGISLATIVE REFORM

Mistrust of tyranny had traditionally prompted Americans to believe that democratic government should be small, should interfere in private affairs only in unique circumstances, and should withdraw when balance had been restored. But in the late 1800s this viewpoint weakened when problems resulting from economic change seemed to overwhelm individual effort. Corporations pursued government aid and protection for their enterprises. Discontented farmers sought government regulation of railroads and other monopolistic businesses. And city dwellers, accustomed to favors performed by political machines, came to expect government to act on their behalf. Before 1900, state governments had been concerned largely with railroads and economic growth; the federal government had focused primarily on tariffs and the currency. But after 1900, issues of regulation, both economic and social, demanded attention. More than in the past, public opinion, roused by muckraking media, influenced change.

Middle-class Progressive reformers rejected the laissez-faire principle of government. Increasingly aware that a simple, inflexible government was inadequate in a complex industrial age, they reasoned that public authority needed to counteract inefficiency and exploitation. But before activists could effectively use such power, they would have to reclaim government from politicians whose greed they believed had soiled the democratic system. Thus eliminating corruption from government was one central thrust of Progressive activity.

Restructuring Government

Prior to the Progressive era, reformers had attacked corruption in cities by trying to regulate government through such structural reforms as civil service, nonpartisan elections, and close scrutiny of public expenditures. After 1900, campaigns to make cities run more efficiently resulted in city-manager and commission forms of government, in which urban officials were chosen for professional expertise rather than for political connections. But reforming city management was not sufficient to realize the improvements reformers sought, and they turned their attention to state and federal governments for support.

At the state level, faith in a reform-minded executive prompted Progressives to support a number of skillful and charismatic governors. In the West, California's Hiram Johnson, who attacked business and political corruption, was an example of such a governor. With Johnson's inspiration, California passed laws regulating utilities and child labor, as well as workers' compensation for state employees. In the South, Georgia's Hoke Smith achieved railroad regulation, juvenile courts, and better-funded public education—though he also supported voting restrictions that disfranchised blacks.

Wisconsin's Robert M. La Follette was one of the most dynamic Progressive governors. A small-town lawyer, La Follette rose through the state Republican Party to become

▲ Robert M. La Follette (1855–1925) was one of the most dynamic of Progressive politicians. As governor of Wisconsin, he sponsored a program of political reform and business regulation known as the Wisconsin Plan. In 1906 he entered the U.S. Senate and continued to champion Progressive reform. The National Progressive Republican League, which La Follette founded in 1911, became the core of the Progressive Party. *(State Historical Society of Wisconsin)*

governor in 1900. In office, he initiated a multipronged reform program, including direct primaries, more equitable taxes, and regulation of railroads. He also appointed commissions staffed by experts, who supplied him with data that he used in speeches to arouse support for his policies. After three terms as governor, La Follette became a U.S. senator and carried his ideals into national politics. "Battling Bob" displayed a rare ability to approach reform scientifically while still exciting people with moving rhetoric. His goal, he proclaimed, was "not to 'smash' corporations, but to drive them out of politics, and then to treat them exactly the same as other people are treated."

Crusades against corrupt politics made the system more democratic. By 1916 all but three states had direct primaries, and many had adopted the initiative, referendum, and recall. Political reformers achieved a major goal in 1913 with adoption of the Seventeenth Amendment to the Constitution, which provided for direct election of U.S. senators, replacing election by state legislatures. Such measures, however, did not always achieve the desired ends. Party bosses, better organized and more experienced than reformers, were still able to control elections, and special-interest groups spent large sums to influence the voting. Moreover, courts usually aided rather than reined in entrenched power.

State laws resulting from Progressive efforts to improve labor conditions had more effect than did political

Labor Reform

reforms, because middle-class and working-class reformers could agree on the need for them. At the instigation of middle-class/working-class coalitions, many states enacted factory inspection laws, and by 1916 nearly two-thirds of the states required compensation for victims of industrial accidents. An alliance of labor and humanitarian groups induced some legislatures to grant aid to mothers with dependent children. Under pressure from the National Child Labor Committee, nearly every state set a minimum age for employment (varying from twelve to sixteen) and limited the hours that employers could make children work. Labor laws did not work perfectly, however. They seldom provided for the close inspection of factories that enforcement required. And families that needed extra income evaded child labor restrictions by falsifying their children's ages to employers.

Several middle- and working-class groups also united behind measures that restricted working hours for women and that aided retirees. After the Supreme Court, in *Muller v. Oregon*, upheld Oregon's ten-hour limit in 1908, more states passed laws protecting female workers. Meanwhile, in 1914 efforts of the American Association for Old Age Security showed signs of success when Arizona established old-age pensions. Judges struck down the law, but demand for pensions continued, and in the 1920s many states enacted laws to provide for needy elderly people.

Opening up government and protecting women and children brought together reform coalitions. But when an

Prohibition

issue involved regulating behavior, such as drinking habits and sexual conduct, differences emerged. One group of reformers used both morality and social control as a basis for their agenda. For example, the Anti-Saloon League, formed in 1893, intensified the long-standing campaign against drunkenness and its costs to society. This organization allied with the

Woman's Christian Temperance Union (founded in 1874) to publicize alcoholism's role in causing liver disease and other health problems. The League was especially successful in shifting attention from the immorality of drunkenness to using law enforcement to break the alleged link between the drinking that saloons encouraged and the accidents, poverty, and poor productivity that were consequences of drinking.

Against the wishes of many working-class residents who valued individual freedom, the war on saloons prompted many states and localities to restrict liquor consumption. By 1900 almost one-fourth of the nation's population lived in "dry" communities (which prohibited the sale of liquor). But consumption of alcohol increased after 1900 as a result of the influx of immigrants whose cultures included social drinking, convincing prohibitionists that a nationwide ban was the best solution. They enlisted support from such notables as Supreme Court Justice Louis D. Brandeis and former president William Howard Taft, and in 1918 Congress passed the Eighteenth Amendment (ratified in 1919 and implemented in 1920), outlawing the manufacture, sale, and transportation of intoxicating liquors. Not all prohibitionists were Progressive reformers, and not all Progressives were prohibitionists. Nevertheless, the Eighteenth Amendment can be seen as an expression of the Progressive goal to protect family and workplace through reform legislation.

Moral outrage erupted when muckraking journalists charged that international gangs were kidnapping young women and forcing them into prostitution, a practice called white slavery. Accusations were exaggerated, but they alarmed some moralists who falsely perceived a link between immigration and prostitution, and who feared that prostitutes were producing genetically inferior children. Although some women voluntarily entered "the profession" because it offered much higher income than any other form of work available to them and other women occasionally performed sexual favors in return for male gifts, those fearful about the social consequences of prostitution prodded governments to investigate and pass corrective legislation. The Chicago Vice Commission, for example, undertook a "scientific" survey of dance halls and illicit sex, and published its findings as *The Social Evil in Chicago* in 1911. The report concluded that poverty, gullibility, and desperation drove women into prostitution.

Such investigations found rising numbers of prostitutes but failed to prove that criminal organizations deliberately lured women into "the trade." Reformers nonetheless believed they could attack prostitution by punishing both those who promoted it and those who practiced it. In 1910 Congress passed the White Slave Traffic Act (Mann Act), prohibiting interstate and international transportation of a woman for immoral purposes. By 1915 nearly every state had outlawed brothels and solicitation of sex. Such laws ostensibly protected young women from exploitation, but in reality they failed to address the more serious problem of sexual violence that women suffered at the hands of family members, presumed friends, and employers.

Like prohibition, the Mann Act reflected growing sentiment that government could improve behavior by restricting it. Middle-class reformers believed that the source of evil was neither original sin nor human nature but the social environment. If evil was created by human will, it followed that it could be eradicated by human effort. Intervention in the form of laws could help create a heaven on earth. The new working classes, however, resented such meddling as unwarranted attempts to control them. Thus, when Chicagoans voted on a referendum to make their city dry shortly before the Eighteenth Amendment was passed, three-fourths of the city's immigrant voters opposed it, and the measure went down to defeat.

NEW IDEAS IN SOCIAL INSTITUTIONS

In addition to legislative paths, reform impulses opened new vistas in the ways social institutions were organized. Preoccupation with efficiency and scientific management infiltrated the realms of education, law, religion, and the social sciences. Darwin's theory of evolution had challenged traditional beliefs in a God-created world; immigration had created complex social diversity; and technology had made old habits of production obsolete. Thoughtful people in several professions grappled with how to respond to the new era yet preserve what was best from the past.

Changing attitudes about childhood and new patterns of school attendance altered approaches to education. As late as 1870, when families needed children at home to do farm work, Americans attended school for an average of only a few months a year for four years. By 1900, however, the urban-industrial economy and its expanding middle class had helped to create a more widespread appreciation of children's innocence and advanced the goal of sheltering youngsters from the dangers of society by channeling them toward a protected physical and emotional growth. Those concerned about children's development believed that youngsters required particular forms of education and other activity appropriate to a child's biological and cultural development.

Controlling Prostitution

John Dewey and Progressive Education

Thus schools shared with, and even replaced, the home as the best environment for promoting children's development. Educators argued that schooling produced better adult citizens and workers. In the 1870s and 1880s, states passed laws that required children to attend school to age fourteen, and swelling populations of immigrant and migrant children jammed schoolrooms. Meanwhile, the number of public high schools grew from five hundred in 1870 to ten thousand in 1910. By 1900 educational reformers, such as psychologist G. Stanley Hall and philosopher John Dewey, asserted that schools needed to prepare children for a modern world. They insisted that personal development should be the focus of the curriculum and the school the center of the community.

Progressive education, based on Dewey's *The School and Society* (1899) and *Democracy and Education* (1916), was a uniquely American phenomenon. Dewey believed that learning should involve real-life problems and that children should be taught to use intelligence and ingenuity as instruments for controlling their environments. From kindergarten through high school, Dewey asserted, children needed to learn through direct experience, not by rote memorization. Dewey and his wife, Alice, put these ideas into practice in their own Laboratory School located at the University of Chicago.

A more practical curriculum became the driving principle behind reform in higher education as well. Previously, the purpose of American colleges and universities had resembled that of European counterparts: to train a select few for careers in law, medicine, and religion. But in the late 1800s, institutions of higher learning multiplied as states eager to establish their own universities used federal funds from the Morrill Acts of 1862 and 1890 to establish new schools. The number of private institutions also expanded. Between 1870 and 1910, the total of American colleges and universities grew from 563 to nearly 1,000. Curricula expanded as educators sought to make learning more appealing and to keep pace with technological and social changes. Harvard University, under President Charles W. Eliot, pioneered in substituting electives for required courses and experimenting with new teaching methods. The University of Wisconsin

Growth of Colleges and Universities

▲ These members of the University of Michigan's Class of 1892 represent the student body of a publicly funded college in the late nineteenth century. With their varied curricula, inclusion of women, and increasing enrollments, such schools transformed American higher education in the Progressive era. *(University of Michigan)*

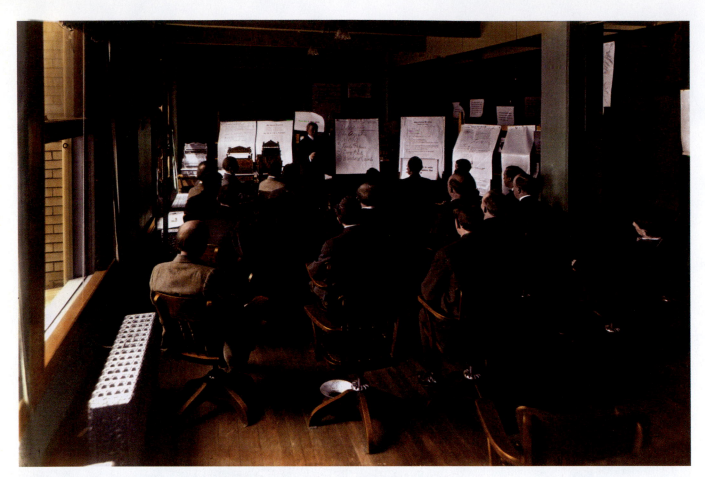

▲ "Business Education at the National Cash Register Company." John H. Patterson, founder of the National Cash Register Company, innovated educational reform of a different sort by promoting the training of salesmen. A social progressive who believed in providing his factories with good light and ventilation, Patterson also pioneered the use of flip charts, seen in this photograph, as means of representing business conditions and of educating his employees. Many of the most forward-looking business executives of the early twentieth century had worked for and learned from Patterson. *(NCR Archive at Dayton History)*

and other state universities achieved distinction in new areas of study, such as political science, economics, and sociology. Many schools, private and public, considered athletics vital to a student's growth, and men's intercollegiate sports became a permanent feature of student life as well as a source of school pride.

Southern states, in keeping with separate-but-equal policies, created segregated land-grant colleges for blacks in addition to institutions for whites. Aided by land-grant funds, such schools as Alabama Agricultural and Mechanical University (A&M), South Carolina State University, and the A&M College for the Colored Race (North Carolina) opened their doors. Separate was a more accurate description of these institutions than equal. African Americans continued to suffer from inferior educational opportunities. Nevertheless, African American men and women found intellectual stimulation in all-black colleges and hoped to use their education to promote the uplifting of their race.

As higher education expanded, so did female enrollments. Between 1890 and 1910, the number of women in colleges and universities swelled from 56,000 to 140,000. Of these, 106,000 attended coeducational institutions (mostly state universities); the rest enrolled in women's colleges, such as Wellesley and Barnard. By 1920, 283,000 women attended college, accounting for 47 percent of total enrollment. But discrimination lingered in admissions and curriculum policies. Women were encouraged (indeed, they usually sought) to take home economics and education courses rather than science and mathematics, and most medical schools, including Harvard and Yale, refused to admit women or imposed stringent quotas. Separate women's medical schools, such as the Women's Medical College of Philadelphia and Women's Medical College of Chicago, trained numerous female physicians, but most of these schools were absorbed or put out of business by larger institutions dominated by men.

American educators justifiably congratulated themselves for increasing enrollments and making instruction more meaningful. By 1920, 78 percent of children between ages five and seventeen were enrolled in public schools; another 8 percent attended private and parochial schools. These figures represented a huge increase over 1870 attendance rates. There were 600,000 college and graduate students in 1920, compared with only 52,000 in 1870. Yet few people looked beyond the numbers to assess how well schools were doing their job. Critical analysis seldom tested the faith that schools could promote equality as well as personal growth and responsible citizenship.

The legal profession also embraced new emphases on experience and scientific principles. Harvard law professor

Progressive Legal Thought

Roscoe Pound and Oliver Wendell Holmes Jr., associate justice of the Supreme Court between 1902 and 1932, led the attack on the traditional view of law as universal and unchanging. "The life of the law," wrote Holmes, sounding like Dewey, "has not been logic; it has been experience." The opinion that law should reflect society's needs challenged the practice of invoking inflexible legal precedents which often obstructed social legislation. Louis D. Brandeis, a lawyer who later joined Holmes on the Supreme Court, insisted that judges' opinions be based on scientifically gathered information about social realities. Using this approach, Brandeis collected extensive data on harmful effects of long working hours to convince the Supreme Court, in *Muller v. Oregon* (1908), to uphold Oregon's ten-hour limit to women's workday.

New legal thinking provoked some resistance. Judges raised on laissez-faire economics and strict interpretation of the Constitution overturned laws that Progressives thought necessary for effective reform. Thus, despite Holmes's forceful dissent, in 1905 the Supreme Court, in *Lochner v. New York*, revoked a New York law limiting bakers' working hours. In this and similar cases, the Court's majority argued that the Fourteenth Amendment protected an individual's right to make contracts without

government interference. Judges weakened other federal regulations by invoking the Tenth Amendment, which prohibited the federal government from interfering in matters reserved to the states.

Courts did uphold some regulatory measures, particularly those intended to safeguard life and limb. A string of decisions, beginning with *Holden v. Hardy* (1898), in which the Supreme Court sustained a Utah law regulating working hours for miners, confirmed the use of state police power to protect health, safety, and morals. Judges also affirmed federal police power and Congress's authority over interstate commerce by upholding federal legislation, such as the Pure Food and Drug Act, the Meat Inspection Act, and the Mann Act. In these instances citizens' welfare took precedence over the Tenth Amendment.

But the concept of general welfare often conflicted with the concept of equal rights when local majorities imposed their will on minorities. Even if one agreed that laws should address society's needs, whose needs should prevail? The United States was (and remains) a mixed nation; gender, race, religion, and ethnicity deeply influenced law. In many localities a native-born Protestant majority imposed Bible reading in public schools (offending Catholics and Jews), required businesses to close on Sundays, limited women's rights, restricted religious practices of Mormons and other groups, prohibited interracial marriage, and enforced racial segregation. Justice Holmes asserted that laws should be made for "people of fundamentally differing views," but fitting such laws to a nation of so many different interest groups has sparked debates that continue to this day.

Social science—the study of society and its institutions—experienced changes similar to those affecting education and law. In economics, a

Social Science

group of scholars used statistics to argue that laws governing economic relationships were not timeless. Instead, they claimed, theory should reflect prevailing social conditions. Richard T. Ely of Johns Hopkins University and the University of Wisconsin, for example, argued that poverty and impersonality resulting from industrialization required intervention by "the united efforts of Church, state, and science." Similarly, a new breed of sociologists led by Lester Ward, Albion Small, and Edward A. Ross agreed, adding that citizens should actively work to cure social ills rather than passively wait for problems to solve themselves.

Meanwhile, historians Frederick Jackson Turner, Charles A. Beard, and Vernon L. Parrington examined the past to explain present American society. Beard, like other Progressives, believed that the Constitution was a flexible document amenable to growth and change, not a sacred code imposed by wise forefathers. His *Economic Interpretation of the Constitution* (1913) argued that a group of merchants and business-oriented lawyers created the Constitution to defend private property. If the Constitution had served special interests in one age, it could be changed to serve broader interests in another age.

In the field of public health, organizations such as the National Consumers League (NCL) joined physicians and social scientists to bring about some of the most far-reaching Progressive reforms. Founded by Florence Kelley in 1899, the NCL pursued activities including protection of female and child laborers, and elimination of potential health hazards. After aiding in the success of *Muller v. Oregon,* the organization became active in sponsoring court cases on behalf of women workers and joined reform lawyers Louis Brandeis and Felix Frankfurter in support of these cases. Local branches united with women's clubs to advance consumer protection measures, such as the licensing of food vendors and inspection of dairies. They also urged city governments to fund neighborhood clinics that provided health education and medical care to the poor.

The Social Gospel served as a response to Social Darwinism, the application of biological natural selection and survival of the fittest to human in-

Eugenics

teractions. But another movement that flourished during the Progressive era, eugenics, sought to apply Darwinian principles to society in a more intrusive way. The brainchild of Francis Galton, an English statistician and cousin of Charles Darwin, eugenics was more of a social philosophy than a science. It rested on the belief that human character and habits could be inherited. If good traits could be inherited, so could bad traits, such as criminality, insanity, and feeblemindedness. Just as some Progressives believed that society had an obligation to intervene and erase poverty and injustice, eugenicists believed that society had an obligation to prevent the reproduction of the mentally defective and the criminally inclined, by preventing such people from marrying and, in extreme cases, by sterilizing them. Inevitably such ideas targeted immigrants and people of color. Supported by such American notables as Alexander Graham Bell, Margaret Sanger, and W. E. B. Du Bois, eugenics was discredited, especially after it became a linchpin of Nazi racial policies, but modern genetic engineering has evolved from some of the eugenics legacy.

Some reformers endorsed eugenics, but others saw immigration restriction as a more acceptable way of controlling the composition of American society. Both a eugenicist and a Progressive (in his ideas about conservation),

Madison Grant's *The Passing of the Great Race* (1916) strongly bolstered theories that immigrants from southern and eastern Europe threatened to weaken American society because they were inferior mentally and morally to earlier Nordic immigrants. Such ideas prompted many people, including some Progressives, to conclude that new laws should curtail the influx of Poles, Italians, Jews, and other eastern and southern Europeans, as well as Asians. Efforts to limit immigration reached fruition in the 1920s, when restrictive legislation drastically closed the door to "new" immigrants.

Thus a new breed of men and women pressed for political reform and institutional change in the two decades before the First World War. Concerned middle-class professionals, confident that new ways of thinking could bring about progress, and representatives of working classes, who experienced social problems first-hand, these people helped broaden government's role to meet the needs of a mature industrial society. But their questioning of prevailing assumptions also unsettled conventional attitudes toward race and gender.

CHALLENGES TO RACIAL AND SEXUAL DISCRIMINATION

The white male reformers of the Progressive era dealt primarily with issues of politics and institutions, and in so doing ignored issues directly affecting former slaves, nonwhite immigrants, Indians, and women. Yet activists within these groups caught the Progressive spirit, challenged entrenched ideas and customs, and made strides toward their own advancement. Their efforts, however, posed a dilemma. Should women and nonwhites aim to imitate white men, with white men's values as well as their rights? Or was there something unique about racial and sexual cultures that they should preserve at the risk of sacrificing broader gains? Both groups fluctuated between attraction to and rejection of the culture that excluded them.

In 1900 nine-tenths of African Americans lived in the South, where repressive Jim Crow laws had multi-

Continued Discrimination for African Americans

plied in the 1880s and 1890s (see page 574). Denied legal and voting rights, and officially segregated in almost all walks of life, southern blacks faced constant exclusion. In 1910 only 8,000 out of 970,000 high-school-age blacks in the South were enrolled in high schools. And blacks met with relentless violence from lynching and countless acts of intimidation. In response, many African Americans moved northward in the 1880s, accelerating their migration after 1900. The conditions they found in places like Chicago,

Cleveland, and Detroit represented relative improvement over rural sharecropping, but job discrimination, inferior schools, and segregated housing still prevailed.

African American leaders differed sharply over how—and whether—to pursue assimilation in their new environments. In the wake of emancipation, ex-slave Frederick Douglass urged "ultimate assimilation through self-assertion, and on no other terms." Others favored separation from white society and supported emigration to Africa or the establishment of all-black communities in Oklahoma Territory and Kansas. Others advocated militancy, believing, as one writer stated, "Our people must die to be saved and in dying must take as many along with them as it is possible to do with the aid of firearms and all other weapons."

Most blacks could neither escape nor conquer white society. They sought other routes to economic and social improvement. Self-help, a strategy articulated by educator Booker T. Washington, offered one popular alternative. Born into slavery in Virginia in 1856, Washington obtained an education and in 1881 founded Tuskegee Institute, an all-black vocational school, in Alabama. There he developed a philosophy that blacks' best hopes for assimilation lay in at least temporarily accommodating to whites. Rather than fighting for political rights, Washington counseled African Americans to work hard, acquire property, and prove they were worthy of respect. Washington voiced his views in a speech at the Atlanta Exposition in 1895. "Dignify and glorify common labor," he urged, in what became known as the Atlanta Compromise. "Agitation of questions of racial equality is the extremest folly." Envisioning a society where blacks and whites would remain apart but share similar goals, Washington observed that "in all things that are purely social we can be as separate as the fingers, yet one as the hand in all matters essential to mutual progress."

Whites welcomed Washington's accommodation policy because it advised patience and reminded black people to stay in their place. Because he said what they wanted to hear, white businesspeople, reformers, and politicians chose to regard Washington as representing all African Americans. Yet though Washington endorsed a separate-but-equal policy, he projected a subtle racial pride that would find more direct expression in black nationalism

Booker T. Washington and Self-Help

▲ Booker T. Washington's Tuskegee Institute helped train young African Americans in useful crafts, such as shoemaking and shoe repair, as illustrated here. At the same time, however, Washington's intentions and the Tuskegee curriculum reinforced what many whites wanted to believe: that blacks were unfit for anything except manual labor. *(Tuskegee University Library)*

in the twentieth century, when some African Americans would advocate control of their own businesses and schools. Washington never argued that blacks were inferior to whites; rather, he asserted that they could enhance their dignity through self-improvement.

Some blacks, however, concluded that Washington endorsed second-class citizenship. His southern-based philosophy did not appeal to educated northern African Americans like newspaper editors William Monroe Trotter and T. Thomas Fortune. In 1905 a group of "anti-Bookerites" convened near Niagara Falls and pledged militant pursuit of such rights as unrestricted voting, economic opportunity, integration, and equality before the law. Representing the Niagara movement was W. E. B. Du Bois, an outspoken critic of the Atlanta Compromise.

W. E. B. Du Bois and the "Talented Tenth"

A New Englander and the first black to receive a Ph.D. degree from Harvard, Du Bois was both a Progressive and a member of the black elite. He held an undergraduate degree from all-black Fisk University and studied in Germany, where he learned about scientific investigation. While a faculty member at Atlanta University, Du Bois compiled fact-filled sociological studies of black urban life and wrote poetically in support of civil rights. He treated Washington politely but could not accept accommodation. "The way for a people to gain their reasonable rights," Du Bois asserted, "is not by voluntarily throwing them away." Instead, blacks must agitate for what was rightfully theirs. Du Bois believed that an intellectual vanguard of cultured, educated blacks, the "Talented Tenth," could use their skill to pursue racial equality. In 1909 he joined with white liberals who also were discontented with Washington's accommodationism to form the National Association for the Advancement of Colored People (NAACP). The organization aimed to end racial discrimination, prevent lynching, and obtain voting rights through legal redress in the courts. By 1914 the NAACP had fifty branch offices and six thousand members.

Within the NAACP and in other ways, African Americans struggled with questions about identity and their place in white society. Du Bois voiced this dilemma poignantly, observing that "one ever feels his twoness—an American, a Negro, two souls, two thoughts, two unreconciled strivings, two warring ideals in one dark body." Somehow blacks had to reconcile that "twoness" by combining racial pride with national identity. As Du Bois wrote in 1903, a black "would not Africanize America, for America has too much to teach the world and Africa. He would not bleach his Negro soul in a flood of white American-

ism, for he knows that Negro blood has a message for the world. He simply wishes to make it possible for a man to be both a Negro and an American." That simple wish would haunt the nation for decades to come.

The dilemma of identity vexed American Indians, but it had an added tribal dimension. Since the 1880s, most Native American reformers had belonged to white-led organizations. In 1911, however, some middle-class Indians formed their own association, the Society of American Indians (SAI), to work for better education, civil rights, and healthcare. It also sponsored "American Indian Days" to cultivate pride and offset the images of savage peoples promulgated in Wild West shows.

Society of American Indians

The SAI's emphasis on racial pride, however, was squeezed between pressures for assimilation on one side and tribal allegiance on the other. Its small membership did not fully represent the diverse and unconnected Indian nations, and its attempt to establish a unifying governing body fizzled. Some tribal governments no longer existed to select representatives, and most SAI members simply promoted their self-interest. At the same time, the goal of achieving acceptance in white society proved elusive. Individual hard work was not enough to overcome white prejudice and condescension, and attempts to redress grievances through legal action faltered for lack of funds. Ultimately, the SAI had little effect on poverty-stricken Indians who seldom knew that the organization even existed. Torn by internal disputes, the association folded in the early 1920s.

Challenges to established social assumptions also raised questions of identity among women. The ensuing quandaries resembled those faced by racial minorities: What tactics should women use to achieve rights? What should be women's role in society? Should they try to achieve equality within a male-dominated society? Or should they assert particular female qualities to create a new place for themselves within society?

"The Woman Movement"

The answers that women found involved a subtle but important shift in their politics. Before 1910, crusaders for women's rights referred to themselves as "the woman movement." This label applied to middle-class women who strived to move beyond the household into higher education and paid professions. Like African American and Indian leaders, women argued that legal and voting rights were indispensable to such moves. They based their claims on the theory that women's special, even superior, traits as guardians of family and morality would humanize all of society. Settlement-house founder Jane Addams, for example, endorsed woman suffrage by asking, "If women have in any sense been responsible for the gentler side of life which softens and blurs some of its harsher conditions, may not they have a duty to perform in our American cities?"

Women's clubs represented a unique dimension of the woman movement. Originating as literary and educational

Women's Clubs

organizations, women's clubs began taking stands on public affairs in the late nineteenth century. Because female activists were generally barred from holding public office (except in a few western states), they asserted traditional female responsibilities for home and family as the rationale for reforming society through an enterprise that historians have called social housekeeping. Rather than advocate reforms like trust-busting and direct primaries, female reformers worked for factory inspection, regulation of children's and women's labor, improved housing and education, and consumer protection.

Such efforts were not confined to white women. Mostly excluded from white women's clubs, African American women had their own club movement, including the Colored Women's Federation, which sought to establish a training school for "colored girls." Founded in 1895, the National Association of Colored Women was the nation's first African American social service organization; it concentrated on establishing nurseries, kindergartens, and retirement homes. Black women also developed reform organizations within Black Baptist and African Methodist Episcopal churches.

Around 1910 some of those concerned with women's place in society began using the term *feminism* to represent their ideas. Whereas the

Feminism

woman movement spoke generally of moral purity and duty to society, feminists emphasized women's rights and self-development as key to economic and sexual independence. Charlotte Perkins Gilman, a major figure in the movement, denounced Victorian notions of womanhood and articulated feminist goals in her numerous writings. Her book *Women and Economics* (1898), for example, declared that domesticity and female innocence were obsolete ,and attacked men's monopoly on economic opportunity. Arguing that paid employees should handle domestic chores, such as cooking, cleaning, and childcare, Gilman asserted that modern women must have access to and take jobs in industry and the professions.

Feminists also supported a single standard of behavior for men and women, and several feminists joined the birth-

▲ The rise of the settlement-house movement and of the Visiting Nurse Association provided young middle-class women with opportunities to aid inner-city working-class neighborhoods and formed the basis of the social work profession. Here a group of visiting nurses prepares to apply their medical training to the disadvantaged.

(Corbis-Bettmann)

Margaret Sanger's Crusade

control movement led by Margaret Sanger. A former visiting nurse who believed in women's rights to sexual pleasure and to determine when to have a child, Sanger helped reverse state and federal "Comstock laws"—named after a nineteenth-century New York moral reformer—which had banned publication and distribution of information about sex and contraception. Although Sanger later gained acceptance, her speeches and actions initially aroused opposition from those who saw birth control as a threat to family and morality. Sanger persevered and in 1921 formed the American Birth Control League, enlisting physicians and social workers to convince judges to allow distribution of birth-control information. Most states still prohibited the sale of contraceptives, but Sanger succeeded in introducing the issue into public debate.

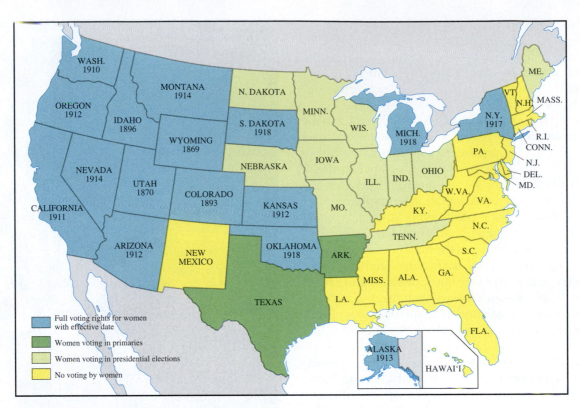

Map 21.1   Woman Suffrage Before 1920

Before Congress passed and the states ratified the Nineteenth Amendment, woman suffrage already existed, but mainly in the West. Several midwestern states allowed women to vote only in presidential elections, but legislatures in the South and Northeast generally refused such rights until forced to do so by constitutional amendment.

During the Progressive era, a generation of feminists, represented by Harriot Stanton Blatch, daughter of

||||||||||||||||||||||||||||||
Woman Suffrage

nineteenth-century suffragist Elizabeth Cady Stanton, carried on women's battle for the vote. Blatch had broad experience in the campaign to obtain the vote for women, having accompanied her mother on speaking tours at home and abroad, and participated in the British women's suffrage movement. In America, Blatch's chief goal was improvement of women's working conditions. She joined the Women's Trade Union League and tried hard to recruit working women into the movement by founding the Equality League of Self Supporting Women in 1907. Declaring that every woman worked, whether she performed paid labor or unpaid housework, Blatch believed that all women's efforts contributed to society's betterment. In her view, achievement rather than wealth and refinement was the best criterion for public status. Thus women should exercise the vote,

not to enhance the power of elites, but to promote and protect women's economic roles.

By the early twentieth century, suffragists had achieved some successes. Nine states, all in the West, allowed women to vote in state and local elections by 1912, and women continued to press for national suffrage (see Map 21.1). Their tactics ranged from moderate but persistent letter-writing and publications of the National American Woman Suffrage Association, led by Carrie Chapman Catt, to spirited meetings and militant marches of the National Woman's Party, led by Alice Paul and Harriot Stanton Blatch. All these activities heightened public awareness. More decisive, however, was women's service during the First World War as factory laborers, medical volunteers, and municipal workers. By convincing legislators that women could shoulder public responsibilities, women's wartime contributions gave final impetus to passage of the national suffrage amendment (the Nineteenth) in 1920.

In spite of these accomplishments, the activities of women's clubs, feminists, and suffragists failed to create an interest group united or powerful enough to overcome men's political, economic, and social control. During the Progressive era, the resolve and energy of leaders like Blatch, Paul, and Catt helped clarify issues that concerned women and finally won women the right to vote, but that victory was only a step, not a conclusion. Discrimination in employment, education, and the law continued to shadow women for decades to come. As feminist Crystal Eastman observed in the aftermath of the suffrage crusade: "Men are saying perhaps, 'Thank God, this everlasting women's fight is over!' But women, if I know them, are saying, 'Now at last we can begin.' . . . Now they can say what they are really after, in common with all the rest of the struggling world, is freedom."

THEODORE ROOSEVELT AND THE REVIVAL OF THE PRESIDENCY

The Progressive era's theme of reform in politics, institutions, and social relations drew attention to government, especially the federal government, as the foremost agent of change. Although the federal government had notable accomplishments during the preceding Gilded Age, its role had been mainly to support rather than to control economic expansion, as when it transferred western public lands and resources to private ownership. Then, in September 1901, the political climate suddenly shifted. The assassination of President William McKinley by anarchist Leon Czolgosz vaulted Theodore Roosevelt, the young vice president (he was forty-two), into the White House. As governor of New York, Roosevelt had angered state Republican bosses by showing sympathy for regulatory legislation, so they rid themselves of him by pushing him into national politics. Little did they anticipate that they provided the steppingstone for the nation's most forceful president since Lincoln, one who bestowed the office with much of its twentieth-century character.

As a youth Roosevelt suffered from asthma and nearsightedness. Driven throughout his life by an obsession to overcome his physical limitations, he exerted what he and his contemporaries called "manliness," meaning a zest for action and display of courage in a "strenuous life." In his teens he became an expert marksman and horseman, and later competed on Harvard's boxing and wrestling teams. In the 1880s he went to live on a Dakota ranch, where he roped cattle and brawled with cowboys. Descended from a Dutch aristocratic family, Roosevelt had the wealth to indulge in such pursuits. But he also inherited a sense of civic responsibility which guided him into a career in public service. He served three terms in the New York State Assembly, sat on the federal Civil Service Commission, served as New York City's police commissioner, and was assistant secretary of the navy. In these offices Roosevelt earned a reputation as a combative, politically crafty leader. In 1898 he thrust himself into the Spanish-American War by organizing a

Theodore Roosevelt

◀ Theodore Roosevelt (1858–1919) liked to think of himself as a great outdoorsman. He loved most the rugged countryside and believed that he and his country should serve as examples of "manliness."

(California Museum of Photography, University of California)

volunteer cavalry brigade, called the Rough Riders, to fight in Cuba. Although his dramatic act had little impact on the war's outcome, it excited public imagination and made him a media hero.

When he assumed the presidency, Roosevelt carried his youthful exuberance into the White House. (A British diplomat once quipped, "You must always remember that the president is about 6.") Considering himself a Progressive, he concurred with his allies that a small, uninvolved government would not suffice in the industrial era. Instead, economic progress necessitated a government powerful enough to guide national affairs broadly. "A simple and poor society," he observed, "can exist as a democracy on the basis of sheer individualism. But a rich and complex society cannot so exist." Especially in economic matters, he wanted the government to act as an umpire, deciding when big business was good and when it was bad. But his brash patriotism and dislike of qualities that he considered effeminate also recalled earlier eras of unbridled expansion, when raw power prevailed in social and economic affairs.

The federal regulation of business that characterized twentieth-century American history began with Roosevelt's presidency. Roosevelt

Regulation of Trusts

turned his attention first to big corporations, where consolidation had created massive, monopolistic trusts. Although labeled a trustbuster, Roosevelt actually considered business consolidation an efficient means to achieve material progress. He believed in distinguishing between good and bad trusts, and preventing bad ones from manipulating markets. Thus he instructed the Justice Department to use antitrust laws to prosecute railroad, meatpacking, and oil trusts, which he believed unscrupulously exploited the public. Roosevelt's policy triumphed in 1904 when the Supreme Court, convinced by the government's arguments, ordered the breakup of Northern Securities Company, the huge railroad combination created by J. P. Morgan and his business allies. Roosevelt chose, however, not to attack other trusts, such as U.S. Steel, another of Morgan's creations.

When prosecution of Northern Securities began, Morgan reportedly collared Roosevelt and offered, "If we have done anything wrong, send your man to my man and they can fix it up." The president refused but was more sympathetic to cooperation between business and government than his rebuff might suggest. Rather than prosecute at every turn, he urged the Bureau of Corporations (part of the newly created Department of Labor and Commerce) to

assist companies in merging and expanding. Through investigation and consultation, the administration cajoled businesses to regulate themselves; corporations often cooperated because government regulation helped them operate more efficiently and reduced overproduction.

Roosevelt also supported regulatory legislation, especially after his resounding electoral victory in 1904, in which he won votes from Progressives and businesspeople alike. After a year of wrangling with railroads and their political allies, Roosevelt persuaded Congress to pass the Hepburn Act (1906), which strengthened the Interstate Commerce Commission (ICC) by giving it greater authority to set railroad freight rates and extending that authority over ferries, express companies, storage facilities, and oil pipelines. In the Elkins Act of 1903, Congress had already allowed the ICC to levy heavy fines against railroads and their customers involved in rebates on published shipping rates. The Hepburn Act still allowed courts to overturn ICC decisions, but, in a break from previous laws, it required shippers to prove they were not in violation of regulations, rather than making the government demonstrate violations.

Knowing that the political process made it difficult to achieve full business regulation, Roosevelt showed willingness to compromise on legislation to ensure the purity of food and

Pure Food and Drug Laws

drugs. For decades reformers had been urging government regulation of processed meat and patent medicines. Public outrage at fraud and adulteration flared in 1906 when Upton Sinclair published *The Jungle*, a fictionalized exposé of Chicago meatpacking plants. Sinclair, a socialist whose objective was to improve working conditions, shocked public sensibilities with his vivid descriptions.

> There would be meat stored in great piles in rooms; and the water from the leaky roofs would drip over it, and thousands of rats would race about on it. It was too dark in these storage places to see well, but a man could run his hand over these piles of meat and sweep off handfuls of dried dung of rats. These rats were a nuisance, and the packers would put poisoned bread out for them; they would die, and then rats, bread, and meat would go into the hoppers together.

After reading the novel, Roosevelt ordered an investigation. Finding Sinclair's descriptions accurate, he supported the Meat Inspection Act, which passed Congress in 1906. Like the Hepburn Act, this law reinforced the principle of government regulation, requiring that government agents monitor the quality of processed meat. But as

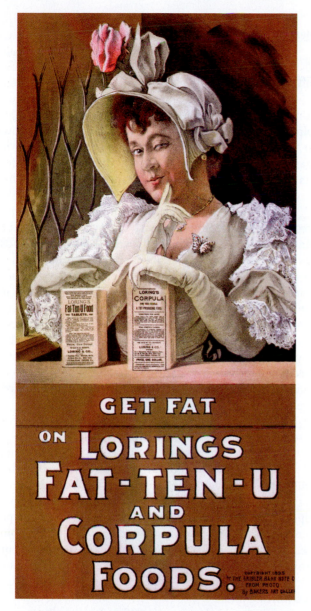

▲ Makers of unregulated patent medicines advertised that their products had exorbitant abilities to cure almost any ailment and remedy any unwanted physical condition. Loring's Fat-Ten-U tablets and Loring's Corpula were two such products. The Pure Food and Drug Act of 1906 did not ban these items but tried to prevent manufacturers from making unsubstantiated claims. *(© Bettmann/Corbis)*

were companies required to provide date-of-processing information on canned meats. Most large meatpackers welcomed the legislation anyway, because it helped them force out smaller competitors and restored foreign confidence in American meat products.

The Pure Food and Drug Act (1906) not only prohibited dangerously adulterated foods but also addressed abuses in the patent medicine industry. Makers of tonics and pills had long been making undue claims about their products' effects and liberally using alcohol and narcotics as ingredients. Ads in popular publications, like one for a "Brain Stimulator and Nerve Tonic" in the Sears, Roebuck catalogue, made wildly exaggerated claims. Although the law did not ban such products, it required that labels list the ingredients—a goal consistent with Progressive confidence that if people knew the truth they would make wiser purchases.

Roosevelt's approach to labor resembled his compromises with business over matters of regulation. When the United Mine Workers struck against Pennsylvania coal-mine owners in 1902 over an eight-hour workday and higher pay, the president employed Progressive tactics of investigation and arbitration. Owners, however, stubbornly refused to recognize the union or to arbitrate grievances. As winter approached and fuel shortages threatened, Roosevelt roused public opinion. He threatened to use federal troops to reopen the mines, thus forcing management to accept arbitration of the dispute by a special commission. The commission decided in favor of higher wages and reduced hours. It also required management to deal with grievance committees elected by the miners, but, in a compromise with management, it did not mandate recognition of the union. The decision, according to Roosevelt, provided a "square deal" for all. The settlement also embodied Roosevelt's belief that the president or his representatives should determine which labor demands were legitimate and which were not. In Roosevelt's mind there were good and bad labor organizations (socialists, for example, were bad), just as there were good and bad business combinations.

Although he angered southern congressmen by inviting Booker T. Washington to the White House to discuss

Race Relations

racial matters, Roosevelt believed in white superiority and was neutral toward blacks only when it helped him politically. An incident in 1906 illustrates this belief. That year, the army transferred a battalion of African American soldiers from Nebraska to Brownsville, Texas. Anglo and Mexican residents resented their presence and banned them from

part of a compromise with meatpackers and their congressional allies, the bill provided that the government, rather than the meatpackers, had to finance inspections, and meatpackers could appeal adverse decisions in court. Nor parks and businesses. They also protested unsuccessfully to Washington. On August 14, a battle between blacks and whites broke out, and a white man was killed. Brownsville residents blamed the soldiers, but when army investigators asked the troops to identify who had participated in the riot, none of the soldiers cooperated. As a result, however, Roosevelt discharged 167 black soldiers without a hearing or trial, and prevented them from receiving their pay and pensions even though there was no evidence against them. Black leaders were outraged. Roosevelt, hoping that blacks would support Republican candidates in the 1906 elections, had stalled before doing anything. But after the elections, he signed the discharge papers and offered no support when a bill was introduced in the Senate to allow the soldiers to reenlist.

Conservation

Roosevelt combined the Progressive impulse for efficiency with his love for the outdoors to make lasting contributions to modern resource conservation. Government involvement in this endeavor, especially the establishment of national parks, had begun in the late nineteenth century. Roosevelt advanced the movement by favoring *conservation* over *preservation*. Thus he not only exercised presidential power to protect such natural wonders as the Olympic Peninsula in Washington and the Grand Canyon in Arizona, as well as such human marvels as the native cliff dwellings in Colorado and Arizona, by declaring them national monuments, but also backed a policy of "wise use" of forests, waterways, and other resources in order to conserve them for future generations. Previously, the government had transferred ownership and control of natural resources on federal land to the states and to private interests. Roosevelt, however, believed the most efficient way to use and conserve resources would be for the federal government to retain management over lands that remained in the public domain.

Roosevelt exerted federal authority over resources in several ways. He created five national parks and fifty-one national bird reservations. He protected waterpower sites from sale to private interests and charged permit fees for users who wanted to produce hydroelectricity. He also supported the Newlands Reclamation Act of 1902, which controlled sale of irrigated federal land in the West (see page 483), and in 1908 he brought the nation's governors to the White House to discuss the efficient use of resources. During his presidency, Roosevelt tripled the number and acreage of national forests, identified a score of national monuments, and supported conservationist Gifford Pinchot in creating the U.S. Forest Service.

Gifford Pinchot

As chief forester of the United States and principal advocate of the "wise use" policy, Pinchot promoted scientific management of the nation's woodlands. He obtained Roosevelt's support for transferring management of the national forests from the Interior Department to his bureau in the Agriculture Department, arguing that forests were crops grown on "tree farms." Under his guidance, the Forest Service charged fees for grazing livestock within the national forests, supervised bidding for the cutting of timber, and hired university-trained foresters as federal employees.

Pinchot and Roosevelt did not seek to lock up—preserve—resources permanently; rather, they wanted to guarantee—conserve—their efficient use and make those who profited from using public lands pay the government for that use. Although antigovernment, pro-development attitudes still prevailed in the West, many of those involved in natural-resource exploitation welcomed such a policy because, like regulation of food and drugs, it enabled them to have better control over products, such as when Roosevelt and Pinchot encouraged large lumber companies to engage in reforestation. As a result of new federal policies, the West and its resources fell under the Progressive spell of management.

Panic of 1907

In 1907 economic crisis forced Roosevelt to compromise his principles and work more closely with big business. That year a financial panic caused by reckless speculation forced some New York banks to close in order to prevent frightened depositors from withdrawing money. J. P. Morgan helped stem the panic by persuading financiers to stop dumping their stocks. In return for Morgan's aid, Roosevelt approved a deal allowing U.S. Steel to absorb the Tennessee Iron and Coal Company—a deal at odds with Roosevelt's trustbusting aims.

But during his last year in office, Roosevelt retreated from the Republican Party's traditional friendliness to big business. He lashed out at irresponsible "malefactors of great wealth" and supported stronger business regulation and heavier taxation of the rich. Having promised that he would not seek reelection, Roosevelt backed his friend, Secretary of War William Howard Taft, for the Republican nomination in 1908, hoping that Taft would continue his initiatives. Democrats nominated William Jennings Bryan for the third time, but the "Great Commoner" lost again. Aided by Roosevelt, who still enjoyed great popularity, Taft won by 1.25 million popular votes and a 2-to-1 margin in the electoral college.

Early in 1909, Roosevelt traveled to Africa to shoot game, leaving Taft to face political problems that Roosevelt had managed to postpone.

Taft Administration

Foremost was the tariff; rates had risen to excessive levels. Honoring Taft's pledge to cut rates, the House passed a bill sponsored by Representative Sereno E. Payne that provided for numerous reductions. Protectionists in the Senate prepared, as in the past, to amend the bill and revise rates upward. But Senate Progressives, led by La Follette, attacked the tariff for benefiting special interests, trapping Taft between reformers who claimed to be preserving Roosevelt's antitrust campaign and protectionists who still dominated the Republican Party. In the end, Senator Aldrich restored many of the cuts the Payne bill had made, and Taft—who believed the bill had some positive provisions and understood that extreme cuts were not politically possible—signed what became known as the Payne-Aldrich Tariff (1909). In the eyes of Progressives, Taft had failed the test of filling Roosevelt's shoes.

Progressive and conservative wings of the Republican Party openly split. Soon after the tariff controversy, a group of insurgents in the House, led by Nebraska's George Norris, challenged Speaker "Uncle Joe" Cannon of Illinois, whose power over committee assignments and the scheduling of debates could make or break a piece of legislation. Taft first supported, then abandoned, the insurgents, who nevertheless managed to liberalize procedures by enlarging the influential Rules Committee and removing selection of its members from Cannon's control. In 1910 Taft also angered conservationists by firing Gifford Pinchot, who had protested Secretary of the Interior Richard A. Ballinger's plans to sell Alaskan coal lands and to reduce federal supervision of western waterpower sites, both of which were intended to aid private development.

In reality Taft was as sympathetic to reform as Roosevelt was. He prosecuted more trusts than Roosevelt, expanded national forest reserves, signed the Mann-Elkins Act (1910), which bolstered regulatory powers of the ICC, and supported such labor reforms as shorter work hours and mine safety legislation. The Sixteenth Amendment, which legalized the federal income tax as a permanent part of federal power, and the Seventeenth Amendment, which provided for direct election of U.S. senators, were initiated during Taft's presidency (and ratified in 1913). Like Roosevelt, Taft compromised with big business, but unlike Roosevelt, he lacked the ability to manipulate the public with spirited rhetoric. Roosevelt had expanded presidential power and infused the presidency with vitality.

"I believe in a strong executive," he once asserted. "I believe in power." Taft, by contrast, believed in the strict restraint of law. He had been a successful lawyer and judge, and returned to the bench as chief justice of the United States between 1921 and 1930. His caution and unwillingness to offend disappointed those accustomed to Roosevelt's magnetism.

In 1910, when Roosevelt returned from Africa, he found his party torn and tormented. Reformers, angered

Candidates in 1912

by Taft's apparent insensitivity to their causes, formed the National Progressive Republican League and rallied behind Robert La Follette for president in 1912, though many hoped Roosevelt would run. Another wing of the party remained loyal to Taft. Disappointed by Taft's performance (particularly his firing of Pinchot), Roosevelt began to speak out. He filled speeches with references to "the welfare of the people" and stronger regulation of business. When La Follette became ill early in 1912, Roosevelt, proclaiming himself fit as a "bull moose," threw his hat into the ring for the Republican presidential nomination.

Taft's supporters controlled the Republican convention and nominated him for a second term. In protest, Roosevelt's supporters bolted the convention to form a third party—the Progressive, or Bull Moose, Party—and nominated the fifty-three-year-old former president. Meanwhile, Democrats took forty-six ballots to select their candidate, New Jersey's Progressive governor Woodrow Wilson. Socialists, by now an organized and growing party, again nominated Eugene V. Debs. The ensuing campaign exposed voters to the most thorough debate on the nature of the American system since 1896.

Central to Theodore Roosevelt's campaign as the Progressive Party's nominee was a scheme called the

New Nationalism Versus New Freedom

New Nationalism, a term coined by reform editor Herbert Croly. The New Nationalism envisioned an era of national unity in which government would coordinate and regulate economic activity. Echoing his statements in the last years of his presidency, Roosevelt asserted that he would establish regulatory commissions of experts who would protect citizens' interests and ensure wise use of economic power. "The effort at prohibiting all combinations has substantially failed," he claimed. "The way out lies . . . in completely controlling them."

Wilson offered a more idealistic proposal, the "New Freedom," based on ideas of Progressive lawyer Louis Brandeis. Wilson argued that concentrated economic

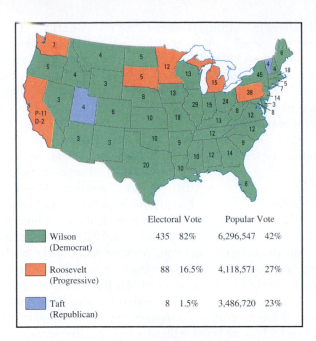

	Electoral Vote		Popular Vote	
Wilson (Democrat)	435	82%	6,296,547	42%
Roosevelt (Progressive)	88	16.5%	4,118,571	27%
Taft (Republican)	8	1.5%	3,486,720	23%

Map 21.2   Presidential Election, 1912
Although he had only a minority of the popular votes, Woodrow Wilson captured so many states that he achieved an easy victory in the electoral college.

power threatened individual liberty and that monopolies should be broken up so that the marketplace could become genuinely open. But he would not restore laissez faire. Like Roosevelt, Wilson would enhance government authority to protect and regulate. "Freedom today," he declared, "is something more than being let alone. Without the watchful . . . resolute interference of the government, there can be no fair play between individuals and such powerful institutions as the trust." Wilson stopped short, however, of advocating the cooperation between business and government inherent in Roosevelt's New Nationalism.

Roosevelt and Wilson stood closer together than their rhetoric implied. Despite his faith in experts as regulators, Roosevelt's belief in individual freedom was as strong as Wilson's. And Wilson was not completely hostile to concentrated economic power. Both men supported equality of opportunity (chiefly for white males), conservation of natural resources, fair wages, and social betterment for all. Neither would hesitate to expand government activity through strong personal leadership and bureaucratic reform.

Amid passionate moral pronouncements from Roosevelt and Wilson, as well as a hard-hitting critique from Debs and a low-key defense of conservatism from Taft,

the popular vote was inconclusive. The victorious Wilson won just 42 percent, though he did capture 435 out of 531 electoral votes (see Map 21.2). Roosevelt received 27 percent of the popular vote. Taft finished third, polling 23 percent of the popular vote and only 8 electoral votes. Debs won 6 percent of the total but no electoral votes. One major outcome was evident, however; three-quarters of the electorate supported some alternative to the view of restrained government that Taft represented. Thus Wilson could proclaim on inauguration day in 1913, "The Nation has been deeply stirred by a solemn passion. . . . The feelings with which we face this new age of right and opportunity sweep across our heartstrings like some air out of God's own presence, where justice and mercy are reconciled and the judge and the brother are one."

WOODROW WILSON AND THE EXTENSION OF PROGRESSIVE REFORM

Woodrow Wilson

The public fondly called Roosevelt "Teddy" and "TR," but Thomas Woodrow Wilson was too aloof ever to be nicknamed "Woody" or "WW." Born in Virginia in 1856 and raised in the South, Wilson was the son of a Presbyterian minister. He earned a B.A. degree at Princeton University, studied law at the University of Virginia, received a Ph.D. degree from Johns Hopkins University, and became a professor of history, jurisprudence, and political economy. Between 1885 and 1908, he published several respected books on American history and government.

Wilson's manner reflected his background. He exuded none of Roosevelt's brashness, yet he was a superb orator who could inspire intense loyalty with religious imagery and eloquent expressions of American ideals. Wilson's convictions led him early into reform. In 1902 he became president of Princeton and upset tradition with curricular reforms and battles against the university's aristocratic elements. But his racist leanings showed themselves when he refused to admit blacks to the college. In 1910 New Jersey's Democrats, eager for respectability, nominated Wilson for governor. After winning the election, Wilson repudiated the party bosses and promoted Progressive legislation. A poor administrator, he often lost his temper and stubbornly refused to compromise. His accomplishments nevertheless attracted national attention and won him the Democratic nomination for president in 1912.

As president, Wilson found it necessary to blend New Freedom competition with New Nationalism regulation;

EXECVTRIX
AVGVSTA
    MINERVA
LVMINARIA !

SALVE
O WOODRECINA
ATHENA
    PROLETARIA!
PRINCETONIENSIS
    POPVLIQVE
DEA
    TVTORLARIA
        !

▲ Depicted here as a stern Roman consul, Woodrow Wilson was a former professor (his university background is represented here by the scholarly owl at his side) who as president used a stubborn moralism to guide the nation toward his ideals.

(Picture Research Consultants & Archives)

Wilson's Policy on Business Regulation

in so doing, he set the direction of future federal economic policy. The corporate merger movement had made restoration of open competition impossible. Wilson could only try to prevent abuses by expanding government's regulatory powers. He thus supported congressional passage in 1914 of the Clayton Anti-Trust Act and a bill creating the Federal Trade Commission (FTC). The Clayton Act corrected deficiencies of the Sherman Anti-Trust Act of 1890 by outlawing such corporate practices as price discrimination (lowering prices in some regions but not in others) and interlocking directorates (management of two or more competing companies by the same executives). The act also aided labor by exempting unions from its anticombination provision, thereby making peaceful strikes, boycotts, and picketing less vulnerable to government interference. The FTC could investigate companies and issue cease-and-desist orders against unfair practices. Accused companies could appeal FTC orders in

court; nevertheless, the FTC represented another step toward consumer protection.

Wilson expanded banking regulation with the Federal Reserve Act (1913), which established the nation's first central banking system since 1836, when the Second Bank of the United States expired. To break the power that banking syndicates like that of J. P. Morgan held over the money supply, the act created twelve district banks to hold reserves of member banks throughout the nation. The district banks, supervised by the Federal Reserve Board, would lend money to member banks at a low interest rate called the discount rate. By adjusting this rate (and thus the amount a bank could afford to borrow), district banks could increase or decrease the amount of money in circulation. In other words, in response to the nation's currency needs, the Federal Reserve Board could loosen or tighten credit, making interest rates fairer, especially for small borrowers.

Wilson and Congress attempted to restore competition in commerce with the Underwood Tariff of 1913. By the

Tariff and Tax Reform

1910s, prices for some consumer goods had become unnaturally high because tariffs discouraged the importation of cheaper foreign materials and manufactured goods. By reducing or eliminating certain tariff rates, the Underwood Tariff encouraged imports. To replace revenues lost because of tariff reductions, the act levied a graduated income tax on U.S. residents—an option made possible when the Sixteenth Amendment was ratified earlier that year. The tax was tame by today's standards. Incomes under $4,000 were exempt; thus almost all factory workers and farmers escaped taxation. Individuals and corporations earning between $4,000 and $20,000 had to pay a 1 percent tax; thereafter rates rose gradually to a maximum of 6 percent on earnings over $500,000.

The outbreak of the First World War (see Chapter 23) and the approaching presidential election campaign prompted Wilson to support stronger reforms in 1916. To aid farmers, the president backed the Federal Farm Loan Act. This measure created twelve federally supported banks (not to be confused with Federal Reserve banks), which could lend money at moderate interest to farmers who belonged to credit institutions—a watered-down version of the subtreasury plan that Populists had proposed a generation earlier (see pages 578–579). To forestall railroad strikes that might disrupt transportation at a time of national emergency, Wilson in 1916 also pushed passage of the Adamson Act, which mandated eight-hour workdays and time-and-a-half overtime pay for railroad laborers. He pleased Progressives by appointing Brandeis, the "people's advocate," to the Supreme Court, though an

Legacy FOR A PEOPLE AND A NATION

Margaret Sanger, Planned Parenthood, and the Birth-Control Controversy

ome reforms of the Progressive era illustrate how earnest intentions to help can become tangled in divisive issues of morality. Such is the legacy of birth-control advocate Margaret Sanger. In 1912 Sanger began writing a column on sex education in the *New York Call* entitled "What Every Girl Should Know." Almost immediately, strict moralists accused her of writing obscene literature because she publicly discussed venereal disease and contraception. The issue of limiting family size, however, became her passion, and she began counseling poor women on New York's Lower East Side about how to avoid the pain of frequent childbirth, miscarriage, and bungled abortion. In 1914 Sanger published the first issue of *The Woman Rebel,* a monthly newspaper that advocated a woman's right to practice birth control. Indicted for distributing obscenity through the mails, she fled to England. There she joined a set of radicals and gave speeches on behalf of family planning and a woman's need to enjoy sexual fulfillment without fear of pregnancy.

Returning to the United States, Sanger opened the country's first birth-control clinic in Brooklyn in 1916. She was arrested, but when a court exempted physicians from a law prohibiting dissemination of contraceptive information, she set up a doctor-run clinic in 1923. Staffed by female doctors and social workers, the Birth Control Clinical Research Bureau acted as a model for other clinics. Sanger also organized the American Birth Control League (1921) and tried to win support from medical and social reformers, including some from the eugenics movement, for legalized birth control. Eventually, her radical views caused her to fall out with some of her allies, and she resigned from the American Birth Control League in 1928.

The movement continued, however, and in 1938 the American Birth Control League and the Birth Control Clinical Research Bureau merged to form the Birth Control Federation of America, renamed the Planned Parenthood Federation of America (PPFA) in 1942. The organization's name defined its mission to strengthen the family and stabilize society with the help of governmental support, rather than to focus more directly on the feminist issue of whether or not a woman should have the right of voluntary motherhood. Throughout the 1940s, the PPFA emphasized family planning through making contraceptives more accessible. In 1970 it began receiving funds under a federal program to provide family-planning services.

In the 1960s, the emergence of new feminist agitation for women's rights and rising concerns about overpopulation moved issues of birth control and abortion into an arena of passionate controversy. Although the PPFA had initially dissociated itself from abortion as a means of family planning, the debate between a woman's "choice" and a fetus's "right to life" drew the organization into the fray, especially after 1973, when the Supreme Court validated women's right to an abortion in *Roe v. Wade.* The national PPFA and its local branches fought legislative and court attempts to make abortions illegal, and in 1989 it helped organize a women's march on Washington for equality and abortion rights. At the same time, some Latino and African American groups attacked the PPFA's stance, charging that legalized abortion was a kind of eugenics program meant to reduce births among nonwhite races.

Because of the PPFA's involvement in abortion politics, several of its clinics have been targets of picketing and even violence by those who believe abortion to be immoral. The PPFA now operates nearly nine hundred health centers providing medical services and education nationwide, and has fulfilled Margaret Sanger's dream of legalized contraception and family planning. But, as with other reforms dealing with issues of morality and individual rights, birth control has left a legacy to a people and a nation of disagreement over whose rights and whose morality should prevail.

anti-Semitic backlash almost blocked Senate approval of the Court's first Jewish justice. In addition, Wilson pleased social reformers by backing laws that regulated child labor and provided workers' compensation for federal employees who suffered work-related injuries or illness.

Amid his reforms, however, Wilson never overcame his racism. Although in 1918 he tried to appoint W. E. B. Du Bois as an army officer to help keep race relations calm (Du Bois, age fifty, failed the physical.). Wilson fired several black federal officials, and his administration preserved racial separation in restrooms, restaurants, and government office buildings. Wilson responded to protesting blacks that "segregation is not a humiliation but a benefit, and ought to be so regarded by you gentlemen." When the pathbreaking but inflammatory film about the Civil War and Reconstruction, *The Birth of a Nation* was released in 1915, Wilson allowed a showing at the White House, though he subsequently prohibited it during the First World War.

In selecting a candidate to oppose Wilson in the presidential election of 1916, Republicans snubbed Theodore Roosevelt in favor of Charles Evans Hughes, Supreme Court justice and former reform governor of New York. Aware of public anxiety over

Election of 1916

the world war raging in Europe since 1914, Wilson ran on a platform of neutrality and Progressivism, using the campaign slogan "He Kept Us Out of War." Hughes advocated greater military preparedness, but Wilson's peace platform resonated with the voters. The election outcome was close. Wilson received 9.1 million votes to Hughes's 8.5 million and barely won in the electoral college, 277 to 254. The Socialist candidate drew only 600,000 votes, down from 901,000 in 1912, largely because Wilson's reforms had won over some Socialists and because the ailing Eugene Debs was no longer the party's standard-bearer.

During Wilson's second term, U.S. involvement in the First World War increased government regulation of the economy. Mobilization and war, he came to believe, required greater coordination of production and cooperation between the public and private sectors. The War Industries Board exemplified this cooperation: private businesses regulated by the board submitted to its control on condition that their profit motives would continue to be satisfied. After the war, Wilson's administration dropped most cooperative and regulatory measures, including farm price supports, guarantees of collective bargaining, and high taxes. This retreat from regulation, prompted in part by the election of a Republican Congress in 1918, stimulated a new era of business ascendancy in the 1920s.

SUMMARY

By 1920 a quarter-century of reform had wrought momentous changes. Government, economy, and society as they had existed in the nineteenth century were gone forever. In their efforts to achieve goals of ending abuses of power, reforming institutions, and applying scientific and efficient management, Progressives established the principle of public intervention to ensure fairness, health, and safety. Concern over poverty and injustice reached new heights. But reformers could not sustain their efforts indefinitely. Although Progressive values lingered after the First World War, a mass-consumer society began to refocus people's attention away from reform to materialism.

Multiple and sometimes contradictory goals characterized the Progressive era. By no means was there a single Progressive movement. Programs on the national level ranged from Roosevelt's faith in big government as a coordinator of big business to Wilson's promise to dissolve economic concentrations and legislate open competition. At state and local levels, reformers pursued causes as varied as neighborhood improvement, government reorganization, public ownership of utilities, and betterment of work-

ing conditions. National associations coordinated efforts on specific issues, but reformers with different goals often worked at cross-purposes. New consciousness about identity confronted women and African Americans, and although women made some inroads into public life, both groups still found themselves in confined social positions and dependent on their own resolve in their quest for dignity and recognition.

In spite of their successes, the failure of many Progressive initiatives indicates the strength of the opposition, as well as weaknesses within the reform movements themselves. As issues such as Americanization, eugenics, prohibition, education, and general moral uplift illustrate, social reform often merged into social control—attempts to impose one group's values on all of society and to regulate behavior of immigrant and nonwhite racial groups. In political matters, courts asserted constitutional and liberty-of-contract doctrines in striking down key Progressive legislation, notably the federal law prohibiting child labor. In states and cities, adoption of the initiative, referendum, and recall did not encourage greater participation in government as had been hoped; those mechanisms either were seldom used or became tools of special interests. Federal regulatory agencies rarely had enough resources for thorough investigations; they had to depend on information from the very companies they policed. Progressives thus failed in many respects to redistribute power. In 1920, as in 1900, government remained under the influence of business, a state of affairs that many people in power considered quite satisfactory.

Yet the reform movements that characterized the Progressive era reshaped the national outlook. Trustbusting, however faulty, made industrialists more sensitive to public opinion, and insurgents in Congress partially diluted the power of dictatorial politicians. Progressive legislation equipped government with tools to protect consumers against price fixing and dangerous products. Social reformers relieved some ills of urban and industrial life. And, perhaps most important, Progressives challenged old ways of thinking. Although the questions they raised about the quality of American life remained unresolved, Progressives made the nation acutely aware of its principles and promises.

SUGGESTIONS FOR FURTHER READING

Francis L. Broderick, *Progressivism at Risk: Electing a President in 1912* (1989)

Nancy F. Cott, *The Grounding of Modern Feminism* (1987)

Steven J. Diner, *A Very Different Age: Americans of the Progressive Era* (1998)

Glenda Gilmore, *Who Were the Progressives?* (2002)

Hugh D. Hindman, *Child Labor: An American History* (2002)

Alice Kessler-Harris, *Out to Work: A History of Wage-Earning Women in the United States,* 20th anniversary ed. (2003)

Michael McGerr, *A Fierce Discontent: The Rise and Fall of the Progressive Movement in America, 1870–1920* (2003)

Patricia A. Schecter, *Ida B. Wells and American Reform, 1880–1930* (2001)

David Tyack, *Seeking Common Ground: Public Schools in a Diverse Society* (2003)

For a more extensive list for further reading, go to college.hmco.com/pic/norton8e.

The Quest for Empire *1865-1914*

evil!" they shouted at Lottie Moon. "Foreign devil!" The Southern Baptist missionary, half a world away from home, braced herself against the cries of the Chinese "rabble" whom she had been determined to convert to Christianity. On that day in the 1880s, she walked "steadily and persistently" through the throng of hecklers, silently vowing to win their acceptance and then their souls.

Born in 1840 in Virginia and educated at what is now Hollins College, Charlotte Diggs Moon volunteered in 1873 for "woman's work" in northern China. There she taught and proselytized, largely among women and children, because women seldom preached to men and men were forbidden to preach to women. This compassionate, pious, and courageous single woman, "putting love into action," worked in China until her death in 1912.

In the 1870s and 1880s, Lottie Moon (Mu Ladi, or 幕拉第) made bold and sometimes dangerous evangelizing trips to isolated Chinese hamlets. "O! The torture of human eyes upon you; scanning every feature, every look, every gesture!" Curious peasant women pinched her, pulled on her skirts, and purred, "How white her hand is!" They peppered her with questions: "How old are you?" "Where do you get money to live on?" Speaking in Chinese, Lottie held high a picture book of Jesus Christ's birth and crucifixion, drawing the crowd's attention to the "foreign doctrine" that she hoped would displace Confucianism, Buddhism, and Taoism.

In the 1890s, a "storm of persecution" directed against foreigners swept China. Because missionaries were upending traditional ways and authority, they became hated targets. One missionary conceded that, in "believing Jesus," girls and women alarmed men who worried that "disobedient wives and daughters" would no longer "worship the idols when told." In the village of Shaling in early 1890, Lottie Moon's Christian converts were beaten and the "foreign devils" ordered to move out. Fearing for her life, she had to flee.

◀ The missionary Lottie Moon (1840–1912) in 1901 with English-language students in Japan, during her refuge from the Boxer Rebellion in China.

(Virginia Baptist Historical Society & University Archives)

CHRONOLOGY

1861–69 ■ Seward sets expansionist course

1867 ■ United States acquires Alaska and Midway

1876 ■ Pro-U.S. Díaz begins thirty-four-year rule in Mexico

1878 ■ United States gains naval rights in Samoa

1885 ■ Strong's *Our Country* celebrates Anglo-Saxon destiny of dominance

1887 ■ United States gains naval rights to Pearl Harbor, Hawai'i
■ McKinley Tariff hurts Hawaiian sugar exports

1893 ■ Economic crisis leads to business failures and mass unemployment
■ Pro-U.S. interests stage successful coup against Queen Lili'uokalani of Hawai'i

1895 ■ Cuban revolution against Spain begins
■ Japan defeats China in war, annexes Korea and Formosa (Taiwan)

1898 ■ United States formally annexes Hawai'i
■ U.S. battleship *Maine* blows up in Havana harbor
■ United States defeats Spain in Spanish-American War

1899 ■ Treaty of Paris enlarges U.S. empire
■ United Fruit Company forms and becomes influential in Central America
■ Philippine insurrection breaks out, led by Emilio Aguinaldo

1901 ■ McKinley assassinated; Theodore Roosevelt becomes president

1903 ■ Panama grants canal rights to United States
■ Platt Amendment subjugates Cuba

1904 ■ Roosevelt Corollary declares United States a hemispheric "police power"

1905 ■ Portsmouth Conference ends Russo-Japanese War

1906 ■ San Francisco School Board segregates Asian schoolchildren
■ United States invades Cuba to quell revolt

1907 ■ "Great White Fleet" makes world tour

1910 ■ Mexican revolution threatens U.S. interests

1914 ■ U.S. troops invade Mexico
■ First World War begins
■ Panama Canal opens

For several months in 1900, during the violent Boxer Rebellion, she had to leave China altogether, as a multinational force (including U.S. troops) intervened to save foreign missionaries, diplomats, and merchants.

Lottie Moon and thousands of other missionaries managed to convert to Christianity only a very small minority of the Chinese people. Although she, like other missionaries, probably never shed the western view that she represented a superior religion and culture, she seldom wavered in her affection for the Chinese people and in her devotion to the foreign missionary project—in her "rejoicing to suffer." In frequent letters and articles directed to a U.S. audience, she lobbied to recruit "a band of ardent, enthusiastic, and experienced Christian women," to stir up "a mighty wave of enthusiasm for Woman's Work for Woman." To this day, the Lottie Moon Christmas Offering in Southern Baptist churches raises millions of dollars for missions abroad.

Like so many other Americans who went overseas in the late nineteenth and early twentieth centuries, Lottie Moon helped spread American culture and influence abroad. In this complex process, other peoples sometimes adopted and sometimes rejected American ways. At the same time, American participants in this cultural expansion and the cultural collisions that it generated became transformed. Lottie Moon, for example, strove to understand the Chinese people and to learn their language. She assumed their dress and abandoned such derogatory phrases as "heathen Chinese" and "great unwashed." She reminded other, less sensitive missionaries that the Chinese rightfully took pride in their own ancient history and thus had no reason to "gape in astonishment at Western civilization."

Lottie Moon also changed—again, in her own words—from "a timid self-distrustful girl into a brave self-reliant woman." As she questioned the Chinese confinement of women, most conspicuous in arranged marriages, foot binding, and sexual segregation, she advanced women's rights. She understood that she could not convert Chinese women unless they had the freedom to listen to her appeals. Bucking the gender ideology of the times, she also uneasily rose to challenge the male domination of America's religious missions. When the Southern Baptist Foreign Mission Board denied woman missionaries the right to vote in meetings, she resigned in protest. The board soon reversed itself.

In later decades, critics labeled the activities of Lottie Moon and other missionaries "cultural imperialism," accusing them of seeking to subvert indigenous traditions and of sparking destructive cultural clashes. Defenders of missionary work, on the other hand, have celebrated their efforts to break down cultural barriers and to bring the world's peoples closer together. Either way, Lottie Moon's story illustrates how Americans in the late nineteenth century interacted with the world in diverse ways, how through their experiences the categories "domestic" and "foreign" came to intersect, and how they expanded abroad not only to seek land, trade, investments, and strategic bases, but also to promote American culture, including the Christian faith.

Between the Civil War and the First World War, an expansionist United States joined the ranks of the great world powers. Before the Civil War, Americans had repeatedly extended the frontier: they bought Louisiana; annexed Florida, Oregon, and Texas; pushed Indians out of the path of white migration westward; seized California and other western areas from Mexico; and acquired southern parts of present-day Arizona and New Mexico from Mexico (the Gadsden Purchase). Americans had also developed a lucrative foreign trade with most of the world and promoted American culture wherever they traveled. They rekindled their expansionist course after the Civil War, building, managing, and protecting an overseas empire.

It was an age of empire. By the 1870s, most of Europe's powers were carving up Africa and large parts of Asia and Oceania for themselves. By 1900 the powers had conquered more than 10 million square miles (one-fifth of the earth's land), and 150 million people. As the century turned, France, Russia, and Germany were spending heavily on modern steel navies, challenging an overextended Great Britain. In Asia, meanwhile, a rapidly modernizing Japan expanded at the expense of both China and Russia.

Engineering advances altered the world's political geography through the Suez Canal (1869), the British Trans-Indian railroad (1870), and the Russian Trans-Siberian Railway (1904), while steamships, machine guns, telegraphs, and malaria drugs greatly facilitated the imperialists' task. Simultaneously, the optimistic spirit that had characterized European political discourse in the 1850s and 1860s gave way to a brooding pessimism and a sense of impending warfare informed by notions of racial conflict and survival of the fittest.

This transformation of world politics did not escape notice by observant Americans; some argued that the United States risked being "left behind" if it failed to join the scramble for territory and markets. Republican senator Henry Cabot Lodge of Massachusetts, claiming that the "great nations" were seizing "the waste areas of the world," advised that "the United States must not fall out of the line of march," because "civilization and the advancement of the [Anglo-Saxon] race" were at stake. Such thinking helped fuel Americans' desire in the years after the Civil War to exert their influence beyond the continental United States, to reach for more space, more land, more markets, more cultural penetration, and more power.

By 1900 the United States had emerged as a great power with particular clout in Latin America, especially as Spain declined and Britain disengaged from the Western Hemisphere. In the Pacific, the new U.S. empire included Hawai'i, American Samoa, and the Philippines. Theodore Roosevelt, who in the 1890s was a leading spokesman for the imperialist cause, would, as president in the decade that followed, seek to consolidate this newfound power.

Most Americans applauded expansionism—the outward movement of goods, ships, dollars, people, and ideas—as a traditional feature of their nation's history. But many became uneasy whenever expansionism gave way to imperialism—the imposition of control over other peoples, undermining their sovereignty and usurping their freedom to make their own decisions. Abroad, native nationalists, commercial competitors, and other imperial nations tried to block the spread of U.S. influence.

- What accounts for the increased importance of foreign policy concerns in American politics in the closing years of the nineteenth century?

- What key arguments were made by American anti-imperialists?

- How did late-nineteenth-century imperialism transform the United States?

▲ As one expression of the theme of economic expansion, this poster, advertising the Uncle Sam stove manu-factured in New York by the Abendroth Bros. company, announces that food links the United States with the rest of the world. Although the foods on the long list are international—potatoes from Ireland and macaroni from Italy, for example—the message here is that the United States itself is "feeding the world." The turkey being removed from the oven seems to be the only uniquely American offering, but many of the items on the list were also pro-duced in the United States. The poster was issued in 1876, which explains the image of the Centennial building in Philadelphia and the patriotic red, white, and blue colors. *(© Collection of The New York Historical Society)*

IMPERIAL DREAMS

Foreign policy assumed a new importance for Americans in the closing years of the nineteenth century. For much of the Gilded Age, they had been preoccupied by internal matters, such as industrialization, the construction of the railroads, and the settlement of the West. Over time, how-ever, increasing numbers of political and business leaders began to look outward, and to advocate a more activist approach to world affairs. The motives of these expansion-ists were complex and varied, but all of them emphasized the supposed benefits of such an approach to the country's domestic health.

That proponents of overseas expansion stressed the benefits that would accrue at home should come as no surprise, for foreign policy has always sprung from the domestic setting of a nation—its needs and moods, ideol-ogy and culture. The leaders who guided America's ex-pansionist foreign relations were the same ones who guided the economic development of the machine age,

forged the transcontinental railroad, built America's bustling cities and giant corporations, and shaped a mass culture. They unabashedly espoused the idea that the United States was an exceptional nation, so different from and superior to others because of its Anglo-Saxon heritage and its God-favored and prosperous history.

Exceptionalism was but one in an intertwined set of ideas that figured prominently in the American march toward empire. Nationalism, capitalism, Social Darwin-ism, and a paternalistic attitude toward foreigners influ-enced American leaders as well. "They are children and we are men in these deep matters of government," future president Woodrow Wilson announced in 1898. The very words he chose reveal the gender and age bias of American attitudes. Where these attitudes intersected with foreign cultures, there came not only adoption but rejection, not only imitation but clash, as Lottie Moon learned.

It would take time for most Americans to grasp the changes under way. "The people" may influence domestic

Foreign Policy Elite

policy directly, but the making of foreign policy is usually dominated by what scholars have labeled the "foreign policy elite"— opinion leaders in politics, journalism, business, agriculture, religion, education, and the military. In the post–Civil War era, this small group, whom Secretary of State Walter Q. Gresham called "the thoughtful men of the country," expressed the opinions that counted. Better read and better traveled than most Americans, more cosmopolitan in outlook, and politically active, they believed that U.S. prosperity and security depended on the exertion of U.S. influence abroad. Increasingly in the late nineteenth century, and especially in the 1890s, the expansionist-minded elite urged both formal and informal imperialism. Ambitious and clannish, the imperialists often met in Washington, D.C., at the homes of historian Henry Adams and of writer and diplomat John Hay (who became secretary of state in 1898) or at the Metropolitan Club. They talked about building a bigger navy and digging a canal across Panama, Central America, or Mexico; establishing colonies; and selling surpluses abroad. Theodore Roosevelt, appointed assistant secretary of the navy in 1897, was among them; so were Senator Henry Cabot Lodge, who joined the Foreign Relations Committee in 1896, and corporate lawyer Elihu Root, who later would serve as both secretary of war and secretary of state. Such well-positioned luminaries kept up the drumbeat for empire.

These American leaders believed that selling, buying, and investing in foreign marketplaces were important to the United States. Why? One reason was profits from foreign sales. "It is my dream," declared the governor of Georgia in 1878, to see "in every valley . . . a cotton factory to convert the raw material of the neighborhood into fabrics which shall warm the limbs of Japanese and Chinese." Fear also helped make the case for foreign trade, as foreign commerce might serve as a safety valve to relieve overproduction, unemployment, economic depression, and the social tension that arose from them. The nation's farms and factories produced more than Americans could consume, all the more so during the 1890s' depression. Surpluses had to be exported, the economist David A. Wells warned, or "we are certain to be smothered in our own grease." Economic ties also permitted political influence to be exerted abroad and helped spread the American way of life, especially capitalism, creating a world more hospitable to Americans. In an era when the most powerful nations in the world were also the greatest traders, vigorous foreign economic expansion symbolized national stature.

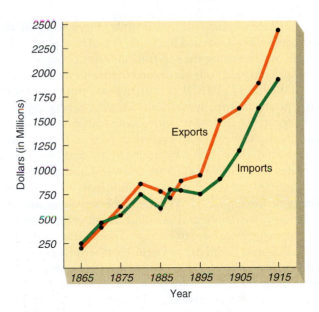

Figure 22.1   U.S. Trade Expansion, 1865–1914

This figure illustrates two key characteristics of U.S. foreign trade: first, that the United States began in the 1870s to enjoy a favorable balance of trade (exporting more than it imported), and second, that U.S. exports expanded tremendously, making the United States one of the world's economic giants.

(Source: Thomas G. Paterson, J. Garry Clifford, and Kenneth J. Hagan, American Foreign Relations: A History, 5th ed. Copyright © 2000 by Houghton Mifflin Company. Used by permission of Houghton Mifflin Company.)

Foreign Trade Expansion

Although most business leaders remained focused on the domestic marketplace, foreign trade figured prominently in the tremendous economic growth of the United States after the Civil War. Foreign commerce in turn stimulated the building of a larger protective navy, the professionalization of the foreign service, calls for more colonies, and a more interventionist foreign policy. In 1865 U.S. exports totaled $234 million; by 1900 they had climbed to $1.5 billion (see Figure 22.1). By 1914, at the outbreak of the First World War, exports had reached $2.5 billion, prompting some Europeans to protest an American "invasion" of goods. In 1874 the United States reversed its historically unfavorable balance of trade (importing more than it exported) and began to enjoy a long-term favorable balance (exporting more than it imported)—though the balance of payments remained in the red. Most of America's products went to Britain, continental Europe, and Canada, but increasing amounts flowed to new markets in Latin America and Asia. Meanwhile, direct American investments abroad reached $3.5 billion by 1914, placing the United States among the top four investor countries.

Agricultural goods accounted for about three-fourths of total exports in 1870 and about two-thirds in 1900, with grain, cotton, meat, and dairy products topping the export list that year. More than half of the annual cotton crop was exported each year. Midwestern farmers transported their crops by railroad to seaboard cities and then on to foreign markets. Farmers' livelihoods thus became tied to world-market conditions and the outcomes of foreign wars. Wisconsin cheesemakers shipped to Britain; the Swift and Armour meat companies exported refrigerated beef to Europe. To sell American grain abroad, James J. Hill of the Great Northern Railroad distributed wheat cookbooks translated into several Asian languages.

In 1913, when the United States outranked both Great Britain and Germany in manufacturing production (see Figure 22.2), manufactured goods led U.S. exports for the first time. Substantial proportions of America's steel, copper, and petroleum were sold abroad, making many workers in those industries dependent on American exports. George Westinghouse marketed his air brakes in Europe; almost as many Singer sewing machines were exported as were sold at home; and Cyrus McCormick's "reaper kings" harvested the wheat of Russian fields.

In promoting the expansion of U.S. influence overseas, many officials championed a nationalism based on

Race Thinking and the Male Ethos

notions of American supremacy. Some, echoing the articulations of European imperialists (who had their own conceptions of national supremacy), found justification for expansionism in racist theories then permeating western thought and politics. For decades, the western scientific establishment had classified humankind by race, and students of physical anthropology drew on phrenology and physiognomy—the analysis of skull size and shape, and the comparison of facial features—to produce a hierarchy of superior and inferior races. One well-known French researcher, for example, claimed that blacks represented a "female race" and "like the woman, the black is deprived of political and scientific intelligence; he has never created a great state . . . he has never accomplished anything in industrial mechanics. But on the other hand he has great virtues of sentiment. Like women he also likes jewelry, dancing, and singing."

The language of U.S. leaders was also weighted with words like *manliness* and *weakling*. Member of Congress, son-in-law of Senator Lodge, and Spanish-American War veteran Augustus P. Gardner extolled the "arena of lust and blood, where true men are to be found." The warrior and president Theodore Roosevelt viewed people of color (or "darkeys," as he called them) as effeminate weaklings who lacked the ability to govern themselves and could not cope with world politics. Americans regularly debased Latin Americans as half-breeds needing close supervision,

Figure 22.2   **The Rise of U.S. Economic Power in the World**
These pie charts showing percentage shares of world manufacturing production for the major nations of the world demonstrate that the United States came to surpass Great Britain in this significant economic measurement of power.

(Source: League of Nations data presented in Aaron L. Friedberg, The Weary Titan: Britain and the Experience of Relative Decline, 1895–1905 *(Princeton, N.J.: Princeton University Press, 1988), p. 26.)*

National Geographic

On a winter day in early 1888, thirty-three members of the elite Cosmos Club in Washington, D.C., convened around a mahogany table to consider "the advisability of organizing a society for the increase and diffusion of geographical knowledge." The result was the National Geographic Society, destined to become the largest non-profit scientific and educational institution in the world.

At the heart of the enterprise would be a magazine designed to win broad support for the society. *National Geographic Magazine* (later simply *National Geographic*) appeared for the first time in October 1888. Early issues were brief, technical, and visually bland, and sales lagged. In 1898, however, Alexander Graham Bell became president of the society and made two key changes: he shifted emphasis from newsstand sales to society membership, reasoning correctly that armchair travelers would flock to join a distinguished fellowship, and he appointed a talented new editor, Gilbert H. Grosvenor, age twenty-three. Grosvenor commissioned articles of general interest and, in an unprecedented move, filled eleven pages of one issue with photographs.

These and other early photos showed people stiffly posed in their native costumes, displayed as anthropological specimens. But they caused a sensation. By 1908 pictures occupied 50 percent of the magazine's space. In 1910 the first color photographs appeared, in a twenty-four-page spread on Korea and China—at that time the largest collection of color photographs ever published in a single issue of any magazine. In later years, *National Geographic* would have several other photographic firsts, including the first natural-color photos of Arctic life and the undersea world.

The society also used membership dues to sponsor expeditions, such as the 1909 journey to the North Pole by Robert Peary and Matthew Henson and, later, Jacques Cousteau's many oceanic explorations and Jane Goodall's up-close observations of wild chimpanzees. The tales of these adventures then appeared in the magazine's pages, along with stunning photographs. By the end of Grosvenor's tenure as editor, in 1954, circulation had grown to more than 2 million.

Grosvenor's winning formula included less-admirable elements. His editors pressured photographers to provide "pictures of pretty girls" to the point at which, as one photographer recalled, "hundreds of bare-breasted women, all from poorer countries, were published at a time of booming subscription rates." Editors also developed a well-earned reputation for avoiding controversial issues and presenting a rosy view of the world. An article about Berlin published just before the start of World War II, for example, contained no criticism of the Nazi regime and no mention of its persecution of Jews. Recent years have seen the magazine take on more newsworthy items—AIDS, stem cell research, Hurricane Katrina, global warming—but in measured, generally nonpolitical tones.

Throughout, the society has continued to expand its reach, moving into the production of books, atlases, globes, and television documentaries. Targeting overseas readers, the society in 1995 launched a Japanese-language edition and subsequently added twenty-five other foreign editions. *National Geographic*, after a century of linking Americans to faraway places, now went in the other direction, connecting readers in many of those locales to the United States.

▲ *National Geographic* had already gone through five different cover formats when Robert Weir Crouch, an English-born Canadian decorative artist came up with a design that cemented the magazine's visual identity. Singular and immediately recognizable, the oak-and-laurel frame on the cover of the February 1910 issue would remain largely unchanged for nearly half a century, though the buff-colored border would be replaced with a golden one.
(National Geographic Society Image Collection)

distressed damsels begging for manly rescue, or children requiring tutelage. The gendered imagery prevalent in U.S. foreign relations joined race thinking to place women, people of color, and nations weaker than the United States in the low ranks of the hierarchy of power and, hence, in a necessarily dependent status justifying U.S. dominance.

Reverend Josiah Strong's popular and influential *Our Country* (1885) celebrated an Anglo-Saxon race destined to lead others. "As America goes, so goes the world," he declared. A few years later, he wrote that "to be a Christian and an Anglo-Saxon and an American . . . is to stand at the very mountaintop of privilege." Social Darwinists saw Americans as a superior people certain to overcome all competition. Secretary of State Thomas F. Bayard (1885–1889) applauded the "overflow of our population and capital" into Mexico to "saturate those regions with Americanism." But, he added, "we do not want them" until "they are fit."

Race thinking—popularized in magazine photos and cartoons, world's fairs, postcards, school textbooks, museums, and political orations—reinforced notions of American greatness, influenced the way U.S. leaders dealt with other peoples, and obviated the need to think about the subtle textures of other societies. The magazine *National Geographic,* which published its first issue in 1888, chronicled with photographs America's new overseas involvements in Asia and the Pacific. Even when smiling faces predominated in these shots, the image portrayed was that of strange, exotic, premodern peoples who had not become "Western." Fairs also put so-called uncivilized people of color on display in the "freak" or "midway" section. Dog-eating Filipinos aroused particular comment at the 1904 St. Louis World's Fair. Such racism downgraded diplomacy and justified domination and war, because self-proclaimed superiors do not negotiate with people ranked as inferiors.

The same thinking permeated attitudes toward immigrants, whose entry into the United States was first restricted in these years. Although the Burlingame Treaty (1868) had provided for free immigration between the United States and China, riots against Chinese immigrants erupted again and again in the American West—in Los Angeles (1871), San Francisco (1877), Denver (1880), and Seattle (1886). A new treaty in 1880 permitted Congress to suspend Chinese immigration to the United States, and it did so two years later. A violent incident occurred in Rock Springs, Wyoming, in 1885, when white coal miners and railway workers rioted and massacred at least twenty-five Chinese.

In 1906 the San Francisco School Board, reflecting the anti-Asian bias of many West Coast Americans, or-

dered the segregation of all Chinese, Koreans, and Japanese in special schools. Tokyo protested the discrimination against its citizens. The following year, President Roosevelt quieted the crisis by striking a "gentleman's agreement" with Tokyo restricting the inflow of Japanese immigrants; San Francisco then rescinded its segregation order. Relations with Tokyo were jolted again in 1913 when the California legislature denied Japanese residents the right to own property in the state.

With a mixture of self-interest and idealism typical of American thinking on foreign policy, expansionists believed that empire benefited both Americans and those who came under their control. When the United States intervened in other lands or lectured weaker states, Americans claimed that in remaking foreign societies they were extending liberty and prosperity to less fortunate people. William Howard Taft, as civil governor of the Philippines (1901–1904), described the United States' mission

The "Civilizing" Impulse

▲ Missionaries Charles and Anna Hartwell, brother and sister, travel in 1901 on their "gospel boat," working out of the Fuzhou mission in China. *(ABCFM Picture Collection: Individuals, Woodhull, Kate C., Courtesy Houghton Library, Harvard College Library)*

in its new colony as lifting Filipinos up "to a point of civilization" that will make them "call the name of the United States blessed." Later, after becoming secretary of war (1904–1908), Taft said about the Chinese that "the more civilized they become . . . the wealthier they become, and the better market they become for us." "The world is to be Christianized and civilized," declared Reverend Josiah Strong. "And what is the process of civilizing but the creating of more and higher wants."

Missionaries dispatched to Africa and Asia, like Lottie Moon, helped spur the transfer of American culture and power abroad—"the peaceful conquest of the world," as Reverend Frederick Gates put it. One organization, the Student Volunteers for Foreign Missions, began in the 1880s on college campuses and by 1914 had placed some 6,000 missionaries abroad. In 1915 a total of 10,000 American missionaries worked overseas. In China by 1915, more than 2,500 American Protestant missionaries—most of them female—labored to preach the gospel, teach school, and administer medical care.

AMBITIONS AND STRATEGIES

The U.S. empire grew gradually, sometimes haltingly, as American leaders defined guiding principles and built institutions to support overseas ambitions. William H. Seward, one of its chief architects, argued relentlessly for extension of the American frontier as senator from New York (1849–1861) and secretary of state (1861–1869). "There is not in the history of the Roman Empire an ambition for aggrandizement so marked as that which characterizes the American people," he once said. Seward envisioned a large, coordinated U.S. empire encompassing Canada, the Caribbean, Cuba, Central America, Mexico, Hawai'i, Iceland, Greenland, and the Pacific islands. This empire would be built not by war but by a natural process of gravitation toward the United States. Commerce would hurry the process, as would a canal across Central America, a transcontinental American railroad to link up with Asian markets, and a telegraph system to speed communications.

Most of Seward's grandiose plans did not reach fruition in his own day. In 1867, for example, he signed a treaty with Denmark to buy the Danish West Indies (Virgin Islands), but his domestic political foes in the Senate and a hurricane that wrecked St. Thomas scuttled his effort. The Virgin Islanders, who had voted for annexation, had to wait until 1917 for official U.S. status. Also doomed to failure was Seward's scheme with unscrupulous Dominican Republic leaders to gain a Caribbean naval base at Samaná Bay. The stench of corruption rising over this unsavory deal-making wafted into the Ulysses S. Grant administration and foiled Grant's initiative in 1870 to buy the entire island nation. The Senate rejected annexation.

Seward's Quest for Empire

Anti-imperialism, not just politics, blocked Seward. Anti-imperialists, such as Senator Carl Schurz and E. L. Godkin, editor of the magazine *The Nation*, argued that the country already had enough unsettled land and that creating a showcase of democracy and prosperity at home would best persuade other peoples to adopt American institutions and principles. Some anti-imperialists, sharing

◄ Beginning in the late nineteenth century, Standard Oil (the forerunner of Exxon Mobil Corporation) sent agents to China to persuade the Chinese to use American-made kerosene in their lamps and cooking stoves. To promote sales, the American entrepreneurs gave away small lamps, which the Chinese called *Mei Foo* (Beautiful Companion). One agent who popularized the lamp was William P. Coltman, shown here with Chinese business associates.

(Exxon Mobil Corporation)

the racism of the times, opposed the annexation of territory populated by dark-skinned people.

Seward did enjoy some successes. In 1866, citing the Monroe Doctrine (see page 242), he sent troops to the border with Mexico and demanded that France abandon its puppet regime there. Also facing angry Mexican nationalists, Napoleon III abandoned the Maximilian monarchy that he had installed by force three years earlier. In 1867 Seward paid Russia $7.2 million for the 591,000 square miles of Alaska—land twice the size of Texas. Some critics lampooned "Seward's Icebox," but the secretary of state extolled the Russian territory's rich natural resources, and the Senate voted overwhelmingly for the treaty. That same year, Seward laid claim to the Midway Islands (two small islands and a coral atoll northwest of Hawai'i) in the Pacific Ocean.

Seward realized his dream of a world knit together by a giant communications system. In 1866, through the persevering efforts of financier Cyrus Field, an underwater transatlantic cable linked European and American telegraph networks. Backed by J. P. Morgan's capital, communications pioneer James A. Scrymser strung telegraph lines to Latin America, entering Chile in 1890. In 1903 a submarine cable reached across the Pacific to the Philippines; three years later, it extended to Japan and China. Information about markets, crises, and war flowed steadily and quickly. Wire telegraphy—like radio (wireless telegraphy) later—shrank the globe. Nellie Bly, a reporter for the *New York World,* accented the impact of new technology in 1890 when she completed a well-publicized trip around the world in seventy-two days. Drawn closer to one another through improved communications and transportation, nations found that faraway events had more and more impact on their prosperity and security. Because of the communications revolution, "every nation elbows other nations to-day," observed Amherst College professor Edwin Grosvenor in 1898.

More and more, American diplomats found that they could enter negotiations with their European counterparts on roughly equal terms—a sure sign that the United States had arrived on the international stage. Seward's successor Hamilton Fish (1869–1887), for example, achieved a diplomatic victory in resolving the knotty problem of the *Alabama* claims. The *Alabama* and other vessels built in Great Britain for the Confederacy during the Civil War had preyed on Union shipping. Senator Charles Sumner demanded that Britain pay $2 billion in damages or cede Canada to the United States, but Fish favored negotiations. In 1871 Britain and America signed the Washing-

International Communications

ton Treaty, whereby the British apologized and agreed to the creation of a tribunal which later awarded the United States $15.5 million.

Washington officials also confronted European powers in a contest over Samoa, a group of beautiful South Pacific islands located 4,000 miles from San Francisco on the trade route to Australia. In 1878 the United States gained exclusive right to a coaling station at Samoa's coveted port of Pago Pago. Eyeing the same prize, Britain and Germany began to cultivate ties with Samoan leaders. Year by year tensions grew, as the powers dispatched warships to Samoa and aggravated factionalism among Samoa's chiefs. War seemed possible. At the eleventh hour, however, Britain, Germany, and the United States met in Berlin in 1889 and, without consulting the Samoans, devised a three-part protectorate that limited Samoa's independence. Ten years later, the three powers partitioned Samoa: the United States received Pago Pago through annexation of part of the islands (now called American Samoa and administered by the U.S. Department of the Interior); Germany took what is today independent Western Samoa; and Britain, for renouncing its claims to Samoa, obtained the Gilbert Islands and Solomon Islands.

With eyes on all parts of the world, even on Africa, where U.S. interests were minimal, ardent expansionists embraced navalism—the campaign to build an imperial navy. Calling attention to the naval buildup by the European powers, notably Germany, they argued for a bigger, modernized navy, adding the "blue water" command of the seas to its traditional role of "brown water" coastline defense and riverine operations. Captain Alfred Thayer Mahan became a major popularizer for this "New Navy." Because foreign trade was vital to the United States, he argued, the nation required an efficient navy to protect its shipping; in turn, a navy required colonies for bases. "Whether they will or no," Mahan wrote, "Americans must now begin to look outward. The growing production of the country demands it." Mahan's lectures at the Naval War College in Newport, Rhode Island, where he served as president, were published as *The Influence of Sea Power upon History* (1890). This book sat on every serious expansionist's shelf, and foreign leaders turned its pages. Theodore Roosevelt and Henry Cabot Lodge eagerly consulted Mahan, sharing his belief in the links between trade, navy, and colonies, and his growing alarm over "the aggressive military spirit" of Germany.

Moving toward naval modernization, Congress in 1883 authorized construction of the first steel-hulled warships. American factories went to work to produce steam

Alfred T. Mahan and Navalism

engines, high-velocity shells, powerful guns, and precision instruments. The navy shifted from sail power to steam and from wood construction to steel. Often named for states and cities to kindle patriotism and local support for naval expansion, New Navy ships, such as the *Maine, Oregon,* and *Boston,* thrust the United States into naval prominence, especially during crises in the 1890s.

CRISES IN THE 1890S: HAWAI'I, VENEZUELA, AND CUBA

In the depression-plagued 1890s, crises in Hawai'i and Cuba gave expansionist Americans opportunities to act on their zealous arguments for what Senator Lodge called a "large policy." Belief that the frontier at home had closed accentuated the expansionist case. In 1893 historian Frederick Jackson Turner postulated that an ever-expanding continental frontier had shaped the American character. That "frontier has gone," Turner pronounced, "and with its going has closed the first period of American history." He did not explicitly say that a new frontier had to be found overseas in order to sustain the American way of life, but he did claim that "American energy will continually demand a wider field for its exercise."

Hawai'i, the Pacific Ocean archipelago of eight major islands located 2,000 miles from the West Coast

Annexation of Hawai'i

of the United States, emerged as a new frontier for Americans. The Hawaiian Islands had long commanded American attention—commercial, missionary religious, naval, and diplomatic. Wide-eyed U.S. expansionists envisioned ships sailing from the eastern seaboard through a Central American canal to Hawai'i and then on to the fabled China market. By 1881 Secretary of State James Blaine had already declared the Hawaiian Islands "essentially a part of the American system." By 1890 Americans owned about three-quarters of Hawai'i's wealth and subordinated its economy to that of the United States through sugar exports that entered the U.S. marketplace duty-free.

In Hawai'i's multiracial society, Chinese and Japanese nationals far outnumbered Americans, who represented a mere 2.1 percent of the population. Prominent Americans on the islands—lawyers, businessmen, and sugar planters, many of them the sons of missionaries—organized secret clubs and military units to contest the royal government. In 1887 they forced the king to accept a constitution that granted foreigners the right to vote and shifted decision-making authority from the monarchy to the legislature. The same year, Hawai'i granted the United States naval rights to Pearl Harbor. Many native

▲ Queen Lili'uokalani (1838–1917), ousted from her throne in 1893 by wealthy revolutionaries, vigorously protested in her autobiography and diary, as well as in interviews, the U.S. annexation of Hawai'i in 1898. For years she defended Hawaiian nationalism and emphasized that American officials in 1893 had conspired with Sanford B. Dole and others to overthrow the native monarchy.
(Courtesy of the Lili'uokalani Trust)

Hawaiians (53 percent of the population in 1890) believed that the *haole* (foreigners)—especially Americans—were taking their country from them.

The McKinley Tariff of 1890 created an economic crisis for Hawai'i that further undermined the native government. The tariff eliminated the duty-free status of Hawaiian sugar exports in the United States. Suffering declining sugar prices and profits, the American island elite pressed for annexation of the islands by the United States so that their sugar would be classified as domestic rather than foreign. When Princess Lili'uokalani assumed the throne in 1891, she sought to roll back the political power of the *haole.* The next year, the white oligarchy—questioning her moral rectitude, fearing Hawaiian nationalism, and reeling from the McKinley Tariff—formed the subversive Annexation Club.

The annexationists struck in January 1893 in collusion with John L. Stevens, the chief American diplomat in Hawai'i, who dispatched troops from the USS *Boston* to occupy Honolulu. The queen, arrested and confined, surrendered. However, rather than yield to the new provisional regime, headed by Sanford B. Dole, son of missionaries and a prominent attorney, she relinquished authority to the U.S. government. Up went the American flag. "The Hawaiian pear is now fully ripe and this is the golden hour to pluck it," a triumphant Stevens informed Washington. Against the queen's protests as well as those of Japan, President Benjamin Harrison hurriedly sent an annexation treaty to the Senate.

Sensing foul play, incoming President Grover Cleveland ordered an investigation, which confirmed a conspiracy by the economic elite in league with Stevens and noted that most Hawaiians opposed annexation. Down came the American flag. But when Hawai'i gained renewed attention as a strategic and commercial way station to Asia and the Philippines during the Spanish-American War, President William McKinley maneuvered annexation through Congress on July 7, 1898, by means of a majority vote (the Newlands Resolution) rather than by a treaty, which would have required a two-thirds count. Under the Organic Act of June 1900, the people of Hawai'i became U.S. citizens with the right to vote in local elections and to send a nonvoting delegate to Congress. Statehood for Hawai'i came in 1959.

The Venezuelan crisis of 1895 also saw the United States in an expansive mood. For decades Venezuela and

Venezuelan Boundary Dispute

Great Britain had quarreled over the border between Venezuela and British Guiana. The disputed territory contained rich gold deposits and the mouth of the Orinoco River, a commercial gateway to northern South America. Venezuela asked for U.S. help. President Cleveland decided that the "mean and hoggish" British had to be warned away. In July 1895, Secretary of State Richard Olney brashly lectured the British that the Monroe Doctrine prohibited European powers from denying self-government to nations in the Western Hemisphere. He aimed his spread-eagle words at an international audience, proclaiming the United States "a civilized state" whose "fiat is law" in the Americas. The United States, he declared, is "master of the situation and practically invulnerable as against any or all other powers." The British, seeking international friends to counter intensifying competition from Germany, quietly retreated from the crisis. In 1896 an Anglo-American arbitration board divided the disputed territory between Britain and Venezuela. The Venezuelans were barely consulted. Thus the United States displayed a trait common to imperialists: disregard for the rights and sensibilities of small nations.

In 1895 came another crisis forced by U.S. policy, this one in Cuba. From 1868 to 1878 the Cubans had battled Spain for their independence. Slavery was abolished but independence denied. While the Cuban economy suffered depression, repressive Spanish rule continued. Insurgents committed to *Cuba libre* waited for another chance, and José Martí, one of the heroes of Cuban history, collected money, arms, and men in the United States.

American financial support of the Cuban cause was but one of the many ways the lives of Americans and

Revolution in Cuba

Cubans intersected. Their cultures, for example, melded. Cubans of all classes had settled in Baltimore, New York, Boston, and Philadelphia. Prominent Cubans on the island had sent their children to schools in the United States. When Cuban expatriates returned home, many came in American clothes, spoke English, had American names, played baseball, and had jettisoned Catholicism for Protestant denominations. Struggling with competing identities, Cubans admired American culture but resented U.S. economic hegemony (predominance).

The Cuban and U.S. economies were also intertwined. American investments of $50 million, mostly in sugar plantations, dominated the Caribbean island. More than 90 percent of Cuba's sugar was exported to the United States, and most island imports came from the United States. Havana's famed cigar factories relocated to Key West and Tampa to evade protectionist U.S. tariff laws. Martí, however, feared that "economic union means political union," for "the nation that buys, commands" and "the nation that sells, serves." Watch out, he warned, for a U.S. "conquering policy" that reduced Latin American countries to "dependencies."

Martí's fears were prophetic. In 1894 the Wilson-Gorman Tariff imposed a duty on Cuban sugar, which had been entering the United States duty-free under the McKinley Tariff. The Cuban economy, highly dependent on exports, plunged into deep crisis, hastening the island's revolution against Spain and its further incorporation into "the American system."

In 1895, from American soil, Martí launched a revolution against Spain that mounted in human and material costs. Rebels burned sugar-cane fields and razed mills, conducting an economic war and using guerrilla tactics to avoid head-on clashes with Spanish soldiers. "It is necessary to burn the hive to disperse the swarm," explained insurgent leader Máximo Gomez. U.S. investments went up in smoke, and Cuban-American trade dwindled. To separate the insurgents from their supporters among the Cuban people, Spanish general Valeriano Weyler instituted a policy of "reconcentration." Some 300,000 Cubans were

◀ On July 1, 1898, U.S. troops stormed Spanish positions on San Juan Hill near Santiago, Cuba. Both sides suffered heavy casualties. A *Harper's* magazine correspondent reported a "ghastly" scene of hundreds killed and thousands wounded. The American painter William Glackens (1870–1938) put to canvas what he saw. Because Santiago surrendered on July 17, propelling the United States to victory in the war, and because Rough Rider Theodore Roosevelt fought at San Juan Hill and later gave a self-congratulatory account of the experience, the human toll has often gone unnoticed.

(The Wadsworth Atheneum Museum of Art, Hartford, Connecticut. Gift of Henry E. Schnakenberg.)

herded into fortified towns and camps, where hunger, starvation, and disease led to tens of thousands of deaths. As reports of atrocity and destruction became headline news in the American yellow press, Americans increasingly sympathized with the insurrectionists. In late 1897, a new government in Madrid modified reconcentration and promised some autonomy for Cuba, but the insurgents continued to gain ground.

President William McKinley had come to office as an imperialist who advocated foreign bases for the New Navy, the export of surplus production, and U.S. supremacy in the Western Hemisphere. Vexed by the turmoil in Cuba, he came to believe that Spain should give up its colony. At one point he explored the purchase of Cuba by the United States for $300 million. Events in early 1898 caused McKinley to lose faith in Madrid's ability to bring peace to Cuba. In January, when antireform pro-Spanish loyalists and army personnel rioted in Havana, Washington ordered the battleship *Maine* to Havana harbor to demonstrate U.S. concern and to protect American citizens.

Sinking of the *Maine*

On February 15 an explosion ripped the *Maine*, killing 266 of 354 American officers and crew. Just a week earlier, William Randolph Hearst's inflammatory *New York Journal* had published a stolen private letter written by the Spanish minister in Washington, Enrique Dupuy de Lôme, who belittled McKinley as "weak and a bidder for the admiration of the crowd" and suggested that Spain would fight on. Congress soon complied unanimously with McKinley's request for $50 million in defense funds. The naval board investigating the *Maine* disaster then reported that a mine had caused the explosion. Vengeful Americans blamed Spain. (Later, official and unofficial studies attributed the sinking to an accidental internal explosion, most likely caused by spontaneous combustion of inadequately ventilated coal bunkers.)

The impact of these events narrowed McKinley's diplomatic options. Though reluctant to go to war, he decided to send Spain an ultimatum. In late March, the United States insisted that Spain accept an armistice, end reconcentration altogether, and designate McKinley as arbiter. Madrid made concessions. It abolished reconcentration and rejected, then accepted, an armistice. The weary president hesitated, but he would no longer tolerate chronic disorder just 90 miles off the U.S. coast. On April 11, McKinley asked Congress for authorization to use force "to secure a full and final termination of hostilities between . . . Spain and . . . Cuba, and to secure in the island the establishment of a stable government,

McKinley's Ultimatum and War Decision

capable of maintaining order." American intervention, he said, meant "hostile constraint upon both the parties to the contest."

McKinley listed the reasons for war: the "cause of humanity"; the protection of American life and property; the "very serious injury to the commerce, trade, and business of our people"; and, referring to the destruction of the *Maine*, the "constant menace to our peace." At the end of his message, McKinley mentioned Spain's recent concessions but made little of them. He did not mention another possible motivation: de Lôme's depiction of him as "weak," a charge also leveled by Assistant Secretary of the Navy Theodore Roosevelt. On April 19, Congress declared Cuba free and independent, and directed the president to use force to remove Spanish authority from the island. The legislators also passed the Teller Amendment, which disclaimed any U.S. intention to annex Cuba or control the island except to ensure its "pacification" (by which they meant the suppression of any actively hostile elements of the population). McKinley beat back a congressional amendment to recognize the rebel government. Believing that the Cubans were not ready for self-government, he argued that they needed a period of American tutoring.

THE SPANISH-AMERICAN WAR AND THE DEBATE OVER EMPIRE

Diplomacy had failed. By the time the Spanish concessions were on the table, events had already pushed the antagonists to the brink. Washington might have been more patient, and Madrid might have faced the fact that its once-grand empire had disintegrated. Still, prospects for compromise appeared dim, because the advancing Cuban insurgents would settle for nothing less than full independence, and no Spanish

government could have given up and remained in office. Nor did the United States welcome a truly independent Cuban government that might attempt to reduce U.S. interests. As historian Louis A. Pérez Jr. has argued, McKinley's decision for war may have been "directed as much against Cuban independence as it was against Spanish sovereignty." Thus came a war some have titled (awkwardly, but accurately) the "Spanish-American-Cuban-Filipino War" so as to represent all the major participants and identify where the war was fought and whose interests were most at stake.

The motives of Americans who favored war were mixed and complex. McKinley's April message expressed a humanitarian impulse to stop the bloodletting, a concern for commerce and property, and the psychological need to end the nightmarish anxiety once and for all. Republican politicians advised McKinley that their party would lose the upcoming congressional elections unless he solved the Cuba question. Many businesspeople, who had been hesitant before the crisis of early 1898, joined many farmers in the belief that ejecting Spain from Cuba would open new markets for surplus production.

Motives for War

Inveterate imperialists saw the war as an opportunity to fulfill expansionist dreams, while conservatives, alarmed

Like soldiers in all wars at all times, ▶ those in the Spanish-American War were keen to receive news from home. Here two unidentified soldiers sit on the ground in front of their tent reading their mail. *(Kansas State Historical Society)*

▲ The Spanish fleet in the Caribbean was commanded by Admiral Pascual Cervera y Topete. His squadron entered Santiago Bay, Cuba, May 19, 1898, where it was immediately blockaded by Admiral William T. Sampson's fleet. On July 3 Cervera, following orders from Madrid, tried a heroic but unsuccessful escape from the U.S. blockade. This painting by Henry Reuterdahl depicts the destruction of the squadron. Cervera survived and became a prisoner of war.

(From The Story of the Spanish-American War of 1898 *as told by W. Newphew King, Lieutenant U.S.N.)*

by Populism and violent labor strikes, welcomed war as a national unifier. One senator commented that "internal discord" was disappearing in the "fervent heat of patriotism." Sensationalism also figured in the march to war, with the yellow press exaggerating stories of Spanish misdeeds. Theodore Roosevelt and others too young to remember the bloody Civil War looked on war as adventure and used masculine rhetoric to trumpet the call to arms.

More than 263,000 regulars and volunteers served in the army and another 25,000 in the navy during the war. Most of them never left the United States. The typical volunteer was young (early twenties), white, unmarried, native-born, and working class. Many were southerners, a fact that helped the cause of reconciliation following the bitter divisions of the Civil War era. Deaths numbered 5,462—but only 379 in combat. The rest fell to yellow fever and typhoid, and most died in the United States, especially in camps in Tennessee, Virginia, and Florida, where in July and August a typhoid epidemic devastated the ranks. About 10,000 African American troops, assigned to segregated regiments, found no relief from racism and Jim Crow, even though black troops played a key role in the victorious battle for Santiago de Cuba. For all, food, sanitary conditions, and medical care were bad.

Still, Roosevelt could hardly contain himself. Although his Rough Riders, a motley unit of Ivy Leaguers and cowboys, proved undisciplined and often ineffective, they nonetheless received good press largely because of Roosevelt's self-serving publicity efforts.

To the surprise of most Americans, the first war news actually came from faraway Asia, from the Spanish colony of the Philippine Islands. Here, too, Madrid faced a rebellion from Filipinos seeking independence. On May 1, 1898, Commodore George Dewey's New Navy ship *Olympia* led an American squadron into Manila Bay and wrecked the outgunned Spanish fleet. Dewey and his sailors had been on alert in Hong Kong since February, when he received orders from imperial-minded Washington to attack the islands if war broke out. Manila ranked with Pearl Harbor and Pago Pago as a choice harbor, and the Philippines sat significantly on the way to China and its potentially huge market.

Facing Americans and rebels in both Cuba and the Philippines, Spanish resistance collapsed rapidly. U.S. ships blockaded Cuban ports to prevent Spain from resupplying its army, which suffered hunger and disease because

Dewey in the Philippines

Cuban insurgents had cut off supplies from the country-side. American troops saw their first ground-war action on June 22, the day several thousand of them landed near Santiago de Cuba and laid siege to the city. On July 3, U.S. warships sank the Spanish Caribbean squadron in Santiago harbor. American forces then assaulted the Spanish colony of Puerto Rico to obtain another Caribbean base for the navy and a strategic site to help protect a Central American canal. Losing on all fronts, Madrid sued for peace.

On August 12, Spain and the United States signed an armistice to end the war. In Paris, in December 1898, American and Spanish negotiators

Treaty of Paris

agreed on the peace terms: independence for Cuba from Spain; cession of the Philippines, Puerto Rico, and the Pacific island of Guam to the United States; and American payment of $20 million to Spain for the territories. The U.S. empire now stretched deep into Asia, and the annexation of Wake Island (1898), Hawai'i (1898), and Samoa (1899) gave American traders, missionaries, and naval promoters other steppingstones to China.

During the war with Spain, the *Washington Post* detected "a new appetite, a yearning to show our strength. . . . The taste of empire is in the mouth of the people." But as the nation debated the Treaty of Paris, anti-imperialists such as author Mark Twain, Nebraska politician William Jennings Bryan, intellectual William Graham Sumner, reformer Jane Addams, industrialist Andrew Carnegie, and Senator George Hoar of Massachusetts argued vigorously against annexation of the Philippines. They were disturbed that a war to free Cuba had led to empire, and they stimulated a momentous debate over the fundamental course in American foreign policy.

Imperial control could be imposed either formally (by military occupation, annexation, or colonialism) or

Anti-Imperialist Arguments

informally (by economic domination, political manipulation, or the threat of intervention). Anti-imperialist ire focused mostly on the formal kind of imperial control, involving an overseas territorial empire comprised of people of color living far from the mainland. Some critics appealed to principle, citing the Declaration of Independence and the Constitution: the conquest of people against their wills violated the right of self-determination. Philosopher William James charged that the United States was throwing away its special place among nations; it was, he warned, about to "puke up its heritage."

Other anti-imperialists feared that the American character was being corrupted by imperialist zeal. Jane Ad-

dams, seeing children play war games in the streets of Chicago, pointed out that they were not freeing Cubans but rather slaying Spaniards. Hoping to build a distinct foreign policy constituency out of networks of women's clubs and organizations, prominent women like Addams championed peace and an end to imperial conquest.

Some anti-imperialists protested that the United States was practicing a double standard—"offering liberty to the Cubans with one hand, cramming liberty down the throats of the Filipinos with the other, but with both feet planted upon the neck of the negro," as an African American politician from Massachusetts put it. Still other anti-imperialists warned that annexing people of color would undermine Anglo-Saxon purity and supremacy at home.

For Samuel Gompers and other anti-imperialist labor leaders, the issue was jobs: they worried that what Gompers called the "half-breeds and semi-barbaric people" of the new colonies would undercut American labor. Might not the new colonials be imported as cheap contract labor to drive down the wages of American workers? Would not exploitation of the weak abroad become contagious and lead to further exploitation of the weak at home? Would not an overseas empire drain interest and resources from pressing domestic problems, delaying reform?

The anti-imperialists entered the debate with many handicaps and never launched an effective campaign. Although they organized the Anti-Imperialist League in November 1898, they differed so profoundly on domestic issues that they found it difficult to speak with one voice on a foreign question. They also appeared inconsistent: Gompers favored the war but not the postwar annexations; Carnegie would accept colonies if they were not acquired by force; Hoar voted for annexation of Hawai'i but not of the Philippines; Bryan backed the Treaty of Paris but only, he said, to hurry the process toward Philippine independence. Finally, possession of the Philippines was an established fact, very hard to undo.

The imperialists answered their critics with appeals to patriotism, destiny, and commerce. They sketched a sce-

Imperialist Arguments

nario of American greatness: merchant ships plying the waters to boundless Asian markets; naval vessels cruising the Pacific to protect American interests; missionaries uplifting inferior peoples. It was America's duty, they insisted, quoting a then-popular Rudyard Kipling poem, to "take up the white man's burden." Furthermore, Filipino insurgents were beginning to resist U.S. rule, and it seemed cowardly to pull out under fire. Germany and Japan, two powerful international competitors, were nosing around the Philippines, apparently ready to seize them if the United States' grip loosened. National honor dictated that Americans keep what they had shed blood to take. Republican Senator Albert Beveridge of Indiana asked, "Shall [history] say that, called by events to captain and command the proudest, ablest, purest race of history in history's noblest work, we declined that great commission?"

In February 1899, by a 57-to-27 vote (just 1 more than the necessary two-thirds majority), the Senate passed the Treaty of Paris, ending the war with Spain. Most Republicans voted yes and most Democrats no. An amendment promising independence as soon as the Filipinos formed a stable government lost by only the tie-breaking ballot of the vice president. Democratic presidential candidate Bryan carried the anti-imperialist case into the election of 1900, warning that repudiation of self-government in the Philippines would weaken the principle at home. But the victorious McKinley refused to apologize for American imperialism, asserting that his policies had served the nation's interests.

ASIAN ENCOUNTERS: WAR IN THE PHILIPPINES, DIPLOMACY IN CHINA

As McKinley knew, however, the Philippine crisis was far from over. He said he intended to "uplift and civilize" the Filipinos, but they denied that they needed U.S. help. Emilio Aguinaldo, the Philippine nationalist leader who had been battling the Spanish for years, believed that American officials had promised independence for his country. But after the victory over Spain, U.S. officers ordered Aguinaldo out of Manila and isolated him from decisions affecting his nation. In early 1899, feeling betrayed by the Treaty of Paris, he proclaimed an independent Philippine Republic and took up arms. U.S. officials soon set their jaws against the rebellion.

In a war fought viciously by both sides, American soldiers burned crops and villages and tortured captives, while Filipino forces staged hit-and-run ambushes that were often brutally effective. Like guerrillas in many later wars, they would strike suddenly and ferociously, and then melt into the jungle or friendly villages. Americans spoke of the "savage" Filipino; one soldier declared that the Philippines "won't be pacified until the niggers [Filipinos] are killed off like the Indians." U.S. troops introduced a variant of the Spanish reconcentration policy—in the province of Batangas, for instance, U.S. troops forced residents to live in designated zones in an effort to separate the insurgents from local support-

Philippine Insurrection and Pacification

ers. Disaster followed. Poor sanitation, starvation, and malaria and cholera killed several thousand people. Outside the secure areas, Americans destroyed food supplies to starve out the rebels. At least one-quarter of the population of Batangas died or fled.

Before the Philippine insurrection was suppressed in 1902, some 20,000 Filipinos had died in combat, and as many as 600,000 had succumbed to starvation and disease. More than 4,000 Americans lay dead. Resistance to U.S. rule, however, did not disappear. The fiercely independent, vehemently anti-Christian, and often violent Muslim Filipinos of Moro Province refused to knuckle under. The U.S. military ordered them to submit or be exterminated. In 1906 the Moros finally met defeat; 600 of them, including many women and children, were slaughtered at the Battle of Bud Dajo. As General Leonard Wood, the Moro provincial governor, wrote the president, "Work of this kind has its disagreeable side."

U.S. officials, with a stern military hand, soon tried to Americanize the Philippines. Architect Daniel Burnham, leader of the City Beautiful movement, planned modern Manila. U.S. authorities instituted a new educational system, with English as the main language of instruction. Thousands of young American educators, many of them motivated by idealism, were recruited to teach in the new schools. The Philippine economy grew while it was an American satellite, and a sedition act silenced critics of U.S. authority by sending them to prison. In 1916 the Jones Act vaguely promised independence once the Philippines established a "stable government." The United States finally ended its rule in 1946 during an intense period of decolonization after the Second World War.

In China, McKinley opted for an approach that emphasized negotiations, with greater success. Outsiders had been pecking away at China since the 1840s, but the Japanese onslaught intensified the international scramble. Taking advantage of the Qing (Manchu) dynasty's weakness, the major imperial powers carved out spheres of influence (regions over which the outside powers claimed political control and exclusive commercial privileges): Germany in Shandong; Russia in Manchuria; France in Yunnan and Hainan; Britain in Kowloon and Hong Kong. Then, in 1895, the same year as the outbreak of the Cuban revolution, Japan claimed victory over China in a short war and assumed control of Formosa and Korea as well as parts of China proper (see Map 22.1). American religious and business leaders petitioned Washington to halt the dismemberment of China before they were closed out.

China and the Open Door Policy

Map 22.1   Imperialism in Asia: Turn of the Century

China and the Pacific region had become imperialist hunting grounds by the turn of the century. The European powers and Japan controlled more areas than the United States, which nonetheless participated in the imperial race by annexing the Philippines, Wake, Guam, Hawai'i, and Samoa; announcing the Open Door policy; and expanding trade. As the spheres of influence in China demonstrate, that besieged nation succumbed to outsiders despite the Open Door policy.

Secretary of State John Hay knew that the United States could not force the imperial powers out of China, but he was determined to protect American commerce and missionaries like Lottie Moon. He knew that missionaries had become targets of Chinese nationalist anger and that American oil and textile companies had been disappointed in the results of their investments in the country. Thus, in September 1899, Hay sent the nations with spheres of influence in China a note asking them to respect the principle of equal trade opportunity—an Open Door. The recipients sent evasive replies, privately complaining that the United States was seeking, for free, the trade rights in China that they had gained at considerable military and administrative cost.

The next year, a Chinese secret society called the Boxers (so named in the western press because some members were martial artists) incited riots that killed foreigners, including missionaries, and laid siege to the foreign legations in Beijing. The Boxers sought ultimately to expel all foreigners from China. The United States, applauded by American merchants and missionaries alike, joined the other imperial powers in sending troops to lift the siege. Hay also sent a second Open Door note in July, which instructed other nations to preserve China's territorial integrity and to honor "equal and impartial trade." Hay's protests notwithstanding, China continued for years to be fertile soil for foreign exploitation, especially by the Japanese.

Although Hay's foray into Asian politics settled little, the Open Door policy became a cornerstone of U.S. diplomacy. The "open door" had actually been a longstanding American principle, for as a trading nation the United States opposed barriers to international commerce and demanded equal access to foreign markets. After 1900, however, when the United States began to emerge as the premier world trader, the Open Door policy became an instrument first to pry open markets and then to dominate them, not just in China but throughout the world. The Open Door also developed as an ideology with several tenets: first, that America's domestic well-being required exports; second, that foreign trade would suffer interruption unless the United States intervened abroad to implant American principles and keep markets open; and third, that the closing of any area to American products, citizens, or ideas threatened the survival of the United States itself.

TR's WORLD

Theodore Roosevelt played an important role in shaping U.S. foreign policy in the McKinley administration. As as-sistant secretary of the navy (1897–1898), as a Spanish-American War hero, and then as vice president in McKinley's second term, Roosevelt worked tirelessly to make the United States a key member of the great power club. He had long had a fascination with power and its uses. He also relished hunting and killing. After an argument with a girlfriend in his youth, he vented his anger by shooting a neighbor's dog. When he killed his first buffalo in the West, he danced crazily around the carcass as his Indian guide watched in amazement. Roosevelt justified the slaughtering of American Indians, if necessary, and took his Rough Riders to Cuba, desperate to get in on the fighting. He was not disappointed. "Did I tell you," he wrote Henry Cabot Lodge afterward, "that I killed a Spaniard with my own hands?"

Like many other Americans of his day, Roosevelt took for granted the superiority of Protestant Anglo-American culture, and he believed in the importance of using American power to shape world affairs (a conviction he summarized by citing the West African proverb "Speak softly and carry a big stick, and you will go far"). In TR's world there were "civilized" and "uncivilized" nations; the former, primarily white and Anglo-Saxon or Teutonic, had a right and a duty to intervene in the affairs of the latter (generally nonwhite, Latin, or Slavic, and therefore "backward") to preserve order and stability. If violent means had to be used to accomplish this task, so be it.

Roosevelt's love of the good fight caused many to rue his ascension to the presidency after McKinley's assassination in September 1901. But there was more to this "cowboy" than mere bluster; he was also an astute analyst of foreign policy and world affairs. TR understood that American power, though growing year by year, remained limited, and that in many parts of the world the United States would have to rely on diplomacy and nonmilitary means to achieve satisfactory outcomes. It would have to work in concert with other powers.

Presidential Authority

Roosevelt sought to centralize foreign policy in the White House. The president had to take charge of foreign relations, he believed, in the same way he took the lead in formulating domestic priorities of reorganization and reform. Congress was too large and unwieldy. As for public opinion, it was, Roosevelt said, "the voice of the devil, or what is still worse, the voice of the fool." This conviction that the executive branch should be supreme in foreign policy was to be shared by most presidents who followed TR in office, down to the present day.

With this bald assertion of presidential and national power, Roosevelt stepped onto the international stage. His

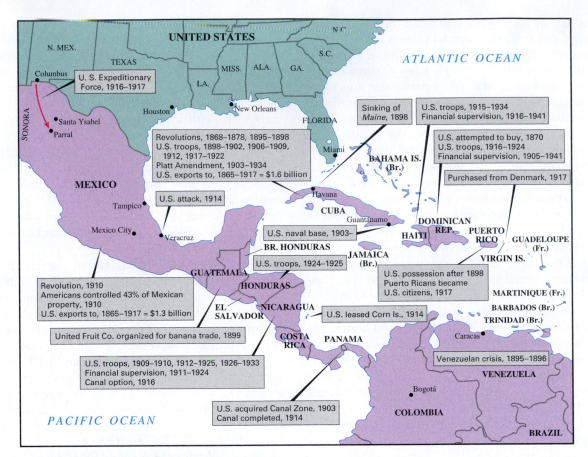

Map 22.2   U.S. Hegemony in the Caribbean and Latin America

Through many interventions, territorial acquisitions, and robust economic expansion, the United States became the predominant power in Latin America in the early twentieth century. The United States often backed up the Roosevelt Corollary's declaration of a "police power" by dispatching troops to Caribbean nations, where they met nationalist opposition.

first efforts were focused on Latin America, where U.S. economic and strategic interests and power towered (see Map 22.2), and on Europe, where repeated political and military disputes persuaded Americans to develop friendlier relations with Great Britain while avoiding entrapment in the continent's troubles, many of which Americans blamed on Germany.

As U.S. economic interests expanded in Latin America, so did U.S. political influence. Exports to Latin America, which exceeded $50 million in the 1870s, had risen to more than $120 million when Roosevelt became president in 1901, and then reached $300 million in 1914. Investments by U.S. citizens in Latin America climbed to a commanding $1.26 billion in 1914. In 1899 two large banana importers had merged to form the United Fruit Company. United Fruit owned much of the land in Central America (more than a million acres in 1913), as well as the railroad and steamship lines, and the firm became an influential economic and political force in the region. The company worked to eradicate yellow fever and malaria at the same time that it manipulated Central American politics, partly by bankrolling favored officeholders.

After the destructive war in Cuba, U.S. citizens and corporations continued to dominate the island's economy, controlling the sugar, mining, tobacco, and utilities industries, and most of the rural lands. Private U.S. investments in Cuba grew from $50 million before the revolution

Cuba and the Platt Amendment

to $220 million by 1913, and U.S. exports to the island rose from $26 million in 1900 to $196 million in 1917. The Teller Amendment outlawed the annexation of Cuba, but officials in Washington soon used the document's call for "pacification" to justify U.S. control. American troops remained there until 1902.

Favoring the "better classes," U.S. authorities restricted voting rights largely to propertied Cuban males, excluding two-thirds of adult men and all women. American officials also forced the Cubans to append to their constitution a frank avowal of U.S. hegemony known as the Platt Amendment. This statement prohibited Cuba from making a treaty with another nation that might impair its independence; in practice, this meant that all treaties had to have U.S. approval. Most important, another Platt Amendment provision granted the United States "the right to intervene" to preserve the island's independence and to maintain domestic order. The amendment also required Cuba to lease a naval base to the United States (at Guantánamo Bay, still under U.S. jurisdiction today). Formalized in a 1903 treaty, the amendment governed Cuban-American relations until 1934. "There is, of course, little or no independence left Cuba under the Platt Amendment," General Wood, military governor of the island until 1902, told President Roosevelt.

The Cubans, like the Filipinos, chafed under U.S. mastery. Widespread demonstrations protested the Platt Amendment, and a rebellion against the Cuban government in 1906 prompted Roosevelt to order another invasion of Cuba. The marines stayed until 1909, returned briefly in 1912, and occupied the island again from 1917 to 1922. All the while, U.S. officials helped to develop a transportation system, expand the public school system, found a national army, and increase sugar production. When Dr. Walter Reed's experiments, based on the theory of the Cuban physician Carlos Juan Finlay, proved that mosquitoes transmitted yellow fever, sanitary engineers controlled the insect and eradicated the disease.

Puerto Rico, the Caribbean island taken as a spoil of war in the Treaty of Paris, also developed under U.S. tutelage. Although no Puerto Rican sat at the negotiating table for that treaty, the Puerto Rican elite at first welcomed the United States as an improvement over Spain. But disillusionment soon set in. The condescending U.S. military governor, General Guy V. Henry, regarded Puerto Ricans as naughty, ill-educated children who needed "kindergarten instruction in controlling themselves without allowing them too much liberty." Some residents warned against the "Yankee peril"; others applauded the "Yankee model" and futilely anticipated statehood.

▲ In a suit and hat, President Theodore Roosevelt occupies the controls of a ninety-five-ton power shovel at a Panama Canal worksite. Roosevelt's November 1906 trip to inspect the massive project was the first time a sitting president left the United States.

(AP/Wide World)

Panama Canal

Panama, meanwhile, became the site of a bold U.S. expansionist venture. In 1869 the world had marveled at the completion of the Suez Canal, a waterway in Northeast Africa that greatly facilitated travel between the Indian Ocean and Mediterranean Sea, and enhanced the power of the British Empire. Surely that feat could be duplicated in the Western Hemisphere, possibly in Panama, a province of Colombia. One expansionist, U.S. navy captain Robert W. Shufeldt, predicted that a new canal would convert "the Gulf of Mexico into an American lake." Business interests joined politicians, diplomats, and navy officers in insisting that the United States control such an interoceanic canal.

To construct such a canal, however, the United States had to overcome daunting obstacles. The Clayton-Bulwer Treaty with Britain (1850) had provided for joint control of a canal. The British, recognizing their diminishing influence in the region and cultivating friendship with the United States as a counterweight to Germany, stepped aside in the Hay-Pauncefote Treaty (1901) to permit a solely U.S.-run canal. When Colombia hesitated to meet Washington's terms, Roosevelt encouraged Panamanian rebels to declare independence and ordered American warships to the isthmus to back them.

In 1903 the new Panama awarded the United States a canal zone and long-term rights to its control. The treaty also guaranteed Panama its independence. (In 1922 the United States paid Colombia $25 million in "conscience money" but did not apologize.) The completion of the Panama Canal in 1914 marked a major technological achievement. During the canal's first year of operation, more than one thousand merchant ships squeezed through its locks.

As for the rest of the Caribbean, Theodore Roosevelt resisted challenges to U.S. hegemony. Worried that

Roosevelt Corollary

Latin American nations' defaults on debts owed to European banks were provoking European intervention (England, Germany, and Italy sent warships to Venezuela in 1902), the president in 1904 issued the Roosevelt Corollary to the Monroe Doctrine. He warned Latin Americans to stabilize their politics and finances. "Chronic wrongdoing," the corollary lectured, might require "intervention by some civilized nation," and "in flagrant cases of such wrongdoing or impotence," the United States would have to assume the role of "an international police power." Laced with presumptions of superiority, Roosevelt's declaration provided the rationale for frequent U.S. interventions in Latin America.

From 1900 to 1917, U.S. presidents ordered American troops to Cuba, Panama, Nicaragua, the Dominican Republic, Mexico, and Haiti to quell civil wars, thwart challenges to U.S. influence, gain ports and bases, and forestall European meddling (see Map 22.2). U.S. authorities ran elections, trained national guards that became politically powerful, and renegotiated foreign debts, shifting them to U.S. banks. They also took over customs houses to control tariff revenues and government budgets (as in the Dominican Republic, from 1905 to 1941).

U.S. officials focused particular attention on Mexico, where long-time dictator Porfirio Díaz (1876–1910)

▲ Francisco "Pancho" Villa presented himself as a selfless Mexican patriot. Americans living along the border thought otherwise, particularly after Villa's forces murdered more than 30 U.S. civilians. American troops pursued Villa more than 300 hundred miles into Mexico but never caught him. *(John O. Hardman Collection)*

U.S.-Mexican Relations

aggressively recruited foreign investors through tax incentives and land grants. American capitalists came to own Mexico's railroads and mines, and invested heavily in petroleum and banking. By the early 1890s, the United States dominated Mexico's foreign trade. By 1910 Americans controlled 43 percent of Mexican property and produced more than half of the country's oil; in the state of Sonora, 186 of 208 mining companies were American owned. The Mexican revolutionaries who ousted Díaz in 1910, like nationalists elsewhere in Latin America, set out to reclaim their nation's sovereignty by ending their economic dependency on the United States.

The revolution descended into a bloody civil war with strong anti-Yankee overtones, and the Mexican government intended to nationalize extensive American-owned properties. Washington leaders worked to thwart this aim, with President Woodrow Wilson twice ordering troops onto Mexican soil: once in 1914, at Veracruz, to avenge a slight to the U.S. uniform and flag, and to overthrow the nationalistic government of President Victoriano Huerta, who was also trying to import German weapons; and again in 1916, in northern Mexico, where General John J. "Black Jack" Pershing spent months pursuing Pancho Villa after the Mexican rebel had raided an American border town. Having failed to capture Villa and facing another nationalistic government led by Venustiano Carranza, U.S. forces departed in January 1917.

As the United States reaffirmed the Monroe Doctrine against European expansion in the hemisphere and demonstrated the power to enforce it, European nations reluctantly honored U.S. hegemony in Latin America. In turn, the United States held to its tradition of standing outside European embroilments. The balance of power in Europe was precarious, and seldom did an American president involve the United States directly. Theodore Roosevelt did help settle a Franco-German clash over Morocco by mediating a settlement at Algeciras, Spain (1906). But the president drew American criticism for entangling the United States in a European problem. Americans endorsed the ultimately futile Hague peace conferences (1899 and 1907) and negotiated various arbitration treaties, but on the whole stayed outside the European arena, except to profit from extensive trade with it.

In East Asia, though, both Roosevelt and his successor, William Howard Taft, took an activist approach.

Peacemaking in East Asia

Both sought to preserve the Open Door and to contain Japan's rising power in the region. Many race-minded Japanese interpreted the U.S. advance into the Pacific as an attempt by whites to gain ascendancy over Asians. Japanese leaders nonetheless urged their citizens to go to America to study it as a model for industrializing and achieving world power. Although some Americans proudly proclaimed the Japanese the "Yankees of the East," the United States gradually had to make concessions to Japan to protect the vulnerable Philippines and to sustain the Open Door policy. Japan continued to plant interests in China and then smashed the Russians in the Russo-Japanese War (1904–1905). President Roosevelt mediated the negotiations at the Portsmouth Conference in New Hampshire and won the Nobel Peace Prize for this effort to preserve a balance of power in Asia and shrink Japan's "big head."

In 1905, in the Taft-Katsura Agreement, the United States conceded Japanese hegemony over Korea in return for Japan's pledge not to undermine the U.S. position in the Philippines. Three years later, in the Root-Takahira Agreement, Washington recognized Japan's interests in Manchuria, whereas Japan again pledged the security of the Pacific possessions held by the United States and endorsed the Open Door in China. Roosevelt also built up American naval power to deter the Japanese; in late 1907 he sent on a world tour the navy's "Great White Fleet" (so named because the ships were painted white for the voyage). Duly impressed, the Japanese began to build a bigger navy of their own.

President Taft, for his part, thought he might counter Japanese advances in Asia through dollar diplomacy—

Dollar Diplomacy

the use of private funds to serve American diplomatic goals and garner profits for American financiers, and at the same time bring reform to less-developed countries. In this case, Taft induced American bankers to join an international consortium to build a railway in China. Taft's venture, however, seemed only to embolden Japan to solidify and extend its holdings in China, where internal discord continued after the nationalist revolution of 1911 overthrew the Qing dynasty.

In 1914, when the First World War broke out in Europe, Japan seized Shandong and some Pacific islands from the Germans. In 1915 Japan issued its Twenty-One Demands, virtually insisting on hegemony over all of China. The Chinese door was being slammed shut, but the United States lacked adequate countervailing power in Asia to block Japan's imperial thrusts. A new president, Woodrow Wilson, worried about how the "white race" could blunt the rise of "the yellow race."

British officials in London shared this concern, though their attention was focused primarily on rising tensions in Europe. A special feature of American-European relations in the TR-Taft years was the flowering of an Anglo-American cooperation that had been growing throughout the late nineteenth century. One outcome of the intense German-British rivalry and the rise of the United States to world power was London's quest for friendship with Washington. Already prepared by racial ideas of Anglo-Saxon kinship, a common language, and respect for representative government and private-property rights, Americans appreciated British support in the 1898 war and the Hay-Pauncefote Treaty, and London's virtual endorsement of the Roosevelt Corollary and withdrawal of British warships from the Caribbean. As Mark Twain said of the two imperialist powers, "We are kin in sin."

Anglo-American Rapprochement

British-American trade and U.S. investment in Britain also secured ties. By 1914 more than 140 American companies operated in Britain, including H. J. Heinz's processed foods and F. W. Woolworth's "penny markets." Many Britons decried an Americanization of British culture. One journalist complained that a Briton "wakes in the morning at the sound of an American alarm clock; rises from his New England sheets, and shaves with . . . a Yankee safety razor. He . . . slips his Waterbury watch into his pocket [and] catches an electric train made in New York. . . . At his office . . . he sits on a Nebraskan swivel chair, before a Michigan roll-top desk." Such exaggerated fears and the always prickly character of the Anglo-American relationship, however, gave way to cooperation in world affairs, most evident in 1917 when the United States threw its weapons and soldiers into the First World War on the British side against Germany.

Legacy FOR A PEOPLE AND A NATION

Guantánamo Bay

Four hundred miles from Miami, near the southeastern corner of Cuba, sits U.S. Naval Base Guantánamo Bay. It is the oldest American base outside the United States, and the only one located in a country with which Washington does not have an open political relationship. The United States has occupied the base for more than a century, since the aftermath of the Spanish-American War, leasing it from Cuba for $4,085 per year (originally $2,000 in gold coins).

From an early point, Cuban leaders expressed dissatisfaction with the deal, and in the aftermath of Fidel Castro's communist takeover in 1959, Guantánamo was a source of constant tension between the two countries. Castro called the 45-square-mile base "a dagger pointed at Cuba's heart" and over the years has pointedly refused to cash the rent checks. He did cash the very first check, though, and Washington has used that fact to argue that his government accepts the terms of the lease.

Since late 2001 "Gitmo," as the base is known to U.S. service members, has contained a detainment camp for persons alleged to be militant combatants captured in Afghanistan and, later, Iraq and elsewhere. The first group of twenty detainees arrived in January 2002, after a twenty-hour flight from Afghanistan. By the end of 2005, the number exceeded five hundred, from more than forty countries. The George W. Bush administration called the detainees "unlawful enemy combatants" rather than "prisoners of war" but promised early on to abide by the Geneva accords governing prisoners of war. But soon there were allegations of abuse and complaints that holding detainees without trial, charges, or any prospect of release was cruel and unlawful. Some detainees committed suicide. For many critics the camp became an international symbol of American heavy-handedness, and even some administration allies said that the controversy surrounding the camp was severely hurting America's image abroad.

In June 2006, the U.S. Supreme Court ruled that President Bush had overstepped his power in setting up the procedures for the Guantánamo detainees without specific authority from Congress. The Court further said that the procedures violated both the Uniform Code of Military Justice and the Geneva accords. Bush responded by saying publicly that he would like to close the Guantánamo camp but that some prisoners were just too "darned dangerous" to release or return to their home governments. The question for a people and a nation thus remained: how would the United States balance its security needs with its commitment to due process and the rule of law?

SUMMARY

In the years from the Civil War to the First World War, expansionism and imperialism elevated the United States to world power status. By 1914 Americans held extensive economic, strategic, and political interests in a world made smaller by modern technology. The victory over Spain in 1898 was but the most dramatic moment in the long process. The outward reach of U.S. foreign policy from Seward to Wilson sparked opposition from domestic critics, other imperialist nations, and foreign nationalists, but expansionists prevailed, and the trend toward empire endured.

From Asia to Latin America, economic and strategic needs and ideology motivated and justified expansion and empire. The belief that the United States needed foreign markets to absorb surplus production in order to save the domestic economy joined missionary zeal in reforming other societies through the promotion of American products and culture. Notions of racial and male supremacy and appeals to national greatness also fed the appetite for foreign adventure and commitments. The greatly augmented navy became a primary means for satisfying American ideas and wants.

Revealing the great diversity of America's intersection with the world, missionaries like Moon in China, generals like Wood in Cuba, companies like Singer in Africa and Heinz in Britain, and politicians like Taft in the Philippines carried American ways, ideas, guns, and goods abroad to a mixed reception. The conspicuous declarations of Olney, Hay, Roosevelt, and other leaders became the guiding texts for U.S. principles and behavior in world affairs. A world power with far-flung interests to protect, the United States had to face a tough test of its self-proclaimed greatness and reconsider its political isolation from Europe when a world war broke out in August 1914.

SUGGESTIONS FOR FURTHER READING

Robert L. Beisner, *Twelve Against Empire: The Anti-Imperialists, 1898–1900* (1968)

Kristin L. Hoganson, *Fighting for American Manhood: How Gender Politics Provoked the Spanish-American and Philippine-American Wars* (1998)

Michael H. Hunt, *Ideology and U.S. Foreign Policy* (1987)

Paul A. Kramer, *The Blood of Government: Race, Empire, the United States, and the Philippines* (2006)

Walter LaFeber, *The American Search for Opportunity, 1865–1913* (1993)

Brian M. Linn, *The Philippine War, 1899–1902* (2000)

Eric T. Love, *Race over Empire: Racism and U.S. Imperialism, 1865–1900* (2004)

Stuart Creighton Miller, *"Benevolent Assimilation": The American Conquest of the Philippines, 1899–1903* (1982)

John Offner, *An Unwanted War: The Diplomacy of the United States and Spain over Cuba, 1895–1898* (1992)

Louis A. Perez Jr., *The War of 1898: The United States and Cuba in History and Historiography* (1998)

For a more extensive list for further reading, go to college.hmco.com/pic/norton8e.

ENLIST

*O*n May 7, 1915, Secretary of State William Jennings Bryan was having lunch with several cabinet members at the Shoreham Hotel in Washington when he received a bulletin: the luxurious British ocean liner *Lusitania* had been sunk, apparently by a German submarine. He rushed to his office, and at 3:06 p.m. came the confirmation from London: "THE LUSITANIA WAS TORPEDOED OFF THE IRISH COAST AND SANK IN HALF AN HOUR. NO NEWS YET OF PASSENGERS." In fact, 1,198 people had perished, including 128 Americans. The giant vessel had taken, not half an hour, but just eighteen minutes to go down. Bryan was deeply distraught but not altogether surprised. The European powers were at war, and he had feared precisely this kind of calamity. Britain had imposed a naval blockade on Germany, and the Germans had responded by launching submarine warfare against Allied shipping. Berlin authorities had proclaimed the North Atlantic a danger zone, and German submarines had already sunk numerous British and Allied ships. As a passenger liner, the *Lusitania* was supposed to be spared, but German officials had placed notices in U.S. newspapers warning that Americans who traveled on British or Allied ships did so at their own risk; passenger liners suspected of carrying munitions or other contraband were subject to attack. For weeks Bryan had urged President Woodrow Wilson to stop Americans from booking passage on British ships; Wilson had refused.

That evening Bryan mused to his wife, "I wonder if that ship carried munitions of war. . . . If she did carry them, it puts a different phase on the whole matter! England has been using our citizens to protect her ammunition!" The *Lusitania*, it soon emerged, *was* carrying munitions, and Bryan set about urging a restrained U.S. response. Desperate to

◀ This poster by Fred Spear, published in Boston not long after the *Lusitania* sinking, captured the anger Americans felt at the loss of 128 of their fellow citizens, among them women and children. Nearly two years before U.S. entry in the war, posters like this one urged Americans to enlist as preparation for the day when they must surely confront the German enemy.

(Library of Congress)

CHRONOLOGY

1914 ■ First World War begins in Europe

1915 ■ Germans sink *Lusitania* off coast of Ireland

1916 ■ After torpedoing the *Sussex,* Germany pledges not to attack merchant ships without warning
■ National Defense Act expands military

1917 ■ Germany declares unrestricted submarine warfare
■ Russian Revolution ousts the czar; Bolsheviks later take power
■ United States enters First World War
■ Selective Service Act creates draft
■ Espionage Act limits First Amendment rights
■ Race riot breaks out in East St. Louis, Illinois

1918 ■ Wilson announces Fourteen Points for new world order
■ Sedition Act further limits free speech
■ U.S. troops at Château-Thierry help blunt German offensive
■ U.S. troops intervene in Russia against Bolsheviks
■ Spanish flu pandemic kills 20 million worldwide
■ Armistice ends First World War

1919 ■ Paris Peace Conference punishes Germany and launches League of Nations
■ May Day bombings help instigate Red Scare
■ American Legion organizes for veterans' benefits and antiradicalism
■ Wilson suffers stroke after speaking tour
■ Senate rejects Treaty of Versailles and U.S. membership in League of Nations
■ *Schenck v. U.S.* upholds Espionage Act

1920 ■ Palmer Raids round up suspected radicals

protest note to Berlin, calling on the German government to end its submarine warfare.

For the next several weeks, as Bryan continued to press his case, he sensed his growing isolation within the administration. When in early June Wilson made it clear that he would not ban Americans from travel on belligerent ships and that he intended to send a second protest note to Germany, Bryan resigned. Privately, Wilson called Bryan a "strange man" who suffered from a "singular sort of moral blindness."

The division between the president and his secretary of state reflected divisions within the American populace over Europe's war. The split could be seen in the reaction to Bryan's resignation. Eastern newspapers charged him with "unspeakable treachery" and of stabbing the country in the back. But in the Midwest and South, Bryan was accorded respect, and he won praise from pacifists and German American groups for his "act of courage." A few weeks later, speaking to a capacity crowd of fifteen thousand at Madison Square Garden (another fifty thousand had been turned away), Bryan was loudly applauded when he warned against "war with any of the belligerent nations." Although many Americans felt, like President Wilson, that honor was more important than peace, others joined Bryan in thinking that some sacrifice of neutral rights was reasonable if the country could thereby stay out of the fighting. The debate would continue up until U.S. entry into the war in 1917, and the tensions would still ripple thereafter.

Like most Americans, Bryan had been stunned by the outbreak of the Great War (as it quickly became known) in 1914. For years the United States had participated in the international competition for colonies, markets, and weapons supremacy. But full-scale war seemed unthinkable. The new machine guns, howitzers, submarines, and dreadnoughts were such awesome death engines that leaders surely would not use them. When they did, lamented one social reformer, "civilization is all gone, and barbarism comes."

For almost three years President Wilson kept America out of the war. During this time, he sought to protect U.S. trade interests and improve the nation's military posture. He lectured the belligerents to rediscover their humanity and to respect international law. But American

keep the United States out of the war, he urged Wilson to couple his condemnation of the German action with an equally tough note to Britain protesting its blockade and to ban Americans from traveling on belligerent ships. Wilson hesitated. Others, including former president Theodore Roosevelt, called the sinking "an act of piracy" and pressed for war. Wilson did not want war, but neither did he accept Bryan's argument that the British and German violations should be treated the same. He sent a strong property, lives, and neutrality fell victim to British and German naval warfare. When, two years after the *Lusitania* went down, the president finally asked Congress for a declaration of war, he did so with his characteristic crusading zeal. America entered the battle not just to win the war but to reform the postwar world: to "make the world safe for democracy."

A year and a half later, the Great War would be over. It exacted a terrible cost on Europe, for a whole generation of young men was cut down—some 10 million soldiers perished. Europeans looked at their gigantic cemeteries and could scarcely believe what had happened. They experienced an acute spiritual loss in the destruction of ideals, confidence, and goodwill. Economically, too, the damage was immense. Most portentous of all for the future of the twentieth century, the Great War toppled four empires of the Old World—German, Austro-Hungarian, Russian, and Ottoman Turkish—and left two others, British and French, drastically weakened.

For the United States the human and material cost was comparatively small, yet Americans could rightly claim to have helped tip the scales in favor of the Allies with their infusion of war materiel and troops, as well as their extension of loans and food supplies. The war years also witnessed a massive international transfer of wealth from Europe across the Atlantic, as the United States went from being the world's largest debtor nation to being its largest creditor nation. The conflict marked the United States' coming of age as a world power. In these and other respects the Great War was a great triumph for Americans.

In other ways, though, World War I was a difficult, painful experience. It accentuated and intensified social divisions. Racial tensions accompanied the northward migration of southern blacks, and pacifists and German Americans were harassed. The federal government, eager to stimulate patriotism, trampled on civil liberties to silence critics. And following a communist revolution in Russia, a Red Scare in America repressed radicals and tarnished America's reputation as a democratic society. After the war, groups that sought to consolidate wartime gains vied with those that wanted to restore the prewar status quo. Although reformers continued to devote themselves to issues like prohibition and woman suffrage, the war experience helped splinter the Progressive movement. Jane Addams

sadly remarked that "the spirit of fighting burns away all those impulses . . . which foster the will to justice."

Abroad, Americans who had marched to battle as if on a crusade grew disillusioned with the peace process. They recoiled from the spectacle of the victors squabbling over the spoils, and they chided Wilson for failing to deliver the "peace without victory" that he had promised. As in the 1790s, the 1840s, and the 1890s, Americans once again engaged in a searching national debate about the fundamentals of their foreign policy. After negotiating the Treaty of Versailles at Paris following World War I, the president urged U.S. membership in the new League of Nations, which he promoted as a vehicle for reforming world politics. The Senate rejected his appeal (the League nonetheless organized without U.S. membership), because many Americans feared that the League might threaten the U.S. empire and entangle Americans in Europe's problems.

- Why did the United States try to remain neutral and then enter the European war in 1917?
- How was American society changed by the war?
- What were the main elements of Woodrow Wilson's postwar vision, and why did he fail to realize them?

PRECARIOUS NEUTRALITY

The war that erupted in August 1914 grew from years of European competition over trade, colonies, allies, and armaments. Two powerful alliance systems had formed: the Triple Alliance of Germany, Austria-Hungary, and Italy, and the Triple Entente of Britain, France, and Russia. All had imperial holdings and ambitions for more, but Germany seemed particularly bold, as it rivaled Great Britain for world leadership. Many Americans saw Germany as a threat to U.S. interests in the Western Hemisphere and viewed Germans as an excessively militaristic people who embraced autocracy and spurned democracy.

Strategists said that Europe enjoyed a balance of power, but crises in the Balkan countries of southeastern Europe triggered a chain of events that shattered the "balance." Slavic nationalists sought to enlarge Serbia, an independent Slavic nation, by annexing regions such as Bosnia, then a province of the Austro-Hungarian Empire (see Map 23.1). On June 28, 1914, Archduke Franz Ferdinand, heir to the Austro-Hungarian throne, was assassinated by a

Outbreak of the First World War

Map 23.1   **Europe Goes to War, Summer 1914**

Bound by alliances and stirred by turmoil in the Balkans, where Serbs repeatedly upended peace, the nations of Europe descended into war in the summer of 1914. Step by step a Balkan crisis escalated into the "Great War."

Serbian nationalist while on a state visit to Sarajevo, the capital of Bosnia. Alarmed by the prospect of an engorged Serbia on its border, Austria-Hungary consulted its Triple Alliance partner Germany, which urged toughness. When Serbia called on its Slavic friend Russia for help, Russia in turn looked for backing from its ally France. In late July, Austria-Hungary declared war against Serbia. Russia then began to mobilize its armies.

Germany—having goaded Austria-Hungary toward war and believing war inevitable—struck first, declaring war against Russia on August 1 and against France two days later. Britain hesitated, but when German forces slashed into neutral Belgium to get at France, London declared war against Germany on August 4. Eventually Turkey (the Ottoman Empire) joined Germany and Austria-Hungary as the Central Powers, and Italy (switching sides) and Japan teamed up with Britain, France, and Russia as the Allies. Japan took advantage of the European war to seize Shandong, Germany's area of influence in China.

President Wilson at first sought to distance America from the conflagration by issuing a proclamation of neutrality—the traditional U.S. policy toward European wars. He also asked Americans to refrain from taking sides, to exhibit "the dignity of self-control." In private, the president said, "We definitely have to be neutral, since otherwise our mixed populations would wage war on each other." The United States, he fervently hoped, would stand apart as a sane, civilized nation in a deranged international system.

Wilson's lofty appeal for American neutrality and unity at home collided with several realities. First, ethnic groups in the United States did take sides. Many German Americans and anti-British Irish Americans (Ireland was then trying to break free from British rule) cheered for the Central Powers. Americans of British and French ancestry, and others with roots in Allied nations, tended to champion the Allied cause. Germany's attack on Belgium confirmed in many people's minds that Germany had become the archetype of unbridled militarism.

Taking Sides

The pro-Allied sympathies of Wilson's administration also weakened the U.S. neutrality proclamation. Honoring Anglo-American rapprochement, Wilson shared the conviction with British leaders that a German victory would destroy free enterprise and government by law. If Germany won the war, he prophesied, "it would change the course of our civilization and make the United States a military nation." Several of Wilson's chief advisers and diplomats—his assistant, Colonel Edward House; ambassador to London Walter Hines Page; and Robert Lansing, a counselor in the State Department who later became secretary of state—held similar anti-German views which often translated into pro-Allied policies.

U.S. economic links with the Allies also rendered neutrality difficult, if not impossible. England had long been one of the nation's best customers. Now the British flooded America with new orders, especially for arms. Sales to the Allies helped pull the American economy out of its recession. Between 1914 and 1916, American exports to England and France grew 365 percent, from $753 million to $2.75 billion. In the same period, however, largely because of Britain's naval blockade, exports to Germany dropped by more than 90 percent, from $345 million to only $29 million. Loans to Britain and France from private American banks—totaling $2.3 billion during the neutrality period—financed much of U.S. trade with the Allies. Germany received only $27 million in the same period. The Wilson administration, which at first frowned on these transactions, came to see them as necessary to the economic health of the United States.

From Germany's perspective, the links between the American economy and the Allies meant that the United States had become the Allied arsenal and bank. Americans, however, faced a dilemma: cutting their economic ties with Britain would constitute a nonneutral act in favor of Germany. Under international law, Britain—which controlled the seas—could buy both contraband (war-related goods) and noncontraband from neutrals. It was Germany's responsibility, not America's, to stop such trade in ways that international law prescribed—that is, by an effective blockade of the enemy's territory, by the seizure of contraband from neutral (American) ships, or by the confiscation of goods from belligerent (British) ships. Germans, of course, judged the huge U.S. trade with the Allies an act of nonneutrality that had to be stopped.

The president and his aides believed, finally, that Wilsonian principles stood a better chance of international acceptance if Britain, rather than the Central Powers, sat astride the postwar world. "Wilsonianism," the cluster of ideas that Wilson espoused, consisted of traditional American principles (such as democracy and the Open Door) and a conviction that the United States was a beacon of freedom to the world. Only the United States could lead the convulsed world into a new, peaceful era of unobstructed commerce, free-market capitalism, democratic politics, and open diplomacy. American Progressivism, it seemed, was to be projected onto the world.

Wilsonianism

"America had the infinite privilege of fulfilling her destiny and saving the world," Wilson claimed. Empires had to be dismantled to honor the principle of self-determination. Armaments had to be reduced. Critics charged that Wilson often violated his own credos in his eagerness to force them on others—as his military interventions in Mexico in 1914, Haiti in 1915, and the Dominican Republic in 1916 testified. All agreed, though, that such ideals served American commercial purposes; in this way idealism and self-interest were married.

To say that American neutrality was never a real possibility given ethnic loyalties, economic ties, and Wilsonian preferences is not to say that Wilson sought to enter the war. He emphatically wanted to keep the United States out. Time and again, he tried to mediate the crisis to prevent one power from crushing another. In early 1917, the president remarked that "we are the only one of the great white nations that is free from war today, and it would be a crime against civilization for us to go in." But go in the United States finally did. Why?

The short answer is that Americans got caught in the Allied–Central Power crossfire. British naval policy aimed

Violations of Neutral Rights

to sever neutral trade with Germany in order to cripple the German economy. The British, "ruling the waves and waiving the rules," declared a blockade of water entrances to Germany and mined the North Sea. They also harassed neutral shipping by seizing cargoes and defining a broad list of contraband (including foodstuffs) that they prohibited neutrals from shipping to Germany. American commerce with Germany dwindled rapidly. Furthermore, to counter German submarines, the British flouted international law by arming their merchant ships and flying neutral (sometimes American) flags. Wilson frequently protested British violations of neutral rights, pointing out that neutrals had the right to sell and ship noncontraband goods to belligerents without interference. But London often deftly defused Washington's criticism by paying for confiscated cargoes, and German provocations made British behavior appear less offensive by comparison.

Unable to win the war on land and determined to lift the blockade and halt American-Allied commerce, Germany looked for victory at sea by using submarines. In February 1915, Berlin declared a war zone around the British Isles, warned neutral vessels to stay out so as not to be attacked by mistake, and advised passengers from neutral nations to stay off Allied ships. President Wilson

informed Germany that the United States would hold it to "strict accountability" for any losses of American life and property.

Wilson was interpreting international law in the strictest possible sense. The law that an attacker had to warn a passenger or merchant ship before attacking, so that passengers and crew could disembark safely into lifeboats, predated the submarine. The Germans thought the slender, frail, and sluggish *Unterseebooten* (U-boats) should not be expected to surface to warn ships, for surfacing would cancel out the U-boats' advantage of surprise and leave them vulnerable to attack. Berlin protested that Wilson was denying it the one weapon that could break the British economic stranglehold, disrupt the Allies' substantial connection with U.S. producers and bankers, and win the war. To all concerned—British, Germans, and Americans— naval warfare became a matter of life and death.

THE DECISION FOR WAR

Ultimately, it was the war at sea that doomed the prospects for U.S. neutrality. In the early months of 1915, German U-boats sank ship after ship, most notably the British liner *Lusitania* on May 7. In mid-August, after a lull following Germany's promise to refrain from attacking passenger liners, another British vessel, the *Arabic*, was sunk off Ireland. Three Americans died. The Germans

► Initially underestimated as a weapon, the German U-boat proved to be frighteningly effective against Allied ships. At the beginning of the war, Germany had about twenty operational submarines in its High Seas Fleet, but officials moved swiftly to speed up production. This photograph shows a German U-boat under construction in 1914.

(Bibliothek für Zeitgeschichte, Stuttgart)

quickly pledged that an unarmed passenger ship would never again be attacked without warning. But the sinking of the *Arabic* fueled debate over American passengers on belligerent vessels. Echoing Bryan's plea from the previous spring (see the chapter-opening vignette), critics asked: why not require Americans to sail on American craft? From August 1914 to March 1917, after all, only 3 Americans died on an American ship (the tanker *Gulflight,* sunk by a German U-boat in May 1915), whereas about 190 were killed on belligerent ships.

In March 1916, a U-boat attack on the *Sussex,* a French vessel crossing the English Channel, took the United States a step closer to war. Four Americans were injured on that ship, which the U-boat commander mistook for a minelayer.

Peace Advocates

Stop the marauding submarines, Wilson lectured Berlin, or the United States will sever diplomatic relations. Again the Germans retreated, pledging not to attack merchant vessels without warning. At about the same time, U.S. relations with Britain soured. The British crushing of the Easter Rebellion in Ireland and further British restriction of U.S. trade with the Central Powers aroused American anger.

As the United States became more entangled in the Great War, many Americans urged Wilson to keep the nation out. In early 1915, Jane Addams, Carrie Chapman Catt, and other suffragists helped found the Woman's Peace Party, the U.S. section of the Women's International League for Peace and Freedom. "The mother half of humanity," claimed women peace advocates, had a special role as "the guardians of life." Later that same year, some pacifist Progressives—including Oswald Garrison Villard, Paul Kellogg, and Lillian Wald—organized an antiwar coalition, the American Union Against Militarism. The businessman Andrew Carnegie, who in 1910 had established the Carnegie Endowment for International Peace, helped finance peace groups. So did Henry Ford, who in late 1915 traveled on a "peace ship" to Europe to propagandize for a negotiated settlement. Socialists like Eugene Debs added their voices to the peace movement.

Antiwar advocates emphasized several points: that war drained a nation of its youth, resources, and reform impulse; that it fostered repression at home; that it violated Christian morality; and that wartime business barons reaped huge profits at the expense of the people. Militarism and conscription, Addams pointed out, were what millions of immigrants had left behind in Europe. Were they now—in the United States—to be forced into the decadent system they had escaped? Although the peace movement was splintered—some wanted to keep the United States out of the conflict but did not endorse the pacifists' claim that intervention could never be justified—it carried political and intellectual weight that Wilson could not ignore, and it articulated several ideas that he shared. In fact, he campaigned on a peace platform in the 1916 presidential election. After his triumph, Wilson futilely labored once again to bring the belligerents to the conference table. In early 1917 he advised them to temper their acquisitive war aims, appealing for "peace without victory."

In Germany, Wilson's overture went unheeded. Since August 1916, leaders in Berlin had debated whether to resume the unrestricted U-boat campaign. Opponents feared a break with the United States, but proponents claimed there was no choice. Only through an all-out attack on Britain's supply shipping, they argued, could Germany win the war before the British blockade and trench warfare in France had exhausted Germany's ability to keep fighting. If the U-boats could sink 600,000 tons of Allied shipping per month, the German admiralty estimated, Britain would be brought to the brink of starvation. True, the United States might enter the war, but that was a risk worth taking. Victory might be achieved before U.S. troops could be ferried across the Atlantic in sizable numbers. It proved a winning argument. In early February 1917, Germany launched unrestricted submarine warfare. All warships and merchant vessels—belligerent or neutral—would be attacked if sighted in the declared war zone. Wilson quickly broke diplomatic relations with Berlin.

Unrestricted Submarine Warfare

This German challenge to American neutral rights and economic interests was soon followed by a German threat to U.S. security. In late February, British intelligence intercepted and passed to U.S. officials a telegram addressed to the German minister in Mexico from German foreign secretary Arthur Zimmermann. Its message: If Mexico joined a military alliance against the United States, Germany would help Mexico recover the territories it had lost in 1848, including several western states. Zimmermann hoped to "set new enemies on America's neck—enemies which give them plenty to take care of over there."

The Zimmermann telegram stiffened Wilson's resolve. Even though Mexico City rejected Germany's offer, the Wilson administration judged Zimmermann's telegram "a conspiracy against this country." Mexico still might let German agents use Mexican soil to propagandize against the United States, if not sabotage American properties. The prospect of a German-Mexican collaboration helped turn the tide of opinion in the American Southwest, where antiwar sentiment had been strong.

Soon afterward, Wilson asked Congress for "armed neutrality" to defend American lives and commerce. He requested authority to arm American merchant ships and to "employ any other instrumentalities or methods that may be necessary." In the midst of the debate, Wilson released Zimmermann's telegram to the press. Americans were outraged. Still, antiwar senators Robert M. La Follette and George Norris, among others, saw the armed-ship bill as a blank check for the president to move the country to war, and they filibustered it to death. Wilson proceeded to arm America's commercial vessels anyway. The action came too late to prevent the sinking of several American ships. War cries echoed across the nation. In late March, an agonized Wilson called Congress into special session.

On April 2, 1917, the president stepped before a hushed Congress. Solemnly he accused the Germans of

|||||||||||||||||||||||||||||||||||

War Message and War Declaration

"warfare against mankind." Passionately and eloquently, Wilson enumerated U.S. grievances: Germany's violation of freedom of the seas, disruption of commerce, interference with Mexico, and breach of human rights by killing innocent Americans. The "Prussian autocracy" had to be punished by "the democracies." Russia was now among the latter, he was pleased to report, because the Russian Revolution had ousted the czar just weeks before. Congress declared war against Germany on April 6 by a vote of 373 to 50 in the House and 82 to 6 in the Senate. (This vote was for war against Germany only; a declaration of war against Austria-Hungary came several months later, on December 7.) Montana's Jeannette Rankin, the first woman ever to sit in Congress, cast a ringing no vote. "Peace is a woman's job," she declared, "because men have a natural fear of being classed as cowards if they oppose war" and because mothers should protect their children from death-dealing weapons.

For principle, for morality, for honor, for commerce, for security, for reform—for all of these reasons, Wilson took the United States into the Great War. The submarine was certainly the culprit that drew a reluctant president and nation into the maelstrom. Yet critics did not attribute the U.S. descent into war to the U-boat alone. They emphasized Wilson's rigid definition of international law, which did not accommodate the submarine's tactics. They faulted his contention that Americans should be entitled to travel anywhere, even on a belligerent ship loaded with contraband. They criticized his policies as nonneutral. But they lost the debate. Most Americans came to accept Wilson's view that the Germans had to be checked to ensure an open, orderly world in which U.S. principles and interests would be safe.

▲ Jeannette Rankin (1880–1973) of Montana was the first woman to sit in the House of Representatives (elected in 1916) and the only member of Congress to vote against U.S. entry into both world wars (in 1917 and 1941). A lifelong pacifist, she led a march in Washington, D.C.—at age eighty-seven—against U.S. participation in the Vietnam War. *(Brown Brothers)*

America went to war to reform world politics, not to destroy Germany. Wilson once claimed that the United States was "pure air blowing in world politics, destroying illusions and cleaning places of morbid miasmic gasses." By early 1917 the president concluded that America would not be able to claim a seat at the postwar peace conference unless it became a combatant. At the peace conference, Wilson intended to promote the principles he thought essential to a stable world order, to advance democracy and the Open Door, and to outlaw revolution and aggression. Wilson tried to preserve part of his country's status as a neutral by designating the United States an "Associated" power rather than a full-fledged Allied nation, but this was akin to a hope of being only partly pregnant.

distinguishing moment in A.F.P

WINNING THE WAR

Even before the U.S. declaration of war, the Wilson administration—encouraged by such groups as the National

Security League and the Navy League, and by mounting public outrage against Germany's submarine warfare—had been strengthening the military under the banner of "preparedness." When the pacifist song "I Didn't Raise My Boy to Be a Soldier" became popular, preparedness proponents retorted, "I Didn't Raise My Boy to Be a Coward." The National Defense Act of 1916 provided for increases in the army and National Guard, and for summer training camps modeled on the one in Plattsburgh, New York, where a slice of America's social and economic elite had trained in 1915 as "citizen-soldiers." The Navy Act of 1916 started the largest naval expansion in American history.

To raise an army after the declaration of war, Congress in May 1917 passed the Selective Service Act, re-

The Draft and the Soldier

quiring all males between the ages of twenty-one and thirty (later changed to eighteen and forty-five) to register. National service, proponents believed, would not only prepare the nation for battle but also instill patriotism and respect for order, democracy, and personal sacrifice. Critics feared it would lead to the militarization of American life.

On June 5, 1917, more than 9.5 million men signed up for the "great national lottery." By war's end, 24 million men had been registered by local draft boards. Of this number, 4.8 million had served in the armed forces, 2 million of that number in France. Among them were hundreds of thousands who had volunteered before December 1917, when the government prohibited enlistment because the military judged voluntarism too inefficient (many volunteers were more useful in civilian factories than in the army) and too competitive (enlistees got to choose the service they wanted, thus setting off recruiting wars). Millions of laborers received deferments from military duty because they worked in war industries or had dependents.

The typical soldier was a draftee in his early to mid-twenties, white, single, American-born, and poorly educated (most had not attended high school, and perhaps 30 percent could not read or write). Tens of thousands of women enlisted in the army Nurse Corps, served as "hello girls" (volunteer bilingual telephone operators) in the army Signal Corps, and became clerks in the navy and Marine Corps. On college campuses, 150,000 students joined the Student Army Training Corps or similar navy and marine units. At officer training camps, the army turned out "ninety-day wonders."

Some 400,000 African Americans also served in the military. Although many southern politicians feared arming African Americans, the army drafted them into segre-

▲ Some fifteen thousand Native Americans served in the military in World War I. Most of them were enlistees who sought escape from restrictive Indian schools and lives of poverty, opportunities to develop new skills, and chances to prove their patriotism. This photo shows Fast Fred Horse, a Rosebud Sioux, as he recuperates in a New York hospital after suffering injury and paralysis during the Meuse-Argonne campaign of fall 1918. Unlike African Americans, Native Americans were not assigned to segregated units during the war. Native Americans participated in all major battles against German forces and suffered a high casualty rate in large part because they served as scouts, messengers, and snipers.

(William Hammond Mathers Museum, Indiana University)

gated units, where they were assigned to menial labor and endured crude abuse and miserable conditions. Ultimately more than 40,000 blacks would see combat in Europe, however, and several black units served with distinction in various divisions of the French army. The all-black 369th Infantry Regiment, for example, spent more time in the trenches—191 days—and received more medals than any other American outfit. The French government awarded the entire regiment the Croix de Guerre.

Although French officers had their share of racial prejudice and often treated the soldiers from their own African colonies poorly, black Americans serving with the French reported a degree of respect and cooperation generally lacking in the American army. They also spoke of getting a much warmer reception from French civilians than they were used to in the United States. The irony was not lost on African American leaders, such as W. E. B. Du Bois. Du Bois had endorsed the support of the National Association for the Advancement of Colored People (NAACP) for the war and echoed its call for blacks to volunteer for the fight so that they might help make the world safe for democracy and help blur the color lines at home.

Not everyone eligible for military service was eager to sign up, however. Approximately 3 million men evaded draft registration. Some were arrested, and others fled to Mexico or Canada, but most stayed at home and were never discovered. Another 338,000 men who had registered and been summoned by their draft boards failed to show up for induction. According to arrest records, most of these "deserters" and the more numerous "evaders" were lower-income agricultural and industrial laborers. Some simply felt overwhelmed by the government bureaucracy and stayed away; others were members of minority or ethnic groups who felt alienated. Although nearly 65,000 draftees initially applied for conscientious-objector status (refusing to bear arms for religious or pacifist reasons), some changed their minds or, like so many others, failed preinduction examinations. Quakers and Mennonites were numerous among the 4,000 inductees actually classified as conscientious objectors (COs). They did not have it easy. General Leonard Wood called COs "enemies of the Republic," and the military harassed them. COs who refused noncombat service, such as in the medical corps, faced imprisonment.

The U.S. troops who shipped out to France would do their fighting under American command. General John J. Pershing, head of the American Expeditionary Forces (AEF), insisted that his "sturdy rookies" remain a separate, independent army. He was not about to turn over his "doughboys" (so termed, apparently, because the large buttons on American uniforms in the 1860s resembled a deep-fried bread of that name) to Allied commanders, who had become wedded to unimaginative and deadly trench warfare, producing a military stalemate and ghastly casualties on the western front. Since the fall of 1914, zigzag trenches fronted by

Trench Warfare

▲ A U.S. soldier of Company K, 110th Infantry Regiment, receives aid during fighting at Verennes, France. *(National Archives)*

barbed wire and mines stretched across France. Between the muddy, stinking trenches lay "no man's land," denuded by artillery fire. When ordered out, soldiers would charge enemy trenches. If machine gun fire did not greet them, poison gas might.

First used by the Germans in April 1915, chlorine gas stimulated overproduction of fluid in the lungs, leading to death by drowning. One British officer tending to troops who had been gassed reported that "quite 200 men passed through my hands. . . . Some died with me, others on the way down. . . . I had to argue with many of them as to whether they were dead or not." Gas in a variety of forms (mustard and phosgene, in addition to chlorine) would continue in use throughout the war, sometimes blistering, sometimes incapacitating, often killing.

The extent of the dying in the trench warfare is hard to comprehend. At the Battle of the Somme in 1916, the British and French suffered 600,000 dead or wounded to earn only 125 square miles; the Germans lost 400,000 men. At Verdun that same year, 336,000 Germans perished, and at Passchendaele in 1917 more than 370,000 British men died to gain about 40 miles of mud and barbed wire. Ambassador Page grew sickened by what Europe had become—"a bankrupt slaughter-house inhabited by unmated women."

The first American units landed in France on June 26, 1917, marched in a Fourth of July parade in Paris, and

Shell Shock

then moved by train toward the front. They soon learned about the horrors caused by advanced weaponry. Some suffered shell shock, a form of mental illness also known as war psychosis. Symptoms included a fixed, empty stare; violent tremors; paralyzed limbs; listlessness; jabbering and screaming; and haunting dreams. The illness could strike anyone; even those soldiers who appeared most manly and courageous cracked after days of incessant shelling and inescapable human carnage. "There was a limit to human endurance," one lieutenant explained. Providing some relief were Red Cross canteens, staffed by women volunteers, which gave soldiers way stations in a strange land and offered haircuts, food, and recreation. Some ten thousand Red Cross nurses also cared for the young warriors, while the American Library Association distributed 10 million books and magazines.

In Paris, where forty large houses of prostitution thrived, it became commonplace to hear that the British were drunkards, the French were whoremongers, and the Americans were both. Venereal disease became a serious problem. French prime minister Georges Clemenceau offered licensed, inspected prostitutes in "special houses" to the American army. When the generous Gallic offer reached Washington, Secretary of War Newton Baker gasped, "For God's sake . . . don't show this to the President or he'll stop the war." By war's end, about 15 percent of America's soldiers had contracted venereal disease, costing the army $50 million and 7 million days of active duty. Periodic inspections, chemical prophylactic treatments, and the threat of court-martial for infected soldiers kept the problem from being even greater.

◀ During the First World War, the War Department promoted a film to combat sexually transmitted diseases. After the war, the New York State Board of Censors declared the film obscene.

(Social Welfare History Archives Center, University of Minnesota)

658 Chapter 23   Americans in the Great War | 1914–1920

The experience of being in Europe enlarged what for many American draftees had been a circumscribed world.

American Units in France

Soldiers filled their diaries and letters with descriptions of the local customs and "ancient" architecture, and noted how the grimy and war-torn French countryside bore little resemblance to the groomed landscapes they had seen in paintings. Some felt both admiration for the spirit of endurance they saw in the populace and irritation that the locals were not more grateful for the Americans' arrival. "Life in France for the American soldier meant marching in the dirt and mud, living in cellars in filth, being wet and cold and fighting," the chief of staff of the Fourth Division remarked. "He had come to help France in the hour of distress and he was glad he came but these French people did not seem to appreciate him at all."

The influx of American men and materiel—and the morale blow they delivered to the Central Powers—decided the outcome of the First World War. With both sides exhausted, the Americans tipped the balance toward the Allies. It took time, though, for the weight of the American military machine to make itself felt. From an early point, the U.S. Navy battled submarines and escorted troop carriers, and pilots in the U.S. Air Service, flying mostly British and French aircraft, saw limited action, mostly against German ground troops and transport. American "aces" like Eddie Rickenbacker took on their German counterparts in aerial "dogfights" and became heroes, as much in France as in their own country. But only ground troops could make a decisive difference, and American units actually did not engage in much combat until after the lull in the fighting during the harsh winter of 1917–1918.

By then, the military and diplomatic situation had changed dramatically, because of an event that was argu-

The Bolshevik Revolution

ably the most important political development of the twentieth century: the Bolshevik Revolution in Russia. In November 1917, the liberal-democratic government of Aleksander Kerensky, which had led the country since the czar's abdication early in the year, was overthrown by radical socialists led by V. I. Lenin. Lenin seized power vowing to change world politics and end imperial rivalries on terms that challenged Woodrow Wilson's. Lenin saw the war as signaling the impending end of capitalism and looked for a global revolution, carried out by workers, that would sweep away the "imperialist order." For western leaders, the prospect of Bolshevik-style revolutions

spreading worldwide was too frightening to contemplate. The ascendancy of the world's laboring classes working in unity would destroy governments everywhere.

In the weeks following their takeover, the Bolsheviks attempted to embarrass the capitalist governments and incite world revolution by publishing several secret agreements among the Allies for dividing up the colonies and other territories of the Central Powers in the event of an Allied victory. Veteran watchers of world affairs found nothing particularly shocking in the documents, and Wilson had known of them, but the disclosures belied the noble rhetoric of Allied war aims. Wilson confided to Colonel House that he really wanted to tell the Bolsheviks to "go to hell," but he accepted the colonel's argument that he would have to address Lenin's claims that there was little to distinguish the two warring sides and that socialism represented the future.

The result was the Fourteen Points, unveiled in January 1918, in which Wilson reaffirmed America's commit-

Fourteen Points

ment to an international system governed by laws and renounced territorial gains as a legitimate war aim. The first five points called for diplomacy "in the public view," freedom of the seas, lower tariffs, reductions in armaments, and the decolonization of empires. The next eight points specified the evacuation of foreign troops from Russia, Belgium, and France, and appealed for self-determination for nationalities in Europe, such as the Poles. For Wilson, the fourteenth point was the most important—the mechanism for achieving all the others: "a general association of nations" or League of Nations.

Wilson's appeal did not impress Lenin, who called for an immediate end to the fighting, the eradication of colonialism, and self-determination for all peoples. Lenin also made a separate peace with Germany—the Treaty of Brest-Litovsk, signed on March 3, 1918. The deal erased centuries of Russian expansion, as Poland, Finland, and the Baltic states were taken from Russia and Ukraine was granted independence. One of Lenin's motives was to allow Russian troops loyal to the Bolsheviks to return home to fight anti-Bolshevik forces, who had launched a civil war to oust the new government.

The emerging feud between Lenin and Wilson contained the seeds of the superpower confrontation that would dominate the international system after 1945. Both men rejected the old diplomacy which they claimed had created the conditions for the current war; both insisted on the need for a new world order. Although each professed adherence to democratic principles, they defined democracy differently. For Lenin, it meant workers everywhere seizing control from the owners of capital and establishing worker-led governments. For Wilson, it meant independent governments operating within capitalist systems and according to republican political practices.

In March 1918, with German troops released from the Russian front and transferred to France, the Germans launched a major offensive. By May they had pushed to within 50 miles of Paris. Late that month, troops of the U.S. First Division helped blunt the German advance at Cantigny (see Map 23.2). In June the Third Division and French forces held positions along the Marne River at

Americans in Battle

Château-Thierry, and the Second Division soon attacked the Germans in the Belleau Wood. American soldiers won the battle after three weeks of fighting, but thousands died or were wounded after they made almost sacrificial frontal assaults against German machine guns.

Allied victory in the Second Battle of the Marne in July 1918 stemmed all German advances. In September, French and American forces took St. Mihiel in a ferocious battle in which American gunners fired 100,000 rounds of phosgene gas shells. Then the Allies began their massive Meuse-Argonne offensive. More than 1 million Americans joined British and French troops in weeks of fierce combat; some 26,000 Americans died before the Allies claimed the Argonne Forest on October 10. For Germany—its

Map 23.2   American Troops at the Western Front, 1918

America's 2 million troops in France met German forces head-on, ensuring the defeat of the Central Powers in 1918.

The Influenza Pandemic of 1918

*I*n the summer and fall of 1918, as World War I neared its end, a terrible plague swept the earth. It was a massive outbreak of influenza, and it would kill more than twice as many as the Great War itself—somewhere between 25 and 40 million people. In the United States, 675,000 people died.

The first cases were identified in midwestern military camps in early March. Soldiers complained of flulike symptoms—headache, sore throat, fever—and many did not recover. At Fort Riley, Kansas, 48 men died. But with the war effort in full swing, few in government or the press took notice. Soldiers shipped out to Europe in large numbers (84,000 in March), some unknowingly carrying the virus in their lungs. The illness appeared on the western front in April. By the end of June, an estimated 8 million Spaniards were infected, thereby giving the disease its name, the Spanish flu.

In August, after a midsummer lull, a second, deadlier form of the influenza began spreading. This time, the epidemic erupted simultaneously in three cities on three continents: Freetown, Sierra Leone, in Africa; Brest, France, the port of entry for many American soldiers; and Boston, Massachusetts. In September, the disease swept down the East Coast to New York, Philadelphia, and beyond. That month, 12,000 Americans died.

It was a flu like no other. People could be healthy at the start of the weekend and dead by the end of it. Some experienced a rapid accumulation of fluid in the lungs and would quite literally drown. Others died more slowly, of secondary infections with bacterial pneumonia. Mortality rates were highest for twenty- to twenty-nine-year-olds—the same group dying in huge numbers in the trenches.

In October, the epidemic hit full force. It spread to Japan, India, Africa, and Latin America. In the United States, 200,000 perished. There was a nationwide shortage of caskets and gravediggers, and funerals were limited to fifteen minutes. Bodies were left in gutters or on front porches, to be picked up by trucks that drove the streets. Stores were forbidden to hold sales; schools and cinemas closed. Army surgeon general Victor Vaughan made a frightening calculation: "If the epidemic continues its mathematical rate of acceleration, civilization could easily disappear from the face of the earth within a few weeks."

Then, suddenly, in November, for reasons still unclear, the epidemic eased, though the dying continued into 1919. In England and Wales, the final toll was 200,000. Samoa lost a quarter of its population, while in India the epidemic may have claimed a staggering 20 million. It was, in historian Roy Porter's words, "the greatest single demographic shock mankind has ever experienced."

World War I had helped spread the disease, but so had technological improvements that in previous decades facilitated global travel. The world was a smaller, more intimate place, often for good but sometimes for ill. Americans, accustomed to thinking that two great oceans could isolate them, were reminded that they were immutably linked to humankind.

The influenza pandemic of 1918 ▶ perhaps started in earnest here, at Camp Funston, Kansas, in the spring of that year. Soldiers were struck with a debilitating illness they called "knock me down fever."

(National Museum of Health & Medicine, Armed Forces Institute of Pathology)

ground and submarine war stymied, its troops and cities mutinous, its allies Turkey and Austria dropping out, its Kaiser abdicated, and facing the prospect of endless American troop reinforcements—peace became imperative. The Germans accepted a punishing armistice that took effect on the morning of November 11, 1918, at the eleventh hour of the eleventh day of the eleventh month.

The cost of the war is impossible to compute, but the scale is clear enough: the belligerents counted 10 million soldiers and 6.6 million civil-

Casualties

ians dead and 21.3 million people wounded. Fifty-three thousand American soldiers died in battle, and another 62,000 died from disease. Many of the latter died from the virulent strain of influenza that ravaged the world in late 1918 and would ultimately claim more victims than the Great War itself. The economic damage was colossal as well, helping to account for the widespread starvation Europe experienced in the winter of 1918–1919. Economic output on the continent dwindled, and transport over any distance was in some countries virtually nonexistent. "We are at the dead season of our fortunes," wrote one British observer. "Never in the lifetime of men now living has the universal element in the soul of man burnt so dimly."

The German, Austro-Hungarian, Ottoman, and Russian empires were no more, themselves casualties of the conflagration. For a time it appeared the Bolshevik Revolution might spread westward, as communist uprisings shook Germany and parts of central Europe. Even before the armistice, revolutionaries temporarily took power in the German cities of Bremen, Hamburg, and Lübeck. In Hungary, a government actually held power for several months, while Austria was racked by left-wing demonstrations. In Moscow, meanwhile, the new Soviet state sought to consolidate its power. "We are sitting upon an open powder magazine," Colonel House worried, "and some day a spark may ignite it."

MOBILIZING THE HOME FRONT

It is not an army that we must shape and train for war," declared President Wilson, "it is a nation." The United States was a belligerent for only nineteen months, but the war had a tremendous impact at home. The federal government moved swiftly to expand its power over the economy to meet war needs and intervened in American life as never before. The vastly enlarged Washington bureaucracy managed the economy, labor force, military, public opinion, and more. Federal expenditures increased tremen-

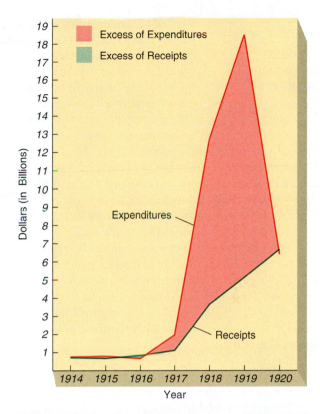

Figure 23.1   The Federal Budget, 1914–1920
During the First World War, the federal government spent more money than it received from increased taxes. It borrowed from banks or sold bonds through Liberty Loan drives. To meet the mounting costs of the war, in other words, the federal government had to resort to deficit spending. Expenditures topped receipts by more than $13 billion in 1919. Given this wartime fiscal pattern, moreover, the U.S. federal debt rose from $1 billion in 1914 to $25 billion in 1919.   (Source: U.S. Department of Commerce, Historical Statistics of the United States: Colonial Times to 1957 [Washington, D.C.: Bureau of the Census, 1960], p. 711.)

dously as the government spent more than $760 million a month from April 1917 to August 1919. As tax revenues lagged behind, the administration resorted to deficit spending (see Figure 23.1). The total cost of the war was difficult to calculate, because future generations would have to pay veterans' benefits and interest on loans. To Progressives of the New Nationalist persuasion, the wartime expansion and centralization of government power were welcome. To others, these changes seemed excessive, leading to concentrated, hence dangerous, federal power.

The federal government and private business became partners during the war. So-called dollar-a-year executives

Business-Government Cooperation

flocked to the nation's capital from major companies, retaining their corporate salaries while serving in official administrative and consulting capacities. Early in the war, the government relied on several industrial committees for advice on purchases and prices. But evidence of self-interested businesspeople cashing in on the national interest aroused public protest. The head of the aluminum advisory committee, for example, was also president of the largest aluminum company. The assorted committees were disbanded in July 1917 in favor of a single manager, the War Industries Board. But the federal government continued to work closely with business through trade associations, which grew significantly to two thousand by 1920. The government also suspended antitrust laws and signed cost-plus contracts, which guaranteed companies a healthy profit and a means to pay higher wages to head off labor strikes. Competitive bidding was virtually abandoned. Under such wartime practices, big business grew bigger.

Hundreds of new government agencies, staffed primarily by businesspeople, placed controls on the economy in order to shift the nation's resources to the Allies, the AEF, and war-related production. The Food Administration, led by engineer and investor Herbert Hoover, launched voluntary programs to increase production and conserve food—Americans were urged to grow "victory gardens" and to eat meatless and wheatless meals—but it also set prices and regulated distribution. The Railroad Administration took over the railway industry. The Fuel Administration controlled coal supplies and rationed gasoline. When strikes threatened the telephone and telegraph companies, the federal government seized and ran them.

The largest of the superagencies was the War Industries Board (WIB), headed by financier Bernard Baruch. At one point, this Wall Streeter told Henry Ford frankly that he would dispatch the military to seize his plants if the automaker did not accept WIB limits on car production. Ford relented. Although the WIB seemed all-powerful, in reality it had to conciliate competing interest groups and compromise with the business executives whose advice it so valued. Designed as a clearing-house for coordinating the national economy, the WIB made purchases, allocated supplies, and fixed prices at levels that business requested. The WIB also ordered the standardization of goods to save materials and streamline production. The varieties of automobile tires, for example, were reduced from 287 to 3.

The performance of the mobilized economy was mixed, but it delivered enough men and materiel to

▲ During the First World War, the U.S. Fuel Administration promoted economic mobilization at home in this poster printed in several languages.

(National Park Service Collection, Ellis Island Immigration Museum. Photo Chermayeff and Geismar MetaForm)

Economic Performance

France to ensure the defeat of the Central Powers. About one-quarter of all American production was diverted to war needs. As farmers enjoyed boom years of higher prices, they put more acreage into production and mechanized as never before. From 1915 to 1920 the number of tractors in American fields jumped tenfold. Gross farm income for the period from 1914 to 1919 increased more than 230 percent. Although manufacturing output leveled off in 1918, some industries realized substantial growth because of wartime demand. Steel reached a peak production of 45 million tons in 1917, twice the prewar figure. As U.S. soldiers popularized American brands in Europe, tobacconists profited from a huge increase in cigarette sales:

from 26 billion cigarettes in 1916 to 48 billion in 1918. Overall, the gross national product in 1920 stood 237 percent higher than in 1914.

The rush to complete massive assignments caused mistakes to be made. Weapons deliveries fell short of demand; the bloated bureaucracy of the War Shipping Board failed to build enough ships. In the severe winter of 1917–1918, millions of Americans could not get coal. Coal companies held back on production to raise prices; railroads did not have enough coal cars; and harbors froze, closing out coal barges. People died from pneumonia and freezing. A Brooklyn man went out in the morning to forage for coal and returned to find his two-month-old daughter frozen to death in her crib.

To help pay its wartime bills, the government dramatically increased taxes. The Revenue Act in 1916 started the process by raising the surtax on high incomes and corporate profits, imposing a federal tax on large estates, and significantly increasing the tax on munitions manufacturers. Still, the government financed only one-third of the war through taxes. The other two-thirds came from loans, including Liberty bonds sold to the American people through aggressive campaigns. The War Revenue Act of 1917 provided for a more steeply graduated personal income tax, a corporate income tax, an excess-profits tax, and increased excise taxes on alcoholic beverages, tobacco, and luxury items.

Although these taxes did curb excessive corporate profiteering, there were loopholes. Sometimes companies inflated costs to conceal profits or paid high salaries and bonuses to their executives. Four officers of Bethlehem Steel, for example, divided bonuses of $2.3 million in 1917 and $2.1 million the next year. Corporate net earnings for 1913 totaled $4 billion; in 1917 they reached $7 billion; and in 1918, after the tax bite and the war's end, they still stood at $4.5 billion. Profits and patriotism went hand in hand in America's war experience. The abrupt cancellation of billions of dollars' worth of contracts at the end of the war, however, caused a brief economic downturn, a short boom, and then an intense decline (see Chapter 24).

For American workers, the full-employment wartime economy increased earnings and gave many of them time-and-a-half pay for overtime work. With the higher cost of living, however, workers saw minimal improvement in their economic

Labor Shortage

standing. Turnover rates were high as workers switched jobs for higher pay and better conditions. Some employers sought to overcome labor shortages by expanding welfare and social programs, and by establishing personnel departments—"specialized human nature engineers to

keep its human machinery frictionless," as General Electric explained.

To meet the labor crisis, the Department of Labor's U.S. Employment Service matched laborers with job vacancies, especially attracting workers from the South and Midwest to war industries in the East. The department also temporarily relaxed the literacy-test and head-tax provisions of immigration law to attract farm labor, miners, and railroad workers from Mexico. Because the labor crisis also generated a housing crisis as workers crammed into cities, the U.S. Housing Corporation and Emergency Fleet Corporation, following British example, built row houses in Newport News, Virginia, and Eddystone, Pennsylvania.

The tight wartime labor market had another consequence: new work opportunities for women. In Connecticut, a special motion picture, *Mr. and Mrs. Hines of Stamford Do Their Bit*, appealed to housewives' patriotism, urging them to take factory jobs. Although the total number of women in the work force increased slightly, the real story was that many changed jobs, sometimes moving into formerly male domains. Some white women left domestic service for factories, shifted from clerking in department stores to stenography and typing, or departed textile mills for employment in firearms plants. At least 20 percent of all workers in the wartime electrical-machinery, airplane, and food industries were women. Some 100,000 women worked in the railroad industry. As white women took advantage of these new opportunities, black women took some of their places in domestic service and in textile factories. For the first time, department stores employed black women as elevator operators and cafeteria waitresses. Most working women were single and remained concentrated in sex-segregated occupations, serving as typists, nurses, teachers, and domestic servants.

Women also participated in the war effort in other ways. As volunteers, they made clothing for refugees and soldiers, served at Red Cross facilities, and taught French to nurses assigned to the war zone. Many worked for the Women's Committee of the Council of National Defense, whose leaders included Ida Tarbell and Carrie Chapman Catt. A vast network of state, county, and town volunteer organizations, the council publicized government mobilization programs, encouraged home gardens, sponsored drives to sell Liberty bonds, and continued the push for social welfare reforms. This patriotic work won praise from men and improved the prospects for passage of the Nineteenth Amendment granting woman suffrage. "We have made partners of women in this war," Wilson said as he endorsed woman suffrage in 1918. "Shall we admit

▲ Stella Young (1896–1989), a Canadian-born woman from Chelsea, Massachusetts, became widely known as the "Doughnut Girl" because of her service during the First World War with the American branch of the Salvation Army, an international organization devoted to social work. She arrived in France in March 1918 and worked in emergency canteens near the battle front, providing U.S. troops with coffee, cocoa, sandwiches, doughnuts, pie, and fruit. Stella Young became famous when this picture of her wearing a khaki uniform and a "doughboy" steel helmet was widely circulated as a postcard. A piece of sheet music was even written about her. She served again in World War II. Chelsea named a city square in her honor in 1968.

(Picture Research Consultants & Archives)

them only to a partnership of suffering and sacrifice . . . and not to a partnership of privilege and right?"

Among African Americans, war mobilization wrought significant change as southern blacks undertook a great migration to northern cities to work in railroad yards, packing houses, steel mills, shipyards, and coal mines. Between 1910 and 1920, Cleveland's black population swelled by more than 300 percent, Detroit's by more than 600 percent, and Chicago's by 150 percent. Much of the increase

occurred between 1916 and 1919. All told, about a half-million African Americans uprooted themselves to move to the North. Families sometimes pooled savings to send one member; others sold their household goods to pay for the journey. Most of the migrants were males—young (in their early twenties), unmarried, and skilled or semiskilled. Wartime jobs in the North provided an escape from low wages, sharecropping, tenancy, crop liens, debt peonage, lynchings, and political disfranchisement. To a friend back in Mississippi, one African American wrote: "I just begin to feel like a man. . . . I don't have to humble to no one. I have registered. Will vote the next election."

To keep factories running smoothly, Wilson instituted the National War Labor Board (NWLB) in early 1918.

National War Labor Board

The NWLB discouraged strikes and lockouts and urged management to negotiate with existing unions. In July, after the Western Union Company fired eight hundred union members for trying to organize the firm's workers and then defied an NWLB request to reinstate the employees, the president nationalized the telegraph lines and put the laborers back to work. That month, too, the NWLB directed General Electric to raise wages and stop discriminating against metal trades union members in Schenectady, New York. On the other hand, in September the NWLB ordered striking Bridgeport, Connecticut, machinists back to munitions factories, threatening to revoke their draft exemptions (granted earlier because they worked in an "essential" industry).

Many labor leaders hoped the war would offer opportunities for recognition and better pay through partnership with government. Samuel Gompers threw the AFL's loyalty to the Wilson administration, promising to deter strikes. He and other moderate labor leaders accepted appointments to federal agencies. The antiwar Socialist Party blasted the AFL for becoming a "fifth wheel on [the] capitalist war chariot," but union membership climbed from roughly 2.5 million in 1916 to more than 4 million in 1919.

The AFL, however, could not curb strikes by the radical Industrial Workers of the World (IWW, also known as "Wobblies") or rebellious AFL locals, especially those controlled by labor activists and socialists. In the nineteen war months, more than six thousand strikes expressed workers' demands for a "living wage" and improved working conditions (many called for an eight-hour workday). Exploiting Wilsonian wartime rhetoric, workers and their unions also sought to create "industrial democracy," a more representative workplace with a role for labor in determining job categories and content, and with workplace representation through shop committees. By 1920, in defiance of the national AFL, labor parties had sprung up in twenty-three states.

CIVIL LIBERTIES UNDER CHALLENGE

Gompers's backing of the call to arms meant a great deal to Wilson and his advisers, and they noted with satisfaction that most newspapers, religious leaders, and public officials were similarly supportive. They were less certain, however, about the attitudes of ordinary Americans. "Woe be to the man that seeks to stand in our way in this day of high resolution," the president warned. An official and unofficial campaign soon began to silence dissenters who questioned Wilson's decision for war or who protested the draft. In the end, the Wilson administration compiled one of the worst civil liberties records in American history.

The targets of governmental and quasi-vigilante repression were the hundreds of thousands of Americans and aliens who refused to support the war: pacifists from all walks of life, conscientious objectors, socialists, radical labor groups, the debt-ridden tenant farmers of Oklahoma who staged the Green Corn Rebellion against the draft, the Non-Partisan League, reformers like Robert La Follette and Jane Addams, and countless others. In the wartime process of debating the question of the right to speak freely in a democracy, the concept of "civil liberties" emerged for the first time in American history as a major public policy issue (see "Legacy for a People and a Nation," page 674).

The centerpiece of the administration's campaign to win support for the war was the Committee on Public In-

The Committee on Public Information

formation (CPI), formed in April 1917 and headed by Progressive journalist George Creel. Employing some of the nation's most talented writers and scholars, the CPI used propaganda to shape and mobilize public opinion. Pamphlets and films demonized the Germans, and CPI "Four-Minute Men" spoke at movie theaters, schools, and churches to pump up a patriotic mood. Encouraged by the CPI to promote American participation in the war, film companies and their trade association, the National Association of the Motion Picture Industry, produced documentaries, newsreels, and anti-German movies, such as *The Kaiser, the Beast of Berlin* (1918) and *To Hell with the Kaiser* (1918).

The committee also urged the press to practice "self-censorship" and encouraged people to spy on their neighbors. Ultrapatriotic groups, such as the Sedition Slammers

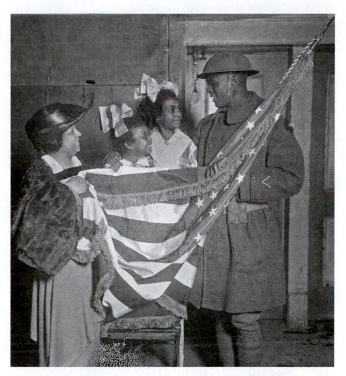

▲ A member of the Eighth Regiment of the Illinois National Guard with his family, circa 1918. Originally organized as a volunteer regiment during the Spanish-American War in 1898, the Eighth Regiment achieved its greatest fame during World War I. The only regiment to be entirely commanded by blacks and headquartered at the only black armory in the U.S., the "Fighting 8th" served with distinction in France, with 143 of its members losing their lives.
(Chicago Historical Society)

and the American Defense Society, used vigilantism. A German American miner in Illinois was wrapped in a flag and lynched. In Hilger, Montana, citizens burned history texts that mentioned Germany. By the end of the war, sixteen states had banned the teaching of the German language. To avoid trouble, the Kaiser-Kuhn grocery in St. Louis changed its name to Pioneer Grocery. Germantown, Nebraska, became Garland, and the townspeople in Berlin, Iowa, henceforth hailed from Lincoln. The German shepherd became the Alsatian shepherd.

Because towns had Liberty Loan quotas to fill, they sometimes bullied "slackers" into purchasing bonds. Nativist advocates of "100% Americanism" exploited the emotional atmosphere to exhort immigrants to throw off their Old World cultures. Companies offered English language and naturalization classes in their factories, and refused jobs and promotions to those who did not make adequate strides toward learning English. Even labor's

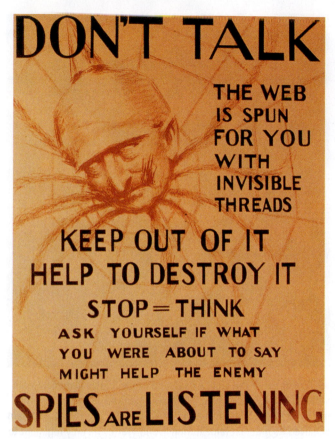

DON'T TALK

THE WEB IS SPUN FOR YOU WITH INVISIBLE THREADS

KEEP OUT OF IT
HELP TO DESTROY IT

STOP = THINK

ASK YOURSELF IF WHAT YOU WERE ABOUT TO SAY MIGHT HELP THE ENEMY

SPIES ARE LISTENING

▲ Through its concerted propaganda effort, the Committee on Public Information helped sell to the American people U.S. participation in the First World War. In this 1917 poster, the committee also warned against German spies, perhaps even German American spies, who might pick up secrets from unsuspecting citizens. *(Private Collection)*

drive for compulsory health insurance, which before the war had gained advocates in several states, including New York and California, became victimized by the poisoned war atmosphere. Many physicians and insurance companies had for years denounced health insurance as "socialistic"; after the United States entered the war, they discredited it as "Made in Germany."

Even institutions that had long prided themselves on tolerance became contaminated by the spirit of coercion. Wellesley College economics professor Emily Greene Balch was fired for her pacifist views (she won the Nobel Peace Prize in 1946). Three Columbia University students were apprehended in mid-1917 for circulating an antiwar petition. Columbia also fired Professor J. M. Cattell, a distinguished psychologist, for his antiwar stand. His colleague Charles Beard, a historian with a prowar perspective, resigned in protest, stating, "If we have to suppress every-

thing we don't like to hear, this country is resting on a pretty wobbly basis." In a number of states, local school boards dismissed teachers who questioned the war.

The Wilson administration also guided through an obliging Congress the Espionage Act (1917) and the Sedition Act (1918). The first statute forbade "false statements" designed to impede the draft or promote military insubordination, and it banned from the mails materials considered treasonous. The Sedition Act made it unlawful to obstruct the sale of war bonds and to use "disloyal, profane, scurrilous, or abusive" language to describe the government, the Constitution, the flag, or the military uniform. These loosely worded laws gave the government wide latitude to crack down on critics. More than two thousand people were prosecuted under the acts, and many others were intimidated into silence.

Espionage and Sedition Acts

Progressives and conservatives alike used the war emergency to throttle the Industrial Workers of the World and the Socialist Party. Government agents raided IWW meetings, and the army marched into western mining and lumber regions to put down IWW strikes. By the end of the war, most of the union's leaders were in jail. In summer 1918, with a government stenographer present, Socialist Party leader Eugene V. Debs delivered a spirited oration extolling socialism and freedom of speech—including the freedom to criticize the Wilson administration for taking America into the war. Federal agents arrested him. Debs told the court what many dissenters—and, later, many jurists and scholars—thought of the Espionage Act: it was "a despotic enactment in flagrant conflict with democratic principles and with the spirit of free institutions." Handed a ten-year sentence, Debs remained in prison until late 1921, when he received a pardon.

The Supreme Court endorsed such convictions. In *Schenck v. U.S.* (1919), the Court unanimously upheld the conviction of a Socialist Party member who had mailed pamphlets urging resistance to the draft. In time of war, Justice Oliver Wendell Holmes wrote, the First Amendment could be restricted: "Free speech would not protect a man falsely shouting 'fire' in a theater and causing panic." If, according to Holmes, words "are of such a nature as to create a clear and present danger that they will bring about the substantial evils that Congress has a right to prevent," free speech could be limited.

RED SCARE, RED SUMMER

The line between wartime suppression of dissent and the postwar Red Scare is not easily drawn. In the name of

Red Scare, Red Summer 667

patriotism, both harassed suspected internal enemies and deprived them of their constitutional rights; both had government sanction. Together they stabbed at the Bill of Rights and wounded radicalism in America. Yet in at least two respects the phenomena were different. Whereas in wartime the main fear had been of subversion, after the armistice it was revolution; and whereas in 1917 the target had often been German Americans, in 1919 it was frequently organized labor. The Russian Revolution and the communist uprisings elsewhere in Europe alarmed many Americans, and the fears grew when in 1919 the Soviet leadership announced the formation of the Communist International (or Comintern), whose purpose was to export revolution throughout the world. Terrified conservatives responded by looking for pro-Bolshevik sympathizers (or "Reds," from the red flag used by communists) in the United States, especially in immigrant groups and labor unions.

Labor Strikes

Labor union leaders emerged out of the war determined to secure higher wages for workers, to meet rising prices, and to retain wartime bargaining rights. Employers instead rescinded benefits they had been forced to grant to labor during the war, including recognition of unions. The result was a rash of labor strikes in 1919, which sparked the Red Scare. All told, more than 3,300 strikes involving 4 million laborers jolted the nation that year, including the Seattle general strike in January. On May 1, a day of celebration for workers around the world, bombs were sent through the mails to prominent Americans. Most of the devices were intercepted and dismantled, but police never captured the conspirators. Most people assumed, not unreasonably, that anarchists and others bent on the destruction of the American way of life were responsible. Next came the Boston police strike in September. Some sniffed a Bolshevik conspiracy, but others thought it ridiculous to label Boston's Irish American, Catholic cops "radicals." The conservative governor of Massachusetts, Calvin Coolidge, gained national attention by proclaiming that nobody had the right to strike against the public safety. State guardsmen soon replaced the striking policemen.

Unrest in the steel industry in September stirred more ominous fears. Many steelworkers worked twelve hours a day, seven days a week, and lived in squalid housing. They looked to local steel unions, organized by the National Committee for Organizing Iron and Steel Workers, to help them improve their lives. When postwar unemployment in the industry climbed and the U.S. Steel Corporation refused to meet with committee representatives, some 350,000 workers walked off the job, demanding the right to collective bargaining, a shorter workday, and a living wage. The steel barons hired strikebreakers and sent agents to club strikers. Worried about both the 1919 strikes and Bolshevism, President Wilson warned against "the poison of disorder" and the "poison of revolt." But in the case of steel, the companies won; the strike collapsed in early 1920.

One of the leaders of the steel strike was William Z. Foster, a former IWW member and militant labor organizer who later joined the Communist Party. His presence in a labor movement seeking bread-and-butter goals permitted political and business leaders to dismiss the steel strike as a foreign threat orchestrated by American radicals. There was in fact no conspiracy, and the American left was badly splintered. Two defectors from the Socialist Party, John Reed and Benjamin Gitlow, founded the Communist Labor Party in 1919. The rival Communist Party of the United States of America, composed largely of aliens, was launched the same year. Neither party commanded many followers—their combined membership probably did not exceed 70,000—and in 1919 the harassed Socialist Party could muster no more than 30,000 members.

Although divisiveness among radicals actually signified weakness, both Progressives and conservatives interpreted the advent of the new parties as strengthening the radical menace. That is certainly how the American Legion saw the question. Organized in May 1919 to lobby for veterans' benefits, the Legion soon preached an antiradicalism that fueled the Red Scare. By 1920, 843,000 Legion members, mostly middle- and upper-class, had become stalwarts of an impassioned Americanism that demanded conformity.

Wilson's attorney general, A. Mitchell Palmer, also insisted that Americans think alike. A Progressive reformer, Quaker, and ambitious politician, Palmer declared that "revolution" was "eating its way into the homes of the American workmen, licking the altars of the churches, leaping into the belfry of the school bell." Palmer appointed J. Edgar Hoover to head the Radical Division of the Department of Justice. The zealous Hoover compiled index cards bearing the names of allegedly radical individuals and organizations. During 1919, agents jailed IWW members, and Palmer saw to it that 249 alien radicals, including the outspoken anarchist Emma Goldman, were deported to Russia.

Again, state and local governments took their cue from the Wilson administration. States passed peacetime sedition acts under which hundreds of people were arrested. Vigilante groups and mobs flourished once again,

American Legion

their numbers swelled by returning veterans. In November 1919, in Centralia, Washington, American Legionnaires broke from a parade to storm the IWW hall. Several were wounded. A number of Wobblies were soon arrested, and one of them, an ex-soldier, was taken from jail by a mob, then beaten, castrated, and shot. The New York State legislature expelled five duly elected Socialist Party members in early 1920.

The Red Scare reached a climax in January 1920 in the Palmer Raids. J. Edgar Hoover planned and directed the operation; government agents in thirty-three cities broke into meeting halls and homes without search warrants. More than four thousand people were jailed and denied counsel. In Boston some four hundred people were kept in detainment on bitterly cold Deer Island; two died of pneumonia, one leaped to his death, and another went insane. Because of court rulings and the courageous efforts of Assistant Secretary of Labor Louis Post, who deliberately held up paperwork, most of the arrestees were released, although in 1920–1921 nearly six hundred aliens were deported.

Palmer Raids

Palmer's disregard for elementary civil liberties drew criticism, with many charging that his tactics violated the Constitution. Many of the arrested "communists" had committed no crimes. When Palmer called for a peacetime sedition act, he alarmed both liberal and conservative leaders. His dire prediction that pro-Soviet radicals would incite violence on May Day 1920 proved mistaken—not a single disturbance occurred anywhere in the country. Palmer, who had taken to calling himself the "Fighting Quaker," was jeered as the "Quaking Fighter."

Palmer also blamed communists for the racial violence that gripped the nation in these years. Here again, the charge was baseless. African Americans realized well before the end of the war that their participation did little to change discriminatory white attitudes. Segregation remained social custom. The Ku Klux Klan was reviving, and racist films like D. W. Griffith's *The Birth of a Nation* (1915) fed prejudice with its celebration of the Klan and its demeaning depiction of blacks. Lynching statistics exposed the wide gap between wartime declarations of humanity and the American practice of inhumanity at home: between 1914 and 1920, 382 blacks were lynched, some of them in military uniform.

Racial Unrest

Northern whites who resented "the Negro invasion" vented their anger in riots, as in East St. Louis, Illinois, in July 1917. The next month, in Houston, where African American soldiers faced white harassment and refused to obey segregation laws, whites and blacks exchanged gunfire. Seventeen whites and two African Americans died, and the army sentenced thirteen black soldiers to death and forty-one to life imprisonment for mutiny. During the bloody "Red Summer" of 1919 (so named by black author James Weldon Johnson for the blood that was spilled), race riots rocked two dozen cities and towns. The worst violence occurred in Chicago, a favorite destination for migrating blacks. In the very hot days of July 1919, a black youth swimming at a segregated white beach was hit by a thrown rock and drowned. Rumors spread, tempers flared, and soon blacks and whites were battling each other. Stabbings, burnings, and shootings went on for days until state police restored some calm. Thirty-eight people died, twenty-three African Americans and fifteen whites.

By the time of this tragedy, a disillusioned W. E. B. Du Bois had already concluded that black support for the war had not diminished whites' adherence to inequality and segregation. That spring he vowed a struggle: "We return. We return from fighting. We return fighting." Or, as poet Claude McKay put it after the Chicago riot in a poem he titled "If We Must Die,"

> Like men we'll face the murderous cowardly pack.
> Pressed to the wall, dying, but fighting back.

The exhortations of Du Bois and McKay reflected a newfound militancy among black veterans and in the growing black communities of the North. Editorials in African American newspapers subjected white politicians, including the president, to increasingly harsh criticism and at the same time implored readers to embrace their own prowess and beauty: "The black man is a power of great potentiality upon whom consciousness of his own strength is about to dawn." The NAACP stepped up its campaign for civil rights and equality, vowing in 1919 to publicize the terrors of the lynch law and to seek legislation to stop "Judge Lynch." Other blacks, doubting the potential for equality, turned instead to a charismatic Jamaican immigrant named Marcus Garvey (see page 685), who called on African Americans to abandon their hopes for integration and to seek a separate black nation.

Black Militancy

The crackdown on laborers and radicals, and the resurgence of racism in 1919, dashed wartime hopes. Although the passage of the Nineteenth Amendment in 1920, guaranteeing women the right to vote, showed that reform could happen, it was the exception to the rule. Unemployment, inflation, racial conflict, labor upheaval, a campaign against free speech—all inspired disillusionment in the immediate postwar years.

◀ An African American is confronted by state militia members during the race riots in Chicago in 1919. The troops were called in after Mayor Bill Thompson determined that the city police could not restore order.

(Chicago Historical Society photo by Jun Fujita)

THE DEFEAT OF PEACE

President Wilson seemed focused on confronting the threat of radicalism more abroad than at home. Throughout the final months of the war he fretted about the Soviet takeover in Russia, and he watched with apprehension the communist uprisings in various parts of central Europe. Months earlier, in mid-1918, Wilson had revealed his ardent anti-Bolshevism when he ordered five thousand American troops to northern Russia and ten thousand more to Siberia, where they joined other Allied contingents in fighting what was now a Russian civil war. They fought on the side of the "Whites" (various counterrevolutionary forces) against the "Reds" (the Bolsheviks). Wilson did not consult Congress. He said the military expeditions would guard Allied supplies and Russian railroads from German seizure, and would also rescue a group of Czechs who wished to return home to fight the Germans.

Worried that the Japanese were building influence in Siberia and closing the Open Door, Wilson also hoped to deter Japan from further advances in Asia. Mostly, though, he wanted to smash the infant Bolshevik government, a challenge to his new world order. Thus he backed an economic blockade of Russia, sent arms to anti-Bolshevik forces, and refused to recognize Lenin's government. The United States also secretly passed military information to anti-Bolshevik forces and used food relief to shore up opponents of the Soviets in the Baltic region. Later, at the Paris Peace Conference, representatives of the new Soviet government were denied a seat. U.S. troops did not leave Russia until spring 1920, after the Bolsheviks had demonstrated their staying power. The actions by Wilson and other Allied leaders in 1918–1920 generated powerful feelings of resentment and suspicion among many Russians.

Wilson faced a monumental task in securing a postwar settlement. When he departed for the Paris Peace Conference in December 1918, he faced obstacles erected by his political enemies, by the Allies, and by himself. Some observers suggested that a cocky Wilson underestimated his task. During the 1918 congressional elections, Wilson committed the blunder of suggesting that patriotism required the election of a Democratic Congress; Republicans had a field day blasting the president for questioning their love of country. The GOP gained control of both houses, signaling trouble for Wilson in two ways. First, a peace treaty would have to be submitted for approval to a potentially hostile Senate. Second, the election results at home diminished Wilson's stature in the eyes of foreign leaders. Wilson aggravated his political problems by not naming a senator to his advisory American Peace Commission. He also refused to take any prominent Republicans with him to Paris or to consult with the Senate Foreign Relations

Committee before the conference. It did not help that the president denounced his critics as "blind and little provincial people."

Wilson was greeted with huge and adoring crowds in Paris, London, and Rome. Behind closed doors, however, the leaders of these countries—Georges Clemenceau of France, David Lloyd George of Britain, and Vittorio Orlando of Italy (with Wilson, the Big Four)—became formidable adversaries. Clemenceau mused, "God gave man the Ten Commandments, and he broke every one. Wilson has given us Fourteen Points. We shall see." After four years of horrible war, the Allies were not about to be cheated out of the fruits of victory. Wilson could wax lyrical about a "peace without victory," but the late-arriving Americans had not suffered the way the peoples of France and Great Britain had suffered. Germany would have to pay, and pay big, for the calamity it had caused.

At the conference, held at the ornate palace of Versailles, the Big Four tried to work out an agreement, mostly behind closed doors. Critics

Paris Peace Conference

quickly pointed out that Wilson had immediately abandoned the first of his Fourteen Points: diplomacy "in the public view." The victors demanded that Germany (which had not been invited to the proceedings) pay a huge reparations bill. Wilson instead called for a small indemnity, fearing that a resentful and economically hobbled Germany might turn to Bolshevism or disrupt the postwar community in some other way. Unable to moderate the Allied position, the president reluctantly gave way, agreeing to a clause blaming the war on the Germans and to the creation of a commission to determine the amount of reparations (later set at $33 billion). Wilson acknowledged that the peace terms were "hard," but he also came to believe that "the German people must be made to hate war."

As for the breaking up of empires and the principle of self-determination, Wilson could deliver on only some of his goals. To the crushing disappointment of much of the world's nonwhite majority, the imperial system emerged largely unscathed, as the conferees created a League-administered "mandate" system which placed former German and Turkish colonies under the control of other imperial nations. Japan gained authority over Germany's colonies in the Pacific, while France and Britain obtained parts of the Middle East—the French obtained what became Lebanon and Syria, while the British received the three former Ottoman provinces that became Iraq. Britain also secured Palestine, on the condition that it uphold its wartime promise to promote "the establishment in Palestine of a national home for the Jewish people" without prejudice to "the civil and religious rights of existing non-Jewish communities"—the so-called Balfour Declaration of 1917.

In other arrangements, Japan replaced Germany as the imperial overlord of China's Shandong Peninsula, and France was permitted occupation rights in Germany's Rhineland. Elsewhere in Europe, Wilson's prescriptions fared better. Out of Austria-Hungary and Russia came the newly independent states of Austria, Hungary, Yugoslavia, Czechoslovakia, and Poland. Wilson and his colleagues also built a *cordon sanitaire* (buffer zone) of new westward-looking nations (Finland, Estonia, Latvia, and Lithuania) around Russia, to quarantine the Bolshevik contagion (see Map 23.3).

Wilson worked hardest on the charter for the League of Nations, the centerpiece of his plans for the postwar world. He envisioned the League

League of Nations and Article 10

as having power over all disputes among states, including those that did not arise from the peace agreement; as such, it could transform international relations. Even so, the great powers would have preponderant say: the organization would have an influential council of five permanent members and elected delegates from smaller states, an assembly of all members, and a World Court.

Wilson identified Article 10 as the "kingpin" of the League covenant: "The Members of the League undertake to respect and preserve as against external aggression the territorial integrity and existing political independence of all Members of the League. In case of any such aggression or in case of any threat or danger of such aggression the Council shall advise upon the means by which this obligation shall be fulfilled." This collective-security provision, along with the entire League charter, became part of the peace treaty because Wilson insisted that there could be no future peace with Germany without a league to oversee it.

German representatives at first refused to sign the punitive treaty but submitted in June 1919. They gave up 13 percent of Germany's territory, 10 percent of its population, all of its colonies, and a huge portion of its national wealth. Many people wondered how the League could function in the poisoned postwar atmosphere of humiliation and revenge. But Wilson waxed euphoric: "The stage is set, the destiny disclosed. It has come about by no plan of our conceiving, but by the hand of God."

Critics in the United States were not so sure. In March 1919, thirty-nine senators (enough to deny the

Map 23.3   Europe Transformed by War and Peace

After President Wilson and the other conferees at the Paris Peace Conference negotiated the Treaty of Versailles, empires were broken up. In eastern Europe in particular, new nations emerged.

IIIIIIIIIIIIIIIIIIIIIIIIIIIIII
Critics of the Treaty

treaty the necessary two-thirds vote) had signed a petition stating that the League's structure did not adequately protect U.S. interests. Wilson denounced his critics as "pygmy" minds, but he persuaded the peace conference to exempt the Monroe Doctrine and domestic matters from League jurisdiction. Having made these concessions to senatorial advice, Wilson would budge no more. Compromises with other nations had been necessary to keep the conference going, he insisted, and the League would rectify wrongs. Could his critics not see that membership in the League would give the United States "leadership in the world"?

By summer, criticism intensified: Wilson had bastardized his own principles. He had conceded Shandong to Japan. He had personally killed a provision affirming the racial equality of all peoples. The treaty did not mention freedom of the seas, and tariffs were not reduced. Reparations on Germany promised to be punishing. Senator La Follette and other critics on the left protested that the League would perpetuate empire. Conservative critics feared that the League would limit American freedom of action in world affairs, stymie U.S. expansion, and intrude on domestic questions. And Article 10 raised serious questions: Would the United States be *obligated* to use armed force to ensure collective security? And what about colonial rebellions, such as in Ireland or India? Would the League feel compelled to crush them? "Were a League of Nations in existence in the days when George Washington fought and won," an Irish American editor wrote, "we would still be an English colony."

Henry Cabot Lodge of Massachusetts led the Senate opposition to the League. A Harvard-educated Ph.D. and partisan Republican who also had an intense personal dislike of Wilson, Lodge packed the Foreign Relations Committee with critics and prolonged public hearings. He introduced several reservations to the treaty, the most important of which held that Congress had to approve any obligation under Article 10.

In September 1919 Wilson embarked on a speaking tour of the United States. Growing more exhausted every day, he dismissed his antagonists as "contemptible quitters." Provoked by Irish American and German American hecklers, he lashed out in Red Scare terms: "Any man who carries a hyphen about him carries a dagger which he is ready to plunge into the vitals of the Republic." While doubts about Article 10 multiplied, Wilson tried to highlight neglected features of the League charter—such as the arbitration of disputes and an international conference to abolish child labor. In Colorado, a day after delivering another passionate speech, the president awoke to nausea and uncontrollable facial twitching. "I just feel as if I am going to pieces," he said. A few days later, he suffered a massive stroke that paralyzed his left side. He became peevish and even more stubborn, increasingly unable to conduct presidential business. More and more, his wife Edith had to select issues for his attention and delegate other matters to his cabinet heads. Advised to placate Lodge and other "Reservationist" senatorial critics so the Versailles treaty would have a chance of being approved by Congress, Wilson rejected "dishonorable compromise." From Senate Democrats he demanded utter loyalty—a vote against all reservations.

▲ In October 1919 President Woodrow Wilson (1856–1924) receives assistance after his massive stroke, which made it difficult for him to maintain his train of thought and manage government affairs. Historians continue to debate the influence of Wilson's poor health on the president's losing battle for U.S. membership in the League of Nations. *(Library of Congress)*

Twice in November the Senate rejected the Treaty of Versailles and thus U.S. membership in the League. In the

Senate Rejection of the Treaty and League

first vote, Democrats joined sixteen "Irreconcilables," mostly Republicans who opposed any treaty whatsoever, to defeat the treaty with reservations (39 for and 55 against). In the second vote, Republicans and Irreconcilables turned down the treaty without reservations (38 for and 53 against). In March 1920 the Senate again voted; this time, a majority (49 for and 35 against) favored the treaty with reservations, but the tally fell short of the two-thirds needed. Had Wilson permitted Democrats to compromise—to accept reservations—he could have achieved his fervent goal of membership in the League, which, despite the U.S. absence, came into being.

At the core of the debate lay a basic issue in American foreign policy: whether the United States would endorse collective security or continue to travel the more solitary path articulated in George Washington's Farewell Address and in the Monroe Doctrine. In a world dominated by imperialist states unwilling to subordinate their strategic ambitions to an international organization, Americans preferred their traditional nonalignment and freedom of choice over binding commitments to collective action. That is why so many of Wilson's critics targeted Article 10. Wilson countered that this argument amounted to embracing the status quo—the European imperialist states are selfish, so the United States should be, too. Acceptance of Article 10 and membership in the League promised something better, he believed, for the United States and for the world; it promised collective security in place of the frail protection of alliances and the instability of a balance of power.

In the end, World War I did not make the world safe for democracy. Wilson failed to create a new world order

An Unsafe World

through reform. Still, the United States emerged from the First World War an even greater world power. By 1920 the United States

had become the world's leading economic power, producing 40 percent of its coal, 70 percent of its petroleum, and half of its pig iron. It also rose to first rank in world trade. American companies took advantage of the war to nudge the Germans and British out of foreign markets, especially in Latin America. Meanwhile, the United States shifted from being a debtor to being a creditor nation, becoming the world's leading banker.

After the disappointment of Versailles, appeals for arms control accelerated, and the peace movement revitalized. At the same time, the military became better armed and more professional. The Reserve Officers Training Corps (ROTC) became permanent; military "colleges" provided upper-echelon training; and the Army Industrial College, founded in 1924, pursued business-military cooperation in the area of logistics and planning. The National Research Council, created in 1916 with government money and Carnegie and Rockefeller funds, continued after the war as an alliance of scientists and businesspeople engaged in research relating to national defense. Tanks, quick-firing guns, armor-piercing explosives, and oxygen masks for high-altitude-flying pilots were just some of the technological advances that emerged from the First World War.

The international system born in these years was unstable and fragmented. Espousing decolonization and taking to heart the Wilsonian principle of self-determination, nationalist leaders active during the First World War, such as Ho Chi Minh of Indochina and Mohandas K. Gandhi of India, vowed to achieve independence for their peoples. Communism became a disruptive force in world politics, and the Soviets bore a grudge against those invaders who had tried to thwart their revolution. The new states in central and eastern Europe proved weak, dependent on outsiders for security. Germans bitterly resented the harsh peace settlement, and German war debts and reparations problems dogged international order for many years. As it entered the 1920s, the international system that Woodrow Wilson had vowed to reform was fraught with unresolved problems.

Legacy FOR A PEOPLE AND A NATION

Freedom of Speech and the ACLU

Although freedom of speech is enshrined in the U.S. Constitution, for more than a century after the nation's founding the concept had little standing in American jurisprudence. Before World War I, those with radical views often met with harsh treatment for exercising what today would be termed their freedom of speech. During the war, however, the Wilson administration's suppression of dissidents led some Americans to reformulate the traditional definition of allowable speech. Two key figures in this movement were Roger Baldwin, a conscientious objector, and woman suffrage activist Crystal Eastman. Baldwin and Eastman were among the first to advance the idea that the content of political speech could be separated from the identity of the speaker and that patriotic Americans could—indeed should—defend the right of others to express political beliefs abhorrent to their own. After working during the war to defend the rights of conscientious objectors, Baldwin and Eastman—joined by activists such as Jane Addams, Helen Keller, and Norman Thomas—formed the American Civil Liberties Union (ACLU).

Since 1920 the ACLU, which today has some 300,000 members in three hundred chapters nationwide, has aimed to protect the basic civil liberties of all Americans and to extend them to those to whom they have traditionally been denied. The organization has been involved in almost every major civil liberties case contested in U.S. courts, among them the John Scopes "monkey trial" (1925), concerning the teaching of evolution at a Tennessee school, and the landmark *Brown v. Board of Education* case (1954) which ended federal tolerance of racial segregation. More recently, the ACLU was involved in a 1997 case in which the Supreme Court decided that the 1996 Communications Act banning "indecent speech" violated First Amendment rights.

Conservatives have long criticized the ACLU for its opposition to official prayers in public schools and its support of the legality of abortion, as well as for what they see as its selectivity in deciding whose freedom of speech to defend. Backers of the organization counter that it has also defended those on the right, such as Oliver North, a key figure in the Iran-contra scandal of the 1980s.

Either way, the principle of free speech is today broadly accepted by Americans, so much so that even ACLU bashers take it for granted. Membership has risen sharply since the terrorist attacks on September 11, 2001, due to concern among some people that government policies have eroded privacy and legal protections, not only for Americans but also for foreign detainees at the Guantánamo Bay detention facility. Ironically, the Wilson administration's crackdown on dissent produced an expanded commitment to freedom of speech for a people and a nation.

SUMMARY

At the close of the First World War, historian Albert Bushnell Hart observed that "it is easy to see that the United States is a new country." Actually, America came out of the war an unsettled mix of the old and the new. The war years marked the emergence of the United States as a world power, and Americans could take justifiable pride in the contribution they had made to the Allied victory. At the same time, the war exposed deep divisions among Americans: white versus black, nativist versus immigrant, capital versus labor, men versus women, radical versus Progressive and conservative, pacifist versus interventionist, nationalist versus internationalist. It is little wonder that Americans—having experienced race riots, labor strikes, disputes over civil liberties, and the League fight—wanted to escape into what President Warren G. Harding called "normalcy."

During the war, the federal government intervened in the economy and influenced people's everyday lives as never before. Centralization of control in Washington, D.C., and mobilization of the home front served as models for the future. Although the Wilson administration shunned reconstruction or reconversion plans (war housing projects, for example, were sold to private investors) and quickly dismantled the many government agencies, the World War I experience of the activist state served as guidance for 1930s reformers battling the Great Depression (see Chapter 25). The partnership of government and business in managing the wartime economy advanced the development of a mass society through the standardization of products and the promotion of efficiency. Wilsonian wartime policies also nourished the concentration of corporate ownership through the suspension of antitrust laws. Business power dominated the next decade. American labor, by contrast, entered lean years, although new labor management practices, including corporate welfare programs, survived.

Although the disillusionment evident after Versailles did not cause the United States to adopt a policy of isolationist withdrawal (see Chapter 26), skepticism about America's ability to right wrongs abroad marked the postwar American mood. The war was grimy and ugly, far less glorious than Wilson's lofty rhetoric had suggested. People recoiled from photographs of shell-shocked faces and of bodies dangling from barbed wire. American soldiers, tired of idealism, craved the latest baseball scores and their regular jobs. Those Progressives who had believed that entry into the war would deliver the millennium later marveled at their naiveté. Many lost their enthusiasm for crusades, and many others turned away in disgust from the bickering of the victors. Some felt betrayed. Journalist William Allen White angrily wrote to a friend that the Allies "have—those damned vultures—taken the heart out of the peace, taken the joy out of the great enterprise of the war, and have made it a sordid malicious miserable thing like all the other wars in the world."

By 1920 Woodrow Wilson's idealism seemed to many Americans to be a spent force, both at home and abroad. Aware of their country's newfound status as a leading world power, they were unsure what this reality meant for the nation, or for their individual lives. With a mixed legacy from the Great War, and a sense of uneasiness, the country entered the new era of the 1920s.

SUGGESTIONS FOR FURTHER READING

John Milton Cooper Jr., *Breaking the Heart of the World: Woodrow Wilson and the Fight for the League of Nations* (2001)

David S. Foglesong, *America's Secret War Against Bolshevism* (1995)

James B. Grossman, *Land of Hope: Chicago, Black Southerners, and the Great Migration* (1989)

Michael Kazin, *A Godly Hero: The Life of William Jennings Bryan* (2006)

Jennifer D. Keene, *Doughboys, the Great War, and the Remaking of America* (2001)

David M. Kennedy, *Over Here: The Home Front in the First World War* (1980)

Thomas J. Knock, *To End All Wars: Woodrow Wilson and the Quest for a New World Order* (1992)

Margaret MacMillan, *Paris 1919: Six Months That Changed the World* (2002)

John A. Thompson, *Woodrow Wilson* (2002)

Robert H. Zieger, *America's Great War: World War I and the American Experience* (2000)

For a more extensive list for further reading, go to college.hmco.com/pic/norton8e.

Beth and Robert Gordon were not very compatible marriage partners. Beth was frumpy and demanding; Robert liked to party. One evening at a nightclub, he met Sally Clark, who liked to party, too. They danced, and when Robert came home, Beth smelled perfume on his suit. The spouses argued, and shortly they divorced. It was not long, however, before Robert found that Sally's appeal had worn off; he missed Beth's intellect and wisdom. Meanwhile, Beth concluded that she needed to change her dowdy image. She bought new clothes and makeup, turning herself into a glamorous beauty. By coincidence, Beth and Robert visited the same summer resort and rekindled their romance. When Robert was injured in an accident, Beth took him home and nursed him back to health, much to Sally's disappointment. In the end, as Beth and Robert remarried, Sally accepted her loss of Robert philosophically, concluding with the wry remark "The only good thing about marriage, anyway, is the alimony."

The experiences of Beth, Robert, and Sally make up the plot of the 1920 motion picture *Why Change Your Wife?*—one of dozens of films directed by Cecil B. DeMille. DeMille succeeded by giving audiences what they wanted to see and what they fantasized about doing. Beth, Robert, and Sally dressed stylishly, went out dancing, listened to phonograph records, rode in cars, and visited resorts. Although DeMille's films and others of the 1920s usually ended by reinforcing marriage, ruling out premarital sex, and supporting the work ethic, they also exuded a new morality. Female lead characters were not mothers tied to the home; both male and female characters shed old-style values for the pursuit of luxury, fun, and the trappings of sexual freedom, just as the actors and actresses themselves, such as Gloria Swanson and Thomas Meighan, the stars of *Why Change Your Wife?* were doing in

◀ Dressed in stylish fashions and indulging in some flirtatious banter, Thomas Meighan and Gloria Swanson, stars of Cecil B. DeMille's romantic comedy *Why Change Your Wife?* represent ways that movies and movie personalities gave the public images, sometimes accurate but often exaggerated, of new social mores in the 1920s. *(Copyright © Courtesy Everett Collection)*

CHRONOLOGY

1920 ■ Volstead Act implements prohibition (Eighteenth Amendment)
■ Nineteenth Amendment ratified, legalizing vote for women in federal elections
■ Harding elected president
■ KDKA transmits first commercial radio broadcast

1920–21 ■ Postwar deflation and depression

1921 ■ Federal Highway Act funds national highway system
■ Emergency Quota Act establishes immigration quotas
■ Sacco and Vanzetti convicted
■ Sheppard-Towner Act allots funds to states to set up maternity and pediatric clinics

1922 ■ Economic recovery raises standards of living
■ *Coronado Coal Company v. United Mine Workers* rules that strikes may be illegal actions in restraint of trade
■ *Bailey v. Drexel Furniture Company* voids restrictions on child labor
■ Federal government ends strikes by railroad shop workers and miners
■ Fordney-McCumber Tariff raises rates on imports

1923 ■ Harding dies; Coolidge assumes presidency
■ *Adkins v. Children's Hospital* overturns a minimum wage law affecting women

1923–24 ■ Government scandals (Teapot Dome) exposed

1924 ■ Snyder Act grants citizenship to all Indians not previously citizens
■ National Origins Act revises immigration quotas
■ Coolidge elected president

1925 ■ Scopes trial highlights battle between religious fundamentalists and modernists

1927 ■ Lindbergh pilots solo transatlantic flight
■ Ruth hits sixty home runs
■ *The Jazz Singer*, first movie with sound, released

1928 ■ Stock market soars
■ Hoover elected president

1929 ■ Stock market crashes; Great Depression begins

their off-screen lives. In this way, *Why Change Your Wife?* was a harbinger, though an inexact one, of a new era.

During the 1920s, consumerism flourished, represented by the products, entertainment, and leisure that film characters and the stars who played them enjoyed. Although poverty beset small farmers, workers in declining industries, and nonwhites in inner cities, most other people enjoyed a high standard of living relative to that of previous generations. Spurred by advertising and installment buying, Americans eagerly acquired radios, automobiles, real estate, and stocks. As in the Gilded Age, the federal government maintained a favorable climate for business. And, in contrast to the Progressive era, few people worried about abuses of private power. Yet state and local governments, extending the reach of public authority, undertook important reforms.

It was an era in which people of all types embraced new technology while trying to preserve values they had long understood. New forms of leisure activity coincided with creativity in the arts and notable advances in science and technology. Changes in work habits, family responsibilities, and healthcare fostered new uses of time and new attitudes about behavior, including encouragements to "think young." While material bounty and expanded consumerism touched the lives of many people, others continued to endure hardship and exclusion. Winds of change also stirred up waves of resistance from those who held tight to traditional beliefs, and cultural divisions came to affect politics. Thus the decade was both appealing and unsettling, prompting enthusiasm and rejection.

An unseen storm lurked on the horizon, however. The glitter of consumer culture that dominated DeMille's films and their audiences' everyday lives blinded Americans to rising debt and uneven prosperity. Just before the decade closed, a devastating depression brought the era to a brutal close.

- How did developments in technology and the workplace stimulate social change during the 1920s?
- What were the benefits and costs of consumerism, and how did people deal with challenges to old-time values?
- What caused the stock market crash and the ensuing deep depression that signaled the end of the era?

BIG BUSINESS TRIUMPHANT

The 1920s began with a jolting economic decline. Shortly after the First World War ended, industrial output dropped as wartime orders dried up. As European agriculture recovered from war, American exports contracted and farm incomes plunged. In the West, railroads and the mining industry suffered. When demobilized soldiers flooded the work force, unemployment, around 2 percent in 1919, passed 12 percent in 1921. Layoffs spread through New England as textile companies abandoned outdated factories for the convenient raw materials and cheap labor of the South. The consequence of all these patterns was that consumer spending dwindled, causing more contraction and joblessness.

Aided by electric energy, a recovery began in 1922 and continued unevenly until 1929. Electric motors enabled

New Economic Expansion

manufacturers to replace steam engines and to produce old and new goods more cheaply and efficiently. Using new metal alloys, such as aluminum, and synthetic materials, such as rayon, producers could turn out an expanded array of consumer goods, including refrigerators, toasters, vacuum cleaners, and clothing. In addition, most urban households now had electric service, enabling them to utilize the new appliances. The growing economy gave Americans more spending money for these products, as well as for restaurants, beauty salons, and movie theaters. But, more important, installment, or time-payment, plans ("A dollar down and a dollar forever," one critic quipped) drove the new consumerism. Of 3.5 million automobiles sold in 1923, some 80 percent were bought on credit.

Economic expansion in the 1920s brought a continuation of the corporate consolidation that had created trusts and holding companies in the late nineteenth century. Although Progressive era trustbusting had achieved some regulation of big business, it had not eliminated oligopoly, the control of an entire industry by one or a few large firms. A few sprawling companies, such as U.S. Steel and General Electric, dominated basic industries, and oligopolies controlled much of marketing, distribution, and finance as well.

Business and professional organizations that had arisen around 1900 also expanded in the 1920s. Retailers and manufacturers formed trade

Associations and "New Lobbying"

associations to swap information and coordinate planning. Farm bureaus promoted scientific agriculture and tried to stabilize markets.

Lawyers, engineers, and social scientists expanded their professional societies. These special-interest groups participated in what is called the "new lobbying." In a complex society in which government was playing an increasingly influential role, hundreds of organizations sought to convince federal and state legislators to support their interests. One Washington, D.C., observer contended that "lobbyists were so thick they were constantly falling over one another."

Government policies helped business thrive, and legislators depended on lobbyists' expertise in making decisions. Prodded by lobbyists, Congress cut taxes on corporations and wealthy individuals in 1921, and passed the Fordney-McCumber Tariff Act (1922) to raise tariff rates. Presidents Warren G. Harding, Calvin Coolidge, and Herbert Hoover appointed cabinet officers who were favorable toward business. Regulatory agencies, such as the Federal Trade Commission and the Interstate Commerce Commission, monitored company activities but, under the influence of lobbyists, cooperated with corporations more than they regulated them.

The Supreme Court, led by Chief Justice William Howard Taft, the former president whom Harding nominated to the Court in 1921, protected business and private property as aggressively as in the Gilded Age, and abandoned its Progressive era antitrust stance. Key decisions sheltered business from government regulation and hindered organized labor's ability to achieve its ends through strikes and legislation. In *Coronado Coal Company v. United Mine Workers* (1922), Taft ruled that a striking union, like a trust, could be prosecuted for illegal restraint of trade, yet in *Maple Floor Association v. U.S.* (1929), the Court decided that trade associations that distributed anti-union information were not acting in restraint of trade. The Court also voided the federal law restricting child labor (*Bailey v. Drexel Furniture Company,* 1922), because it infringed on state power, and overturned a minimum wage law affecting women, because it infringed on liberty of contract (*Adkins v. Children's Hospital,* 1923).

Organized labor suffered other setbacks during the 1920s. Fearful of communism allegedly brought into the

Setbacks for Organized Labor

country by radical immigrants, public opinion turned against workers who disrupted everyday life with strikes. Perpetuating tactics used during the Red Scare of 1919, the Harding administration in 1922 obtained a sweeping court injunction to quash a strike by 400,000 railroad shop workers. The same year, the Justice Department helped end a nationwide strike by 650,000 miners. Courts at both the state and federal level issued injunctions to prevent strikes and permitted businesses to sue unions for damages suffered because of labor actions.

Meanwhile, corporations fought unions in several ways. To prevent labor organization, employers imposed yellow-dog contracts which, as a condition of employment, compelled an employee to agree not to join a union. Companies also countered the appeal of unions by offering pensions, profit sharing, and company-sponsored picnics and sporting events—a policy known as welfare capitalism. State legislators aided employers by prohibiting closed shops (workplaces where unions required that all employees be members of their labor organization) and permitting open shops (in which employers could hire nonunion employees). As a result of court action, welfare capitalism, and ineffective leadership, union membership fell from 5.1 million in 1920 to 3.6 million in 1929.

Agriculture was one sector of the national economy that languished during the 1920s. Pressed into competition

Languishing Agriculture

with growers in other countries and trying to increase productivity by investing in new machines, such as harvesters and tractors, American farmers found themselves further beset by hardship. Irrigation and mechanization had created "factories in the fields," making large-scale farming so efficient that fewer farmers could produce more crops than ever before. As a result, crop prices plunged, big agribusinesses took over, and small landholders and tenants could not make a living. Shortly after the end of the First World War, for example, the price that farmers could get for cotton dropped by two-thirds, and that for hogs and cattle fell by half. Foreign competition made matters worse. Incomes of small farmers (but not agribusinesses) plummeted, and debts rose.

POLITICS AND GOVERNMENT

A series of Republican presidents extended Theodore Roosevelt's notion of government-business cooperation, but they made government a compliant coordinator rather than the active manager Roosevelt had advocated. A symbol of government's goodwill toward business was President Warren G. Harding, elected in 1920 when the populace no longer desired national or international crusades. Democrats had nominated Ohio's Governor James M. Cox, who supported Woodrow Wilson's fading hope for U.S. membership in the League of Nations. But Cox and running mate Franklin D. Roosevelt, governor of New York, failed to excite voters. Harding, who kept his position on the League vague, captured 16 million popular votes to 9 million for Cox. (The total vote in the 1920 presidential election was 36 percent higher than in 1916, reflecting participation of women voters for the first time.)

A popular small-town newspaperman and senator from Ohio, Harding appointed some capable assistants who helped promote business growth, notably Secretary of State Charles Evans Hughes, Secretary of Commerce Herbert Hoover, Secretary of the Treasury Andrew Mellon, and Secretary of Agriculture Henry C. Wallace. Harding also backed some reforms. His administration helped streamline federal spending with the Budget and Accounting Act of 1921 (which created the Bureau of the Budget), supported antilynching legislation (rejected by Congress), and approved bills assisting farm cooperatives and liberalizing farm credit.

Harding, however, had personal weaknesses. As a senator, he had an extramarital liaison with the wife of an

Scandals of the Harding Administration

Ohio merchant. In 1917 he began a relationship with Nan Britton, who was thirty-one years his junior. A daughter was born from the affair in 1919, and Britton reputedly continued to visit Harding in the White House after he became president. Unlike Grover Cleveland, Harding never acknowledged his illegitimate offspring.

Of more consequence than his sexual escapades, Harding appointed cronies who saw office holding as an invitation to personal gain. Charles Forbes, head of the Veterans Bureau, went to federal prison, convicted of fraud and bribery in connection with government contracts. Attorney General Harry Daugherty resigned after being implicated in a kickback scheme involving bootleggers of illegal liquor; he escaped prosecution by refusing to testify against himself. Most notoriously, a congressional inquiry in 1923 and 1924 revealed that Secretary of the Interior Albert Fall had accepted bribes to lease government property to private oil companies. For his role in the affair—called the Teapot Dome scandal after a Wyoming oil reserve that he handed to the Mammoth Oil Company—Fall was fined $100,000 and spent a year in jail, the first cabinet member ever to be so disgraced.

By mid-1923, Harding had become disillusioned. Amid rumors of mismanagement and crime, he told a journalist, "My God, this is a hell of a job. I have no trouble with my enemies. . . . But my friends, my Goddamned friends . . . they're the ones that keep me walking the floor nights." On a speaking tour that summer, Harding became ill and died in San Francisco on August 2. Although his death preceded revelation of the Teapot Dome scandal, some people speculated that, to avoid im-

◀ President Calvin Coolidge liked to hobnob with business leaders but also display his Vermont background. He is shown here at his home in Plymouth, Vermont, in 1925, holding a bucket of maple syrup and sitting with Harvey Firestone (of the tire company) on his right, Henry Ford on his left, and Thomas Edison on Ford's left.

(Calvin Coolidge Memorial Room, Forbes Library, Northampton, MA)

peachment, Harding committed suicide or was poisoned by his wife. Most evidence, however, points to death from natural causes, probably heart disease. Regardless, Harding was widely mourned. A warm, dignified-looking man who relished a good joke and an evening of poker, he seemed suited to a nation recovering from world war and domestic hard times.

Vice President Calvin Coolidge, who now became president, was far less outgoing than his predecessor. Nicknamed "Silent Cal," he once observed that he seldom spoke to people who interviewed him because when he did, "it winds them up for twenty minutes more." As governor of Massachusetts, Coolidge had attracted national attention in 1919 when he used the national guard to end a strike by Boston policemen, an action that won him business support and the vice-presidential nomination in 1920.

Coolidge's presidency coincided with and assisted business prosperity. Respectful of private enterprise and aided by Andrew Mellon, who was retained as treasury secretary, Coolidge's administration reduced federal debt, lowered income-tax rates (especially for the wealthy), and began construction of a national highway system. But Coolidge refused to apply government power to assist

Coolidge Prosperity

struggling farmers. Responding to farmers' complaints of falling prices, Congress twice passed bills to establish government-backed price supports for staple crops (the McNary-Haugen bills of 1927 and 1928). Resembling the subtreasury scheme that Farmers' Alliances had advocated in the 1890s, these bills proposed to establish a system whereby the government would buy surplus farm products and either hold them until prices rose or sell them abroad. Farmers argued that they deserved as much government protection as manufacturers got. Coolidge, however, vetoed the measures both times as improper government interference in the market economy.

"Coolidge prosperity" was the decisive issue in the 1924 presidential election. Both major parties ran candidates who favored private initiative over government intervention. Republicans nominated Coolidge with little dissent. At their national convention, Democrats first debated whether to denounce the revived Ku Klux Klan, voting 542 to 541 against condemnation. They then endured 103 ballots, deadlocked between southern prohibitionists, who supported former treasury secretary William G. McAdoo, and antiprohibition easterners, who backed New York's governor, Alfred E. Smith. They finally compromised on John W. Davis, a New York corporate lawyer.

Remnants of the Progressive movement, along with farm, labor, and socialist groups, formed a new Progressive Party and nominated Robert M. La Follette, the aging Wisconsin reformer. The new party stressed issues of the previous two decades: public ownership of railroads and power plants, conservation of natural resources, aid to farmers, rights for organized labor, and regulation of business. The electorate, however, endorsed Coolidge prosperity. Coolidge beat Davis by 15.7 million to 8.4 million popular votes, and 382 to 136 electoral votes. La Follette finished third, receiving 4.8 million popular votes and 13 electoral votes.

In Congress and the presidency, the urgency for political and economic reform that had moved the genera-

Extensions of Progressive Reform

tion of Progressive reformers faded in the 1920s. Much reform, however, occurred at state and local levels. Following initiatives begun before the First World War, thirty-four states instituted or expanded workers' compensation laws and public welfare programs in the 1920s. In cities, social workers strived for better housing and poverty relief. By 1926 every major city and many smaller ones had planning and zoning commissions to harness physical growth to the common good. As a result of their efforts, a new generation of reformers who later influenced national affairs acquired valuable experience in the nation's statehouses, city halls, and universities.

Some reformers were disturbed by the federal government's generally apathetic Indian policy. Organizations

Indian Affairs and Politics

such as the Indian Rights Association, the Indian Defense Association, and the General Federation of Women's Clubs worked to obtain justice and social services, including better education and return of tribal lands. But most Americans perceived Indians as no longer a threat to whites' ambitions and expected them to assimilate like other minorities. Such assumption overlooked important drawbacks. Severalty, the federal policy created by the Dawes Act of 1887, allotting land to individuals rather than to tribes, failed to make Indians self-supporting. Indian farmers had to suffer poor soil, lack of irrigation, scarce medical care, and cattle thieves. Deeply attached to their land, they showed little inclination to move to cities. Whites still hoped to convert native peoples into "productive" citizens, but in a way that ignored indigenous cultures. Reformers were especially critical of Indian women, who refused to adopt middle-class homemaking habits and balked at sending their children to boarding schools.

Meanwhile, the federal government struggled to clarify Indians' citizenship status. The Dawes Act had conferred citizenship on all Indians who accepted land allotments, but not on those who remained on reservations. Also, the government retained control over Indians that it did not exercise over others. For example, because of alleged drunkenness on reservations, federal law prevented the sale of liquor to Indians even before ratification of prohibition. After several court challenges, Congress finally passed an Indian Citizenship Act (Snyder Act) in 1924, granting full citizenship to all Indians who previously had not received it. In addition, President Hoover reinforced the intent of this measure by stating that citizenship was the best means for Indians to assimilate.

Even after achieving suffrage in 1920 with ratification of the Nineteenth Amendment, politically active women

Women and Politics

remained excluded from local and national power structures. But, like business associations, their voluntary organizations used tactics that advanced modern pressure-group politics. Whether the issue was birth control, peace, education, Indian affairs, or opposition to lynching, women in these associations lobbied legislators to support their causes. For example, the League of Women Voters, reorganized out of the National Woman Suffrage Association, encouraged women to run for office and actively lobbied for laws to improve conditions for employed women, the mentally ill, and the urban poor.

In 1921 action by women's groups persuaded Congress to pass the Sheppard-Towner Act, which allotted funds to states to create maternity and pediatric clinics as means of reducing infant mortality. (The measure ended in 1929, when Congress, under pressure from private physicians, canceled funding.) The Cable Act of 1922 reversed the law under which an American woman who married a foreigner assumed her husband's citizenship, allowing such a woman to retain U.S. citizenship. At the state level, too, women achieved rights, such as the ability to serve on juries.

As new voters, however, women faced daunting tasks in achieving their goals and overcoming internal differences. Women in the National Association of Colored Women, for example, fought for the rights of minority women and men without support from either the National Woman's Party or the newly organized League of Women Voters. Some groups, such as the National Woman's Party, pressed for an equal rights amendment to ensure women's equality with men under the law. But such activity alienated the National Consumers League, the Women's Trade Union League, the League of Women Voters, and other organizations that supported special protective legislation to limit hours and improve conditions for employed women. But, like men, women of all types sought participation in the new era's consumerism.

A CONSUMER SOCIETY

The consumerism depicted in *Why Change Your Wife?* reflected important economic changes affecting the nation.

TABLE 24.1	Consumerism in the 1920s	
1900		
2 bicycles	$	70.00
Wringer and washboard		5.00
Brushes and brooms		5.00
Sewing machine (mechanical)		25.00
TOTAL	$	105.00
1928		
Automobile	$	700.00
Radio		75.00
Phonograph		50.00
Washing machine		150.00
Vacuum cleaner		50.00
Sewing machine (electric)		60.00
Other electrical equipment		25.00
Telephone (per year)		35.00
TOTAL		$1,145.00

Source: From an article in *Survey Magazine* in 1928 reprinted in *Another Part of the Twenties,* by Paul Carter. Copyright 1977 by Columbia University Press. Reprinted with permission of the publisher.

Between 1919 and 1929, the gross national product—the total value of all goods and services produced in the United States—swelled by 40 percent. Wages and salaries also grew (though not as drastically), while the cost of living remained relatively stable. People had more purchasing power, and they spent as Americans had never spent before (see Table 24.1). Technology's benefits reached more people than ever before. By 1929, two-thirds of all Americans lived in dwellings that had electricity, compared with one-sixth in 1912. In 1929 one-fourth of all families owned vacuum cleaners, and one-fifth had toasters. Many could afford these goods as well as radios, beauty products, and movie tickets, because more than one family member earned wages or because the breadwinner took a second job. Nevertheless, new products and services were available to more than just the rich, especially to people of other classes living in cities. For example, indoor plumbing and electricity became more common in private residences, and canned foods and ready-made clothes were more affordable.

The automobile stood as vanguard of the era's material wonders. During the 1920s, automobile registrations

Effects of the Automobile

soared from 8 million to 23 million, and by 1929 there was one car on the road for every five Americans. Mass production and competition made cars affordable even to some working-class families. A Ford Model T cost less than $300, and a Chevrolet sold for $700 by 1926—

when factory workers earned about $1,300 a year and clerical workers about $2,300. Used cars cost less. At those prices, people could consider the car a necessity rather than a luxury. "There is no such thing as a 'pleasure automobile,'" proclaimed one newspaper ad in 1925. "You might as well talk of 'pleasure fresh air,' or of 'pleasure beef steak.' . . . The automobile increases length of life, increases happiness, represents above all other achievements the progress and the civilization of our age."

Cars altered American life as much as railroads had seventy-five years earlier. Those who could afford autos acquired a new "riding habit" and abandoned crowded, inconvenient streetcars. Streets became cleaner as autos replaced the horses that had dumped tons of manure every day. Women who learned to drive achieved newfound independence, taking touring trips with female friends, conquering muddy roads, and making repairs when their vehicles broke down. Families created "homes on wheels," packing food and camping equipment to "get away from it all." By 1927 most autos were enclosed (they previously had open tops), offering young people new private space for courtship and sex. A vast choice of models (there were 108 automobile manufacturers in 1923) and colors allowed owners to express personal tastes. Most important, the car was the ultimate social equalizer. As one writer observed in 1924, "It is hard to convince Steve Popovich, or Antonio Branca, or plain John Smith that he is being ground into the dust by Capital when at will he may drive the same highways, view the same scenery, and get as much enjoyment from his trip as the modern Midas."

Americans' passion for driving necessitated extensive road construction and abundant fuel supplies. Since the late 1800s, farmers and bicyclists had been lobbying for improved roads. After the First World War, motorists joined the campaign, and in the 1920s government aid made "automobility" truly feasible. In 1921 Congress passed the Federal Highway Act, providing funds for state roads, and in 1923 the Bureau of Public Roads planned a national highway system. Roadbuilding in turn inspired such technological developments as mechanized road graders and concrete mixers. The oil-refining industry, which produced gasoline, became vast and powerful. In 1920 the United States produced about 65 percent of the world's oil. Automobiles also forced public officials to pay more attention to safety and traffic control. General Electric Company produced the first timed stop-and-go traffic light in 1924.

Advertising, an essential component of consumerism, acquired new prominence. By 1929 more money was spent

▲ During the 1920s, the desire to own an automobile spread to members of all classes, races, and ethnic groups. Low prices and available credit enabled this family from Beaumont, Texas, to own a "touring car." *(Tyrrell Historical Library)*

Advertising

on advertising automobiles and other goods and services than on all types of formal education. Blending psychological theory with practical cynicism, advertising theorists confidently asserted that any person's tastes could be manipulated, and marketers developed new techniques to achieve their ends. For example, cosmetics manufacturers like Max Factor, Helena Rubenstein, and African American entrepreneur Madame C. J. Walker used movie stars and beauty advice in magazines to induce women to buy their products. Other advertisers hired baseball star Babe Ruth and football's Red Grange to endorse food and sporting goods.

Radio became one of consumer society's most influential advertising and entertainment media. By 1929 over 10 million families owned radios,

Radio

and Americans spent $850 million a year on radio equipment. In the early 1920s, Congress decided that broadcasting should be a private enterprise, not a tax-supported public service as in Great Britain. As a result,

American radio programming consisted mainly of entertainment rather than educational content, because entertainment attracted larger audiences and therefore higher profits from advertisers. Station KDKA in Pittsburgh, owned by Westinghouse Electric Company, pioneered commercial radio in 1920, broadcasting results of the 1920 presidential election. Then, in 1922, an AT&T-run station in New York City broadcast recurring advertisements— "commercials"—for a Long Island real estate developer. Other stations began airing commercials; by the end of 1922 there were 508 such stations. In 1929 the National Broadcasting Company began to assemble a network of stations and soon was charging advertisers $10,000 to sponsor an hour-long show.

Like automobiles, radio transformed American society. In 1924 the presidential nominating conventions of both political parties were the first to be broadcast, enabling candidates and issues to reach more Americans simultaneously than ever before. And, as a result of its mass marketing and standardized programming, radio had the effect of blurring ethnic boundaries and creating—at least in one way—a homogeneous "American" culture, an effect

VICTROLA
REG. U.S. PAT. OFF.

All you need to enjoy the world's best
music—a Victrola and Victor Records

Victor Talking Machine Co., Camden, N. J.

"HIS MASTER'S VOICE"
REG. U.S. PAT. OFF.

▲ The spread of electric service to households gave families access to new forms of entertainment, such as recorded music. The Victrola Talking Machine Company, with its trademark of a little fox terrier looking into the horn of a gramophone, became one of the world's most recognized advertisers, even after it was purchased by RCA in 1929. *(Picture Research Consultants & Archives)*

that television and other mass media expanded throughout the twentieth century.

CITIES, MIGRANTS, AND SUBURBS

Consumerism signified not merely an economically mature nation but also an urbanized one. The 1920 federal census revealed that, for the first time, a majority of Americans lived in urban areas (defined as places with 2,500 or more people); the city had become the focus of national experience. In addition to growth in metropolises like Chicago and New York, manufacturing and services helped propel expansion in dozens of regional centers. Industries like steel, oil, and auto production energized Birmingham, Houston, and Detroit; services and retail trades boosted expansion in Seattle, Atlanta, and Minneapolis. Explosive

growth also occurred in warm-climate cities—notably Miami and San Diego—where promises of comfort and profit attracted thousands of real estate speculators.

As cities grew, the agrarian way of life waned. During the 1920s, 6 million Americans left their farms for the city. Young farm people who felt stifled when they compared their existence with the flashy openness of urban life moved to regional centers like Kansas City and Indianapolis or to the West. Between 1920 and 1930, California's population increased 67 percent, and California became a highly urbanized state while retaining its status as a leader in agricultural production. Meanwhile, streams of rural southerners moved to that region's industrial cities or rode railroads northward to Chicago and Cleveland.

African Americans, in what has come to be called the Great Migration, made up a sizable portion of people

African American Migration

on the move during the 1920s. Pushed from cotton farming by a boll weevil plague and lured by industrial jobs, 1.5 million blacks moved, doubling the African American populations of New York, Chicago, Detroit, and Houston. Black communities were also growing in Los Angeles, San Francisco, and San Diego. In cities, however, racial biases blocked opportunity. Forced by low wages and discrimination to seek the cheapest housing, black newcomers squeezed into low-rent ghettos like Chicago's South Side, New York's Harlem, and Los Angeles's Central Avenue. On the West Coast, however, black home ownership rates were higher than in the Northeast and Midwest. Many, for example, took advantage of Los Angeles's "bungalow boom," in which they could purchase a small, one-story house for as little as $900. But unlike white migrants, who were free to move out of the inner city when they could afford to, blacks everywhere found better neighborhoods closed to them. They could either crowd further into already densely populated black neighborhoods or spill into nearby white neighborhoods, a process that sparked resistance and violence. Fears of such "invasion" prompted neighborhood associations to adopt restrictive covenants, whereby white homeowners pledged not to sell or rent property to blacks.

In response to discrimination, threats, and violence, thousands of urban blacks joined movements that glorified racial independence. The most

Marcus Garvey

influential of these black nationalist groups was the Universal Negro Improvement Association (UNIA), headquartered in Harlem and led by Marcus Garvey, a Jamaican immigrant who believed blacks should separate from corrupt white society. Proclaiming, "I am the equal of any white man," Garvey spread his message with mass meetings and parades. He also promoted black-owned businesses that would manufacture and sell products to black consumers, and he incorporated the Negro Factories Corporation to finance such companies. Garvey's newspaper, *Negro World,* preached black independence, and he founded the Black Star steamship line to transport manufactured goods and raw materials among black businesses in North America, the Caribbean, and Africa.

The UNIA declined in the mid-1920s after mismanagement forced dissolution of the Negro Factories Corporation, and Garvey was deported for mail fraud involving the bankrupt Black Star line. He had been charged with trying to sell stock in the company by advertising a ship that it did not own. His prosecution, however, was politically motivated. Middle-class black leaders, such as W. E. B. Du Bois, and several clergymen opposed the UNIA, fearing that its extremism would undermine their efforts and influence. The U.S. Bureau of Investigation had been mon-itoring Garvey's radical activities since 1919, and in 1923 eight prominent blacks petitioned the attorney general to deport Garvey. Du Bois also had been incensed when word leaked out in 1922 that Garvey had met secretly with the leader of the Ku Klux Klan. Nevertheless, for several years the UNIA attracted a large following (contemporaries estimated 500,000; Garvey claimed 6 million), especially in the cities, and Garvey's speeches instilled in many African Americans a heightened sense of racial pride.

The newest immigrants to urban America came from Mexico and Puerto Rico, where, as in rural North America, declining fortunes pushed people off the land. During the 1910s, Anglo farmers' associations encouraged Mexican immigration as a source of cheap agricultural labor, and by the 1920s Mexican migrants constituted three-fourths of farm labor in the American West. Growers treated Mexican laborers as slaves, paying them extremely low wages. Resembling other new

Newcomers from Mexico and Puerto Rico

▲ Over half a million Mexicans immigrated to the United States during the 1920s. Many of them traveled in families and worked together in the fields and orchards of California and other western states. This family is shown pitting apricots in Los Angeles County in 1924.

(Seaver Center for Western History Research, Natural History Museum of Los Angeles County)

Links TO THE WORLD

Pan American Airways

ir transportation and airmail service between the United States and Latin America began in the 1920s, but establishing the connections was not easy at first, because of anti-American hostility in the region. In 1926 the U.S. government, fearful that German aircraft might drop bombs on the Panama Canal if the United States were ever again to go to war with Germany, signed a treaty with Panama giving American airplanes exclusive rights to operate in Panamanian airports. But America's hero of the air, Charles Lindbergh (see pages 698–699), and a formerly obscure pilot, Juan Trippe, played key roles in changing sentiments and expanding American air service to other parts of Latin America.

Trippe dreamed of creating an international airline. With help from his father-in-law, a banking partner of J. P. Morgan, he established Pan American Airways (informally known as Pan Am) in 1927, invested in modern airplane technology, and won a contract to carry mail between Florida and Cuba. In December of that year, still basking in fame from his transatlantic heroics, Lindbergh flew to Mexico and used his charm to persuade the Mexicans to accept airline links to the United States. The next year, Lindbergh joined Pan Am and began flying company planes to destinations in Central and South America. Welcomed wildly everywhere he landed, Lindbergh helped Trippe initiate mail and passenger service to Panama, Mexico, and other Latin American countries in 1929. Trippe advertised to wealthy Americans the opportunity to escape prohibition and enjoy Caribbean beaches by taking Pan Am flights to Havana and beyond, and he offered in-flight meals to travelers.

Needing landing facilities in order to operate, Pan Am built some of the airports that became essential connections between Latin America and the rest of the world. Trippe's employees created aerial maps that provided navigational aids for many years. Pan Am not only linked Latin America more closely with the United States but also helped unite parts of Latin America that had previously been divided by impenetrable mountain ranges. Yet Pan Am was also willing to resort to almost any tactic to build an airport and to start service. Thus it cooperated with unsavory dictators, engaged in bribery, and violated human rights, in one case helping Bolivian police to corral local Indians behind barbed wire for several days in order to clear land for a new airport.

Still, Pan Am both enabled Americans (mostly the wealthy) to travel abroad more conveniently and brought more foreigners to the United States. In 1942 one of its aircraft became the first to fly around the world. In the 1940s, the company began offering flights to Europe and Africa, and in 1950 changed its name to Pan American World Air-

ways to emphasize its global character. Until its demise in 1991, Pan Am provided a leading link between the United States and the rest of the world.

▲ Providing air transport connections to the Caribbean, Central America, and South America, Pan American Airways established the first major passenger and cargo links between the United States and other nations. By the early 1930s, flights were so numerous that the timetable announced in this illustration consisted of twelve pages. *(The Pan American Heritage Web Site)*

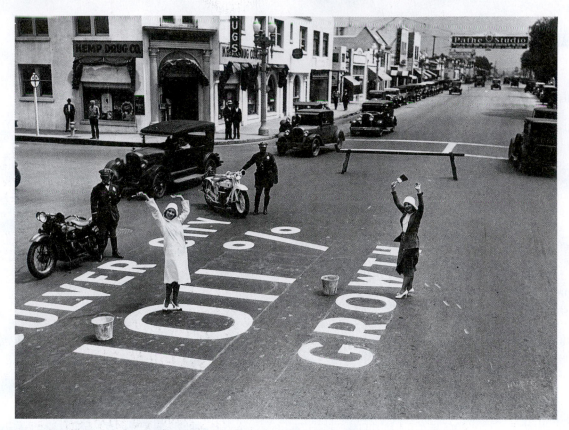

▲ Wide highways, cheap land, and affordable housing allowed automobile commuters to move to the urban periphery. In this photo, young women wearing 1920s flapper-style outfits celebrate the phenomenal growth of Culver City, outside Los Angeles. Notice the strong presence of the motor car. *(Security Pacific National Bank Collection, Los Angeles Public Library)*

immigrant groups, Mexican newcomers generally lacked resources and skills, and men outnumbered women. Although some achieved middle-class status as shopkeepers and professionals, most crowded into low-rent districts in growing cities like Denver, San Antonio, Los Angeles, and Tucson, where they suffered poor sanitation, poor police protection, and poor schools. Both rural and urban Mexicans moved back and forth between their homeland and the United States, seeking available jobs and creating a way of life that Mexicans called *sin fronteras*—without borders.

The 1920s also witnessed an influx of Puerto Ricans to the mainland. Puerto Rico had been a U.S. possession since 1898, and its natives were granted U.S. citizenship in 1916. As a shift in the island's economy from sugar to coffee production created a labor surplus, Puerto Ricans moved to New York and other cities, attracted by contracts from employers seeking cheap labor. In the cities, they created *barrios* (communities) and found jobs in fac-

tories, hotels, restaurants, and domestic service. Puerto Ricans maintained traditional customs and developed businesses—*bodegas* (grocery stores), cafés, boarding houses—and social organizations to help them adapt to American society. As with Mexicans, educated Puerto Rican elites—doctors, lawyers, business owners—became community leaders.

As urbanization peaked, suburban growth accelerated. Although towns had sprouted around major cities since

Growth of Suburbs

the nation's earliest years, prosperity and automobile transportation in the 1920s made suburbs more accessible to those wishing to flee congested urban neighborhoods. Between 1920 and 1930, suburbs of Chicago (such as Oak Park and Evanston), Cleveland (Shaker Heights), and Los Angeles (Burbank and Inglewood) grew five to ten times faster than did the nearby central cities. They sparked an outburst of home construction; Los Angeles builders alone erected 250,000 homes for auto-owning suburbanites. Although some suburbs, such as Highland Park (near Detroit) and East Chicago, were industrial satellites, most were middle- and upper-class bedroom communities.

Increasingly, suburbs resisted annexation to core cities. Suburbanites wanted to escape big-city crime, grime, and taxes, and they fought to preserve control over their own police, schools, and water and gas services. Particularly in the Northeast and Midwest, the suburbs' fierce independence choked off expansion by the central cities and prevented them from access to the resources and tax bases of wealthier suburban residents. Suburban expansion had other costs, too, as automobiles and the dispersal of population spread the environmental problems of city life—trash, pollution, noise—across the entire metropolitan area.

Together, cities and suburbs fostered the mass culture that gave the decade its character. Most of the consumers who jammed shops, movie houses, and sporting arenas, and who embraced fads like crossword puzzles and miniature golf, lived in or around cities. These were the places where people defied older morals by patronizing speakeasies (illegal saloons during prohibition), wearing outlandish clothes, and dancing to jazz. Yet the ideal of small-town society survived. While millions thronged cityward, Americans reminisced about the simplicity of a world gone by, however mythical that world might have been. This was the dilemma the modern nation faced: how does one anchor oneself in a world of rampant materialism and rapid social change?

NEW RHYTHMS OF EVERYDAY LIFE

Amid changes to modern consumer society, Americans developed new patterns of everyday life. One pattern involved uses of time. People increasingly split their day into distinct time compartments: work, family, and leisure. For many, time on the job shrank as mechanization and higher productivity enabled employers to shorten the workweek for many industrial laborers from six days to five and a half. White-collar employees often worked a forty-hour week, enjoyed a full weekend off, and received annual vacations as a standard job benefit.

Family time is hard to measure, but certain trends are clear. Family size decreased between 1920 and 1930 as birth control became more widely practiced. Among American women who married in the 1870s and 1880s, well over half who survived to age fifty had five or more children; of their counterparts who married in the 1920s, however, just 20 percent had five or more children. Lower birth rates and longer life expectancy meant that adults were devoting a smaller portion of their lives to raising children and having more time for nonfamily activities. Meanwhile, the divorce rate rose. In 1920 there was 1 divorce for every 7.5 marriages; by 1929 the national ratio was 1 in 6, and in many cities it was 2 in 7.

At home, housewives still worked long hours cleaning, cooking, and raising children, but machines now lightened some of their tasks and enabled them to use time differently than their forebears had. Especially in middle-class households, electric irons and washing machines simplified some chores. Gas- and oil-powered central heating and hot-water heaters eliminated the hauling of wood, coal, and water, the upkeep of a kitchen fire, and the removal of ashes.

Household Management

Even as technology and economic change made some tasks simpler, they also created new demands on a mother's time. Daughters of working-class families stayed in school longer, and alternative forms of employment caused a shortage of domestic servants, with the result that the pool of those who helped housewives with cleaning, cooking, and childcare shrank. In addition, the availability of washing machines, hot water, vacuum cleaners, and commercial soap put greater pressure on housewives to keep everything clean. Advertisers of these products tried to make women feel guilty for not devoting enough attention to cleaning the home. No longer a producer of food and clothing, as her ancestors had been, a housewife instead became the chief shopper, responsible for making sure her family spent money wisely. And the automobile made the wife a family's chief chauffeur. One survey found that urban housewives spent on average seven and one-half hours per week driving to shop and to transport children.

New emphasis on nutrition added a scientific dimension to housewives' responsibilities. With the discovery of vitamins between 1915 and 1930, nutritionists began advocating consumption of certain foods to prevent illness. Giant companies scrambled to advertise their products as filled with vitamins and minerals beneficial to growth and health. Producers of milk, canned fruits and vegetables, and other foods exploited the vitamin craze with claims that were hard to dispute because little was known about these invisible, tasteless ingredients. Welch's Grape Juice, for example, avoided mentioning the excess sugars in its product when it advertised that it was "Rich in Health Values" and "the laxative properties you cannot do without." Even chocolate candy manufacturers plugged their bars as vitamin packed.

Health and Life Expectancy

Your Children ___
___ is their food safe ?

YOU, as a conscientious mother, buy the best food for your children, prepare it with scrupulous care and cook it correctly. Yet, in spite of all, you may be giving your children food which is not wholesome—possibly dangerous!

For even the best food becomes unsafe to eat unless it is *kept at the proper degree of cold*, which medical authorities agree should be 50 degrees or less—always. Above that temperature, bacteria multiply, food is contaminated—becomes a menace to health.

There is only one way to be sure that your children's food is fresh and healthful—correct refrigeration. There is one refrigerator that assures you of scientifically perfect refrigeration at all times—the General Electric. Faithfully, quietly, day and night, it maintains a

temperature safely below the danger point—50 degrees.

The General Electric is ideal for the home. Its simple mechanism which you never need to oil, is mounted on top

of the cabinet and hermetically sealed in a steel casing. It has a simple and accessible temperature control, makes a generous supply of ice cubes, creates no radio interference. It has the only *all-steel*, warp-proof cabinet—easily-cleaned, sanitary.

Your dealer will be glad to explain the spaced payment plan, which makes it so easy to own this faithful watchman of the family health. Let him help you select the particular model that fits your needs. If there is not a dealer near you, write Electric Refrigeration Dept., General Electric Co., Hanna Building, Cleveland, Ohio, for booklet Q-9.

An unmatched record
There are now more than 300,000 homes enjoying the comfort and protection of *General Electric Refrigerators*—and not one of the owners has ever had to pay a single dollar for repairs or service.

The price of this new all-steel refrigerator—the small-family model—is now
$215 AT THE FACTORY

GENERAL ⊕ ELECTRIC
ALL-STEEL REFRIGERATOR

▲ While electric appliances gave mothers and housewives more convenient ways to carry out their roles, producers tried to sell their products by creating guilt among women who were concerned about their families' safety. Here, the General Electric Company warns a mother that she needs a GE refrigerator if she is to be "conscientious" and "scrupulous" about giving her children wholesome and healthy food. *(Picture Research Consultants & Archives)*

Better diets and improved hygiene made Americans generally healthier. Life expectancy at birth increased from fifty-four to sixty years between 1920 and 1930, and infant mortality decreased by two-thirds. Public sanitation and research in bacteriology combined to reduce risks of life-threatening diseases, such as tuberculosis and diphtheria. But medical progress did not benefit all groups equally; race and class mattered in health trends as they did in everything else. Rates of infant mortality were 50 to 100 percent higher among nonwhites than among whites, and tuberculosis in inner-city slums remained alarmingly

common. Moreover, fatalities from car accidents rose 150 percent, and deaths from heart disease and cancer—diseases of old age—increased 15 percent. Nevertheless, Americans in general were living longer: the total population over age sixty-five grew 35 percent between 1920 and 1930, while the rest of the population increased only 15 percent.

As the numbers of elderly increased, their worsening economic status stirred interest in pensions and other forms of old-age assistance. Industrialism put premiums on youth and agility, pushing older people into poverty from forced retirement and reduced income. Recognizing the needs of aging citizens, most European countries established state-supported pension systems in the early 1900s. Many Americans, however, believed that individuals should prepare for old age by saving in their youth; pensions, they felt, smacked of socialism. As late as 1923, the Pennsylvania Chamber of Commerce labeled old-age assistance "un-American and socialistic . . . an entering wedge of communistic propaganda."

Older Americans and Retirement

Yet conditions were alarming. Most inmates in state poorhouses were older people, and almost one-third of Americans age sixty-five and older depended financially on someone else. Few employers, including the federal government, provided for retired employees. Noting that the government fed retired horses until they died, one postal worker complained, "For the purpose of drawing a pension, it would have been better had I been a horse than a human being." Resistance to pension plans finally broke at the state level in the 1920s. Led by physician Isaac Max Rubinow and journalist Abraham Epstein, reformers persuaded voluntary associations, labor unions, and legislators to endorse old-age assistance through pensions, insurance, and retirement homes. By 1933 almost every state provided at least minimal support to needy elderly people, and a path had been opened for a national program of old-age insurance.

As Americans encountered new influences in their time away from work and family, altered habits and values were inevitable. Aided by new fabrics and chemical dyes, clothes became a means of self-expression as women and men wore more casual and gaily colored styles than their parents would have considered. The line between acceptable and inappropriate behavior blurred as smoking, drinking, and frankness about sex became fashionable. Birth control gained a large following in respectable circles. Newspapers, magazines, motion pictures, and popular songs (such as "Hot Lips" and

Social Values

"Burning Kisses") made certain that Americans did not suffer from "sex starvation." A typical movie ad promised "brilliant men, beautiful jazz babies, champagne baths, midnight revels, petting parties in the purple dawn, all ending in one terrific smashing climax that makes you gasp."

Other trends weakened inherited customs. Because state child-labor laws and compulsory-attendance rules kept children in school longer than ever before, peer groups rather than parents played an influential role in socializing youngsters. In earlier eras, different age groups had often shared the same activities: children interacted with adults in fields and kitchens, and young apprentices toiled in workshops beside journeymen and craftsmen. Now, graded school classes, sports, and clubs constantly brought together children of the same age, separating them from the company and influence of adults. Meanwhile, parents tended to rely less on traditions of childcare and more on experts who wrote manuals on how best to raise children.

Furthermore, the ways that young males and females interacted with each other underwent fundamental changes. Between 1890 and the mid-1920s, ritualized middle- and upper-class courtship, consisting of men's formally "calling on" women and of chaperoned social engagements, faded in favor of "dating," without adult supervision, in which a man "asked out" a woman and, usually, spent money on her. The more liberal practice arose from new freedoms and opportunities of urban life, and spread from the working class to the middle and upper classes. Employed unmarried young people, living away from family restraints, were eager to go on dates to new commercial amusements, such as movies and nightclubs, and when automobiles became the major mode of transportation, as they did in the 1920s, they made dating even more extensive. A woman's job, however, seldom provided sufficient income for her to afford these entertainments, but she could enjoy them if a man "treated" and escorted her. Companionship, romance, and, at times, sexual exploitation accompanied the practice, especially when a woman was expected to give sexual favors in return for being treated. A date thus ironically weakened a woman's prerogative at the same time that it expanded her opportunities. Under the courtship system, a woman had control over who could "call" on her and who could not. But once she entered a system in which a man's money enabled her to fulfill her desire for entertainment and independence, a young woman might find herself faced with difficult moral choices.

The practice of dating burgeoned because, after the First World War, women continued to stream into the labor force. By 1930, 10.8 million women held paying jobs, an increase of 2 million since war's end. Although the proportion of women working in agriculture shrank, proportions in categories of urban jobs grew or held steady (see Figure 24.1). The sex segregation that had long characterized workplaces persisted; most women took jobs that men seldom sought and vice versa. Thus, over 1 million women held jobs as teachers and nurses. In the clerical

Women in the Work Force

Figure 24.1   **Changing Dimensions of Paid Female Labor, 1910–1930**
These charts reveal the extraordinary growth in clerical and professional occupations among employed women and the accompanying decline in agricultural labor in the early twentieth century. Notice that manufacturing employment peaked in 1920 and that domestic service fluctuated as white immigrant women began to move out of these jobs and were replaced by women of color.

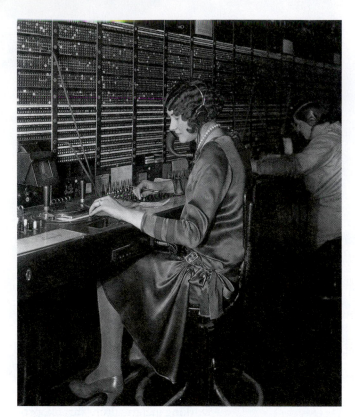

▲ The expansion of service-sector jobs and new technology opened new opportunities for women in the 1920s. This telephone operator handled scores of phone calls and monitored a huge switchboard at the same time. Her dress and jewelry contrasted with the simpler styles worn by factory women, who had to be more careful in working with dangerous machines. *(George Eastman House)*

proportion of the work force rose by 30 percent during the 1920s, and the number of employed married women swelled from 1.9 million to 3.1 million. These figures omit countless widowed, divorced, and abandoned women who held jobs and who, like married women, often had children to support.

The proportion of nonwhite women in paid labor was double that of white women. Often they entered the workforce because their husbands were unemployed or underemployed. The majority of employed African American women held domestic jobs doing cooking, cleaning, and laundry. The few who held factory jobs, such as in cigarette factories and meatpacking plants, performed the least desirable, lowest-paying tasks. Some opportunities opened for educated black women in social work, teaching, and nursing, but these women also faced discrimination and low incomes. More than white mothers, employed black mothers called on a family network of grandmothers and aunts to help with childcare.

Employment of Minority Women

Economic necessity also drew thousands of other minority women into the labor force. Mexican women increasingly entered into wage labor, although their tradition resisted female employment. Exact figures are difficult to uncover, but it is certain that many Mexican women in the Southwest worked as domestic servants, operatives in garment factories, and agricultural laborers. Next to black women, Japanese American women were the most likely to hold paying jobs. They, too, worked as field hands and domestics, jobs in which they encountered racial bias and low pay.

Employed or not, some women remade the image of femininity. In contrast to the heavy, floor-length dresses and long hair of previous generations, the short skirts and bobbed hair of the 1920s "flapper" symbolized new independence and sexual freedom. Although few women lived the flapper life, the look became fashionable among office workers and store clerks as well as college coeds. As Cecil B. DeMille's movies showed, chaste models of female behavior were eclipsed by movie temptresses, such as Clara Bow, known as the "It Girl," and Gloria Swanson, notorious for torrid love affairs on and off the screen. Many women were asserting a new social equality with men. One observer described "the new woman" as intriguingly independent.

Alternative Images of Femininity

category, some 2.2 million women were typists, bookkeepers, and filing clerks, a tenfold increase since 1920. Another 736,000 were store clerks, and growing numbers could be found in the personal service category as waitresses and hairdressers. Although almost 2 million women worked in manufacturing, their numbers grew very little over the decade. Wherever women were employed, their wages seldom exceeded half of those paid to men.

Although women worked outside the home for a variety of reasons, their families' economic needs were paramount. The consumerism of the 1920s tempted working-class and middle-class families to satisfy their wants and needs by living beyond their means or by expanding their income with women's wages. In previous eras, most people whose earnings supplemented those of the primary breadwinner had been young and single. Even though the vast majority of married women did not hold paying jobs (only 12 percent were employed in 1930), married women as a

She takes a man's point of view as her mother never could. . . . She will never make you a hatband or knit you a necktie, but she'll drive you from the station . . . in her own little sports car. She'll don knickers and go skiing with you, . . . she'll dive as well as you, perhaps better, she'll dance as long as you care to, and she'll take everything you say the way you mean it.

The era's openness regarding sexuality also enabled the underground homosexual culture to surface a little more than in previous eras. In nontraditional city neighborhoods, such as New York's Greenwich Village and Harlem, cheap rents and an apparent tolerance for alternate lifestyles attracted gay men and lesbians, who patronized dance halls, speakeasies, cafés, and other gathering places. Establishments that catered to a gay clientele remained targets for police raids, however, demonstrating that gays and lesbians could not expect acceptance from the rest of society.

Gay and Lesbian Culture

These trends represented a break with the more restrained culture of the nineteenth century. But social change rarely proceeds smoothly. As the decade wore on, various groups mobilized to defend older values.

LINES OF DEFENSE

Early in 1920, the leader of a newly formed organization, using a tactic adopted by modern businesses, hired two public relations experts to recruit members. The experts, Edward Clarke and Elizabeth Tyler, canvassed communities in the South, Southwest, and Midwest, where they found countless people eager to pay a $10 membership fee and $6 for a white uniform. Clarke and Tyler pocketed $2.50 from each membership they sold. Their success helped build the organization to 5 million members and four thousand chapters by 1923.

No ordinary civic club like the Lions or Kiwanis, this was the Ku Klux Klan, a revived version of the hooded order that had terrorized southern communities after the Civil War. More than its predecessor, the new KKK vowed to protect female purity as well as racial and ethnic purity. As one pamphlet distributed by Clarke and Tyler declared, "Every criminal, every gambler, every thug, every libertine, every girl ruiner, every home wrecker, every wife beater, every dope peddler, every moonshiner, every white slaver, every Rome-controlled newspaper, every black spider—is fighting the Klan. Think it over, which side are you on?"

Ku Klux Klan

Reconstituted in 1915 by William J. Simmons, an Atlanta, Georgia, evangelist and insurance salesman, the Klan adopted the hoods, intimidating tactics, and mystical terminology of its forerunner (its leader was the Imperial Wizard; its book of rituals, the Kloran). But Klan of the early 1920s had broader objectives than the old. It fanned outward from the Deep South and for a time wielded political power in places as diverse as Oregon, where Portland's mayor was a Klan member, and Indiana, where Klansmen held the governorship and several seats in the legislature. Its membership included many from the urban middle class who were fearful of losing social and economic gains achieved from postwar prosperity and nervous about a new youth culture that seemed to be eluding family control. It included a women's adjunct, Women of the Ku Klux Klan, consisting of an estimated half-million members.

One phrase summed up Klan goals: "Native, white, Protestant supremacy." Native meant no immigration, no "mongrelization" of American culture. According to Imperial Wizard Hiram Wesley Evans, white supremacy was a matter of survival. "The world," he warned, "has been so made so that each race must fight for its life, must conquer, accept slavery, or die. The Klansman believes the whites will not become slaves, and he does not intend to die before his time." Evans praised Protestantism for promoting "unhampered individual development," and he accused the Catholic Church of discouraging assimilation and enslaving people to priests and a foreign pope.

Using threatening assemblies, violence, and political and economic pressure, the Klan menaced many communities in the early 1920s. Klansmen meted out vigilante justice to suspected bootleggers, wife beaters, and adulterers; forced schools to stop teaching the theory of evolution; campaigned against Catholic and Jewish political candidates; pledged members not to buy from merchants who did not share their views; and fueled racial tensions against Mexicans in Texas border cities. Although men firmly controlled Klan activities, women not only joined male members in efforts to promote native white Protestantism but also, with male approval, worked for moral reform and enforcement of prohibition. Because the KKK vowed to protect the "virtue" of women, housewives and other women sometimes appealed to the Klan for help in punishing abusive, immoral, or irresponsible husbands and fathers when legal authorities would not intervene. Rather than an arrest and trial, the Klan's method of justice was a flogging.

By 1925, however, the Invisible Empire was weakening, as scandal undermined its moral base. In 1925 Indiana grand dragon David Stephenson was convicted of second-degree murder after he kidnapped and raped a woman who later died either from taking poison or from infection

▲ When Nicola Sacco and Bartolomeo Vanzetti were convicted of murder and robbery in 1921, people who believed that the men's anarchist political beliefs had caused the judge and jury to be overly biased tried to raise money for court appeals. Contributors received buttons to wear in support of the two Italian immigrants. Efforts by sympathizers, both in the U.S. and abroad, failed, however, and Sacco and Vanzetti were executed in August of 1927. *(© Bettmann/Corbis)*

caused by bites on her body. More generally, the Klan's negative, exclusive brand of patriotism and purity could not compete in a pluralistic society.

The KKK had no monopoly on bigotry in the 1920s; intolerance pervaded American society. Nativists had urged an end to free immigration since the 1880s. They charged that Catholic and Jewish immigrants clogged city slums, flouted community norms, and stubbornly embraced alien religious and political beliefs. Fear of immigrant radicals also fueled a dramatic trial in 1921, when two Italian anarchists, Nicola Sacco and Bartolomeo Vanzetti, were convicted of murdering a paymaster and guard in Braintree, Massachusetts. Evidence for their guilt was flimsy, but Judge Webster Thayer openly sided with the prosecution, privately calling the defendants "anarchistic bastards."

Guided by such sentiments, the movement to restrict immigration gathered support. Labor leaders warned that floods of alien workers would depress wages and raise unemployment. Business executives, who formerly had opposed restrictions

Immigration Quotas

because they desired cheap immigrant laborers, changed their minds, having realized that they could keep wages low by mechanizing. Even some humanitarian reformers supported restriction as a means of reducing poverty and easing assimilation. Drawing support from such groups, Congress reversed previous policy and, in the Emergency Quota Act of 1921, set yearly immigration allocations for each nationality. Reflecting preference for Anglo-Saxon Protestant immigrants and prejudice against Catholics and Jews from southern and eastern Europe, Congress stipulated that annual immigration of a given nationality could not exceed 3 percent of the number of immigrants from that nation residing in the United States in 1910. The act thereby discriminated against immigrants from southern and eastern Europe, whose numbers were small in 1910 relative to those from northern Europe.

The Quota Act was a temporary measure, and in 1924 Congress replaced it with the National Origins Act. This law limited annual immigration to 150,000 people and set quotas at 2 percent of each nationality residing in the United States in 1890, except for Asians, who were banned completely. (Chinese had been excluded by legislation in 1882.) The act further restricted southern and eastern Europeans, because even fewer of those groups lived in the United States in 1890 than in 1910. The law did, however, allow wives and children of U.S. citizens to enter as nonquota immigrants. In 1927 a revised National Origins Act apportioned new quotas to begin in 1929. It retained the annual limit of 150,000 but redefined quotas to be distributed among European countries in proportion to the "national-origins" (country of birth or descent) of American inhabitants in 1920. People coming from the Western Hemisphere did not fall under the quotas (except for those whom the Labor Department defined as potential paupers), and soon they became the largest immigrant groups (see Figure 24.2).

Whereas nativists tried to establish ethnic and racial purity, the pursuit of spiritual purity stirred religious fundamentalists. Millions of Americans sought certainty and salvation from what they perceived as the irreverence of a materialistic, hedonistic society by following evangelical denominations of Protestantism that interpreted the Bible literally. Resolutely believing that God's miracles created the world and its living creatures, they condemned the theory of evolution as heresy, and argued that wherever fundamentalists constituted a majority of a community, as they did in many places, they should be able to determine what would be taught in schools. Their enemies were "modernists," who used reasoning from social sciences, such

Fundamentalism

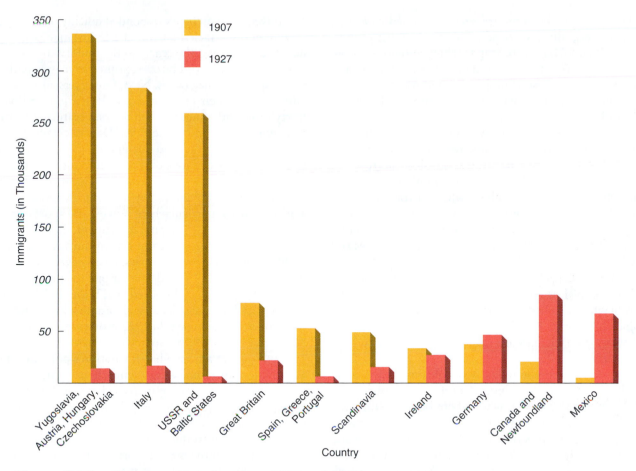

Figure 24.2   **Sources of Immigration, 1907 and 1927**
Immigration peaked in 1907 and 1908, when newcomers from southern and eastern Europe poured into the United States. After immigration restriction laws were passed in the 1920s, the greatest number of immigrants came from the Western Hemisphere (Canada and Mexico), which was exempted from the quotas, and the number coming from eastern and southern Europe shrank.

as psychology and anthropology, to interpret behavior. To modernists, God was important to the study of culture and history, but science was responsible for advancing knowledge.

In 1925 Christian fundamentalism clashed with modernism in a celebrated case in Dayton, Tennessee. Early that year, the state legislature had passed a law forbidding public school instructors from teaching the theory that humans had evolved from lower forms of life rather than having descended from Adam and Eve. Shortly thereafter, high-school teacher John Thomas Scopes volunteered to serve in a test case and was arrested for violating the law. Scopes's trial that summer became a headline event. William Jennings Bryan, former secretary of state and three-time presiden-

Scopes Trial

tial candidate, argued for the prosecution, and a team of civil liberties lawyers headed by Clarence Darrow represented Scopes. News correspondents crowded into town, and radio stations broadcast the trial.

Although Scopes was convicted—clearly he had broken the law—modernists claimed victory. The testimony, they believed, showed fundamentalism to be illogical. The trial's climax was Bryan's taking the witness stand as an expert on the Bible. Responding to Darrow's probing, Bryan asserted that Eve really had been created from Adam's rib, that the Tower of Babel was responsible for the diversity of languages, and that Jonah had actually been swallowed by a big fish. Spectators in Dayton cheered Bryan for his testimony, but the liberal press mocked him and his allies. Nevertheless, fundamentalists were not discouraged. For example, the Southern Baptist Convention, the fastest-growing Protestant sect, continued to attract members and, along with other fundamentalist groups, pressured school boards to stop teaching about evolution. Advocates for what they believed to be basic values of family and conduct, these churches created an independent subculture, with their own schools, camps, radio ministries, and missionary societies.

Religious fervor spread wherever people struggling with economic insecurity became nervous about modernism's attack on old-time religion.

|||||||||||||||||||||||||||||||
Religious Revivalism

Cities housed countless Pentecostal churches, which attracted blacks and whites who were swayed by their pageantry and depiction of a personal Savior. Using modern advertising techniques and elaborately staged broadcasts on radio, magnetic "revivalist" preachers, such as the flamboyant Aimee Semple McPherson of Los Angeles, former baseball player Billy Sunday who preached on nationwide travels, and Father Divine, an African American who amassed an interracial following from his base on Long Island, stirred revivalist fervor.

Revivalism represented only one means of sustaining old-fashioned values and finding comfort in a fast-moving consumer society. Millions who did not belong to the KKK firmly believed that nonwhites and immigrants were inferior people who imperiled national welfare. Clergy and teachers of all faiths condemned dancing, new dress styles, and sex in movies and in parked cars. Many urban dwellers supported prohibition, believing that eliminating the temptation of drink would help win the battle against poverty, vice, and corruption. Yet even while mourning a lost past, most Americans sincerely sought some kind of balance as they tried to adjust to the modern order in one way or another. Few refrained from listening to the radio and seeing movies like *Why Change Your Wife?*—activities that proved less corrupting than critics feared. More than ever, Americans sought fellowship in civic organizations, such as Rotary, Elks, and women's clubs. Perhaps most important, more people were finding release in recreation and new uses of leisure time.

THE AGE OF PLAY

Americans in the 1920s embraced commercial entertainment as never before. In 1919 they spent $2.5 billion on leisure activities; by 1929 such expenditures topped $4.3 billion, a figure not again equaled until after the Second World War. Spectator amusements—movies, music, and sports—accounted for 21 percent of the 1929 total; the rest involved participatory recreation, such as games, hobbies,

and travel. Entrepreneurs responded quickly to an appetite for fads and spectacles. Early in the 1920s, mahjong, a Chinese tile game, was the craze. In the mid-1920s, devotees popularized crossword puzzles, printed in mass-circulation newspapers and magazines. Next, funseekers adopted miniature golf as their new fad. By 1930 the nation boasted thirty thousand miniature golf courses featuring tiny castles, windmills, and waterfalls. Dance crazes like the Charleston were practiced throughout the country, aided by live and recorded music on radio and the growing popularity of jazz.

In addition to indulging actively, Americans were avid spectators, particularly of movies and sports. In total capital investment, motion pictures

|||||||||||||||||||||||||||||||
Movies and Sports

became one of the nation's leading industries. Nearly every community had at least one theater, whether a hundred-seat Bijou on Main Street or a big-city "picture palace" with ornate lobbies and thousands of cushioned seats. In 1922 movies attracted 40 million viewers weekly; by decade's end the number neared 100 million—at a time when the nation's population was 120 million and total weekly church attendance was 60 million. New technology increased movies' appeal. Between 1922 and 1927, the Technicolor Corporation developed a means of producing movies in color. This process, along with the introduction of sound in *The Jazz Singer* in 1927, made movies even more exciting and realistic.

Responding to tastes of mass audiences, the movie industry produced escapist entertainment. Although DeMille's romantic comedies like *Why Change Your Wife?* were entertaining, his most popular films—*The Ten Commandments* (1923) and *The King of Kings* (1927)—were biblical. Lurid dramas like *Souls for Sale* (1923) and *A Woman Who Sinned* (1924) also drew big audiences, as did slapstick comedies starring Harold Lloyd and Charlie Chaplin. Movie content was tame by current standards, however. In 1927 producers, bowing to pressure from legislators and religious leaders, instituted self-censorship, forbidding nudity, rough language, and plots that did not end with justice and morality triumphant. Movies also reproduced social prejudices. Although white actresses and actors played roles as glamour queens and action heroes, what few black actors there were had to take roles as maids and butlers.

Spectator sports also boomed. Each year millions packed stadiums and parks to cheer athletic events. In an age when technology and mass production had robbed experiences and objects of their uniqueness, sports provided some of the unpredictability and drama that people craved. Newspapers and radio magnified this tension, feed-

▲ Excluded from playing in white-dominated professional baseball, African Americans organized their own teams and leagues. The Indianapolis ABCs, named after the American Brewing Company, was one of the more successful teams in the Negro National League during the 1920s, and featured some of the best black baseball players of the era, including Oscar Charleston, Elwood "Bingo" DeMoss, and "Cannonball" Dick Redding. *(National Baseball Hall of Fame, Cooperstown, NY)*

ing sports news to an eager public and glorifying events with such dramatic narrative that sports promoters did not need to buy advertising.

Baseball's drawn-out suspense, variety of plays, and potential for keeping statistics attracted a huge following. After the "Black Sox scandal" of 1919, when eight members of the Chicago White Sox were banned from the game for allegedly throwing the World Series to the Cincinnati Reds (even though a jury acquitted them), baseball regained respectability by transforming itself. Discovering that home runs excited fans, the leagues redesigned the ball to make it livelier. Game attendance skyrocketed. A record 300,000 people attended the six-game 1921 World Series between the New York Giants and New York Yankees. Millions gathered regularly to watch local teams, and even more listened to professional games on the radio. Although African American ballplayers were prohibited from playing in the major leagues, they formed their own teams, and in 1920 the first successful Negro League was founded in Kansas City, Missouri, with Andrew "Rube"

Foster as its president. The league consisted of eight teams from places such as Chicago, Kansas City, and Indianapolis, and several rival leagues were formed in the following years.

Sports, movies, and the news created a galaxy of heroes. As technology and mass society made the individual less significant, people clung to heroic personalities as a means of identifying with the unique. Athletes like Bill Tilden in tennis, Gertrude Ederle in swimming (in 1926 she became the first woman to swim across the English Channel), and Bobby Jones in golf were household words. The power and action of boxing, football, and baseball produced the most popular sports heroes. Heavyweight champion Jack Dempsey, the "Manassa (Colorado) Mauler," attracted the first of several million-dollar gates in his fight with French boxer Georges Carpentier in 1921. Harold "Red" Grange, running back for the University of Illinois football team, thrilled fans and sportswriters with his speed and agility.

Sports Heroes

▲ Standing beside his plane, the "Spirit of St. Louis," shortly before takeoff on his solo trans-atlantic flight, young Charles Lindbergh exhibits the self-reliance and determination that made him one of the most revered heroes of the 1920s. Lindbergh's feat signified a blend of new technology with old-fashioned individual effort. *(Picture Research Consultants & Archives)*.

Baseball's foremost hero was George Herman "Babe" Ruth, who began his career as a pitcher but found he could use his prodigious strength to better advantage hitting home runs. Ruth hit twenty-nine homers in 1919, fifty-four in 1920 (the year the Boston Red Sox traded him to the New York Yankees), fifty-nine in 1921, and sixty in 1927—each year a record. His talent and boyish grin endeared him to millions. Known for overindulgence in food, drink, and sex, he charmed fans into forgiving his excesses by appearing at public events and visiting hospitalized children.

Beyond sports, Americans also fulfilled their yearning for romance and adventure through movie idols. The

Movie Stars and Public Heroes

films and personal lives of Douglas Fairbanks, Gloria Swanson, and Charlie Chaplin were discussed in parlors and pool halls across the country. One of the decade's most adored movie personalities was Rudolph Valentino, whose suave manner made women swoon and men imitate his pomaded hairdo and slick sideburns. Valentino's image exploited the era's sexual liberalism and flirtation with wickedness. In his most famous film, Valentino played a

passionate sheik who carried away beautiful women to his tent, combining the roles of abductor and seducer. When he died at thirty-one of complications from ulcers and appendicitis, the press turned his funeral into a public extravaganza. Mourners lined up for a mile to file past his coffin.

The era's most celebrated hero, however, was Charles A. Lindbergh, an indomitable aviator who in May 1927 flew a plane solo from New York to Paris. The flight seized the attention of practically every American, as newspaper and telegraph reports followed Lindbergh's progress. After the pilot landed successfully, President Coolidge dispatched a warship to bring "Lucky Lindy" back home. Celebrants sent Lindbergh 55,000 telegrams and dropped 1,800 tons of shredded paper on him during a triumphant homecoming parade. Among countless prizes, Lindbergh received the Distinguished Flying Cross and the Congressional Medal of Honor. Promoters offered him millions of dollars to tour the world and $700,000 for a movie contract. Through it all, Lindbergh, nicknamed "The Lone Eagle," remained dignified, even aloof. Although his flight and its aftermath symbolized the new combination of technology and mass culture of the 1920s, Lindbergh himself epitomized individual achievement, self-reliance, and courage—old-fashioned values that attracted public allegiance amid the media frenzy.

In their quest for fun and self-expression, some Americans became lawbreakers by refusing to give up drinking. The Eighteenth Amend-

Prohibition

ment (1919), which prohibited the manufacture, sale, and transportation of alcoholic beverages, and the federal law that implemented it (the Volstead Act of 1920) worked well at first. Per capita consumption of liquor dropped, as did arrests for drunkenness, and the price of illegal booze rose above what average workers could afford. But federal and state authorities for the most part refrained from enforcing the new law. In 1922 Congress gave the Prohibition Bureau only three thousand employees and less than $7 million for nationwide enforcement, and by 1927 most state budgets omitted funds to enforce prohibition.

After 1925 the so-called noble experiment of prohibition broke down as thousands of people made their own wine and gin illegally, and bootleg importers along the country's borders and shorelines easily evaded the few patrols that attempted to intercept them. Moreover, drinking, like gambling and prostitution, was a business with willing customers, and criminal organizations quickly capitalized on public demand. The most notorious of such mobs belonged to Al Capone, a burly tough who seized control of illegal liquor and vice in Chicago, maintaining power over politicians and the vice business through intimidation, bribery, and violence. But Capone contended, in a statement revealing of the era, "Prohibition is a business. All I do is supply a public demand." Americans wanted their liquor and beer, and until 1931, when a federal court convicted and imprisoned him for income-tax evasion (the only charge for which authorities could obtain hard evidence), Capone supplied them. Reflecting on the contradictions inherent in prohibition, columnist Walter Lippmann wrote in 1931, "The high level of lawlessness is maintained by the fact that Americans desire to do so many things which they also desire to prohibit."

CULTURAL CURRENTS

Along with the consumerism of the 1920s, hardship and crassness spawned unease, and intellectuals like Lippmann were quick to point to the era's hypocrisies. Serious writers and artists felt at odds with society, and their rejection of materialism and conformity was both biting and bitter.

Several writers from the so-called Lost Generation, including novelist Ernest Hemingway and poets Ezra

Literature of Alienation

Pound and T. S. Eliot, abandoned the United States for Europe. Others, like novelists William Faulkner and Sinclair Lewis, remained in America but, like the expatriates, expressed disillusionment with the materialism that they witnessed. F. Scott Fitzgerald's novels *This Side of Paradise* (1920) and *The Great Gatsby* (1925); Lewis's *Babbitt* (1922), *Arrowsmith* (1925), and *Elmer Gantry* (1927); and Eugene O'Neill's plays scorned Americans' preoccupation with money. Edith Wharton explored the clash of old and new moralities in novels such as *The Age of Innocence* (1920). Ellen Glasgow, one of the South's leading literary figures, lamented the trend toward impersonality in *Barren Ground* (1925). John Dos Passos's *Three Soldiers* (1921) and Hemingway's *A Farewell to Arms* (1929) interwove antiwar sentiment with critiques of the emptiness in modern relationships.

Discontent quite different from that of white authors inspired a new generation of African American artists.

Harlem Renaissance

Middle-class, educated, and proud of their African heritage, black writers rejected white culture and exalted the militantly assertive "New Negro." Most of them lived in New York's Harlem; in this "Negro Mecca," black intellectuals and artists, aided by a few white patrons, celebrated black culture during what became known as the Harlem Renaissance.

The popular 1921 musical comedy *Shuffle Along* is often credited with launching the Harlem Renaissance. The musical showcased talented African American artists, such as lyricist Noble Sissle, composer Eubie Blake, and singers Florence Mills, Josephine Baker, and Mabel Mercer. Harlem in the 1920s also fostered a number of gifted writers, among them poets Langston Hughes, Countee Cullen, and Claude McKay; novelists Zora Neale Hurston, Jessie Fauset, and Jean Toomer; and essayist Alain Locke. The movement also included such visual artists as painter Aaron Douglas and sculptress Augusta Savage. Lesser-known writers from other parts of the country also flourished during the decade. They included novelist Sutton E. Griggs of Houston and Memphis, and journalist and historian Drusilla Dunjee Houston from Oklahoma.

These artists and intellectuals grappled with notions of identity. Though cherishing their African heritage and the black folk culture of the slave South, they realized that blacks had to come to terms with themselves as free Americans. Thus Alain Locke urged that the New Negro should become "a collaborator and participant in American civilization." But Langston Hughes wrote, "We younger

This painting by African American artist Archibald Motley represented the "Ash-Can" style, which considered no subject too undignified to paint, as well as the sensual relationship between jazz music and dancing in African American culture.

(Collection of Archie Motley and Valerie Gerrard Browne. Photo courtesy of The Art Institute of Chicago)

Negro artists who create now intend to express our individual dark-skinned selves without fear or shame. If white people are pleased, we are glad. If they are not, it doesn't matter. We know we are beautiful."

The Jazz Age, as the 1920s is sometimes called, owes its name to the music of black culture. Evolving from African and black American folk music, early jazz communicated exuberance, humor, and autonomy that African Americans seldom experienced in their public and political lives. With its emotional rhythms and improvisation, jazz blurred the distinction between composer and performer and created intimacy between performer and audience. As African Americans moved northward and westward, jazz traveled with them; they created centers of their music in Kansas City, Chicago, and San Diego. Urban dance halls and nightclubs, some of which included interracial audiences of blacks, whites, Latinos, and Asians, featured gifted jazz performers like trumpeter Louis Armstrong, trombonist Kid Ory, and blues singer Bessie Smith, who enjoyed wide fame thanks to phonograph records and radio. Music recorded by black artists and aimed at black consumers (sometimes called "race records") gave African Americans a place in commercial culture. More important, jazz endowed America with its own distinctive art form.

In many ways the 1920s were the most creative years the nation had yet experienced. Painters such as Georgia O'Keeffe, Aaron Douglas, and John Marin forged a

Jazz

uniquely American style of visual art. Composer Henry Cowell pioneered electronic music, and Aaron Copland built orchestral works around native folk motifs. George Gershwin blended jazz rhythms, classical forms, and folk melodies in serious works (*Rhapsody in Blue,* 1924, and *Piano Concerto in F,* 1925), musical dramas (*Funny Face,* 1927), and hit tunes, such as "The Man I Love." In architecture, skyscrapers, including the art deco Chrysler Building of New York designed by William van Allen, drew worldwide attention to American forms. At the beginning of the decade, essayist Harold Stearns had complained that "the most . . . pathetic fact in the social life of America today is emotional and aesthetic starvation." By 1929 that contention had been disproved.

THE ELECTION OF 1928 AND THE END OF THE NEW ERA

Intellectuals' uneasiness about materialism seldom affected the confident rhetoric of politics. Herbert Hoover voiced that confidence when he accepted the Republican nomination for president in 1928. "We in America today," Hoover boasted, "are nearer to the final triumph over poverty than ever before in the history of any land. . . . We have not yet reached the goal, but, given a chance to go forward with the policies of the last eight years, we shall soon, with the help of God, be in sight of the day when poverty will be banished from this nation."

Hoover was an apt Republican candidate in 1928 (Coolidge chose not to seek reelection) because he fused the traditional value of individual

Herbert Hoover

hard work with modern emphasis on corporate action. A Quaker from Iowa, orphaned at age ten, Hoover worked his way through Stanford University and became a wealthy mining engineer. During and after the First World War, he distinguished himself as U.S. food administrator and head of food relief for Europe.

As secretary of commerce under Harding and Coolidge, Hoover promoted what has been called "associationalism." Recognizing the extent to which nationwide associations dominated commerce and industry, Hoover wanted to stimulate cooperation between business and government. He took every opportunity to make the Commerce Department a center for the promotion of business, encouraging the formation of trade associations, holding conferences, and issuing reports, all aimed at improving productivity and profits. His active leadership prompted one observer to quip that Hoover was "Secretary of Commerce and assistant secretary of everything else."

As their candidate, Democrats in 1928 chose New York's governor Alfred E. Smith, whose background contrasted sharply with Hoover's.

Al Smith

Hoover had rural, native-born, Protestant, and business roots, and had never run for public office. Smith was an urbane, gregarious politician of Irish stock with a career embedded in New York City's Tammany Hall political machine. His relish for the give-and-take of city streets is apparent in his response to a heckler during the campaign. When the heckler shouted, "Tell them all you know, Al. It won't take long!" Smith unflinchingly retorted, "I'll tell them all we both know, and it won't take any longer!"

Smith was the first Roman Catholic to run for president on a major party ticket. His religion enhanced his appeal among urban ethnics, who were voting in increasing numbers, but intense anti-Catholic sentiments lost him southern and rural votes. Smith had compiled a strong record on Progressive reform and civil rights during his governorship, but his campaign failed to build a coalition of farmers and city dwellers because he stressed issues unlikely to unite these groups, particularly his opposition to prohibition.

Smith waged a spirited campaign, directly confronting anti-Catholic critics, but Hoover, who emphasized national prosperity under Republican administrations, won the popular vote by 21 million to 15 million and the electoral vote by 444 to 87. Smith's candidacy nevertheless had beneficial effects on the Democratic Party. By luring millions of foreign-stock voters to the polls, he carried the nation's twelve largest cities, which formerly had given majorities to Republican candidates. For the next forty years, the Democratic Party solidified this urban base, which in conjunction with its traditional strength in the South made the party a formidable force in national elections.

At his inaugural Hoover proclaimed a New Day, "bright with hope." His cabinet, composed mostly of businessmen committed to the existing

Hoover's Administration

order, included six millionaires. To the lower ranks of government Hoover appointed young professionals who agreed with him that a scientific approach could solve national problems. If Hoover was optimistic, so were most Americans. The belief was widespread that success resulted from individual effort and that unemployment and poverty suggested personal weakness. Prevailing opinion also held that fluctuations of the business cycle were natural and therefore not to be tampered with by government.

This trust dissolved on October 24, 1929, later known as Black Thursday, when stock market prices suddenly plunged, wiping out $10 billion in

Stock Market Crash

value (worth around $100 billion today). Panic selling set in. Prices of many stocks hit record lows; some sellers could find no buyers. Stunned crowds gathered outside the frantic New York Stock Exchange. At noon, leading bankers met at the headquarters of J. P. Morgan and Company. To restore faith, they put up $20 million and ceremoniously began buying stocks. The mood brightened, and some stocks rallied. The bankers, it seemed, had saved the day.

But as news of Black Thursday spread, frightened investors decided to sell stocks rather than risk further losses. On Black Tuesday, October 29, prices plummeted again. Hoover, who had never approved of what he called "the fever of speculation," assured Americans that "the crisis will be over in sixty days." Three months later, he still believed that "the worst is over without a doubt." He shared the popular assumptions that the stock market's ills could be quarantined and that the economy was strong enough to endure until the market righted itself. Instead, the crash ultimately helped to unleash a devastating worldwide depression.

In hindsight, it is easy to see that the depression began long before the stock market crash. Prosperity in the 1920s was not as widespread as optimists believed. Agriculture

▲ As the stock market tumbled on October 24, 1929, a crowd of concerned investors gathered outside the New York Stock Exchange on Wall Street, unprepared for an unprecedented economic decline that would send the country into a tailspin for the next decade. *(Corbis-Bettmann)*

had been languishing for decades, and many areas, especially in the South, had been excluded from the new bounty of consumer society. Racial minorities suffered from economic as well as social discrimination in both urban and rural settings. Industries such as mining and textiles failed to sustain profits throughout most of the decade, and even the high-flying automotive and household goods industries had been stagnant since 1926. The fever of speculation that concerned Hoover had included rash investment in California and Florida real estate, as well as in the stock market, and had masked much of what was unhealthy in the national economy.

More generally, the economic weakness that underlay the Great Depression had several interrelated causes.

Declining Demand

One was declining demand. Since mid-1928, demand for new housing had faltered, leading to declining sales of building materials and unemployment among construction workers. Growth industries, such as automobiles and electric appliances, had been able to expand as long as consumers bought their products. Expansion, however, could not continue unabated. When demand leveled off, factory owners had to cut back production and their workforce. Retailers had amassed large inventories that were going unsold, and in turn they started ordering less from manufacturers. Farm prices continued to sag, leaving farmers with less income to purchase new machinery and goods. As wages and employment fell, families could not afford things they needed and wanted. Thus by 1929 a sizable population of under-consumers was causing serious repercussions.

Underconsumption also resulted from widening divisions in income distribution. As the rich grew richer, middle- and lower-income Americans made modest gains at best. Although average per capita disposable income (income after taxes) rose about 9 percent between 1920 and 1929, income of the wealthiest 1 percent rose 75 percent, accounting for most of the increase. Much of this increase was put into stock market investments, not consumer goods.

Furthermore, in their eagerness to boost profits, many businesses overloaded themselves with debt. To obtain

Corporate Debt and Stock Market Speculation

loans, they misrepresented their assets in ways that hid their inability to repay if forced to do so. Such practices, overlooked by lending agencies, put the nation's banking system on precarious footing. When one part of the edifice collapsed, the entire structure crumbled.

Risky stock market speculation also precipitated the depression. Individuals and corporations had bought millions of stock shares on margin, meaning that they invested by placing a down payment of only a fraction of a stock's actual price and then used stocks they had bought, but not fully paid for, as collateral for more stock purchases. When stock prices stopped rising, people tried to minimize losses by selling holdings they had bought on margin. But numerous investors selling at the same time caused prices to drop. As stock values collapsed, brokers demanded full payment for stocks bought on margin. Investors attempted to comply by withdrawing savings from banks or selling stocks at a loss for whatever they could get. Cash-short bankers pressured businesses to pay back their loans, tightening the vise further. The more obligations went unmet, the more the system tottered. Inevitably, banks and investment companies collapsed.

International economic conditions also contributed to the depression. During the First World War and postwar reconstruction, Americans loaned billions of dollars to European nations. By the late 1920s, however, American investors were keeping their money at home, investing instead in the stock market. Europeans, unable to borrow more funds and unable to sell goods in the American market because of high tariffs, began to buy less from the United States. Moreover, the Allied nations depended on German war reparations to pay their own war debts to the United States, and the German government depended on American bank loans to pay those reparations. When the crash choked off American loans, the Germans could not meet obligations to the Allies, and in turn the Allies were unable to pay war debts to the United States. The western economy ground to a halt.

International Economic Troubles

Failure of Federal Policies

Federal policies also underlay the crisis. The government refrained from regulating speculation and only occasionally scolded bankers and businesspeople. In keeping with government support of business expansion, the Federal Reserve Board pursued easy credit policies before the crash, charging low discount rates (interest rates on its loans to member banks) even though such loans were financing the speculative mania.

Partly because of optimism and partly because of the relatively unsophisticated state of economic analysis, neither experts nor people on the street realized what really had happened in 1929. Conventional wisdom, based on experiences from previous depressions, held that little could be done to correct economic problems; they simply had to run their course. So in 1929 people waited for the tailspin to ease, never realizing that the "new era" had come to an end and that the economy, politics, and society would have to be rebuilt.

Legacy FOR A PEOPLE AND A NATION

Intercollegiate Athletics

In 1924 scandals of brutality, academic fraud, and illegal payments to recruits prompted the Carnegie Foundation for the Advancement of Higher Education to undertake a five-year investigation of college sports. Its 1929 report condemned coaches and alumni supporters for violating the amateur code and recommended the abolition of varsity football. The report had minimal effect, however. As the career of Red Grange illustrated, football had become immensely popular during the 1920s, and scores of colleges and universities built stadiums and arenas to attract spectators, bolster alumni allegiance, enhance revenues, and promote school spirit.

For most of the twentieth century and into the twenty-first, big-time intercollegiate athletics, with professional coaches and highly recruited student athletes, ranked as one of the nation's major commercial entertainments. At the same time, American institutions have struggled to reconcile conflicts between the commercialism of athletic competition on one hand and the academic mission and the ideal of athletic amateurism on the other. No other country developed as extensive a link between high-caliber competitive athletics and higher education as the United States. Supposedly, cultivation of the mind is the objective of higher education. But the economic potential of college sports coupled with expanding athletic departments—including administrators, staffs, and tutors, as well as coaches and trainers—has created programs that compete with and sometimes overshadow the academic mission of the institutions that sponsor intercollegiate athletics.

Since the 1920s, recruiting scandals, academic fraud, and felonious behavior have sparked controversy in college sports. In 1952, after revelations of point-shaving (fixing the outcome) of basketball games involving several colleges in New York City and elsewhere, the American Council on Education undertook a study of college sports similar to that of the Carnegie Foundation a generation earlier. Its recommendations, including the elimination of football bowl games, went largely unheeded. In 1991 further abuses, especially in academics, prompted the Knight Foundation Commission on Intercollegiate Athletics to conduct a study that urged college presidents to take the lead in reforming intercollegiate athletics. Few significant changes resulted, even after a follow-up study in 2001. The most sweeping reforms followed court rulings in the 1990s, mandating under Title IX of the Educational Amendments Act of 1972 that women's sports be treated equally with men's sports. Enforcement, however, provoked a backlash that resulted in suggested changes to prevent men's teams from being cut in order to satisfy Title IX requirements. In recent years, the National College Athletic Association (NCAA) has initiated efforts to regulate academic standards in college athletics in addition to its voluminous rules on recruitment and amateurism, but its success depends on cooperation from member institutions. As long as millions of dollars are involved and sports remain a vital component of college as well as national culture, the system established in the 1920s shows the ability to withstand most pressures for change.

SUMMARY

Two critical events, the end of the First World War and the beginning of the Great Depression, marked the boundaries of the 1920s. In the war's aftermath, traditional customs and values weakened as women and men sought new forms of self-expression and gratification. A host of new effects from modern science and technology—automobiles, such conveniences as electric appliances, and broadened exposure from mass media, such as radio—touched the lives of rich and poor alike. Sports and movies made entertainment more accessible. Moreover, the decade's freewheeling consumerism enabled ordinary Americans to emulate wealthier people not only by purchasing more but also by trying to get rich through stock market speculation. The depression that set in following the stock market crash stifled these habits, at least for a while.

Beneath the "new era" lurked two important phenomena rooted in previous eras. One was the continued prejudice and ethnic tensions that had long tainted the American dream. As prohibitionists, Klansmen, and immigration restrictionists made their voices heard, they encouraged discrimination against racial minorities and slurs against supposedly inferior ethnic groups. Meanwhile, the distinguishing forces of twentieth-century life—technological change, bureaucratization, mass culture, and growth of the middle class—accelerated, making the decade truly "new." Both phenomena would recur as major themes in the nation's history for the rest of the twentieth century.

SUGGESTIONS FOR FURTHER READING

Lynn Dumenil, *The Modern Temper: American Culture and Society in the 1920s* (1995)

James R. Grossman, *Land of Hope: Chicago, Black Southerners, and the Great Migration* (1989)

Maury Klein, *Rainbow's End: The Crash of 1929* (2003)

Roland Marchand, *Advertising the American Dream: Making Way for Modernity, 1920–1940* (1985)

David Montgomery, *The Fall of the House of Labor: The Workplace, the State, and American Activism, 1865–1925* (1987)

Mae M. Ngai, *Impossible Subjects: Illegal Aliens and the Making of Modern America* (2004)

George Sanchez, *Becoming Mexican American: Ethnicity, Culture and Identity in Chicano Los Angeles, 1900–1945* (1993)

Susan Thistle, *From Marriage to the Market: The Transformation of Women's Lives and Work* (2006)

Michael Miller Topp, *The Sacco and Vanzetti Case: A Brief History With Documents* (2005)

For a more extensive list for further reading, go to college.hmco.com/pic/norton8e.

The Great Depression and the New Deal
1929-1941

*I*n 1931 the rain stopped in the Great Plains. Montana and North Dakota became as arid as the Sonora Desert. Temperatures reached 115 degrees in Iowa. The soil baked. Farmers watched rich black dirt turn to gray dust.

Then the winds began to blow. Farmers had stripped the Plains of native grasses in the 1920s, using tractors to put millions of acres of new land into production. Now, with nothing to hold the earth, it began to blow away. The dust storms began in 1934—and worsened in 1935. Dust obscured the noonday sun; some days it was pitch black at noon. Cattle, blinded by blowing grit, ran in circles until they died. A seven-year-old boy in Smith Center, Kansas, suffocated in a dust drift. Boiling clouds of dust filled the skies in parts of Kansas, Colorado, Oklahoma, Texas, and New Mexico—the Dust Bowl.

In late 1937, on a farm near Stigler, Oklahoma, Marvin Montgomery counted up his assets: $53 and a car—a 1929 Hudson he had just bought. "The drought and such as that, it just got so hard," he said later. "I decided it would help me to change countries." So, on December 29, 1937, Montgomery and his wife and four children—along with their furniture, bedding, pots, and pans—squeezed into the Hudson. "I had that old car loaded to the full capacity," Montgomery told a congressional committee conducting hearings in a migratory labor camp in 1940, "on top, the sides, and everywhere else." Traveling west on Route 66, the Montgomerys headed for California.

They were not alone. At least a third of farms in the Dust Bowl were abandoned in the 1930s, and many families made the westward trek, lured by circulars and newspaper advertisements promising work in the fields of California. Some 300,000 people migrated

◀ This 1939 photograph, titled "Mother and Children on the Road," was taken in Tule Lake, California, by Farm Security Administration photographer Dorothea Lange. The FSA used photos like this one to build public support for New Deal programs to assist migrant workers and the rural poor. *(Library of Congress)*

CHRONOLOGY

1929 ■ Stock market crash (October); Great Depression begins

1930 ■ Hawley-Smoot Tariff raises rates on imports

1931 ■ "Scottsboro Boys" arrested in Alabama

1932 ■ Banks fail throughout nation
- ■ Bonus Army marches on Washington
- ■ Hoover's Reconstruction Finance Corporation tries to stabilize banks, insurance companies, railroads
- ■ Roosevelt elected president

1933 ■ 13 million Americans unemployed
- ■ "First Hundred Days" of Roosevelt administration offer major legislation for economic recovery and poor relief
- ■ National bank holiday halts run on banks
- ■ Agricultural Adjustment Act (AAA) encourages decreased farm production
- ■ National Industrial Recovery Act (NIRA) attempts to spur industrial growth
- ■ Tennessee Valley Authority (TVA) established

1934 ■ Long starts Share Our Wealth Society
- ■ Townsend proposes old-age pension plan
- ■ Indian Reorganization (Wheeler-Howard) Act restores lands to tribal ownership

1935 ■ National Labor Relations (Wagner) Act guarantees workers' right to unionize
- ■ Social Security Act establishes insurance for the aged, the unemployed, and needy children
- ■ Works Progress Administration (WPA) creates jobs in public works projects
- ■ Revenue (Wealth Tax) Act raises taxes on business and the wealthy

1936 ■ 9 million Americans unemployed
- ■ United Auto Workers win sit-down strike against General Motors

1937 ■ Roosevelt's court-packing plan fails
- ■ Memorial Day massacre of striking steelworkers
- ■ "Roosevelt recession" begins

1938 ■ 10.4 million Americans unemployed
- ■ 80 million movie tickets sold each week

1939 ■ Marian Anderson performs at Lincoln Memorial
- ■ Social Security amendments add benefits for spouses and widows

to California in the 1930s. Most of these were not displaced and poverty-stricken farm families like the Montgomerys; many were white-collar workers seeking better opportunities in California's cities. It was the plight of families like the Montgomerys, however, captured in federal government–sponsored Farm Security Administration (FSA) photographs and immortalized in John Steinbeck's bestselling 1938 novel *The Grapes of Wrath*, that came to represent the human suffering of the Great Depression.

The Montgomerys' trip was not easy. The family ran out of money somewhere in Arizona and worked in the cotton fields there for five weeks before they moved on. Once in California, "I hoed beets some; hoed some cotton, and I picked some spuds," Montgomery reported, but wages were low, and migrant families found little welcome. As they took over the agricultural labor formerly done by Mexicans and Mexican Americans, they learned that, by doing fieldwork, they had forfeited their "whiteness" in the eyes of many rural Californians. "Negroes and 'Okies' upstairs," read a sign in a San Joaquin valley movie theater.

Most migrants to rural California lived in squalid makeshift camps, but the Montgomerys were lucky. They got space in housing provided for farm workers by the Farm Security Administration. The FSA camp at Shafter in Kern County had 240 tents and 40 small houses. For nine months the Montgomery family of six lived in a fourteen-by-sixteen-foot tent, which rented for 10 cents a day plus four hours of volunteer labor a month. Then they proudly moved into an FSA house, "with water, lights, and everything, yes sir; and a little garden spot furnished." Montgomery, homesick for the farm, told the congressional committee that he hoped to return to Oklahoma, but his seventeen-year-old son, Harvey, saw a different future. "I like California," he said. "I would rather stay out here." And soon there were plentiful employment opportunities in California, not only for Harvey Montgomery but for many other newcomers, in aircraft factories and shipyards mobilizing for the Second World War.

The Montgomerys' experience shows the human costs of the Great Depression, but statistics are necessary to give a sense of its magnitude. In the 1930s, as nations worldwide plunged into depression, the United States confronted a crisis of enormous proportions. Between 1929 and 1933, the gross national product was cut in half. Corporate profits fell from $10 billion to $1 billion; 100,000 businesses shut their doors altogether. As businesses failed or cut back, they laid off workers. Every day, thousands of men and women lost their jobs. Four million workers were unemployed in January 1930; by November the number had jumped to 6 million. When President Herbert Hoover left office in 1933, 13 million workers—about one-fourth of the labor force—were idle, and millions more had only part-time work. There was no national safety net: no welfare system, no unemployment compensation, no Social Security. And, as banks failed by the thousands, with no federally guaranteed deposit insurance, families' savings simply disappeared.

Herbert Hoover, who had been elected president in the prosperity and optimism of the late 1920s, looked first to private enterprise for solutions. By the end of his term, he had extended the federal government's role in managing an economic crisis further than any of his predecessors. Still, the economy had not improved, and, as the depression deepened, the mood of the country became increasingly desperate. The economic catastrophe exacerbated existing racial and class tensions, and law and order seemed to be breaking down. In Germany, the international economic crisis propelled Adolf Hitler to power. Although America's leaders did not really expect the United States to turn to fascism, they also knew that the German people had not anticipated Hitler's rise either. By late 1932 the depression seemed more than just "hard times." Many feared it was a crisis of capitalism, even of democracy itself.

In 1932 voters turned Hoover out of office, replacing him with a man who promised a New Deal and projected hope in a time of despair. Franklin Delano Roosevelt seemed willing to experiment, and although his scattershot approach did not end the economic depression (only the massive mobilization for World War II did that), New Deal programs did alleviate suffering. For the first time, the federal government assumed responsibility for the nation's economy and the welfare of its citizens. New federal agencies regulated a financial system badly in need of reform; Franklin Roosevelt's administration gave legitimacy to labor unions and collective bargaining. Social Security guaranteed assistance to many of America's elderly citizens and to others who could not support themselves. In the process, the federal government strengthened its power in relation to states and local authorities.

As it transformed the role and power of the federal government, however, the New Deal maintained America's existing economic and social systems. Although some Americans saw the depression crisis as an opportunity for major economic change—even revolution—Roosevelt's goal was to save capitalism. New Deal programs increased federal government regulation of the economy, but they did not fundamentally alter the existing capitalist system or the distribution of wealth. And, despite pressure (even within his own administration) to attack the social system that denied equality to African Americans, Roosevelt never directly challenged legal segregation in the South—in part because he relied on the votes of southern white Democrats to pass New Deal legislation.

Despite its limits, the New Deal preserved America's democratic experiment through a time of uncertainty and crisis. By the end of the decade, the widening force of world war shifted America's focus from domestic to foreign policy. But the changes set in motion by the New Deal continued to transform the United States for decades to come.

- How did economic hard times during the 1930s affect Americans, and what differences were there in the experiences of specific groups and regions?
- How and why did the power of the federal government expand during the Great Depression?
- What were the successes and the failures of the New Deal?

HOOVER AND HARD TIMES, 1929–1933

By the early 1930s, as the depression continued to deepen, tens of millions of Americans were desperately poor. In the cities, hungry men and women lined up at soup kitchens. People survived on potatoes, crackers, or dandelion greens; some scratched through garbage cans for bits of food. In West Virginia and Kentucky, hunger was so widespread—and resources so limited—that the American Friends Service Committee distributed food only to those who were at least 10 percent below the normal weight for their height. In November 1932, *The Nation* told its readers that one-sixth of the American population risked starvation over the coming winter. Social workers in New York reported there was "no food at all" in the homes of many of the city's black children. In Albany, New York, a ten-year-old girl died of starvation in her elementary school classroom.

Families, unable to pay rent, were evicted. The new homeless poured into shantytowns, called "Hoovervilles" in ironic tribute to the formerly popular president. Over a million men took to the road or the rails in desperate search of any sort of work. Teenage boys and girls (the latter called "sisters of the road") also left destitute families to strike out on their own. With uncertain futures, many young couples delayed marriage; the average age at marriage rose by more than two years during the 1930s. Married people put off having children, and in 1933 the birth rate sank below replacement rates. (Contraceptive sales, with condoms costing at least $1 per dozen, did not fall during the depression.) More than 25 percent of women who were between the ages of twenty and thirty during the Great Depression never had children.

Farmers were hit especially hard by the economic crisis. The agricultural sector, which employed almost one-quarter of American workers, had never shared in the good times of the 1920s. But as urbanites cut back on spending and foreign competitors dumped agricultural surpluses into the global market, farm prices hit rock bottom. Farmers tried to compensate for lower prices by producing more, thus adding to the surplus and depressing prices even further. By 1932, a bushel of wheat that cost North Dakota farmers 77 cents to produce brought only 33 cents. Throughout the nation, cash-strapped farmers could not pay their property taxes or mortgages. Banks, facing their own ruin, foreclosed. In Mississippi, it was reported in 1932, on a single day in April approximately one-fourth of all the farmland in the state was being auctioned off to meet debts. By the middle of the decade, the ecological crisis of the Dust Bowl would drive thousands of farmers from their land.

Unlike farmers, America's industrial workers had seen a slow but steady rise in their standard of living during the 1920s. In 1929 almost every urban American who wanted a job had one, and workers' spending on consumer goods had bolstered the nation's economic growth. But as Americans had less money to spend, sales of manufactured goods plummeted and factories closed—more than seventy thousand had gone out of business by 1933. As car sales

Farmers and Industrial Workers

dropped from 4.5 million in 1929 to 1 million in 1933, Ford laid off more than two-thirds of its Detroit workers. The remaining workers at U.S. Steel, America's first billion-dollar corporation, were put on "short hours"; the huge steel company had no full-time workers in 1933. Almost one-quarter of industrial workers were unemployed, and those who managed to hang onto a job saw the average wage fall by almost one-third.

For workers on the lowest rungs of the employment ladder, the depression was a crushing blow. In the South, where opportunities were already most limited for African Americans, jobs that many white men had considered below their dignity before the depression—street cleaner, bellhop, garbage collector—seemed suddenly desirable. In 1930 a short-lived fascist-style organization, the Black Shirts, recruited 40,000 members with the slogan "No Jobs for Niggers Until Every White Man Has a Job!" Northern blacks did not fare much better. As industry cut production, African Americans were the first fired. An Urban League survey of 106 cities found black unemployment rates averaged 30 to 60 percent higher than rates for whites. By 1932, African American unemployment reached almost 50 percent.

Marginal Workers

Mexican Americans and Mexican nationals trying to make a living in the American Southwest also felt the twin impacts of economic depression and racism. Their wages on California farms fell from a miserable 35 cents an hour in 1929 to a cruel 14 cents an hour by 1932. Throughout the Southwest, Anglo-Americans claimed that foreign workers were stealing their jobs. Campaigns against "foreigners" hurt not only Mexican immigrants but also American citizens of Hispanic background whose families had lived in the Southwest for centuries, long before the land belonged to the United States. In 1931 the Labor Department announced plans to deport illegal immigrants to free jobs for American citizens. This policy fell hardest on people of Mexican origin. Even those who had immigrated legally often lacked full documentation. Officials often ignored the fact that children born in the United States were U.S. citizens. The U.S. government officially deported 82,000 Mexicans between 1929 and 1935, but a much larger number—almost half a million people—repatriated to Mexico during the 1930s. Some left voluntarily, but many were coerced or tricked into believing they had no choice.

Even before the economic crisis, women of all classes and races were barred from many jobs and were paid significantly less than men. As the economy worsened, discrimination increased. Most Americans already believed

◀ As hard times grew worse, families were evicted from their houses or apartments. In desperation, many moved into shantytowns—called Hoovervilles, after the now-unpopular president—on the outskirts of the nation's cities. These shacks, photographed in October 1931, are in Seattle's Hooverville. Despite the squalor of the surroundings, someone has done laundry and hung it to dry in the sun.

(University of Washington Libraries, Seattle, Washington).

that men should be breadwinners and women homemakers. With widespread male unemployment, it was easy to believe that women who worked took jobs from men. In fact, men laid off from U.S. Steel would not likely have been hired as elementary school teachers, secretaries, "salesgirls," or maids. Nonetheless, when a 1936 Gallup poll asked whether wives should work if their husbands had jobs, 82 percent of the respondents (including 75 percent of the women) answered no. Such beliefs translated into policy. Of fifteen hundred urban school systems surveyed in 1930 and 1931, 77 percent refused to hire married women as teachers, and 63 percent fired female teachers who married while employed.

The depression had a mixed impact on women workers. At first, women lost jobs more quickly than men. Women in low-wage manufacturing jobs were laid off before male employees, who were presumed to be supporting families. Hard times hit domestic workers especially hard, as middle-class families economized by dispensing with household help. Almost one-quarter of women in domestic service—a high percentage of them African American—were unemployed by January 1931. And, as jobs disappeared, women of color lost even these poorly paid positions to white women who were newly willing to do domestic labor. Despite discrimination and a poor economy, however, the number of women working outside the home rose during the 1930s. "Women's

jobs," such as teaching, clerical work, and switchboard operating, were not hit as hard as "men's jobs" in heavy industry, and women—including married women who previously did not work for wages—increasingly sought employment to keep their families afloat during hard times. Still, by 1940 only 15.2 percent of married women worked outside the home.

Although unemployment rates climbed to 25 percent, most Americans did not lose their homes or their jobs during the depression. Professional and white-collar workers did not fare as badly as industrial workers and farmers. Many middle-class families, however, while never hungry or homeless, "made do" with less. "Use it up, wear it out, make it do, or do without," the saying went, and middle-class women cut back on household expenses by canning food or making their own clothes. Newspapers offered imaginative suggestions for cooking cheap cuts of meat ("Liverburgers") or for using "extenders," cheap ingredients to make food go further ("Cracker-Stuffed Cabbage"). Although most families' incomes fell, the impact was cushioned by the falling cost of consumer goods, especially food. In early 1933, for example, a café in Omaha offered a ten-course meal, complete with a rose for ladies and a cigar for gentlemen, for 60 cents.

As housewives scrambled to make do, men who could no longer provide well for their families often blamed themselves for their "failures." But even for the relatively affluent, the psychological impact of the depression was

Middle-Class Workers and Families

▲ As the economic depression deepened, Americans had less money to spend, even on necessities, and manufacturers of consumer goods struggled to sell their products and stay in business. In this 1932 *Ladies' Home Journal* advertisement, Armour Foods tried to convince housewives who were making do with less that it was economical— "often as low as 10¢ a serving"—to purchase a whole ham instead of cheaper cuts of meat. *(Picture Research Consultants & Archives)*

inescapable. The human toll of the depression was visible everywhere, and no one took economic security for granted any more. Suffering was never equal, but all Americans had to contend with years of uncertainty and with fears about the future of their family and their nation.

Although Herbert Hoover, "the Great Engineer," had a reputation as a problem solver, the economic crisis was not easily solved, and no one, including Hoover, really knew what to do. Experts and leaders disagreed about the causes of the depression, and they disagreed about the proper course of action as well. Many prominent business leaders believed that financial panics and depressions, no matter how painful, were part of a natural and ultimately beneficial "business cycle." Economic depressions, according to this theory, brought down inflated

Hoover's Limited Solutions

prices and cleared the way for real economic growth. As one banker told a Senate committee investigating the rising unemployment rates, "You are always going to have, once in so many years, difficulties in business, times that are prosperous and times that are not prosperous. There is no commission or any brain in the world that can prevent it."

Herbert Hoover disagreed. "The economic fatalist," he said, "believes that these crises are inevitable. . . . I would remind these pessimists that exactly the same thing was once said of typhoid, cholera, and smallpox." Hoover had great faith in "associationalism": business and professional organizations, coordinated by the federal government, working together to solve the nation's problems. The federal government's role was limited to gathering information and serving as a clearing-house for ideas and plans that state and local governments, along with private industry, could then choose—voluntarily—to implement.

While many Americans thought that Hoover was doing nothing to fight the economic downturn, in truth he stretched his beliefs about the proper role of government to their limit. He tried voluntarism, exhortation, and limited government intervention. First, he sought voluntary pledges from hundreds of business groups to keep wages stable and renew economic investment. But when individual businessmen looked at their own bottom lines, few could live up to those promises.

As unemployment climbed, Hoover continued to encourage voluntary responses to mounting need, creating the President's Organization on Unemployment Relief (POUR) to generate private contributions to aid the destitute. Although 1932 saw record charitable contributions, they were nowhere near adequate. By mid-1932 one-quarter of New York's private charities, funds exhausted, had closed their doors. Atlanta's Central Relief Committee could provide only $1.30 per family per week to those seeking help. State and city officials found their treasuries drying up, too. Hoover, however, held firm. "It is not the function of the government to relieve individuals of their responsibilities to their neighbors," he insisted.

Hoover feared that government "relief" would destroy the spirit of self-reliance among the poor. Thus he authorized federal funds to feed the drought-stricken livestock of Arkansas farmers but rejected a smaller grant to provide food for impoverished farm families. Many Americans were becoming angry at Hoover's seeming insensitivity. When Hoover, trying to restore confidence to the increasingly anxious nation, said, "What this country needs is a good big laugh. . . . If someone could get off a good joke every ten days, I think our troubles would be over," the resulting jokes were not exactly what he had in mind.

"Business is improving," one man tells another. "Is Hoover dead?" asks his companion. In the two short years since his election, Hoover had become the most hated man in America.

Hoover eventually endorsed limited federal action to combat the economic crisis, but it was much too little. Federal public works projects, such as the Grand Coulee Dam in Washington, created some jobs. The Federal Farm Board, established under the Agricultural Marketing Act of 1929, supported crop prices by lending money to cooperatives to buy crops and keep them off the market. But the board soon ran short of money, and unsold surpluses jammed warehouses.

Hoover also signed into law the Hawley-Smoot Tariff (1930), which was meant to support American farmers and manufacturers by raising import duties on foreign goods to a staggering 40 percent. Instead it hampered international trade as other nations created their own protective tariffs. And, as other nations sold fewer goods to the United States, they had less money to repay their U.S. debts or buy American products. Fearing the collapse of the international monetary system, Hoover in 1931 announced a moratorium on the payment of First World War debts and reparations.

In January 1932, the administration took its most forceful action. The Reconstruction Finance Corporation (RFC) provided federal loans to banks, insurance companies, and railroads, an action Hoover hoped would shore up those industries and halt the disinvestment in the American economy. New York mayor Fiorello La Guardia called this provision of taxpayers' dollars to private industry "a millionaire's dole." But with the RFC Hoover had compromised his ideological principles. This was direct government intervention, not "voluntarism." If he would support direct assistance to private industries, why not direct relief to the millions of unemployed?

More and more Americans had begun to ask that question. Although most met the crisis with bewilderment or quiet despair, social unrest and violence began to surface as the depression deepened. In scattered incidents, farmers and unemployed workers took direct action against what they saw as the causes of their plight. Others lashed out in anger, scapegoating those even weaker than themselves. Increasing violence raised the specter of popular revolt, and Chicago mayor Anton Cermak told Congress that if the federal government did not send his citizens aid, it would have to send troops instead.

Throughout the nation, tens of thousands of farmers took the law into their own hands. Angry crowds forced

Protest and Social Unrest

auctioneers to accept just a few dollars for foreclosed property, and then returned it to the original owners. Farmers also tried to stop produce from reaching the market. In August 1932, a new group, the Farmers' Holiday Association, encouraged farmers to take a "holiday"—to hold back agricultural products as a way to limit supply and drive prices up. In the Midwest, farmers barricaded roads with spiked logs and telegraph poles to stop other farmers' trucks, and then dumped the contents in roadside ditches. In Iowa, strikers shot four other farmers who tried to run a roadblock.

In the cities, too, protest grew. The most militant actions came from Unemployed Councils, local groups similar to unions for unemployed workers that were created and led by Communist Party members. Communist leaders believed that the depression demonstrated capitalism's failure and offered an opportunity for revolution. Few of the quarter-million Americans who joined the local Unemployed Councils sought revolution, but they did demand action. "Fight, Don't Starve," read banners in a Chicago demonstration. Demonstrations often turned ugly. When three thousand members of Detroit Unemployment Councils marched on Ford's River Rouge plant in 1932, Ford security guards opened fire on the crowd, killing four men and wounding fifty. Battles between protesters and police broke out in cities from the East Coast to the West Coast but rarely were covered as national news.

As social unrest spread, so, too, did racial violence. Vigilante committees offered bounties in an attempt to force African American workers off the Illinois Central Railroad's payroll: $25 for maiming and $100 for killing black workers. Ten men were murdered and at least seven more wounded. With the worsening economy, the Ku Klux Klan reemerged, and at least 140 attempted lynchings were recorded between January 1930 and February 1933. In most cases local authorities were able to prevent the lynchings, but white mobs tortured, hanged, and mutilated thirty-eight black men during the early years of the Great Depression. Racial violence was not restricted to the South; lynchings took place in Pennsylvania, Minnesota, Colorado, and Ohio as well.

The worst public confrontation shook the nation in the summer of 1932. More than fifteen thousand unemployed World War I veterans and their families converged on the nation's capital as Congress debated a bill authorizing immediate payment of cash "bonuses" that veterans had been scheduled to receive in 1945. Calling themselves the Bonus Expeditionary Force, or Bonus Army, they set up a sprawling "Hooverville" shantytown in Anacostia Flats, just across

Bonus Army

In the summer of 1932, unemployed veterans of the First World War gathered in Washington, D.C. to demand payment of their soldiers' bonuses. After Congress rejected the appeal of the "Bonus Army," some refused to leave and President Hoover sent U.S. Army troops to force them out. Here, police battle Bonus Marchers in July 1932.

(National Archives)

the river from the Capitol. Concerned about the impact on the federal budget, President Hoover opposed the bonus bill, and after much debate the Senate voted it down. "We were heroes in 1917, but we're bums today," one veteran shouted after the Senate vote.

Most of the Bonus Marchers left Washington after this defeat, but several thousand stayed on. Some were simply destitute, with nowhere to go; others stayed to press their case. The president called them "insurrectionists" and set a deadline for their departure. On July 28, Hoover sent in the U.S. Army, led by General Douglas MacArthur. Four infantry companies, four troops of cavalry, a machine gun squadron, and six tanks converged on the veterans and their families. What followed shocked the nation. Men and women were chased down by horsemen; children were tear-gassed; shacks were set afire. The next day, newspapers carried photographs of U.S. troops attacking their own citizens. Hoover was unrepentant, insisting in a campaign speech, "Thank God we still have a government that knows how to deal with a mob."

While desperation-driven social unrest raised fears of revolution, some saw an even greater danger in the growing disillusionment with democracy itself. As the depression worsened, the appeal of a strong leader—someone who would take decisive action, unencumbered by constitutionally mandated checks and balances—grew. In early 1933, media magnate William Randolph Hearst released the film *Gabriel over the White House*, in which a political hack of a president is possessed by the archangel Gabriel and, divinely inspired, assumes dictatorial powers to end the misery of the Great Depression. More significantly, in February 1933 the U.S. Senate passed a resolution calling for newly elected president Franklin D. Roosevelt to assume "unlimited power." The rise to power of Hitler and his National Socialist Party in depression-ravaged Germany was an obvious parallel, adding to the sense of crisis that would come to a head in early 1933.

FRANKLIN D. ROOSEVELT AND THE LAUNCHING OF THE NEW DEAL

In the presidential campaign of 1932, voters were presented with a clear choice. In the face of the Great Depression, incumbent Herbert Hoover held to a platform of limited federal intervention. Democratic challenger Franklin Delano Roosevelt insisted that the federal government had to play a much greater role. He supported direct relief payments for the unemployed, declaring that such governmental aid was not charity, but instead "a matter of social duty." He pledged "a new deal for the American people." During the campaign, he was never very explicit about the outlines of his New Deal. His most concrete proposals, in fact, were sometimes contradictory (in a nation without national news media, this was less a problem than it would be today). But all understood that he had committed to use the power of the federal government to combat the economic crisis that was paralyzing the nation. Voters chose Roosevelt over Hoover overwhelmingly: Roosevelt's 22.8 million popular votes far outdistanced Hoover's 15.8 million (see Map 25.1). Third-party Socialist candidate Norman Thomas drew nearly 1 million votes.

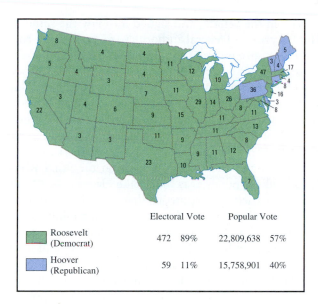

Map 25.1   Presidential Election, 1932
One factor above all decided the 1932 presidential election: the Great Depression. Roosevelt won 42 states and Hoover 6.

	Electoral Vote		Popular Vote	
▮ Roosevelt (Democrat)	472	89%	22,809,638	57%
▮ Hoover (Republican)	59	11%	15,758,901	40%

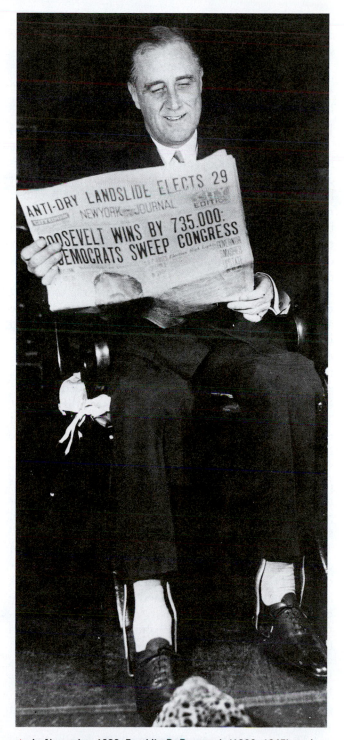

▲ In November 1930, Franklin D. Roosevelt (1882–1945) read the good news. Reelected governor of New York by 735,000 votes, he immediately became a leading contender for the Democratic presidential nomination. Notice Roosevelt's leg braces, rarely shown because of an unwritten agreement by photographers to shoot him from the waist up. *(© Bettmann/Corbis)*

Franklin Roosevelt, the twentieth-century president most beloved by America's "common people," had been born into a world of old money and upper-class privilege. The talented son of a politically prominent family, he seemed destined for political success. After graduating from Harvard College and Columbia Law School, he had married Eleanor Roosevelt, Theodore Roosevelt's niece and his own fifth cousin, once removed. He served in the New York State legislature, was appointed assistant secretary of the navy by Woodrow Wilson, and, at the age of thirty-eight, ran for vice president in 1920 on the Democratic Party's losing ticket.

Then, in 1921, Roosevelt was stricken with polio. For two years he was bedridden, fighting one of the most feared diseases of the early twentieth century. He lost the use of his legs but gained, according to his wife Eleanor, a new strength of character that would serve him well as he reached out to depression-scarred America. As Roosevelt explained it, "If you had spent two years in bed trying to wiggle your big toe, after that anything would seem easy." By 1928 Roosevelt was sufficiently recovered to run for—and win—the governorship of New York, and then to accept the Democratic Party's presidential nomination in 1932.

Elected in November 1932, Roosevelt would not take office until March 4, 1933. (The Twentieth Amendment to the Constitution—the so-called Lame Duck Amendment, ratified in 1933—shifted all future inaugurations to January 20.) In this long interregnum, the American banking system reached the verge of collapse.

The origins of the banking crisis lay in the flush years of World War I and the 1920s, when American banks

Banking Crisis

made countless risky loans. After real-estate and stock market bubbles burst in 1929 and agricultural prices collapsed, many of these loans went bad. As a result, many banks lacked sufficient funds to cover their customers' deposits. Fearful of losing their savings in a bank collapse, depositors pulled money out of banks and put it into gold or under mattresses. "Bank runs," in which crowds of angry, frightened customers lined up to demand their money, became a common sight in economically ravaged towns throughout the nation.

By the 1932 election, the bank crisis was escalating rapidly. Hoover, the lame-duck president, refused to take action without Roosevelt's support, while Roosevelt called Hoover's request for support "cheeky" and refused to endorse actions he could not control. Meanwhile, the situation worsened. By Roosevelt's inauguration on March 4, every state in the Union had either suspended banking operations or restricted depositors' access to their money. The new president understood that this was more than a test of his administration. The total collapse of the U.S. banking system would threaten the nation's survival.

Roosevelt (who reportedly saw the film *Gabriel over the White House* several times before his inauguration) used his inaugural address to promise the American people decisive action. Standing in a cold rain on the Capitol steps, he vowed to face the crisis "frankly and boldly." The lines we best remember from his speech are words of comfort: "Let me assert my firm belief," the new president told the thousands gathered on the Capitol grounds and the millions gathered around their radios, "that the only thing we have to fear is fear itself—nameless, unreasoning, unjustified terror." But the only loud cheers that day came when Roosevelt invoked "the analogue of war," asserting that, if need be, "I shall ask the Congress for the one remaining instrument to meet the crisis—broad Executive power to wage a war against the emergency, as great as the power that would be given to me if we were in fact invaded by a foreign foe."

The next day Roosevelt, using powers legally granted by the World War I Trading with the Enemy Act, closed the nation's banks for a four-day "holiday" and summoned Congress to an emergency session. He immediately introduced the Emergency Banking Relief Bill, which was passed sight unseen by unanimous House vote, approved

73 to 7 in the Senate, and signed into law the same day. This bill provided federal authority to reopen solvent banks and reorganize the rest, and authorized federal money to shore up private banks. In his inaugural address, Roosevelt had attacked "unscrupulous money changers," and many critics of the failed banking system had hoped he planned to remove the banks from private hands. Instead, as one North Dakota congressman complained, "the President drove the money changers out of the Capitol on March 4th and they were all back on the 9th." Roosevelt's banking policy was much like Hoover's—a fundamentally conservative approach that upheld the status quo.

The banking bill could save the U.S. banking system only if Americans were confident enough to deposit money in the reopened banks. So Roosevelt, in the first of his radio "Fireside Chats," asked the support of the American people. "We have provided the machinery to restore our financial system," he said. "It is up to you to support and make it work." The next morning, when the banks opened their doors, people lined up—but this time, most waited to deposit money. It was an enormous triumph for the new president. It also demonstrated that Roosevelt, though unafraid to take bold action, was not as radical as some wished or as others feared.

During the ninety-nine-day-long special session of Congress, dubbed by journalists "The First Hundred

First Hundred Days

Days," the federal government took on dramatically new roles. Roosevelt, aided by a group of advisers—lawyers, university professors, and social workers, who were collectively nicknamed "the Brain Trust"—and by the enormously capable First Lady, set out to revive the American economy. These "New Dealers" had no single, coherent plan, and Roosevelt's economic policies fluctuated between attempts to balance the budget and massive deficit spending (spending more than is taken in in taxes and borrowing the difference). But with a strong mandate for action and the support of a Democrat-controlled Congress, the new administration produced a flood of legislation. The first priority was economic recovery. Two basic strategies emerged during the First Hundred Days. New Dealers experimented with national economic planning, and they created a range of "relief" programs to help those in need.

At the heart of the New Deal experiment in planning were the National Industrial Recovery Act (NIRA) and

National Industrial Recovery Act

the Agricultural Adjustment Act (AAA). The NIRA was based on the belief that "destructive competition" had worsened industry's economic woes. Skirting antitrust regulation, the NIRA authorized competing businesses to cooperate in crafting industrywide codes. Thus automobile manufacturers, for example, would cooperate to limit production, establish industrywide prices, and set workers' wages. Competition among manufacturers would no longer drive down prices and wages. With wages and prices stabilized, the theory went, consumer spending would increase, thus allowing industries to rehire workers. Significantly, Section 7(a) guaranteed industrial workers the right to "organize and bargain collectively"—in other words, to unionize.

Individual businesses' participation in this program, administered by the National Recovery Administration (NRA), was voluntary—with one catch. Businesses that adhered to the industrywide codes could display the Blue Eagle, the NRA symbol; the government urged consumers to boycott businesses that did not fly the Blue Eagle. This voluntary program, though larger in scale than any previous government–private sector cooperation, was not very different from Hoover-era "associationalism."

From the beginning, the NRA faced serious problems. As small-business owners had feared, big business easily dominated the NRA-mandated cartels. NRA staff lacked the training and experience to stand up to the representatives of corporate America. The twenty-six-year-old NRA staffer who oversaw the creation of the petroleum industry code was "helped" by twenty highly paid oil industry lawyers. The majority of the 541 codes eventually approved by the NRA reflected the interests of major corporations, not small-business owners, labor, or consumers. Most fundamentally, the NRA did not deliver economic recovery. In 1935 the Supreme Court put an end to the fragile, floundering system. Using an old-fashioned (what Roosevelt called a "horse-and-buggy") definition of interstate commerce, the Supreme Court found that the NRA extended federal power past its constitutional bounds.

The Agricultural Adjustment Act (AAA) had a more enduring effect on the United States. Establishing a national system of crop controls, the AAA offered subsidies to farmers who agreed to limit production of specific crops. (Overproduction drove crop prices down.) The subsidies, funded by taxing the processors of agricultural goods, were meant to give farmers the same purchasing power they had had during the prosperous period before World War I. But to reduce production in 1933, the nation's farmers agreed to destroy 8.5 million piglets and to plow under crops in the fields. Although limiting production did raise agricultural prices, millions of hungry Amer-

Agricultural Adjustment Act

YEARS OF DUST
RESETTLEMENT ADMINISTRATION
Rescues Victims
Restores Land to Proper Use

▲ Under the Agricultural Adjustment Act, farmers received government payments for not planting crops or for destroying crops they had already planted. Some farmers, however, needed help of a different kind. The Resettlement Administration, established by executive order in 1935, was authorized to resettle destitute farm families from areas of soil erosion, flooding, and stream pollution to homestead communities. This poster was done by Ben Shahn. *(Library of Congress)*

icans found it difficult to understand the economic theory behind this waste of food.

Government crop subsidies had unintended consequences: they were a disaster for tenant farmers and sharecroppers. Despite government hopes to the contrary, as landlords cut production they turned tenant farmers off their land. In the South the number of sharecropper farms dropped by almost one-third between 1930 and 1940. The result was a homeless population of dispossessed Americans—many of them African American—heading to cities and towns throughout the nation. But the subsidies did help many. In the depression-ravaged Dakotas, for example, government payments accounted for almost three-quarters of the total farm income for 1934.

In 1936 the Supreme Court found that the AAA, like the NRA, was unconstitutional. But the AAA (unlike the NRA) was too popular with its constituency, American farmers, to disappear. The legislation was rewritten to meet the Supreme Court's objections, and farm subsidies continue into the twenty-first century.

With millions of Americans in desperate poverty, Roosevelt also moved quickly to implement poor relief:

Relief Programs

$3 billion in federal dollars were allocated in 1935. New Dealers, however—like many other Americans—disapproved of direct relief payments. "Give a man a dole and you save his body and destroy his spirit; give him a job and pay him an assured

wage and you save both the body and the spirit," wrote Harry Hopkins, Roosevelt's trusted adviser and head of the president's major relief agency, the Federal Emergency Relief Administration (FERA). Thus New Deal programs emphasized "work relief." By January 1934, the Civil Works Administration had hired 4 million people, most earning $15 a week. And the Civilian Conservation Corps (CCC) paid unmarried young men (young women were not eligible) $1 a day to do hard outdoor labor: building dams and reservoirs, creating trails in national parks. The program was segregated by race but brought together young men from very different backgrounds. By 1942 the CCC had employed 2.5 million men, including 80,000 Native Americans who worked on western Indian reservations.

Work relief programs rarely addressed the needs of poor women. Mothers of young children were usually classified as "unemployable" and were offered relief instead of

TABLE 25.1   New Deal Achievements

Year	Labor	Agriculture and Environment	Business and Industrial Recovery	Relief	Reform
1933	Section 7(a) of NIRA	Agricultural Adjustment Act Farm Credit Act	Emergency Banking Relief Act Economy Act Beer-Wine Revenue Act Banking Act of 1933 (guaranteed deposits) National Industrial Recovery Act	Civilian Conservation Corps Federal Emergency Relief Act Home Owners Refinancing Act Public Works Administration Civil Works Administration	TVA Federal Securities Act
1934	National Labor Relations Board	Taylor Grazing Act			Securities Exchange Act
1935	National Labor Relations (Wagner) Act	Resettlement Administration Rural Electrification Administration		Works Progress Administration National Youth Administration	Social Security Act Public Utility Holding Company Act Revenue Act (wealth tax)
1937		Farm Security Administration		National Housing Act	
1938	Fair Labor Standards Act	Agricultural Adjustment Act of 1938			

Source: Adapted from Charles Sellers, Henry May, and Neil R. McMillen, *A Synopsis of American History*, 6th ed. Copyright © 1985 by Houghton Mifflin Company. Reprinted by permission.

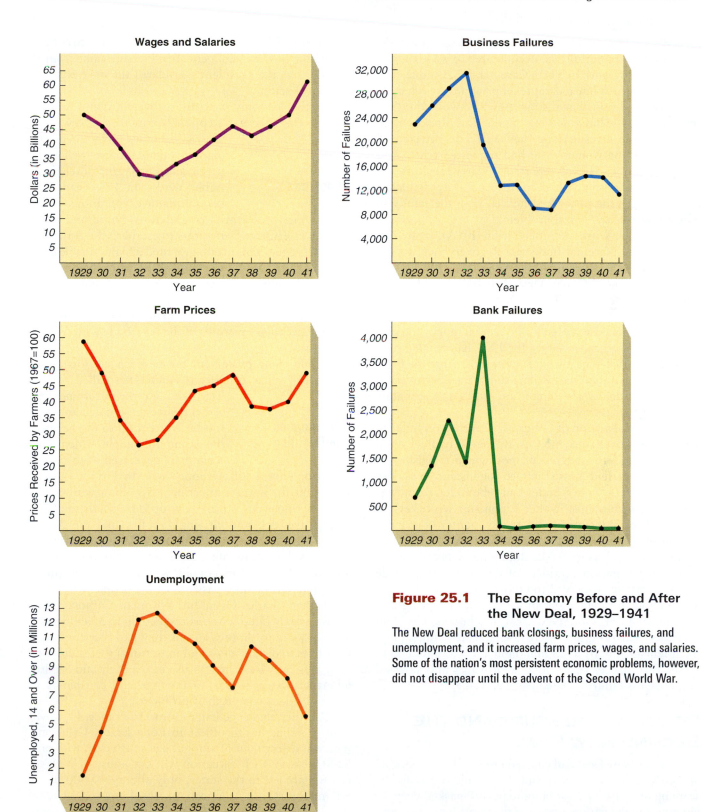

Figure 25.1   The Economy Before and After the New Deal, 1929–1941

The New Deal reduced bank closings, business failures, and unemployment, and it increased farm prices, wages, and salaries. Some of the nation's most persistent economic problems, however, did not disappear until the advent of the Second World War.

jobs. But, as historian Linda Gordon explains, "mother's-aid" grants were pitifully small compared to wages in federal works programs. In North Carolina, for example, they were one-sixth. While federal relief programs rejected the poor-law tradition that distinguished between the "deserving" and the "undeserving" poor, local officials often did not. "The investigators, they were like detectives," complained one woman who had requested relief. And journalist Lorena Hickok reported to Harry Hopkins that "a woman who isn't a good housekeeper is apt to have a pretty rough time of it. And heaven help the family in which there is any 'moral problem'."

The Public Works Administration (PWA), created by Title II of the National Industrial Recovery Act, appropriated $3.3 billion for public works in 1933. PWA workers built the Grand Coulee Dam (begun during Hoover's administration) and the Triborough Bridge in New York City, as well as hundreds of public buildings. But the PWA's main purpose was to pump federal money into the economy. As federal revenues for 1932 had totaled only $1.9 billion, this huge appropriation shows that the Roosevelt administration was willing to use the controversial technique of deficit spending in an attempt to stimulate the economy.

The special session of Congress adjourned on June 16, 1933. In just over three months, Roosevelt had delivered fifteen messages to Congress proposing major legislation, and Congress had passed fifteen significant laws (see Table 25.1). The United States had rebounded from near collapse. As columnist Walter Lippmann wrote, at the time of Roosevelt's inauguration the country was a collection of "disorderly panic-stricken mobs and factions. In the hundred days from March to June we became again an organized nation confident of our power to provide for our own security and to control our own destiny." Throughout the remainder of 1933 and the spring and summer of 1934, more New Deal bills became law. And as New Deal programs were implemented, unemployment fell steadily from 13 million in 1933 to 9 million in 1936. Farm prices rose, along with wages and salaries, and business failures abated (see Figure 25.1).

POLITICAL PRESSURE AND THE SECOND NEW DEAL

Roosevelt's New Deal had enjoyed unprecedented popular and congressional support, but that would not last. The seeming unity of the First Hundred Days masked deep divides within the nation, and once the immediate crisis was averted, the struggle over solutions began in earnest. As some tried to stop the expansion of government power, others pushed for increased governmental action to combat continuing poverty and inequality. Pressure came from all directions as the president considered the next phase of New Deal action.

As the economy partially recovered, many wealthy business leaders began to publicly criticize the New Deal.

Business Opposition

They condemned government regulation and taxation, as well as the use of deficit financing for relief and public works. In 1934 leaders of several major corporations joined with former presidential candidate Al Smith and disaffected conservative Democrats to establish the American Liberty League. This group mounted a highly visible campaign against New Deal "radicalism." In an attempt to turn southern whites against the New Deal and so splinter the Democratic Party, the Liberty League also secretly channeled funds to a racist group in the South, which circulated incendiary pictures of the First Lady with African Americans.

While many prominent business leaders fought the New Deal, other Americans (sometimes called "populists") thought the government favored business too much and paid too little attention to the needs of

Demagogues and Populists

the common people. Unemployment had decreased—but 9 million people were still without work. In 1934 a wave of strikes hit the nation, affecting 1.5 million workers. In 1935 enormous dust storms enveloped the southern plains, killing livestock and driving families like the Montgomerys from their land. Millions of Americans still suffered. As their dissatisfaction mounted, so, too, did the appeal of various demagogues, who played to the prejudices and unreasoning passions of the people.

Father Charles Coughlin, a Roman Catholic priest whose weekly radio sermons reached up to 30 million listeners, spoke to those who felt they had lost control of their lives to distant elites and impersonal forces. Increasingly anti–New Deal, he was also increasingly anti-Semitic, telling his listeners that an international conspiracy of Jewish bankers caused their problems.

Another challenge came from Dr. Francis E. Townsend, a public health officer in Long Beach, California, who was thrown out of work at age sixty-seven with only $100 in savings. His situation was not unusual. With social welfare left to the states, only about 400,000 of the 6.6 million elderly Americans received any sort of state-supplied pension. And as employment and savings disappeared with the depression, many older people fell into desperate poverty. Townsend proposed that Americans over the age of sixty should receive a government pension of $200 a month, financed by a new "transaction" (sales) tax. In fact, Townsend's plan was fiscally impossible (almost three-quarters of working Americans earned $200 a month or less) and profoundly regressive (because sales tax rates are the same for everyone, they take a larger share of income from those who earn least). Thus Townsend actually sought a massive transfer of income from the working poor to the nonworking elderly. Nonetheless, 20 million Americans, or 1 in 5 adults—concerned about the plight of the elderly and not about details of funding—signed petitions supporting this plan.

Then there was Huey Long, perhaps the most successful populist demagogue in American history. Long was elected governor of Louisiana in 1928 with the slogan "Every Man a King, But No One Wears a Crown." As a U.S. senator, Long initially supported the New Deal but soon decided that Roosevelt had fallen captive to big business. Long countered in 1934 with the Share Our Wealth Society, advocating the seizure (by taxation) of all income exceeding $1 million a year and of wealth in excess of $5 million per family. From these funds, the government would provide each American family an annual income of $2,000 and a one-time homestead allowance of $5,000. (Long's plan was fiscally impossible but definitely not regressive.) By mid-1935 Long's movement claimed 7 million members, and few doubted that he aspired to the presidency. But Long was killed by a bodyguard's bullet during an assassination attempt in September 1935.

The political left also gained ground as hard times continued. Socialists and communists alike criticized the

||||||||||||||||||||||||||||||

Left-Wing Critics

New Deal for trying to save capitalism instead of working to lessen the inequality of power and wealth in American society. In California, muckraker and socialist Upton Sinclair won the Democratic gubernatorial nomination in 1934 with the slogan "End Poverty in California." That year in Wisconsin, the left-wing Progressive Party provided seven of the state's ten representatives to Congress, as voters reelected Robert La Follette to the Senate and gave his brother Philip the state governorship. Even the U.S. Communist Party found new support as it campaigned for social welfare and relief. Changing its strategy to disclaim any intention of overthrowing the U.S. government, the party proclaimed that "Communism Is Twentieth Century Americanism" and began to cooperate with left-wing labor unions, student groups, and writers' organizations in a "Popular Front" against fascism abroad and racism at home. In the late 1920s, attempting to appeal to African Americans, it established the League of Struggle for Negro Rights to fight lynching, and from 1931 on provided critical legal and financial support to the "Scottsboro Boys," who were falsely accused of raping two white women in Alabama (see page 733). As one black worker who became a communist organizer in Alabama explained, the Communist Party "fought selflessly and tirelessly to undo the wrongs perpetrated upon my race. Here was no dilly-dallying, no pussyfooting on the question of

◄ In the 1930s, Senator Huey Long (center) had a mass following and presidential ambitions. But he was assassinated in 1935, the evening this photograph was taken. When Long was shot, he fell into the arms of James O'Connor (left), a political crony. Louisiana governor O. K. Allen (right) seized a pistol and dashed into the corridor in pursuit of the murderer, shouting, "If there's shooting, I want to be in on it." *(Wide World Photos, Inc.)*

full equality of the Negro people." In 1938, at its high point for the decade, the party had 55,000 members.

It was not only external critics who pushed Roosevelt to focus on social justice. His administration—largely due to Eleanor Roosevelt's influ-

Shaping the Second New Deal

ence—included many progressive activists. Frances Perkins, America's first woman cabinet member, came from a social work background, as did Roosevelt's close adviser Harold Ickes. A group of women social reformers who coalesced around the First Lady became important figures in government and in the Democratic Party. And African Americans had an unprecedented voice in this White House. By 1936 at least fifty black Americans held relatively important positions in New Deal agencies and cabinet-level departments. Journalists called these officials—who met on Friday evenings at the home of Mary McLeod Bethune, a distinguished educator who served as Director of Negro Affairs for the National Youth Administration—the "black cabinet." Finally, Eleanor Roosevelt herself worked tirelessly to put social justice issues at the center of the New Deal agenda.

As Roosevelt faced the election of 1936, he understood that he had to appeal to Americans who had seemingly contradictory desires. Those who had been hit hard by the depression looked to the New Deal for help and for social justice. If that help was not forthcoming, Roosevelt would lose their support. Other Americans—not the poorest, but those with a tenuous hold on the middle class—were afraid of the continued chaos and disorder. They wanted security and stability. Still others, with more to lose, were frightened by the populist promises of people like Long and Coughlin. They wanted the New Deal to preserve American capitalism. With these lessons in mind, Roosevelt took the initiative once more.

During the period historians call the Second New Deal, Roosevelt introduced a range of progressive programs aimed at providing, as he said in a 1935 address to Congress, "greater security for the average man than he has ever known before in the history of America." The first triumph of the Second New Deal was an innocuous-sounding but momentous law that Roosevelt called "the Big Bill." The Emergency Relief Appropriation Act provided $4 billion in new deficit spending, primarily to create massive public works programs for the jobless. It also established the Resettlement Administration, which resettled destitute families and organized rural homestead communities and suburban greenbelt towns for low-income workers; the Rural Electrification Administration, which brought electricity to isolated rural areas; and the National Youth Administration, which sponsored work-relief programs for young adults and part-time jobs for students.

The largest and best-known program funded by the Emergency Relief Appropriation Act was the Works Prog-

Works Progress Administration

ress Administration (WPA), later renamed the Work Projects Administration. The WPA employed more than 8.5 million people who built 650,000 miles of highways and roads, and 125,000 public buildings, as well as bridges, reservoirs, irrigation systems, sewage treatment plants, parks, playgrounds, and swimming pools

Mary McLeod Bethune, pictured here with her friend and supporter Eleanor Roosevelt, became the first African American woman to head a federal agency as director of the Division of Negro Affairs for the National Youth Administration.

(© Bettmann/Corbis)

▲ In 1930, 90 percent of American farms did not have electricity. This 1936 cover from *Fortune* magazine celebrates the work of the Rural Electrification Administration, which brought power to some of America's most remote regions. *(Fortune magazine, March 1936)*

throughout the nation. Many WPA projects helped local communities: WPA workers built or renovated schools and hospitals, operated nurseries for preschool children, and taught 1.5 million adults to read and write.

The WPA also employed artists, musicians, writers, and actors for a wide range of cultural programs. The WPA's Federal Theater Project brought vaudeville, circuses, and theater, including African American and Yiddish plays, to cities and towns across the country. Its Arts Project hired painters and sculptors to teach their crafts in rural schools, and commissioned artists to decorate post office walls with murals depicting ordinary life in America past and present. The Federal Music Project employed 15,000 musicians in government-sponsored orchestras and collected folk songs from around the nation. Perhaps the most ambitious of the New Deal's cultural programs was the WPA's Federal Writers' Project (FWP), which hired talented authors, such as John Steinbeck and Richard Wright. FWP writers created guidebooks for every state and territory, and they wrote about the plain people of the United States. More than 2,000 elderly men and women who

had been freed from slavery by the Civil War told their stories to FWP writers, who collected these "slave narratives"; life stories of sharecroppers and textile workers were published as *These Are Our Lives* (1939). These and other WPA arts projects were controversial, for many of the WPA artists, musicians, actors, and writers sympathized with the political struggles of workers and farmers. Critics assailed them as left-wing propaganda, and in fact some of these artists were communists. However, the goal of this "Popular Front" culture was not to overthrow the government, but to recover a tradition of American radicalism through remembering, and celebrating artistically, the lives and labor of America's plain folk.

Social Security Act

Big Bill programs and agencies were part of a short-term "emergency" strategy meant to address the immediate needs of the nation. Roosevelt's long-term strategy centered around the second major piece of Second New Deal legislation, the Social Security Act. The Social Security Act created, for the first time, a federal system to provide for the social welfare of American citizens. Its key provision was a federal pension system in which eligible workers paid mandatory Social Security taxes on their wages and their employers contributed an equivalent amount; these workers then received federal retirement benefits. The Social Security Act also created several welfare programs, including a cooperative federal-state system of unemployment compensation and Aid to Dependent Children (later renamed Aid to Families with Dependent Children, AFDC) for needy children in families without fathers present. Over the course of the twentieth century, benefits provided through the Social Security system would save tens of millions of Americans, especially the elderly, from poverty and despair.

Compared with the national systems of social security already in place in most western European nations, the U.S. Social Security system was fairly conservative. First, the government did not pay for old-age benefits; workers and their bosses did. Second, the tax was regressive in that the more workers earned, the less they were taxed proportionally. Finally, the law did not cover agricultural labor, domestic service, and "casual labor not in the course of the employer's trade or business" (for example, janitorial work at a hospital). Thus a disproportionately high number of people of color, who worked as farm laborers, as domestic servants, and in service jobs in hospitals and restaurants, received no benefits. The act also excluded public-sector employees, so that many teachers, nurses, librarians, and social workers, the majority of whom were women, went uncovered. (Although the original Social Security Act provided no retirement benefits for

▲ The Works Progress Administration commissioned twenty-six artists to create a mural depicting scenes of life in modern California for San Francisco's Coit Tower, which had been completed in 1933. "The Woman with Cala Lilies," a detail from the large fresco that filled the lobby, was painted by Maxine Albro. *(Coit Tower, San Francisco)*

giants down to size" through antitrust suits and heavy corporate taxes. He also supported the Wealth Tax Act, which some critics saw as the president's attempt to "steal Huey Long's thunder." The tax act helped achieve a slight redistribution of income by raising the income taxes of the wealthy (see Figure 25.2). It also imposed a new tax on business profits and increased taxes on inheritances, large gifts, and profits from the sale of property.

In November 1936, Roosevelt won the presidency by a landslide, defeating Republican nominee Governor Alf Landon of Kansas by a margin of 27.8 to 16.7 million votes. The Democrats also won huge majorities in the House and Senate. The Democratic victory was so overwhelming that some worried the two-party system might collapse. In fact, Roosevelt and the Democrats had forged a powerful "New Deal coalition." This new alliance pulled together groups from very different backgrounds and with different interests: the urban working class (especially immigrants from southern and eastern Europe and their sons and daughters), organized labor, the eleven states of the Confederacy (the "Solid South"), and northern blacks. By this time, the African American population in northern cities was large enough to constitute voting blocks, and New Deal benefits drew them away from the Republican Party, which they had long supported as the party of Lincoln. This New Deal coalition gave the Democratic Party dominance in the two-party system and ensured that Democrats would occupy the White House for most of the next thirty years.

LABOR

During the worst years of the depression, American workers continued to organize and to struggle for the rights of labor. Management, however, resisted unionization vigorously. Many employers refused to recognize unions, and some hired armed thugs to intimidate workers. One business publication declared that "a few hundred funerals will have a quieting influence." As employers refused to negotiate with union representatives, workers walked off the job. Employers tried to replace striking workers with strikebreakers—and workers tried to keep the strikebreakers from crossing their picket lines. The situation often turned violent. Local police or National Guard troops frequently intervened on the side of management, smashing workers' picket lines. As strikes spread throughout the nation, violence erupted in the steel, automobile, and textile industries, among lumber workers in the Pacific Northwest, and among teamsters in the Midwest. In 1934 police met a longshoremen's strike with violence on the

spouses or widows of covered workers, Congress added these benefits in 1939.) Despite these limitations, the Social Security Act was a highly significant development. With its passage, the federal government took some responsibility for the economic security of the aged, the temporarily unemployed, dependent children, and people with disabilities.

As the election of 1936 approached, Roosevelt adopted the populist language of his critics. He made

Roosevelt's Populist Strategies

scathing attacks on big business. Denouncing "entrenched greed" and the "unjust concentration of wealth and power," he proposed that government should "cut the

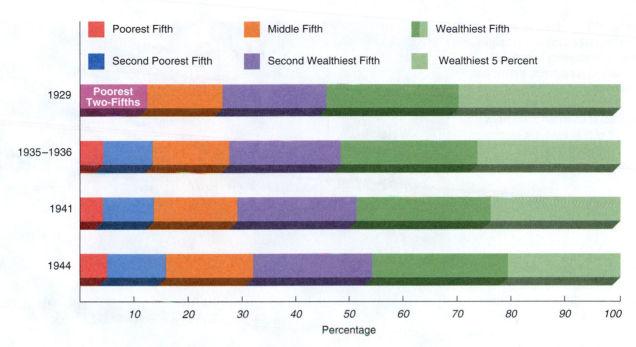

Figure 25.2   **Distribution of Total Family Income Among the American People, 1929–1944 (percentage)**

Although the New Deal provided economic relief to the American people, it did not, as its critics so often charged, significantly redistribute income downward from the rich to the poor.

(Source: Adapted from U.S. Bureau of the Census, Historical Statistics of the United States, Colonial Times to 1970, *2 parts [Washington, D.C.: U.S. Government Printing Office, 1975], Part 1, p. 301.)*

docks of San Francisco; 2 union members were killed, and workers' anger spread to other industries. Eventually 130,000 workers joined the general strike.

Workers pushed the Roosevelt administration for support, which came in the 1935 National Labor Relations (Wagner) Act. This act guaranteed workers the right to organize unions and to bargain collectively. It outlawed "unfair labor practices," such as firing workers who joined unions, prohibited management from sponsoring company unions, and required employers to bargain with labor's elected union representatives to set wages, hours, and working conditions. Critical for its success, the Wagner Act created a mechanism for enforcement: the National Labor Relations Board (NLRB). Although labor-management conflict continued, by the end of the decade the NLRB played a key role in mediating disputes. With federal protection, union membership grew. Organizers in the coalfields told miners that "President Roosevelt wants you to join the union," and join they

did—along with workers in dozens of industries. In 1929 union membership stood at 3.6 million; in mid-1938 it surpassed 7 million.

The Wagner Act further alienated business leaders from the New Deal. "No Obedience," proclaimed an editorial in a leading business magazine. The business-sponsored Liberty League insisted—incorrectly—that the Supreme Court would soon find the Wagner Act unconstitutional.

Conflict existed not only between labor and management, but also within the labor movement itself. The rapid growth and increasing militancy of the movement exacerbated an existing division between "craft" and "industrial" unions in the United States. Craft unions represented labor's elite: the skilled workers in a particular trade, such as carpentry. Industrial unions represented all the workers, skilled and

Rivalry Between Craft and Industrial Unions

During the 1937 sit-down strike by automobile workers in Flint, Michigan, a women's "emergency brigade" of wives, mothers, daughters, sisters, and sweethearts demonstrated daily at the plant. When the police tried to force the men out of Chevrolet Plant No. 9 by filling it with teargas, the women used these clubs to smash the plant's windows and let in fresh air.

(AP Images)

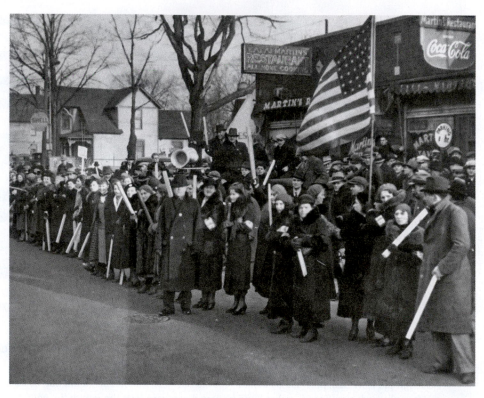

unskilled, in a given industry, such as automobile manufacture. In the 1930s, it was the industrial unions that had grown dramatically.

Craft unions dominated the American Federation of Labor, the powerful umbrella organization for specific unions. Most AFL leaders offered little support for industrial organizing. Many looked down on the industrial workers, disproportionately immigrants from southern and eastern Europe—"the rubbish at labor's door," in the words of the Teamsters' president. Skilled workers had economic interests different from those of the great mass of unskilled workers, and more conservative craft unionists were often alarmed at what they saw as the radicalism of industrial unions.

In 1935 the industrial unionists made their move. John L. Lewis, head of the United Mine Workers and the nation's most prominent labor leader, resigned as vice president of the AFL. He and other industrial unionists created the Committee for Industrial Organization (CIO); the AFL responded by suspending all CIO unions. In 1938 the slightly renamed Congress of Industrial Organizations had 3.7 million members, slightly more than the AFL's 3.4 million. Unlike the AFL, the CIO included women and people of color in its membership. Union membership gave these "marginal" workers greater employment security and the benefits of collective bargaining.

The most decisive labor conflict of the decade came in late 1936, when the United Auto Workers (UAW), an industrial union, demanded recognition from General Motors (GM), Chrysler, and Ford. When GM refused, UAW organizers responded with a relatively new tactic: a "sit-down strike." On De-

Sit-Down Strikes

cember 30, 1936, workers at the Fisher Body plant in Flint, Michigan, went on strike *inside* the Fisher One factory. They refused to leave the building, thus immobilizing a key part of the GM production system. GM tried to force the workers out by turning off the heat. When police attempted to take back the plant, strikers hurled steel bolts, coffee mugs, and bottles. The police tried tear gas. Strikers turned the plant's water hoses on the police.

As the sit-down strike spread to adjacent plants, auto production plummeted. General Motors obtained a court order to evacuate the plant, but the strikers stood firm, risking imprisonment and fines. In a critical decision, Michigan's governor refused to send in the National Guard to clear workers from the buildings. After forty-four days, the UAW triumphed. GM agreed to recognize the union, and Chrysler quickly followed. Ford held out until 1941.

On the heels of this triumph, however, came a grim reminder of the costs of labor's struggle. On Memorial Day 1937, a group of picnicking workers and their families marched toward the Republic Steel plant in Chicago, intending to show support for strikers on a picket line in front of the plant. Police blocked their route and ordered them to disperse. One of the marchers threw something at the police, and the police attacked. Ten men were killed,

Memorial Day Massacre

seven of them shot in the back. Thirty marchers were wounded, including a woman and three children. Many Americans, fed up with labor strife and violence, showed little sympathy for the workers. The antilabor *Chicago Tribune* blamed the marchers and praised police for repelling "a trained military unit of a revolutionary body."

At great cost, organized labor made great gains during the 1930s. Gradually violence receded, as the National Labor Relations Board proved effective in mediating disputes. And unionized workers—about 23 percent of the nonagricultural work force—saw their standard of living rise. By 1941 the average steelworker could afford to buy a new coat for himself and his wife every six years and, every other year, a pair of shoes for each of his children.

FEDERAL POWER AND THE NATIONALIZATION OF CULTURE

In the 1930s, national culture, politics, and policies played an increasingly important role in the lives of Americans from different regions, classes, and ethnic backgrounds, as the reach of the national mass media grew and the power of the federal government expanded. This happened in large part because the power of the federal government expanded. During the decade-long economic crisis, political power moved from the state and local level to the White House and Congress. Individual Americans, in new ways, found their lives bound up with the federal government. In 1930, with the single exception of the post office, Americans had little direct contact with the federal government. By the end of the 1930s, almost 35 percent of the population had received some sort of federal government benefit, whether crop subsidies through the federal AAA or a WPA job or relief payments through FERA. As political analyst Michael Barone argues, "The New Deal changed American life by changing the relationship between Americans and their government." Americans in the 1930s began to look to the federal government to play a major and active role in the life of the nation.

The New Deal changed the American West more than any other region, as federally sponsored construction of dams and other public works projects reshaped the region's economy and environment. During the 1930s, the federal Bureau of Reclamation, an obscure agency created by the Newlands Reclamation Act of 1902 to provide irrigation for small farms and ranches, expanded its mandate dramatically to build large multipurpose dams that controlled entire river systems. The Central Valley Project dammed the Sacramento River and its tributaries. The

New Deal in the West

Boulder Dam (later renamed for Herbert Hoover) harnessed the Colorado River, providing water to southern California municipalities and using hydroelectric power to produce electricity for Los Angeles and southern Arizona. The water from these dams opened new areas to agriculture and allowed western cities to expand; the cheap electricity they produced attracted industry to the region. Large factory farms consolidated their hold in the region with water from these massive projects, which were paid for by taxpayers across the nation and by regional consumers of municipal water and electricity. These federally managed projects also gave the federal government an unprecedented role in the West. Especially after the completion of Washington State's Grand Coulee Dam in 1941, the federal government controlled both a great deal of water and hydroelectric power in the region. And in the West, control of water meant control over the region's future.

The federal government also brought millions of acres of western land under its control in the 1930s. Attempting to combat the environmental disaster of the Dust Bowl and to keep crop and livestock prices from falling further, federal programs worked to limit agricultural production. To reduce pressure on the land from overgrazing, the federal government bought 8 million cattle from farmers in a six-month period in 1934–1935 and transported the healthy cattle out of the region. In 1934 the Taylor Grazing Act imposed new restrictions on ranchers' use of public lands for grazing stock. Federal stock reduction programs probably saved the western cattle industry, but they destroyed the traditional economy of the Navajos by forcing them to reduce the size of their sheep herds on their federally protected reservation lands. The large farms and ranches of the West benefited immensely from federal subsidies and crop supports through the AAA, but such programs also increased federal government control in the region. As western historian Richard White argues, by the end of the 1930s, "federal bureaucracies were quite literally remaking the American West."

New federal activism extended to the West's people as well. Over the past several decades, federal policy toward Native Americans, especially those on western Indian reservations, had been disastrous. The Bureau of Indian Affairs (BIA) was riddled with corruption; in its attempts to "assimilate" Native Americans, it had separated children from their parents, suppressed native languages, and outlawed tribal religious practices. Such BIA-enforced assimilation was not successful. Division of tribal lands had failed to promote individual land ownership—almost half of those living on reservations in 1933

New Deal for Native Americans

As the commissioner of Indian affairs, John Collier *(right)* reversed long-standing U.S. policy, insisting that "the cultural history of Indians is in all respects to be considered equal to that of any non-Indian group." However, some of the reforms he introduced were at odds with traditional practices, as in the case of the Hopis, whose tradition of independent villages did not fit the model of centralized tribal control mandated by the Indian Reorganization Act. Here, Hopi leaders Loma Haftowa *(left)* and Chaf Towa *(middle)* join Collier at the opening ceremonies for the new Department of the Interior building in Washington, D.C. *(Wide World Photos, Inc.)*

owned no land. In the early 1930s, Native Americans were the poorest group in the nation, plagued by epidemics and malnutrition, with an infant mortality rate twice that of white Americans.

In 1933 Roosevelt named one of the BIA's most vocal critics to head the agency. John Collier, founder of the American Indian Defense Agency, meant to completely reverse the course of America's Indian policy, and his initiatives had many positive results. The Indian Reorganization Act (1934) went a long way toward ending the forced assimilation of native peoples and restoring Indian lands to tribal ownership. It also gave federal recognition to tribal governments. Indian tribes had regained their status as semisovereign nations, guaranteed "internal sovereignty" in all matters not specifically limited by acts of Congress.

Not all Indian peoples supported the IRA. Some saw it as a "back-to-the-blanket" measure based on romantic notions of "authentic" Indian culture. The tribal government structure specified by the IRA was culturally alien— and quite perplexing—to tribes such as the Papagos, whose language had no word for "representative." The Navajo nation also refused to ratify the IRA; in a terrible case of bad timing, the vote took place during the federally mandated destruction of Navajo sheep herds. Eventually, however, 181 tribes organized under the IRA. Collier had succeeded in reversing some of the destructive policies of the past, and the IRA laid the groundwork for future economic development and limited political autonomy among native peoples.

New Dealers did not set out to transform the American West, but they did intend to transform the American

New Deal in the South

South. Well before the Great Depression, the South was mired in widespread and debilitating poverty. In 1929 the South's per capita income of $365 per year was less than half of the West's $921. More than half of the region's farm families were tenants or sharecroppers with no land of their own. "Sickness, misery, and unnecessary death," in the words of a contemporary study, plagued the southern poor. Almost 15 percent of South Carolina's people could not read or write.

Roosevelt, who sought a cure for his polio in the pools of Warm Springs, Georgia, had seen southern poverty firsthand and understood its human costs. But in describing the South as "the Nation's No. 1 economic problem" in 1938, he was referring to the economic theory that underlay many New Deal programs. As long as its people were too poor to participate in the nation's mass consumer economy, the South would be a drag on national economic recovery.

The largest federal intervention in the South was the Tennessee Valley Authority (TVA), authorized by Congress during Roosevelt's First Hundred Days. The TVA was created to develop a water and hydroelectric power project similar to the multipurpose dams of the West; dams would not only control flooding but also produce electric power for the region (see Map 25.2). However, confronted with the poverty and hopelessness of the Ten-

Map 25.2   The Tennessee Valley Authority
To control flooding and generate electricity, the Tennessee Valley Authority constructed dams along the Tennessee River and its tributaries from Paducah, Kentucky, to Knoxville, Tennessee.

nessee River Valley region (which included parts of Virginia, North Carolina, Tennessee, Georgia, Alabama, Mississippi, and Kentucky), the TVA quickly extended its focus. Through the TVA, the federal government promoted economic development, helped bring electricity to rural areas, restored fields worn out from overuse, and fought the curse of malaria.

Although it benefited many poor southerners, over time the TVA proved to be a monumental environmental disaster. TVA strip mining caused soil erosion. Its coal-burning generators released sulfur oxides, which combined with water vapor to produce acid rain. Above all, the TVA degraded the water by dumping untreated sewage, toxic chemicals, and metal pollutants from strip mining into streams and rivers.

During the 1930s, the Roosevelt administration faced a very difficult political situation in the South. The southern senators whose support Roosevelt so desperately needed benefited from the flow of federal dollars to their states. But they were also suspicious of federal intervention and determined to preserve states' rights. Especially when federal action threatened the South's racial hier-

archy, they resisted passionately. As the nation's poorest and least educated region, the South would not easily be integrated into the national culture and economy. But New Deal programs began that process and in so doing improved the lives of at least some of the region's people.

It was not only federal government programs that broke down regional boundaries and fostered national connections during the 1930s. The national mass medium of radio helped millions survive hard times, and America's national popular culture played a critical role in the life of Americans throughout the 1930s.

Mass Media and Popular Culture

The sound of the radio filled the days and nights of the depression era. Manufacturers rushed to produce cheaper models, and by 1937 Americans were buying radios at the rate of twenty-eight a minute. By the end of the decade, 27.5 million households owned radios, and families listened on average five hours a day. Roosevelt understood the importance of the radio in American life, going directly to the American people with radio "Fireside Chats" throughout his presidency. Americans, in fact,

The 1936 Olympic Games

The 1936 Olympic Games that were scheduled to take place in Berlin, under the Nazi regime, created a dilemma for the United States and other nations. Should they go to Berlin? Would participation in the Nazi-orchestrated spectacle lend credence to Hitler's regime? Or would victories won by other nations undermine Hitler's claims about the superiority of Germany's "Aryan race"?

Although the modern Olympic Games had been founded in 1896 with high hopes that they might help unite the nations of the world in peace and understanding, international politics were never far from the surface. Germany had been excluded from the 1920 and 1924 games following its aggression and defeat in World War I, and the International Olympic Committee's choice (in 1931) of Berlin for the XI Olympiad was intended to welcome Germany back into the world community. However, with Hitler's rise to power in 1933, Germany determined to use the games as propaganda for the Nazi state and to demonstrate the superiority of its pure "Aryan" athletes. Soon thereafter, campaigns to boycott the Berlin Olympics emerged in several nations, including Great Britain, Sweden, France, Czechoslovakia, and the United States.

The American people were divided over the question of a boycott. Some U.S. Jewish groups led campaigns against U.S. participation in Berlin, while others took no public position, concerned that their actions might lead to increased anti-Semitic violence within Germany. Jewish athletes made individual decisions about whether or not to boycott the Olympics. But the debate over the Berlin Olympics revealed pockets of American anti-Semitism. The president of the American Olympic Committee, Avery Brundage, attributed the boycott movement to a "conspiracy" of Jews and communists, and instructed American athletes not to get involved in the "present Jew-Nazi altercation." African Americans, overwhelmingly, opposed boycotting the games.

Well aware of Hitler's attitudes toward "mongrel" peoples, many looked forward to demonstrating on the tracks and fields of Berlin just how wrong Hitler's notions of Aryan superiority were. Some also pointed out the hypocrisy of American officials who criticized Germany while ignoring U.S. discrimination against black athletes.

In the end, the United States sent 312 athletes to Berlin; 18 were African American. These athletes won 14 medals, almost one-quarter of the U.S. total of 56. Track and field star Jesse Owens came home with 4 gold medals. Jewish athletes won 13 medals in the 1936 Olympics; one of those athletes was American. But German athletes won 89 medals to U.S. athletes' 56, and despite the initial controversy, the XI Olympiad was a public relations triumph for Germany. The *New York Times*, impressed by the spectacle of the games and the hospitality of the Germans, proclaimed that the XI Olympiad had put Germany "back in the fold of nations."

The idealistic vision of nations linked together through peaceful athletic competition hit a low point at the 1936 Olympics. The 1940 Olympic Games, scheduled for Tokyo, were cancelled because of the escalating world war.

The eleventh summer Olympic Games in Berlin were carefully crafted as propaganda for the Nazi state. And the spectacle of the 1936 games, as represented in this poster, was impressive. But on the athletic fields, Nazi claims of Aryan superiority were challenged by athletes such as African American Jesse Owens, who is shown breaking the Olympic record in the 200-meter race.

(Above: © Leonard de Selva/Corbis; Right: © Corbis-Bettmann)

put him eleventh in a ranking of America's top "radio personalities" in 1938.

The radio offered Americans many things. In a time of uncertainty, radio gave citizens immediate access—as never before—to the political news of the day and to the actual voices of their elected leaders. During hard times, radio offered escape: for children, the adventures of *Flash Gordon* and *Jack Armstrong, The All-American Boy;* for housewives, new soap operas, such as *The Romance of Helen Trent* and *Young Widder Brown.* Entire families gathered to listen to the comedy of ex-vaudevillians George Burns and Gracie Allen, and Jack Benny.

Radio also gave people a chance to participate—however vicariously—in events they could never have experienced before: listeners were carried to New York City for performances of the Metropolitan Opera on Saturday afternoons; to the Moana Hotel on the beach at Waikiki through the live broadcast of *Hawaii Calls;* to major league baseball games (begun by the St. Louis Cardinals in 1935) in distant cities. Millions shared the horror of the kidnapping of aviator Charles Lindbergh's son in 1932; black Americans in the urban North and rural South shared the triumphs of African American boxer Joe Louis ("the Brown Bomber"). Radio lessened the isolation of individuals and communities. It helped create a more homogeneous mass culture, as children throughout the nation acted out the same stories they had learned from the radio, but by offering a set of shared experiences, it also lessened the gulfs among Americans from different regions and class backgrounds.

The shared popular culture of 1930s America also centered on Hollywood movies. The film industry suffered in the initial years of the depression—almost one-third of all movie theaters closed, and ticket prices fell from 30 cents to 20 cents—but it rebounded after 1933. In a nation of fewer than 130 million people, between 80 and 90 million movie tickets were sold each week by the mid-1930s. Film's power to influence American attitudes was clearly demonstrated when sales of undershirts plummeted after Clark Gable took off his shirt to reveal a bare chest in *It Happened One Night.* As the depression continued, many Americans sought escape from grim realities at the movies. Comedies were especially popular, from the slapstick of the Marx Brothers to the sophisticated banter of *My Man Godfrey* or *It Happened One Night.* However, the appeal of upbeat movies was in the context of economic hard times. The song "Who's Afraid of the Big Bad Wolf?" from Disney's *Three Little Pigs,* was a big hit in 1933—as the economy hit bottom.

Yet as a cycle of gangster movies (including *Little Caesar* and *Scarface*) drew crowds in the early 1930s, many Americans worried about the effect of such films.

▲ *King Kong* broke all box-office records in 1933, as Americans flocked to see the giant ape fighting off airplanes from the top of New York's new Empire State Building—the tallest building in the world. *(Granger Collection)*

Crime seemed to be glamorized, no matter that the gangster hero always met death or destruction. Faced with a boycott organized by the Roman Catholic Legion of Decency, in 1934 the film industry established a production code that would determine what American film audiences saw—and did not see—for decades. "The vulgar, the cheap, and the tawdry is out," pledged the head of the Production Code Administration. "There is no room on the screen at any time for pictures which offend against common decency."

Finally, in an unintended consequence, federal policies intended to channel jobs to male heads of households strengthened the power of national popular culture. During Roosevelt's first two years in office, 1.5 million youths lost jobs; many young people who would have gone to work at the age of fourteen in better times decided to stay in school. By the end of the decade, three-quarters of American youth went to high school—up from one-half in 1920—and graduation rates doubled. School was free, classrooms were warm, and education seemed to promise a better future. The exuberant, fad-driven peer cultures that had developed in 1920s high schools and colleges were no more, but consumer-oriented youth culture had not died out. And as more young people went to high school, more participated in that national youth culture. Increasingly, young people listened to the same music. More than ever before, they adopted the same styles of clothing, of dance, of speech. Paradoxically, the hard times of the depression did not destroy youth culture; instead, they caused youth culture to spread more widely among America's young.

THE LIMITS OF THE NEW DEAL

Roosevelt began his second term with great optimism and a strong mandate for reform. Almost immediately, however, the president's own actions undermined his New Deal agenda. Labor strife and racial issues divided the American people. As fascism spread in Europe, the world inched toward war, and domestic initiatives lost ground to foreign affairs and defense. By the end of 1938, New Deal reform had ground to a halt, but it had already had a profound impact on the United States.

Following his landslide electoral victory in 1936, Roosevelt set out to safeguard his progressive agenda. The

Court-Packing Plan

greatest danger he saw was from the U.S. Supreme Court. In ruling unconstitutional both the National Industrial Recovery Act (in 1935) and the Agricultural Adjustment Act (in 1936), the Court rejected not only specific provisions of hastily drafted New Deal legislation but also the expansion of presidential and federal power such legislation entailed. Only three of the nine justices were consistently sympathetic to New Deal "emergency" measures, and Roosevelt was convinced the Court would invalidate most of the Second New Deal legislation. Citing the advanced age and heavy workload of the nine justices, he asked Congress for authority to appoint up to six new justices to the Supreme Court. But in an era that had seen the rise to power of Hitler, Mussolini, and Stalin, many Americans saw Roosevelt's plan as an attack on constitutional government. Even those sympathetic to the New Deal worried about politicizing the Court. "Assuming, which is not at all impossible," wrote prominent journalist William Allen White, "a reactionary president, as charming, as eloquent and as irresistible as Roosevelt, with power to change the court, and we should be in the

devil's own fix." Congress rebelled, and Roosevelt experienced his first major congressional defeat.

The episode had a final, ironic twist. During the long public debate over court packing, the ideological center of the Supreme Court shifted. Key swing-vote justices began to vote in favor of liberal, pro–New Deal rulings. In short order the Court upheld both the Wagner Act (*NLRB v. Jones & Laughlin Steel Corp.*), ruling that Congress's power to regulate interstate commerce also involved the power to regulate the production of goods for interstate commerce, and the Social Security Act. Moreover, a new judicial pension program encouraged older judges to retire, and the president appointed seven new associate justices in the next four years, including such notables as Hugo Black, Felix Frankfurter, and William O. Douglas. In the end, Roosevelt got what he wanted from the Supreme Court, but the court-packing plan damaged his political credibility.

Another New Deal setback was the renewed economic recession of 1937–1939, sometimes called the Roosevelt

Roosevelt Recession

recession. Despite his use of deficit spending, Roosevelt had never abandoned his commitment to a balanced budget. In 1937, confident that the depression had largely been cured, he began to cut back government spending. At the same time, the Federal Reserve Board, concerned about a 3.6 percent inflation rate, tightened credit. The two actions sent the economy into a tailspin: unemployment climbed from 7.7 million in 1937 to 10.4 million in 1938. Soon Roosevelt resumed deficit financing.

The New Deal was in trouble in 1937 and 1938, and New Dealers struggled over the direction of liberal reform. Some urged vigorous trustbusting; others advocated the resurrection of national economic planning as it had existed under the National Recovery Administration. But in the end Roosevelt rejected these alternatives and chose deficit financing as a means of stimulating consumer demand and creating jobs. And in 1939, with conflict over the world war that had begun in Europe commanding more and more of the nation's attention, the New Deal came to an end. Roosevelt sacrificed further domestic reforms in return for conservative support for his programs of military rearmament and preparedness.

No president had ever served more than two terms, and many Americans speculated about whether Franklin

Election of 1940

Roosevelt would run for a third term in 1940. Roosevelt seemed undecided until that spring, when Adolf Hitler's military advances in Europe apparently convinced him to stay on. Roosevelt

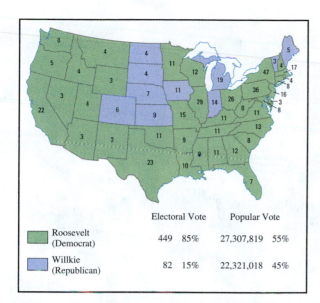

Map 25.3   Presidential Election, 1940
Roosevelt won an unprecedented third term in the 1940 presidential election. He did not repeat his landslide 1936 victory, in which he won all but two states. But he did capture 38 states in 1940 to Republican Wendell Willkie's 10.

	Electoral Vote		Popular Vote	
Roosevelt (Democrat)	449	85%	27,307,819	55%
Willkie (Republican)	82	15%	22,321,018	45%

headed off the predictable attacks from his opponent, Republican Wendell Willkie, by expanding military and naval contracts and thus reducing unemployment. Roosevelt also promised Americans, "Your boys are not going to be sent into any foreign wars."

Roosevelt did not win this election in a landslide, as he had in 1936 (see Map 25.3). But the New Deal coalition held. Once again Roosevelt won in the cities, supported by blue-collar workers, ethnic Americans, and African Americans. He also carried every state in the South. Although New Deal reform was over at home, Roosevelt was still riding a wave of public approval.

While the New Deal directly touched the lives of a great many Americans, not all benefited equally. More than anything else, differences were based on race. The New Deal fell short of equality for people of color for two major reasons.

Race and the Limits of the New Deal

First was the relationship between local and national power. National programs were implemented at the local level, and where local custom conflicted with national intent, as in the South and West, local custom won. In the South, African Americans received lower relief payments than whites and were paid lower wages in WPA jobs. The situation was similar in the Southwest. In Tucson, Arizona,

for example, Federal Emergency Relief Agency officials divided applicants into four groups—Anglos, Mexican Americans, Mexican immigrants, and Indians—and allocated relief payments in descending order.

Such discriminatory practices were rooted not only in racism but also in the economic interests of whites/Anglos. The majority of African American and Mexican American workers were paid so poorly that they *earned* less than impoverished whites got for "relief." Why would these workers take low-paying private jobs if government relief or government work programs provided more income? Local communities understood that federal programs threatened a political, social, and economic system based on racial hierarchies.

The case of the Scottsboro Boys illustrates the power of racism in the conflict between local and national power in 1930s America. One night in March 1931, a fight broke out between groups of young black and white "hobos" on a Southern Railroad freight train as it passed through Alabama. The black youths won the fight and tossed the whites off the train. Not long afterward, a posse stopped the train, arrested the black youths, and threw them in the Scottsboro, Alabama, jail. The posse also discovered two white women "riding the rails," who claimed that the young men had raped them. Word spread, and the youths were barely saved from a lynch mob. Medical evidence later showed that the women were lying. But within two weeks, eight of the so-called Scottsboro Boys were convicted of rape by all-white juries and sentenced to death. The ninth, a boy of thirteen, was saved from the death penalty by one vote. The case—so clearly a product of southern racism—became a cause célèbre, both in the nation and, through the efforts of the Communist Party, around the world.

The Supreme Court intervened, ruling that Alabama deprived black defendants of equal protection under the law by systematically excluding African Americans from juries and that the defendants had been denied counsel. Alabama, however, staged new trials. Five of the young men were convicted (four would be paroled by 1950, and one escaped from prison). Despite federal action through the Supreme Court, Alabama prevailed. Southern resistance to federal intervention, centered around issues of race, would not yield easily to federal power.

Second, the gains made by people of color under the New Deal were limited by the political realities of southern resistance. Roosevelt needed the support of southern Democrats to pass his legislative program, and they were willing to hold him hostage over race. For example, in 1938 southern Democrats blocked an antilynching bill with a six-week-long filibuster in the Senate. Roosevelt

Marchers in Washington (January 1, 1934) demand freedom for the "Scottsboro Boys," who were falsely accused and convicted of raping two white women in Alabama, and call on President Roosevelt for "Equal Rights for Negroes." The case of the Scottsboro Boys came to symbolize not only the racism and violence of the Jim Crow South, but also the discriminatory policies and practices that harmed African Americans throughout the nation. *(© Corbis/Bettmann)*

refused to use his political capital to break the filibuster and pass the bill. Politically, he had much to lose and little to gain. He knew that blacks would not desert the Democratic Party, but without southern senators, his legislative agenda was dead. Roosevelt wanted all Americans to enjoy the benefits of democracy, but he had no strong commitment to the cause of civil rights. As the NAACP's Roy Wilkins put it, "Mr. Roosevelt was no friend of the Negro. He wasn't an enemy, but he wasn't a friend."

Why, then, did African Americans support Roosevelt and the New Deal? Because, despite discriminatory poli-

African American Support

cies, the New Deal helped African Americans. By the end of the 1930s, almost one-third of African American households survived on income from a WPA job. African Americans held some significant positions in the Roosevelt administration. Finally, there was the First Lady. When the acclaimed black contralto Marian Anderson was barred from performing in Washington's Constitution Hall by its owners, the Daughters of the American Revolution, Eleanor Roosevelt arranged for Anderson to sing at the Lincoln Memorial on Easter Sunday 1939. Such public commitment to racial equality was enormously important to African American citizens.

Despite widespread support for Roosevelt and the New Deal, many African Americans were well aware of the limits of New Deal reform. Some concluded that they could depend only on themselves and organized self-help and direct-action movements. In 1934 black tenant farmers and sharecroppers joined with poor whites to form the Southern Tenant Farmers' Union. In the North, the militant Harlem Tenants League fought rent increases and evictions, and African American consumers began to boycott white merchants who refused to hire blacks as clerks. Their slogan was "Don't Buy Where You Can't Work." And the Brotherhood of Sleeping Car Porters, under the astute leadership of A. Philip Randolph, fought for the rights of black workers. Such actions, along with the limited benefits of New Deal programs, helped to improve the lives of black Americans during the 1930s.

Any analysis of the New Deal must begin with Franklin Delano Roosevelt himself. Assessments of Roo-

An Assessment of the New Deal

sevelt varied widely during his presidency: he was passionately hated, and just as passionately loved. Roosevelt personified the presidency for the American people. When he spoke directly to Americans in his Fireside Chats, hundreds of thousands wrote to him, sharing their problems, asking for his help, offering their advice.

▲ Robert Abbott, owner of the African American newspaper *The Chicago Defender*, and newspaper employees prepare to hand out food so needy families could celebrate Thanksgiving in 1931. *The Chicago Defender* was a strong voice for African Americans, and Abbott chronicled the devastating effects of the depression on the nation's black citizens. *(The Chicago Defender)*

Eleanor Roosevelt, the nation's First Lady, played a crucial and unprecedented role in the Roosevelt administration. As First Lady, she worked tirelessly for social justice and human rights, bringing reformers, trade unionists, and advocates for the rights of women and African Americans to the White House. Described by some as the conscience of the New Deal, she took public positions—especially on African American civil rights—far more progressive than those of her husband's administration. In some ways she served as a lightning rod, deflecting conservative criticism from her husband to herself. But her public stances also cemented the allegiance of other groups, African Americans in particular, to the New Deal.

Most historians and political scientists consider Franklin Roosevelt a truly great president, citing his courage and buoyant self-confidence, his willingness to experiment, and his capacity to inspire the nation during the most somber days of the depression. Some, who see the New Deal as a squandered opportunity for true political and economic change, charge that Roosevelt lacked vision and courage. They judge Roosevelt by goals that were not his own: Roosevelt was a pragmatist whose goal was to preserve the system. But even scholars who criticize Roosevelt's performance agree that he transformed the presidency. "Only Washington, who made the office, and Jackson, who remade it, did more than Roosevelt to raise it to its present condition of strength, dignity, and independence," claims political scientist Clinton Rossiter. Some find this transformation troubling, tracing the roots of "the imperial presidency" to the Roosevelt administration.

During his more than twelve years in office, Roosevelt strengthened not only the presidency but also the federal government. In the past, the federal government had exercised little control over the economy. Through New Deal programs, the government greatly added to its regulatory responsibilities, including overseeing the nation's financial systems. For the first time the federal government assumed a responsibility to offer relief to the jobless and the needy, and for the first time it used deficit spending to stimulate the economy. Millions of Americans benefited from government programs that are still operating today. The New Deal laid the foundation of the Social Security system on which subsequent presidential administrations would build.

New Deal programs pumped money into the economy and saved millions of Americans from hunger and misery. However, as late as 1939, more than 10 million men and women were still jobless, and the nation's unemployment rate stood at 19 percent. In the end it was not the New Deal, but massive government spending during the Second World War that brought full economic recovery. In 1941, as a result of mobilization for war, unemployment declined to 10 percent, and in 1944, at the height of the war, only 1 percent of the labor force was jobless. World War II, not the New Deal, would reinvigorate the American economy.

Legacy FOR A PEOPLE AND A NATION

Social Security

The New Deal's Social Security system has created a more secure and enjoyable old age for millions of Americans who might otherwise have lived in poverty. Although Social Security initially excluded some of America's neediest citizens, such as farm and domestic workers, amendments to the law have expanded eligibility. Today, almost 99 percent of American workers are covered by Social Security. Social Security has dramatically reduced the poverty rate among the nation's elderly, and payments provide critical support for the disabled and dependent children.

Despite its successes, today's Social Security system faces an uncertain future. Its troubles are due in part to decisions made during the 1930s. President Franklin Roosevelt did not want Social Security to be confused with poor relief. Therefore, he rejected the European model of government-funded pensions and instead created a system financed by payments from workers and their employers—a system based on individual accounts. This system, however, presented a short-term problem. If benefits came from their own contributions, workers who began receiving Social Security payments in 1940 would have received less than $1 a month. Therefore, Social Security payments from current workers paid the benefits of those already retired.

Over the years, this system of financing has become increasingly unstable, as an ever larger pool of retirees has to be supported by those currently in the work force. People are living longer. In 1935, when the system was created, average life expectancy was lower than sixty-five years, the age one could begin to collect benefits. Today, on average, American men live almost sixteen years past the retirement age of sixty-five, and women come close to twenty years past retirement age. In 1935 there were 16 current workers paying into the system for each person receiving retirement benefits. In 2000 there were fewer than 3.5 workers per retiree. Almost 77 million baby boomers born in the 1940s, 1950s, and 1960s will retire in the first decades of the twenty-first century. Unless the system is reformed, many argue, the retirement of the baby-boom cohort could even bankrupt the system

While the stock market was rising rapidly during the 1990s, some proposed that, because Social Security paid only a fraction of what individuals might have earned by investing their Social Security tax payments in the stock market, Americans be allowed to do just that. Some opponents declared this proposal too risky; others simply pointed to the structure of Social Security retirement. If current workers kept their money to invest, where would benefits for current retirees come from? The stock market's huge decline in the first years of the twenty-first century (and the losses sustained by private pension funds) slowed the push for privatization, and President George W. Bush's privatization initiative gained little congressional support. But, with the oldest baby boomers beginning to retire, questions about the future of the Social Security system will become increasingly important in the years to come.

SUMMARY

In the 1930s, a major economic crisis threatened the future of the nation. By 1933 almost one-quarter of America's workers were unemployed. Millions of people did not have enough to eat or adequate places to live. Herbert Hoover, elected president in 1928, believed that government should play only a limited role in managing and regulating the nation's economy. He tried to solve the nation's economic problems through a voluntary partnership of businesses and the federal government known as associationalism. In the 1932 presidential election, voters turned to the candidate who promised them a "New Deal." President Franklin Delano Roosevelt acted decisively to stabilize America's capitalist system and then worked to ameliorate its harshest impacts on the nation's people.

The New Deal was a liberal reform program that developed within the parameters of America's capitalist and democratic system. Most fundamentally, it expanded the role and power of the federal government. Because of New Deal reforms, banks, utilities, stock markets, farms, and most businesses operated in accord with rules set by the federal government. The federal government guaranteed workers' right to join unions without fear of employer reprisals, and federal law required employers to negotiate with workers' unions to set wages, hours, and working conditions. Many unemployed workers, elderly and disabled Americans, and dependent children were protected by a national welfare system administered through the federal government. And the president, through the power of the mass media and his own charisma, became an important presence in the lives of ordinary Americans.

The New Deal faced challenges from many directions. As the depression wore on, populist demagogues blamed scapegoats or offered overly simple explanations for the plight of the American people. Business leaders attacked the New Deal for its new regulation of business and its support of organized labor. As the federal government expanded its role throughout the nation, tensions between national and local authority sometimes flared up, and differences in regional ways of life and in social and economic structures presented challenges to national policy-makers. Both the West and the South were transformed by federal government action, but citizens of both regions were suspicious of federal intervention, and white southerners strongly resisted any attempt to challenge the racial system of Jim Crow. The political realities of a fragile New Deal coalition and strong opposition shaped—and limited—New Deal programs of the 1930s and the social welfare systems with which Americans still live today.

It was the economic boom created by America's entry into World War II, not the New Deal, that ended the Great Depression. However, New Deal programs helped many of America's people live better, more secure lives. And the New Deal fundamentally changed the way that the U.S. government would deal with future economic downturns and with the needs of its citizens in good times and in bad.

SUGGESTIONS FOR FURTHER READING

Anthony J. Badger, *The New Deal: The Depression Years, 1933–1940* (1989)

Alan Brinkley, *The End of Reform: New Deal Liberalism in Recession and War* (1995)

Alan Brinkley, *Voices of Protest: Huey Long, Father Coughlin, and the Great Depression* (1982)

Lizabeth Cohen, *Making a New Deal: Industrial Workers in Chicago* (1990)

Blanche Wiesen Cook, *Eleanor Roosevelt,* Vols. 1 and 2 (1992, 1999)

Sidney Fine, *Sitdown: The General Motors Strike of 1936–37* (1969)

James E. Goodman, *Stories of Scottsboro* (1994)

David M. Kennedy, *Freedom from Fear: The American People in Depression and War* (1999)

Robert McElvaine, The *Great Depression: America, 1929–1941* (1984)

Donald Worster, *Dust Bowl: The Southern Plains in the 1930s* (2004)

For a more extensive list for further reading, go to college.hmco.com/pic/norton8e.

The United States in a Troubled World *1920-1941*

*I*n 1921 the Rockefeller Foundation declared war on the mosquito in Latin America. As the carrier of yellow fever, the biting insect *Aedes aegypti* transmitted a deadly virus that caused severe headaches, vomiting, jaundice (yellow skin), and, for many, death. With clearance from the U.S. Department of State, the foundation dedicated several million dollars for projects to control yellow fever in Latin America, beginning with Mexico. Learning from the pioneering work of Carlos Juan Finlay of Cuba, Oswaldo Cruz of Brazil, and U.S. Army surgeon Walter Reed, scientists sought to destroy the mosquito in its larval stage, before it became an egg-laying adult.

Nothing less than U.S. dominance in the hemisphere seemed at stake. U.S. diplomats, military officers, and business executives agreed with foundation officials that the disease threatened public health, which in turn disturbed political and economic order. When outbreaks occurred, ports were closed and quarantined, disrupting trade and immigration. The infection struck down American officials, merchants, investors, and soldiers stationed abroad. Workers became incapacitated, reducing productivity. Throughout Latin America, insufficient official attention to yellow-fever epidemics stirred public discontent against regimes the United States supported. When the Panama Canal opened its gates to ships from around the world in 1914, some leaders feared that the death-dealing disease would spread, even reinfecting the United States, which had suffered its last epidemic in 1905.

In Veracruz, a Mexican province of significant U.S. economic activity, where American troops had invaded in 1914, a yellow-fever outbreak in 1920 killed 235 people. The next year, gradually overcoming strong local anti-U.S. feelings, Rockefeller personnel

◀ **Officials of the Brazilian Federal Health Service, in cooperation with the Rockefeller Foundation, spray houses in Bahía to control mosquitoes during a campaign in the 1920s to battle yellow fever.**
(Courtesy of the Rockefeller Archive Center)

CHRONOLOGY

1921–22 ■ Washington Conference limits naval arms
■ Rockefeller Foundation begins battle against yellow fever in Latin America

1922 ■ Mussolini comes to power in Italy

1924 ■ Dawes Plan eases German reparations

1928 ■ Kellogg-Briand Pact outlaws war

1929 ■ Great Depression begins
■ Young Plan reduces German reparations

1930 ■ Hawley-Smoot Tariff raises duties

1931 ■ Japan seizes Manchuria

1933 ■ Adolf Hitler becomes chancellor of Germany
■ United States extends diplomatic recognition to Soviet Union
■ United States announces Good Neighbor policy for Latin America

1934 ■ Fulgencio Batista comes to power in Cuba

1935 ■ Italy invades Ethiopia
■ Congress passes first Neutrality Act

1936 ■ Germany reoccupies Rhineland
■ Spanish Civil War breaks out

1937 ■ Sino-Japanese War breaks out
■ Roosevelt makes "quarantine speech" against aggressors

1938 ■ Mexico nationalizes American-owned oil companies
■ Munich Conference grants part of Czechoslovakia to Germany

1939 ■ Germany and Soviet Union sign nonaggression pact
■ Germany invades Poland; Second World War begins

1940 ■ Germany invades Denmark, Norway, Belgium, the Netherlands, and France
■ Selective Training and Service Act starts first U.S. peacetime draft

1941 ■ Lend-Lease Act gives aid to Allies
■ Germany attacks Soviet Union
■ United States freezes Japanese assets
■ Roosevelt and Churchill sign Atlantic Charter
■ Japanese flotilla attacks Pearl Harbor, Hawai'i; United States enters Second World War

painstakingly inspected breeding places in houses and deposited larvae-eating fish in public waterworks. In 1924 La Fundación Rockefeller declared yellow fever eradicated in Mexico. Elsewhere in Latin America, the foundation's antimosquito campaign proved successful in maritime and urban areas but less so in rural and jungle regions. Rockefeller Foundation efforts in the 1920s and 1930s also carried political effects: strengthening central governments by providing a national public health infrastructure and helping diminish anti-U.S. sentiment in a region known for virulent anti-Yankeeism.

The Rockefeller Foundation's drive to eradicate the mosquito offers insights into Americans' fervent but futile effort to build a stable international order after the First World War. The United States did not cut itself off from international affairs, despite the tag "isolationist" which is sometimes still applied to U.S. foreign relations during the interwar decades. Americans remained very active in world affairs in the 1920s and 1930s—from gunboats on Chinese rivers, to negotiations in European financial centers, to marine occupations in Haiti and Nicaragua, to oil wells in the Middle East, to campaigns against diseases in Africa and Latin America. President Wilson had it right when he said after the First World War that the United States had "become a determining factor in the history of mankind, and after you have become a determining factor you cannot remain isolated, whether you want to or not."

Even so, a majority of Americans came out of World War I deeply suspicious of foreign entanglements, of using collective action to address the world's ills. The most apt description of interwar U.S. foreign policy is "independent internationalism." In other words, the United States was active on a global scale but retained its independence of action, its traditional unilateralism. Notwithstanding the nation's far-flung overseas projects—colonies, spheres of influence, naval bases, investments, trade, missionary activity, humanitarian projects—many Americans did think of themselves as isolationists, by which they meant that they wanted no part of Europe's political squabbles, military alliances and interventions, or the League of Nations, which might drag them unwillingly into war. More internationalist-minded Americans—a group that included most senior officials—were equally desirous of staying out of any future European war but were more willing than isolationists to work to shape the world to their liking.

Such a world would be peaceful and stable, the better to facilitate American prosperity and security. In the interwar years, American diplomats increasingly sought to exercise the power of the United States through conferences, humanitarian programs, cultural penetration ("Americanization"), moral lectures and calls for peace, nonrecognition of disapproved regimes, arms control, and economic and financial ties under the Open Door principle. In Latin America, for example, U.S. leaders downgraded military interventions to fashion a Good Neighbor policy.

But a stable world order proved elusive. Some nations schemed to disrupt it, and severe economic problems undercut it. Public health projects saved countless lives but could not address the low living standards and staggering poverty of dependent peoples around the globe. The debts and reparations bills left over from the First World War bedeviled the 1920s, and the Great Depression of the 1930s shattered world trade and finance. The depression threatened America's prominence in international markets; it also spawned totalitarianism and political extremism, militarism, and war in Europe and Asia. As Nazi Germany marched toward world war, the United States tried to protect itself from the conflict by adopting a policy of neutrality. At the same time, the United States sought to defend its interests in Asia against Japanese aggression by invoking the Open Door policy.

In the late 1930s, and especially after the outbreak of European war in September 1939, many Americans came to agree with President Franklin D. Roosevelt that Germany and Japan imperiled the U.S. national interest because they were building exclusive, self-sufficient spheres of influence based on military power and economic domination. Roosevelt first pushed for American military preparedness and then for the abandonment of neutrality in favor of aiding Britain and France. A German victory in Europe, he reasoned, would undermine western political principles, destroy traditional economic ties, threaten U.S. influence in the Western Hemisphere, and place at the pinnacle of European power a fanatical man—Adolf Hitler—whose ambitions and barbarities seemed limitless.

At the same time, Japan seemed determined to dismember America's Asian friend China, to destroy the Open Door principle by creating a closed economic sphere in Asia, and to endanger a U.S. colony—the Philippines. To deter Japanese expansion in the Pacific, the United States ultimately cut off supplies of vital American products, such as oil. But economic warfare only intensified antagonisms. Japan's surprise attack on Pearl Harbor, Hawai'i, in December 1941 finally brought the United States into the Second World War.

- Why and by what means did Americans try to facilitate a stable world order in the interwar period?
- How did the Roosevelt administration respond to the growing Nazi German threat in the second half of the 1930s?
- Why did the United States enter World War II?

SEARCHING FOR PEACE AND ORDER IN THE 1920S

The First World War left Europe in a shambles. Between 1914 and 1921, Europe suffered tens of millions of casualties from world war, civil wars, massacres, epidemics, and famine. Germany and France both lost 10 percent of their workers. Crops, livestock, factories, trains, forests, bridges—little was spared. The American Relief Administration and private charities delivered food to needy Europeans, including Russians wracked by famine in 1921 and 1922. Americans hoped not only to feed desperate Europeans but also to dampen any appeal political radicalism might have for them. As Secretary of State Charles Evans Hughes put it in the early 1920s, "There will be no permanent peace unless economic satisfactions are enjoyed." Hughes and other leaders expected American economic expansion to promote international stability—that is, out of economic prosperity would spring a world free from ideological extremes, revolution, arms races, aggression, and war.

Collective security, as envisioned by Woodrow Wilson (see page 670), elicited far less enthusiasm among Hughes and other Republican leaders. Senator Henry Cabot Lodge gloated in 1920 that "we have destroyed Mr. Wilson's League of Nations and . . . we have torn up Wilsonism by the roots." Not quite. The Geneva-headquartered League of Nations, envisioned as a peacemaker, did prove feeble, not just because the United States did not join, but also because members failed to utilize the new organization to settle important disputes. Still, starting in the mid-1920s, American officials participated discreetly in League meetings on public health, prostitution, drug and arms trafficking, counterfeiting of currency, and other questions. American jurists served on the Permanent Court of International Justice (World Court), though the United States also refused to join that League body. The Rockefeller Foundation, meanwhile, donated $100,000 a year to the League to support its work in public health.

Wilson's legacy was felt in other ways as well. In the United States, peace societies worked for international stability, many of them keeping alive the Wilsonian preference for a world body. During the interwar years, peace groups, such as the

Peace Groups

Fellowship of Reconciliation and the National Council for Prevention of War, drew widespread public support. Women peace advocates gravitated to several of their own organizations because they lacked influence in the male-dominated groups and because of the popular assumption that women—as life givers and nurturing mothers—had a unique aversion to violence and war. Carrie Chapman Catt's moderate National Conference on the Cure and Cause of War, formed in 1924, and the more radical U.S. section of the Women's International League for Peace and Freedom (WILPF), organized in 1915 under the leadership of Jane Addams and Emily Greene Balch, became the largest women's peace groups. When Addams won the Nobel Peace Prize in 1931, she transferred her award money to the League of Nations.

Most peace groups pointed to the carnage of the First World War and the futility of war as a solution to international problems, but they differed over strategies to ensure world order. Some urged cooperation with the League of Nations and the World Court. Others championed the arbitration of disputes, disarmament and arms reduction, the outlawing of war, and strict neutrality during wars. The WILPF called for an end to U.S. economic imperialism, which, the organization claimed, compelled the United States to intervene militarily in Latin America to protect U.S. business interests. The Women's Peace Union (organized in 1921) lobbied for a constitutional amendment to require a national referendum on a declaration of war. The Carnegie Endowment for International Peace (founded in 1910) promoted peace education through publications. Quakers, YMCA officials, and Social Gospel clergy in 1917 created the American Friends Service Committee to identify pacifist alternatives to warmaking. All in all, peaceseekers believed that their various reform activities could and must deliver a world without war.

War Is a Crime Against Humanity

Gassed ; Near Dun-sur-Meuse, in the Woods, France

To you who are filled with horror at the sufferings of war-ridden mankind ;

To you who remember that ten million men were slaughtered in the last war ;

To you who have the courage to face the reality of war, stripped of its sentimental "glory" ;

We make this appeal :—

Eight years since the signing of the Armistice! And peace is still hard beset by preparations for war. In another war men, women and children would be more wantonly, more cruelly massacred, by death rays, gas, disease germs, and machines more fiendish than those used in the last war. Those whom you love must share in its universal destruction.

Can You Afford Not To Give Your Utmost To Cleanse The World Of This Black Plague Of Needless Death and Suffering?

Send your contribution to an uncompromising Peace organization

THE WOMEN'S PEACE UNION
39 Pearl Street, New York

▲ The Women's Peace Union (WPU) distributed this flier in the 1920s to remind Americans of the human costs of the First World War. One of many peace societies active in the interwar years, the WPU lobbied for a constitutional amendment requiring a national referendum on a declaration of war. In the 1930s, Representative Louis Ludlow (Democrat from Indiana) worked to pass such a measure in Congress, but he failed.

(Schwimmer-Lloyd Collection, Freida Langer Lazarus Papers. The New York Public Library, Astor, Lenox, and Tilden Foundations)

Peace advocates influenced Warren G. Harding's administration to convene the Washington Naval Conference of November 1921–February 1922. Delegates from Britain, Japan, France, Italy, China, Portugal, Belgium, and the Netherlands joined a U.S. team led by Secretary of State Charles Evans Hughes to discuss limits on naval armaments. Britain, the United States, and Japan were fac-

Washington Naval Conference

▲ French foreign minister Aristide Briand (1862–1932) *(left)* and U.S. secretary of state Charles Evans Hughes (1862–1948) join other diplomats at the Washington Naval Conference of 1921–1922, where they negotiated a naval arms control agreement. Years later, Briand helped craft the Kellogg-Briand Pact outlawing war. A graduate of Brown University and Columbia Law School, Hughes also served on the Supreme Court at two different times: 1910–1916 (associate justice) and 1930–1941 (chief justice). Conservative and reserved (Theodore Roosevelt called him "the bearded iceberg"), Hughes argued that the United States must be internationalist, leading the world to respect law and order. *(National Archives)*

5:3:1.75). These totals were agreed to in the Five-Power Treaty, which also set a ten-year moratorium on the construction of capital ships (battleships and aircraft carriers). The governments also pledged not to build new fortifications in their Pacific possessions (such as the Philippines).

Next, the Nine-Power Treaty reaffirmed the Open Door in China, recognizing Chinese sovereignty. Finally, in the Four-Power Treaty, the United States, Britain, Japan, and France agreed to respect one another's Pacific possessions. The three treaties did not limit submarines, destroyers, or cruisers, nor did they provide enforcement powers for the Open Door declaration. Still, the conference was a major achievement for Hughes. He achieved genuine arms limitation and at the same time improved America's strategic position vis-à-vis Japan in the Pacific.

Peace advocates also welcomed the Locarno Pact of 1925, a set of agreements among European nations that sought to reduce tensions between Germany and France, and the Kellogg-Briand Pact of 1928. In the latter document, named for its chief promoters, U.S. secretary of state Frank B. Kellogg and French premier Aristide Briand, sixty-two nations agreed to "condemn recourse to war for the solution of international controversies, and renounce it as an instrument of national policy." The accord passed the Senate 85 to 1, but many lawmakers considered it little more than a statement of moral preference because it lacked enforcement provisions. Although weak—skeptics called it a mere "international kiss"—the Kellogg-Briand Pact reflected popular opinion that war was barbaric and wasteful, and the agreement stimulated serious public discussion of peace and war. But arms limitations, peace pacts, and efforts by peace groups and international institutions all failed to muzzle the dogs of war, which fed on the economic troubles that upended world order.

Kellogg-Briand Pact

ing a naval arms race whose huge military spending endangered economic rehabilitation. American leaders also worried that an expansionist Japan, with the world's third largest navy, would overtake the United States, ranked second behind Britain.

Hughes opened the conference by making a stunning announcement: he proposed to achieve real disarmament by offering to scrap thirty major U.S. ships, totaling 846,000 tons. He then turned to the shocked British and Japanese delegations and urged them to do away with somewhat smaller amounts. The final limit, Hughes declared, should be 500,000 tons each for the Americans and the British; 300,000 tons for the Japanese; and 175,000 tons each for the French and the Italians (that is, a ratio of

THE WORLD ECONOMY, CULTURAL EXPANSION, AND GREAT DEPRESSION

While Europe struggled to recover from the ravages of the First World War, the international economy wobbled and then, in the early 1930s, collapsed. The Great Depression set off a political chain reaction that carried the world to war. Cordell Hull, secretary of state under President Franklin D. Roosevelt from 1933 to 1944, often pointed out that political extremism and militarism sprang from maimed economies. "We cannot have a peaceful

John D. Rockefeller Jr. (1874–1960) *(second from right)* traveled to China in 1921 for the dedication of the Peking Union Medical College, a project of the Rockefeller Foundation, the philanthropic organization founded in 1913 by oil industrialist John D. Rockefeller Sr. At the center of this photograph is Xu Shi Chang (1855–1939), China's president.

(Courtesy of the Rockefeller Archive Center)

world," he warned, "until we rebuild the international economic structure." Hull proved right.

For leaders like Hughes and Hull, who believed that economic expansion by the United States would stabilize world politics, America's prominent position in the international economy seemed opportune. Because of World War I, the United States became a creditor nation and the financial capital of the world (see Figure 26.1). From 1914 to 1930, private investments abroad grew fivefold, to more than $17 billion. By the late 1920s, the United States produced nearly half of the world's industrial goods and ranked first among exporters ($5.2 billion worth of shipments in 1929). For example, General Electric invested heavily in Germany, American companies began to exploit Venezuela's rich petroleum resources, and U.S. firms began to challenge British control of oil resources in the Middle East. Britain and Germany lost ground to American businesses in Latin America, where Standard Oil operated in eight nations and where the United Fruit Company became a huge landowner.

America's economic prominence facilitated the export of American culture. Hollywood movies saturated the global market and stimulated interest in American ways and products. In Britain, where American silent and talkie films dominated, one woman from a mining town recalled seeing on the screen "all these marvelous [American] film stars. Everything was bright. I just wanted to go there and be like them." Although some foreigners warned against Americanization, others aped American mass-production

Economic and Cultural Expansion

methods and emphasis on efficiency and modernization. Coca-Cola opened a bottling plant in Essen, Germany; Ford built an automobile assembly plant in Cologne; and General Motors built one for trucks near Berlin. German writer Hans Joachim claimed that this cultural adoption might help deliver a peaceful, democratic world because "our interest in elevators, radio towers, and jazz was . . . an attitude that wanted to convert the flame thrower into a vacuum cleaner."

Germans marveled at Henry Ford's economic success and industrial techniques ("Fordismus"), buying out copies of his translated autobiography, *My Life and Work* (1922). In the 1930s, Nazi leader Adolf Hitler sent German car designers to Detroit before he launched the Volkswagen. Further advertising the American capitalist model were the Phelps-Stokes Fund, exporting to black Africa Booker T. Washington's Tuskegee philosophy of education, and the Rockefeller Foundation, battling diseases in Latin America and Africa, supporting colleges to train doctors in Lebanon and China, and funding medical research and nurses' training in Europe.

The U.S. government assisted this cultural and economic expansion. The Webb-Pomerene Act (1918) excluded from antitrust prosecution those combinations set up for export trade; the Edge Act (1919) permitted American banks to open foreign-branch banks; and the overseas offices of the Department of Commerce gathered and disseminated valuable market information. The federal

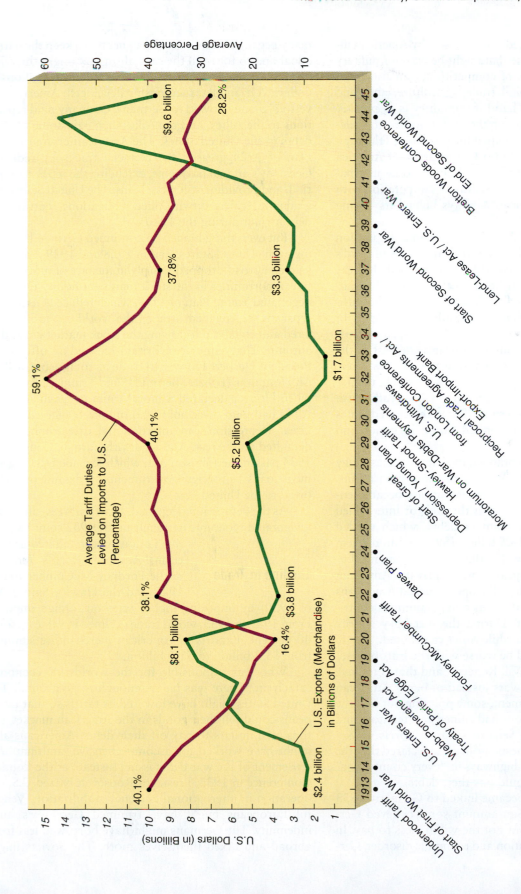

Figure 26.1   The United States in the World Economy

In the 1920s and 1930s, global depression and war scuttled the United States' hope for a stable economic order. This graph suggests, moreover, that high American tariffs meant lower exports, further impeding world trade. The Reciprocal Trade Agreements program initiated in the early 1930s was designed to ease tariff wars with other nations.

(Source: U.S. Bureau of the Census, Historical Statistics of the United States, Colonial Times to 1970 [Washington, D.C., 1975].)

government also stimulated foreign loans by American investors, discouraging those that might be used for military purposes. "In these days of competition," an American diplomat explained, "capital, trade, agriculture, labor, and statecraft all go hand in hand if a country is to profit." U.S. government support for the expansion of the telecommunications industry helped International Telegraph and Telephone (IT&T), Radio Corporation of America (RCA), and the Associated Press (AP) become international giants by 1930. The U.S. Navy's cooperation with Juan Trippe's Pan American Airways helped its "flying boats" reach Asia.

Europeans watched American economic expansion with wariness. Even as they snapped up copies of Ford's autobiography, many old-world elites worried that the populist consumerism that he and other U.S. industrialists championed portended social upheaval and the withering of established habits. As a result, the prospect of mass consumerism became a politically charged class issue. When the French Popular Front government in the 1930s sought to raise the purchasing power of workers through wage increases and a shorter workweek, the notion was condemned by conservatives for its radicalism and revolutionary spirit—a spirit that in the United States had generated a consumption-led boom in goods and services in the 1920s.

Some Europeans also branded the United States stingy for its handling of World War I debts and reparations.

War Debts and German Reparations

Twenty-eight nations became entangled in the web of inter-Allied government debts, which totaled $26.5 billion ($9.6 billion of them owed to the U.S. government). Europeans owed private American creditors another $3 billion. Europeans urged Americans to erase the government debts as a magnanimous contribution to the war effort. During the war, they angrily charged, Europe had bled while America profited. "There is only one way we could be worse with the Europeans," remarked the humorist Will Rogers, "and that is to have helped them out in two wars instead of one." American leaders insisted on repayment, some pointing out that the victorious European nations had gained vast territory and resources as war spoils. Senator George Norris of Nebraska, emphasizing domestic priorities, declared that the United States could build highways in "every county seat" if only the Europeans would pay their debts.

The debts question became linked to Germany's $33 billion reparations bill—an amount some believed Germany had the capacity but not the willingness to pay. In any case, hobbled by inflation and economic disorder, Germany began to default on its payments. To keep the nation afloat and to forestall the radicalism that might thrive on economic troubles, American bankers loaned millions of dollars. A triangular relationship developed: American investors' money flowed to Germany, Germany paid reparations to the Allies, and the Allies then paid some of their debts to the United States. The American-crafted Dawes Plan of 1924 greased the financial tracks by reducing Germany's annual payments, extending the repayment period, and providing still more loans. The United States also gradually scaled down Allied obligations, cutting the debt by half during the 1920s.

But everything hinged on continued German borrowing in the United States, and in 1928 and 1929 American lending abroad dropped sharply in the face of more lucrative opportunities in the stock market at home. The U.S.-negotiated Young Plan of 1929, which reduced Germany's reparations, salvaged little as the world economy sputtered and collapsed following the stock market crash that autumn. That same year, Britain rejected an offer from President Herbert Hoover to trade its total debt for British Honduras (Belize), Bermuda, and Trinidad. By 1931, when Hoover declared a moratorium on payments, the Allies had paid back only $2.6 billion. Staggered by the Great Depression—an international catastrophe—they defaulted on the rest. Annoyed with Europe, Congress in 1934 passed the Johnson Act, which forbade U.S. government loans to foreign governments in default on debts owed to the United States.

As the depression deepened, tariff wars revealed a reinvigorated economic nationalism. By 1932 some twenty-five nations had retaliated against rising American tariffs (created in the Fordney-McCumber Act of 1922 and the Hawley-Smoot Act of 1930) by imposing higher rates on foreign imports. From 1929 to 1933, world trade declined in value by some 40 percent. Exports of American merchandise slumped from $5.2 billion to $1.7 billion.

Decline in Trade

Who was responsible for the worldwide economic cataclysm? There was blame enough to go around. The United States might have lowered its tariffs so that Europeans could sell their goods in the American market and thus earn dollars to pay off their debts. Americans also might have worked for a comprehensive, multinational settlement of the war debts issue. Instead, at the London Conference in 1933, President Roosevelt barred U.S. cooperation in international currency stabilization. Vengeful Europeans might have trimmed Germany's huge indemnity. The Germans might have borrowed less from abroad and taxed themselves more. The Soviets might have agreed to pay rather than repudiate Russia's $4 billion debt.

For Secretary of State Hull, finding a way out of the crisis depended on reviving world trade. Increased trade, he insisted, would not only help the United States pull itself out of the economic doldrums but also boost the chances for global peace. Calling the protective tariff the "king of evils," he successfully pressed Congress to pass the Reciprocal Trade Agreements Act in 1934. This important legislation empowered the president to reduce U.S. tariffs by as much as 50 percent through special agreements with foreign countries. The central feature of the act was the most-favored-nation principle, whereby the United States was entitled to the lowest tariff rate set by any nation with which it had an agreement. If, for example, Belgium and the United States granted each other most-favored-nation status, and Belgium then negotiated an agreement with Germany that reduced the Belgian tariff on German typewriters, American typewriters would receive the same low rate.

In 1934 Hull also helped create the Export-Import Bank, a government agency that provided loans to foreigners for the purchase of American goods. The bank stimulated trade and became a diplomatic weapon, allowing the United States to exact concessions through the approval or denial of loans. But in the short term, Hull's ambitious programs—examples of America's independent internationalism—brought only mixed results.

Economic imperatives also lay behind another major policy decision in these years: the move by the Roosevelt administration to extend diplomatic recognition to the Soviet Union. Throughout the 1920s the Republicans had refused to open diplomatic relations with the Soviet government, which had failed to pay $600 million for confiscated American-owned property and had repudiated preexisting Russian debts. To many Americans, the communists ranked as godless, radical malcontents bent on destroying the American way of life through world revolution. Nonetheless, in the late 1920s American businesses, such as General Electric and International Harvester, entered the Soviet marketplace, and Henry Ford signed a contract to build an automobile plant there. By 1930 the Soviet Union had become the largest buyer of American farm and industrial equipment.

Upon entering the White House, Roosevelt concluded that nonrecognition had failed to alter the Soviet system, and he speculated that closer Soviet-American relations might help the economy and also deter Japanese expansion. In 1933 Roosevelt granted U.S. diplomatic recogni-

U.S. Recognition of the Soviet Union

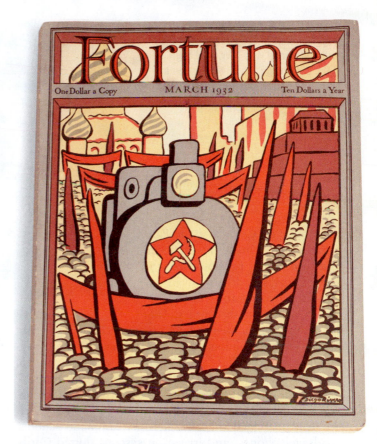

▲ In the early 1930s, treatments of the Soviet Union in the American press were generally mild and polite. The March 1932 issue of Henry Luce's *Fortune* magazine, appearing a year before the U.S. government extended recognition to the Soviet Union, featured this cover illustration by Diego Rivera and a special thirty-page section entitled "Russia, Russia, Russia." One appendix explicated the teachings of Karl Marx, while another listed dozens of U.S. businesses that had sold more than $1 million worth of goods to the Soviet Union in 1930, among them Ford, Westinghouse, Caterpillar, John Deere, American Express, and RCA. *(The Michael Barson Collection/Past Perfect)*

tion to the Soviet Union in return for Soviet agreement to discuss the debts question, to forgo subversive activities in the United States, and to grant Americans in the Soviet Union religious freedom and legal rights.

U.S. DOMINANCE IN LATIN AMERICA

One of the assumptions behind Hughes's Washington Treaty system of 1921–1922 was that certain powers would be responsible for maintaining order in their regions—Japan in East Asia, for example, and the United States in Latin America. Through the Platt Amendment,

Among the U.S. companies with large holdings in Latin America in the interwar period was F. W. McLaughlin & Co. of Chicago. Here, workers on a private company wharf in Santos, Brazil, prepare to load coffee for shipment to the United States.

(© Curt Teich Postcard Archives, Lake County Museum)

PRIVATE WHARF, W. F. McLAUGHLIN & CO., SANTOS, BRAZIL.

the Roosevelt Corollary, the Panama Canal, military intervention, and economic preeminence the United States had thrown an imperial net over Latin America in the early twentieth century. U.S. dominance in the hemisphere grew apace after the First World War. A prominent State Department officer patronizingly remarked that Latin Americans were incapable of political progress because of their "low racial quality." They were, however, "very easy people to deal with if properly managed."

And managed they were. American-made schools, roads, telephones, and irrigation systems dotted Caribbean and Central American nations. American "money doctors" in Colombia and Peru helped reform tariff and tax laws, and invited U.S. companies to build public works. Washington forced private high-interest loans on the Dominican Republic and Haiti as ways to wield influence there. In El Salvador, Honduras, and Costa Rica, the State Department pressed governments to silence anti-imperialist intellectuals. For a time, Republican administrations curtailed U.S. military intervention in the hemisphere, withdrawing troops from the Dominican Republic (1924) and Nicaragua (1925) that had been committed in the previous decade. But the marines returned to Nicaragua in 1926 to end fighting between conservative and liberal Nicaraguans and to protect American property. In Haiti, the U.S. troop commitment made under Woodrow Wilson in 1915 lasted until 1934, with the soldiers there to keep pro-Washington governments in power. All the while, U.S. authorities maintained Puerto Rico as a colony (see Map 26.1).

By 1929 direct American investments in Latin America (excluding bonds and securities) totaled $3.5 billion, and U.S. exports dominated the trade of the area. Country after country experienced the repercussions of U.S. economic and political decisions.

American Economic Muscle

For example, the price that Americans set for Chilean copper determined the health of Chile's economy. North American oil executives bribed Venezuelan politicians for tax breaks.

Latin American nationalists protested that their resources were being drained away as profits for U.S. companies, leaving too many nations in a disadvantageous position. A distinguished Argentine writer, Manuel Ugarte, asserted that the United States had become a new Rome, which annexed wealth rather than territory, and that unapologetic Americans believed they were bringing not only material improvements but also the blessings of liberty to Latin American neighbors.

Criticism of U.S. imperialism in the region mounted in the interwar years. In 1928, at the Havana Inter-American conference, U.S. officials unsuccessfully tried to kill a resolution stating that "no state has a right to intervene in the internal affairs of another." Two years later, a prominent Chilean newspaper warned that the American "Colossus" had "financial might" without "equal in history" and that its aim was "Americas for the Americans— of the North." In the United States, Senator William Borah of Idaho urged that Latin Americans be granted the right of self-determination, letting them decide their own futures. Business leaders feared that Latin American nationalists would direct their anti-Yankee feelings against American-owned property. Some Americans also became troubled by the double standard that prevailed. Hoover's secretary of state, Henry L. Stimson, acknowledged the problem in 1932 when he was protesting Japanese incursions in China: "If we landed a single soldier among those South Americans now . . . it would put me absolutely in the wrong in China, where Japan has done all

Map 26.1   The United States and Latin America Between the Wars

The United States often intervened in other nations to maintain its hegemonic power in Latin America, where nationalists resented outside meddling in their sovereign affairs. The Good Neighbor policy decreased U.S. military interventions, but U.S. economic interests remained strong in the hemisphere.

this monstrous work under the guise of protecting her nationals with a landing force."

Renouncing unpopular military intervention, the United States shifted to other methods to maintain its influence in Latin America: Pan-Americanism (a concept dating back some fifty years, which aimed to bring about closer ties between North and South America); support for strong local leaders; the training of national guards; economic and cultural penetration; Export-Import Bank loans; financial supervision; and political subversion. Although this general approach predated his presidency, Franklin Roosevelt gave it a name in 1933: the Good Neighbor policy. It meant that the United States would be less blatant in its domination—less willing to defend exploitative business practices, less eager to launch military expeditions, and less reluctant to consult with Latin Americans.

Good Neighbor Policy

"Give them a share," Roosevelt said, as he took several measures to show he meant business. Most notably, he ordered home the U.S. military forces that had been stationed in Haiti (since 1915) and Nicaragua (since 1912, with a hiatus in 1925–1926), and he restored some sovereignty to Panama and increased that nation's income from the canal. Such acts greatly enhanced Roosevelt's popularity in Latin America, and his image was further boosted when, in a series of pan-American conferences, he joined in pledging that no nation in the hemisphere would intervene in the "internal or external affairs" of any other.

Here Roosevelt promised more than he was prepared to deliver. His administration continued to support and bolster dictators in the region, believing that they would promote stability and preserve U.S. economic interests. ("He may be an S.O.B.," Roosevelt supposedly remarked of the Dominican Republic's ruthless leader Rafael Leonidas Trujillo, "but he is our S.O.B.") And, when a revolution brought a radical government to power in Cuba in 1933, FDR proved unwilling to let the matter be. Although he refrained from sending U.S. ground troops to Cuba, he instructed the American ambassador in Havana to work with conservative Cubans to replace the new government with a regime more friendly to U.S. interests. With Washington's support, army sergeant Fulgencio Batista took power in 1934.

During the Batista era, which lasted until Fidel Castro dethroned Batista in 1959, Cuba attracted and protected U.S. investments while it aligned itself with U.S. foreign policy goals. In return, the United States provided military aid and Export-Import Bank loans, abrogated the unpopular Platt Amendment, and gave Cuban sugar a favored position in the U.S. market. Cuba became further incorporated into the North American consumer culture, and American tourists flocked to Havana's nightlife of rum, rhumba, prostitution, and gambling. Nationalistic Cubans protested that their nation had become a mere extension—a dependency—of the United States.

In Mexico, Roosevelt again showed a level of restraint that his predecessors had lacked. Since Woodrow Wilson sent troops to Mexico in 1914 and again in 1916, U.S.-Mexican relations had endured several difficult periods as the two governments wrangled over the rights of U.S. economic interests. Still, throughout the post–World War I period the United States stood as Mexico's chief trading partner, accounting for 61 percent of Mexico's imports and taking 52 percent of its exports in 1934. That year, however, a new government under Lázaro Cárdenas pledged "Mexico for the Mexicans" and promptly strengthened trade unions so they could strike against foreign corporations.

Clash with Mexican Nationalism

In 1937 workers struck foreign oil companies for higher wages and recognition, but the companies, including Standard Oil, rejected union appeals, hoping to send a message across the hemisphere that economic nationalism could never succeed. In a statement of economic independence the following year, the Cárdenas government boldly expropriated the property of all foreign-owned petroleum companies, calculating that the approaching war in Europe would restrain the United States from attacking Mexico. The United States countered by reducing purchases of Mexican silver and promoting a multinational business boycott against the nation. But Roosevelt rejected appeals from some business leaders that he intervene militarily and instead decided to compromise, in part because he feared that the Mexicans would increase oil sales to Germany and Japan. Negotiations were long and difficult, but in 1942 an agreement was reached whereby the United States conceded that Mexico owned its raw materials and could treat them as it saw fit, and Mexico compensated the companies for their lost property.

All in all, then, under Roosevelt the Good Neighbor policy can be said to have gone a considerable distance toward living up to its name—or at least the United States was now a Markedly Better Neighbor. Even as it remained the dominant power in the hemisphere, its newfound restraint created hopes among Latin Americans that a new era had dawned. Yet the more sober-minded nationalists in the region knew that Washington might be acting differently were it not for the deepening tensions in Europe and

◄ Ambassador Josephus Daniels (1862–1948) *(second from left)* and Mexican president Lázaro Cárdenas (1895–1970) *(second from right)* enjoy a cordial moment during the often stormy relations between the United States and Mexico in the 1930s. When Cárdenas attempted to regain control of his nation's oil resources from multinational corporations through expropriation, Daniels defended him as a "New Dealer" seeking to improve his country's living standards. Accepting Daniels's description and calling Cárdenas "one of the few Latin leaders who was actually preaching and trying to practice democracy," President Roosevelt compromised with Mexico in 1941.

(Library of Congress)

Asia. These threats created a sense that all the nations in the Western Hemisphere should stand together.

THE COURSE TO WAR IN EUROPE

The main threat came from a revitalized Germany. On March 5, 1933, one day after the inauguration of Franklin Roosevelt, Germany's parliament granted dictatorial powers to the new chancellor, Adolf Hitler, leader of the Nazi Party. The act marked the culmination of a stunning rise to power for Hitler, whose Nazis very likely would have remained a fringe party had the Great Depression not hit Germany with such force. Production plummeted 40 percent, and unemployment ballooned to 6 million, meaning that two workers out of five did not have jobs. Together with a disintegrating banking system, which robbed millions of their savings, as well as widespread resentment among Germans over the Versailles peace settlement, the plummeting employment figures brought mass discontent to the country. While the communists preached a workers' revolution, German business executives and property owners threw their support to Hitler and the Nazis, many of them believing they could manipulate him once he had thwarted the communists. They were wrong.

Like Benito Mussolini, who had gained control of Italy in 1922, Hitler was a fascist. Fascism (called Nazism, or National Socialism, in Germany) was a collection of ideas and prejudices that celebrated supremacy of the state over the individual; of dictatorship over democracy; of authoritarianism over freedom of speech; of a regulated, state-oriented economy over a free-market economy; and of militarism and war over peace. The Nazis vowed not only to revive German economic and military strength but also to cripple communism and "purify" the German "race" by destroying Jews and other people, such as homosexuals and Gypsies, whom Hitler disparaged as inferiors. The Nuremberg Laws of 1935 stripped Jews of citizenship and outlawed intermarriage with Germans. Teachers, doctors, and other professionals could not practice their craft, and half of all German Jews were without work.

Determined to get Germany out from under the Versailles treaty system, Hitler withdrew Germany from the League of Nations, ended reparations payments, and began to rearm. While secretly laying plans for the conquest of neighboring states, he watched admiringly as Mussolini's troops invaded the African nation of Ethiopia in 1935. The next year Hitler ordered his own goose-stepping troopers into the Rhineland, an area that the Versailles treaty had demilitarized. When Germany's timid neighbor France did not resist this act, Hitler crowed, "The world belongs to the man with guts!"

Soon the aggressors joined hands. In 1936 Italy and Germany formed an alliance called the Rome-Berlin Axis. Shortly thereafter, Germany and Japan united against the Soviet Union in the Anti-Comintern Pact. To these events Britain and France responded with a policy

German Aggression Under Hitler

of appeasement, hoping to curb Hitler's expansionist appetite by permitting him a few territorial nibbles. The policy of appeasing Hitler, though not altogether unreasonable in terms of what could be known at the time, proved disastrous, for the hate-filled German leader continually raised his demands.

Hitler also made his presence felt in Spain, where a civil war broke out in 1936. Beginning in July, the Loyalists defended Spain's elected republican government against Francisco Franco's fascist movement. The U.S. government was officially neutral, but about three thousand American volunteers, known as the Abraham Lincoln Battalion of the "International Brigades," joined the fight on the side of the Loyalist republicans, which also had the backing of the Soviet Union. Many American Catholics, meanwhile, believed Franco would promote social stability and therefore should be supported, a view also held by some State Department officials. Hitler and Mussolini sent military aid to Franco, who won in 1939, tightening the grip of fascism on the European continent.

Early in 1938, Hitler once again tested the limits of European tolerance when he sent soldiers into Austria to annex the nation of his birth. Then, in September, he seized the largely German-speaking Sudeten region of Czechoslovakia. Appeasement reached its apex that month when France and Britain, without consulting the Czechs, agreed at Munich to allow Hitler this territorial bite, in exchange for a pledge that he would not take more. British prime minister Neville Chamberlain returned home to proclaim "peace in our time," confident that Hitler was satiated. In March 1939 Hitler swallowed the rest of Czechoslovakia (see Map 26.3).

Americans had watched this buildup of tension in Europe with apprehension. Many sought to distance

Isolationist Views in the United States

themselves from the tumult by embracing isolationism, whose key elements were abhorrence of war and fervent opposition to U.S. alliances with other nations. Americans had learned powerful negative lessons from the First World War: that war damages reform movements, undermines civil liberties, dangerously expands federal and presidential power, disrupts the economy, and accentuates racial and class tensions. A 1937 Gallup poll found that nearly two-thirds of the respondents thought U.S. participation in World War I had been a mistake.

Conservative isolationists feared higher taxes and increased executive power if the nation went to war again. Liberal isolationists worried that domestic problems might go unresolved as the nation spent more on the military. Many isolationists predicted that, in attempting to spread

democracy abroad or to police the world, Americans would lose their freedoms at home. The vast majority of isolationists opposed fascism and condemned aggression, but they did not think the United States should have to do what Europeans themselves refused to do: block Hitler. Isolationist sentiment was strongest in the Midwest and among anti-British ethnic groups, especially Americans of German or Irish descent, but it was a nationwide phenomenon that cut across socioeconomic, ethnic, party, and sectional lines, and it attracted a majority of the American people.

Some isolationists charged that corporate "merchants of death" had promoted war and were assisting the aggressors. A congressional commit-

Nye Committee Hearings

tee headed by Senator Gerald P. Nye held hearings from 1934 to 1936 on the role of business and financiers in the U.S. decision to enter the First World War. The Nye committee did not prove that American munitions makers had dragged the nation into that war, but it did uncover evidence that corporations practicing "rotten commercialism" had bribed foreign politicians to bolster arms sales in the 1920s and 1930s, and had lobbied against arms control.

Isolationists grew suspicious of American business ties with Nazi Germany and fascist Italy which might endanger U.S. neutrality. Twenty-six of the top one hundred American corporations, including DuPont, Standard Oil, and General Motors, had contractual agreements in 1937 with German firms. And after Italy attacked Ethiopia in 1935, American petroleum, copper, scrap iron, and steel exports to Italy increased substantially, despite Roosevelt's call for a moral embargo on such commerce. A Dow Chemical official stated, "We do not inquire into the uses of the products. We are interested in selling them." Not all American executives thought this way. The Wall Street law firm of Sullivan and Cromwell, for example, severed lucrative ties with Germany to protest the Nazi persecution of Jews.

Reflecting the popular desire for distance from Europe's disputes, Roosevelt signed a series of neutrality acts. Congress sought to protect the nation by outlawing the kinds of contacts that had compromised U.S. neutrality during World War I. The Neutrality Act of 1935 prohibited arms shipments to either side in a war, once the president had declared the existence of belligerency. Roosevelt had wanted the authority to name the aggressor and apply an arms embargo against it alone, but Congress would not grant the president such discretionary power. The Neutrality Act of 1936 forbade loans to belligerents. After a joint resolution in 1937 declared the United States neutral in the Spanish Civil War, Roosevelt embargoed arms shipments to both sides. The Neutrality Act of 1937 introduced the cash-and-carry principle: warring nations wishing to trade with the United States would have to pay cash for their nonmilitary purchases and carry the goods from U.S. ports in their own ships. The act also forbade Americans from traveling on the ships of belligerent nations.

President Roosevelt shared isolationist views in the early 1930s. Although prior to World War I he was an

|||||||||||||||||||||||||||||||
Roosevelt's Evolving Views

expansionist and interventionist like his older cousin Theodore, during the interwar period FDR talked less about preparedness and more about disarmament and the horrors of war, less about policing the world and more about handling problems at home. In a passionate speech delivered in August 1936 at Chautauqua, New York, Roosevelt expressed prevailing isolationist opinion and made a pitch for the pacifist vote in the upcoming election: "I have seen war. . . . I have seen blood running from the wounded. I have seen men coughing out their gassed lungs. . . . I have seen the agony of mothers and wives. I hate war." The United States, he promised, would remain unentangled in the European conflict. During the crisis over Czechoslovakia in 1938, Roosevelt endorsed appeasement and greeted the Munich accord with a "universal sense of relief."

All the while, Roosevelt grew troubled by the arrogant behavior of Germany, Italy, and Japan—aggressors that he tagged the "three bandit nations." He condemned the Nazi persecution of the Jews and Japan's expansionist actions in East Asia. Privately he chastised the British and French for failing to collar Hitler. Yet he himself also moved cautiously in confronting the German leader. In November 1938, Hitler launched *Kristallnacht* (or "Crystal Night," so named for the shattered glass that littered the streets after the attack on Jewish synagogues, businesses, and homes) and sent tens of thousands of Jews to concentration camps. Roosevelt expressed his shock, recalled the U.S. ambassador to Germany, and allowed 15,000 refugees on visitor permits to remain longer in the United States. But he would not do more, such as break trade relations with Hitler or push Congress to loosen tough immigration laws enacted in the 1920s. Congress, for its part, rejected all measures, including a bill to admit 20,000 children under the age of fourteen. Motivated by economic concerns and widespread anti-Semitism, more than 80 percent of Americans supported Congress's decision to uphold immigration restrictions.

Even the tragic voyage of the *St. Louis* did not change government policy. The vessel left Hamburg in mid-1939 carrying 930 desperate Jewish refugees who lacked proper immigration documents. Denied entry to Havana, the *St. Louis* headed for Miami, where Coast Guard cutters prevented it from docking. The ship was forced to return to Europe. Some of those refugees took shelter in countries that later were overrun by Hitler's legions. "The cruise of the *St. Louis*," wrote the *New York Times*, "cries to high heaven of man's inhumanity to man."

Quietly, though, Roosevelt had begun moving to ready the country for war. In early 1938 he successfully pressured the House of Representatives to defeat a constitutional amendment proposed by Indiana Democrat Louis Ludlow to require a majority vote in a national referendum before a congressional declaration of war could go into effect (unless the United States were attacked). Later that year, in the wake of the Munich crisis, Roosevelt asked Congress for funds to build up the air force, which he believed essential to deter aggression. In January 1939 the president secretly decided to sell bombers to France, saying privately that "our frontier is on the Rhine." Although

▲ German leader Adolf Hitler (1889–1945) is surrounded in this propagandistic painting by images that came to symbolize hate, genocide, and war: Nazi flags with emblems of the swastika, the iron cross on the dictator's pocket, Nazi troops in loyal salute. The anti-Semitic Hitler denounced the United States as a "Jewish rubbish heap" of "inferiority and decadence" that was "incapable of conducting war." *(U.S. Army Center of Military History)*

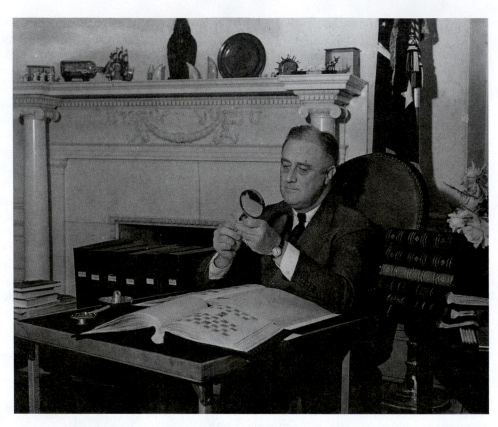

President Franklin D. Roosevelt relaxes with his favorite hobby, stamp collecting, from which he said he learned history and geography. During World War II he once showed British prime minister Winston Churchill a stamp from "one of your colonies." Churchill asked, "Which one?" Roosevelt replied, "One of your last. . . . You won't have them much longer, you know."

(Franklin D. Roosevelt Library)

the more than five hundred combat planes delivered to France did not deter war, French orders spurred growth of the U.S. aircraft industry.

For Roosevelt and for other Western leaders, Hitler's swallowing of the whole of Czechoslovakia in March 1939 proved a turning point, forcing them to face a stark new reality. Until now, they had been able to explain away Hitler's actions by saying he was only trying to reunite German-speaking peoples. That argument no longer worked. Leaders in Paris and London realized that, if the German leader was to be stopped, it would have to be by force. When Hitler began eyeing his neighbor Poland, London and Paris announced they would stand by the Poles. Undaunted, Berlin signed a nonaggression pact with Moscow in August 1939. Soviet leader Joseph Stalin believed that the West's appeasement of Hitler had left him no choice but to cut a deal with Berlin. But Stalin also coveted territory: a top-secret protocol attached to the pact carved eastern Europe into German and Soviet zones, and permitted the Soviets to grab the eastern half of Poland and the three Baltic states of Lithuania, Estonia, and Latvia, formerly part of the Russian Empire.

In the early morning hours of September 1, German tank columns rolled into Poland. German fighting planes

Poland and the Outbreak of World War II

covered the advance, thereby launching a new type of warfare, the *blitzkrieg* (lightning war)—highly mobile land forces and armor combined with tactical aircraft. Within forty-eight hours, Britain and France responded by declaring war on Ger-

many. "It's come at last," Franklin Roosevelt murmured. "God help us all."

When Europe descended into the abyss of war in September 1939, Roosevelt declared neutrality and pressed for repeal of the arms embargo. Isolationist senator Arthur Vandenberg of Michigan roared back that the United States could not be "an arsenal for one belligerent without becoming a target for the other." After much debate, however, Congress in November lifted the embargo on contraband and approved cash-and-carry exports of arms. Using "methods short of war," Roosevelt thus began to aid the Allies. Hitler sneered that a "half Judaized . . . half Negrified" United States was "incapable of conducting war."

JAPAN, CHINA, AND A NEW ORDER IN ASIA

While Europe succumbed to political turmoil and war, Asia suffered the aggressive march of Japan. The United States had interests at stake in Asia: the Philippines and Pacific islands, religious missions, trade and investments, and the Open Door in China. In traditional missionary fashion, Americans also believed that they were China's special friend and protector. "With God's help," Senator Kenneth Wherry of Nebraska once proclaimed, "we will lift Shanghai up and up, ever up, until it is just like Kansas City." Pearl Buck's bestselling novel *The Good Earth* (1931), made into a widely distributed film six years later, countered prevailing images of the very different— and thus deviant—"heathen Chinee" by representing the Chinese as noble, persevering peasants. The daughter of Presbyterian missionaries, Buck helped shift negative American images of China to positive ones. By contrast, the aggressive Japan loomed as a threat to American attitudes and interests. The Tokyo government seemed bent on subjugating China and unhinging the Open Door doctrine of equal trade and investment opportunity.

The Chinese themselves were uneasy about the U.S. presence in Asia. Like the Japanese, they wished to reduce the influence of westerners. The Chinese Revolution of 1911 still rumbled in the 1920s, as antiforeign riots damaged American property and imperiled American missionaries. Chinese nationalists criticized Americans for the imperialist practice of extraterritoriality (the exemption from Chinese legal jurisdiction of foreigners accused of crimes), and they demanded an end to this affront to Chinese sovereignty.

In the late 1920s, civil war broke out in China when Jiang Jieshi (Chiang Kai-shek) ousted Mao Zedong and

Jiang Jieshi

his communist followers from the ruling Guomindang Party. Americans applauded this display of anti-Bolshevism and Jiang's conversion to Christianity in 1930. Jiang's new wife, Soong Meiling, also won their hearts. American-educated, Madame Jiang spoke flawless English, dressed in western fashion, and cultivated ties with prominent Americans. Warming to Jiang, U.S. officials abandoned one imperial vestige by signing a treaty in 1928 restoring control of tariffs to the Chinese. U.S. gunboats and marines still remained in China to protect American citizens and property.

The Japanese grew increasingly suspicious of U.S. ties with China. In the early twentieth century, Japanese-American relations steadily deteriorated as Japan gained influence in Manchuria, Shandong, and Korea. The Japanese sought not only to oust western imperialists from Asia but also to dominate Asian territories that produced the raw materials that their import-dependent island nation required. The Japanese also resented the discriminatory immigration law of 1924, which excluded them from emigrating to the United States and declared they were "aliens ineligible to citizenship." Secretary Hughes urged Congress not to pass the act; when it rejected his counsel, he sadly called the law "a lasting injury" to Japanese-American relations. Despite the Washington Conference treaties, naval competition continued, and there was also rivalry in the commercial arena. In the United States the

importation of inexpensive Japanese goods, especially textiles, spawned "Buy America" campaigns and boycotts.

Relations further soured in 1931 after the Japanese military seized Manchuria from China (see Map 26.2),

Manchurian Crisis

weakened by civil war and unable to resist. Larger than Texas, Manchuria served Japan both as a buffer against the Soviets and as a vital source of coal, iron, timber, and food. More than half of Japan's foreign investments rested in Manchuria. "We are seeking room that will let us breathe," said a

▲ After the outbreak of the Sino-Japanese War (termed the "China Incident" by Japan) in 1937, Japanese postcard publishers churned out large numbers of postcards showing the newly conquered territories, or weaponry, or scenes of army life. Soldiers would send the postcards back to family members in Japan. This image appeared on the cover of a packet of eight postcards in the late 1930s. The text reads, "China Incident Postcard—Fourth Set."

(Eric Politzer/Curt Teich Postcard Archives, Lake County Museum)

Map 26.2   Japanese Expansion Before Pearl Harbor
The Japanese quest for predominance began at the turn of the century and intensified in the 1930s. China suffered the most at the hands of Tokyo's military. Vulnerable U.S. possessions in Asia and the Pacific proved no obstacle to Japan's ambitions for a Greater East Asia Co-Prosperity Sphere.

Japanese politician, arguing that his heavily populated island nation (65 million people in an area slightly smaller than California) needed to expand in order to survive. Although the seizure of Manchuria violated the Nine-Power Treaty and the Kellogg-Briand Pact, the United States did not have the power to compel Japanese withdrawal, and the League of Nations did little but condemn the Tokyo government. The American response came as a moral lecture known as the Stimson Doctrine: the United States would not recognize any impairment of China's sovereignty or of the Open Door policy, Secretary Stimson declared in 1932. He himself later described his policy as largely "bluff."

Japan continued to pressure China. In mid-1937, owing to Japanese provocation, the Sino-Japanese War erupted. Japanese forces seized Beijing and cities along the coast. The gruesome bombing of Shanghai intensified

anti-Japanese sentiment in the United States. Senator Norris, an isolationist who moved further away from isolationism with each Japanese thrust, condemned the Japanese as "disgraceful, ignoble, barbarous, and cruel, even beyond the power of language to describe." In an effort to help China by permitting it to buy American arms, Roosevelt refused to declare the existence of war, thus avoiding activation of the Neutrality Acts.

In a speech denouncing the aggressors on October 5, 1937, the president called for a "quarantine" to curb the "epidemic of world lawlessness." People who thought Washington had been too gentle with Japan cheered. Isolationists warned that the president was edging toward war. On December 12, Japanese aircraft sank the American gunboat *Panay*, an escort for

Roosevelt's Quarantine Speech

Standard Oil Company tankers on the Yangtze River. Two American sailors died during the attack. Roosevelt was much relieved when Tokyo apologized and offered to pay for damages.

Japan's declaration of a "New Order" in Asia, in the words of one American official, "banged, barred, and bolted" the Open Door. Alarmed, the Roosevelt administration during the late 1930s gave loans and sold military equipment to Jiang's Chinese government. Secretary Hull declared a moral embargo on the shipment of airplanes to Japan. Meanwhile, the U.S. Navy continued to grow, aided by a billion-dollar congressional appropriation in 1938. In mid-1939 the United States abrogated its trade treaty with Tokyo, yet Americans continued to ship oil, cotton, and machinery to Japan. The administration hesitated to initiate economic sanctions because such pressure might spark a Japanese-American war at a time when Germany posed a more serious threat and the United States was unprepared for war. When war broke out in Europe in the late summer of 1939, Japanese-American relations were stalemated.

U.S. ENTRY INTO WORLD WAR II

A stalemate was just fine with many Americans if it served to keep the United States out of war. But how long could the country stay out? Roosevelt remarked in 1939 that the United States could not "draw a line of defense around this country and live completely and solely to ourselves." Thomas Jefferson had tried that with his 1807 embargo— "the damned thing didn't work," and "we got into the War of 1812." America, the president insisted, could not insulate itself from world war. Polls showed that Americans strongly favored the Allies and that most supported aid to Britain and France, but the great majority emphatically wanted the United States to remain at peace. Troubled by this conflicting advice—oppose Hitler, aid the Allies, but stay out of the war—the president gradually moved the nation from neutrality to undeclared war against Germany and then, after the Japanese attack on Pearl Harbor, to full-scale war itself.

Because the stakes were so high, Americans vigorously debated the direction of their foreign policy from 1939 through 1941. Unprecedented numbers of Americans spoke out on foreign affairs and joined organizations that addressed the issues. Spine-chilling events and the widespread use of radio, the nation's chief source of news, helped stimulate this high level of public interest. So did ethnic affiliations with the various belligerents and victims of aggression. The American Legion, the League of Women Voters, labor unions, and local chapters of the Committee to Defend America by Aiding the Allies and of the isolationist America First Committee (both organized in 1940) provided outlets for citizen participation in the national debate. African American churches organized anti-Italian boycotts to protest Mussolini's pummeling of Ethiopia.

In March 1940, the Soviet Union invaded Finland. In April, Germany conquered Denmark and Norway (see Map 26.3). "The small countries are smashed up, one by one, like matchwood," sighed Winston Churchill, who became Britain's prime minister on May 10, 1940, the day Germany attacked Belgium, the Netherlands, and France. German divisions ultimately pushed French and British forces back to the English Channel. At Dunkirk, France, between May 26 and June 6, more

◀ Guns, tanks, and bombs were the principal weapons of the war, but there were other, subtler forms of warfare as well. Words, posters, and films waged a constant battle for the hearts and minds of the citizenry of each belligerent nation just as surely as military weapons engaged the enemy. This scene of the South Downs in England sought to arouse feelings for an idealized pastoral Britain. *(Frank Newbould)*

Map 26.3   The German Advance
Hitler's drive to dominate Europe pushed German troops deep into France and the Soviet Union. Great Britain took a beating but held on with the help of American economic and military aid before the United States itself entered the Second World War in late 1941.

than 300,000 Allied soldiers frantically escaped to Britain on a flotilla of small boats. The Germans occupied Paris a week later. A new French government located in the town of Vichy decided to collaborate with the conquering Nazis and, on June 22, surrendered France to Berlin. With France knocked out of the war, the German Luftwaffe (air force) launched massive bombing raids against Great Britain in preparation for a full-scale invasion. Stunned Americans asked whether Washington or New York could be the Luftwaffe's next target.

Alarmed by the swift defeat of one European nation after another, Americans gradually shed their isolationist sentiment. Some liberals left the isolationist fold; it became more and more the province of conservatives. Emotions ran high. Roosevelt called the isolationists "ostriches" and

charged that some were pro-Nazi subversives. Assuring Americans that New Deal reforms would not have to be sacrificed to achieve military preparedness, the president began to aid the beleaguered Allies to prevent the fall of Britain. In May 1940 he ordered the sale of old surplus military equipment to Britain and France. In July he cultivated bipartisan support by naming Republicans Henry L. Stimson and Frank Knox, ardent backers of aid to the Allies, secretaries of war and the navy, respectively. In September, by executive agreement, the president traded fifty over-age American destroyers for leases to eight British military bases, including Newfoundland, Bermuda, and Jamaica.

Two weeks later, Roosevelt signed into law the hotly debated and narrowly passed Selective Training and

Radio News

In radio's early years, stations broadcast little news. Network executives believed their job was to entertain Americans and that current affairs should be left to newspapers. Yet radio could do something that no previous medium of communication could do: it could report not merely what had happened, but what was happening as it happened.

Franklin Roosevelt was among the first to grasp radio's potential in this regard. As governor of New York, he occasionally went on the air, and after becoming president, he commenced his Fireside Chats. With a voice perfectly suited to the medium, he reassured Americans suffering through the depression that, although current conditions were grim, the government was working hard to help them. So successful were these broadcasts that, in the words of one journalist, "The President has only to look toward a radio to bring Congress to terms."

Across the Atlantic, another leader also understood well the power of radio. Adolf Hitler determined early that he would use German radio to carry speeches directly to the people. His message: Germany had been wronged by enemies abroad and by Marxists and Jews at home. But the Nazis under Hitler's direction would lead the country back to its former greatness. As "Sieg Heil!" thundered over the airwaves, millions of Germans came to see Hitler as their salvation.

In 1938, as events in Europe reached a crisis, American radio networks increased their news coverage. When Hitler annexed Austria in March, NBC and CBS broke into scheduled programs to deliver news bulletins. Then, on the evening of Saturday, March 13, CBS went its rival one better by broadcasting the first international news roundup, a half-hour show featuring live reports on the annexation from the major capitals of Europe. A new era in American radio was born. In the words of author Joseph Persico, what made the broadcast revolutionary "was the listener's sensation of being on the scene" in far-off Europe.

When leaders from France and Britain met with Hitler in Munich later that year, millions of Americans listened with rapt attention to live radio updates. Correspondents soon became well known, none more so than Edward R. Murrow of CBS. During the Nazi air blitz of London in 1940–1941, Murrow's rich, understated, nicotine-scorched voice kept Americans spellbound. "This—is London," he would begin each broadcast, then proceed to give graphic accounts that tried, as he put it, to "report suffering to people [Americans] who have not suffered."

Murrow was resolutely pro-Allies, and there is little doubt his reports strengthened the interventionist voices in Washington by emphasizing Winston Churchill's greatness and England's bravery. More than that, though, radio reports from Europe made Americans feel more closely linked than before to people living thousands of miles and an ocean away. As American writer Archibald MacLeish said of Murrow's broadcasts, "Without rhetoric, without dramatics, without more emotion than needed be, you destroyed the superstition of distance and of time."

▲ Edward R. Murrow at his typewriter in wartime London.
(Library of Congress)

First Peacetime Military Draft

Service Act, the first peacetime military draft in American history. The act called for the registration of all men between the ages of twenty-one and thirty-five. Soon more than 16 million men had signed up, and draft notices began to be delivered. Meanwhile, Roosevelt won reelection in November 1940 with promises of peace: "Your boys are not going to be sent into any foreign wars." Republican candidate Wendell Willkie, who in the emerging spirit of bipartisanship had not made an issue of foreign policy, snapped, "That hypocritical son of a bitch! This is going to beat me!" And it did.

Roosevelt claimed that the United States could stay out of the war by enabling the British to win. The United States, he said, must become the "great arsenal of democracy." In January 1941, Congress debated the president's Lend-Lease bill. Because Britain was broke, the president explained, the United States should lend rather than sell weapons, much as a neighbor lends a garden hose to fight a fire. Most lawmakers needed little persuasion. In March 1941, with pro-British sentiment running high, the House passed the Lend-Lease Act by 317 votes to 71; the Senate followed with a 60-to-31 tally. The initial appropriation was $7 billion, but by the end of the war the amount had reached $50 billion, more than $31 billion of it for Britain.

To ensure the safe delivery of Lend-Lease goods, Roosevelt ordered the U.S. Navy to patrol halfway across the Atlantic, and he sent American troops to Greenland. In July, arguing that Iceland was also essential to the defense of the Western Hemisphere, the president dispatched marines there. He also sent Lend-Lease aid to the Soviet Union, which Hitler had attacked in June (thereby shattering the 1939 Nazi-Soviet nonaggression pact). If the Soviets could hold off two hundred German divisions in the east, Roosevelt calculated, Britain would gain some breathing time. Churchill, who had long thundered against communists, now applauded aid to the Soviets: "If Hitler invaded Hell, I would make at least a favorable reference to the Devil in the House of Commons."

In August 1941, Churchill and Roosevelt met for four days on a British battleship off the coast of Newfoundland. They got along well, trading naval stories and enjoying the fact that Churchill was half American (his mother was from New York). The two leaders issued the Atlantic Charter, a set of war aims reminiscent of Wilsonianism: collective security, disarmament, self-determination, economic cooperation, and freedom of the seas. Churchill later recalled

Atlantic Charter

that the president told him in Newfoundland that he could not ask Congress for a declaration of war against Germany, but "he would wage war" and "become more and more provocative."

Within days, German and American ships came into direct contact in the Atlantic. On September 4, a German submarine launched torpedoes at (but did not hit) the American destroyer *Greer*. Henceforth, Roosevelt said, the U.S. Navy would have authority to fire first when under threat. He also announced a policy that he already had promised Churchill in private: American warships would convoy British merchant ships across the ocean. Thus the United States entered into an undeclared naval war with Germany. When in early October a German submarine torpedoed the U.S. destroyer *Kearny* off the coast of Iceland, the president announced that "the shooting has started. And history has recorded who fired the first shot." Later that month, when the destroyer *Reuben James* went down with the loss of more than one hundred American lives, Congress scrapped the cash-and-carry policy and further revised the Neutrality Acts to permit transport of munitions to Britain on armed American merchant ships. The United States was edging very close to being a belligerent.

It seems ironic, therefore, that the Second World War came to the United States by way of Asia. Roosevelt had wanted to avoid war with Japan in order to concentrate American resources on the defeat of Germany. In September 1940, after Germany, Italy, and Japan had signed the Tripartite Pact (to form the Axis powers), Roosevelt slapped an embargo on shipments of aviation fuel and scrap metal to Japan. Because the president believed the Japanese would consider a cutoff of oil a life-or-death matter, he did not embargo that vital commodity. But after Japanese troops occupied French Indochina in July 1941, Washington froze Japanese assets in the United States, virtually ending trade (including oil) with Japan. "The oil gauge and the clock stood side by side" for Japan, wrote one observer.

U.S. Demands on Japan

Tokyo recommended a summit meeting between President Roosevelt and Prime Minister Prince Konoye, but the United States rejected the idea. American officials insisted that the Japanese first agree to respect China's sovereignty and territorial integrity, and to honor the Open Door policy—in short, to get out of China. According to polls taken in fall 1941, the American people seemed willing to risk war with Japan to thwart further aggression. For Roosevelt, Europe still claimed first priority, but he supported Secretary Hull's hard-line policy against Japan's pursuit of the Greater East Asia Co-Prosperity Sphere—

▲ President Franklin D. Roosevelt *(left)* and British prime minister Winston Churchill (1874–1965) confer on board a ship near Newfoundland during their summit meeting of August 1941. During the conference, they signed the Atlantic Charter. On his return to Great Britain, Churchill told his advisers that Roosevelt had promised to "wage war" against Germany and do "everything" to "force an incident." *(Franklin D. Roosevelt Library)*

the name Tokyo gave to the vast Asian region it intended to dominate.

Roosevelt told his advisers to string out ongoing Japanese-American talks to gain time—time to fortify the Philippines and check the fascists in Europe. By breaking the Japanese diplomatic code and deciphering intercepted messages through Operation MAGIC, American officials learned that Tokyo's patience with diplomacy was fast dissipating. In late November, the Japanese rejected American demands that they withdraw from Indochina. An intercepted message that American experts decoded on December 3 instructed the Japanese embassy in Washington to burn codes and destroy cipher machines—a step suggesting that war was coming.

The Japanese plotted a daring raid on Pearl Harbor in Hawai'i. An armada of sixty Japanese ships, with a core of six carriers bearing 360 airplanes, crossed 3,000 miles of the Pacific Ocean. To avoid detection, every ship maintained radio silence.

Surprise Attack on Pearl Harbor

In the early morning of December 7, some 230 miles northwest of Honolulu, the carriers unleashed their planes, each stamped with a red sun representing the Japanese flag. They swept down on the unsuspecting American naval base and nearby airfields, dropping torpedoes and bombs and strafing buildings.

The battleship USS *Arizona* fell victim to a Japanese bomb that ignited explosives below deck, killing more

▲ The stricken USS *West Virginia* was one of eight battleships caught in the surprise Japanese attack at Pearl Harbor, Hawai'i, on December 7, 1941. In this photograph, sailors on a launch attempt to rescue a crew member from the water as oil burns around the sinking ship. *(U.S. Army)*

than 1,000 sailors. The USS *Nevada* tried to escape the inferno by heading out to sea, but a second wave of aerial attackers struck the ship. Altogether the invaders sank or damaged eight battleships and many smaller vessels, and smashed more than 160 aircraft on the ground. Huddled in an air-raid shelter, sixteen-year-old Mary Ann Ramsey watched the injured come in "with filthy black oil covering shredded flesh. With the first sailor, so horribly burned, personal fear left me; he brought me the full tragedy of the day." A total of 2,403 died; 1,178 were wounded. By chance, three aircraft carriers at sea escaped the disaster. The Pearl Harbor tragedy, from the perspective of the war's

outcome, amounted to a military inconvenience more than a disaster.

How could the stunning attack on Pearl Harbor have happened? After all, American cryptanalysts had broken

Explaining Pearl Harbor

the Japanese diplomatic code. Although the intercepted Japanese messages told policymakers that war lay ahead, the intercepts never revealed naval or military plans and never mentioned Pearl Harbor specifically. Roosevelt did not, as some critics charged, conspire to leave the fleet vulnerable to attack so that the United States could enter the

Second World War through the "back door" of Asia. The base at Pearl Harbor was not on red alert because a message sent from Washington warning of the imminence of war had been too casually transmitted by a slow method and had arrived too late. Base commanders were too relaxed, believing Hawai'i too far from Japan to be a target for all-out attack. Like Roosevelt's advisers, they expected an assault on British Malaya, Thailand, or the Philippines (see Map 26.2). The Pearl Harbor calamity stemmed from mistakes and insufficient information, not from conspiracy.

On December 8, referring to the previous day as "a date which will live in infamy," Roosevelt asked Congress for a declaration of war against Japan. He noted that the Japanese had also, almost simultaneously, attacked Malaya, Hong Kong, Guam, the Philippines, Wake, and Midway, and he expressed the prevailing sense of revenge when he vowed that Americans would never forget "the character of the onslaught against us." A unanimous vote in the Senate and a 388-to-1 vote in the House thrust America into war. Representative Jeannette Rankin of Montana voted no, repeating her vote against entry into the First World War. Britain declared war on Japan, but the Soviet Union did not. Three days later, Germany and Italy, honoring the Tripartite Pact they had signed with Japan in September 1940, declared war against the United States. "Hitler's fate was sealed," Churchill later wrote. "Mussolini's fate was sealed. As for the Japanese, they would be ground to powder. . . . I went to bed and slept the sleep of the saved and thankful."

A fundamental clash of systems explains why war came. Germany and Japan preferred a world divided into closed spheres of influence. The United States sought a liberal capitalist world order in which all nations enjoyed freedom of trade and investment. American principles manifested respect for human rights; fascists in Europe and militarists in Asia defiantly trampled such rights. The United States prided itself on its democratic system; Germany and Japan embraced authoritarian regimes backed by the military. When the United States protested against German and Japanese expansion, Berlin and Tokyo charged that Washington was applying a double standard, conveniently ignoring its own sphere of influence in Latin America and its own history of military and economic aggrandizement. Americans rejected such comparisons and claimed that their expansionism had benefited not just themselves but the rest of the world. So many incompatible objectives and outlooks obstructed diplomacy and made war likely.

Likely, but perhaps not inevitable. At least with respect to the Japanese, there is the tantalizing question of whether a more flexible American negotiating posture in the fall of 1941 might have averted a U.S.-Japanese war. Privately, after all, American planners admitted that they were largely powerless to affect Japan's moves in China; they further conceded among themselves that any Japanese withdrawal from China would take many months to carry out. So why the public insistence that Japan had to get out, and get out now? Why not assent, grudgingly, to the Japanese presence in China and also reopen at least limited trade with the Tokyo government, in order to forestall further Japanese expansion in Southeast Asia? Such a policy would have delayed any showdown with Japan, allowed continued concentration on the European war, and also given Washington more time to rearm. Writes historian David M. Kennedy, "Whether under those circumstances a Japanese-American war might have been avoided altogether is among the weightiest of might-have-beens, with implications for the nature and timing of America's struggle against Hitler and for the shape of postwar Europe as well as Asia." It was not to be, though, and the United States now prepared to wage war in two theaters half a world apart.

Avoidable War?

Legacy FOR A PEOPLE AND A NATION

Presidential Deception of the Public

Before U-652 launched two torpedoes at the *Greer,* heading for Iceland on September 4, 1941, the U.S. destroyer had stalked the German submarine for hours. Twice the *Greer* signaled the U-boat's location to British patrol bombers, one of which dropped depth charges on the submarine. After the torpedo attack, which missed its mark, the *Greer* also released depth charges. But when President Roosevelt described the encounter in a dramatic radio Fireside Chat on September 11, he declared that the German submarine, without warning, had fired the first shot, and he protested German "piracy" as a violation of the principle of freedom of the seas.

Roosevelt misled the American people about the events of September 4. The incident had little to do with freedom of the seas—a principle relating to neutral merchant ships, not to U.S. warships operating in a war zone. Roosevelt's words amounted to a call to arms, yet he never asked Congress for a declaration of war against Germany. The president believed that he had to deceive Americans in order to move them toward noble positions that they would ultimately see as necessary. The practice worked: polls showed that most Americans approved Roosevelt's shoot-on-sight policy following the *Greer* incident.

Over time, however, questions were raised—even by those who agreed that Germany had to be stopped. Critics have seen in Roosevelt's methods a danger to the democratic process, which cannot work in an environment of dishonesty and a usurping of congressional powers. In the 1960s, during the Vietnam War, Senator J. William Fulbright of Arkansas recalled the *Greer* incident: "FDR's deviousness in a good cause made it easier for LBJ to practice the same kind of deviousness in a bad cause." In the mid-1980s, Reagan administration officials consciously and publicly lied about U.S. arms sales to Iran and about covert aid to Nicaraguan rebels, and after the March 2003 U.S. invasion of Iraq, there were charges that President George W. Bush and his aides did the same in claiming that Iraq had weapons of mass destruction and that its leader, Saddam Hussein, intended to use them. Bush, critics charged, had used "weapons of mass deception" to justify the invasion of Iraq.

Following Roosevelt, presidents have found it easier to exaggerate, distort, withhold, or even lie about the facts of foreign relations in order to shape a public opinion favorable to their policies. One result: the growth of the "imperial presidency"—the president's grabbing of power from Congress and use of questionable means to reach his objectives. The practice of deception—for an end the president calls noble—was one of Roosevelt's legacies for a people and a nation.

SUMMARY

In the 1920s and 1930s, Americans proved unable to create a peaceful and prosperous world order. The Washington Conference treaties failed to curb a naval arms race or to protect China, and both the Dawes Plan and the Kellogg-Briand Pact proved ineffective. Philanthropic activities fell short of need, and the process of cultural Americanization provided no panacea. In the era of the Great Depression, U.S. trade policies, shifting from protectionist tariffs to reciprocal trade agreements, only minimally improved U.S. or international commerce. Recognition of the Soviet Union barely improved relations. Most ominous of all, the aggressors Germany and Japan ignored repeated U.S. protests, from the Stimson Doctrine onward; as the 1930s progressed, the United States became more entangled in the crises in Europe and Asia. Even where American power and policies seemed to work to satisfy Good Neighbor goals—in Latin America—nationalist resentments simmered and Mexico challenged U.S. dominance.

During the late 1930s and early 1940s, President Roosevelt hesitantly but steadily moved the United States from neutrality to aid for the Allies, to belligerency, and finally to a declaration of war after the attack on Pearl Harbor. Congress gradually revised and retired the Neutrality Acts in the face of growing danger and receding isolationism. Independent internationalism and economic and nonmilitary means to peace gave way to alliance building and war.

The Second World War offered yet another opportunity for Americans to set things right in the world. As publisher Henry Luce wrote in *American Century* (1941), the United States must "exert upon the world the full impact of our influence, for such purposes as we see fit and by such means as we see fit." As they had so many times before, Americans flocked to the colors. Isolationists joined the president in spirited calls for victory. "We are going to win the war, and we are going to win the peace that follows," Roosevelt predicted.

SUGGESTIONS FOR FURTHER READING

Patrick Cohrs, *The Unfinished Peace After World War I: America, Britain and the Stabilization of Europe, 1919–1932* (2006)

Frank Costigliola, *Awkward Dominion: American Political, Economic, and Cultural Relations with Europe* (1984)

Robert Dallek, *Franklin D. Roosevelt and American Foreign Policy* (1995)

Justus D. Doenecke, *Storm on the Horizon: The Challenge to American Intervention, 1939–1941* (2000)

Akira Iriye, *The Origins of the Second World War in Asia and the Pacific* (1987)

David M. Kennedy, *Freedom from Fear: The American People in Depression and War, 1929–1945* (1999)

Walter LaFeber, *Inevitable Revolutions: The United States in Central America*, 2d and extended ed. (1993)

Fredrick B. Pike, *FDR's Good Neighbor Policy* (1995)

Emily S. Rosenberg, *Spreading the American Dream: American Economic and Cultural Expansion, 1890–1945* (1982)

Linda A. Schott, *Reconstructing Women's Thoughts: The Women's International League for Peace and Freedom Before World War II* (1997)

For a more extensive list for further reading, go to college.hmco.com/pic/norton8e.

The Second World War at Home and Abroad *1941-1945*

*W*illiam Dean Wilson was only sixteen in 1942 when U.S. Marine Corps recruiters came to Shiprock, New Mexico, where he was a student at the Navajo boarding school, but he was eager to fight the war. Five years too young to be drafted and a year too young to volunteer for the marines, he lied about his age. His parents did not want him to drop out of school and go to war, but he removed the note reading, "Parents will not consent" from his recruiting file and was inducted into the Marine Corps.

Despite his youth, Wilson was recruited for one of the most important projects of the war. Battles were won or lost because nations broke the codes in which their enemies transmitted messages. The marines sought to use a code based on Diné, the Navajo language, which is extremely complex because of its syntax and tonal qualities. In 1942 it did not exist in written form, and there were fewer than thirty non-Navajos in the world—none of them Japanese—who could understand it. Unlike written ciphers, this code promised to be unbreakable.

Wilson and his fellow Navajo recruits trained as radio operators and helped devise a basic code. Navajo words represented the first letter of their English translations; thus *wol-la-chee* ("ant") stood for the letter *A*. Each also memorized a special dictionary of Navajo words that represented 413 basic military terms and concepts. *Dah-he-tih-hi* ("hummingbird") meant fighter plane; *ne-he-mah*, "our mother," was the United States; *beh-na-ali-tsosie*, "slant-eye," stood for Japan.

By the time Wilson's seventeenth birthday arrived, he was fighting in the Pacific. Beginning with the Battle of Guadalcanal, he and others from the corps of 420 code talkers

◀ Navajo "code talkers," who were U.S. Marines, were among the first assault forces to land on Pacific beaches. Dodging enemy fire, they set up radio equipment and transmitted vital information to headquarters, including enemy sightings and targets for American shelling. The Japanese never broke the special Navajo code. The artist is Colonel C. H. Waterhouse, U.S. Marine Corps (retired).

(U.S. Marine Corps Art Collection/Colonel C. H. Waterhouse)

CHRONOLOGY

1941 ■ Japan attacks Pearl Harbor
■ United States enters World War II

1942 ■ War Production Board created to oversee conversion to military production
■ Allies losing war in Pacific to Japan; U.S. victory at Battle of Midway in June is turning point
■ Office of Price Administration creates rationing system for food and consumer goods
■ United States pursues "Europe First" war policy; Allies reject Stalin's demands for a second front and invade North Africa
■ West Coast Japanese Americans relocated to internment camps
■ Manhattan Project set up to create atomic bomb
■ Congress of Racial Equality established

1943 ■ Soviet army defeats German troops at Stalingrad
■ Congress passes War Labor Disputes (Smith-Connally) Act following coal miners' strike
■ "Zoot suit riots" in Los Angeles; race riots break out in Detroit, Harlem, and other cities
■ Allies invade Italy
■ Roosevelt, Churchill, and Stalin meet at Teheran Conference

1944 ■ Allied troops land at Normandy on D-Day, June 6
■ Roosevelt elected to fourth term as president
■ United States retakes Philippines

1945 ■ Roosevelt, Stalin, and Churchill meet at Yalta Conference
■ British and U.S. forces firebomb Dresden, Germany
■ Battles of Iwo Jima and Okinawa result in heavy Japanese and American losses
■ Roosevelt dies; Truman becomes president
■ Germany surrenders; Allied forces liberate Nazi death camps
■ Potsdam Conference calls for Japan's "unconditional surrender"
■ United States uses atomic bombs on Hiroshima and Nagasaki
■ Japan surrenders

took part in every assault the marines conducted in the Pacific from 1942 to 1945. Usually, two code talkers were assigned to a battalion, one going ashore with the assault forces and the other remaining on ship to receive messages. Often under hostile fire, code talkers set up their radio equipment and began transmitting, reporting sightings of enemy forces and directing shelling by American detachments. Their work required great courage, and it paid off. "Were it not for the Navajos," declared Major Howard Conner, Fifth Marine Division signal officer, "the Marines would never have taken Iwo Jima. The entire operation was directed by Navajo code. . . . I had six Navajo radio sets operating around the clock. In that period alone they sent and received over eight hundred messages without an error."

As it did for millions of other American fighting men and women, wartime service changed the Navajo code talkers' lives, broadening their horizons and often deepening their ambitions. Many became community leaders. William Dean Wilson, for example, became a tribal judge. From "the service," recalled Raymond Nakai, a navy veteran who became chairman of the Navajo nation, "the Navajo got a glimpse of what the rest of the world is doing." But in 1945 most Navajo war veterans were happy to return to their homes and traditional culture. And, in accordance with Navajo ritual, the returning veterans participated in purification ceremonies to dispel the ghosts of the battlefield and invoke blessings for the future.

The Second World War marked a turning point in the lives of millions of Americans, as well as in the history of the United States. Most deeply affected were those who fought the war, on the beaches and battlefields, in the skies and at sea. For forty-five months Americans fought abroad to subdue the German, Italian, and Japanese aggressors. Although the war began badly for the United States, by mid-1942 the Allies had halted the Axis powers' advance. In June 1944, American troops, together with Canadian, British, and Free French units, launched a massive invasion across the English Channel, landing at Normandy and pushing into Germany by the following spring. Battered by merciless bombing raids, leaderless after Adolf Hitler's suicide, and pressed by a Soviet advance from the east, the Nazis capitulated in May 1945.

In the Pacific, Americans drove Japanese forces back, island by island, toward Japan. America's devastating conventional bombing of Japanese cities, followed by the atomic bombs that demolished Hiroshima and Nagasaki in August 1945, led to the surrender of Japan. Throughout the war, the "Grand Alliance"—Britain, the Soviet Union, and the United States—stuck together to defeat Germany. But they disagreed about how best to fight the war and had profound differences over how to shape the postwar world. Prospects for postwar international cooperation seemed bleak, and the advent of the atomic age frightened everyone.

The war was fought far from the United States, but it had a major impact on American society. America's leaders sought to fight the war on the "production front" as well as on the battlefield and committed the United States to become the "arsenal of democracy," producing vast quantities of arms for the war against the Axis. All sectors of the economy—industry, finance, agriculture, labor—were mobilized. America's big businesses got even bigger, as did its central government, labor unions, and farms. The federal government had the monumental task of coordinating activity in these spheres, as well as in two new ones: higher education and science.

During the war, nearly one of every ten Americans moved permanently to another state. Most headed for war-production centers, especially cities in the North and on the West Coast. Japanese Americans moved, too, but involuntarily, as they were rounded up by the army and placed in internment camps. And while the war offered new economic and political opportunities for African Americans, encouraging them to demand their full rights as citizens, competition for jobs and housing created the conditions for an epidemic of race riots. For women, the war offered new job opportunities in the armed forces and in war industries.

On the home front, the American people united behind the war effort, collecting scrap iron, rubber, and newspapers for recycling, and planting "victory gardens." Although commodities such as food and gasoline were rationed, the war had brought prosperity back to the United States. At war's end, although many Americans grieved for loved ones lost in battle and worried about

the stability of the emerging postwar order, the United States had unprecedented power and unmatched prosperity among the world's nations.

- What military, diplomatic, and social factors influenced decisions about how to fight the Second World War?
- Was the generation of Americans that fought World War II "the greatest generation"?
- How did World War II transform the United States?

THE UNITED STATES AT WAR

As Japanese bombs fell in the U.S. territory of Hawai'i, American antiwar sentiment evaporated. Franklin Roosevelt summoned the nation to war with Japan on December 8, proclaiming that "the American people in their righteous might will win through to absolute victory." When Germany formally declared war on the United States three days later, America joined British and Soviet Allied nations in the ongoing war against the Axis powers of Japan, Germany, and Italy. The American public's shift from caution—even isolationism—to fervent support for war was sudden and dramatic. Some former critics of intervention, seeking a persuasive explanation, turned to the popular children's story *Ferdinand the Bull*. Ferdinand, though huge and powerful, just liked to "sit and smell the flowers"—until the day he was stung by a bee. It was a comforting tale, but inaccurate. As the world went to war, the United States had not been, like Ferdinand, just "smell[ing] the flowers." America's embargo of shipments to Japan and refusal to accept Japan's expansionist policies had brought the two nations to the brink of war, and the United States was deeply involved in an undeclared naval war with Germany well before Japan's attack on Pearl Harbor. By December 1941, Roosevelt had long since instituted an unprecedented peacetime draft, created war mobilization agencies, and commissioned war plans for simultaneous struggle in Europe and the Pacific. America's entry into World War II was not a surprise.

Nonetheless, the nation was not ready for war. Throughout the 1930s, military funding had been a low priority. In September 1939 (when Hitler invaded Poland and began the Second World War), the U.S. Army ranked forty-fifth in size among the world's armies and could fully equip only one-third of its 227,000 men. A peacetime draft instituted in 1940 expanded the U.S.

A Nation Unprepared

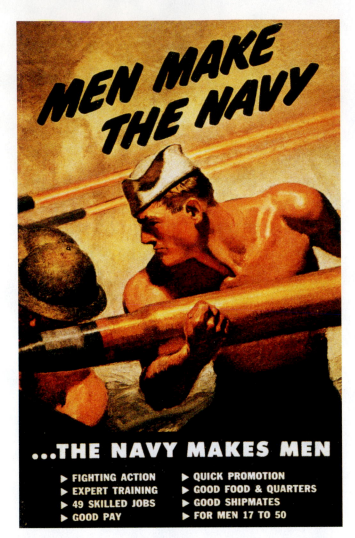

MEN MAKE THE NAVY

...THE NAVY MAKES MEN

▶ FIGHTING ACTION   ▶ QUICK PROMOTION
▶ EXPERT TRAINING   ▶ GOOD FOOD & QUARTERS
▶ 49 SKILLED JOBS   ▶ GOOD SHIPMATES
▶ GOOD PAY   ▶ FOR MEN 17 TO 50

▲ "MEN MAKE THE NAVY," proclaims this U.S. Navy recruiting booklet, which encourages men to enlist by highlighting the good pay, food, and shipmates, as well as the possibility of "fighting action." One hundred thousand women also responded to the navy's recruiting efforts by joining the WAVES. *(Private Collection)*

Africa. German U-boats controlled the Atlantic from the Arctic to the Caribbean. Within months of America's entry into the war, German submarines sank 216 vessels—some so close to American shores that people could see the glow of burning ships.

In the Pacific, the war was largely America's to fight. The Soviets had not declared war on Japan, and although

War in the Pacific

British troops protected Great Britain's Asian colonies, there were too few to make much difference. By late spring of 1942 Japan had captured most of the European colonial possessions in Southeast Asia: the Dutch East Indies (Indonesia), French Indochina (Vietnam), and the British colonies of Malaya, Burma, Western New Guinea, Hong Kong, and Singapore. In the American Philippines, the struggle went on longer, but also in vain. The Japanese attacked the Philippines hours after their success at Pearl Harbor and, finding the entire force of B-17 bombers sitting on the airfields, destroyed U.S. air capability in the region. American and Filipino troops retreated to the Bataan Peninsula, hoping to hold the main island, Luzon, but Japanese forces were superior. In March 1942, under orders from Roosevelt, General Douglas MacArthur, the commander of U.S. forces in the Far East, departed the Philippines for Australia, proclaiming, "I shall return."

Left behind were almost eighty thousand American and Filipino troops. Starving and weakened by disease, they held on for almost another month before surrendering. Those who survived long enough to surrender faced worse horror. The Japanese troops, lacking supplies themselves, were unprepared to deal with such a large number of prisoners, and most believed the prisoners had forfeited honorable treatment by surrendering. In what came to be known as the Bataan Death March, the Japanese force-marched their captives to prison camps 80 miles away. Guards denied the prisoners food and water, and bayoneted or beat to death those who fell behind. As many as ten thousand Filipinos and six hundred Americans died on the march. Filipino civilians suffered horribly. Tens of thousands of refugees and prisoners of war died under Japanese occupation.

As losses mounted, the United States began to strike back. On April 18, sixteen American B-25s appeared in the skies over Japan. The Doolittle raid (named after the mission's leader) did little harm to Japan, but it had an enormous psychological impact on Japanese leaders. The image of American bombers over Japan's home islands pushed Japanese commander Yamamoto to bold action. Instead of consolidating control close to home, Yamamoto concluded, Japan must move quickly to lure the weak-

military to 2 million men, but Roosevelt's 1941 survey of war preparedness, the "Victory Plan," estimated that the United States could not be ready to fight before June 1943.

In December 1941, U.S. victory must have seemed unlikely. In Europe, the Allies were losing the war (see Map 26.3). Hitler had claimed Austria, Czechoslovakia, Poland, the Netherlands, Denmark, and Norway. Romania was lost, then Greece and Bulgaria. France had fallen in 1940. Britain fought on, but German planes rained bombs on London. More than 3 million soldiers under German command had penetrated deep into the Soviet Union and

Map 27.1   The Pacific War

The strategy of the United States was to "island-hop" — from Hawai'i in 1942 to Iwo Jima and Okinawa in 1945. Naval battles were also decisive, notably the Battles of the Coral Sea and Midway in 1942. The war in the Pacific ended with Japan's surrender on August 15, 1945 (V-J Day).

(Source: Thomas G. Paterson, J. Garry Clifford, Kenneth J. Hagan, American Foreign Policy: A History, Vol. 2, 3d revised ed. Copyright © 1991 by D. C. Heath and Company. Used by permission of Houghton Mifflin Company.)

ened United States into a "decisive battle." The target was Midway—two tiny islands about 1,000 miles northwest of Honolulu, where the U.S. Navy had a base. If Japan could take Midway—not implausible, given Japan's string of victories—it would have a secure defensive perimeter far from the home islands (see Map 27.1). By using Guam, the Philippines, and perhaps even Australia as hostages, Japan believed, it could negotiate a favorable peace agreement with the United States.

General Yamamoto did not know that America's MAGIC code-breaking machines could decipher Japanese messages. This time, surprise was on the side of the United States, as the Japanese fleet found the U.S. Navy and its carrier-based dive bombers lying in wait. The Battle of Midway in June 1942 was a turning point in the Pacific war. Japanese strategists had hoped that the United

States, discouraged by Japan's early victories, would withdraw and leave Japan to control the Pacific. That outcome was no longer a possibility. Now Japan was on the defensive.

Despite the importance of these early Pacific battles, America's war strategy was "Europe First." Germany, American war planners recognized, was a greater danger to the United States than Japan. If Germany conquered the Soviet Union, they believed, it might directly threaten the United States. Roosevelt also feared that the Soviet Union, suffering almost unimaginable losses as its military battled Hitler's invading army, might pursue a separate peace with Germany and so undo the Allied coalition. Therefore, the United States would work first with Britain and

"Europe First" Strategy

the USSR to defeat Germany, then deal with an isolated Japan.

British prime minister Winston Churchill and Soviet premier Joseph Stalin disagreed vehemently, however, over how to wage the war against Germany. By late 1941, before the fierce Russian winter stalled their onslaught, German troops had nearly reached Moscow and Leningrad (present-day St. Petersburg) and had slashed deeply into Ukraine, taking Kiev. Over a million Soviet soldiers had died defending their country. Stalin pressed for British and American troops to attack Germany from the west, through France, to draw German troops away from the Soviet front. Roosevelt believed "with heart and *mind*" that Stalin was right and promised to open a "second front" to Germany's west before the end of 1942. Churchill, however, blocked this plan. He had not forgotten Stalin's nonaggression pact with Hitler (see page 754). More fundamentally, in large part because of experience with the agonies of prolonged trench warfare in World War I, British military commanders did not want a large-scale invasion of Europe. Churchill wanted to win control of the North Atlantic shipping lanes first and promoted air attacks on Germany. He also pushed for a smaller, safer attack on Axis positions in North Africa; halting the Germans there would protect British imperial possessions in the Mediterranean and the oil-rich Middle East.

Against his advisers' advice, Roosevelt accepted Churchill's plan. The U.S. military was not yet ready for a major campaign, and Roosevelt needed to show the American public some success in the European war. Thus, instead of coming to the rescue of the USSR, the British and Americans made a joint landing in North Africa in November 1942. American troops, facing relatively light resistance, won quick victories in Algeria and Morocco. In Egypt, the British confronted General Erwin Rommel and his Afrika Korps in a struggle for control of the Suez Canal and the Middle East oil fields. Rommel's army, trapped between British and American troops, surrendered after six months. And in Russia, against all odds, the Soviet army hung on, fighting block by block for control of Stalingrad in the deadly cold, to defeat the German Sixth Army in early 1943. Stalingrad, like Midway, was a major turning point in the war. By the spring of 1943, Germany, like Japan, was on the defensive. But relations among the Allies remained precarious. The Soviet Union had lost 1.1 million men in the Battle of Stalingrad. The United States and Britain, however, continued to resist Stalin's demand that they immediately open a second front. The death toll, already in the millions, continued to mount.

THE PRODUCTION FRONT AND AMERICAN WORKERS

In late December 1940—almost a year before the United States entered the war—Franklin Roosevelt pledged that America would serve as the world's "great arsenal of democracy," making the machines that would win the war for the Allies. After Pearl Harbor, U.S. strategy remained much the same. The United States would prevail through a "crushing superiority of equipment," Roosevelt told Congress. Although the war would be fought on the battlefields of Europe and the Pacific, the nation's strategic advantage lay on the "production front" at home.

Goals for military production were staggering. In 1940, with war looming, American factories had built only 3,807 airplanes. Following Pearl Harbor, Roosevelt asked for 60,000 aircraft in 1942 and double that number in 1943. Plans called for the manufacture of 16 million tons of shipping and 120,000 tanks. The military needed supplies to train and equip a force that would grow to almost 16 million men. Thus, for the duration of the war, military production took precedence over the manufacture of civilian goods. Automobile plants built tanks and airplanes instead of cars; dress factories sewed military uniforms. The War Production Board, established by Roosevelt in early 1942, had the enormous task of allocating resources and coordinating production among thousands of independent factories.

During the war, American businesses overwhelmingly cooperated with government war-production plans.

Businesses, Universities, and the War Effort

Patriotism was one reason, but generous incentives were another. Major American industries had at first resisted government pressure to shift to military production. In 1940, as the United States produced armaments for the Allies, the American economy began to recover from the depression. Rising consumer spending built industrial confidence. Auto manufacturers, for example, expected to sell 4 million cars in 1941, a more than 25 percent increase over 1939. The massive retooling necessary to produce planes or tanks instead of cars would be enormously expensive and leave manufacturers totally dependent on a single client—the federal government. Moreover, many major industrialists, such as General Motors head Alfred Sloan, remained suspicious of Roosevelt and what they saw as his antibusiness policies.

Government, however, met business more than halfway. The federal government paid for expensive retooling and factory expansions; it guaranteed profits by allowing

PRODUCING MORE FOR VICTORY

GM
GENERAL MOTORS

Folks

"UNITED WE STAND"

JULY, 1942
VOL. 3   NO. 7

Dayton Presents Arms for Victory
Pageant "Plowshares"...Pages 2-5

▲ Unprepared to fight a war of such magnitude, the U.S. government turned to the nation's largest and most efficient corporations to produce the planes and ships and guns that would make America the "great arsenal of democracy," and General Motors received 8 percent of the value of all government war contracts. With no new cars to sell, GM continued to advertise in national magazines, proclaiming "Victory Is Our Business." Pictured here is GM's in-house magazine for employees, reminding these "production soldiers" of the importance of their work.

(Courtesy, Collection of Peter Kreitler/General Motors)

corporations to charge the government for production costs plus a fixed profit; it created generous tax write-offs and exemptions from antitrust laws. War mobilization did not require America's businesses to sacrifice profits. Instead, corporations doubled their net profits between 1939 and 1943. As Secretary of War Henry Stimson explained, when a "capitalist country" goes to war, it must "let business make money out of the process or business won't work."

Most military contracts went to America's largest corporations, which had the facilities and experience to guarantee rapid, efficient production. From mid-1940 through September 1944 the government awarded contracts totaling $175 billion, with about two-thirds going to the top hundred corporations. General Motors alone received 8 percent of the total. This approach made sense for a nation that wanted enormous quantities of war goods manufactured in the shortest possible time; most small businesses just did not have the necessary capacity. However, wartime government contracts further consolidated American manufacturing in the hands of a few giant corporations.

Wartime needs also created a new relationship between science and the U.S. military. Millions of dollars went to fund research programs at America's largest universities: $117 million to Massachusetts Institute of Technology alone. Such federally sponsored research programs developed new technologies of warfare, such as vastly improved radar systems and the proximity fuse. The most important government-sponsored scientific research program was the Manhattan Project, a $2 billion secret effort to build an atomic bomb. Roosevelt had been convinced by scientists fleeing the Nazis in 1939 that Germany was working to create an atomic weapon, and he resolved to beat them at their own efforts. The Manhattan Project achieved the world's first sustained nuclear chain reaction in 1942 at the University of Chicago, and in 1943 the federal government set up a secret community for atomic scientists and their families at Los Alamos, New Mexico. In this remote, sparsely populated, and beautiful setting, some of America's most talented scientists worked with Jewish refugees from Nazi Germany to develop the weapon that would change the world.

Manhattan Project

New Opportunities for Workers

America's new defense factories, running around the clock, required millions of workers. At first workers were plentiful: 9 million Americans were still unemployed in 1940 when war mobilization began, and 3 million remained without work in December 1941. But during the war, the armed forces took almost 16 million men out of the potential civilian labor pool, forcing industry to look elsewhere for workers. Women, African Americans, Mexican Americans, poor whites from the isolated mountain hollows of Appalachia and the tenant farms of the Deep South—all streamed into jobs in defense plants.

In some cases, federal action eased their path. In 1941, as the federal government poured billions of dollars into war industries, many industries refused to hire

African Americans. "The Negro will be considered only as janitors and other similar capacities," one executive notified black applicants. A. Philip Randolph, head of the Brotherhood of Sleeping Car Porters, proposed a march on Washington, D.C., to demand equal access to defense industry jobs. Roosevelt, fearing that the march might provoke race riots and also that communists might infiltrate the movement, offered the March on Washington movement a deal. In exchange for canceling the march, the president issued Executive Order No. 8802, which prohibited discrimination in war industries and government jobs. The Fair Employment Practices Committee (FEPC) was established to ensure that its provisions were respected. Although enforcement was uneven, hundreds of thousands of black Americans migrated from the South to the industrial cities of the North and West on the strength of this official guarantee of job equality.

Mexican workers also filled wartime jobs in the United States. Although the U.S. government had deported Mexicans as unemployment rose during the Great Depression, about 200,000 Mexican farm workers, or *braceros,* were offered short-term contracts to fill agricultural jobs left vacant as Americans sought well-paid war work. Mexican and Mexican American workers alike faced discrimination and segregation, but they seized the economic opportunities newly available to them. In 1941 not a single Mexican American worked in the Los Angeles shipyards; by 1944, 17,000 were employed there.

Early in the war production boom, employers insisted that women were not suited for industrial jobs. But

Women at Work

as labor shortages began to threaten the war effort, employers did an about-face. "Almost overnight," said Mary Anderson, head of the Women's Bureau of the Department of Labor, "women were reclassified by industrialists from a marginal to a basic labor supply for munitions making." Posters and billboards urged women to "Do the Job HE Left Behind." The government's War Manpower Commission glorified the invented worker "Rosie the Riveter," who was featured on posters, in magazines, and in the recruiting jingle "Rosie's got a boyfriend, Charlie / Charlie, he's a marine / Rosie is protecting Charlie / Working overtime on the riveting machine."

Rosie the Riveter was an inspiring image, but she did not accurately represent women in the American work force. Only 16 percent of women workers held jobs in defense plants, and only 4.4 percent of "skilled" jobs (such as riveting) were held by women. Nonetheless, during the war years, more than 6 million women entered the labor force, and the number of working women increased by

57 percent. More than 400,000 African American women left domestic service for higher-paying industrial jobs, often with union benefits. Seven million women moved to war-production areas, such as southern California, home of both shipyards and aircraft factories. And the majority of women workers who did not hold war-production jobs—whether they took traditional "women's jobs" as clerical workers or filled traditionally male jobs as bus drivers or even "lumberjills," as men left for military service or better-paid factory jobs—kept the American economy going and freed other workers for the demanding work in war-production plants.

Workers in defense plants were often expected to work ten days for every day off or to accept difficult night shifts. Recognizing the importance of keeping people on the job, both businesses and the federal government provided workers new forms of support. The West Coast Kaiser shipyards offered not only high pay, but also childcare, subsidized housing, and healthcare: the Kaiser Permanente Medical Care Program, a forerunner of the health maintenance organization (HMO), supplied medical care to workers for a weekly payroll deduction of 50 cents. The federal government also funded childcare centers and before- and after-school programs. At its peak, 130,000 preschoolers and 320,000 school-age children were enrolled in federally sponsored childcare.

Because industrial production was key to America's war strategy, the federal government attempted to make

Organized Labor During Wartime

sure that labor strikes, so common in the 1930s, would not interrupt production. Less than a week after Pearl Harbor, a White House labor-management conference agreed to a no-strike/no-lockout pledge. In 1942 Roosevelt created the National War Labor Board (NWLB) to settle labor disputes. The NWLB forged a temporary compromise between labor union demands for a "closed shop," in which only union members could work, and management's desire for "open" shops. Workers could not be required to join a union, but unions could enroll as many members as possible. Between 1940 and 1945, union membership ballooned from 8.5 million to 14.75 million.

However, the government did not hesitate to restrict union power if it threatened war production. When coal miners in the United Mine Workers union went on strike in 1943, following an attempt by the NWLB to limit wage increases to a cost-of-living adjustment, lack of coal halted railroads and shut down steel mills. Few Americans supported this strike. An air force pilot said, "I'd just as soon shoot down one of those strikers as shoot

War production plans called for defense factories to build 120,000 new aircraft in 1943. Here, women workers take on "men's jobs" at Vultee Aircraft Corporation, using riveting guns and bucking bars to build the center section of wings for training planes. *(© Corbis)*

440-foot-long cargo ships that transported the tanks and guns and bullets overseas—from 355 to 56 days. (As a publicity stunt, Kaiser's Richmond shipyard, near San Francisco, built one Liberty ship in 4 days, 15 hours, and 26 minutes.) The ships were not well made; welded hulls sometimes split in rough seas, and one ship foundered while still docked at the pier. However, as the United States struggled to produce cargo ships faster than German U-boats could sink them, speed of production was more important than quality.

A visitor to the Willow Run plant described "the roar of the machinery, the special din of the riveting gun absolutely deafening nearby, the throbbing crash of the giant metal presses . . . the far-reaching line of half-born skyships growing wings under swarms of workers." His words reveal the might of American industry but also offer a glimpse of the experience of workers, who did dirty, repetitive, and physically exhausting work day after day "for the duration." Although American propaganda during the war badly overstated the contributions of well-paid war workers as being equal to those of men in combat, the American production front played a critical role in winning the war.

LIFE ON THE HOME FRONT

The United States was the only major combatant in World War II that did not experience warfare directly (Hawai'i was a U.S. territory and the Philippines a U.S. possession, but neither was part of the nation proper). Americans worried about loved ones fighting in distant places; they grieved over the loss of sons and brothers and fathers and husbands and friends. Their lives were disrupted. But the United States, protected by two oceans

down Japs—they're doing as much to lose the war for us." As antilabor sentiment grew, Congress passed the War Labor Disputes (Smith-Connally) Act. This act gave the president authority to seize and operate any strike-bound plant deemed necessary to the national security, but it also contained broad, punitive provisions that created criminal penalties for leading strikes and tried to constrain union power by prohibiting contributions to political campaigns during time of war.

For close to four years, American factories operated twenty-four hours a day, seven days a week, fighting the war on the production front.

Success on the Production Front

Between 1940 and 1945, American factories turned out roughly 300,000 airplanes; 102,000 armored vehicles; 77,000 ships; 20 million small arms; 40 billion bullets; and 6 million tons of bombs. By war's end, the United States was producing 40 percent of the world's weaponry. This amazing feat depended on transforming formerly skilled work in industries like shipbuilding into an assembly-line process of mass production. Henry Ford, now seventy-eight years old, created a massive bomber plant on farmland along Willow Run Creek not far from Detroit. Willow Run's assembly lines, almost a mile long, turned out B-24 Liberator bombers at the rate of one an hour. On the West Coast, William Kaiser used mass-production techniques to cut construction time for Liberty ships—the huge, from its enemies, was spared the war that other nations experienced. Bombs did not fall on American cities; invading armies did not burn and rape and kill. Instead, war mobilization ended the Great Depression and brought prosperity. American civilians experienced the paradox of good times amid global conflagration.

Although the war was distant, it was a constant presence in the lives of Americans on "the home front."

Supporting the War Effort

Civilians supported the war effort in many ways, though Americans were never so unified or committed to shared sacrifice as the images of "the greatest generation" that were widespread in popular history and popular culture in the early twenty-first century suggest. During the war, however, families planted 20 million "victory gardens" to free up food supplies for the armed forces. Housewives saved fat from cooking and returned it to butchers, for cooking fat yielded glycerin to make black powder used in shells or bullets. Children collected scrap metal, aware that the iron in one old shovel blade was enough for four hand grenades and that every tin can helped make a tank or Liberty ship.

Many consumer goods were rationed or unavailable. To save wool for military use, the War Production Board basically redesigned men's suits, narrowing lapels, shortening jackets, and dispensing with vests and pant cuffs. Bathing suits, the WPB specified, must shrink by 10 percent. When silk and nylon were diverted from stockings to parachutes, women used makeup on their legs and drew in the "stocking" seam with eyebrow pencil. The Office of Price Administration (OPA), created by Congress in 1942, established a nationwide rationing system for such consumer goods as sugar, coffee, and gasoline. By early 1943, the OPA had instituted a point system for rationing food. Feeding a family required complex calculations. Every citizen—regardless of age—received two ration books each month. Blue stamps were for canned fruits and vegetables; red for meat, fish, and dairy. To buy a pound of meat, for example, consumers had to pay its cost in dollars and in points. With only 48 blue points and 64 red points per person per month, in September 1944 a small bottle of ketchup "cost" 20 blue points, while "creamery butter" cost 20 red points and sirloin steak 13 red points a pound. Pork shoulder, however, required only dollars. Sugar was tightly rationed, and people saved for months to make a birthday cake or holiday dessert. A black market existed, but most Americans understood that sugar produced alcohol for weapons manufacture and meat went to feed "our boys" overseas.

Despite near-unanimous support for the war, government leaders worried that, over time, public willingness

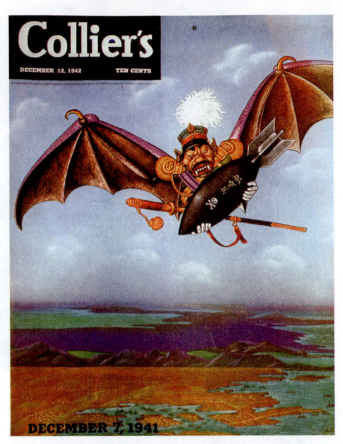

▲ In the days following the attack on Pearl Harbor, the Japanese were often pictured as subhuman—buck-toothed, nearsighted rodents and other vermin. Racial stereotyping would affect how both the Americans and the Japanese waged war. The Americans badly underestimated the Japanese, leaving themselves open for the surprise attack on Pearl Harbor and American forces in the Philippines. And the Japanese, believing Americans were barbarians who lacked a sense of honor, mistakenly expected that the United States would withdraw from East Asia once confronted with Japanese power and determination. *(Collier's, December 12, 1942)*

Propaganda and Popular Culture

to sacrifice might lag. In 1942 Roosevelt created the Office of War Information (OWI), which took charge of domestic propaganda and hired Hollywood filmmakers and New York copywriters to sell the war at home. OWI posters exhorted Americans to save and sacrifice, and reminded them to watch what they said, for "loose lips sink ships."

Popular culture also reinforced wartime messages. A *Saturday Evening Post* advertisement for vacuum cleaners (unavailable for the duration) urged women war workers to fight "for freedom and all that means to women everywhere. You're fighting for a little house of your own, and a husband to meet every night at the door. You're fighting for the right to bring up your children without the shadow of fear." Popular songs urged Americans to "Remember December 7th" or to "Accentuate the Positive." Others made fun of America's enemies ("You're a sap, Mr. Jap / You make a Yankee cranky / You're a sap, Mr. Jap / Uncle Sam is gonna spanky") or, like "Cleanin' My Rifle (and Dreamin' of You)," dealt with the hardship of wartime separation.

Movies drew 90 million viewers a week in 1944—out of a total population of 132 million. Hollywood sought to meet Eleanor Roosevelt's challenge to "Keep 'em laughing." *A WAVE, a WAC, and a Marine* promised "no battle scenes, no message, just barrels of fun and jive to make you happy you're alive." Others, such as *Bataan* or *Wake Island,* portrayed actual—if sanitized—events in the war. Even at the most frivolous comedies, however, the war was always present. Theaters held "plasma premieres," offering free admission to those who donated a half-pint of blood to the Red Cross. Audiences rose to sing "The Star Spangled Banner," then watched newsreels featuring carefully censored footage of recent combat before the feature film began. On D-Day, June 6, 1944, as Allied troops landed at Normandy, theater managers across the nation led audiences in the Lord's Prayer or the Twenty-third Psalm ("The Lord is my shepherd . . ."). It was in movie theaters that Americans saw the horror of Nazi death camps in May 1945. The Universal newsreel narrator ordered audiences, "Don't turn away. Look."

The war demanded sacrifices from Americans, but it also rewarded them with new highs in personal income.

Wartime Prosperity

Between 1939 and the end of the war, per capita income rose from $691 to $1,515. Wages and salaries increased more than 135 percent from 1940 to 1945. OPA-administered price controls kept inflation down so that wage increases did not disappear to higher costs. And with little to buy, savings rose.

Fighting World War II cost the United States approximately $304 billion (more than $3 trillion in today's dollars). Instead of financing the war primarily through taxation, the government relied on deficit spending, borrowing money in the form of war bonds sold to patriotic citizens and financial institutions. The national debt skyrocketed, from $49 billion in 1941 to $259 billion in 1945 (and was not paid off until 1970). However, wartime revenue acts increased the number of Americans paying personal income tax from 4 million to 42.6 million—at rates ranging from 6 to 94 percent—and introduced a new system in which employers "withheld" taxes from employee paychecks. For the first time, individual Americans paid more in taxes than corporations.

Despite hardships and fears, the war offered home-front Americans new opportunities, and millions of Americans took them. More than 15 million civilians moved during the war (see Map 27.2). More than half moved to another state, and half that number moved to another region. Seven hundred thousand black Americans left the South during the war years; in 1943, ten thousand black migrants poured into Los Angeles every month. People who had never traveled farther than the next county found themselves on the other side of the country—or of the world. People moved for defense jobs or to be close to loved ones at stateside military postings. Southerners moved north, northerners moved south, and 1.5 million people moved to California.

A Nation in Motion

The rapid influx of war workers to major cities and small towns strained community resources. Migrants crowded into substandard housing—even woodsheds, tents, or cellars—and into trailer parks without adequate sanitary facilities. Disease spread: scabies and ringworm, polio, tuberculosis. Many long-term residents found the newcomers—especially the unmarried male war workers—a rough bunch. In the small town of Lawrence, Kansas, civic leaders bragged of the economic boost a new war plant gave the town but fretted over the appearance of bars, "dirty windowed dispensaries" that sold alcohol to the war workers.

In and around Detroit, where car factories now produced tanks and planes, established residents called war workers freshly arrived from southern Appalachia "hillbillies" and "white trash." A new joke circulated: "How many states are there in the Union? Forty-five. Tennessee and Kentucky moved to Michigan, and Michigan went to hell." Many of these migrants knew little about urban life. One young man from rural Tennessee, unfamiliar with traffic lights and street signs, navigated by counting the number of trees between his home and the war plant where he worked. Some Appalachian "trailer-ites" appalled their neighbors by building outdoor privies or burying garbage in their yards.

As people from different backgrounds confronted one another under difficult conditions, tensions rose. Widespread racism made things worse. In 1943 almost 250 racial conflicts exploded in forty-seven cities. Outright racial warfare bloodied the streets of Detroit in June. White mobs, undeterred by police, roamed the city attacking blacks. Blacks hurled rocks at police and dragged white passengers off streetcars. At

Racial Conflicts

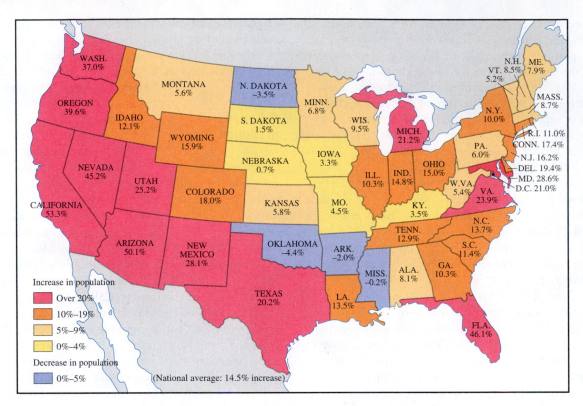

Map 27.2   A Nation on the Move, 1940–1950

American migration during the 1940s was the largest on record to that time. The farm population dropped dramatically as men, women, and children moved to war-production areas and to army and navy bases, particularly on the West Coast. Well over 30 million Americans (civilian and military) migrated during the war. Many returned to their rural homes after the war, but 12 million migrants stayed in their new locations. Notice the population increases on the West Coast, as well as in the Southwest and Florida.

the end of thirty hours of rioting, twenty-five blacks and nine whites lay dead. Surveying the damage, an elderly black woman said, "There ain't no North anymore. Everything now is South."

The heightened racial and ethnic tensions of wartime also led to riots in Los Angeles in 1943. Young Mexican American gang members, or *pachucos,* had adopted the zoot suit: a long jacket with wide padded shoulders, loose pants "pegged" below the knee, a wide-brimmed hat, and dangling watch chain. With cloth rationed, wearing pants requiring five yards of fabric was a political statement, and some young men wore the zoot suit as a purposeful rejection of wartime ideals of service and sacrifice. Although in fact a high percentage of Mexican Americans served in the armed forces, many white servicemen believed otherwise. Racial tensions were not far from the surface in overcrowded L.A., and rumors that *pachucos*

had attacked white sailors quickly led to violence. For four days, mobs of white men—mainly soldiers and sailors—roamed the streets attacking zoot-suiters and stripping them of their clothes. The city of Los Angeles outlawed zoot suits and arrested men who wore them. The "zoot suit riots" ended only when naval personnel were removed from the city.

The dislocations of war also had profound impacts on the nation's families. Despite policies that exempted

Families in Wartime

married men and fathers from the draft during most of the war, almost 3 million families were broken up. Young children grew up not knowing their father. The divorce rate of 16 per 1,000 marriages in 1940 almost doubled to 27 per 1,000 in 1944. At the same time, hundreds of thousands of men and women were getting married.

▲ Members of the Vega family pose for the camera in uniforms of the Marine Corps, National Guard, and U.S. Navy.

(Los Angeles Public Library)

The number of marriages rose from 73 per 1,000 unmarried women in 1939 to 93 in 1942. Some couples scrambled to get married before the man was sent overseas; others sought military deferments. The birth rate climbed as well: 2.4 million babies were born in 1939 and 3.1 million in 1943. Many were "goodbye babies," conceived to guarantee the continuation of the family if the father died in war.

On college campuses, some virtually stripped of male students, women complained, along with the song lyrics, "There is no available male." But other young women found an abundance of male company, sparking concern about wartime threats to sexual morality. *Youth in Crisis,* a 1943 newsreel, featured a girl with "experience far beyond her age" necking with a soldier on the street. These "victory girls" or "cuddle bunnies" were said to support the war effort by giving their all to men in uniform. Many young men and women, caught up in the emotional intensity of war, behaved as they never would in peacetime.

Often that meant hasty marriages to virtual strangers, especially if a baby was on the way. Taboos against unwed motherhood remained strong, however, and babies born outside marriage increased only from 0.7 percent to 1 percent of all births. Wartime mobility also increased opportunities for young men and women to explore sexual attraction to members of the same sex, and gay communities grew in such cities as San Francisco.

In many ways, the war reinforced traditional gender roles that had been weakened during the depression, when many men lost the role of breadwinner. Now men defended their nation while women "kept the home fires burning." Some women took "men's jobs," but those few who did so from patriotism rather than need understood their work to be "for the duration"—the home-front equivalent to men's wartime military service. Even so, women who worked were frequently blamed for neglecting their children and creating an "epidemic" of juvenile delinquency—evidenced by the "victory girl." Nonetheless, millions of women took on new responsibilities in wartime, whether on the factory floor or within their family. Many husbands returned to find that the lives of their wives and children seemed complete without them, and some women realized how much they had enjoyed their greater freedom and independence.

THE LIMITS OF AMERICAN IDEALS

During the war, the U.S. government worked hard to explain to its citizens the reasons for their sacrifices. In 1941 Roosevelt had pledged America to defend "four essential human freedoms"—freedom of speech, freedom of religion, freedom from want, and freedom from fear—and government-sponsored films contrasted democracy and totalitarianism, freedom and fascism, equality and oppression.

Despite such confident proclamations, as America fought the totalitarian regimes of the Axis powers, the nation confronted questions with no easy answers: What limits on civil liberties were justified in the interest of national security? How freely could information flow to the nation's citizens without revealing military secrets to the enemy and costing American lives? How could the United States protect itself against the threat of spies or saboteurs, especially from German, Italian, or Japanese citizens living in the United States? And what about America's ongoing domestic problems—particularly the problem of race? Could the nation address its own citizens' demands for reform as it fought the war against the Axis? The answers to these questions often revealed tensions between the nation's democratic ideals and its wartime practices.

War Brides

During and immediately after World War II, more than 60,000 American servicemen married women from other nations, both those the United States had fought alongside and those it had fought against. The U.S. government promised these servicemen that it would deliver their wives and babies to their doorstep, free of charge.

The U.S. Army's "Operation War Bride," which would eventually transport more than 70,000 women and children, began in Britain in early 1946. The first group of war brides—455 British women and their 132 children—arrived in the United States on February 4, 1946. As the former World War II transport *Argentina* sailed into New York harbor in the predawn darkness, the Statue of Liberty was specially illuminated to greet them. Women who had sung, "There'll Always Be an England" as they set sail from Southampton, England, gathered on the deck to attempt "The Star-Spangled Banner." These women, many of them teenagers, had left their homes and families behind to join their new husbands in a strange land. Mrs. Edna Olds Butler, "nearly seventeen," practiced a southern accent in hopes that her new in-laws in Roanoke Rapids, North Carolina, would be able to understand her. Two young British women

had married African American soldiers, and one carried with her a letter from her husband promising that she would be the "white queen of Atlanta."

War brides fanned out to every state of the Union. Women from war-destroyed cities were impressed by the material abundance of American society and pleased by the warm welcome they received. But America's racial prejudice shocked Shanghai native Helen Chia Wong, wife of Staff Sgt. Albert Wong of the Fourteenth Air Force Service Command, when she and her husband were turned away from a house by a rental agent with the explanation "The neighbors wouldn't like it." The file of one young woman who sought passage back to England showed another kind of distress. An American official recorded that she was "too shocked to bring her baby up on the black tracks of a West Virginia [coal] mining town as against her own home in English countryside of rose-covered fences." It was not always easy, but most of the war brides settled into their new families and communities, becoming part of their new nation and helping to forge an intimate link between America and other nations of the world.

▲ The army's "Operation War Bride" (sometimes called "Operation Mother-in-Law" or "the Diaper Run") began in Britain in early 1946. Employing eleven former World War II troopships, including the *Queen Mary,* the U.S. government relocated the wives and babies of U.S. servicemen from dozens of nations to the United States. These English war brides, with babies their fathers have not yet seen, are waiting to be reunited with their husbands in Massachusetts, Missouri, and Iowa. *(© Bettmann/Corbis)*

For the most part, America handled the issue of civil liberties well. American leaders embraced a "strategy of truth," declaring that citizens of a democratic nation required a truthful accounting of the war's progress. However, the government closely controlled information about military matters. Censorship was serious business, as even seemingly unimportant details might tip off enemies about troop movements or invasion plans. Government-created propaganda sometimes dehumanized the enemy. Nonetheless, the American government resorted to hate mongering much less frequently than during the First World War.

More complex was the question of how to handle dissent and how to guard against the possibility that enemy agents were operating within the nation's borders. The Alien Registration (Smith) Act, passed in 1940, made it unlawful to advocate the overthrow of the U.S. government by force or violence, or to join any organization that did so. After Pearl Harbor, the government used this authority to take thousands of Germans, Italians, and other Europeans into custody as suspected spies and potential traitors. During the war, the government interned 14,426 Europeans in Enemy Alien Camps. Fearing subversion, the government also prohibited ten thousand Italian Americans from living or working in restricted zones along the California coast, including San Francisco and Monterey Bay.

In March 1942, Roosevelt ordered that all 112,000 foreign-born Japanese and Japanese Americans living in

Internment of Japanese Americans

California, Oregon, and the state of Washington (the vast majority of the mainland population) be removed from the West Coast to "relocation centers" for the duration of the war. Each of the Italian and German nationals interned by the U.S. government faced specific, individual charges. That was not the case for Japanese nationals and Japanese Americans. They were imprisoned as a group, under suspicion solely because they were of Japanese descent.

American anger at Japan's "sneak attack" on Pearl Harbor fueled the calls for internment, as did fears that West Coast cities might yet come under enemy attack. Long-standing racism was evident, as the chief of the Western Defense Command warned, "The Japanese race is an enemy race." Finally, people in economic competition with Japanese Americans strongly supported internment. Although Japanese nationals were forbidden to gain U.S. citizenship or own property, American-born Nissei (second generation) and Sansei (third generation), all U.S. citizens, were increasingly successful in business and agriculture. The relocation order forced Japanese Americans

▲ In February 1942 President Franklin D. Roosevelt ordered that all Japanese resident aliens and Japanese Americans living on the West Coast—about 110,000 people—be confined in remote "internment camps." Residents were not allowed to take photographs, but many tried to illustrate their experiences. This watercolor, "First Impressions of Manzanar," shows internees' constant struggle against the harsh desert climate, with its high winds, swirling dust, and extreme temperatures. Manzanar War Relocation Camp was located in California, at the foot of the Sierra Nevadas. The eight guard towers that surrounded the camp were manned by military police with submachine guns.

(Gift of Tango Takamura, Department of Special Collections Charles E. Young Research Library, UCLA)

to sell property valued at $500 million for a fraction of its worth. West Coast Japanese Americans also lost their positions in the truck-garden, floral, and fishing industries.

The internees were sent to flood-damaged lands at Relocation, Arkansas; to the intermountain terrain of Wyoming and the desert of western Arizona; and to other arid and desolate spots in the West. The camps were bleak and demoralizing. Behind barbed wire stood tarpapered wooden barracks where entire families lived in a single room furnished only with cots, blankets, and a bare light bulb. Toilets and dining and bathing facilities were communal; privacy was almost nonexistent. In such difficult circumstances, people nonetheless attempted to sustain community life, setting up schools for the children and clubs for adults.

Betrayed by their government, almost 6,000 internees renounced U.S. citizenship and demanded to be sent to Japan. Some sought legal remedy, but the Supreme Court upheld the government's action in *Korematsu v. U.S.* (1944). Still others sought to demonstrate their loyalty. The all–Japanese American 442nd Regimental Combat Team, drawn heavily from young men in internment camps, was the most decorated unit of its size. Suffering heavy casualties in Italy and France, members of the 442nd were awarded a Congressional Medal of Honor, 47 Distinguished Service Crosses, 350 Silver Stars, and more than 3,600 Purple Hearts. In 1988 Congress issued a public apology and largely symbolic payment of $20,000 to each of the 60,000 surviving Japanese American internees.

As America mobilized for war, some African American leaders attempted to force the nation to confront the uncomfortable parallels between the racist doctrines of the Nazis and the persistence of Jim Crow segregation in the United States. Proclaiming a "Double V" campaign (victory at home and abroad), groups such as the National Association for the Advancement of Colored People (NAACP) hoped to "persuade, embarrass, compel and shame our government and our nation . . . into a more enlightened attitude toward a tenth of its people." Membership in civil rights organizations soared. The NAACP, 50,000 strong in 1940, had 450,000 members by 1946. And in 1942 civil rights activists, influenced by the philosophy of India's Mohandas Gandhi, founded the Congress of Racial Equality (CORE), which stressed "nonviolent direct action" and staged sit-ins to desegregate restaurants and movie theaters in Chicago and Washington, D.C.

African Americans and "Double V"

Military service was a key issue for African Americans, who understood the traditional link between the duty to defend one's country and the rights of full citizenship. But the U.S. military remained segregated by race and strongly resisted efforts to use black units as combat troops. As late as 1943, less than 6 percent of the armed forces were African American, compared with more than 10 percent of the population. The marines at first refused to accept African Americans at all, and the navy approximated segregation by assigning black men to service positions in which they would rarely interact with nonblacks as equals or superiors.

Why did the United States fight a war for democracy with a segregated military? The U.S. military understood that its sole priority was to stop the Axis and win the war, and the federal government and War Department decided that the midst of world war was no time to try to integrate the armed forces. The majority of Americans (approximately 89 percent of Americans were white) opposed integration, many of them vehemently. As a sign of how deeply racist beliefs penetrated the United States, the Red Cross segregated blood plasma during the war.

A Segregated Military

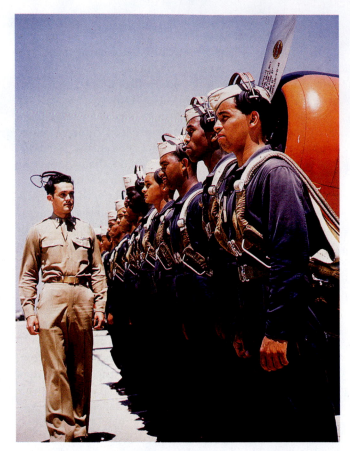

▲ During World War II, for the first time, the War Department sanctioned the training and use of African American pilots. These members of the 99th Pursuit Squadron—known as "Tuskegee Airmen" because they trained at Alabama's all-black Tuskegee Institute—joined combat over North Africa in June 1943. Like most African American units in the racially segregated armed forces, the men of the 99th Pursuit Squadron were under the command of white officers. *(National Archives)*

In most southern states, racial segregation was not simply custom; it was the law. Integration of military installations and training camps, the majority of which were in the South, would have provoked a crisis as federal power contradicted state law. Pointing to outbreaks of racial violence in southern training camps as evidence, government and military officials argued that wartime integration would almost certainly provoke even more racial violence, create disorder within the military, and hinder America's war effort. Such resistance might have been short-term, but the War Department did not take that chance. Justifying its decision, the War Department argued that it could not "act outside the law, nor contrary to the will of the majority of the citizens of the Nation." General George C. Marshall, Army Chief of Staff, proclaimed that it was not the job of the army to "solve a social problem that has perplexed the American people throughout the history of this nation. . . . The army is not a sociological laboratory." Hopes for racial justice, so long deferred, were another casualty of the war.

Despite such discrimination, many African Americans stood up for their rights. Lt. Jackie Robinson refused to move to the back of the bus while training at the army's Camp Hood, Texas, in 1944—and faced court-martial, even though military regulations forbade racial discrimination on military vehicles, regardless of local law or custom. Black sailors disobeyed orders to return to work after surviving an explosion that destroyed two ships, killed 320 men, and shattered windows 35 miles away—an explosion caused by the navy practice of assigning men who were completely untrained in handling high explosives to load bombs from the munitions depot at Port Chicago, near San Francisco, onto Liberty ships. When they were court-martialed for mutiny, future Supreme Court justice and chief counsel for the NAACP Thurgood Marshall asked why only black sailors did this work. He proclaimed, "This is not fifty men on trial for mutiny. This is the Navy on trial for its whole vicious policy toward Negroes."

As the war wore on, African American servicemen did fight on the front lines, and fought well. The Marine Corps commandant in the Pacific proclaimed that "Negro Ma-

rines are no longer on trial. They are Marines, period." The "Tuskegee Airmen," pilots trained at the Tuskegee Institute in Alabama, saw heroic service in all-black units, such as the Ninety-ninth Pursuit Squadron, which won eighty Distinguished Flying Crosses. After the war, African Americans—as some white Americans had feared—called on their wartime service to claim the full rights of citizenship. Black men and women shared fully in the benefits offered to veterans under the GI Bill (see page 827). African Americans' wartime experiences were mixed, but the war was a turning point in the movement for equal rights.

America and the Holocaust

America's inaction in the face of what we now call the Holocaust is a tragic failure, though the consequences are clearer in retrospect than they were at the time. As the United States turned away refugees on the *St. Louis* (page 753) in early 1939 and refused to relax its immigration quotas to admit European Jews and others fleeing Hitler's Germany, almost no one foresaw that the future would bring death camps like Auschwitz or Treblinka. Americans knew they were turning away people fleeing dire persecution, and while anti-Semitism played a significant role in that decision, it was not unusual to refuse those seeking refuge, especially in the midst of a major economic crisis that seemed to be worsening.

As early as 1942, American newspapers reported the "mass slaughter" of Jews and other "undesirables" (Gypsies, homosexuals, the physically and mentally handicapped) under Hitler. Many Americans, having been taken in by manufactured atrocity tales during World War I,

◀ Millions of civilians were starved, gassed, machine gunned, or worked to death by their Nazi jailers during the war. Here, U.S. Army troops force Nazi Party members to exhume the bodies of two hundred Russian officers and others who were shot by the SS near Wuelfel, while the residents of Hannover watch. Allied troops often compelled local townspeople to watch exhumations of mass graves, attempting to make them confront the atrocities that many insisted they never knew were happening.

(United States Holocaust Memorial Museum)

wrongly discounted these stories. But Roosevelt knew about the existence of Nazi death camps capable of killing up to two thousand people an hour using the gas Zyklon-B.

In 1943 British and American representatives met in Bermuda to discuss the situation but took no concrete action. Many Allied officials, though horrified, saw Hitler's "Final Solution" as just one part of a larger, worldwide holocaust in which tens of millions were dying. Appalled by the reluctance to act, Secretary of the Treasury Henry Morgenthau Jr. charged that the State Department's foot dragging made the United States an accessory to murder. "The matter of rescuing the Jews from extermination is a trust too great to remain in the hands of men who are indifferent, callous, and perhaps even hostile," he wrote bitterly in 1944. Later that year, stirred by Morgenthau's well-documented plea, Roosevelt created the War Refugee Board, which set up refugee camps in Europe and played a crucial role in saving 200,000 Jews from death. But, lamented one American official, "by that time it was too damned late to do too much." By war's end, the Nazis had systematically murdered almost 11 million people.

LIFE IN THE MILITARY

More than 15 million men and approximately 350,000 women served in the U.S. armed forces during World War II. Eighteen percent of American families had a father, son, or brother in the armed forces. Some of these men (and all of the women) volunteered, eager to defend their nation. But most who served—more than 10 million—were draftees. By presidential order, the military stopped accepting volunteers in December 1942. Faced with the challenge of filling a broad range of military positions while maintaining war production and the civilian economy, the Selective Service system and the new War Manpower Commission attempted to centralize control over the allocation of manpower. Their efforts were often defeated as tensions between local and national control remained strong throughout the war. Most Americans, however, believed that the draft operated fairly. Compared with the Civil War and the Vietnam War, the draft reached broadly and mostly equitably through the American population during World War II.

The Selective Service Act did allow deferments, but they did not disproportionately benefit the well-to-do.

Selective Service

Almost 10,000 Princeton students or alumni served—as did all 4 of Franklin and Eleanor Roosevelt's sons—while throughout the nation judges offered minor criminal offenders the choice of the military or jail. The small number of college deferments was more than balanced by deferments for a long list of "critical occupations," including not only war industry workers but also almost 2 million agricultural workers. Most exemptions from military service were for men deemed physically or mentally unqualified to serve. Army physicians discovered what a toll the depression had taken on the nation's youth as draftees arrived with rotted teeth and deteriorated eyesight—signs of malnutrition. Army dentists pulled 15 million teeth and fitted men with dentures; optometrists prescribed 2.5 million pairs of glasses. Hundreds of thousands of men with venereal diseases were cured by sulfa drugs, developed in 1942. Military examiners also found evidence of the impact of racism and poverty. Half of African American draftees had no schooling beyond the sixth grade, and up to one-third were functionally illiterate. Forty-six percent of African Americans and almost one-third of European-Americans called for the draft were classified "4-F"—unfit for service.

Nonetheless, almost 12 percent of America's total population served in the military. Regiments were created rapidly, throwing together men from very different backgrounds. Regional differences were profound, and northerners and southerners often—literally—could not understand one another. Ethnic differences complicated things further. Although African Americans and Japanese Americans served in their own separate units, Hispanics, Native Americans, and Chinese Americans served in "white" units. Furthermore, the differences among "whites"—the "Italian" kid from Brooklyn and the one from rural Mississippi (or rural Montana)—were profound. The result was often tension, but many Americans became less prejudiced and less provincial as they served with men unlike themselves.

Although military service was widespread, the burdens of combat were not equally shared. Although women served their nation honorably and often courageously, women's roles in the U.S. military were much more restricted than in the British or Soviet militaries, where women served as anti-aircraft gunners and in other combat-related positions. U.S. women served as nurses, in communications offices, and as typists or cooks. The recruiting slogan for the WACs (Women's Army Corps) was "Release a Man for Combat." However, most men in the armed forces never saw combat either; one-quarter never left the United States. The United States had the lowest "teeth-to-tail" ratio of any of the combatants, with each combat soldier backed up by eight or more support personnel. Japan's ratio was

Fighting the War

close to one to one. One-third of U.S. military personnel served in clerical positions, with well educated men most likely to be slotted into noncombat positions. African Americans, though assigned dirty and dangerous tasks, were largely kept from combat service. In World War II, lower-class, less-educated white men bore the brunt of the fighting.

For those who fought, combat in World War II was as horrible as anything humans have experienced. Home-front audiences for the war films Hollywood churned out saw men die bravely, shot cleanly through the heart and comforted by their buddies in their last moments. What men experienced was carnage. Less than 10 percent of casualties were caused by bullets. Most men were killed or wounded by mortars, bombs, or grenades. Seventy-five thousand American men remained missing in action at the end of the war, blown into fragments of flesh too small to identify. Combat meant days and weeks of unrelenting rain in malarial jungles, sliding down a mud-slicked hill to land in a pile of putrid corpses. It meant drowning in the waters of the frigid North Atlantic amid burning wreckage of a torpedoed ship. It meant using flamethrowers that burned at 2,000 degrees Fahrenheit on other human beings. It meant being violently ill on a landing craft steering through floating body parts of those who had attempted the landing first, knowing that if you tripped you would likely drown under the sixty-eight-pound weight of your pack, and that if you made it ashore you would likely be blown apart by artillery shells. Service was "for the duration" of the war. Only death, serious injury, or victory offered release. In this hard world, men fought to victory.

In forty-five months of war, close to 300,000 American servicemen died in combat. Almost 1 million American troops were wounded, half of them seriously. Medical advances, such as the development of penicillin and the use of blood plasma to prevent shock, helped wounded men survive—but many never fully recovered from those wounds. Between 20 and 30 percent of combat casualties were psychoneurotic, as men were pushed past the limits of endurance. The federal government strictly censored images of American combat deaths for most of the war, consigning them to a secret file known as "the chamber of horrors." Americans at home rarely understood what combat had been like, and many men, upon return, never talked about their experiences in the war.

WINNING THE WAR

Axis hopes for victory depended on a short war. Leaders in Germany and Japan knew that, if the United States

had time to fully mobilize, flooding the theaters of war with armaments and reinforcing Allied troops with fresh, trained men, the war was lost. However, powerful factions in the Japanese military and German leadership believed that the United States would concede if it met with early, decisive defeats. As Hitler, blinded by racial arrogance, had stated shortly after declaring war on the United States, "I don't see much future for the Americans. . . . It's a decayed country. . . . American society [is] half Judaized, and the other half Negrified. How can one expect a State like that to hold together." By mid-1942 the Axis powers understood that they had underestimated not only American resolve but also the willingness of other Allies to sacrifice unimaginable numbers of their citizens to stop the Axis advance (see Map 27.3). The chance of an Axis victory grew increasingly slim as the months passed, but though the outcome was virtually certain after spring 1943, two years of bloody fighting lay ahead.

As the war continued, the Allies concentrated on defeating the aggressors, but their suspicions of one another undermined cooperation. The Soviets continued to press Britain and the United States to open a second front to the west of Germany and so draw German troops away from the USSR. The United States and Britain, however, continued to delay. Stalin was not mollified by the massive "thousand-bomber" raids on Germany begun by Britain's Royal Air Force in 1942, nor by the Allied invasion of Italy in the summer of 1943. With the alliance badly strained, Roosevelt sought reconciliation through personal diplomacy. The three Allied leaders met in Teheran, Iran, in December 1943. Stalin dismissed Churchill's repetitious justifications for further delaying a second front that would draw German troops away from the Soviet Union. Roosevelt had had enough, too; he also rejected Churchill's proposal for another peripheral attack, this time through the Balkans to Vienna. The three finally agreed to launch Operation Overlord—the cross-Channel invasion of France—in early 1944. And the Soviet Union promised to aid the Allies against Japan once Germany was defeated.

Tensions Among the Allies

The second front opened in the dark morning hours of June 6, 1944: D-Day. In the largest amphibious landing in history, more than 140,000 Allied troops under the command of American general Dwight D. Eisenhower scrambled ashore at Normandy, France. Thousands of ships ferried the men within one hundred yards of the sandy beaches. Landing craft and soldiers immediately encountered the enemy; they triggered mines and were pinned down by fire from

War in Europe

Map 27.3

The Allies on the Offensive in Europe, 1942–1945

The United States pursued a "Europe First" policy: first defeat Germany, then focus on Japan. American military efforts began in North Africa in late 1942 and ended in Germany in 1945 on May 8 (V-E Day).

▲ U.S. troops land at Normandy during the D-Day invasion on June 6, 1944. Men drowned as they lost their footing in the rough surf and were pulled under by the weight of their 68-pound packs; others were torn by artillery or machine gun fire from German gun batteries on the cliffs that rose steeply from the beaches. About 2500 Allied troops died in the D-Day invasion. Together, Allied and German troops suffered more than 450,000 casualties (killed, missing, or wounded) during the Battle of Normandy, which lasted until the end of August. *(Robert Capa/ Magnum Photos, Inc.)*

cliffside pillboxes. Meanwhile, 15,500 Allied airborne troops, along with thousands of dummies meant to confuse the German defense, dropped from aircraft. Although heavy aerial and naval bombardment and the clandestine work of saboteurs had softened the German defenses, the fighting was ferocious.

By the end of June 11, 170,000 more Allied troops were fighting in France. They spread across the countryside, liberating France and Belgium by the end of August. Almost 54,000 Allied troops died in that struggle, and up to 20,000 French civilians were killed, most by Allied bombing. In September the Allies pushed into Germany. German armored divisions counterattacked in Belgium's Ardennes Forest in December, hoping to push on to

Antwerp to halt the flow of Allied supplies through that Belgian port. After weeks of heavy fighting in what has come to be called the Battle of the Bulge—because of a "bulge" 60 miles deep and 40 miles wide where German troops had pushed back the Allied line—the Allies gained control in late January 1945.

By that point, "strategic" bombing (though not nearly as precise as was publicly claimed) had destroyed Germany's war-production capacity and devastated its economy. In early 1945, the British and Americans began "morale" bombing, killing tens of thousands of civilians in aerial attacks on Berlin and then Dresden. Meanwhile, battle-hardened Soviet troops marched through Poland and cut a path to Berlin. American forces crossed the

Rhine River in March 1945 and captured the heavily industrial Ruhr valley. Several units peeled off to enter Austria and Czechoslovakia, where they met up with Soviet soldiers.

Even as Allied forces faced the last, desperate resistance from German troops in the Battle of the Bulge, Allied leaders began planning the peace. In early 1945, Franklin Roosevelt, by this time very ill, called for a summit meeting to discuss a host of political questions—including what to do with Germany. The three Allied leaders met at Yalta, in the Russian Crimea, in February 1945. Each had definite goals for the shape of the postwar world. Britain, its formerly powerful empire now vulnerable and shrinking, sought to protect its colonial possessions and to limit Soviet power. The Soviet Union, with 21 million dead, wanted Germany to pay reparations to fund its massive rebuilding effort. The Soviets hoped to expand their sphere of influence throughout eastern Europe and to guarantee their national security; Germany, Stalin insisted, must be permanently weakened. Two German invasions in a quarter-century were more than enough.

The United States, like the other powers, hoped to expand its influence and to control the peace. To that end, Roosevelt lobbied for the United Nations Organization, approved in principle the previous year at Dumbarton Oaks in Washington, D.C., through which the United States hoped to exercise influence. The lessons of World War I also shaped American proposals; seeking long-term peace and stability, the United States hoped to avoid the debts-reparations fiasco that had plagued Europe after the First World War. U.S. goals included

Yalta Conference

self-determination for liberated peoples; gradual and orderly decolonization; and management of world affairs by what Roosevelt had once called the Four Policemen: the Soviet Union, Great Britain, the United States, and China. (Roosevelt hoped China might help stabilize Asia after the war; the United States abolished the Chinese Exclusion Act in 1943 in an attempt to consolidate ties between the two nations.) The United States was also determined to limit Soviet influence in the postwar world. Obviously, there was much about which to disagree.

Military positions at the time of the Yalta conference helped shape the negotiations. Soviet troops occupied eastern European nations that they had liberated, including Poland, where Moscow had installed a pro-Soviet regime despite a British-supported Polish government-in-exile in London. With Soviet troops in place in eastern Europe, Britain and the United States were limited in what they could negotiate regarding these lands. As for Germany, the Big Three agreed that some eastern German territory would be transferred to Poland and the remainder divided into four zones—the fourth zone to be administered by France, which Britain had pressed to be included in plans for postwar control of Germany, so as to reduce the Soviet zone from one-third to one-quarter. Berlin, within the Soviet zone, would also be divided among the four victors. Yalta marked the high point of the Grand Alliance; in the tradition of diplomatic give-

The three Allied leaders—Winston ▶ Churchill, Franklin D. Roosevelt, and Joseph Stalin—met at Yalta in February 1945. Having been president for twelve years, Roosevelt showed signs of age and fatigue. Two months later, he died of a massive cerebral hemorrhage. *(Franklin D. Roosevelt Library)*

and-take, each of the Allies came away with something it wanted. In exchange for U.S. promises to support Soviet claims on territory lost to Japan in the Russo-Japanese War of 1904–1905, Stalin agreed to sign a treaty of friendship with Jiang Jieshi (Chiang Kai-shek), America's ally in China, rather than with the communist Mao Zedong (Mao Tse-tung), and to declare war on Japan two or three months after Hitler's defeat.

Franklin D. Roosevelt, reelected to an unprecedented fourth term in November 1944, did not live to see the war's end. He died on April 12, and Vice President Harry S. Truman became president and commander-in-chief. Truman, a senator from Missouri who had replaced former vice president Henry Wallace as Roosevelt's running mate in 1944, was inexperienced in foreign policy. He was not even informed about the top-secret atomic weapons project until after he became president. The day after Roosevelt's death, Truman sought out old friends, Democrats and Republicans, in Congress, to ask their help in this "terrible job." Shortly afterward, he told reporters, "Boys, if you ever pray, pray for me now. I don't know whether you fellows ever had a load of hay fall on you, but when they told me yesterday what had happened, I felt like the moon, the stars, and all the planets had fallen on me." Eighteen days into Truman's presidency, Adolf Hitler killed him-

Harry Truman

self in a bunker in bomb-ravaged Berlin. On May 8 Germany surrendered.

As the great powers jockeyed for influence after Germany's surrender, the Grand Alliance began to crumble. At the Potsdam Conference in mid-July, Truman—a novice at international diplomacy—was less patient with the Soviets than Roosevelt had been. And Truman learned during the conference that a test of the new atomic weapon had been successful. The United States, possessing such a weapon, no longer needed the Soviet Union's help in fighting the Pacific war. Roosevelt had secretly promised Stalin territory from Japan's wartime holdings in exchange for help in defeating Japan; the bomb made those concessions unnecessary. The Allies did agree that Japan must surrender unconditionally. But with the defeat of Hitler and the end of the European war, the wartime bonds between the Allies were strained to breaking.

In the Pacific, the war continued. Since halting the Japanese advance in the Battle of Midway in June 1942, American strategy had been to "island-hop" toward Japan, skipping the most strongly fortified islands whenever possible and taking the weaker ones, aiming to strand the Japanese armies on their island outposts. To cut off supplies being shipped from Japan's home islands, Americans also targeted the Japanese merchant marine. Allied and Japanese forces fought savagely for control of tiny specks of land scattered throughout the Pacific. By 1944, Allied troops—from the United States, Britain,

War in the Pacific

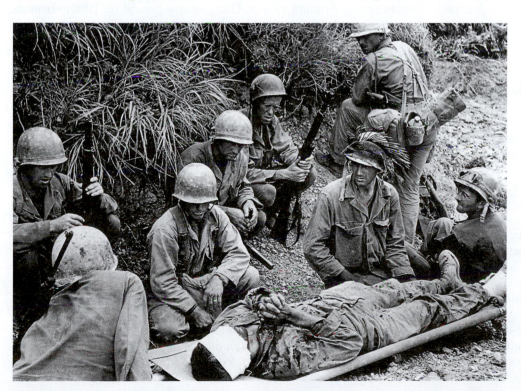

◀ On Okinawa, a wounded GI prays while awaiting evacuation to a field hospital. Medical advances, such as the discovery of penicillin and the use of glucose saline solution to replace lost blood, greatly improved the survival rate for those wounded in combat. But where combat was especially horrific, as it was on Okinawa, psychiatric casualties might outnumber combat deaths three to one.

(W. Eugene Smith/Timepix/Getty Images)

Australia, and New Zealand—had secured the Solomon, Gilbert, Marshall, and Mariana Islands. General Douglas MacArthur landed at Leyte to retake the Philippines for the United States in October 1944.

In February 1945, while the Big Three were meeting at Yalta, U.S. and Japanese troops battled for Iwo Jima, an island less than 5 miles long, located about 700 miles south of Tokyo. Twenty-one thousand Japanese defenders occupied the island's high ground. Hidden in a network of caves, trenches, and underground tunnels, they were protected from the aerial bombardment that U.S. forces used to clear the way for an amphibious landing. The stark volcanic island offered no cover, and marines were slaughtered as they came ashore. For twenty days, U.S. forces fought their way, yard by yard, up Mount Suribachi, the highest and most heavily fortified point on Iwo Jima. The struggle for Iwo Jima cost the lives of 6,821 Americans and more than 20,000 Japanese—some of whom committed suicide rather than surrender. Only 200 Japanese survived.

A month later, American troops landed on Okinawa, an island in the Ryukyus chain at the southern tip of Japan, from which Allied forces planned to invade the main Japanese islands. Fighting raged for two months; death was everywhere. The monsoon rains began in May, turning battlefields into seas of mud filled with decaying corpses. The supporting fleet endured waves of mass kamikaze (suicide) attacks, in which Japanese pilots intentionally crashed bomb-laden planes into American ships. Almost 5,000 seamen perished in these attacks. On Okinawa, 7,374 American soldiers and marines died in battle. Almost the entire Japanese garrison of 100,000 was killed. More than one-quarter of Okinawa's people, or approximately 80,000 civilians, perished as the two powers struggled over their island.

Even with American forces entrenched just 350 miles from Japan's main islands, Japanese leaders still refused to admit defeat. A powerful military faction was determined to avoid the humiliation of an unconditional surrender and to preserve the emperor's sovereignty. They hung on even while American bombers leveled their cities. On the night of March 9, 1945, 333 American B-29 Superfortresses dropped a mixture of explosives and incendiary devices on a 4-by-3-mile area of Tokyo. Attempting to demonstrate the strategic value of airpower, they created a firestorm, a blaze so fierce that it sucked all the oxygen from the air, creating hurricane-force winds and growing so hot it could melt concrete and steel. Almost 100,000 people were incinerated, suffocated, or boiled to death in canals where

Bombing of Japan

they had taken refuge from the fire. Over the following five months, American bombers attacked sixty-six Japanese cities, leaving 8 million people homeless, killing almost 900,000.

Japan, at the same time, was attempting to bomb the U.S. mainland. Thousands of bomb-bearing high-altitude balloons, constructed out of rice paper and potato-flour paste by schoolgirls, were launched into the jet stream. Those that did reach the United States fell on unpopulated areas, occasionally starting forest fires. The only mainland U.S. casualties in the war were five children and an adult on a Sunday school picnic in Oregon who accidentally detonated a balloon bomb that they found in the underbrush. As General Yamamoto had realized at the war's beginning, American resources would far outlast Japan's.

Early in the summer of 1945, Japan began to send out peace feelers through the Soviets. Japan was not, however, willing to accept the "unconditional surrender" terms on which the Allied leaders had agreed at Potsdam, and Truman and his advisers chose not to pursue a negotiated peace. By this time, U.S. troops were mobilizing for an invasion of the Japanese home islands. The experiences of Iwo Jima and Okinawa weighed heavily in the planning; Japanese troops had fought on, well past any hope of victory, and death tolls for Japanese and American troops alike had been enormous. News of the success of the Manhattan Project offered another option, and President Truman took it. Using atomic bombs on Japan, Truman believed, would end the war quickly and save American lives.

Historians still debate Truman's decision to use the atomic bomb. Why would he not negotiate surrender terms? Was Japan on the verge of an unconditional surrender, as some argue? Or was the antisurrender faction of Japanese military leaders strong enough to prevail? Truman knew the bomb could give the United States both real and psychological power in negotiating the peace; how much did his desire to demonstrate the bomb's power to the Soviet Union, or to prevent the Soviets from playing a major role in the last stages of the Pacific war, influence his decision? Did racism or a desire for retaliation play a role? How large were the projected casualty figures for invasion on which Truman based his decision, and were they accurate? No matter the answers to these ongoing debates, bombing (whether conventional or atomic) fit the established U.S. strategy of using machines rather than men whenever possible.

The decision to use the bomb did not seem as momentous to Truman as it does in retrospect. The moral line had already been crossed, as the move to wholesale bombing of civilian populations continued throughout the war: The

▲ This scorched watch, found in the rubble at Hiroshima, stopped at the time of the blast—8:16. The shock waves and fires caused by the atomic bomb leveled great expanses of the city. Radiation released by the bomb caused lingering deaths for thousands who survived the explosion. The photo of Hiroshima shown above was taken eight months after the attack. *(Watch: John Launois/Black Star; Hiroshima: U.S. Air Force)*

Japanese had bombed the Chinese city of Shanghai in 1937. Germans had "terror-bombed" Warsaw, Rotterdam, and London. British and American bombers had purposely created firestorms in German cities; on a single night in February 1945, 225,000 people perished in the bombing of Dresden. The American bombing of Japanese cities—accomplished with conventional weapons—had already killed close to a million people and destroyed 56 square miles of Tokyo alone. What distinguished the atomic bombs from conventional bombs was their power and their efficiency—not that they killed huge numbers of innocent civilians in unspeakably awful ways.

On July 26, 1945, the Allies delivered an ultimatum to Japan: promising that the Japanese people would not be "enslaved," the Potsdam Declaration called for the Japanese to surrender unconditionally or face "prompt and utter destruction." Tokyo radio announced that the government would respond with *mokusatsu* (literally, "kill with silence," or ignore the ultimatum). On August 6, 1945, a B-29 bomber named after the pilot's mother, the

Enola Gay, dropped an atomic bomb above the city of Hiroshima. A flash of dazzling light shot across the sky; then a huge, purplish mushroom cloud boiled forty thousand feet into the atmosphere. Much of the city was leveled by the blast. The bomb ignited a firestorm, and thousands who survived the initial blast burned to death. Approximately 130,000 people were killed. Tens of thousands more would suffer the effects of radiation poisoning.

American planes continued their devastating conventional bombing. On August 8, the Soviet Union declared war on Japan. On August 9, a second American atomic bomb fell on Nagasaki, killing at least 60,000 people. Five days later, on August 14, Japan surrendered. Recent histories argue that the Soviet declaration of war played a much more significant role in Japan's decision to surrender than America's use of atomic weapons. In the end, the Allies promised that the Japanese emperor could remain as the nation's titular head. Formal surrender ceremonies were held September 2 aboard the battleship *Missouri* in Tokyo Bay. The Second World War was over.

Legacy FOR A PEOPLE AND A NATION

Nuclear Proliferation

Virtually from the moment of the Hiroshima and Nagasaki atomic bombings, American strategists grappled with the problem of erecting barriers to membership in the "nuclear club." The early focus was on the Soviet Union. How long, analysts wondered, before Stalin gets the bomb? On September 23, 1949, came the answer, as President Truman informed a shocked American public that the Soviets had successfully tested an atomic device.

In the years thereafter, membership in the nuclear club grew, through a combination of huge national investments, espionage, and a black market of willing western suppliers of needed raw materials and technologies. There were successful detonations by Great Britain (1952), France (1960), China (1964), India (1974), and Pakistan (1998). Israel crossed the nuclear weapon threshold on the eve of the 1967 Six-Day War but to this day has always refused to confirm or deny that it has the bomb. More recently, creditable reports indicate that North Korea has a small nuclear arsenal and that Iran is working to get one.

If this is a sizable number of nuclear states, it is far fewer than experts predicted in the 1960s. "If three nations made nuclear weapons in the 1970s," one senior British analyst warned then, "ten might do so in the 1980s and thirty in the 1990s." It did not happen, and the main reason is that the 5 existing nuclear powers committed themselves in the mid-1960s—for a complex set of self-interested reasons—to promoting nonproliferation. Subsequently, the rate of proliferation steadily declined; all told, 22 of 31 states that started down the nuclear path changed course and renounced the bomb. By late 2006, the Treaty on the Non-Proliferation of Nuclear Weapons (NPT), enacted on July 1, 1968, had 187 signatories and was widely hailed as one of the great international agreements of the post-1945 era.

Skeptics took a different view. They noted that 3 states outside the NPT (Israel, India, and Pakistan) became nuclear powers, and they charged the "original five" with hypocrisy, for doing everything possible to prevent others from obtaining nuclear arms while keeping large stockpiles for themselves. With the world in 2007 awash in some 27,000 nuclear weapons (97 percent belonging to the United States and Russia), critics feared a new kind of proliferation, in which a terrorist group or other nonstate actor got its hands on one or more bombs. In that nightmare scenario, they warned, the de facto post-Nagasaki international moratorium on the use of nuclear weapons would soon be—literally—blown away.

SUMMARY

Hitler once prophesied, "We may be destroyed, but if we are, we shall drag a world with us—a world in flames." In that, at least, Hitler was right. World War II devastated much of the globe. In Asia and in Europe, ghostlike people wandered through rubble, searching desperately for food. One out of nine people in the Soviet Union had perished: a total of at least 21 million civilian and military war dead. The Chinese calculated their war losses at 10 million; the Germans and Austrians at 6 million; the Japanese at 2.5 million. Up to 1 million died of famine in Japanese-controlled Indochina. Almost 11 million people had been systematically murdered in Nazi death camps. Across the globe, the Second World War killed at least 55 million people.

Waging war required the cooperation of Allied nations with very different goals and interests. Tensions among them remained high throughout the war, as the United States and Britain resisted Stalin's demands that they open a second front to draw German soldiers away from the Soviet Union. The United States, meanwhile, was fighting a brutal war in the Pacific, pushing Japanese forces back toward their home islands. By the time Japan surrendered in August 1945, the strains between the Soviet Union and its English-speaking Allies made postwar peace and stability unlikely.

American men and machines were a critical part of the Allied war effort. Although Americans did not join in the perfect unity and shared sacrifice suggested by current descriptions of "the greatest generation," American servicemen covered the globe, from the Arctic to the tropics. And on the home front, Americans worked around the clock to make the weapons that would win the war. Although they made sacrifices during the war—including almost 300,000 who gave their lives—many Americans found that the war had changed their lives for the better. Mobilization for war ended the Great Depression, reducing unemployment practically to zero. War jobs demanded workers, and Americans moved in huge numbers to war-production centers. The influx of workers strained the resources of existing communities and sometimes led to social friction and even violence. But many Americans—African Americans, Mexican Americans, women, poor whites from the South—found new opportunities for employment in well-paid war jobs.

The federal government, in order to manage the nation's war efforts, became a stronger presence in the lives of individual Americans—regulating business and employment; overseeing military conscription, training, and deployment; and even controlling what people could buy to eat or to wear. The Second World War was a powerful engine of social change.

Americans emerged from World War II fully confident that theirs was the greatest country in the world. It was certainly the most powerful. At war's end, only the United States had the capital and economic resources to spur international recovery; only the United States was more prosperous and more secure than when war began. In the coming struggle to fashion a new world out of the ashes of the old, soon to be called the Cold War, the United States held a commanding position. For better or worse—and clearly there were elements of each—the Second World War was a turning point in the nation's history.

SUGGESTIONS FOR FURTHER READING

Michael C. C. Adams, *The Best War Ever: America and World War II* (1993)

Roger Daniels, *Prisoners Without Trial: Japanese Americans in World War II* (1993)

Tsuyoshi Hasegawa, *Racing the Enemy: Stalin, Truman, and the Surrender of Japan* (2005)

David M. Kennedy, *Freedom from Fear: The American People in Depression and War, 1929–1945* (1999)

Warren F. Kimball, *Forged in War: Roosevelt, Churchill, and the Second World War* (1997)

Nelson Lichtenstein, *Labor's War at Home: The CIO in World War II* (1983)

Gerald F. Linderman, *The World Within War: America's Combat Experience in World War II* (1997)

Leisa Meyers, *Creating G.I. Jane: Sexuality and Power in the Women's Army Corps During World War II* (1996)

George Roeder, Jr., *The Censored War: American Visual Experience During World War II* (1993)

Ronald Takaki, *Double Victory: A Multicultural History of America in World War II* (2000)

For a more extensive list for further reading, go to college.hmco.com/pic/norton8e.

The Cold War and American Globalism *1945-1961*

O n July 16, 1945, the "Deer" Team leader parachuted into northern Vietnam, near Kimlung, a village in a valley of rice paddies. Colonel Allison Thomas could not know that the end of the Second World War was just weeks away, but he and the other five members of his Office of Strategic Services (OSS) unit knew their mission: to work with the Vietminh, a nationalist Vietnamese organization, to sabotage Japanese forces that in March had seized Vietnam from France. After disentangling himself from the banyan tree into which his parachute had slammed him, Thomas spoke a "few flowery sentences" to two hundred Vietminh soldiers assembled near a banner proclaiming, "Welcome to Our American Friends." Ho Chi Minh, head of the Vietminh, ill but speaking in good English, cordially greeted the OSS team and offered supper. The next day Ho denounced the French but remarked that "we welcome 10 million Americans." "Forget the Communist Bogy," Thomas radioed OSS headquarters in China.

A communist who had worked for decades to win his nation's independence from France, Ho joined the French Communist Party after World War I and sought to use it as a vehicle for Vietnamese independence. For the next two decades, living in China, the Soviet Union, and elsewhere, he patiently planned and fought to free his nation from French colonialism. During World War II, Ho's Vietminh warriors harassed both French and Japanese forces and rescued downed American pilots. In March 1945 Ho met with U.S. officials in China, where he read the *Encyclopaedia Americana* and *Time* magazine at an Office of War Information facility. Receiving no aid from his ideological allies in the Soviet Union, Ho hoped that the United States would favor his nation's long quest for liberation from colonialism.

Other OSS personnel soon parachuted into Kimlung, including a male nurse who diagnosed Ho's ailments as malaria and dysentery. Quinine and sulfa drugs restored his

◀ The Vietnamese nationalist Ho Chi Minh (1890–1969) meets with OSS "Deer" Team members in 1945. On the far left is Ho's military aide Vo Nguyen Giap. *(Private Collection)*

CHRONOLOGY

1945 ■ Roosevelt dies; Truman becomes president
    ■ Atomic bombings of Japan

1946 ■ Kennan's "long telegram" criticizes USSR
    ■ Vietnamese war against France erupts

1947 ■ Truman Doctrine seeks aid for Greece and
       Turkey
    ■ Marshall offers Europe economic assistance
    ■ National Security Act reorganizes government

1948 ■ Communists take power in Czechoslovakia
    ■ Truman recognizes Israel
    ■ United States organizes Berlin airlift

1949 ■ NATO founded as anti-Soviet alliance
    ■ Soviet Union explodes atomic bomb
    ■ Mao's communists win power in China

1950 ■ NSC-68 recommends major military buildup
    ■ Korean War starts in June; China enters in fall

1951 ■ United States signs Mutual Security Treaty
       with Japan

1953 ■ Eisenhower becomes president
    ■ Stalin dies
    ■ United States helps restore shah to power in
       Iran
    ■ Korean War ends

1954 ■ Geneva accords partition Vietnam
    ■ CIA-led coup overthrows Arbenz in
       Guatemala

1955 ■ Soviets create Warsaw Pact

1956 ■ Soviets crush uprising in Hungary
    ■ Suez crisis sparks war in Middle East

1957 ■ Soviets fire first ICBM and launch *Sputnik*

1958 ■ U.S. troops land in Lebanon
    ■ Berlin crisis

1959 ■ Castro ousts Batista in Cuba

1960 ■ Eighteen African colonies become independent
    ■ Vietcong organized in South Vietnam

eigners' presence as a sign of U.S. anticolonial and anti-Japanese sentiments. In early August the Deer Team began to give Vietminh soldiers weapons training. During many conversations with the OSS members, Ho said he hoped young Vietnamese could study in the United States and that American technicians could help build an independent Vietnam. Citing history, Ho remarked that "your statesmen make eloquent speeches about . . . self-determination. We are self-determined. Why not help us? Am I any different from . . . your George Washington?"

A second OSS unit, the "Mercy" Team, headed by Captain Archimedes Patti, arrived in the city of Hanoi on August 22. When Patti met Ho—"this wisp of a man," as Patti put it—the Vietminh leader applauded America's assistance and called for future "collaboration." But, unbeknownst to these OSS members, who believed that President Franklin D. Roosevelt's general sympathy for eventual Vietnamese independence remained U.S. policy, the new Truman administration in Washington had decided to let France decide the fate of Vietnam. That change in policy explains why Ho never received answers to the several letters and telegrams he sent to Washington—the first dated August 30, 1945.

On September 2, 1945, amid great fanfare in Hanoi, with OSS personnel present, an emotional Ho Chi Minh read his declaration of independence for the Democratic Republic of Vietnam: "All men are created equal; they are endowed by their Creator with certain unalienable Rights; among these are Life, Liberty, and the pursuit of Happiness." Having borrowed from the internationally renowned American document of 1776, Ho then itemized Vietnamese grievances against France. At one point in the ceremonies, two American P-38 aircraft swooped down over the square. Many in the crowd cheered, interpreting the flyby as U.S. endorsement of Vietnamese independence. Actually, the pilots had no orders to make a political statement; they just wanted to see what was happening.

By early autumn both OSS teams had departed Vietnam. In a last meeting with Captain Patti, Ho expressed his sadness that the United States had armed the French to reestablish their colonial rule in Vietnam. Sure, Ho said, U.S. officials in Washington judged him a "Moscow puppet" because he was a communist. But Ho claimed that he drew inspiration from the American struggle for inde-

health, but Ho remained frail. As a sign of friendship, the Americans in Vietnam named Ho "OSS Agent 19." Everywhere the Americans went, impoverished villagers thanked them with gifts of food and clothing, despite the devastating famine of 1944–1945 in which at least a million Vietnamese died. The villagers interpreted the forpendence and that he was foremost "a free agent," a nationalist. If necessary, Ho insisted, the Vietnamese would go it alone, with or without American or Soviet help. And they did—first against the French and eventually against more than half a million U.S. troops in what became America's longest war. How different world history would have been had President Harry S Truman responded favorably to Ho Chi Minh's last letter to Washington, dated February 16, 1946, which asked the United States "as guardians and champions of World Justice to take a decisive step in support of our independence."

Because Ho Chi Minh and many of his nationalist followers had declared themselves communists, U.S. leaders rejected their appeal. Endorsing the containment doctrine to draw the line against communism everywhere, American presidents from Truman to George H. W. Bush believed that a ruthless Soviet Union was directing a worldwide communist conspiracy against peace, free-market capitalism, and political democracy. Soviet leaders from Joseph Stalin to Mikhail Gorbachev protested that a militarized, economically aggressive United States sought nothing less than world domination. This protracted contest between the United States and the Soviet Union acquired the name Cold War.

The primary feature of world affairs for more than four decades, the Cold War was fundamentally a bipolar contest between the United States and the Soviet Union over spheres of influence and world power. Decisions made in Washington and Moscow dominated world politics as the capitalist "West" squared off against the communist "East." The contest dominated international relations and eventually took the lives of millions, cost trillions of dollars, spawned doomsday fears, and destabilized one nation after another. On occasion the two superpowers negotiated at summit conferences and signed agreements to temper their dangerous arms race; at other times they went to the brink of war and armed allies to fight vicious Third World conflicts. Sometimes these allies had their own ideas and ambitions, and they often proved adept at resisting pressure applied on them by one or both of the superpowers. Over time, American and Soviet leaders came to realize that, notwithstanding the immense military might at their disposal, their power to effect change was in key respects limited.

Vietnam was part of the Third World, a general term for those nations that during the Cold War era wore neither the "West" (the "First World") nor the "East" (the "Second World") label. Sometimes called "developing countries," Third World nations were on the whole nonwhite, nonindustrialized, and located in the southern half of the globe—in Asia, Africa, the Middle East, and Latin America. Many had been colonies of European nations or Japan, and they were vulnerable to the Cold War rivalry that intruded on them. U.S. leaders often interpreted their anticolonialism, political instability, and restrictions on foreign-owned property as Soviet or communist inspired, or capable of being exploited by Moscow—in short, as Cold War matters rather than as expressions of profound indigenous nationalism. As an example, Vietnam became one among many sites where Cold War fears and Third World aspirations intersected, prompting American intervention. Such intervention bespoke a globalist foreign policy, meaning that U.S. officials now regarded the entire world as the appropriate sphere for America's influence.

Critics in the United States challenged the architects of the Cold War, questioning their exaggerations of threats from abroad, meddlesome interventions in the Third World, and expensive militarization of foreign policy. But when leaders like Truman described the Cold War in extremist terms as a life-and-death struggle against a monstrous enemy, legitimate criticism became suspect and dissenters were discredited. Critics' searching questions about America's global, interventionist foreign policy and its reliance on nuclear weapons were drowned out by charges that dissenters were "soft on communism," if not un-American. Decision makers in the United States successfully cultivated a Cold War consensus that stifled debate and shaped the mindset of generations of Americans.

- Why did relations between the Soviet Union and the United States turn hostile soon after their victory in World War II?

- When and why did the Cold War expand from a struggle over the future of Europe and central Asia to one encompassing virtually the entire globe?

- By what means did the Truman and Eisenhower administrations seek to expand America's global influence in the late 1940s and the 1950s?

THE WEEKLY NEWSMAGAZINE

THE BIG THREE
One job done.

PONY EDITION
SPECIALLY PRINTED
FOR AIR TRANSPORT
•
Editorial content
unchanged from
the regular
edition

▲ The wartime Grand Alliance of the United States, Britain, and the Soviet Union was never without tension, but it succeeded in producing a victory over the Axis powers. This cover of *Time* magazine from May 14, 1945, celebrates the defeat of Nazi Germany. It was a high point in Soviet-American relations, but it would not last.

(Time Life Pictures/Time Life Picture Collection/Getty Images)

FROM ALLIES TO ADVERSARIES

The Second World War had a deeply unsettling effect on the international system. At its end, Germany was in ruins. Great Britain was badly overstrained and exhausted; France, having endured five years of Nazi occupation, was rent by internal division. Italy also emerged drastically weakened, and, in Asia, Japan was decimated and under occupation, and China was headed toward a renewed civil war. Throughout Europe and Asia, factories, transportation, and communications links had been reduced to rubble. Agricultural production plummeted,

and displaced persons wandered about in search of food and family. How would the devastated economic world be pieced back together? The United States and the Soviet Union, though allies in the war, offered very different answers and models. The collapse of Germany and Japan, moreover, had created power vacuums that drew the two major powers into collision as they sought influence in countries where the Axis aggressors had once held sway. And the political turmoil that many nations experienced after the war also spurred Soviet-American competition. For example, in Greece and China, where civil wars raged between leftists and conservative regimes, the two powers supported different sides.

The international system also experienced instability because empires were disintegrating, creating the new Third World. Financial constraints and nationalist rebellions forced the imperial states to set their colonies free. Britain exited India (and Pakistan) in 1947 and Burma and Sri Lanka (Ceylon) in 1948. The Philippines gained independence from the United States in 1946. After four years of battling nationalists in Indonesia, the Dutch left in 1949. In the Middle East, Lebanon (1943), Syria (1946), and Jordan (1946) gained independence, while in Palestine British officials faced growing pressure from Zionists intent on creating a Jewish homeland and from Arab leaders opposed to the prospect. In Iraq, too, nationalist agitation increased against the British-installed government. Washington and Moscow paid close attention to this anticolonial ferment, seeing these new or emerging Third World states as potential allies that might provide military bases, resources, and markets. Not all new nations were willing to play along; some chose nonalignment in the Cold War. "We do not intend to be the playthings of others," declared India's leader, Jawaharlal Nehru.

Decolonization

Driven by different ideologies and different economic and strategic needs in this volatile international climate, the United States and the Soviet Union assessed their most pressing tasks in very different terms. The Soviets, though committed to seeking ultimate victory over the capitalist countries, were most concerned about preventing another invasion of their homeland. It was a homeland much less secure than the United States, for reasons both geographic and historical. Its land mass was huge—three times as large as that of the United States—but it had only 10,000 miles of seacoast, much of which was under ice for a large part of the year. Russian leaders both before and after the revolution

Stalin's Aims

had made increased maritime access a chief foreign policy aim.

What is more, the geographical frontiers of the USSR were hard to defend. Siberia, vital for its mineral resources, lay 6,000 miles east of Moscow and was vulnerable to encroachment by Japan and China. In the west, the border with Poland had generated violent clashes ever since World War I, and eastern Europe had been the launching pad for Hitler's invasion in 1941: the resulting war cost the lives of at least 21 million Russians and caused massive physical destruction. Henceforth, Soviet leaders determined, they could have no dangers along their western borders.

Overall, however, Soviet territorial objectives were limited. Although many Americans were quick to compare Stalin to Hitler, Stalin did not have the Nazi leader's grandiose plans for world hegemony. In general, his aims resembled those of the czars before him: he wanted to push the USSR's borders to include the Baltic states of Estonia, Latvia, and Lithuania, as well as the eastern part of prewar Poland. Fearful of a revived Germany, he sought to ensure pro-Soviet governments in eastern Europe. To the south, Stalin wanted to have a presence in northern Iran, and he pressed the Turks to grant him naval bases and free access out of the Black Sea. Economically, the Soviet government promoted economic independence more than trade with other countries; suspicious of their European neighbors, they did not promote rapid rebuilding of the war-ravaged economies of the region or, more generally, expanded world trade.

The leadership in the United States, by contrast, came out of the war extremely confident about the immediate

U.S. Economic and Strategic Needs

security of the country's borders. Separated from the other world powers by two vast oceans, the American home base had been virtually immune from attack during the fighting—only an occasional shell from a submarine or a hostile balloon reached the shores of the continental United States. American casualties were fewer than those of any of the other major combatants—hugely so in comparison with the Soviet Union. With its fixed capital intact, its resources more plentiful than ever, and in lone possession of the atomic bomb, the United States was the strongest power in the world at war's end.

Yet this was no time for complacency, Washington officials reminded one another. Some other power—almost certainly the USSR—could take advantage of the political and economic instability in war-torn Europe and Asia, and eventually seize control of these areas, with dire implications for America's physical and economic security. To prevent this eventuality, officials in Washington sought forward bases overseas, in order to keep an airborne enemy at bay. To further enhance U.S. security, American planners, in direct contrast to their Soviet counterparts, sought the quick reconstruction of nations—including the former enemies Germany and Japan—and a world economy based on free trade. Such a system, they reasoned, was essential to preserve America's economic well-being.

The Soviets, on the other hand, refused to join the new World Bank and International Monetary Fund (IMF), created at the July 1944 Bretton Woods Conference by forty-four nations to stabilize trade and finance. They held that the United States dominated both institutions and used them to promote private investment and open international commerce, which Moscow saw as capitalist tools of exploitation. With the United States as its largest donor, the World Bank opened its doors in 1945 and began to make loans to help members finance reconstruction projects; the IMF, also heavily backed by the United States, helped members meet their balance-of-payments problems through currency loans.

The personalities of the two countries' leaders also mattered. Joseph Stalin, though hostile to the western

Stalin and Truman

powers and capable of utter ruthlessness against his own people (his periodic purges since the 1930s had taken the lives of millions), had no wish for an immediate war. With the huge Russian losses in World War II, he was all too aware of his country's weakness vis-à-vis the United States. For a time at least, he appears to have believed he could achieve his aspirations peacefully, through continued cooperation with the Americans and the British. Over the long term, though, he envisaged more conflict. Stalin believed that Germany and Japan would rise again to threaten the USSR, probably by the 1960s, and his suspicion of the other capitalist powers knew no bounds. Many have concluded that Stalin was clinically paranoid: the first to do so, a leading Russian neuropathologist in 1927, died a few days later! As historian David Reynolds has noted, this paranoia, coupled with Stalin's xenophobia (fear of anything foreign) and his Marxist-Leninist ideology, created in the Soviet leader a mental map of "them" versus "us" that decisively influenced his approach to world affairs.

Harry Truman had none of Stalin's capacity for deception or ruthlessness, but to a lesser degree he, too, was prone to a "them" versus "us" world-view. Truman often glossed over nuances, ambiguities, and counterevidence; he preferred the simple answer stated in either/or terms. As

Winston Churchill, who admired Truman's decisiveness, once observed, the president "takes no notice of delicate ground, he just plants his foot firmly on it." Truman constantly exaggerated, as when he declared in his undelivered farewell address that he had "knocked the socks off the communists" in Korea. Shortly after Roosevelt's death in early 1945, Truman met the Soviet commissar of foreign affairs, V. M. Molotov, at the White House. When the president sharply protested that the Soviets were not fulfilling the Yalta agreement on Poland, Molotov stormed out. Truman had self-consciously developed what he called his "tough method," and he bragged after the encounter that "I gave it to him straight 'one-two to the jaw.'" Truman's display of toughness became a trademark of American Cold War diplomacy.

At what point did the Cold War actually begin? No precise start date can be given. The origins must be thought

The Beginning of the Cold War

of as a process, one that arguably began in 1917 with the Bolshevik Revolution and the western powers' hostile response, but in a more meaningful sense began in mid-1945, as World War II drew to a close. By the spring of 1947, certainly, the struggle had begun.

One of the first Soviet-American clashes came in Poland in 1945, when the Soviets refused to allow the Polish government-in-exile in London to be a part of the communist government that Moscow sponsored. The Soviets also snuffed out civil liberties in the former Nazi satellite of Romania, justifying their actions by pointing to what they claimed was an equivalent U.S. manipulation of Italy. Moscow initially allowed free elections in Hungary and Czechoslovakia, but as the Cold War accelerated and U.S. influence in Europe expanded, the Soviets encouraged communist coups in Hungary (1947) and Czechoslovakia (1948). Yugoslavia stood as a unique case: its independent communist government, led by Josip Broz Tito, successfully broke with Stalin in 1948.

To defend their actions, Moscow officials pointed out that the United States was reviving their traditional enemy, Germany. Twice in the lifetime of Soviet leaders Germany had wrought enormous suffering on Russia, and Stalin and his associates were determined to prevent a third occurrence. The Soviets also protested that the United States was meddling in eastern Europe. They cited clandestine American meetings with anti-Soviet groups, repeated calls for elections likely to produce anti-Soviet regimes, and the use of loans to gain political influence (financial diplomacy). Moscow charged that the United States was pursuing a double standard—intervening in the affairs of eastern Europe but demanding that the Soviet Union stay out of Latin America and Asia. Americans called for free elections in the Soviet sphere, Moscow noted, but not in the U.S. sphere in Latin America, where several military dictatorships ruled.

The atomic bomb also divided the two major powers. The Soviets believed that the United States was practicing

Atomic Diplomacy

"atomic diplomacy"—maintaining a nuclear monopoly to scare the Soviets into diplomatic concessions. Secretary of State James F. Byrnes thought that the atomic bomb gave the United States bargaining power and could serve as a deterrent to Soviet expansion, but Secretary of War Henry L. Stimson thought otherwise in 1945. If Americans continued to have "this weapon rather ostentatiously on our hip," he warned Truman, the Soviets' "suspicions and their distrust of our purposes and motives will increase."

In this atmosphere of suspicion and distrust, Truman refused to turn over the weapon to an international control authority. In 1946 he backed the Baruch Plan, named after its author, financier Bernard Baruch. Largely a propaganda ploy, this proposal provided for U.S. abandonment of its atomic monopoly only after the world's fissionable materials were brought under the authority of an international agency. The Soviets retorted that this plan would require them to shut down their atomic-bomb development project while the United States continued its own. Washington and Moscow soon became locked in an expensive and frightening nuclear arms race.

By the middle of 1946, the wartime Grand Alliance was but a fading memory; that year, Soviets and Americans clashed on every front. When the United States turned down a Soviet request for a reconstruction loan but gave a loan to Britain, Moscow upbraided Washington for using its dollars to manipulate foreign governments. The two Cold War powers also backed different groups in Iran, where the United States helped bring the pro-West shah to the throne. Unable to agree on the unification of Germany, the former allies built up their zones independently.

After Stalin gave a speech in February 1946 that depicted the world as threatened by capitalist acquisitiveness,

Warnings from Kennan and Churchill

the American chargé d'affaires in Moscow, George F. Kennan, sent a pessimistic "long telegram" to Washington. Kennan asserted that Soviet fanaticism made even a temporary understanding impossible. His widely circulated report fed a growing belief among American officials that only toughness would work with the Soviets. The following month, Winston Churchill de-

These permanent members could not prohibit discussion of any issue, but they could exercise a veto against any proposed action. To be effective on the major issues of war and peace, therefore, the U.N. needed great-power cooperation of the type that had existed in wartime but was a distant memory by mid-1946. Of the fifty-one founding states, twenty-two came from the Americas and another fifteen from Europe, which in effect gave the United States a large majority in the assembly. In retaliation, Moscow began to exercise its veto in the Security Council.

Some high-level U.S. officials were dismayed by the administration's harsh anti-Soviet posture. Secretary of Commerce Henry A. Wallace, who had been Roosevelt's vice president before Truman, charged that Truman's get-tough policy was substituting atomic and economic coercion for diplomacy. Wallace told a Madison Square Garden audience in September 1946 that "'getting tough' never brought anything real and lasting—whether for schoolyard bullies or businessmen or world powers. The tougher we get, the tougher the Russians will get." Truman soon fired Wallace from the cabinet, blasting him privately as "a real Commy and a dangerous man" and boasting that he, Truman, had now "run the crackpots out of the Democratic Party."

East-West tensions escalated further in early 1947, when the British requested American help in Greece to defend their conservative client-government (a government dependent on the economic or military support of a more powerful country) in a civil war against leftists. In his March 12, 1947, speech to Congress, Truman requested $400 million in aid to Greece and Turkey. He had a selling job to do. The Republican Eightieth Congress wanted less, not more, spending; many of its members had little respect for the Democratic president whose administration the voters had repudiated in the 1946 elections by giving the GOP ("Grand Old Party," the Republican Party) majorities in both houses of Congress. Republican senator Arthur Vandenberg of Michigan, a bipartisan leader who backed Truman's request, bluntly told the president that he would have to "scare hell out of the American people" to gain congressional approval.

Truman Doctrine

With that advice in mind, the president delivered a speech laced with alarmist language intended to stake out the American role in the postwar world. Truman claimed that communism, feeding on economic dislocations, imperiled the world. "If Greece should fall under the control of an armed minority," he gravely concluded in an early version of the domino theory (see page 812), "the effect upon its neighbor, Turkey, would be immediate and serious.

▲ On March 5, 1946, former British prime minister Winston S. Churchill (1874–1965) delivered a speech, which he intended for a worldwide audience, at Westminster College in Fulton, Missouri. President Harry S Truman *(right)* had encouraged Churchill *(seated)* to speak on two themes: the need to block Soviet expansion and the need to form an Anglo-American partnership. Always eloquent and provocative, Churchill denounced the Soviets for drawing an "iron curtain" across eastern Europe. This speech became one of the landmark statements of the Cold War. *(Harry S. Truman Library)*

livered a stirring speech in Fulton, Missouri. The former British prime minister warned that a Soviet-erected "iron curtain" had cut off eastern European countries from the West. With an approving Truman sitting on the stage, Churchill called for Anglo-American partnership to resist the new menace.

The growing Soviet-American tensions had major implications for the functioning of the United Nations. The delegates who gathered in San Francisco in April 1945 to sign the U.N. charter had agreed on an organization that would include a General Assembly of all member states, as well as a smaller Security Council which would take the lead on issues of peace and security. Five great powers were given permanent seats on the council—the United States, the Soviet Union, Great Britain, China, and France.

Confusion and disorder might well spread throughout the entire Middle East." Truman articulated what became known as the Truman Doctrine: "I believe that it must be the policy of the United States to support free peoples who are resisting attempted subjugation by armed minorities or by outside pressures."

Critics correctly pointed out that the Soviet Union was little involved in the Greek civil war, that the communists in Greece were more pro-Tito than pro-Stalin, and that the resistance movement had noncommunist as well as communist members. Nor was the Soviet Union threatening Turkey at the time. Others suggested that such aid should be channeled through the United Nations. Truman countered that, should communists gain control of Greece, they might open the door to Soviet power in the Mediterranean. After much debate, the Senate approved Truman's request by 67 to 23 votes. Using U.S. dollars and military advisers, the Greek government defeated the insurgents in 1949, and Turkey became a staunch U.S. ally on the Soviets' border.

In the months after Truman's speech, the term *Cold War* slipped into the lexicon as a description of the Soviet-American relationship. Less than two years had passed since the glorious victory over the Axis powers, and the two Grand Alliance members now found themselves locked in a tense struggle for world dominance. It would last almost half a century. Could the confrontation have been avoided? Not altogether, it seems clear. Even before World War II had ended, perceptive observers anticipated that the United States and the USSR would seek to fill the power vacuum that would exist after the armistice, and that friction would result. The two countries had a history of hostility and tension, and both were militarily powerful. Most of all, the two nations were divided by sharply differing political economies with widely divergent needs and by a deep ideological chasm. Some kind of confrontation was destined to occur.

It is far less clear that the conflict had to result in a Cold War. The "cold peace" that had prevailed from the revolution in 1917 through World War II could conceivably have been maintained into the postwar years as well. Neither side's leadership wanted war. Both hoped—at least in the initial months—that a spirit of cooperation could be maintained. The Cold War resulted from decisions by individual human beings who might well have chosen differently, who might have done more, for example, to maintain diplomatic dialogue, to seek negotiated solutions to complex international problems. For decades,

Inevitable Cold War?

many Americans would wonder if the high price they were paying for victory in the superpower confrontation was necessary.

CONTAINMENT IN ACTION

Having committed themselves to countering Soviet and communist expansion, the Truman team had to figure out just how to fight the Cold War. The policy they chose, containment, was in place before the term was coined. George Kennan, having moved from the U.S. embassy in Moscow to the State Department in Washington, published an influential statement of the containment doctrine. Writing as "Mr. X" in the July 1947 issue of the magazine *Foreign Affairs,* Kennan advocated a "policy of firm containment, designed to confront the Russians with unalterable counterforce at every point where they show signs of encroaching upon the interests of a peaceful and stable world." Such counterforce, Kennan argued, would check Soviet expansion and eventually foster a "mellowing" of Soviet behavior. Along with the Truman Doctrine, Kennan's "X" article became a key manifesto of Cold War policy.

Lippmann's Critique

The veteran journalist Walter Lippmann took issue with the containment doctrine in his slim but powerful book *The Cold War* (1947), calling it a "strategic monstrosity" that failed to distinguish between areas vital and peripheral to U.S. security. If American leaders defined every place on earth as strategically important, Lippmann reasoned, the nation's patience and resources soon would be drained. Nor did Lippmann share Truman's conviction that the Soviet Union was plotting to take over the world. The president, he asserted, put too little emphasis on diplomacy. Ironically, Kennan himself agreed with much of Lippmann's critique, and he soon began to distance himself from the doctrine he had helped to create.

Invoking the containment doctrine, the United States in 1947 and 1948 began to build an international economic and defensive network to protect American prosperity and security, and to advance U.S. hegemony. In western Europe, the region of primary concern, American diplomats pursued a range of objectives, including economic reconstruction and fostering a political environment friendly to the United States. They sought the ouster of communists from governments, as occurred in 1947 in France and Italy, and blockage of "third force" or neutralist tendencies. To maintain political stability in key capitals, U.S. officials worked to keep the decolonization of

▲ Under official postwar relief and recovery programs, including the Marshall Plan, the United States shipped billions of dollars' worth of food and equipment to western European nations struggling to overcome the destruction of the Second World War. Private efforts, such as this one in 1950, also succeeded. The people of Jersey City, New Jersey, sent this snowplow to the mountainous village of Capracotta, Italy. *(Corbis-Bettmann).*

European empires orderly. In Germany, they advocated the unification of the western zones. At the same time, American culture—consumer goods, music, consumption ethic, and production techniques—permeated European societies. Some Europeans resisted Americanization, but transatlantic ties strengthened.

The first instrument designed to achieve U.S. goals in western Europe was the Marshall Plan. European nations, still reeling economically and unstable politically, lacked the dollars to buy vital American-made goods. Americans, who had already spent billions of dollars on European relief and recovery by 1947, remembered all too well the troubles of the 1930s: global depression, political extremism, and war born of economic discontent. Such cataclysms could not be allowed to happen again; communism must not replace fascism. Western Europe, said one State Department diplomat, was "the keystone in the arch which supports the kind of a world which we have to have in order to conduct our lives."

Marshall Plan

In June 1947, Secretary of State George C. Marshall announced that the United States would finance a massive European recovery program. Launched in 1948, the Marshall Plan sent $12.4 billion to western Europe before the program ended in 1951 (see Map 28.1). To stimulate business at home, the legislation required that Europeans spend the foreign-aid dollars in the United States on American-made products. The Marshall Plan proved a mixed success; some scholars today even argue that Europe could have revived without it. The program caused inflation, failed to solve a balance-of-payments problem, took only tentative steps toward economic integration, and further divided Europe between "East" and "West." But the program spurred impressive western European industrial production and investment, and started the region toward self-sustaining economic growth. From the American perspective, moreover, the plan succeeded because it helped contain communism.

To streamline the administration of U.S. defense, Truman worked with Congress on the National Security

Map 28.1   Divided Europe

After the Second World War, Europe broke into two competing camps. When the United States launched the Marshall Plan in 1948, the Soviet Union countered with its own economic plan the following year. When the United States created NATO in 1949, the Soviet Union answered with the Warsaw Pact in 1955. On the whole, these two camps held firm until the late 1980s.

Act of July 1947. The act created the Office of Secretary of Defense (which became the Department of Defense two years later) to oversee all branches of the armed services, the National Security Council (NSC) of high-level officials to advise the president, and the Central Intelligence Agency (CIA) to conduct spy operations and information gathering overseas. By the early 1950s the CIA had become a significant element in national security policy and had expanded its functions to include covert (secret) operations aimed at overthrowing unfriendly foreign leaders and, as a high-ranking American official put it, a "Department of Dirty Tricks" to stir up economic trouble in "the camp of the enemy." Taken together, the components of the National Security Act gave the president increased powers with which to conduct foreign policy.

In the wake of the Marshall Plan and the National Security Act, Stalin hardened his Cold War posture. He forbade communist satellite governments in eastern Europe to accept Marshall Plan aid and ordered communist parties in western Europe to work to thwart the plan. He also created the Cominform, an organization designed to coordinate communist activities around the world. It was a classic example of what historian Herbert Butterfield called the "security dilemma": whereas American planners saw the Marshall Plan as helping their European friends achieve security against a potential Soviet threat, in Stalin's mind it raised anew the specter of capitalist penetration. He responded by tightening his grip on eastern Europe—most notably, he engineered a coup in Czechoslovakia in February 1948 that ensured full Soviet control of the country—which in turn created more anxiety in the United States. In this way the U.S.-Soviet relationship became a downward spiral that seemed to gain in velocity with each passing month.

The German problem remained especially intractable. In June 1948, the Americans, French, and British agreed to fuse their German zones, including their three sectors of Berlin. They sought to integrate West Germany (the Federal Republic of Germany) into the western European economy, complete with a reformed German currency. Fearing a resurgent Germany tied to the American Cold War camp, the Soviets cut off western land access to the jointly occupied city of Berlin, located well inside the Soviet zone. In response to this bold move, President Truman ordered a massive airlift of food, fuel, and other supplies to Berlin. Their spoiling effort blunted, the Sovi-

ets finally lifted the blockade in May 1949 and founded the German Democratic Republic, or East Germany.

The successful airlift was a big victory for Harry Truman, and it may have saved his political career: he surprised pundits by narrowly defeating Republican Thomas E. Dewey in the presidential election that occurred in the middle of the crisis in November 1948. Safely elected, Truman took the major step of formalizing what was already in essence a military alliance among the United States, Canada, and the nations of western Europe. In April 1949, twelve nations signed a mutual defense treaty, agreeing that an attack on any one of them would be considered an attack on all, and establishing the North Atlantic Treaty Organization (NATO; see Map 28.1).

The treaty aroused considerable domestic debate, for not since 1778 had the United States entered a formal European military alliance, and some critics, such as Senator Robert A. Taft, Republican of Ohio, claimed that NATO would provoke rather than deter war. Other critics argued that the Soviet threat was political, not military. Administration officials themselves did not anticipate a Soviet military thrust against western Europe, but they responded that, should the Soviets ever probe westward, NATO would function as a "tripwire," bringing the full force of the United States to bear on the Soviet Union. Truman officials also hoped that NATO would keep western Europeans from embracing communism or even neutralism in the Cold War. The Senate ratified the treaty by 82 votes to 13, and the United States soon began to spend billions of dollars under the Mutual Defense Assistance Act.

By the summer of 1949, Truman and his advisers were basking in the successes of their foreign policy. Containment was working splendidly, they and many outside observers had concluded. West Germany was on the road to recovery. The Berlin blockade had been defeated, and NATO had been formed. In western Europe, the threat posed by communist parties seemed lessened. True, there was trouble in China, where the communists under Mao Zedong were winning that country's civil war. But that struggle would likely wax and wane for years or even decades to come, and besides, Truman could not be held responsible for events there. Just possibly, some dared to think, Harry Truman was on his way to winning the Cold War.

Then, suddenly, in late September, came the "twin shocks," two momentous developments that made Americans feel in even greater danger than ever before—two decades later, they were still dealing with the reverberations. First, an American

▲ Richard Edes Harrison's illustration of the Soviet Union's detonation of an atomic bomb appeared in the October 1949 issue of *Life* magazine. A leading journalist-cartographer of the mid-twentieth century, Harrison was known for incorporating a global perspective in his work. Here he uses a single cloud of smoke to suggest the potentially far-reaching effects of an isolated bomb explosion. *(Library of Congress)*

reconnaissance aircraft detected unusually high radioactivity in the atmosphere. The news stunned U.S. officials: the Soviets had exploded an atomic device. With the American nuclear monopoly erased, western Europe seemed more vulnerable. At the same time, the communists in China completed their conquest—the end came more quickly than many expected. Now the world's largest and most populous countries were ruled by communists, and one of them had the atomic bomb. The bipartisan foreign policy of 1945–1948 broke down, as Republicans, bitter over Truman's reelection, declared that traitors in America must have given Stalin the bomb and allowed China to be "lost."

Rejecting calls by Kennan and others for high-level negotiations, Truman in early 1950 gave the go-ahead to begin production of a hydrogen bomb, the "Super," and ordered his national security team to undertake a thorough review of policy. Kennan bemoaned the militarization of the Cold War and was replaced at the State Department by Paul Nitze. The National Security Council delivered to the president in April 1950 a significant top-secret document tagged NSC-68. Predicting continued tension with

expansionistic communists all over the world and describing "a shrinking world of polarized power," the report, whose primary author was Nitze, appealed for a much enlarged military budget and the mobilization of public opinion to support such an increase. The Cold War was about to become a vastly more expensive, more far-reaching affair.

THE COLD WAR IN ASIA

Although Europe was the principal battleground in the early Cold War, Asia gradually became ensnared in the conflict as well. Indeed, it was in Asia that the consequences of an expansive containment doctrine would exact its heaviest price on the United States, in the form of large-scale and bloody wars in Korea and Vietnam. Though always less important to both superpowers than Europe, Asia would be the continent where the Cold War most often turned hot.

From the start, Japan was crucial to U.S. strategy. Much to Stalin's dismay, the United States monopolized Japan's reconstruction through a military occupation directed by General Douglas MacArthur, who envisioned turning the Pacific Ocean into "an Anglo-Saxon lake." Truman did not like "Mr. Prima Donna, Brass Hat" MacArthur, but the general initiated "a democratic revolution from above," as the Japanese called it, that reflected Washington's wishes. MacArthur wrote a democratic constitution, gave women voting rights, revitalized the economy, and destroyed the nation's weapons. U.S. authorities also helped Americanize Japan through censorship; films that hinted at criticism of the United States (for the destruction of Hiroshima, for example) or that depicted traditional Japanese customs, such as suicide, arranged marriages, and swordplay, were banned. In 1951 the United States and Japan signed a separate peace that restored Japan's sovereignty and ended the occupation. A Mutual Security Treaty that year provided for the stationing of U.S. forces on Japanese soil, including a base on Okinawa.

The administration had less success in China. The United States had long backed the Nationalists of Jiang

Chinese Civil War

Jieshi (Chiang Kai-shek) against Mao Zedong's communists. But after the Second World War, Generalissimo Jiang became an unreliable partner who rejected U.S. advice. His government had become corrupt, inefficient, and out of touch with discontented peasants, whom the communists enlisted with promises of land reform. Jiang also subverted American efforts to negotiate a cease-fire and a coalition government.

◄ Mao Zedong was a military theoretician who also involved himself in day-to-day military decision making. He was responsible for, or at least approved, all of the major strategic moves the communists made on their way to power. This image shows him applauding soldiers and other supporters on Tiananmen Square in Beijing.

(Sovfoto/Eastfoto)

"We picked a bad horse," Truman admitted, privately denouncing the Nationalists as "grafters and crooks." Still, seeing Jiang as the only alternative to Mao, Truman backed him to the end.

American officials divided on the question of whether Mao was a puppet of the Soviet Union. Some considered him an Asian Tito—communist but independent—but most believed him to be part of an international communist movement that might give the Soviets a springboard into Asia. Thus, when the Chinese communists made secret overtures to the United States to begin diplomatic talks in 1945 and again in 1949, American officials rebuffed them. Mao decided to "lean" to the Soviet side in the Cold War. Because China always maintained a fierce independence that rankled the Soviets, before long a Sino-Soviet schism opened. Indeed, Mao deeply resented the Soviets' refusal to aid the communists during the civil war.

Then came Mao's victory in September 1949. Jiang fled to the island of Formosa (Taiwan), and in Beijing (formerly Peking) Mao proclaimed the People's Republic of China (PRC). Truman hesitated to extend diplomatic recognition to the new government, even after the British prime minister asked him, "Are we to cut ourselves off from all contact with one-sixth of the inhabitants of the world?" U.S. officials became alarmed by the 1950 Sino-Soviet treaty of friendship and by the harassment of Americans and their property in China. Truman also chose nonrecognition because a vocal group of Republican critics, the so-called China lobby, was winning headlines by asking the question "Who lost China?" The publisher

Henry Luce, Senator William Knowland of California, and Representative Walter Judd of Minnesota pinned Jiang's defeat on Truman. The president stoutly answered that the self-defeating Jiang, despite billions of dollars in American aid, had proven a poor instrument of the containment doctrine. The administration nonetheless took the politically safe route and rejected recognition. (Not until 1979 did official Sino-American relations resume.)

Mao's victory in China drew urgent American attention to Indochina, the southeast Asian peninsula that had

Vietnam's Quest for Independence

been held by France for the better part of a century. The Japanese had wrested control over Indochina during World War II, but even then Vietnamese nationalists dedicated to independence grew in strength. One leading nationalist, Ho Chi Minh, hoped to use Japan's defeat to assert Vietnamese independence, and he asked for U.S. support. American officials had few kind things to say about French colonial policy, and many were pessimistic that France could achieve a military solution to the conflict. Nevertheless, they rejected Ho's appeals in favor of a restoration of French rule, mostly to ensure France's cooperation in the emerging Soviet-American confrontation. Paris warned that American support of the Vietnamese independence movement would alienate French public opinion and strengthen the French Communist Party, perhaps even drive France into the arms of the USSR. In addition, the Truman administration was wary of Ho Chi Minh's communist politics. Ho, the State Department declared, was an "agent of international communism" who, it was assumed, would assist Soviet and, after 1949, Chinese expansionism. Overlooking the native roots of the nationalist rebellion against French colonialism, and the tenacious Vietnamese resistance to foreign intruders, Washington officials interpreted events in Indochina through a Cold War lens.

Even so, when war between the Vietminh and France broke out in 1946, the United States initially took a hands-off approach. But when Jiang's regime collapsed in China three years later, the Truman administration made two crucial decisions—both of them in early 1950, before the Korean War. First, in February, Washington recognized the French puppet government of Bao Dai, a playboy and former emperor who had collaborated with the French and Japanese. In the eyes of many Vietnamese, the United States thus became in essence a colonial power, an ally of the hated French. Second, in May, the administration agreed to send weapons and other assistance to sustain the French in Indochina. From 1945 to 1954, the United States gave $2 billion of the $5 billion that France spent to keep Vietnam within its empire—to no avail (see Chapters 30 and 31). How Vietnam ultimately became the site of America's longest war, and how the world's most powerful nation failed to subdue a peasant people who suffered enormous losses, is one of the most remarkable and tragic stories of modern history.

THE KOREAN WAR

Before Vietnam, however, the United States would fight another large-scale military conflict, in Korea. In the early morning of June 25, 1950, a large military force of the Democratic People's Republic of Korea (North Korea) moved across the 38th parallel into the Republic of Korea (South Korea). Colonized by Japan since 1910, Korea had been divided in two by the victorious powers after Japan's defeat in 1945. Although the Soviets had armed the North and the Americans had armed the South (U.S. aid had reached $100 million a year), the Korean War began as a civil war. Virtually from the moment of the division, the two parts had been skirmishing along their supposedly temporary border while antigovernment (and anti-U.S.) guerrilla fighting flared in the South.

Both the North's communist leader, Kim Il Sung, and the South's president, Syngman Rhee, sought to reunify their nation. Kim's military in particular gained strength when tens of thousands of battle-tested Koreans returned home in 1949 after serving in Mao's army. Displaying the Cold War mentality of the time, however, President Truman claimed that the Soviets had masterminded the North Korean attack. "Communism was acting in Korea just as Hitler, Mussolini, and the Japanese had acted," he said, recalling Axis aggression.

Actually, Kim had to press a doubting Joseph Stalin,

Map 28.2   The Korean War, 1950–1953

Beginning as a civil war between North and South, this war became international when the United States, under the auspices of the United Nations, and the People's Republic of China intervened with their military forces.

(Source: Adapted from Thomas G. Paterson, J. Garry Clifford, and Kenneth J. Hagan, American Foreign Relations: A History, vol. 2, 5th ed. Copyright © 2000 by Houghton Mifflin Company.)

who only reluctantly approved the attack after Kim predicted an easy, early victory and after Mao backed Kim. Whatever Stalin's reasoning, his support for Kim's venture remained lukewarm. When the U.N. Security Council voted to defend South Korea against the invasion from the north, the Soviet representative was not even present to veto the resolution, because the Soviets were boycotting the United Nations to protest its refusal to grant membership to the People's Republic of China. During the war, Moscow gave limited aid to North Korea and China, which grew angry at Stalin for reneging on promised Soviet airpower. Stalin, all too aware of his strategic inferiority vis-à-vis the United States, did not want to be dragged into a costly war.

▲ Chinese soldiers guard marching American prisoners of the Korean War during the cold winter of 1950. *(Xinhua, New China News Agency)*

The president first ordered General Douglas MacArthur to send arms and troops to South Korea. He did

U.S. Forces Intervene

not seek congressional approval—he and his aides feared that lawmakers would initiate a lengthy debate—and thereby set the precedent of waging war on executive authority alone. Worried that Mao might use the occasion to take Formosa, Truman also directed the Seventh Fleet to patrol the waters between the Chinese mainland and Jiang's sanctuary on Formosa, thus inserting the United States again into Chinese politics. After the Security Council voted to assist South Korea, MacArthur became commander of U.N. forces in Korea. Sixteen nations contributed troops to the U.N. command, but 40 percent were South Korean and about 50 percent American. In the war's early weeks, North Korean tanks and superior firepower sent the South Korean army into chaotic retreat. The first American soldiers, taking heavy casualties, could not stop the North Korean advance. Within weeks, the South Kore-

ans and Americans had been pushed into the tiny Pusan perimeter at the tip of South Korea (see Map 28.2).

General MacArthur planned a daring operation: an amphibious landing at heavily fortified Inchon, several hundred miles behind North Korean lines. After U.S. guns and bombs pounded Inchon, marines sprinted ashore on September 15, 1950. The operation was a brilliant success, and the troops soon liberated the South Korean capital of Seoul and pushed the North Koreans back to the 38th parallel. Even before Inchon, Truman had redefined the U.S. war goal, changing it from the containment of North Korea to the reunification of Korea by force. Communism not only would be stopped; it would be rolled back.

In September, Truman authorized U.N. forces to cross the 38th parallel. These troops drove deep into

Chinese Entry into the War

North Korea, and American aircraft began strikes against bridges on the Yalu River, the border between North Korea and China. The Chinese watched warily, fearing that the Americans would next stab at the People's Republic. Mao publicly warned that China could not permit the bombing of its transportation links with Korea and would not accept the annihilation of North Korea itself. MacArthur shrugged off the warnings, and Washington officials agreed with the strong-willed general, drawing further confidence from the fact that, as MacArthur had predicted, the Soviets were not preparing for war.

MacArthur was right about the Soviets, but wrong about the Chinese. Mao, concluding that the "Americans would run more rampant" unless stopped, on October 25 sent Chinese soldiers into the war near the Yalu. Perhaps to lure American forces into a trap or to signal willingness to begin negotiations, they pulled back after a brief and successful offensive against South Korean troops. Then, after MacArthur sent the U.S. Eighth Army northward, tens of thousands of Chinese troops counterattacked on November 26, surprising American forces and driving them pell-mell southward. One U.S. officer termed it "a sight that hasn't been seen for hundreds of years: the men of a whole United States Army fleeing from a battlefield, abandoning their wounded, running for their lives."

By early 1951 the front had stabilized around the 38th parallel. A stalemate set in. Both Washington and Moscow welcomed negotiations, but MacArthur had other ideas. The theatrical general recklessly called for an attack on China and for Jiang's return to the mainland. Now was the time, he insisted, to smash communism by destroying its Asian flank. Denouncing the concept of limited war (war without nuclear weapons, confined to one place), MacArthur hinted that the president was practicing appeasement. In April, backed by the Joint Chiefs of Staff (the heads of the various armed services), Truman fired MacArthur. The general, who had not set foot in the United States for more than a decade, returned home a hero, with ticker-tape parades and cheers on the lecture circuit. Truman's popularity sagged, but he weathered scattered demands for his impeachment.

Truman's Firing of MacArthur

Armistice talks began in July 1951, but the fighting and dying went on for two more years. The most contentious point in the negotiations was the fate of prisoners of war (POWs). Defying the Geneva Prisoners of War Convention (1949), U.S. officials announced that only those North Korean and Chinese POWs who wished to go home would be returned. Responding to the American statement that there would be no forced repatriation, the North Koreans denounced forced retention. Both sides undertook "reeducation" or "brainwashing" programs to persuade POWs to resist repatriation.

As the POW issue stalled negotiations, U.S. officials made deliberately vague public statements about using atomic weapons in Korea. American bombers obliterated dams (whose rushing waters then destroyed rice fields), factories, airfields, and bridges in North Korea. Casualties on all sides mounted. Not until July 1953 was an armistice signed. Stalin's death in March and the advent of new leaders in both Moscow and Washington helped ease the way to a settlement that all sides welcomed. The combatants agreed to hand over the POW question to a special panel of neutral nations, which later gave prisoners their choice of staying or leaving. (In the end, 70,000 of about 100,000 North Korean and 5,600 of 20,700 Chinese POWs elected to return home; 21 American and 325 South Korean POWs of some 11,000 decided to stay in North Korea.) The North Korean–South Korean borderline was set near the 38th parallel, the prewar boundary, and a demilitarized zone was created between the two Koreas.

Peace Agreement

American casualties totaled 54,246 dead and 103,284 wounded. Close to 5 million Asians died in the war: 2 million North Korean civilians and 500,000 soldiers; 1 million South Korean civilians and 100,000 soldiers; and at least 1 million Chinese soldiers—ranking Korea as one of the costliest wars of the twentieth century.

The Korean War carried major domestic political consequences. The failure to achieve victory and the public's impatience with a stalemated war undoubtedly helped to elect Republican Dwight Eisenhower to the presidency in 1952, as the former general promised to "go to Korea" to end the war. The powers of the presidency grew as Congress repeatedly deferred to Truman. The president had never asked Congress for a declaration of war, believing that, as commander-in-chief, he had the authority to send troops wherever he wished. He saw no need to consult Congress—except when he wanted the $69.5 billion Korean War bill paid. In addition, the war, which occurred in the midst of the "who lost China?" debate, inflamed antileftist politics in the United States. Republican lawmakers, including Wisconsin senator Joseph McCarthy, accused Truman and Secretary of State Dean Acheson of being "soft on communism" in failing first to prevent, and then to go all-out to win, the war; their verbal attacks strengthened the administration's determination to take an uncompromising position in the negotiations.

Consequences of the War

The impact on foreign policy was even greater. The Sino-American hostility generated by the war ensured that there would be no U.S. reconciliation with the Beijing government and that South Korea and Formosa would become major recipients of American foreign aid. The alliance with Japan strengthened as the island's economy boomed after filling large procurement orders from the United States. Australia and New Zealand joined the United States in a mutual defense agreement, the ANZUS Treaty (1951). The U.S. Army sent four divisions to Europe, and the administration initiated plans to rearm West Germany. The Korean War also persuaded Truman to do what he had been unwilling to do before the outbreak of hostilities—approve NSC-68. Indeed, the military budget shot up from $14 billion in 1949 to $44 billion in 1953; it remained between $35 billion and $44 billion a year throughout the 1950s. The Soviet Union sought to match this military buildup, and the result was a major arms race between the two nations. In sum, Truman's legacy was a highly militarized U.S. foreign policy active on a global scale.

UNRELENTING COLD WAR

The new foreign policy team of President Eisenhower and Secretary of State John Foster Dulles largely sustained Truman's Cold War policies. Both brought abundant experience in foreign affairs to their posts. Eisenhower had lived and traveled in Europe, Asia, and Latin America and, as a general during the Second World War, had ne-gotiated with world leaders. After the war, he had served as army chief of staff and NATO supreme commander. Dulles had been closely involved with U.S. diplomacy since the first decade of the century. "Foster has been studying to be secretary of state since he was five years old," Eisenhower observed. He relied heavily on Dulles to be his emissary abroad. The secretary of state spent so much time traveling to world capitals that critics exclaimed, "Don't do something, Foster, just stand there!"

Eisenhower and Dulles accepted the Cold War consensus about the threat of communism and the need for global vigilance. Although Democrats promoted an image of Eisenhower as a bumbling, passive, aging hero, deferring most foreign policy matters to Dulles, the president in fact commanded the policymaking process and on occasion tamed the more hawkish proposals of Dulles and Vice President Richard Nixon. Even so, the secretary of state's influence was considerable. Few Cold Warriors rivaled Dulles's impassioned anticommunism, often expressed in biblical terms. A graduate of Princeton and George Washington Universities, Dulles had assisted Woodrow Wilson at Versailles and later became a senior partner in a prestigious Wall Street law firm and an officer of the Federal Council of Churches. Though polished and articulate, Dulles impressed people as arrogant, stubborn, and hectoring—and averse to compromise, an essential ingredient in successful diplomacy. Behind closed doors Dulles could show a different side, one considerably more flexible and pragmatic, but there is little evidence that he saw much utility in negotiations, at least where communists were involved. His assertion that neutrality was an "immoral and short-sighted conception" did not sit well with Third World leaders, who resented being told they had to choose between East and West.

Eisenhower and Dulles

◄ President Eisenhower *(left)* confers with Secretary of State John Foster Dulles (1888–1959), known for his strong anti-communism and his often self-righteous, lecturing style. Dulles once remarked that the United States "is almost the only country strong enough and powerful enough to be moral." *(© Bettmann/Corbis).*

Like the president, Dulles conceded much to the anticommunist McCarthyites, who claimed that the State Department was infested with communists (see pages 835–836). The State Department's chief security officer, a McCarthy follower, targeted homosexuals and other "incompatibles," and made few distinctions between New Dealers and communists. Dulles thus forced many talented officers out of the Foreign Service with unsubstantiated charges that they were disloyal. Among them were Asia specialists whose expertise was thus denied to the American leaders who were steadily expanding the U.S. presence on that continent. "The wrong done," the journalist Theodore A. White wrote, "was to poke out the eyes and ears of the State Department on Asian affairs, to blind American foreign policy."

Dulles said that he considered containment too defensive a stance toward communism. He called instead

"Massive Retaliation"

for "liberation," although he never explained precisely how the countries of eastern Europe could be freed from Soviet control. "Massive retaliation" was the administration's plan for the nuclear obliteration of the Soviet state or its assumed client, the People's Republic of China, if either one took aggressive actions. Eisenhower said that it "simply means the ability to blow hell out of them in a hurry if they start anything." The ability of the United States to make such a threat was thought to provide "deterrence," the prevention of hostile Soviet behavior.

In their "New Look" for the American military, Eisenhower and Dulles emphasized airpower and nuclear weaponry. The president's preference for heavy weapons stemmed in part from his desire to trim the federal budget ("more bang for the buck," as the saying went). Galvanized by the successful test of the world's first hydrogen bomb in November 1952, Eisenhower oversaw a massive stockpiling of nuclear weapons—from 1,200 at the start of his presidency to 22,229 at the end. Backed by its huge military arsenal, the United States could practice "brinkmanship": not backing down in a crisis, even if it meant taking the nation to the brink of war. Eisenhower also popularized the "domino theory": that small, weak, neighboring nations would fall to communism like a row of dominoes if they were not propped up by the United States.

Eisenhower increasingly utilized the Central Intelligence Agency as an instrument of foreign policy. Headed by Allen Dulles, brother of the sec-

CIA as Foreign Policy Instrument

retary of state, the CIA put foreign leaders (such as King Hussein of Jordan) on its payroll; subsidized foreign labor unions, newspapers,

and political parties (such as the conservative Liberal Democratic Party of Japan); planted false stories in newspapers through its "disinformation" projects; and trained foreign military officers in counterrevolutionary methods. It hired American journalists and professors; secretly funded the National Student Association to spur contacts with foreign student leaders; used business executives as "fronts"; and conducted experiments on unsuspecting Americans to determine the effects of "mind control" drugs (the MKULTRA program). The CIA also launched covert operations (including assassination schemes) to subvert or destroy governments in the Third World. The CIA helped overthrow the governments of Iran (1953) and Guatemala (1954) but failed in attempts to topple regimes in Indonesia (1958) and Cuba (1961).

The CIA and other components of the American intelligence community followed the principle of plausible deniability: covert operations should be conducted in such a way, and the decisions that launched them concealed so well, that the president could deny any knowledge of them. Thus President Eisenhower disavowed any U.S. role in Guatemala, even though he had ordered the operation. He and his successor, John F. Kennedy, also denied that they had instructed the CIA to assassinate Cuba's Fidel Castro, whose regime after 1959 became stridently anti-American.

It did not take leaders in Moscow long to become aware of Eisenhower's expanded use of covert action, as

Nuclear Buildup

well as his stockpiling of nuclear weapons. They increased their own intelligence activity and tested their first H-bomb in 1953. Four years later, they shocked Americans by firing the world's first intercontinental ballistic missile (ICBM) and then propelling the satellite *Sputnik* into orbit in outer space. Americans felt more vulnerable to air attack and inferior in rocket technology, even though in 1957 the United States had 2,460 strategic weapons and a nuclear stockpile of 5,543, compared with the Soviet Union's 102 and 650. As President Eisenhower said, "If we were to release our nuclear stockpile on the Soviet Union, the main danger would arise not from retaliation but from fallout in the earth's atmosphere." The administration enlarged its fleet of long-range bombers (B-52s) and deployed intermediate-range missiles in Europe, targeted against the Soviet Union. At the end of 1960 the United States began adding Polaris missile–bearing submarines to its navy. To foster future technological advancement, the National Aeronautics and Space Administration (NASA) was created in 1958.

Overall, though, Eisenhower sought to avoid any kind of military confrontation with the Soviet Union and China;

The People-to-People Campaign

Not long after the start of the Cold War, U.S. officials determined that the Soviet-American confrontation was as much psychological and ideological as military and economic. One result was the People-to-People campaign, a state-private venture initiated by the United States Information Agency (USIA) in 1956, which aimed to win the "hearts and minds" of people around the world. In this program, American propaganda experts sought to channel the energies of ordinary Americans, businesses, civic organizations, labor groups, and women's clubs to promote confidence abroad in the basic goodness of the American people and, by extension, their government. In addition, the campaign was designed to raise morale at home by giving Americans a sense of personal participation in the Cold War struggle. The People-to-People campaign, one USIA pamphlet said, made "every man an ambassador."

Campaign activities resembled the home-front mobilization efforts of World War II. If, during the war, Americans were exhorted by the Office of War Information to purchase war bonds, now they were told that $30 could send a ninety-nine-volume portable library of American books to schools and libraries overseas. Publishers donated magazines and books for free distribution to foreign countries— *Woman's Day,* for example, volunteered six thousand copies of the magazine per month. People-to-People committees organized sister-city affiliations and "pen-pal" letter exchanges, hosted exchange students, and organized traveling "People-to-People delegations" representing their various communities. The travelers were urged to behave like goodwill ambassadors when abroad and to "help overcome any feeling that America is a land that thinks money can buy everything." They were to "appreciate [foreigners'] manners and customs, not to insist on imitations of the American way of doing things."

To extol everyday life in the United States, Camp Fire Girls in more than three thousand communities took photographs on the theme "This is our home. This is how we live. These are my People." The photographs, assembled in albums, were sent to girls in Latin America, Africa, Asia, and the Middle East. The Hobbies Committee, meanwhile, connected people with interests in radio, photography, coins, stamps, and horticulture. One group represented dog owners, in the belief that "dogs make good ambassadors and are capable of hurdling the barriers of language and ideologies in the quest for peace."

Just what effect the People-to-People campaign had on foreign images of the United States is hard to say. The persistence to this day of the widespread impression that Americans are a provincial, materialistic people suggests that skepticism is in order. But alongside this negative image is a more positive one that sees Americans as admirably open, friendly, optimistic, and pragmatic; if the campaign did not erase the former impression, it may have helped foster the latter. Whatever role the People-to-People campaign played in the larger Cold War struggle, it certainly achieved one of its chief objectives: to link ordinary Americans more closely to people in other parts of the world.

▲ This Alice Nast painting of two girls—one from the United States and one from Taiwan—was commissioned by the Kansas City chapter of People to People and the Kansas City/Tainan Sister City Committee. The painting was presented to the mayor of Tainan in September 1994, prior to the 11th Worldwide Conference of the People-to-People International. *(People to People)*

notwithstanding Dulles's tough talk of "liberation" and "massive retaliation," the administration was content to follow Truman's lead and emphasize the *containment* of communism. Eisenhower rejected opportunities to use nuclear weapons, and he proved more reluctant than many other Cold War presidents to send American soldiers into battle. He preferred to fight the Soviets at the level of propaganda. Convinced that the struggle against Moscow would in large measure be decided in the arena of international public opinion, he wanted to win the "hearts and minds" of people overseas. The "People-to-People" campaign, launched in 1956, sought to use ordinary Americans and nongovernmental organizations to enhance the international image of the United States and its people.

Likewise, American cultural exchanges and participation in trade fairs in the Eisenhower years were used to create a favorable atmosphere abroad for U.S. political, economic, and military policies. Sometimes the propaganda war was waged on the Soviets' own turf. In 1959 Vice President Richard Nixon traveled to Moscow to open an American products fair. In the display of a modern American kitchen, part of a model six-room ranch-style house, Nixon extolled capitalist consumerism, while Soviet premier Nikita Khrushchev, Stalin's successor, touted the merits of communism. The encounter became famous as the "kitchen debate."

Eisenhower showed his restraint in 1956 when turmoil rocked parts of eastern Europe. In February, Khrushchev

Rebellion in Hungary

called for "peaceful coexistence" between capitalists and communists, denounced Stalin, and suggested that Moscow would tolerate different brands of communism. Revolts against Soviet power promptly erupted in Poland and Hungary, testing Khrushchev's new permissiveness. After a new Hungarian government in 1956 announced its withdrawal from the Warsaw Pact (the Soviet military alliance formed in 1955 with communist countries of eastern Europe), Soviet troops and tanks battled students and workers in the streets of Budapest and crushed the rebellion.

Although the Eisenhower administration's propaganda had been encouraging liberation efforts, U.S. officials found themselves unable to aid the rebels without igniting a world war. They stood by, promising only to welcome Hungarian immigrants in greater numbers than American quota laws allowed. Even so, the West could have reaped some propaganda advantage from this display of Soviet brute force had not British, French, and Israeli troops—U.S. allies—invaded Egypt during the Suez crisis just before the Soviets smashed the Hungarian uprising (see page 820).

Hardly had the turmoil subsided when the divided city of Berlin once again became a Cold War flash point. The Soviets railed against the placement in West Germany of American bombers capable of carrying nuclear warheads, and they complained that West Berlin had become an escape route for disaffected East Germans. In 1958 Khrushchev announced that the Soviet Union would recognize East German control of all of Berlin unless the United States and its allies began talks on German reunification and rearmament. The United States refused to give up its hold on West Berlin or to break West German ties with NATO. Khrushchev backed away from his ultimatum but promised to press the issue again.

Khrushchev hoped to do just that at a summit meeting planned for Paris in mid-1960. But two weeks before

U-2 Incident

the conference, on May 1, a U-2 spy plane carrying high-powered cameras crashed 1,200 miles inside the Soviet Union. Moscow claimed credit for shooting down the plane, which the Soviets put on display along with Francis Gary Powers, the captured CIA pilot, and the pictures he had been snapping of Soviet military sites. Khrushchev demanded an apology for the U.S. violation of Soviet airspace. When Washington refused, the Soviets walked out of the Paris summit—"a graveyard of lost opportunities," as a Soviet official put it.

While sparring over Europe, both sides kept a wary eye on the People's Republic of China, which denounced the Soviet call for peaceful coexistence. Despite evidence of a widening Sino-Soviet split, most American officials still treated communism as a monolithic world movement. The isolation separating Beijing and Washington stymied communication and made continued conflict between China and the United States likely. In 1954, in a dispute over Jinmen (Quemoy) and Mazu (Matsu), two tiny islands off the Chinese coast, the United States and the People's Republic of China lurched toward the brink. Taiwan's Jiang Jieshi used these islands as bases from which to raid the mainland. Communist China's guns bombarded the islands in 1954. Thinking that U.S. credibility was at stake, Eisenhower decided to defend the outposts; he even hinted that he might use nuclear weapons. Why massive retaliation over such an insignificant issue? "Let's keep the Reds guessing," advised John Foster Dulles. "But what if they guessed wrong?" critics replied.

In early 1955, Congress passed the Formosa Resolution, authorizing the president to deploy American forces

Formosa Resolution

to defend Formosa and adjoining islands. In so doing, Congress formally surrendered to the president what it had informally given up at the time of the Korea decision in

1950: the constitutional power to declare war. Although the crisis passed in April 1955, war loomed again in 1958 over Jinmen and Mazu. But this time, after Washington strongly cautioned him not to use force against the mainland, Jiang withdrew some troops from the islands. China then relaxed its bombardments. One consequence accelerated the arms race: Eisenhower's nuclear threats persuaded the Chinese that they, too, needed nuclear arms. In 1964 China exploded its first nuclear bomb.

THE STRUGGLE FOR THE THIRD WORLD

Like Truman before him and all Cold War presidents after him, Eisenhower worried most about the fate of western Europe. Over time, however, his administration focused more and more attention on the threat of communist expansion in Africa, Asia, Latin America, and the Middle East. In much of the Third World, the process of decolonization that began during the First World War accelerated after the Second World War, when the economically wracked imperial countries proved incapable of resisting their colonies' demands for freedom. A cavalcade of new nations cast off their colonial bonds (see Map 28.3). In 1960 alone, eighteen new African nations did so. From 1943 to 1994, a total of 125 countries became independent (the figure includes the former Soviet republics that departed the USSR in 1991). The emergence of so many new states in the 1940s and after, and the instability associated with the transfer of authority, shook the foundations of the international system. Power was redistributed, creating "near chaos," said one U.S. government report. In the traditional U.S. sphere of influence, Latin America, nationalists once again challenged Washington's dominance.

By the late 1940s, when Cold War lines were drawn fairly tightly in Europe, Soviet-American rivalry shifted increasingly to the Third World.

Interests in the Third World

Much was at stake. The new nations could buy American goods and technology, supply strategic raw materials, and invite investments (more than one-third of America's private foreign investments were in Third World countries in 1959). And they could build cultural ties with the United States. Both great powers, moreover, looked to these new states for votes in the United Nations and sought sites within their borders for military and intelligence bases. But, often poor and unstable—and rife with tribal, ethnic, and class rivalries—many new nations sought to end the economic, military, and cultural hegemony of the West. Many learned to play off the two superpowers against each other to garner more aid and arms. U.S. interventions—military and otherwise—in the Third World, American leaders believed, became necessary to impress Moscow with Washington's might and to resolve and counter the nationalism and radical anticapitalist social change that threatened American strategic and economic interests.

To thwart nationalist, radical, and communist challenges, the United States directed massive resources—foreign aid, propaganda, development projects—toward the Third World. By 1961 more than 90 percent of U.S. foreign aid was going to developing nations. Washington also allied with native elites and with undemocratic but anticommunist regimes, meddled in civil wars, and unleashed CIA covert operations. These American interventions often generated resentment among the local populace. When some of the larger Third World states—notably India, Ghana, Egypt, and Indonesia—refused to take sides in the Cold War, Secretary of State Dulles declared that neutralism was a step on the road to communism. Both he and Eisenhower insisted that every nation should take a side in the life-and-death Cold War struggle.

American leaders argued that technologically "backward" Third World countries needed western-induced capitalist development and modernization in order to enjoy economic growth, social harmony, and political moderation. Often these U.S. officials also ascribed stereotyped race-, age-, and gender-based characteristics to Third World peoples, seeing them as dependent, emotional, and irrational, and therefore dependent on the fatherly tutelage of the United States. Cubans, CIA director Allen Dulles told the National Security Council in early 1959, "had to be treated more or less like children. They had to be led rather than rebuffed. If they were rebuffed, like children, they were capable of almost anything."

At other times American officials used gendered language, suggesting that Third World countries were weak women—passive and servile, unable to resist the menacing appeals of communists and neutralists. In speaking of India, for example—a neutralist nation that Americans deemed effeminate and submissive—Eisenhower condescendingly described it as a place where "emotion rather than reason seems to dictate policy."

Race attitudes and segregation practices in the United States especially influenced U.S. relations with Third World countries.

Racism and Segregation as U.S. Handicaps

In 1955 G. L. Mehta, the Indian ambassador to the United States, was refused service in the whites-only section of a restaurant at Houston International Airport. The insult stung deeply, as did many similar indignities experienced by other Third World diplomats. Fearing damaged relations with India, a large nation whose allegiance the United States sought in the

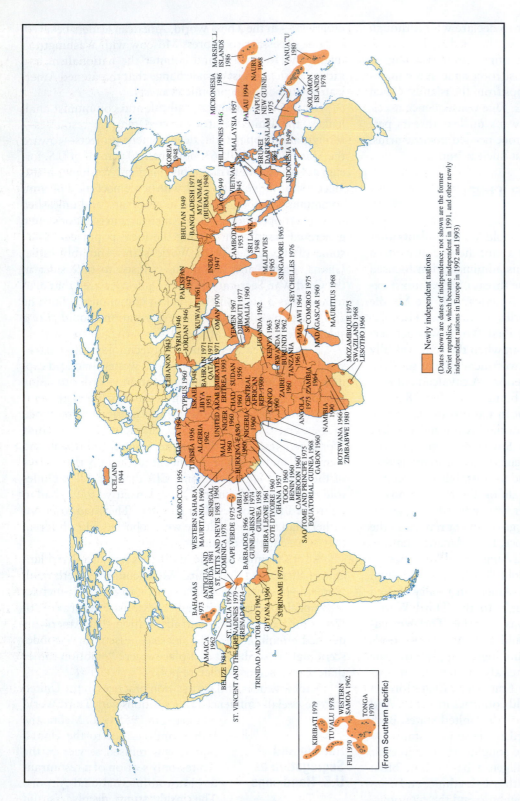

Map 28.3   **The Rise of the Third World: Newly Independent Nations Since 1943**

Accelerated by the Second World War, decolonization liberated many peoples from imperial rule. New nations emerged in the postwar international system dominated by the Cold War rivalry of the United States and the Soviet Union. Many newly independent states became targets of great-power intrigue but chose nonalignment in the Cold War.

Cold War, John Foster Dulles apologized to Mehta. The secretary thought racial segregation in the United States was a "major international hazard," spoiling American efforts to win friends in Third World countries and giving the Soviets a propaganda advantage. American practices and ideals did not align.

Thus, when the U.S. attorney general appealed to the Supreme Court to strike down segregation in public schools, he underlined that the humiliation of dark-skinned diplomats "furnished grist for the Communist propaganda mills." When the Court announced its *Brown* decision in 1954 (see page 838), the government quickly broadcast news of the desegregation order around the world in thirty-five languages on its Voice of America overseas radio network. But the problem did not go away. For example, after the 1957 Little Rock crisis (see page 840), Dulles remarked that racial bigotry was "ruining our foreign policy. The effect of this in Asia and Africa will be worse for us than Hungary was for the Russians." Still, when an office of the Department of State decided to counter Soviet propaganda by creating for the 1958 World's Fair in Brussels an exhibit titled "The Unfinished Work"—on race relations in the United States and strides taken toward desegregation—southern conservatives kicked up such a furor that the Eisenhower administration closed the display.

American hostility toward revolution also obstructed the quest for influence in the Third World. In the twentieth century, the United States openly opposed revolutions in Mexico, China, Russia, Cuba, Vietnam, Nicaragua,

and Iran, among other nations. Americans celebrated the Spirit of '76 but grew intolerant of revolutionary disorder because many Third World revolutions arose against America's Cold War allies and threatened American investments, markets, and military bases. Preferring, like most other great powers in history, to maintain the status quo, the United States usually supported its European allies or the conservative, propertied classes in the Third World. In 1960, for example, when forty-three African and Asian states sponsored a U.N. resolution endorsing decolonization, the United States abstained from the vote.

Yet the American approach also had its element of idealism. Believing that Third World peoples craved mod-

Development and Modernization

ernization and that the American economic model of private enterprise and cooperation among business, labor, and government was best for them, American policymakers launched various "development" projects. Such projects held out the promise of sustained economic growth, prosperity, and stability, which the benefactors hoped would undermine radicalism. In the 1950s, the Carnegie, Ford, and Rockefeller Foundations worked with the U.S. Agency for International Development (AID) to sponsor a Green Revolution, a dramatic increase in agricultural production—for example, by the use of hybrid seeds. The Rockefeller Foundation supported foreign universities' efforts to train national leaders committed to nonradical development; from 1958 to 1969 the philanthropic agency spent $25 million in Nigeria. Before Dean Rusk became secretary of state in 1961, he served as president of the Rockefeller Foundation.

To persuade Third World peoples to abandon radical doctrines and neutralism, American

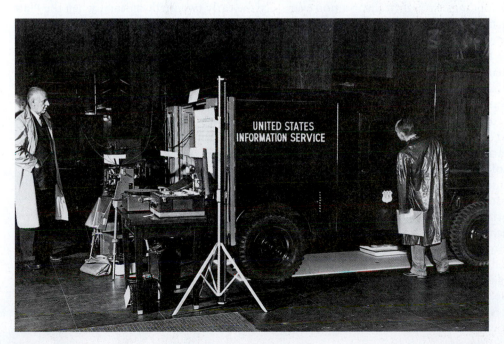

◄ In the 1950s, these specially outfitted jeeps (equipped with projectors, screens, and films) served America's overseas information program in what the State Department called "isolated areas." Believing that social modernization and economic progress would counter leftist and communist ideas, U.S. propaganda officials dispatched these "mobile motion picture units" to such places as rural Mexico, seeking to reach people with films on U.S. sports, music, health, and agriculture. *(National Archives)*

leaders, often in cooperation with the business-sponsored Advertising Council, directed propaganda at developing nations. The United States Information Agency (USIA), founded in 1953, used films, radio broadcasts, the magazine *Free World,* exhibitions, exchange programs, and libraries (in 162 cities worldwide by 1961) to trumpet the theme of "People's Capitalism." Citing America's economic success—contrasted with "slave-labor" conditions in the Soviet Union—the message showcased well-paid American workers, political democracy, and religious freedom. To counter ugly pictures of segregation and white attacks on African Americans and civil rights activists in the South, the USIA applauded success stories of individual African Americans, such as boxers Floyd Patterson and Sugar Ray Robinson. In 1960 alone, some 13.8 million people visited U.S. pavilions abroad, including 1 million at the consumer-products exhibit "Tradeways to Peace and Prosperity" in Damascus, Syria.

Undoubtedly the American way of life had appeal for some Third World peoples. They, too, wanted to enjoy American consumer goods, rock music, economic status, and educational opportunities. Hollywood movies offered enticing glimpses of middle-class materialism, and American films dominated many overseas markets. Blue jeans, advertising billboards, and soft drinks flooded foreign societies. But if foreigners often envied Americans, they also resented them for having so much and wasting so much, while poorer peoples went without. The popular American novel *The Ugly American* (1958) spotlighted the "golden ghettoes" where American diplomats lived in compounds separated from their poorer surroundings by high walls. The people of many countries, moreover, resented the ample profits that U.S. corporations extracted from them. Americans often received blame for the persistent poverty of the developing world, even though the leaders of those nations made decisions that hindered their own progress, such as pouring millions of dollars into their militaries while their people needed food. Nonetheless, anti-American resentments could be measured in the late 1950s in attacks on USIA libraries in Calcutta, India; Beirut, Lebanon; and Bogotá, Colombia.

When the more benign techniques of containment—aid, trade, cultural relations—proved insufficient to get Third World nations to line up on the American side in the Cold War, the Eisenhower administration often showed a willingness to press harder, by covert or overt means. Guatemala was an early test case. In 1951 leftist Jacobo Arbenz Guzmán was elected president of Guatemala, a poor country whose largest landowner was the American-

Intervention in Guatemala

owned United Fruit Company. United Fruit was an economic power throughout Latin America, where it owned 3 million acres of land and operated railroads, ports, ships, and telecommunications facilities. To fulfill his promise of land reform, Arbenz expropriated United Fruit's uncultivated land and offered compensation. The company dismissed the offer and charged that Arbenz posed a communist threat—a charge that CIA officials had already floated because Arbenz employed some communists in his government. The CIA began a secret plot to overthrow Arbenz. He turned to Moscow for military aid, thus reinforcing American suspicions. The CIA airlifted arms into Guatemala, dropping them at United Fruit facilities, and in mid-1954, CIA-supported Guatemalans struck from Honduras. U.S. planes bombed the capital city, and the invaders drove Arbenz from power. The new pro-American regime returned United Fruit's land, but an ensuing civil war staggered the Central American nation for decades.

Eisenhower also watched with apprehension as turmoil gripped Cuba in the late 1950s. In early 1959, Fidel Castro's rebels, or *barbudos* ("bearded ones"), driven by profound anti-American nationalism, ousted Fulgencio Batista, a longtime U.S. ally who had welcomed North American investors, U.S. military advisers, and tourists to the Caribbean island. Batista's corrupt, dictatorial regime had helped turn Havana into a haven for gambling and prostitution run by organized crime. Cubans had resented U.S. domination ever since the early twentieth century, when the Platt Amendment had compromised their independence. Curbing U.S. influence became a rallying cry of the Cuban revolution, all the more so after the CIA conspired secretly but futilely to block Castro's rise to power in 1958. From the start Castro sought to roll back the influence of American business, which had invested some $1 billion on the island, and to break the U.S. grasp on Cuban trade.

The Cuban Revolution and Fidel Castro

Castro's increasing authoritarianism, anti-Yankee declarations, and growing popularity in the hemisphere alarmed Washington. In early 1960, after Cuba signed a trade treaty with the Soviet Union, Eisenhower ordered the CIA to organize an invasion force of Cuban exiles to overthrow the Castro government. The agency also began to plot an assassination of the Cuban leader. When the president drastically cut U.S. purchases of Cuban sugar, Castro seized all North American–owned companies that had not yet been nationalized. Threatened by U.S. decisions designed to bring him and his revolution down, Castro appealed to the Soviet Union, which offered loans

In the years 1948–1950, hundreds of thousands of Jewish refugees arrived in the state of Israel. Legendary war photographer Robert Capa snapped this picture of refugees arriving on a boat in Haifa in 1949. A few years later, while on assignment for *Life* magazine, Capa would be killed by a land mine in Indochina. *(Robert Capa/ Magnum Photos, Inc.)*

and expanded trade. Just before leaving office in early 1961, Eisenhower broke diplomatic relations with Cuba and advised president-elect John F. Kennedy to advance plans for the invasion, which came—and failed—in early 1961 (see page 862).

In the Middle East, meanwhile, the Eisenhower administration confronted challenges posed by ongoing tensions between Arabs and Jews, and by nationalist leaders in Iran and Egypt (see Map 33.2). Prior to the end of World War II, only France and Britain among the great powers had been much concerned with this region of the world; they had effectively dominated the area during the prior three decades. But the dissolution of empires and the rise of Cold War tensions drew Washington into the region, as did the deepening tensions in British-held Palestine. From 1945 to 1947, Britain tried to enlist U.S. officials in the effort to find a solution to the vexing question of how to split Palestine between the Arabs and Jews who lived there. The Truman administration rejected London's solicitations, and the British, despairing at the violence between Arabs and Jews and at the rising number of British deaths, in 1947 turned the issue over to the United Nations, which voted to partition Palestine into separate Arab and Jewish states. Arab leaders opposed the decision, but in May 1948 Jewish leaders announced the creation of Israel.

The United States, which had lobbied hard to secure the U.N. vote, extended recognition to the new state mere minutes after the act of foundation. A moral conviction

Arab-Israeli Conflict

that Jews deserved a homeland after the suffering of the Holocaust, and that Zionism was a worthy movement that would create a democratic Israel, influenced Truman's decision, as did the belief that Jewish votes might swing some states to the Democrats in the 1948 election. These beliefs trumped some senior officials' concerns that Arab oil producers might turn against the United States and that close Soviet-Israeli ties could turn Israel into a pro-Soviet bastion in the Middle East. The Soviet Union did promptly recognize the new nation, but Israeli leaders kept Moscow at arm's length, in part because they had more pressing concerns. Palestinian Arabs, displaced from land they considered theirs, joined with Israel's Arab neighbors to make immediate war on the new state. The Israelis stopped the offensive in bloody fighting over the next six months until a U.N.-backed truce was called.

In the years thereafter, American policy in the Middle East centered on ensuring Israel's survival and cementing ties with Arab oil producers. U.S. oil holdings were extensive: American companies produced about half of the region's petroleum in the 1950s. Eisenhower consequently sought to avoid actions that might alienate Arab states, such as drawing too close to Israel, and he cultivated close relations with oil-rich Iran. Its ruling shah had granted American oil companies a 40 percent interest in a new petroleum consortium in return for CIA help in the successful overthrow, in 1953, of his rival, Mohammed Mossadegh, who had attempted to nationalize foreign oil interests. Nor was it only about petroleum: Iran's position on the Soviet border made the shah a particularly valuable friend.

American officials faced a more formidable foe in Egypt, in the form of Gamal Abdul Nasser, a towering figure in a pan-Arabic movement to reduce western interests in the Middle East. Nasser vowed to expel the British from the Suez Canal and the Israelis from Palestine. The United States wished neither to anger the Arabs, for fear of losing valuable oil supplies, nor to alienate its ally Israel, which was supported at home by politically active American Jews. But when Nasser declared neutrality in the Cold War, Dulles lost patience.

In 1956 the United States abruptly reneged on its offer to Egypt to help finance the Aswan Dam, a project

Suez Crisis

to provide inexpensive electricity and water for thirsty Nile valley farmland. Secretary Dulles's blunt economic pressure backfired, for Nasser responded by nationalizing the British-owned Suez Canal, intending to use its profits to build the dam. At a mass rally in Alexandria, Nasser expressed the profound nationalism typical of Third World peoples shedding an imperial past: "Tonight our Egyptian canal will be run by Egyptians. Egyptians!" Fully 75 percent of western Europe's oil came from the Middle East, most of it transported through the Suez Canal. Fearing an interruption in this vital trade, the British and French conspired with Israel to bring down Nasser. On October 29, 1956, the Israelis invaded Suez, joined two days later by British and French forces.

Eisenhower fumed. America's allies had not consulted him, and the attack had shifted attention from Soviet intervention in Hungary. The president also feared that the invasion would cause Nasser to seek help from the Soviets, inviting them into the Middle East. Eisenhower sternly demanded that London, Paris, and Tel Aviv pull their troops out, and they did. Egypt took possession of the canal, the Soviets built the Aswan Dam, and Nasser became a hero to Third World peoples. French and British influence in the region declined sharply. To counter Nasser, the United States determined to "build up" as an "Arab rival" the conservative King Ibn Saud of Saudi Arabia. Although the monarch renewed America's lease of an air base, few Arabs respected the notoriously corrupt Saud.

Washington officials worried that a "vacuum" existed in the Middle East—and that the Soviets might fill it.

Eisenhower Doctrine

Nasserites insisted that there was no vacuum but rather a growing Arab nationalism that provided the best defense against communism. In an effort to improve the deteriorating western position in the Middle East and to protect American interests there, the president proclaimed the Eisenhower Doctrine in 1957. The United States would intervene in the Middle East, he declared, if any government threatened by a communist takeover asked for help.

In 1958 fourteen thousand American troops scrambled ashore in Lebanon to quell an internal political dispute that Washington feared might be exploited by pro-Nasser groups or communists. Concentrating the troops in the area of Beirut, Eisenhower said their mission was "not primarily to fight" but merely to show the flag. The restrained use of U.S. military power served to defuse the crisis, as Lebanese officials agreed to work for a peaceful transition to a new leadership. In Dulles's view, the intervention also served to "reassure many small nations that they could call on us in a time of crisis."

Cold War concerns also drove Eisenhower's policy toward Vietnam, where nationalists battled the French for independence. Despite a substantial U.S. aid program initiated under Truman, the French lost steadily to the Vietminh. Finally, in early 1954, Ho's forces surrounded the French fortress at Dienbienphu in northwest Vietnam (see Map 30.2). Although some of Eisenhower's advisers recommended a massive American air strike against Vietminh positions, perhaps even using tactical atomic weapons, the president moved cautiously. The United States had been advising and bankrolling the French, but it had not committed its own forces to the war. If American airpower did not save the French, would ground troops be required next, and in hostile terrain? As one high-level doubter remarked, "One cannot go over Niagara Falls in a barrel only slightly."

Worrying aloud about a communist victory, Eisenhower pressed the British to help form a coalition to address the Indochinese crisis, but they refused. At home, influential members of Congress—including Lyndon Baines Johnson of Texas, who as president would wage large-scale war in Vietnam—told Eisenhower they wanted "no more Koreas" and warned him against any U.S. military commitment, especially in the absence of cooperation from America's allies. Some felt very uneasy about supporting colonialism. The issue became moot on May 7, when the weary French defenders at Dienbienphu surrendered.

Peace talks, already under way in Geneva, brought Cold War and nationalist contenders together—the United

Geneva Accords on Vietnam

States, the Soviet Union, Britain, the People's Republic of China, Laos, Cambodia, and the competing Vietnamese regimes of Bao Dai and Ho Chi Minh. John Foster Dulles, a reluctant participant, feared the communists would get the better of any agreement, yet in the end the Vietminh received less than their dominant military position suggested they should. The 1954 Geneva accords, signed by France and Ho's Democratic Republic of Vietnam, temporarily divided Vietnam at the 17th parallel;

◀ French soldiers assemble one of the eight tanks that were flown into Dienbienphu in parts. In the background are the airstrip and fortifications of the garrison. The tanks proved largely ineffectual in the fighting that followed. *(Everette Dixie Reece/George Eastman House)*

Ho's government was confined to the North, Bao Dai's to the South. Only after pressure from the Chinese and the Soviets, who feared U.S. intervention in Vietnam without an agreement, did Ho's government agree to this compromise. The 17th parallel was meant to serve as a military truce line, not a national boundary; the country was scheduled to be reunified after national elections in 1956. Meanwhile, neither North nor South was to join a military alliance or permit foreign military bases on its soil.

Confident that the Geneva agreements ultimately would mean communist victory, the United States from an early point set about trying to undermine them. Soon after the conference, a CIA team entered Vietnam and undertook secret operations against the North, including commando raids across the 17th parallel. In the South, the United States helped Ngo Dinh Diem push Bao Dai aside and inaugurate the Republic of Vietnam. A Catholic in a Buddhist nation, Diem was a dedicated nationalist and anticommunist, but he had little mass support. He staged a fraudulent election in South Vietnam that gave him 99 percent of the vote (in Saigon he received 200,000 more votes than there were registered voters). When Ho and some in the world community pressed for national elections in keeping with the Geneva agreements, Diem and

Eisenhower refused, fearing that the popular Vietminh leader would win. From 1955 to 1961, the Diem government received more than $1 billion in American aid, most of it military. American advisers organized and trained Diem's army, and American agriculturalists worked to improve crops. Diem's Saigon regime became dependent on the United States for its very existence, and the culture of South Vietnam became increasingly Americanized.

Diem proved a difficult ally. He acted dictatorially, abolishing village elections and appointing to public office people beholden to him. He threw dissenters in jail and shut down newspapers that criticized his regime. When U.S. officials periodically urged him to implement meaningful land reform, he blithely ignored them. Non-communists and communists alike began to strike back at Diem's repressive government. In Hanoi, Ho's government initially focused on solidifying its control on the North, but in the late 1950s it began to send aid to southern insurgents, who embarked on a program of terror, assassinating hundreds of Diem's village officials. In late 1960, southern communists, acting at the direction of Hanoi, organized the National Liberation Front (NLF), known as the Vietcong. The Vietcong in turn attracted other anti-Diem groups in the South. And the Eisenhower administration, all too aware of Diem's shortcomings and his unwillingness to follow American advice, continued to affirm its commitment to the preservation of an independent, noncommunist South Vietnam.

National Liberation Front

Legacy FOR A PEOPLE AND A NATION

The National Security State

To build a cathedral, someone has observed, you first need a religion, and a religion needs inspiring texts that command authority. For decades, America's Cold War religion has been national security; its texts, the Truman Doctrine, the "X" article, and NSC-68; and its cathedral, the national security state. The word *state* in this case means "civil government." During the Cold War, embracing preparedness for total war, the U.S. government essentially transformed itself into a huge military headquarters that interlocked with corporations and universities. Preaching the doctrine of national security, moreover, members of Congress strove to gain lucrative defense contracts for their districts.

Overseen by the president and his advisory body, the National Security Council, the national security state has had as its core what the National Security Act of 1947 called the National Military Establishment; in 1949 it became the Department of Defense. This department ranks as a leading employer; its payroll by 2007 included 1.4 million people on active duty and almost 600,000 civilian personnel, giving it more employees than Exxon-Mobil, Ford, General Motors, and GE combined. Almost 700,000 of these troops and civilians served overseas, in 177 countries covering every time zone. Although spending for national defense declined in the years after the end of the Cold War, it never fell below $290 billion. In the aftermath of the 9/11 terrorist attacks and the invasion of Iraq, the military budget rose again, reaching $439 billion in 2007. That figure represents the approximate size of the entire economy of Poland and the Netherlands, and equals the combined military spending of the twenty-five countries with the next-largest defense budgets. Nor does that sum include tens of billions of dollars in supplementary funds allocated by Congress to pay for operations in Afghanistan and Iraq.

Joining the Department of Defense as instruments of national security policy were the Joint Chiefs of Staff, the Central Intelligence Agency, and dozens more government bodies. The focus of all these entities was on finding the best means to combat real and potential threats from foreign governments. But what about threats from within? The terrorist attacks of September 2001 made starkly clear that enemies existed who, while perhaps beholden to a foreign entity—it need not be a government—launched their attacks from inside the nation's borders. Accordingly, in 2002 President George W. Bush proposed the creation of a Department of Homeland Security, which would have 170,000 employees and would include all or part of twenty-two agencies, including the Coast Guard, the Customs Service, the Federal Emergency Management Administration (FEMA), and the Internal Revenue Service. It would involve the biggest overhaul of the federal bureaucracy since the Department of Defense was created, and it signified a more expansive notion of national security. By 2006, the number of DHS employees had risen to 190,000.

In 1961 President Eisenhower warned against a "military-industrial complex," while others feared a "garrison state" or a "warfare state." Despite the warnings, by the start of the twenty-first century, the national security state remained vigorous, a lasting legacy of the early Cold War period for a people and a nation.

SUMMARY

The United States emerged from the Second World War as the preeminent world power. Confident in the nation's immediate physical security, Washington officials nevertheless worried that the unstable international system, an unfriendly Soviet Union, and the decolonizing Third World could upset American plans for the postwar peace. Locked with the Soviet Union in a "Cold War," U.S. leaders marshaled their nation's superior resources to influence and cajole other countries. Foreign economic aid, atomic diplomacy, military alliances, client states, covert operations, interventions, propaganda, cultural infiltration—these and more became the instruments for waging the Cold War, a war that began as a conflict over the future of Europe but soon spread to encompass the globe.

America's claim to international leadership was welcomed by many in western Europe and elsewhere who feared Stalin's intentions and those of his successors in the Soviet Union. The reconstruction of former enemies Japan and (West) Germany helped those nations recover swiftly and become staunch members of the western alliance. But U.S. policy also sparked resistance. Communist countries condemned financial and atomic diplomacy, while Third World nations, many of them newly independent, sought to undermine America's European allies and sometimes identified the United States as an imperial coconspirator. On occasion even America's allies bristled at a United States that boldly proclaimed itself economic master and global policeman, and haughtily touted its hegemonic status.

At home, liberal and radical critics protested that Presidents Truman and Eisenhower exaggerated the communist threat, wasting U.S. assets on immoral foreign ventures; crippled legitimate nationalist aspirations; and displayed racial bias. Still, these presidents and their successors held firm to the mission of creating a nonradical, capitalist, free-trade international order in the mold of domestic America. Determined to contain Soviet expansion, fearful of domestic charges of being "soft on communism," they worked to enlarge the U.S. sphere of influence and shape the world. In their years of nurturing allies and applying the containment doctrine worldwide, Truman and Eisenhower held the line—against the Soviet Union and the People's Republic of China, and against nonalignment, communism, nationalism, and revolution everywhere. One consequence was a dramatic increase in presidential power in the realm of foreign affairs—what the historian Arthur M. Schlesinger Jr. called "the Imperial Presidency"—as Congress ceded constitutional power.

Putting itself at odds with many in the Third World, the United States usually stood with its European allies to slow decolonization and to preach evolution rather than revolution. The globalist perspective of the United States prompted Americans to interpret many troubles in the developing world as Cold War conflicts, inspired if not directed by Soviet-backed communists. The intensity of the Cold War obscured for Americans the indigenous roots of most Third World troubles, as the wars in Korea and Vietnam attested. Nor could the United States abide developing nations' drive for economic independence—for gaining control of their own raw materials and economies. Deeply intertwined in the global economy as importer, exporter, and investor, the United States read challenges from this "periphery" as threats to the American standard of living and a way of life characterized by private enterprise. The Third World, in short, challenged U.S. strategic power by forming a third force in the Cold War, and it challenged American economic power by

seeking a new economic order of shared interests. Overall, the rise of the Third World introduced new actors to the world stage, challenging the bipolarity of the international system and diffusing power.

All the while, the threat of nuclear war unsettled Americans and foreigners alike. In the film *Godzilla* (1956), a prehistoric monster, revived by atomic bomb tests, rampages through Tokyo. Stanley Kramer's popular but disturbing movie *On the Beach* (1959), based on Nevil Shute's bestselling 1957 novel, depicts a nuclear holocaust in which the last humans on earth choose to swallow government-issued poison tablets so that they can die before H-bomb radiation sickness kills them. Such doomsday or Armageddon attitudes contrasted sharply with official U.S. government assurances that Americans would survive a nuclear war. In *On the Beach*, a dying wife asks her husband, "Couldn't anyone have stopped it?" His answer: "Some kinds of silliness you just can't stop." Eisenhower did not halt it, even though he told Khrushchev in 1959 that "we really should come to some sort of agreement in order to stop this fruitless, really wasteful rivalry."

SUGGESTIONS FOR FURTHER READING

Campbell Craig, *Destroying the Village: Eisenhower and Thermonuclear War* (1998)

Nick Cullather, *Secret History: The CIA's Classified Account of Its Operations in Guatemala, 1952–1954* (1999)

Mary L. Dudziak, *Cold War Civil Rights: Race and the Image of American Democracy* (2000)

John Lewis Gaddis, *Strategies of Containment*, 2nd ed. (2005)

Walter LaFeber, *America, Russia, and the Cold War, 1945–2006*, 10th ed. (2006)

Douglas Little, *American Orientalism: The United States and the Middle East Since 1945* (2002)

Fredrik Logevall, *The Origins of the Vietnam War* (2001)

Robert J. McMahon, *The Limits of Empire: The United States and Southeast Asia Since World War II* (1999)

Geoffrey Roberts, *Stalin's Wars: From World War to Cold War, 1939–1953* (2007)

Marc Trachtenberg, *A Constructed Peace: The Making of the European Settlement, 1945–1963* (1999)

For a more extensive list for further reading, go to college.hmco.com/pic/norton8e.

Evenings after supper, when the hot, sticky heat of the Georgia summer days had started to ebb, most of the families on Nancy Circle went out for a walk. The parents stood chatting, watching the children play swing-the-statue or hide-and-seek.

In 1959 the twenty houses on Nancy Circle were just a couple of years old. Some lots still looked raw, but in that climate grass grew quickly, and the few remaining vacant lots were covered over with kudzu. The small houses stood on land that had once belonged to the Cherokees, in a development carved from the old Campbell plantation, not far from the site where, during the Civil War, Confederate troops had made their final attempt to prevent General William Tecumseh Sherman's Union Army from launching its attack on Atlanta. Slaves had picked cotton there a century before, but no African Americans lived in the suburban homes. Sometimes an elderly black man came by on a mule cart, selling vegetables.

Nancy Circle was part of a new suburban development in Smyrna, Georgia, just northwest of Atlanta, but few of the people who lived there worked in the city. Most, instead, traveled the other direction, to the massive Lockheed Georgia airplane plant that had been created, in large part, by Cold War defense spending. This suburb was born of the union of Cold War and baby boom: families with small children lived there. With three small bedrooms, two baths, a kitchen, a combined living-dining room, and a garage for about $17,000, the houses on Nancy Circle were ones that young families could afford.

On Nancy Circle, children ran in and out of each other's houses, and women gathered to drink coffee and gossip in the morning. The men left early for work. There were several aerospace engineers, three career military men (one of whom was rumored to be

◀ A four-year-old boy stares at military aircraft, the real version of the toy he holds in his hand. The Cold War growth of defense industry plants, such as Lockheed Georgia near Atlanta, meant that many children grew up in suburbs shaken by sonic booms from military aircraft being tested overhead. *(© Bettmann/Corbis)*

CHRONOLOGY

1945 ■ World War II ends

1946 ■ Marriage and birth rates skyrocket
■ More than 1 million veterans enroll in colleges under GI Bill
■ More than 5 million U.S. workers go on strike

1947 ■ Taft-Hartley Act limits power of unions
■ Truman orders loyalty investigation of 3 million government employees
■ Mass-production techniques used to build Levittown houses

1948 ■ Truman issues executive order desegregating armed forces and federal government
■ Truman elected president

1949 ■ Soviet Union explodes atomic bomb

1950 ■ Korean War begins
■ McCarthy alleges communists in government
■ "Treaty of Detroit" creates model for new labor-management relations

1951 ■ Race riots in Cicero, Illinois, as white residents oppose residential integration

1952 ■ Eisenhower elected president

1953 ■ Korean War ends
■ Congress adopts termination policy for Native American tribes
■ Rosenbergs executed as atomic spies

1954 ■ *Brown v. Board of Education* decision reverses "separate but equal" doctrine
■ Senate condemns McCarthy

1955 ■ Montgomery bus boycott begins

1956 ■ Highway Act launches interstate highway system
■ Eisenhower reelected
■ Elvis Presley appears on *Ed Sullivan Show*

1957 ■ King elected first president of Southern Christian Leadership Conference
■ School desegregation crisis in Little Rock, Arkansas
■ Congress passes Civil Rights Act
■ Soviet Union launches *Sputnik*

1958 ■ Congress passes National Defense Education Act

1959 ■ Alaska and Hawai'i become forty-ninth and fiftieth states

in military intelligence), an auto mechanic, and a musician. Only two women held paid jobs. One had almost-grown children and taught second grade; the other was divorced and worked as a secretary. She dyed her hair blonde and drove a convertible. People were suspicious of her but liked her sister, born with dwarfism, who had left her job in a North Carolina textile mill to move to Nancy Circle and help care for her nephew. Two war brides—one Japanese and one German—lived in the neighborhood. The Japanese woman spoke little English, and people worried that she was unhappy. The German woman taught the girls in the neighborhood to do Swedish embroidery and to crochet.

The people who lived on Nancy Circle read national magazines that criticized the homogeneity and conformity of suburban life, but it didn't feel that way to them. On this single street, people from deep Appalachia or the small farms of south Georgia lived side by side with people who had grown up in crowded city apartments or dilapidated boarding houses; a Pennsylvania Dutch family brought Southern Baptist neighbors to join the new Lutheran church they'd helped found; and women who'd done graduate work baked Christmas cookies with women who had not finished high school. These new suburbanites were creating for themselves a new world and a new middle-class culture. They had grown up with the Great Depression and world war; now, on this suburban street, they believed they had found good lives.

Of all the major nations in the world, only the United States had emerged from World War II stronger and more prosperous than when the war began. Europe and Asia had been devastated, but America's farms and cities and factories were intact. U.S. production capacity had increased during the war, and despite social tensions and inequalities, the fight against fascism gave Americans a unity of purpose. Victory seemed to confirm their struggles. But sixteen years of depression and war shadowed the U.S. victory, and memories of these experiences would continue to shape the choices Americans made in their private lives, their domestic policies, and their relations with the world.

In the postwar era, the actions of the federal government and the choices made by individual Americans began a profound reconfiguration of American society. Postwar social policies that sent millions of veterans to college on the GI Bill, linked the nation with high-speed interstate highways, fostered the growth of suburbs and the Sunbelt, and disrupted regional isolation helped to create a national middle-class culture that encompassed an unprecedented majority of the nation's citizens. Countless individual decisions—to go to college, to marry young, to have a large family, to move to the suburbs, to start a business—were made possible by these federal initiatives. The cumulative weight of these individual decisions would change the meanings of class and ethnicity in American society. Americans in the postwar era defined a new American Dream—one that centered on the family, on a new level of material comfort and consumption, and on a shared sense of belonging to a common culture. Elite cultural critics roundly denounced this ideal of suburban comfort as "conformism," but many Americans found satisfaction in this new way of life.

Almost one-quarter of the American people did not share in the postwar prosperity—but they were ever less visible to the middle-class majority. Rural poverty continued, and inner cities became increasingly impoverished as more-affluent Americans moved to the suburbs and new migrants—poor black and white southerners, new immigrants from Mexico and Puerto Rico, and Native Americans resettled by the federal government from tribal lands—arrived.

As class and ethnicity became less important in suburbia, race continued to divide the American people. African Americans faced racism and discrimination throughout the nation, but the war had been a turning point in the struggle for equal rights. During this period, African Americans increasingly took direct action, and in 1955 the year-long Montgomery bus boycott launched the modern civil rights movement. Their initiatives led to important federal actions to protect the civil rights of black Americans, including the Supreme Court's school desegregation decision in *Brown v. Board of Education*.

After the dramatic accomplishments of the New Deal, the national politics of the postwar era were circumscribed. Truman pledged to expand the New Deal but was stymied by a conservative Congress. General Dwight D. Eisenhower, elected in 1952 as the first Republican president in twenty years, offered a solid Republican platform, seeking—though rarely attaining—a balanced budget, reduced taxes, and lower levels of government spending. Both men focused primarily on the foreign policy challenges of the Cold War. The most significant domestic political ferment, in fact, was a byproduct of the Cold War: a ferocious anticommunism that narrowed the boundaries of acceptable dissent.

The economic boom that began with the end of the war lasted twenty-five years, bringing new prosperity to the American people. Although fears—of nuclear war, of returning hard times—lingered, prosperity bred complacency by the late 1950s. At decade's end, people sought satisfaction in their families and in the consumer pleasures newly available to so many.

- How did the Cold War affect American society and politics?
- How did federal government actions following World War II change the nation?
- During the 1950s, many people began to think of their country as a middle-class nation. Were they correct?

SHAPING POSTWAR AMERICA

As Americans celebrated the end of World War II and mourned those who would never return, many feared the challenges that lay ahead. It seemed almost inevitable that the economy would plunge back into depression—and in the immediate aftermath of the war, unemployment rose and a wave of strikes rocked the nation. But economists who made dire predictions were wrong. In the postwar years the American economy flourished, and Americans' standard of living improved. And the GI Bill and other new federal programs created opportunities for Americans that changed the nation in fundamental ways.

As the end of the war approached and the American war machine slowed, factories began to lay off workers.

Postwar Economic Uncertainty

At Ford Motor Company's massive Willow Run plant outside Detroit, where nine thousand Liberator bombers had been produced, most workers were let go in the spring of 1945. Ten days after the victory over Japan, 1.8 million people nationwide received pink slips, and 640,000 filed for unemployment compensation. More than 15 million GIs awaited demobilization; how were they to be absorbed into the shrinking job base?

Anticipating a postwar crisis, the federal government planned for demobilization even while some of the war's most difficult battles lay ahead. In the spring of 1944—a year before V-E Day—Congress unanimously passed the Servicemen's Readjustment Act, known as the GI Bill of Rights. The GI Bill showed the nation's gratitude to the men who fought. But it also attempted to keep the flood of demobilized veterans (almost all of them male) from swamping the U.S. economy: year-long unemployment benefits allowed veterans to be absorbed gradually into civilian employment, and higher-education benefits were designed to keep men in college and out of the job market. In winter 1945, congressional Democrats introduced a national Full Employment Act guaranteeing work to all who were able and willing, through public-sector employment if necessary. By the time conservatives in Congress had finished with the bill and Truman signed it into law in early 1946, key provisions regarding guaranteed work had virtually disappeared. But the act did reaffirm the federal government's responsibility for managing the economy and created a Council of Economic Advisers to help the president prevent economic downturns.

Conversion to a peacetime economy hit workers hard, especially as the end of wartime price controls sent inflation skyrocketing. Workers had accepted wartime limits on wages, but they would not stand by as unemployment threatened and their paychecks were eaten away. More than 5 million workers walked off the job in the year following Japan's surrender. Unions shut down the coal, automobile, steel, and electric industries, and halted railroad and maritime transportation. The strikes were so disruptive that Americans began hoarding food and gasoline.

Postwar Strikes and the Taft-Hartley Act

By spring 1946, Americans were losing patience with the strikes and with the Democratic administration, which they saw as partly responsible. When unions threatened a national railway strike, President Truman made a dramatic appearance before a joint session of Congress. If strikers in an industry deemed vital to national security refused a presidential order to return to work, he announced, he would ask Congress to immediately draft into the armed forces "all workers who are on strike against their government." The Democratic Party, Truman made clear, would not offer unlimited support to organized labor.

Making the most of public anger at the strikes, in 1947 a group of pro-business Republicans and their conservative Democratic allies worked to restrict the power of labor unions. The Taft-Hartley Act permitted states to enact right-to-work laws that outlawed "closed shops," in which all workers were required to join the union if a majority of their number favored a union shop. The law also mandated an eighty-day cooling-off period before unions initiated strikes that imperiled national security. These restrictions limited unions' ability to expand their membership, especially in the South and West, where states passed right-to-work laws. Although Truman had used the power of the presidency to avert a national railroad strike, he did not want to see union power so limited. But Congress passed the Taft-Hartley Act over Truman's veto.

Despite widespread fears, economic depression did not return. The first year of adjustment to a peacetime economy was difficult, but the economy recovered quickly, fueled by consumer spending. Although Americans had brought home steady paychecks during the war, there was little on which to spend them. No new cars, for example, had been built since 1942. Americans had saved their money for four years—and when new cars and appliances appeared at war's end, they were ready to buy. Companies like General Motors, which flouted conventional wisdom about a coming depression and expanded its operations just after the war, found millions of eager buyers. And because most other factories around the world were in ruins, U.S. corporations expanded their global dominance. America's leading corporations rode this postwar boom, increasing dramatically in size. Many created huge conglomerates. International Telegraph and Telephone (IT&T), for instance, bought up companies in several fields, including suburban development, insurance, and hotels. In keeping with the thrust of America's postwar boom, the country's ten largest corporations were in automobiles (GM, Ford, Chrysler); oil (Standard Oil of New Jersey, Mobil, Texaco); and electronics and communications (GE, IBM, IT&T, AT&T).

Economic Growth

In the agricultural sector, new machines, such as mechanical cotton, tobacco, and grape pickers, and crop-dusting planes, revolutionized farming, and the increased use of fertilizers and pesticides raised the total value of farm output from $24.6 billion in 1945 to $38.4 billion in 1961. At the same time, the productivity of farm labor tripled. Large investors were drawn to agriculture by its increased profitability, and the average size of farms increased from 195 to 306 acres.

Economic growth was also fueled by government programs, such as the GI Bill, which pumped money into the economy. By 1949, veterans had received close to $4 billion in unemployment compensation. But the GI Bill did more than help forestall economic collapse. It offered veterans low-interest loans to buy a house or start a business, and—perhaps most significantly—stipends to cover college or technical school tuition and living expenses. As individ-

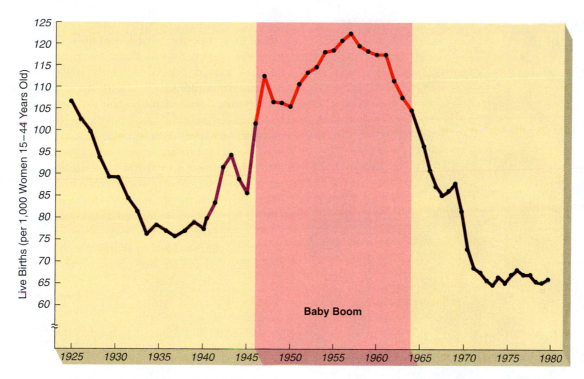

Figure 29.1   Birth Rate, 1945–1964

The birth rate began to rise in 1942 and 1943, but it skyrocketed during the postwar years beginning in 1946, reaching its peak in 1957. From 1954 to 1964, the United States recorded more than 4 million births every year.

(Source: Adapted from *U.S. Bureau of the Census,* Historical Statistics of the United States, Colonial Times to 1970, *Bicentennial Edition [Washington, D.C.: U.S. Government Printing Office, 1975], p. 49.)*

uals grasped these opportunities, they changed their own lives and the shape of American society.

Before the war, higher education was for the affluent; only about 7.5 percent of young Americans went to college. With GI benefits, almost half of America's returning veterans sought some form of higher education. The resulting increase in the number of well-educated or technically trained workers benefited the American economy. And although University of Chicago president Robert Maynard Hutchins protested that the GI Bill would turn universities into "educational hobo jungles," the flood of students and federal dollars into the nation's colleges and universities created a golden age for higher education.

Education obtained through the GI Bill created social mobility: children of barely literate menial laborers became white-collar professionals. And postwar universities, like the military, brought together people from vastly different backgrounds. The GI Bill fostered the emergence of a national middle-class culture, for as colleges exposed people to new ideas and to new experiences, their students tended to become less provincial, less rooted in ethnic or regional cultures.

During the Great Depression, young people had delayed marriage, and America's birth rate had plummeted.

Baby Boom

Marriage and birth rates began to rise as war brought economic recovery. But the end of the war brought a boom. In 1946 the U.S. marriage rate was higher than that of any record-keeping nation (except Hungary) in the history of the twentieth century. The birth rate soared, reversing the downward trend of the past 150 years. "Take the 3,548,000 babies born in 1950," wrote Sylvia F. Porter in her syndicated newspaper column. "Bundle them into a batch, bounce them all over the bountiful land that is America. What do you get?" Porter's answer: "Boom. The biggest, boomiest boom ever known in history. Just imagine how much these extra people, these new markets, will absorb—in food, clothing, in gadgets, in housing, in services. Our factories must expand just to keep pace." Although the baby boom peaked in 1957, more than 4 million babies were born every year until 1965 (see Figure 29.1). As this vast cohort grew older, it had successive impacts on housing, nursery schools, grade schools, and high schools, fads and

▲ Housing was so tight in the years following World War II that many young couples had to move in with one set of their parents— or accept some unusual housing options. Former marine lieutenant Willard Pedrick and his family made their home in a Quonset hut on the campus of Northwestern University in Evanston, Illinois, where Pedrick was an associate professor in the economics department.

(© Bettmann/Corbis)

popular music, colleges and universities, the job market, and retirement funds, including Social Security.

Where were all these baby-boom families to live? Scarcely any new housing had been built since the 1920s. Almost 2 million families were doubled up with relatives in 1948; 50,000 people were living in Quonset huts, and in Chicago housing was so tight that 250 used trolley cars were sold as homes.

A combination of market forces, government actions, and individual decisions solved the housing crisis and, in so doing, changed the way large numbers of Americans lived. In the postwar years, white Amer-

Suburbanization

icans moved to the suburbs. Their reasons varied. Some moved to escape the crowds and noise of the city. People from rural areas moved closer to city jobs. Some white families moved out of urban neighborhoods because African American families were moving in. Many new suburbanites wanted more political influence and more control over their children's education. Most who moved to the suburbs, however, simply wanted to own their own home—and suburban developments were where the affordable housing was. Although suburban development predated World War II, the massive migration of 18 million Americans to the suburbs from cities, small towns, and farms between 1950 and 1960 was on a wholly different scale (see Table 29.1).

In the years following World War II, suburban developers applied techniques of mass production to create acres of modest suburban houses in what had recently been pastures and fields. In 1947 builder William Levitt adapted Henry Ford's assembly-line methods to revolutionize home building. By 1949, instead of 4 or 5 custom homes per year, Levitt's company built 180 houses a week. They were very basic—four and a half rooms on a 60-by-100-foot lot, all with identical floorplans—the Model Ts of houses. But the same floorplan could be disguised by four different exteriors, and by rotating seven paint colors Levitt guaranteed that only 1 in every 28 houses would be identical. In the Levittown on Long Island, a tree was planted every 28 feet (two and a half trees per house). The basic house, appliances included, sold for $7,990. Other homebuilders quickly adopted Levitt's techniques.

Suburban development could never have happened on such a large scale, however, without federal policies that encouraged it. Federal Housing Administration (FHA) mortgage insurance made low-interest GI mortgages and loans possible. New highways also promoted suburban development. Congress authorized construction of a 37,000-mile chain of highways in 1947 and in 1956 passed the Highway Act to create a 42,500-mile interstate highway system. Intended to facilitate commerce and rapid mobilization of the military in case of a threat to national security, these highways also allowed workers to live farther and farther from their jobs in central cities.

Postwar federal programs did not benefit all Americans equally. First, federal policies often assisted men at the expense of women. The federal Selective Service Act guaranteed veterans (overwhelmingly men) priority in postwar employment over the war workers who had replaced them. As industry laid off civilian workers to make room for veterans, women lost their jobs at a rate 75 percent

Inequality in Benefits

TABLE 29.1	Geographic Distribution of the U.S. Population, 1930–1970 (in percentages)		
Year	Central Cities	Suburbs	Rural Areas and Small Towns
1930	31.8	18.0	50.2
1940	31.6	19.5	48.9
1950	32.3	23.8	43.9
1960	32.6	30.7	36.7
1970	31.4	37.6	31.0

Source: Adapted from U.S. Bureau of the Census, Decennial Censuses, 1930–1970 (Washington, D.C.: U.S. Government Printing Office).

higher than men. Many women stayed in the work force but were pushed into less well-paying jobs. Universities made room for veterans on the GI Bill by excluding qualified women students; a much smaller percentage of college degrees went to women after the war than before.

Inequities were also based on race. Like European American veterans, African American, Native American, Mexican American, and Asian American veterans received educational benefits and hiring preference in civil service jobs following the war. But war workers from these groups were among the first laid off as factories made room for white, male veterans. Federal housing policies also exacerbated racial inequality. Federal loan officers and bankers often labeled African American or racially mixed neighborhoods "high risk" for lending, denying mortgages to members of racial minorities regardless of individual creditworthiness. This practice, called "redlining" because such neighborhoods were outlined in red on lenders' maps, kept African Americans and many Hispanics from buying into the great economic explosion of the postwar era. White families who bought homes with federally guaranteed mortgages saw their small investments grow dramatically over the years. Discriminatory policies denied most African Americans and other people of color that opportunity.

DOMESTIC POLITICS IN THE COLD WAR ERA

Although the major social and economic transformations of the postwar era were due in great part to federal policies and programs, domestic politics were not at the forefront of American life. Foreign affairs were usually paramount, as Democratic president Harry Truman and Republican president Dwight D. Eisenhower both faced significant challenges in the expanding Cold War. Domestically, Truman attempted to build on the New Deal's liberal agenda, while Eisenhower called for balanced budgets and business-friendly policies. But neither administration approached the level of political and legislative activism of the 1930s New Deal.

Harry Truman, the plain-spoken former haberdasher from Missouri, had never expected to be president. In

Harry S Truman and Postwar Liberalism

1944, when Franklin Roosevelt asked him to join the Democratic ticket as the vice-presidential candidate, he almost refused. Roosevelt, the master politician, played hardball. "If he wants to break up the Democratic Party in the middle of the war, that's his responsibility," the president said flatly. "Oh shit," said Truman, "if that's the situation, I'll have to say yes." But the president, with his hands full as America entered its fourth year of war, had little time for his new vice president and left Truman in the dark about everything from the Manhattan Project to plans for postwar domestic policy. When Roosevelt died, suddenly, in April 1945, Truman was unprepared to take his place.

Truman stepped forward, however, placing a sign on his desk that proclaimed, "The Buck Stops Here." Most of Truman's presidency focused on foreign relations, as he led the nation through the last months of World War II and into the new Cold War with the Soviet Union. Domestically, he oversaw the process of reconversion from war to peace and attempted to keep a liberal agenda—the legacy of Roosevelt's New Deal—alive.

In his 1944 State of the Union address, President Roosevelt had offered Americans a "Second Bill of Rights": the right to employment, healthcare, education, food, and housing. This declaration of government responsibility for the welfare of the nation and its citizens was the cornerstone of postwar liberalism. Truman's legislative program sought to maintain the federal government's active role in guaranteeing social welfare, promoting social justice,

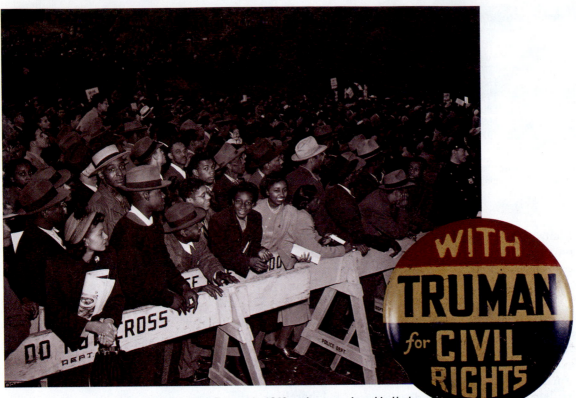

▲ A large crowd gathered to hear President Truman in 1948, as he campaigned in Harlem. African American voters were an increasingly important political force in the postwar era, and Truman was the first presidential candidate to go to Harlem seeking support. Truman had political reasons for appealing to black voters, but he also felt a moral obligation to support their struggle for civil rights. *(Left: Chicago Historical Society; Right: Collection of Janice L. and David J. Frent)*

managing the economy, and regulating the power of business corporations. Truman proposed an increase in the minimum wage and national housing legislation offering loans for mortgages, and he supported the Full Employment Act. To pay for his proposed social welfare programs, Truman gambled that full employment would generate sufficient tax revenue and that consumer spending would fuel economic growth.

The gamble on economic growth paid off, but Truman quickly learned the limits of his political influence. The conservative coalition of Republicans and southern Democrats that had stalled Roosevelt's New Deal legislation in the late 1930s was even less inclined to support Truman. Congress gutted the Full Employment Act, refused to raise the minimum wage, and passed the antiunion Taft-Hartley Act over Truman's veto. With powerful congressional opposition, Truman had little chance of major legislative accomplishments. But his inexperience contributed to the political impasse. "To err is Truman," people began to joke. As Truman presided over

the rocky transition from wartime to peacetime economy, he had to deal with massive inflation (briefly hitting 35 percent), shortages of consumer goods, and a wave of postwar strikes that slowed production of eagerly awaited consumer goods and drove prices up further. Truman's approval rating plunged from 87 percent in late 1945 to 32 percent in 1946.

By 1948 it seemed that Republicans would win the White House in November. A confident Republican Party nominated Thomas Dewey, the man Roosevelt had defeated in 1944, as its presidential candidate. The Republicans were counting on schisms in the Democratic Party to give them victory. Two years before, Truman had fired Henry A. Wallace, the only remaining New Dealer in the cabinet, for publicly criticizing U.S. foreign policy. In 1948 Wallace ran for president on the Progressive Party ticket, advocating friendly relations with the Soviet Union, racial desegregation, and nationalization of basic industries. A fourth

1948 Election

party, the Dixiecrats (States' Rights Democratic Party), was organized by white southerners who walked out of the 1948 Democratic convention when it adopted a pro-civil rights plank; they nominated the fiercely segregationist governor Strom Thurmond of South Carolina. If Wallace's candidacy did not destroy Truman's chances, experts said, the Dixiecrats certainly would.

Truman, however, refused to give up. He resorted to red-baiting, denouncing "Henry Wallace and his communists" at every opportunity. Most important, he directly appealed to the burgeoning population of African American voters in northern cities, becoming the first presidential candidate to campaign in Harlem. In the end, Truman prevailed. The Progressive and Dixiecrat Parties attracted far fewer voters than had been predicted; most Democrats saw Truman—in contrast to Thurmond or Wallace—as an appealing moderate. African American voters made the difference, giving Truman the electoral votes of key northern states. Roosevelt's New Deal coalition—African Americans, union members, northern urban voters, and most southern whites—had endured.

Truman began his new term brimming with confidence. It was time, he believed, for government to fulfill

Truman's Fair Deal

its responsibility to provide economic security for the poor and the elderly. As he worked on his 1949 State of the Union message, he penciled in his intentions: "I expect to give every segment of our population a fair deal." Truman, unlike Roosevelt, pushed forward legislation to support the civil rights of African Americans, including the antilynching bill that Roosevelt had given only lukewarm support. He proposed a national health insurance program and federal aid for education. Once again, however, little of Truman's legislative agenda came to fruition. A filibuster by southern conservatives in Congress destroyed his civil rights legislation; the American Medical Association denounced his health insurance plan as "socialized medicine"; and the Roman Catholic Church opposed aid to education because it would not include parochial schools.

When the postwar peace proved short-lived and Truman ordered troops to Korea in June 1950, there was much grumbling among Americans as the nation again mobilized for war. People remembered the shortages of the last war and stocked up on sugar, coffee, and canned goods. Fueled by panic buying, inflation began to rise. Many reservists and national guardsmen resented being called to active duty. An unpopular war and charges of influence peddling by some of Truman's cronies pushed the president's public approval rating to an all-time low of 23 percent in 1951, where it stayed for a year.

"It's Time for a Change" was the Republican presidential campaign slogan in 1952, and voters agreed,

Eisenhower's Dynamic Conservatism

especially when the Republican candidate was General Dwight D. Eisenhower. Americans hoped that the immensely popular World War II hero could end the Korean War. And Eisenhower appealed to moderates in both parties (in fact, the Democrats had tried to recruit him as their presidential candidate).

With a Republican in the White House for the first time in twenty years, conservatives hoped to roll back such New Deal liberal programs as the mandatory Social Security system. Eisenhower, however, had no such intention, in part because it was politically almost impossible to dismantle New Deal and Fair Deal programs without harming a great many Americans. Eisenhower, as a moderate Republican, adopted an approach that he called "dynamic conservatism": being "conservative when it comes to money and liberal when it comes to human beings." On the liberal side, in 1954 Eisenhower signed into law amendments to the Social Security Act that raised benefits and added 7.5 million workers, mostly self-employed farmers, to the Social Security rolls. The Eisenhower administration also increased government funding for education—though increases were motivated by Cold War fears, not liberal principles. When the Soviet Union launched *Sputnik*, the first earth-orbiting satellite, in 1957 (and America's first launch exploded seconds after liftoff), improving science and technology education became an issue of national security. Congress responded in 1958 with the National Defense Education Act (NDEA), which funded enrichment of elementary and high-school programs in mathematics, foreign languages, and the sciences, and offered fellowships and loans to college students. This attempt to win the "battle of brainpower" increased the educational opportunities available to young Americans.

Overall, however, Eisenhower's was unabashedly "an Administration representing business and industry," as

Growth of the Military-Industrial Complex

Interior Secretary Douglas McKay acknowledged. The Eisenhower administration's tax reform bill raised business depreciation allowances, and the Atomic Energy Act of 1954 granted private companies the right to own reactors and nuclear materials to produce electricity. Eisenhower also tried to reduce the federal budget. In fact, he balanced only three of his eight budgets, turning to deficit spending to cushion the impact of three recessions (in 1953–1954, 1957–1958, and 1960–1961) and to fund the tremendous cost of America's global activities. In 1959 federal expenditures climbed to $92 billion, about half of which went to the military, much of that for developing new weapons.

Just before leaving office in early 1961, at the end of his second term, Eisenhower went on national radio and television to deliver his farewell address to the nation. Because of the Cold War, he observed, the United States had begun to maintain a large standing army—3.5 million men. And ever greater percentages of the nation's budget went to developing and building weapons of war. Condemning the new "conjunction of an immense military establishment and a large arms industry," Eisenhower warned, "The total influence—economic, political, even spiritual—is felt in every city, every statehouse, every office of the federal government" and threatened the nation's democratic process. Eisenhower, the former five-star general and war hero, urged Americans to "guard against . . . the military-industrial complex."

During Eisenhower's presidency, both liberal Democrats and moderate Republicans seemed satisfied to be occupying what historian Arthur M. Schlesinger Jr. called "the vital center." And with the Cold War between the United States and the Soviet Union portrayed as a battle between good and evil, a struggle for the future of the world, criticism of American society seemed suspect—even unpatriotic. British journalist Godfrey Hodgson described this time as an era of "consensus," when Americans were "confident to the verge of complacency about the perfectibility of American society, anxious to the point of paranoia about the threat of communism."

COLD WAR FEARS AND ANTICOMMUNISM

International relations had a profound influence on America's domestic politics in the years following World War II. Americans were frightened by the Cold War tensions between the United States and the Soviet Union—and there were legitimate reasons for fear. Reasonable fears, however, spilled over into anticommunist demagoguery and witch hunts. Fear allowed the trampling of civil liberties, the suppression of dissent, and the persecution of thousands of innocent Americans.

Anticommunism was not new in American society. A Red Scare had swept the nation following the Russian Revolution of 1917, and opponents of America's labor movement had used charges of communism to block unionization through the 1930s. Many saw the Soviet Union's virtual takeover of eastern Europe in the late 1940s as an alarming parallel to Nazi Germany's takeover of neighboring states. People remembered the failure of "appeasement" at Munich and worried that the United States was "too soft" in its policy toward the Soviet Union.

In addition, top U.S. government officials knew that the Soviet Union was spying on the United States (the United States also had spies within the Soviet Union). A top-secret project, code-named "Venona," decrypted almost three thousand Soviet telegraphic cables that proved Soviet spies had infiltrated U.S. government agencies and nuclear programs. Intelligence officials resolved to prosecute Soviet spies, but they kept their evidence from the American public so that the Soviets would not realize their codes had been compromised.

Espionage and Nuclear Fears

Fear of nuclear war also contributed to American anticommunism. For four years, the United States alone possessed what seemed the ultimate weapon, but in 1949 the Soviet Union exploded its own atomic device. President Truman, initiating a national atomic civil defense program shortly thereafter, told Americans, "I cannot tell you when or where the attack will come or that it will come at all. I can only remind you that we must be ready when it does come." Children practiced "duck-and-cover" positions in their school classrooms, learning how to shield their faces from the atomic flash and flying debris in the event of an attack. *Life* magazine featured backyard fallout shelters. As the stakes of the global struggle increased, Americans worried that the United States was newly vulnerable to attack on its own soil.

Politics of Anticommunism

At the height of the Cold War, American leaders, including Presidents Truman and Eisenhower, did not always draw a sufficient line between prudent attempts to prevent Soviet spies from infiltrating important government agencies and anticommunist scare-mongering for political gain. Truman purposely invoked "the communist threat" to gain support for aid to Greece and Turkey in 1947. Republican politicians "red-baited" Democratic opponents, eventually targeting the Truman administration as a whole. In 1947 President Truman ordered investigations into the loyalty of more than 3 million U.S. government employees. As anticommunist hysteria grew, the government began discharging people deemed "security risks," among them alcoholics, homosexuals, and debtors thought susceptible to blackmail. In most cases there was no evidence of disloyalty.

Leading the anticommunist crusade was the House Un-American Activities Committee (popularly known as HUAC). Created in 1938 to investigate "subversive and

The Cold War shaped American popular culture as well as foreign policy. Cartoonist Jay Ward's "Rocky and His Friends" premiered on television in 1959. In the first forty-segment episode, "Jet Fuel Formula," Rocky the Flying Squirrel and Bullwinkle J. Moose—urged on by American military leaders—tried to recreate their secret formula for lunar propulsion while evading the tricks and explosive traps of Boris Badenov and Natasha Fatale, spies who's supposed "Pottsylvanian" origins did nothing to mask their heavy Russian accents.

(Bruce Stawicki/http://artist4hire.net)

un-American propaganda," the viciously anti–New Deal committee had lost credibility then by charging that film stars—including eight-year-old Shirley Temple—were dupes of the Communist Party. In 1947, in a shameless publicity-grabbing tactic, HUAC attacked Hollywood again, using Federal Bureau of Investigation (FBI) files and the testimony of people like Screen Actors Guild president Ronald Reagan (who was also a secret informant for the FBI, complete with code name). Members of a group of screenwriters and directors known as the "Hollywood Ten" were sent to prison for contempt of Congress when they refused to "name names" of suspected communists for HUAC. At least a dozen other Hollywood figures committed suicide. Studios panicked and blacklisted hundreds of actors, screenwriters, directors, even makeup artists, who were suspected of communist affiliations. With no evidence of wrongdoing, these men and women had their careers—and sometimes their lives—ruined.

University professors became targets of the growing "witch hunt" in 1949, when HUAC demanded lists of the textbooks used in courses at eighty-one universities. When the board of regents at the University of California, Berkeley, instituted a loyalty oath for faculty, firing twenty-six who resisted on principle, protests from faculty members across the nation forced

McCarthyism and the Growing "Witch Hunt"

the regents to back down. But many professors, afraid of the reach of HUAC, began to downplay controversial material in their courses. In the labor movement, the CIO expelled eleven unions, with more than 900,000 members, for alleged communist domination. The red panic reached its nadir in February 1950, when a relatively obscure U.S. senator came before an audience in Wheeling, West Virginia, to charge that the U.S. State Department was "thoroughly infested with Communists." Republican senator Joseph R. McCarthy of Wisconsin was not an especially credible source. He made charges and then retracted them, claiming first that there were 205 communists in the State Department, then 57, then 81. He had a severe drinking problem; downing a water glass full of Scotch in a single gulp, he would follow it with a quarter-pound stick of butter, hoping to counteract the effects of the liquor. He had a record of dishonesty as a lawyer and judge in his hometown of Appleton, Wisconsin. But McCarthy crystallized the anxieties many felt as they faced a new and difficult era in American life, and the anticommunist excesses of this era came to be known as McCarthyism.

With HUAC and McCarthy on the attack, Americans began pointing accusing fingers at one another. The anticommunist crusade was embraced by labor union officials, religious leaders, and the media, as well as by politicians. A bootblack at the Pentagon was questioned by the FBI seventy times because he had given $10 during the 1930s to a defense fund for the Scottsboro Boys, who had been represented by an attorney from the Communist Party.

▲ In 1954 Senator Joseph R. McCarthy, surrounded by his own newspaper headlines, adorns the cover of *Time* magazine. His downfall came later that year, during the televised Army-McCarthy hearings. McCarthy's wild accusations and abusive treatment of witnesses disgusted millions of viewers. *(© 1954 Time Inc.)*

Women in New York who lobbied for the continuation of wartime daycare programs were denounced as communists by the *New York World Telegram*. "Reds, phonies, and 'parlor pinks,'" in Truman's words, seemed to lurk everywhere.

In such a climate, most public figures found it too risky to stand up against McCarthyist tactics. And most Democrats did support the domestic Cold War and its anticommunist actions. In 1950, with bipartisan support, Congress passed the Internal Security (McCarran) Act, which required members of "Communist-front" organizations to register with the government and prohibited them from holding government jobs or traveling abroad. In 1954 the Senate unanimously passed the Communist Control Act (there were two dissenting votes in the

Anticommunism in Congress

House), which effectively made membership in the Communist Party illegal. Its chief sponsor, Democratic senator Hubert H. Humphrey of Minnesota, told his colleagues just before he cast his vote, "We have closed all of the doors. The rats will not get out of the trap."

The anticommunist fervor was fueled by spectacular and controversial trials of Americans accused of passing secrets to the Soviet Union. In 1948 Congressman Richard Nixon of California, a member of HUAC, was propelled onto the national stage when he accused former State Department official Alger Hiss of espionage. In 1950 Hiss was convicted of lying about his contacts with Soviet agents. That same year, Ethel and Julius Rosenberg were arrested for passing atomic secrets to the Soviets; they were found guilty of treason and executed in 1953. For decades, many historians believed that the Rosenbergs were primarily victims of a witch hunt. In fact, there was strong evidence of Julius Rosenberg's guilt in cables decrypted by the Venona Project (as well as evidence that Ethel Rosenberg was less involved than had been charged), but this evidence was not presented at their trial for reasons of national security. The cables remained top secret until 1995, when a Clinton administration initiative opened the files to historians.

Some of the worst excesses of Cold War anticommunism waned when Senator McCarthy was discredited on national television in 1954. McCarthy himself was a master at using the press, making sensational accusations—front-page material—just before reporters' deadlines. When the evidence did not pan out or McCarthy's charges proved untrue, retractions appeared in the back pages of the newspapers. Even journalists who knew McCarthy was unreliable continued to report his charges. Sensational stories sell papers, and McCarthy became a celebrity.

Waning of the Red Scare

But McCarthy badly misunderstood the power of television. His crucial mistake was taking on the U.S. Army in front of millions of television viewers. At issue was the senator's wild accusation that the army was shielding and promoting communists; he cited the case of one army dentist. The so-called Army-McCarthy hearings, held by a Senate subcommittee in 1954, became a showcase for the senator's abusive treatment of witnesses. McCarthy, apparently drunk, alternately ranted and slurred his words. Finally, after he maligned a young lawyer who was not even involved in the hearings, army counsel Joseph Welch protested, "Have you no sense of decency, sir?" The gallery erupted in applause, and McCarthy's career as a witch-hunter was over. In December 1954, the Senate voted to "condemn" McCarthy for sullying the dignity of the Senate. He remained a senator, but exhaustion and alcohol took their toll, and he died in 1957 at the age of forty-eight. With McCarthy discredited, the most virulent strand of anticommunism had run its course. However, the use of fear tactics for political gain, and the narrowing of American freedoms and liberties, were chilling domestic legacies of the Cold War.

THE STRUGGLE FOR CIVIL RIGHTS

The Cold War—at home and abroad—also shaped African American struggles for social justice and the nation's responses to them. As the Soviet Union was quick to point out, the United States could hardly pose as the leader of the free world or condemn the denial of human rights in eastern Europe and the Soviet Union if it practiced segregation at home. Nor could the United States convince new African and Asian nations of its dedication to human rights if African Americans were subjected to segregation, discrimination, disfranchisement, and racial violence. Some African American leaders, in fact, understood their struggle for equal rights in the United States as part of a larger, international movement. To win the support of nonaligned nations, the United States would have to live up to its own ideals. At the same time, many Americans viewed social criticism of any kind as a Soviet-inspired attempt to weaken the United States in the ongoing Cold War. The Federal Bureau of Investigation and local law enforcement agencies commonly used such anticommunist fears to justify attacks on civil rights activists. In this heated environment, African Americans struggled to seize the political initiative.

Americans had seen the Second World War as a struggle for democracy and against hatred. African Americans who had helped win the war were determined that their lives in postwar America would be better because of their sacrifices. Moreover, politicians like Harry Truman were beginning to pay attention to black aspirations, especially as black voters in some urban-industrial states began to strongly influence the political balance of power.

Growing Black Political Power

President Truman had compelling political reasons for supporting African American civil rights. But he also felt a moral obligation to do something, for he genuinely believed it was only fair that every American, regardless of race, should enjoy the full rights of citizenship. Truman was disturbed by a resurgence of racial terrorism, as a revived Ku Klux Klan was burning crosses and murdering blacks who sought civil rights and racial justice in

▲ Jackie Robinson cracked the color line in major league baseball when he joined the Brooklyn Dodgers for the 1947 season. Sliding safely into third base, Robinson displays the aggressive style that won him rookie-of-the-year honors. He was later elected to the Baseball Hall of Fame. *(Hy Peskin, Life Magazine © Time Inc.)*

the aftermath of World War II. But what really horrified Truman was the report that police in Aiken, South Carolina, had gouged out the eyes of a black sergeant just three hours after he had been discharged from the army. Several weeks after this atrocity, in December 1946, Truman signed an executive order establishing the President's Committee on Civil Rights. The committee's report, *To Secure These Rights,* would become the civil rights movement agenda for the next twenty years. It called for antilynching and antisegregation legislation, and for laws guaranteeing voting rights and equal employment opportunity. For the first time since Reconstruction, a president had acknowledged the federal government's responsibility to protect blacks and to strive for racial equality.

Truman took this responsibility seriously, and in 1948 he issued two executive orders declaring an end to racial discrimination in the federal government. One proclaimed a policy of "fair employment throughout the federal establishment" and created the Employment Board of the Civil Service Commission to hear charges of discrimination. The other ordered the racial desegregation of the armed forces and appointed a committee to oversee this process. Despite strong opposition to desegregation within the military, segregated units were being phased out by the beginning of the Korean War.

Such actions were possible in part because of changing social attitudes and experiences in postwar America. A new and visible black middle class was emerging, composed of college-educated activists, war veterans, and union workers. White awareness of social injustice had been increased by Gunnar Myrdal's social science study *An American Dilemma* (1944) and by Richard Wright's novel *Native Son* (1940) and autobiography *Black Boy* (1945). Blacks and whites also worked together in CIO unions and service organizations, such as the National Council of Churches. In 1947 a black baseball player, Jackie Robinson, broke the major league color barrier and electrified Brooklyn Dodgers fans with his spectacular hitting and base running.

African Americans were successfully challenging racial discrimination in the courts. In 1939 the NAACP had established its Legal Defense and

Supreme Court Victories and School Desegregation

Educational Fund under Thurgood Marshall. By the 1940s, Marshall (who in 1967 would become the first African American Supreme Court justice) and his colleagues carried forward the plan devised by Charles Hamilton Houston to destroy the separate-but-equal doctrine established in *Plessy v. Ferguson* (1896) by insisting on its literal interpretation. In higher education, the NAACP calculated, the cost of true equality in racially separate schools would be prohibitive. "You can't build a cyclotron for one student," the president of the University of Oklahoma acknowledged. As a result of NAACP lawsuits, African American students won admission to professional and graduate schools at several formerly segregated state universities. The NAACP also won major victories through the Supreme Court in *Smith v. Allwright* (1944), which outlawed the whites-only primaries held by the Democratic Party in some southern states; *Morgan v. Virginia* (1946), which struck down segregation in interstate bus transportation; and *Shelley v. Kraemer* (1948), in which the Court held that racially restrictive covenants (private agreements among white homeowners not to sell to blacks) could not legally be enforced.

Even so, segregation was still standard practice in the 1950s, and blacks continued to suffer disfranchisement, job discrimination, and violence, including the 1951 bombing murder of the Florida state director of the NAACP and his wife. But in 1954 the NAACP won a historic victory that stunned the white South and energized African Americans to challenge segregation on several fronts. *Brown v. Board of Education of Topeka*, which Thurgood Marshall argued before the high court, incorporated school desegregation cases from several states. The Court's unanimous decision was written by Chief Justice Earl Warren, who, as California's attorney general, had pushed for the internment of Japanese Americans during World War II and had come to regret that action. The Court concluded that "in the field of public education the doctrine of 'separate but equal' has no place. Separate educational facilities are inherently unequal." But the ruling that overturned *Plessy v. Ferguson* did not demand immediate compliance. A year later, the Court finally ordered school desegregation, but only "with all deliberate speed."

By the mid-1950s, African Americans were increasingly engaged in a grassroots struggle for civil rights, and

Montgomery Bus Boycott

that struggle, through news reporting and television, attracted the attention of the nation. In 1955 Rosa Parks, a department store seamstress and long-time NAACP activist, was arrested when she refused to give up her seat to a white man on a public bus in Montgomery, Alabama. Her arrest gave local black women's organizations and civil rights groups a cause around which to organize a boycott of the city's bus system. They selected Martin Luther King Jr., a recently ordained minister who had just arrived in Montgomery, as their leader. King launched the boycott with a moving speech, declaring, "If we are wrong, the Constitution is wrong. If we are wrong, God Almighty is wrong. If we are wrong, Jesus of Nazareth was merely a utopian dreamer. . . . If we are wrong, justice is a lie."

Martin Luther King Jr. was a twenty-six-year-old Baptist minister with a recent Ph.D. from Boston University. Committed to the transforming potential of Christian love and schooled in the teachings of India's leader Mohandas K. Gandhi, King believed in nonviolent protest and civil disobedience. By refusing to obey unjust and racist laws, he hoped to focus the nation's attention on the immorality of Jim Crow. King persisted in this struggle even as opponents bombed his house and he was jailed for "conspiring" to boycott.

During the year-long Montgomery bus boycott, blacks young and old rallied in their churches, sang hymns, and prayed that the nation would awaken to the evils of segregation and racial discrimination. They maintained their boycott through heavy rains and the steamy heat of summer, often walking miles a day. One elderly black woman, offered a ride to work by a white reporter, told him, "No, my feets is tired, but my soul is rested." With the bus company near bankruptcy and downtown merchants suffering from declining sales, city officials adopted ha-

▲ For leading the movement to gain equality for blacks riding city buses in Montgomery, Alabama, Martin Luther King Jr. (1929–1968) and other African Americans, including twenty-three other ministers, were indicted by an all-white jury for violating an old law banning boycotts. In late March 1956, King was convicted and fined $500. A crowd of well-wishers cheered a smiling King (here with his wife, Coretta) outside the courthouse, where King proudly declared, "The protest goes on!" King's arrest and conviction made the bus boycott front-page news across America. (© Bettmann/Corbis)

rassment tactics to bring an end to the boycott. But the black people of Montgomery persevered. Thirteen months after the boycott began, the Supreme Court declared Alabama's bus segregation laws unconstitutional.

As the civil rights movement won significant victories, white reactions varied. Some communities in border states like Kansas and Maryland quietly implemented the school desegregation order, and many southern moderates advocated a gradual rollback of segregation. But others urged defiance. The Klan experienced another resurgence, and white violence against blacks increased. In August 1955, Emmett Till, a fourteen-year-old from Chicago, was murdered by white men in Mississippi who took offense at the way he spoke to a white woman. Business and professional people created White Citizens' Councils for the express purpose of resisting the school desegregation order. Known familiarly as "uptown Ku Klux Klans," the councils brought their economic power to bear against black civil rights activists. In keeping with the program of "massive resis-

White Resistance

tance" proposed by Virginia's U.S. senator, Harry F. Byrd Sr., they pushed through state laws that provided private-school tuition for white children who left public schools to avoid integration and, in Virginia, refused state funding to integrated schools. When FBI director J. Edgar Hoover briefed President Eisenhower on southern racial tensions in 1956, he warned of communist influences among the civil rights activists and even suggested that, if the Citizens' Councils did not worsen the racial situation, their actions might "control the rising tension."

White resistance to civil rights also gained strength in large northern cities. Chicago's African American population had increased from 275,000 in 1940 to 800,000 in 1960. These newcomers found good jobs in industry, and their increased numbers gave them political power. But they faced racism and segregation in the North as well. In 1951 in Cicero, a town adjoining Chicago, several thousand whites who were determined to keep blacks from moving into their neighborhood provoked a race riot. So racially divided was Chicago that the U.S. Commission on Civil Rights in 1959 described it as "the most residentially segregated city in the nation." Detroit and other northern cities were not far behind. And because children attended neighborhood schools, education in the North was in fact often segregated as well, though not by law, as it had been in the South.

Unlike Truman, President Eisenhower wanted to avoid dealing with civil rights, preferring gradual and voluntary change in race relations over executive orders and court mandates. Although the president disapproved of racial segregation, he objected to "compulsory federal law," believing instead that race relations would improve "only if [desegregation] starts locally." He also feared that the ugly public confrontations likely to follow rapid desegregation would jeopardize Republican inroads in the South. Thus Eisenhower did not state forthrightly that the federal government would enforce the *Brown* decision as the nation's law. In short, instead of leading, he spoke ambiguously and thereby tacitly encouraged white resistance. In 1956, 101 congressmen and senators from eleven southern states, all Democrats, issued "The Southern Manifesto." This document condemned the *Brown* decision as an "unwarranted exercise of power by the Court" which violated the principle of states' rights and commended those states that sought to "resist forced integration by any lawful means."

Federal Authority and States' Rights

Events in Little Rock, Arkansas, forced the president to stop sidestepping the issue. In September 1957, Arkansas governor Orval E. Faubus defied a court-supported desegregation plan for Little Rock's Central High School. Faubus went on television the night before school began and told Arkansans that "blood would run in the streets" if black students tried to enter the high school the next day. He deployed 250 Arkansas National Guard troops to block their entrance. Eight black teenagers tried to enter Central High on the second day of school but were turned away by the National Guard. The ninth, separated from the others, was surrounded by jeering whites and narrowly escaped the mob with the help of a sympathetic white woman.

The "Little Rock Nine" entered Central High for the first time more than two weeks after school began, after a federal judge intervened. An angry crowd surrounded the school, and television broadcast the scene to the nation and the world. Eisenhower, fearing violence and angry at what he saw as Faubus's attempt to provoke a crisis, nationalized the Arkansas National Guard (placing it under federal, not state, control) and dispatched 1,000 army paratroopers to Little Rock. Troops guarded the students for the rest of the year. Eisenhower's use of federal power in Little Rock was a critical step in America's struggle over racial equality, for he had directly confronted the conflict between federal authority and states' rights. However, state power triumphed the following year, when Faubus closed all public high schools in Little Rock rather than desegregate them.

Nonetheless, federal action continued. In 1957 Congress passed the first Civil Rights Act since Reconstruction, creating the United States Commission on Civil Rights to investigate systemic discrimination, such as in voting. Although this measure, like a voting rights act passed three years later, was not fully effective, it was another federal recognition of the centrality of civil rights. Most important, however, was the growing strength of a new, grassroots civil rights activism. In 1957 Martin Luther King Jr. became the first president of the Southern Christian Leadership Conference (SCLC), organized to coordinate civil rights activities. With the success in Montgomery and the gains won through the Supreme Court and the Truman administration, African Americans were poised to launch a major national movement for civil rights in the years to come.

CREATING A MIDDLE-CLASS NATION

Even as African Americans encountered massive resistance in their struggles for civil rights during the 1950s, in other ways the United States was becoming a more inclusive society. More Americans than ever before participated in a broad middle-class and suburban culture, and divisions among Americans based on class, ethnicity, religion, and regional identity became less important. National prosperity offered ever greater numbers of Americans material comfort and economic security through entrance into an economic middle class. Old European ethnic identities were fading, as an ever smaller percentage of America's people were first- or second-generation immigrants.

In the new suburbs, people from different backgrounds worked together to create communities and build schools, churches, and other institutions. Middle-class Americans, like those on Nancy Circle, increasingly looked to powerful national media rather than to regional or ethnic traditions for advice on matters ranging from how to celebrate Thanksgiving to what car to buy to how to raise children. New opportunities for consumption—whether the fads of a powerful teenage culture or the suburban ranch-style house—also tied Americans from different backgrounds together. In the postwar years, a new middle-class way of life was transforming the United States.

During the 1950s, sustained economic growth created unprecedented levels of prosperity and economic security for a broad range of America's people (see Figure 29.2). Several factors contributed to the economic boom. In great part it was driven by consumer spending. Americans eagerly bought consumer goods that had not been available during the war, and industries expanded production to meet consumer demand. Government spending also played an important role. As the Cold War deepened, the government poured money into defense industries, creating jobs and stimulating the economy.

Prosperity for More Americans

Cold War military and aerospace spending changed American society and culture in unintended ways. The professional middle class grew because the government's weapons development and space programs required highly educated scientists, engineers, and other white-collar workers. And as universities received billions of dollars to fund such research, universities expanded, playing a variety of new roles in American life. The results of such government-funded research were not limited to military applications or the space race; the transistor, invented during the 1950s, made possible both the computer revolution and the transistor radio, which was critically important to 1950s youth culture.

A new era of labor relations also helped bring economic prosperity to more Americans. By 1950, labor and management created a new, more stable relationship. In peaceful negotiations, the United Auto Workers (UAW) and General Motors led the way for other corporations in providing workers with health insurance, pension plans, and guaranteed cost-of-living adjustments, or COLAs, to

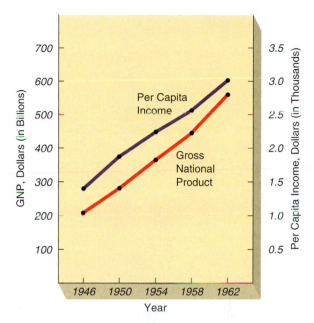

Figure 29.2   **Gross National Product and Per Capita Income, 1946–1962**

Both gross national product and per capita income soared during the economic boom from 1946 to 1962.

(Source: *Adapted from U.S. Bureau of the Census,* Historical Statistics of the United States, Colonial Times to 1970, *Bicentennial Edition [Washington, D.C.: U.S. Government Printing Office, 1975], p. 224.)

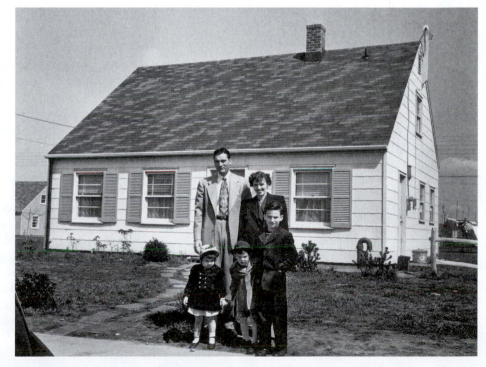

Bernard Levey, a truck supervisor, stands with his family in front of their new home in Levittown, PA. This house, with four and a half rooms, sold for under $8,000.

(Bernard Hoffman//Time Life Pictures/Getty Images)

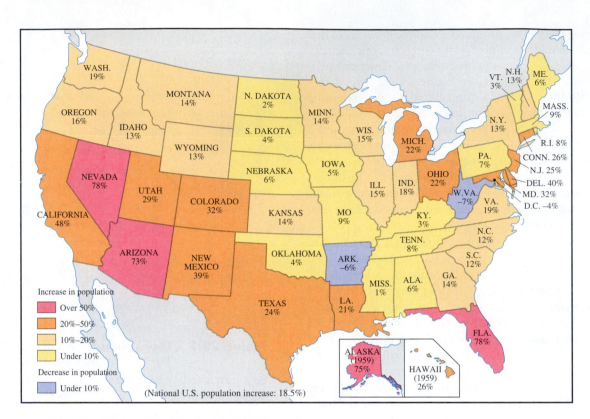

Map 29.1   Rise of the Sunbelt, 1950–1960

The years after the Second World War saw a continuation of the migration of Americans to the Sunbelt states of the Southwest and the West Coast.

protect wages from inflation. The 1950 agreement that *Fortune* magazine called "The Treaty of Detroit" gave GM's workers a five-year contract, with regular wage increases tied to corporate productivity. This was a turning point for the labor movement. In exchange for wages and benefits, organized labor gave up its demands for greater control in corporate affairs. And with wage increases tied to corporate productivity, labor cast its lot with management: workplace stability and efficiency, not strikes, would bring higher wages. During the 1950s, wages and benefits often rivaled those of college-educated professionals and propelled union families into the ranks of the economic middle class.

Just as labor agreements helped create prosperity for union members and their families, government policies helped bring the nation's poorest region into the American economic mainstream. In the 1930s, Roosevelt had called the South "the nation's No. 1 economic problem."

Sunbelt and Economic Growth

During World War II, new defense industry plants and military training camps channeled federal money to the region, stimulating economic growth. In the postwar era, huge levels of defense spending, especially for the nation's aerospace industry, continued to shift economic development from the Northeast and Midwest to the South and Southwest—the Sunbelt (see Map 29.1). Government actions—including generous tax breaks for oil companies, siting of military bases, and awarding of defense and aerospace contracts—were crucial to the region's new prosperity.

The Sunbelt's spectacular growth was also due to agribusiness, the oil industry, real-estate development, and recreation. Sunbelt states aggressively—and successfully—sought foreign investment. Industry was drawn to the South by right-to-work laws, which outlawed closed shops, and by low taxes and low heating bills. The development of air conditioning was also crucial, for it made bearable even the hottest summer days. Houston, Phoenix, Los Angeles, San Diego, Dallas, and Miami all boomed; the population of Houston, a center of the aerospace industry and also of oil and petrochemical production, more than tripled between 1940 and 1960. California absorbed no less than one-fifth of the nation's entire population increase in the 1950s. By 1963 it was the most populous state in the Union.

By the 1950s, it seemed that America was becoming a middle-class nation. Unionized blue-collar workers gained

A New Middle-Class Culture

middle-class incomes, and veterans with GI Bill college educations swelled the growing managerial and professional class. In 1956, for the first time, the United States had more white-collar than blue-collar workers, and in 1957 there were 61 percent more salaried middle-class workers than just a decade earlier. Also for the first time, a majority of families—60 percent—had incomes in the middle-class range (approximately $3,000 to $9,000 a year in the mid-1950s).

However, middle-class identity was not simply a matter of economics. Half of teenagers whose fathers did unskilled menial labor or whose mothers had only a sixth-grade education, a major 1952 survey discovered, believed their family was "middle class" (not working class or lower class). Paradoxically, the strength of unions in the postwar era contributed to a decline in working-class identity: as large numbers of blue-collar workers participated fully in the suburban middle-class culture, the lines separating working class and middle class seemed less important. Increasingly, a family's standard of living mattered more than what sort of work made the standard of living possible. People of color did not share equally in America's postwar prosperity and were usually invisible in American representations of "the good life." However, many middle-income African Americans, Latinos, and Asian Americans did participate in the broad middle-class culture.

The emergence of a national middle-class culture was possible in part because America's population was more

Whiteness and National Culture

homogeneous in the 1950s than before or since. In the nineteenth and early twentieth centuries, the United States had restricted or prohibited immigration from Asia, Africa, and Latin America while accepting millions of Europeans to America's shores. This large-scale European immigration had been shut off in the 1920s, so that by 1960 only 5.7 percent of Americans were foreign-born (compared with approximately 15 percent in 1910 and 12.4 percent in 2005). In 1950, 88 percent of Americans were of European

ancestry (compared with 69 percent in 2000); 10 percent of the population was African American; 2 percent was Hispanic; and Native Americans and Asian Americans each accounted for about one-fifth of 1 percent. But almost all European-Americans were at least a generation removed from immigration. Instead of "Italians" or "Russians" or "Jews," they were increasingly likely to describe themselves as "white." In 1959 the addition of two new states, Alaska and Hawai'i, brought more people of native, Asian, or Pacific origin to the U.S. population.

Although the new suburbs were peopled mostly by white families, these suburbs were usually more diverse than the communities from which their residents had come. America's small towns and urban ethnic enclaves were quite homogeneous and usually intolerant of difference and of challenges to traditional ways. In the suburbs, people from different backgrounds came together: migrants from the city and the country; from different regions of the nation, different ethnic cultures, and different religious backgrounds. It was in the suburbs, paradoxically, that many people encountered different customs and beliefs. But as they joined with neighbors to forge new communities, the new suburbanites frequently adopted the norms of the developing national middle class. They traded the provincial homogeneity of specific ethnic or regional cultures for a new sort of homogeneity: a national middle-class culture.

Because many white Americans were new to the middle class, they were uncertain about what behaviors were

Television

proper and expected of them. They found instruction, in part, in the national mass media. Women's magazines helped housewives replace the ethnic and regional dishes with which they had grown up with "American" recipes created from national brandname products—such as casseroles made with Campbell's Cream of Mushroom soup. Television also fostered America's shared national culture and taught Americans how to be middle class. Although television sets cost about $300—the equivalent of $2,000 today—almost half of American homes had TVs by 1953. Television ownership rose to 90 percent by 1960, when more American households had a television set than a washing machine or an electric iron.

On television, suburban families like the Andersons (*Father Knows Best*) and the Cleavers (*Leave It to Beaver*) ate dinner at a properly set dining room table. The mothers were always well groomed; June Cleaver did housework in a carefully ironed dress. When children faced moral dilemmas, parents gently but firmly guided them toward correct decisions. Every crisis was resolved through paternal wisdom—and a little humor. In these families, no one ever yelled or hit. These popular family situation comedies portrayed and reinforced the suburban middle-class ideal that so many American families sought.

The "middle-classness" of television programming was due in part to the economics of the television industry. Advertising paid for television programming, and the corporations that bought advertising did not want to offend potential consumers. Thus, although African American musician Nat King Cole drew millions of viewers to his NBC television show, it never found a sponsor. National corporations were afraid that being linked to a black performer like Cole would hurt their sales among whites—especially in the South. Because African Americans made up only about 10 percent of the population and many had little disposable income, they had little power in this economics-driven system. The *Nat King Cole Show* was canceled within a year; it was a decade before the networks again tried to anchor a show around a black performer.

Television's reach extended beyond the suburbs. People from the inner cities and from isolated rural areas also watched family sitcoms or laughed at the antics of Milton Berle and Lucille Ball. With only network television available— ABC, CBS, and NBC (and, until 1956, DuMont)—at any one time 70 percent or more of all viewers might be watching the same popular program. (In the early twenty-first century the most popular shows might attract 12 percent of the viewing audience.) Television gave Americans a shared set of experiences; it also helped create a more homogeneous, white-focused, middle-class culture.

Linked by a shared national culture, Americans also found common ground in a new abundance of consumer

Consumer Culture

goods. After decades of scarcity, Americans had what seemed a dazzling array of consumer goods from which to choose, and they embraced them with unmatched exuberance. Even the most utilitarian objects got two-tone paint jobs or rocket-ship details; there was an optimism and vulgar joy in the popularity of turquoise refrigerators, furniture shaped like boomerangs, and cars designed to resemble fighter jets. In this consumer society, people used consumer choices to express their personal identity and to claim status within the broad boundaries of the middle class. Cars more than anything else embodied the consumer fantasies and exuberance of newly prosperous Americans. Expensive Cadillacs were the first to develop tail fins, and fins soon soared from midrange Chevys, Fords, and Plymouths as well. Americans spent $65 billion on automobiles in 1955—a figure equivalent to almost 20 percent of the gross national product. To pay for all those cars—and for suburban houses with modern appliances—America's consumer debt rose from $5.7 billion in 1945 to $58 billion in 1961.

Admiral's "Up-Side-Down" refrigerator boasted a full-size freezer that would hold up to 120 pounds of frozen food, making life easier for the modern housewife. It also captured the new consumer exuberance: even the inside of this refrigerator is colorful!

(Picture Research Consultants & Archives)

In the same years, Americans turned in unprecedented numbers to organized religion. Membership (primarily

Religion

in mainline Christian churches) doubled between the end of World War II and the beginning of the 1960s. The uncertainties of the nuclear age likely contributed to the resurgence of religion, and some Americans may have sought spiritual consolation in the wake of the immensely destructive world war. The increasingly important national mass media played a role, as preachers like Billy Graham created national congregations from television audiences, preaching a message that combined the promise of salvation with Cold War patriotism. But along with religious teachings, local churches and synagogues offered new suburbanites a sense of community. They welcomed newcomers, celebrated life's rituals, and supported the sick and the bereaved who were often far from their extended families and old communities. It is difficult to measure the depth of religious belief in postwar America, but church fellowship halls were near the center of the new postwar middle-class culture.

MEN, WOMEN, AND YOUTH AT MIDCENTURY

Most of all, Americans pursued "the good life" and sought refuge from the tensions of the Cold War world through their homes and families. Having survived the Great Depression and a world war, many sought fulfillment in private life rather than public engagement; they saw their commitment to home and family as an expression of faith in the future. However, despite the real satisfactions that many Americans found in family life, both men and women found their life choices limited by powerful social pressures to conform to narrowly defined gender roles.

During the 1950s, few Americans remained single, and most people married very young. By 1959, almost

Marriage and Families

half of American brides had yet to reach their nineteenth birthday; their husbands were usually only a year or so older. This trend toward early marriage was endorsed by experts and approved by most parents, in part as a way to prevent premarital sex. As Americans accepted psychotherapeutic insights in the years following the war, they worried not only that premarital sex might leave the young woman pregnant or ruin her "reputation," but also that the experience could so damage her psychologically that she could never adjust to "normal" marital relations. One popular women's magazine argued, "When two people

are ready for sexual intercourse at the fully human level they are ready for marriage. . . . Not to do so is moral cowardice. And society has no right to stand in their way."

Many young couples—still teenagers—found autonomy and freedom from parental authority by marrying and setting up their own household. Most newlyweds quickly had babies— an average of three—completing their family while still in their twenties. Birth control (condoms and diaphragms) was widely available and widely used, for most couples planned the size of their family. But almost all married couples, regardless of race or class, wanted a large family. Two children were the American ideal in 1940; by 1960, most couples wanted four. And though many families looked nothing like television's June, Ward, Wally, and Beaver Cleaver, 88 percent of children under eighteen lived with two parents (in 2000, the figure was 69 percent). Fewer children were born outside marriage then; only 3.9 percent of births were to unmarried women in 1950 (compared with more than one-third of births in 2000). Divorce rates were also lower. As late as 1960, there were only 9 divorces per 1,000 married couples.

In these 1950s families, men and women usually took distinct and different roles, with male breadwinners

Gender Roles in 1950s Families

and female homemakers. This division of labor, contemporary commentators insisted, was based on the timeless and essential differences between the sexes. In fact, the economic and social structure and the cultural values of postwar American society largely determined what choices were available to American men and women.

During the 1950s, it was possible for many families to live in modest middle-class comfort on one (male) salary. There were strong incentives for women to stay at home, especially while children were young. Good childcare was rarely available, and fewer families lived close to the grandparents or other relatives who had traditionally helped with the children. A new cohort of childcare experts, including Dr. Spock, whose 1946 *Baby and Child Care* sold millions of copies, insisted that a mother's full-time attention was necessary for her children's well-being. Because of hiring discrimination, women who could afford to stay home often did not find the jobs available to them attractive enough to justify a double shift, with paid employment simply added to their responsibilities for cooking and housework. Many women thus chose to devote their considerable energies to family life. America's schools and religious institutions also benefited immensely from their volunteer labor.

A great number of women, however, found that their lives did not completely match the ideal of 1950s family

‖‖‖‖‖‖‖‖‖‖‖‖‖‖‖‖‖
Women and Work

life. Suburban domesticity left many women feeling isolated, cut off from the larger world of experiences that their husbands still inhabited. The popular belief that one should find complete emotional satisfaction in private life put unrealistic pressures on marriages and family relationships. And finally, despite near-universal celebration of women's domestic roles, many women found themselves managing both job and family responsibilities (see Figure 29.3). Twice as many women were employed in 1960 as in 1940, including 39 percent of women with children between the ages of six and seventeen. A majority of these women worked part-time for some specific family goal: a new car; college tuition for the children. They did not see these jobs as violating their primary role as housewife; these jobs were in service to the family, not a means to independence from it.

Whether she worked to supplement a middle-class income, to feed her children, or to support herself, however, a woman faced discrimination in the world of work. Want ads were divided into "Help Wanted—Male" and "Help Wanted—Female" categories. Female full-time workers earned, on average, just 60 percent of what male full-time workers were paid and were restricted to less well-paid "female" fields, as maids, secretaries, teachers, and nurses. Women with exceptional talent or ambition often found their aspirations blocked. A popular book, *Modern Woman: The Lost Sex*, explained that ambitious women and "feminists" suffered from "penis envy." Textbooks for college psychology and sociology courses warned women not to "compete" with men; magazine articles described "career women" as a "third sex." Medical schools commonly limited the admission of women to 5 percent of each class. In 1960 less than 4 percent of lawyers and judges were female. When future Supreme Court Justice Ruth Bader Ginsburg graduated at the top of her Columbia Law School class in 1959, she could not find a job.

While academics and mass media critics alike stressed the importance of "proper" female roles, they devoted

‖‖‖‖‖‖‖‖‖‖‖‖‖‖‖‖‖‖‖‖‖‖
"Crisis of Masculinity"

equal attention to the plight of the American male. American men faced a "crisis of masculinity," proclaimed the nation's mass-circulation magazines, quoting an array of psychological experts. In a bestselling book, sociologist William H. Whyte explained that postwar corporate employees had become "organization men," succeeding through cooperation and conformity, not through individual initiative and risk. Women, too, were blamed for men's crisis: women's "natural" desire for security and comfort, experts insisted, was stifling men's

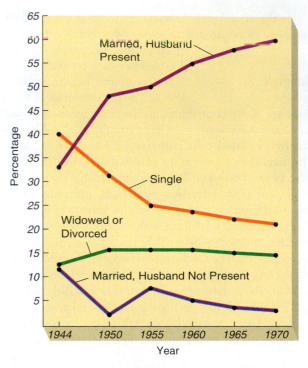

Figure 29.3 **Marital Distribution of the Female Labor Force, 1944–1970**

The composition of the female labor force changed dramatically from 1944 to 1970. In 1944, 41 percent of women in the labor force were single; in 1970, only 22 percent were single. During the same years, the percentage of the female labor force who had a husband in the home jumped from 34 to 59. The percentage who were widowed or divorced remained about the same from 1944 to 1970.

(Source: *Adapted from U.S. Bureau of the Census,* Historical Statistics of the United States, Colonial Times to 1970, *Bicentennial Edition [Washington, D.C.: U.S. Government Printing Office, 1975], p. 133.)*

natural instinct for adventure. Some even linked concerns about masculinity to the Cold War, arguing that, unless America's men recovered masculinity diminished by white-collar work or a suburban, family-centered existence, the nation's future was at risk. At the same time, however, men who did not conform to current standards of male responsibility—husband, father, breadwinner—were forcefully condemned, sometimes in the same magazines that preached the crisis of masculinity. One influential book advocated mandatory psychotherapy for men who reached thirty without having married; such single men were open to charges of "emotional immaturity" or "latent homosexuality."

Sexuality was complicated terrain in postwar America. Only heterosexual intercourse within marriage was

Sexuality

deemed socially acceptable, and consequences for sexual misconduct could be severe. Women who became pregnant outside marriage were often ostracized by friends and family, and expelled from schools or colleges. Homosexuality was grounds for dismissal from a job, expulsion from college, even jail. At the same time, a great many Americans were breaking the sexual rules of the era. In his major works on human sexuality, *Sexual Behavior in the Human Male* (1948) and *Sexual Behavior in the Human Female* (1953), Dr. Alfred Kinsey, director of the Institute for Sex Research at Indiana University, informed Americans that, despite the fact that more than 80 percent of his female sample disapproved of premarital sex on "moral grounds," half of these women had had premarital sex. He also reported that at least 37 percent of American men had had "some homosexual experience." Americans made bestsellers of Kinsey's dry, quantitative studies—as many rushed to condemn him. One congressman charged Kinsey with "hurling the insult of the century against our mothers, wives, daughters and sisters"; the *Chicago Tribune* called him a "menace to society." Although Kinsey's population samples did not provide a completely accurate picture of American sexual behavior, his findings made many Americans aware that they were not alone in breaking certain rules.

Another challenge to the sexual rules of 1950s America came from Hugh Hefner, who launched *Playboy* magazine in 1953. Within three years, the magazine had a circulation of 1 million. Hefner saw *Playboy* as an attack on America's "ferocious anti-sexuality [and] dark antieroticism" and his nude "playmates" as a means for men to combat what he considered the increasingly "blurred distinctions between the sexes" in a family-centered suburban culture.

As children grew up in relative stability and prosperity, a distinctive "youth culture" developed. Youth culture was really a set of subcultures; the

Youth Culture

culture of white, middle-class, suburban youth was not the same as that of black, urban teens or even of the white working class. Youth culture was, however, distinct from the culture of adults. Its customs and rituals were created within peer groups and shaped by national media—teen magazines, movies, radio, advertising, music—targeted toward this huge potential audience.

The sheer numbers of "baby boom" youth made them a force in American society. People sometimes described the baby-boom generation as "a pig in a python," and as this group moved from childhood to youth, communities successively built elementary schools, junior high schools, and high schools. America's corporations quickly learned the power of youth, as children's fads launched multimillion-dollar industries. Slinky, selling for a dollar, began loping down people's stairs in 1947; Mr. Potato Head—probably the first toy advertised on television—had $4 million in sales in 1952. In the mid-1950s, when Walt Disney's television show *Disneyland* featured Davy Crockett, "King of the Wild Frontier," every child in America (and more than a few adults) just *had* to have a coonskin cap. When the price of raccoon fur skyrocketed from 25 cents to $8 a pound, many children had to make do with a Davy Crockett lunchbox or toothbrush instead. As these baby-boom children grew up, their buying power shaped American popular culture.

By 1960, America's 18 million teenagers were spending $10 billion a year. Seventy-two percent of movie tickets in the 1950s were sold to teenagers, and Hollywood catered to this audience with a flood of teen films, ranging from forgettable B-movies like *The Cool and the Crazy* and *Senior Prom* to controversial and influential movies, such as James Dean's *Rebel Without a Cause*. Adults worried that teens would be drawn to romantic images of delinquency in *Rebel Without a Cause*, and teenage boys did copy Dean's rebellious look. The film, however, blamed parents for teenage confusion, drawing heavily on popular psychological theories about sexuality and the "crisis of masculinity." "What can you do when you have to be a man?" James Dean's character implored his father.

Movies helped shape teen fads and fashions, but nothing defined youth culture as much as its music. Young Americans were electrified by the driving energy and beat of Bill Haley and the Comets, Chuck Berry, Little Richard, and Buddy Holly. Elvis Presley's 1956 appearance on TV's *Ed Sullivan Show* touched off a frenzy of teen adulation—and a flood of letters from parents scandalized by his "gyrations." As one reviewer noted, "When Presley executes his bumps and grinds, it must be remembered that even the 12-year-old's curiosity may be overstimulated." Although few white musicians acknowledged the debt, the roots of rock 'n' roll lay in African American rhythm and blues. The raw energy and sometimes sexually suggestive lyrics of early rock music faded as the music industry sought white performers, like Pat Boone, to do blander, more acceptable "cover" versions of music by black artists.

The distinct youth culture that developed in the 1950s made many adults uneasy. Parents worried that the common practice of "going steady" made it more likely that teens would "go too far" sexually. Juvenile delinquency was a major concern. Crime rates for young people had, in fact, risen dramatically in the years following World

Barbie

Barbie, the "all-American doll," is—like many Americans—an immigrant. Although Barbie was introduced in 1959 by the American toy company Mattel, her origins lie in Germany, where she went by the name Lilli.

As many mothers at the time suspected, noting the new doll's figure (equivalent to 39-21-31 in human proportions), Barbie's background was not completely respectable. The German Lilli doll was a toy for adult men, not little girls. She was based on a character that cartoonist Reinhard Beuthien drew to fill some empty space in the June 24, 1952, edition of the German tabloid *Das Bild.* The cartoon was meant to appear just once, but Lilli was so popular that she became a regular feature. Soon Lilli appeared in three-dimensional form as *Bild* Lilli, an eleven-and-a-half-inch-tall blonde doll—with the figure Barbie would make famous. Dressed in a variety of sexy outfits, Lilli was sold in tobacco shops and bars as a "novelty gift" for men.

Lilli came to America with Ruth Handler, one of the founders and codirectors of the Mattel toy company. In a time when girls were given baby dolls, Handler imagined a grown-up doll that girls could dress as they did their paper dolls. When she glimpsed Lilli while on vacation in Europe, Handler bought three—and gave one to her daughter Barbara, after whom Lilli would be renamed. Mattel bought the rights to Lilli (the doll and the cartoon, which Mattel quietly retired) and unveiled Barbie in March 1959. Despite mothers' hesitations about buying a doll that looked like Barbie, within the year Mattel had sold 351,000 Barbies at $3 each (or about $17 in 2000 dollars). The billionth Barbie was sold in 1997.

Within the United States, Barbie has been controversial—at least among adults. Some have worried that Barbie's wildly unrealistic figure fosters girls' dissatisfaction with their own body—a serious problem in a culture plagued with eating disorders. Others claim that, despite Barbie's 1980s "Girls Can Do

Anything" makeover, Barbie represents a model of empty-headed femininity, focused on endless consumption. And many have criticized the ways in which blonde, blue-eyed Barbie failed to represent the diversity of America's people, especially as Mattel's early attempts at racial and ethnic diversity (such as "Colored Francie," introduced in 1967) created dolls with the same Caucasian features as the original Barbie, except with darker skin coloring and hair.

In recent years, Barbie has played a role in important international issues. In 2002 international labor-rights groups called for a boycott of Barbie. They cited studies showing that half of all Barbies are made by exploited young women workers in mainland China: of the $10 retail cost of an average Barbie, Chinese factories receive only 35 cents per doll to pay for all their costs, including labor. Barbie has also played a role in international relations. Saudi Arabia banned sales of Barbie in 2003, arguing that her skimpy outfits and the values she represents are not suitable for a Muslim nation. And a poll found that, following the beginning of the United States' war in Iraq, people in other nations said they were less likely to buy Barbie because she was so closely identified with America.

Even so, the eleven-and-a-half-inch doll remains popular throughout the world, sold in more than 150 countries. Today, the average American girl has ten Barbies—and the typical German girl owns five. Over the years, for better or worse, Barbie has continued to link the United States and the rest of the world.

Before Barbie became an American ▶
child's toy, she was "Lilli," a German
sex symbol. Mattel transformed the doll
into a wholesome American teenager
with a new wardrobe to match.

(Spielzeug Museum, Munich).

oriented popular culture, comic books in particular. In 1955 *Life* magazine reported, "Some American parents, without quite knowing what it is their kids are up to, are worried that it's something they shouldn't be." Most youthful behavior, however—from going steady to fads in music and dress—fit squarely into the consumer culture that youth shared with their parents. "Rebellious youth" rarely questioned the logic of postwar American culture.

Despite the growing reach and power of this middle-class culture, there were pockets of cultural dissent. Beat (a word that suggested both "down and out" and "beatific") writers rejected both middle-class social decorum and contemporary literary conventions. Jack Kerouac, author of *On The Road*, traced his inspiration to "weariness with all forms of the modern industrial state." The Beat Generation embraced spontaneity in their art, in their lives sought freedom from the demands of everyday life, and enjoyed a more open sexuality and drug use. Perhaps the most significant beat work was Allen Ginsberg's angry, incantational poem "Howl" (1956), the subject of an obscenity trial whose verdict opened American publishing to a much broader range of works. The mainstream press made fun of the beats, dubbing them and their followers "beatniks" (after *Sputnik*, suggesting their un-Americanness). Although they attracted little attention in the 1950s, they laid the groundwork for the 1960s counterculture.

Challenges to Middle-Class Culture

THE LIMITS OF THE MIDDLE-CLASS NATION

During the 1950s, America's popular culture and mass media celebrated the opportunities available to the nation's people. At the same time, a host of influential critics rushed to condemn the new middle-class culture as a wasteland of conformity, homogeneity, and ugly consumerism.

These critics were not lone figures crying out in the wilderness. Americans, obsessed with self-criticism even as most participated wholeheartedly in the celebratory "consensus" culture of their age, rushed to buy books like John Keats's *The Crack in the Picture Window* (1957), which portrayed three families—the "Drones," the "Amiables," and the "Fecunds"—who lived in identical suburban tract houses "vomited" up by developers and sacrificed their remaining individuality in the quest for consumer goods. Some of the most popular fiction of the postwar era, such as J. D. Salinger's *The Catcher in the*

Critics of Conformity

▲ Elvis Presley "gyrates" during a live performance in 1956. Many adults were horrified ("sexhibitionist," *Time* magazine sneered), but Elvis was selling $75,000 worth of records a day in April 1956.

(Picture Research Consultants & Archives)

War II, but that was partly because there were so many young people, and they were under greater scrutiny than before. Much juvenile delinquency consisted of "status" crimes—curfew violations, sexual experimentation, underage drinking—activities that were criminal because of the person's age, not because of the action itself. Congress held extensive hearings on juvenile delinquency, with experts testifying to the corrupting power of youth-

During tho Second World War, DDT was used to protect American troops from bug-borne diseases and was hailed as a miracle insecticide. The use of DDT spread in postwar America, but little attention was paid to its often-fatal consequences for birds, mammals, and fish. In 1945, even as children ran alongside, this truck sprayed DDT as part of a mosquito-control program at New York's Jones Beach State Park.

(© Bettmann/Corbis)

Rye and Norman Mailer's *The Naked and the Dead,* was profoundly critical of American society. Americans even made bestsellers of difficult academic works, such as David Riesman's *The Lonely Crowd* (1950) and William H. Whyte's *The Organization Man* (1955), both of which criticized the rise of conformity in American life. Versions of these critiques also appeared in mass-circulation magazines like *Ladies' Home Journal* and *Reader's Digest.* Steeped in such cultural criticism, many Americans even understood *Invasion of the Body Snatchers*—a 1956 film in which zombielike aliens grown in huge pods gradually replace a town's human inhabitants—as criticism of suburban conformity and the bland homogeneity of postwar culture.

Most of these critics were attempting to understand large-scale and significant changes in American society. Americans were contending with some loss of autonomy in work as large corporations replaced smaller businesses; they experienced the homogenizing force of mass production and a national consumer culture; they saw distinctions among ethnic groups and even among socioeconomic classes decline in importance. Many wanted to understand these social dislocations better. Critics of the new culture, however, were often elitist and antidemocratic. Many saw only bland conformity and sterility in the emerging middle-class suburban culture and so missed something important. Identical houses did not produce identical souls; instead, inexpensive suburban housing gave healthier, and perhaps happier, lives to millions who had grown up in dank, dark tenements or ramshackle farmhouses without indoor plumbing. In retrospect, however, other criticisms are obvious.

First, the new consumer culture encouraged wasteful habits and harmed the environment. *Business Week* noted

Environmental Degradation

during the 1950s that corporations need not rely on "planned obsolescence," purposely designing a product to wear out so that consumers would have to replace it. Americans replaced products because they were "out of date," not because they did not work, and automakers, encouraging the trend, revamped designs every year. New and inexpensive plastic products and detergents made consumers' lives easier—but were not biodegradable. And America's new consumer society used an ever larger share of the world's resources. By the 1960s, the United States, with only 5 percent of the world's population, consumed more than one-third of its goods and services.

The rapid economic growth that made the middle-class consumer culture possible exacted environmental costs. Steel mills, coal-powered generators, and internal-combustion car engines burning lead-based gasoline polluted the atmosphere and imperiled people's health. As suburbanites commuted greater distances to their jobs, and neighborhoods were built without public transportation or shopping within walking distance of people's homes, Americans relied on private automobiles, consuming the nonrenewable resources of oil and gasoline, and filling cities and suburbs with smog. Vast quantities of water were diverted from lakes and rivers to meet the needs of America's burgeoning Sunbelt cities, including the swimming pools and golf courses that dotted parched Arizona and southern California.

Defense contractors and farmers were among the country's worst polluters. Refuse from nuclear weapons facilities at Hanford, Washington, and at Colorado's

Rocky Flats arsenal poisoned soil and water resources for years. Agriculture began employing massive amounts of pesticides and other chemicals. DDT, a chemical used on Pacific islands during the war to kill mosquitoes and lice, was used widely in the United States from 1945 until after 1962, when wildlife biologist Rachel Carson specifically indicted DDT for the deaths of mammals, birds, and fish in her bestselling book *Silent Spring*.

In the midst of prosperity, few understood the consequences of the economic transformation taking place. The nation was moving toward a postindustrial economy in which providing goods and services to consumers was more important than producing goods. Therefore, though union members prospered during the 1950s, union membership grew slowly—because most new jobs were being created not in heavy industries that hired blue-collar workers but in the union-resistant white-collar service trades. Technological advances increased productivity, as automated electronic processes replaced slower mechanical ones—but they pushed people out of relatively well paid blue-collar jobs into the growing and less well-paid service sector.

Largely oblivious to the environmental degradation and work-sector shifts that accompanied economic growth and consumerism, the new middle-class culture also largely ignored those who did not belong to its ranks. Race remained a major dividing line in American society,

Continuing Racism

even as fewer Americans were excluded because of ethnic identity. Racial discrimination stood unchallenged in most of 1950s America. Suburbs, both North and South, were almost always racially segregated. Many white Americans had little or no contact in their daily lives with people of different races—not only because of residential segregation but also because the relatively small populations of nonwhite Americans were not dispersed equally throughout the nation. In 1960 there were 68 people of Chinese descent and 519 African Americans living in Vermont; 181 Native Americans lived in West Virginia; and Mississippi had just 178 Japanese American residents. Most white Americans in the 1950s—especially those outside the South, where there was a large African American population—gave little thought to race. They did not think of the emerging middle-class culture as "white," but as "American," marginalizing people of color in image as in reality (see Map 29.2).

The new middle-class culture was also indifferent to the plight of the poor. In an age of abundance, more than one in five Americans lived in poverty. One-fifth of the poor were people of color, including almost half of the nation's

Percent Races Other Than White

- 30 or more
- 20—29
- 10—19
- Less than 10
- Not applicable

Map 29.2   Racial Composition of the United States, 1950 and 2000

Compared with present-day America, most states were fairly racially homogeneous in 1950. The exception was the Deep South, where most African Americans still lived.

(Source: Adapted from "Demographic Trends in the Twentieth Century," U.S. Census Bureau; www.census.gov/population/www/censusdata /hiscendata.html.)

African American population and more than half of all Native Americans. Two-thirds of the poor lived in households headed by a person with an eighth-grade education or less, one-fourth in households headed by a single woman. More than one-third of the poor were under age eighteen; one-fourth were over age sixty-five. Social Security payments helped the elderly, but many retirees were not yet covered, and medical costs drove many older

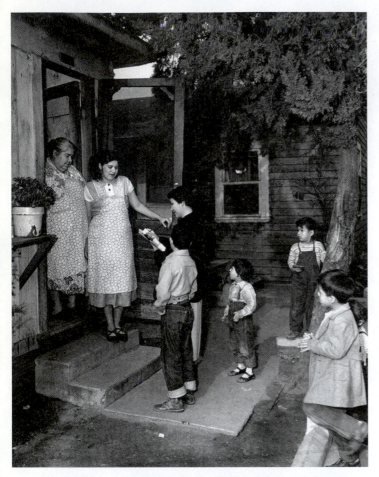

▲ A volunteer from the Community Service Organization (CSO) registers a Mexican American mother and daughter as part of a massive voter registration drive in postwar Los Angeles. Women played a critical role in the CSO, which was founded in 1947 to address Mexican American civil rights issues, including education and labor, in East Los Angeles.

(Los Angeles Daily News Collection, Department of Special Collections, University Research Library, UCLA)

Americans into poverty. Few of these people had much reason for hope.

As millions of Americans (most of them white) were settling in the suburbs, the poor were ever more concentrated in the inner cities. African American migrants from the South were joined by poor whites from the southern Appalachians, many of whom moved to Chicago, Cincinnati, Baltimore, and Detroit. Meanwhile, Latin Americans were arriving in growing numbers from Mexico, the Dominican Republic, Colombia, Ecuador, and Cuba.

Poverty in an Age of Abundance

According to the 1960 census, over a half-million Mexican Americans had migrated to the barrios of the Los Angeles–Long Beach area since 1940. And New York City's Puerto Rican population exploded from 70,000 in 1940 to 613,000 in 1960.

All of these newcomers to the cities came seeking better lives and greater opportunities. Because of the strong economy and low unemployment rate, many did gain a higher standard of living. But discrimination limited their advances, and they endured crowded and decrepit housing and poor schools. In addition, the federal programs that helped middle-class Americans sometimes made the lives of the poor worse. For example, the National Housing Act of 1949, passed to make available "a decent home . . . for every American family," provided for "urban redevelopment." Redevelopment meant slum clearance. Many poor people lost what housing they had as entire neighborhoods were leveled and replaced with luxury high-rise buildings, parking lots, and even highways.

Rural poverty was a long-standing problem in America, but the growth of large agribusinesses pushed more tenant farmers and owners of small farms off the land. From 1945 to 1961 the nation's farm population declined from 24.4 million to 14.8 million. When the harvesting of cotton in the South was mechanized in the 1940s and 1950s, more than 4 million people were displaced. Southern tobacco growers dismissed their tenant farmers, bought tractors to plow the land, and hired migratory workers to harvest the crops. Many of these displaced farmers traded southern rural poverty for northern urban poverty. And in the West and Southwest, Mexican citizens continued to serve as cheap migrant labor under the *bracero* program. Almost 1 million Mexican workers came legally to the United States in 1959; many more were undocumented workers. Entire families labored, enduring conditions little better than in the Great Depression.

Native Americans were America's poorest people, with an average annual income barely half that of the poverty level. Conditions for native peoples were made worse by a federal policy implemented during the Eisenhower administration: termination. Termination reversed the Indian Reorganization Act of 1934, allowing Indians to terminate their tribal status and so remove reservation lands from federal protection that prohibited their sale. Sixty-one tribes were terminated between 1954 and 1960. Termination could take place only with a tribe's agreement, but pressure was sometimes intense—especially when reservation land was rich in natural resources. The Klamaths of Oregon, for example, lived on a reservation rich in ponderosa pine, which lumber interests coveted. Enticed by cash payments, almost four-fifths of the Klamaths ac-

After the war, American Indians lost sacred land to both big corporations and the federal government. In 1948 George Gillette *(left)*, chairman of the Fort Berthold, North Dakota, Indian Tribal Council, covers his face and weeps as Secretary of the Interior J. A. Krug signs a contract buying 155,000 acres of tribal land for a reservoir. *(Wide World Photos, Inc.)*

cepted termination and voted to sell their shares of the forest land. With termination, their way of life collapsed. Many Indians left reservation land for the city, joining the influx of other poor Americans seeking jobs and new lives. By the time termination was halted in the 1960s, observers compared the situation of Native Americans to the devastation their forebears had endured in the nineteenth century. Like most of the poor, these Americans were invisible to the growing middle class in the suburbs.

Overall, Americans who had lived through the devastation of the Great Depression and World War II enjoyed the relative prosperity and economic security of the postwar era. But those who had made it to the comfortable middle class often ignored the plight of those left behind. It would be their children—the generation of the baby boom, many reared in suburban comfort—who would see racism, poverty, and the self-satisfaction of postwar suburban culture as a failure of American ideals.

SUMMARY

As the experiences of economic depression and world war receded, Americans worked to create good lives for themselves and their families. People married and had children in record numbers. Millions of veterans used the GI Bill to attend college, buy homes, and start businesses. Although American leaders feared that the nation would lapse back into economic depression after wartime government spending ended, consumer spending brought economic growth. The sustained economic growth of the postwar era lifted a majority of Americans into an expanding middle class.

The Cold War presidencies of Truman and Eisenhower focused on international relations and a global struggle against communism, rather than on domestic politics. Within the United States, Cold War fears provoked an extreme anticommunism that stifled political dissent and diminished Americans' civil liberties and freedoms.

The continuing African American struggle for civil rights drew national attention during the Montgomery bus boycott, reminding whites that not all Americans enjoyed equality. African Americans won important victories in

Legacy FOR A PEOPLE AND A NATION

The Pledge of Allegiance

The Pledge of Allegiance that Americans recite in school classrooms and sports stadiums throughout the nation today was shaped by America's Cold War struggle against the Soviet Union. Congress added the phrase "under God" to the existing pledge in 1954, as part of an attempt to emphasize the difference between the god-fearing United States and the "godless communists" of the Soviet Union.

The Pledge of Allegiance was not always an important part of American public life. The original version was written in 1892 by Francis Bellamy, editor of *The Youth's Companion,* to commemorate the four hundredth anniversary of Columbus's arrival in North America. On October 11, 1892, more than 11 million schoolchildren recited the words "I pledge allegiance to my flag and the Republic for which it stands; one nation indivisible, with liberty and justice for all." In 1942 Congress officially adopted a revised version of this pledge as an act of wartime patriotism. The Supreme Court ruled in 1943, however, that schoolchildren could not be forced to say the "Pledge to the Flag."

During the Cold War years, the pledge became more and more important as a way to demonstrate loyalty to the United States. Cold War fears lent force to a campaign by the Knights of Columbus, a Catholic men's service organization, to include "under God" in the pledge. Supporting the bill, President Eisenhower proclaimed that

in this way we are reaffirming the transcendence of religious faith in America's heritage and future; in this way we shall constantly strengthen those spiritual weapons which forever will be our country's most powerful resource in peace and war. From this day forward, the millions of our schoolchildren will daily proclaim in every city and town, every village and every rural schoolhouse, the dedication of our nation and our people to the Almighty.

Some Americans, citing the doctrine of separation of church and state, have protested the inclusion of "under God" in the nation's pledge. In June 2002, the Ninth District Court (covering California and eight other western states) touched off a major controversy by ruling that the 1954 version of the pledge was unconstitutional because it conveyed a "state endorsement" of a religious belief. Questions about the proper role of religion in American life are sure to remain controversial, a legacy for a people and a nation as America's people become even more diverse in the twenty-first century.

the Supreme Court, including the landmark decision in *Brown v. Board of Education,* and both Truman and Eisenhower used federal power to guarantee the rights of black Americans. With these victories, a national civil rights movement began to coalesce, and racial tensions within the nation increased.

Despite continued racial divisions, the United States became in many ways a more inclusive nation in the 1950s, as a majority of Americans participated in a national, consumer-oriented, middle-class culture. This culture largely ignored the poverty that remained in the nation's cities and rural areas, and contributed to rapidly increasing economic degradation. But for the growing number of middle-class Americans who, for the first time, lived in modest material comfort, the American dream seemed a reality.

SUGGESTIONS FOR FURTHER READING

Taylor Branch, *Parting the Waters: America in the King Years, 1954–1963* (1988)

Lizabeth Cohen, *A Consumer's Republic: The Politics of Mass Consumption in Postwar America* (2003)

Stephanie Coontz, *The Way We Never Were: American Families and the Nostalgia Trap* (1992)

Mary Dudziak, *Cold War Civil Rights: Race and the Image of American Democracy* (2000)

James Gregory, *The Southern Diaspora: How the Great Migrations of Black and White Southerners Transformed the Nation* (2007)

Thomas Hine, *Populuxe* (1986)

Grace Palladino, *Teenagers* (1996)

James T. Patterson, *Grand Expectations: The United States, 1945–1974* (1996)

Ellen W. Schrecker, *Many Are the Crimes: McCarthyism in America* (1998)

Thomas J. Sugrue, *The Origins of the Urban Crisis: Race and Inequality in Postwar Detroit* (1996)

For a more extensive list for further reading, go to college.hmco.com/pic/norton8e.

The Tumultuous Sixties *1960-1968*

*I*t was late at night, and Ezell Blair had a big exam the next day. But there he was with his friends in the dormitory, talking—as they so often did—about injustice, and discrimination, and about living in a nation that proclaimed equality for all but denied full citizenship to some of its people because of the color of their skin. They were complaining about all the do-nothing adults, condemning pretty much the entire black community of Greensboro—and not for the first time—when Franklin McCain said, as if he meant it, "It's time to fish or cut bait." And Joe McNeil said, "Yes, we're a bunch of hypocrites. Come on, let's do it. Let's do it tomorrow." McCain's roommate, David Richmond, agreed. Blair hesitated. "I was thinking about my grades," he said later, just "trying to deal with that architecture and engineering course I was taking."

But Blair was outvoted. The next day, February 1, 1960, after their classes at North Carolina Agricultural and Technical College were over, the four freshmen walked into town. At the F. W. Woolworth's on South Elm Street, one of the most profitable stores in the national chain, each bought a few small things, mostly school supplies. Then, nervously, they sat down on the vinyl-covered stools at the lunch counter and tried to order coffee. These young men—seventeen and eighteen years old—were prepared to be arrested, even physically attacked. But nothing happened. The counter help ignored them as long as possible; they never got their coffee. When one worker finally reminded them, "We don't serve colored here," the four made their point: they had already been served just a few feet away when they made their purchases. Why not at the lunch counter? An elderly white woman came up to the boys and told them

◄ When four freshmen from North Carolina Agricultural and Technical College sat down and tried to order coffee at the whites-only Woolworth's lunch counter in Greensboro, North Carolina, they did not know if they would be met with arrest or even violence. This photograph is from the second day of the sit-in, when the young men were joined by classmates. Two of the original four, Joseph McNeil and Franklin McCain, are on the left. *(© Corbis-Bettmann)*

CHRONOLOGY

1960 ■ Sit-ins begin in Greensboro
   ■ Birth-control pill approved
   ■ John F. Kennedy elected president
   ■ Young Americans for Freedom write Sharon Statement

1961 ■ Freedom Rides protest segregation in transportation

1962 ■ Students for a Democratic Society issues Port Huron Statement
   ■ Cuban missile crisis courts nuclear war

1963 ■ Civil rights March on Washington for Jobs and Freedom draws more than 250,000
   ■ South Vietnamese leader Diem assassinated following U.S.-sanctioned coup d'état
   ■ John F. Kennedy assassinated; Lyndon B. Johnson becomes president

1964 ■ Civil Rights Act passed by Congress
   ■ Race riots break out in first of the "long, hot summers"
   ■ Gulf of Tonkin Resolution passed by Congress
   ■ Free Speech Movement begins at University of California, Berkeley
   ■ Lyndon B. Johnson elected president

1965 ■ Lyndon Johnson launches Great Society programs
   ■ United States commits ground troops to Vietnam and initiates bombing campaign
   ■ Voting Rights Act outlaws practices preventing most African Americans from voting in southern states
   ■ Immigration and Nationality Act lowers barriers to immigration from Asia and Latin America
   ■ Malcolm X assassinated

1966 ■ National Organization for Women founded

1967 ■ "Summer of love" in San Francisco's Haight-Ashbury district
   ■ Race riots erupt in Newark, Detroit, and other cities

1968 ■ Tet Offensive deepens fear of losing war in Vietnam
   ■ Martin Luther King Jr. assassinated
   ■ Robert Kennedy assassinated
   ■ Violence erupts at Democratic National Convention
   ■ Richard Nixon elected president

how proud she was of them. "We got so much courage and so much pride" from that "little old lady," McCain said later. But still nothing happened. The store closed; the manager turned out the lights. After sitting in near darkness for about forty-five minutes, the four men who had begun the sit-in movement got up and walked from the store.

The next day they returned, but they were not alone. Twenty fellow students joined the sit-in. By February 3, sixty-three of the sixty-five seats were taken. On February 4, students from other colleges arrived, and the sit-in spread to the S. H. Kress store across the street. By February 7, there were sit-ins in Winston-Salem; by February 8, in Charlotte; on February 9, sit-ins began in Raleigh. By the third week in February, students were picketing Woolworth's stores in the North, and at lunch counters throughout the South, well-dressed young men and women sat, politely asking to be served. On July 26, 1960, they won. F. W. Woolworth's ended segregation, not only in Greensboro but in all its stores.

When these four college freshmen sat down at the Woolworth's lunch counter in Greensboro, they signaled the beginning of a decade of public activism rarely matched in American history. During the 1960s, millions of Americans—many of them young people—took to the streets. Some marched for civil rights or against the war in Vietnam; others lashed out in anger over the circumstances of their lives. Passion over the events of the day revitalized democracy—and threatened to tear the nation apart.

John F. Kennedy, the nation's youngest president, told Americans as he took office in 1961, "The torch has been passed to a new generation." Despite his inspirational language, Kennedy had only modest success implementing his domestic agenda. As he began his third year as president, pushed by the bravery of civil rights activists and the intransigence of their white opponents, Kennedy began to offer more active support for civil rights and to propose more ambitious domestic policies. But Kennedy was assassinated in November 1963. His death seemed, to many, the end of an era of hope.

Lyndon Johnson, Kennedy's successor, called on the memory of the martyred president to launch an ambitious program of civil rights and other liberal legislation. Johnson meant to use the power of the federal government to eliminate poverty and to guarantee equal rights to all America's people. He called his vision the Great Society.

Despite liberal triumphs in Washington, D.C., and real gains by the African American civil rights movement, social tensions escalated during the mid-1960s. A revitalized conservative movement emerged, and Franklin Roosevelt's old New Deal coalition fractured as white southerners abandoned the Democratic Party. Many African Americans, especially in the North, were angry that poverty and racial discrimination persisted despite the passage of landmark civil rights laws, and their discontent exploded during the "long, hot summers" of the mid-1960s. White youth culture, which seemed intent on rejecting everything an older generation had worked for, created a division that Americans came to call "the generation gap."

Developments overseas also contributed to a growing national instability. After the Cuban missile crisis of 1962 brought the Soviet Union and the United States close to nuclear disaster, President John F. Kennedy and Soviet leader Nikita Khrushchev moved to reduce bilateral tensions in 1963, with the result that Cold War pressures in Europe lessened appreciably. In the rest of the world, however, the superpowers continued their frantic competition. Throughout the 1960s, the United States used a variety of approaches—including foreign aid, CIA covert actions, military assaults, cultural penetration, economic sanctions, and diplomacy—in its attempts to win the Cold War, draw unaligned nations into its orbit, and defuse revolutionary nationalism. In Vietnam, Kennedy chose to expand U.S. involvement significantly. Johnson "Americanized" the war, increasing U.S. troops to more than half a million in 1968.

By 1968 the war in Vietnam had divided the American people and undermined Johnson's Great Society. With the assassinations of Martin Luther King Jr. and Robert Kennedy—two of America's brightest leaders—that spring, with cities in flames, and with tanks in the streets of Chicago in August, the fate of the nation seemed to hang in the balance.

- What were the successes and failures of American liberalism in the 1960s?
- Why did the United States expand its participation in the war in Vietnam and continue in the war so long?
- By 1968, many believed the fate of the nation hung in the balance. What did they think was at stake? What divided Americans, and how did they express their differences?

KENNEDY AND THE COLD WAR

President John F. Kennedy was, as writer Norman Mailer observed, "our leading man." Young, handsome, and vigorous, the new chief executive was the first president born in the twentieth century. Kennedy had a genuinely inquiring mind, and as a patron of the arts he brought wit and sophistication to the White House. He was born to wealth and politics: his Irish American grandfather had been mayor of Boston, and his millionaire father, Joseph P. Kennedy, had served as ambassador to Great Britain. In 1946 the young Kennedy, having returned from the Second World War a naval hero (the boat he commanded had been rammed and sunk by a Japanese destroyer in 1943, and Kennedy had saved his crew), continued the family tradition by campaigning to represent Boston in the U.S. House of Representatives. He won easily, served three terms in the House, and in 1952 was elected to the Senate.

As a Democrat, Kennedy inherited the New Deal commitment to America's social welfare system. He generally cast liberal votes in line with the pro-labor sentiments of his low-income, blue-collar constituents. But he avoided controversial issues, such as civil rights and the censure of Joseph McCarthy. Kennedy won a Pulitzer Prize for his *Profiles in Courage* (1956), a study of politicians who had acted on principle, but he shaded the truth when he claimed sole authorship of the book, which had been written largely by aide Theodore Sorensen (though based on more than one hundred pages of notes dictated by Kennedy). In foreign policy, Senator Kennedy endorsed the Cold War policy of containment, and his interest in world affairs deepened as the 1950s progressed. His record as a legislator was not impressive, but he enjoyed an enthusiastic following, especially after his landslide reelection to the Senate in 1958.

Kennedy and his handlers worked hard to cultivate an image of him as a happy and healthy family man. To some

John Fitzgerald Kennedy

▲ Many Americans were enchanted with the youthful and photogenic Kennedys. Here the president and his family pose outside the Palm Beach, Florida, home of the president's father after a private Easter Service, April 14, 1963. *(AP Images)*

War II. After the war, Kennedy was diagnosed with Addison's disease, an adrenalin deficiency that required daily injections of cortisone in order to be contained. At the time, the disease was thought to be terminal; though Kennedy survived, he was often in acute pain. As president he would require plenty of bed rest and frequent therapeutic swims in the White House pool.

Kennedy's rhetoric and style captured the imagination of many Americans. Yet his election victory over Republican Richard Nixon in 1960 was extraordinarily narrow—118,000 votes out of nearly 69 million cast. Kennedy achieved only mixed success in the South, but he ran well in the Northeast and Midwest. His Roman Catholic faith hurt him in some states, where voters feared he would take direction from the pope, but helped in states with large Catholic populations. As the sitting vice president, Nixon was saddled with the handicaps of incumbency; he had to answer for sagging economic figures and the Soviet downing of a U-2 spy plane. Nixon also looked disagreeable on TV; in televised debates against the telegenic Kennedy, he looked alternately nervous and surly, and the camera made him appear unshaven. Perhaps worse, Eisenhower gave Nixon only a tepid endorsement. Asked to list Nixon's significant decisions as vice president, Eisenhower replied, "If you give me a week, I might think of one."

Election of 1960

In a departure from the Eisenhower administration's staid, conservative image, the new president surrounded himself with mostly young advisers of intellectual verve, who proclaimed that they had fresh ideas for invigorating the nation; writer David Halberstam called them "the best and the brightest." Secretary of Defense Robert McNamara (age forty-four) had been an assistant professor at Harvard at twenty-four and later the whiz-kid president of the Ford Motor Company. Kennedy's special assistant for national security affairs, McGeorge Bundy (age forty-one) had become a Harvard dean at thirty-four with only a bachelor's degree. Secretary of State Dean Rusk, the old man in the group at fifty-two, had been a Rhodes scholar in his youth. Kennedy himself was only forty-three, and his brother Robert, the attorney general, was thirty-five.

It was no accident that most of these "best and brightest" operated in the realm of foreign policy. From the start, Kennedy gave top priority to waging the Cold War. In the campaign he had criticized Eisenhower's foreign policy as unimaginative, accusing him of missing chances to reduce the threat of nuclear war with the Soviet Union and of weakening America's standing in the Third World. Kennedy and his advisers exuded confidence that they would change things. As national security adviser Mc-

extent it was a ruse. He was a chronic womanizer, and his liaisons continued even after he married Jacqueline Bouvier in 1953. Nor was he the picture of physical vitality that his war-hero status and youthful handsomeness seemed to project. As a child he had almost died of scarlet fever, and he spent large portions of his early years in bed, suffering from one ailment after another. He developed severe back problems, made worse by his fighting experience in World

George Bundy put it, "The United States is the engine of mankind, and the rest of the world is the caboose." Kennedy's inaugural address suggested no halfway measures: "Let every nation know that we shall pay any price, bear any burden, meet any hardship, support any friend, oppose any foe to assure the survival and the success of liberty."

In reality, Kennedy in office would not be prepared to pay any price or bear any burden in the struggle against communism. He came to understand, sooner than many of his advisers, that there were limits to American power abroad; overall he showed himself to be cautious and pragmatic in foreign policy. More than his predecessor, he proved willing to initiate dialogue with the Soviets, sometimes using his brother Robert as a secret back channel to Moscow. Yet Kennedy also sought victory in the Cold War. After Soviet leader Nikita Khrushchev endorsed "wars of national liberation," such as the one in Vietnam, Kennedy called for "peaceful revolution" based on the concept of nation building. The administration set out to help developing nations through the early stages of nationhood with aid programs aimed at improving agriculture, transportation, and communications. Kennedy thus oversaw the creation of the multibillion-dollar Alliance for Progress in 1961 to spur economic development in Latin America. In the same year he also created the Peace Corps, dispatching thousands of American teachers, agricultural specialists, and health workers, many of them right out of college, to assist authorities in developing nations.

Nation Building in the Third World

Cynics then and later dismissed the Alliance and the Peace Corps as Cold War tools by which Kennedy sought to counter anti-Americanism and defeat communism in the developing world. The programs did have those aims, but both were also born of genuine humanitarianism. The Peace Corps in particular embodied both the idealistic, can-do spirit of the 1960s and Americans' long pursuit of moral leadership in the world. "More than any other entity," historian Elizabeth Cobbs Hoffman has written, "the Peace Corps broached an age-old dilemma of U.S. foreign policy: how to reconcile the imperatives and temptations of power politics with the ideals of freedom and self-determination for all nations."

It was one thing to broach the dilemma, and quite another to resolve it. Kennedy and his aides considered themselves to be supportive of social revolution in the Third World, but they could not imagine the legitimacy of communist involvement in any such uprising, or that developing countries might wish to be neutral in the East-West struggle. In addition to largely benevolent programs like the Peace Corps, therefore, the administration also relied on the more insidious concept of counterinsurgency to defeat revolutionaries who challenged pro-American Third World governments. American military and technical advisers trained native troops and police forces to quell unrest.

Nation building and counterinsurgency encountered numerous problems. The Alliance for Progress was only partly successful; infant mortality rates improved, but Latin American economies registered unimpressive growth rates, and class divisions continued to widen, exacerbating political unrest. Americans assumed that the U.S. model of capitalism and representative government could be transferred successfully to foreign cultures. But although many foreign peoples welcomed U.S. economic assistance and craved American material culture, they resented meddling by outsiders. And because aid was usually funneled through a self-interested elite, it often failed to reach the very poor. To people who preferred the relatively quick solutions of a managed economy, moreover, the American emphasis on private enterprise seemed inappropriate.

Nor did the new president have success in relations with the Soviet Union. A summit meeting with Soviet leader Nikita Khrushchev in Vienna in June 1961 went poorly, with the two leaders disagreeing over the preconditions for peace and stability in the world. Consequently, the administration's first year witnessed little movement on controlling the nuclear arms race or even on getting a superpower ban on testing nuclear weapons in the atmosphere or underground. The latter objective mattered a great deal to Kennedy, who saw a test ban as a prerequisite to preventing additional nations from getting the terrifying weapon. Instead, both superpowers continued testing and accelerated their arms production. In 1961 the U.S. military budget shot up 15 percent; by mid-1964, U.S. nuclear weapons had increased by 150 percent. Government advice to citizens to build fallout shelters in their backyards intensified public fear of devastating war.

Soviet-American Tensions

If war occurred, many believed it would be over the persistent problem of Berlin. In mid-1961 Khrushchev ratcheted up the tension by demanding an end to western occupation of West Berlin and a reunification of East and West Germany. Kennedy replied that the United States would stand by its commitment to West Berlin and West Germany. In August the Soviets, at the urging of the East German regime, erected a concrete and barbed-wire barricade across the divided city to halt the exodus of East Germans into the more prosperous and politically free West Berlin. The Berlin Wall inspired protests throughout the noncommunist world, but Kennedy privately sighed that "a wall is a hell of a lot better than a war." The ugly barrier shut off the flow of refugees, and the crisis passed.

Yet Kennedy knew that Khrushchev would continue to press for advantage in various parts of the globe. The president was particularly rankled by the growing Soviet assistance to the Cuban government of Fidel Castro. Kennedy once acknowledged that most American allies thought the United States had a "fixation" with Cuba; whether true of the country as a whole, he himself certainly did. The Eisenhower administration had contested the Cuban revolution and bequeathed to the Kennedy administration a partially developed CIA plan to overthrow Fidel Castro: CIA-trained Cuban exiles would land and secure a beachhead; the Cuban people would rise up against Castro and welcome a new government brought in from the United States.

Bay of Pigs Invasion

Kennedy approved the plan, and the attack took place on April 17, 1961, as twelve hundred exiles landed at the swampy Bay of Pigs in Cuba. But no discontented Cubans were there to greet them, only troops loyal to the Castro government. The invaders were quickly surrounded and captured. Kennedy had tried to keep the U.S. participation in the operation hidden—for this reason he refused to provide air cover for the attackers—but the CIA's role swiftly became public. Anti-American sentiment shot up throughout Latin America. Castro, concluding that the United States would not take defeat well and might launch another invasion, looked even more toward the Soviet Union for a military and economic lifeline.

Embarrassed by the Bay of Pigs fiasco, Kennedy vowed to bring Castro down. The CIA soon hatched a project called Operation Mongoose to disrupt the island's trade, support raids on Cuba from Miami, and plot to kill Castro. The agency's assassination schemes included providing Castro with cigars laced with explosives and deadly poison, and an attempt to harpoon him while he was snorkeling at a Caribbean resort. The United States also tightened its economic blockade and undertook military maneuvers in the Caribbean. The Joint Chiefs of Staff sketched plans to spark a rebellion in Cuba that would be followed by an invasion of U.S. troops. "If I had been in Moscow or Havana at that time," defense secretary Robert McNamara later remarked, "I would have believed the Americans were preparing for an invasion."

▲ The October 29 meeting of the "ExComm," or Executive Committee (the only meeting photographed). To President Kennedy's immediate right is Secretary of State Dean Rusk; to his left, in front of the Presidential Seal on the wall, is Secretary of Defense Robert McNamara. Presidential adviser Theodore Sorensen *(near side, third from right)* later wrote, "I saw first-hand how brutally physical and mental fatigue can numb the good sense as well as the senses of normally articulate men." *(John F. Kennedy Library)*

McNamara knew whereof he spoke, for both Castro and Khrushchev believed an invasion was coming. This

Cuban Missile Crisis

was one reason for the Soviet leader's risky decision in 1962 to secretly deploy nuclear missiles in Cuba: he hoped the presence of such weapons on the island would deter any attack. But Khrushchev also had other motives. Installing atomic weaponry in Cuba would instantly improve the Soviet position in the nuclear balance of power, he believed, and might also force Kennedy to resolve the German problem once and for all. Khrushchev still wanted to oust the West from Berlin, and he also worried that Washington might provide West Germany with nuclear weapons. What better way to prevent such a move than to put Soviet missiles just 90 miles off the coast of Florida? With Castro's support, Khrushchev moved to install the weapons. The world soon faced brinkmanship at its most frightening.

In mid-October 1962, a U-2 plane flying over Cuba photographed the missile sites. The president immediately organized a special Executive Committee (ExComm) of advisers to find a way to force the missiles and their nuclear warheads out of Cuba. Options that the ExComm considered ranged from full-scale invasion to limited bombing to quiet diplomacy. McNamara proposed the formula that the president ultimately accepted: a naval quarantine of Cuba.

Kennedy addressed the nation on television on October 22 and demanded that the Soviets retreat. U.S. warships began crisscrossing the Caribbean, while B-52s with nuclear bombs took to the skies. Khrushchev replied that the missiles would be withdrawn if the United States pledged never to attack Cuba. And he added that American Jupiter missiles aimed at the Soviet Union must be removed from Turkey. Edgy advisers predicted war, and for several days the world teetered on the brink of disaster. Then, on October 28, came a compromise. The United States promised not to invade Cuba, secretly pledging to withdraw the Jupiters from Turkey in exchange for the withdrawal of Soviet offensive forces from Cuba. Fearing accidents or some provocative action by Castro that might start a "real fire," Khrushchev decided to settle without consulting the Cubans. The missiles were removed from the island.

Many observers then and later called it Kennedy's finest hour. Tapes of the ExComm meetings recorded during the crisis reveal a deeply engaged, calmly authoritative commander-in-chief, committed to removing the missiles peacefully if possible. Critics claim that Kennedy helped cause the crisis in the first place with his anti-Cuban projects; some contend that quiet diplomacy could have achieved the same result, without the extraordinary tension. Other skeptics assert that Kennedy rejected a diplomatic solution because he feared the Republicans would ride the missiles to victory in the upcoming midterm elections. Still, it cannot be denied that the president handled the crisis skillfully, exercising both restraint and flexibility. At this most tense moment of the Cold War, Kennedy had proven equal to the task.

The Cuban missile crisis was a watershed in the Soviet-American relationship. Both Kennedy and Khrushchev acted with greater prudence in its aftermath, taking determined steps toward improved bilateral relations. Much of the hostility drained out of the relationship. In June 1963 Kennedy spoke in conciliatory terms during a commencement address at American University, urging cautious Soviet-American steps toward disarmament. In August the adversaries signed a treaty banning nuclear tests in the atmosphere, the oceans, and outer space. They also installed a coded wire-telegraph "hot line" staffed around the clock by translators and technicians, to allow near-instant communication between the capitals. Both sides refrained from further confrontation in Berlin.

Individually these steps were small, but together they reversed the trend of the previous years and began to build much-needed mutual trust. One could even argue that, by the autumn of 1963, the Cold War in Europe was drawing to a close. Both sides, it seemed, were prepared to accept the status quo of a divided continent and a fortified border. At the same time, though, the arms race continued and in some respects accelerated, and the superpower competition in the Third World showed little sign of cooling down.

MARCHING FOR FREEDOM

From the beginning of his presidency, John Kennedy believed that the Cold War was the most important issue facing the American people. But in the early 1960s, young civil rights activists seized the national stage and demanded that the force of the federal government be mobilized behind them. They won victories in their struggle for racial justice, but their gains were paid for in blood.

The Woolworth's lunch counter sit-in begun by the four freshmen from North Carolina A&T marked a turn-

Students and the Movement

ing point in the African American struggle for civil rights. In 1960, six years after the *Brown* decision had declared "separate but equal" unconstitutional, only 10 percent of southern public schools had begun desegregation. Fewer than one in four adult black Americans in the South had access to the voting booth, and water fountains in public places were still labeled "White Only" and "Colored Only." But one year after the young men had sat down at the all-white lunch counter in Greensboro, more than seventy thousand Americans—most of them college students—had participated in the sit-in movement. City by city, they challenged Jim Crow segregation at lunch counters in the South and protested at the northern branches of national chains that practiced segregation in their southern stores.

The young people who created the Student Nonviolent Coordinating Committee (SNCC) in the spring of 1960 to help coordinate the sit-in movement were, like Martin Luther King Jr., committed to nonviolence. In the years to come, SNCC stalwarts—including lifelong activist Diane Nash; future NAACP chair Julian Bond; future Washington, D.C., mayor Marion Barry; and future member of the U.S. House of Representatives John Lewis—would risk their lives in the struggle for social justice.

On May 4, 1961, thirteen members of the Congress of Racial Equality (CORE), a nonviolent civil rights or-

Freedom Rides and Voter Registration

ganization formed during World War II, purchased bus tickets in Washington, D.C., for a 1,500-mile trip through the South to New Orleans. This racially integrated group, calling themselves Freedom Riders, meant to demonstrate that, despite Supreme Court rulings ordering the desegregation of interstate buses and bus stations, Jim Crow still ruled in the South. These men and women knew they were risking their lives, and some suffered injuries from which they never recovered. One bus was firebombed outside Anniston, Alabama. Riders were badly beaten in Birmingham. In Montgomery, after reinforcements replaced the injured, a mob of more than a thousand whites attacked riders on another bus with baseball bats and steel bars. Police were nowhere to be seen; Montgomery's police commissioner declared, "We have no intention of standing guard for a bunch of troublemakers coming into our city."

News of the violent attacks made headlines around the world. In the Soviet Union, commentators pointed out the "savage nature of American freedom and democracy." One southern business leader, in Tokyo to promote Birmingham as a site for international business development, saw Japanese interest evaporate when photographs of the Birmingham attacks appeared in Tokyo newspapers.

In America, the violence—reported by the national news media—forced many to confront the reality of racial discrimination and hatred in their nation. Middle- and upper-class white southerners had participated in the

"massive resistance" to integration following the *Brown* decision, and many white southerners, even racial moderates, remained highly suspicious of interference by the "Yankee" federal government almost a century after the Civil War. The Freedom Rides made some think differently. The *Atlanta Journal* editorialized: "[I]t is time for the decent people . . . to muzzle the jackals." The national and international outcry pushed a reluctant President Kennedy to act. In a direct challenge to southern doctrines of states' rights, Kennedy sent federal marshals to Alabama to safeguard the Freedom Riders and their supporters. At the same time, bowing to white southern pressure, he allowed the Freedom Riders to be arrested in Mississippi.

While some activists pursued these "direct action" tactics, others worked to build black political power in the South. Beginning in 1961, thousands of SNCC volunteers, many of them high school and college students, risked their lives walking the dusty back roads of Mississippi and Georgia, encouraging African Americans to register to vote. Some SNCC volunteers were white, and some were from the North, but many were black southerners, and many were from low-income families. These volunteers understood from experience how racism, powerlessness, and poverty intersected in the lives of African Americans.

President Kennedy was generally sympathetic— though not terribly committed—to the civil rights move-

Kennedy and Civil Rights

ment, and he realized that racial oppression hurt the United States in the Cold War struggle for international opinion. However, like Franklin D. Roosevelt, he also understood that, if he alienated conservative southern Democrats in Congress, his legislative programs would founder. Thus he appointed five die-hard segregationists to the federal bench in the Deep South and delayed issuing an executive order forbidding segregation in federally subsidized housing (a pledge made in the 1960 campaign) until late 1962. Furthermore, he allowed FBI director J. Edgar Hoover to harass Martin Luther King and other civil rights leaders, using wiretaps and surveillance to gather personal information and circulating rumors of communist connections and of personal improprieties in efforts to discredit their leadership.

But grassroots civil rights activism—and the violence of white mobs—relentlessly forced Kennedy's hand. In September 1962, the president ordered 500 U.S. marshals to protect James Meredith, the first African American student to attend the University of Mississippi. In response, thousands of whites attacked the marshals with guns, gasoline bombs, bricks, and pipes. The mob killed two men and seriously wounded 160 federal marshals. The marshals did not back down, nor did James Meredith. He broke the color line at "Ole Miss."

In 1961 the Freedom Riders had captured the attention of the nation and the larger Cold War world, and forced the hand of the president. Martin Luther King Jr., having risen through the Montgomery bus boycott to leadership in the movement, understood the implications of these events. He and his allies, still committed to principles of nonviolence, concluded that the only way to move to the next stage of the struggle for civil rights was to provoke a crisis that would attract national and international attention, and create pressure for further change. King and his Southern Christian Leadership Conference (SCLC) began to plan a 1963 campaign in the most violently racist city in America: Birmingham, Alabama. Fully aware that their nonviolent protests would draw violent response, they called their plan Project C—for "confrontation." King wanted all Americans to see the racist hate and violence that marred their nation.

Birmingham and the Children's Crusade

Through most of April 1963, nonviolent protests in Birmingham led to hundreds of arrests. Then, on May 2, in a highly controversial action, King and the parents of Birmingham raised the stakes. They put children, some as young as six, on the front lines of protest. As about a thousand black children marched for civil rights, police commissioner Eugene "Bull" Connor ordered his police to train "monitor" water guns—powerful enough to strip bark from a tree at 100 feet—on them. The water guns mowed the children down, and then police loosed attack dogs. It was all captured on television, as the nation watched in horror. President Kennedy, once again, was pushed into action. He demanded that Birmingham's white business and political elite negotiate a settlement. Under pressure, they agreed. The Birmingham movement had won a concrete victory. Even more, activists had pushed civil rights to the fore of President Kennedy's political agenda.

The Kennedy administration also confronted the defiant governor of Alabama, George C. Wallace. On June 11, Wallace fulfilled a promise to "bar the schoolhouse door" himself to prevent the desegregation of the University of Alabama. Hearing echoes of Wallace's January 1963 inaugural pledge "Segregation now, segregation tomorrow, segregation forever!" and facing a nation rocked by hundreds of civil rights protests, many of them met with white mob violence, Kennedy committed the power of the federal government to guarantee racial justice—even over the opposition of individual states. The next evening, June 12,

"Segregation Forever!"

in a televised address, Kennedy told the American people, "Now the time has come for this nation to fulfill its promise." A few hours later, thirty-seven-year-old civil rights leader Medgar Evers was murdered—in front of his children—in his driveway in Jackson, Mississippi. The next week, the president asked Congress to pass a comprehensive civil rights bill that would end legal discrimination on the basis of race in the entire United States.

On August 28, 1963, a quarter-million Americans gathered in the steamy heat on the Washington Mall. They came from all over America to show Congress their support for Kennedy's civil rights bill; many also wanted federal action to guarantee work opportunities. Behind the scenes, organizers from the major civil rights groups—SCLC, CORE, SNCC, the NAACP, the Urban League, and A. Philip Randolph's Brotherhood of Sleeping Car Porters—grappled with growing tensions within the movement. SNCC activists saw Kennedy's proposed legislation as too little, too late, and wanted radical action. King and other older leaders counseled the virtues of moderation. The movement was beginning to splinter.

March on Washington

Those divisions were not completely hidden. SNCC's John Lewis told the assembled crowd that SNCC members had come to the march "with a great sense of misgiving" and asked, "Where is the political party that will make it unnecessary to march on Washington?" What most Americans saw, however, was a celebration of unity. Black and white celebrities joined hands; folk singers sang songs of freedom. Television networks cut away from afternoon soap operas as Martin Luther King Jr., in southern-preacher cadences, prophesied a day when "all God's children, black men and white men, Jews and Gentiles, Protestants and Catholics, will be able to join hands and sing in the words of the old Negro spiritual, 'Free at last! Free at last! Thank God Almighty, we are free at last!'" The 1963 March on Washington for Jobs and Freedom was a moment of triumph, powerfully demonstrating to the nation the determination of its African American citizens to secure equality and justice. But the struggle was far from over. Just days later, white supremacists bombed the Sixteenth Street Baptist Church in Birmingham, killing four black girls.

In the face of violence, the struggle for racial justice continued. During the summer of 1964, more than one thousand white students joined the voter mobilization project in Mississippi. These workers formed Freedom Schools, teaching literacy

Freedom Summer

A historic moment for the civil rights movement was the March on Washington of August 28, 1963. The Reverend Martin Luther King Jr. *(center)* joined a quarter-million black people and white people in their march for racial equality. Addressing civil rights supporters, and the nation, from the steps of the Lincoln Memorial, King delivered his "I Have a Dream" speech.

(R. W. Kelley, Life *magazine © Time, Inc.)*

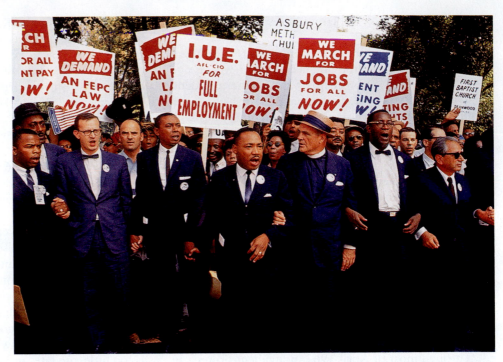

and constitutional rights, and helped organize the Mississippi Freedom Democratic Party as an alternative to the regular, white-only Democratic Party. Key SNCC organizers also believed that large numbers of white volunteers would focus national attention on Mississippi repression and violence. Not all went smoothly: local black activists were sometimes frustrated when well-educated white volunteers stepped into decision-making roles, and tensions over interracial sexual relationships complicated an already difficult situation. Far worse, project workers were arrested over a thousand times and were shot at, bombed, and beaten. On June 21, local black activist James Cheney and two white volunteers, Michael Schwerner and Andrew Goodman, were murdered by a Klan mob. Four days later, before their bodies had been found, Walter Cronkite told the nightly news audience that all of America was watching Mississippi. CBS played footage of black and white workers holding hands, singing "We Shall Overcome." That summer, black and white activists risked their lives together, challenging the racial caste system of the Deep South.

LIBERALISM AND THE GREAT SOCIETY

By 1963, with civil rights at the top of his domestic agenda, Kennedy seemed to be taking a new path. Campaigning in 1960, he had promised to lead Americans into a "New Frontier," a society in which the federal government would work to eradicate poverty, restore the nation's cities, guarantee healthcare to the elderly, and provide decent schools for all America's children. But few of Kennedy's domestic initiatives were passed into law, in part because Kennedy

did not use his political capital to support them. Lacking a popular mandate in the 1960 election, fearful of alienating southern Democrats in Congress, and without a strong vision of domestic reform, Kennedy let his administration's social policy agenda languish.

Instead, Kennedy focused on less controversial attempts to fine-tune the American economy, believing that continued economic growth and prosperity would solve America's social problems. Kennedy's vision was perhaps best realized in America's space program. As the Soviets drew ahead in the Cold War space race, Kennedy vowed in 1961 to put a man on the moon before decade's end. With billions in new funding, the National Aeronautics and Space Administration (NASA) began the Apollo program. And in February 1962, astronaut John Glenn orbited the earth in the space capsule *Friendship 7*.

The nation would not learn what sort of president John Kennedy might have become. On November 22, 1963, Kennedy visited Texas, the

Kennedy Assassination

home state of his vice president, Lyndon Johnson. In Dallas, riding with his wife, Jackie, in an open-top limousine, Kennedy was cheered by thousands of people lining the motorcade's route. Suddenly shots rang out. The president crumpled, shot in the head. Tears ran down the cheeks of CBS anchorman Walter Cronkite as he told the nation their president was dead. The word spread quickly, in whispered messages to classroom teachers, by somber announcements in factories and offices, through the stunned faces of people on the street.

That same day police captured a suspect: Lee Harvey Oswald, a former U.S. marine (dishonorably discharged) who had once attempted to gain Soviet citizenship. Just two days later, in full view of millions of TV viewers, Oswald himself was shot dead by shady nightclub owner Jack Ruby. Americans, already in shock, were baffled. What was Ruby's motive? Was he silencing Oswald to prevent him from implicating others? The seven-member Warren Commission, headed by U.S. Supreme Court Chief Justice Earl Warren, concluded that Oswald had acted alone. But debates still rage over whether Oswald was a lone assassin or part of a larger conspiracy.

For four days the tragedy played uninterrupted on American television. Millions of Americans watched their president's funeral: the brave young widow behind a black veil; a riderless horse; three-year-old "John-John" saluting his father's casket. In one awful moment in Dallas, the reality of the Kennedy presidency had been transformed into myth, the man into martyr. People would

remember Kennedy less for any specific accomplishment than for his youthful enthusiasm, his inspirational rhetoric, and the romance he brought to American political life. In a peculiar way, he accomplished more in death than in life. In the postassassination atmosphere of grief and remorse, Lyndon Johnson, sworn in as president aboard *Air Force One,* invoked Kennedy's memory to push through the most ambitious program of legislation since the New Deal.

The new president was a big and passionate man, different from his predecessor in almost every respect. While

Johnson and the Great Society

Kennedy had been raised to wealth and privilege and was educated at Harvard, Johnson had grown up in modest circumstances in the Texas hill country and was graduated from Southwest Texas State Teachers' College. He was as earthy as Kennedy was elegant, prone to colorful curses and willing to use his physical size to his advantage. Advisers and aides reported that he expected them to follow him into the bathroom and conduct business while he showered or used the toilet. But Johnson had been in

▲ Poverty in America was not only an urban problem, and President Johnson visited poverty-stricken areas throughout the nation during the summer of 1964. Here he talks with the Marlow family of Rocky Mount, North Carolina, on the steps of their farmhouse. *(© Bettmann/Corbis)*

national politics most of his adult life. He filled an empty congressional seat from Texas in 1937, and as Senate majority leader from 1954 to 1960, he had learned how to manipulate people and wield power to achieve his ends. Now, as president, he used these political skills in an attempt to unite and reassure the nation. "Let us here highly resolve," he told a joint session of Congress five days after the assassination, "that John Fitzgerald Kennedy did not live—or die—in vain."

Johnson, a liberal in the style of Franklin D. Roosevelt, believed that the federal government must work actively to improve the lives of Americans. In a 1964 commencement address at the University of Michigan, he described his vision of a nation built on "abundance and liberty for all . . . demand[ing] an end to poverty and racial injustice . . . where every child can find knowledge to enrich his mind and to enlarge his talents . . . where every man can renew contact with nature . . . where men are more concerned with the quality of their goals than the quantity of their goods." Johnson called this vision "The Great Society."

Johnson made civil rights his top legislative priority, and in July he signed into law the Civil Rights Act of 1964. This legislation ended *legal*

Civil Rights Act

discrimination on the basis of race, color, religion, national origin, in federal programs, voting, employment, and public accommodation; sex discrimination in employment was also banned. The original bill did not include sex discrimination; that provision was introduced by a southern congressman who hoped it would engender so much opposition that the bill as a whole would fail. However, when a bipartisan group of women members of the House of Representatives took up the cause, the bill was passed—with sex as a protected category. Significantly, the Civil Rights Act of 1964 created mechanisms for enforcement, giving the government authority to withhold federal funds from public agencies or federal contractors that discriminated and establishing the Equal Employment Opportunity Commission (EEOC) to investigate and judge claims of job discrimination. However, the EEOC paid little attention to sex discrimination, and in response, in 1966 supporters of women's equality formed the National Organization for Women (NOW). It would be one element in a broad movement for women's rights and equality that would take off in the next decade (see page 895).

Many Americans did not believe that it was the federal government's job to end racial discrimination or to fight poverty. Many white southerners, especially, resented federal intervention in what they considered local customs.

And throughout the nation, millions of conservative Americans believed that since the New Deal the federal government had been overstepping its constitutional boundaries. They sought a return to local control and states' rights in the face of growing federal power. In the 1964 election, this conservative vision was championed by the Republican candidate, Arizona senator Barry Goldwater.

Goldwater had not only voted against the 1964 Civil Rights Act; he also opposed the national Social Security system. Like many conservatives,

Election of 1964

he believed that individual *liberty,* not equality, was the most important American value. Goldwater also believed that the United States needed a more powerful national military to fight communism; in campaign speeches he suggested that the United States should use tactical nuclear weapons against its enemies. "Extremism in the defense of liberty is no vice," he told delegates at the 1964 Republican National Convention.

Goldwater's campaign slogan, "In your heart you know he's right," was turned against him by Lyndon Johnson supporters: "In your heart you know he's right . . . far right," one punned. Another version warned of Goldwater's willingness to use nuclear weapons: "In your heart you know he might." Johnson campaigned on his record, with an unemployment rate under 4 percent and economic growth at better than 6 percent. But he knew that his support of civil rights had broken apart the New Deal coalition. Shortly after signing the Civil Rights Act of 1964, he told an aide, "I think we just delivered the south to the Republican Party for my lifetime and yours."

The tension between Johnson's support of civil rights and his need for southern Democratic support came to a head at the 1964 Democratic National Convention. Two delegations had arrived from Mississippi, each demanding to be seated. The Democratic Party's official delegation was exclusively white; the Mississippi Freedom Democratic Party (MFDP) sent a racially mixed delegation to represent a state in which discriminatory literacy tests and violence disenfranchised its black citizens. The white representatives from southern states threatened to stage a public walkout if the MFDP delegates were seated. MFDP delegate Fannie Lou Hamer offered powerful testimony to the convention's credentials committee, concluding, "[If] the Freedom Party is not seated now, I question America." Johnson tried to engineer a compromise, but the MFDP had no interest in political deals. "We didn't come all this way for no two seats," Hamer said, and the delegation walked out.

Johnson lost the MFDP, and he also lost the Deep South—the first Democrat since the Civil War to do so. Yet

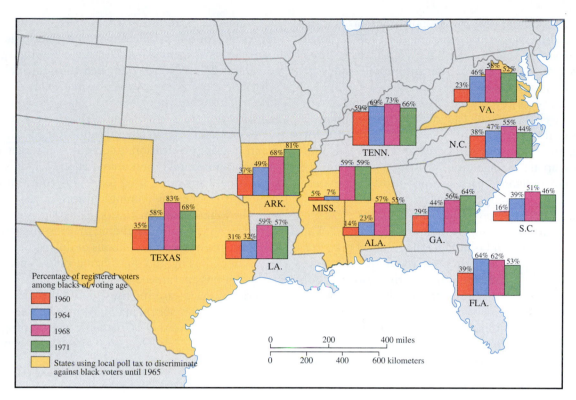

Map 30.1   African American Voting Rights, 1960–1971

After passage of the 1965 Voting Rights Act, African American registration skyrocketed in Mississippi and Alabama, and rose substantially in other southern states.

(Source: *Harold W. Stanley,* Voter Mobilization and the Politics of Race: The South and Universal Suffrage, 1952–1984. *Praeger Publishers, p. 97. Copyright © 1987 by Greenwood Publishing Group. Reproduced with permission of Greenwood Publishing Group, Inc., Westport, CT.)*

he won the election by a landslide, and American voters also gave him the most liberal Congress in American history. With the mandate provided by a record 61.1 percent of the popular vote, Johnson launched his Great Society. Congress responded to Johnson's election with the most sweeping reform legislation since 1935.

Civil rights remained a critical issue. In late 1964, the SCLC put voting rights at the top of its agenda. Martin Luther King Jr. and other leaders turned to Selma, Alabama—a town with a history of vicious response to civil rights protest—seeking another public confrontation that would mobilize national support and federal action. That confrontation came on March 6, when state troopers turned electric cattle prods, chains, and tear gas against peaceful marchers as they crossed the Edmund Pettus Bridge on the way to Montgomery. On March 15, the president addressed Congress and the nation, offering full support for a second monumental civil rights bill, the Voting

Rights Act. This act outlawed practices that had prevented most black citizens in the Deep South from voting and provided for federal oversight of elections in districts where there was evidence of past discrimination (see Map 30.1). Within two years, the percentage of African Americans registered to vote in Mississippi jumped from 7 percent to almost 60 percent. Black elected officials became increasingly common in southern states over the following decade.

Seeking to improve the quality of American life, the Johnson administration established new student loan and grant programs to help low- and moderate-income Americans attend college, and created the National Endowment for the Arts and the National Endowment for the Humanities. The Immigration Act of 1965 ended the racially based quotas that had shaped American immigration

Improving American Life

policy for decades. And Johnson supported important consumer protection legislation, including the 1966 National Traffic and Motor Vehicle Safety Act, which was inspired by Ralph Nader's exposé of the automobile industry, *Unsafe at Any Speed* (1965).

Environmentalists found an ally in the Johnson administration as well. First Lady Claudia Alta Taylor Johnson (known to all as "Lady Bird") successfully pushed for legislation to restrict the billboards and junkyards that had sprung up along the nation's new interstate highway system. Johnson signed "preservation" legislation to protect America's remaining wilderness and supported laws addressing environmental pollution.

At the heart of Johnson's Great Society was the War on Poverty. Johnson and other liberals believed that, in a time of great economic affluence, the nation had the resources for programs that could end "poverty, ignorance and hunger as intractable, permanent features of American society." Beginning in 1964, the Johnson administration passed more than a score of major legislative acts meant to do so (see Table 30.1).

War on Poverty

Johnson's goal, in his words, was "to offer the forgotten fifth of our people opportunity, not doles." Thus many new laws focused on increasing opportunity. Billions of federal dollars were channeled to municipalities and school districts to improve opportunities for the poverty-stricken, from preschoolers (Head Start) to high schoolers (Upward Bound) to young adults (Job Corps). The Model Cities program offered federal funds to upgrade employment, housing, education, and health in targeted urban neighborhoods, and Community Action Programs involved poor Americans in creating local grassroots antipoverty programs for their own communities.

The Johnson administration also tried to ensure basic economic safeguards, expanding the existing Food Stamp program and earmarking billions of dollars for constructing public housing and subsidizing rents. Two new federal programs guaranteed healthcare for specific groups of Americans: Medicare for those sixty-five and older, and Medicaid for the poor. Finally, Aid to Families with Dependent Children (AFDC), the basic welfare program created during the New Deal, expanded both benefits and eligibility.

TABLE 30.1	Great Society Achievements, 1964–1966		
	1964	**1965**	**1966**
Civil Rights	Civil Rights Act Equal Employment Commission Twenty-fourth Amendment	Voting Rights Act	
War on Poverty	Economic Opportunity Act Office of Economic Opportunity Job Corps Legal Services for the Poor VISTA		Model Cities
Education		Elementary and Secondary Education Act Head Start Upward Bound	
Environment		Water Quality Act Air Quality Act	Clean Water Restoration Act

New Government Agencies		Department of Housing and
		   Urban Development
		National Endowments for the
		   Arts and Humanities
			Department of
			   Transportation

Other		Medicare and Medicaid Immigration and Nationality Act	

The Great Society of the mid-1960s saw the biggest burst of reform legislation since the New Deal of the 1930s.

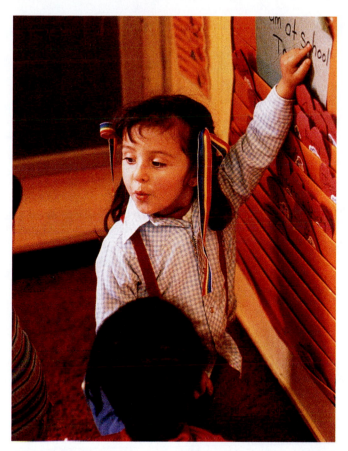

▲ This three-year-old Hispanic girl learns to read in a Head Start program. One of several programs established by the 1964 Economic Opportunity Act, Head Start prepared preschoolers from low-income families for grade school. *(E. Crews/The Image Works)*

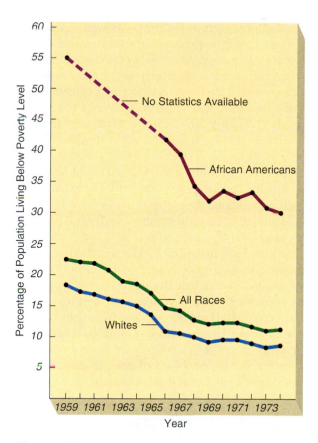

Figure 30.1   Poverty in America for Whites, African Americans, and All Races, 1959–1974

Because of rising levels of economic prosperity, combined with the impact of Great Society programs, the percentage of Americans living in poverty in 1974 was half as high as in 1959. African Americans still were far more likely than white Americans to be poor. In 1959 more than half of all blacks (55.1 percent) were poor; in 1974 the figure remained high (30.3 percent). The government did not record data on African American poverty for the years 1960 through 1965.

The War on Poverty was controversial from its beginnings. Leftists believed that the government was doing too little to change fundamental structural inequality. Conservatives argued that Great Society programs created dependency among America's poor. Policy analysts noted that specific programs were ill conceived and badly implemented. Even supporters acknowledged that programs were vastly underfunded and marred by political compromises. Responding to criticisms, Joseph Califano, one of the "generals" in the War on Poverty, claimed, "Whatever historians of the Great Society say twenty years later, they must admit we tried, and I believe they will conclude that America is a better place because we did."

Decades later, most historians judge the War on Poverty a mixed success. War on Poverty programs improved the quality of housing, healthcare, and nutrition available to the nation's poor. Between 1965 and 1970, federal spending for Social Security, healthcare, welfare, and education more than doubled, and the trend continued into the next decade. By 1975, for instance, the number of eligible Americans receiving food stamps had increased from 600,000 (in 1965) to 17 million. Poverty among the elderly fell from about 40 percent in 1960 to 16 percent in 1974, due largely to increased Social Security benefits and to Medicare. The War on Poverty undoubtedly improved the quality of life for many low-income Americans (see Figure 30.1).

But War on Poverty programs less successfully addressed the root causes of poverty. Neither the Job Corps nor Community Action Programs showed significant results. Economic growth, not Johnson administration policies, was primarily responsible for the dramatic decrease in government-measured poverty during the 1960s—from 22.4 percent of Americans in 1959 to 11 percent in 1973. And one structural determinant of poverty remained unchanged: 11 million Americans in female-headed households remained poor at the end of the decade—the same number as in 1963.

Political compromises that shaped Great Society programs also created long-term problems. For example, Congress accommodated the interests of doctors and hospitals in its Medicare legislation by allowing federal reimbursements of hospitals' "reasonable costs" and doctors' "reasonable charges" in treating elderly patients. With no incentives for doctors or hospitals to hold prices down, the cost of healthcare rose dramatically. National healthcare expenditures as a percentage of the gross national product rose by almost 44 percent from 1960 to 1971. Johnson's Great Society was not an unqualified success, but it was a moment in which many Americans believed they could solve the problems of poverty and disease and discrimination—and that it was necessary to try.

JOHNSON AND VIETNAM

Johnson's domestic ambitions were threatened from an early point by turmoil overseas. In foreign policy, he held firmly to ideas about U.S. superiority and the menace of communism. He saw the world in simple, bipolar terms— them against us—and he saw a lot of "them." But, mostly, he preferred not to see the world beyond America's shores at all. International affairs had never much interested him, and he had little appreciation for foreign cultures. Once, on a visit to Thailand while vice president, he flew into a rage when an aide gently advised him that the Thai people recoil from physical contact with strangers. Dammit, Johnson exploded, he shook hands with people everywhere, and they loved it. At the Taj Mahal in India, Johnson tested the monument's echo with a Texas cowboy yell. And on a trip to Senegal he ordered that an American bed, a special showerhead, and cases of Cutty Sark be sent along with him. "Foreigners," Johnson quipped early in his administration, only half-jokingly, "are not like the folks I am used to."

Yet Johnson knew from the start that foreign policy, especially regarding Vietnam, would demand a good deal of his attention. Since the late 1950s, hostilities in Vietnam had increased, as Ho Chi Minh's North assisted the Vietcong guerrillas in the South to advance the reunifica-

Kennedy's Legacy in Vietnam

tion of the country under a communist government. President Kennedy had stepped up aid dollars to the Diem regime in Saigon, increased the airdropping of raiding teams into North Vietnam, and launched crop destruction by herbicides to starve the Vietcong and expose their hiding places. Kennedy also strengthened the U.S. military presence in South Vietnam, to the point that by 1963 more than sixteen thousand military advisers were in the country, some authorized to take part in combat alongside the U.S.-equipped Army of the Republic of Vietnam (ARVN).

Meanwhile, opposition to Diem's repressive regime increased, and not just by communists. Peasants objected to programs that removed them from their villages for their own safety, and Buddhist monks, protesting the Roman Catholic Diem's religious persecution, poured gasoline over their robes and ignited themselves in the streets of Saigon. Although Diem was personally honest, he countenanced corruption in his government and concentrated power in the hands of family and friends. He jailed critics to silence them. Eventually U.S. officials, with Kennedy's approval, encouraged ambitious South Vietnamese generals to remove Diem. On November 1, 1963, the generals struck, murdering Diem. Just a few weeks later, Kennedy himself was assassinated.

The timing of Kennedy's murder ensured that Vietnam would be the most controversial aspect of his legacy. Just what would have happened in Southeast Asia had Kennedy returned from Texas alive can never be known, of course, and the speculation is made more difficult by his contradictory record on the conflict. He expanded U.S. involvement and approved a coup against Diem, but despite the urgings of top advisers he refused to commit American ground forces to the struggle. Over time he became increasingly skeptical about South Vietnam's prospects and hinted that he would end the American commitment after winning reelection in 1964. Some authors have gone further and argued that he was ending U.S. involvement even at the time of his death, but the evidence for this claim is thin. More likely, Kennedy arrived in Dallas that fateful day still uncertain about how to solve the Vietnam problem, postponing the truly difficult choices until later.

Lyndon Johnson viewed his Vietnam options through the lens of the impending 1964 election. He wanted to do nothing that could complicate his aim of winning the presidency in his own right, and that meant keeping Vietnam on the back burner. Yet Johnson also sought victory, or at least that he would not lose the war, which in practice amounted to the same thing. As a result, throughout 1964 the administration secretly laid

Tonkin Gulf Incident and Resolution

Map 30.2   Southeast Asia and the Vietnam War

To prevent communists from coming to power in Vietnam, Cambodia, and Laos in the 1960s, the United States intervened massively in Southeast Asia. The interventions failed, and the remaining American troops made a hasty exit from Vietnam in 1975, when the victorious Vietcong and North Vietnamese took Saigon and renamed it Ho Chi Minh City.

plans to expand the war to North Vietnam and never seriously considered negotiating a settlement.

In early August 1964, an incident in the Gulf of Tonkin, off the coast of North Vietnam, drew Johnson's involvement (see Map 30.2). Twice in three days, U.S. destroyers reported coming under attack from North Vietnamese patrol boats. Despite a lack of evidence that the second attack occurred, Johnson ordered retaliatory air strikes against selected North Vietnamese patrol boat bases and an oil depot. He also directed aides to rework a long-existing congressional resolution on the use of force. By a vote of 416 to 0 in the House and 88 to 2 in the Senate, Congress quickly passed the Gulf of Tonkin Resolution, which gave the president the authority to "take all necessary measures to repel any armed attack against the forces of the United States and to prevent further aggression." In so doing, Congress essentially surrendered its warmaking powers to the executive branch. The resolution, Secretary of Defense McNamara later noted, served "to open the floodgates."

President Johnson, delighted with the broad authority the resolution gave him, used a different metaphor. "Like grandma's nightshirt," he quipped, "it covered everything." He also appreciated what the Gulf of Tonkin affair did for his political standing—his public approval ratings went up dramatically, and his show of force effectively removed Vietnam as a campaign issue for GOP presidential nominee Barry Goldwater. On the ground in South Vietnam, however, the outlook remained grim in the final weeks of 1964, as the Vietcong continued to make gains. U.S. officials responded by laying secret plans for an escalation of American involvement.

Decision for Escalation

In February 1965, in response to Vietcong attacks on American installations in South Vietnam which killed thirty-two Americans, Johnson ordered Operation Rolling Thunder, a bombing program planned the previous fall, which continued, more or less uninterrupted, until October 1968. Then, on March 8, the first U.S. combat battalions came ashore near Danang. The North Vietnamese, however, would not give up. They hid in shelters and rebuilt roads and bridges with a perseverance that frustrated and awed American decision makers. They also increased infiltration into the South. In Saigon, meanwhile, coups and countercoups by self-serving military leaders undermined U.S. efforts to turn the war effort around. "I don't think we ought to take this government seriously," Ambassador Henry Cabot Lodge told a White House meeting. "There is simply no one who can do anything."

In July 1965, Johnson convened a series of high-level discussions about U.S. policy in the war. Although these

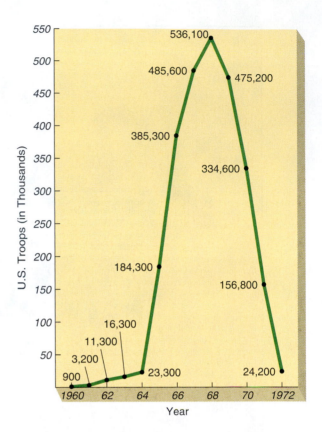

Figure 30.2   **U.S. Troops in Vietnam, 1960–1972**

These numbers show the Americanization of the Vietnam War under President Johnson, who ordered vast increases in troop levels. President Nixon reversed the escalation, so that by the time of the cease-fire in early 1973 fewer than 25,000 American troops remained in Vietnam. Data are for December 31 of each year. *(Source: U.S. Department of Defense.)*

deliberations had about them the character of a charade—Johnson wanted history to record that he agonized over a choice he had in fact already made—they did confirm that the American commitment would be more or less open-ended. On July 28, Johnson publicly announced a significant troop increase, disclosing that others would follow. By the end of 1965, more than 180,000 U.S. ground troops were in South Vietnam. In 1966 the figure climbed to 385,000. In 1967 alone, U.S. warplanes flew 108,000 sorties and dropped 226,000 tons of bombs on North Vietnam. In 1968 U.S. troop strength reached 536,100 (see Figure 30.2). Each American escalation brought not victory, but a new North Vietnamese escalation. The Soviet Union and China responded to the stepped-up U.S. involvement by increasing their material assistance to the Hanoi government.

The initiation of Rolling Thunder and the U.S. troop commitment "Americanized" the war. What could have been seen as a civil war between North and South, or a war of national reunification, was now clearly an American war against the communist Hanoi government.

Opposition to Americanization

This "Americanization" of the war in Vietnam came despite deep misgivings on the part of influential and informed voices at home and abroad. In the key months of decision, Democratic leaders in the Senate, major newspapers such as the *New York Times* and the *Wall Street Journal*, and prominent columnists like Walter Lippmann warned against deepening involvement. So did some within the administration, including Vice President Hubert H. Humphrey and Undersecretary of State George W. Ball. Abroad, virtually all of America's allies—including France, Britain, Canada, and Japan—cautioned against escalation and urged a political settlement, on the grounds that no military solution favorable to the United States was possible. Remarkably, top U.S. officials themselves shared this deep pessimism. Most of them knew that the odds of success were small. They certainly hoped that the new measures would cause Hanoi to end the insurgency in the South, but it cannot be said they were confident.

Why, then, did America's leaders choose war? At stake was "credibility." They feared that, if the United States failed to prevail in Vietnam, friends and foes around the world would find American power less credible. The Soviets and Chinese would be emboldened to challenge U.S. interests elsewhere in the world, and allied governments might conclude that they could not depend on Washington. For at least some key players, too, including the president himself, domestic political credibility and personal credibility were also on the line. Johnson worried that failure in Vietnam would harm his domestic agenda; even more, he feared the personal humiliation that he imagined would inevitably accompany a defeat—and for him, a negotiated withdrawal constituted defeat. As for the stated objective of helping a South Vietnamese ally repulse external aggression, that, too, figured into the equation, but not as much as it would have had the Saigon government—racked with infighting among senior leaders and possessing little popular support—done more to assist in its own defense.

Even as Johnson Americanized the Vietnam War, he sought to keep the publicity surrounding the action as low as possible. Thus he rejected the Joint Chiefs' view that U.S. reserve forces should be mobilized and a national emergency declared. This decision not to call up reserve

American Soldiers in Vietnam

units had a momentous impact on the makeup of the American fighting force sent to Vietnam. It forced the military establishment to rely more heavily on the draft, which in turn meant that Vietnam became a young man's war—the average age of soldiers was twenty-two, as compared with twenty-six in World War II. It also became a war of the poor and the working class. Through the years of heavy escalation (1965–1968), college students could get deferments, as could teachers and engineers. (In 1969 the draft was changed so that some students were called up through a lottery system.) The poorest and least educated young men were less likely to be able to avoid the draft and also more likely to volunteer. The armed services recruited hard in poor communities, many of them heavily African American and Latino, advertising the military as an avenue of training and advancement; very often, the pitch worked. Once in uniform, those with fewer skills were far more likely to see combat, and hence to die.

Infantrymen on maneuvers carried heavy rucksacks into thick jungle growth, where every step was precarious. Booby traps and land mines were a constant threat. Insects swarmed, and leeches sucked at weary bodies. Boots and human skin rotted from the rains, which alternated with withering suns. "It was as if the sun and the land itself were in league with the Vietcong," recalled marine officer Philip Caputo in *A Rumor of War* (1977), "wearing us down, driving us mad, killing us." The enemy, meanwhile, was hard to find, often burrowed into elaborate underground tunnels or melded into the population, where any Vietnamese might be a Vietcong.

The American forces fought well, and their entry into the conflict in 1965 helped stave off a South Vietnamese defeat. In that sense, Americanization achieved its most immediate and basic objective. But if the stepped-up fighting that year demonstrated to Hanoi leaders that the war would not swiftly be won, it also showed the same thing to their counterparts in Washington. As the North Vietnamese matched each American escalation with one of their own, the war became a stalemate. The U.S. commander, General William Westmoreland, proved mistaken in his belief that a strategy of attrition represented the key to victory—the enemy had a seemingly endless supply of recruits to throw into battle. Under Westmoreland's strategy, the measure of success became the "body count"—that is, the number of North Vietnamese and Vietcong corpses found after battle. From the start, the counts were subject to manipulation by officers eager to convince superiors of the success of an operation. Worse, the American reliance on massive military and other technology—including carpet bombing, napalm (jellied gasoline), and crop defoliants that destroyed entire forests—alienated many South Vietnamese and brought new recruits to the Vietcong.

▲ **Wounded American soldiers after a battle in Vietnam.** *(Larry Burrows/*Life *magazine © Time Warner, Inc.)*

Increasingly, Americans divided into those who supported the war and those who did not. As television coverage brought the war—its body counts and body bags, its burned villages and weeping refugees—into homes every night, the number of opponents grew. On college campuses, professors and students organized debates and lectures on American policy. Sometimes going around the clock, these intense public discussions became a form of protest, called "teach-ins" after the sit-ins of the civil rights movement. The big campus and street demonstrations were still to come, but pacifist groups, such as the American Friends Service Committee and the Women's International League for Peace and Freedom, organized early protests.

In early 1966 Senator William Fulbright held televised public hearings on whether the national interest was being served by pursuing the war. What exactly was the threat? senators asked. To the surprise of some, George F. Kennan testified that his containment doctrine was meant for Europe, not the volatile environment of Southeast Asia. America's "preoccupation" with Vietnam, Kennan asserted, was undermining its global obligations. Whether many minds were changed by the Fulbright hearings is hard to say, but they constituted the first in-depth national discussion of the U.S. commitment in Vietnam. They provoked Americans to think about the conflict and the nation's role in it. No longer could anyone doubt that there were deep divisions on Vietnam among public officials, or that two of them, Lyndon Johnson and William Fulbright, had broken completely over the war.

Defense secretary Robert McNamara, who despite private misgivings championed the Americanization of the war in 1965, became increasingly troubled by the killing and destructiveness of the bombing. Already in November 1965 he expressed skepticism that victory could ever be achieved, and in the months thereafter he agonized over how the United States looked in the eyes of the world. American credibility, far from being protected by the staunch commitment to the war, was suffering grievous damage, McNamara feared. "The picture of the world's greatest superpower killing or seriously injuring 1,000 noncombatants a week, while trying to pound a tiny backward nation into submission on an issue whose merits are hotly disputed, is not a pretty one," he told Johnson in mid-1967.

But Johnson was in no mood to listen or reconsider. Determined to prevail in Vietnam, he dug in, snapping at

Divisions at Home

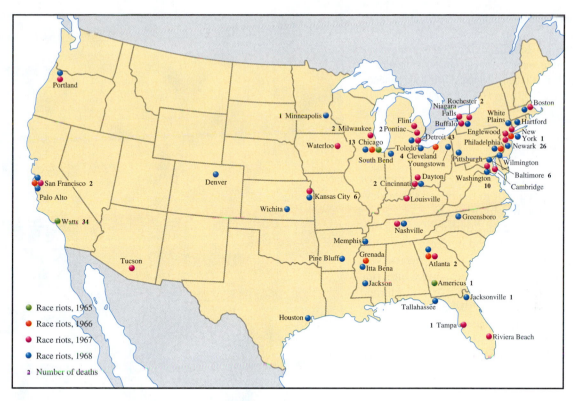

Map 30.3   Race Riots, 1965–1968
The first major race riot of the 1960s exploded in the Los Angeles neighborhood of Watts in 1965. The bloodiest riots of 1967 were in Newark, New Jersey, and Detroit. Scores of riots erupted in the aftermath of Martin Luther King Jr.'s assassination in 1968.

"those little shits on the campuses." Although on occasion he halted the bombing to encourage Ho Chi Minh to negotiate (on America's terms), and to disarm critics, such pauses often were accompanied by increases in American troop strength. And the United States sometimes resumed or accelerated the bombing just when a diplomatic breakthrough seemed possible. Hanoi demanded a complete suspension of bombing raids before sitting down at the conference table. And Ho could not accept American terms, which amounted to abandonment of his lifelong dream of an independent, unified Vietnam.

A NATION DIVIDED

As Johnson struggled to overcome an implacable foe in Vietnam, his liberal vision of a Great Society faced challenges at home. The divisions among Americans over policy in Vietnam were only one fissure in a society that was fracturing along many different lines: black and white, youth and age, radical and conservative.

Even as the civil rights movement was winning important victories in the mid-1960s, many African Ameri-

Urban Unrest

cans had given up on the promise of liberal reform. In 1964, shortly after President Johnson signed the landmark Civil Rights Act, racial violence erupted in northern cities. Angry residents of Harlem took to the streets after a white police officer shot a black teenager. The following summer, in the predominantly black Watts section of Los Angeles, crowds burned, looted, and battled police for five days and nights. The riot, which began when a white police officer attempted to arrest a black resident on suspicion of drunken driving, left thirty-four dead and more than one thousand injured. In July 1967, twenty-six people were killed in street battles between African Americans and police and army troops in Newark, New Jersey. A week later, in Detroit, forty-three died as 3 square miles of the city went up in flames. In 1967 alone, there were 167 violent outbreaks in 128 cities (see Map 30.3).

The "long, hot summers" of urban unrest in the 1960s differed from almost all previous race riots. Past riots were typically started by whites. Here, black residents exploded in anger and frustration over the conditions of their

During award ceremonies at the 1968 Olympic Games in Mexico City, American sprinters Tommie Smith *(center)* and John Carlos *(right)* extend gloved hands skyward to protest racial inequality and express Black Power. In retaliation, Olympic officials suspended Smith and Carlos. *(Wide World Photos, Inc.)* ▶

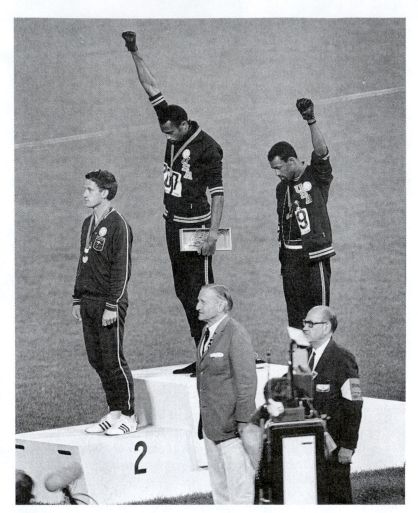

lives. They looted and burned stores, most of them white-owned. But in the process they devastated their own neighborhoods.

In 1968 the National Advisory Commission on Civil Disorders, chaired by Governor Otto Kerner of Illinois, warned that America was "moving towards two societies, one white, one black—separate and unequal," and blamed white racism for the riots. "What white Americans have never fully understood—but what the Negro can never forget—is that white society is deeply implicated in the ghetto. White institutions created it, white institutions maintain it, and white society condones it," concluded the Kerner Commission. Some white Americans rejected this interpretation. Others, shocked at what appeared to be senseless violence, wondered why African Americans were venting their frustration so destructively just when they were making real progress in the civil rights struggle.

The answer stemmed in part from regional differences. The civil rights movement had focused mostly on fighting *legal* disenfranchisement and discrimination in the South. But northern African Americans also suffered racial discrimination. Increasingly concentrated in the deteriorating ghettos of inner cities, most northern African Americans lived in societies as segregated as any in the Deep South. They faced discrimination in housing, in the availability of credit and mortgages, and in employment. The median income of northern blacks was little more than half that of northern whites, and their unemployment rate was twice as high. Many northern blacks had given up on the civil rights movement, and few believed that Great Society liberalism would solve their plight.

In this climate, a new voice urged blacks to seize their freedom "by any means necessary." Malcolm X, a

|||||||||||||||||||||||||||||

Black Power

onetime pimp and street hustler who had converted while in prison to the Nation of Islam faith, offered African Americans a new di-

rection of leadership. Members of the Nation of Islam, commonly known as Black Muslims, espoused black pride and separatism from white society. Their faith, combining elements of traditional Islam with a belief that whites were subhuman "devils" whose race would soon be destroyed, also emphasized the importance of sobriety, thrift, and social responsibility. By the early 1960s, Malcolm X had become the Black Muslims' chief spokesperson, and his advice was straightforward: "If someone puts a hand on you, send him to the cemetery." But Malcolm X was murdered in early 1965 by members of the Nation of Islam who believed he had betrayed their cause by breaking with the Black Muslims to start his own, more racially tolerant organization. In death, Malcolm X became a powerful symbol of black defiance and self-respect.

A year after Malcolm X's death, Stokely Carmichael, SNCC chairman, denounced "the betrayal of black dreams by white America." To be truly free from white oppression, Carmichael proclaimed, blacks had to "stand up and take over"—to elect black candidates, to organize their own schools, to control their own institutions, to embrace "Black Power." That year, SNCC expelled its white members and repudiated both nonviolence and integration. CORE followed suit in 1967.

The best known black radicals of the era were the Black Panthers, an organization formed in Oakland, California, in 1966. Blending black separatism and revolutionary communism, the Panthers dedicated themselves to destroying both capitalism and "the military arm of our oppressors," the police in the ghettos. In direct contrast to earlier, nonviolent civil rights protesters, who had worn suits and ties or dresses to demonstrate their respectability, male Panthers dressed in commando gear, carried weapons, and talked about killing "pigs"—and did kill eleven officers by 1970. Police responded in kind; most infamously, Chicago police murdered local Panther leader Fred Hampton in his bed. However, the group also worked to improve life in their neighborhoods by instituting free breakfast and healthcare programs for ghetto children, offering courses in African American history, and demanding jobs and decent housing for the poor. The Panthers' platform attracted many young African Americans, while their public embrace of violence frightened many whites. Radicalism, however, was not limited to black nationalist groups. Before the end of the decade, a vocal minority of America's young would join in calls for revolution.

By the mid-1960s, 41 percent of the American population was under the age of twenty. These young people

Youth and Politics

spent more time in the world of peer culture than had any previous generation, as three-quarters of them graduated from high school (up from one-fifth in the 1920s) and almost half of them went to college (up from 16 percent in 1940). As this large baby-boom generation came of age, many young people took seriously the idea that they must provide democratic leadership for their nation. Black college students had begun the sit-in movement, infusing new life into the struggle for African American civil rights. Some white college students—from both political left and right—also committed themselves to changing the system.

In the fall of 1960, a group of conservative college students came together at the family estate of William F. Buckley in Sharon, Connecticut, to create Young Americans for Freedom (YAF). Their manifesto, the "Sharon Statement," endorsed Cold War anticommunism and a vision of limited government power directly opposed to New Deal liberalism and its heritage. "In this time of moral and political crises," they wrote, "it is the responsibility of

the youth of America to affirm certain eternal truths. . . . [F]oremost among the transcendent values is the individual's use of his God-given free will." The YAF planned to capture the Republican Party and move it to the political right; Goldwater's selection as the Republican candidate for president in 1964 demonstrated their early success.

At the other end of the political spectrum, an emerging "New Left" soon joined conservative youth in rejecting liberalism. Whereas conservatives believed that liberalism's activist government encroached on individual liberty, these young Americans believed that liberalism was not enough, that it could never offer true democracy and equality to all America's people. At a meeting in Port Huron, Michigan, in 1962, founding members of Students for a Democratic Society (SDS) proclaimed, "We are people of this generation, bred in at least modest comfort, housed now in the universities, looking uncomfortably to the world we inherit." Their "Port Huron Statement" condemned racism, poverty in the midst of plenty, and the Cold War. Calling for "participatory democracy," SDS sought to wrest power from the corporations, the military, and the politicians and return it to "the people."

The first indication of the new power of activist white youth came at the University of California, Berkeley. In the fall of 1964, the univer-

Free Speech Movement

sity administration banned political activity—including recruiting volunteers for civil rights work in Mississippi—from its traditional place along a university-owned sidewalk bordering the campus. When the administration called police to arrest a CORE worker who defied the order, some four thousand students surrounded the police car. Berkeley graduate student and Mississippi Freedom Summer veteran Mario Savio ignited the movement, telling students, "You've got to put your bodies upon the levers . . . [and] you've got to indicate to the people who run it, to the people who own it, that unless you're free, the machine will be prevented from working at all."

Student political groups, left and right, came together to create the Free Speech Movement (FSM). The FSM did win back the right to political speech, but not before state police had arrested almost eight hundred student protesters. Berkeley students took two lessons from the Free Speech Movement. Many saw the administration's actions as a failure of America's democratic promises, and they were radicalized by the experience. But the victory of the FSM also demonstrated to students their potential power. By the end of the decade, the activism born at Berkeley would spread to hundreds of college and university campuses (see Map 30.4).

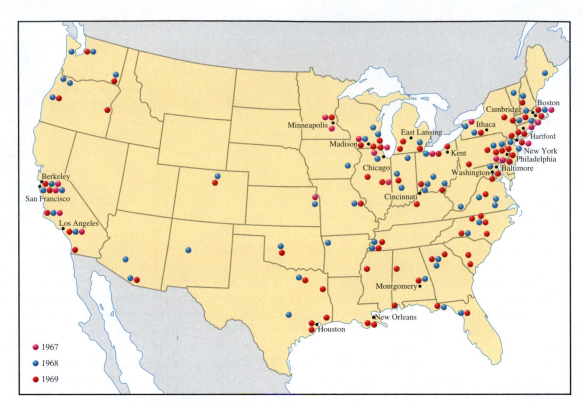

Berkeley
San Francisco
Los Angeles
Houston
New Orleans
Montgomery
Cincinnati
Chicago
Madison
Minneapolis
East Lansing
Kent
Ithaca
Cambridge
Boston
Hartford
New York
Philadelphia
Washington
Baltimore

● 1967
● 1968
● 1969

Map 30.4   Disturbances on College and University Campuses, 1967–1969

Students on campuses from coast to coast protested against the Vietnam War. Some protests were peaceful; others erupted into violent confrontations between protesters and police or the National Guard.

Many student protesters in the 1960s sought greater control over their lives as students, demanding more rele-

|||||||||||||||||||||||||||
Student Activism

vant class offerings, more freedom in selecting their courses of study, and a greater voice in the running of universities. A major target of protest was the doctrine of in loco parentis, which until the late 1960s put universities legally "in the place of parents" to their students, allowing control over student behavior that went well beyond the laws of the land. The impact of in loco parentis fell heaviest on women, who were subject to strict curfew regulations called parietals, while men had no such rules. Protesters demanded an end to discrimination on the basis of sex, but rejected in loco parentis for other reasons as well. A group at the University of Kansas demanded that the administration explain how its statement that "college students are assumed to have maturity of judgment necessary for adult responsibility" squared with the minute regulation of students' nonacademic lives. One young man complained that "a

high school dropout selling cabbage in a supermarket" had more rights and freedoms than successful university students. Increasingly, students insisted they should be allowed the full rights and responsibilities of citizens in a democratic society.

It was the war in Vietnam, however, that mobilized a nationwide student movement. Believing that it was the

|||||||||||||||||||||||||||||||
Youth and the War in Vietnam

democratic responsibility of citizens to learn about and speak out on issues of vital national importance, university students and faculty held "teach-ins" about U.S.

involvement in Vietnam as the war escalated in 1965. Students for a Democratic Society sponsored the first major antiwar march that year, drawing twenty thousand protesters to Washington, D.C. Local SDS chapters grew steadily as opposition to the war increased. On campuses throughout the nation, students adopted tactics developed in the civil rights movement, picketing ROTC buildings and protesting military research and recruiting done on

◀ Hundreds of thousands of young people came together for the Woodstock Music and Art Fair in August 1969. In its coverage, *Time* magazine warned adults that "the children of the welfare state and the atom bomb do indeed march to the beat of a different drummer, as well as to the tune of an electric guitarist," but the local sheriff called them "the nicest bunch of kids I've ever dealt with." *(Pictorial Press)*

their campuses. However, despite the visibility of campus antiwar protests, most students did not yet oppose the war: in 1967, only 30 percent of male college students declared themselves "doves" on Vietnam, while 67 percent proclaimed themselves "hawks." And many young men were, in fact, in Vietnam fighting the war. But as the war continued to escalate, an increasing number of America's youth came to distrust the government that turned a deaf ear to their protests, as well as the university administrations that seemed more a source of arbitrary authority than of democratic education.

But the large baby-boom generation would change the nation's culture more than its politics. Although many young people protested the war and marched for social justice, most did not. The sixties' "youth culture" was never homogeneous. Fraternity and sorority life stayed strong on most campuses, even as radicalism flourished. And although there was some crossover, black, white, and Latino youth had different cultural styles: different music, different clothes, even different versions of a youth dialect often incomprehensible to adults. Nonetheless, as potential consumers, young people as a group exercised tremendous cultural authority. Their music and their styles drove Amer-

Youth Culture and the Counterculture

ican popular culture in the late 1960s.

The most unifying element of youth culture was the importance placed on music. The Beatles had electrified American teenagers—73 million viewers watched their first television appearance on the *Ed Sullivan Show* in 1964. Bob Dylan promised revolutionary answers in "Blowin' in the Wind"; Janis Joplin brought the sexual power of the blues to white youth; James Brown and Aretha Franklin proclaimed black pride; and the psychedelic rock of Jefferson Airplane and the Grateful Dead—along with hallucinogenic drugs—redefined reality. That new reality took brief form in the Woodstock Festival in upstate New York in 1969, as more than 400,000 people reveled in the music and in a world of their own making, living in rain and mud for four days without shelter and without violence.

Some young people hoped to turn youth rebellion into something more than a consumer-based lifestyle, rejecting what they saw as hypocritical middle-class values. They attempted to craft an alternative way of life, or counterculture, liberated from competitive materialism and celebrating the legitimacy of pleasure. "Sex, drugs, and rock 'n' roll" became a mantra of sorts, offering these "hippies," or "freaks," a path to a new consciousness. Many did the hard work of creating communes and intentional communities, whether in cities or in hidden stretches of rural America. Although the New Left criticized the counterculture as apolitical, many freaks did envision revolutionary change. As John Sinclair, manager of the rock band MC5, explained, mind-blowing experiences with sex, drugs, or

The British Invasion

The British invasion began in earnest on February 7, 1964. London and Paris had already fallen, reported *Life* magazine, and New York was soon to follow. Three thousand screaming American teenagers were waiting when Pan Am's *Yankee Clipper* touched down at Kennedy Airport with four British "moptops" aboard. "I Want to Hold Your Hand" was already at the top of the U.S. charts, and the Beatles' conquest of America was quick. Seventy-three million people—the largest television audience in history—watched them on the *Ed Sullivan Show* the following Sunday night.

Although the Beatles led the invasion, they did not conquer America alone. The Rolling Stones' first U.S. hit single also came in 1964. The Dave Clark Five appeared on *Ed Sullivan* eighteen times. And there was a whole list of others, some now forgotten, some not: Freddie and the Dreamers, Herman's Hermits, the Animals, the Yardbirds, the Hollies, the Kinks, Gerry and the Pacemakers, Chad and Jeremy, Petula Clark.

The British invasion was, at least in part, the triumphal return of American music, part of a transatlantic exchange that reinvigorated both nations. American rock 'n' roll had lost much of its early energy by the early 1960s, and in England, the London-centered popular music industry was pumping out a highly produced, saccharine version of American pop. But other forms of American music had made their way across the Atlantic, often carried by travelers through port cities like Liverpool, where the Beatles were born. By the late 1950s, young musicians in England's provincial cities were listening to the music of African American bluesmen Muddy Waters and Howlin' Wolf; they were playing cover versions of the early rock 'n' roll of Buddy Holly and Chuck Berry; and they were experimenting with skiffle, a sort of jazz- and blues-influenced folk music played mostly with improvised instruments. None of this music had a large popular audience in the United States, where *Billboard* magazine's number one hit for 1960 was Percy Faith's "Theme from *A Summer Place*" (a movie starring Sandra Dee and Troy Donahue), and the Singing Nun was at the top of the charts just before the Beatles arrived.

Young British musicians, including John Lennon, Eric Clapton, and Mick Jagger, re-created American musical forms and reinvented rock 'n' roll. By the mid-1960s, the Beatles and the other bands of the British invasion were at the heart of a youth culture that transcended the boundaries of nations. This music not only connected Britain and America but also reached across the Atlantic and the Pacific to link America's youth with young people throughout the world.

The Beatles perform on the *Ed Sullivan Show* in February 1964. Although Britain's Queen Mother thought the Beatles "young, fresh, and vital," American parents were appalled when the "long" Beatles haircut swept the nation.

(AP/Wide World Photos, Inc.)

music were far more likely to change young people's minds than earnest speeches: "Rather than go up there and make some speech about our moral commitment in Vietnam, you just make 'em so freaky they'd never want to go into the army in the first place."

The nascent counterculture had first burst on the national consciousness during the summer of 1967, when tens of thousands of young people poured into the Haight-Ashbury district of San Francisco, the heart of America's psychedelic culture, for the "summer of love." As an older generation of "straight" (or Establishment) Americans watched with horror, white youth came to look—and act—more and more like the counterculture. Coats and ties disappeared, as did stockings—and bras. Young men grew long hair, and parents throughout the nation complained, "You can't tell the boys from the girls." Millions used marijuana or hallucinogenic drugs, read underground newspapers, and thought of themselves as alienated from "straight" culture even though they were attending high school or college and not completely "dropping out" of the Establishment.

Some of the most lasting cultural changes involved attitudes about sex. The mass media were fascinated with "free love," and some people did embrace a truly promiscuous sexuality. More important, however, premarital sex no longer destroyed a woman's "reputation." The birth-control pill, distributed since 1960 and widely available to single women by the late 1960s, greatly lessened the risk of unplanned pregnancy, and venereal diseases were easily cured by a basic course of antibiotics. The number of couples living together—"without benefit of matrimony," as the phrase went at the time—increased 900 percent from 1960 to 1970; many young people no longer tried to hide the fact that they were sexually active. Still, 68 percent of American adults disapproved of premarital sex in 1969.

Adults were baffled and often angered by the behavior of youth. A generation that had grown up in the hard decades of depression and war, many of whom saw middle-class respectability as crucial to success and stability, just did not understand. How could young people put such promising futures at risk by having sex without marriage, taking drugs, or opposing the American government over the war in Vietnam?

1968

By the beginning of 1968, it seemed that the nation was coming apart. Divided over the war in Vietnam, frustrated by the slow pace of social change or angry over the racial violence that wracked America's cities, Americans looked

for solutions as the nation faced the most serious domestic crisis of the postwar era.

The year opened with a major attack in Vietnam. On January 31, 1968, the first day of the Vietnamese New Year (Tet), Vietcong and North Vietnamese forces struck all across South Vietnam, capturing provincial capitals (see Map 30.2). During the carefully planned offensive, the Saigon airport, the presidential palace, and the ARVN headquarters came under attack. Even the American embassy compound in the city was penetrated by Vietcong soldiers, who occupied its courtyard for six hours. U.S. and South Vietnamese units eventually regained much of the ground they had lost, inflicting heavy casualties and devastating numerous villages.

The Tet Offensive

Although the Tet Offensive did not achieve the resounding battlefield victory that Hanoi strategists had hoped for, the heavy fighting called into question American military leaders' confident predictions in earlier months that the war would soon be won. Had not the Vietcong and North Vietnamese demonstrated that they could strike when and where they wished? If America's airpower, dollars, and half a million troops could not now defeat the Vietcong, could they ever do so? Had the American public been deceived? In February, the highly respected CBS television anchorman Walter Cronkite went to Vietnam to find out. The military brass in Saigon assured him that "we had the enemy just where we wanted him." The newsman recalled, "Tell that to the Marines, I thought—the Marines in the body bags on that helicopter."

Top presidential advisers sounded notes of despair. Clark Clifford, who had succeeded Robert McNamara as secretary of defense, told Johnson that the war—"a sinkhole"—could not be won, even with the 206,000 additional soldiers requested by Westmoreland. Aware that the nation was suffering a financial crisis prompted by rampant deficit spending to sustain the war and other global commitments, they knew that taking the initiative in Vietnam would cost billions more, further derail the budget, panic foreign owners of dollars, and wreck the economy. Clifford heard from his associates in the business community; "These men now feel we are in a hopeless bog," he told the president. To "maintain public support for the war without the support of these men" was impossible.

Controversy over the war split the Democratic Party, just as a presidential election loomed in November. Senator Eugene McCarthy of Minnesota and Robert F. Kennedy (now a senator from New York), both strong opponents of Johnson's war

Johnson's Exit

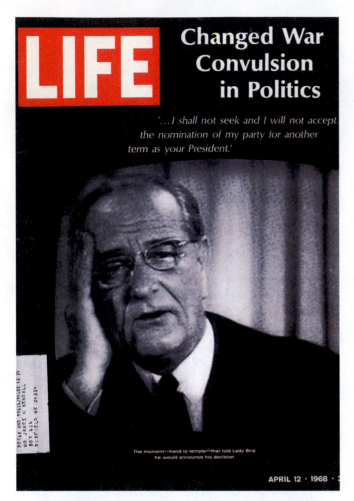

LIFE

Changed War Convulsion in Politics

'...I shall not seek and I will not accept the nomination of my party for another term as your President.'

The moment—hand to temple—that told Lady Bird he would announce his decision

APRIL 12 · 1968 ·

▲ *Life* magazine captures the moment when President Lyndon Johnson, in a televised address, told the nation he would not seek another term as president of the United States. Johnson's face shows the toll taken by his years in the White House, as the war in Vietnam gradually destroyed his presidency and divided the nation.

(Time Life Pictures/Time Life Picture Collection/Getty Images)

policies, forcefully challenged the president in early primaries. Strained by exhausting sessions with skeptical advisers, troubled by the economic implications of escalation, and sensing that more resources would not bring victory, Johnson changed course. During a March 31 television address he announced a halt to most of the bombing, asked Hanoi to begin negotiations, and stunned his listeners by withdrawing from the presidential race. He had become a casualty of the war, his presidency doomed by a seemingly interminable struggle 10,000 miles from Washington. Peace talks began in May in Paris, but the war ground on.

Less than a week after Johnson's shocking announcement, Martin Luther King Jr. was murdered in Memphis, where he had traveled to support striking sanitation workers. It is still not clear why James Earl Ray, a white forty-year-old drifter and petty criminal, shot King—or whether he acted alone or as part of a conspiracy. By 1968 King, the senior statesman of the civil rights movement, had become an outspoken critic of the Vietnam War and of American capitalism. Although some Americans hated what he stood for, he was widely respected and honored. Most Americans mourned his death, even as black rage and grief exploded into riots in 130 cities. Once again, ghetto neighborhoods burned; thirty-four blacks and five whites died. The violence provoked a backlash from whites—primarily urban, working-class people who were tired of violence and quickly losing whatever sympathy they might have had for black Americans' increasingly radical demands. In Chicago, Mayor Richard Daley ordered police to shoot rioters.

Assassinations

An already shaken nation watched in disbelief as another leader fell to violence only two months later. Antiwar Democratic presidential candidate Robert Kennedy was shot and killed as he celebrated his victory in the California primary. His assassin, Sirhan Sirhan, an Arab nationalist, targeted Kennedy because of his support for Israel.

Chicago Democratic National Convention

Violence erupted again in August at the Democratic National Convention in Chicago. Thousands of protesters converged on the city: students who'd gone "Clean for Gene," cutting long hair and donning "respectable" clothes to campaign for antiwar candidate Eugene McCarthy; members of America's counterculture drawn by a promise from the anarchist group, the Yippies, of a "Festival of Life" to counter the "Convention of Death"; members of antiwar groups that ranged from radical to mainstream. Mayor Daley, resolving that no one would disrupt "his" convention, assigned twelve thousand police to twelve-hour shifts and had twelve thousand army troops with bazookas, rifles, and flamethrowers on call as backup. Police attacked peaceful antiwar protesters and journalists. "The whole world is watching," chanted the protesters, as club-swinging police indiscriminately beat people to the ground, and Americans gathered around their television sets, despairing over the future of their nation.

Although American eyes were focused on the clashes in Chicago, upheavals burst forth around the world that

▲ A military truck with civilians waving Czech flags drives past a Soviet truck in Prague on August 21, 1968, shortly after Warsaw Pact troops invaded Czechoslovakia. More than one hundred people were killed in the clashes, and several Prague Spring leaders, including Alexander Dubček, were arrested and taken to Moscow. Dubček's attempts to create "socialism with a human face" are often seen as historical and ideological forerunners to Mikhail Gorbachev's reform policies in the 1980s in the Soviet Union. *(Hulton Archive/Getty Images)*

Global Protest

spring and summer. In France, university students protested both rigid academic policies and the Vietnam War. They received support from French workers, who occupied their factories and paralyzed public transport; the turmoil contributed to the collapse of Charles de Gaulle's government the following year. In Italy, Germany, England, Ireland, Sweden, Canada, Mexico, Chile, Japan, and South Korea, students also protested—sometimes violently—against universities, governments, and the Vietnam War. In Czechoslovakia, hundreds of thousands of demonstrators flooded the streets of Prague, demanding democracy and an end to repression by the Soviet-controlled government. This so-called Prague Spring developed into a full-scale national rebellion before being crushed by Soviet tanks.

Why so many uprisings occurred in so many places simultaneously is not altogether clear. Sheer numbers had an impact. The postwar baby boom experienced by many nations produced by the late 1960s a huge mass of teenagers and young adults, many of whom had grown up in relative prosperity, with high expectations for the future. The expanded reach of global media also mattered. Technological advances allowed the nearly instantaneous transmittal of televised images around the world, so protests in one country could readily inspire similar actions in others. Although the worldwide demonstrations might have occurred even without the Vietnam War, television news footage showing the wealthiest and most industrialized nation carpet-bombing a poor and developing one—whose leader was the charismatic revolutionary Ho Chi Minh—surely helped fuel the agitation.

The presidential election of 1968, coming at the end of such a difficult year, did little to heal the nation. Democratic nominee Hubert Humphrey, Johnson's vice president, seemed a continuation of the old politics. Republican candidate

Nixon's Election

Richard Nixon, no newcomer to the political scene, called for "law and order"—a phrase some understood as racist code words—to appeal to those who were angry about racial violence and tired of social unrest. Promising to "bring us together," he reached out to those he called "the great, quite forgotten majority—the nonshouters and the nondemonstrators, the millions who ask principally to go their own way in decency and dignity." On Vietnam, Nixon vowed he would "end the war and win the peace." Governor George Wallace of Alabama, who only five years before had vowed, "Segregation forever!" and who proposed using nuclear weapons on Vietnam, ran as a third-party candidate. Wallace carried five southern states, drawing almost 14 percent of the popular vote, and Nixon was elected president with the slimmest of margins (see Map 30.5). Divisions among Americans deepened.

Yet on Christmas Eve 1968—in a step toward fulfilling the pledge John Kennedy had made at the opening of a tumultuous decade—*Apollo 8* entered lunar orbit. Looking down on a troubled world, the astronauts broadcast photographs of the earth seen from space, a fragile blue orb floating in darkness. As people around the world listened, the astronauts read aloud the opening passages of Genesis, "In the beginning, God created the heaven and the earth . . . and God saw that it was good," and many listeners found themselves in tears.

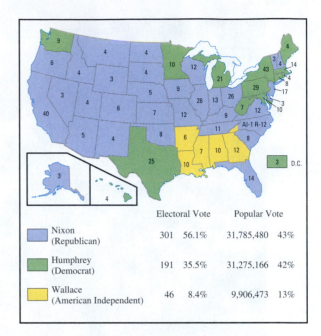

		Electoral Vote		Popular Vote	
▉	Nixon (Republican)	301	56.1%	31,785,480	43%
▉	Humphrey (Democrat)	191	35.5%	31,275,166	42%
▉	Wallace (American Independent)	46	8.4%	9,906,473	13%

Map 30.5   Presidential Election, 1968

The popular vote was almost evenly split between Richard M. Nixon and Hubert Humphrey, but Nixon won 31 states to Humphrey's 14 and triumphed easily in electoral votes. George Wallace, the American Independent Party candidate, won 5 states in the Deep South.

SUMMARY

The 1960s began with high hopes for a more democratic America. Civil rights volunteers, often risking their lives, carried the quest for racial equality to all parts of the nation. Gradually, the nation's leaders put their support behind the movement, and the 1964 Civil Rights Act and the 1965 Voting Rights Act were major landmarks in the quest for a more just society. America was shaken by the assassination of President John Kennedy in 1963, but under President Johnson, the liberal vision of government power used to create a better life for the nation's citizens reached new heights, as a flood of legislation was enacted in hopes of creating a Great Society.

But throughout this period, the nation was troubled by threats to its stability. The Cold War between the United States and the USSR grew in size and scope during the 1960s. The world came close to nuclear war in the 1962 Cuban missile crisis. Cold War geopolitics led the United States to become more and more involved in the ongoing war in Vietnam. Determined not to let Vietnam "fall" to communists, the United States sent military forces to prevent the victory of communist Vietnamese nationalists led by Ho Chi Minh in that nation's civil war. By 1968 there were more than half a million American ground troops in Vietnam. America's war in Vietnam divided the country, undermined Great Society domestic programs, and destroyed the presidency of Lyndon Johnson.

Despite real gains in civil rights and in attempts to promote justice and end poverty, divisions among Americans deepened. Many African Americans turned away from the civil rights movement, seeking more immediate change in their lives. Poor African American neighborhoods burned as riots spread through the nation. Integrationists and civil rights advocates fought both separatist Black Power militants and white segregationists. Vocal young people—and some of their elders—questioned whether democracy truly existed in the United States. Large numbers of the nation's

Legacy FOR A PEOPLE AND A NATION

The Immigration Act of 1965

When President Johnson signed the 1965 Immigration Act in a ceremony at the foot of the Statue of Liberty, he stated, "This bill that we sign today is not a revolutionary bill. It does not affect the lives of millions. It will not reshape the structure of our daily lives, or really add importantly to our wealth and power." Johnson believed that the act was important in an era of struggle over the role of race in American society because it "repair[ed] a very deep and painful flaw in the fabric of American justice" by ending national-origins quotas that all but excluded "Polynesians, orientals, and Negroes" (as Hawai'i's senator Hiram Fong pointed out in 1963). Nevertheless, the president and his advisers saw it as primarily symbolic. They were wrong. This relatively obscure act may have had greater long-term impact on Americans' lives than any other piece of Great Society legislation.

The 1965 Immigration Act ended blatant discrimination against potential immigrants from Asia, Africa, and various Third World nations by substituting Eastern and Western Hemispheric "caps" for national quotas and establishing a policy of family reunification that allowed immediate relatives of U.S. citizens to immigrate to the United States regardless of numerical ceilings on immigration. The architects of the Immigration Act did not expect the scale or the sources of immigration to change, but world events decreed otherwise. Political instability, including wars in southeast Asia and civil conflict in Latin America and Africa, along with rapidly growing population in many of the world's poorer nations, created a large pool of potential immigrants who were drawn by the continuing prosperity of the United States. Immigration rates skyrocketed.

By the 1990s, immigration accounted for almost 60 percent of America's population growth. By 2000, more Americans were foreign-born than at any time since the 1930s—and their numbers continued to grow. No longer were most immigrants from western Europe. The majorities came from Mexico, the Philippines, Vietnam, China, the Dominican Republic, Korea, India, the former USSR, Jamaica, and Iran.

More than two-thirds of the new immigrants settled in six states—New York, California, Florida, New Jersey, Illinois, and Texas—but many found their way to parts of America that had previously been much more homogeneous. By the late twentieth century, Spanish-language signs appeared in South Carolina, and Hmong farmers from the mountains of southeast Asia offered their produce at the farmers' market in Missoula, Montana. The legacy of the 1965 Immigration Act was unintended but profound: the people and the nation are today much more diverse than they otherwise would have been.

white youth embraced another form of rebellion, claiming membership in a "counterculture" that rejected white middle-class respectability. With great passion, Americans struggled over the future of their nation.

1968 was a year of crisis, of assassinations and violence in the streets. The decade that had started with such promise was moving toward its end in fierce political polarization.

SUGGESTIONS FOR FURTHER READING

Beth Bailey, *Sex in the Heartland* (1999)

David Farber, *Chicago '68* (1988)

Lawrence Freedman, *Kennedy's Wars: Berlin, Cuba, Laos, and Vietnam* (2000)

George C. Herring, *LBJ and Vietnam: A Different Kind of War* (1994)

Michael Kazin and Maurice Isserman, *America Divided: The Civil War of the 1960s* (1999)

Fredrik Logevall, *Choosing War: The Lost Chance for Peace and the Escalation of War in Vietnam* (1999)

Lisa McGirr, *Suburban Warriors: The Origins of the New American Right* (2001)

Charles Payne, *I've Got the Light of Freedom: The Organizing Tradition and the Mississippi Freedom Struggle* (1995)

For a more extensive list for further reading, go to college.hmco.com/pic/norton8e.

CHAPTER

31

Continuing Divisions and New Limits

1969-1980

*J*n 1969 Daniel Ellsberg was a thirty-eight-year-old former aide to Assistant Secretary of Defense John McNaughton. At the Pentagon Ellsberg had worked on a top-secret study of U.S. decision making in Vietnam requested by Secretary of Defense Robert S. McNamara. When he left office following the election of Richard Nixon, Ellsberg gained access to a copy of the study being stored at the Rand Corporation, where he intended to resume his pregovernment career as a researcher. He spent the next six months poring over the forty-seven volumes and seven thousand pages that made up what would come to be called the Pentagon Papers.

Initially supportive of U.S. military intervention in Vietnam, Ellsberg had in the last years of his government career grown deeply disillusioned. A Harvard-trained Ph.D., former marine officer, and Cold Warrior with a moral fervor to preserve America's nuclear strength, he had spent nearly two years in South Vietnam, from 1965 to 1967, assessing the war's progress for his superiors in Washington. Several times he had gone on combat patrols and come under enemy fire, and he had interviewed military officials, U.S. diplomats, and Vietnamese leaders. The war, he concluded, was in multiple respects—military, political, moral—a lost enterprise.

Ellsberg was at first reluctant to act on that conviction and disassociate himself from the policy. "Like so many," he later recalled, "I put personal loyalty to the president . . . above all else." But when in 1969 it became clear that the incoming Nixon administration had no intention of ending the war, he decided on a bold course of action:

◀ Daniel Ellsberg talks to reporters on January 17, 1973, after the opening session of his trial. Behind him is codefendant Anthony Russo, Ellsberg's colleague at the Rand Corporation who had assisted in the secret photocopying of the Pentagon Papers. The government indicted Ellsberg and Russo on charges of espionage, theft, and conspiracy, but in May 1973 a federal court judge dismissed all charges against them because of improper government conduct. *(© Corbis-Bettmann)*

CHRONOLOGY

1969 ■ Stonewall Inn uprising begins gay liberation movement
   ■ *Apollo 11* Astronaut Neil Armstrong becomes first person to walk on moon's surface
   ■ National Chicano Liberation Youth Conference held in Denver
   ■ "Indians of All Tribes" occupy Alcatraz Island
   ■ Nixon administration begins affirmative-action plan

1970 ■ United States invades Cambodia
   ■ Students at Kent State and Jackson State Universities shot by National Guard troops
   ■ First Earth Day celebrated
   ■ Environmental Protection Agency created

1971 ■ Pentagon Papers published

1972 ■ Nixon visits China and Soviet Union
   ■ CREEP stages Watergate break-in
   ■ Congress approves ERA and passes Title IX, which creates growth in women's athletics

1973 ■ Peace agreement in Paris ends U.S. involvement in Vietnam
   ■ OPEC increases oil prices, creating U.S. energy crisis
   ■ *Roe v. Wade* legalizes abortion
   ■ Agnew resigns; Ford named vice president

1974 ■ Nixon resigns under threat of impeachment; Ford becomes president

1975 ■ In deepening economic recession, unemployment hits 8.5 percent
   ■ New York City saved from bankruptcy by federal loan guarantees
   ■ Congress passes Indian Self-Determination and Education Assistance Act in response to Native American activists

1976 ■ Carter elected president

1978 ■ *Regents of the University of California v. Bakke* outlaws quotas but upholds affirmative action
   ■ California voters approve Proposition 13

1979 ■ Three Mile Island nuclear accident raises fears
   ■ Camp David accords signed by Israel and Egypt
   ■ American hostages seized in Iran
   ■ Soviet Union invades Afghanistan
   ■ Consumer debt doubles from 1975 to hit $315 billion

he would make the Pentagon Papers public, even though doing so might land him in prison. The study, he believed, showed incontrovertibly that presidents had repeatedly escalated the American commitment in Vietnam despite uniformly pessimistic estimates from their advisers—and that they had repeatedly lied to the public about what they were doing and the results achieved. Perhaps, Ellsberg thought, disclosure of this information would generate sufficient uproar to force a dramatic change in policy.

With the assistance of a Rand colleague, Ellsberg surreptitiously photocopied the entire study, then spent months pleading with antiwar senators and representatives to release it. When they refused, he went to the press. On June 13, 1971, the world first learned of the Pentagon Papers through a front-page article in the *New York Times*. Numerous other newspapers soon began publishing excerpts as well.

Ellsberg's act of leaking a top-secret study became intensely controversial, particularly with Nixon's decision to try to stop the papers' publication—among the first such efforts to muzzle the press since the American Revolution—and to discredit Ellsberg and deter other leakers through the illegal actions of a group of petty operatives. To many Americans, Ellsberg was a hero whose defiant act might at least indirectly shorten an illegitimate war. To many others, he was a publicity-seeking traitor. These divergent views reflected the deep schisms in American society during the latter stages of the Vietnam era.

The 1970s would be, for Americans, a decade of division and an age of limits. The violence and chaos of 1968 continued in Richard Nixon's first years as president. Opposition to the war in Vietnam became more extreme. As government deceptions were exposed, the American people were ever more divided over U.S. policy in Vietnam. The movements for racial equality and social justice that had flowered in the 1960s also became more radical by the early 1970s. Although some continued to work for racial integration, many activists embraced cultural nationalism, which emphasized the differences among Americans and sought separatist cultures and societies. Even the women's movement, which was the strongest social movement of the 1970s and won great victories against sex discrimination, had a polarizing effect. Opponents, many of them women, understood feminism as an attack on their chosen way of life and mobilized a conservative grassroots movement that had great political importance over the subsequent decades.

This divided America faced great challenges abroad and at home. To some of these challenges leaders responded boldly and imaginatively. Richard Nixon and his national security adviser, Henry Kissinger, understood that, in foreign affairs, America's capacity to effect change was limited. They grasped that the United States and the Soviet Union, weakened by the huge costs of their competition and challenged by other nations, faced an international system in which power had become diffused. Accordingly, even as they stubbornly and futilely pursued victory in Vietnam, Nixon and Kissinger worked to improve relations with the People's Republic of China and the Soviet Union. In an increasingly multipolar system, they reasoned, the maintenance of world order depended on stable relations among the great powers. Through the opening to China and through improved relations with the USSR, the two men helped reduce the threat of great-power war.

Ultimately, however, exposure of Richard Nixon's illegal acts in the political scandal known as "Watergate" shook the faith of Americans not already disillusioned by presidential deception over the war in Vietnam. By the time Nixon, under threat of impeachment, submitted his resignation, the American people were cynical about politics and skeptical of military and executive leaders. Neither of Nixon's successors, Gerald Ford or Jimmy Carter, though both honorable men, was able to regain the faith of the American people. Despite some domestic successes, Carter's presidency was undermined by international events beyond his control. In the Middle East—a region of increasing importance in U.S. foreign policy—Carter helped broker a peace deal between Egypt and Israel but proved powerless to end a lengthy crisis in Iran involving American hostages. Meanwhile, the Soviet invasion of Afghanistan in 1979 revived Cold War tensions.

Adding to Carter's woes was a deepening economic crisis that defied traditional remedies. Suddenly in the 1970s, middle-class Americans saw their savings disappearing to double-digit inflation and their seemingly secure jobs vanishing overnight. The economic crisis was caused in large part by changes in the global economy and inter-

national trade, made worse by the oil embargo launched by Arab members of the Organization of Petroleum Exporting Countries in 1973. Americans realized anew that they were vulnerable to decisions made in far-off lands—decisions the United States could not control.

- How did American foreign policy change as a result of involvement in Vietnam?
- Why did Americans see this era as an age of limits?
- Some historians describe the period between 1968 and 1980 as a time when many Americans lost faith—in their government, in the possibility of joining together in a society that offered equality to all, in the possibility of consensus instead of conflict. Do you agree, or were the struggles and divisions of this era similar to those of previous decades?

THE NEW POLITICS OF IDENTITY

By the end of the 1960s, as divisions continued to deepen among the American people, movements for social justice and racial equality had become stronger, louder, and often more radical. The civil rights movement, begun in a quest for equal rights and integration, splintered, as many young African Americans turned away from the tactics of nonviolence, rejected integration in favor of separatism, and embraced a distinct African American culture. Mexican Americans and Native Americans, inspired by the civil rights movement to struggle against their own marginalization in American society, had created powerful "Brown Power" and "Red Power" movements by the early 1970s. Like young African Americans, they demanded not only equal rights but also recognition of their distinct cultures. These movements fueled the development of a new "identity politics." Advocates of identity politics believed that differences among American racial and ethnic groups were critically important. Group identity, these Americans argued, must be the basis for political action. And government and social leaders must stop imagining the American public as individuals and instead address the needs of different identity-based groups.

By 1970, most African American activists no longer sought political power and racial justice through the universalist claim of the civil rights movement that "We are all the same but for the color of our skin." Instead, they emphasized the distinctiveness of black culture and society. These ideas attracted a large following,

African American Cultural Nationalism

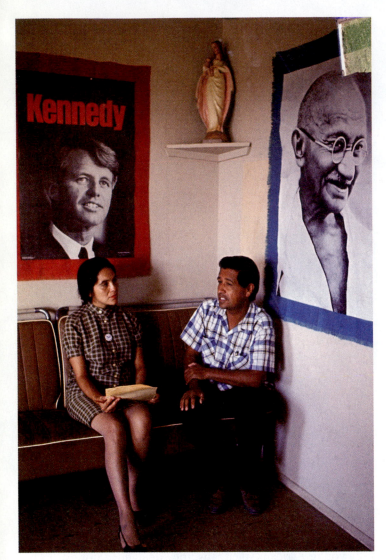

▲ United Farm Workers leaders César Chávez and Dolores Huerta talk during the 1968 grape pickers' strike. The statue of the Virgin Mary, poster for presidential candidate Robert Kennedy, and photograph of Mahatma Gandhi suggest the guiding religious, political, and philosophical understandings of the movement.

(Arthur Schatz/Time Life Pictures/Getty Images)

even among older, less radical people. Many black Americans, powerfully disillusioned by the racism that outlasted the end of legal segregation, had come to believe that integration would mean subordination in a white-dominated society that had no respect for their history and cultural traditions.

In the early 1970s, though mainstream groups like the NAACP continued to seek political and social equal-ity through the nation's courts and ballot boxes, many African Americans (like the white youth of the counter-culture) looked to culture rather than to narrow political action for social change. Rejecting current European American standards of beauty, young people let their hair grow into "naturals" and "Afros"; they claimed the power of black "soul." Seeking strength in their own histories and cultural heritages, black college students and young faculty members fought successfully to create black studies departments in American universities. African traditions were reclaimed—or sometimes created. The new holiday Kwanzaa, created in 1966 by Maulana Karenga, professor of black studies at California State University, Long Beach, offered celebration of a shared African heritage. Many African Americans found a new pride in their history and culture; the most radical activists gave up on the notion of a larger "American" culture altogether.

In 1970 the nation's 9 million Mexican Americans (4.3 percent of America's total population) were heavily con-centrated in the Southwest and California. Although these Americans were officially classified as white by the federal government—all Hispanics were counted as white in the federal census—discrimination in hiring, pay, housing, schools, and the courts was commonplace. In cities, poor Mexican Americans lived in run-down barrios. In rural areas, poverty was widespread. Almost half of Mexican Americans were functionally illiterate, and even among the young, high school drop-out rates were astronomical: in 1974, only 21 percent of Mexican American males graduated high school. Although growing numbers of Mexican Americans were middle class, almost one-quarter of Mexican American families remained below the poverty level in the 1970s. Especially dire was the plight of migrant farm workers.

Mexican American Activism

The national Mexican American movement for social justice began with these migrant workers. From 1965 through 1970, labor organizers César Chávez and Dolores Huerta led migrant workers, the majority of whom were of Mexican ancestry, in a strike (*huelga*) against large grape growers in California's San Joaquin Valley. Chávez and the AFL-CIO–affiliated United Farm Workers (UFW) drew national attention to the working conditions of migrant laborers. Grape growers paid workers as little as 10 cents an hour (the minimum wage in 1965 was $1.25) and often lodged them in squalid housing without running water or indoor toilets. A national consumer boycott of table grapes brought the growers to the bargaining table, and in 1970 the UFW won its fight for better wages and working conditions. The UFW's roots in the Mexican and Mexican American communities were critical to its success. The union resembled nineteenth-century Mexican *mutualistas,* or cooperative associations, as much as it did a traditional American labor union. Its members founded cooperative groceries, a Spanish-language newspaper, and a theater group; they called on the Virgin de Guadalupe for assistance in their struggle.

During the same period, more radical struggles were also beginning. In northern New Mexico, Reies Tijerina created the Alianza Federal de Mercedes (Federal Alliance of Grants) to fight for the return of land that the organization claimed belonged to local *hispano* villagers, whose ancestors had occupied the territory before it was claimed by the United States, under the 1848 Treaty of Guadalupe Hidalgo. In Denver, former boxer Rudolfo "Corky" González drew Mexican American youth to his "Crusade for Justice"; more than one thousand young people gathered there for the National Chicano Liberation Youth Conference in 1969. They adopted a manifesto, *El Plan Espiritual de Aztlán,* which condemned the "brutal 'Gringo' invasion of our territories" and declared "the Independence of our . . . Nation."

Chicano Movement

These young activists called for the liberation of "La Raza" (from *La Raza de Bronze,* "the brown people") from the oppressive force of American society and culture, not for equal rights through integration. They also rejected a hyphenated "Mexican-American" identity. The "Mexican American," they explained in *El Plan Espiritual de Aztlán,* "lacks respect for his culture and ethnic heritage . . . [and] seeks assimilation as a way out of his 'degraded' social status." These young people called themselves "Chicanos" or "Chicanas"—a term drawn from barrio slang and associated with *pachucos,* the hip, rebellious, and sometimes criminal young men who symbolized much of what "respectable" Mexican Americans despised.

Many middle-class Mexican Americans and members of the older generations never embraced the term *Chicano* or the separatist, cultural nationalist agenda of *el movimiento.* Throughout the 1970s, however, younger activists continued to seek "Brown Power" based on a separate and distinct Chicano/Chicana culture. They succeeded in introducing Chicano studies into local high school and college curricula and in creating a strong and unifying sense of cultural identity for Mexican American youth. Some activists made clear political gains as well, founding La Raza Unida (RUP), a Southwest-based political party that registered tens of thousands of voters and won several lo-

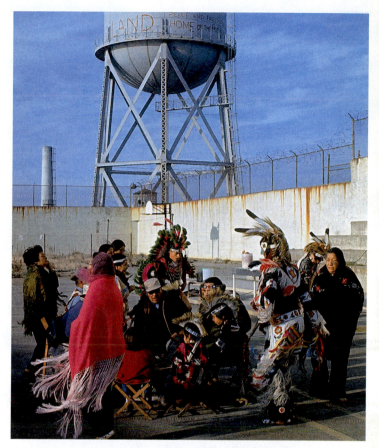

▲ Calling their movement "Red Power," these American Indian activists dance in 1969 while "reclaiming" Alcatraz Island in San Francisco Bay. Arguing that an 1868 Sioux treaty entitled them to possession of unused federal lands, the group occupied the island until mid-1971. *(Ralph Crane,* Life *magazine © Time, Inc.)*

cal elections. The Chicano movement was never as influential nationally as the African American civil rights movement or the Black Power movement. However, it effectively challenged discrimination on the local level and created a basis for political action as the Mexican American (and broader Latino) population of the United States grew dramatically over the following decades.

Between 1968 and 1975, Native American activists forced American society to hear their demands and to reform U.S. government policies toward native peoples. Like African Americans and Mexican Americans, young Native American activists were greatly influenced by cultural nationalist beliefs. Many young activists, seeking a return to the "old ways," joined with "traditionalists"

Native American Activism

among their elders to challenge tribal leaders who advocated assimilation and cooperation with federal agencies.

In November 1969 a small group of activists, calling themselves "Indians of All Tribes," occupied Alcatraz Island in San Francisco Bay, demanding that the land be returned to native peoples for an Indian cultural center. The protest, which lasted nineteen months and eventually involved more than four hundred people from fifty different tribes, marked the consolidation of a "pan-Indian" approach to activism. Before Alcatraz, protests tended to be reservation based and concerned with specific local issues. Many of the Alcatraz activists were urban Indians, products in part of government policies that led Native Americans to leave reservations and seek jobs in the nation's cities. They were interested in claiming a shared "Indian" identity that transcended tribal differences. Although the protesters did not succeed in reclaiming Alcatraz Island, they drew national attention to their struggle and inspired the growing "Red Power" movement. In 1972 members of the radical American Indian Movement occupied a Bureau of Indian Affairs office in Washington, D.C., and then in 1973 a trading post at Wounded Knee, South Dakota, where U.S. Army troops had massacred three hundred Sioux men, women, and children in 1890.

At the same time, more moderate activists, working through such pan-tribal organizations as the National Congress of American Indians and the Native American Rights Fund, lobbied Congress for greater rights and resources to govern themselves and to strengthen their tribal cultures. In response to those demands, Congress and the federal courts returned millions of acres of land to tribal ownership, and in 1975 Congress passed the Indian Self-Determination and Education Assistance Act. Despite these successes, conditions for most Native Americans remained grim during the 1970s and 1980s: American Indians had a higher rate of tuberculosis, alcoholism, and suicide than any other group. Nine of ten lived in substandard housing, and unemployment rates for Indians were almost 40 percent.

As activists from various groups made all Americans increasingly aware of discrimination and inequality, policymakers struggled to frame remedies. As early as 1965, President Johnson had acknowledged the limits of civil rights legislation. "You do not take a person who, for years, has been hobbled by chains and liberate him, bring him up to the starting line of a race and then say, 'you are free to compete with all the others,'" Johnson told an audience at Howard University, "and still justly believe that you have been completely fair." In this speech, Johnson called for "not just

Affirmative Action

legal equality . . . but equality as a fact and equality as a result." Here Johnson joined his belief that the federal government must help *individuals* attain the skills necessary to compete in American society to a new concept: equality could be measured by *group* outcomes or results.

Practical issues also contributed to the shift in emphasis from individual opportunity to group outcomes. The 1964 Civil Rights Act had outlawed discrimination but seemingly had stipulated that action could be taken only when an employer "intentionally engaged" in discrimination against an individual. This individual, case-by-case approach to equal rights created a nightmare for the Equal Employment Opportunity Commission (EEOC). The tens of thousands of cases filed suggested a pervasive pattern of racial and sexual discrimination in American education and employment, but each required proof of "intentional" actions against an individual. Some people were beginning to argue that it was possible, instead, to prove discrimination by "results"—by the relative number of African Americans or women, for example, an employer had hired or promoted.

In 1969 the Nixon administration implemented the first major government affirmative-action program to promote "equality of results." The Philadelphia Plan (so called because it targeted government contracts in that city) required businesses contracting with the federal government to show (in the words of President Nixon) "affirmative action to meet the goals of increasing minority employment" and set specific numerical "goals," or quotas, for employers. Affirmative action for women and members of racial and ethnic minorities was soon required by all major government contracts, and many large corporations and educational institutions began their own programs.

Supporters saw affirmative action as a remedy for the lasting effects of past discrimination. Critics (some of whom were supporters of racial and sexual equality) argued that attempts to create proportional representation for women and minorities meant discrimination against other individuals who had not created past discrimination, and that group-based remedies violated the principle that individuals should be judged on their own merits. As affirmative-action programs began to have an impact in hiring and university admissions, bringing members of underrepresented groups into college classrooms, law firms, schoolrooms, construction companies, police stations, and firehouses nationwide, a deepening recession made jobs scarce. Thus increasing the number of minorities and women hired often meant reducing the number of white men. White working-class men were most adversely affected by the policy, and many resented it.

THE WOMEN'S MOVEMENT AND GAY LIBERATION

During the 1950s, even as more and more women joined the paid work force and participated in the political life of the nation, American society and culture emphasized women's private roles as wives and mothers. The women's movement that had won American women the vote in the 1920s had all but disappeared. But during the 1960s, a "second wave" of the American women's movement emerged, and by the 1970s mainstream and radical activists waged a multifront battle for "women's liberation."

In 1963, the surprise popularity of Betty Friedan's *The Feminine Mystique* signaled that there was ample fuel for a revived women's movement. Writing as a housewife and mother (though she had a long history of political activism as well), Friedan described "the problem with no name," the dissatisfaction of educated, middle-class wives and mothers like herself, who—looking at their nice homes and families—wondered guiltily if that was all there was to life. This "problem" was not new; the vague sense of dissatisfaction plaguing housewives had been a staple topic for women's magazines in the 1950s. But Friedan, instead of blaming individual women for failing to adapt to women's proper role, blamed the role itself and the society that created it.

The organized, liberal wing of the women's movement emerged in 1966, with the founding of the National Organization for Women (NOW).

Liberal and Radical Feminism

NOW, made up primarily of educated, professional women, was a traditional lobbying group; its goal was to pressure the EEOC to enforce the 1964 Civil Rights Act. Racial discrimination was the EEOC's focus, and discrimination on the basis of sex was such a low priority that the topic could be treated as a joke. When a reporter asked EEOC chair Franklin Roosevelt Jr., "What about sex?" Roosevelt laughed, "Don't get me started. I'm all for it." Women who faced workplace discrimination were not amused by such comments, and by 1970, NOW had one hundred chapters with more than three thousand members nationwide.

Another strand of the women's movement developed from the nation's increasingly radical movements for social change and justice. Many women, as they worked for civil rights or against the war in Vietnam, found themselves treated as second-class citizens—making coffee, not policy. As they analyzed inequality in America's social and political structure, these young women began to discuss their own oppression, and the oppression of all women, in American society. In 1968 a group of women gathered outside the Miss America Pageant in Atlantic City to protest the "degrading mindless-boob girlie symbol" represented by the beauty pageant. Although nothing was burned, the pejorative 1970s term for feminists, "bra-burners," came from this event, in which women threw items of "enslavement" (girdles, high heels, curlers, and bras) into a "Freedom Trashcan."

The feminism embraced by these young activists and others who challenged women's oppression was never a single, coherent set of beliefs. Some argued that the world should be governed by peaceful, noncompetitive values, which they believed were intrinsically female; others claimed that society imposed gender roles and that there were no innate differences between men and women. Most radical feminists, however, practiced what they called "personal politics." They believed, as feminist author Charlotte Bunch explained, that "there is no private domain of a person's life that is not political, and there is no political issue that is not ultimately personal." Some of these young women began to meet in "consciousness-raising" groups to discuss how, in their personal, everyday lives, women were subordinated by men and by a patriarchal society. In the early 1970s, women throughout the nation came together, in suburban kitchens, college dorm rooms, and churches or synagogues, to create their own consciousness-raising groups, exploring topics such as power relationships in romance and marriage, sexuality, abortion, healthcare, work, and family.

During the 1970s, the diverse groups that made up the women's movement claimed significant achievements.

Accomplishments of the Women's Movement

Feminists worked for reforms that touched all aspects of American life: the right of a married woman to obtain credit in her own name; the right of an unmarried woman to obtain birth control; the right of women to serve on juries; the end of sex-segregated help wanted ads. They sought to change attitudes about rape and procedures for dealing with rape victims, such as the claim by a psychiatrist at the University of Kansas student health center in 1970: "A woman sometimes plays a big part in provoking her attacker by . . . her overall attitude and appearance." But by the end of the decade, activists working on the state and local level had established rape crisis centers, educated local police and hospital officials about procedures for protecting survivors of rape, and even changed laws.

As most of the medical establishment paid little attention to women's desires to understand—and take control of—their own sexual and reproductive health, the Boston Women's Health Collective published *Our Bodies,*

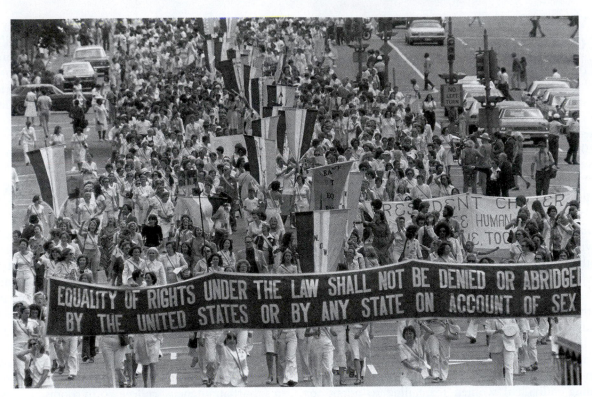

▲ On August 26, 1977, supporters of the Equal Rights Amendment (ERA) march down Pennsylvania Avenue following a ceremony in the White House Rose Garden that had proclaimed it "Women's Equality Day." The ERA initially had broad support from both Democrats and Republicans, but was ratified by only thirty-five of the necessary thirty-eight states.   *(AP Images)*

Ourselves in 1971 (the original edition sold more than 3 million copies). And women who sought the right to safe and legal abortions won a major victory in 1973 when the Supreme Court, in a 7-to-2 decision on *Roe v. Wade*, ruled that privacy rights protected a woman's choice to end a pregnancy.

NOW and many other women's organizations worked together to promote an Equal Rights Amendment that would end all discriminatory treatment on the basis of sex, the same amendment first proposed by the National Woman's Party in the 1920s. On March 22, 1972, Congress approved the amendment, stating simply that "equality of rights under the law shall not be denied or abridged by the United States or by any State on account of sex." By the end of the year, 22 states (of the 38 necessary to amend the Constitution) had ratified the ERA. Also in 1972, Congress passed Title IX of the Higher Education Act, which prevented federal funds from going to any college or university that discriminated against women. As a result, universities began to channel money to women's athletics, and women's participation in sports boomed.

Women's applications to graduate programs also boomed. In 1970 only 8.4 percent of medical school graduates and 5.4 percent of law school graduates were women. By 1979, 23 percent of the graduating class of America's medical schools was female, and 28.5 percent of new lawyers were women. During the 1970s, women greatly increased their roles in religious organizations, including the Church of Christ, the Unitarian and Episcopalian churches, and Reform and Conservative Judaism. Some denominations began to ordain women. Colleges and universities established women's studies departments, and by 1980 more than thirty thousand college courses focused on the study of women or gender relations.

The women's movement encompassed a broad range of women, but it was met by powerful opposition, much

Opposition to the Women's Movement

of it from women. Many women believed that middle-class feminists did not understand the realities of their world. They had no desire to be "equal" if that meant giving up traditional gender roles in marriage or going out to work at low-wage, physically exhausting jobs. African American women and Latinas, many of whom had been active in movements for the liberation of their peoples and some of whom had helped create second-wave feminism, often came to regard feminism as a "white" movement that ignored their cultural traditions and needs; some believed that the women's movement diverted time and energy away from the fight for racial equality.

Organized opposition to feminism came primarily from conservative, often religiously motivated men and women. As one conservative Christian writer claimed, "The Bible clearly states that the wife is to submit to her husband's leadership . . . just as she would to Christ her Lord." Such beliefs, along with fears about changing gender roles and expectations, fueled the STOP-ERA movement led by Phyllis Schlafly, a lawyer and prominent conservative political activist. Schlafly argued that ERA supporters were "a bunch of bitter women seeking a constitutional cure for their personal problems." She attacked the women's movement as "a total assault on the role of the American woman as wife and mother, and on the family as the basic unit of society." Schlafly and her supporters argued that the ERA would foster federal intervention in personal life, decriminalize rape, force Americans to use unisex toilets, and make women subject to the military draft.

Many women saw feminism as an attack on the choices they had made and felt that by opposing the ERA they were defending their traditional roles. In fighting the ERA, tens of thousands of women became politically experienced; they fed a growing grassroots conservative movement that would come into its own in the 1980s. And by the mid-1970s, the STOP-ERA movement had stalled the Equal Rights Amendment. Despite Congress's extension of the ratification deadline, the amendment would fall three states short of ratification and expire in 1982.

In the early 1970s, gay men and lesbians faced widespread discrimination. Consensual sexual intercourse between people of the same sex was illegal in almost every state, and until 1973 homosexuality was labeled a mental disorder by the American Psychiatric Association. Homosexual couples did not receive partnership benefits, such as health insurance; they could not marry or adopt children. The issue of gay and lesbian rights divided even progressive organizations: in 1970 the New York City chapter of NOW expelled its lesbian officers. As open racism declined, gay men and women remained targets of discrimination in

Gay Liberation

hiring and endured public ridicule, harassment, and physical attacks.

Gay men and lesbians, unlike most members of racial minorities, could conceal the identity that made them vulnerable to discrimination and harassment. Remaining "in the closet" offered individuals some protection, but that option also made it very difficult to organize a political movement. There were small "homophile" organizations, such as the Mattachine Society (named for the Société Mattachine, a medieval musical organization whose members performed in masks, to evoke the "masked" lives of gay Americans) and the Daughters of Bilitis (after a work of love poems between women), which had worked for gay rights since the 1950s. But the symbolic beginning of the gay liberation movement came on June 28, 1969, when New York City police raided the Stonewall Inn, a gay bar in Greenwich Village, for violating the New York City law that made it illegal for more than three homosexual patrons to occupy a bar at the same time. That night, for the first time, patrons stood up to the police. As word spread through New York's gay community, hundreds more joined the confrontation. The next morning, New Yorkers found a new slogan spray-painted on neighborhood walls: "Gay Power."

Inspired by the Stonewall riot, some men and women worked openly and militantly for gay rights. They focused on a dual agenda: legal equality and the promotion of Gay Pride. In a version of the identity politics adopted by racial and ethnic communities, some rejected the notion of fitting into straight (heterosexual) culture and helped create distinctive gay communities. "Look out, straights," wrote gay liberation activist Martha Shelley in 1970. "We're gonna make our own revolution." By 1973, there were about eight hundred gay organizations in the United States. Centered in big cities and on college campuses, most organizations tried to create supportive environments for gay men and lesbians to come "out of the closet." Once "out," they could use their numbers ("We are everywhere" was a popular slogan) to push for political reform, such as nondiscrimination statutes similar to those that protected women and racial minority groups. By the end of the decade, gay men and lesbians were a public political force in cities including New York, Miami, and San Francisco, and played an increasingly visible role in the social and political life of the nation.

THE END IN VIETNAM

Of all the divisions in American politics and society at the end of the 1960s, none was as pervasive as that over the war in Vietnam. "I'm not going to end up like LBJ,"

Richard Nixon vowed after winning the 1968 presidential election, recalling that the war had destroyed Johnson's political career. "I'm going to stop that war. Fast." But he did not. He understood that the conflict was generating deep divisions at home and hurting the nation's image abroad, yet—like officials in the Johnson administration—he feared that a precipitous withdrawal would harm American credibility on the world stage. Anxious to get American troops out of Vietnam, Nixon was at the same time no less committed than his predecessors to preserving an independent, noncommunist South Vietnam. To accomplish these aims, he set upon a policy that at once contracted and expanded the war.

A centerpiece of Nixon's policy was "Vietnamization"—the building up of South Vietnamese forces to replace U.S. forces. Nixon hoped that

Invasion of Cambodia

such a policy would quiet domestic opposition and also advance the peace talks under way in Paris since May 1968. Accordingly, the president began to withdraw American troops from Vietnam, decreasing their number from 543,000 in the spring of 1969 to 156,800 by the end of 1971, and to 60,000 by the fall of 1972. Vietnamization did help limit domestic dissent, but it did nothing to end the stalemate in the Paris negotiations. Even as he embarked on this troop withdrawal, therefore, Nixon intensified the bombing of North Vietnam and enemy supply depots in neighboring Cambodia, hoping to pound Hanoi into concessions (see Map 30.2 on page 873).

The bombing of neutral Cambodia commenced in March 1969. Over the next fourteen months, B-52 pilots flew 3,600 missions and dropped over 100,000 tons of bombs on that country. At first the administration went to great lengths to keep the bombing campaign secret. When the North Vietnamese refused to buckle, Nixon turned up the heat: in April 1970 South Vietnamese and U.S. forces invaded Cambodia in search of arms depots and North Vietnamese army sanctuaries. The president announced publicly that he would not allow "the world's most powerful nation" to act "like a pitiful, helpless giant."

Instantly, the antiwar movement rose up, as students on about 450 college campuses went out on strike and hundreds of thousands of demonstrators gathered in various cities to

Protests and Counter-demonstrations

protest the administration's policies. The crisis atmosphere intensified further on May 4, when National Guardsmen in Ohio fired into a crowd of fleeing students at Kent State University, killing 4 young people and wounding 11. Ten days later,

police and state highway patrolmen armed with automatic weapons blasted a women's dormitory at Jackson State, a historically black university in Mississippi, killing 2 students and wounding 9 others. The police claimed they had been shot at, but no evidence of sniping could be found. In Congress, where opposition to the war had been building over the previous months, Nixon's widening of the war sparked outrage, and in June the Senate terminated the Tonkin Gulf Resolution of 1964. After two months, U.S. troops withdrew from Cambodia, having accomplished little.

Americans still, however, remained divided on the war. Although a majority told pollsters they thought the original American troop commitment to Vietnam to have been a mistake, 50 percent said they believed Nixon's claim that the Cambodia invasion would shorten the war. Angered by the sight of demonstrating college students, many voiced support for the president and the war effort. In Washington, an "Honor America Day" program attracted more than 200,000 people who heard Billy Graham and Bob Hope laud administration policy. Nevertheless, though Nixon welcomed these expressions of support, the tumult over the invasion served to reduce his options on the war. Henceforth, solid majorities could be expected to oppose any new missions for U.S. ground troops in Southeast Asia.

Nixon's troubles at home mounted in June 1971, when the *New York Times* began to publish the Pentagon Papers, the top-secret official study of U.S. decisions in the Vietnam War. Nixon secured an injunction to prevent publication, but the Supreme Court overturned the order. Americans learned from this study that political and military leaders frequently had lied to the public about their aims and strategies in Southeast Asia.

Equally troubling, to both opponents and supporters of the war, was the growing evidence of decay within the armed forces. Morale and discipline among troops had been on

Morale Problems in Military

the decline even before Nixon took office, and there were growing reports of drug addiction, desertion, racial discord, even the murder of unpopular officers by enlisted men (a practice called "fragging"). Stories of atrocities committed by U.S. troops also began to make their way home. The court-martial and conviction in 1971 of Lieutenant William Calley, who was charged with overseeing the killing of more than three hundred unarmed South Vietnamese civilians in the hamlet of My Lai in 1968, got particular attention. An army photographer captured the horror in graphic pictures. For many, the massacre signified the dehumanizing impact of the war on those who fought it.

▲ Aftermath of the My Lai massacre, March 16, 1968, photographed by U.S. Army photographer Ronald Haeberle of the 11th Infantry Brigade, Americal Division. *(Ron Haeberle/Life magazine © Time Inc.)*

The Nixon administration, meanwhile, stepped up its efforts to pressure Hanoi into a settlement. Johnson had lacked the will to "go to the brink," Nixon told Kissinger, "I have the will in spades." When the North Vietnamese launched a major offensive across the border into South Vietnam in March 1972, Nixon responded with a massive aerial onslaught against North Vietnam. In December 1972, after an apparent peace agreement collapsed when the South Vietnamese refused to moderate their position, the United States launched a massive air strike on the North—the so-called Christmas bombing.

A diplomatic agreement was, however, close. Months earlier, Kissinger and his North Vietnamese counterpart in the negotiations, Le Duc Tho, had resolved many of the outstanding issues. Most notably, Kissinger agreed that North Vietnamese troops could remain in the South after the settlement, while Tho abandoned Hanoi's insistence that the Saigon government of Nguyen Van Thieu be removed. Nixon had instructed Kissinger to make concessions because the president was eager to improve relations with the Soviet Union and China, to win back the alle-

Paris Peace Accords

giance of America's allies, and to restore stability at home. On January 27, 1973, Kissinger and Le Duc Tho signed a cease-fire agreement in Paris, and Nixon compelled a reluctant Thieu to accept it by threatening to cut off U.S. aid while at the same time promising to defend the South if the North violated the agreement. In the accord, the United States promised to withdraw all of its troops within sixty days. North Vietnamese troops would be allowed to stay in South Vietnam, and a coalition government that included the Vietcong eventually would be formed in the South.

The United States pulled its troops out of Vietnam, leaving behind some military advisers. Soon, both North and South violated the cease-fire, and full-scale war erupted once more. The feeble South Vietnamese government, despite holding a clear superiority in the number of tanks and combat-ready troops, could not hold out. Just before its surrender, hundreds of Americans and Vietnamese who had worked for them were hastily evacuated from Saigon. On April 29, 1975, the South Vietnamese government collapsed, and Vietnam was reunified under a communist government based in Hanoi. Shortly thereafter, Saigon was renamed Ho Chi Minh City for the persevering patriot who had died in 1969.

The overall costs of the war were immense. More than 58,000 Americans and between 1.5 and 2 million Vietnamese had died. Civilian deaths in Cambodia and Laos numbered in the hundreds of thousands. The war cost the United States at least $170 billion, and billions more

Costs of the Vietnam War

would be paid out in veterans' benefits. The vast sums spent on the war became unavailable for investment in domestic programs. Instead, the nation suffered inflation and retreat from reform, as well as political schism and abuses of executive power. The war also delayed accommodation with the Soviet Union and the People's Republic of China, fueled friction with allies, and alienated Third World nations.

In 1975 communists assumed control and formed repressive governments in Vietnam, Cambodia, and Laos, but beyond Indochina the domino effect once predicted by U.S. officials never occurred. Acute hunger afflicted the people of those devastated lands. Soon refugees—"boat people"—crowded aboard unsafe vessels in an attempt to escape their battered homelands. Many emigrated to the United States, where they were received with mixed feelings by Americans reluctant to be reminded of defeat in Asia. But many Americans faced the fact that the United States, which had relentlessly bombed, burned, and defoliated once-rich agricultural lands, bore considerable responsibility for the plight of the southeast Asian peoples.

Americans seemed both angry and confused about the nation's war experience. As historian William Appleman Williams observed, for the first time Americans had had their overseas sphere of influence pushed back, violently, and they were suffering from a serious case of "empire shock." Hawkish observers

Debate over the Lessons of Vietnam

claimed that America's failure in Vietnam undermined the nation's credibility and tempted enemies to exploit opportunities at the expense of U.S. interests. They pointed to a "Vietnam syndrome"—a resulting American suspicion of foreign entanglements—which they feared would inhibit the future exercise of U.S. power. America lost in Vietnam, they asserted, because Americans had lost their guts at home.

Dovish analysts drew different conclusions, denying that the military had suffered undue restrictions. Some blamed the war on an imperial presidency that had permitted strong-willed men to act without restraint and on a weak Congress that had conceded too much power to the executive branch. Make the president adhere to the checks-and-balances system—make him go to Congress for a declaration of war—these critics counseled, and America

▲ Dedicated in 1993 in Washington, D.C., the Vietnam Women's Memorial honors the several thousand military women who served in Vietnam, many of them as nurses who volunteered for duty. One nurse, Judy Marron, remembered treating wounded soldiers round the clock: "There were days when the stress and strain and blood and guts almost had to equal the frontlines." This bronze sculpture, by Glenna Goodacre, stands near the long wall on which are etched the names of Americans who died in Vietnam. *(Brad Markel/Liaison Agency)*

would become less interventionist. This view found expression in the War Powers Act of 1973, which sought to limit the president's warmaking freedom. Henceforth, Congress would have to approve any commitment of U.S. forces to combat action lasting more than sixty days. In the same year, the draft (which had been shifted to a lottery system in 1969), came to an end; the U.S. military would henceforth be a volunteer army.

Public discussion of the lessons of the Vietnam War was also stimulated by veterans' calls for help in dealing

Vietnam Veterans

with posttraumatic stress disorder, which afflicted thousands of the 2.8 million Vietnam veterans. Once home, they suffered nightmares and extreme nervousness. Doctors reported that the disorder stemmed primarily from the soldiers' having seen so many children, women, and elderly people killed. Some GIs inadvertently killed these people; some killed them vengefully and later felt guilt. Other veterans heightened public awareness of the war by publicizing their deteriorating health from the effects of the defoliant Agent Orange and other herbicides they had handled or were accidentally sprayed with in Vietnam. The Vietnam Veterans Memorial, erected in Washington, D.C., in 1982, has kept the issue alive, as have many oral history projects of veterans conducted by school and college students in classes to this day.

NIXON, KISSINGER, AND THE WORLD

Even as Nixon and Kissinger tried to achieve victory in Vietnam, they understood that the United States had overreached in the 1960s with a military commitment that had caused massive bloodshed, deep domestic divisions, and economic dislocation. The difficulties of the war signified to them that American power was limited and, in relative terms, in decline. This reality necessitated a new approach to the Cold War, and both moved quickly to reorient American policy. In particular, they believed the United States had to adapt to a new, multipolar international system; no longer could that system be defined simply by the Soviet-American rivalry. Western Europe was becoming a major player in its own right, as was Japan. The Middle East loomed increasingly large, due in large part to America's growing dependence on oil from the region. Above all, Americans had to come to grips with the reality of China by rethinking the policy of hostile isolation followed since the communist takeover in 1949.

They were an unlikely duo—the reclusive, ambitious Californian, born of Quaker parents, and the sociable, dynamic Jewish intellectual who had fled Nazi Germany as a child. Nixon, ten years older, was more or less a career politician, while Kissinger had made his name as a Harvard professor and foreign policy consultant. Whereas Nixon was a staunch Republican, Kissinger would have been quite prepared to join Hubert Humphrey's administration had the Democrat prevailed in the election. What the two men had in common was a tendency toward paranoia about rivals and a capacity to think in large conceptual terms about America's place in the world.

In July 1969 Nixon and Kissinger acknowledged the limits of American power and resources when they announced the Nixon Doctrine. The United States, they said, would continue to provide economic aid to allies in Asia and elsewhere, but these allies should no longer count on American troops. It was

Nixon Doctrine

an admission that Washington could no longer afford to sustain its many overseas commitments and therefore would have to rely more on regional allies—including, it turned out, many authoritarian regimes—to maintain an anticommunist world order. Although Nixon did not say so, his doctrine amounted to a partial retreat from the 1947 Truman Doctrine, with its promise to support noncommunist governments facing internal or external threats to their existence.

If the Nixon Doctrine was one pillar of the new foreign policy, the other was détente: measured cooperation with the Soviets through negotiations within a general environment of rivalry, drawn from the French word for "relaxation." Détente's primary purpose, like that of the containment doctrine it resembled, was to check Soviet expansion and limit the Soviet arms buildup, though now that goal would be accomplished through diplomacy and mutual concessions. The second part of the strategy sought to curb revolution and radicalism in the Third World so as to quash threats to American interests. More specifically, the Cold War and limited wars like that in Vietnam were costing too much; expanded trade with friendlier Soviets and Chinese might reduce the huge U.S. balance-of-payments deficit. And improving relations with both communist giants, at a time when Sino-Soviet tensions were increasing, might exacerbate feuding between the two, weakening communism.

Détente

The Soviet Union's leadership had its own reasons for wanting détente. The Cold War was a drain on its resources, too, and by the late 1960s defense needs and consumer demands were increasingly at odds. Improved ties with Washington would also allow the USSR to focus more on its increasingly fractious relations with China and might generate serious progress on outstanding European issues, including the status of Germany and Berlin. Some ideologues in the Moscow leadership remained deeply suspicious of cozying up to the American capitalists, but they did not prevail over advocates of change. Thus in May 1972 the United States and the USSR agreed in the ABM Treaty (officially the Treaty on the Limitation of Anti-Ballistic Missile Systems) to slow the costly arms race by limiting the construction and deployment of intercontinental ballistic missiles and antiballistic missile defenses.

While cultivating détente with the Soviet Union, the United States took dramatic steps to end more than two decades of Sino-American hostility. The Chinese welcomed the change because they wanted to spur trade and hoped that friendlier Sino-American relations would make their onetime ally and now enemy, the Soviet Union, more cautious. Nixon reasoned

Opening to China

▲ "This was the week that changed the world," Richard Nixon said of his visit to China in February 1972. Many historians agree and consider the China opening Nixon's greatest achievement as president. When he and wife Pat visited the Great Wall the president reportedly remarked: "This is a great wall." *(Chicago Historical Society)*

the same way: "We're using the Chinese thaw to get the Russians shook." In early 1972 Nixon made a historic trip to "Red China," where he and the venerable Chinese leaders Mao Zedong and Zhou Enlai agreed to disagree on a number of issues, except one: the Soviet Union should not be permitted to make gains in Asia. Sino-American relations improved slightly, and official diplomatic recognition and the exchange of ambassadors came in 1979.

The opening to communist China and the policy of détente with the Soviet Union reflected Nixon's and Kissinger's belief in the importance of maintaining stability among the great powers. In the Third World, too, they sought stability, though there they hoped to get it not by change but by maintaining the status quo. As it happened, events in the Third World would provide the Nixon-Kissinger approach with its greatest test, and not merely because of Vietnam.

In the Middle East the situation had grown more volatile in the aftermath of the Arab-Israeli Six-Day War

Wars in the Middle East

in 1967. In that conflict, Israel had scored victories against Egypt and Syria, seizing the Sinai Peninsula and the Gaza Strip from Egypt, the West Bank and East Jerusalem from Jordan, and the Golan Heights from Syria (see Map 33.2). Instantly, Israel's regional position was transformed, as it gained 28,000 square miles and could henceforth defend itself more easily against invading military forces. But the victory came at a price. Gaza and the West Bank were the ancestral home of hundreds of thousands of Palestinians and the more recent home of additional hundreds of thousands of Palestinian refugees from the 1948 Arab-Israeli conflict (see Chapter 28). Suddenly Israel found itself governing large numbers of people who wanted nothing more than to see Israel destroyed. When the Israelis began to establish Jewish settlements in their newly won areas, Arab resentment grew even stronger. Terrorists associated with the Palestinian Liberation Organization (PLO) made hit-

OPEC and the 1973 Oil Embargo

If one date can be said to have marked the relative decline of American power in the Cold War era and the arrival of the Arab nations of the Middle East as important players on the world stage, it would be October 20, 1973. That day, the Arab members of the Organization of Petroleum Exporting Countries (OPEC)—Saudi Arabia, Iraq, Kuwait, Libya, and Algeria—imposed a total embargo on oil shipments to the United States and to other allies of Israel. The move was in retaliation against U.S. support of Israel in the two-week-old Yom Kippur War. The embargo followed a decision by the members three days earlier to unilaterally raise oil prices, from $3.01 to $5.12 per barrel. In December, the five Arab countries, joined by Iran, raised prices again, to $11.65 per barrel, close to a fourfold increase from early October. "This decision," said National Security Adviser Henry Kissinger of the price hike, "was one of the pivotal events in the history of this century."

If Kissinger exaggerated, it was not by much. Gasoline prices surged across America, and some dealers ran low on supplies. Frustrated Americans endured endless lines at the pumps and shivered in underheated homes. Letters to newspaper editors expressed anger not merely at the Arab governments but also at the major oil companies, whose profits soared. When the embargo was lifted after five months, in April 1974, oil prices stayed high, and the aftereffects of the embargo would linger through the decade.

Like no other event could, it confirmed the extent to which Americans no longer exercised full control over their own economic destiny.

Just twenty years before, in the early 1950s, Americans had produced at home all the oil they needed. Detroit automakers had no difficulty selling ever larger gas-guzzlers with ever more outrageous tail fins. By the early 1960s, the picture had begun to change, as American factories and automobiles then were dependent on foreign sources for one out of every six barrels of oil they used. By 1972, the figure had gone up to about two out of six, or more than 30 percent. Although in absolute terms the amount was massive—U.S. motorists consumed one of every seven barrels used in the world each day—few Americans worried. Hence the shock of the embargo. As author Daniel Yergin has put it, "The shortfall struck at fundamental beliefs in the endless abundance of resources, convictions so deeply rooted in the American character and experience that a large part of the public did not even know, up until October 1973, that the United States imported any oil at all."

Although Americans resumed their wasteful ways after the embargo ended, an important change had occurred, whether people understood it or not. The United States had become a dependent nation, its economic future linked to decisions by Arab leaders half a world away.

◀ In 1976 OPEC sharply raised the price of oil a second time, prompting this editorial cartoon by Don Wright of the *Miami News*.

(Don Wright in the Miami News, *1976, Tribune Media Services)*

and-run raids on Jewish settlements, hijacked jetliners, and murdered Israeli athletes at the 1972 Olympic Games in Munich, West Germany. The Israelis retaliated by assassinating PLO leaders.

In October 1973, on the Jewish High Holy Day of Yom Kippur, Egypt and Syria attacked Israel. Their motives were complex, but primarily they sought revenge for the 1967 defeat. Caught by surprise, Israel reeled before launching an effective counteroffensive against Soviet-armed Egyptian forces in the Sinai. In an attempt to punish Americans for their pro-Israel stance, the Organization of Petroleum Exporting Countries (OPEC), a group of mostly Arab nations that had joined together to raise the price of oil, embargoed shipments of oil to the United States and other supporters of Israel. An energy crisis and dramatically higher oil prices rocked the nation. Soon Kissinger arranged a cease-fire in the war, but not until March 1974 did OPEC lift the oil embargo. The next year Kissinger persuaded Egypt and Israel to accept a U.N. peacekeeping force in the Sinai. But peace did not come to the region, for Palestinians and other Arabs still vowed to destroy Israel, and Israelis insisted on building more Jewish settlements in occupied lands.

In Latin America, meanwhile, the Nixon administration sought to preserve stability and to thwart radical leftist challenges to authoritarian rule. In Chile, after voters in 1970

Antiradicalism in Latin America and Africa

elected a Marxist president, Salvador Allende, the CIA began secret operations to disrupt Chile and encouraged military officers to stage a coup. In 1973 a military junta ousted Allende and installed an authoritarian regime under General Augusto Pinochet. (Allende was subsequently murdered.) Washington publicly denied any role in the affair that implanted iron-fisted tyranny in Chile for two decades.

In Africa as well, Washington preferred the status quo. Nixon backed the white-minority regime in Rhodesia (now Zimbabwe) and activated the CIA in a failed effort to defeat a Soviet- and Cuban-backed faction in newly independent Angola's civil war. In South Africa, Nixon tolerated the white rulers who imposed the segregationist policy of apartheid on blacks and mixed-race "coloureds" (85 percent of the population), keeping them poor, disfranchised, and ghettoized in prisonlike townships. After the leftist government came to power in Angola, however, Washington took a keener interest in the rest of Africa, building economic ties and sending arms to friendly black nations, such as Kenya and the Congo. The administration also began to distance the

United States from the white governments of Rhodesia and South Africa. America had to "prevent the radicalization of Africa," said Kissinger.

PRESIDENTIAL POLITICS AND THE CRISIS OF LEADERSHIP

Richard Nixon took pride in his foreign policy accomplishments, but they were overshadowed by his failures at home. He betrayed the public trust and broke laws, large and small. His misconduct, combined with Americans' growing belief that their leaders had lied to them repeatedly about the war in Vietnam, shook Americans' faith in government. This new mistrust joined with conservatives' traditional suspicion of big, activist government to create a crisis of leadership and undermine liberal policies that had governed the nation since the New Deal, even in the Eisenhower era. The profound suspicion of presidential leadership and government action that enveloped the nation by the end of the Watergate hearings would limit what Gerald Ford and Jimmy Carter, Nixon's successors to the presidency, could accomplish.

Richard Nixon was one of America's most complex presidents. Brilliant, driven, politically cunning, able to address changing global realities with creativity—Nixon was also crude, prejudiced against Jews and African Americans, happy to use dirty tricks and the power of the presidency against those he considered his enemies, and driven by a sense of resentment that bordered on paranoia. Despite his tenacity and intelligence, Nixon—the son of a grocer from an agricultural region of southern California—was never accepted by the sophisticated northeastern liberal elite. (After Nixon's election, *Washingtonian* magazine joked that "cottage cheese with ketchup" had replaced elegant desserts at White House dinners.) Nixon loathed the liberal establishment, which loathed him back, and his presidency was driven by that hatred as much as by any strong philosophical commitment to conservative principles.

Nixon's Domestic Agenda

Nixon's domestic policy initiatives have long confused historians. Much of his agenda was liberal, expanding federal programs to improve society. The Nixon administration pioneered affirmative action. It doubled the budgets of the new National Endowment for the Humanities (NEH) and National Endowment for the Arts (NEA). Nixon supported the ERA, signed major environmental legislation, created the Occupational Safety and Health Administration (OSHA), actively attempted to manage the economy using deficit spending, and even proposed a guaranteed minimum income for all Americans.

At the same time, Nixon pursued a conservative agenda. One of his major legislative goals was "devolution," or shifting federal government authority to states and localities. He promoted revenue-sharing programs that distributed federal funds back to the states to use as they saw fit, thus appealing to those who were angry about, as they saw it, paying high taxes to support liberal "giveaway" programs for poor and minority Americans. As president, Nixon worked to equate the Republican Party with law and order and the Democrats with permissiveness, crime, drugs, radicalism, and the "hippie lifestyle." To capitalize on the backlash against the 1960s movements for social change and consolidate the support of those he called "the silent majority," Nixon fostered division, using his outspoken vice president, Spiro Agnew, to attack war protesters and critics as "naughty children," "effete . . . snobs," and "ideological eunuchs." He appointed four conservative justices to the Supreme Court: Warren Burger, Harry Blackmun, Lewis Powell Jr., and William Rehnquist.

With such a confusing record, was Nixon liberal, conservative, or simply pragmatic? Much of his "liberal" agenda was not so much liberal as it was tricky—a term commonly applied to Nixon at the time. Instead of attacking liberal programs and the entrenched government bureaucracies that administered them, he attempted to undermine them while appearing to offer support. For example, when the Nixon administration proposed a guaranteed minimum income for all Americans, including the working poor, his larger goal was to dismantle the federal welfare system and destroy its liberal bureaucracy of social workers (no longer necessary under Nixon's model). And though Nixon doubled funding for the NEA, he redirected awards from the northeastern art establishment—the "elite" that he thought of as an enemy—toward local and regional art groups that sponsored popular art forms, such as representational painting or folk music.

In addition, recognizing the possibility of attracting white southerners to the Republican Party, Nixon pursued a highly pragmatic "southern strategy." He nominated two southerners for positions on the Supreme Court—one of whom had a segregationist record—and when Congress declined to confirm either nominee, Nixon protested angrily, saying, "I understand the bitter feelings of millions of Americans who live in the South." After the Supreme Court upheld a school desegregation plan that required a North Carolina school system—still highly segregated fifteen years after the *Brown* decision—to achieve racial integration by removing both black and white children from their neighborhood schools and busing them to schools elsewhere in the county (*Swann v. Charlotte-Mecklenburg*, 1971), Nixon denounced busing as a reckless and extreme remedy.

Nixon was almost sure of reelection in 1972. His Democratic opponent was George McGovern, a progressive senator from South Dakota and strong opponent of the Vietnam War. McGovern appealed to the left and essentially wrote off the middle, declaring, "I am not a centrist candidate." Alabama governor George Wallace, running on a third-party ticket, withdrew from the race after an assassination attempt left him paralyzed. The Nixon campaign, however, was taking no chances. On June 17, four months before the election, five men were caught breaking into the Democratic National Committee's offices at the Watergate apartment and office complex in Washington, D.C. The men were associated with the Committee to Re-elect the President, known as CREEP. The break-in got little attention at the time, and Nixon was swept into office in November with 60 percent of the popular vote. McGovern carried only Massachusetts and the District of Columbia. But even as Nixon triumphed, his downfall had begun.

Enemies and Dirty Tricks

From the beginning of his presidency, Nixon was obsessed with the idea that, in a time of national turmoil, he was surrounded by enemies. He made "enemies lists," hundreds of names long, that included all black members of Congress and the presidents of most Ivy League universities. The Nixon administration worked, in the words of one of its members, to "use the available federal machinery to screw our political enemies." On Nixon's order, his aide Charles Colson (best known for his maxim "When you've got them by the balls, their hearts and minds will follow") formed a secret group called the Plumbers. Their first job was to break into the office of the psychiatrist treating Daniel Ellsberg, the former Pentagon employee who had gone public with the Pentagon Papers, looking for material to discredit him. The Plumbers expanded their "dirty tricks" operations during the 1972 presidential primaries and campaign, bugging phones, infiltrating campaign staffs, even writing and distributing anonymous letters falsely accusing Democratic candidates of sexual misconduct. They had already bugged the Democratic National Committee offices and were going back to plant more surveillance equipment when they were caught by the D.C. police at the Watergate complex.

Nixon was not directly involved in the Watergate affair. But instead of distancing himself and firing those

Watergate Cover-up and Investigation

responsible, he chose to cover up their connection to the break-ins. He had the CIA stop the FBI's investigation, citing reasons of national security. At this point, Nixon had obstructed justice—a felony and, under the Constitution, an impeachable crime—but he had also, it seemed, halted the investigation. However, two young, relatively unknown reporters for the *Washington Post,* Carl Bernstein and Bob Woodward, would not give up on the story. Aided by an anonymous, highly placed government official whom they code-named Deep Throat (the title of a notorious 1972 X-rated film), they began to follow a money trail that led straight to the White House. (W. Mark Felt, who was second-in-command at the FBI in the early 1970s, publicly identified himself as Watergate's Deep Throat in 2005.)

The Watergate cover-up continued to unravel under the scrutiny of both the courts and Congress. From May to August 1973, the Senate held televised public hearings on the Watergate affair. White House Counsel John Dean, fearful that he was being made the fall guy for the entire Watergate fiasco, gave damning testimony. Then, on July 13, a White House aide told the Senate Committee that Nixon regularly recorded his conversations in the Oval Office. These tape recordings were the "smoking gun" that could prove Nixon's direct involvement in the cover-up—but Nixon refused to turn the tapes over to Congress.

As Nixon and Congress fought over the tapes, Nixon faced scandals on other fronts. In October 1973, Vice

Impeachment and Resignation

President Spiro Agnew resigned, following charges that he had accepted bribes while governor of Maryland. Following constitutional procedures, Nixon appointed and Congress approved Michigan's Gerald Ford, the House minority leader, as Agnew's replacement. Meanwhile, Nixon's staff was increasingly concerned about his excessive drinking and seeming mental instability. Then, on October 24, 1973, the House of Representatives began impeachment proceedings against the president.

Under court order, Nixon began to release edited portions of the Oval Office tapes to Congress. Although the first tapes revealed no criminal activity, the public was shocked by Nixon's constant obscenities and racist slurs. Finally, in July 1974, the Supreme Court ruled that Nixon must release all the tapes. Despite "mysterious" erasures

▲ Resigning in disgrace as impeachment for his role in the Watergate cover-up became a certainty, Richard Nixon flashes the "V for victory" sign as he leaves the White House for the last time.
(Nixon Presidential Materials Project, National Archives and Record Administration)

on two key tapes, the House Judiciary Committee found evidence to impeach Nixon on three grounds: obstruction of justice, abuse of power, and contempt of Congress. On August 9, 1974, facing certain impeachment and conviction, Richard Nixon became the first president of the United States to resign his office.

The Watergate scandal shook the confidence of American citizens in their government. It also prompted Congress to reevaluate the balance of power between the executive and legislative branches. Beginning in 1973, Congress passed several major bills aimed at restricting presidential power. They included not only the War Powers Act, but also the 1974 Budget and Impoundment Control Act, which made it impossible for the president to disregard congressional spending mandates.

Gerald Ford, the nation's first unelected president, faced a nation awash in cynicism. The presidency was

Ford's Presidency

discredited. The economy was in decline. The nation's people were divided. Ford was a decent and honorable man who did his best to end what he called "the long national nightmare." In one of his first official acts as president he issued a full pardon to Richard Nixon, forestalling any attempts to bring criminal charges. Ford's approval ratings plummeted from 71 to 41 percent. Some suggested, with no evidence, that he had struck some sort of sordid deal with Nixon. Ford insisted, for decades, that he had simply acted in the interest of the nation, but shortly before his death in late 2006 he told a reporter that, though few knew it, he and Nixon had been good friends and "I didn't want to see my real friend have the stigma" of criminal charges.

Ford accomplished little domestically during his two and a half years in office. The Democrats gained a large margin in the 1974 congressional elections, and, after Watergate, Congress was willing to exercise its power. Ford almost routinely vetoed its bills—39 in one year—but Congress often overrode his veto. In addition, Ford, during the course of his brief presidency, was the object of constant mockery. In political cartoons, comedy monologues, and especially on the new hit television show *Saturday Night Live,* he was portrayed as a buffoon and a klutz. When he slipped on the steps exiting *Air Force One,* footage appeared on major newscasts. The irony of portraying Ford—who had turned down a chance to play in the National Football League in order to attend Yale Law School—as physically inept was extraordinary. But, as Ford understood, these portrayals began to give the impression that he was a "stumbler," in danger of making blunders of all kinds. Ford caught the fallout of disrespect that Nixon's actions had unleashed. No longer would respect for the office of the presidency prevent the mass media from reporting presidential slips, stumbles, frailties, or misconduct. Ford was the first president to discover how much the rules had changed.

Jimmy Carter, who was elected in 1976 by a slim margin, initially benefited from Americans' suspicion of political leadership. Carter was a one-term governor of Georgia, one of the new southern leaders who were committed to racial equality and integration. He had grown up in the rural Georgia town of Plains, where his family owned a peanut farm, graduated from the Naval Academy, then served as an engineer in the navy's nuclear submarine program. Carter, a deeply religious born-again Christian, made a virtue of his lack of political

Carter as "Outsider" President

experience. Promising the American people, "I will never lie to you," he emphasized his distance from Washington and the political corruption of recent times.

From his inauguration, when he broke with the convention of a motorcade and walked down Pennsylvania Avenue holding hands with his wife and close adviser, Rosalynn, and their young daughter, Amy, Carter rejected the trappings of the imperial presidency and emphasized his populist, outsider appeal. But the outsider status that gained him the presidency would be one of Carter's major drawbacks as president. Though an astute policymaker, he scorned the deal making that was necessary to pass legislation in Congress.

Carter faced problems that would have challenged any leader: the economy continued to decline, energy shortages had not abated, the American people distrusted their government. More than any other American leader of the post–World War II era, Carter was willing to tell the American people things they did not want to hear. As shortages of natural gas forced schools and businesses to close during the bitterly cold winter of 1977, Carter went on television—wearing a cardigan sweater—to speak to the American people about the new era of limits and called for "sacrifice." Carter put energy conservation measures into effect at the White House and government buildings, and proposed to Congress a detailed energy plan that emphasized conservation. In the defining speech of his presidency, as the nation struggled with a sense of uncertainty and unease, Carter told Americans that the nation suffered from a crisis of the spirit. He talked about the false lures of "self-indulgence and consumption," about "paralysis and stagnation and drift." And he called for a "new commitment to the path of common purpose." But he was unable to offer practical solutions for what was then described as a national malaise.

Carter did score some noteworthy domestic accomplishments. He worked to ease burdensome government regulations without destroying consumer and worker safeguards, and created the Departments of Energy and Education. He also created environmental protections, establishing a $1.6 billion "superfund" to clean up abandoned chemical-waste sites and placing more than 100 million acres of Alaskan land under the federal government's protection as national parks, national forests, and wildlife refuges.

ECONOMIC CRISIS

Americans' loss of confidence in their political leaders was intensified by a growing economic crisis. Since World War II, except for a few brief downturns, prosperity had been a fundamental condition of American life. A steadily rising gross national product, based largely on growing rates of productivity, had propelled large numbers of Americans into the economically comfortable middle class. Prosperity had made possible the great liberal initiatives of the 1960s and improved the lives of America's poor and elderly citizens. But in the early 1970s, that long period of economic expansion and prosperity came to an end. Almost every economic indicator drove home bad news. In 1974 alone, the gross national product dropped 2 full percentage points. Industrial production fell 9 percent. Inflation—the increase in costs of goods and services—skyrocketed, and unemployment grew.

Throughout most of the 1970s, the U.S. economy floundered in a condition that economists dubbed "stag-

|||||||||||||||||||||||||||||||||

Stagflation and Its Causes

flation": a stagnant economy characterized by high unemployment combined with out-of-control inflation (see Figure 31.1). Stagflation was almost impossible to manage with traditional economic remedies. When the federal government increased spending to stimulate the economy and so reduce unemployment, inflation grew. When the federal government tried to rein in inflation by cutting government spending or tightening the money supply, the recession deepened and unemployment rates skyrocketed.

The causes of the economic crisis were complex. Federal management of the economy was in part to blame: President Johnson had reversed conventional economic wisdom and created inflationary pressure by insisting that the United States could have both "guns and butter," as he waged a very expensive war in Vietnam while greatly expanding domestic spending in his Great Society programs. But fundamental problems also came from America's changing role in the global economy. After World War II, with most leading industrial nations in ruins, the United States had stood alone at the pinnacle of the global economy. But the war-ravaged nations—often with major economic assistance from the United States—rebuilt their productive capacities with new, technologically advanced industrial plants. By the early 1970s, both of America's major wartime adversaries, Japan and Germany, had become major economic powers—and major competitors in global trade. In 1971, for the first time since the end of the nineteenth century, the United States imported more goods than it exported, beginning an era of American trade deficits.

American corporate actions also contributed to the growing trade imbalance. During the years of global dominance, few American companies had reinvested profits in

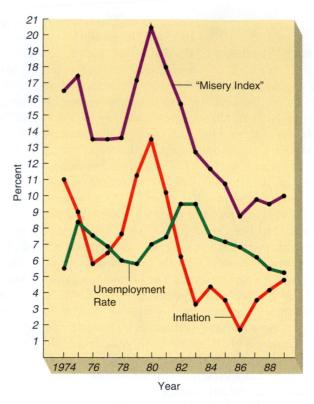

Figure 31.1   "Misery Index" (Unemployment Plus Inflation), 1974–1989

Americans' economic discomfort directly determined their political behavior. When the "misery index" was high in 1976 and 1980, Americans voted for a change in presidents. When economic discomfort declined in 1984 and 1988, Ronald Reagan and George Bush were the political beneficiaries.

(Source: *Adapted from* Economic Report of the President, *1992 [Washington, D.C.: 1992], pp. 340, 365.)*

improving production techniques or educating workers. Consequently, American productivity—that is, the average output of goods per hour of labor—had begun to decline. As workers' productivity declined, however, their wages rarely did. The combination of falling productivity and high labor costs meant that American goods became more and more expensive—both for American consumers and for consumers in other nations. Even worse, without significant competition from foreign manufacturers, American companies had allowed the quality of their goods to decline. From 1966 to 1973, for example, American car and truck manufacturers had to recall almost 30 million vehicles because of serious defects.

America's global economic vulnerability was driven home by the energy crisis that began in 1973. Americans had grown up with cheap and abundant energy, and their lifestyles showed it. American passenger cars got an average of 13.4 miles per gallon in 1973, when a gallon of gas cost 38 cents (about $1.40 in 2006 dollars); neither home heating nor household appliances were designed to be energy-efficient. The country, however, depended on imported oil for almost one-third of its energy supply. When OPEC cut off oil shipments to the United States, U.S. oil prices rose 350 percent. The increases reverberated through the economy: heating costs, shipping costs, and manufacturing costs increased, and so did the cost of goods and services. Inflation jumped from 3 percent in early 1973 to 11 percent in 1974. Sales of gas-guzzling American cars plummeted as people rushed to buy energy-efficient subcompacts from Japan and Europe. American car manufacturers, stuck with machinery for producing large cars, were hit hard. GM laid off 6 percent of its domestic work force and put an even larger number on rolling unpaid leaves. As the ailing automobile industry quit buying steel, glass, and rubber, manufacturers of these goods laid off workers, too.

American political leaders tried desperately to manage the economic crisis, but their actions often exacerbated it instead. As America's rising trade deficit undermined international confidence in the dollar, the Nixon administration ended the dollar's link to the gold standard; free-floating exchange rates increased the price of foreign goods in the United States and stimulated inflation. President Ford created a voluntary program, Whip Inflation Now (complete with red and white "WIN" buttons), in 1974 to encourage grassroots anti-inflation efforts. Following the tenets of monetary theory, which held that, with less money available to "chase" the supply of goods, price increases would gradually slow down, ending the inflationary spiral, Ford curbed federal spending and encouraged the Federal Reserve Board to tighten credit—and prompted the worst recession in forty years. In 1975 unemployment climbed to 8.5 percent.

Attempts to Fix the Economy

Carter first attempted to bring unemployment rates down by stimulating the economy, but inflation careened out of control; he then tried to slow the economy down—and prompted a major recession during the election year of 1980. In fact, Carter's larger economic policies, including his 1978 deregulation of airline, trucking, banking, and communications industries, would eventually foster economic growth—but not soon enough. After almost a decade of decline, Americans were losing faith in the American economy and in the ability of their political leaders to manage it.

The economic crisis of the 1970s accelerated the nation's transition from an industrial to a service economy. During the 1970s, the American economy "deindustrialized." Automobile companies laid off workers. Massive steel plants shut down, leaving entire communities devastated. Other manufacturing concerns moved overseas, seeking lower labor costs and fewer government regulations. New jobs were created—27 million of them—but they were overwhelmingly in what economists called the "service sector": retail sales, restaurants, and other service providers. As heavy industries collapsed, formerly highly paid, unionized workers took jobs in the growing but not unionized service sector. These jobs—such as warehouse work or retail sales, for example—paid much lower wages and often lacked healthcare and other important benefits.

Impacts of the Economic Crisis

Formerly successful blue-collar workers saw their middle-class standards of life slipping away. More married women joined the work force because they had to—though some were drawn by new opportunities. Even in the best of times the economy would have been hard pressed to produce jobs for the millions of baby boomers who joined the labor market in the 1970s. Young people graduating from high school or college in the 1970s, raised with high expectations, suddenly found very limited possibilities—if they found jobs at all.

The economic crisis also helped to shift the economic and population centers of the nation. As the old industrial regions of the North and Midwest went into decline, people fled the "snow belt" or the "rust belt," speeding up the Sunbelt boom already in progress (see Map 31.1). The Sunbelt was where the jobs were. The federal government had invested heavily in the South and West during the postwar era, especially in military and defense industries, and in the infrastructures necessary for them. Never a major center for heavy manufactures, the Sunbelt was primed for the rapid growth of modern industries and services—aerospace, defense, electronics, transportation, research, banking and finance, and leisure. City and state governments competed to lure businesses and investment dollars, in part by preventing the growth of unions. Atlanta, Houston, and other southern cities marketed themselves as cosmopolitan, sophisticated, and racially tolerant; they bought sports teams and built museums.

This population shift south and west, combined with the flight of middle-class taxpayers to the suburbs, created disaster in northern and midwestern cities. New York City, close to financial collapse by late 1975, was saved only when the House and Senate Banking Committees approved federal loan guarantees. Cleveland defaulted on its debts

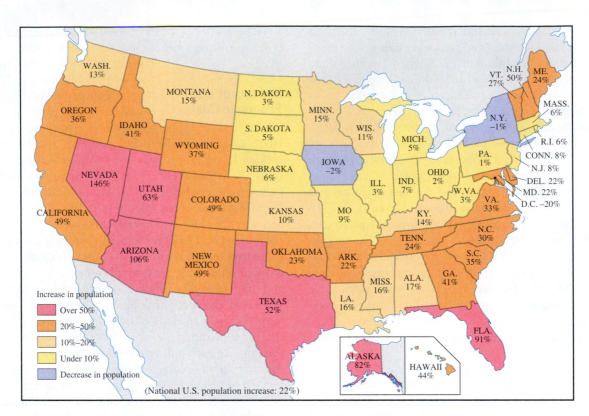

Map 31.1   The Continued Shift to the Sunbelt in the 1970s and 1980s

Throughout the 1970s and 1980s, Americans continued to leave economically declining areas of the North and East in pursuit of opportunity in the Sunbelt. States in the Sunbelt and in the West had the largest population increases. *(Source: "Shift to the Sunbelt," Newsweek, September 10, 1990.)*

in 1978, the first major city to do so since Detroit declared bankruptcy in 1933.

Even as stagflation and Sunbelt growth transformed American politics, a "tax revolt" movement emerged in the rapidly growing American West. In California, inflation had driven property taxes up rapidly, hitting middle-class taxpayers hard. In this era of economic decline and post-Watergate suspicion, angry taxpayers saw government as the problem. Instead of calling for wealthy citizens and major corporations to pay a larger share of taxes, voters rebelled against taxation itself. California's Proposition 13, passed by a landslide in 1978, rolled back property taxes and restricted future increases. Within months of Proposition 13's passage, thirty-seven states cut property taxes, and twenty-eight lowered their state income-tax rates.

The impact of Proposition 13 and similar initiatives was initially cushioned by state budget surpluses, but as those surpluses turned to deficits, states cut services—

Tax Revolts

closing fire stations and public libraries, ending or limiting mental health services and programs for the disabled. Public schools were hit especially hard. The tax revolt movement signaled the growth of a new conservatism; voters who wanted lower taxes and smaller government would help bring Ronald Reagan to the White House in the election of 1980.

The runaway inflation of the 1970s also changed how Americans managed their money. Before this era, home mortgages and auto loans were the only kind of major debt most Americans would venture. National credit cards had become common only in the late 1960s, and few Americans—especially those who remembered the Great Depression—were willing to spend money they did not have. In the 1970s, however, thriftiness stopped making sense. Double-digit inflation rates meant double-digit declines in the purchasing power of a dollar. It was economically smarter to buy goods before their prices

Credit and Investment

went up—even if it meant borrowing the money. Because debt was paid off later with devalued dollars, the consumer came out ahead. In 1975 consumer debt hit a high of $167 billion; it almost doubled, to $315 billion, by 1979.

The 1970s were also the decade in which average Americans became investors rather than savers. Throughout the 1970s, because of regulations created during the Great Depression, the interest rates that banks could pay on individual savings accounts were capped. An average savings account bearing 5 percent interest actually *lost* more than 20 percent of its value from 1970 through 1980 because of inflation. That same money, invested at market rates, would have grown dramatically. Fidelity Investments, a mutual fund company, saw a business opportunity: its money market accounts combined many smaller investments to purchase large-denomination Treasury bills and certificates of deposit, thus allowing small investors to get the high interest rates normally available only to major investors. Money flooded out of passbook accounts and into money funds, and money market investments grew from $1.7 billion in 1974 to $200 billion in 1982. At the same time, deregulation of the New York Stock Exchange spawned discount brokerage houses, whose low commission rates made it affordable for middle-class investors to trade stocks.

AN ERA OF CULTURAL TRANSFORMATION

The 1970s have been dismissed as a cultural wasteland, an era in which the nation confronted new limits without much passion or creativity. But it was during the 1970s, as Americans struggled with economic recession, governmental betrayal, and social division, that major strands of late-twentieth-century culture were developed or consolidated. The current environmental movement, the growth of technology, the rise of born-again Christianity and a "therapeutic culture," contemporary forms of sexuality and the family, and America's emphasis on diversity all have roots in this odd decade sandwiched between the political vibrancy of the 1960s and the conservatism of the 1980s.

Just as Americans were forced to confront the end of postwar prosperity, a series of ecological crises drove

Environmentalism

home the limits on natural resources and the fragility of the environment. In 1969 a major oil spill took place off the coast of Santa Barbara, California; that same year, the polluted Cuyahoga River, flowing through Cleveland, caught fire. Although the energy crisis of the 1970s was due to an oil

▲ Celebrants of the first Earth Day, on April 22, 1970, gather in an urban park. More than 20 million Americans across the nation participated in local teach-ins, celebrations, and protests to draw attention to environmental issues. By 1990 Earth Day was celebrated globally, drawing 200 million participants from 141 countries. *(Ken Regan)*

embargo, not a scarcity of oil, it drove home the real limits of the world's supplies of oil and natural gas. In 1979 human error contributed to a nuclear accident at the Three Mile Island nuclear power plant near Harrisburg, Pennsylvania, and in 1980 President Carter declared a federal emergency at New York State's Love Canal, which had served as a dump site for a local chemical manufacturer, after it was discovered that 30 percent of local residents had suffered chromosome damage. Public activism during the 1970s produced major environmental regulations and initiatives, from the Environmental Protection Agency (EPA), created (under strong public pressure) in 1970 by the Nixon administration, to eighteen major environmental laws enacted by Congress during the decade.

When almost 20 million Americans—half of them schoolchildren—gathered in local communities to celebrate the first Earth Day on April 22, 1970, they signaled the triumph of a relatively new understanding of environmentalism. Traditional concerns about preserving "unspoiled" wilderness had joined with a new focus on "ecology," which stressed the connections between the earth and all living organisms, including humans. Central to this movement was a recognition that the earth's resources were finite and must be both conserved and protected from the consequences of human action, such as pollution. In 1971 biologist Barry Commoner insisted, "The present course of environmental degradation . . . is so serious, that, if continued, it will destroy the capability of the environment to support a reasonably civilized human society." Many of those concerned about the strain on earth's resources also identified rapid global population growth as a problem, and state public health offices frequently dispensed contraceptives as a way to stem this new "epidemic."

During these years, Americans became increasingly uneasy about the science and technology that had been

Technology

one source of America's might. In a triumph of technology, American astronaut Neil Armstrong stepped onto the lunar surface on July 20, 1969, as people worldwide watched the grainy television transmission and heard, indistinctly, his first words— "That's one small step for a man, one giant step for mankind." But the advances that could take a man to the moon seemed unable to cope with earthbound problems of poverty, crime, pollution, and urban decay; and the failure of technological warfare to deliver victory in Vietnam came at the same time antiwar protesters were questioning the morality of using such technology. Some Americans joined a movement for "appropriate technology" and human-scale development, but the nation was profoundly dependent on complex technological systems. And it was during the 1970s that the foundation was laid for America's computer revolution. The integrated circuit was created in 1970, and by 1975 the MITS Altair 8800— operated by toggle switches that entered individual binary numbers, boasting 256 bytes of memory, and requiring about thirty hours to assemble—could be mail-ordered from Albuquerque, New Mexico.

As Americans confronted material limits, they increasingly sought spiritual fulfillment and well-being. Some turned to religion, though not to traditional mainstream Protestantism.

Religion and the Therapeutic Culture

Methodist, Presbyterian, and Episcopalian churches all lost members during this era, while membership in evangelical and fundamentalist Christian churches grew dramatically. Protestant evangelicals, professing a personal relationship with their sav-

ior, described themselves as "born again" and emphasized the immediate, daily presence of God in their lives. Even some Catholics, such as the Mexican Americans who embraced the *cursillo* movement (a "little course" in faith), sought a more personal relationship with God. Other Americans looked to the variety of beliefs and practices described as "New Age." The New Age movement drew from and often combined versions of nonwestern spiritual and religious practices, including Zen Buddhism, yoga, and shamanism, along with insights from western psychology and a form of spiritually oriented environmentalism.

Also in the 1970s, America saw the full emergence of a "therapeutic" culture. Although some Americans were disgusted with the self-centeredness of the "Me-Decade," bestselling books by therapists and self-help gurus insisted that individual feelings offered the ultimate measure of truth; emotional honesty and self-awareness were social goods surpassing the bonds of community, friendship, or family. Self-help books with titles like *I Ain't Much Baby—But I'm All I've Got,* or *I'm OK—You're OK* (first published in 1967, it became a bestseller in the mid-1970s) made up 15 percent of all bestselling books during the decade.

One such self-help book was *The Joy of Sex* (1972), which sold 3.8 million copies in two years. Sex became

Sexuality and the Family

much more visible in America's public culture during the 1970s, as network television loosened its regulation of sexual content. At the beginning of the 1960s, married couples in television shows were required to occupy twin beds; in the 1970s, hit television shows included *Three's Company,* a situation comedy based on the then-scandalous premise that a single man shared an apartment with two beautiful female roommates—and got away with it only by pretending to their suspicious landlord that he was gay. *Charlie's Angels,* another major television hit, capitalized on what people called the "jiggle factor," and displayed (for the time) lots of bare female flesh. A major youth fad of the era was "streaking," running naked through public places. Donna Summers's 1975 disco hit "Love to Love You Baby" contained sixteen minutes of sexual moaning. And though very few Americans participated in heterosexual orgies at New York City's Plato's Retreat, many knew about them through a *Time* magazine feature story.

Sexual behaviors had also changed. The seventies were the era of singles bars and gay bathhouses, and some Americans led sexual lives virtually unrestrained by the old rules. For most Americans, however, the major changes brought about by the "sexual revolution" were a broader public acceptance of premarital sex and a limited acceptance of homosexuality, especially among more educated Americans. More and more heterosexual young people "lived together" without marriage during the 1970s; the census bureau even coined the term *POSSLQ* ("persons of opposite sex sharing living quarters") to describe the relationship. When First Lady Betty Ford said on *60 Minutes* that she would not be surprised if her then-seventeen-year-old daughter Susan began a sexual relationship, it was clear that much had changed in the course of a decade.

Changes in sexual mores and in the roles possible for women helped to alter the shape of the American family as well. Both men and women married later than in recent decades, and American women had fewer children. By the end of the 1970s, the birth rate had dropped almost 40 percent from its 1957 peak. Almost one-quarter of young single women in 1980 said that they did not plan to have children. And a steadily rising percentage of babies were born to unmarried women, as the number of families headed by never-married women rose 400 percent during the 1970s. The divorce rate also rose, in part because states implemented "no fault" divorce, which did not require evidence of adultery, physical cruelty, abandonment, or other wrongdoing. Although families seemed less stable in the 1970s than in the previous postwar decades, Americans also developed a greater acceptance of various family forms (the blended family of television's *Brady Bunch,* for example), and many young couples sought greater equality between the sexes in romantic relationships or marriages.

The racial-justice and identity movements of the late 1960s and 1970s made all Americans more aware of differences among the nation's peoples—

||||||||||||||||||||||||||||||

Diversity

an awareness made stronger by the great influx of new immigrants, not from Europe but from Latin America and Asia. It was a challenge, however, to figure out how to acknowledge the new importance of "difference" in public policy. The solution developed in the 1970s was the idea of "diversity." Difference was not a problem but a strength; the nation should not seek policies to diminish differences among its peoples but should instead seek to foster the "diversity" of its schools, workplaces, and public culture.

One major move in this direction came in the 1978 Supreme Court decision *Regents of the University of California v. Bakke.* Allan Bakke, a thirty-three-year-old white man with a strong academic record, had been denied admission to the medical school of the University of California at Davis. Bakke sued, charging that he had been denied "equal protection" of the law because the medical school's affirmative-action program reserved 16 percent of its slots for racial-minority candidates, who were held to lower standards than other applicants. The case set off furious debates nationwide over the legitimacy of affirmative action. In 1978 the Supreme Court, in a split decision, decided in favor of Bakke. Four justices argued that any race-based decision violated the Civil Rights Act of 1964; four saw affirmative-action programs as constitutionally acceptable remedies for past discrimination. The deciding vote, though for Bakke, contained an important qualification. A "diverse student body," Justice Lewis Powell wrote, is "a constitutionally permissible goal for an institution of higher education." To achieve the positive quality of "diversity," educational institutions could take race into account when making decisions about admissions.

RENEWED COLD WAR AND MIDDLE EAST CRISIS

When Jimmy Carter took office in 1977, he asked Americans to put their "inordinate fear of Communism" behind them. With reformist zeal, Carter vowed to reduce the U.S. military presence overseas, to cut back arms sales (which had reached the unprecedented height of $10 billion per year under Nixon), and to slow the nuclear arms race. At the time, more than 400,000 American military personnel were stationed abroad, the United States had military links with ninety-two nations, and the CIA was active on every continent. Carter promised to avoid new Vietnams through an activist preventive diplomacy in the Third World and to give more attention to environmental issues as well as relations between rich and poor nations. He especially determined to improve human rights abroad—the freedom to vote, worship, travel, speak out, and get a fair trial. Like his predecessors, however, Carter identified revolutionary nationalism as a threat to America's prominent global position.

Carter spoke and acted inconsistently, in part because in the post-Vietnam years no consensus existed in foreign

||||||||||||||||||||||||||||||

Carter's Divided Administration

policy and in part because his advisers squabbled among themselves. One source of the problem was the stern-faced Zbigniew Brzezinski, a Polish-born political scientist who became Carter's national security adviser. An old-fashioned Cold Warrior, Brzezinski blamed foreign crises on Soviet expansionism. Carter gradually listened more to Brzezinski than to Secretary of State Cyrus Vance, an experienced public servant who advocated quiet diplomacy. Vocal neoconservative intellectuals, such as Norman Podhoretz, editor of *Commentary* magazine, and the Committee on the Present Danger, founded in 1976 by such Cold War hawks as Paul Nitze, who had composed NSC-68 in 1950, criticized Carter for any relaxation of the Cold War and demanded that he jettison détente.

Nitze got his wish. Under Carter détente deteriorated, and the Cold War deepened. But it did not happen right away. Initially, Carter maintained fairly good relations with Moscow and was able to score some foreign policy successes around the world. In Panama, where citizens longed for control over the Canal Zone, which they believed had been wrongfully taken from them in 1903, Carter reenergized negotiations that had begun after anti-American riots in Panama in 1964. The United States signed two treaties with Panama in 1977. One provided for the return of the Canal Zone to Panama in 2000, and the other guaranteed the United States the right to defend the canal after that time. With conservatives denouncing the deal as a sellout, the Senate narrowly endorsed both agreements in 1978. The majority agreed with Carter's argument that relinquishing the canal was the best way to improve U.S. relations with Latin America.

Important though it was, the Panama agreement paled next to what must be considered the crowning accomplishment of Carter's presidency: the Camp David accords, the first mediated peace treaty between Israel and an Arab nation. Through tenacious personal diplomacy at a Camp David, Maryland, meeting in September 1978 with Egyptian and Israeli leaders, the president persuaded Israel and Egypt to agree to a peace treaty, gained Israel's promise to withdraw from the Sinai Peninsula, and forged a provisional agreement that provided for continued negotiations on the future status of the Palestinian people living in the occupied territories of Jordan's West Bank and Egypt's Gaza Strip (see Map 33.2). Other Arab states denounced the agreement for not requiring Israel to relin-

Camp David Accords

▲ Egyptian president Anwar al-Sadat, U.S. President Jimmy Carter, and Israeli Prime Minister Menachem Begin sit together outside the White House on March 26, 1979, ready to sign the peace treaty based on the Camp David Accords of September 1978. The treaty ended the long-standing state of war between Egypt and Israel. *(© Wally McNamee/CORBIS)*

quish all occupied territories and for not guaranteeing a Palestinian homeland. But the accord at least ended warfare along one frontier in that troubled area of the world. On March 26, 1979, Israeli prime minister Menachem Begin and Egyptian president Anwar al-Sadat signed the formal treaty on the White House lawn, with a beaming Carter looking on.

Carter's moment of diplomatic triumph did not last long, for soon other foreign policy problems pressed in. Relations with Moscow had deteriorated, with U.S. and Soviet officials sparring over the Kremlin's reluctance to lift restrictions on Jewish emigration from the USSR, and over the Soviet decision to deploy new intermediate-range ballistic missiles aimed at western Europe. Then, in December 1979, the Soviets invaded Afghanistan. A remote, mountainous country, Afghanistan had been a source of great-power conflict because of its strategic position. In the nineteenth century it was the fulcrum of the Great Game, the contest between Britain and Russia for control of Central Asia and India. Following World War II, Afghanistan settled into a pattern of ethnic and factional squabbling; few in the West paid attention until the country spiraled into anarchy in the 1970s. In late 1979, the Red Army bludgeoned its way into Afghanistan to shore up a faltering communist government under siege by Muslim rebels. Moscow officials calculated that they could be in and out of the country before anyone really noticed, including the Americans.

Soviet Invasion of Afghanistan

To their dismay, Carter not only noticed but reacted forcefully. He suspended shipments of grain and high-technology equipment to the Soviet Union, withdrew a major new arms control treaty from Senate consideration, and initiated an international boycott of the 1980 Summer Olympics in Moscow. He also secretly authorized the CIA to distribute aid, including arms and military support, to the Mujahidin (Islamic guerillas) fighting the communist government and sanctioned military aid to their backer, Pakistan. Announcing the Carter Doctrine, the president asserted that the United States would intervene, unilaterally and militarily if necessary, should Soviet aggression threaten the petroleum-rich Persian Gulf. This string of measures represented a victory of the hawkish Brzezinski over the pro-détente Vance. Indeed, Carter seemed more ardent than Brzezinski in his denunciations of the Kremlin. He warned aides that the Soviets, unless checked, would likely attack elsewhere in the Middle East, but declassified documents confirm what critics at the time said: that the Soviet invasion was limited in scope and did not presage a push southwest to the Persian Gulf.

Iranian Hostage Crisis

Carter's aggressive rhetoric on Afghanistan may be partly explained by the fact that he simultaneously faced a tough foreign policy test in neighboring Iran. The shah, long the recipient of American favor, had been driven from his throne by a broad coalition of Iranians, many of whom resented that their traditional ways had been dislocated by the shah's attempts at modernization. American analysts failed to perceive the volatility that this dislocation generated and were caught off guard when riots led by anti-American Muslim clerics erupted in late 1978. The shah went into exile, and in April 1979 Islamic revolutionaries, led by the Ayatollah Khomeini, an elderly cleric who denounced the United States as the stronghold of capitalism and western materialism, proclaimed a Shi'ite Islamic Republic. In November, with the exiled shah in the United States for medical treatment, mobs stormed the U.S. embassy in Teheran. They took American personnel as hostages, demanding the return of the shah to stand trial. The Iranians eventually released a few American prisoners, but fifty-two others languished under Iranian guard. They suffered solitary confinement, beatings, and terrifying mock executions.

Unable to gain the hostages' freedom through diplomatic intermediaries, Carter said that he felt "the same kind of impotence that a powerful person feels when his child is kidnapped." He took steps to isolate Iran economically, freezing Iranian assets in the United States. When the hostage takers paraded their blindfolded captives before television cameras, Americans felt taunted and humiliated. In April 1980, frustrated and at a low ebb in public opinion polls, Carter broke diplomatic relations with Iran and ordered a daring rescue mission. But the rescue effort miscarried after equipment failure in the sandy Iranian desert, and during the hasty withdrawal two aircraft collided, killing eight American soldiers. The hostages were not freed until January 1981, after Carter left office and the United States unfroze Iranian assets and promised not to intervene again in Iran's internal affairs.

The Iranian revolution, together with the rise of the Mujahidin in Afghanistan, signified the emergence of Islamic fundamentalism as a force in world affairs. Socialism and capitalism, the great answers that the two superpowers offered to the problems of modernization, had failed to solve the problems in Central Asia and the Middle East, let alone satisfy the passions and expectations they had aroused. Nor had they assuaged deeply held feelings of humiliation generated by centuries of western domination. As a result, Islamic orthodoxy found growing support for its message: that secular leaders such as Nasser in Egypt

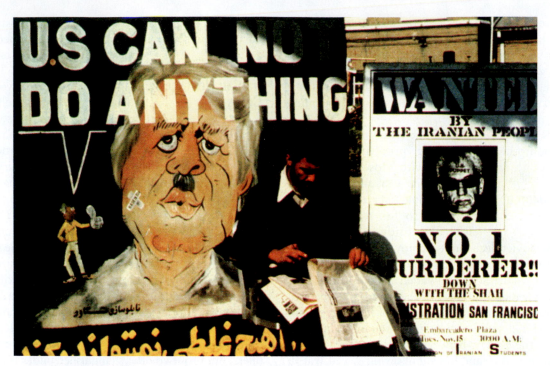

▲ An Iranian is pictured reading a newspaper not long before mobs in Teheran stormed the American embassy and took more than fifty Americans hostage. Behind him are posters mocking U.S. President Carter and denouncing the shah. *(Picture Research Consultants & Archives)*

and the shah in Iran had taken their peoples down the wrong path, necessitating a return to conservative Islamic values and Islamic law. The Iranian revolution in particular expressed a deep and complex mixture of discontents within many Islamic societies.

U.S. officials took some consolation from the fact that Iran faced growing friction from the avowedly secular

Rise of Saddam Hussein

government in neighboring Iraq. Ruled by the Ba'athist Party (a secular and quasi-socialist party with branches in several Arab countries), Iraq had already won favor in Washington for its ruthless pursuit and execution of Iraqi communists. When a Ba'athist leader named Saddam Hussein took over as president of Iraq in 1979 and began threatening the Teheran government, U.S. officials were not displeased; to them, Saddam seemed likely to offset the Iranian danger in the Persian Gulf region. As border clashes between Iraqi and Iranian forces escalated in 1980, culminating in the outbreak of large-scale war in September, Washington policymakers took an officially neutral position but soon tilted toward Iraq.

Jimmy Carter's record in foreign affairs sparked considerable criticism from both left and right. He had earned some diplomatic successes in the Middle East, Africa, and Latin America, but the revived Cold War and the prolonged Iranian hostage crisis had hurt the administration politically. Contrary to Carter's goals, more American military personnel were stationed overseas in 1980 than in 1976; the defense budget climbed and sales of arms abroad grew to $15.3 billion in 1980. On human rights, the president proved inconsistent. He practiced a double standard by applying the human-rights test to some nations (the Soviet Union, Argentina, and Chile) but not to U.S. allies (South Korea, the shah's Iran, and the Philippines). Still, if inconsistent, Carter's human-rights policy was not unimportant: he gained the release and saved the lives of some political prisoners, and he popularized and institutionalized concern for human rights around the world. But Carter did not satisfy Americans who wanted a post-Vietnam restoration of the economic dominance and military edge that the United States once enjoyed. He lost the 1980 election to the hawkish Ronald Reagan, former Hollywood actor and governor of California.

Legacy FOR A PEOPLE AND A NATION

The All-Volunteer Force

On June 30, 1973, the United States ended its military draft. From that date on, the nation relied on an all-volunteer force (AVF). The draft had been in effect, with only a brief interruption in the late 1940s, since the United States had begun to mobilize in 1940 for World War II. Never before had the United States had a peacetime draft. But as the country took on new roles of global leadership after the war, and as the dark shadow of the Cold War grew, the draft became an accepted part of American life. In 1973 more than 50 million American men had been inducted into the nation's military since the end of World War II.

Richard Nixon had promised to end the draft during his presidential campaign in 1968. It was an astute political move, for the draft had become a focus for widespread protest during the failing—and increasingly unpopular—war in Vietnam. Ending the draft was not feasible during the war, but Nixon kept his promise and began planning for an all-volunteer force as soon as he took office. Many Americans supported the shift because they believed it would be more difficult for a president to send an all-volunteer military to war because he or she could not rely on a draft to compel people to fight a war they did not support.

The military, however, was not enthusiastic about Nixon's plan. The war in Vietnam had shattered morale and left much of the nation's military—particularly the army—in disarray. Public opinion of the military was at an all-time low. How were they to attract volunteers?

The army, as the largest of the four services, had to draw the largest number of volunteers. It faced a difficult task. Reform was the first step: getting rid of make-work ("chickenshit") tasks and enhancing military professionalism. The army also turned to state-of-the-art market research and advertising. Discovering that many young men were afraid they would lose their individuality in the army, the army's advertising agency launched a new campaign. Instead of the traditional poster of Uncle Sam proclaiming, "I Want You," the new volunteer army claimed, "Today's Army Wants to Join You."

The AVF had a rough beginning. The army had to recruit about 225,000 new soldiers each year (compared to about 80,000 per year in 2006) and had difficulty attracting enough capable young men and women. Within a decade, however, America's military boasted a higher rate of high school graduates and higher mental "quality" (as measured by standardized tests) than the comparable age population in the United States. During an era of relative peace, many young men and women found opportunities for education and training through military service. Military service was particularly attractive to capable but economically disadvantaged young people, a high percentage of whom were African American.

The move to a volunteer force had major legacies for the American people. The military understood that, without a draft, it would have to turn to women in order to fill the ranks. The proportion of women in the military increased from 1.9 percent in 1972 to about 15 percent currently, and the roles they were allowed to fill widened dramatically. At the same time, the nation's understanding of military service changed. No longer was it seen as an obligation of (male) citizenship. Instead, it was a voluntary choice. The implications seemed less urgent in peacetime. But in time of war, the legacy of the move to an AVF is highly charged. What does it mean when only a small number of volunteers bears the burden of warfare and most Americans never have to consider the possibility of going to war?

SUMMARY

The 1970s were a difficult decade for Americans. From the crisis year of 1968 on, it seemed that Americans were ever more polarized—over the war in Vietnam, over the best path to racial equality and equal rights for all Americans, over the meaning of equality, and over the meaning of America itself. As many activists for social justice turned to "cultural nationalism," or group-identity politics, notions of American unity seemed a relic of the past. And though a new women's movement won great victories against sex discrimination, a powerful opposition movement arose in response.

During this era, Americans became increasingly disillusioned with politics and presidential leadership. Richard Nixon's abuses of power in the Watergate scandal and cover-up, combined with growing awareness that the administration had lied to its citizens repeatedly about America's role in Vietnam, produced a profound suspicion of government. A major economic crisis ended the post-World War II expansion that had fueled the growth of the middle class and social reform programs alike, and Americans struggled with the psychological impact of a new age of limits and with the effects of stagflation: rising unemployment rates coupled with high rates of inflation.

Overseas, a string of setbacks—defeat in Vietnam, the oil embargo, and the Iranian hostage crisis—signified the waning of American power during the 1970s. The nation seemed increasingly unable to have its own way on the world stage. Détente with the Soviet Union had flourished for a time, as both superpowers sought to adjust to the new geopolitical realities; however, by 1980 Cold War tensions were again on the rise. But if the nation's most important bilateral relationship remained that with the USSR, an important change, not always perceptible at the time, was under way: more and more, the focus of U.S. foreign policy was on the Middle East.

Plagued by political, economic, and foreign policy crises, America ended the 1970s bruised, battered, and frustrated. The age of liberalism was long over; the elements for a conservative resurgence were in place.

SUGGESTIONS FOR FURTHER READING

Donald T. Critchlow, *Phyllis Schlafly and Grassroots Conservatism: A Woman's Crusade* (2005)

Daniel Ellsberg, *Secrets: A Memoir of Vietnam and the Pentagon Papers* (2002)

David Farber, *Taken Hostage: The Iran Hostage Crisis and America's First Encounter with Radical Islam* (2004)

Ian F. Haney-Lopez, *Racism on Trial: The Chicano Fight for Justice* (2003)

Richard Reeves, *President Nixon: Alone in the White House* (2001)

Ruth Rosen, *The World Split Open: How the Modern Women's Movement Changed America* (2000)

Hal Rothman, *The Greening of a Nation: Environmentalism in the U.S. Since 1945* (1997)

Bruce Schulman, *The Seventies: The Great Shift in American Culture, Society, and Politics* (2001)

John D. Skrentny, *The Minority Rights Revolution* (2002)

Odd Arne Westad, *The Global Cold War: Third World Interventions and the Making of Our Times* (2005)

For a more extensive list for further reading, go to college.hmco.com/pic/norton8e.

Conservatism Revived *1980-1992*

*I*t was hot and there was a lot of desert," Luisa Orellana remembered, as she described crossing the border from Mexico into the United States in the early 1980s. "All of us started running, each one with a child in our arms. My mother was praying the rosary the whole time and suddenly the sky opened up and started raining. It rained so hard we couldn't see where we were going, but it helped because the Border Patrol couldn't see us either."

Three months earlier Luisa's father had been murdered. Tanis Stanislaus Orellana had worked in El Salvador with Archbishop Óscar Romero, the most powerful critic of the ruling military dictatorship whose death squads were responsible for the murder of about thirty thousand Salvadorans between 1979 and 1981. In 1980 Romero had been assassinated—shot, publicly, as he consecrated the Eucharist during Mass. The civil war that followed lasted twelve years; an estimated 1 million Salvadorans sought refuge in other nations from the death squads and the torture, rape, and murder that had become commonplace in their own country.

Luisa's father, along with other church officials, had been targeted. After his murder, his widow took her children, including teenage Luisa, and fled their home, leaving behind almost everything they owned. They took the bus through Guatemala, crossed illegally into Mexico, and, given shelter by one church after another, made their way from Chiapas to Mexico City to Agua Prieta, on the U.S.-Mexico border.

From Agua Prieta, Luisa and her family ran for two miles through blinding rain. They crossed into Douglas, Arizona, cold, wet, hungry, and scared, seeking refuge. They were met there by members of the Sanctuary movement, Americans who believed that the U.S. government's refugee policy, which offered asylum to those who fled violent repression and the threat of death or torture, must include those who escaped the deadly

◀ Social worker Sarah Martinez assisted refugees from Central America at Los Angeles's Rescate Refugee Center during the 1980s. Martinez was also a refugee; she fled her homeland of El Salvador after a Salvadoran death squad murdered her husband, a university professor, and she was imprisoned and tortured. *(AP Images)*

CHRONOLOGY

1980 ■ Reagan elected president

1981 ■ AIDS first observed in United States
■ Economic problems continue; prime interest rate reaches 21.5 percent
■ Reagan breaks air traffic controllers' strike
■ "Reaganomics" plan of budget and tax cuts approved by Congress

1982 ■ Unemployment reaches 10.8 percent, highest rate since Great Depression
■ ERA dies after Stop-ERA campaign prevents ratification in key states

1983 ■ Reagan introduces SDI
■ Terrorists kill U.S. marines in Lebanon
■ U.S. invasion of Grenada

1984 ■ Reagan aids contras despite congressional ban
■ Economic recovery; unemployment rate drops and economy grows without inflation
■ Reagan reelected
■ Gorbachev promotes reforms in USSR

1986 ■ Iran-contra scandal erupts

1987 ■ Stock market drops 508 points in one day
■ Palestinian intifada begins

1988 ■ George H. W. Bush elected president

1989 ■ Tiananmen Square massacre in China
■ Berlin Wall torn down
■ U.S. troops invade Panama
■ Gulf between rich and poor at highest point since 1920s

1990 ■ Americans with Disabilities Act passed
■ Communist regimes in eastern Europe collapse
■ Iraq invades Kuwait
■ South Africa begins to dismantle apartheid

1991 ■ Persian Gulf War
■ USSR dissolves into independent states
■ United States enters recession

1992 ■ Annual federal budget deficit reaches high of $300 billion at end of Bush presidency

The originators of the U.S. Sanctuary movement used church networks and human rights groups throughout Central America to investigate and verify the refugees' stories of rape, torture, and murder. Faced with the human toll of such violence, they believed it necessary to protect human rights and to save those they could from torture and death. Many members of the Sanctuary movement belonged to faith-based communities, although secular institutions, including public and private universities and the state of New Mexico, also participated. Some members of the movement went to prison for their work, charged with transporting or harboring fugitives.

Luisa and her family went from the sanctuary offered by Tucson churches, which were at the center of the movement, to live in the basement of a Catholic church in Spokane, Washington. In 1989 the U.S. government granted protection and work permits to the Central American refugees who had sought refuge in the United States. Luisa stayed in the state of Washington, where she became a teacher of English as a second language. When she looks back to the Sanctuary movement and the people who helped her family, she says, "They were like saints. They risked their lives to save ours."

Luisa Orellana and her family were part of the "new immigration" that began in the early 1970s and grew throughout the 1980s, as record numbers of immigrants came to the United States from Asia, Mexico, Central and South America, and the Caribbean. These immigrants came under a wide range of circumstances; many from Central America, Vietnam, the Soviet Union, and Cuba were political refugees granted asylum in the United States. The Orellanas found safety and peace in the United States, but not all immigrants—or all Americans—fared so well in the 1980s. The decade saw increasing divisions between rich and poor in America. A host of social problems—drugs, violence, homelessness, the growing AIDS epidemic—made life even more difficult for the urban poor. But for those on the other side of the economic divide, the 1980s were an era of luxury and ostentation. One of the most poignant images from the time was of a homeless man huddled just outside the Reagan White House—the two Americas, divided by a widening gulf.

The election of Ronald Reagan in 1980 began a twelve-year period of Republican rule, as Reagan was

civil wars that ravaged much of Central America in the 1980s. Officially, however, the U.S. government designated them "economic refugees" and denied them asylum.

▲ On a snowy November day, a homeless man makes his bed on park benches in Lafayette Square, across the street from the White House. This 1987 photograph symbolized the stark contrasts between dire poverty and great wealth in 1980s America. *(© Corbis-Bettmann)*

succeeded by his vice president, George Bush, in 1988. Reagan was a popular president who seemed to restore the confidence and optimism that had been shaken by the social, economic, and political crises of the 1970s. Throughout the 1980s, Reagan drew support from a wide variety of Americans: wealthy people who liked his pro-business economic policies; the religious New Right who sought the creation of "God's America"; white middle- and working-class Americans attracted by Reagan's charisma and his embrace of "old-fashioned" values.

Reagan supported social issues that were important to the New Right: he was anti-abortion; he embraced causes such as prayer in schools; he reversed the GOP's position in support of the Equal Rights Amendment, which would expire in 1983 after the necessary three-quarters of U.S. states failed to approve it. Most important, Reagan appointed judges to the Supreme Court and to the federal bench whose judicial rulings strengthened social-conservative agendas. Nonetheless, the Reagan administration focused primarily on the agendas of political and economic conservatives: reducing the size and power of the federal government and creating favorable conditions for business and industry. The U.S. economy recovered from the stagflation that had plagued the nation in the 1970s, and through much of the 1980s, it boomed. But corruption flourished in financial institutions freed from

government oversight, and taxpayers paid the bill for bailouts. By the end of the Reagan-Bush era, a combination of tax cuts and massive increases in defense spending left a budget deficit five times larger than when Reagan took office.

The most dramatic events of the Reagan-Bush years were not domestic, however, but international. In the span of a decade, the Cold War intensified drastically and then ended. The key figure in the intensification was Reagan, who entered office promising to reassert America's military might and stand up to the Soviet Union, and he delivered on both counts. The key figure in ending the Cold War was Soviet leader Mikhail Gorbachev, who came to power in 1985 determined to address the USSR's long-term economic decline and needed a more amicable superpower relationship to do so. Gorbachev, though no revolutionary—he hoped to reform the Soviet system, not eradicate it—lost control of events as a wave of revolutions in eastern Europe toppled one communist regime after another. In 1991 the Soviet Union itself disappeared, and the United States found itself the world's lone superpower. The Persian Gulf War of that same year demonstrated America's unrivaled world power, and also the unprecedented importance of the Middle East in U.S. foreign policy.

- Ronald Reagan, campaigning for president in 1984, told voters, "It's morning again in America." How would Americans from different backgrounds judge the accuracy of his claim?
- What issues, beliefs, backgrounds, and economic realities divided Americans in the 1980s, and how do those divisions shape the culture and politics of contemporary America?
- Why did the Cold War intensify and then wane during the decade of the 1980s?

REAGAN AND THE CONSERVATIVE RESURGENCE

The 1970s had been a hard decade for Americans: defeat in Vietnam; the resignation of a president in disgrace; the energy crisis; economic "stagflation" and the Iranian hostage crisis. In the election year of 1980, President Carter's public approval rating stood at 21 percent, even lower than

Richard Nixon's during the depths of Watergate. The nation was divided and dispirited as people who had grown accustomed to seemingly endless economic growth and unquestioned world power confronted new limits at home and abroad. The time was ripe for a challenge to Carter's presidential leadership, to the Democratic Party, and to the liberal approaches that had, in the main, governed the United States since Franklin Roosevelt's New Deal.

In 1980 several conservative Republican politicians ran for the White House. Foremost among them was Ronald Reagan, former movie star and two-term governor of California. In the 1940s, as president of the Screen Actors Guild in Hollywood, Reagan had been a New Deal Democrat. But in the 1950s, as a corporate spokesman for General Electric, he became increasingly conservative. In 1964 Reagan's televised speech in support of Republican presidential candidate Barry Goldwater catapulted him to the forefront of conservative politics. America, Reagan said, had come to "a time for choosing" between free enterprise and big government, between individual liberty and "the ant heap of totalitarianism."

Ronald Reagan

Elected governor of California just two years later, Reagan became well known for his right-wing rhetoric: America should "level Vietnam, pave it, paint stripes on it, and make a parking lot out of it," Reagan claimed. And in 1969, when student protesters occupied "People's Park" near the University of California in Berkeley, he threatened a "bloodbath" and dispatched National Guard troops in full riot gear. Reagan was often pragmatic, however, about policy decisions. He denounced welfare but presided over reform of the state's social welfare bureaucracy. And he signed one of the nation's most liberal abortion laws.

In the 1980 election, Reagan, in stark contrast to incumbent Jimmy Carter, offered an optimistic vision for America's future. With his Hollywood charm and strong conservative credentials, he succeeded in forging very different sorts of American conservatives into a new political coalition. Reagan built on a natural constituency of political conservatives. These strong anticommunists wanted to strengthen national defense; they also believed the federal government should play a more limited role in the nation's domestic life and wished to roll back the liberal programs begun under the New Deal in the 1930s and the Great Society in the 1960s. Reagan also reached out to less ideologically oriented economic conservatives, gaining their support by promising economic deregulation and tax policies that would benefit corporations, wealthy investors, and entrepreneurs. He

The New Conservative Coalition

also attracted a relatively new cohort of neoconservatives, a small but influential group composed primarily of academics and intellectuals, many of them former Democrats who believed the party had lost its way after Vietnam and who rejected the old conservatism as backward looking. The neoconservatives took particular interest in foreign policy and embraced the Reagan campaign's aggressively anti-Soviet posture.

In a major accomplishment, Reagan managed to unite these political, economic, and neoconservatives with two new constituencies. He tapped into the sentiments that fueled the tax revolt movement of the 1970s, drawing voters from traditionally Democratic constituencies, such as labor unions and urban ethnic groups. Many middle- and working-class whites resented their hard-earned money's going to what they saw as tax-funded welfare for people who did not work; some had reacted angrily to government programs, such as busing children to achieve racial integration of schools, meant to combat racial inequities. Many also thought that Reagan's joke that there was nothing more frightening than finding a government official on the doorstep saying, "I'm from the government and I'm here to help," rang true. These "Reagan Democrats" found the Republican critique of tax-funded social programs and "big government" appealing, even though Reagan's proposed economic policies would benefit the wealthy at their expense.

Finally, in the largest leap, Reagan tied these groups to the religiously based New Right, an increasingly powerful movement of social conservatives. "When political conservative leaders began to . . . strike an alliance with social conservatives—the pro-life people, the anti-ERA people, the evangelical and born-again Christians, the people concerned about gay rights, prayer in the schools, sex in the movies or whatever," explained conservative fundraiser Richard Viguerie, "that's when this whole movement began to come alive."

On election day, Reagan and his running mate, George Bush, claimed victory with 51 percent of the popular vote. Jimmy Carter carried only six states. Reagan's victory in 1980 began more than a decade of Republican power in Washington: Reagan served two terms as president, followed by his vice president, George Bush, who was elected as Reagan's successor in 1988. Reagan, as much as any president since Franklin Roosevelt, defined the era over which he presided.

Reagan's Conservative Agenda

Reagan, as president, was not especially focused on the details of governing or the specifics of policies and programs. When outgoing president Jimmy Carter briefed him on urgent issues of foreign and domestic policy, Rea-

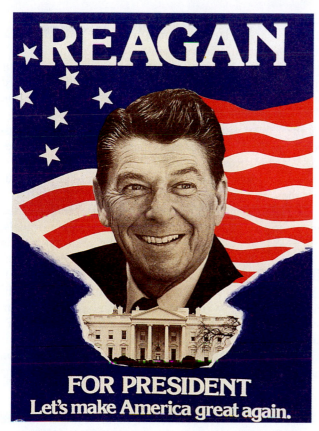

▲ Ronald Reagan, the Republican presidential candidate in 1980, campaigned for "family values," an aggressive anti-Soviet foreign and military policy, and tax cuts. He also exuded optimism and appealed to Americans' patriotism. This poster issued by the Republican National Committee included Reagan's favorite campaign slogan, "Let's make America great again." *(Collection of David J. and Janice L. Frent)*

gan listened politely but took not a single note and asked no questions. Critics argued that his lack of knowledge could prove dangerous—as when he insisted that intercontinental ballistic missiles carrying nuclear warheads could be called back once launched, or when he said that "approximately 80 percent of our air pollution stems from hydrocarbons released by vegetation."

But supporters insisted that Reagan was a great president in large part because he focused on the big picture. When he spoke to the American people, he offered what seemed to be simple truths—and he did it with the straightforwardness of a true believer and the warmth and humor of an experienced actor. Although many—even among Reagan supporters—winced at his willingness to reduce complex policy issues to simple (and often misleading) stories, Reagan was to most Americans the "Great Communicator." He won admiration for his courage after he

was seriously wounded in an assassination attempt just sixty-nine days into his presidency. Reagan quipped to doctors preparing to remove the bullet lodged near his heart, "I hope you're all Republicans."

Most important, Reagan had a clear vision for America's future. He and his advisers wanted nothing less than to roll back the liberalism of the past fifty years that had made government responsible for the health of the nation's economy and for the social welfare of its citizens. In the words of David Stockman, a Reagan appointee who headed the Office of Management and Budget, the administration meant to "create a minimalist government" and sever "the umbilical cords of dependency that run from Washington to every nook and cranny of the nation."

Reagan, like traditional conservatives, believed that America's social problems could not be solved by the federal government. But he also tapped into a broader, and less coherent, backlash against the social policies and programs of the Great Society. Many Americans who struggled to make ends meet during the economic crises of the 1970s and early 1980s resented paying taxes that, they believed, went to fund government "handouts" to people who did not work. Lasting racial tensions also fueled public resentment: Reagan fed a stereotype of welfare recipients as unwed, black, teenage mothers who kept having babies to collect larger checks. Even before he became president, Reagan played to these resentments with fabricated tales of a Chicago "welfare queen" who collected government checks under eighty different false names.

Attacks on Social Welfare Programs

In 1981 the administration cut funding for social welfare programs by $25 billion. But "welfare" (Aid to Families with Dependent Children and food stamp programs) was a small part of the budget compared with Social Security and Medicare—social welfare programs that benefited Americans of all income levels, not just the poor. Major budget cuts for these popular, broadly based programs proved impossible. The Reagan administration did shrink the *proportion* of the federal budget devoted to social welfare programs (including Social Security and Medicare) from 28 to 22 percent by the late 1980s—but only because of a $1.2 trillion increase in defense spending.

Reagan also attacked federal environmental, health, and safety regulations that he believed reduced business profits and discouraged economic growth. Administration officials claimed that removing the stifling hand of government regulation would restore the energy and creativity of America's free-market

Pro-Business Policies and the Environment

system. However, they did not so much end government's role as deploy government power to aid corporate America. The president went so far as to appoint opponents of federal regulations to head agencies charged with enforcing them—letting foxes guard the chicken coop, critics charged.

Environmentalists were appalled when Reagan appointed James Watt, a well-known antienvironmentalist, as secretary of the interior. Watt was a leader in the "Sagebrush Rebellion," which sought the return of publicly owned lands in the West, such as national forests, from federal to state control. Land control issues were complicated: the federal government controlled more than half of western lands—including 83 percent of the land in Nevada, 66 percent in Utah, and 50 percent in Wyoming—and many westerners believed that eastern policymakers did not understand the realities of western life. But states' ability to control land within their borders was not the sole issue; Watt and his group wanted to open western public lands to private businesses for logging, mining, and ranching.

Watt also dismissed the need to protect national resources and public wilderness lands for future generations, telling members of Congress during his 1981 Senate confirmation hearing, "I don't know how many generations we can count on until the Lord returns." As interior secretary, Watt allowed private corporations to acquire oil, mineral, and timber rights to federal lands for minuscule payments. He was forced to resign in 1983 after he dismissively referred to a federal advisory panel as "a black . . . a woman, two Jews, and a cripple." Even before Watt's resignation, his appointment had backfired, as his actions reenergized the nation's environmental movement and even provoked opposition from business leaders who understood that uncontrolled strip-mining and clear-cut logging of western lands could destroy lucrative tourism and recreation industries in western states.

As part of its pro-business agenda, the Reagan administration undercut organized labor's ability to negotiate wages and working conditions.

Attacks on Organized Labor

Union power was already waning; labor union membership declined in the 1970s as jobs in heavy industry disappeared, and efforts to unionize the high-growth electronics and service sectors of the economy had not succeeded. Reagan's policies made hard times for unions worse. Setting the tone for his administration, in August 1981 Reagan intervened in a strike by the Professional Air Traffic Controllers Organization (PATCO). The air traffic controllers—federal employees, for whom striking was illegal—had walked out in protest over working conditions that they believed compromised the safety of American air travel. Only forty-eight hours into the strike, Reagan fired the 11,350 strikers and stipulated that they could never be rehired by the Federal Aviation Administration.

With the support of an anti-union secretary of labor and appointees to the National Labor Relations Board who consistently voted for management and against labor, businesses took an increasingly hard line with labor during the 1980s, and unions failed to mount an effective opposition. Yet an estimated 44 percent of union families had voted for Reagan in 1980, drawn to his geniality, espousal of old-fashioned values, and vigorous anticommunist rhetoric.

Although much of Reagan's domestic agenda focused on traditional conservative political and economic goals, the New Right and its agenda played an increasingly important role in Reagan-era social policy. It is surprising that the strongly religious New Right was drawn to Reagan, a divorced man without strong ties to religion or, seemingly, his own children. But the non-church-going Reagan lent his support to New Right social issues: he endorsed the anti-abortion cause, and his White House issued a report supporting prayer in public schools.

The New Right

Reagan's judicial nominations also pleased the religious New Right. The Senate, in a bipartisan vote, refused to confirm Supreme Court nominee Robert Bork after eighty-seven hours of antagonistic hearings. Congress eventually confirmed Anthony M. Kennedy instead. Reagan also appointed Anton Scalia, who would become a key conservative force on the Court, and Sandra Day O'Connor (the first woman appointee), and elevated Nixon appointee William Rehnquist to chief justice.

All these appointments made the Court more conservative. In 1986, for example, the Supreme Court upheld a Georgia law that punished consensual anal or oral sex between men with up to twenty years in jail (*Bowers v. Hardwick*); in 1989 justices ruled that a Missouri law restricting the right to an abortion was constitutional (*Webster v. Reproductive Health Services*), thus encouraging further challenges to *Roe v. Wade*. In federal courts, Justice Department lawyers argued New Right positions on such social issues, and Reagan's 378 appointees to the federal bench usually ruled accordingly. Overall, however, the Reagan administration did not push a conservative social agenda as strongly as some members of the new Republican coalition had hoped.

REAGANOMICS

The centerpiece of Reagan's domestic agenda was the economic program that took his name: Reaganomics. The

U.S. economy was in bad shape at the beginning of the 1980s. Stagflation had proved resistant to traditional economic remedies: when the government increased spending to stimulate a stagnant economy, inflation skyrocketed; when it cut spending or tightened the money supply to reduce inflation, the economy plunged deeper into recession, and unemployment rates jumped. Everyone agreed that something had to be done to break the cycle, but few thought that government intervention would work. Even some Democrats, such as Colorado senator Gary Hart, voiced a "nonideological skepticism about the old, Rooseveltian solutions to social problems."

Reagan offered the American people a simple answer to economic woes. Instead of focusing on the complexities of global competition, deindustrialization, and OPEC's control of oil, Reagan argued that U.S. economic problems were caused by government intrusion in the "free-market" economic system. At fault were intrusive government regulation of business and industry, expensive government social programs that offered "handouts" to nonproductive citizens, high taxes, and deficit spending—in short, government itself. The Reagan administration's economic agenda was closely tied to its larger conservative ideology of limited government: it sought to "unshackle" the free-enterprise system from government regulation and control, to slash spending on social programs, to limit government's use of taxes to redistribute income among the American people, and to balance the budget by reducing the role of the federal government.

Reagan's economic policy was based largely on supply-side economics, the theory that tax cuts (rather than government spending) will

Supply-Side Economics

create economic growth. Economist Arthur Laffer had proposed one key concept for supply-siders, sketching his soon-to-be-famous Laffer curve on a cocktail napkin for a *Wall Street Journal* writer and President Gerald Ford's chief of staff (and the future vice president) Dick Cheney in 1974. According to Laffer's theory, at some point rising tax rates discourage people from engaging in taxable activities (such as investing their money): if profits from investments simply disappear to taxes, what is the incentive to invest? As people invest less, the economy slows. Even though tax rates remain high, the government collects less in tax revenue because the economy stalls. Cutting taxes, on the other hand, reverses the cycle and increases tax revenues.

Although economists at the time accepted the larger principle behind Laffer's curve, almost none believed that U.S. tax rates approached the point of disincentive. Even conservative economists were highly suspicious of supply-

side principles. Reagan and his staff, however—on the basis of the unproven assumption that both corporate and personal tax rates in the United States had reached a level that discouraged investment—sought a massive tax cut. They argued that American corporations and individuals would invest funds freed up by lower tax rates, producing new plants, new jobs, and new products. Economic growth would more than make up for the tax revenues lost. And as prosperity returned, the profits at the top would "trickle down" to the middle classes and even to the poor.

Reagan's economic program was most fully developed by David Stockman, head of the Office of Management and Budget. Stockman proposed a five-year plan to balance the federal budget through economic growth (created by tax cuts) and deep cuts, primarily in social programs. Congress cooperated with a three-year, $750 billion tax cut, at that point the largest ever in American history. Cutting the federal budget, however, proved more difficult. Stockman's plan for balancing the budget assumed $100 billion in cuts from government programs, including Social Security and Medicare—and Congress was not about to cut Social Security and Medicare benefits. Reagan, meanwhile, canceled out gains from domestic spending cuts by dramatically increasing annual defense spending.

Major tax cuts, big increases in defense spending, small cuts in social programs: the numbers did not add up. The annual federal budget deficit exploded—from $59 billion in 1980 to more than $100 billion in 1982 to almost $300 billion by the end of George Bush's presidency in 1992. The federal government borrowed money to make up the difference, transforming the United States from the world's largest creditor nation to its largest debtor (see Figure 32.1). The national debt grew to almost $3 trillion. Because an ever greater share of the federal budget went to pay the interest on this ballooning debt, less was available for federal programs, foreign or domestic.

Reaganomics attempted to stimulate the economy—but economic growth would not solve the persistent problem of inflation. Here the Federal

Harsh Medicine for Inflation

Reserve Bank, an autonomous federal agency, stepped in. In 1981 the Federal Reserve Bank raised interest rates for bank loans to an unprecedented 21.5 percent, battling inflation by tightening the money supply and slowing the economy down. The nation plunged into recession. During the last three months of the year, the gross national product (GNP) fell 5 percent, and sales of cars and houses dropped sharply. With declining economic activity, unemployment soared to 8 percent, the highest level in almost six years.

By late 1982, unemployment had reached 10.8 percent, the highest rate since 1940. For African Americans,

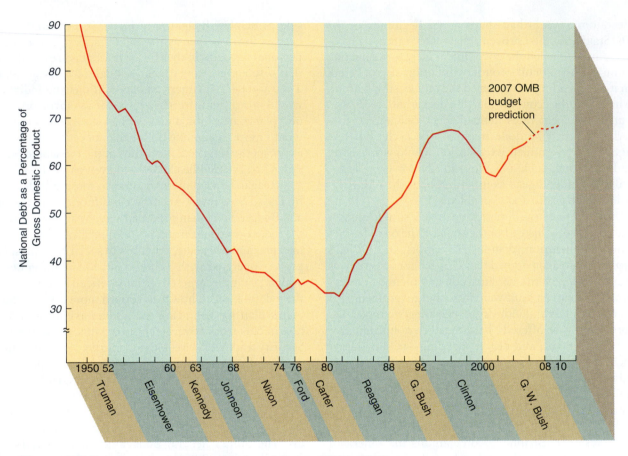

Figure 32.1   **America's Rising National Debt, 1974–1989**
America's national debt, which rose sporadically throughout the 1970s, soared to record heights during the 1980s. Under President Reagan, large defense expenditures and tax cuts caused the national debt to grow by $1.5 trillion.

(Source: Adapted from U.S. Bureau of the Census, Statistical Abstract of the United States *[Washington, D.C.: 1992], p. 315.)*

it was 20 percent. Many of the unemployed were blue-collar workers in ailing "smokestack industries," such as steel and automobiles. Reagan and his advisers promised that consumers would lift the economy out of the recession by spending their tax cuts. But as late as April 1983, unemployment still stood at 10 percent, and people were angry. Jobless steelworkers paraded through McKeesport, Pennsylvania, carrying a coffin that bore the epitaph "American Dream." Agriculture, too, was faltering and near collapse. Farmers suffered not only from falling crop prices due to overproduction, but also from floods, droughts, and burdensome debts which they had incurred at high interest rates. Many lost their property through mortgage foreclosures and farm auctions. Others filed for bankruptcy. As the recession deepened, poverty rose to its highest level since 1965.

It was harsh medicine, but the Federal Reserve Bank's plan to end stagflation worked. High interest rates helped drop inflation from 12 percent in 1980 to less than 7 percent in 1982. The economy also benefited from OPEC's 1981 decision, after eight years of engineering an artificial scarcity, to increase oil production, thus lowering prices. In 1984 the GNP rose 7 percent, the sharpest increase since 1951, and midyear unemployment fell to a four-year low of 7 percent. The economy was booming, but without sparking inflation.

By the presidential election of 1984, the recession was only a memory. Reagan got credit for the recovery, though it had little to do with his supply-side policies. In fact, the Democratic candidate, former vice president Walter Mondale, repeat-

"Morning in America"

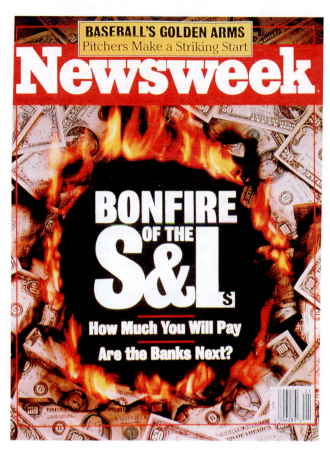

BASEBALL'S GOLDEN ARMS
Pitchers Make a Striking Start

Newsweek

BONFIRE OF THE S&Ls

How Much You Will Pay

Are the Banks Next?

▲ The 1980s savings-and-loan crisis led to the greatest collapse of U.S. financial institutions since the Great Depression. The federal bailout of S&Ls would cost American taxpayers at least $124 billion.

edly hammered at Reagan's economic policies. Insisting that the rapidly growing budget deficit would have dire consequences for the American economy, he said (honestly, but probably not very astutely) that he would raise taxes. And he focused on themes of fairness and compassion; not all Americans, Mondale told the American public, were prospering in Reagan's America. Reagan, in contrast, proclaimed, "It's morning again in America." Television ads showed heartwarming images of American life, as an off-screen narrator told viewers, "Life is better. America is back. And people have a sense of pride they never felt they'd feel again." Reagan won in a landslide, with 59 percent of the vote. Mondale, with running mate Geraldine Ferraro—U.S. congresswoman from New York and the first woman vice-presidential candidate—carried only his home state of Minnesota.

Supply-side economics was not the only policy that transformed America's economy in the 1980s. Deregula-

Deregulation

tion, begun under Jimmy Carter and expanded vastly under Reagan (the *Federal Register,* which contains all federal regulations, shrank from 87,012 pages in 1980 to 47,418 pages in 1986), created new opportunities for American business and industry. The 1978 deregulation of the airline industry lowered ticket prices both short-term and long-term; airline tickets cost almost 45 percent less in the early twenty-first century (in constant dollars) than in 1978. Deregulation of telecommunications industries created serious competition for the giant AT&T, and long-distance calling became inexpensive.

The Reagan administration loosened regulation of the American banking and finance industries and purposely cut the enforcement ability of the Securities and Exchange Commission (SEC), which oversees Wall Street. In the early 1980s, Congress deregulated the nation's savings-and-loan institutions (S&Ls), organizations previously required to invest depositors' savings in thirty-year, fixed-rate mortgages secured by property within a 50-mile radius of the S&L's main office. Stagflation had already left many S&Ls insolvent, but the 1980s legislation created conditions for a collapse. By ending government oversight of investment practices, while guaranteeing to cover losses from bad S&L investments, Congress left no penalties for failure. S&Ls increasingly put depositors' money into high-risk investments and engaged in shady—even criminal—deals.

High-risk investments carried the day on Wall Street as well, as Michael Milken, a reclusive bond trader for

Junk Bonds and Merger Mania

the firm Drexel Firestone, pioneered the "junk bond" industry and created wildly lucrative investment possibilities. Milken offered financing to debt-ridden or otherwise weak corporations that could not get traditional, low-interest bank loans to fund expansion, using bond issues that paid investors high interest rates because they were high-risk (thus "junk" bonds). Many of these corporations, Milken realized, were attractive targets for takeover by other corporations or investors—who, in turn, could finance takeovers with junk bonds. Such "predators" could use the first corporation's existing debt as a tax write-off, sell off unprofitable units, and lay off employees to create a more efficient—and thus more profitable—corporation. Investors in the original junk bonds could make huge profits by selling their shares to the corporate raiders.

By the mid-1980s, it was no longer only weak corporations that were targeted for these "hostile takeovers"; hundreds of major corporations—including giants Walt Disney and Conoco—fell prey to merger mania. Profits for investors were staggering, and by 1987 Milken, the guru of junk bonds, was earning $550 million a year—about $1,046 a minute—in salary; counting investment returns, Milken's income was about $1 billion a year.

What were the results of such practices? Heightened competition and corporate downsizing often created more-efficient businesses and industries. Deregulation helped smaller and often innovative corporations challenge the virtual monopolies of giant corporations in fields like tele-communications. And through much of the 1980s, following the "Reagan recession," the American economy boomed. Although the stock market plunged 508 points on a single day in October 1987—losing 22.6 percent of its value, or almost double the percentage loss in the crash of 1929—it rebounded quickly. The high-risk boom of the 1980s did, however, have significant costs. Corporate downsizing meant layoffs for white-collar workers and management personnel, many of whom (especially those past middle age) had difficulty finding comparable positions. The wave of mergers and takeovers left American corporations as a whole more burdened by debt than before. It also helped to consolidate sectors of the economy—such as the media—under the control of an ever smaller number of players.

The high-risk, deregulated boom of the 1980s, furthermore, was rotten with corruption. By the late 1980s, insider trading scandals—in which people used "inside" information about corporations, which was not available to the general public, to make huge profits trading stocks—rocked financial markets and sent some of the most prominent figures on Wall Street to jail (albeit comfortable, "country club" jails). Savings and loans lost billions of dollars in bad investments, sometimes turning to fraud to cover them up. Scandal reached all the way to the White House: Vice President Bush's son Neil was involved in shady S&L deals. The Reagan-Bush administration's bailout of the S&L industry cost taxpayers half a trillion dollars.

The Rich Get Richer

Finally, during the 1980s, the rich got richer, and the poor got poorer (see Figure 32.2). Merger mania and the financial market bonanza contributed, as the number of Americans reporting an annual income of $500,000 increased tenfold between 1980 and 1989. According to the Economic Policy Institute, the average compensation of a corporate executive officer increased from approximately 35 times an average worker's pay in 1978 to 71 times workers' average pay in 1989 (in 2005 the ratio

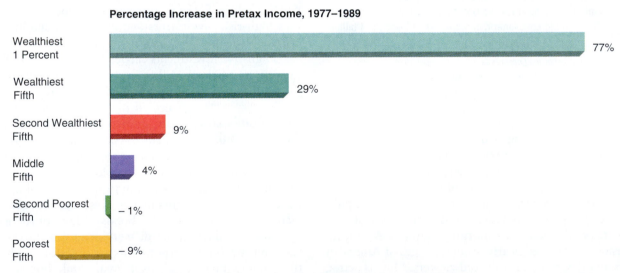

Percentage Increase in Pretax Income, 1977–1989

- Wealthiest 1 Percent — 77%
- Wealthiest Fifth — 29%
- Second Wealthiest Fifth — 9%
- Middle Fifth — 4%
- Second Poorest Fifth — −1%
- Poorest Fifth — −9%

Figure 32.2   While the Rich Got Richer in the 1980s, the Poor Got Poorer

Between 1977 and 1989, the richest 1 percent of American families reaped most of the gains from economic growth. In fact, the average pretax income of families in the top percentage rose 77 percent. At the same time, the typical family saw its income edge up only 4 percent. And the bottom 40 percent of families had actual declines in income.

(Source: Data from the New York Times, March 5, 1992.)

was 262 to 1). In 1987 the United States had forty-nine billionaires—up from one in 1978. While the number of very wealthy Americans grew, middle-class incomes were stagnant.

Most of the new inequality was due to Reagan's economic policies, which benefited the wealthy at the expense of middle- and lower-income Americans. Reagan's tax policies decreased the "total effective tax rates"—income taxes plus Social Security taxes—for the top 1 percent of American families by 14.4 percent. But they increased tax rates for the poorest 20 percent of families by 16 percent. By 1990, the richest 1 percent of Americans controlled 40 percent of the nation's wealth; fully 80 percent of wealth was controlled by the top 20 percent. Not since the 1920s had America seen such economic inequality.

REAGAN AND THE WORLD

A key element in Reagan's winning strategy in the 1980 election was his forthright call for the United States to assert itself on the world stage. Though lacking a firm grasp of world issues, history, and geography—friends and associates often marveled at his ability to get even elementary facts wrong—Reagan adhered to a few core principles. One was a deep and abiding anticommunism which had dictated his world-view for decades and which formed the foundation of his presidential campaign. A second was an underlying optimism about the ability of American power and values to bring positive change in the world. Reagan liked to quote Thomas Paine of the American Revolution: "We have it in our power to begin the world over again." Yet Reagan was also a political pragmatist, particularly as time went on and his administration became mired in scandal. Together, these elements of the president's personality help explain both his aggressive anticommunist foreign policy and his willingness to respond positively in his second term to Soviet leader Mikhail Gorbachev's call for "new thinking" in world affairs.

Initially, toughness vis-à-vis Moscow was the watchword. Embracing the strident anticommunism that char-

Soviet-American Tension

acterized U.S. foreign policy in the early Cold War, Reagan and his advisers rejected both the détente of the Nixon years and the Carter administration's focus on extending human rights abroad. Where Nixon and Carter perceived an increasingly multipolar international system, the Reagan team reverted to a bipolar perspective defined by the Soviet-American relationship. Young neoconservatives, such as Richard Perle and Paul Wolfowitz, who held mid-level positions in the administration, provided much of

the intellectual ballast and moral fervor for this shift toward confrontation with Moscow.

In his first presidential press conference Reagan described a malevolent Soviet Union, whose leaders thought they had "the right to commit any crime, to lie, to cheat." When Poland's pro-Soviet leaders in 1981 cracked down on an independent labor organization, Solidarity, Washington responded by restricting Soviet-American trade and hurled angry words at Moscow. In March 1983, Reagan told an audience of evangelical Christians in Florida that the Soviets were "the focus of evil in the modern world . . . an evil empire." That same year, Reagan restricted commercial flights to the Soviet Union after a Soviet fighter pilot mistakenly shot down a South Korean commercial jet that had strayed some 300 miles off course into Soviet airspace. The world was shocked by the death of 269 passengers, and Reagan exploited the tragedy to score Cold War points.

A key Reagan tenet held that a substantial military buildup would thwart the Soviet threat and intimidate Moscow. Accordingly, the administration launched the largest peacetime arms buildup in American history, driving up the federal debt. In 1985, when the military budget hit $294.7 billion (a doubling since 1980), the Pentagon was spending an average of $28 million an hour. Assigning low priority to arms control talks, Reagan announced in 1983 his desire for a space-based defense shield against incoming ballistic missiles: the Strategic Defense Initiative (SDI). His critics tagged it "Star Wars" and said such a system could never be made to work scientifically—some enemy missiles would always get through the shield. Moreover, the critics warned, SDI would have the effect of elevating the arms race to dangerous new levels. But Reagan was undaunted, and in the years that followed, SDI research and development consumed tens of billions of dollars.

Because he attributed Third World disorders to Soviet intrigue, the president declared the Reagan Doctrine: the

Reagan Doctrine

United States would openly support anticommunist movements— "freedom fighters"—wherever they were battling the Soviets or Soviet-backed governments. In Afghanistan, the president continued Jimmy Carter's policy of providing covert assistance, through Pakistan, to the Mujahidin rebels in their war against the Soviet occupation. CIA director William J. Casey made numerous trips to Pakistan to coordinate the flow of arms and other assistance. When the Soviets stepped up the war in 1985, the Reagan administration responded by sending more high-tech weapons. Particularly important were the anti-aircraft Stinger missiles. Easily transportable and fired by a single soldier, the Stingers turned the tide in the Afghan war by making Soviet jets and helicopters vulnerable below fifteen thousand feet.

The administration also applied the Reagan Doctrine aggressively in the Caribbean and Central America. Senior officials believed that the Soviets and Castro's Cuba were fomenting disorder in the region (see Map 32.1). Accordingly, in October 1983 the president sent U.S. troops into the tiny Caribbean island of Grenada to oust a pro-Marxist government that appeared to be forging ties with Moscow and Havana. In El Salvador, he provided military and economic assistance to a military-dominated government engaged in a struggle with left-wing revolutionaries. The regime used (or could not control) right-wing death squads, from which Luisa Orellana and her family fled. By the end of the decade they had killed forty thousand dissidents and other citizens, as well as several American missionaries who had been working with landless peasants. By the end of the decade the United States had spent more than $6 billion there in a counterinsurgency war. In January 1992 the Salvadoran combatants finally negotiated a U.N.-sponsored peace.

The Reagan administration also meddled in the Nicaraguan civil war. In 1979 leftist insurgents in Nicaragua

Contra War in Nicaragua

overthrew Anastasio Somoza, a long-time ally of the United States and member of the dictatorial family that had ruled the Central American nation since the mid-1930s. The revolutionaries called themselves Sandinistas in honor of César Augusto Sandino—who had headed the nationalistic, anti-imperialist Nicaraguan opposition against U.S. occupation in the 1930s, battled U.S. marines, and was finally assassinated by Somoza henchmen—and they denounced the tradition of U.S. imperialism in their country. When the Sandinistas aided rebels in El Salvador, bought Soviet weapons, and invited Cubans to work in Nicaragua's hospitals and schools and help reorganize the Nicaraguan army, Reagan officials charged that Nicaragua was becoming a Soviet client. In 1981 the CIA began to train, arm, and direct more than ten thousand counterrevolutionaries, known as contras, to overthrow the Nicaraguan government.

The U.S. interventions in El Salvador and Nicaragua sparked a debate much like the earlier one over Vietnam. Many Americans, including Democratic leaders in Congress, were skeptical about the communist threat to the region and warned that Nicaragua could become another Vietnam. Congress in 1984 voted to stop U.S. military aid to the contras. Secretly, the Reagan administration lined up other countries, including Saudi Arabia, Panama, and

South Korea, to funnel money and weapons to the contras, and in 1985 Reagan imposed an economic embargo against Nicaragua. The president might have opted for a diplomatic solution, but he rejected a plan proposed by Costa Rica's president Oscar Arias Sánchez in 1987 to obtain a cease-fire in Central America through negotiations and cutbacks in military aid to all rebel forces. (Arias won the 1987 Nobel Peace Prize.) Three years later, after Reagan had left office, all of the Central American presidents at last brokered a settlement; in the national election that followed, the Sandinistas lost to a U.S.-funded party. After nearly a decade of civil war, thirty thousand Nicaraguans had died, and the ravaged economy had dwindled to one of the poorest in the hemisphere.

Reagan's obsession with defeating the Sandinistas almost caused his political undoing. In November 1986 it

Iran-Contra Scandal

became known that the president's national security adviser, John M. Poindexter, and an aide, marine lieutenant colonel Oliver North, in collusion with CIA director Casey, had covertly sold weapons to Iran as part of a largely unsuccessful attempt to win the release of several Americans being held hostage by Islamic fundamentalist groups in the Middle East. During the same period, Washington had been condemning Iran as a terrorist nation and demanding that America's allies not trade with the Islamic state. Still more damaging was the revelation that money from the Iran arms deal had been illegally diverted to a fund to aid the contras—this after Congress had unambiguously rejected providing such aid. North later admitted that he had illegally destroyed government documents and lied to Congress to keep the operation clandestine.

Although Reagan survived the scandal—it remained unclear just what he did and did not know about the operation—his presidency suffered a major blow. His personal popularity declined, and an emboldened Congress began to reassert its authority over foreign affairs. In late 1992, outgoing president George Bush pardoned several former government officials who had been convicted of lying to Congress. Critics smelled a cover-up, for Bush himself, as vice president, had participated in high-level meetings on Iran-contra deals. As for North, his conviction was overturned on a technicality. In view of its deliberate thwarting of congressional authority, the Iran-contra secret network, the scholar William LeoGrande has argued, "posed a greater threat to democracy in the United States than Nicaragua ever did."

The Iran-contra scandal also pointed to the increased importance in U.S. foreign policy of the Middle East and

Map 32.1   The United States in the Caribbean and Central America

The United States has often intervened in the Caribbean and Central America. Geographical proximity, economic stakes, political disputes, security links, trade in illicit drugs, and Cuba's alliance with the Soviet Union and defiance of the United States have kept North American eyes fixed on events in the region.

U.S. Interests in the Middle East

terrorism (see Map 33.2). As before, the United States had as its main goals in the Middle East preserving access to oil and supporting its ally Israel, while at the same time checking Soviet influence in the region. In the 1980s, though, American leaders faced new pressures, in the form of a deepened Israeli-Palestinian conflict and an anti-American and anti-Israeli Islamic fundamentalist movement that began to spread after the ouster of the shah of Iran in 1979.

The 1979 Camp David accords between Israel and Egypt had raised hopes of a lasting settlement involving self-government for the Palestinian Arabs living in the Israeli-occupied Gaza Strip and West Bank. It did not happen, as Israel and the Palestinian Liberation Organization (PLO) remained at odds. In 1982, in retaliation for Palestinian shelling of Israel from Lebanon, Israeli troops invaded Lebanon, reaching the capital, Beirut, and inflicting massive damage. The beleaguered PLO and various Lebanese factions called on Syria to contain the Israelis. Thousands of civilians died in the multifaceted conflict, and a million people became refugees. Reagan made no effort to halt the Israeli offensive, but he agreed to send U.S. marines to Lebanon to join a peacekeeping force. Soon the American troops became embroiled in a war between Christian and Muslim factions, as the latter accused the marines of helping the Christian-dominated government rather than acting as neutral peacekeepers. In October 1983, terrorist bombs demolished a barracks, killing 241 American servicemen. Four months later, Reagan recognized failure and pulled the remaining marines out.

The attack on the marine barracks showed the growing danger of terrorism to the United States and other western countries. In the 1980s, numerous otherwise powerless groups, many of them associated with the Palestinian cause or with Islamic fundamentalism, relied on terrorist acts to further their political aims. Often they targeted American citizens and property, on account of Washington's support of Israel and U.S. involvement in the Lebanese civil war. Of the 690 hijackings, kidnappings, bombings, and shootings around the world in 1985, for example, 217 were against Americans. Most of these actions originated in Iran, Libya, Lebanon, and the Gaza Strip. In June 1985, for example, Shi'ite Muslim terrorists from Lebanon hijacked an American jetliner, killed one passenger, and held thirty-nine Americans hostage for seventeen days. Three years later, a Pan American passenger plane was destroyed over Scotland, probably by pro-Iranian terrorists who concealed the bomb in a cassette player.

Terrorism

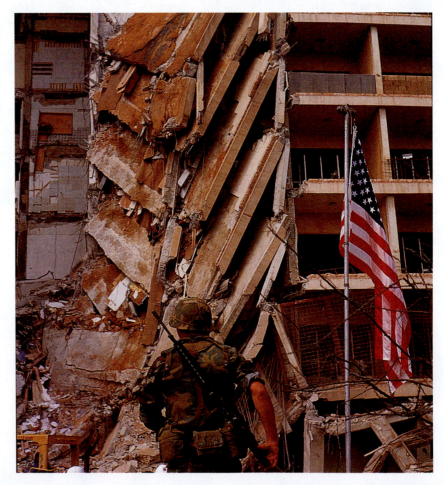

On April 18, 1983, a car bomb placed by terrorists demolished the U.S. embassy in Beirut, Lebanon, killing 63 people, 17 of them Americans. An American soldier stands guard near the destroyed building. Then, in October of the same year, terrorist bombs leveled a military barracks, killing 241 American personnel. A few months later, President Reagan withdrew U.S. marines from a multinational peacekeeping force that had been dispatched to Lebanon to calm a war waged there by Israel against PLO and Syrian forces.

(Bill Pierce/Sygma)

Washington, firmly allied with Israel, continued to propose peace plans designed to persuade the Israelis to give back occupied territories and the Arabs to give up attempts to push the Jews out of the Middle East (the "land-for-peace" formula). As the peace process stalled in 1987, Palestinians living in the West Bank began an *intifada* (Arabic for "uprising") against Israeli forces. Israel refused to negotiate, but the United States decided to talk with PLO chief Yasir Arafat after he renounced terrorism and accepted Israel's right to live in peace and security. For the PLO to recognize Israel and, in effect, for the United States to recognize the PLO were major developments in the Arab-Israeli conflict, even as a lasting settlement remained elusive.

In South Africa, too, American diplomacy became more aggressive as the decade progressed. At first, the Reagan administration followed a policy of "constructive engagement"—asking the increasingly isolated government to reform its apartheid system, designed to preserve white supremacy. But many Americans demanded economic sanctions: cutting off imports from South Africa and pressuring some 350 American companies—top among them Texaco, General Motors, Ford, and Goodyear—to cease operations there. Some American cities and states passed divestment laws, withdrawing dollars (such as pension funds used to buy stock) from American companies active in South Africa. Public protest and congressional legislation forced the Reagan administration in 1986 to impose economic restrictions against South Africa. Within two years, about half of the American companies in South Africa had pulled out.

Many on the right were unhappy with the South Africa sanctions policy—they believed the main black opposition group, the African National Congress (ANC), was dominated by communists, and they doubted the efficacy of sanctions—and the more extreme among them soon found another reason to be disenchanted with Reagan. A new Soviet leader, Mikhail S. Gorbachev, had come to power, and Reagan, his own popularity declining somewhat, showed a newfound willingness to enter negotiations with the "evil empire." Gorbachev called for a friendlier superpower relationship and a new, more cooperative world system. At a 1985 Geneva summit meeting between the two men, Reagan agreed in principle with Gorbachev's contention that strategic weapons should be substantially reduced, and at a 1986 Reykjavik, Iceland, meeting they came very close to a major reduction agreement. SDI, however, stood in the way: Gorbachev insisted that the initiative be shelved, and Rea-

Enter Gorbachev

▲ In one of several summit meetings, top Soviet leader Mikhail Gorbachev (b. 1931) and President Ronald Reagan (1911–2004) met in Moscow in May 1988 in hopes of signing a Strategic Arms Reduction Talks (START) agreement. The chemistry of warm friendship that Reagan later claimed characterized his personal relationship with Gorbachev fell short of producing cuts in dangerous strategic weapons. But their cordial interaction encouraged the diplomatic dialogue that helped end the Cold War.

(Ronald Reagan Presidential Library)

gan refused to part with it, despite continuing scientific objections that the plan would cost billions of dollars and never work.

But Reagan and Gorbachev got along well, despite the language barrier and their differing personalities. Reagan's penchant for telling stories rather than discussing the intricacies of policy did not trouble the detail-oriented Gorbachev. As General Colin Powell commented, though the Soviet leader was far superior to Reagan in mastery of specifics, he never exhibited even a trace of condescension. He understood that Reagan was, as Powell put it, "the embodiment of his people's down-to-earth character, practicality, and optimism." And Reagan toned down his strident anti-Soviet rhetoric, particularly as his more hawkish advisers left the administration in the late 1980s.

The turnaround in Soviet-American relations stemmed more from changes abroad than from Reagan's decisions.

Perestroika and *Glasnost*

As Reagan said near the end of his presidency, he had been "dropped into a grand historical moment." Under the dynamic Gorbachev, a younger generation of Soviet leaders came to power in 1985. They began to modernize the highly bureaucratized, decaying economy through a reform program known as *perestroika* ("restructuring") and to liberalize the authoritarian political system through *glasnost* ("openness"). For these reforms to work, however, Soviet military expenditures had to be reduced and foreign aid decreased.

In 1987 Gorbachev and Reagan signed the Intermediate-Range Nuclear Forces (INF) Treaty banning all land-based intermediate-range nuclear missiles in Europe. Soon began the destruction of 2,800 missiles, including Soviet missiles targeted at western Europe and NATO missiles aimed at the Soviet Union. Gorbachev also unilaterally reduced his nation's armed forces, helped settle regional conflicts, and began the withdrawal of Soviet troops from Afghanistan. After more than forty chilling years, the Cold War was coming to an end.

AMERICAN SOCIETY IN THE 1980S

As the Cold War waned, so, too, did the power of the belief in an America united by a set of shared, middle-class values. Although the ideal of shared values was never a reality, it had exercised a powerful hold in the nation's public culture from World War II well into the 1960s. By the 1980s, after years of social struggle and division, few Americans believed in the reality of that vision; many rejected it as undesirable. And though the 1980s were never as contentious and violent as the era of social protest in the 1960s and early 1970s, deep social and cultural divides existed among Americans. A newly powerful group of Christian conservatives challenged the secular culture of the American majority. A growing class of affluent, well-educated Americans seemed a society apart from the urban poor, whom sociologists and journalists began calling "the underclass." At the same time, the composition of the American population was changing dramatically, as people immigrated to the United States from more different nations than ever before.

As late as 1980, many Americans believed that the 1925 Scopes trial over the teaching of evolution had been the last gasp of fundamentalist Christianity in the United States. They were wrong. Since the 1960s, America's mainline liberal Protestant churches—Episcopalian, Pres-

Growth of the Religious Right

byterian, Methodist—had been losing members, while Southern Baptists and other denominations that offered the spiritual experience of being "born again" through belief in Jesus Christ and that accepted the literal truth of the Bible (fundamentalism) had grown rapidly. Fundamentalist preachers reached out to vast audiences through television: by the late 1970s, televangelist Oral Roberts was drawing an audience of 3.9 million. Close to 20 percent of Americans identified themselves as fundamentalist Christians in 1980.

Most fundamentalist Christian churches stayed out of the social and political conflicts of the 1960s and early 1970s, arguing that preaching the "pure saving gospel of Jesus Christ" was more important. But in the late 1970s—motivated by what they saw as the betrayal of God's will in an increasingly permissive American society—some influential preachers began to mobilize their flocks for political struggle. In a "Washington for Jesus" rally in 1980, fundamentalist leader Pat Robertson told crowds, "We have enough votes to run the country. . . . And when the people say, 'We've had enough,' we are going to take over." The Moral Majority, founded in 1979 by Jerry Falwell, sought to create a "Christian America," in part by supporting political candidates on the local and national levels. Falwell's defense of socially conservative "family values" and his condemnation of feminism (he called NOW the "National Order of Witches"), homosexuality, pornography, and abortion resonated with many Americans.

Throughout the 1980s, the coalition of conservative Christians known as the New Right waged campaigns against America's secular culture. Rejecting the idea associated with multiculturalism that different cultures and lifestyle choices were equally valid, the New Right worked to establish what they believed to be "God's law" as the basis for American society. Concerned Women for America, founded by Beverly LaHayes in 1979, attempted to have elementary school readers containing "unacceptable" religious beliefs (including excerpts from *The Diary of Anne Frank* and *The Wizard of Oz*) removed from school classrooms. In 1989 the American Family Association protested network television shows including *Cheers* (a popular comedy set in a Boston neighborhood bar) and *Nightline*. Fundamentalist Christian groups once again began to challenge the teaching of evolutionary theory in public schools. The Reagan administration frequently turned to James Dobson, founder of the conservative Focus on the Family organization, for policy advice. Conservative Christians also joined with Roman Catholics, Mormons, and other religious opponents of abortion in the anti-abortion or "prolife" movement, which had sprung up in the wake of the Supreme Court's 1973 decision in *Roe v. Wade*.

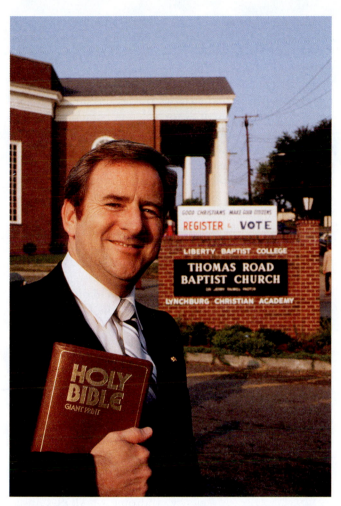

▲ Holding his Bible, the Reverend Jerry Falwell stands before his church in Lynchburg, Virginia, on a Sunday morning before services. An evangelical preacher whose "Old Time Gospel Hour" program reached 15 million Americans, Falwell encouraged his congregation—and the religious right in general—to show their political power in the 1980 presidential election. *(© Wally McNamee/Corbis)*

Although the New Right often found an ally in the Reagan White House, many other Americans vigorously

"Culture Wars"

opposed a movement that they saw as preaching a doctrine of intolerance and threatening basic freedoms—including freedom of religion for those whose beliefs did not accord with the conservative Christianity of the New Right. In 1982 politically progressive television producer Norman Lear, influential former congresswoman Barbara Jordan, and other prominent figures from the fields of business, religion, politics, and entertainment founded People for the American Way to support American civil liberties and free-

doms, the separation of church and state, and the values of tolerance and diversity. The struggle between the religious right and their opponents for the future of the nation came to be known as the "culture wars."

It was not only organized groups, however, that opposed the agenda of the religious right. Many beliefs of Christian fundamentalists ran counter to the way most Americans lived—especially when it came to women's roles. The women's movement, like the civil rights movement, had brought about significant changes in American society. By the 1980s, a generation of girls had grown up expecting freedoms and opportunities that their mothers never had. Legislation such as the Civil Rights Act of 1964 and Title IX had opened both academic and athletic programs to girls and women. In 1960 there were thirty-eight male lawyers for every female lawyer in the United States; by 1983, the ratio was 5.5 to 1. By 1985, more than half of married women with children under three worked outside the home—many from economic necessity. The religious right's insistence that women's place was in the home, subordinated to her husband, contradicted not only the gains made toward sexual equality in American society but also the reality of many women's lives.

As Americans fought the "culture wars" of the 1980s, another major social divide threatened the na-

The New Inequality

tion. A 1988 national report on race relations looked back to the 1968 Kerner Commission report to claim, "America is again becoming two separate societies," white and black. It argued that African Americans endured poverty, segregation, and crime in inner-city ghettos while most whites lived comfortably in suburban enclaves. In fact, America's separate societies of comfort and hardship were not wholly determined by race. The majority of America's poor were white, and the black middle class was strong and expanding. But people of color made up a disproportionate share of America's poor. In 1980, 33 percent of blacks and 26 percent of Latinos lived in poverty, compared with 10 percent of whites (see Figure 32.3).

Reasons for poverty varied. For people of color, the legacies of racism played a role. The changing job structure was partly responsible, as the overall number of well-paid jobs for both skilled and unskilled workers decreased, replaced by lower-paid service jobs. New York alone had 234,000 fewer blue-collar workers in 1980 than at the beginning of the 1970s. In addition, families headed by a single mother were more likely to be poor—five times more likely than families of the same race maintained by a married couple. By 1990, a high rate of unwed pregnancy and a rising divorce rate meant that about one-quarter of all

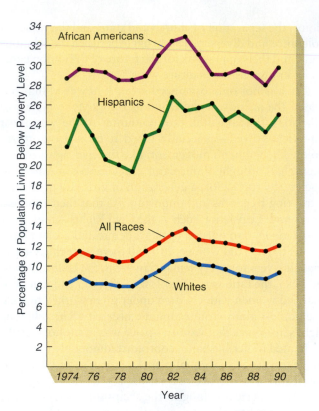

Figure 32.3   Poverty in America by Race, 1974–1990

Poverty in America rose in the early 1980s but subsided afterward. Many people of color, however, experienced little relief during the decade. Notice that the percentage of African Americans living below the poverty level was three times higher than that for whites. It was also much higher for Hispanics.

(Source: *Adapted from U.S. Bureau of the Census,* Statistical Abstract of the United States [Washington, D.C.: 1992], p. 461.)

children lived in a household without a father. Racial differences were significant: by 1992, 59 percent of African American children and 17 percent of white children lived in female-headed households, and almost half of black children lived in poverty.

As inequality increased, so, too, did social pathology. In impoverished and often hopeless inner-city neighbor-

Social Crises in American Cities

hoods, violent crime—particularly homicides and gang warfare—grew alarmingly, as did school dropout rates, crime rates, and child abuse. Some people tried to find escape in hard drugs, especially crack, a derivative of cocaine, which first struck New York City's poorest neighborhoods in

1985. Crack's legacy included destroyed families, abused children, and heavily armed teenage drug dealers. Gang shootouts over drugs were deadly: the toll in Los Angeles in 1987 was 387 deaths, more than half of them innocent bystanders. Shocked by the violence, many states instituted mandatory prison sentences for possessing small amounts of crack, making penalties for a gram of crack equivalent to those for 100 grams of cocaine, the drug of choice for more-affluent, white Americans during the 1980s. Such policies increased America's prison population almost fourfold from 1980 to the mid-1990s, with black and Latino youth arrested in disproportionate numbers. By 2000, young black men were more likely to have been arrested than to have graduated from a four-year college.

Rates of homelessness also grew during the 1980s, in part because of major cuts to low-income housing subsidies. Some of the homeless were impoverished families; many of the people living on the streets had problems with drugs or alcohol. About one-third of the homeless were former psychiatric patients discharged from psychiatric wards in a burst of enthusiasm for "deinstitutionalization." By 1985, 80 percent of the total number of beds in state mental hospitals had been eliminated on the premise that small neighborhood programs would be more responsive to people's needs than large state hospitals. Such local programs failed to materialize. Without adequate medical supervision and medication, many of America's mentally ill citizens wandered the streets.

Another social crisis confronting Americans in the 1980s was the global spread of acquired immune deficiency syndrome, or AIDS. Caused

The AIDS Epidemic

by the human immunodeficiency virus (HIV), which attacks cells in the immune system, AIDS leaves its victims susceptible to deadly infections and cancers. The human immunodeficiency virus itself is spread through the exchange of blood or body fluids, often through sexual intercourse or needle sharing by intravenous drug users.

AIDS was first diagnosed in the United States in 1981. Between 1981 and 1988, of the 57,000 AIDS cases reported, nearly 32,000 resulted in death. Politicians were slow to devote resources to combating AIDS, in part because it was initially perceived as a "gay man's disease" which did not threaten other Americans. "A man reaps what he sows," declared the Reverend Jerry Falwell of the Moral Majority. AIDS, along with other sexually transmitted diseases, such as genital herpes and chlamydia, ended an era defined by penicillin and "the pill," in which sex was freed from the threat of serious disease or unwanted pregnancy.

▲ In the 1980s there was an alarming spread of sexually transmitted diseases, especially acquired immune deficiency syndrome (AIDS). Campaigns for "safe sex," such as this New York City subway ad, urged people to use condoms.

(Reprinted with permission of Saatchi & Saatchi)

As America confronted the spreading AIDS epidemic, as well as what seemed to be epidemics of drug addiction, violence, and urban despair, some Americans were living extraordinarily well. "Greed is all right," Wall Street financier Ivan Boesky told students at the University of California, Berkeley, the center of 1960s campus protest, and he was met with cheers and laughter. For the rich, the 1980s were an era of ostentation. New York entrepreneur Donald Trump's $29 million yacht had gold-plated bathroom fixtures. Publisher Malcolm Forbes flew eight hundred guests to Morocco for his seventieth birthday; with an honor guard of three hundred Berber horsemen and six hundred acrobats, jugglers, and belly dancers to entertain the guests, the party cost $2 million.

An Era of Ostentation

With Wall Street booming, just-graduated M.B.A.s were offered starting salaries of $80,000 and new graduates from top law schools the same. Nineteen eighty-four was the "Year of the Yuppie"—Young Urban Professional—proclaimed *Newsweek* magazine. *Yuppie* was a derogatory term from the beginning (as was *Buppie,* for Black Urban Professional), but it described the lives of many ambitious and successful young Americans who worked hard in demanding careers and who created an identifiable lifestyle defined by consumer goods: BMWs, Sub-Zero refrigerators, Armani suits, Häagen-Dazs ice cream. Americans in the 1980s seemed fascinated with tales of the super-rich (making *Dallas* a top-rated television show) and with Yuppie lifestyles (chronicled on the popular show *thirtysomething*). But Yuppies also represented those who got ahead without caring about those left behind. As Yuppies led the way in gentrifying urban neighborhoods, displacing poorer residents, graffiti began to appear in New York: "Die, Yuppie Scum."

The divisions affecting American society in the 1980s were complicated by the arrival of large numbers of new immigrants from regions not formerly strongly represented in the U.S. ethnic mix. Between 1970 and 1990 the United States absorbed more than 13 million new arrivals, most from Latin America and Asia. Before the immigration act reforms of 1965, Americans of Asian ancestry had made up less than 1 percent of the nation's total population; that percentage more than tripled, to almost 3 percent, by 1990.

New Immigrants from Asia

The composition of this small slice of America's population also changed dramatically. Before 1965, the majority of Asian Americans were of Japanese ancestry (about 52 percent in 1960), followed by Chinese and Filipino. In contrast, in the 1960s and 1970s, the highest rates of immigration were from nations not previously represented in the U.S. population. There were only 603 Vietnamese residents of the United States in 1964. By 1990, the United States had absorbed almost 800,000 refugees from Indochina, casualties of the war in Vietnam and surrounding nations. Immigrants flooded in from South Korea, Thailand, India, Pakistan, Bangladesh, Indonesia, Singapore, Laos, Cambodia, and Vietnam. Japanese Americans became a much smaller portion of the Asian American population, at 15 percent surpassed by Chinese and Filipino Americans and rivaled by the Vietnamese.

Immigrants from Asia tended to be either highly skilled or unskilled. Unsettled conditions in the Philippines in the 1970s and 1980s created an exodus of well-educated Filipinos to the United States. India's economy was not able to support its abundance of well-trained physicians and healthcare workers, who increasingly found employment in the United States and elsewhere. Korea, Taiwan, and China also lost skilled and educated workers to the United States. Other immigrants from China, however, had few job skills and spoke little or no English. Large numbers of new immigrants crowded into neighborhoods like New York City's Chinatown, where women worked long hours under terrible conditions in the city's nonunion garment industry. Immigrants from southeast Asia were the most

Applicants for visas wait in line ▶ at the U.S. embassy in New Delhi, India. In 1985, 140,000 people were on the waiting list for one of 20,000 annual immigrant visas. Many poorer nations, such as India, experienced a "brain drain" of highly educated people to the United States and western Europe.

(Sandro Tucci/Time Life Pictures/Getty Images)

likely to be unskilled and to live in poverty in the United States, though some found opportunities for success.

But even highly educated immigrants often found their options limited. A 1983 study found that Korean immigrants or Korean Americans owned three-quarters of the approximately twelve hundred greengroceries in New York City. Though often cited as a great immigrant success story, Korean greengrocers usually had descended the professional ladder: 78 percent of them had college or professional degrees.

Although immigration from Asia was high, unprecedented rates of immigration coupled with a high birth rate made Latinos the fastest-growing group of Americans. New immigrants from Mexico joined Mexican Americans and other Spanish-surnamed Americans, many of whose families had lived in the United States for generations. In 1970 Latinos comprised 4.5 percent of the nation's population; that percentage jumped to 9 percent by 1990, when one out of three Los Angelenos and Miamians were Hispanic, as were 48 percent of the population of San Antonio and 70 percent of El Paso. Mexican Americans, concentrated in California and the Southwest, made up the majority of this population, but Puerto Ricans, Cubans, Dominicans, and other immigrants from the Caribbean also lived in the United States, clustered principally in East Coast cities.

During the 1980s, people from Guatemala and El Salvador, like Luisa Orellana, fled civil war and government violence, and many found their way to the United States. Although the U.S. government commonly refused to grant them political asylum (about 113,000 Cubans received political refugee status during the 1980s, compared with

The Growing Latino Population

fewer than 1,400 El Salvadorans), a national Sanctuary movement of Christian churches defied the law to protect refugees from deportation back to places where they risked violence or death. Economic troubles in Mexico and throughout Central and South America also produced a flood of a different sort of refugee: undocumented workers who crossed the poorly guarded 2,000-mile border between the United States and Mexico, seeking economic opportunities. Some were sojourners, who moved back and forth across the border. A majority meant to stay. These new Americans created a new hybrid culture that became an important part of the American mosaic. "We want to be here," explained Daniel Villanueva, a TV executive in Los Angeles, "but without losing our language and our culture. They are a richness, a treasure that we don't care to lose."

The incorporation of so many newcomers into American society was not always easy, as many Americans believed new arrivals threatened their jobs and economic security, and nativist violence and simple bigotry increased. In 1982 twenty-seven-year-old Vincent Chin was beaten to death in Detroit by an unemployed auto worker and his uncle. American auto plants were losing in competition with Japanese imports, and the two men seemingly mistook the Chinese American Chin for Japanese, reportedly shouting at him, "It's because of you little [expletive deleted] that we're out of work." In New York, Philadelphia, and Los Angeles, inner-city African Americans boycotted Korean groceries. Riots broke out in Los Angeles schools between black students and newly arrived Mexicans. In Dade County, Florida, voters passed an antibilingual measure that led to the removal of Spanish-language signs on public transportation, while at the state and national level people debated initiatives declaring English the "official" language of the United States. Public school classrooms, however, struggled with practical issues: in 1992 more than one thousand school districts in the United States enrolled students from at least eight different language groups.

Concerned about the flow of illegal aliens into the United States, Congress passed the Immigration Reform and Control (Simpson-Rodino) Act in 1986. The act's purpose was to discourage illegal immigration by imposing sanctions on employers who hired undocumented workers, but it also provided amnesty to millions who had immigrated illegally before 1982. As immigration continued at a high rate into the 1990s, however, it would further transform the face of America, offering both the richness of diverse cultures and the potential for continued social conflict.

THE END OF THE COLD WAR AND GLOBAL DISORDER

The departure of Ronald Reagan from the presidency coincided with a set of changes in world affairs that would lead in short order to the end of the Cold War and the dawn of a new international system. Reagan's vice president, George Herbert Walker Bush, would become president and oversee the transition. The scion of a Wall Street banker who had been a U.S. senator from Connecticut, Bush had attended an exclusive boarding school and then gone on to Yale. An upper-class, eastern Establishment figure of the type that was becoming increasingly rare in the Republican Party, he had the advantage over his rivals for the presidential nomination in that he had been a loyal vice president. And he possessed a formidable résumé—he had been ambassador to the United Nations, chairman of the Republican Party, special envoy to China, and director of the CIA. He had also been a war hero, flying fifty-eight combat missions in the Pacific in World War II and receiving the Distinguished Flying Cross.

Bush entered the 1988 presidential campaign trailing his Democratic opponent, Massachusetts governor Michael

George Herbert Walker Bush

Dukakis, by a wide margin. Republican operatives turned that around by waging one of the most negative campaigns in American history. Most notoriously, the Bush camp aired a television commercial featuring a black convicted murderer, Willie Horton, who had terrorized a Maryland couple, raping the woman, while on weekend furlough—a temporary release program begun under Dukakis's Re-

publican predecessor but associated in the ad with the implication that Dukakis was "soft on crime." The Republicans also falsely suggested that Dukakis had a history of psychiatric problems. His patriotism was questioned, as was that of his wife, who was wrongly accused of having burned an American flag while protesting the Vietnam War. These personal attacks generally did not come from Bush himself, but neither did he disavow them. Dukakis, meanwhile, did not engage in personal attacks on Bush but ran an uninspired campaign. On election day, Bush won by 8 percentage points in the popular vote and received 426 electoral votes to Dukakis's 112. The Democrats, however, retained control of both houses of Congress.

From the start, Bush focused most of his attention on foreign policy, but he was by nature cautious and reactive in world affairs, much to the chagrin of neoconservatives, even in the face of huge changes in the international system. Mikhail Gorbachev's reforms in the Soviet Union were now taking on a life of their own, stimulating reforms in eastern Europe that ultimately led to revolution. In 1989 many thousands of people in East Germany, Poland, Hungary, Czechoslovakia, and Romania, longing for personal freedom, startled the world by repudiating their communist governments and staging mass protests against a despised ideology. In November 1989, Germans scaled the Berlin Wall and then tore it down; the following October, the two Germanys reunited after forty-five years of separation. By then, the other communist governments in eastern Europe had either fallen or were about to do so.

Challenges to communist rule in China met with less success. In June 1989, hundreds—perhaps thousands—of

Pro-Democracy Movements

unarmed students and other citizens who for weeks had been holding peaceful pro-democracy rallies in Beijing's Tiananmen Square were slaughtered by Chinese armed forces. The Bush administration, anxious to preserve influence in Beijing, did no more than denounce the action, allowing the Chinese government, whose successful economic reforms had won much admiration in the 1980s, to emphatically reject political liberalization.

Elsewhere, however, the forces of democratization proved too powerful to resist. In South Africa, a new government under F. W. de Klerk, responding to increased domestic and international pressure, began a cautious retreat from the apartheid system. In February 1990, de Klerk legalized all political parties in South Africa, including the ANC, and ordered the release of Nelson Mandela, a hero to black South Africans, after a twenty-seven-year imprisonment. Then, in a staged process lasting several years, the government repealed its apartheid laws and

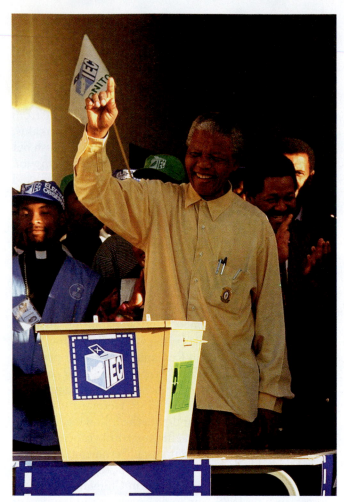

▲ African National Congress (ANC) leader Nelson Mandela gestures after casting his vote at Ohlange High School hall in Inanda, on April 27, 1994, for South Africa's first all-race elections. When results were announced later in the week, Mandela had been elected South Africa's first black president. *(John Parkin/AP Images)*

opened up the vote to all citizens, regardless of color. Mandela, who became South Africa's first black president in 1994, called the transformation of his country "a small miracle."

In 1990 the Soviet Union itself began to disintegrate. First the Baltic states of Lithuania, Latvia, and Estonia declared independence from Moscow's rule. The following year, the Soviet Union itself ceased to exist, disintegrating into independent successor states—Russia, Ukraine, Tajikistan, and many others (see Map 32.2). Muscled aside by Russian reformers who thought he was moving too

Collapse of Soviet Power

slowly toward democracy and free-market economics, Gorbachev himself lost power. The breakup of the Soviet empire, the dismantling of the Warsaw Pact (the Soviet military alliance formed in 1955 with communist countries of eastern Europe), the repudiation of communism by its own leaders, German reunification, and a significantly reduced risk of nuclear war signaled the end of the Cold War. The Soviet-American rivalry that for half a century had dominated international politics—and circumscribed domestic prospects in both countries—was over.

The United States and its allies had won. The containment policy followed by nine presidents—from Truman through Bush—had had many critics over the years, on both the left and the right, but it had succeeded on a most basic level: it had contained communism for four-plus decades without blowing up the world and without obliterating freedom at home. Two systems competed in this East-West confrontation, and that of the West had clearly triumphed—as anyone who experienced life in both a NATO country and a Warsaw Pact nation quickly realized. Next to the glitz and bustle and well-stocked store shelves of the former were the drab housing projects, polluted skies, and scarce consumer goods of the latter. Over time, the Soviet socialist economy proved less and less able to compete with the American free-market one, less and less able to cope with the demands of the Soviet and eastern European citizenry.

Yet the Soviet empire might have survived for years more had it not been for Gorbachev, one of the most influential figures of the twentieth century. His ascension to the top of the Soviet leadership was the single most important event in the final phase of the Cold War, and it is hard to imagine the far-reaching changes of the 1985–1990 period without his influence. Through a series of unexpected overtures and decisions, Gorbachev fundamentally transformed the nature of the superpower relationship in a way that could scarcely have been anticipated a few years before. Ronald Reagan's role was less central but still vitally important, not so much because of his hard-line policies in his first term as because of his later willingness to enter into serious negotiations and to treat Gorbachev more as a partner than as an adversary. George H. W. Bush, too, followed this general approach. In this way, just as personalities mattered in starting the Cold War, so they mattered in ending it.

The victory in the Cold War elicited little celebration among Americans. The struggle had exacted a heavy price in money and lives. The confrontation may never have become a hot war on a global level, but the period after 1945 nevertheless witnessed numerous bloody Cold War–related conflicts claim-

Costs of Victory

Map 32.2   The End of the Cold War in Europe

When Mikhail Gorbachev came to power in the Soviet Union in 1985, he initiated reforms that ultimately undermined the communist regimes in eastern Europe and East Germany, and led to the breakup of the Soviet Union itself, ensuring an end to the Cold War.

ing millions of lives. In the Vietnam War alone, between 1.5 million and 2 million people died, more than 58,000 of them Americans. Military budgets, meanwhile, had eaten up billions upon billions of dollars that could have been allocated to domestic programs. Some Americans wondered whether the steep price had been necessary, whether the communist threat had ever been as grave as officials, from the late 1940s on, had claimed.

Bush proclaimed a "new world order," but for him and his advisers the question was: what happens next? As the Cold War closed, they struggled futilely to describe the dimensions of an international system that they said would be based on democracy, free trade, and the rule of law. The administration signed important arms reduction treaties with the Soviet Union in 1991 and with the post-breakup Russia in 1993, leading to major reductions in nuclear weapons on both sides, but the United States sustained a large defense budget and continued to station large numbers of military forces overseas. As a result, Ameri-

cans were denied the "peace dividend" that they hoped would reduce taxes and free up funds to address domestic problems.

In Central America, the Bush administration cooled the zeal with which Reagan had meddled, because the interventions had largely failed, and, with the Cold War over, anticommunism seemed irrelevant. Still, like so many presidents before him, Bush showed no reluctance to intervene forcefully and unilaterally in the region to further U.S. aims. In December 1989, American troops invaded Panama to oust military leader Manuel Noriega. A long-time drug trafficker, Noriega had stayed in Washington's favor in the mid-1980s by providing logistical support for the contras in nearby Nicaragua, but in the early 1990s, exposés of his sordid record, which provoked protests in Panama, changed Bush's mind. Noriega was captured in the invasion and taken to Miami, where, in 1992, he was convicted of drug trafficking and imprisoned. Devastated Panama, meanwhile, became all the more dependent on the United States, which offered little reconstruction aid.

The strongest test of Bush's foreign policy came in the Middle East. The Iran-Iraq War had ended inconclusively in August 1988, after eight years of fighting and almost 400,000 dead. The Reagan administration had assisted the Iraqi war effort with weapons and intelligence, as had many other NATO countries. In mid-1990 Iraqi president Saddam Hussein, facing massive war debts and growing domestic discontent, invaded neighboring Kuwait, hoping thereby to enhance his regional power and his oil revenues and also shore up domestic support. He counted on Washington to look the other way. Instead, George Bush condemned the invasion and vowed to defend Kuwait. He was outraged by Hussein's act of aggression and also feared that Iraq might threaten U.S. oil supplies, not merely in Kuwait but also in petroleum-rich Saudi Arabia next door.

Saddam Hussein's Gamble

Within weeks, Bush had convinced virtually every important government, including most of the Arab and Islamic states, to sign on to an economic boycott of Iraq. Then, in Operation Desert Shield, Bush dispatched more than 500,000 U.S. forces to the region, where they were joined by more than 200,000 from the allies. Likening Saddam to Hitler and declaring the moment the first post–Cold War "test of our mettle," Bush rallied a deeply divided Congress to authorize "all necessary means" to oust Iraq from Kuwait (a vote of 250 to 183 in the House and 52 to 47 in the Senate). Although Bush did not invoke the 1973 War Powers Act, numerous observers saw his seeking a congressional resolution of ap-

proval as reinforcing the intent of the act. Many Americans believed that economic sanctions imposed on Iraq should be given more time to work, but Bush would not wait. "This will not be another Vietnam," the president said, by which he meant it would not be a lengthy and frustrating affair. Victory would come swiftly and cleanly.

Operation Desert Storm began on January 16, 1991, with the greatest air armada in history pummeling Iraqi targets. American cruise missiles reinforced round-the-clock bombing raids on Baghdad, Iraq's capital. It was a television war, in which CNN reporters broadcast live from a Baghdad hotel while bombs were falling in the city, and millions of Americans sat transfixed in their living rooms, eyes glued to the TV. In late February, coalition forces under General Norman Schwartzkopf launched a ground war that quickly routed the Iraqis from Kuwait. When the war ended on March 1, at least 40,000 Iraqis had been killed, while the death toll for allied troops stood at 240 (148 of them Americans). Almost one-quarter of the American dead were killed by "friendly fire"—by weapons fired by U.S. or allied troops.

Operation Desert Storm

Bush rejected a call from some of his advisers to take Baghdad and topple Hussein's regime. Coalition members would not have agreed to such a plan—it would go beyond the original objective of forcing Iraq out of Kuwait—and it was also not clear who in Iraq would replace the dictator. Some also warned that the drive to Baghdad could

In the Persian Gulf War of early 1991, Operation Desert Storm forced Iraqi troops out of Kuwait. Much of that nation's oil industry was destroyed by bombs and by the retreating Iraqis, who torched oil facilities as they left. Oil wells burned for months, darkening the sky over these American forces and causing environmental damage.

(Bruno Barbey/Magnum Photos, Inc.)

CNN

When Ted Turner launched CNN, his Cable News Network, on June 1, 1980, few people took it seriously. CNN, with a staff of three hundred—mostly young, mostly inexperienced—operated out of the basement of a converted country club in Atlanta. Dismissed by critics as the Chicken Noodle Network, CNN was at first best known for its on-air errors, as when a cleaning woman walked onto the set and emptied anchor Bernard Shaw's trash during his live newscast. But by 1992, against all expectations, CNN was seen in more than 150 nations worldwide, and *Time* magazine named Ted Turner its "Man of the Year" for realizing media theorist Marshall McLuhan's vision of the world as a "global village" united by mass media.

Throughout the 1980s, CNN steadily built relations with local news outlets in nations throughout the world. As critical—and sometimes unanticipated—events reshaped the world, CNN reported live from Tiananmen Square and from the Berlin Wall in 1989. Millions watched as CNN reporters broadcast live from Baghdad in the early hours of the Gulf War in 1991. CNN changed not only viewers' experience of these events but diplomacy itself. When the Soviet Union wanted to denounce the 1989 U.S. invasion of Panama, officials called CNN's Moscow bureau instead of the U.S. embassy. During the Gulf War, Saddam Hussein reportedly kept televisions in his bunker tuned to CNN, and U.S. generals relied on its broadcasts to judge the effectiveness of missile attacks. In 1992 President George H. W. Bush noted, "I learn more from CNN than I do from the CIA."

Although Turner's twenty-four-hour news network had a global mission, its American origins were often apparent. During the U.S. invasion of Panama, CNN cautioned correspondents not to refer to the American military forces as "our" troops. Turner himself once sent his staff a memo insisting that anyone who used the word *foreign* instead of *international* would be fined $100. What CNN offered was not so much international news, but a global experience: people throughout the world joined in watching the major moments in contemporary history as they unfolded. America's CNN created new links among the world's people. But, as *Time* magazine noted (while praising Turner as the "Prince of the Global Village"), such connections "did not produce instantaneous brotherhood, just a slowly dawning awareness of the implications of a world transfixed by a single TV image."

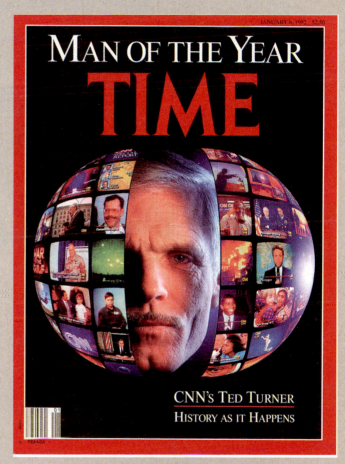

▲ "I am the right man in the right place at the right time," Ted Turner declared at the time of CNN's founding in 1980. "Not me alone, but all the people who think the world can be brought together by telecommunications." Just over a decade later Turner was rewarded for his visionary idea by being named *Time* magazine's "Man of the Year" for 1991. *(Time & Life Pictures/Getty Images)*

▲ President George Bush signs the Americans with Disabilities Act (ADA) on the White House lawn, July 26, 1990. As he lifted his pen, the president said: "Let the shameful wall of exclusion finally come tumbling down." *(© Ron Sachs/CNP/Corbis)*

bog down, subjecting U.S. forces to a costly and drawn-out campaign. So Saddam Hussein survived in power, though with his authority curtailed. The U.N. maintained an arms and economic embargo, and the Security Council issued Resolution 687, demanding that Iraq provide full disclosure of all aspects of its program to develop weapons of mass destruction and ballistic missiles with a range greater than 150 kilometers. In Resolution 688, the Security Council condemned a brutal crackdown by the Iraqi regime against Kurds in northern Iraq and Shi'ite Muslims in the south and demanded access for humanitarian groups. The United States, Britain, and France seized on Resolution 688 to create a northern "no-fly zone" prohibiting Iraqi aircraft flights. A similar no-fly zone was set up in southern Iraq in 1992 and expanded in 1996.

Although in time some would question President Bush's decision to stop short of Baghdad, initially there

Domestic Problems

were few objections. In the wake of Desert Storm the president's popularity in the polls soared to 91 percent, beating the previous high of 89 percent set by Harry Truman in June 1945 after the surrender of Germany. Cocky White House advisers thought Bush could ride his popularity right through the 1992 election and beyond. In the afterglow of military victory it seemed a good bet, particularly as Bush could also claim achievements on the domestic front that seemed to affirm his inauguration-day pledge to lead a "kinder, gentler nation."

In 1990, for example, Bush had signed the Americans with Disabilities Act. This act, which applied to companies with twenty-five or more employees and covered 87 percent of all wage earners, banned job discrimination against those with disabilities who can, with reasonable accommodation, perform the essential tasks required by the job. It also required that "reasonable accommodations," such as wheelchair ramps, be made available to people with disabilities. Also in 1990, the president, much to the disappointment of conservatives, who opposed increased regulation, signed the Clean Air Act, which sought to reduce acid rain by limiting emissions from factories and automobiles. And in 1991, after many months of contentious debate, Bush and Congress agreed on a civil rights bill to protect against job discrimination.

Yet not long after reaching their historic highs, Bush's poll numbers started falling and kept falling, largely because of the president's ineffectual response to the weakening American economy. He was slow to grasp the implications of the heavy burden of national debt and the massive federal deficit which had been out of control for nearly a decade. When the nation entered into a full-fledged recession in the months after the Gulf War, Bush did not respond, beyond proclaiming that things were not really that bad. Echoed his treasury secretary Nicholas Brady, "I don't think it's the end of the world even if we have a recession. We'll pull out of it again. It's no big deal."

For millions of ordinary Americans, it was a big deal. Business shrank, despite low interest rates that theoretically should have encouraged investment. Real-estate prices plummeted. American products faced steadily tougher competition from products made overseas, especially in Japan and elsewhere in Asia. As unemployment climbed to 8 percent, consumer confidence sank. By late 1991, fewer than 40 percent of the American people felt comfortable with the way the country was going. Many demanded that the federal government address neglected problems, such as the rising cost of healthcare.

Bush's credibility was diminished further by confirmation hearings for Clarence Thomas, whom Bush nominated to the Supreme Court in the fall of 1991. The Bush administration hoped that those who opposed the nomination of yet another conservative to the high court might nonetheless support the addition of an African American justice. But in October, Anita Hill, an African American law professor at the University of Oklahoma, charged that Thomas had sexually harassed her when she worked for him during the early 1980s. The Judiciary Committee hearings, carried live on television, turned ugly, and some Republican members suggested that Hill was either lying or mentally ill. Thomas described himself as the "victim" of a "high-tech lynching," and African American groups were passionately divided over the Hill-Thomas testimony. However, Hill's testimony focused the nation's attention on issues of power, gender, sex, and the workplace. And the Senate's confirmation of Thomas, along with the attacks on Hill, angered many, further increasing the gender gap in American politics.

Clarence Thomas Nomination

As George H. W. Bush and the Republicans entered the election year of 1992, the glow of military victory in the Gulf War had faded completely.

SUMMARY

When Ronald Reagan left the White House in 1988, succeeded by his vice president, George Bush, the *New York Times* summed up his presidency: "Ronald Reagan leaves no Vietnam War, no Watergate, no hostage crisis. But he leaves huge question marks—and much to do." George H. W. Bush met the foreign policy promises of the 1980s, as the Soviet Union collapsed and America achieved victory in the decades-long Cold War. He also led the United States into war with Iraq—a war that ended in swift and decisive victory but left Saddam Hussein in power.

During the 1980s, the United States moved from deep recession to economic prosperity. However, deep tax cuts and massive increases in defense spending created huge budget deficits, increasing the national debt from $994 billion to more than $2.9 trillion. This enormous debt would limit the options of subsequent presidential administrations. Pro-business policies, such as deregulation, created opportunities for the development of new technologies and prompted economic growth but also opened the door to corruption and fraud. Policies that benefited the wealthy at the expense of middle-class or poor Americans widened the gulf between the rich and everyone else. The social pathologies of drug addiction, crime, and violence grew, especially in the nation's most impoverished areas. The legacies of the 1980s included thousands of children born addicted to crack, who would live the rest of their lives with mental and physical impairments, and prisons that overflowed with young men.

The 1980s also saw the coalescence of the "culture wars" between fundamentalist Christians who sought to "restore" America to God and opponents who championed separation of church and state, and embraced liberal values. The nation shifted politically to the right, though the coalitions of economic and social conservatives that

Legacy FOR A PEOPLE AND A NATION

The Americans with Disabilities Act

The Americans with Disabilities Act (ADA), passed by large bipartisan majorities in Congress and signed into law by President George Bush on July 26, 1990, built on the legacy of America's civil rights movement; President Bush called it "the world's first comprehensive declaration of equality for people with disabilities." But the ADA did more than prohibit discrimination against people with physical and mental disabilities. It mandated that public and private entities—including schools, stores, restaurants and hotels, libraries and other government buildings, and public transportation authorities—provide "reasonable accommodations" to allow people with disabilities to participate fully in the life of their communities and their nation.

In less than two decades, the equal-access provisions of the ADA have changed the landscape of America. Steep curbs and stairs once blocked access to wheelchair users; now ramps and lifts are common. Buses "kneel" for passengers with limited mobility; crosswalks and elevators use audible signals for the sight-impaired. At colleges and universities, qualified students (including those with learning disabilities) receive a wide range of assistance or accommodation. The National Park Service's "accessibility" program has enabled people with a whole spectrum of disabilities to travel into the Grand Canyon and on trails in many parks. Lee Page, a wheelchair user and sports fan from Virginia, described the impact of ADA standards for sports stadiums: "We were able to see over the standing spectators as the anthem was sung. I could see the flag and everything that was happening down on the field. . . . I finally felt like a part of the crowd."

At the same time that the ADA has offered greater opportunity to many Americans, regulations covering employment have generated some difficult legal questions. Which conditions are covered by the ADA? (The Supreme Court has ruled that asymptomatic HIV infection is a covered disability and carpal tunnel syndrome is not.) Employers may not discriminate against qualified people who can, with "reasonable" accommodation, perform the "essential" tasks of a job—but what is "reasonable" and what is "essential"? The specific provisions of the ADA will likely continue to be contested and redefined in the courts. But as Attorney General Janet Reno noted, as she celebrated the tenth anniversary of the ADA with a ceremony at Warm Springs, Georgia, where President Franklin Roosevelt had sought therapy for the effects of polio, the true legacy of the ADA is the determination "to find the best in everyone and to give everyone equal opportunity."

supported Reagan were fragile and did not guarantee continued Republican dominance.

Finally, during the 1980s, the face of America changed. A society that many had thought of as white and black became ever more diverse. The nation's Latino population grew in size and visibility. New immigrants from Asia arrived in large numbers; though still a small part of the population, they would play an increasingly important role in American society. During the Reagan-Bush years, America had become both more divided and more diverse. In the years to come, Americans and their leaders would struggle with the legacies of the "Reagan era."

SUGGESTIONS FOR FURTHER READING

Elijah Anderson, *Streetwise: Race, Class, and Change in an Urban Community* (1992)

A. J. Bacevich et al., *The Gulf War of 1991 Reconsidered* (2003)

Lou Cannon, *President Reagan: The Role of a Lifetime* (2000)

Robert M. Collins, *Transforming America: Politics and Culture During the Reagan Years* (2006)

Jack F. Matlock, *Reagan and Gorbachev: How the Cold War Ended* (2004)

John Micklethwait and Adrian Wooldridge, *The Right Nation: Conservative Power in America* (2004)

James A. Morone, *Hellfire Nation: The Politics of Sin in American History* (2003)

James Patterson, *The Restless Giant: The United States from Watergate to Bush vs. Gore* (2005)

For a more extensive list for further reading, go to college.hmco.com/pic/norton8e.

Into the Global Millennium

America Since 1992

*α*t 8:46 a.m. on that fateful Tuesday morning, Jan Demczur, a window washer, stepped into an elevator in the North Tower of the World Trade Center in New York City. The elevator started to climb, but before it reached its next landing, one of the six occupants recalled, "We felt a muted thud. The whole building shook. And the elevator swung from side to side like a pendulum." None of the occupants knew it, but American Airlines Flight 175 had just crashed into the building, at a speed of 440 miles per hour.

The elevator started plunging. Someone pushed the emergency stop button, and the descent stopped. For several minutes, nothing happened. Then a voice came over the intercom to deliver a blunt message: there had been an explosion. The line went dead, as smoke began to seep through the elevator's doors. Using the wooden handle of Demczur's squeegee, several of the men forced open the doors but discovered they were on the fiftieth floor, five hundred feet above the ground, where this elevator did not stop. In front of them was a wall.

Demczur, a Polish immigrant who once worked as a builder, saw that the wall was made of Sheetrock, a plasterboard he knew could be cut. Using the squeegee, he started to scrape the metal edge against the wall, back and forth, over and over again. When the blade broke and fell down the shaft, he used a short metal handle that he had in his bucket. It took more than an hour, but the six men took turns scraping and poking, and finally burst through to a men's bathroom. Startled firefighters guided them to a stairwell. After an agonizingly slow descent through the heavy smoke, they finally burst onto the street at 10:23 a.m. Five minutes later the tower collapsed.

It was September 11, 2001.

◄ "The Tribute of Light," dedicated to the memory of the victims of the World Trade Center terrorist attacks, lights up the sky above Lower Manhattan on March 11, 2002, the six-month anniversary of the attacks. The Brooklyn Bridge is seen in the foreground. *(Daniel P. Derella/AP./Wide World Photos, Inc.)*

Only later that day did Demczur learn what had happened: terrorists had hijacked four airliners and turned them into missiles. Two had been flown into the World Trade Center; one had slammed into the Pentagon in Washington, D.C.; and one had crashed in a field in rural Pennsylvania after passengers tried to wrest control of the plane from the hijackers. Both World Trade Center towers had collapsed, killing close to three thousand people, including Demczur's close friend Roko Camaj, a window washer from Albania.

It was the deadliest attack the United States had ever suffered on its soil, and it would lead to far-ranging changes in American life. But the events of the day sent shock waves well beyond the country's shores, indeed around the globe, and made starkly clear just how interconnected the world had become at the dawn of the twenty-first century. At the World Trade Center alone, nearly five hundred foreigners from more than eighty countries lost their lives. Sixty-seven Britons died, twenty-one Jamaicans, and twenty-seven Japanese. Mexico lost seventeen of its citizens; India lost thirty-four. Sixteen Canadians perished, as did fifteen Australians and seven Haitians. The tiny Caribbean nation of Trinidad and Tobago counted fifteen deaths.

The list of victims revealed the extraordinary diversity of people who inhabited New York, showing the city once again to be a melange of world cultures. According to a chaplain at "ground zero," the victims' families communicated their grief in well over a hundred languages. Many of the victims were, like Demczur and Camaj, immigrants who had come to New York to seek a better life for themselves and their families; others were there on temporary work visas. But all helped to make the World Trade Center a kind of global city within a city, where some 50,000 people worked and another 140,000 visited on any given day.

A symbol of U.S. financial power, the World Trade Center towers were also—as their very name suggested—a symbol of the globalization of world trade that had been a central phenomenon of the 1980s and 1990s. The towers housed the offices and Wall Street infrastructure of more than four hundred businesses, including some of the world's leading financial institutions—Bank of America,

Switzerland's Credit Suisse Group, Germany's Deutsche Bank, and Japan's Dai-Ichi Kangyo Bank.

Globalization had become one of the buzzwords of the 1990s and by most definitions went beyond trade and investment to include the web of connections—in commerce, communications, and culture—that increasingly bound the world together. The terrorists, who were tied to a radical Islamic group called Al Qaeda, sought to strike a blow at that globalization, yet their attack was also an expression of it. In other words, Al Qaeda depended on the same international technological, economic, and travel infrastructure that had fueled global integration. Cell phones, computers, intercontinental air travel—the plotters made full use of these instruments of globalization in preparing to carry out their attack, then turned four modern jetliners into lethal weapons.

Islamic militants had actually struck at the World Trade Center before, in 1993, detonating a massive bomb in the center's underground parking garage and causing significant damage. But Americans at the time paid only fleeting attention. With the demise of Soviet communism and the end of the Cold War, most were intent on focusing inward. President Bill Clinton had come into office in 1993 determined to concentrate less on foreign policy and more on such domestic issues as healthcare and deficit reduction. Convinced that advances in digital technology would fundamentally change how Americans did business at home and abroad, Clinton sought to harness the forces of globalization to America's benefit.

For a broad majority of the American people, the last decade of the century offered good times. The stock market soared, unemployment dropped, and more Americans than ever before owned their own homes. But the 1990s were also marked by violence and cultural conflict—the first multiethnic uprising in Los Angeles, domestic terrorism in Oklahoma City, shootings by students at their schools, hate crimes that shocked the nation.

These were also years of political volatility and divisions. From the first days of Clinton's presidency, conservative Republicans blocked the Democrats' legislative programs. With a conservative agenda of limited government and "family values," the GOP routed Democrats in the 1994 midterm elections. But Republicans overestimated their power, alienating many voters by forcing the federal government to shut down during the winter of 1995–1996 in a standoff over the federal budget, and Clinton was reelected in 1996. However, scandal plagued the Clinton White House, and in 1999 Clinton was impeached by the House of Representatives, which alleged that he had committed perjury and obstructed justice. Clinton survived the crisis; the Senate failed to convict him, and his popularity figures remained high. But his ability to lead the nation was compromised and his presidency tarnished.

Clinton's successor, George W. Bush, successful in an extremely close and controversial election, responded to the 9/11 attacks by declaring a "war on terrorism." In so doing, he committed his administration and the nation to a complex and dangerous campaign of undefined scope and duration. Twice within eighteen months, Bush ordered U.S. forces into large-scale military action, first in Afghanistan, where Al Qaeda had its headquarters with the blessing of the ruling Taliban regime, then in Iraq to oust the government of Saddam Hussein. Both operations initially went well militarily, as the Taliban and the Iraqi government were quickly beaten. Al Qaeda, however, did not cease to be a threat, and in Afghanistan fighting eventually resumed. In Iraq, U.S. occupying forces battled a large-scale insurgency. Bush saw his high approval ratings begin to drop, and though he won reelection in 2004, his second term was undermined by continued bloodshed in Iraq and scandal at home.

- What was "The New Economy" of the 1990s, and how did it contribute to the globalization of business?
- Did the attacks of September 11, 2001 change America in fundamental ways? Explain.
- Why did the United States invade Iraq in 2003, and why did its occupying forces subsequently face a drawn-out and bloody insurgency?

SOCIAL STRAINS AND NEW POLITICAL DIRECTIONS

Although the 1990s would be remembered as an era of relative peace and prosperity, the decade did not start that way. Stories on the evening news portrayed a divided and troubled nation. Scourges of drugs, homelessness, and crime plagued America's cities. Racial tensions had worsened; the gulf between rich and poor had grown more pronounced. The economy, slowing since 1989, had tipped into recession. Public disillusionment with political leaders ran strong, but members of an otherwise ineffective and scandal-ridden Congress had voted themselves a pay raise. As the 1992 presidential election year began, Americans were frustrated and looking for a change.

The racial tensions that troubled the nation erupted in the South Central neighborhood of Los Angeles in 1992. Like most such outbreaks of violence, there was an immediate cause. A jury (with no African American members) had acquitted four white police officers charged with beating a black man, Rodney King, who had fled a pursuing police car at speeds exceeding 110 miles per hour. A bystander's video of the beating had been played so often on CNN, the new twenty-four-hour news network, that CNN's vice president called it "wallpaper." Thus the local event became a national story, the beating a symbol of continuing racism in American society. Within hours of the verdict, fires were burning in South Central.

Violence in Los Angeles

The roots of this violence, however, went deeper. Well-paid jobs had disappeared in the deindustrialization of the 1970s and 1980s, as Firestone, Goodyear, and Bethlehem Steel, along with more than a hundred other manufacturing and industrial plants, shut their doors. By the early 1990s, almost one-third of South Central residents lived in poverty—a rate 75 percent higher than for the city as a whole.

Tensions increased as new immigrants sought a foothold in the area—Latino immigrants from Mexico and Central America who competed with African American residents for scarce jobs; Korean immigrants establishing small businesses, such as grocery stores. Outside the legitimate economy, the 40 Crips (an African American gang) and the 18th Street gang (Latino) struggled over territory in South Central as the crack epidemic further decimated the neighborhood and the homicide rate soared. The police did not succeed in controlling gang violence, and their tactics alienated neighborhood residents. Relations between African Americans and Korean immigrants were especially strained. Many African American and Latino residents saw high prices in Korean-owned shops as exploitation and claimed that shopkeepers treated them disrespectfully, while Korean shopkeepers complained of frequent shoplifting, robberies, even beatings.

The violence in Los Angeles (what the Korean community called Sa-I-Gu, or 4/29, for the date it began) was a multiethnic uprising that left at least fifty-three people dead, some victims of random violence, some targeted because of their race or ethnicity, some killed by law enforcement, a few victims of accidents in the overwhelming chaos. Almost a billion dollars' worth of property was destroyed, including 2,300 stores owned by Koreans or Korean Americans. More than sixteen thousand people were arrested, half of them Latinos, many of them recent immigrants.

Americans were shocked by the events in L.A. They were also increasingly worried about the economy. During the Bush administration, the economy had grown slowly or not at all, the worst showing since the Great Depression of the 1930s. Some city and state governments faced bankruptcy. In 1978 California's Proposition 13—the first in a series of "tax revolts" across the nation—had cut property taxes while the population boomed, and the state government, out of money in mid-1992, paid its workers and bills in IOUs. California was not alone; thirty states were in financial trouble in the early 1990s. Many businesses, deeply burdened with debt, closed down or cut back. Factory employment was at its lowest level since the recession of 1982, and corporate downsizing meant that well-educated white-collar workers were losing jobs as well. In 1991 median household incomes hit the most severe decline since the 1973 recession; in 1992 the number of poor people in America reached the highest level since 1964.

Economic Troubles and the 1992 Election

As economic woes continued, President George H. W. Bush's approval rating fell—down to half of its high point of 91 percent after the Persian Gulf War. Americans seized on a news story about the president's amazed reaction to a grocery store price scanner—though Bush was admiring the prototype for a new scanning mechanism at a trade fair and not encountering a supermarket scanner for the first time—as evidence that the president was out of touch with the everyday lives and problems of American citizens who had to do their own shopping. Despite the credit Bush gained for foreign policy—the end of the Cold War and the quick victory in the Gulf War—economic woes and a lack of what he once called the "vision thing" left him vulnerable in the 1992 presidential election.

Democratic nominee Bill Clinton, the governor of Arkansas, offered a profound contrast to George Bush. Clinton's campaign headquarters bore signs with the four-word reminder "It's the economy, stupid." In a town hall-format presidential debate, a woman asked how the economic troubles had affected each candidate, and Clinton moved from behind the podium to ask her, "Tell me how it's affected you again? You know people who've lost their jobs and lost their homes?" George Bush was caught on camera looking at his watch.

On election day, Americans denied George Bush a second term. Ross Perot, a Texas billionaire who claimed he would bring economic common sense to the federal government, claimed almost 20 percent of the popular vote—the highest percentage for a third-party candidate in eighty years—but did not carry a single state. Clinton and his running mate, Tennessee Senator Al Gore, with 43 percent of the popular vote, swept New England, the West Coast, and much of the industrial Midwest, even making inroads into what had become an almost solidly Republican South and drawing "Reagan Democrats" back to the fold. The American people were voting for change, and their discontent carried over to congressional elections. Democrats remained in control of both houses, but incumbents did not fare well. The 103rd Congress had 110 new representatives and 11 new senators.

Bill Clinton was one of the most paradoxical presidents in American history. A journalist described him in

William Jefferson Clinton

a 1996 *New York Times* article as "one of the biggest, most talented, articulate, intelligent, open, colorful characters ever to inhabit the White House," while noting that Clinton "can also be an undisciplined, fumbling, obtuse, defensive, self-justifying rogue. . . . He is breathtakingly bright while capable of doing really dumb things." Clinton was a larger-than-life figure, a born politician from a small town called Hope who had wanted to be president most of his life. In college at Georgetown University in Washington, D.C., during the 1960s he had protested the Vietnam War and (like many of his generation) had maneuvered to keep himself from being sent to Vietnam. Clinton had won a Rhodes scholarship to Oxford, earned his law degree from Yale, and returned to his home state of Arkansas, where he was elected governor in 1978 at the age of thirty-two.

In 1975 Clinton had married Hillary Rodham, whom he met when they were both law students at Yale. Rodham Clinton, who made Law Review at Yale (an honor not shared by her husband), was the first First Lady to have a significant career of her own during her married life, and she spoke of balancing her commitments to her professional life with those to her husband and their daughter, Chelsea. Although Clinton boasted during the campaign that his slogan might be "Buy one, get one free," Rodham Clinton was quickly attacked by conservatives and antifeminists. After she told a hostile interviewer, "I suppose I could have stayed home and baked cookies and had teas. But what I decided to do was pursue my profession, which I entered

◀ Presidential candidate Bill Clinton campaigns in Jackson, Mississippi in 1992. Describing Clinton's campaign appearance the night before the election, a *New York Times* journalist wrote: "Bill Clinton, a middling amateur saxophonist, is playing his true instrument, the crowd." *(Ira Wyman)*

before my husband was in public life," the *New York Post* called her "a buffoon, an insult to most women."

Politically, Bill Clinton was a "new Democrat." He, along with other members of the new Democratic Leadership Council, advocated a more centrist—though still socially progressive—position for the Democratic Party. Clinton and his colleagues asked whether large government bureaucracies were still appropriate tools for addressing social problems in modern America. They emphasized private-sector economic development rather than public jobs programs, focusing on job training and other policies that they believed would promote opportunity, not dependency. They championed a global outlook in both foreign policy and economic development. Finally, they emphasized an ethic of "mutual responsibility" and "inclusiveness." Some Democrats found Clinton's policies too conservative. However, the political right attacked Clinton with a vehemence unmatched since the attacks on Franklin Roosevelt's New Deal, and the political struggles of the 1990s were exceptionally partisan and rancorous.

A New Democrat's Promise and Pitfalls

Clinton began his presidency with a great sense of promise. "Profound and powerful forces are shaking and remaking our world," he proclaimed in his inaugural address. "Well, my fellow citizens, this is our time. Let us embrace it." Clinton plunged into an ambitious program of reform and revitalization, beginning with his goal of appointing a cabinet that "looks like America" in all its diversity. But almost immediately he ran into trouble. Republicans, determined not to allow Clinton the traditional "honeymoon" period, maneuvered him into fulfilling a campaign pledge to end the ban on gays in the military before he had secured congressional or widespread military support. Amid great public controversy, Clinton finally accepted a "don't ask, don't tell" compromise that alienated liberals and conservatives, the gay community and the military.

Clinton's major goal was to make healthcare affordable and accessible for all Americans, including the millions who had no insurance coverage. But special interests mobilized in opposition: the insurance industry worried about lost profits; the business community feared higher taxes to support the uninsured; the medical community was concerned about more regulation, lower government reimbursement rates, and reduced healthcare quality. The administration's healthcare task force, cochaired by Hillary Rodham Clinton, could not create a political coalition strong enough to defeat these forces. Within a year, the centerpiece of Clinton's fledgling presidency had failed.

With Clinton beleaguered, new-style Republicans seized the chance to challenge the new Democrat. In September 1994, shortly before the midterm congressional elections, more than three hundred Republican candidates for the House of Representatives endorsed the "Contract with America." Developed under the leadership of Georgia congressman Newt Gingrich, the "Contract" promised "the end of government that is too big, too intrusive, and too easy with the public's money [and] the beginning of a Congress that respects the values and shares the faith of the American family." It called for a balanced-budget amendment to the Constitution, reduction of the capital gains tax, a two-year limit on welfare payments (while making unmarried mothers under eighteen ineligible), and increased defense spending.

"Republican Revolution"

In the midterm elections, the Republican Party mobilized socially conservative voters to score a major victory. Republicans took control of both houses of Congress for the first time since 1954 and made huge gains in state legislatures and governorships. Ideological passions ran high, and many Republicans believed that their ongoing attempts to weaken federal power and to dismantle the welfare state would now succeed.

The Republicans of the 104th Congress, however, miscalculated. Although many Americans applauded the idea of cutting government spending, they opposed cuts to most specific programs, including Medicare and Medicaid, education and college loans, highway construction, farm subsidies, veterans' benefits, and Social Security. Republicans made a bigger mistake when they issued President Clinton an ultimatum on the federal budget. Clinton refused to accept their terms; Republicans refused to pass a continuing resolution to provide interim funding; and the government was forced to suspend all nonessential action during the winter of 1995–1996. An angry public blamed the Republicans.

Such struggles showed Clinton's resolve, but they also led him to make compromises that moved American politics to the right. For example, he signed the 1996 Personal Responsibility and Work Opportunity Act, a welfare reform measure that eliminated the provision in the 1935 Social Security Act guaranteeing cash assistance for poor children (Aid to Families with Dependent Children). The law mandated that heads of families on welfare must find work within two years—though states could exempt up to 20 percent of recipients—and limited welfare benefits to five years

Political Compromise and the Election of 1996

over an individual's lifetime. It also made many legal immigrants ineligible for welfare. The Telecommunications Act of 1996, signed by Clinton, reduced diversity in America's media by permitting companies to own more television and radio stations.

Clinton and Gore were reelected in 1996 (defeating Republican Bob Dole and Reform Party candidate Ross Perot), in part because Clinton stole some of the conservatives' thunder. He declared that "the era of big government is over" and invoked family values, a centerpiece of the Republican campaign. Sometimes Clinton's actions were true compromises with conservative interests; other times he attempted to reclaim issues from the conservatives, as when he redefined family values as "fighting for the family-leave law or the assault-weapons ban or . . . trying to keep tobacco out of the hands of kids." And despite scandal and gridlock and ideological chasms that divided politicians and the American people alike, Clinton's election-year promise to "build a bridge to the future" seemed plausible in a time of increasing prosperity.

"THE NEW ECONOMY" AND GLOBALIZATION

Just how much credit Clinton deserved for the improved economic figures in mid-decade is a matter of debate. Presidents typically get too much blame when the economy struggles and too much credit when times are good. The roots of the 1990s boom were in the 1970s, when American corporations began investing in new technologies, retooling plants to become more energy-efficient, and cutting labor costs. Specifically, companies reduced the influence of organized labor by moving operations, some to the South and West, where unions were weak, and some out of the United States entirely, to countries like China and Mexico, where labor was cheap and pollution controls were lax.

Even more important than the restructuring of existing corporations was the emergence of a powerful new sector of the economy associated with digital technology. The rapid

Digital Revolution development of what came to be called "information technology"—computers, fax machines, cell phones, and the Internet—had a huge economic impact in the 1980s and 1990s. New companies and industries sprang up, many headquartered in the "Silicon Valley" near San Francisco. By the second half of the 1990s, the Forbes list of the 400 Richest Americans featured high-tech leaders like Bill Gates of Microsoft, who became the wealthiest person in the world with worth approaching $100 billion, as his company produced the software for operating most personal

▲ Apple cofounder and CEO Steve Jobs holds an iPod digital audio player on the cover of *Newsweek* in July 2004. Developed by Apple engineers in 2001 to take advantage of the pending revolution in digital music, the iPod was launched that October, barely a month after 9/11. The initial price: $399.00. Technical refinements improved the product and lowered the price, and sales surged. As of April 2007 more than 100 million units had been sold worldwide.

computers. The high-tech industry had considerable spillover effects on the broader economy, generating improved productivity, new jobs, and sustained economic growth.

The heart of this technological revolution was the microprocessor. Introduced in 1970 by Intel, the microprocessor miniaturized the central processing unit of a computer, meaning that small machines could now perform calculations previously requiring large machines. In the next decades the power of these integrated circuits increased by a factor of seven thousand. Computing chores that took a week in the early 1970s took one minute by

2000; the cost of storing one megabyte of information, or enough for a 320-page book, fell from more than $5,000 in 1975 to 17 cents in 1999. The implications for business were enormous.

Analysts dubbed this technology-driven sector "The New Economy," and it would have emerged whether or not Bill Clinton had won the White House. Yet Clinton and his advisers had some responsibility for the dramatic upturn. With the U.S. budget deficit topping $500 billion, they made the politically risky move of abandoning the middle-class tax cut and making deficit reduction a top priority. White House officials rightly concluded that, if the deficit could be brought under control, interest rates would be reduced and the economy would rebound. And that is what happened. The budget deficit started to come down (by 1997 it had been erased), a development that lowered interest rates, which in turn helped boost investment. Stock prices soared to unprecedented levels, and the gross national product rose by an average of 3.5 to 4 percent annually.

Clinton perceived early on that the technology revolution would shrink the world and make it more interconnected. He was convinced that, with the demise of Soviet communism, capitalism was spreading around the globe—if not full-blown capitalism, at least the introduction of market forces, freer trade, and widespread deregulation.

Globalization of Business

Globalization was not a new phenomenon—it had been under way for a century—but now it had unprecedented momentum. Journalist Thomas L. Friedman asserted that the post-Cold War world was "the age of globalization," characterized by the integration of markets, finance, and technologies. U.S. officials lowered trade and investment barriers, completing the North American Free Trade Agreement (NAFTA) with Canada and Mexico in 1993, and in 1994 concluding the Uruguay Round of the General Agreement on Tariffs and Trade (GATT), which lowered tariffs significantly for the seventy member nations that accounted for about 80 percent of world trade. The administration also endorsed the creation in 1995 of the World Trade Organization (WTO), to administer and enforce agreements made at the Uruguay Round. In a sign of how important trade had become to the administration's foreign agenda, the president formed a National Economic Council to complement the National Security Council and established a "war room" in the Commerce Department to promote trade missions around the world.

Multinational corporations were the hallmark of this global economy. By 2000 there were 63,000 parent com-

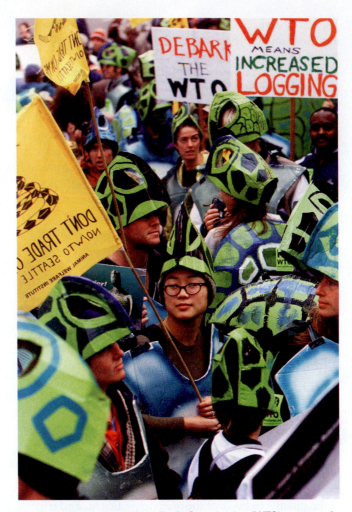

▲ Protesting that the World Trade Organization (WTO) possessed the dangerous power to challenge any nation's environmental laws if the WTO deemed them barriers to trade, chanting demonstrators marched in the streets of Seattle on November 29, 1999. Critics of the WTO have claimed that sea turtles and dolphins had already been victimized by the organization. Demonstrators identified the WTO as an example of globalization gone wrong. The WTO meeting went on, but the results proved meager because nations could not agree on rules governing dumping, subsidies for farm goods, genetically altered foods, and lower tariffs on high-tech goods. *(AP Photo/Beth A. Keiser)*

panies worldwide and 690,000 foreign affiliates. Some, like Nike and Gap, Inc., subcontracted production of certain merchandise to whichever developing countries had the lowest labor costs. Such arrangements created a "new international division of labor" and generated a boom in world exports, which, at $5.4 trillion in 1998, had doubled in two decades. U.S. exports climbed steadily, reaching $680 billion in 1998, but imports rose even higher, to

$907 billion in the same year (for a trade deficit of $227 billion). Sometimes the multinationals directly affected foreign policy, as when Clinton in 1995 extended full diplomatic recognition to Vietnam partly in response to pressure from such corporations as Coca-Cola, Citigroup, General Motors, and United Airlines, which wanted to enter that emerging market.

While the administration promoted open markets, labor unions argued that free-trade agreements exacerbated the trade deficit and often

Critics of Globalization

exported American jobs. Average real wages for American workers declined steadily after 1973, from $320 per week to $260 by the mid-1990s, a drop that labor leaders blamed on the inability of laid-off workers in import-competing industries to find jobs at their previous pay. Other critics extended this argument to the global level, maintaining that globalization was widening the gap between rich and poor countries, creating a mass of "slave laborers" in poor countries who endured working conditions that would never be tolerated in the West. Environmentalists charged that globalization also exported pollution and toxic waste into countries unprepared to deal with them, and warned of increased loss of biodiversity and the depletion of natural resources the world over. Still other critics warned that the power of multinational corporations and the global financial markets threatened both national sovereignty and traditional cultures.

Antiglobalization fervor reached a peak in the fall of 1999, when thousands of protesters disrupted a meeting of WTO ministers in Seattle. Hundreds were arrested. In the months that followed, there were smaller but sizable protests at meetings of the International Monetary Fund (IMF), which controls international credit and exchange rates, and the World Bank, which issues funds for development projects in numerous countries. In July 2001, some fifty thousand demonstrators descended on Genoa, Italy, to protest a meeting of the IMF and World Bank. Clashes with police resulted in one death and hundreds of injuries.

Activists also targeted individual corporations, such as the Gap, Starbucks, Nike, and, especially, McDon-

Target: McDonald's

ald's, which by 1995 was serving 30 million customers a day in some twenty thousand franchises in over one hundred countries. Critics assailed the company's slaughterhouse techniques, its alleged exploitation of low-skilled workers, and its high-fat menu, as well as its role in a global culture that they denounced as increasingly homoge-

▲ McDonald's restaurants circled the globe by the early twenty-first century, exemplifying the globalization of American culture. This Ukrainian woman in Kiev seems to enjoy both her hamburger and a conversation with the human symbol of the fast-food chain, Ronald McDonald. *(Wide World Photos, Inc.)*

neous and sterile, a so-called McWorld. Starting in 1996 and continuing for the next six years, McDonald's endured hundreds of often-violent protests, including bombings in Rome, Prague, London, Macao, Rio de Janeiro, and Jakarta.

Others decried both the violence and the underlying arguments of the antiglobalization campaigners. True, some economists acknowledged, statistics showed that global inequality had grown in recent years. But if one included quality-of-life measurements, such as literacy and health, global inequality had actually declined. In the United States, some studies found, wage and job losses for workers were caused not primarily by globalization factors, such as imports, production outsourcing, and immigration, but by technological change that made production processes more efficient and reduced the need for unskilled labor. Other researchers saw no evidence that governments' sovereignty had been seriously compromised as a result of globalization or that there was a "race to the bottom" in environmental standards. For them, the essential point was incontrovertible: poor countries that increased their economic openness enjoyed higher growth rates, and no country had prospered by turning its back on the world economy.

Others pointed out that the big franchise operations were not homogenizing global culture to the degree that critics claimed. McDonald's, they said, supposedly a prime mover of "McWorld," tailored its menu and operating practices to local tastes. And although American movies, TV programs, music, computer software, and other "intellectual property" often dominated world markets in the 1990s, foreign competition also made itself felt in America. Millions of American children were gripped by the Japanese fad game Pokemon, and if satellite television established a worldwide following for Michael Jordan and the Chicago Bulls, it did the same for soccer's David Beckham and Manchester United. An influx of foreign players added to the international appeal of both the National Basketball Association and Major League Baseball, while in the National Hockey League some 20 percent of players by the late 1990s hailed from Europe.

Yet if it was erroneous to glibly equate globalization with Americanization, it remained true that the United States occupied a uniquely power-

Clinton's Diplomacy

ful position on the world stage. The demise of the Soviet Union had created a one-superpower world, in which the United States stood far above other powers in terms of political and military as well as economic might. The "unipolar moment" was the phrase one commentator used in urging an aggressive U.S. posture. Yet in his first term Clinton was far more wary in handling the traditional aspects of foreign policy—great-power diplomacy, arms control, regional disputes—than in facilitating American cultural and trade expansion. He was deeply suspicious of foreign military involvements. The Vietnam debacle had taught him that the American public had limited patience for wars lacking clear-cut national interest, a lesson he found confirmed by George Bush's failure to gain lasting political strength from the Gulf War victory.

This mistrust of foreign interventions was cemented for Clinton by the difficulties he inherited from Bush in Somalia. In 1992 Bush had sent U.S. marines to the East African nation as part of a U.N. effort to ensure that humanitarian supplies reached starving Somalis. But in the summer of 1993, when Americans came under deadly attack from forces loyal to a local warlord, Clinton withdrew U.S. troops. And he did not intervene in Rwanda, where in 1994 the majority Hutus butchered 800,000 of the minority Tutsis in a brutal civil war.

That Somalia and Rwanda were on the policy agenda at all testified to the growing importance of humanitarian

Balkan Crisis

concerns in post–Cold War U.S. policy. Many administration officials argued for using America's power to contain ethnic hatreds, support human rights, and promote democracy around the world. The notion faced a severe test in the Balkans, which erupted in a series of ethnic wars. Bosnian Muslims, Serbs, and Croats were soon killing one another by the tens of thousands. Clinton, critical of Europe's reluctance to act in its own backyard, talked tough against Serbian aggression and atrocities in Bosnia-Herzegovina, especially the Serbs' cruel "ethnic cleansing" of Muslims through massacres and rape camps. On occasion he ordered U.S. airpower to strike Serb positions, but he put primary emphasis on diplomacy. In late 1995, after American diplomats brokered an agreement among the belligerents for a new multiethnic state in Bosnia-Herzegovina, a fragile peace took hold.

But Yugoslav president Slobodan Milosevic did not stop the anti-Muslim and anti-Croat fervor. When Serb forces moved to violently rid Serbia's southern province of Kosovo of its majority ethnic Albanians, Clinton was pressed to intervene. Initially he was reluctant; the ghosts of Vietnam were ever present in Oval Office deliberations. But reports of Serbian atrocities against the Muslim Kosovars and a major refugee crisis generated by the Yugoslavian military action stirred world opinion and finally caused the administration to act. In 1999 NATO forces led by the United States launched a massive aerial bombardment of Serbia. Milosevic withdrew his brutal military from Kosovo, where U.S. troops joined a U.N. peacekeeping force. That same year, the International War Crimes Tribunal indicted Milosevic and his top aides for atrocities.

In the Middle East, Clinton took an active role in trying to bring the PLO and Israel together to settle their differences. In September 1993 the

Agreements in the Middle East

PLO's Yasir Arafat and Israel's prime minister, Yitzhak Rabin, signed an agreement at the White House for Palestinian self-rule in the Gaza Strip and the West Bank's Jericho. The following year Israel signed a peace accord with Jordan, further reducing the chances of another full-scale Arab-Israeli war. Radical anti-Arafat Palestinians, however, continued to stage bloody terrorist attacks on Israelis, while extremist Israelis killed Palestinians and, in November 1995, Rabin himself. Only after American-conducted negotiations and renewed violence in the West Bank did Israel agree in early 1997 to withdraw its forces from the Palestinian city of Hebron. Thereafter the peace process alternately sagged and spurted.

▲ In spring 1999, as NATO bombing raids pounded Serbia (Yugoslavia) and Serb military positions in Kosovo to punish Serbia for killing and displacing ethnic Albanians, the number of Kosovar refugees increased dramatically. Desperate and hungry, they fled to neighboring nations. Here, in a NATO-run refugee camp outside Skopje, Macedonia, U.S. marines distribute food to some of the 850,000 forced to leave their Kosovo homes. *(Wide World Photos, Inc.)*

The same could be said of international efforts to protect the environment, which gathered pace in the 1990s. The George H. W. Bush administration had opposed many of the provisions of the 1992 Rio de Janeiro Treaty protecting the diversity of plant and animal species, on the grounds that the likely economic consequences would be too severe. For the same reason the administration had blocked efforts to draft stricter rules to reduce global warming. Clinton, urged on by Vice President Al Gore, an ardent environmentalist, took a more proactive posture. Most notably, his administration signed the 1997 Kyoto protocol, which aimed to combat emissions of carbon dioxide and other gases that most scientists believe trap heat in the atmosphere. The treaty required the United States to reduce its emissions by 2012 to 7 percent below its 1990 levels. But facing strong congressional opposition, Clinton never submitted the protocol for ratification to the Republican-controlled Senate.

Far less publicized than the Israeli-Palestinian conflict or the debate over Kyoto was the growing adminis-

Bin Laden and Al Qaeda

tration concern about the threat to U.S. interests posed by Islamic fundamentalism. In particular, senior officials worried about the rise of Al Qaeda (Arabic for "the base"), an international terrorist network led by Osama bin Laden, which was dedicated to purging Muslim countries of what it saw as the profane influence of the West and installing fundamentalist Islamic regimes.

The son of a Yemen-born construction tycoon in Saudi Arabia, bin Laden had supported the Afghan Mujahidin in their struggle against Soviet occupation. He then founded Al Qaeda and began financing terrorist projects with the fortune he received on his father's death. U.S. officials grew steadily more concerned, particularly as it became clear that bin Laden intended to go after American targets. In 1995 a car bomb in Riyadh killed 7 people, 5 of them Americans. In 1998 simultaneous bombings at the American embassies in Kenya and Tanzania killed 224 people, including 12 Americans. In Yemen in

2000, a small boat laden with explosives hit the destroyer *USS Cole,* killing 17 American sailors. Although bin Laden was understood to have masterminded and financed these attacks, he eluded U.S. attempts to apprehend him. In 1998 Clinton approved a plan to assassinate bin Laden at an Al Qaeda camp in Afghanistan, but the attempt failed.

PARADOXES OF PROSPERITY

Despite conflicts abroad and partisan struggles in Washington, the majority of Americans experienced the late 1990s as a time of unprecedented peace and prosperity, fueled by the dizzying rise of the stock market. The Dow Jones Industrial Average increased almost twelvefold in the last two decades of the twentieth century. Between 1991 and 1999 alone, it climbed from 3,169 to a high of 11,497 (see Figure 33.1). The booming market benefited the middle class as well as the wealthy, for the mutual funds created during the 1970s and other new investment vehicles, such as 401(k) retirement plans, had drawn a majority of

Americans into the stock market. In 1952 only 4 percent of American households owned stocks. That percentage soared to almost 60 percent by the year 2000.

At the end of the 1990s, the unemployment rate stood at 4.3 percent—the lowest peacetime rate since 1957. Plentiful jobs made it easier to implement welfare reform, and welfare rolls were cut almost in half. The standard of living rose for all income groups: both the richest 5 percent and the least well-off 20 percent of American households saw their incomes rise almost 25 percent. But as that meant an average gain of $50,000 for the top 5 percent and only $2,880 for the bottom 20 percent, the gap between rich and poor continued to grow. Still, by the end of the decade more than two-thirds of Americans were homeowners—the highest percentage in history. Differences among groups were significant but declining: 52 percent of families earning less than the median income were homeowners in 2000, as were 48 percent of people of color. Teen pregnancy began to decline. Infant mortality dropped to the lowest rate in American history. Violent crime decreased; murder rates hit a thirty-year low.

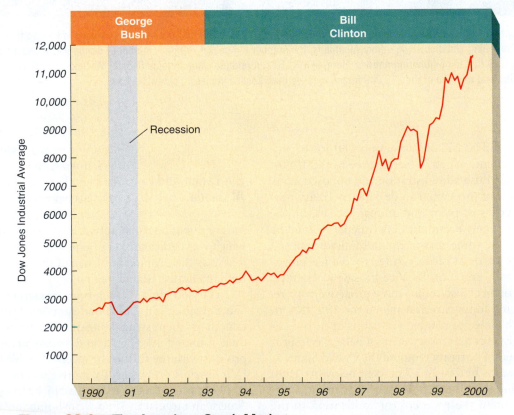

Figure 33.1   **The American Stock Market**

This graph of the Dow Jones Industrial Average, climbing steadily in the bull market of the 1990s, illustrates the great economic expansion of the decade. *(Source: Adapted from Dow Jones & Company.)*

Despite these positive signs, there were new and unexpected crises. On April 19, 1995, 168 children, women,

Oklahoma City Bombing

and men were killed in a powerful bomb blast that destroyed the nine-story Alfred P. Murrah Federal Building in downtown Oklahoma City. At first, many thought the bomb had come from abroad, perhaps set off by Middle Eastern terrorists. But a charred piece of truck axle located two blocks from the explosion, with the vehicle identification number still legible, proved otherwise. The bomber was Timothy McVeigh, a native-born white American and a veteran of the Persian Gulf War. He sought revenge for the deaths of members of the Branch Davidian religious sect, whom he believed the FBI had deliberately slaughtered in a standoff over firearms charges on that date two years before in Waco, Texas.

In the months that followed, reporters and government investigators discovered networks of militias, tax resisters, and various white-supremacist groups throughout the nation. These groups were united by distrust of the federal government. Many saw federal gun control laws, such as the Brady Bill, signed into law in 1993, as a dangerous usurpation of citizens' right to bear arms. Members of these groups believed that the federal government was controlled by "sinister forces," including Zionists, cultural elitists, Queen Elizabeth, and the United Nations. After McVeigh's act of domestic terrorism these groups lost members but also turned to the new Internet to spread their beliefs.

Other forms of violence also haunted America. On April 20, 1999, eighteen-year-old Eric Harris and

Violence and Hate Crimes

seventeen-year-old Dylan Klebold opened fire on classmates and teachers at Columbine High School in Littleton, Colorado, killing thirteen before turning their guns on themselves. No clear reason why two academically successful students in a middle-class suburb would commit mass murder ever emerged. And the Columbine massacre was not an isolated event: students in Paducah, Kentucky; Springfield, Oregon; and Jonesboro, Arkansas, massacred classmates

In the late 1990s, two hate crimes shocked the nation. In 1998 James Byrd Jr., a forty-nine-year-old black man, was murdered by three white supremacists who dragged him for miles by a chain from the back of a pickup truck in Jasper, Texas. Later that year, Matthew Shepherd, a gay college student, died after being beaten unconscious and left tied to a wooden fence in freezing weather outside Laramie, Wyoming. His killers said they were "humili-

▲ On April 20, 1999, students evacuated Columbine High School in Littleton, Colorado, after two schoolmates went on a shooting rampage, killing twelve students and a teacher before killing themselves. *(Wide World Photos, Inc.)*

ated" when he flirted with them at a bar. Some argued that these murders demonstrated the strength of racism and homophobia in American society, while others saw the horror that most Americans expressed at these murders as a sign of positive change.

Throughout the Clinton years, scandals and rumors of scandal plagued the White House. The independent

Scandal in the Clinton White House

counsel's office (independent counsels were appointed by a judicial board independent from the Justice Department to investigate possible misdeeds of high government officials) would eventually spend $72 million investigating allegations of wrongdoing by Hillary and Bill Clinton. Independent counsel Kenneth Starr, a conservative Republican and former judge, was originally charged with investigating Whitewater, a 1970s Arkansas real-estate deal in which the Clintons had invested. He turned up no evidence against the Clintons in his Whitewater investigation. However, Starr expanded the range of his investigation.

Early in Clinton's presidency, former Arkansas state employee Paula Jones had brought charges of sexual harassment against the president. Clinton denied the charges, which were eventually dropped. But when asked during questioning before a grand jury whether he had engaged in sexual relations with twenty-two-year-old White House intern Monica Lewinsky, Clinton said no. Speaking to the American people, Clinton angrily declared, "I did not have sexual relations with that woman, Miss Lewinsky." Starr, however, produced proof of the sexual relationship, including DNA evidence: a navy blue dress of Lewinsky's, stained with Clinton's semen.

In a 445-page report to Congress, Starr outlined eleven possible grounds for impeachment of the president, accusing Clinton of lying under oath, obstruction of justice, witness tampering, and abuse of power. On December 19, 1998, the House voted on four articles of impeachment against Clinton; largely along party lines, the House passed two of the articles, one alleging that the president had committed perjury in his grand jury testimony, the other that he had obstructed justice. Clinton became only the second president—and the first in 130 years—to face a trial in the Senate, which has the constitutional responsibility to decide (by two-thirds vote) whether to remove a president from office.

Impeachment

But the American people did not want Clinton removed from office. Polls showed that large majorities approved of the president's job performance, even as many condemned his personal behavior. And many did not believe that his actions rose to the level of "high crimes and misdemeanors" (normally acts such as treason) required by the Constitution as grounds for impeachment. The Republican-controlled Senate, responding at least in part to popular opinion, voted against the charge of perjury 55 to 45 and, to the charge of obstructing justice, 50 to 50, thus clearing Clinton, because a two-thirds majority is required for conviction.

Clinton, of course, bears responsibility for his own actions. However, how those actions became grounds for impeachment, with the explicit sexual details contained in the Starr Report circulated by Internet around the world, is part of a larger story. Clinton was not the first president to engage in illicit sex. President John F. Kennedy had numerous and well-known sexual affairs, including one

Political Partisanship, the Media, and Celebrity Culture

with a nineteen-year-old intern. But after the Watergate scandals of the early 1970s, the mass media were no longer willing to turn a blind eye to presidential misconduct. The fiercely competitive twenty-four-hour news networks that began with CNN in 1980 relied on scandal, spectacle, and crisis to lure viewers. Public officials also contributed to the blurring of lines between public and private, celebrity and statesman. Clinton, for example, had appeared on MTV during his first campaign and answered a question about his preference in underwear (boxers).

The partisan political wars of the 1990s created a take-no-prisoners climate in which no politician's missteps would be overlooked. As fallout from the Clinton impeachment, both Republican Speaker of the House Newt Gingrich and his successor, Robert Livingston, resigned when faced with evidence of their own extramarital affairs. Finally, as former Clinton aide Sidney Blumenthal writes, the impeachment struggle was about more than presidential perjury and sexual infidelity. It was part of the "culture wars" that divided the American people: "a monumental battle over very large political questions about the Constitution, about cultural mores and the position of women in American society, and about the character of the American people. It was, ultimately, a struggle about the identity of the country."

Clinton's legislative accomplishments during his two terms in office were modest but included programs that made life easier for American families. The Family and Medical Leave Act guaranteed 91 million workers the right to take time off to care for ailing relatives or newborn children. The Health Insurance Portability and Accountability Act ensured that, when Americans changed jobs, they would not lose health insurance because of pre-existing medical conditions. Government became more efficient: the federal government operated with 365,000 fewer employees by the end of Clinton's term, and Vice President Gore led an initiative that eliminated sixteen thousand pages of federal regulations. Clinton created national parks and monuments that protected 3.2 million acres of American land and made unprecedented progress cleaning up toxic waste dumps throughout the nation.

Clinton's Legislative Record

Vice President Al Gore was the favorite in the 2000 presidential election. The son of a prominent senator from Tennessee, Gore had graduated cum laude from Harvard in 1969 and, despite his reservations about the war, had enlisted in the army and served in Vietnam. He had served six terms in Congress and in the Clinton administration had played a greater role than any vice president

The Bush-Gore Race

in American history. After eight years of prosperity and relative peace, he had a strong platform on which to run. Gore, however, failed to inspire voters. Earnest and highly intelligent, he appeared to many to be a well-informed policy wonk rather than a charismatic leader.

Gore's Republican opponent was best known nationally as the son of George H. W. Bush, the forty-first president of the United States. An indifferent student, George W. Bush had graduated from Yale in 1968 and pulled strings to jump ahead of a one-and-a-half-year waiting list for the Texas Air National Guard, thus avoiding service in Vietnam. After a difficult period, which included a rocky career in the oil business, at the age of forty Bush gave up alcohol and embraced Christianity. His fortunes improved while his father was president, and in 1994 he was elected to the first of two terms as governor of Texas.

As a presidential candidate, Bush made up for his limited foreign policy knowledge, often garbled syntax, and lack of interest in the intricacies of public policy with a direct, confident style that connected with many Americans. Unlike Gore, who peppered his stump speeches with statistics and programmatic initiatives, Bush spoke of his relationship with God and his commitment to conservative social values, styling himself a "compassionate conservative." Supported heavily by prominent Republicans and business leaders, Bush amassed the largest campaign war chest in history ($67 million, compared with Gore's $28 million).

Finally, in 2000, consumer rights activist Ralph Nader ran on the Green Party ticket. Condemning globalization and environmental despoliation, he attacked both Bush and Gore, calling them "Tweedledee and Tweedledum." Nader drew support from left-liberal voters who would have been more likely to vote for Gore and possibly helped tip some states to Bush.

On election day 2000, Al Gore narrowly won the popular vote (see Map 33.1). But he did not win the presidency. It all came down to Florida (where Bush's brother Jeb was governor) and its twenty-five electoral votes. According to the initial tally, Bush narrowly edged Gore out in Florida, but by so close a margin that a recount was legally required. Charges and countercharges flew. In several heavily African American counties, tens of thousands of votes were not counted because voters failed to fully dislodge the "chads," or small perforated squares, when punching the old-fashioned paper ballots. Lawyers struggled over whether "hanging chads" (partially detached) and "pregnant chads" (punched but not detached) were sufficient signs of voter intent. In Palm Beach County, many elderly Jewish residents were confused by a poorly

The Contested Election of 2000

designed ballot. Thinking they were selecting Gore, they voted instead for the allegedly anti-Semitic Pat Buchanan. After thirty-six days of confusion, with court cases at the state and federal levels, the Supreme Court voted 5 to 4 along narrowly partisan lines to end the recount process. Florida's electoral votes—and the presidency—went to George Bush.

In the 2000 election, Gore won the West Coast, Northeast, and industrial Midwest. The South, Rocky Mountain West (except New Mexico), and heartland went to Bush. More than 90 percent of black voters selected Gore, as did 63 percent of Latinos and 55 percent of Asian Americans. Bush won 60 percent of the white vote, and, overall, 95 percent of his supporters were white. The gender gap was 12 points: 54 percent of women voted for Gore, as opposed to 42 percent of men (see Figure 33.2). And the struggles over the election outcome had further polarized the nation. As Bush waited for the January inaugural, critics and comics began referring to him as the "president-select."

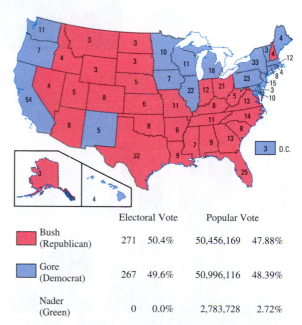

	Electoral Vote		Popular Vote	
Bush (Republican)	271	50.4%	50,456,169	47.88%
Gore (Democrat)	267	49.6%	50,996,116	48.39%
Nader (Green)	0	0.0%	2,783,728	2.72%

Map 33.1   Presidential Election, 2000
Democratic candidate Al Gore won the popular vote, but George W. Bush succeeded in gaining electoral victory by four votes. Among white males, Bush ran extremely well, while Gore won a majority of minority and women voters. Ralph Nader's Green Party won less than 3 percent of the national vote, but his votes in Florida may have detracted from the Gore tally, helping Bush win the critical electoral votes.

(Source: Carol Berkin et al., Making America, Third Edition. Used by permission of Houghton Mifflin Company.)

▶ Supporters of Democratic presidential candidate Al Gore and Republican candidate George Bush confront each other in front of the U.S. Supreme Court as attorneys prepare to argue the postelection legal case *Bush v. Gore.* The Supreme Court's 5-4 decision to end the Florida recount would give the presidency to George Bush.

(© Reuters/Corbis)

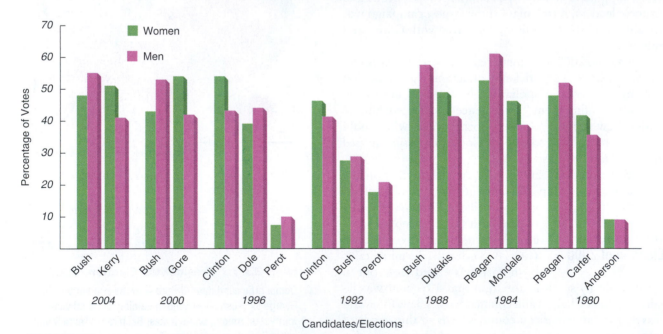

Figure 33.2   **The Gender Gap in American Presidential Elections**

The gender gap, or the difference in voting patterns between men and women, was first identified in 1980 by National Organization for Women president Eleanor Smeal and has been recognized as an important force in American politics ever since. In virtually every presidential election portrayed here, greater percentages of women (no matter their race or ethnicity, income, level of education, or marital status) than men voted for the Democratic candidate.

(Source: Based on data from the Center for American Women and Politics.)

SEPTEMBER 11 AND THE WAR ON TERRORISM

In view of the close election and bitter Florida controversy, many believed that Bush would govern from the center. Some also thought that he was philosophically centrist, as his father had been, and that he had moved to the right only to ensure turnout among conservative evangelical Christians, who made up an increasingly large part of the Republican base. From the administration's first days, however, Bush governed from the right, arguably further to the right than any administration of modern times. As the head of the Heritage Foundation, a conservative Washington think tank, enthused, the new team was "more Reaganite than the Reagan administration."

The centerpiece of the Bush agenda was a massive tax cut, to be financed by the predicted budget surplus.

Bush's Tax Plan

"A surplus in tax revenue, after all, means that taxpayers have been overcharged," the president said. "And usually when you've been overcharged, you expect to get something back." Critics replied that a massive cut would wipe out the surplus and that the Bush plan favored the wealthy, but Bush persisted, using his party's control of Congress to push through the largest tax cut in U.S. history—$1.3 trillion. To the dismay of environmentalists, he also reiterated his campaign proposal to drill for oil in America's last wilderness, the Arctic National Wildlife Refuge, and chose a secretary of the interior with close ties to the energy industry who favored scaling back regulations protecting the environment.

In international affairs, the administration moved swiftly to chart a more unilateralist course than its predecessors. Given America's preponderant power, senior Bush officials reasoned, it did not need the help of others in the international system; accordingly they attached less importance to consultation and cooperation than had the Clinton administration. Soon after taking office, Bush announced that the United States would exit the 1972 Anti-Ballistic Missile Treaty with Russia to develop a National Missile Defense system (forbidden under the treaty) broadly similar to Reagan's "Star Wars" plan. Such a system, Bush said, would protect the United States from missile threats by potentially hostile nations, such as North Korea, Iraq, and Iran. The White House also renounced the 1997 Kyoto protocol on controlling global warming and registered opposition to a carefully negotiated protocol to strengthen the 1972 Biological and Toxin Weapons Convention. All three decisions caused consternation in Europe, as did the administration's hands-off policy toward the Israeli-Palestinian peace process.

Then came September 11. On that sunny Tuesday morning, nineteen hijackers seized control of four commercial jets that had taken off from East Coast airports. At 8:46 a.m. one plane crashed into the 110-story North Tower of the World Trade Center in New York City, causing a huge explosion and fire. At 9:03 a.m., a second plane flew into the South Tower. In less than two hours, both buildings collapsed, killing thousands of office workers, firefighters, and police officers. At 9:43, the third plane crashed into the Pentagon, leaving a huge hole in its west side. The fourth plane was also headed toward Washington, but several passengers—learning of the World Trade Center attacks through cell-phone conversations—stormed the cockpit; in the scuffle that followed, the plane crashed in Somerset County, Pennsylvania, killing all aboard.

9/11

More than three thousand people died, making this the deadliest act of terrorism in history. Not since the Japanese assault on Pearl Harbor in 1941 had the United States experienced such a devastating attack on its soil. The hijackers—fifteen Saudi Arabians, two Emiratis, one Lebanese, and, leading them, an Egyptian—had ties to Al Qaeda, Osama bin Laden's radical Islamic organization. Some officials in the Clinton and Bush administrations had warned that an attack by Al Qaeda was inevitable: when Clinton's national security adviser met with his successor, Condoleezza Rice, shortly before Bush's inauguration, he told her, "You're going to spend more time during your four years on terrorism generally and Al Qaeda specifically than any issue." Broadly speaking, however, neither administration made counterterrorism a top foreign policy priority.

In an instant, counterterrorism was priority number one. President Bush decided immediately, indeed before 9/11 had become 9/12, to respond with large-scale military force. Al Qaeda operated out of Afghanistan with the blessing of the ruling Taliban, a repressive Islamic fundamentalist group that had gained power in 1996 in the turmoil following the defeat of the Soviet-backed government in 1989. In early October, the United States launched a sustained bombing campaign against Taliban and Al Qaeda positions, and sent special operations forces to help a resistance organization based in northern Afghanistan. Within two months, the Taliban had been driven from power, although bin Laden as well as top Taliban leaders eluded capture.

Afghanistan War

As administration officials were quick to acknowledge, the swift military victory did not end the terrorist threat. Bush spoke of a long and difficult struggle that he called a war against evil forces, in which the nations of the world were either with the United States or against it. Some questioned whether a "war on terrorism" could ever be won in a meaningful sense, given that the foe was a nonstate actor weak in the traditional measures of power—territory and governmental power—and with little to lose. A war against such an adversary could have no definable end, observers noted, and they questioned whether Bush, by speaking in such unambiguous terms, was setting himself and the nation up for eventual failure. Most Americans, however, were ready to believe. Stunned by September 11, they experienced a renewed sense of national unity and pride. Flag sales soared, and Bush's approval ratings skyrocketed. Citizenship applications from immigrants rose dramatically.

But the new patriotism had a dark side. Just as the outbreak of the Cold War half a century earlier had brought a search for domestic traitors, the war on terrorism incorporated a hunt for potential Al Qaeda supporters at home. Congress passed the USA PATRIOT Act (Uniting and Strengthening America by Providing Appropriate Tools Required to Intercept and Obstruct Terrorism), making it easier for law enforcement to conduct searches, wiretap telephones, and obtain electronic records on individuals. Attorney General John Ashcroft approved giving FBI agents new powers to monitor the Internet, mosques, and rallies. Civil libertarians charged that the Justice Department had overstepped sensible boundaries, and some judges ruled against the tactics. Yet, according to a June 2002 Gallup poll, 80 percent of Americans were willing to give up some freedoms for security.

PATRIOT Act

In surveys weeks after the attacks, 71 percent of respondents said that they felt depressed, and one-third said that they had trouble sleeping. The figures dropped thereafter, but anxiety remained. The discovery of anthrax-laden letters in several East Coast cities heightened fears about vulnerability to bioterrorism, particularly after post offices and government buildings were closed and five people died. Investigators found no evidence to connect the letters to the 9/11 hijackings, but also no good clues as to who the perpetrator might be, despite conducting more than five thousand interviews and pursuing hundreds of leads.

Yet continuity was as evident as change. People continued shopping in malls, visiting amusement parks, purchasing cars and homes. Employees still showed up for work, even in skyscrapers, and still gossiped around the lunch table. Although airline bookings dropped significantly in the early weeks (causing severe economic problems for many airlines), people still took to the skies. Some even complained about the new security measures at airports. In Washington, the partisanship that had all but disappeared after 9/11 returned, as Democrats and Republicans sparred over judicial appointments, energy policy, and the proposed new Department of Homeland Security. Approved by Congress in November 2002, the department was designed to coordinate intelligence and consolidate defenses against terrorism. Incorporating parts of eight cabinet departments and twenty-two agencies, it was the first new department since the Department of Veterans Affairs in 1989.

Economically, the months before September 11 witnessed a collapse of the so-called dot-coms, the Internet companies that had been the darlings of Wall Street in the 1990s. In the course of 2001 some five hundred dot-coms declared bankruptcy or closed, and analysts warned of worse to come. There were other economic warning signs as well, notably a meager 0.2 percent growth rate in the nation's goods and services for the second quarter of 2001—the slowest growth in eight years. Corporate revenues were also down.

Economic Uncertainty

Economic concerns deepened after 9/11 with a four-day closing of Wall Street and a subsequent sharp drop in stock prices. The week after the markets reopened, the Dow Jones Industrial Average plunged 14.26 percent—the fourth largest weekly drop in percentage terms since 1900. The markets eventually rebounded, but questions remained about the economy's overall health. Such was Bush's political strength after 9/11, however, that neither this economic uncertainty nor the failure to capture Osama bin Laden and top Taliban leaders dented his popularity. In the midterm elections of 2002, the Republicans retook the Senate and added to their majority in the House.

Overseas, the president's standing was not nearly so high. Immediately after September 11, there was an outpouring of support from people everywhere. "We are all Americans now," said the French newspaper *Le Monde* the day after the attacks. Moments of silence in honor of the victims were held in many countries, and governments all over the world announced that they would cooperate with Washington in the struggle against terrorism. But within a year, attitudes had changed dramatically. Bush's bellicose stance and good-versus-evil terminology had put off many foreign observers from the start, but they initially swallowed their objections. But when the president started hinting that America might unilaterally strike Saddam Hussein's Iraq or deal forcefully with North Korea or Iran—the three countries of Bush's "axis of evil"—many allied governments registered strong objections.

International Responses

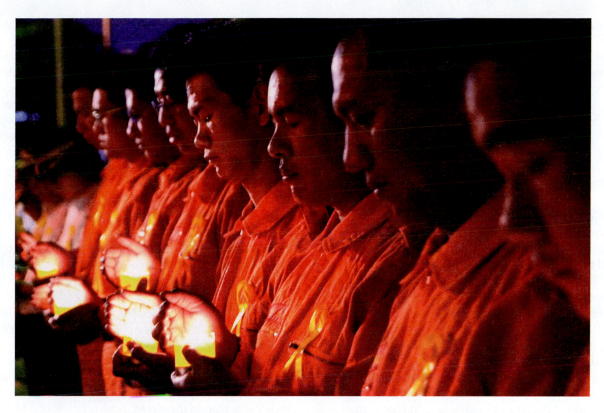

▲ The attacks on 9/11 brought forth an outpouring of sympathy for the victims and their families, and for the United States generally, from people around the world. Here firefighters in Taipei, Taiwan, attend a prayer service during a global day of mourning. *(AFP/Getty)*

At issue was not merely the prospect of an American attack on one of these countries but the underlying rationale that would accompany it. Bush and other top officials were in effect saying that the strategy of containment and deterrence that had guided U.S. foreign policy for more than fifty years was outmoded. In an age of terrorism, they maintained, the United States would not wait for a potential security threat to become real; henceforth, it would strike first. "In the world we have entered, the only path to safety is the path of action and this nation will act," Bush declared. Americans had to be "ready for preemptive action when necessary to defend our liberty and to defend our lives." Critics of the strategy, among them many world leaders, called it recklessly aggressive and contrary to international law, and they wondered what would happen if dictators around the world began claiming the same right of preemption.

WAR AND OCCUPATION IN IRAQ

But Bush was determined, particularly on Iraq. Several of his top advisers, including Secretary of Defense Donald Rumsfeld and Vice President Dick Cheney, had wanted to oust Saddam Hussein for years, indeed since the end of the Gulf War in 1991; for them it was a piece of unfinished business. Before 9/11, however, these Iraq hawks were stymied by officials who sought in effect to maintain the Bush, Sr.–Clinton policy of keeping Saddam Hussein contained through a mix of sanctions and military coercion, such as periodic air strikes to enforce the no-fly zones in the north and south. Secretary of State Colin Powell, the first African American to hold that position and a figure of growing influence in the administration's early months, talked only of improving the sanctions policy, and National Security adviser Condoleezza Rice—the first African American and first woman to hold *that* post—made it "extremely clear" to colleagues that there would be no move to oust the Iraqi dictator militarily.

No sooner had the Twin Towers fallen, however, than President Bush began contemplating a move against Saddam. Along with Cheney and Rumsfeld, Bush saw an opportunity to fold Iraq into the larger war on terrorism—this despite the fact that counterterrorism experts saw no link between Saddam and Al Qaeda. For a time Powell succeeded in keeping the focus on Afghanistan, but little by little the thinking in the White House shifted. In November 2001 Bush ordered the Pentagon to initiate war planning for Iraq; by spring 2002 a secret consensus had been reached: Saddam Hussein would be removed by force.

In September Bush challenged the United Nations to immediately enforce its resolutions against Iraq, or the United States would be compelled to act on its own. In the weeks that followed, he and his aides offered sometimes-shifting reasons for getting tough with Iraq, if necessary through military action. They said that Saddam was a major threat to the United States and its allies, a leader who possessed and would use banned biological and chemical "weapons of mass destruction" (WMDs) and who actively sought to acquire nuclear weapons. They claimed, contrary to their own intelligence estimates, that he had ties to Al Qaeda and could be linked to the 9/11 attacks. They said that he brutalized his own people and generated regional instability with his tyrannous rule.

Why Iraq?

Beneath the surface lurked other motivations. Neoconservatives, enjoying influence in Washington for the first time since the Reagan years, saw in Iraq a chance to use U.S. power to reshape the region in America's image, to oppose tyranny and spread democracy. Ousting Saddam, they said, would enhance the security of Israel, America's key ally in the Middle East, and would likely start a chain reaction that would extend democracy throughout the region. White House political strategists, meanwhile, thinking in mundane but for them crucial terms, believed that a swift and decisive removal of a hated dictator would cement Republican domination in Washington and virtually assure Bush's reelection two years hence. Oil, too, entered the picture, though not quite in the way many antiwar activists assumed: for Bush and his aides, it was not so much about access to Iraqi oil as about preventing an Iraq armed with WMDs from destabilizing an oil-rich region.

Like his father in 1991, Bush claimed he did not need congressional authorization to launch military action against Iraq; also like his father, he nevertheless sought such backing. In early October 2002, the House of Representatives voted 296 to 133 and the Senate 77 to 23 to authorize the use of force against Iraq. The lopsided vote was misleading; many who voted in favor were unwilling to defy a president so close to a midterm election, even though they opposed military action without U.N. sanction. Vietnam veteran and Nebraska Republican senator

Congressional Approval

Chuck Hagel protested that "many of those who want to rush this country into war and think it would be quick and easy don't know anything about war." Both inside and outside Congress, critics complained that the president had not presented evidence that Saddam Hussein constituted an imminent threat or was connected to the 9/11 attacks. Bush switched to a less hawkish and unilateral stance, and in so doing gained U.N. backing: in early November, the U.N. Security Council unanimously approved Resolution 1441, imposing rigorous new arms inspections on Iraq.

Behind the scenes, though, the Security Council was deeply divided over what should happen next. In late January 2003, the weapons inspector's report castigated Iraq for failing to carry out "the disarmament that was demanded of it" but also said it was too soon to tell whether the inspections would succeed. Whereas U.S. and British officials emphasized the first point and said the time for diplomacy was up, France, Russia, and China emphasized the second point and called for more inspections. Some at the world body also warned that toppling the regime could cause an explosion of sectarian bloodshed between Iraq's Sunni Muslims and the majority Shi'ites who had suffered so grievously under the Sunni Saddam's rule. As the U.N. debate continued, and as massive antiwar demonstrations took place around the world, Bush sent about 250,000 soldiers to the region. Britain sent about 45,000 troops.

In late February, the United States floated a draft resolution to the U.N. that proposed issuing an ultimatum to Iraq, but only three of the fifteen Security Council members affirmed support. Faced with an embarrassing political defeat, Bush abandoned the resolution and all further diplomatic efforts on March 17, when he ordered Saddam Hussein to leave Iraq within forty-eight hours or face an attack. Saddam ignored the ultimatum, and on March 19 the United States and Britain launched an aerial bombardment of Baghdad and other areas. A ground invasion followed a few days later (see Map 33.2). The Iraqis initially offered stiff resistance, but soon the advancing forces gained momentum. On April 9, Baghdad fell to American troops.

Fall of Baghdad

The military victory was swift and decisive, the result of sixteen months of careful planning, smooth cooperation among the services, and precisely executed operations. Barely had the celebrations begun, however, before trouble started. So careful in making military preparations, senior policymakers showed scant interest in planning for postwar Iraq. The State Department's extensive studies were ignored, as Bush assigned responsibility for the postwar effort to the Pentagon. From consistently voicing the worst-case scenarios in making the case for war, top officials

Map 33.2   The Middle East

Extremely volatile and often at war, the nations of the Middle East maintained precarious relations with the United States. To protect its interests, the United States extended large amounts of economic and military aid, and sold huge quantities of weapons to the area. At times, Washington ordered U.S. troops to the region. The Arab-Israeli dispute particularly upended order, although the peace process moved forward intermittently.

▲ A man cries for help after explosions outside the Imam Ali shrine in Najaf, Iraq, one of the holiest sites for Shia Muslims, in September 2003. The immediate vicinity of the shrine would be the scene of frequent attacks in the months and years thereafter, one of which caused damage to two of the minarets. On August 10, 2006, a suicide bomber wearing an explosive harness blew himself up near the shrine, killing forty people and injuring more than fifty. *(Kate Books/Polaris)*

did the opposite in preparing for the peace, emphasizing best-case outcomes regarding how Iraqis would react to "liberation" (with joy), how many U.S. troops would be required to secure the country (not very many), and how quickly a stable Iraq would emerge (in short order).

Thus, when violence, lawlessness, and looting erupted almost immediately, American planners seemed powerless to respond. The plight of ordinary Iraqis deteriorated as the occupation authority proved no more able to provide services than to maintain order. In Baghdad, electricity worked only a few hours each day, and telephone service was nonexistent. Garbage piled up in the streets, and hospitals had far too few workers to care for the influx of wounded and sick. Several decisions by the Coalition Governing Council (CPA), headed by Ambassador Paul Bremer, contributed to the lawlessness—notably Bremer's decision in May to disband the Iraqi army, which left tens of thousands of men, angry

Insurgency

and armed, out of work. A multisided insurgency made up of Saddam loyalists, Iraqi nationalists of various stripes, and foreign Islamic revolutionaries took shape; soon, U.S. occupying forces faced frequent ambushes and hit-and-run attacks. By October 2003 more troops had died from these attacks than had perished in the initial invasion the previous spring.

The mounting chaos in Iraq and the failure to find any weapons of mass destruction led critics to question the validity of the war. The much-derided sanctions and U.N. inspections, it was now clear, had in fact been remarkably successful in rendering Saddam a largely toothless tyrant, with a hollow military and no chemical or biological weapons. Prewar claims of a "rush to war" resounded once again. Even many defenders of the invasion castigated the administration for its failure to anticipate the occupation problems and, once it learned of them, being tentative and slow-footed in responding. In the spring of 2004, graphic photos showing Iraqi detainees being abused and tortured by American guards at Abu Ghraib prison were broadcast around the world, generating international condemnation and adding fuel to the insurgency.

President Bush, facing reelection that fall, expressed disgust at the Abu Ghraib images and fended off charges

Election of 2004

that he and his top aides knew of and condoned the abuse. The White House also made much of the dissolution of the CPA in late June and the transfer of sovereignty to an interim Iraqi government—developments, it predicted, that would soon take the steam out of the insurgency. Many were skeptical, but voters that fall were prepared to give Bush the benefit of the doubt. His Democratic opponent, Senator John Kerry of Massachusetts, a Vietnam veteran who had reluctantly voted for the Iraq resolution in October 2002, had difficulty finding his campaign footing and never articulated a clear alternative strategy on the war. With the electorate deeply split, Bush won reelection with 51 percent of the popular vote to Kerry's 48 percent, and 279 electoral votes to Kerry's 252. The GOP also increased its majorities in the House and Senate.

White House aides crowed that the result validated the administration's foreign and domestic policies. Bush told the American people that he would use this "mandate" to make major changes in U.S. domestic policy. In his State of the Union address in early February 2005, Bush focused on his plan to partially privatize the Social Security system. This plan failed, as both Democratic and Republican members of Congress argued that it would not work, either economically or politically. The president did have success, however, in his efforts to reshape the Supreme Court. Conservative U.S. Circuit Court judge John Roberts was confirmed as chief justice following the death of Chief Justice William Rehnquist, and another strong conservative, Samuel Alito, became junior associate justice following the resignation of Sandra Day O'Connor. This conservative reorientation of the Supreme Court, along with the war in Iraq, are likely to be George Bush's major presidential legacies.

In the months following the 2004 election, the increasing evidence that the war in Iraq had little chance of success, by any definition, began to undermine the American people's confidence in President Bush and his administration. Growing perceptions of administrative incompetence were exacerbated when a major hurricane hit the Gulf Coast and New Orleans in late August 2005. Hurricane Katrina was the sixth most powerful Atlantic hurricane on record, with winds reaching 100 miles from its center. Katrina had fallen from force 5 (the highest rating) to force 3 by the time it slammed into New Orleans, but the high winds and storm surge destroyed the levees that kept low-lying parts of the city from being swamped by water from Lake Pontchartrain and surrounding canals. Floodwaters covered 80 percent of the city, and more than eighteen hundred people died in the storm and the floods that followed.

Tens of thousands of people who lacked the resources to evacuate the city sought shelter at the Superdome. Supplies of food and water quickly ran low, and toilets backed up; people wrapped the dead in blankets and waited for rescue. Those outside the Gulf region, watching the suffering crowd of poor, black New Orleanians stranded at the Superdome, began a soul-searching conversation about what Democratic party leader Howard Dean called the "ugly truth": that poverty remains linked to race in this nation. Quickly, however, public attention shifted to charges of administrative mismanagement and the seeming indifference of the president. "Nothing about the President's demeanor yesterday," reported the *New York Times* shortly after the hurricane, "which seemed casual to the point of carelessness—suggested that he understood the depth of the current crisis." Despite the federal government's failure to manage the crisis in New Orleans, President Bush cheered on Federal Emergency Management Association (FEMA) director Michael Brown with the words "Brownie, you're doing a heck of a job." In fact, poor planning on local, state, and federal levels compounded the human suffering caused by Katrina and made Americans wonder how well the nation was prepared, four years after the 9/11 attacks, to meet a major crisis. Many, looking at Katrina in the context of the continuing war in Iraq, questioned the competence of the Bush administration.

Internationally, too, Bush faced growing criticism, not only on account of Iraq and Abu Ghraib, but also be-

America Isolated

cause of his administration's continued lack of engagement in the Israeli-Palestinian dispute and what observers saw as its continuing disdain for the messy compromises of diplomacy. The White House, critics said, rightly sought to prevent North Korea and Iran from joining the nuclear club but seemed incapable of working imaginatively and multilaterally to make it happen. In Europe, where most editorial observers had hoped for a Kerry victory, Bush continued to be depicted as a gun-slinging cowboy whose moralistic rhetoric and aggressive policies threatened world peace. According to a Pew survey in June 2006, the percentage of the public expressing confidence in Bush's leadership in international affairs had fallen to 30 in Britain, 25 in Germany, 15 in France, and 7 in Spain.

Iraq, though, remained the chief problem. The bill for the war now exceeded $1 billion per week and appeared certain to continue rising. In March 2005, the number of American war dead reached 1,500; that October, the figure hit 2,000; and in December 2006, it reached 3,000. The insurgents, too, suffered major casualties but showed no sign of weakening. Meanwhile, estimates of Iraqi civilian deaths since the invasion ranged by mid-2006 from a low of 60,000 to a high of 655,000. These Iraqi casualties resulted from insurgent suicide attacks and U.S. bombing of suspected insurgent hideouts, as well as from increasing sectarian violence between Sunnis and Shi'ites. In July 2006 alone, according to an authoritative tally, more than 3,400 civilians were killed, most of them from this sectarian conflict. In January 2007, the Iraq Health Ministry reported 17,310 civilian deaths over the previous six months.

The Bush administration denied that Iraq had degenerated into civil war or that the struggle had become a Vietnam-like quagmire, but it seemed to have little clue how to bring the fighting to an end. Far from helping to reduce the threat of terrorism to Americans and others, the Iraq invasion seemed only to have increased it, as the Al Qaeda presence in the country (nonexistent before the war) became pronounced and as the ongoing struggle in Afghanistan suffered comparative neglect.

In Congress and the press, calls for withdrawal from Iraq multiplied, but skeptics cautioned that disengagement would make things worse: it would cause an explosion of sectarian bloodshed and, almost certainly, a collapse of the Baghdad government. The power and regional influence of neighboring Iran would increase, and American credibility would be undermined throughout the Middle East. Some commentators instead called for a major increase in the number of U.S. forces in Iraq, but it was not clear where these troops would be found in the overstretched American military or whether they would do much good on the ground. The 2006 midterm election was at least in part a referendum on the war, and the voters made their feeling clear: 55 percent nationally voted for Democratic candidates, and the party seized control of both houses of Congress. Not a single Democratic incumbent in either house suffered defeat.

AMERICANS IN THE FIRST DECADE OF THE NEW MILLENNIUM

At the beginning of the twenty-first century, the United States is a nation of extraordinary diversity. For much of the twentieth century, however, it had seemed that the United States was moving in the opposite direction. Very few immigrants had been allowed into the United States from the 1920s through 1965. New technologies, such as radio and television, had a homogenizing effect at first, for these mass media were dependent on reaching the broadest possible audience—a mass market. Although local and ethnic traditions persisted, more and more Americans participated in a shared mass culture. During the last third of the twentieth century, however, those homogenizing trends were reversed. Immigration reform in the mid-1960s opened American borders to large numbers of people from a wider variety of nations than ever before. New technologies—the Internet, and cable and satellite television, with their proliferation of channels—replaced mass markets with niche markets. Everything from television shows to cosmetics to cars could be targeted toward specific groups defined by age, ethnicity, class, gender, or lifestyle choices. These changes did not simply make American society more fragmented. Instead, they helped to make Americans' understandings of identity more fluid and more complex.

In the 2000 U.S. government census, for the first time Americans were allowed to identify themselves as belonging to more than one race. New census categories recognized that notions of biological "race" were problematic. Why could a white woman bear a "black" child when a black woman could not bear a white child? The change also acknowledged the growing number of Americans born to parents of different racial backgrounds, as American mixed-race and mixed-ethnicity marriages grew from less than 1 percent in 1970 to 5.4 percent at the turn of the millennium. Critics, however, worried that, because census data are used to gather information about social conditions in the United States and as a basis for allocating resources, the new "multiracial" option would reduce the visibility and clout of minority groups. Thus the federal government counted those who identified both as white and as members of a racial or ethnic minority as belonging to the minority group. Under this system, the official population of some groups increased: more Americans than ever before, for example, identified themselves as at least partly Native American. Others rejected racial and ethnic categories altogether: 20 million people identified themselves simply as "American," up more than 50 percent since 1990.

Race and Ethnicity in Recent America

On October 17, 2006, the United States officially passed the 300 million population mark (it hit 100 million in 1915 and 200 million in 1967), and its people were increasingly diverse. During the 1990s, the population of people of color grew twelve times as fast as the white

Map 33.3   Mapping America's Diversity

Aggregate figures (more than 12 percent of the U.S. population was African American and about 4 percent Asian American in 2000, for example) convey America's ethnic and racial diversity. However, as this map shows, members of racial and ethnic groups are not distributed evenly throughout the nation.

(Source: Adapted from the New York Times National Edition, April 1, 2001, "Portrait of a Nation," p. 18. Copyright © 2001 by The New York Times Co. Reprinted with permission.)

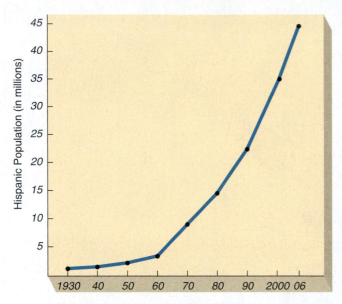

Figure 33.3   **The Growth of the U.S. Hispanic Population**

"Hispanic" combines people from a wide variety of national origins or ancestries—including all the nations of Central and South America, Mexico, Cuba, Puerto Rico, the Dominican Republic, Spain—as well as those who identify as Californio, Tejano, Nuevo Mexicano, and Mestizo.

(Source: Adapted from the U.S. Department of Commerce, Economics and Statistics Information, Bureau of the Census, 1993 report "We, the American . . . Hispanics"; also recent Census Bureau figures for the Hispanic population.)

▲ This twenty-first-century American family shows the increasing complexity of racial and ethnic identities. The father is Chinese, Irish, French, German, and Swedish; the mother, Italian, Irish, and Japanese. *(Terrence Mielse/Newsweek)*

population, fueled by both immigration and birth rates. In 2003 Latinos moved past African Americans to become the second largest ethnic or racial group in the nation (after non-Hispanic whites), making the United States the fifth largest "Latino" country in world (see Figure 33.3). Immigration from Asia also remained high, and in 2006, 5 percent of the U.S. population was Asian or Asian American.

These rapid demographic changes have altered the face of America. At a Dairy Queen in the far southern suburbs of Atlanta, 6 miles from the Gone with the Wind Historical District, teenage children of immigrants from India and Pakistan serve Blizzards and Brownie Earthquakes. In the small town of Ligonier, Indiana, the formerly empty main street now boasts three Mexican restaurants and a Mexican western-wear shop; Mexican immigrants drawn in the 1990s by plentiful industrial jobs cross paths with the newest immigrants, Yemenis, some in traditional dress, and with Amish families in horse-drawn buggies.

Although many of America's schools and neighborhoods remain racially segregated and public debates about

the consequences of illegal immigration are heated, American popular culture has embraced the influences of this new multiethnic population. Economics were important: the buying power of the growing Latino population exceeded $798 billion in 2006, and average income for Asian American households topped that for all other groups. But American audiences also crossed racial and ethnic lines. Golfer Tiger Woods became a symbol of this new hybrid, multiethnic nation: of African, European, Native American, Thai, and Chinese descent, he calls himself "Cablinasian" (CAucasian-BLack-INdian-ASIAN).

Americans were divided over the meaning of other changes as well—especially the changing shape of American families (see Figure 33.4). The

The Changing American Family

median age at marriage continued to rise, reaching 27.1 for men and 25.8 for women in 2006 (for women who pursued graduate degrees, the median age at first marriage was almost 30). The number of people living together without marriage also increased. In 2006, when households composed of married couples slipped below 50 percent for the first time, unmarried, opposite-sex partners made up about 5 percent of households, and same-sex couples accounted for slightly less than 1 percent. One-third of female-partner households and one-fifth of male-partner households had children, and in 2002 the American Academy of Pedi-

▲ Rescuers save a family from floodwaters in Bay St. Louis, Mississippi after Hurricane Katrina. Katrina destroyed not only New Orleans, but much of the U.S. Gulf Coast from Louisiana into Alabama. The federal government designated 90,000 square miles as disaster area. More than 1,800 people lost their lives in the storm. *(AP Photo/Ben Sklar)*

atrics endorsed adoption by gay couples. A vocal antigay movement coexisted with rising support for the legal equality of gay, lesbian, transgendered, and bisexual Americans. Although many states and private corporations extended domestic-partner benefits to gay couples, the federal Defense of Marriage Act, passed by Congress in 1996, defined marriage as "only" a union between one man and one woman, and state legislatures continue to grapple with the issue.

Early in the twenty-first century, one-third of all American children and more than two-thirds of African American children were born to unmarried women. (In Britain, the rate was 42 percent.) In the majority of married-couple families with children under eighteen, both parents held jobs. Although almost one-third of families with children had only one parent present—usually the mother—children also lived in blended families created by second marriages or moved back and forth between households of parents who had joint custody. Based on current statistical analysis, for couples who married in the mid-1990s the woman's level of education was the clearest predictor of divorce: if the woman graduated from a four-year college, the couple

had a 25 percent likelihood of divorce; if she had not, the rate jumped to 50 percent.

In 2006 the leading edge of the baby-boom generation turned 60; the median age of the American population was 36.2, up from 29.5 in 1967. Although baby boomers are not aging in the same manner as their parents and grandparents—"Sixty is the new forty," the saying goes—the large and growing proportion of older people will have a major impact on American society. As life expectancy increases, the growing number of elderly Americans will put enormous pressure on the nation's healthcare system and family structure—who will care for people as they can no longer live independently?—and strain the Social Security and Medicare systems.

Other health issues have become increasingly important as well. In a rapid change over the course of a decade, more than 65 percent of American adults are now overweight or obese—conditions linked to hypertension, cardiovascular disease, and diabetes. In 1995 no state had an adult obesity rate that hit 20 percent. By 2005, only four states were under that 20 percent marker, and Louisiana, Mississippi, and West Virginia topped 30 percent. On the

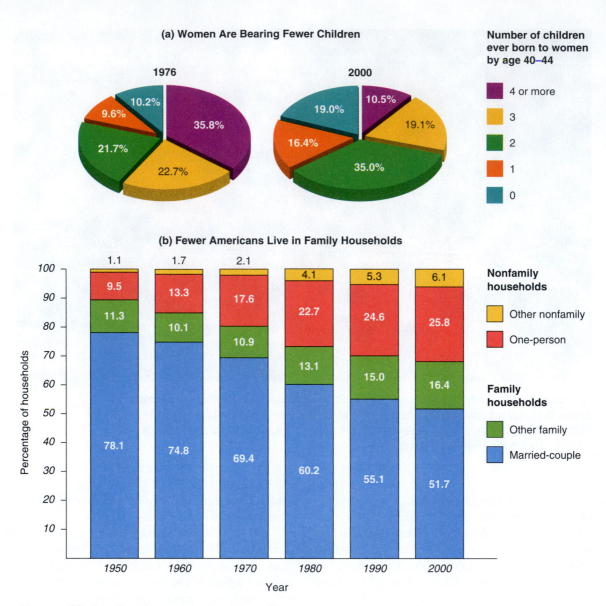

(a) Women Are Bearing Fewer Children

Number of children ever born to women by age 40–44

- 4 or more
- 3
- 2
- 1
- 0

(b) Fewer Americans Live in Family Households

Nonfamily households
- Other nonfamily
- One-person

Family households
- Other family
- Married-couple

Figure 33.4   The Changing American Family
American households became smaller in the latter part of the twentieth century, as more people lived alone and women had, on average, fewer children.

(Source: Adapted from U.S. Bureau of the Census, http://www.census.gov/prod/2002pubs/censr-4.pdf and http://www.census.gov/population/pop-profile/2000/chap04.pdf.)

other hand, cigarette smoking continues a slow but steady decline. About one-fifth of American adults smoked in 2005, down from about one-third of adults in 1980. Approximately 440,000 people die each year from illness caused by smoking, and medical costs and lost productivity total about $157 billion a year. With clearer understanding of the danger of second-hand smoke, local governments have increasingly banned smoking in public spaces, including restaurants and bars.

As scientists and medical researchers continue to struggle to find cures for devastating diseases like cancer and AIDS, rapid advances in the field of biogenetics offer great new possibilities and, for many Americans, raise ethical or philosophical conundrums. During in vitro fertilizations—in which sperm and egg combine in a sterile dish and the fertilized egg or eggs

Medicine, Science, and Religion

are then transferred to the uterus—five- or six-cell blastocytes are formed by the initial division of fertilized eggs. These blastocytes contain stem cells, unspecialized cells that can be induced to become cells with specialized functions. For example, stem cells might become insulin-producing cells of the pancreas, and thus a cure for diabetes; or they might become dopamine-producing neurons, offering therapy for Parkinson's disease, a progressive disorder of the nervous system affecting over 1 million Americans. President Bush in 2001 called embryonic stem cell research "the leading edge of a series of moral hazards," because extracting stem cells destroys the blastocyte's "potential for life," and limited federally funded research to the existing seventy-eight stem cell lines, the majority of which turned out not to be viable for research. In 2006 he vetoed a bipartisan congressional bill that expanded the number of stem cell lines available for federally funded research. Like many issues in America today, the controversy over stem cells is often treated as a conflict between religion and science. However, the majority of Americans support stem cell research, arguing that the moral good of curing diseases that devastate the lives of many men, women, and children outweighs the moral good of preserving the potential life of blastocytes.

At the same time, many Americans see a fundamental conflict between religious belief and scientific study. Fundamentalist Christians have struggled to prevent the teaching of evolution in the nation's science classes or to introduce parallel instruction of biblical "creationism" or theories of "intelligent design," which hold that an intelligent creator lies behind the development of life on earth. The percentage of Americans who accept the scientific evidence for evolution is lower than that in any other major nation in the world, with the sole exception of Turkey.

The twentieth century had seen more momentous change than any previous century—change that brought

Century of Change

enormous benefits to human beings, change that threatened the very existence of the human species. Research in the physical and biological sciences had provided insight into the structure of matter and of the universe. Technology—the application of science—had made startling advances that benefited Americans in nearly every aspect of life: better health, more wealth, more mobility, less drudgery, greater access to information.

Through these advances, Americans at the start of the new century were more connected to the rest of humankind than ever before. This interconnection was perhaps the most powerful product of globalization. A commodities trader in Chicago in March 2003 could send an e-mail to her fiancé in Tokyo while she spoke on the phone to a trader in Frankfurt and kept one eye on CNN's real-time coverage of the air war over Baghdad; within a minute or two she could receive a reply from her fiancé saying that he missed her, too. If she felt sufficiently lovesick, she could board an airplane and be in Japan the following day.

The world had shrunk to the size of an airplane ticket. In 1955, 51 million people a year traveled by plane. By the turn of the century, 1.6 billion were airborne every year, and 530 million—or about 1.5 million each day—crossed international borders. This permeability of national boundaries brought many benefits, as did the integration of markets and the global spread of information that occurred alongside it.

But there was a flip side to this growing connectivity, which even advocates of globalization perceived. The

Globalization and World Health

rapid increase in international air travel was a particularly potent force for the dissemination of global disease, as flying made it possible for people to reach the other side of the world in far less time than the incubation period for many ailments. In early 2003, a respiratory illness known as severe acute respiratory syndrome (SARS) emerged in China and threatened to spread rapidly across the globe. Thirteen labs in ten countries worked day and night to map the genome, whereupon efforts to devise a diagnostic test for the virus began. SARS did not develop into a worldwide epidemic, but health authorities were put on notice: international cooperation would be essential to combat the health threats intensified by globalization and the rapidity of world travel.

Environmental degradation also created major global health threats. In 2003 the World Health Organization (WHO) estimated that nearly one-quarter of the global burden of disease and injury was related to environmental disruption and decline. For example, some 90 percent of diarrheal diseases (such as cholera), which were killing 3 million people a year, resulted from contaminated water. WHO also pointed to globalization and environmental disruption as contributing to the fact that, in the final two decades of the twentieth century, more than thirty infectious diseases were identified in humans for the first time—including AIDS, Ebola virus, hantavirus, and hepatitis C and E. Environmentalists, meanwhile, insisted that the growing interaction of national economies was having a deleterious impact on the ecosystem through climate change, ozone depletion, hazardous waste, and damage to fisheries.

The Global AIDS Epidemic

AIDS, first reported in the United States in 1981, has become a global epidemic. Researchers now believe that the first infection with HIV, the human immunodeficiency virus that causes AIDS, may have appeared in West Africa around 1930. HIV/AIDS began spreading rapidly in the late 1970s, in part as a byproduct of globalization. Increasingly commonplace international travel allowed for sexual transmission of HIV between populations; the international heroin trade that grew in the 1970s stimulated intravenous drug use, another means of transmission; and the international circulation of blood for transfusions in medical procedures also contributed to the virus's spread. In 2003 the World Health Organization estimated that 58 million people worldwide were living with HIV/AIDS and that 23 million had died from the disease.

Globally, AIDS claims 350 lives per hour, and though altered behavior and new drug therapies have slowed the progress of the disease in North America and western Europe, infection and death rates continue to grow rapidly in sub-Saharan Africa, Thailand, eastern Europe and the former Soviet Union, and Latin America, especially the Caribbean. In the African nation of Malawi, 1 in 6 adults is HIV-positive, and the nation expects to lose almost one-quarter of its work force to AIDS in the next decade. Half of current teenagers in the hardest-hit African nations will eventually die of AIDS; more than 14 million children across the globe have been orphaned by the disease.

The human suffering is staggering. However, U.S. worries about the global spread of AIDS are not based solely on humanitarian concerns. In 2000 the U.S. National Intelligence Council concluded that AIDS and other new and reemerging infectious diseases must be treated as threats to the health of U.S. citizens and to global security, stating, "These diseases will endanger U.S. citizens at home and abroad, threaten U.S. armed forces deployed overseas, and exacerbate social and political instability in key countries and regions in which the United States has significant interests." In nations already facing shortages of food and clean water, and riven by war and ethnic conflict, AIDS has further undermined both individual and governmental ability to cope with crisis; political instability and social disorder result.

In 2002 U.N. secretary general Kofi Annan estimated that between $7 billion and $10 billion are needed each year to combat the spread of AIDS—and of tuberculosis and malaria, both of which have reemerged as major threats to world health. President Bush called for major increases in U.S. spending to combat AIDS internationally, but many believe the United States must take more responsibility for combating the epidemic. In the era of globalization, diseases do not stop at borders or respect wealth and power. The links between Americans and the rest of the world's peoples cannot be denied.

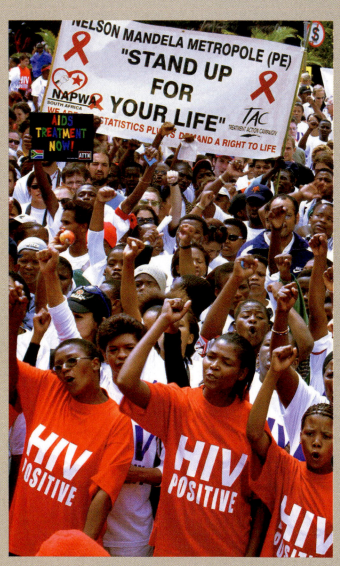

▲ Activists protest outside Parliament in Cape Town, South Africa, calling on South African president Thabo Mbeki to make the struggle against AIDS a national priority. An estimated 20 percent of South Africans between the ages of fifteen and forty-nine are HIV-positive.

(AP/Wide World Photos, Inc.)

▲ Melinda and Bill Gates hold babies as they visit the Manhica Research Center in Mozambique in 2003. The Center was one of the recipients of a $168 million grant for malaria research funded by the Bill and Melinda Gates Foundation. Bill and Melinda Gates co-chair the foundation, whose mission is to "reduce inequities and improve lives around the world." It is active in all fifty U.S. states and one hundred other nations; in 2006 it made grants of more than one and a half billion dollars. *(© Naashon Zalk/Corbis)*

But if the interaction between national economies and the rapid increase in person-to-person contacts were

International Response to Disease

responsible for many health and other problems, they also were essential in mobilizing the world to find solutions. Whereas it took centuries to identify the cause of cholera and two years to identify the virus that causes AIDS, in the case of SARS, thirteen labs in ten countries put everything else aside and in a matter of weeks determined that the coronavirus was responsible. Within a month, laboratories from Vancouver to Atlanta to Singapore had mapped the genome, whereupon efforts to devise a diagnostic test for the virus began. Thus, although the disease spread internationally with unprecedented speed, so did the response. Speed of communication allowed for a coordinated international effort at finding the cause

of SARS and also allowed individual countries, including the United States, to adopt measures that succeeded, in the early months at least, in keeping the epidemic out.

Even in the interconnected world of the new millennium, then, national borders still mattered. There were limits to their permeability. In the wake of 9/11, indeed, the process of integration was to some degree reversed. To prevent future terrorist attacks, the United States and other countries imposed tighter security measures on air travelers, imported goods, immigration, and information flows. Some economists predicted these measures would stall the global movement toward integration of markets; in the short term they certainly did, but the long-term outlook was less clear. Trade and investment shrank in 2001, but they were falling before September 11 as a result of economic slowdowns in the world's biggest economies, including the United States, Europe, and Japan.

TABLE 33.1	U.S. Military Personnel on Active Duty in Foreign Countries, 2005[1]		
Region/Country[2]	**Personnel**	**Region/Country[2]**	**Personnel**
United States and Territories		Thailand	116
Continental U.S.	894, 921	**North Africa, Near East, and South Asia**	
Alaska	18,980	Bahrain	1,482
Hawai'i	33,816	Diego Garcia	773
Guam	2, 931	Egypt	424
Puerto Rico	211	Iraq	207,000
Europe		Israel	43
Belgium*	1,388	Oman	36
Bosnia and Herzegovina	261	Pakistan	195
France*	56	Qatar	387
Germany*	66,000	Saudi Arabia	269
Greece*	431	United Arab Emirates	72
Greenland*	144	**Sub-Saharan Africa**	
Iceland*	1,257	Kenya	32
Italy*	11,428	South Africa	33
Macedonia	40	**Western Hemisphere**	
Netherlands*	579	Brazil	39
Norway*	74	Canada	145
Portugal*	990	Chile	29
Russia	44	Colombia	96
Serbia (includes Kosovo)	1,909	Cuba (Guantánamo)	950
Spain*	1,634	Honduras	416
Turkey*	1,738	Peru	36
United Kingdom*	10,536	Venezuela	21
East Asia and Pacific		**Total foreign countries[2]**	**271,381**
Australia	140	**Ashore**	**247,341**
China (includes Hong Kong)	71	**Afloat**	**24,040**
Japan	35,050	**Total worldwide[2]**	**1,605,414**
Korea, Rep. of	29,982	**Ashore**	**1,249,616**
Philippines	44	**Afloat**	**128,398**
Singapore	159		

*NATO countries
[1]Only countries with 35 or more U.S. military personnel are listed.
[2]Includes all regions/countries, not simply those listed.

Source: U.S. Department of Defense, Defense Manpower Data Center.

Moreover, the falloff in international economic activity in the months after the attacks was not massive.

In military and diplomatic terms, though, 9/11 made a deep and lasting impression. The attacks that day brought home what Americans had only dimly perceived before then: that globalization had shrunk the natural buffers that distance and two oceans provided the United States. Al Qaeda, it was clear, had used the increasingly open, integrated, globalized world to give itself new power and reach. It had shown that small cells of terrorists could become true transnational threats—thriving around the world without any single state sponsor or home base. According to American intelligence, Al Qaeda operated in more than ninety countries—including the United States.

Confronting Terrorism

How would one go about vanquishing such a foe? Was a decisive victory even possible? These remained open questions five years after the World Trade Center collapsed. Unchallenged militarily and seeing no rival great power, the United States felt few constraints about intervening in Afghanistan and then Iraq, but the problems in Iraq showed that it could take scant comfort from this superiority. It continued to spend colossal sums on its military, more indeed than the rest of the world combined. (Including the supplemental appropriations for Iraq and Afghanistan, the Pentagon in 2006 spent more than $500 billion, or roughly $60 million dollars per hour.) America had taken on military commitments all over the globe, from the Balkans and Iraq to Afghanistan and Korea (see Table 33.1). Its armed forces looked colossal, but its obligations looked even larger.

Legacy FOR A PEOPLE AND A NATION

The Internet

"Google it"—the phrase, essentially unknown before the new century, had within its first years become a household expression like "Xerox it" or "FedEx it." Google was the hugely popular Internet search engine that had gone from obscurity in the mid-1990s to a point where it responded, more or less instantly, to 200 million queries per day from around the world—almost 40 percent of all Internet search requests.

Google's phenomenal rise was one sign among many of how the Internet had become, by the early years of the twenty-first century, an ordinary, expected part of many Americans' daily lives. For younger people in particular, the Internet was something to be taken for granted, like refrigerators, microwaves, stereos, and televisions.

Yet the widespread use of the Internet was a recent phenomenon, even though its history went back some four decades. In the mid-1960s, the U.S. military's Advanced Research Projects Agency (ARPA) hoped to create a communications network for government and university researchers spread out across the nation. In 1969 the first portions of the experimental system, called ARPANET, went online at UCLA; the University of California, Santa Barbara; Stanford Research Institute; and the University of Utah. By 1971, twenty-three computers were connected, and gradually the numbers grew, reaching close to a thousand by 1984. This system, which by the late 1980s had been renamed the Internet, transmitted only words, but in 1990 computer scientists developed the World Wide Web, which used the Internet to send graphic and multimedia information as well. Then in 1993 the first commercial "browser" to aid navigation through the Web hit the market. It was followed in 1994 and 1995 by two superior browsers: Netscape and Internet Explorer. The prospect of millions of computers connected worldwide had become a reality.

By early 2007, there were more than a billion Internet users worldwide, including 200 million Americans. Thanks to technological advances and to the new forms of "broadband" access that provided high-speed connections, these users could do an astonishing array of things online. They could send and receive e-mail, join online discussion groups, read newspapers, book vacations, download movies and music, purchase everything from books to private jets, even do their banking—all through a small computer in their home. For the American people in the new globally connected millennium, there could be no more fitting legacy of the twentieth century than the Internet.

SUMMARY

The 1990s were, for most Americans, good times. A digitized revolution in communications and information—as fundamental as the revolution brought about by electricity and the combustion engine a century earlier, or the steam engine a century before that—was generating prosperity and transforming life in America and around the globe. The longest economic expansion in American history—from 1991 to 2001—meant that most Americans who wanted jobs had them, that the stock market boomed, that the nation had a budget surplus instead of a deficit, and that more Americans than ever before owned their own homes. And America was not only prosperous; it was powerful. With the Soviet Union gone and no other formidable rival on the horizon, the United States stood as the world's lone superpower, its economic and military power daunting to friend and foe alike.

Yet, although America seemed at the apex of power and prosperity, unsettling events troubled the nation. Localized and ethnic conflicts in the Balkans, the Middle East, Central Asia, and Africa crowded the international agenda, as did human rights and the natural environment. At home, high-profile acts of violence—the domestic terrorist attack in Oklahoma City in 1995; a rash of school shootings—captured headlines, even as the crime rate dropped. And scandal further undermined the faith of Americans in their government, as President Bill Clinton was impeached by the House of Representatives.

Just minutes before midnight on December 31, 1999, President Clinton called on the American people not to fear the future, but to "welcome it, create it, and embrace it." The challenges of the future would be greater than Americans imagined as they welcomed the new millennium that night. In 2000 the contested presidential election was decided by the Supreme Court in a partisan 5-to-4 vote; in 2001 the ten-year economic expansion came to an end.

Then, on September 11 of that year, radical Islamic terrorists attacked the World Trade Center and the Pentagon, killing thousands and altering many aspects of American life. The new president, George W. Bush, declared a "war on terrorism," one with both foreign and domestic components. While U.S. air and ground forces went after targets in Afghanistan, Congress moved to create the Department of Homeland Security and passed the PATRIOT Act, expanding the federal government's powers of surveillance. In March 2003, Bush took the nation into war in Iraq, not expecting what followed: a full-fledged insurgency by disaffected Iraqis against U.S. occupying forces and sectarian violence between Sunnis and Shi'ites. To counter a troubled economy, Bush pushed through tax cuts each of his first three years in office, something no wartime president had ever done.

The world that Americans found in the first years of the twenty-first century was much different from the one they had looked forward to with confidence and high hopes as they celebrated the coming of the new millennium on New Year's Eve 1999. The horror of the terror attacks of September 11, 2001, shook America to its core. Throughout the nation, people declared that life would never again be the same. And it was not, not for those who had lost loved ones that day or for a people now forcibly aware of the powerful and inescapable links that bind their nation to the rest of the world's nations and peoples. But, as Americans attempted to cope with the aftermath of 9/11, crafting new foreign and domestic policies, the resilience of the American people was clear. For Americans continued to struggle over these plans and policies, over the direction of their nation, with the passion and commitment that keeps democracy alive.

SUGGESTIONS FOR FURTHER READING

Daniel Benjamin and Steven Simon, *The Sacred Age of Terror* (2002)

Barbara Ehrenreich, *Nickled and Dimed: On (Not) Getting by in America* (2002)

David Halberstam, *War in a Time of Peace: Bush, Clinton, and the Generals* (2001)

John F. Harris, *The Survivor: Bill Clinton in the White House* (2005)

Jennifer L. Hochschild, *Facing up to the American Dream: Race, Class, and the Soul of the Nation* (1995)

James Mann, *Rise of the Vulcans: The History of Bush's War Cabinet* (2004)

Alejandro Portes and Reuben G. Rumbaut, *Immigrant America: A Portrait,* 3d ed. (2006)

Thomas E. Ricks, *Fiasco: The American Military Adventure in Iraq* (2006)

Joseph E. Stiglitz, *Globalization and Its Discontents* (2002)

For a more extensive list for further reading, go to college.hmco.com/pic/norton8e.

DECLARATION OF INDEPENDENCE IN CONGRESS, JULY 4, 1776

When, in the course of human events, it becomes necessary for one people to dissolve the political bonds which have connected them with another, and to assume, among the powers of the earth, the separate and equal station to which the laws of nature and of nature's God entitle them, a decent respect to the opinions of mankind requires that they should declare the causes which impel them to the separation.

We hold these truths to be self-evident: That all men are created equal; that they are endowed by their Creator with certain unalienable rights; that among these are life, liberty, and the pursuit of happiness; that, to secure these rights, governments are instituted among men, deriving their just powers from the consent of the governed; that whenever any form of government becomes destructive of these ends, it is the right of the people to alter or to abolish it, and to institute new government, laying its foundation on such principles, and organizing its powers in such form, as to them shall seem most likely to effect their safety and happiness. Prudence, indeed, will dictate that governments long established should not be changed for light and transient causes; and accordingly all experience hath shown that mankind are more disposed to suffer, while evils are sufferable, than to right themselves by abolishing the forms to which they are accustomed. But when a long train of abuses and usurpations, pursuing invariably the same object, evinces a design to reduce them under absolute despotism, it is their right, it is their duty, to throw off such government, and to provide new guards for their future security. Such has been the patient sufferance of these colonies; and such is now the necessity which constrains them to alter their former systems of government. The history of the present King of Great Britain is a history of repeated injuries and usurpations, all having in direct object the establishment of an absolute tyranny over these states. To prove this, let facts be submitted to a candid world.

He has refused his assent to laws, the most wholesome and necessary for the public good.

He has forbidden his governors to pass laws of immediate and pressing importance, unless suspended in their operation till his assent should be obtained; and, when so suspended, he has utterly neglected to attend to them.

He has refused to pass other laws for the accommodation of large districts of people, unless those people would relinquish the right of representation in the legislature, a right inestimable to them, and formidable to tyrants only.

He has called together legislative bodies at places unusual, uncomfortable, and distant from the depository of their public records, for the sole purpose of fatiguing them into compliance with his measures.

He has dissolved representative houses repeatedly, for opposing, with manly firmness, his invasions on the rights of the people.

He has refused for a long time, after such dissolutions, to cause others to be elected; whereby the legislative powers, incapable of annihilation, have returned to the people at large for their exercise; the state remaining, in the mean time, exposed to all the dangers of invasions from without and convulsions within.

He has endeavored to prevent the population of these states; for that purpose obstructing the laws for naturalization of foreigners; refusing to pass others to encourage their migration hither, and raising the conditions of new appropriations of lands.

He has obstructed the administration of justice, by refusing his assent to laws for establishing judiciary powers.

He has made judges dependent on his will alone, for the tenure of their offices, and the amount and payment of their salaries.

He has erected a multitude of new offices, and sent hither swarms of officers to harass our people and eat out their substance.

He has kept among us, in times of peace, standing armies, without the consent of our legislatures.

He has affected to render the military independent of, and superior to, the civil power.

He has combined with others to subject us to a jurisdiction foreign to our constitution, and unacknowledged by our laws, giving his assent to their acts of pretended legislation:

For quartering large bodies of armed troops among us;

For protecting them, by a mock trial, from punishment for any murders which they should commit on the inhabitants of these states;

For cutting off our trade with all parts of the world;

For imposing taxes on us without our consent;

For depriving us, in many cases, of the benefits of trial by jury;

For transporting us beyond seas, to be tried for pretended offenses;

For abolishing the free system of English laws in a neighboring province, establishing therein an arbitrary government, and enlarging its boundaries, so as to render it at once an example and fit instrument for introducing the same absolute rule into these colonies;

For taking away our charters, abolishing our most valuable laws, and altering fundamentally the forms of our governments;

For suspending our own legislatures, and declaring themselves invested with power to legislate for us in all cases whatsoever.

He has abdicated government here, by declaring us out of his protection and waging war against us.

He has plundered our seas, ravaged our coasts, burned our towns, and destroyed the lives of our people.

He is at this time transporting large armies of foreign mercenaries to complete the works of death, desolation, and tyranny already begun with circumstances of cruelty and perfidy scarcely paralleled in the most barbarous ages, and totally unworthy the head of a civilized nation.

He has constrained our fellow-citizens, taken captive on the high seas, to bear arms against their country, to become the executioners of their friends and brethren, or to fall themselves by their hands.

He has excited domestic insurrection among us, and has endeavored to bring on the inhabitants of our frontiers the merciless Indian savages, whose known rule of warfare is an undistinguished destruction of all ages, sexes, and conditions.

In every stage of these oppressions we have petitioned for redress in the most humble terms; our repeated petitions have been answered only by repeated injury. A prince, whose character is thus marked by every act which may define a tyrant, is unfit to be the ruler of a free people.

Nor have we been wanting in our attentions to our British brethren. We have warned them, from time to time, of attempts by their legislature to extend an unwarrantable jurisdiction over us. We have reminded them of the circumstances of our emigration and settlement here. We have appealed to their native justice and magnanimity; and we have conjured them, by the ties of our common kindred, to disavow these usurpations, which would inevitably interrupt our connections and correspondence. They, too, have been deaf to the voice of justice and of consanguinity. We must, therefore, acquiesce in the necessity which denounces our separation, and hold them, as we hold the rest of mankind, enemies in war, in peace friends.

We, therefore, the representatives of the United States of America, in General Congress assembled, appealing to the Supreme Judge of the world for the rectitude of our intentions, do, in the name and by the authority of the good people of these colonies, solemnly publish and declare, that these United Colonies are, and of right ought to be, FREE AND INDEPENDENT STATES; that they are absolved from all allegiance to the British crown, and that all political connection between them and the state of Great Britain is, and ought to be, totally dissolved; and that, as free and independent states, they have full power to levy war, conclude peace, contract alliances, establish commerce, and do all other acts and things which independent states may of right do. And for the support of this declaration, with a firm reliance on the protection of Divine Providence, we mutually pledge to each other our lives, our fortunes, and our sacred honor.

ARTICLES OF CONFEDERATION

Whereas the Delegates of the United States of America in Congress assembled did on the fifteenth day of November in the Year of our Lord One Thousand Seven Hundred and Seventy seven, and in the Second Year of the Independence of America agree to certain articles of Confederation and perpetual Union between the States of Newhampshire, Massachusetts Bay, Rhode Island and Providence Plantations, Connecticut, New York, New Jersey, Pennsylvania, Delaware, Maryland, Virginia, North Carolina, South Carolina and Georgia in the Words following, viz. "Articles of Confederation and perpetual Union between the states of Newhampshire, Massachusetts Bay, Rhode Island and Providence Plantations, Connecticut, New York, New Jersey, Pennsylvania, Delaware, Maryland, Virginia, North Carolina, South Carolina and Georgia.

Article I   The Stile of this confederacy shall be "The United States of America."

Article II   Each state retains its sovereignty, freedom and independence, and every Power, Jurisdiction and right, which is not by this confederation expressly delegated to the United States, in Congress assembled.

Article III   The said states hereby severally enter into a firm league of friendship with each other, for their common defence, the security of their Liberties, and their mutual and general welfare, binding themselves to assist each other, against all force offered to, or attacks made upon them, or any of them, on account of religion, sovereignty, trade, or any other pretence whatever.

Article IV   The better to secure and perpetuate mutual friendship and intercourse among the people of the different states in this union, the free inhabitants of each of these states, paupers, vagabonds and fugitives from Justice excepted, shall be entitled to all privileges and immunities of free citizens in the several states; and the people of each state shall have free ingress and regress to and from any other state, and shall enjoy therein all the privileges of trade and commerce, subject to the same duties, impositions and restrictions as the inhabitants thereof respectively, provided that such restriction shall not extend so far as to prevent the removal of property imported into any state, to any other state of which the Owner is an inhabitant; provided also that no imposition, duties or restriction shall be laid by any state, on the property of the united states, or either of them.

If any Person guilty of, or charged with treason, felony, or other high misdemeanor in any state, shall flee from Justice, and be found in any of the united states, he shall upon demand of the Governor or executive power, of the state from which he fled, be delivered up and removed to the state having jurisdiction of his offence.

Full faith and credit shall be given in each of these states to the records, acts and judicial proceedings of the courts and magistrates of every other state.

Article V   For the more convenient management of the general interests of the united states, delegates shall be annually appointed in such manner as the legislature of each state shall direct, to meet in Congress on the first Monday in November, in every year, with a power reserved to each state, to recall its delegates, or any of them, at any time within the year, and to send others in their stead, for the remainder of the Year.

No state shall be represented in Congress by less than two, nor by more than seven Members; and no person shall be capable of being a delegate for more than three years in any term of six years; nor shall any person, being a delegate, be capable of holding any office under the united states, for which he, or another for his benefit receives any salary, fees or emolument of any kind.

Each state shall maintain its own delegates in a meeting of the states, and while they act as members of the committee of the states.

In determining questions in the united states, in Congress assembled, each state shall have one vote.

Freedom of speech and debate in Congress shall not be impeached or questioned in any Court, or place out of Congress, and the members of congress shall be protected in their persons from arrests and imprisonments, during the time of their going to and from, and attendance on congress, except for treason, felony, or breach of the peace.

Article VI   No state without the Consent of the united states in congress assembled, shall send any embassy to, or receive any embassy from, or enter into any conference, agreement, or alliance or treaty with any King, prince or state; nor shall any person holding any office of profit or trust under the united states, or any of them, accept of any present, emolument, office or title of any kind whatever from any king, prince or foreign state; nor shall the united states in congress assembled, or any of them, grant any title of nobility.

No two or more states shall enter into any treaty, confederation or alliance whatever between them, without the consent of the united states in congress assembled, specifying accurately the purposes for which the same is to be entered into, and how long it shall continue.

No state shall lay any imposts or duties, which may interfere with any stipulations in treaties, entered into by the united states in congress assembled, with any king, prince or state, in pursuance of any treaties already proposed by congress, to the courts of France and Spain.

No vessels of war shall be kept up in time of peace by any state, except such number only, as shall be deemed necessary by the united states in congress assembled, for the defence of such state, or its trade; nor shall any body of forces be kept up by any state, in time of peace, except such number only, as in the judgment of the united states, in congress assembled, shall be deemed requisite to garrison the forts necessary for the defence of such state; but every state shall always keep up a well regulated and disciplined militia, sufficiently armed and accoutred, and shall provide and constantly have ready for use, in public stores, a due number of field pieces and tents, and a proper quantity of arms, ammunition and camp equipage.

No state shall engage in any war without the consent of the united states in congress assembled, unless such state be actually invaded by enemies, or shall have received certain advice of a resolution being formed by some nation of Indians to invade such state, and the danger is so imminent as not to admit of a delay, till the united states in congress assembled can be consulted: nor shall any state grant commissions to any ships or vessels of war, nor letters of marque or reprisal, except it be after a declaration of war by the united states in congress assembled, and then only against the kingdom or state and the subjects thereof, against which war has been so declared, and under such regulations as shall be established by the united states in congress assembled, unless such state be infested by pirates, in which case vessels of war may be fitted out for that occasion, and kept so long as the danger shall continue, or until the united states in congress assembled shall determine otherwise.

Article VII   When land-forces are raised by any state for the common defence, all officers of or under the rank of colonel, shall be appointed by the legislature of each state respectively by whom such forces shall be raised, or in such manner as such state shall direct, and all vacancies shall be filled up by the state which first made the appointment.

Article VIII   All charges of war, and all other expences that shall be incurred for the common defence or general welfare, and allowed by the united states in congress assembled, shall be defrayed out of a common treasury, which shall be supplied by the several states, in proportion to the value of all land within each state, granted to or surveyed for any Person, as such land and the buildings and improvements thereon shall be estimated according to such mode as the united states in congress assembled, shall from time to time direct and appoint. The taxes for paying that proportion shall be laid and levied by the authority and direction of the legislatures of the several states within the time agreed upon by the united states in congress assembled.

Article IX   The united states in congress assembled, shall have the sole and exclusive right and power of determining on peace and war, except in the cases mentioned in the sixth article—of sending and receiving ambassadors—entering into treaties and alliances, provided that no treaty of commerce shall be made whereby the legislative power of the respective states shall be restrained from imposing such imposts and duties on foreigners, as their own people are subjected to, or from prohibiting the exportation or importation of any species of goods or commodities whatsoever—of establishing rules for deciding in all cases, what captures on land or water shall be legal, and in what manner prizes taken by land or naval forces in the service of the united states shall be divided or appropriated—of granting letters of marque and reprisal in times of peace—appointing courts for the trial of piracies and felonies committed on the high seas and establishing courts for receiving and determining final appeals in all cases of captures, provided that no member of congress shall be appointed a judge of any of the said courts.

The united states in congress assembled shall also be the last resort on appeal in all disputes and differences now subsisting or that hereafter may arise between two or more states concerning boundary, jurisdiction or any other cause whatever; which authority shall always be exercised in the manner following. Whenever the legislative or executive authority or lawful agent of any state in controversy with another shall present a petition to congress, stating the matter in question and praying for a hearing, notice thereof shall be given by order of congress to the legislative or executive authority of the other state in controversy, and a day assigned for the appearance of the parties by their lawful agents, who shall then be directed to appoint by joint consent, commissioners or judges to constitute a court for hearing and determining the matter in question: but if they cannot agree, congress shall name three persons out of each of the united states, and from the list of such persons each party shall alternately strike out one, the petitioners beginning, until the number shall be reduced to thirteen; and from that number not less than seven, nor more than nine names as congress shall direct, shall in the presence of congress be drawn out by lot, and the persons whose names shall be so drawn or any five of them, shall be commissioners or judges, to hear and finally determine the controversy, so always as a major part of the judges who shall hear the cause shall agree in the determination: and if either party shall neglect to attend at the day appointed, without shewing reasons, which congress shall judge sufficient, or being present shall refuse to strike, the congress shall proceed to nominate three persons out of each state, and the secretary of congress shall strike in behalf of such party absent or refusing; and the judgment and sentence of the court to be appointed, in the manner before prescribed, shall be final and conclusive; and if any of the parties shall refuse to submit to the authority of such court, or to appear to defend their claim or cause, the court shall nevertheless proceed to pronounce sentence, or judgment, which shall in like manner be final and decisive, the judgment or sentence and other proceedings being in either case transmitted to congress, and lodged among the acts of congress for the security of the parties concerned: provided that every commissioner, before he sits in judgment, shall take an oath to be administered by one of the judges of the supreme or superior court of the state, where the cause shall be tried, "well and truly to hear and determine the matter in question, according to the best of his judgment, without favour, affection or hope of reward:" provided also that no state shall be deprived of territory for the benefit of the united states.

All controversies concerning the private right of soil claimed under different grants of two or more states, whose jurisdictions as they may respect such lands, and the states which passed such grants are adjusted, the said grants or either of them being at the same time claimed to have originated antecedent to such settlement of jurisdiction, shall on the petition of either party to the congress of the united states, be finally determined as near as may be in the same manner as is before prescribed for deciding disputes respecting territorial jurisdiction between different states.

The united states in congress assembled shall also have the sole and exclusive right and power of regulating the alloy and value of coin struck by their own authority, or by that of the respective states—fixing the standard of weights and measures throughout the united states—regulating the trade and managing all affairs with the Indians, not members of any of the states, provided that the legislative right of any state within its own limits be not infringed or violated—establishing and regulating post-offices from one state to another, throughout all the united states, and exacting such postage on the papers passing thro' the same as may be requisite to defray the expences of the said office—appointing all officers of the land forces, in the service of the united states, excepting regimental officers—appointing all the officers of the naval forces, and commissioning all officers whatever in the service of the united states—making rules for the government and regulation of the said land and naval forces, and directing their operations.

The united states in congress assembled shall have authority to appoint a committee, to sit in the recess of congress, to be denominated "A Committee of the States," and to consist of one delegate from each state; and to appoint such other committees and civil officers as may be necessary for managing the general affairs of the united states under their direction—to appoint one of their number to preside, provided that no person be allowed to serve in the office of president more than one year in any term of three years; to ascertain the necessary sums of Money to be raised for the service of the united states, and to appropriate and apply the same for defraying the public expences—to borrow money, or emit bills on the credit of the united states, transmitting every half year to the respective states an account of the sums of money so borrowed or emitted—to build and equip a navy—to agree upon the number of land forces, and to make requisitions from each state for its quota, in proportion to the number of white inhabitants in such state; which requisition shall be binding, and thereupon the legislature of each state shall appoint the regimental officers, raise the men and cloath, arm and equip them in a soldier like manner, at the expence of the united states, and the officers and men so cloathed, armed and equipped shall march to the place appointed, and within the time agreed on by the united states in congress assembled: But if the united states in congress assembled shall, on consideration of circumstances judge proper that any state should not raise men, or should raise a smaller number than its quota, and that any other state should raise a greater number of men than the quota thereof, such extra number shall be raised, officered, cloathed, armed and equipped in the same manner as the quota of such state, unless the legislature of such state shall judge that such extra number cannot be safely spared out of the same, in which case they shall raise, officer, cloath, arm and equip as many of such extra number as they judge can be safely spared. And the officers and men so cloathed, armed and equipped, shall march to the place appointed, and within the time agreed on by the united states in congress assembled.

The united states in congress assembled shall never engage in a war, nor grant letters of marque and reprisal in time of peace, nor enter into any treaties or alliances, nor coin money, nor regulate the value thereof, nor ascertain the sums and expences necessary for the defence and welfare of the united states, or any of them, nor emit bills, nor borrow money on the credit of the united states, nor appropriate money, nor agree upon the number of vessels of war, to be built or purchased, or the number of land or sea forces to be raised, nor appoint a commander in chief of the army or navy, unless nine states assent to the same: nor shall a question on any other point, except for adjourning from day to day be determined, unless by the votes of a majority of the united states in congress assembled.

The congress of the united states shall have power to adjourn to any time within the year, and to any place within the united states, so that no period of adjournment be for a longer duration than the space of six Months, and shall publish the Journal of their proceedings monthly, except such parts thereof relating to treaties, alliances or military operations as in their judgment require secresy; and the yeas and nays of the delegates of each state on any question shall be entered on the Journal, when it is desired by any delegate; and the delegates of a state, or any of them, as his or their request shall be furnished with a transcript of the said Journal, except such parts as are above excepted, to lay before the legislatures of the several states.

Article X   The committee of the states, or any nine of them, shall be authorised to execute, in the recess of congress, such of the powers of congress as the united states in congress assembled, by the consent of nine states, shall from time to time think expedient to vest them with; provided that no power be delegated to the said committee, for the exercise of which, by the articles of confederation, the voice of nine states in the congress of the united states assembled is requisite.

Article XI   Canada acceding to this confederation, and joining in the measures of the united states, shall be admitted into, and entitled to all the advantages of this union: but no other colony shall be admitted into the same, unless such admission be agreed to by nine states.

Article XII   All bills of credit emitted, monies borrowed and debts contracted by, or under the authority of congress, before the assembling of the united states, in pursuance of the present confederation, shall be deemed and considered as a charge against the united states, for payment and satisfaction whereof the said united states, and the public faith are hereby solemnly pledged.

Article XIII   Every state shall abide by the determinations of the united states in congress assembled, on all questions which by this confederation are submitted to them. And the Articles of this confederation shall be inviolably observed by every state, and the union shall be perpetual; nor shall any alteration at any time hereafter be made in any of them; unless such alteration be agreed to in a congress of the united states, and be afterwards confirmed by the legislatures of every state.

AND WHEREAS it hath pleased the Great Governor of the World to incline the hearts of the legislatures we respectively represent in congress, to approve of, and to authorize us to ratify the said articles of confederation and perpetual union. Know Ye that we the under-signed delegates, by virtue of the power and authority to us given for that purpose, do by these presents, in the name and in behalf of our respective constituents, fully and entirely ratify and confirm each and every of the said articles of confederation and perpetual union, and all and singular the matters and things therein contained: And we do further solemnly plight and engage the faith of our respective constituents, that they shall abide by the determinations of the united states in congress assembled, on all questions, which by the said confederation are submitted to them. And that the articles thereof shall be inviolably observed by the states we respectively represent, and that the union shall be perpetual. In Witness whereof we have hereunto set our hands in Congress. Done at Philadelphia in the state of Pennsylvania the ninth Day of July in the Year of our Lord one Thousand seven Hundred and Seventy-eight, and in the third year of the independence of America.

CONSTITUTION OF THE UNITED STATES OF AMERICA AND AMENDMENTS*

Preamble

We the people of the United States, in order to form a more perfect union, establish justice, insure domestic tranquillity, provide for the common defense, promote the general welfare, and secure the blessings of liberty to ourselves and our posterity, do ordain and establish this Constitution for the United States of America.

Article I

Section 1   All legislative powers herein granted shall be vested in a Congress of the United States, which shall consist of a Senate and a House of Representatives.

Section 2   The House of Representatives shall be composed of members chosen every second year by the people of the several States, and the electors in each State shall have the qualifications requisite for electors of the most numerous branch of the State Legislature.

No person shall be a Representative who shall not have attained to the age of twenty-five years, and been seven years a citizen of the United States, and who shall not, when elected, be an inhabitant of that State in which he shall be chosen.

Representatives and direct taxes shall be apportioned among the several States which may be included within this Union, according to their respective numbers, *which shall be determined by adding to the whole number of free persons, including those bound to service for a term of years and excluding Indians not taxed, three-fifths of all other persons.* The actual enumeration shall be made within three years after the first meeting of the Congress of the United States, and within every subsequent term of ten years, in such manner as they shall by law direct. The number of Representatives shall not exceed one for every thirty thousand, but each State shall have at least one Representative; *and until such enumeration shall be made, the State of New Hampshire shall be entitled to choose three, Massachusetts eight, Rhode Island and Providence Plantations one, Connecticut five, New York six, New Jersey four, Pennsylvania eight, Delaware one, Maryland six, Virginia ten, North Carolina five, South Carolina five, and Georgia three.*

When vacancies happen in the representation from any State, the Executive authority thereof shall issue writs of election to fill such vacancies.

The House of Representatives shall choose their Speaker and other officers; and shall have the sole power of impeachment.

Section 3   The Senate of the United States shall be composed of two Senators from each State, *chosen by the legislature thereof,* for six years; and each Senator shall have one vote.

Immediately after they shall be assembled in consequence of the first election, they shall be divided as equally as may be into three classes. The seats of the Senators of the first class shall be vacated at the expiration of the second year, of the second class at the expiration of the fourth year, and of the third class at the expiration of the sixth year, so that one-third may be chosen every second year; *and if vacancies happen by resignation or otherwise, during the recess of the legislature of any State, the Executive thereof may make temporary appointments until the next meeting of the legislature, which shall then fill such vacancies.*

No person shall be a Senator who shall not have attained to the age of thirty years, and been nine years a citizen of the United States, and who shall not, when elected, be an inhabitant of that State for which he shall be chosen.

The Vice-President of the United States shall be President of the Senate, but shall have no vote, unless they be equally divided.

The Senate shall choose their other officers, and also a President *pro tempore,* in the absence of the Vice-President, or when he shall exercise the office of President of the United States.

The Senate shall have the sole power to try all impeachments. When sitting for that purpose, they shall be on oath or affirmation. When the President of the United States is tried, the Chief Justice shall preside: and no person shall be convicted without the concurrence of two-thirds of the members present.

Judgment in cases of impeachment shall not extend further than to removal from the office, and disqualification to hold and enjoy any office of honor, trust or profit under the United States: but the party convicted shall nevertheless be liable and subject to indictment, trial, judgment and punishment, according to law.

Section 4   The times, places and manner of holding elections for Senators and Representatives shall be prescribed in each State by the legislature thereof; but the Congress may at any time by law make or alter such regulations, except as to the places of choosing Senators.

The Congress shall assemble at least once in every year, and such meeting *shall be on the first Monday in December, unless they shall by law appoint a different day.*

Section 5   Each house shall be the judge of the elections, returns and qualifications of its own members, and a majority of each shall constitute a quorum to do business; but a smaller number may adjourn from day to day, and may be authorized to compel the attendance of absent members, in such manner, and under such penalties, as each house may provide.

Each house may determine the rules of its proceedings, punish its members for disorderly behavior, and with the concurrence of two-thirds, expel a member.

Each house shall keep a journal of its proceedings, and from time to time publish the same, excepting such parts as may in their judgment require secrecy; and the yeas and nays of the members of either house on any question shall, at the desire of one-fifth of those present, be entered on the journal.

*Passages no longer in effect are printed in italic type.

Neither house, during the session of Congress, shall, without the consent of the other, adjourn for more than three days, nor to any other place than that in which the two houses shall be sitting.

Section 6   The Senators and Representatives shall receive a compensation for their services, to be ascertained by law and paid out of the treasury of the United States. They shall in all cases except treason, felony and breach of the peace, be privileged from arrest during their attendance at the session of their respective houses, and in going to and returning from the same; and for any speech or debate in either house, they shall not be questioned in any other place.

No Senator or Representative shall, during the time for which he was elected, be appointed to any civil office under the authority of the United States, which shall have been created, or the emoluments whereof shall have been increased, during such time; and no person holding any office under the United States shall be a member of either house during his continuance in office.

Section 7   All bills for raising revenue shall originate in the House of Representatives; but the Senate may propose or concur with amendments as on other bills.

Every bill which shall have passed the House of Representatives and the Senate, shall, before it become a law, be presented to the President of the United States; if he approve he shall sign it, but if not he shall return it with objections to that house in which it originated, who shall enter the objections at large on their journal, and proceed to reconsider it. If after such reconsideration two-thirds of that house shall agree to pass the bill, it shall be sent, together with the objections, to the other house, by which it shall likewise be reconsidered, and, if approved by two-thirds of that house, it shall become a law. But in all such cases the votes of both houses shall be determined by yeas and nays, and the names of the persons voting for and against the bill shall be entered on the journal of each house respectively. If any bill shall not be returned by the President within ten days (Sundays excepted) after it shall have been presented to him, the same shall be a law, in like manner as if he had signed it, unless the Congress by their adjournment prevent its return, in which case it shall not be a law.

Every order, resolution, or vote to which the concurrence of the Senate and House of Representatives may be necessary (except on a question of adjournment) shall be presented to the President of the United States; and before the same shall take effect, shall be approved by him, or being disapproved by him, shall be repassed by two-thirds of the Senate and House of Representatives, according to the rules and limitations prescribed in the case of a bill.

Section 8   The Congress shall have power

To lay and collect taxes, duties, imposts, and excises, to pay the debts and provide for the common defense and general welfare of the United States; but all duties, imposts and excises shall be uniform throughout the United States;

To borrow money on the credit of the United States;

To regulate commerce with foreign nations, and among the several States, and with the Indian tribes;

To establish an uniform rule of naturalization, and uniform laws on the subject of bankruptcies throughout the United States;

To coin money, regulate the value thereof, and of foreign coin, and fix the standard of weights and measures;

To provide for the punishment of counterfeiting the securities and current coin of the United States;

To establish post offices and post roads;

To promote the progress of science and useful arts by securing for limited times to authors and inventors the exclusive right to their respective writings and discoveries;

To constitute tribunals inferior to the Supreme Court;

To define and punish piracies and felonies committed on the high seas and offenses against the law of nations;

To declare war, grant letters of marque and reprisal, and make rules concerning captures on land and water;

To raise and support armies, but no appropriation of money to that use shall be for a longer term than two years;

To provide and maintain a navy;

To make rules for the government and regulation of the land and naval forces;

To provide for calling forth the militia to execute the laws of the Union, suppress insurrections, and repel invasions;

To provide for organizing, arming, and disciplining the militia, and for governing such part of them as may be employed in the service of the United States, reserving to the States respectively the appointment of the officers, and the authority of training the militia according to the discipline prescribed by Congress;

To exercise exclusive legislation in all cases whatsoever, over such district (not exceeding ten miles square) as may, by cession of particular States, and the acceptance of Congress, become the seat of government of the United States, and to exercise like authority over all places purchased by the consent of the legislature of the State, in which the same shall be, for erection of forts, magazines, arsenals, dockyards, and other needful buildings; —and

To make all laws which shall be necessary and proper for carrying into execution the foregoing powers, and all other powers vested by this Constitution in the government of the United States, or in any department or officer thereof.

Section 9   *The migration or importation of such persons as any of the States now existing shall think proper to admit shall not be prohibited by the Congress prior to the year 1808; but a tax or duty may be imposed on such importation, not exceeding $10 for each person.*

The privilege of the writ of habeas corpus shall not be suspended, unless when in cases of rebellion or invasion the public safety may require it.

No bill of attainder or ex post facto law shall be passed.

No capitation, or other direct, tax shall be laid, unless in proportion to the census or enumeration herein before directed to be taken.

No tax or duty shall be laid on articles exported from any State.

No preference shall be given by any regulation of commerce or revenue to the ports of one State over those of another; nor shall vessels bound to, or from, one State, be obliged to enter, clear, or pay duties in another.

No money shall be drawn from the treasury, but in consequence of appropriations made by law; and a regular statement and account of the receipts and expenditures of all public money shall be published from time to time.

No title of nobility shall be granted by the United States: and no person holding any office of profit or trust under them, shall, without the consent of the Congress, accept of any present, emolument, office, or title, of any kind whatever, from any king, prince, or foreign state.

Section 10   No State shall enter into any treaty, alliance, or confederation; grant letters of marque and reprisal; coin money; emit bills of credit; make anything but gold and silver coin a tender in payment of debts; pass any bill of attainder, ex post facto law, or law impairing the obligation of contracts, or grant any title of nobility.

No State shall, without the consent of Congress, lay any imposts or duties on imports or exports, except what may be absolutely necessary for executing its inspection laws: and the net produce of all duties and imposts, laid by any State on imports or exports, shall be for the use of the treasury of the United States; and all such laws shall be subject to the revision and control of the Congress.

No State shall, without the consent of Congress, lay any duty of tonnage, keep troops or ships of war in time of peace, enter into any agreement or compact with another State, or with a foreign power, or engage in war, unless actually invaded, or in such imminent danger as will not admit of delay.

Article II

Section 1   The executive power shall be vested in a President of the United States of America. He shall hold his office during the term of four years, and, together with the Vice-President, chosen for the same term, be elected as follows:

Each State shall appoint, in such manner as the legislature thereof may direct, a number of electors, equal to the whole number of Senators and Representatives to which the State may be entitled in the Congress; but no Senator or Representative, or person holding an office of trust or profit under the United States, shall be appointed an elector.

The electors shall meet in their respective States, and vote by ballot for two persons, of whom one at least shall not be an inhabitant of the same State with themselves. And they shall make a list of all the persons voted for, and of the number of votes for each; which list they shall sign and certify, and transmit sealed to the seat of government of the United States, directed to the President of the Senate. The President of the Senate shall,

in the presence of the Senate and House of Representatives, open all the certificates, and the votes shall then be counted. The person having the greatest number of votes shall be the President, if such number be a majority of the whole number of electors appointed; and if there be more than one who have such majority, and have an equal number of votes, then the House of Representatives shall immediately choose by ballot one of them for President; and if no person have a majority, then from the five highest on the list said house shall in like manner choose the President. But in choosing the President the votes shall be taken by States, the representation from each State having one vote; a quorum for this purpose shall consist of a member or members from two-thirds of the States, and a majority of all the States shall be necessary to a choice. In every case, after the choice of the President, the person having the greatest number of votes of the electors shall be the Vice-President. But if there should remain two or more who have equal votes, the Senate shall choose from them by ballot the Vice-President.

The Congress may determine the time of choosing the electors and the day on which they shall give their votes; which day shall be the same throughout the United States.

No person except a natural-born citizen, *or a citizen of the United States at the time of the adoption of this Constitution,* shall be eligible to the office of President; neither shall any person be eligible to that office who shall not have attained to the age of thirty-five years, and been fourteen years a resident within the United States.

In cases of the removal of the President from office or of his death, resignation, or inability to discharge the powers and duties of the said office, the same shall devolve on the Vice-President, and the Congress may by law provide for the case of removal, death, resignation, or inability, both of the President and Vice-President, declaring what officer shall then act as President, and such officer shall act accordingly, until the disability be removed, or a President shall be elected.

The President shall, at stated times, receive for his services a compensation, which shall neither be increased nor diminished during the period for which he shall have been elected, and he shall not receive within that period any other emolument from the United States, or any of them.

Before he enter on the execution of his office, he shall take the following oath or affirmation:—"I do solemnly swear (or affirm) that I will faithfully execute the office of the President of the United States, and will to the best of my ability preserve, protect and defend the Constitution of the United States."

Section 2   The President shall be commander in chief of the army and navy of the United States, and of the militia of the several States, when called into the actual service of the United States; he may require the opinion, in writing, of the principal officer in each of the executive departments, upon any subject relating to the duties of their respective offices, and he shall have power to grant reprieves and pardons for offenses against the United States, except in cases of impeachment.

He shall have power, by and with the advice and consent of the Senate, to make treaties, provided two-thirds of the Senators present concur; and he shall nominate, and by and with the advice and consent of the Senate, shall appoint ambassadors, other public ministers and consuls, judges of the Supreme Court, and all other officers of the United States, whose appointments are not herein otherwise provided for, and which shall be established by law: but Congress may by law vest the appointment of such inferior officers, as they think proper, in the President alone, in the courts of law, or in the heads of departments.

The President shall have power to fill up all vacancies that may happen during the recess of the Senate, by granting commissions which shall expire at the end of their next session.

Section 3   He shall from time to time give to the Congress information of the state of the Union, and recommend to their consideration such measures as he shall judge necessary and expedient; he may, on extraordinary occasions, convene both houses, or either of them, and in case of disagreement between them, with respect to the time of adjournment, he may adjourn them to such time as he shall think proper; he shall receive ambassadors and other public ministers; he shall take care that the laws be faithfully executed, and shall commission all the officers of the United States.

Section 4   The President, Vice-President and all civil officers of the United States shall be removed from office on impeachment for, and on conviction of, treason, bribery, or other high crimes and misdemeanors.

Article III

Section 1   The judicial power of the United States shall be vested in one Supreme Court, and in such inferior courts as the Congress may from time to time ordain and establish. The judges, both of the Supreme and inferior courts, shall hold their offices during good behavior, and shall, at stated times, receive for their services a compensation which shall not be diminished during their continuance in office.

Section 2   The judicial power shall extend to all cases, in law and equity, arising under this Constitution, the laws of the United States, and treaties made, or which shall be made, under their authority;—to all cases affecting ambassadors, other public ministers and consuls;—to all cases of admiralty and maritime jurisdiction;—to controversies to which the United States shall be a party;—to controversies between two or more States;— between a State and citizens of another State;—between citizens of different States;—between citizens of the same State claiming lands under grants of different States, and between a State, or the citizens thereof, and foreign states, citizens or subjects.

In all cases affecting ambassadors, other public ministers and consuls, and those in which a State shall be party, the Supreme Court shall have original jurisdiction. In all the other cases before mentioned, the Supreme Court shall have appellate jurisdiction, both as to law and fact, with such exceptions, and under such regulations, as the Congress shall make.

The trial of all crimes, except in cases of impeachment, shall be by jury; and such trial shall be held in the State where said crimes shall have been committed; but when not committed within any State, the trial shall be at such place or places as the Congress may by law have directed.

Section 3   Treason against the United States shall consist only in levying war against them, or in adhering to their enemies, giving them aid and comfort. No person shall be convicted of treason unless on the testimony of two witnesses to the same overt act, or on confession in open court.

The Congress shall have power to declare the punishment of treason, but no attainder of treason shall work corruption of blood, or forfeiture except during the life of the person attainted.

Article IV

Section 1   Full faith and credit shall be given in each State to the public acts, records, and judicial proceedings of every other State. And the Congress may by general laws prescribe the manner in which such acts, records, and proceedings shall be proved, and the effect thereof.

Section 2   The citizens of each State shall be entitled to all privileges and immunities of citizens in the several States.

A person charged in any State with treason, felony, or other crime, who shall flee from justice, and be found in another State, shall on demand of the executive authority of the State from which he fled, be delivered up, to be removed to the State having jurisdiction of the crime.

No person held to service or labor in one State, under the laws thereof, escaping into another, shall, in consequence of any law or regulation therein, be discharged from such service or labor, but shall be delivered up on claim of the party to whom such service or labor may be due.

Section 3   New States may be admitted by the Congress into this Union; but no new State shall be formed or erected within the jurisdiction of any other State; nor any State be formed by the junction of two or more States, or parts of States, without the consent of the legislatures of the States concerned as well as of the Congress.

The Congress shall have power to dispose of and make all needful rules and regulations respecting the territory or other property belonging to the United States; and nothing in this Constitution shall be so construed as to prejudice any claims of the United States, or of any particular State.

Section 4   The United States shall guarantee to every State in this Union a republican form of government, and shall protect each of them against invasion; and on application of the legislature, or of the executive (when the legislature cannot be convened), against domestic violence.

Article V

The Congress, whenever two-thirds of both houses shall deem it necessary, shall propose amendments to this Constitution, or, on the application of the legislatures of two-thirds of the several States, shall call a convention for proposing amendments, which, in either case, shall be valid to all intents and purposes, as part of this Constitution, when ratified by the legislatures of three-fourths of the several States, or by conventions in three-fourths thereof, as the one or the other mode of ratification may be proposed by the Congress; provided *that no amendments which may be made prior to the year one thousand eight hundred and eight shall in any manner affect the first and fourth clauses in the ninth section of the first article;* and that no State, without its consent, shall be deprived of its equal suffrage in the Senate.

Article VI

All debts contracted and engagements entered into, before the adoption of this Constitution, shall be as valid against the United States under this Constitution, as under the Confederation.

This Constitution, and the laws of the United States which shall be made in pursuance thereof; and all treaties made, or which shall be made, under the authority of the United States, shall be the supreme law of the land; and the judges in every State shall be bound thereby, anything in the Constitution or laws of any State to the contrary notwithstanding.

The Senators and Representatives before mentioned, and the members of the several State legislatures, and all executive and judicial officers, both of the United States and of the several States, shall be bound by oath or affirmation to support this Constitution; but no religious test shall ever be required as a qualification to any office or public trust under the United States.

Article VII

The ratification of the conventions of nine States shall be sufficient for the establishment of this Constitution between the States so ratifying the same.

Done in Convention by the unanimous consent of the States present, the seventeenth day of September in the year of our Lord one thousand seven hundred and eighty-seven and of the Independence of the United States of America the twelfth. In witness whereof we have hereunto subscribed our names.

Amendments to the Constitution*

Amendment I

Congress shall make no law respecting an establishment of religion, or prohibiting the free exercise thereof; or abridging the freedom of speech, or of the press; or the right of the people peaceably to assemble, and to petition the government for a redress of grievances.

*The first ten Amendments (the Bill of Rights) were adopted in 1791.

Amendment II

A well-regulated militia being necessary to the security of a free State, the right of the people to keep and bear arms shall not be infringed.

Amendment III

No soldier shall, in time of peace, be quartered in any house without the consent of the owner, nor in time of war, but in a manner to be prescribed by law.

Amendment IV

The right of the people to be secure in their persons, houses, papers, and effects, against unreasonable searches and seizures, shall not be violated, and no warrants shall issue but upon probable cause, supported by oath or affirmation, and particularly describing the place to be searched, and the persons or things to be seized.

Amendment V

No person shall be held to answer for a capital, or otherwise infamous crime, unless on a presentment or indictment of a grand jury, except in cases arising in the land or naval forces, or in the militia, when in actual service in time of war or public danger; nor shall any person be subject for the same offense to be twice put in jeopardy of life or limb; nor shall be compelled in any criminal case to be a witness against himself, nor be deprived of life, liberty, or property, without due process of law; nor shall private property be taken for public use without just compensation.

Amendment VI

In all criminal prosecutions, the accused shall enjoy the right to a speedy and public trial, by an impartial jury of the State and district wherein the crime shall have been committed, which district shall have been previously ascertained by law, and to be informed of the nature and cause of the accusation; to be confronted with the witnesses against him; to have compulsory process for obtaining witnesses in his favor, and to have the assistance of counsel for his defense.

Amendment VII

In suits at common law, where the value in controversy shall exceed twenty dollars, the right of trial by jury shall be preserved, and no fact tried by a jury shall be otherwise reexamined in any court of the United States, than according to the rules of the common law.

Amendment VIII

Excessive bail shall not be required, nor excessive fines imposed, nor cruel and unusual punishments inflicted.

Amendment IX

The enumeration in the Constitution, of certain rights, shall not be construed to deny or disparage others retained by the people.

Amendment X

The powers not delegated to the United States by the Constitution, nor prohibited by it to the States, are reserved to the States respectively, or to the people.

Amendment XI

[Adopted 1798]

The judicial power of the United States shall not be construed to extend to any suit in law or equity, commenced or prosecuted against one of the United States by citizens of another State, or by citizens or subjects of any foreign state.

Amendment XII

[Adopted 1804]

The electors shall meet in their respective States, and vote by ballot for President and Vice-President, one of whom, at least, shall not be an inhabitant of the same State with themselves; they shall name in their ballots the person voted for as President, and in distinct ballots the person voted for as Vice-President, and they shall make distinct lists of all persons voted for as President, and of all persons voted for as Vice-President, and of the number of votes for each, which lists they shall sign and certify, and transmit sealed to the seat of government of the United States, directed to the President of the Senate;—the President of the Senate shall, in the presence of the Senate and House of Representatives, open all the certificates and the votes shall then be counted;—the person having the greatest number of votes for President shall be the President, if such number be a majority of the whole number of electors appointed; and if no person have such majority, then from the persons having the highest numbers not exceeding three on the list of those voted for as President, the House of Representatives shall choose immediately, by ballot, the President. But in choosing the President, the votes shall be taken by States, the representation from each State having one vote; a quorum for this purpose shall consist of a member or members from two-thirds of the States, and a majority of all the States shall be necessary to a choice. And if the House of Representatives shall not choose a President whenever the right of choice shall devolve upon them, before *the fourth day of March* next following, then the Vice-President shall act as President, as in the case of the death or other constitutional disability of the President.

The person having the greatest number of votes as Vice-President shall be the Vice-President, if such number be a majority of the whole number of electors appointed; and if no person have a majority, then from the two highest numbers on the list the Senate shall choose the Vice-President; a quorum for the purpose shall consist of two-thirds of the whole number of Senators, and a majority of the whole number shall be necessary to a choice. But no person constitutionally ineligible to the office of President shall be eligible to that of Vice-President of the United States.

Amendment XIII

[Adopted 1865]

Section 1   Neither slavery nor involuntary servitude, except as a punishment for crime whereof the party shall have been duly convicted, shall exist within the United States, or any place subject to their jurisdiction.

Section 2   Congress shall have power to enforce this article by appropriate legislation.

Amendment XIV

[Adopted 1868]

Section 1   All persons born or naturalized in the United States, and subject to the jurisdiction thereof, are citizens of the United States and of the State wherein they reside. No State shall make or enforce any law which shall abridge the privileges or immunities of citizens of the United States; nor shall any State deprive any person of life, liberty, or property, without due process of law; nor deny to any person within its jurisdiction the equal protection of the laws.

Section 2   Representatives shall be apportioned among the several States according to their respective numbers, counting the whole number of persons in each State, excluding Indians not taxed. But when the right to vote at any election for the choice of Electors for President and Vice-President of the United States, Representatives in Congress, the executive and judicial officers of a State, or the members of the legislature thereof, is denied to any of the male inhabitants of such State, being twenty-one years of age and citizens of the United States, or in any way abridged, except for participation in rebellion, or other crime, the basis of representation therein shall be reduced in the proportion which the number of such male citizens shall bear to the whole number of male citizens twenty-one years of age in such State.

Section 3   No person shall be a Senator or Representative in Congress, or Elector of President and Vice-President, or hold any office, civil or military, under the United States, or under any State, who, having previously taken an oath, as a member of Congress, or as an officer of the United States, or as a member of any State legislature, or as an executive or judicial officer of any State, to support the Constitution of the United States, shall have engaged in insurrection or rebellion against the same, or given aid or comfort to the enemies thereof. Congress may, by a vote of two-thirds of each house, remove such disability.

Section 4   The validity of the public debt of the United States, authorized by law, including debts incurred for payment of pensions and bounties for services in suppressing insurrection or rebellion, shall not be questioned. But neither the United States nor any State shall assume or pay any debt or obligation incurred in aid of insurrection or rebellion against the United States, or any claim for the loss of emancipation of any slave; but all such debts, obligations, and claims shall be held illegal and void.

Section 5 The Congress shall have power to enforce, by appropriate legislation, the provisions of this article.

Amendment XV

[Adopted 1870]

Section 1 The right of citizens of the United States to vote shall not be denied or abridged by the United States or by any State on account of race, color, or previous condition of servitude.

Section 2 The Congress shall have power to enforce this article by appropriate legislation.

Amendment XVI

[Adopted 1913]

The Congress shall have power to lay and collect taxes on incomes, from whatever source derived, without apportionment among the several States, and without regard to any census or enumeration.

Amendment XVII

[Adopted 1913]

Section 1 The Senate of the United States shall be composed of two Senators from each State, elected by the people thereof, for six years; and each Senator shall have one vote. The electors in each State shall have the qualifications requisite for electors of [voters for] the most numerous branch of the State legislatures.

Section 2 When vacancies happen in the representation of any State in the Senate, the executive authority of such State shall issue writs of election to fill such vacancies: Provided, that the Legislature of any State may empower the executive thereof to make temporary appointments until the people fill the vacancies by election as the Legislature may direct.

Section 3 This amendment shall not be so construed as to affect the election or term of any Senator chosen before it becomes valid as part of the Constitution.

Amendment XVIII

[Adopted 1919; Repealed 1933]

Section 1 After one year from the ratification of this article the manufacture, sale, or transportation of intoxicating liquors within, the importation thereof into, or the exportation thereof from the United States and all territory subject to the jurisdiction thereof, for beverage purposes, is hereby prohibited.

Section 2 The Congress and the several States shall have concurrent power to enforce this article by appropriate legislation.

Section 3 This article shall be inoperative unless it shall have been ratified as an amendment to the Constitution by the legislatures of the several States, as provided by the Constitution, within seven years from the date of the submission thereof to the States by the Congress.

Amendment XIX

[Adopted 1920]

Section 1 The right of citizens of the United States to vote shall not be denied or abridged by the United States or by any State on account of sex.

Section 2 The Congress shall have power to enforce this article by appropriate legislation.

Amendment XX

[Adopted 1933]

Section 1 The terms of the President and Vice-President shall end at noon on the 20th day of January, and the terms of Senators and Representatives at noon on the 3rd day of January, of the years in which such terms would have ended if this article had not been ratified; and the terms of their successors shall then begin.

Section 2 The Congress shall assemble at least once in every year, and such meeting shall begin at noon on the 3d day of January, unless they shall by law appoint a different day.

Section 3 If, at the time fixed for the beginning of the term of the President, the President-elect shall have died, the Vice-President–elect shall become President. If a President shall not have been chosen before the time fixed for the beginning of his term, or if the President-elect shall have failed to qualify, then the Vice-President–elect shall act as President until a President shall have qualified; and the Congress may by law provide for the case wherein neither a President-elect nor a Vice-President–elect shall have qualified, declaring who shall then act as President, or the manner in which one who is to act shall be selected, and such persons shall act accordingly until a President or Vice-President shall have qualified.

Section 4 The Congress may by law provide for the case of the death of any of the persons from whom the House of Representatives may choose a President whenever the right of choice shall have devolved upon them, and for the case of the death of any of the persons from whom the Senate may choose a Vice-President whenever the right of choice shall have devolved upon them.

Section 5 Sections 1 and 2 shall take effect on the 15th day of October following the ratification of this article.

Section 6 This article shall be inoperative unless it shall have been ratified as an amendment to the Constitution by the Legislatures of three-fourths of the several States within seven years from the date of its submission.

Amendment XXI

[Adopted 1933]

Section 1   The eighteenth article of amendment to the Constitution of the United States is hereby repealed.

Section 2   The transportation or importation into any State, Territory, or Possession of the United States for delivery or use therein of intoxicating liquors, in violation of the laws thereof, is hereby prohibited.

Section 3   This article shall be inoperative unless it shall have been ratified as an amendment to the Constitution by conventions in the several States, as provided in the Constitution, within seven years from the date of submission thereof to the States by the Congress.

Amendment XXII

[Adopted 1951]

Section 1   No person shall be elected to the office of President more than twice, and no person who has held the office of President, or acted as President, for more than two years of a term to which some other person was elected President shall be elected to the office of President more than once. But this article shall not apply to any person holding the office of President when this article was proposed by the Congress, and shall not prevent any person who may be holding the office of President, or acting as President, during the term within which this article becomes operative from holding the office of President or acting as President during the remainder of such term.

Section 2   This article shall be inoperative unless it shall have been ratified as an amendment to the Constitution by the legislatures of three-fourths of the several States within seven years from the date of its submission to the States by the Congress.

Amendment XXIII

[Adopted 1961]

Section 1   The District constituting the seat of Government of the United States shall appoint in such manner as the Congress may direct:

A number of electors of President and Vice-President equal to the whole number of Senators and Representatives in Congress to which the District would be entitled if it were a State, but in no event more than the least populous State; they shall be in addition to those appointed by the States, but they shall be considered for the purposes of the election of President and Vice-President, to be electors appointed by a State; and they shall meet in the District and perform such duties as provided by the twelfth article of amendment.

Section 2   The Congress shall have the power to enforce this article by appropriate legislation.

Amendment XXIV

[Adopted 1964]

Section 1   The right of citizens of the United States to vote in any primary or other election for President or Vice-President, for electors for President or Vice-President, or for Senator or Representative in Congress, shall not be denied or abridged by the United States or any State by reason of failure to pay any poll tax or other tax.

Section 2   The Congress shall have the power to enforce this article by appropriate legislation.

Amendment XXV

[Adopted 1967]

Section 1   In case of the removal of the President from office or of his death or resignation, the Vice-President shall become President.

Section 2   Whenever there is a vacancy in the office of the Vice-President, the President shall nominate a Vice-President who shall take office upon confirmation by a majority vote of both Houses of Congress.

Section 3   Whenever the President transmits to the President pro tempore of the Senate and the Speaker of the House of Representatives his written declaration that he is unable to discharge the powers and duties of his office, and until he transmits to them a written declaration to the contrary, such powers and duties shall be discharged by the Vice-President as Acting President.

Section 4   Whenever the Vice-President and a majority of either the principal officers of the executive departments or of such other body as Congress may by law provide, transmit to the President pro tempore of the Senate and the Speaker of the House of Representatives their written declaration that the President is unable to discharge the powers and duties of his office, the Vice-President shall immediately assume the powers and duties of the office as Acting President.

Thereafter, when the President transmits to the President pro tempore of the Senate and the Speaker of the House of Representatives his written declaration that no inability exists, he shall resume the powers and duties of his office unless the Vice-President and a majority of either the principal officers of the executive department[s] or of such other body as Congress may by law provide, transmit within four days to the President pro tempore of the Senate and the Speaker of the House of Representatives their written declaration that the President is unable to discharge the powers and duties of his office. Thereupon Congress shall decide the issue, assembling within forty-eight hours for that purpose if not in session. If the Congress, within twenty-one days after receipt of the latter written declaration, or, if Congress is not in session, within twenty-one days after Congress is required to assemble, determines by two-thirds vote of both Houses that the President is unable to discharge the powers and duties of his office, the Vice-President shall continue to discharge the same as Acting President; otherwise, the President shall resume the powers and duties of his office.

Amendment XXVI

[Adopted 1971]

Section 1 The right of citizens of the United States, who are eighteen years of age or older, to vote shall not be denied or abridged by the United States or by any State on account of age.

Section 2 The Congress shall have power to enforce this article by appropriate legislation.

Amendment XXVII

[Adopted 1992]

No law, varying the compensation for the services of the Senators and Representatives, shall take effect, until an election of Representatives shall have intervened.

1. *President*	George Washington	1789–1797	
Vice President	John Adams	1789–1797	
2. *President*	John Adams	1797–1801	
Vice President	Thomas Jefferson	1797–1801	
3. *President*	Thomas Jefferson	1801–1809	
Vice President	Aaron Burr	1801–1805	
Vice President	George Clinton	1805–1809	
4. *President*	James Madison	1809–1817	
Vice President	George Clinton	1809–1813	
Vice President	Elbridge Gerry	1813–1817	
5. *President*	James Monroe	1817–1825	
Vice President	Daniel Tompkins	1817–1825	
6. *President*	John Quincy Adams	1825–1829	
Vice President	John C. Calhoun	1825–1829	
7. *President*	Andrew Jackson	1829–1837	
Vice President	John C. Calhoun	1829–1833	
Vice President	Martin Van Buren	1833–1837	
8. *President*	Martin Van Buren	1837–1841	
Vice President	Richard M. Johnson	1837–1841	
9. *President*	William H. Harrison	1841	
Vice President	John Tyler	1841	
10. *President*	John Tyler	1841–1845	
Vice President	None		
11. *President*	James K. Polk	1845–1849	
Vice President	George M. Dallas	1845–1849	
12. *President*	Zachary Taylor	1849–1850	
Vice President	Millard Fillmore	1849–1850	
13. *President*	Millard Fillmore	1850–1853	
Vice President	None		
14. *President*	Franklin Pierce	1853–1857	
Vice President	William R. King	1853–1857	
15. *President*	James Buchanan	1857–1861	
Vice President	John C. Breckinridge	1857–1861	
16. *President*	Abraham Lincoln	1861–1865	
Vice President	Hannibal Hamlin	1861–1865	
Vice President	Andrew Johnson	1865	
17. *President*	Andrew Johnson	1865–1869	
Vice President	None		
18. *President*	Ulysses S. Grant	1869–1877	
Vice President	Schuyler Colfax	1869–1873	
Vice President	Henry Wilson	1873–1877	
19. *President*	Rutherford B. Hayes	1877–1881	
Vice President	William A. Wheeler	1877–1881	
20. *President*	James A. Garfield	1881	
Vice President	Chester A. Arthur	1881	
21. *President*	Chester A. Arthur	1881–1885	
Vice President	None		
22. *President*	Grover Cleveland	1885–1889	
Vice President	Thomas A. Hendricks	1885–1889	
23. *President*	Benjamin Harrison	1889–1893	
Vice President	Levi P. Morton	1889–1893	
24. *President*	Grover Cleveland	1893–1897	
Vice President	Adlai E. Stevenson	1893–1897	
25. *President*	William McKinley	1897–1901	
Vice President	Garret A. Hobart	1897–1901	
Vice President	Theodore Roosevelt	1901	
26. *President*	Theodore Roosevelt	1901–1909	
Vice President	Charles Fairbanks	1905–1909	
27. *President*	William H. Taft	1909–1913	
Vice President	James S. Sherman	1909–1913	
28. *President*	Woodrow Wilson	1913–1921	
Vice President	Thomas R. Marshall	1913–1921	
29. *President*	Warren G. Harding	1921–1923	
Vice President	Calvin Coolidge	1921–1923	
30. *President*	Calvin Coolidge	1923–1929	
Vice President	Charles G. Dawes	1925–1929	
31. *President*	Herbert C. Hoover	1929–1933	
Vice President	Charles Curtis	1929–1933	
32. *President*	Franklin D. Roosevelt	1933–1945	
Vice President	John N. Garner	1933–1941	
Vice President	Henry A. Wallace	1941–1945	
Vice President	Harry S Truman	1945	
33. *President*	Harry S Truman	1945–1953	
Vice President	Alben W. Barkley	1949–1953	
34. *President*	Dwight D. Eisenhower	1953–1961	
Vice President	Richard M. Nixon	1953–1961	

35. *President*	John F. Kennedy	1961–1963
Vice President	Lyndon B. Johnson	1961–1963
36. *President*	Lyndon B. Johnson	1963–1969
Vice President	Hubert H. Humphrey	1965–1969
37. *President*	Richard M. Nixon	1969–1974
Vice President	Spiro T. Agnew	1969–1973
Vice President	Gerald R. Ford	1973–1974
38. *President*	Gerald R. Ford	1974–1977
Vice President	Nelson A. Rockefeller	1974–1977
39. *President*	James E. Carter	1977–1981
Vice President	Walter F. Mondale	1977–1981

40. *President*	Ronald W. Reagan	1981–1989
Vice President	George H. W. Bush	1981–1989
41. *President*	George H. W. Bush	1989–1993
Vice President	J. Danforth Quayle	1989–1993
42. *President*	William J. Clinton	1993–2001
Vice President	Albert Gore	1993–2001
43. *President*	George W. Bush	2001–
Vice President	Richard B. Cheney	2001–